Employment Discrimination Law

Third Edition

1998 Supplement

Other BNA Books Authored by the ABA Section of Labor & Employment Law

Covenants Not to Compete: A State-by-State Survey

The Developing Labor Law

Discipline and Discharge in Arbitration

Employee Benefits Law

Employee Duty of Loyalty: A State-by-State Survey

Equal Employment Law Update

Elkouri and Elkouri: How Arbitration Works

International Labor and Employment Laws

Labor Arbitration: A Practical Guide for Advocates

Labor Arbitration: Cases and Materials for Advocates

Labor Arbitrator Development: A Handbook

Occupational Safety and Health Law

The Railway Labor Act

Trade Secrets: A State-by-State Survey

1998 Supplement to Lindemann & Grossman's

Employment Discrimination Law

Third Edition

Editor-in-Chief
W. Carl Jordan
Vinson & Elkins L.L.P.
Houston, TX

Associate Editors

Catherine Hagen
O'Melveny & Myers
Newport Beach, CA

Cathy Ventrell-Monsees
Chevy Chase, MD

Coordinator, Union Reviewers
Nora L. Macey
Macey, Macey and Swanson
Indianapolis, IN

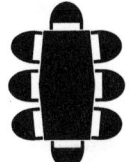

Equal Employment Opportunity Committee
Section of Labor and Employment Law
American Bar Association

The Bureau of National Affairs, Inc., Washington, D.C.

Copyright © 1998
American Bar Association
Chicago, IL

Library of Congress Cataloging-in-Publication Data

Employment discrimination law / Barbara Lindemann . . . [et al]. -- 3rd ed.
    p. cm.
Includes index.
    ISBN 0-87179-791-7 (set). -- ISBN 1-57018-064-4 (vol. 1). -- ISBN 1-57018-065-2 (vol. 2)
    1. Discrimination in employment--Law and legislation--United States. I. Lindemann, Barbara, 1935-
KF3464.E445   1996
344.7301'133--dc21

96-48048
CIP

The materials contained herein represent the opinions of the authors and editors and should not be construed to be those of either the American Bar Association or the Section of Labor and Employment Law. Nothing contained herein is to be considered as the rendering of legal advice for specific cases, and readers are responsible for obtaining such advice from their own legal counsel. These materials and any forms and agreements herein are intended for educational and informational purposes only.

International Standard Book Number: 1-57018-127-6
Printed in the United States of America

BOARD OF EDITORS

EDITOR-IN-CHIEF

W. CARL JORDAN
Vinson & Elkins L.L.P.
Houston, TX

ASSOCIATE EDITORS

CATHERINE HAGEN
O'Melveny & Myers LLP
Newport Beach, CA

CATHY VENTRELL-MONSEES
Chevy Chase, MD

COORDINATOR, UNION REVIEWERS

NORA L. MACEY
Macey, Macey and Swanson
Indianapolis, IN

CHAPTER CHAIRS AND LIST OF CONTRIBUTORS

Chapter 1

Chair

W. CARL JORDAN
Vinson & Elkins L.L.P.
Houston, TX

Chapter 2

Chairs

THOMAS H. BARNARD
Ulmer & Berne LLP
Cleveland, OH

KENNETH KOWALSKI
Cleveland State University
Cleveland, OH

CHRISTOPHER V. BACON
Vinson & Elkins L.L.P.
Houston, TX

Ch. 2 *(cont'd)* **Contributors**

WAYNE O. ADAMS III
Johnson, Smith, Pence, Densborn,
 Wright & Heath
Indianapolis, IN

ROMAN ARCE
Marshall & Melhorn
Toledo, OH

SALLY M. BARKER
Schuchat, Cook & Werner
St. Louis, MO

MERRITT BUMPASS
Thompson Hine & Flory LLP
Cleveland, OH

MICHAEL K. K. CHOY
Haskell Slaughter & Young, L.L.C.
Birmingham, AL

TRACEY DIAMOND
ELLEN MARTIN
Patterson, Belknap, Webb & Tyler
New York, NY

JOHN A. HNAT
Ulmer & Berne LLP
Cleveland, OH

MICHAEL G. KANE
Cashdan & Golden
Washington, DC

JAMES K. L. LAWRENCE
Frost & Jacobs
Cincinnati, OH

CHRISTOPHER H. MILLS
Collier, Jacob & Mills
Somerset, NJ

WILLIAM C. STROCK
Haynes and Boone, LLP
Dallas, TX

Chapter 3

Chairs

ELLIOT GORDON, JR.
Santa Monica, CA

JULES SMITH
Blitman and King, LLP
Rochester, NY

Chapter 4

Chair

NEAL D. MOLLEN
Paul, Hastings, Janofsky & Walker LLP
Washington, DC

Contributors

SUSAN K. KRELL
TASOS PANDERIS
Jackson, Lewis, Schnitzler
  & Krupman
Hartford, CT

CARL S. YALLER
Glass, Molders, Pottery,
  Plastics & Allied Workers
Media, PA

Chapters 5 and 7

Chairs

WALTER COCHRAN-BOND
Cochran-Bond & Connon, LLP
Los Angeles, CA

LOUIS P. MALONE
O'Donoghue & O'Donoghue
Washington, DC

Contributors

MARCIA E. GRECKY
Corporate Express
Denver, CO

WILLIAM J. KLEMICK
Eckert Seamans Cherin & Mellott
Pittsburgh, PA

LOUIS K. OBDYKE IV
Small, Craig & Werkenthin
Austin, TX

NANCY E. RAFUSE
Paul, Hastings, Janofsky
  & Walker LLP
Atlanta, GA

DEBORAH J. SAGER
Proskauer Rose LLP
Los Angeles, CA

LEE ANNE STEINBERG
Mitchell, Silberberg
  & Knupp LLP
Los Angeles, CA

MICHAEL A. STRAUTMANIS
Chicago, IL

DEBORAH A. SUDBURY
Jones, Day, Reavis & Pogue
Atlanta, GA

Chapter 8

Chairs

KEITH M. PYBURN, JR.
McCalla, Thompson, Pyburn,
  Hymowitz & Shapiro
New Orleans, LA

JEFFREY IVAN PASEK
Cozen and O'Connor
Philadelphia, PA

Ch. 8 *(cont'd)*

Contributors

JENNIFER BURR ALTABEF
Locke Purnell Rain & Harrell
Dallas, TX

SALLY M. BARKER
Schuchat, Cook & Werner
St. Louis, MO

STEPHEN S. EBERLY
Vorys, Sater, Seymour and Pease
Cincinnati, OH

KIM F. EBERT
Locke Reynolds
Indianapolis, IN

ALLEN I. FAGIN
JONATHAN M. GLASSMAN
Proskauer Rose LLP
New York, NY

L. ANTHONY GEORGE
Jackson & Kelly
Denver, CO

KRISTIN M. HUOTARI
DeWitt, Ross & Stevens
Madison, WI

EDWARD R. LEVIN
Schmeltzer, Aptaker & Shepard
Washington, DC

TIMOTHY D. LOUDON
SCOTT S. MOORE
Berens & Tate
Omaha, NE

MARC STERN

ELVIGE C. RICHARDS
Carver, Darden, Koretzky, Tessier,
  Finn, Blossman & Areaux
New Orleans, LA

LON R. WILLIAMS
JASON P. WYLIE
Law, Snakard & Gambill
Fort Worth, TX

Chapter 9

Chairs

C. GEOFFREY WEIRICH
Paul, Hastings, Janofsky
  & Walker LLP
Atlanta, GA

FRANK H. STEWART
Taft, Stettinius & Hollister
Cincinnati, OH

SALLY P. DUNAWAY
AARP Foundation Litigation
Washington, DC

GERARD JOHN DEWOLF
New York State United Teachers
Albany, NY

Contributors

A. CRAIG CLELAND
Paul, Hastings, Janofsky
  & Walker LLP
Atlanta, GA

ANDREW B. COHEN
AGNES M. SCHIPPER
Moore & Van Allen, PLLC
Durham, NC

RICHARD L. CONNORS
Stinson, Mag & Fizzell, PC
Kansas City, MO

DAVID K. FRAM
National Employment Law
  Institute
Washington, DC

RUSSELL H. GARDNER
LARRY R. SEEGULL
Piper & Marbury L.L.P.
Baltimore, MD

INTRA L. GERMANIS
W. GLENN MERTEN
Paul, Hastings, Janofsky
  & Walker LLP
Washington, DC

SCOTT C. LABARRE
National Federation of the Blind
  of Colorado
Denver, CO

CAROLYN H. LADD
Jackson, Lewis, Schnitzler & Krupman
Seattle, WA

MICHAEL C. LUEDER
DAVID H. PECK
MARK J. STEPANIAK
Taft, Stettinius & Hollister, LLP
Cincinnati, OH

MEGAN P. NORRIS
Miller, Canfield, Paddock
  and Stone, P.L.C.
Detroit, MI

MELISSA A. ROMIG
BRADD N. SIEGEL
Porter, Wright, Morris & Arthur
Columbus, OH

STACEY L. SHAWN
T.J. WRAY
Fulbright & Jaworski L.L.P.
Houston, TX

Chapter 10

Chair

PROF. DAVID BURCHAM
Loyola Law School
Los Angeles, CA

Contributor

CARL S. YALLER
Glass, Molders, Pottery, Plastics & Allied Workers
Media, PA

Chapter 11

Chairs

CHARLES A. POWELL IV
Constangy, Brooks & Smith, LLC
Birmingham, AL

PROF. MARK ADAMS
Valparaiso University School of Law
Valparaiso, IN

Contributors

ROBERT M. DOHRMANN
Schwartz, Steinsapir, Dohrmann
  and Sommers
Los Angeles, CA

GREGORY A. HEARING
Thompson, Sizemore & Gonzalez
Tampa, FL

REBECCA KOZLOFF
KATHRYN E. UNDERWOOD
STEVEN D. WHEELESS
Steptoe & Johnson LLP
Phoenix, AZ

JOHN W. SHEFFIELD
Johnston, Barton, Proctor & Powell
Birmingham, AL

Chapter 12

Chair

CHARLES A. POWELL IV
Constangy, Brooks & Smith, LLC
Birmingham, AL

Contributors

ROBERT M. DOHRMANN
Schwartz, Steinsapir, Dohrmann
  and Sommers
Los Angeles, CA

MARCIA MORALES HOWARD
McGuire, Woods, Battle
  & Boothe
Jacksonville, FL

MARY S. WELCH
Akin, Gump, Strauss, Hauer
  & Feld, LLP
Washington, DC

Chapter 13

Chairs

MARK STEVEN SNYDERMAN
The Coca-Cola Company
Atlanta, GA

HELEN NORTON
Washington, DC

WOODY N. PETERSON
Dickstein Shapiro Morin
 & Oshinsky LLP
Washington, DC

Contributors

FRANCIS J. CONNELL III
Drinker Biddle & Reath LLP
Philadelphia, PA

PAUL E. ILASH

ELIZABETH A. MATTHEWS
Dickstein Shapiro Morin
 & Oshinsky LLP
Washington, DC

JONATHAN D. QUANDER

Chapter 14

Chairs

RICHARD D. GLOVSKY
PETER M. KELLEY
Glovsky & Associates
Boston, MA

Contributor

AMANDA O'REILLY
City of Boston Law Department
Boston, MA

Chapter 15

Chairs

JANA HOWARD CAREY
TODD J. HORN
Venable, Baetjer & Howard
Baltimore, MD

HELEN NORTON
Washington, DC

Ch. 15 *(cont'd)*

SALLY M. BARKER
Schuchat, Cook & Werner
St. Louis, MO

Contributors

REBECCA EPSTEIN

EDWARD EVANS

Chapter 16

Chairs

GEORGE P. PARKER, JR.
Strasburger & Price, L.L.P.
San Antonio, TX

LAURIE A. MCCANN
AARP Foundation Litigation
Washington, DC

Contributors

RICHARD J. ANTONELLI
REBECCA J. DICK-HURWITZ
Buchanan Ingersoll, PC
Pittsburgh, PA

G. RANDALL AYERS
LOUISE BROCK
CHERYL BRUNER
ROBERT REID
Dinsmore & Shohl LLP
Cincinnati, OH

PATRICIA A. BARBIERI
Roche Pharmaceuticals
Nutley, NJ

ANNE E. BENDERNAGEL
Barbara Ryniker Evans
 & Associates
New Orleans, LA

ELISE MAYERS BOUCHNER
GREGORY GUIDRY
Onebane, Bernard, Torian, Diaz,
 McNamara & Abell, PLC
Lafayette, LA

LISA BRUNO
ALBERT CALILLE
Ameritech
Detroit, MI

LESLIE SELIG BYRD
VICTORIA M. GARCIA
JUDY K. JETELINA
KELLY M. KILLIAN
LAURA M. MERRITT
RAQUEL G. PEREZ
PENELOPE ROBINSON
Strasburger & Price, L.L.P.
San Antonio, TX

HOLLY CLAGHORN
Thompson & Knight, PC
Austin, TX

ROBERT A. COLON
Woods, Oviatt, Gilman, Sturman
 & Clark LLP
Rochester, NY

DESHA DARDENNE
GEORGE PHILLIP SHULER III
Chaffe, McCall & Associates
New Orleans, LA

Contributors

Lisa D'Avolio
Richard G. Kass
Rains & Pogrebin, PC
Mineola, NY

Kathleen A. Devine
Sonia Rivera-Suire
Robert Shaw-Meadow
San Antonio, TX

Lisa A. Dreishmire
Dean J. Schaner
Haynes and Boone, LLP
Houston, TX

Herbert C. Ehrhardt
Butler, Snow, O'Mara, Stevens
  & Cannada, PLLC
Jackson, MS

Mark R. Flora
Carr, Flora, Carroll & Driscoll
El Paso, TX

Adam P. Forman
Testa, Hurwitz & Thibeault, LLP
Boston, MA

David I. Gindler
Bryan Cave LLP
Los Angeles, CA

Mark A. Gloade
Cheryl R. Saban
Paul, Hastings, Janofsky
  & Walker LLP
New York, NY

Lacey L. Gourley
Strasburger & Price, L.L.P.
Austin, TX

Thomas M. J. Hathaway
Brady Hathaway PC
Detroit, MI

J. Kevin Hennessy
Banta, Cox & Hennessy
Chicago, IL

Sam Jensen
Erickson & Sederstrom, P.C.
Omaha, NE

Judith J. Johnson
Mississippi College School
  of Law
Jackson, MS

Kimberly J. Korando
Smith, Anderson, Blount, Dorsett,
  Mitchell & Jernigan, L.L.P.
Raleigh, NC

Diane Krejsa
University of Maryland
College Park, MD

Charles D. Maurer
New York, NY

Inez M. McBride
Matthews & Branscomb, PC
San Antonio, TX

Helen McDonald
Matthew Edmund Swaya
Lane Powell Spears Lubersky LLP
Seattle, WA

Paige Waldrop Mills
Wyatt, Tarrant & Combs
Nashville, TN

Michael J. Moberg
Ogletree, Deakins, Nash, Smoak
  & Stewart, LLP
Greenville, SC

Carl F. Muller
Warren & Young
Ashtabula, OH

Ch. 16 *(cont'd)*

Peter K. Newman
Thompson Hine & Flory LLP
Cincinnati, OH

Robert S. Nichols
Beverly B. Swallows
Strasburger & Price, L.L.P.
Corpus Christi, TX

Gregory Parker Rogers
Taft, Stettinius & Hollister
Cincinnati, OH

James M. Samples
Faegre & Benson LLP
Minneapolis, MN

Michael W. Sculnick
Vedder, Price, Kaufman
 & Kammholz
Chicago, IL

Timothy L. Stalnaker
Timothy L. Stalnaker, LC
Chesterfield, MO

Amy C. Strauss
Benesch, Friedlander, Coplan
 & Aronoff, LLP
Cleveland, OH

Jim Odell Stuckey II
Nelson Mullins Riley
 & Scarborough, L.L.P.
Columbia, SC

Miguel A. Torres
El Paso, TX

Jayne A. Wright
Fruit of the Loom, Inc.
Bowling Green, KY

Chapter 17

Chairs

E. Jeffrey Grube
Paul, Hastings, Janofsky
 & Walker LLP
San Francisco, CA

Theodore E. Karatinos
Seeley & Karatinos, PA
St. Petersburg, FL

Contributors

Marcia Nelson Jackson
Akin, Gump, Strauss, Hauer
 & Feld, LLP
Los Angeles, CA

Shannon P. Wright
Los Angeles, CA

Carl S. Yaller
Glass, Molders, Pottery, Plastics
 & Allied Workers
Media, PA

Chapter 18

Chair

CHARLES S. MISHKIND
Miller, Canfield, Paddock and Stone, P.L.C.
Grand Rapids, MI

Contributors

BRIDGETTE BATES-SKAFF
MICHAEL CAMAROTA
YVONNE HADDAD
SHERRY KATZ-CRANK
PAUL MACHESKY
BRUCE OLSON
JOHN STECCO
VINCENT WOLTJER
Miller, Canfield, Paddock and Stone, P.L.C.
Grand Rapids, MI

CARL S. YALLER
Glass, Molders, Pottery, Plastics & Allied Workers
Media, PA

Chapter 19

Chairs

CHARLES S. MISHKIND
Miller, Canfield, Paddock and Stone, P.L.C.
Grand Rapids, MI

S. MARK WANN
MARCIE FYKE
Maxey, Wann, Begley & Fyke, PLLC
Jackson, MS

ERIC L. SIEGEL
The Siegel Law Firm
Washington, DC

Contributors

SALLY M. BARKER
Schuchat, Cook & Werner
St. Louis, MO

MARTIN BROOK
BRUCE OLSON
ROBBI SACKVILLE
MICHELLE SMITH
Miller, Canfield, Paddock and Stone, P.L.C.
Grand Rapids, MI

GUY ZUZOVSKY
The Siegel Law Firm
Washington, DC

Chapter 20

Chairs

RICHARD K. WALKER
Streich Lang
Phoenix, AZ

VANESSA M. CLEM
Vinson & Elkins L.L.P.
Houston, TX

DAVID B. KILLALEA
Dickstein Shapiro Morin
 & Oshinsky LLP
Washington, DC

Contributors

THOMAS D. ARN
STEVEN G. BIDDLE
SUZANNE E. BRODERICK
MARY JO FOSTER
ROBERT K. JONES
ROBERT W. HEGLIN
PETER C. PRYNKIEWICZ
Streich Lang
Phoenix, AZ

PAULA BRUNER
JENNIFER GOLDSTEIN
PAUL RAMSHAW
SUSAN STARR
JOHN SUHRE
NANCY WEEKS
EEOC
Washington, DC

ELIZABETH MATTHEWS
Dickstein Shapiro Morin
 & Oshinsky, LLP
Washington, DC

PHYLLIS M. POLLARD
JULIE SPRINGER
Scott, Douglass, Luton
 and McConico, L.L.P.
Austin, TX

Chapter 21

Chairs

LEONARD COURT
Crowe & Dunlevy
Oklahoma City, OK

DON D. SESSIONS
Don D. Sessions, APLC
Mission Viejo, CA

Chapters 22 and 25

Chairs

MAURICE WEXLER
Baker, Donelson, Bearman
   & Caldwell
Memphis, TN

NICHOLAS R. FEMIA
O'Donoghue & O'Donoghue
Washington, DC

Contributors

DAVID L. BEARMAN
STEPHEN D. GOODWIN
Baker, Donelson, Bearman
   & Caldwell
Memphis, TN

CLIFFORD FREED
Frank and Rosen
Seattle, WA

ROBIN T. SARRAZIN
Federal Express Corp.
Memphis, TN

Chapter 23

Chair

MICHAEL G. MCCLORY
Bullard, Korshoj, Smith & Jernstedt
Portland, OR

Contributors

GREGORY R. CROCHET
Kutak Rock
Atlanta, GA

DOUGLAS M. LARSEN
Baker, Manock & Jensen
Fresno, CA

MICHELLE E. LENTZNER
Portland, OR

NANETTE L. WESLEY
Wyatt, Tarrant & Combs
Memphis, TN

Chapter 24

Chairs

J. ALFRED SOUTHERLAND
Ogletree, Deakins, Nash, Smoak & Stewart, P.C.
Houston, TX

PROF. MARK L. ADAMS
Valparaiso University School of Law
Valparaiso, IN

CHRISTOPHER V. BACON
Vinson & Elkins L.L.P.
Houston, TX

Contributors

MERRITT B. CHASTAIN III
SHAWN K. JACKSON
KATE MCCORMICK
MICHAEL D. MITCHELL
MATTHEW R. PEARSON
ANTHONY G. STERGIO
Ogletree, Deakins, Nash, Smoak & Stewart, PC
Houston, TX

Chapter 26

Chair

JAMES A. ODLUM
Mundell, Odlum, Haws & Reider, LLP
San Bernadino, CA

Contributors

LISA GARCIA
Mundell, Odlum, Haws
 & Reider, LLP
San Bernadino, CA

RICHARD J. SWANSON
Macey, Macey and Swanson
Indianapolis, IN

Chapter 27

Chair

LAURA ALLEN
Hughes, Hubbard & Reed LLP
New York, NY

Chapter 28

Chairs

STUART B. JOHNSTON, JR.
JULIE I. UNGERMAN
Vinson & Elkins L.L.P.
Dallas, TX

Chapter 29

Chairs

FRED WILLIAM ALVAREZ
Wilson Sonsini Goodrich
  & Rosati
Palo Alto, CA

CHRISTOPHER V. BACON
Vinson & Elkins L.L.P.
Houston, TX

Contributors

SUE BRENNEMEN
Indianapolis, IN

KRISTEN GARCIA DUMONT
Pillsbury Madison & Sutro LLP
Palo Alto, CA

EMILY J. GOULD
Heller, Ehrman, White & McAuliffe
San Francisco, CA

ALICE K. HAYASHI
CHRISTOPHER D. WATKINS
Pillsbury Madison & Sutro LLP
San Francisco, CA

ANN E. POLUS
Cooley Godward, LLP
San Francisco, CA

RICHARD J. SWANSON
Macey, Macey and Swanson
Indianapolis, IN

ELIZABETH C. WATSON
Gibson, Dunn & Crutcher LLP
Los Angeles, CA

Chapter 30

Chairs

DONALD R. LIVINGSTON
Akin, Gump, Strauss,
  Hauer & Feld, LLP
Washington, DC

DEBRA A. MILLENSON
United States Department
  of Labor, Office of Solicitor
Washington, DC

Ch. 30 *(cont'd)*

Contributors

ROBERT M. DOHRMANN
Schwartz, Steinsapir, Dohrmann
 and Sommers
Los Angeles, CA

JAMES J. MURPHY
Akin, Gump, Strauss, Hauer
 & Feld, L.L.P.
Washington, DC

Chapter 31

Chairs

HOPE B. EASTMAN
DAVID M. ROTHENSTEIN
Paley, Rothman, Goldstein, Rosenberg & Cooper
Bethesda, MD

Contributor

RICHARD L. DAVIS

Chapter 32

Chairs

ROBERT L. IVEY
Vinson & Elkins L.L.P.
Houston, TX

GERARD JOHN DEWOLF
New York State United Teachers
Albany, NY

JOHN D. GIANSELLO
Orrick, Herrington & Sutcliff
New York, NY

LOUIS GRAZIANO
EEOC
New York, NY

Chapter 33

Chair

FRED WILLIAM ALVAREZ
Wilson Sonsini Goodrich & Rosati
Palo Alto, CA

Contributors

KRISTEN GARCIA DUMONT
Pillsbury Madison & Sutro LLP
Palo Alto, CA

ANN E. POLUS
Cooley Godward, LLP
San Francisco, CA

EMILY J. GOULD
Heller, Ehrman, White
 & McAuliffe
San Francisco, CA

ELIZABETH C. WATSON
Gibson, Dunn & Crutcher LLP
Los Angeles, CA

ALICE K. HAYASHI
CHRISTOPHER D. WATKINS
Pillsbury Madison & Sutro LLP
San Francisco, CA

Chapter 34

Chair

PROF. CHARLES A. SHANOR
Emory University
Atlanta, GA

Chapter 36

Chairs

KATHLEEN KINNEY
Malibu, CA

MARGARET LEE HERBERT
EEOC
Chicago, IL

Contributors

DONALD J. HORTON
Andrews & Kurth
Houston, TX

MARK J. O'BERTI

Chapter 37

Chairs

Thomas L. Pfister
Latham & Watkins
Los Angeles, CA

Joseph M. Sellers
Cohen, Milstein, Hausseld
 & Toll
Washington, DC

Joe R. Whatley, Jr.
Cooper, Mitch, Crawford, Kuykendall & Whatley, L.L.C.
Birmingham, AL

Contributors

Lisa R. Dewey
Mary E. Gately
Margaret E. Johnson
Edward J. Reed
Amy Schaner Stanley
Christine E. Webber
Kimberly E. Wolod
Washington, DC

Daniel L. Martens
Latham & Watkins
Los Angeles, CA

Chapter 38

Chairs

Philip J. Pfeiffer
Fulbright & Jaworski L.L.P.
San Antonio, TX

Linda Dardarian
Saperstein, Goldstein, Demchak
 & Baller
Oakland, CA

Contributors

Julia Turner Baumhart
Dickenson, Wright, Moon,
 Van Dusen & Freeman
Bloomfield Hills, MI

John C. Burgin, Jr.
Kramer, Rayson, Leake, Rodgers
 & Morgan
Knoxville, TN

Rebecca Dean
Foster, Pepper & Sheffelman
Seattle, WA

Bruce S. Harrison
Shawe & Rosenthal
Baltimore, MD

Contributors

David M. Korn
Phelps Dunbar, L.L.P.
New Orleans, LA

Anne E. Lewis
Monroe & Lemann
New Orleans, LA

Amy Liebermann
Stoll, Keenon & Park, LLP
Lexington, KY

Michael R. Lied
Husch & Eppenberger
Peoria, IL

Laura A. Lindner
Ross & Hardies
Chicago, IL

Terence H. Murphy
Flett, Lieber, Rooney
 & Schorling
Pittsburgh, PA

Victoria Phipps
Conoco, Inc.
Houston, TX

David B. Ritter
Altheimer & Gray
Chicago, IL

Thomas M. Winn III
Woods, Rogers & Hazlegrove, P.L.C.
Roanoke, VA

Linda L. Yoder
Shipman & Goodwin
Hartford, CT

Chapter 39

Chair

Neal D. Mollen
Paul, Hastings, Janofsky & Walker LLP
Washington, DC

Contributors

Sarah H. Lamar
Hunter, MacLean, Exely & Dunn
Savannah, GA

Kurt E. Pletcher
Paul, Hastings, Janofsky
 & Walker LLP
Washington, DC

Richard J. Swanson
Macey, Macey and Swanson
Indianapolis, IN

Chapter 40

Chairs

LAURA ALLEN
Hughes Hubbard & Reed LLP
New York, NY

GARY T. LESTER
Houston, Texas

Contributors

ROBERT M. DOHRMANN
Schwartz, Steinsapir, Dohrmann
and Sommers
Los Angeles, CA

SHARONA HOFFMAN
Houston, TX

CATHERINE S. WEIL
Albertsons, Inc.
Fort Worth, TX

Chapter 41

Chair

MICHAEL L. WOLFRAM
Morgan, Lewis & Bockius LLP
Los Angeles, CA

Contributors

VICKI L. BEATTY
Meyer, Darragh, Buckler,
Bebenek & Eck
Pittsburgh, PA

WILLIAM K. HARVEY
Jackson, Shields, Yeiser
& Cantrell
Cordova, TN

JASON HEDICAN
CAROLYN S. NESTINGEN
Briggs and Morgan
Minneapolis, MN

MATTHEW B.E. HUGHES
Marshall & Gonzalez, L.L.P.
Houston, TX

GEORGE L. LENARD
Harris, Dowell, Fisher
& Harris, L.C.
Chesterfield, MD

BARRI NOVOM
RAUL PEREZ
ERIC M. STEINERT
Morgan, Lewis & Bockius LLP
Los Angeles, CA

TYLER M. PAETKAU
Sheppard, Mullin, Richter
  & Hampton LLP
San Francisco, CA

RICHARD J. SWANSON
Macey, Macey and Swanson
Indianapolis, IN

Chapter 42

Chair

CHARLES A. POWELL IV
Constangy, Brooks & Smith, LLC
Birmingham, AL

Contributors

JEFFREY S. DUNLAP
STEPHANIE DUCHESS TRUDEAU
Ulmer & Berne LLP
Cleveland, OH

JONATHAN C. HANCOCK
McKnight Hudson Lewis Ford
  & Harrison LLP
Memphis, TN

JEFFREY S. KOEHLINGER
Dow Elanco
Indianapolis, IN

SUSAN L. MOSES
Smith & Hilbig
Torrance, CA

PAMELA H. PLOOR
Quarles & Brady
Milwaukee, WI

JAMES G. RAMSEY
Falls, Ramsey & Veach
Nashville, TN

RICHARD J. SWANSON
Macey, Macey and Swanson
Indianapolis, IN

Chapter 43

Chair

PAMELA L. HEMMINGER
Gibson, Dunn & Crutcher LLP
Los Angeles, CA

Contributor

KATHLEEN M. VANDERZIEL
Gibson, Dunn & Crutcher LLP
Los Angeles, CA

FOREWORD

Since 1945 the ABA Section of Labor and Employment Law has had as its state purposes (1) to study and report upon continuing developments in the law affecting labor relations, (2) to assist the professional growth and development of practitioners in the field of employment and labor relations law, and (3) to promote justice, human welfare, industrial peace, and the recognition of the supremacy of law in labor-management relations.

Through the publication of books such as Employment Discrimination Law, and through annual and committee meeting programs designed to provide a forum for the exchange of ideas, the Section has built a library of comprehensive legal works intended for the use of the Section membership as well as the bar generally.

The Section of Labor and Employment Law is pleased to provide this supplement to its classic treatise on employment discrimination law as part of its library of books published by BNA Books, a Division of The Bureau of National Affairs, Inc. The combined efforts of many individual authors from the Committee on Equal Employment Opportunity of the Section are reflected in this supplement.

The Section wishes to express its appreciation to the committee, and in particular to the editor-in-chief, W. Carl Jordan, the associate editors, Catherine Hagen and Cathy Ventrell-Monsees, and coordinator, union reviewers, Nora Macey. This group has tried to accomplish two primary objectives: (1) to be equally balanced and nonpartisan in their viewpoints, and (2) to ensure the book is of significant value to the practitioner, student, and sophisticated nonlawyer.

The views expressed herein do not necessarily represent the views of the American Bar Association, or its Section of Labor and Employment Law, or any other organization, but are simply the collective, but not necessarily the individual, views of the authors. Information on the affiliation of government employees who contributed to this work is for informational purposes and does not constitute any official endorsement of the information provided herein.

Stephen E. Tallent
Chair

Max Zimny
Chair-Elect

Section of Labor
and Employment Law
American Bar Association

September 1998

PREFACE

This supplement is the result of the collective efforts of many individuals who have made generous contributions of their time and resources to this project. Most of these persons are acknowledged in the Board of Editors listing that appears in the preceding pages. A few whose names do not appear, but who nevertheless made special and significant contributions, are credited below. While considerable effort has been made to acknowledge everyone who contributed, some omissions are inevitable. To any who contributed but have not been named, your efforts are valued and appreciated.

The protocol employed in preparing this supplement was similar to that used for the Main Edition. Co-editors were appointed from the plaintiff/public and defense bars for most chapters, and by the union bar for several of the chapters. These co-editors, with the assistance of many additional volunteers drawn mainly from the EEO Committee, conducted the research and prepared initial chapter drafts. The senior editorial team then reviewed the chapters for general accuracy and objectivity. As editor-in-chief, the ultimate accountability for what material has been included or excluded, as well as the substantive content of each chapter, is mine. It should be noted, nevertheless, that the final product reflects a consensus of the views of practitioners of diverse perspectives, rather than the individual views of any particular person.

This supplement attempts to report the more important developments in the field, beginning with the cases decided after June 1994 through at least July 1996 and, for Supreme Court decisions, through the 1997–98 term. Numerous chapters, due to the conscientious efforts of their editors to make them as current as possible, also include lower court cases subsequent to July 1996. Some chapters are brief, reflecting the relative maturity of the subject areas that they treat or simply a dearth of more recent case law that would add to the discussion contained in the Main Edition. Other chapters are lengthy (e.g., those dealing with disability and age discrimination), reflecting the wide range of issues encompassed within and the complexities of their subject matters, which we concluded warranted more extensive reporting and discussion of the decisional law.

I take this opportunity to express my gratitude to each person who contributed in any way to the writing and publication of the supplement. I am particularly indebted to the other senior editors. Catherine Hagen, at O'Melveny & Myers, and Cathy Ventrell-Monsees were my partners in this project from the beginning. We worked together at the outset to assemble the chapter editorial teams and coordinated editorial efforts through the conclusion of the project. Cathy Hagen (with assistance from Kathleen Kinney and George Turner) did the initial edit on approximately half of the chapter drafts. Cathy and her colleagues' efforts were Herculean, and this book would not have been possible without them. Cathy Ventrell-Monsees reviewed each chapter and made many editorial suggestions, most of which were incorporated verbatim. As the senior editor from the plaintiff/public bar, her insights and contributions both balanced and enriched our final product. Nora Macey oversaw the union bar's editorial review of every chapter and was personally responsible for reviewing many of the chapters. The comments and suggestions contributed by Nora and those who assisted her were extremely valuable.

Special thanks are owed to several other individuals, most of whose names do not appear on the Board of Editors. I am fortunate to have a colleague like Christopher Bacon, whose enthusiasm for this project never waned notwithstanding the many weekends he devoted to supplementing and doing initial edits on numerous chapter drafts. Diane Goode and Tara Henke, legal assistants in our offices, devoted untold hours to formatting, checking, and updating citations. Carole Horton-Howe, a paralegal at O'Melveny & Myers, provided similar assistance to Cathy Hagen. My long-time secretary and administrative assistant, Sylvia Hall, did her usual outstanding job of coordinating communications and providing administrative support. Bonnie Blackburn, a document specialist, was responsible for final formatting and word processing for each chapter. I am also very appreciative of the encouragement and support that my law firm, Vinson & Elkins, has given to this project.

Tim Darby and Anne Scott at BNA were unfaltering in their encouragement and support of our efforts. They provided helpful guidance and suggestions throughout the project.

I would be neglectful by not thanking the past and current leadership of the Labor and Employment Law Section of the American Bar Association, and its Equal Employment Opportunity Committee, for the opportunity to participate in this work. Too often the rigors of representing our respective client constituencies deflect our attention from the noble purposes and hopes embodied within those laws that our practices encompass. Participation in an endeavor such as this requires us to reflect upon our chosen field of practice from a different perspective than what we routinely see as advocates. In doing so, it elevates both our thought processes and spirits. This, of course, is entirely consistent with the mission of the EEO Committee.

My final thanks go to Lisa, whose patience, understanding and encouragement have always been without limit. These qualities notwithstanding, I am confident that she and our children (Kimberly, Hillary, Christopher, and Nicholas) share in my happiness, and relief, upon the completion of this book.

W. CARL JORDAN

September 1998

TABLE OF CONTENTS

	Main Edition (Vol. I)	Supplement
CONTRIBUTORS	—	v
FOREWORD	—	xxvii
PREFACE	—	xxix
FOREWORD TO THE THIRD EDITION	ix	—
FOREWORD TO THE SECOND EDITION	xi	—
ACKNOWLEDGMENTS	xix	—
CHAPTER 1. AN OVERVIEW	1	1

FIRST CATEGORY OF DISCRIMINATION—DISPARATE TREATMENT

	Main	Supp.
CHAPTER 2. DISPARATE TREATMENT	9	5
I. The Theory	9	5
II. Proof of Disparate Treatment in the Individual Case	10	5
A. The *McDonnell Douglas-Burdine-Hicks* Analysis: Proof of Disparate Treatment Through Circumstantial Evidence	11	5
1. The Prima Facie Case	13	6
2. The Employer's Burden of Producing Evidence	17	8
3. Plaintiff's Proof of Pretext	22	10
a. Direct Evidence	28	13
b. Comparative Evidence	30	14
c. Statistics	34	14
d. Other Evidence	35	15
4. The Order of Proof	37	—
5. Instructing the Jury	38	16
B. Proof of Disparate Treatment Through Direct Evidence	39	—

	Main Edition	Supplement
C. Proof of Disparate Treatment in Mixed-Motive Cases	40	17
III. Disparate Treatment Class Actions and Pattern-or-Practice Cases	44	—

SECOND CATEGORY OF DISCRIMINATION—PRESENT EFFECTS OF PAST DISCRIMINATION

	Main Edition	Supplement
CHAPTER 3. SENIORITY	51	23
I. Statutory Authority	51	—
II. Seniority and Transfer Rights	51	23
A. An Historical Perspective	51	—
B. The Bona Fide Seniority System Defense	54	23
C. Challenging Seniority Systems After *Teamsters*	57	—
1. What Constitutes a "Seniority System"	57	—
2. Bona Fides or Lack Thereof	60	—
a. The Standards for Evaluating Seniority Systems	60	—
b. Application of the Four-Factor Test	62	—
D. Timeliness of Challenges to Seniority Systems	66	—
III. Seniority and the Remedial Power of Courts	66	—
A. Constructive Seniority as a Remedy for Identifiable Victims of Discrimination	67	—
B. Remedies for Unlawful Restrictions on Transfer and Promotion	69	—
C. Seniority and Affirmative Action	72	—

THIRD CATEGORY OF DISCRIMINATION—ADVERSE IMPACT

	Main Edition	Supplement
CHAPTER 4. ADVERSE IMPACT	81	27
I. Overview	81	27
II. Historical Development and Statutory Authority	83	27

			Main Edition	Supplement
	A.	The Plaintiff's Prima Facie Case	88	27
		1. The Threshold Showing of Adverse Impact Required	89	29
		2. The Appropriate Method of Comparison	95	30
		a. The Relevant Labor Market	95	30
		b. Selection Rates or Rejection Rates?	97	—
		c. "Bottom-Line" Statistics	99	30
		3. Responses to the Plaintiff's Statistical Evidence	103	32
	B.	Business Necessity and Job Relatedness	106	32
	C.	Demonstration of Alternative Selection Devices Having Less Adverse Impact	111	—
III.	Remedies		113	34
Chapter 5.	**Scored Tests**		**115**	**37**
I.	Introduction		115	37
II.	Overview of Coverage and Relevant Statutory Provisions		120	37
	A.	Title VII	120	37
		1. Section 703(h)	120	—
		2. Demographic Norming	121	—
		3. State Licensing Examinations	122	37
	B.	The ADA	123	—
III.	The Uniform Guidelines on Employee Selection Procedures		124	39
	A.	History of the Uniform Guidelines	124	—
	B.	Basic Features of the Uniform Guidelines	126	39
	C.	The Weight to Be Accorded Administrative Guidelines on Employer Testing	129	40
IV.	Allocation of Proof in Testing Cases		133	41
V.	Validation of Tests With Adverse Impact: Defendant's Proof of Job Relatedness		135	42
	A.	Standard of Proof of Job Relatedness	135	42
	B.	Choice of Validation Strategy	137	44
		1. Criterion-Related Validation	140	44
		a. The Appropriate Criteria	140	44

	Main Edition	Supplement
b. Selection of the Criterion Measure	143	—
c. The Necessary Correlation	144	44
2. Content Validation	147	44
3. Construct Validation	153	47
C. Differential, Single-Group, and Situational Validity	153	—
D. Validity Problems in the Application of Scored Tests	158	47
1. Rank-Ordering	159	47
2. Cutoff Scores	161	49
VI. Remedies	163	50
VII. Practical Litigation Issues and Considerations	165	51
A. The Industrial Psychologist as a "Privileged" Trial Preparation Expert	165	—
B. The Industrial Psychologist as an Expert Witness	166	51
1. Selection of the Expert	166	51
a. Plaintiffs	166	—
b. Defendants	166	—
c. Both	167	—
2. Pretrial Use of the Expert	167	—
3. Trial Role of the Expert	168	—
a. Direct Examination of an Expert	168	—
b. Cross-Examination of the Expert	169	—
4. Role of the Expert After Trial	169	—
C. Use of Test Questions	169	—
D. The Job Analysis	171	—
CHAPTER 6. NONSCORED OBJECTIVE CRITERIA	173	53
I. General Analytical Considerations	173	—
II. Specific Educational, Experience, Performance, and Licensure Requirements	175	—
A. Educational Requirements	175	—
B. Experience Requirements	178	—
C. Performance and Licensure Requirements	183	—
III. Arrest and Conviction Records	185	—
A. Arrest Records	185	—
B. Convictions	187	—

	Main Edition	Supplement
C. Less-Than-Honorable Discharges	190	—
IV. Garnishments and Other Financial Criteria	191	—
V. Miscellaneous Criteria	193	—
A. Reference Checks	193	—
B. Drug Use	194	—
C. Residency Requirements	195	—
CHAPTER 7. SUBJECTIVE CRITERIA	197	55
I. Overview	197	55
II. Types of Jobs for Which Selection Is Being Considered	202	—
A. Blue-Collar Jobs	203	—
B. White-Collar Jobs	203	—
III. Factors to Consider in Structuring, Attacking, or Defending Subjective Criteria	209	55
A. Whether the Decisionmaker Has Considered a Carefully Prepared Job Analysis	210	56
B. Whether Raters Operate Under Specific Safeguards and Guidelines	211	56
C. Whether the Employer Uses Criteria Based Upon Observable Behaviors or Performances, Rather Than Personal Traits or Vague or Attitudinal Terms	213	57
D. Whether the Evaluator Is a Member of the Protected Group	214	57
E. Whether the Employer Uses Objective Factors in Conjunction With Subjective Decisionmaking	214	57
F. Whether the Employer Provides Notice of Job Opportunities	215	58

FOURTH CATEGORY OF DISCRIMINATION—REASONABLE ACCOMMODATION

	Main Edition	Supplement
CHAPTER 8. RELIGION	219	61
I. What Is Protected as Religion	219	61

	Main Edition	Supplement
II. The Employer's Duty to Accommodate	224	62
A. The Source of and Rationale for the Duty	224	—
B. The Constitutionality of the Duty	225	—
C. The Extent of the Duty to Accommodate	226	62
1. The Elements of Proof	226	62
2. The Scope of the Duty to Accommodate	227	62
a. Framework for Analysis	227	62
b. The Extent of Accommodation Required	231	64
3. Specific Accommodations	234	66
a. Work Scheduling	234	66
b. Employment Testing and Preemployment Inquiries	240	67
c. Union Membership	241	67
d. Personal Appearance	243	67
e. Other Common Employer Accommodation Issues	244	68
III. Disparate Treatment	246	69
IV. Harassment	247	69
V. Permissible Religious Discrimination—Special Exemptions	248	70
A. Educational and Religious Institutions Under § 702	248	70
B. Educational Institutions Under § 703(e)(2)	252	71
C. Religion as a Bona Fide Occupational Qualification	253	—
VI. Recent Legislation	255	71
CHAPTER 9. DISABILITY	257	73
I. Overview of Disability Law	257	73
II. Coverage of the Major Statutes	259	74
A. ADA	259	—
1. Structure of the ADA	259	—
2. Title I—Employment	261	—
B. The Rehabilitation Act	262	74
1. Federal Government Employers—§ 501	263	74

			Main Edition	Supplement
	2.	Federal Contractors—§ 503	264	75
	3.	Recipients of Federal Financial Assistance and Federal Agencies—§ 504	264	75
C.	State and Local Laws		266	77
D.	The Veterans' Readjustment Assistance Act		268	77
E.	Protection Under the Constitution		269	78
	1.	Disability as a Suspect or Quasi-Suspect Class	269	78
	2.	Due Process Protection	269	79
III. The Major Substantive Protections Offered by the ADA and the Rehabilitation Act			271	79
A.	"Individuals With Disabilities"		273	79
	1.	Is the Condition an "Impairment"?	274	79
	2.	Does the Impairment "Substantially Limit" a Major Life Activity?	276	82
	3.	What Qualifies as a "Major Life Activity"?	278	84
	4.	Explicitly Excluded Conditions	280	—
B.	"Qualified" Individuals With Disabilities and "Essential Job Functions"		281	84
	1.	An Individualized Inquiry	283	84
	2.	Delineating a Job's Essential Functions	285	85
		a. Are Employees Actually Required to Perform the Function at Issue?	285	85
		b. Would Removing That Function Fundamentally Change the Job?	285	85
		c. Proof	286	85
	3.	Special Issues	288	89
		a. Jobs With Multiple Functions	288	—
		b. Essential Functions of the Changing Job	289	—
		c. Attendance as an Essential Function	289	89
	4.	The Role of Medical Evidence	292	—
IV. Prohibited Conduct			293	90
A.	Discrimination		293	90

		Main Edition	Supplement
1.	Limiting, Segregating, or Classifying Candidates	293	90
2.	Utilizing Discriminatory Tests, Standards, or Selection Criteria	294	91
3.	Improperly Conducting Medical Examinations or Inquiries	295	92
	a. Preemployment Medical Examinations and Inquiries	295	92
	b. Entrance Medical Examinations	296	93
	c. Medical Examinations and Inquiries for Existing Employees	296	94
	d. Physical Agility Tests and Job Demonstrations	297	—
4.	Discriminatory Contractual Arrangements	297	94
5.	Discriminatory Benefit Plans	298	95
B. Failure to Make Reasonable Accommodation		300	99
1.	General Guidelines	300	99
2.	Examples of Reasonable Accommodations	302	100
	a. Readily Accessible Facilities	302	100
	b. Job Restructuring	302	100
	c. Reassignment	305	104
	d. Employment Tests	307	110
	e. Policies and Training Materials	308	111
	f. Readers, Interpreters, and Other Helpers or Aids	308	114
	g. Allowing the Individual to Provide His or Her Own Accommodation	309	—
3.	What Accommodations Are Not "Reasonable"?	310	115
4.	Significance of Collective Bargaining and Other Agreements	311	120
5.	The Process of Determining Reasonable Accommodation	313	121
V. Defenses		316	127
A. Job Relatedness and Business Necessity		316	127
B. Undue Hardship		317	129

	Main Edition	Supplement
C. Direct Threat to Health or Safety	320	132
D. Special Issues	323	135
1. Contagious Diseases and AIDS	323	135
2. Drug or Alcohol Impairment	326	136
VI. Proof	330	139
VII. Enforcement Issues	334	142
A. ADA	334	142
1. Agency Proceedings	334	142
2. Private Suits	335	143
3. Alternative Dispute Resolution	335	144
4. Attorney's Fees	335	144
B. Rehabilitation Act	336	145
1. Federal Government Employers—§ 501	336	145
2. Federal Contractors—§ 503	337	146
3. Recipients of Federal Financial Assistance and Federal Agencies—§ 504	337	146
a. Agency Enforcement	338	—
b. Private Enforcement	337	146
C. State and Local Laws	339	—
Appendix	—	147

SPECIFIC BASES FOR DISCRIMINATION

	Main Edition	Supplement
CHAPTER 10. RACE AND COLOR	343	155
I. Discrimination Based on Race-Linked Characteristics	343	155
II. Discrimination Based on Grooming and Cultural Identification	345	—
III. Association Discrimination	345	—
IV. Segregated Employment and Employment Facilities	346	—
V. Racial Harassment	347	155
VI. "Race Plus"	350	156
VII. Defenses to Race and Color Discrimination	350	156

	Main Edition	Supplement
CHAPTER 11. NATIONAL ORIGIN AND CITIZENSHIP	351	157
I. Introduction	351	157
II. Sources of Protection	355	158
A. Title VII	355	158
1. Defining "National Origin"	355	158
2. National Origin Versus Citizenship	358	158
a. Title VII's Coverage of Noncitizens	358	—
b. Title VII's Lack of Protection Against Citizenship Discrimination	359	158
3. Extraterritorial Application of Title VII to U.S. Employers and Employees	361	—
B. The Fourteenth Amendment and the 1871 Civil Rights Act	362	159
C. The 1866 Civil Rights Act	365	159
D. The Immigration Reform and Control Act of 1986 (IRCA)	367	159
1. IRCA's Antidiscrimination Provisions	367	—
2. Administrative Enforcement of, and Exhaustion for, Charges of Discrimination Brought Under IRCA	370	159
III. Language and Accent	372	160
A. Fluency Requirements	372	160
B. English-Only Rules	374	160
C. Accents	378	163
IV. Height and Weight Standards	380	—
V. Foreign Education and Training	381	—
VI. Exceptions	381	163
A. Security Clearance	381	—
B. Bona Fide Occupational Qualification	382	163
C. Treaty Obligations	383	163
CHAPTER 12. NATIVE AMERICANS	387	165
I. Antidiscrimination Protection of Native Americans	387	—
II. Preferential Treatment of Native Americans	387	—
A. Section 703(i) Exemption	387	—

	Main Edition	Supplement
B. Other Statutory Preferences	389	—
III. Liability of Indian Tribes	391	165
A. Section 701(b) Exemption	391	165
B. Exemption From Other Antidiscrimination Statutes	391	166
CHAPTER 13. SEX	393	167
I. Bona Fide Occupational Qualification (BFOQ)	393	167
A. Statutory Authority and EEOC Guidelines	393	—
B. Required Elements of the BFOQ Defense	396	167
1. Direct Relationship Between Sex and Ability to Perform the Job	397	167
2. Essence of the Business	399	—
3. No Reasonable Alternative	402	167
C. The Theories of BFOQ	404	168
1. Safety	404	—
2. Privacy	405	168
3. Customer Preference	408	—
4. Role Models	409	169
D. State Protective Laws	410	—
1. The History of State Protective Laws	410	—
2. Constitutional and Statutory Authority and EEOC Guidelines	411	—
3. "Beneficial" State Protective Legislation	414	—
II. Seniority Systems and Lines of Progression	416	169
A. The Intentional Discrimination Requirement	416	169
B. What Constitutes a "Seniority System"?	418	169
C. When Did the Alleged Discrimination Occur?	419	—
III. Sex Discrimination in Executive and Professional Employment	420	170
A. The Glass Ceiling	421	170
B. Sex Stereotyping	422	—
C. Second-Guessing the Employer	423	171
IV. Fringe Benefits	425	172

		Main Edition	Supplement
A.	Statutory Authority and EEOC Guidelines	425	—
B.	Retirement Plans	427	172
	1. Contributions and Benefits	427	172
	2. Retirement Eligibility Age	433	—
C.	Death Benefit Plans	434	—
D.	Insurance, Medical, and Disability Plans	434	172
V. Pregnancy, Childbirth, and Parenting		437	173
A.	General Theory	437	173
	1. The *Gilbert* and *Satty* Decisions	438	—
	2. The Pregnancy Discrimination Act	440	173
B.	Mandatory Maternity Leaves	444	—
C.	Right to Voluntary Leave	445	174
	1. Title VII	445	174
	a. Pregnancy and Childbirth-Related Disability Leave	445	—
	b. Parenting Leave	448	174
	c. Reinstatement After Leave	448	174
	2. The Family and Medical Leave Act	450	—
D.	Benefits	451	—
	1. State Disability Insurance	451	—
	2. State Unemployment Compensation	452	—
	3. Employer Health and Disability Benefits	453	—
E.	The Fertile or Pregnant Employee in a Hazardous Work Area	454	—
VI. Sex Plus		456	174
A.	Overview	456	—
B.	Sex Plus Marriage and Family	458	174
C.	Sex Plus Race	461	175
D.	Sex Plus Appearance and Grooming Standards	462	176
VII. Transsexuality		466	177
VIII. Height, Weight, and Physical Agility Requirements		468	177

CHAPTER 14. SEXUAL ORIENTATION 475   179

I.	Title VII	475	179
II.	State Statutes and Initiatives	478	179

	Main Edition	Supplement
III. Constitutional Issues and Federal Statutes Applicable to Public Employment	480	180
A. Civil Service Reform Act of 1978	480	—
B. Due Process and Equal Protection	481	180
C. First Amendment	483	181
IV. Special Issues Regarding Service in the Armed Forces	484	181

CHAPTER 15. EQUAL PAY

	Main Edition	Supplement
CHAPTER 15. EQUAL PAY	489	185
I. Overview	489	—
II. The Equal Pay Act's Coverage	491	185
A. The Parties	491	185
B. FLSA Exemptions	493	—
III. The Relevant Comparison	494	186
A. "Wages"	494	186
B. "Employees of the Opposite Sex"	494	—
C. "Within Any Establishment"	495	186
D. "Equal Work"	496	—
IV. Determining the Equality of Jobs	497	187
A. The Applicable Standard	497	187
B. Equal Skill, Effort, and Responsibility	502	187
C. Performed Under Similar Working Conditions	509	—
V. Statutory Defenses	510	188
A. "Differences . . . Pursuant to . . . a Seniority System"	511	188
B. "Differences . . . Pursuant to . . . a Merit System"	512	189
C. "Differences . . . Pursuant to . . . a System Which Measures Earnings by Quantity or Quality of Production"	513	—
D. "Differences . . . Pursuant to . . . a Differential Based on Any Other Factor Other Than Sex"	513	189
1. Training Programs	515	—
2. Market Rate	516	190
3. Other	519	190
VI. Enforcement Mechanisms	523	191

	Main Edition	Supplement
A. Administrative Enforcement	523	—
B. Judicial Enforcement	524	191
1. Relief Available	524	191
2. Timeliness of Suit	529	191
3. Jury Trial	530	—
4. Collective Actions	531	—
VII. "Comparable Worth"	531	192
A. The Bennett Amendment	532	—
B. The Prima Facie Case	534	192
1. Disparate Treatment	534	—
2. Perpetuation of Past Discrimination	538	—
3. Adverse Impact	540	—
C. Recommendations to Employers on Minimizing Compensation Discrimination Exposure	542	—
D. Recommendations to Plaintiffs on Bringing Comparable Worth-Type Cases	543	—
CHAPTER 16. AGE	**545**	**193**
I. Jurisdiction	545	193
A. Protected Individuals	545	193
1. Generally	545	193
2. Exemptions for Certain Military Personnel and Executives	546	194
3. Exclusion of Independent Contractors and Partners in a Bona Fide Partnership	547	194
B. Covered Employers	549	195
1. Private Employers	549	195
2. The Federal Government	552	198
3. State and Local Governments	553	198
4. Labor Organizations and Employment Agencies	555	200
5. Apprenticeship Programs	556	—
II. Prohibited Practices	556	200
III. Procedure	559	201
A. Background	559	—

	Main Edition	Supplement
B. Filing With the EEOC	559	201
1. The Charge	560	201
2. 180/300-Day Time Limit	562	202
3. Determining When Discrimination Has Occurred	563	202
4. Tolling of the Limitations Period	565	204
C. Filing a Charge With the State FEP Agency	569	205
D. EEOC Conciliation	571	206
E. Bringing Suit Under the ADEA	573	206
1. Right of Private Action	573	206
2. Time for Filing Suit	575	207
3. Scope of Suit	576	208
F. Representative Actions	577	209
1. Standards for Determining Representativeness	579	209
2. Notice to Potential Opt-In Plaintiffs	580	209
3. The Original EEOC Charge May Be Sufficient for Opt Ins	581	210
4. ADEA Trial Structure for Representative Actions	582	211
5. Federal Employees Must Follow Rule 23 Procedures	582	—
G. Jury Trial	583	211
IV. Proof	585	212
A. Disparate Treatment	586	212
1. The Prima Facie Case	586	212
a. Plaintiff's Qualifications	587	213
b. Someone "Younger"	588	214
2. Defendant's Articulation of a Legitimate, Nondiscriminatory Reason	589	215
3. Plaintiff's Proof of Pretext	591	216
4. Cases of Mixed Motives	596	223
B. Adverse Impact	597	223
C. Reductions in Force	599	224
a. "Olive Grading"	605	—
b. "Fast Downhill"	605	—
c. Inconsistent Data	606	—
d. "Playing Doctor"	606	—

	Main Edition	Supplement
e. Age-Related Comments	606	—
f. "Least Painful"	606	—
D. Summary Judgment	607	230
1. Stray Remarks	607	230
2. Older Decisionmaker	609	234
3. Same Decisionmaker	609	234
4. "Before and After" Age Statistics	609	235
5. The Prima Facie Case in RIF Cases	610	235
6. Decisions Tied to Salary	611	237
7. Other Undisputed Reasons	612	237
V. Affirmative Defenses	612	238
A. Statutory Provisions	612	—
B. Reasonable Factors Other Than Age and Good Cause	614	238
C. Bona Fide Occupational Qualification (BFOQ)	615	—
D. Bona Fide Employee Benefit Plan	618	238
1. Early Retirement Incentives	619	238
2. Pensions	623	239
3. Severance Benefits	624	240
4. Disability Benefits	625	240
5. Health Insurance	626	—
E. Bona Fide Seniority System	626	240
F. Settlement and Release	626	241
G. Good Faith Reliance on Administrative Actions	630	—
VI. Remedies	631	242
A. Statutory Provisions	631	—
B. Equitable Relief	632	242
1. Injunctions	632	242
2. Reinstatement and Instatement	633	243
C. Back Pay	635	243
D. Front Pay	639	245
E. Liquidated Damages	642	246
F. Compensatory Damages	644	—
G. Punitive Damages	645	247
H. Attorney's Fees	645	248
I. Prejudgment Interest	646	248
J. Taxation of ADEA Damages Awards	647	—

	Main Edition	Supplement
CHAPTER 17. RETALIATION	649	251
I. An Overview of the Two Clauses of § 704(a)	649	251
II. The Participation Clause	651	252
III. The Opposition Clause	655	253
A. The Requirement That the Employment Practice Opposed Be "Made An Unlawful Employment Practice by [Title VII]"	655	253
B. Whether Ambiguous Protests Constitute Protected Opposition	658	254
C. Weighing the Disruption and Protection of Various Forms of Opposition	660	254
1. Picketing and Demonstrations Outside the Workplace	661	—
2. Serious, Public Opposition to the Employer's Goals	662	—
3. Work on the Employee's Complaint Rather Than Assigned Tasks	663	—
4. Intra-Office Disruption	663	254
D. The Special Role of Management and EEO Officers	665	255
IV. Type of Adverse Treatment Cognizable Under § 704(a)	668	255
V. Proof	672	258
A. "False Motives" ("Pretext") Cases	673	258
B. "Mixed Motive" Cases	677	260
VI. Special Issues Pertaining to Relief in Retaliation Cases	679	261
A. Reinstatement	679	261
B. Preliminary Injunctive Relief Available to the EEOC in § 704(a) Cases Pending Completion of the Administrative Process—§ 706(f)(2)	680	—
VII. Alternative Causes of Action	681	261
A. Private Employers	682	261
1. The Civil Rights Act of 1866— 42 U.S.C. § 1981	682	261
2. The Civil Rights Act of 1871— 42 U.S.C. §§ 1983, 1985(3), and 1986	683	—

	Main Edition	Supplement
3. National Labor Relations Act—29 U.S.C. §§ 157 and 158(a)(1)	684	262
4. Other Federal Avenues	685	—
5. Common Law Duties—State Law	686	—
B. State and Local Government Employers	687	262
1. Section 1983	687	262
2. First Amendment Right of Free Speech	688	262
3. First Amendment Rights to Petition for Redress of Grievances and Assembly	691	266
C. Federal Employees	692	—
1. Covered by Title VII	692	—
2. Not Covered by Title VII	693	—

SPECIFIC EMPLOYMENT ISSUES

	Main Edition	Supplement
CHAPTER 18. HIRING	697	269
I. General Considerations	697	—
II. Creating the Applicant Pool	698	269
A. Word-of-Mouth Recruitment	699	—
B. Nepotism	703	269
C. Recruitment Sources	706	270
D. Walk-In Applications	707	270
E. Job Opportunity Advertising	708	—
F. Chilling	710	270
III. Selecting From the Applicant Pool	713	270
A. Selection Criteria	713	270
B. Proof of Hiring Discrimination	714	271
C. Preemployment Inquiries	715	272
D. Issues of Standing	717	273
IV. Initial Job Assignments	718	273
CHAPTER 19. PROMOTION	721	275
I. Publicizing the Opening	721	275
II. Plaintiff's Qualifications	725	277

	Main Edition	Supplement
III. Experience Requirements and Seniority	732	281
IV. Subjective Criteria	733	282
V. Statistical Proof: The Qualified Potential Applicant Pool	736	283
VI. Remedies	741	284

Chapter 20. Sexual and Other Forms of Harassment

	Main Edition	Supplement
Chapter 20. Sexual and Other Forms of Harassment	745	285
I. An Overview and Historical Perspective	745	—
II. Harassment on Bases Other Than Sex	749	285
A. Introduction	749	285
B. Race, Color, and National Origin	750	285
C. Religion	755	285
1. Activity	755	—
2. Membership	755	285
D. Age	757	286
E. Disability	758	287
III. Quid Pro Quo Harassment	759	287
A. The Framework for Analyzing Quid Pro Quo Claims	759	—
B. The Prima Facie Case	759	287
1. The Basis: Membership in a Protected Class	761	—
2. The Activity: Unwelcome Sexual Advances	761	—
a. The Advance Must Be "Sexual"	761	—
b. The Advance Must Be "Unwelcome"	763	—
3. The Issue: The Adverse Employment Action	768	287
4. The Causal Connection	771	289
a. On the Basis of Sex	771	289
b. The Link Between Harassment and the Adverse Employment Action	773	291
5. Employer Responsibility	775	292
C. The Employer's Rebuttal	777	293
1. Disputing Elements of the Prima Facie Case	777	—

	Main Edition	Supplement
2. Articulating a Legitimate Nondiscriminatory Reason	778	293
D. The Complainant's Proof of Pretext	779	293
IV. Hostile Environment Harassment	780	294
A. An Overview of Environmental Harassment Claims	780	—
B. The Prima Facie Case	783	294
1. The Basis: Membership in a Protected Group	784	294
2. The Activity: Unwelcome Conduct	785	295
3. The Issue: Affecting a Term or Condition of Employment	793	296
a. The Effect on Conditions of Employment Must Be "Severe or Pervasive"	793	296
b. The Standard and Perspective for Evaluating the Conduct	800	297
4. The Causal Connection: On the Basis of Sex	808	300
5. Employer Responsibility	811	301
a. Employer Liability for Hostile Environment Harassment by Supervisors	812	301
b. Employer Liability for Hostile Environment Harassment by Co-Workers	822	304
c. Employer Liability for Hostile Environment Harassment by Nonemployees	825	305
C. The Employer's Rebuttal	827	—
1. Disputing Elements of the Prima Facie Case	827	—
2. Rebutting Employer Responsibility	828	—
D. The "Harassment Defense" to Performance Deficiencies	829	—
V. Claims by Third Parties and "Reverse" Claims by the Harasser	830	306
A. Overview of Third-Party Claims	830	—
B. Third-Party Claims Based on Implicit Quid Pro Quo Harassment	831	306

	Main Edition	Supplement
C. Third-Party Hostile Environment Claims	834	307
1. Third-Party Hostile Environment Claims Based on Nonconsensual Conduct	834	—
2. Third-Party Hostile Environment Claims Based on Underlying Consensual Conduct	835	307
D. "Reverse" Harassment Claims	836	307
CHAPTER 21. DISCHARGE	837	309
I. Introduction	837	—
II. Constructive Discharge	838	309
III. Disparate Treatment Discharge Cases	846	318
A. The Allocation of Proof	846	318
B. The Plaintiff's Prima Facie Case	847	318
C. The Employer's Legitimate Nondiscriminatory Reason and the Plaintiff's Burden to Show Pretext for Discrimination	853	—
IV. Adverse Impact Discharge Cases	857	—
V. Techniques for Litigating Discharge Cases	860	—
A. Suggestions to Plaintiffs	860	—
B. Suggestions to Defendants	861	—

UNION AND EMPLOYMENT AGENCY RESPONDENTS

	Main Edition	Supplement
CHAPTER 22. UNIONS	871	321
I. A Union's Liability for Its Own Discrimination	871	321
A. Liability of a Union in Its Role as Employer	871	321
B. Liability of a Union in Its Role as Union	872	322
1. Membership	872	322
2. Referrals	873	—
3. Union Office	877	323
4. Apprenticeship Programs	877	323
5. Duty of Fair Representation	878	323
a. Handling of Grievances	880	323

	Main Edition	Supplement
b. Grievance Settlements	885	324
c. Bargaining Obligations	886	—
6. Failure to Accommodate	887	325
a. Religious Beliefs and Practices	887	—
b. Disabilities	888	325
7. Liability for the Acts of Union Agents	889	326
8. Liability of Regional and International Unions	889	326
II. Joint Union-Employer Liability	892	326
A. Joint Liability for Discrimination Caused by the Provisions of a Collective Bargaining Agreement	892	326
B. Joint Liability for Acquiescing in Employer Discrimination Not Based on Provisions of a Collective Bargaining Agreement	895	—
C. A Union's Liability for Inducing Employer Discrimination	896	—
D. Employer Liability for Union Discrimination	896	—
E. Procedural Issues in Cases of Joint Liability	897	327
1. Contribution	897	327
2. Joinder of Unions as Co-Defendants in Suits Against Employers	899	327
3. Joinder of Employers as Co-Defendants in Suits Against Unions	900	—
4. Realignment of the Parties	900	—
5. Settlement	901	—
III. Other Procedural Problems Involving the Role of Unions in Employment Discrimination Cases	901	328
A. A Union as Plaintiff	901	—
B. A Union as Class Representative	902	—
C. A Union as Intervenor	904	328
D. Suits Under Executive Order 11246 Against Unions	904	—
IV. Union Challenges to Employer Actions Taken Pursuant to Conciliation Agreements and Court or Government Directives	904	—

	Main Edition	Supplement
A. Joinder or Concurrence of the Union	904	—
B. Grievance Arbitration by Unions	905	—
C. Lawsuits by Unions	906	—
CHAPTER 23. EMPLOYMENT AGENCIES	907	329
I. Overview	907	—
II. Definition of an Employment Agency	908	329
III. Unlawful Practices	912	330
A. Initial Processing of Applicants	912	330
B. Accepting Discriminatory Job Orders	913	331
C. Discriminatory Referrals	915	331
D. Agency Employee Complaints	916	332
E. EEOC Investigations of Alleged Unlawful Practices	916	332
IV. Remedies	917	—

OTHER SOURCES OF PROTECTION AND PROBLEMS OF AFFIRMATIVE ACTION

	Main Edition	Supplement
CHAPTER 24. THE CIVIL RIGHTS ACTS OF 1866 AND 1871	921	335
I. Introduction	921	—
II. Scope and Coverage of the Civil Rights Act of 1866, 42 U.S.C. § 1981	921	337
A. Statutory Authority	921	337
B. Cognizable Defendants Under § 1981	923	337
1. Private Entities	923	337
2. The Federal Government	923	338
3. State and Local Governments	924	338
C. Bases of Discrimination Prohibited by § 1981	925	339
1. Race Discrimination	925	339
2. Retaliation	926	340
3. Other Bases of Discrimination	928	341
a. National Origin and Religion	928	341
b. Alienage	929	—

	Main Edition	Supplement
c. Sex	929	341
d. Disability [New Topic]	—	341
e. Age [New Topic]	—	341
III. Scope and Coverage of Civil Rights Act of 1871, 42 U.S.C. § 1983	929	341
A. Statutory Authority	929	—
B. Cognizable Defendants Under § 1983	930	341
1. The State Action Requirement and Private Discrimination	930	341
2. The Federal Government	933	—
3. State and Local Governments	934	342
a. Local Governments	934	342
b. State Governments	938	343
4. State and Local Governmental Officials in Their Individual Capacities	943	343
C. Bases of Discrimination Prohibited by § 1983	946	344
1. Equal Protection	946	344
2. Speech	949	346
3. Due Process	951	—
IV. Scope and Coverage of Civil Rights Act of 1871, 42 U.S.C. §§ 1985 and 1986	956	346
A. Statutory Authority	956	—
B. Cognizable Defendants	958	346
1. The Applicability of § 1985 to Private Discrimination	958	346
2. The Conspiracy Requirement	961	346
3. Federal and State Governments	964	347
C. Bases of Discrimination Prohibited by §§ 1985 and 1986	965	347
V. Litigation, Proof, Procedure, and Remedies	969	348
A. Jurisdiction and Venue	969	—
B. Timeliness	970	348
C. Procedural Prerequisites	971	—
D. Proof	972	348
E. Remedies	973	349
F. Jury Trial	976	—
G. Res Judicata	976	350

		Main Edition	Supplement
Chapter 25.	National Labor Relations Act	979	351
I.	Introduction	979	—
II.	Remedies Against Unions	980	351
	A. General Statutory Obligations	980	—
	B. Denial of Access to Board Remedies	982	—
	C. Challenges to Certification	983	351
	D. Unfair Labor Practice Remedies for Breach of the Duty of Fair Representation	987	—
	E. Unions That Resist Employer Efforts to Remedy Discrimination	988	—
III.	Employer Discrimination	989	351
	A. Overview	989	—
	B. Concerted Activity Protesting Alleged Discrimination	991	351
	C. Employer's Duty to Bargain and Furnish Union With Information on Composition of Workforce	994	352
Chapter 26.	Related Causes of Action	999	355
I.	Introduction	999	—
II.	Procedural Issues in Combining Common Law and Federal Statutory Claims	999	355
	A. Supplemental Jurisdiction	999	—
	B. Preemption	1000	355
	C. Federal Court Acceptance of State Court Determinations	1003	—
	D. Exclusivity of the State Statutory Remedy	1004	—
III.	Contract and Tort Causes of Action That Limit the "Employment-at-Will" Doctrine	1004	356
	A. Contract Theory	1004	356
	1. Generally	1004	—
	2. Employment Policies/Oral Representations as the Basis for a Contract	1005	356
	3. Employment Policies/Oral Representations in Conjunction With Other Factors as the Basis for a Contract	1009	358

		Main Edition	Supplement
4. Promissory Estoppel		1011	360
5. Breach of Implied Covenant of Good Faith and Fair Dealing		1012	360
B. Tort Theories		1013	361
1. Generally		1013	—
2. Breach of Implied Covenant of Good Faith and Fair Dealing		1013	—
3. Public Policy		1014	361
IV. Other Common Law Tort Theories		1021	364
A. Intentional Infliction of Emotional Distress		1021	364
B. Defamation		1024	365
C. Misrepresentation or Fraud		1027	367
D. Interference With Contractual Relations		1029	368
E. Negligence		1031	369
F. Invasion of Privacy		1033	369
V. Applicability of Workers' Compensation Laws		1033	369
CHAPTER 27. REVERSE DISCRIMINATION AND AFFIRMATIVE ACTION		1035	371
I. Introduction		1035	371
II. Reverse Discrimination Outside the Context of Affirmative Action Programs		1037	372
A. Prohibited Bases for Discrimination		1038	372
1. Race		1038	372
2. Other Bases		1040	375
B. Proof of Reverse Discrimination		1041	377
III. Reverse Discrimination Pursuant to Affirmative Action Programs		1043	379
A. Affirmative Action Under the Equal Protection Clause		1044	379
1. Voluntary State and Local Government Plans		1044	379
a. Race-Based Plans		1044	379
b. Sex-Based Plans		1052	386
2. Congressionally Sanctioned Affirmative Action		1053	—
B. Voluntary Affirmative Action Plans Under Title VII		1058	387

	Main Edition	Supplement
1. Legality of Affirmative Action Under Title VII	1058	—
2. Requirements for a Valid Plan	1059	387
a. The Supreme Court's Evolving View—From *Weber* to *Johnson*	1059	—
b. The Necessary Factual Predicate	1064	387
c. Permissible Scope of a Voluntary Plan	1067	389
d. Consent Decrees	1071	393
3. The Effect of the Civil Rights Act of 1991	1074	394
a. *Martin v. Wilks*	1074	394
b. Burden of Proof	1074	395
c. Race-Norming	1077	396
d. Enhanced Damages	1078	396

CHAPTER 28. FEDERAL CONTRACTOR AFFIRMATIVE ACTION COMPLIANCE

	Main Edition	Supplement
CHAPTER 28. FEDERAL CONTRACTOR AFFIRMATIVE ACTION COMPLIANCE	1081	397
I. Coverage and Exemptions	1083	399
A. Contracts and Covered Subcontracts	1083	399
1. Prime Contracts	1083	399
2. Subcontracts	1085	399
3. Extension of Coverage to Related Entities	1087	—
4. Successor Liability	1088	—
B. Coverage Thresholds	1088	400
1. Basic Threshold	1089	400
2. AAP Threshold	1091	—
II. Executive Order 11246	1092	—
A. Mandates of the Order	1092	—
B. Components of the Executive Order 11246 Affirmative Action Program for Supply and Service Contractors	1093	—
1. Narrative Sections	1095	—
a. Suggested Precautions	1095	—
b. Required Narrative Sections	1100	—
2. Statistical Sections	1102	—
a. Workforce Analysis	1102	—

	Main Edition	Supplement
b. Job Group Analysis	1104	—
c. Availability Analysis	1106	—
d. Utilization Analysis	1110	—
e. Development of Goals to Correct Underutilization	1112	—
3. Good Faith Efforts	1114	—
4. Analysis of Hiring, Promotion, and Termination Practices	1115	—
C. Construction Contractors	1118	—
III. Section 503 of the Rehabilitation Act of 1973	1120	401
IV. The Vietnam Era Veterans' Readjustment Assistance Act	1120	—
V. Affirmative Action Programs for Veterans and Individuals With Disabilities	1121	402
VI. Compliance Review and Complaint Investigation Process: Desk Audit Letter Through Exit Conference	1125	403
A. Selection for Review	1126	405
1. Equal Employment Data System	1126	—
2. Pre-Award Review	1126	405
3. Discrimination Complaint	1127	406
B. Contractor Precompliance Review Preparation	1130	—
C. The Desk Audit	1140	—
1. Purpose of the Desk Audit	1140	—
2. The OFCCP's Activities Preceding the Desk Audit	1140	—
a. Initial Contact With Contractor	1140	—
b. The Scheduling Letter	1141	—
c. Contact With EEOC, State and Local FEP Agencies, and VETS	1141	—
d. Review of Previous Compliance Actions	1142	—
3. The Contractor's Response to the Scheduling Letter	1142	—
4. The OFCCP's Initial Review of the AAP and Supporting Data	1143	—
a. Currency and Completeness	1143	—

	Main Edition	Supplement
b. Review of the Executive Order AAP for Reasonableness	1143	—
c. Review of Executive Order AAP for Acceptability	1144	—
d. Review of Executive Order Support Data for Acceptability	1144	—
e. Review, for Acceptability, of AAPs for Individuals With Disabilities and Veterans	1146	—
5. Overview of Personnel Activity, EEO Trends, and Workforce Structure/Personnel Practices	1147	—
a. Summary of Personnel Activity	1147	—
b. EEO Trend Analysis	1147	—
c. Workforce Structure/Personnel Practices	1147	—
6. Preliminary Discrimination Analyses	1148	—
a. General Considerations	1148	—
b. Review of the Workforce Analysis	1148	—
c. Audits of Impact Ratio Analyses (IRAs) of Personnel Activity	1150	—
d. Compensation Analyses	1151	—
e. Summary of Potential Discrimination Problems and On-Site Investigative Plan	1152	—
7. Suggested Contractor Techniques for Preparing the Desk Audit Package	1152	—
D. The On-Site Review	1153	406
1. Scope	1153	—
2. Notice of the On-Site Review	1153	—
3. Components of the On-Site Review	1154	406
a. Entrance Conference	1154	—
b. Human Resources Meeting	1155	—
c. Facility Tour	1156	—
d. Investigation of Potential Discrimination	1156	—
e. Management Interviews	1156	—
f. Employee Interviews	1157	—

			Main Edition	Supplement
		g. Hiring/Recruiting/Compensation Manager Interview	1159	—
		h. Document Review	1159	—
		i. Predetermination Notice and Response	1161	—
		j. Exit Conference	1161	—
	4.	Additional Considerations for Managing the On-Site Review	1162	—
	5.	On-Site Investigation of Potential Discrimination	1164	—
		a. Employment Discrimination Theories	1164	—
		b. Investigation of Individual Discrimination	1164	—
		c. Investigation of Pattern-or-Practice of Discrimination	1166	—
		d. The Contractor's Response to the Predetermination Notice and Individual Discrimination Findings	1170	—
	6.	Notice of Violations, Contractor Responses, Conciliation Agreements, and Letters of Commitment	1171	407
	7.	Notices of Review Completion	1174	—
VII.	Enforcement Procedures and Sanctions for Noncompliance		1174	407
	A.	Administrative Enforcement	1175	407
	B.	Cancellation, Debarment, and Other Sanctions Following Administrative Hearing	1178	407
	C.	Judicial Enforcement	1182	—
		1. Justice Department Actions	1182	—
		2. No Private Enforcement Against Contractors	1182	—
		3. Third-Party Standing to Sue the OFCCP	1183	—
		4. Suits Against Unions	1185	—
VIII.	Disclosure of Information to Third Parties Pursuant to the Freedom of Information Act		1186	—
	A.	General Provisions	1186	—

	Main Edition	Supplement
B. OFCCP Guidelines for Disclosure	1187	—
C. Contractor Objections to Disclosure	1189	—
D. Suits to Compel and Prohibit Disclosure of Documents in Possession of the OFCCP	1190	—
IX. Validity of the Executive Order and Resulting Actions	1193	408
A. Validity of the Executive Order and Implementing Regulations	1194	—
1. Validity of Particular Regulations	1196	—
2. Validity of the Affirmative Action Requirement	1197	—
B. Validity of the Back-Pay Remedy	1201	408

PROCEDURE

	Main Edition (Vol. II)	Supplement
CHAPTER 29. EEOC ADMINISTRATIVE PROCESS	1205	411
I. Structure and Statutes Enforced	1205	—
A. Structure of the EEOC	1205	—
B. Statutes Enforced	1206	—
1. Title VII	1206	—
2. ADEA and EPA	1206	—
3. ADA	1206	—
II. General Administrative Powers	1207	—
A. Rulemaking Powers	1207	—
B. EEOC Posting Requirements	1209	—
C. Records and Reports	1209	—
1. Reports Required Under Title VII	1210	—
2. Records to Be Made or Kept	1212	—
3. Preservation of Records Made or Kept	1212	—
III. The EEOC Enforcement Process	1214	411
A. Evolution of the Current System	1214	—
B. Place for Filing Charge and Venue	1217	—
C. The Intake and Initial Investigation of a Charge	1217	411

			Main Edition	Supplement
	D.	Assignment of a Charge Number	1220	—
	E.	Deferral and Contracts With State and Local Agencies	1221	—
	F.	Service of the Charge on the Respondent	1223	—
	G.	Administrative Closures	1225	—
		1. Withdrawal	1225	—
		2. Failure to Locate/Failure to Cooperate	1226	—
		3. Other Administrative Closures	1226	—
	H.	Negotiated Settlement Prior to Determination	1226	412
	I.	Investigations and Determinations	1230	412
		1. The Assignment Process and the Respondent's Position Statement	1230	—
		2. Requests for Information (RFIs) and On-Site Reviews	1230	412
		3. Fact-Finding Conference	1232	—
		4. Adverse Inference Rule	1232	—
		5. Scope of the Investigation	1233	—
		6. Determination Counseling and the Investigative Memorandum	1233	412
		7. EEOC Letters of Determination and EEOC Decisions	1234	412
		8. Reconsideration	1236	413
	J.	The Conciliation Process	1237	—
	K.	Issuance of Notice of Right to Sue Under Title VII and the ADA	1239	—
	L.	Role of Attorneys	1240	—
		1. During the Administrative Enforcement Process	1240	—
		2. In Court	1242	—
	M.	The Systemic Program	1243	—
	N.	Interagency Coordination	1245	—
IV.	EEOC Investigation and Subpoena Powers		1247	413
	A.	Statutory Authority Under Title VII and the ADA	1247	413
		1. Title VII and the ADA	1247	413
		2. The ADEA and the EPA	1248	—
	B.	The "Valid Charge" Requirement Under Title VII and the ADA	1249	413

	Main Edition	Supplement
C. Permissible Scope of Inquiry	1251	415
V. Access to EEOC Files and Admissibility of the EEOC Determination	1257	417
A. Access to EEOC Files	1257	417
1. Statutory Framework	1257	417
a. Title VII and the ADA	1257	—
b. The Freedom of Information Act	1259	417
2. The EEOC's Procedure on Disclosure of Files	1263	—
3. What the EEOC May and Must Remove From the File Prior to Disclosure to a Party	1264	—
4. Federal Employees' Procedures	1265	418
B. Admissibility Into Evidence of EEOC Findings	1265	418
VI. Advice to Respondents on Responding to a Charge of Employment Discrimination	1267	—
A. Initial Response Upon Service of the Charge	1267	—
B. The Employer's Initial Investigation	1268	—
C. Settlement Options	1269	—
D. The Position Statement	1269	—
E. The Fact-Finding Conference	1272	—
CHAPTER 30. TITLE VII COVERAGE	1275	419
I. Overview	1275	419
II. The Substantive and Formal Elements of a Charge of Discrimination	1275	419
A. Substantive Elements	1275	—
B. Formal Requirements	1276	419
III. Charging Parties	1280	420
A. Statutory Provisions	1280	—
B. Charges Filed by Persons Who Are Members of the Protected Group in Question and Who Are Affected by an Adverse Employment Decision or Practice	1282	420
1. Is the Complainant Personally Aggrieved?	1282	420

		Main Edition	Supple- ment
	2. Is the Complainant Protected by Title VII?	1283	421
	a. Undocumented Aliens	1283	—
	b. Independent Contractors and Other Nonemployees	1284	421
	c. "Personal Staff" Exemption	1287	424
	d. Former Employees	1288	425
C.	Charges Filed by Persons Who Are Members of the Protected Group in Question But Who Are Not Affected by an Adverse Employment Decision or Practice	1289	—
D.	Charges Filed by Persons Who Are Not Members of the Protected Group in Question, But Who Still Claim to Be Aggrieved	1291	425
	1. Charges Alleging an Independent Violation	1292	425
	2. Charges "on Behalf of" a Person Aggrieved	1294	426
E.	Charges Filed by an Organization Itself Claiming to Be an Aggrieved Person	1297	426
F.	Testers	1299	427
G.	Commissioner Charges	1301	427
IV. Respondents		1304	427
A.	Employer	1304	427
	1. Definition	1304	428
	a. Who May Be Counted as "Employees"	1305	428
	b. How the Counting Is Done	1307	430
	2. Requirement of a Covered Issue	1308	—
	3. Determining Who Is the "Employer"	1309	430
	a. "Single Employer" Theory	1309	431
	b. "Joint Employer" Theory	1312	432
	c. The "Agent" Theory	1314	433
B.	Unions and Apprenticeship Programs	1317	434
C.	Employment Agencies	1320	434
V. Certain Exemptions and Exclusions		1321	434

		Main Edition	Supplement
A.	Bona Fide Private Membership Clubs	1321	434
B.	Exemption of Elected Officials, Policymaking Appointees, and Their Advisors	1324	435
C.	Aliens Employed Within and Without the United States	1328	—
D.	Extraterritorial Employment by U.S. Companies	1329	—
E.	Coverage of Foreign Employers	1329	435
	1. Foreign Employers Operating in the United States	1329	435
	2. Extraterritorial Activities of Foreign Employers	1332	436
F.	National Security Exemption	1333	—

CHAPTER 31. TIMELINESS ... 1335 437

			Main Edition	Supplement
I.	Overview		1335	—
	A.	History	1335	—
	B.	Scope	1337	—
II.	Timeliness of Filing the EEOC Charge		1337	437
	A.	The 180/300-Day Limitations Periods	1337	437
		1. EEOC Deferral Procedure	1339	—
		2. The Circumstances Under Which Prior Resort to a State or Local Agency Is Required	1340	—
		a. State Law Must Authorize an Appropriate Agency to Prosecute the Claim of Discrimination	1340	—
		b. No Need for Deferral With Respect to Every Incident	1341	—
		3. Deferral Mistakes by Charging Parties; Cure of Such Mistakes	1342	—
		4. Availability of the 300-Day Filing Period	1344	437
		5. Effect of State Action or Inaction on Title VII Rights	1346	—
		a. State Inaction	1346	—

	Main Edition	Supplement
b. State Action	1346	—
B. When Has Discrimination Occurred?	1347	437
1. Individual Acts	1347	437
2. Application of Policies	1350	438
3. Continuing Violations	1351	439
a. A Series of Acts With at Least One Act Within the Charge-Filing Period	1353	—
b. Maintenance of a System or Policy That Discriminates	1355	—
c. The Present Effects of Past Discrimination	1360	—
d. Alternative Analytical Approaches	1360	—
C. Tolling of the Charge-Filing Period	1363	441
1. A Jurisdictional Prerequisite, or a Statute of Limitations That May Be Tolled for Equitable Reasons?	1363	441
2. The Effect of Estoppel or Tolling	1364	—
3. Tolling Because of Resort to Another Forum	1364	442
4. Other Grounds for Estoppel or Tolling	1365	442
III. Timeliness of Filing Suit	1370	446
A. Statutory and Regulatory Framework	1370	—
B. Time of Issuing Notice of Right to Sue	1371	446
1. The EEOC Is Not Required to Issue Notice Within a Specified Period After the Charge Is Filed	1371	—
2. Preliminary Relief Before Receiving Right-to-Sue Notice	1372	—
3. Premature Issuance of Right-to-Sue Notices and Premature Filing of Suit	1373	446
C. Timely Court Filing	1375	446
1. Form of Right-to-Sue Notice and Multiple Notices	1375	—
2. What Triggers Commencement of the 90-Day Period	1376	446
3. What Constitutes a "Filing"	1378	447
4. Tolling	1380	449
5. Laches and Related Issues	1382	449

	Main Edition	Supplement
CHAPTER 32. ELECTION AND EXHAUSTION OF REMEDIES	1385	451
I. Introduction	1385	—
II. Election of Remedies	1385	451
A. Preclusion Issues Resulting From Prior Resort to Another Forum	1385	451
1. Preclusive Effect of Prior State Proceedings	1386	451
a. State Court Judgments and Reviewed State Administrative Decisions	1386	451
b. Unreviewed State Administrative Decisions	1394	451
2. Preclusive Effect of Prior Federal Proceedings	1395	452
3. Preclusive Effect of Prior Arbitration Decisions	1398	453
4. Preclusive Effect of Jury Findings on Nonjury Claims	1400	453
5. Preclusive Effect of Consent Decrees	1401	—
6. Preclusion Issues in Class Actions	1401	454
7. Preclusive Effect of Prior Sworn Statements [New Topic]	—	454
B. Contractual Election of Arbitration	1402	455
C. Practical Considerations in Preparing and Negotiating Arbitration Agreements	1407	457
1. FAA Coverage	1408	457
2. Consideration	1409	—
3. Persons and Entities Covered	1409	457
4. Scope of Claims Covered	1410	—
5. Discovery	1411	—
6. Punitive Damages	1412	457
7. Statute of Limitations	1413	458
8. Consultation With, and Representation by, Counsel	1413	—
9. Fraudulent Inducement Claims	1413	—
10. Adhesion-Contract Issues	1414	458
11. Manifestation of Intent to Arbitrate	1415	459
12. Appellate Review	1416	460

	Main Edition	Supplement
III. Exhaustion of Remedies	1416	460
A. Duty of Nonfederal Employees to Exhaust State Administrative Remedies or Contractual Remedies Under a Collective Bargaining Agreement	1416	460
B. Duty of Federal Employees to Exhaust State Administrative Remedies or Contractual Remedies Under a Collective Bargaining Agreement	1417	—
CHAPTER 33. LITIGATION PROCEDURE	1419	461
I. Effect of Deficiencies in EEOC Administrative Process on Charging Party's Right to Sue	1419	461
A. EEOC Errors in Charge Filing	1421	462
B. EEOC Errors in Processing Charge/Failing to Defer Charge	1422	463
C. EEOC Failure to Serve Charge on Respondent	1422	—
D. EEOC Failure to Investigate and/or Conciliate	1423	463
E. Charge Not Under Oath	1424	464
F. EEOC Failure to Issue Notice of Right to Sue When Charging Party Is Entitled to It	1425	465
II. Suit Against Parties Not Named in EEOC Charge	1426	465
A. Introduction	1426	465
B. Circumstances in Which Joinder of an Unnamed Party Has Been Permitted	1430	467
1. Joinder Where Injustice Would Otherwise Result to Plaintiff and Defendant Named in EEOC Charge	1430	467
2. Joinder of Parties Necessary for Purposes of Modifying Seniority Provisions of Collective Bargaining Agreements	1433	—

	Main Edition	Supplement
3. Joinder Where There Is an Agency Relationship or Substantial Identity Between the Named Party and the Unnamed Defendant	1434	468
4. Joinder Where Named Party Since Has Been Acquired, Merged With, or Succeeded by a Different Entity	1437	—
C. Necessary and Indispensable Parties	1438	—
1. Necessary Parties	1439	—
2. Indispensable Parties	1440	—
D. Joinder of One Defendant by Another	1442	—
III. Scope of EEOC Charge as Limiting the Scope of a Title VII Lawsuit	1443	470
A. The Problem	1443	—
B. The *Sanchez* Doctrine	1444	—
C. Application of the *Sanchez* Doctrine	1447	470
1. Basic Rationale	1447	470
2. Issues Rooted in the Same Basis of Discrimination	1448	471
3. Suit Alleging a Basis of Discrimination Different From That Specified in the Charge	1450	471
4. Incidents Occurring Subsequent to the Filing of the EEOC Charge	1451	471
5. The Suit Alleges Classwide Discrimination But the Charge Relates to Individual Treatment	1454	472
IV. Mootness	1455	472
V. Venue	1460	473
VI. Summary Judgment	1463	474
VII. Jury Trial	1469	475
CHAPTER 34. EEOC LITIGATION	1471	477
I. Introduction and Historical Perspective	1471	—
II. Administrative Prerequisites to Suit	1472	477
A. Administrative Prerequisites to Suit Under § 706 and the ADEA	1472	477
1. A Timely Charge	1474	477

	Main Edition	Supplement
2. Notice of the Charge	1476	—
3. Investigation	1477	478
4. Reasonable Cause Determination	1481	478
5. Conciliation	1483	479
B. Administrative Prerequisites to Pattern-or-Practice Suits Under § 707	1487	480
III. EEOC Internal Processes	1488	480
A. Statutory Authority	1488	—
B. Organization of the Office of General Counsel	1489	480
1. Structure	1489	—
2. Processing EEOC Suits Under § 706(f)(1)	1490	480
3. Processing EEOC Intervention in Private Suits	1492	—
4. Processing Actions for Preliminary Relief	1492	480
5. Processing Pattern-or-Practice Suits Under § 707	1493	—
6. Processing Proceedings to Enforce Decrees Under § 706(i)	1494	—
IV. EEOC Suits in the Nature of Class Actions	1494	481
V. Statutes of Limitations and Laches	1495	482
A. Statutes of Limitations	1495	482
1. Title VII	1495	482
2. ADEA and Equal Pay Act	1496	482
B. Laches	1496	483
VI. Scope of the Litigation	1501	483
A. Additional Defendants	1501	—
B. Expansion of Basis and Issue	1502	483
C. Geographic Scope	1506	—
VII. The Relationship Between EEOC Suits and Private Suits	1507	483
A. The EEOC's Right to File Suit in Addition to a Private Suit	1507	483
B. Rights of Charging Parties When EEOC Has Filed Suit	1510	484
C. Permissive Intervention by EEOC in a Pending Action	1510	—

	Main Edition	Supplement
1. Conditions Precedent to Permissive Intervention	1511	—
2. Factors Considered	1512	—
VIII. Preliminary Relief	1516	485
A. Statutory Authority	1516	—
B. Procedure	1516	—
C. Standards for Relief	1517	485
IX. Discovery Against the EEOC	1519	485
X. Settlement	1521	485
XI. Decree Enforcement	1522	486
XII. EEOC Liability for Attorney's Fees and Costs	1524	487
CHAPTER 35. JUSTICE DEPARTMENT LITIGATION	1525	489
I. Overview	1525	—
II. Justice Department Public Sector Suits	1526	—
A. The 1972 Amendments	1526	—
B. Justice Department Authority Under § 706	1526	—
C. Justice Department Authority Under § 707	1528	—
III. Jurisdictional Prerequisites to Justice Department Litigation	1529	—
A. Under § 706	1529	—
B. Under § 707	1530	—
1. Administrative Prerequisites to Suit	1530	—
2. The Requirement of a Continuing Violation	1531	—
IV. Enforcement of Government Contract Provisions Prohibiting Employment Discrimination	1531	—
V. Justice Department Jurisdiction Under Other Statutes	1532	—
A. The Americans with Disabilities Act	1532	—
B. The Omnibus Crime Control and Safe Streets Act	1533	—
C. Immigration Reform and Control Act	1533	—

	Main Edition	Supplement
CHAPTER 36. FEDERAL EMPLOYEE LITIGATION	1537	491
I. Introduction and Historical Overview	1537	491
A. 1964–1972: No Coverage of Federal Employees Under Title VII	1540	—
B. The Equal Employment Opportunity Act of 1972: Title VII Was Amended to Cover Certain Federal Employees	1542	—
C. The Civil Service Reform Act of 1978 (CSRA): Administrative Enforcement of § 717 Was Restructured	1543	—
D. The Civil Rights Act of 1991: New Remedies, a Limitations Period, and Expanded Coverage of § 717	1545	491
E. The Congressional Accountability Act of 1995: New Protection for Employees of Congress	1546	—
II. Administrative Enforcement	1547	492
A. Employees Covered by § 717	1547	492
1. General Overview of Procedures and Timeliness	1547	—
2. Individual Complaints	1549	492
a. Individual Discrimination Complaints Not Appealable to the MSPB ("Pure EEO Cases")	1549	492
b. Individual Discrimination Complaints Appealable to the MSPB ("Mixed Cases")	1552	492
3. Class Complaints	1557	493
4. Employees Covered by Collective Bargaining Agreements	1559	493
5. Retaliation	1561	494
6. Affirmative Action	1561	494
B. Employees of Congress	1563	—
C. Employees of the Judicial Branch	1565	—
III. Litigation Procedure	1566	495
A. Administrative Exhaustion	1566	495
B. Timeliness	1568	495
C. Trial de Novo	1571	496

TABLE OF CONTENTS lxxv

	Main Edition	Supplement
D. Class Actions	1573	497
E. Exclusivity of Remedy	1574	—
F. Scope of Relief	1576	497
G. Attorney's Fees	1576	497
H. Federal Officials as Defendants	1577	497
CHAPTER 37. CLASS ACTIONS	1581	499
I. The Application of Rule 23 to Title VII Class Actions	1581	499
A. Basic Requirements	1581	—
B. An Historical Perspective—The Across-the-Board Approach	1582	—
C. Across-the-Board Class Actions After *Falcon*	1584	499
D. Application of Rule 23 Requirements After the 1991 Amendments to Title VII [New Topic]	—	500
II. The "Nexus" Requirements of Rule 23(a): Commonality, Typicality, and Adequacy of Representation	1587	502
A. Nexus Between Claims Asserted	1588	502
1. General Principles	1588	—
2. Adverse Impact Claims	1591	502
3. Disparate Treatment Claims	1593	503
4. Reasonable Accommodation Claims	1595	504
5. Claims for Compensatory Damages [New Topic]	—	505
B. Nexus Between Job Classifications	1596	506
C. Nexus Between Organizational Units or Geographical Facilities	1597	506
III. Special Issues Pertaining to Adequacy of Representation	1599	507
A. Adequacy of Plaintiff's Counsel	1599	507
B. Adequacy of the Named Plaintiff	1600	507
IV. Numerosity	1605	508
V. Rule 23(b) Requirements	1609	511
VI. Organizations as Class Representatives	1614	514
VII. Jurisdictional Requirements	1615	515

	Main Edition	Supplement
A. Exhausting the EEOC Administrative Process	1615	—
B. Intervention	1617	515
C. Tolling the Limitations Period	1618	515
D. The Employer in Bankruptcy	1619	516
VIII. The Class Determination Hearing	1620	517
A. Setting and Timing of the Hearing	1620	517
B. Inquiry Into the Merits—Prohibited, Permitted, or Required?	1621	—
C. Preclass-Determination Discovery	1626	—
IX. Rule 23(d)—Discretionary Orders	1627	517
X. Procedural Devices for Resolving Class Monetary Claims	1629	518
A. Bifurcation	1629	518
B. Appointment of a Special Master	1632	521
C. Proof-of-Claim Forms	1633	522
XI. Settlement	1635	522
A. Precertification Settlements	1635	522
B. Settlement Procedure and Court Approval	1636	523
C. Distribution of Settlement Proceeds	1639	—
D. Collateral Attack on Consent Decrees	1641	524
XII. Appeals	1642	524

DISCOVERY AND PROOF

CHAPTER 38. DISCOVERY	1649	529
I. Introduction	1649	529
II. Strategy Considerations	1651	530
A. Plaintiffs	1651	530
B. Defendants	1659	533
III. Limitations on Discovery	1662	534
A. Discovery Sought by Plaintiffs	1662	534
1. Privileged Materials	1662	534
2. Burdensome or Irrelevant Discovery	1670	539
B. Discovery Sought by Defendants	1676	540
1. Privileged Materials	1676	—
2. Burdensome or Irrelevant Discovery	1678	—

		Main Edition	Supplement
CHAPTER 39. STATISTICAL PROOF		1687	545
I. Introduction		1687	545
II. Types of Statistical Proof		1689	545
	A. Selection Rate Comparisons	1690	546
	B. Potential Selection Rate Comparisons	1691	546
	C. Population/Workforce Comparisons	1694	547
	D. Regression Analyses	1697	547
	E. Other Kinds of Statistical Comparisons	1700	548
	F. The Bottom-Line Concept	1701	548
III. Sources of Statistics		1703	549
	A. Applicant Flow Data	1704	549
	B. Population/Labor Market Data	1709	552
	1. Qualified Labor Market Data	1709	552
	2. Qualified and Interested Labor Market Data	1711	—
	3. General Population Data	1712	553
	4. Employer's Workforce Data	1714	554
IV. Proper Geographic Scope of Statistics		1717	554
V. The Proper Time Frame for Statistics		1724	555
VI. The Proper Weight to Be Given Statistical Proof		1728	555
	A. Degree of the Disparity	1728	558
	B. Size of the Statistical Sample	1734	559
	C. Conflicting Statistical Conclusions	1735	—

REMEDIES

	Main Edition	Supplement
CHAPTER 40. INJUNCTIVE AND AFFIRMATIVE RELIEF	1741	563
I. Statutory Authority and Objectives	1741	—
II. Enjoining Practices Found Unlawful	1744	563
III. Relief for Identifiable Victims of Unlawful Employment Practices	1750	566
IV. Affirmative Relief Benefiting Persons Other Than Identified Victims of Discrimination	1758	579

	Main Edition	Supplement
A. Race- or Gender-Neutral Affirmative Relief	1758	—
B. Race- or Gender-Conscious Affirmative Relief	1760	579
V. Monitoring the Court Decree	1766	580
VI. Preliminary Injunctions	1769	583
A. Rule 65 Preliminary Relief	1769	583
B. Section 706(f)(2) Preliminary Relief	1773	586
CHAPTER 41. MONETARY RELIEF	1775	587
I. Back Pay	1775	587
A. A Discriminatee's Right to Back Pay in General	1775	587
B. Calculation of the Back-Pay Award	1779	588
1. Elements of a Back-Pay Award	1779	588
a. Wages and Salary	1780	588
b. Fringe Benefits	1781	589
c. Interest	1784	589
d. Mitigation Expenses	1787	592
2. The Period of Recovery	1788	592
a. Commencement of the Back-Pay Period	1788	592
b. Termination of the Back-Pay Period	1790	593
3. Deductions and Offsets	1804	600
a. Actual Interim Earnings	1805	600
b. Separation Payments	1809	601
c. Periods of Unavailability	1810	602
d. Taxes	1811	602
II. Front Pay	1815	602
III. Compensatory and Punitive Damages	1821	606
A. Statutory Bases for Compensatory and Punitive Damages	1821	606
1. Title VII	1821	606
2. Civil Rights Acts of 1866 and 1871	1825	607
a. Private Employers	1825	—
b. Public Employers	1826	607
3. Title IX	1827	—

	Main Edition	Supplement
B. The Entitlement to, and Calculation of, Compensatory Damages	1828	607
C. The Entitlement to, and Calculation of, Punitive Damages	1833	609
IV. Liquidated Damages	1835	611
V. Right to Jury Trial	1839	612
VI. Defenses to Monetary Relief	1841	613
A. The Mixed-Motive Defense	1841	613
B. Conformity With Government Rules and Regulations	1842	615
C. Equitable Defenses to Back-Pay and Front-Pay Relief	1844	616
1. Laches	1844	616
2. Good Faith	1847	616
3. Unclean Hands	1847	617
VII. Individual Back-Pay Claims in Collective Proceedings	1848	617
A. Determining Individual Back-Pay Damages	1848	617
1. When Did the Period of Liability Commence?	1849	617
2. How Many Available Positions Did Class Members Lose?	1850	617
3. Which Class Members Experienced Discrimination?	1852	618
4. What Deductions Should Be Taken From Each Class Member's Damages?	1855	618
B. Dividing a Classwide Award Among Class Members	1856	619
CHAPTER 42. ATTORNEY'S FEES	1859	621
I. The Prevailing Plaintiff's Right to Attorney's Fees	1859	621
A. Statutory Authorization	1859	—
1. Title VII	1859	—
2. 42 U.S.C. § 1988	1859	—

	Main Edition	Supplement
3. The Age Discrimination in Employment Act and the Equal Pay Act	1859	—
4. Equal Access to Justice Act	1860	—
5. Americans with Disabilities Act	1861	—
B. The General Fee Rule for Prevailing Plaintiffs	1861	621
1. Who Is a Prevailing Plaintiff?	1861	621
a. The Relevance of Minimal Success	1861	621
b. The Attorney's Entitlement to Fees	1865	625
c. The Forum	1865	625
2. Discretion in Denying Attorney's Fees	1866	626
C. Awards to Prevailing Plaintiffs in Actions Against State Governments	1871	—
D. Awards to Prevailing Plaintiffs in Suits Against the Federal Government	1871	627
E. Awards to Prevailing Plaintiffs Before Administrative Agencies	1872	—
F. Awards to Prevailing Plaintiffs Represented by Public Interest Law Firms	1874	—
G. Awards to Prevailing Plaintiffs in Negotiated Settlements	1875	—
H. Awards for Interim Success	1877	—
I. Awards to Prevailing Plaintiffs for Services on Appeal	1880	628
J. Awards to Prevailing Plaintiffs for Time Spent on the Fee Claim	1880	628
K. Awards of Costs	1881	629
II. Computation of Attorney's Fees for Prevailing Plaintiffs	1883	630
A. General Principles	1883	630
1. The *Johnson* Criteria	1883	—
2. The "Lodestar" Evolution	1886	—
3. Lodestar Enhancements?	1889	—
4. The Primacy of the Lodestar	1893	630
B. Applying the General Criteria	1894	630
1. Lodestar Components	1894	630
a. Rates	1894	630
b. Hours	1896	631
c. The Partially Prevailing Plaintiff	1897	631

	Main Edition	Supplement
2. Adjustments to the Lodestar	1899	632
a. Contingency	1899	632
b. Results Achieved	1900	632
c. Delay	1903	633
d. Quality	1902	—
C. Procedure	1904	633
1. Discovery	1904	—
2. Documentation	1906	—
3. Hearing	1906	633
4. Timing	1907	—
III. The Prevailing Defendant's Right to Attorney's Fees	1907	633
IV. Intervenors and Attorney's Fees	1913	—
A. Prevailing Intervenors	1913	—
B. Unsuccessful Intervenors	1914	—
CHAPTER 43. SETTLEMENT	1915	635
I. Validity of Waivers of Discrimination Claims	1915	635
A. Knowing and Voluntary Waivers of Past Claims Are Valid	1916	635
1. Waivers of Past Claims Are Valid	1916	—
2. The Waiver Must Be Knowing and Voluntary	1917	635
B. Waivers of Future Claims Are Invalid	1921	637
C. Extinguishment of Claims of Nonparties by Entry of Consent Decree	1922	—
II. Waiver of Age Discrimination Claims After the Older Workers Benefit Protection Act	1923	639
A. Waivers as Part of Settlement of EEOC Charge or Court Action	1924	640
B. Prelitigation Releases	1925	640
C. Unresolved Issues	1926	643
III. Terms of the Settlement Agreement	1927	644
A. The Defendant-Employer's Perspective	1927	644
1. General and Special Releases	1928	644
2. Dismissals and Withdrawals of Charges or Complaints	1930	—

	Main Edition	Supplement
3. Covenants Not to File Charges or to Assist in the Future Prosecution of Claims	1930	644
4. Confidentiality	1932	—
5. Acknowledgment Concerning Legal Advice and Voluntariness	1933	—
6. Additional Provisions	1934	—
B. The Plaintiff-Employee's Perspective	1935	—
1. General and Special Releases	1935	—
2. Monetary and Other Benefits	1935	—
3. References	1936	—
C. Class Actions	1936	—
D. Attorney's Fees and Retainer Agreements	1936	—
IV. Tax Considerations	1937	645
V. Rule 68 Offers of Judgment	1938	646
VI. "Busted" Settlements	1941	647
TABLE OF CASES	1947	649
INDEX	2151	—
TABLE OF LAWS AND RULES CONSTRUED	2233	—

Chapter 1

AN OVERVIEW

Since the writing of the Main Edition of this treatise, the courts and administrative agencies have continued to shape the law under the various federal employment discrimination statutes. The Civil Rights Act of 1991 and the Americans with Disabilities Act were in their infancies when the Main Edition was prepared. Since then, the federal courts have continued to construct, brick by brick, a cogent body of law upon these recently laid statutory foundations. Neither has the flow of judicial decisions in the more mature areas of employment discrimination law slowed in the last few years. Indeed, both the pace and scope of recent decisions from the federal trial courts, circuits, and Supreme Court in all areas of employment discrimination law are reminiscent of the years during which Title VII and the ADEA were reaching toward maturity. For example, during its last term, the Supreme Court issued decisions, resolving conflicts among the lower courts, concerning standards for determining employer liability under Title VII for sexual harassment,[1] the status of same-sex harassment under Title VII,[2] the status of asymptomatic HIV under the Americans with Disabilities Act,[3] and the consequences of noncompliance with the waiver provisions contained in the Older Workers' Benefits Protection Act.[4] This supplement attempts to report the more important developments in the field, beginning with cases decided after June 1994 through at least July 1996 and, for Supreme Court decisions, through the 1997–98 term.

The structure and format of this supplement tracks that of the Main Edition. The first portion of the supplement contains chapters on the major theories, bases, and issues of discrimination, while

---
[1]Faragher v. City of Boca Raton, 118 S. Ct. 2275, 77 FEP 14 (1998); Burlington Indus., Inc. v. Ellerth, 118 S. Ct. 2257, 77 FEP 1 (1998).
[2]Oncale v. Sundowner Offshore Servs., Inc., 118 S. Ct. 998, 76 FEP 221 (1998).
[3]Bragdon v. Abbott, 118 S. Ct. 2196, 8 AD 239 (1998).
[4]Oubre v. Entergy Operations, Inc., 118 S. Ct. 838, 75 FEP 1255 (1998).

the latter portion contains chapters on topics such as affirmative action, other sources of legal protection, administrative enforcement, litigation procedure, remedies, and settlement.[5]

---

[5]Identification of those specific chapters that fall into these general categories can be found at the end of Chapter 1 (An Overview) of the Main Edition.

Part 1

First Category of Discrimination—Disparate Treatment

CHAPTER 2

DISPARATE TREATMENT

I. THE THEORY

Disparate treatment due to cronyism does not violate Title VII.[1]
Treatment that might be considered favorable to a person in the protected classification could still constitute actionable disparate treatment.[2]

II. PROOF OF DISPARATE TREATMENT IN THE INDIVIDUAL CASE

A. The *McDonnell Douglas-Burdine* Analysis: Proof of Disparate Treatment Through Circumstantial Evidence

While the three-part framework for proving and analyzing disparate treatment cases set forth in *McDonnell Douglas Corp. v. Green*,[3] *Texas Department of Community Affairs v. Burdine*,[4] and *St. Mary's Honor Center v. Hicks*[5] continues to be utilized in the vast majority of disparate treatment cases, commentators have criticized its tendency to inject unnecessary formality and complexity into discrimination litigation.[6]

---

[1]Foster v. Dalton, 71 F.3d 52, 69 FEP 1402 (1st Cir. 1995) (white male selected for promotion was old friend of officer).
[2]Calabritto v. Dillon, 920 F. Supp. 370, 73 FEP 675 (E.D.N.Y. 1996) (since hazardous assignments could be a method of career advancement and increased pay, paternalistic treatment of female investigators by sparing them from such assignments would be actionable disparate treatment if decision makers were aware of and condoned the practice), *aff'd,* 107 F.3d 2 (2d Cir. 1997).
[3]411 U.S. 792, 5 FEP 965 (1973).
[4]450 U.S. 248, 25 FEP 113 (1981).
[5]509 U.S. 502, 62 FEP 96 (1993).
[6]Deborah C. Malamud, *The Last Minuet: Disparate Treatment After Hicks,* 93 MICH. L. REV. 2229, 2311–24 (1995) (calling for abandonment of *McDonnell Douglas-Burdine* framework); *Development in the Law—Employment Discrimination,* 109 HARV. L. REV. 1568, 1602 (1996) ("The entire area of shifting burdens is replete with confusion, and guidance is needed desperately.").

1. The Prima Facie Case

Courts continue to opt for a flexible application of the elements of a prima facie case.[7] For example, in *O'Connor v. Consolidated Coin Caterers Corp.*,[8] the Supreme Court held that a plaintiff could meet the fourth element of the prima facie case of age discrimination by showing that he was replaced by someone substantially younger even though the replacement was still in the protected class.

While *O'Connor* could be read to affect only age discrimination cases, since other types of discrimination usually present a purely dichotomous situation in which a person is either within a protected class or not, at least one court has extended *O'Connor* to cases involving other types of discrimination.[9] Taking a broad view of *O'Connor*, the Seventh Circuit reasoned that the focus should be on the larger question of "whether the plaintiff established a logical reason to believe that the decision rests on a legally forbidden ground."[10] Viewed in this fashion, the *McDonnell Douglas* test presents not a *sine qua non* for presenting a claim of discrimination but rather a "plaintiff's guide" to presenting evidence sufficient to lead to an inference of discrimination.[11]

Often the analysis of the prima facie case turns on whether the person to whom the plaintiff seeks to be compared is similarly situated. Some courts require the plaintiff to show that other employees alleged to have been treated more favorably were nearly identical in all or almost all respects.[12]

---

[7]Chertkova v. Connecticut Gen. Life Ins. Co., 92 F.3d 81, 91, 71 FEP 1006 (2d Cir. 1996) (error to ritualistically require plaintiff to show that a replacement was sought for his or her position; other evidence, including pattern of baseless criticism by superiors, the threat of termination for failure to meet ambiguous standards, and insults by superiors during training sessions, sufficient to permit inference of discrimination).

[8]517 U.S. 308, 70 FEP 486 (1996).

[9]Carson v. Bethlehem Steel Corp., 82 F.3d 157, 159, 70 FEP 921 (7th Cir. 1996) (white plaintiff did not need to show that she was replaced by a minority employee).

[10]*Id.* at 159.

[11]Kastel v. Winnetka Bd. of Educ., 946 F. Supp. 1329, 1337 (N.D. Ill. 1996).

[12]Cheek v. Peabody Coal Co., 97 F.3d 200, 204, 71 FEP 1775 (7th Cir. 1996) (woman suspended for excessive absenteeism could not support fourth prong of prima facie case as she presented no evidence to support her allegation that males with medical problems similar to her own received more favorable treatment and proffered no evidence of males with a similar absenteeism record who were not similarly disciplined); Mayberry v. Vought Aircraft Co., 55 F.3d 1086, 1090, 68 FEP 401

Other courts hold plaintiffs to a lesser standard of similarity at the prima facie stage.[13]

(5th Cir. 1995) (in a work-rule violation case, plaintiff can establish prima facie case either by showing that he did not violate the rule or by showing that white employees were treated differently under "nearly identical" circumstances; here plaintiff failed to show that whites who also scrapped parts but were not disciplined had a history of poor work performance, nor did he show the cost of the parts they scrapped, both of which were factors in whether employees would be disciplined for scrapping parts); Pierce v. Commonwealth Life Ins. Co., 40 F.3d 796, 802, 66 FEP 600 (6th Cir. 1994) (plaintiff supervisor demoted and transferred for sexual harassment unable to make prima facie case since proposed comparable was a nonsupervisory employee and, therefore, not nearly identical); Henderson v. Corrections Corp. of Am., 918 F. Supp. 204, 211, 71 FEP 1250 (E.D. Tenn. 1996) (plaintiff terminated from position as corrections officer after publicly disparaging employer did not establish that other employees not disciplined were similarly situated since other employees who had appeared on television programs talked only about union activities and did not trash employer); Marthel v. Bridgestone/Firestone, Inc., 926 F. Supp. 1293, 1301 (M.D. Tenn. 1996) (plaintiff attempting to satisfy fourth prong of prima facie case by showing that comparable nonprotected employees were treated more favorably must demonstrate relevant aspects of his employment situation nearly identical to those of the other employees, including that he and they shared the same supervisor and engaged in the same conduct); Fredrick v. Goodyear Tire & Rubber Co., 71 FEP 1842, 1847 (S.D. Tex. 1996) (summary judgment granted when plaintiff, demoted from store manager position for consistently failing to open his store on time, did not present sufficient evidence that other nonminority store managers regularly failed to open their stores); Phillips v. Holladay Prop. Servs., Inc., 937 F. Supp. 32, 37, 75 FEP 375 (D.D.C. 1996) (plaintiff who did not offer evidence that same supervisor who fired her treated white male employee more favorably nor evidence of white employee's disciplinary record failed to establish prima facie case), aff'd, 1997 WL 411695 (D.C. Cir., June 19, 1997); Lewis v. Zilog, Inc., 908 F. Supp. 931, 954, 69 FEP 337 (N.D. Ga. 1995) (plaintiff did not meet burden of establishing prima facie case since she could not show that misconduct of comparable male employees was nearly identical to the conduct for which she was disciplined); Darnell v. Northern Can Sys., Inc., 937 F. Supp. 668, 671–72, 67 FEP 419 (N.D. Ohio 1995) (plaintiff not similarly situated to male who had more extensive experience in packer position to which he was permitted to bump instead of plaintiff), opinion clarified, 1996 WL 343448 (N.D. Ohio, Apr. 23, 1996).

[13]Harrison v. Metropolitan Gov't of Nashville, 80 F.3d 1107, 1115, 73 FEP 109 (6th Cir.) (in discriminatory discipline case, plaintiff need not show "precise equivalency in culpability between employees"; plaintiff need only show misconduct of other employees of comparable seriousness), cert. denied, 117 S. Ct. 169 (1996); Ensley-Gaines v. Runyon, 100 F.3d 1220, 1226, 72 FEP 602 (6th Cir. 1996) (plaintiff need only demonstrate that nonpregnant employee similar in ability or inability to work treated more favorably); Batson v. Powell, 912 F. Supp. 565, 573–74 (D.D.C. 1996) (plaintiffs' prima facie showing that they were treated dissimilarly to similarly situated male guards satisfied by evidence that male guards allowed options in complying with uniform dress policy not allowed to female guards); Petsch-Schmid v. Boston Edison Co., 914 F. Supp. 697, 705 n.17, 6 AD 291 (D. Mass. 1996) (prima facie case established by evidence of males with similar salaries and responsibilities who received lesser discipline for work problems at least as severe as those for

2. The Employer's Burden of Producing Evidence

Courts continue to refrain from passing judgment as to the overall "legitimacy" or "reasonableness" of the employer's stated reasons for its actions, especially in discipline and discharge cases.[14] In cases involving alleged employee misconduct, courts have held that in order to satisfy its burden of production, the employer need only show that it honestly believed that a work rule was violated and not that the infraction actually occurred.[15] Courts continue to accept employers' explanations based on subjective criteria.[16] Employers continue to proffer a wide range of justifications for

---

which plaintiff was terminated, though none of the male comparables were supervised by same person as supervised plaintiff since the employer had implemented companywide policy of discipline designed to be used by all supervisors); Hammett v. Lankenau Hosp., 72 FEP 442, 443 n.2 (E.D. Pa. 1996) (plaintiff only needed to show that similarly situated white employees retained after her discharge and not that white employees had as poor a work record as she had); Brennan v. National Tel. Directory Corp., 881 F. Supp. 986, 994, 67 FEP 922 (E.D. Pa. 1995) (plaintiff satisfied prima facie case burden, which is not onerous, by showing that men working with her not terminated; additionally, even if required to show similarly situated males treated more favorably, plaintiff presented genuine issue of material fact since she showed that male who was also discharged received notice and counseling prior to discharge, while she was informed of her six violations all at once while on maternity leave and was never counseled); Henry v. Gehl Corp., 867 F. Supp. 960, 964, 68 FEP 175 (D. Kan. 1994) (prima facie case satisfied by evidence that male telemarketers with production and attendance records similar to plaintiff's not as severely disciplined and given more opportunities to improve).

[14]Montgomery v. Brookshire, 880 F. Supp. 483, 486–87 (W.D. Tex. 1995) (employer's stated reason for terminating plaintiff satisfies burden of production, despite plaintiff's challenge to the reasonableness of the employer's action).

[15]Johnson v. J.C. Penney Co., 876 F. Supp. 135, 139 (N.D. Tex. 1995) (the relevant question is whether employer believed that plaintiff sexually harassed coworkers, not whether he actually did); Sunstrom v. Schering-Plough Corp., 856 F. Supp. 1265, 1272 (E.D. Tenn. 1994) (even if plaintiff, a former sales representative, did not falsify company records as charged, the employer successfully rebutted prima facie case of disparate treatment by showing that it honestly believed that the plaintiff committed the infraction).

[16]EEOC v. Insurance Co. of N. Am., 49 F.3d 1418, 67 FEP 411 (9th Cir. 1995) (employer's explanation that plaintiff was overqualified for the position satisfies burden of production); Binder v. Long Island Lighting Co., 57 F.3d 193, 67 FEP 1783 (2d Cir. 1995) (employer's proffered justification, i.e., a policy against "underemployment," satisfies employer's burden of production); Nelson v. Pulaski County Sheriff's Dep't, 859 F. Supp. 1228, 1232, 65 FEP 1563, 1566 (E.D. Ark. 1994) (interviewer's good faith suspicions about circumstances of plaintiff's discharge from military and of his resignation from prison job, though unfounded, together with observation that plaintiff changed jobs frequently, constitute legitimate, nondiscriminatory reasons for not granting plaintiff an interview).

taking adverse employment actions, including lesser work performance than other candidates,[17] misconduct,[18] need to eliminate jobs,[19] other economic factors,[20] poor work performance,[21] insubordination,[22] personality factors,[23] being overqualified for the job,[24] or a combination of such factors.[25]

---

[17]Torre v. Federated Mut. Ins. Co., 897 F. Supp. 1332, 1372–73, 68 FEP 1850 (D. Kan. 1995) (employer chose a co-worker of plaintiff to receive monthly performance bonus because co-worker provided particularly good service to a client), *aff'd,* 124 F.3d 218 (10th Cir. 1997).

[18]Wixson v. Dowagiac Nursing Home, 87 F.3d 164, 71 FEP 186, 191 (6th Cir. 1996) (one plaintiff was fired for disclosing confidential patient information and the other for failing to return from leave at the agreed-upon time); Sunstrom v. Schering-Plough Corp., 856 F. Supp. 1265, 1268–69 (E.D. Tenn. 1994) (employer "honestly believed" that plaintiff, a sales representative, falsified company records in order to exaggerate her sales activity); Evans v. Bally's Health & Tennis, Inc., 64 FEP 33 (D. Md. 1994) (employer maintained that it had evidence that four separate female employees had complained about plaintiff's harassing behavior).

[19]Kunzman v. Enron Corp., 902 F. Supp. 882, 901, 73 FEP 803 (N.D. Iowa 1995) (reduction-in-force).

[20]Johnson v. University of Wis., 70 F.3d 469, 479, 69 FEP 644 (7th Cir. 1995) (university presented legitimate, nondiscriminatory reason for equalizing pay rates of plaintiff, who had originally been paid at a higher rate than her male colleague); Castner v. United States Dep't of Energy, 897 F. Supp. 481, 482, 68 FEP 1642, 1643 (D. Or. 1995) (hiring freeze permitting hiring of only persons already employed with agency was legitimate, nondiscriminatory reason for not hiring plaintiff, who was not so employed at time of application).

[21]Roush v. KFC Nat'l Mgmt. Co., 10 F.3d 392, 396, 63 FEP 609 (6th Cir. 1993) (plaintiff's performance was inadequate because she did not follow company procedures, did not properly prioritize her work, spent too much time talking on the telephone, and her work area was disorganized), *cert. denied,* 513 U.S. 808 (1994).

[22]Montgomery v. Brookshire, 880 F. Supp. 483, 486 (W.D. Tex. 1995) (plaintiff, a deputy sheriff, was terminated because he told the sheriff, "If you force me to make a choice, my family comes first, and the Sheriff's Department can go to Hell.").

[23]Manzer v. Diamond Shamrock Chems. Co., 29 F.3d 1078, 1082, 65 FEP 585 (6th Cir. 1994) (plaintiff was fired in part for being argumentative and confrontational with superiors and co-workers and being generally considered "obnoxious and unreliable").

[24]Binder v. Long Island Lighting Co., 57 F.3d 193, 197, 67 FEP 1783 (2d Cir. 1995) (defendant's failure to hire plaintiff was made out of a "genuine desire to avoid placing [plaintiff] in a job in which he might be frustrated, exhibit low morale and perform poorly"); EEOC v. Insurance Co. of N. Am., 49 F.3d 1418, 1420–21, 67 FEP 411 (9th Cir. 1995) (defendant failed to hire plaintiff out of fear that someone with plaintiff's extensive background in the loss control field would become too involved in uncomplicated risks, and would therefore waste time on the job).

[25]Tyler v. Runyon, 70 F.3d 458, 467, 5 AD 31 (7th Cir. 1995) (postal service's reasons for not providing training as a window clerk to plaintiff, that there was no need for window clerks at that time and that plaintiff had little seniority, held to satisfy its burden); Evans v. McClain of Ga., Inc., 934 F. Supp. 1383, 1389 (M.D.

3. Plaintiff's Proof of Pretext

The question raised most often concerning *St. Mary's Honor Center v. Hicks*[26] is whether summary judgment for the employer should be precluded if a plaintiff presents sufficient evidence to allow a finding of pretext but has no additional evidence of discriminatory intent.[27] At least half of the circuits have held that evidence of pretext combined with evidence of a prima facie case will always be sufficient to defeat a motion for summary judgment. In *Sheridan v. E.I. DuPont de Nemours & Co.*,[28] the Third Circuit held that the disbelief of an employer's reasons plus evidence of a prima facie case will always sustain a finding of intentional discrimination.

A similar position has been taken by the Fourth,[29] Sixth,[30]

Ga. 1996) (plaintiff was fired for intimidating employees, telling employees they were targeted to be fired, failing to order parts on time, insubordination, and making threats), *rev'd,* 131 F.3d 957 (11th Cir. 1997).

[26] 509 U.S. 502, 62 FEP 96 (1993).

[27] Deborah C. Malamud, *The Last Minuet: Disparate Treatment After Hicks,* 93 MICH. L. REV. 2229, 2276 (1995) ("A review of cases at the pretrial stage reveals that *McDonnell Douglas-Burdine* figures most centrally in summary judgment practice.").

[28] 100 F.3d 1061, 1066–67, 72 FEP 518 (3d Cir. 1996), *cert. denied,* 117 S. Ct. 2532 (1997). As pointed out by the partial concurrence and partial dissent, the majority decision does not use the word "always." *Id.* at 1078. Nevertheless, in holding that a court may not pretermit the jury's ability to draw the inference of discrimination from evidence that could rationally support a finding that the employer's proffered reasons are unworthy of credence, the majority essentially held that when the record contains sufficient evidence that the employer's proffered reason is not true, summary judgment should always be denied.

[29] Mitchell v. Data Gen. Corp., 12 F.3d 1310, 1316, 63 FEP 816 (4th Cir. 1993) (summary judgment can be defeated by the presentation of evidence sufficient to establish a prima facie case and a showing of a factual issue about the defendant's proffered explanation). *But see* Runnebaum v. NationsBank of Md., N.A., 123 F.3d 156, 164, 7 AD 216 (4th Cir. 1997) (en banc), which raises some doubt as to the Fourth Circuit's stand on this issue. In dicta, the en banc court stated that *Hicks* held that a prima facie case coupled with disbelief of the employer's asserted justification for an adverse employment action may not be sufficient to establish a violation or to forestall summary judgment.

[30] EEOC v. Yenkin-Majestic Paint Corp., 112 F.3d 831, 835, 73 FEP 1317 (6th Cir. 1997) (prima facie case and proof that employer's proffered reasons not actual reasons for discharge sufficient to support inference of intentional discrimination; no additional proof of discriminatory animus required); Ensley-Gaines v. Runyon, 100 F.3d 1220, 1227, 72 FEP 602 (6th Cir. 1996) (since plaintiff presented evidence that defendant's reasons were false or pretextual, reasonable trier of fact could infer intentional discrimination).

Seventh,[31] Ninth,[32] Tenth,[33] and District of Columbia[34] Circuits.

Other circuits have held that evidence of pretext only will not necessarily be sufficient to support a finding of discrimination. The latest circuit to take this view of *Hicks,* at least in the context of a determination rendered by a trial court following a bench trial, is the Second Circuit in *Fisher v. Vassar College.*[35] Agreeing with a panel decision that had overturned the district court's finding of discrimination in a denial of tenure case,[36] the en banc court held

---

[31]Wohl v. Spectrum Mfg., Inc., 94 F.3d 353, 355, 71 FEP 1081 (7th Cir. 1996) (plaintiff can defeat summary judgment by producing evidence that employer proffered a phony reason for firing employee); Testerman v. EDS Tech. Prods. Corp., 98 F.3d 297, 72 FEP 959 (7th Cir. 1996) (if plaintiff could cast employer's asserted reasons for terminating into doubt, summary judgment would be improper); Perdomo v. Browner, 67 F.3d 140, 146, 68 FEP 1751 (7th Cir. 1995) (inference of discrimination permitted based upon a finding that employer proffered spurious reason for decision). *But see* Sample v. Aldi, 61 F.3d 544, 549, 68 FEP 759 (7th Cir. 1995) (plaintiff must create an issue of fact as to each reason proffered by defendant; if at least one reason remains unquestioned and standing alone it would justify the action, summary judgment proper); Russell v. Acme-Evans Co., 51 F.3d 64, 69, 67 FEP 559 (7th Cir. 1995) (that plaintiff was successful in challenging some of the reasons advanced by defendant for the adverse action does not defeat summary judgment if at least one of the reasons is not questioned).

[32]Warren v. City of Carlsbad, 58 F.3d 439, 443 (9th Cir. 1995) (plaintiff's burden at summary judgment stage is to produce facts that either directly show discriminatory motive or show that city's explanation for denial of promotion not credible), *cert. denied,* 516 U.S. 1171 (1996); Washington v. Garrett, 10 F.3d 1421, 1433, 63 FEP 540 (9th Cir. 1993) (a question is always presented for the fact finder if the plaintiff establishes a prima facie case and genuine factual issues as to the truth of the employer's explanation).

[33]Randle v. City of Aurora, 69 F.3d 441, 69 FEP 489 (10th Cir. 1995) (plaintiff can withstand summary judgment by establishing prima facie case and evidence of pretext). Elsewhere in the opinion, however, the court did point out an exception to this rule, stating that if a plaintiff conceded that the real reason for the adverse employment decision concealed by the employer's pretextual proffer was itself not a discriminatory motivation, the defendant would be entitled to judgment because the concession by plaintiff of a nondiscriminatory motive would preclude an inference of discriminatory intent.

[34]Kolstad v. American Dental Ass'n, 108 F.3d 1431, 1436–37, 73 FEP 625 (D.C. Cir. 1997) (because the plaintiff introduced sufficient evidence for the jury to conclude she had proven both a prima facie case and that defendant's reasons were pretextual, the jury could also have reasonably concluded that the plaintiff proved intentional discrimination); Barbour v. Merrill, 48 F.3d 1270, 1277, 67 FEP 369 (D.C. Cir. 1995) (rejection of employer's proffered reason for decision sufficient to permit finding of discrimination), *cert. granted,* 516 U.S. 1086, *cert. dismissed,* 516 U.S. 1155 (1996).

[35]114 F.3d 1332, 74 FEP 109 (2d Cir. 1997) (en banc), *cert. denied,* 118 S. Ct. 851 (1998).

[36]Fisher v. Vassar College, 70 F.3d 1420, 70 FEP 1155 (2d Cir. 1995).

that a finding of discrimination, like any other factual determination, can be reviewed for clear error even when it is supported by a finding of pretext that is itself sustainable.[37] The First[38] and Fifth[39] Circuits have also held that evidence of pretext alone will not necessarily support a finding of discrimination.

The Eleventh Circuit has acknowledged an intra-circuit conflict on the correct interpretation of *Hicks*.[40] Most recently, an Eleventh Circuit panel held that plaintiffs who presented sufficient evidence to create a question of fact as to the employer's truthfulness should survive at least at the summary judgment stage.[41] The Eighth Circuit has also gone back and forth on the issue of whether

---

[37]*Fisher,* 114 F.3d at 1340.

[38]Barbour v. Dynamics Research Corp., 63 F.3d 32, 39 (1st Cir. 1995) (plaintiff's argument that summary judgment precluded by his showing that the employer's reasons are not worthy of credence foreclosed by *Woods*), *cert. denied,* 516 U.S. 1113 (1996); Woods v. Friction Materials, Inc., 30 F.3d 255, 261 n.3, 65 FEP 1109 (1st Cir. 1994) (concluding that a jury could not infer age discrimination if the employer's articulated nondiscriminatory reason was that the employee lacked necessary work skills when, in fact, the employer sought to conceal its own acts of embezzlement). *Cf.* Woodman v. Haemonetics Corp., 51 F.3d 1087, 1093, 67 FEP 838 (1st Cir. 1995) (summary judgment precluded where evidence of pretext, together with an admission that the employer wanted younger employees, held sufficient to generate a suspicion of mendacity adequate to permit inference of intentional discrimination).

[39]Rhodes v. Guiberson Oil Tools, 75 F.3d 989, 993–94, 69 FEP 1720 (5th Cir. 1996) (en banc) (evidence of pretext "will often, perhaps usually" permit an inference of discrimination). Because the actual holding of the en banc court in *Rhodes* was that the evidence submitted at trial to prove pretext was adequate to support the jury's finding of discriminatory intent, the court's pronouncement on the effect of evidence of pretext has been characterized as dicta. Combs v. Plantation Patterns, 106 F.3d 1519, 1536, 73 FEP 232 (11th Cir. 1997), *cert. denied,* 118 S. Ct. 685 (1998).

[40]Mayfield v. Patterson Pump Co., 101 F.3d 1371, 1376 n.4, 72 FEP 1153 (11th Cir. 1996). *Compare* Isenbergh v. Knight-Ridder Newspaper Sales, Inc., 97 F.3d 436, 72 FEP 735 (11th Cir. 1996) (prior to stating its holding that the lack of a question presented on the issue of pretext justified granting defendant's motion for judgment as a matter of law, the court at some length explained why evidence of pretext might not be enough to support a judgment for a plaintiff), *cert. denied,* 117 S. Ct. 2511 (1997), *and* Walker v. NationsBank of Fla., N.A., 53 F.3d 1548, 1558, 68 FEP 314 (11th Cir. 1995) (affirming granting of directed verdict on grounds that plaintiff's evidence, though sufficient to permit fact finder to disbelieve defendant's proffered reasons for termination, failed to raise suspicion of mendacity sufficient to permit finding of discrimination), *with* Howard v. BP Oil Co., 32 F.3d 520, 527 (11th Cir. 1994) (fact finder's rejection of defendant's proffered reasons was sufficient circumstantial evidence on which to base a finding of discrimination), *and* Hairston v. Gainesville Sun Publ'g Co., 9 F.3d 913, 921, 63 FEP 838 (11th Cir. 1993) (summary judgment reversed since there existed evidence that the employer's proffered reasons were mere pretext).

[41]Combs v. Plantation Patterns, 106 F.3d 1519, 73 FEP 232 (11th Cir. 1997), *cert. denied,* 118 S. Ct. 685 (1998).

evidence of pretext, without more, will preclude summary judgment.[42] The more recent Eighth Circuit cases, however, have recognized that proof of pretext does not always support an inference of discrimination.[43]

a. Direct Evidence. Courts continue to give little weight to biased remarks by nondecision makers and to stray remarks by decision makers that do not pertain to the plaintiff.[44] Statements

---

[42]*See* Rothmeier v. Investment Advisers, Inc., 85 F.3d 1328, 1336, 71 FEP 1458 (8th Cir. 1996) (acknowledging that the court's post-*Hicks* decisions on the issue of whether evidence of pretext is enough to defeat summary judgment "have not been models of apparent consistency"). *Compare* Krenik v. County of Le Sueur, 47 F.3d 953, 958, 67 FEP 312 (8th Cir. 1995) (plaintiff must show evidence of pretext *and* evidence of intentional discrimination), *and* Hutson v. McDonnell Douglas Corp., 63 F.3d 771, 777, 68 FEP 1209 (8th Cir. 1995), *and* Nelson v. Boatmen's Bancshares, Inc., 26 F.3d 796, 801, 64 FEP 1799 (8th Cir. 1994) (same), *with* Gaworski v. ITT Commercial Fin. Corp., 17 F.3d 1104, 1109, 64 FEP 382 (8th Cir.) (if there is sufficient evidence for jury to reject proffered reasons, then the evidence is sufficient for the jury to determine whether intentional discrimination occurred), *cert. denied,* 513 U.S. 946 (1994), *and* Kobrin v. University of Minn., 34 F.3d 698, 703, 65 FEP 1624 (8th Cir. 1994) (same).

[43]*See* Ryther v. KARE 11, 108 F.3d 832, 73 FEP 373 (8th Cir.), *cert. denied,* 117 S. Ct. 2510 (1997); Rothmeier v. Investment Advisers, Inc., 85 F.3d 1328, 71 FEP 1458 (8th Cir. 1996).

[44]Geir v. Medtronic, Inc., 99 F.3d 238, 72 FEP 249, 251–52 (7th Cir. 1996) (supervisor's statement that plaintiff should have children during particular time of year is not direct evidence of pregnancy discrimination because it was not made contemporaneous with the discharge or causally related to the discharge decisionmaking process); Trotter v. Board of Trustees of Univ. of Ala., 91 F.3d 1449, 1453–54, 71 FEP 1175 (11th Cir. 1996) (supervisor's racist statements not direct evidence of discrimination because she was not involved in the challenged decision); Cheek v. Peabody Coal Co., 97 F.3d 200, 203, 71 FEP 1775 (7th Cir. 1996) (supervisors' statements that they did not want women but had to accept them were not direct evidence of discrimination where statements were uttered some 15 years prior to the employment decision and there was no nexus between the remarks and the contested employment actions); Kelly v. Boeing Petroleum Servs., Inc., 61 F.3d 350, 357, 4 AD 1284 (5th Cir. 1995) (in disability discrimination case, comments regarding race, sex, and other categories besides disability were irrelevant particularly because person making comments was not a decision maker); Bright v. Standard Register Co., 66 F.3d 171, 172–73, 68 FEP 1694 (8th Cir. 1995) (union president's statement that he thought the company planned to get rid of old people was a stray remark). *But cf.* Wells v. New Cherokee Corp., 58 F.3d 233, 235–37, 68 FEP 284 (6th Cir. 1995) (discriminatory statements by person without final decisionmaking authority admissible where there was evidence he consulted with person making the ultimate decision); Odima v. Westin Tucson Hotel, 53 F.3d 1484, 1490–91, 67 FEP 1222 (9th Cir. 1995) (comment "Go back to Africa where you come from. We don't have any job for you here." was direct evidence where declarant was in plaintiff's chain of command and she had the practical, if not formal, authority to block him from obtaining position).

by decision makers that do relate to the plaintiff, however, are much more likely to be considered direct evidence of discrimination.[45]

  b. *Comparative Evidence.* The critical issue continues to be whether the comparisons are apt in light of all the circumstances.[46]

  c. *Statistics.* In individual disparate treatment cases, courts continue to find that statistics that do not compare persons comparably situated to the plaintiff lack probative value.[47]

---

[45]Schnidrig v. Columbia Mach., Inc., 80 F.3d 1406, 1410, 71 FEP 1763 (9th Cir.) (along with evidence of statements made by board members indicating that the board wanted somebody younger for the position, plaintiff produced evidence of shorthand notes taken at board meetings indicating the same; such direct evidence shifts burden to defendant to articulate nondiscriminatory motives), *cert. denied,* 117 S. Ct. 295 (1996); Haynes v. W.D. Caye & Co., 52 F.3d 928, 930, 67 FEP 1755 (11th Cir. 1995) (summary judgment inappropriate where company's president stated that "women were simply not tough enough to do the job"); Brinkley-Obu v. Hughes Training, Inc., 36 F.3d 336, 354, 65 FEP 1840 (4th Cir. 1994) (supervisor's comment that plaintiff had to choose "between having a career and being a woman" was direct evidence of discrimination); Stacks v. Southwestern Bell Yellow Pages, Inc., 27 F.3d 1316, 1318, 65 FEP 341 (8th Cir. 1994) (judgment for plaintiff where supervisor, who was closely involved in the decisionmaking process, stated, among other things, that "women in sales were the worst thing that had happened to this company").
[46]*See, e.g.,* Pierce v. Commonwealth Life Ins. Co., 40 F.3d 796, 802, 66 FEP 600 (6th Cir. 1994) (supervisor who was punished for violating the company's sexual harassment policy could not maintain his claim of reverse discrimination where he was not similarly situated to a female nonsupervisory employee who also engaged in sexual harassment but was not punished); Perkins v. Brigham & Women's Hosp., 78 F.3d 747, 751, 70 FEP 568 (1st Cir. 1996) (fired African-American employee not similarly situated to white employee who also engaged in sexual misconduct because plaintiff's conduct was more severe and plaintiff had a history of disciplinary actions); EEOC v. Our Lady of the Resurrection Med. Ctr., 77 F.3d 145, 151, 70 FEP 104 (7th Cir. 1996) (even though plaintiff and male employee both failed to take the first certification for which they were eligible, plaintiff was not similarly situated to male employee because plaintiff did not notify her supervisor); Kuhn v. Ball State Univ., 78 F.3d 330, 332, 70 FEP 449 (7th Cir. 1996) (one anecdote of an employer's treatment of a similarly situated employee is insufficient); Byrd v. Ronayne, 61 F.3d 1026, 1032–33, 68 FEP 769 (1st Cir. 1995) (client complaints for which plaintiff was discharged were more frequent and serious than complaints about a male employee who was not discharged).
[47]Furr v. Seagate Tech., Inc., 82 F.3d 980, 986, 70 FEP 1325 (10th Cir. 1996) (statistical evidence is not evidence of discrimination unless it compares similarly situated persons and attempts to eliminate nondiscriminatory explanations for the statistical disparities), *cert. denied,* 117 S. Ct. 684 (1997); Hartsel v. Keys, 87 F.3d 795, 799, 72 FEP 951 (6th Cir. 1996) (statistical evidence of no female department heads fails to create fact issue to show individual disparate treatment for failure to promote female to department head position because no evidence presented of pattern or practice and male applicant admittedly had more advanced computer skills,

d. Other Evidence. Plaintiffs may demonstrate pretext by presenting statements by supervisors and managers that exhibit bias yet fall short of direct evidence,[48] evidence that the rationale asserted by the employer for the decision in question is without factual basis or is implausible on its face,[49] or evidence that

---

which were required for the job), *cert. denied,* 117 S. Ct. 683 (1997); Hutson v. McDonnell Douglas Corp., 63 F.3d 771, 777, 68 FEP 1209 (8th Cir. 1995) (evidence showing a higher percentage of layoffs among older employees not probative of discrimination because it failed to analyze treatment of comparable employees); Fisher v. Vassar College, 70 F.3d 1420, 1443–45, 70 FEP 1155 (2d Cir. 1995) (district court's reliance on plaintiff's inadequately small and factually "flawed" statistical evidence held clear error justifying reversal of bench trial verdict for plaintiff), *opinion amended,* 114 F.3d 1332 (2d Cir. 1997), *cert. denied,* 118 S. Ct. 851 (1998).

[48]Antol v. Perry, 82 F.3d 1291, 1301, 70 FEP 993 (3d Cir. 1996) (repeated references to applicant for promotion as "spasm head" by supervisor involved in decisionmaking process supported an inference of discrimination under the Rehabilitation Act); Stemmons v. Missouri Dep't of Corrections, 82 F.3d 817, 820–21, 70 FEP 1215 (8th Cir. 1996) (comments and conduct of department of corrections officials and interviewers undermined proffered reason for denying plaintiff a promotion and supported jury verdict in favor of plaintiff).

[49]Williams v. Bristol-Myers Squibb Co., 85 F.3d 270, 275, 70 FEP 1639 (7th Cir. 1996) (court reversed grant of summary judgment in age discrimination case where employer's proffered rationale for adverse employment decision was based upon employer's strained interpretation of its own code of conduct and an unpersuasive comparison of plaintiff's offenses to those of younger people whom employer fired); Tomka v. Seiler Corp., 66 F.3d 1295, 1308–10, 68 FEP 1508 (2d Cir. 1995) (summary judgment reversed on retaliatory discharge claim when evidence created ambiguity regarding employer's communication with employee regarding need to provide medical documentation for leave of absence following alleged sexual assaults by male co-workers; employer's investigation and response to alleged sexual assaults reported by employee also raised concerns about true reasons for employer's termination of employee's salary and benefits one month after she complained of assaults); Dunning v. Simmons Airlines, Inc., 62 F.3d 863, 869–72, 68 FEP 785 (7th Cir. 1995) (trial court disbelieved supervisor's claim that there were no light-duty jobs available for pregnant employee); Evans v. Connecticut, 935 F. Supp. 145, 158–60, 73 FEP 131 (D. Conn. 1996) (in addition to utilizing statistical evidence, trial court found pretext in Title VII race discrimination case where reasons proffered by defendants for taking challenged action were in many respects insignificant to actual decisionmakers, where there were serious discrepancies in defendants' stated reasons for the decision and serious deficiencies in defendants' proffer of evidence, and where the decisionmaker ultimately responsible for the challenged employment action admitted that his decision to terminate plaintiff was basically subjective and revealed that he harbored serious subjective bias toward minorities), *opinion amended,* 967 F. Supp. 673 (D. Conn. 1997); Terry v. Gallegos, 926 F. Supp. 679, 703–05 (W.D. Tenn. 1996) (employer stated that it did not select employee for position because employee did not apply; proffered reason was contradicted by employer's own policy of permitting employees to be promoted without applying for position after completing candidate program); Eldred v. Consolidated Freightways Corp., 898 F. Supp. 928, 938–39, 71 FEP 33 (D. Mass. 1995) (employer's articulated reason for failing

the employer changed its rationale or acted irregularly in some other way.[50]

5. Instructing the Jury

The Seventh Circuit has proposed a one sentence jury instruction for ADEA cases. In *Gehring v. Case Corp.*,[51] the court stated that the phrase "determining factor" has no useful role to play in jury instructions under the ADEA because often there are more factors than age at work when an employer makes an employment decision.[52] The court suggested the following jury instruction because it uses familiar words, avoids double negatives, and can be tailored to the circumstances of the claim: "You [the fact finder]

---

to promote employee—lack of aggressiveness—was a "smoke screen" where employer promoted other male employees whose evaluations noted a lack of aggressiveness); Long v. Ringling Bros.-Barnum & Bailey Combined Shows, Inc., 882 F. Supp. 1553, 1559–60, 67 FEP 1685 (D. Md. 1995) (employer's articulated reason for not hiring the plaintiff was that insufficient time existed for plaintiff to complete two months of necessary training; court found this reason to be pretextual where plaintiff offered evidence that employer had no set time period for training, employer's own employee testified that plaintiff's experience would probably shorten the time period necessary for training, and neither the advertisement describing the position nor the order form placed with the employer's recruiting agency made any reference to the two-month training period as a prerequisite for employment); DeNardo v. Clarence House Imports, Ltd., 870 F. Supp. 227, 232–33, 70 FEP 1539 (N.D. Ill. 1994) (when employer claimed termination of pregnant employee was the result of financial trouble, employee created genuine issue of material fact by setting forth evidence that the employer hired another person within two months of employee's termination to perform virtually the same duties as terminated employee).

[50]Antol v. Perry, 82 F.3d 1291, 1301, 70 FEP 993 (3d Cir. 1996) (employer's failure to follow its own affirmative action plan and its employees' resistance to plan's implementation were factors creating a material issue regarding whether employer's articulated reason was pretextual); Thurman v. Yellow Freight Sys., Inc., 90 F.3d 1160, 1167, 72 FEP 657 (6th Cir.) ("An employer's changing rationale for making an adverse employment decision can be evidence of pretext.") (citing Edwards v. U.S. Postal Serv., 909 F.3d 320, 324 (8th Cir. 1990)), *opinion amended,* 97 F.3d 833 (6th Cir. 1996) (en banc); Kobrin v. Univ. of Minn., 34 F.3d 698, 703, 65 FEP 1624 (8th Cir. 1994) ("substantial changes over time in the employer's proffered reason for its employment decision support a finding of pretext") (citing Briscoe v. Fred's Dollar Store, Inc., 24 F.3d 1026, 1028, 64 FEP 1185 (8th Cir. 1994)); *cf.* Fischbach v. District of Columbia Dep't of Corrections, 86 F.3d 1180, 1183–85, 71 FEP 316 (D.C. Cir. 1996) (although employer failed to follow its own prescribed procedures in selection process, the court held such a failure was not pretextual where the process utilized was reasonable and was the employer's usual practice).

[51]43 F.3d 340, 344, 66 FEP 1373 (7th Cir. 1994), *cert. denied,* 515 U.S. 1159 (1995).

[52]*Id.*

must decide whether the employer would have fired [demoted, laid off] the employee if the employee had been younger than 40 and everything else had remained the same."[53] In other words, the jury must determine whether age was the "but for" cause of the employer's adverse decision.[54]

C. Proof of Disparate Treatment in Mixed-Motive Cases

The plaintiff has a relatively high hurdle to surmount before being entitled to the benefit of the *Price Waterhouse* instruction.[55]

---

[53]*Id.*

[54]*See* Fuka v. Thomson Consumer Electronics, 82 F.3d 1397, 1402, 71 FEP 1417 (7th Cir 1996) (to succeed on a claim under the ADEA, the plaintiff must show that an adverse employment action would not have occurred "but for" the employer's motive to discriminate on the basis of age); Carson v. Bethlehem Steel Corp., 82 F.3d 157, 159, 70 FEP 921 (7th Cir. 1996) (the central question in any employment discrimination case is whether the employer would have taken the same action had the employee been of a different age and everything else had remained the same); Umpleby v. Potter & Brumfield, Inc., 69 F.3d 209, 213, 72 FEP 1047 (7th Cir. 1995) (the plaintiff in an ADEA action is required to prove that the same employment decision would not have been made if the plaintiff was younger than 40).

[55]*See, e.g.,* Tomsic v. State Farm Mut. Auto. Ins. Co., 85 F.3d 1472, 1479, 71 FEP 137 (10th Cir. 1996) (remarks by decisionmaker reflecting "stereotyped views of women and of marriage" were mere expressions of "personal opinion" and thus "constitute[d] circumstantial or indirect evidence, and not direct evidence"); Smith v. F.W. Morse & Co., 76 F.3d 413, 421, 69 FEP 1687 (1st Cir. 1996) ("Absent the evidentiary equivalent of a 'smoking gun,' the plaintiff must attempt to prove her case by resort to a burden-shifting framework."); Nitschke v. McDonnell Douglas Corp., 68 F.3d 249, 253, 71 FEP 99 (8th Cir. 1995) (same); Fuller v. Phipps, 67 F.3d 1137, 1141, 69 FEP 111 (4th Cir. 1995) ("What is required . . . is evidence of conduct or statements that both reflect directly the alleged discriminatory attitude and that bear directly on the contested employment decision."); Mooney v. Aramco Servs. Co., 54 F.3d 1207, 1218, 68 FEP 421 (5th Cir. 1995) (employees not entitled to mixed-motive instruction because statements proffered by plaintiff as direct evidence of age discrimination did not provide proof of discriminatory animus "without inference or presumption"); Hutson v. McDonnell Douglas Corp., 63 F.3d 771, 780, 68 FEP 1209 (8th Cir. 1995) ("[W]hen the plaintiff relies on a discriminatory 'attitude' in the workplace to justify *Price Waterhouse* analysis, there must be a showing of a causal relationship between that attitude and the adverse employment action."); Armbruster v. Unisys Corp., 32 F.3d 768, 778, 65 FEP 828 (3d Cir. 1994) ("[T]he evidence required to come within the *Price Waterhouse* framework must directly reflect a discriminatory or retaliatory animus on the part of a person involved in the decisionmaking process."); Manzer v. Diamond Shamrock Chems. Co., 29 F.3d 1078, 1081, 65 FEP 585 (6th Cir. 1994) ("Because this evidence [requiring an inference] is, at most, circumstantial evidence of discrimination, *Price Waterhouse* is not applicable."). *But cf.* Cram v. Lamson & Sessions Co., 49 F.3d 466, 471, 67 FEP 449 (8th Cir. 1995) (the evidence may be circumstantial but must be "tied directly to the alleged discriminatory animus").

Most courts require that a plaintiff produce direct evidence of discrimination.[56] One court has criticized this approach noting that

---

[56]For recent cases in which the courts utilizing this approach found "direct evidence" of discrimination, see Wilson v. Susquehanna Township Police Dep't, 55 F.3d 126, 67 FEP 1345 (3d Cir. 1995) (police chief's remark that there would be no women supervisors while he was in charge, combined with evidence that a woman had never been appointed to a supervisory position and that male officers had shown pornographic videos at work, was sufficient to compel mixed-motive analysis); Hennessy v. Penril Datacomm Networks, Inc., 69 F.3d 1344, 1348–50, 69 FEP 398 (7th Cir. 1995) (supervisor's comment that he was surprised to find plaintiff pregnant because he thought she was a "career woman," and company president's statement that he did not like to hire female salespeople "because they get pregnant," constituted direct evidence); Haynes v. W.C. Caye & Co., 52 F.3d 928, 930, 67 FEP 1537 (11th Cir. 1995) (supervisor's statements that women were not "tough enough" to supervise collections and that "it would require a man to do the job" were direct evidence of sex discrimination); Robinson v. PPG Indus., Inc., 23 F.3d 1159, 1164–65, 64 FEP 1690 (7th Cir. 1994) (statements of supervisor who ranked employees prior to reduction in force, implying that employer would not keep employees until they reached age 65, "could be construed as a corporate goal to boot employees out before they retired" and thus constituted direct evidence of discrimination); Hearn v. General Elec. Co., 927 F. Supp. 1486, 1499, 71 FEP 435 (M.D. Ala. 1996) (male manager's statement that "I don't like working for a . . . woman and I don't want one working for me" was direct evidence of gender discrimination).

For cases in which the courts did not consider the proffered evidence sufficiently "direct" to entitle the plaintiff to the *Price Waterhouse* instruction, see de La Cruz v. New York City Human Resources Admin., 82 F.3d 16, 23, 70 FEP 893 (2d Cir. 1996) (supervisor's comments to Hispanic plaintiff, in the context of an allegedly discriminatory transfer, that his problems were "cultural" and that plaintiff and his new Hispanic supervisor would "understand each other better" were not direct evidence of national origin discrimination, where plaintiff's English language skills were shown to be deficient), cert. denied, ___ U.S. ___ (1996); Fuller v. Phipps, 67 F.3d 1137, 1141, 69 FEP 111 (4th Cir. 1995) (statistics reflecting low number of African-Americans hired and plaintiff's superior qualifications were insufficient to constitute direct evidence of a discriminatory attitude); Nitschke v. McDonnell Douglas Corp., 68 F.3d 249, 253, 71 FEP 99 (8th Cir. 1995) (document written by company president referring to the need to hire and retain best young talent was not direct evidence of discrimination, as it was written six years before plaintiff's termination and company president was not involved in decision to terminate plaintiff); Philipp v. ANR Freight Sys., Inc., 61 F.3d 669, 675, 70 FEP 1347 (8th Cir. 1995) (references to plaintiff as an "old man" and statements by former company officials who were not employed when the challenged reduction in force was implemented did not justify mixed-motive analysis); Bialas v. Greyhound Lines, Inc., 59 F.3d 759, 762–64, 68 FEP 552 (8th Cir. 1995) (memorandum that did not directly address employees' age, but rather the fact that some managers resisted company's reorganization, written by a manager who did not take part in the terminations at issue, did not constitute direct evidence of discrimination); Kriss v. Sprint Communications Co., 58 F.3d 1276, 1281–82, 68 FEP 1382 (8th Cir. 1995) (decisionmaker's statements that certain sales representatives were not ready to "run with the stallions," that a high-ranking female manager was "ugly," and that another female employee was a "bitch" were "little more than 'stray remarks in the workplace' and 'statements by decision-makers

direct evidence is not required so long as the plaintiff submits "enough evidence that, if believed, could reasonably allow a jury to conclude that the adverse employment consequences were 'because of' an impermissible factor."[57]

---

unrelated to the decisional process itself' "); Armbruster v. Unisys Corp., 32 F.3d 768, 778, 65 FEP 828 (3d Cir. 1994) (statement that employer could "not afford to keep people over 50 [years of age] and 50 [thousand dollars per year]" was insufficient to merit mixed-motive instruction, where the speaker was not involved in decisionmaking process); Clark v. Hess Trucking Co., 879 F. Supp. 524, 530, 69 FEP 195 (W.D. Pa. 1995) (vice president's use of racially offensive language in conversation with plaintiff was not direct evidence of discrimination, where plaintiff was unable to demonstrate that vice president participated in decision to terminate him); Reiff v. Interim Personnel, Inc., 906 F. Supp. 1280, 1288, 5 AD 740 (D. Minn. 1995) (supervisor's alleged concern over rising insurance costs due to plaintiff's disability did not constitute direct evidence of discrimination because plaintiff failed to demonstrate a "specific link" between the alleged discriminatory animus and the challenged decision); Maidenbaum v. Bally's Park Place, Inc., 870 F. Supp. 1254, 1261–62, 68 FEP 1245 (D.N.J. 1994) (memorandum that listed employees' ages and the revocation of a seniority-based termination policy four days before plaintiffs were laid off did not constitute direct evidence of age discrimination), *aff'd without opinion*, 67 F.3d 291, 69 FEP 320 (3d Cir. 1995).

[57]Tyler v. Bethlehem Steel Corp., 958 F.2d 1176, 1187, 59 FEP 875 (2d Cir.), *cert. denied,* 506 U.S. 826 (1992) (direct evidence of discrimination is not a "precondition" for a mixed-motive case). *See also* Cram v. Lamson & Sessions Co., 49 F.3d 466, 471, 67 FEP 449 (8th Cir. 1995) (the evidence may be circumstantial but must be "tied directly to the alleged discriminatory animus").

Part 2

Second Category of Discrimination—Present Effects of Past Discrimination

Chapter 3

SENIORITY

II. Seniority and Transfer Rights

B. The Bona Fide Seniority System Defense

Section 703(h) continues to immunize bona fide seniority systems from disparate impact challenges under Title VII.[1]

Courts have interpreted the Age Discrimination in Employment Act's bona fide seniority system defense[2] similarly to § 703(h) as a bar to disparate impact challenges to the operation or effect of seniority systems.[3] The interplay between the ADEA and seniority systems is discussed more fully in Chapter 16 (Age).

---

[1] *See* Sanchez v. City of Santa Ana, 928 F. Supp. 1494, 1502 n.6, 1503–05 (C.D. Cal. 1995) (§ 703(h) barred challenge to city police force's promotional system that gave "seniority point additives" and to portion of merit pay plan that rewarded length of service); Fontelroy v. Day & Zimmermann, Inc., 1995 WL 530666 (D. Kan. Sept. 7, 1995) (court rejected disparate impact challenge to layoff plan based on unit or classification seniority rather than plant seniority), *aff'd,* 83 F.3d 431 (10th Cir. 1996).
[2] 29 U.S.C. § 623(f)(2).
[3] *See* Hiatt v. Union Pac. R.R., 65 F.3d 838, 842–43, 68 FEP 1160 (10th Cir. 1995) (court rejected disparate impact challenge under ADEA by railroad brakemen who were given promotions to conductor mandated by federal law but could not carry their seniority with them and therefore were forced to perform undesirable work; their treatment was driven by a neutral seniority system, and nothing obligated the railroad to dovetail seniority in the two groups or otherwise give the promoted brakemen preferential treatment), *cert. denied,* 116 S. Ct. 917 (1996); EEOC v. Newport Mesa Unified Sch. Dist., 893 F. Supp. 927, 933–34, 68 FEP 657 (C.D. Cal. 1995) (as a result of collective bargaining agreement that provided greater pay based on past experience, school district preferred hiring less experienced and thus less expensive teachers; court rejected EEOC's argument that district should be required to offer more experienced teachers lower pay than provided for in the collective bargaining agreement on the ground that the agreement was protected by the bona fide seniority system defense of the ADEA).

Part 3

Third Category of Discrimination—Adverse Impact

CHAPTER 4

ADVERSE IMPACT

I. Overview

Although a plaintiff can, and frequently will, combine disparate treatment and adverse impact claims as alternative theories of liability, the two are mutually exclusive; the former theory applies to intentional discrimination, the latter to attacks on rules "fair in form, but discriminatory in operation."[1] Thus, if a challenged rule or practice is expressly based on a protected characteristic such as race or sex, no adverse impact challenge is possible. For example, in *Healey v. Southwood Psychiatric Hospital*,[2] the plaintiff challenged a hospital practice of making sex-based shift assignments. The court noted that the hospital "uses sex as an explicit factor in assigning . . . shifts," and held that "[a]nalysis under disparate impact is not appropriate where plaintiff claims injury based on a facially discriminatory policy."[3]

II. Historical Development and Statutory Authority

A. The Plaintiff's Prima Facie Case

Although plaintiffs typically will offer some sort of formalized statistical analysis in support of their prima facie case, courts continue to recognize that this will not always be necessary. For example, in *EEOC v. Steamship Clerks Local 1066*,[4] the plaintiffs challenged a "sponsorship" rule for admission to membership in the union. In establishing their prima facie case, the plaintiffs relied on the following facts: (1) all 30 of the new members admitted

---

[1] Griggs v. Duke Power Co., 401 U.S. 424, 431, 3 FEP 175 (1971).
[2] 78 F.3d 128, 70 FEP 439 (3d Cir. 1996).
[3] *Id.* at 131.
[4] 48 F.3d 594, 67 FEP 629 (1st Cir.), *cert. denied,* 116 S. Ct. 65 (1995).

to the union between 1980 and 1986 were white; (2) all of these new members were either sons or brothers of existing members (who were all white); and (3) during the relevant period, African-Americans and Hispanics comprised between 8 and 27 percent of the relevant labor market. Attacking the sufficiency of this prima facie showing, the union claimed that absent some "formal statistical analysis" these facts (which were undisputed) were inadequate. The First Circuit rejected this view as "untenable."[5] "[T]hough one would normally expect sound statistical analyses to assist a plaintiff in making out a prima facie case, . . . the absence of such analyses, by itself, does not automatically doom the plaintiff's efforts . . . . To hold otherwise would effectively subordinate the whole of Title VII, in every last disparate impact case, to the sometimes vagarious sway of statistical proof."[6]

A plaintiff, however, does retain the burden of proving that members of the protected group are disproportionately disadvantaged by the employer's policy. In *Long v. First Union Corp. of Virginia*,[7] for example, the court rejected the position taken by the EEOC in its guidelines[8] that an adverse impact is demonstrated as a matter of law whenever the employer adopts an English-only policy.[9] Similarly, in *Alford v. City of Montgomery*,[10] the plaintiff's disparate impact claim failed because she was unable to show that the employer's threshold requirements for promotion had adversely affected any other African-Americans or women.

Although there will be circumstances in which the statistical disparity will be sufficiently plain to make sophisticated statistical analyses unnecessary, it typically will not be appropriate for a court to take judicial notice of such a disparity. In *York v. American Telephone & Telegraph*,[11] the plaintiff sought a position as an operating engineer in one of the employer's power plants. She was rejected because she did not have sufficient operational experience to satisfy the employer's job requirements. The plaintiff challenged

---

[5] *Id.* at 606.
[6] *Id.*
[7] 894 F. Supp. 933, 68 FEP 917 (E.D. Va. 1995), *aff'd mem.*, 86 F.3d 1151, 71 FEP 736 (4th Cir. 1996).
[8] 29 C.F.R. § 1607(a) and (b).
[9] Long v. First Union Corp. of Va., 894 F. Supp. at 939.
[10] 879 F. Supp. 1143 (M.D. Ala. 1995), *aff'd mem.*, 79 F.3d 1160 (11th Cir. 1996).
[11] 95 F.3d 948, 73 FEP 1654 (10th Cir. 1996).

the experience requirement and asked the court to take judicial notice that "few if any women in the Oklahoma City area would be able to satisfy a two-year experience requirement."[12] The Tenth Circuit held that the district court's refusal to do so was not an abuse of discretion because the number of women in the area able to satisfy the requirement is neither generally known nor readily determinable—the standard for judicial notice under Federal Rule of Evidence 201(b).

1. The Threshold Showing of Adverse Impact

In *Watson v. Fort Worth Bank & Trust*,[13] the Supreme Court noted that the "80 percent rule" contained in the Uniform Guidelines on Employee Selection Procedures[14] had been subject to substantial academic criticism and that, at best, it provides a "rule of thumb" for measuring the impact of an employer practice.[15] Since *Watson*, however, some courts have continued to apply the 80 percent or "four fifths" rule as a basis for finding disparate impact.[16] Other courts, however, have been more reticent in using the test. In *Jones v. Pepsi-Cola Metropolitan Bottling Co.*,[17] for example, the court held that the plaintiff's reliance on the four fifths rule was inappropriate because the sample size was relatively small (189) and because the plaintiff's analysis "does not combine the 4/5ths test [80 percent rule] with standard deviation or other statistical evidence."[18] In keeping with *Watson*, other recent cases evince a judicial preference for standard deviation analysis.[19]

---

[12]*Id.* at 958.
[13]487 U.S. 977, 47 FEP 102 (1988).
[14]29 U.S.C. §§ 1607.1, 1607.4(D).
[15]487 U.S. at 995 n.3.
[16]Fickling v. New York State Dep't of Civil Serv., 909 F. Supp. 185, 189 (S.D.N.Y. 1995) (calling the 80% rule a "widely accepted benchmark for assessing disparate impact"); Sanchez v. City of Santa Ana, 928 F. Supp. 1494 (C.D. Cal. 1995) (police department's adjustment of passing score to eliminate disparate impact with respect to pass/fail did not ameliorate test's disparate impact with respect to hiring since candidates were selected based on relative test score ranking), *order issued,* 1996 WL 364765 (C.D. Cal. Jan. 23, 1996); Palmer v. Kroger Co., 1994 U.S. Dist. LEXIS 8283 (E.D. Mich. Mar. 14, 1994) (applying 80% rule).
[17]871 F. Supp. 305 (E.D. Mich. 1994).
[18]*Id.* at 311.
[19]*See, e.g.,* NAACP v. Town of East Haven, 70 F.3d 219, 221, 69 FEP 500 (2d Cir. 1995); Clark v. Pennsylvania, 885 F. Supp. 694, 69 FEP 1379 (E.D. Pa. 1995).

2. The Appropriate Method of Comparison

a. The Relevant Labor Market. Although the Civil Rights Act of 1991[20] was intended to overrule certain aspects of *Wards Cove Packing Co. v. Atonio*,[21] courts continue to follow the "relevant labor market" analysis described in that case, i.e., that the proper comparison in an adverse impact case is between the composition of the "qualified persons in the labor market and the persons holding at-issue jobs."[22] In *Vitug v. Multistate Tax Commission*,[23] for example, the plaintiff attacked the employer's word-of-mouth recruiting and use of subjective evaluations, but failed to make the necessary showing of causation because he did not compare the employer's hiring and promotion rates for those in the protected classes to data reflecting the demographic makeup of the relevant labor market.[24]

c. "Bottom-Line" Statistics. (i.) The bottom-line defense. The Supreme Court decision in *Connecticut v. Teal* virtually eliminated the bottom-line defense when a component in the employer's selection process has an adverse impact on a particular group.[25] Employers may still defend against such claims, if the test is not a pass/fail barrier, by challenging the significance of plaintiff's statistics or by demonstrating the business necessity and job relatedness of the selection method.[26]

(ii.) The bottom-line offense. Following the Supreme Court's decision in *Wards Cove Packing Co. v. Atonio*,[27] courts have continued to hold that a plaintiff generally cannot establish a prima facie case under an adverse impact theory by showing only that the cumulative impact of the employer's selection procedures results in an adverse impact on members of a protected class. Rather, a plaintiff generally must identify a particular part of the selection

---

[20] Pub. L. No. 102-166, 1991 U.S.C.C.A.N. (105 Stat.) 1071 (codified as 42 U.S.C. § 1981 note).

[21] 490 U.S. 642, 49 FEP 1519 (1989).

[22] *Id.* at 650.

[23] 88 F.3d 506, 71 FEP 1445 (7th Cir. 1996).

[24] *Accord* Forehand v. Florida State Hosp. at Chattahoochee, 89 F.3d 1562, 1574, 71 FEP 905 (11th Cir. 1996) (same); Edwards v. Wallace Community College, 49 F.3d 1517, 1520, 67 FEP 949 (11th Cir. 1995).

[25] 457 U.S. 440, 29 FEP 1 (1982).

[26] *See* Sections II.A.3 and II.B *infra*.

[27] 490 U.S. 642, 49 FEP 1519 (1989).

process that causes the adverse impact.[28] Where the particular components in the selection process "are not capable of separation," however, the Civil Rights Act of 1991 permits the plaintiff to make out a prima facie case based on adverse impact at the bottom line.[29]

The court in *Graffam v. Scott Paper Co.* held that the components of the employer's selection process were not separable.[30] There, the plaintiff established a prima facie case of adverse impact by showing that the reduction in force at the defendant's paper mill resulted in an "overall rate of retention of 61% of employees age fifty and older, and an overall rate of retention of 91% of employees under age fifty."[31] In selecting employees for layoff, the company developed a process beginning with the identification by department of job functions and positions to be eliminated.[32] The department heads then divided the jobs in their departments into "job groups," i.e., job clusters that shared comparable skills. The employees in each group were then assessed using a point system.[33] The company selected incumbents for layoff based on their respective ratings.[34]

---

[28] EEOC v. Steamship Clerks Local 1066, 48 F.3d 594, 601, 67 FEP 629 (1st Cir.) ("[T]he plaintiff must identify the challenged employment practice or policy, and pinpoint the defendant's use of it."), *cert. denied,* 116 S. Ct. 65 (1995); Anderson v. Douglas & Lomason Co., 26 F.3d 1277, 1284, 65 FEP 417 (5th Cir. 1994) (court refused to analyze plaintiff's claim under adverse impact theory where plaintiff could not identify a specific aspect of the decisionmaking process that had a causal connection to the alleged imbalance in the workforce), *cert. denied,* 513 U.S. 1149 (1995); Diehl v. Xerox Corp., 933 F. Supp. 1157, 1167, 71 FEP 723 (W.D.N.Y. 1996) ("In order to establish a prima facie case of disparate impact discrimination, plaintiffs must demonstrate that Xerox utilized a specific employment practice which disparately impacted them on the basis of their age and gender."); Donnelly v. Rhode Island Bd. of Governors for Higher Educ., 929 F. Supp. 583, 588, 71 FEP 363 (D.R.I. 1996) (to establish a prima facie case, employee must prove that a particular employment practice has an adverse impact on a group and that there is a causal relationship between the identified practice and the adverse impact), *aff'd on other grounds,* 110 F.3d 2, 73 FEP 972 (1st Cir. 1997); Matthews v. Runyon, 860 F. Supp. 1347, 1355, 67 FEP 1515 (E.D. Wis. 1994) (plaintiff is "responsible for isolating and identifying the specific employment practices that are allegedly responsible for any observed statistical disparities") (internal citations and quotations omitted).

[29] 42 U.S.C. § 2000e-2(k)(1)(B).

[30] 870 F. Supp. 389, 66 FEP 1007 (D. Me. 1994), *aff'd,* 60 F.3d 809, 71 FEP 736 (1st Cir. 1995).

[31] *Id.* at 392.

[32] *Id.* at 400.

[33] *Id.* at 400–01.

[34] *Id.* at 401.

3. Responses to the Plaintiff's Statistical Evidence

Courts continue to recognize that a statistical sample may be too small to produce a reliable analysis.[35] In *EEOC v. Steamship Clerks Local 1066*,[36] however, the court rejected the claim that the sample size (30 new members admitted under an allegedly unlawful membership policy) was too small to permit meaningful analysis. It suggested, without extended explanation, that the concern over small sample sizes is limited to challenges to "screening test[s] for admission to employment."[37] In other cases, the court said, "in weighing the probative value of statistical evidence, 'even small samples are not per se unacceptable'."[38]

B. Business Necessity and Job Relatedness

Courts have yet to sort out the implications of the Civil Rights Act of 1991[39] on the "business necessity/job relatedness" inquiry in adverse impact cases. As the Eighth Circuit recently recalled in *Houghton v. SIPCO, Inc.*,[40] under *Wards Cove*, "there [was] no requirement that the challenged practice be 'essential' or 'indispensable' to the employer's business for it to pass muster: this degree of scrutiny would be almost impossible for most employers to meet."[41] Whether, or how, this standard was changed by the 1991 Act is the subject of continued debate.

The language of the 1991 Act, which requires that the challenged practice be "consistent with business necessity," does little

---

[35] *See, e.g.,* Vitug v. Multistate Tax Comm'n, 88 F.3d 506, 71 FEP 1445 (7th Cir. 1995) (no meaningful statistical comparison is possible when the employer has filled only four of the relevant jobs); Balele v. Klauser, 1996 U.S. App. LEXIS 1012 (7th Cir. Jan. 11, 1996) (sample size of 19 is too small to produce meaningful statistical analysis).

[36] 48 F.3d 594, 67 FEP 629 (1st Cir.), *cert. denied,* 116 S. Ct. 65 (1995).

[37] *Id.* at 604.

[38] *Id.* (quoting Freeman v. Package Mach. Co., 865 F.2d 1331, 1342 n.5, 49 FEP 1139 (1st Cir. 1988)).

[39] Pub. L. No. 102-166, 1991 U.S.C.C.A.N. (105 Stat.) 1071 (codified as 42 USC § 1981 note).

[40] 38 F.3d 953, 66 FEP 97 (8th Cir. 1994).

[41] *Id.* at 959 (quoting *Wards Cove,* 490 U.S. at 659). Of course, even the presumably less onerous *Wards Cove* standard is no guarantee of employer success. *See* Melendez v. Illinois Bell Tel. Co., 79 F.3d 661, 70 FEP 589 (7th Cir. 1996) (concluding that employer had failed to satisfy *Wards Cove* "legitimate business reasons" standard in validating standardized test for managerial candidates in case filed before the effective date of the Civil Rights Act of 1991).

to suggest whether a new standard should apply, and if so what that standard might be. One district court recently noted that the new statutory phrase is laden with ambiguity; "[t]wo things are consistent with one another if they are in harmony as opposed to being in conflict."[42] "On the other hand, something is a necessity if it is required or compelled."[43] Presumably, a thing can be "consistent with" business necessity without being, in *Wards Cove's* words, " 'essential' or 'indispensable' to the employer's business."

The legislative history is of limited assistance. The Act explicitly embraced an "interpretative memorandum" authored by then-Senator Danforth as the only reliable legislative history on the meaning of the term "business necessity."[44] That memorandum, in turn, states only that Congress used the term "to reflect the [business necessity] concept [ ] enunciated in *Griggs v. Duke Power* and in other Supreme Court decisions prior" to *Wards Cove Packing Co. v. Atonio.*[45] This hardly resolves the matter since there is substantial disagreement over the meaning of pre-*Wards Cove* decisions.[46]

This has left lower courts without much guidance. The district court in *Donnelly v. Rhode Island Board of Governors for Higher Education*[47] gave several reasons for rejecting the notion that Congress intended the business necessity defense to be applicable only when the employer could show that the challenged practice was an indispensable prerequisite to continued operation. First, the court noted that one of the early drafts of the 1991 amendments used the phrase "required by business necessity"—something the court believed to be closer to an "indispensability" test than the "consistent with" language actually adopted.[48] When Congress later substituted the phrase "consistent with" for "required by," the court decided, it

---

[42]Donnelly v. Rhode Island Bd. of Governors for Higher Educ., 929 F.Supp. 583, 593, 71 FEP 363 (D.R.I. 1996), *aff'd on other grounds*, 110 F.3d 2, 73 FEP 972 (1st Cir. 1997).

[43]*Id.*

[44]*See* note following 42 U.S.C. § 1981, citing the memorandum reprinted at 137 Cong. Rec. S15276 (daily ed. Oct. 25, 1991). The entire provision states that "[n]o statements other than the interpretive memorandum appearing [at this cite] shall be considered legislative history of, or relied upon in any way as legislative history in construing or applying, any provision of this Act . . . that relates to *Wards Cove*-business necessity/cumulation/alternative business practice."

[45]490 U.S. 642, 49 FEP 1519 (1989).

[46]*See* Section II.B of the Main Edition.

[47]929 F. Supp. 583, 71 FEP 363 (D.R.I. 1996), *aff'd on other grounds*, 110 F.3d 2, 73 FEP 972 (1st Cir. 1997).

[48]*Id.* at 593.

strongly suggested that a less perfect nexus to continued operation was envisioned by Congress. The court also noted that a plaintiff can overcome the employer's proof of "business necessity" by showing that an alternative business practice would serve the employer's interests as well without an adverse impact (or with a reduced impact).[49] If "business necessity" actually meant that the challenged practice had to be an indispensable prerequisite to continued operation, by definition no "alternate practice" would be possible and the alternative business practice language would be meaningless.[50] The *Donnelly* court concluded that an employer has satisfied its business necessity burden if it shows that the challenged practice "is reasonably necessary to achieve an important business purpose."[51]

Other courts, without much explanation, have articulated the standard for meeting the business necessity defense in different ways. One district court merely opined that the employer's policy must only serve "a legitimate business need."[52] The Eighth Circuit, on the other hand, simply announced that the business necessity defense requires that an employer show that the challenged standard is "necessary to safe and effective job performance,"[53] but then held that "[t]he lack of a precise or universally perfect fit between a job requirement and actual effective performance is not fatal to a claim of business necessity, particularly when the public health and safety are at stake."[54] This lack of consistent phraseology in articulating the employer's burden for rebutting a prima facie case based on business necessity thus continues to lend confusion to this area.

III. Remedies

In *Eldredge v. Carpenters Local 46 Northern California Counties Joint Apprenticeship & Training Committee*,[55] the Ninth Circuit

---

[49] 42 U.S.C. § 2000e-2(k)(1)(C).
[50] 929 F. Supp. at 593.
[51] *Id.* at 594; Long v. First Union Corp. of Va., 894 F. Supp. 933, 68 FEP 917 (E.D. Va. 1995), *aff'd,* 86 F.3d 1151, 71 FEP 736 (4th Cir. 1996).
[52] Smith v. City of Des Moines, 99 F.3d 1466, 1471, 6 AD 14 (8th Cir. 1996).
[53] *Id.* at 1473.
[54] *Id.*
[55] 94 F.3d 1366, 71 FEP 1385 (9th Cir. 1996), *cert. denied,* 117 S. Ct. 1470 (1997).

held that the district court's refusal to adopt a proposed 20 percent set-aside remedy for positions in an apprenticeship program was an abuse of discretion given the union's long-standing "egregious and obstinate" conduct.[56]

In *EEOC v. Steamship Clerks Local No. 1066*,[57] the First Circuit held that the district court had abused its discretion by proceeding directly from its determination of liability to issuing an award of injunctive relief without affording either party notice. The appellate court noted, however, that the defendant had no absolute right to an evidentiary hearing; "due process does not necessarily require any particular kind of hearing," and litigants "have no absolute right to present their arguments in whatever way they may prefer, or to expostulate for as long as they may choose."[58]

The preliminary injunctive authority of trial courts pending resolution on the merits was at issue in *NAACP v. Town of East Haven*.[59] Presented with what it found to be substantial evidence of discriminatory hiring practices and a motion for preliminary injunctive relief, the district court refused to enter a requested injunction prohibiting the city from hiring any police officers or firefighters at least until the underlying action was resolved on the merits, concluding that it could not enter an order of the sort requested because of considerations of public safety. The Second Circuit vacated the trial court's order. It noted that the town of East Haven had carried substantial staffing shortages for years prior to the litigation without apparent impact on public safety and that the town had not been moving aggressively to fill the vacant positions in the years prior to the request for injunctive relief. The appellate court remanded for reconsideration.

---

[56]*Id.* at 1371.
[57]48 F.3d 594, 67 FEP 629 (1st Cir.), *cert. denied*, 116 S. Ct. 65 (1995).
[58]*Id.* at 609.
[59]70 F.3d 219, 69 FEP 500 (2d Cir. 1995).

Chapter 5

SCORED TESTS

I. Introduction

Recent cases suggest that employers continue to be moving away from tests that attempt to measure basic cognitive aptitude and toward examinations that test specific job knowledge and functions.[1] Increasingly, courts include in their decisions a detailed discussion of the steps taken during test development including, in particular, the development of a thorough job analysis.[2]

II. Overview of Coverage and Relevant Statutory Provisions

A. Title VII

3. State Licensing Examinations

While some courts continue to hold that state licensing boards are not employers within the meaning of Title VII,[3] the Northern

---

[1]Rudder v. District of Columbia, 890 F. Supp. 23, 47 (D.D.C. 1995) (upholding three-part firefighter test assessing job knowledge, behavioral characteristics, and a simulated fire scene), *aff'd without opinion,* 99 F.3d 448 (D.C. Cir. 1996); United Black Firefighters Ass'n v. City of Akron, 66 FEP 1452, 1461 (N.D. Ohio 1994) (job knowledge component of firefighter test found to be job related), *aff'd without opinion,* 81 F.3d 161 (6th Cir. 1996); Adams v. City of Chicago, 1996 WL 137660, at *11 (N.D. Ill. Mar. 25, 1996) (police promotion exam that included in-basket simulation and oral "briefing" component).

[2]Brown v. City of Chicago, 917 F. Supp. 577, 579–80 (N.D. Ill. 1996) (outside consultant prepared examination for police lieutenant position after interviews, ride-alongs, station house observations, and reviews by senior police officials); Adams v. City of Chicago, 1996 WL 137660, at *7 (detailing steps taken by industrial psychologist in developing a police promotion examination).

[3]McFarland v. Folsom, 854 F. Supp. 862, 879 (M.D. Ala. 1994) (the Alabama Bar Association is not an employer under Title VII).

District of Illinois ruled that the reach of Title VII extends to private associations that certify the achievement of a level of expertise. In *Morrison v. American Board of Psychiatry & Neurology, Inc.*,[4] the court followed the rationale adopted by the District of Columbia and the Seventh Circuits[5] that entities meeting the Title VII definition of "employer"[6] may violate the Act if they are in a position to interfere with the employment relationship between a Title VII plaintiff and a third party.[7] The court in *Morrison* found that the defendant board was not a licensing agency, because it did not issue licenses required for the practice of psychiatry but merely certified the achievement of a level of expertise.[8] The court then held, in accordance with the decision in *Association of Mexican-American Educators v. California*,[9] that the board was subject to Title VII based on the plaintiff's allegation that "the lack of certification will significantly inhibit [the plaintiff's] future employment prospects."[10]

---

[4]908 F. Supp. 582, 584–86, 69 FEP 1217 (N.D. Ill. 1996).
[5]Doe v. St. Joseph Hosp., 788 F.2d 411, 422–25, 40 FEP 820 (7th Cir. 1986) (a hospital's discriminatory withholding of staff privileges may violate Title VII if it interferes with a physician's ability to serve and retain patients); Sibley Memorial Hosp. v. Wilson, 488 F.2d 1338, 1341, 6 FEP 1029 (D.C. Cir. 1973) (private duty nurse may challenge hospital's registry and referral system under Title VII as discriminating on the basis of sex). *See also* Gomez v. Alexian Bros. Hosp., 698 F.2d 1019, 1021–22, 30 FEP 1705 (9th Cir. 1983) (physician whose professional corporation sought a contract to run hospital's emergency room may state a Title VII claim against a hospital that is subject to Title VII and has the power to interfere with the plaintiff's employment opportunities with the professional corporation).
[6]42 U.S.C. § 2000e(b) (a person engaged in an industry affecting commerce who has 15 or more employees and any agent of such person).
[7]The *Morrison* court also disagreed with the exception that other courts have afforded licensing agencies, rejecting the argument that there should be a public policy exception because licensing agencies perform a "policing function of public importance." The court reasoned:

> If Title VII bars a party from placing a discriminatory impediment between an individual and his or her employment relationship with a third party, it is certainly inconsistent to conclude that because the function of a licensing board is to impose restrictions for the public good it should not be held liable for doing so in a discriminatory manner.

908 F. Supp. at 585–86 n.11.
[8]*Id.* at 586.
[9]836 F. Supp 1534, 1550–51, 62 FEP 1390 (N.D. Cal. 1993). *See* Section II.A.3 of the Main Edition.
[10]908 F. Supp. at 586.

State licensing agencies also have been subjected to suit under 42 U.S.C. § 1983 on due process[11] or equal protection grounds.[12] The *Morrison* decision recognized a cause of action under 42 U.S.C. § 1981.[13] Under either legal theory, a plaintiff would have to establish intentional discrimination.[14]

III. THE UNIFORM GUIDELINES ON EMPLOYEE SELECTION PROCEDURES

B. Basic Features of the Uniform Guidelines[15]

Courts continue to approve of the Uniform Guidelines' support for the three methods used in conducting validation studies—"criterion-related," "content," and "construct" validity.[16] Establishing a test as being job related by one of these methods is sufficient.[17] However, an assessment of which method is appropriate to validate a particular test may be required.[18]

---

[11]McFarland v. Folsom, 854 F. Supp. at 884 (there may be a due process right to have a licensing examination graded correctly); Partin v. Arkansas State Bd. of Law Examiners, 863 F. Supp. 924, 927–28 (E.D. Ark. 1994) (court abstained from ruling on a due process challenge to disqualification from bar admission due to felony arrests on the ground that the action by the state board of law examiners was fundamentally judicial in nature), *aff'd,* 56 F.3d 69 (8th Cir.), *cert. denied,* 116 S. Ct. 308 (1995).

[12]McFarland v. Folsom, 854 F. Supp. at 879–84 (equal protection challenge to bar examination dismissed due to insufficient facts to prove an intent to discriminate based on race).

[13]Morrison v. American Bd. of Psychiatry & Neurology, 908 F. Supp. at 587–89 (permitted § 1981 claim alleging board examination to be a race-based impediment between the plaintiff and the plaintiff's future job opportunities).

[14]*See* Chapter 24 (The Civil Rights Acts of 1866 and 1871) in the Main Edition.

[15]Uniform Guidelines on Employee Selection Procedures, 29 C.F.R. pt. 1607 (Uniform Guidelines).

[16]Association of Mexican-American Educators v. California, 937 F. Supp. 1397, 1411 (N.D. Cal. 1996); Fickling v. New York State Dep't of Civil Serv., 909 F. Supp. 185, 189 (S.D.N.Y. 1995); Nash v. Consolidated City of Jacksonville, 895 F. Supp. 1536, 1545 (M.D. Fla. 1995), *aff'd,* 85 F.3d 643 (11th Cir. 1996); Rudder v. District of Columbia, 890 F. Supp. 23, 41 (D.D.C. 1995), *aff'd without opinion,* 99 F.3d 448 (D.C. Cir. 1996); Sims v. Montgomery County Comm'n, 890 F. Supp. 1520, 1526 (M.D. Ala. 1995).

[17]Association of Mexican-American Educators v. California, 937 F. Supp. at 1411 (rejecting plaintiffs' argument that written test required for teacher credential shown to be content valid also must be validated by criterion-related or construct validation).

[18]*Id.*

The Sixth Circuit has endorsed the Uniform Guidelines' requirement[19] that employers make a reasonable effort to become aware of alternative selection procedures that may have a lesser adverse impact and include, as a part of a validation study, an investigation of suitable alternative selection procedures and alternative methods of using the selection procedure being studied.[20] Other courts have noted that the defendants explored alternative ways to make a test that is the most effective while having the least adverse impact.[21] Most courts, however, continue to place the burden on the plaintiff to demonstrate an alternative selection procedure that would have comparable utility and less adverse impact.[22]

C. The Weight to Be Accorded Administrative Guidelines on Employer Testing

Courts continue to give deference to the standards set forth in the Uniform Guidelines[23] and to note that these standards have become "accepted benchmarks."[24] However, a district court has indicated that Title VII does not require "strict adherence to the 'intricate details' of the Guidelines."[25]

---

[19]29 C.F.R. § 1607.3(B).

[20]Brunet v. City of Columbus, 1 F.3d 390, 412, 64 FEP 1215 (6th Cir. 1993) (district court committed error by not exploring alternatives to strict rank-order hiring or examining whether the defendant complied with its obligation under the Uniform Guidelines to explore such alternatives before implementing strict rank-ordering), *cert. denied sub nom.* Brunet v. Turner, 510 U.S. 1164 (1994).

[21]Rudder v. District of Columbia, 890 F. Supp. at 37 (test developers placed more emphasis on test component that assessed behavioral characteristics to reduce adverse impact without compromising the validity of the test battery); Adams v. City of Chicago, 1996 WL 137660, at *12 (N.D. Ill. Mar. 25, 1996) (test developer conducted computer simulation to determine whether a different scheme of weighting three test components might produce less adverse impact).

[22]*See* discussion at Section IV *infra*.

[23]Sims v. Montgomery County Comm'n, 890 F. Supp. 1520, 1532 (M.D. Ala. 1995) (court deferred to Uniform Guidelines' use of the four fifths rule in assessing adverse impact).

[24]Fickling v. New York State Dep't of Civil Serv., 909 F. Supp. 185, 188 (S.D.N.Y. 1995) (Uniform Guidelines' four fifths rule recognized as a widely accepted benchmark for assessing adverse impact).

[25]Rudder v. District of Columbia, 890 F. Supp. 23, 40 (D.D.C. 1995), *aff'd without opinion*, 99 F.3d 448 (D.C. Cir. 1996). *See also* Association of Mexican-American Educators v. California, 937 F. Supp. 1397, 1419–20 (N.D. Cal. 1996) (defendants' validity evidence not perfect but not required to be under either legal or scientific standards).

IV. ALLOCATION OF PROOF IN TESTING CASES

The vast majority of testing cases continue to rely upon the adverse impact theory of discrimination rather than a showing of disparate treatment. However, in a case where the plaintiff presented evidence that her supervisor was aware that the civil service examination used to determine promotions yielded no African-American employees eligible for interviews, the court found that the plaintiff had established a prima facie case of disparate treatment.[26] Plaintiff's evidence was sufficient to raise the inference that the supervisor chose to use the civil service exam method, rather than an available alternative method, knowing that it would eliminate African-American candidates.[27]

Courts continue to analyze adverse impact cases using the burden-shifting framework set forth in *Griggs v. Duke Power Co.*[28] and *Albemarle Paper Co. v. Moody.*[29] Once an employer establishes that a test is job related, most courts have held that the plaintiff bears the burden of proving that any suggested alternative employment practice with a lesser adverse impact is equally effective as the challenged practice.[30]

Some courts require employers to conduct an investigation into viable alternative employment selection practices with a lesser or no adverse impact. In *Brunet v. City of Columbia*,[31] the Sixth Circuit

---

[26]Clark v. Pennsylvania, 885 F. Supp. 694, 708–09, 69 FEP 1379 (E.D. Penn. 1995).

[27]*Id.*

[28]401 U.S. 424, 432, 3 FEP 175 (1971).

[29]422 U.S. 405, 425, 10 FEP 1181 (1975).

[30]Association of Mexican-American Educators v. California, 937 F. Supp. at 1426–28 (alternatives proposed by plaintiff were not adequate substitutes); Sanchez v. City of Santa Ana, 928 F. Supp. 1494, 1510–12 (C.D. Cal. 1995) (alternative practices not shown to be equally effective as the city's chosen practice in achieving its legitimate employment goals); Nash v. Consolidated City of Jacksonville, 895 F. Supp. 1536, 1552–53 (M.D. Fla. 1995) (alternative that is equally valid and has less adverse impact not shown), *aff'd without opinion,* 85 F.3d 643 (11th Cir. 1996); Rudder v. District of Columbia, 890 F. Supp. 23, 46 (D.D.C. 1995) (plaintiffs failed to meet burden by showing existence of an equally effective, nondiscriminatory alternative), *aff'd without opinion,* 99 F.3d 448 (D.C. Cir. 1996); Brown v. City of Chicago, 917 F. Supp. at 585 (plaintiffs failed to show that city refused to use an available, legal, and equally valid alternative selection device); Adams v. City of Chicago, 1996 WL 137660, at *16 (N.D. Ill. Mar. 25, 1996) (use of performance evaluations not a reliable alternative).

[31]1 F.3d 390, 412, 64 FEP 1215 (6th Cir. 1993), *cert. denied sub nom.* Brunet v. Tucker, 510 U.S. 1164 (1994).

held that the district court erred by not exploring alternatives to strict rank-order hiring where the city ranked candidates based on equal weighting of a physical capability test and a cognitive ability test and one test was found to be more predictive of job success than the other. The court relied on the directive in the Uniform Guidelines that an employer is "obligated to conduct its own investigation of viable alternatives with lesser or no impact" on members of a protected class before implementing strict rank-order hiring.[32]

In *Melendez v. Illinois Bell Telephone Co.*,[33] the Seventh Circuit clarified the prima facie burden on an individual plaintiff who challenges a selection procedure under the adverse impact theory. It held that the plaintiff was required to demonstrate that he was not hired or promoted as a direct result of a test having an adverse impact but that he need not establish that he was qualified for the position as part of his prima facie case.

V. Validation of Tests With Adverse Impact: Defendant's Proof of Job Relatedness

A. Standard of Proof of Job Relatedness

Courts continue to struggle with two recurring issues related to the 1991 amendments addressing adverse impact and the parties' respective burdens of proof. First, if the plaintiffs carry their burden of proving adverse impact, then the defendant has the burden of "demonstrating that the challenged practice is job related for the position in question and consistent with business necessity."[34] Some plaintiffs have argued that this statutory language requires a showing that the employment practice at issue is essential to the conduct of the employer's business. At least one district court has rejected this argument as inconsistent with the history and intent of the 1991 Act. In *Donnelly v. Rhode Island Board of*

---

[32]*Id.* (emphasis omitted), citing Uniform Guidelines, 29 C.F.R. § 1607.3B and Officers for Justice v. Civil Service Comm'n, 979 F.2d 721, 728, 62 FEP 868 (9th Cir. 1992). While the court focused on the employer's failure to investigate alternatives, the underlying problem appears to be the employer's failure to validate its use of the two tests. *See* Uniform Guidelines, 29 C.F.R. § 1604.5G.

[33]79 F.3d 661, 667–68, 70 FEP 589 (7th Cir. 1996).

[34]42 U.S.C. § 2000e-2(k)(1)(A)(i).

Governors,[35] the court found that the apparent intent of Congress when enacting the 1991 Act was to codify the concepts of business necessity and job relatedness as they existed prior to the decision in *Wards Cove Packing Co. v. Atonio*[36] and held:

> [A]lthough the statute reintroduces some of the confusion that existed before *Wards Cove,* it does indicate that the term "consistent with business necessity" requires something less than a showing that the challenged practice is essential to the conduct of the employer's business but something more than a showing that it serves a legitimate business purpose. What it appears to require is proof that the challenged practice is reasonably necessary to achieve an important business objective.[37]

The second issue raised by the amendments is whether the burden of proof provisions may be applied retroactively. In cases filed after the effective date of the 1991 Act, plaintiffs may seek to challenge not only the current administration of the test at issue, but also the employer's pre-Act use of the test. Plaintiffs presumably will seek to hold the defendant to the burden of proving job relatedness as defined in the 1991 Act. Defendants, on the other hand, presumably will argue that pre-Act use of the test should be governed by the allocation of burdens outlined in *Wards Cove,* which places the lighter burden of production on the employer. While the Supreme Court has addressed the retroactivity of the 1991 Act in *Landgraf v. USI Film Products,*[38] the decision did not address directly the retroactivity of the burden of proof provisions. The courts continue to be split on this issue.[39]

---

[35]929 F. Supp. 583, 593, 71 FEP 363 (D.R.I. 1996).
[36]490 U.S. 642, 49 FEP 1519 (1989).
[37]929 F. Supp. at 593. *See* Section II.B in Chapter 4.
[38]511 U.S. 244, 64 FEP 820 (1994).
[39]*Compare* Association of Mexican-American Educators v. California, 937 F. Supp. 1397, 1405–06 (N.D. Cal. 1996) (burden of proof established by 1991 Act applied retroactively) *and* Graffam v. Scott Paper Co., 870 F. Supp. 389, 394, 66 FEP 1007 (D. Me. 1994) (burden of proof in 1991 Act applies to cases filed after, or which were pending as of, the Act's effective date), *aff'd without opinion,* 60 F.3d 809 (1st Cir. 1995), *with* Melendez v. Illinois Bell Tel. Co., 79 F.3d 661, 667 n.5, 70 FEP 589 (7th Cir. 1996) (applying pre-1991 standards to adverse impact claims based on pre-Act conduct) *and* EEOC v. Steamship Clerks Local 1066, 48 F.3d 594, 601 n.5, 67 FEP 629 (1st Cir.) ("because the EEOC sued before the Act became law, the boggard of retroactive application hovers" over its adverse impact challenge), *cert. denied,* 116 S. Ct. 65 (1995).

B. Choice of Validation Strategy

1. Criterion-Related Validation

A district court held that an employer failed to prove job relatedness for a test that purported to predict future job success where, among other things, the employer never undertook a predictive validity study using the criterion-related validation method.[40] However, for a minimum competency exam that is not designed to predict a candidate's job performance, another court held that criterion-related validity is not required.[41]

a. The Appropriate Criteria. In a reduction-in-force case, the district court approved of the employer's choice of seven criteria to be used in an assessment center to determine which employees would be retained because the testimony from department heads familiar with the jobs at issue established that the criteria were representative of the skills needed in each department.[42]

c. The Necessary Correlation. The Seventh Circuit found insufficient a criterion-related validity study that demonstrated that the test at issue predicted job performance at a rate only 3 percent greater than chance alone.[43]

2. Content Validation

While courts have not required every job function to be measured in order for an exam to be content valid, courts continue to require the exam to test: (1) a representative sample or a sufficient amount of knowledge, skills, and abilities identified by a job analysis, and (2) the critical functions of the job. The critical functions can be determined by an accurate rating of the importance of the knowledge, skills, and abilities.

In *Fickling v. New York State Department of Civil Service,*[44] the district court concluded that the department's exam for wel-

---
[40]Fickling v. New York State Dep't of Civil Serv., 909 F. Supp. 185, 191 (S.D.N.Y. 1995).
[41]Association of Mexican-American Educators v. California, 937 F. Supp. at 1411.
[42]Graffam v. Scott Paper Co., 870 F. Supp. 389, 402, 66 FEP 1007 (D. Me. 1994), *aff'd without opinion,* 60 F.3d 809 (1st Cir. 1995).
[43]Melendez v. Illinois Bell Tel. Co., 79 F.3d 661, 669, 70 FEP 589 (7th Cir. 1996); *contra* Chapter 5, at note 3 in the Main Edition.
[44]909 F. Supp. 185, 192 (S.D.N.Y. 1995).

fare eligibility examiners was not content valid, in part, because it only tested 13 of the 49 areas of knowledge, skills, and abilities identified in the job analysis and therefore was not representative of the job requirements. The job analysis also failed to rate the importance of the knowledge, skills, and abilities tested resulting in an exam that did not necessarily test the most important aspects of job performance.[45]

In contrast, the court in *Sanchez v. City of Santa Ana*[46] found a test to be content valid where a considerable number of areas of knowledge, skills, and abilities were tested and the test covered a "substantial proportion" of the performance domain of the job.

The courts continue to analyze content validity using the factors set forth in the Second Circuit decision in *Guardians Ass'n of the New York City Police Department v. Civil Service Commission.*[47] Many of the post-*Guardian* decisions focus heavily on the requirement of a "suitable job analysis." For example, in *Nash v. Consolidated City of Jacksonville*,[48] the court found that the city properly identified the critical work behavior and produced a test that was job related, because it conducted a thorough job analysis. A determination of which work behaviors are *critical* can be accomplished by rating the areas of knowledge, skills, and abilities identified through the job analysis.[49]

Similarly, in *Rudder v. District of Columbia,*[50] the District of Columbia conducted a sufficient analysis of the position of firefighter. The analysis consisted of interviews, preparation of a task narrative, questionnaires, and a six-phase development of the job knowledge test.

The defendant in *Legault v. aRusso,*[51] on the other hand, did not adequately analyze the position of firefighter, and the court found that its test was not content valid. In *Legault,* the fire chief

---

[45]*Id.* at 190.
[46]928 F. Supp. 1494, 1509 (C.D. Cal. 1995).
[47]630 F.2d 79, 95, 23 FEP 909 (2d Cir. 1980), *cert. denied,* 452 U.S. 940 (1981); *see* discussion in Chapter 5, Section V.B.2 in the Main Edition.
[48]895 F. Supp. 1536, 1545–46 (M.D. Fla. 1995), *aff'd without opinion,* 85 F.3d 643 (11th Cir. 1996).
[49]*See, e.g.,* Fickling v. New York State Dep't of Civil Serv., 909 F. Supp. 185, 190 (S.D.N.Y. 1995).
[50]890 F. Supp. 23, 32 (D.D.C. 1995), *aff'd without opinion,* 99 F.3d 448 (D.C. Cir. 1996).
[51]842 F. Supp. 1479, 1488, 64 FEP 170 (D.N.H. 1994).

relied on a several-year-old job description of a firefighter's general duties and did not break down the job into component tasks or skills. The court rejected the argument that the test was valid simply because other cities used similar selection practices or because the test simulated things that were normally experienced by a firefighter.

The "competency in test construction" factor articulated in *Guardians* has not been discussed at length in recent cases. However, courts have required the employer to present *some* credible evidence that the test was constructed with reasonable competence in order to prove content validity.[52]

At least one case suggests that the content validity of a test may require an ongoing assessment process. In *Fickling v. New York State Department of Civil Service*,[53] the job analysis was performed in 1975, and the department had never conducted a predictive validity study in all the years the test was given. The *Fickling* court found that the "content of the old examinations was no longer wholly related to the content of the job in 1989 and 1990."

The use of job simulations in testing applicants has found success because such tests are not "far removed from the content and context of the candidate's actual work behavior."[54] For example, in *Rudder v. District of Columbia*,[55] a promotional exam for firefighters included a fire scene simulation that was found to test knowledge of strategies for attacking a fire, the ability to develop a plan of attack, and the giving of orders to subordinates. Although the fire scene simulation had an adverse impact on African-Americans, it was found to be representative of important aspects of job performance and hence content valid.

Although some courts previously required tests to be criterion-related valid in addition to content valid, recent decisions have held that an examination need only be validated by one of these methods. For example, in *Association of Mexican-American Educators v.*

---

[52]*See* Fickling v. New York State Dep't of Civil Serv., 909 F. Supp. at 190.
[53]*Id.* at 191.
[54]Firefighters Inst. for Racial Equality v. City of St. Louis, 616 F.2d 350, 360, 21 FEP 1140 (8th Cir. 1980), *cert. denied*, 452 U.S. 938 (1981).
[55]890 F. Supp. 23, 43 (D.D.C. 1995), *aff'd without opinion*, 99 F.3d 448 (D.C. Cir. 1996).

California,[56] because the state proved that the examination was a basic test of educational skills rather than one designed to predict a candidate's performance as a teacher, the court ruled that it was sufficient to show content validity and the state did not also have to prove construct or criterion-related validity.

3. Construct Validation

In *Association of Mexican-American Educators v. California*,[57] the plaintiffs argued that a showing of construct validity was necessary to establish the job relatedness of the written test used by California as a prerequisite for obtaining a teacher credential. Relying on the Uniform Guidelines,[58] the plaintiffs argued that since the test measured general mental aptitude rather than specific skills, content validation was not sufficient. The court rejected this argument, holding that the test was not designed to measure "a candidate's general mental aptitude, intelligence, or any other construct," but rather seeks to measure "specific, well-defined skills in reading, mathematics, and writing."[59]

D. Validity Problems in the Application of Scored Tests

1. Rank-Ordering

The courts continue to hold that employers who use ranking, especially strict rank-ordering, are required to demonstrate both that the test itself is valid and that the test is a valid means of differentiating among passing candidates.[60]

In *Nash v. Consolidated City of Jacksonville*,[61] firefighters were placed on a promotion list in order of their test scores. The test

---

[56] 937 F. Supp. 1397, 1411 (N.D. Cal. 1996).
[57] *Id.* at 1411–12.
[58] 29 C.F.R. § 1607.14(C)(1).
[59] 937 F. Supp. 1397, 1412 (N.D. Cal. 1996).
[60] The Uniform Guidelines provide that "[i]f a user decides to use a selection procedure on a ranking basis, and that method of use has a greater adverse impact than use on an appropriate pass/fail basis . . ., the user should have sufficient evidence of validity and utility to support the use on a ranking basis." 29 C.F.R. § 1607.5G. *See also id.* at §§ 1607.3B, 1607.14B(6), 1607.14C(9), 1607.15B(10), and 1607.15C(7).
[61] 895 F. Supp. 1536, 1549–51 (M.D. Fla. 1995), *aff'd without opinion,* 85 F.3d 643 (11th Cir. 1996).

was found to be content valid. While the court approved the use of the test for rank-ordering, it recognized that:

> Content validity is not an all or nothing matter; it comes in degrees. A test may have enough validity for making gross distinctions between those qualified and unqualified for a job, yet may be totally inadequate to yield passing grades that show positive correlation with job performance.[62]

In *Brunet v. City of Columbus*,[63] the Sixth Circuit found that the city had validated its use of two content valid tests to rank firefighter candidates by conducting a concurrent criterion-related validity study that showed a linear relationship between test scores and job performance. In a subsequent appeal, the Sixth Circuit also upheld an equal weighting of these cognitive and physical tests.[64]

While courts are hesitant to approve rank-ordering without specific evidence of correlation between test scores and job performance, where an employer uses rank-ordering based on validated test scores, courts have struck down deviations from strict rank-order selection used to achieve affirmative action goals. In *Dallas Fire Fighters v. City of Dallas*,[65] nonminority firefighters sued the city for its policy of promoting minorities out of rank order pursuant to the city's voluntary affirmative action plan. Firefighters took a validated promotional exam and were placed on an eligibility list according to their scores on the exam. Normally, employees were promoted as vacancies occurred by going down the eligibility list. However, the city's affirmative action plan permitted it to skip over nonminority candidates to give an appointment

---

[62]*Id.* at 1549, quoting Guardians Ass'n of New York City Police Dep't v. Civil Serv. Comm'n of New York, 630 F.2d 79, 100, 23 FEP 909 (2d Cir. 1980), *cert. denied*, 452 U.S. 940 (1981).

[63]1 F.3d 390, 411, 64 FEP 1215 (6th Cir. 1993), *cert. denied sub nom.* Brunet v. Turner, 510 U.S. 1164 (1994).

[64]Brunet v. City of Columbus, 58 F.3d 251, 255–57, 68 FEP 518 (6th Cir. 1995). Employers may be able to capitalize on a growing body of empirical evidence that "shows that test scores, particularly on content-validated job knowledge tests, relate in a linear fashion to job performance, which means the higher the test score, the higher the probability of being a successful job performer." Adams v. City of Chicago, 1996 WL 137660, at *15 (N.D. Ill. Mar. 25, 1996) (finding for purposes of plaintiff's motion for preliminary injunction that success on the test was related to job success).

[65]885 F. Supp. 915, 923, 927 (N.D. Tex. 1995).

to a lower ranked minority candidate. The *Dallas* court found these "skip" promotions to violate the Equal Protection Clause, because the promotion goals were tied to a single, arbitrary percentage rather than a goal related to minority representation in the feeder pool.[66] The court found a violation of Title VII on this same ground as well, and also because race or gender was used as the sole factor, not as one of several factors, in deciding whether to grant a skip promotion.[67]

However, deviation from rank-ordering is permitted if found to remedy past discrimination. The Seventh Circuit, in *Erwin v. Daley*,[68] recognized that a number of courts have "upheld the use of out of rank order promotions as a remedy in the face of a statistical disparity and a showing of past discrimination." And, in *McNamara v. City of Chicago*,[69] the court held that the city's promotion of minority employees out of rank-order pursuant to its affirmative action plan did not violate Title VII or § 1981.

Courts continue to approve the use of "banding" as a selection technique. "Banding" is considered a more "reasonable" method of ranking employees due to the fact that job performance is most likely unaffected by a difference of a few points. For example, the court in *Sims v. Montgomery County Commission*[70] approved a settlement that mandated the use of banding candidates based on their scores on content valid tests. The court recognized that banding "has the advantage of explicitly considering the Uniform Guidelines' warning to avoid overinterpreting small score differences."[71]

2. *Cutoff Scores*

Increasingly, courts are examining not just the validity of the test itself, but also the validity of the passing or "cutoff" scores. The Uniform Guidelines provide that "[w]here cutoff scores are used, they should normally be set so as to be reasonable and consistent with normal expectations of acceptable proficiency within

---

[66]*Id.* at 923.
[67]*Id.* at 927.
[68]92 F.3d 521, 527 (7th Cir. 1996), *petition for cert. pending*.
[69]867 F. Supp. 739, 748–52 (N.D. Ill. 1994).
[70]890 F. Supp. 1520, 1526 (M.D. Ala. 1995).
[71]*Id.*

the work force."[72] Employers, therefore, may have to justify both the test's composition and the minimum passing scores.

In *Association of Mexican-American Educators v. California*,[73] a class of minority would-be school teachers challenged the cutoff score used by the state of California for a basic educational skills test as being set at an unreasonably high level. The court found that the cutoff score represented professionally acceptable judgments about the required knowledge, skills, and abilities for teaching jobs.

VI. REMEDIES

Although race-conscious remedies continue to be used to remedy prior testing discrimination, when challenged, such remedies are subject to strict scrutiny.[74] Courts may consider whether testing procedures are validated in determining whether a remedy that provides for race-based promotions or hiring of minority candidates is narrowly tailored.[75] However, there is some disagreement about the significance of a proper validation study. While courts have emphasized that an employer may not indefinitely rely upon race-based promotions as an alternative to developing properly validated selection procedures,[76] at least one court has held that

---

[72]29 C.F.R. § 1607.5H. *See also id* at §§ 1607.3B, 1607.14B(6), 1607.15B(10), and 1607.15C(7).

[73]937 F. Supp. 1397, 1426 (N.D. Cal. 1996).

[74]*See generally* Chapter 27 (Reverse Discrimination and Affirmative Action) in the Main Edition.

[75]Aiken v. City of Memphis, 37 F.3d 1155, 1164, 65 FEP 1757 (6th Cir. 1994) (city's failure to develop validated promotional procedures years after initial disparate impact challenges cannot be used as excuse to justify race-based promotions).

[76]Ensley Branch, NAACP v. Seibels, 31 F.3d 1548, 1572 (11th Cir. 1994) (employer could not "indefinitely administer racially discriminatory tests and then attempt to cure the resulting injury to blacks with race-conscious affirmative action"); Aiken v. City of Memphis, 37 F.3d at 1164 (remanding for a determination of whether out-of-rank promotions were a narrowly tailored remedy in light of the city's failure to utilize or develop validated promotional procedures or to limit the duration of the remedy). *See also* Koski v. Gainer, 1995 U.S. Dist. LEXIS 14604, *51–54 (N.D. Ill. Oct. 5, 1995) (affirmative action plan not narrowly tailored where racially differential cutoff scores used to offset adverse impact of unvalidated written tests).

validation of a promotional test was itself evidence that out-of-rank promotions were not a narrowly tailored remedy.[77]

Remedies requiring employers to select among candidates within the same "band," or range of scores, continue to be approved.[78]

VII. PRACTICAL LITIGATION ISSUES AND CONSIDERATIONS

B. The Industrial Psychologist as an Expert Witness

1. Selection of the Expert

The comparative credibility of the parties' experts continues to be critical to the outcome of many testing cases.[79]

C. Use of Test Questions

Some courts continue to engage in analysis of specific test questions, despite employer claims of confidentiality.[80]

---

[77]Dallas Fire Fighters Ass'n v. City of Dallas, 885 F. Supp. 915, 922 (N.D. Tex. 1995) (noting that "[c]ontinued use of the skip promotion remedy may foster the misguided belief that minorities cannot compete on their own even on a validated test").

[78]Sims v. Montgomery County Comm'n, 890 F. Supp. 1520, 1529, 1532–33 (M.D. Ala. 1995) (finding that consent decree requiring all promotional procedures to use banding was narrowly tailored remedy to ensure that all applicants were considered on the basis of their qualifications). *But see* Dallas Fire Fighters Ass'n v. City of Dallas, 885 F. Supp at 922 n.13 (rejecting employer's after-the-fact use of banding to explain out-of-rank promotions of minority candidates as "smack[ing] of hindsight justification").

[79]*See, e.g.,* Melendez v. Illinois Bell Tel. Co., 79 F.3d 661, 669, 70 FEP 589 (7th Cir. 1996) (crediting testimony by plaintiff's expert that test was not job related where, although expert had not previously validated an employment test, he had a doctorate in social psychology and had published in the area of statistical analysis); Rudder v. District of Columbia, 890 F. Supp. 23, 30–31 (D.D.C. 1995) (rejecting testimony of plaintiff's expert as "extremely biased" where expert accepted test results only where they showed adverse impact and at one point paused before answering a question so that he could answer in a manner consistent with his "burden"), *aff'd without opinion,* 99 F.3d 448 (D.C. Cir. 1996).

[80]Melendez v. Illinois Bell Tel. Co., 79 F.3d at 666 (upholding Rule 11 sanctions imposed on employer for failure to produce test questions after it was discovered that there were at least two different versions of the test); Nash v. Consolidated

D. The Job Analysis

Developing and maintaining documentation on job analysis continues to be essential to establishing that a test is content valid.[81]

City of Jacksonville, 895 F. Supp. 1536, 1547–48 (M.D. Fla. 1995) (court "thoroughly reviewed each and every question" on the exam to determine content validity), *aff'd,* 85 F.3d 643 (11th Cir. 1996).

[81]*Compare* Fickling v. New York State Dep't of Civil Serv., 909 F. Supp. 185, 190–91 (S.D.N.Y. 1995) (employer's lack of documentation that a thorough job analysis had been performed precluded a finding that written exam was content valid) *and* Legault v. aRusso, 842 F. Supp. 1479, 1488, 64 FEP 170 (D.N.H. 1994) (in absence of proper job analysis, employer's anecdotal evidence that testing procedures were job related was "grossly deficient") *with* Nash v. Consolidated City of Jacksonville, 895 F. Supp. at 1547–48 (extensive job analysis conducted in conformity with Uniform Guidelines supported finding that test was content valid) *and* Rudder v. District of Columbia, 890 F. Supp. at 41–42 (same).

CHAPTER 6

NONSCORED OBJECTIVE CRITERIA

There have been no significant changes or developments in the law since publication of the Main Edition.

Chapter 7

SUBJECTIVE CRITERIA

I. Overview

Courts continue to recognize that the use of subjective criteria alone in making an employment-related decision is not "per se" discriminatory[1]; however, the use of subjective criteria, coupled with unfettered discretion, can support a plaintiff's claim of pretext so as to overcome the employer's rebuttal of the plaintiff's prima facie case.[2]

The use of appropriate statistics to demonstrate the impact of subjective criteria on a protected individual or claim continues to be an effective plaintiffs' tool.[3]

III. Factors to Consider in Structuring, Attacking, or Defending Subjective Criteria

The courts continue to distinguish between the treatment of subjective criteria under disparate impact and disparate treatment

---

[1]Amirmokri v. Baltimore Gas & Elec., 60 F.3d 1126, 1130, 60 FEP 809, 810 (4th Cir. 1995) (even if complainant's education and outside experience were objectively superior, employer may properly rely on objective factor of performance evaluations as well as subjective factors such as good interpersonal skills and ability to lead a team to overcome plaintiff's prima facie case of national origin discrimination).

[2]EEOC v. Rodriguez, 66 FEP 1649 (E.D. Cal. 1994) (use of standardless criteria in hiring automobile salesperson, which varied from decisionmaker to decisionmaker, supports claim of discrimination in hiring based on race); Eldred v. Consolidated Freightways Corp., 898 F. Supp. 928, 939, 71 FEP 33, 38 (D. Mass. 1995) (reliance on subjective criteria to support defendant's claim of a legitimate nondiscriminatory reason for adverse employment action found pretextual).

[3]Fisher v. Vassar College, 70 F.3d 1420, 1443, 70 FEP 1155 (2d Cir. 1995) (in tenure denial case, district court properly relied on statistical evidence to support plaintiff's claim of disparate treatment; however, appellate court found that actual statistics offered by plaintiff were built on gerrymandered data constituting statistical fallacies), *amended,* 1995 U.S. App. LEXIS 38412, *and modified, en banc,* 114 F.3d 1332, 74 FEP 109 (2d Cir. 1997), *petition for cert. pending.*

analyses. Under disparate treatment theory, the question is whether the facially neutral subjective criteria—valid or not—were actually used by the employer or whether the decision was more likely the result of class-based considerations.[4] Under disparate impact theory, an employer is only obligated to demonstrate that a subjective selection mechanism is job related for the position in question and consistent with business necessity if a particular subjective employment practice is shown to have a disparate impact upon a protected class.[5] However, the care, or lack of care, with which subjective criteria are established and applied to employment decisions will enhance or undermine the credibility of the employer in asserting this defense to a disparate impact claim.

A. Whether the Decisionmaker Has Considered a Carefully Prepared Job Analysis

Courts continue to recognize that employers are not required to introduce formal validation studies to predict actual on-the-job performance.[6] However, a job analysis is required under any of the three formal validation methods described in the EEOC's Uniform Guidelines on Employee Selection Procedures.[7]

B. Whether Raters Operate Under Specific Safeguards and Guidelines

In the disparate impact context, courts continue to look at whether the individual raters had specific instructions in weighing the job relatedness and business necessity of a subjective selection mechanism.[8]

In the disparate treatment context, written criteria for selection continues to be helpful in defending against a claim of discrimination.[9]

---

[4]*See, e.g.,* Perdomo v. Browner, 67 F.3d 140, 144–46, 68 FEP 1751, 1753–55 (7th Cir. 1995).

[5]42 U.S.C § 2000e-2(k)(1)(A)(i).

[6]Rudder v. District of Columbia, 890 F. Supp. 23, 45 n.14 (D.D.C. 1995), *aff'd without opinion,* 99 F.3d 448 (D.C. Cir. 1996), quoting Watson v. Fort Worth Bank & Trust, 487 U.S. 977, 998, 47 FEP 102 (1988).

[7]*Id.* at 41; 29 C.F.R. §§ 1607.14B(2), 1607.14C(2), and 1607.14D(2).

[8]Graffam v. Scott Paper Co., 870 F. Supp. 389, 400–04, 66 FEP 1007, 1015–20 (D. Me. 1994), *aff'd,* 60 F.3d 809, 71 FEP 736 (1st Cir. 1995).

[9]Howard v. BP Oil, Inc., 32 F.3d 520, 526 (11th Cir. 1994), *aff'd,* 102 F.3d 555 (11th Cir. 1996).

C. Whether the Employer Uses Criteria Based Upon Observable Behaviors or Performances, Rather Than Personal Traits or Vague or Attitudinal Terms

Selection mechanisms that use subjective criteria and have an adverse impact on a protected class may be defended using professional validation studies. Selection mechanisms that rely on personal traits and attitudinal terms arguably cannot be validated using content validation but may be subject to "construct validation,"[10] although this may be impracticable in many employment cases.[11] Thus, it may be dangerous for an employer to use vague "constructs" to select employees if such use has an adverse impact on a protected group, because such criteria will be difficult to formally validate.

D. Whether the Evaluator Is a Member of the Protected Group

In disparate impact cases, which by definition involve unintentional discrimination through the use of facially neutral selection mechanisms, the membership of an evaluator in the protected group should technically be irrelevant. Some courts, however, consider whether the job analysis that led to the selection mechanism included interviews with members of protected groups.[12]

In a disparate treatment case, on the other hand, where the question is whether the decisionmaker is hiding the use of improper considerations behind a pretext of subjective selection characteristics, the membership of the evaluator in the protected class has been found to be one factor weighing against a finding of pretext.[13]

E. Whether the Employer Uses Objective Factors in Conjunction With Subjective Decisionmaking

In a disparate impact case, the plaintiff must demonstrate that a particular employment practice has a disparate impact, unless

---

[10]29 U.S.C. § 1607.14D.

[11]Guardians Ass'n of New York City Police Dep't, Inc. v. Civil Serv. Comm'n of New York, 630 F.2d 79, 92, 23 FEP 909, 921 (2d Cir. 1980), *cert. denied sub nom.* Civil Serv. Comm'n of City of New York v. Guardians Ass'n of New York City Police Dep't, 452 U.S. 940, 25 FEP 1683 (1981).

[12]Rudder v. District of Columbia, 890 F. Supp. 23, 41–43 (D.D.C. 1995), *aff'd*, 99 F.3d 448 (D.C. Cir. 1996).

[13]*See* discussion in Chapter 7, Section III.D, in the Main Edition, and cases cited therein (note 68).

the plaintiff can show that the elements of the employer's decision-making process are not capable of separate analysis.[14] If the challenged employment practice is purely subjective, and that particular practice is shown to have a disparate impact, then the use of objective considerations in other parts of the selection process will be technically irrelevant. If the challenged employment practice involves both subjective and objective criteria, the objective criteria may assist in showing that the process as a whole is job related and consistent with business necessity.[15]

F. Whether the Employer Provides Notice of Job Opportunities

While not relevant to establishing the job relatedness and business necessity of an employment practice shown to have an adverse impact on a protected group, the extent to which an employer uses special recruiting or other programs that cause the pool of protected class candidates to be atypical of the normal pool is a factor to consider in determining whether a particular practice actually has an adverse impact on that class.[16]

---

[14] 42 U.S.C. § 2000e-2(k)(1)(B)(i).
[15] Rudder v. District of Columbia, 890 F. Supp. 23, 41–43 (D.D.C. 1995), *aff'd*, 99 F.3d 448 (D.C. Cir. 1996).
[16] 29 C.F.R. § 1607.4E.

Part 4

Fourth Category of Discrimination—Reasonable Accommodation

Chapter 8

RELIGION

I. What Is Protected as Religion

Courts handling of the definition of religion in the context of the military service exemption[1] and the First Amendment[2] may also provide guidance concerning the parameters of legally protected religion under Title VII.

Often, courts have assumed the existence of a "bona fide religious belief" without delving further, and have decided the controversy on other grounds.[3] Where the existence of a bona fide religious belief is attacked as lacking sincerity, courts continue to find that a modest showing of sincerity is sufficient.[4]

---

[1]Roby v. United States Dep't of Navy, 76 F.3d 1052, 1055–56 (9th Cir. 1996) (finding that only sincerely and deeply held religious beliefs qualify for a religious discharge from the military).

[2]Snyder v. Murray City Corp., 902 F. Supp. 1444, 1449–50 (plaintiff's request to present a prayer at a city council meeting was properly denied because the "prayer" was political and not religious in nature), *amended by* 902 F. Supp. 1455 (D. Utah 1995); Howard v. United States, 864 F. Supp. 1019, 1021, 1024 (D. Colo. 1994) (in finding that the beliefs of "a self-proclaimed Satanist" fell within the protections of the First Amendment, the court assumed that these beliefs were religious in nature, but inquired as to the sincerity of plaintiff's beliefs, based on his attendance at Hare Krishna meetings and other religious ceremonies, and his own conflicting representations of his beliefs).

[3]Cary v. Carmichael, 908 F. Supp. 1334, 1343, 72 FEP 1178 (E.D. Va. 1995) (plaintiff's claim of religious discrimination was dismissed on a variety of grounds, although the court assumed that plaintiff's refusal to sign forms related to drug testing was based on a bona fide religious belief); Hover v. Florida Power & Light Co., 67 FEP 34, 36, 38–39 (S.D. Fla. 1994) (court dismissed case on reasonable accommodations grounds without determining whether plaintiff's fear of using his Social Security number on employment forms was based on a bona fide religious belief).

[4]Shpargel v. Stage & Co., 914 F. Supp. 1468, 1475, 5 AD 1558 (E.D. Mich. 1996) (plaintiff had attended Yom Kippur services in the past and wanted to attend the services).

II. THE EMPLOYER'S DUTY TO ACCOMMODATE

C. The Extent of the Duty to Accommodate

1. The Elements of Proof

A prima facie case of religious discrimination is established by showing that "(1) the employee has a bona fide religious belief that conflicts with an employment requirement; (2) the employee informed the employer of this belief; and (3) the employee was disciplined for failing to comply with the conflicting employment requirement."[5] The Eighth Circuit has followed the Ninth Circuit in holding that an employee need not explicitly ask for an accommodation based on religion; rather, an employer need have "only enough information about an employee's religious needs to permit the employer to understand the existence of a conflict between the employee's religious practices and the employer's job requirements."[6] In addition, one court has held that a plaintiff can establish a prima facie case even when he has acceded to the objectionable employment policy if he reasonably could have inferred that he would have been disciplined for failing to comply with the assignment. Actual discipline or discharge was not necessary.[7]

Once the plaintiff establishes a prima facie case, the burden shifts to the employer to prove that it attempted to accommodate and that it was unable to do so without "undue hardship."[8]

2. The Scope of the Duty to Accommodate

a. Framework for Analysis. Courts continue to follow the analysis of the Supreme Court in *Ansonia Board of Education v.*

---

[5]Wilson v. U.S. West Communications, 58 F.3d 1337, 1340, 68 FEP 341 (8th Cir. 1995); EEOC v. BJ Servs. Co., 921 F. Supp. 1509, 1513 (N.D. Tex. 1995) (same); Shpargel v. Stage & Co., 914 F. Supp. at 1475 (same).

[6]Brown v. Polk County, 61 F.3d 650, 654, 68 FEP 648 (8th Cir. 1995) (en banc) (quoting Heller v. EBB Auto Co., 8 F.3d 1433, 1439, 63 FEP 505 (9th Cir. 1993)), *cert. denied,* 116 S. Ct. 1042 (1996).

[7]Rodriguez v. City of Chicago, 69 FEP 993, 995 (N.D. Ill. 1996) (police officer opposed to abortion who was assigned to protect abortion clinic during demonstrations established prima facie case even though he did not allege he had been discharged, disciplined, or otherwise damaged).

[8]EEOC v. BJ Servs. Co., 921 F. Supp. 1509, 1513 (N.D. Tex. 1995); Cary v. Carmichael, 908 F. Supp. 1334, 1346, 72 FEP 1178 (E.D. Va. 1995).

Philbrook.[9] The distinction between whether an accommodation is reasonable and whether it poses an undue hardship was demonstrated in two separate decisions in *Graves v. Nordstrom, Inc.,*[10] where the employer had offered an employee a 2½-hour work break on Saturdays[11] in order to attend religious services. The court first held that this accommodation was not reasonable, because it did not eliminate Graves's religious conflict, which prohibited all work on Saturdays. The court later found, however, that a factual issue existed as to whether Graves's proposed accommodation would pose an undue hardship on the employer.[12]

Even when an employer has made no attempt to accommodate, the employer may successfully defend a claim by showing no reasonable accommodations were possible. For example, in *Hover v. Florida Power & Light Co.,*[13] the employer made no attempt to accommodate an employee who considered his Social Security number as a "mark of the beast." The court found that using no number, or a fictitious number (as the employee suggested) on various tax and employment documents would have violated federal regulations and subjected the employer to fines. The court therefore concluded that no accommodation was viable and that the employer had not violated Title VII.[14] As a general rule, however, an employer should explore and, if possible, offer some accommodation.[15]

---

[9]479 U.S. 60, 67, 42 FEP 359 (1986). *Accord* Cowan v. Gilless, 81 F.3d 160 (6th Cir. 1996) (unpublished) (employer met initial burden by presenting evidence that it allowed employee to get a substitute, through use of the employer's bulletin board if necessary, when she was scheduled to work on Sabbath); Wilson v. U.S. West Communications, 58 F.3d 1337, 1342, 68 FEP 341 (8th Cir. 1995) (when employer demonstrated that it offered reasonable accommodation of allowing employee to wear button protesting abortion but required that she keep button covered, statutory inquiry ended; employer need not show that the employee's proposed accommodations would cause undue hardship).

[10]*Compare* 1994 WL 721589, at *2–3 (N.D. Cal. 1994) (court granted plaintiff's motion for summary judgment on reasonable accomodation issue) *with* 1995 WL 55336, at *2–3 (N.D. Cal. 1995) (court denied motions for summary judgment on undue hardship issue).

[11]1994 WL 721589, at *1–3.

[12]1995 WL 55336, at *2–3.

[13]67 FEP 34 (S.D. Fla. 1994).

[14]*Id.* at 38–39.

[15]Brown v. Polk County, 61 F.3d 650, 654–55, 68 FEP 648 (8th Cir. 1995) (en banc) (where employer made no attempt to accommodate, employer can only prevail if it shows accommodation was not possible without undue hardship), *cert. denied,* 116 S. Ct. 1042 (1996); Reid v. Kraft Gen. Foods, Inc., 67 FEP 1367,

Employers appear to have a duty to accommodate even if the employee has not requested any particular form of accommodation.[16] Courts continue to hold that an employee has no duty to suggest proposed accommodations.[17] The would-be plaintiff continues to have a duty to cooperate with accommodation measures suggested by the employer unless doing so would compromise his or her religious beliefs.[18]

b. The Extent of Accommodation Required. The courts continue to apply the principles established in *Trans World Airlines, Inc. v. Hardison*[19] concerning the extent of the duty to reasonably accommodate.[20]

1372 (E.D. Pa. 1995) (denying employer's motion for summary judgment where, on two occasions, employer held firm in its position that female applicant must wear pants).

[16]Brown v. Polk County, 61 F.3d at 654 (rejecting employer's argument that employee could not claim Title VII's protections because he had never explicitly requested an accommodation; employer was aware of employee's religious beliefs, which triggered the duty to reasonably accommodate).

[17]Cary v. Carmichael, 908 F. Supp. 1334, 1347, 72 FEP 1178 (E.D. Va. 1995) (no duty to propose accommodations but plaintiff did have a duty to cooperate).

[18]Wilson v. U.S. West Communications, 58 F.3d 1337, 1341–42, 68 FEP 341 (8th Cir. 1995) (employer offer to allow employee to wear covered antiabortion button while in workplace was reasonable accommodation and employee proposal that co-workers be instructed to ignore button was "antithetical to the concept of reasonable accommodation"); Beadle v. Hillsborough County Sheriff's Dep't, 29 F.3d 589, 593, 65 FEP 1069 (11th Cir. 1994) (Seventh Day Adventist failed to satisfy duty to cooperate where he failed to take advantage of opportunity to advertise his need to swap shifts at meetings and on bulletin boards), *cert. denied,* 115 S. Ct. 2001 (1995); Cary v. Carmichael, 908 F. Supp. at 1349–50 (employee refused to explain why his religion prevented him from signing consent form for drug testing, making it impossible for his employer to accommodate him).

[19]432 U.S. 63, 14 FEP 1697 (1977).

[20]*Generally:* EEOC v. United Parcel Serv., 94 F.3d 314, 318, 71 FEP 1301 (7th Cir. 1996) (employer may respond to prima facie case by proving either that it was unable to provide a reasonable accommodation without undue hardship or that it offered a reasonable accommodation that was not accepted by the employee).

Employer failed to accommodate: Opuku-Boateng v. California, 95 F.3d 1461, 1469, 71 FEP 1849 (9th Cir. 1996) (employer failed to establish reasonable accommodation and undue hardship in accommodating employee's religious holidays by failing to show hardship on plaintiff's co-workers or that accommodation required more than a de minimis cost), *cert. denied,* 65 U.S.L.W. 3764 (1997); EEOC v. Ilona of Hungary, Inc., 885 F. Supp. 1111, 1124, 71 FEP 1874 (N.D. Ill. 1995) (where the loss to employer resulting from accommodating absence of employees for religious reasons would have been inefficiency resulting from absence, loss was de minimis), *aff'd in part & rev'd in part,* 108 F.3d 1569, 1576 (7th Cir. 1996); Vetter v. Farmland Indus., Inc., 901 F. Supp. 1446, 1456 (N.D. Iowa 1995) (employee's

An employer has no obligation to make an accommodation that would be in violation of federal regulations[21] or the seniority provisions of a collective bargaining agreement.[22] However, the mere possibility that a proposed accommodation might violate a labor agreement appears insufficient to relieve the employer from seeking an acceptable means of providing an accommodation.[23]

---

request to live outside of sales territory, because he desired to live in an active Jewish community, would not impose an undue burden on employer); Reid v. Kraft Gen. Foods, Inc., 67 FEP 1367, 1372 (E.D. Pa. 1995) (until employer satisfies its initial obligation to offer reasonable accommodation, the employee does not breach his duty to cooperate); Shpargel v. Stage & Co., 914 F. Supp. 1468, 1476, 5 AD 1558 (E.D. Mich. 1996) (where employer did not allow employee to work with other available employees to complete his task in a timely fashion so that he could observe religious holiday and this accommodation would not have increased the employer's costs, employer did not demonstrate that it had offered a reasonable accommodation).

Employer reasonably accommodated or accommodation required undue hardship: Wilson v. U.S. West Communications, 58 F.3d 1337, 1341–42, 68 FEP 341 (8th Cir. 1995) (employer's proposal that plaintiff cover antiabortion button while at work represented reasonable accommodation); Beadle v. City of Tampa, 42 F.3d 633, 636–38, 66 FEP 1540 (11th Cir.) (requiring department to grant shift exceptions to officer would have resulted in greater than de minimis cost and thus employer was not required to accommodate Sabbath observance), *cert. denied,* 115 S. Ct. 2600 (1995); Brown v. Polk County, 61 F.3d 650, 655, 68 FEP 348 (8th Cir. 1995) (en banc) (allowing employee to direct a secretary to type his Bible study notes amounted to more than a de minimis cost to employer as work secretary would otherwise be doing would have to be postponed), *cert. denied,* 116 S. Ct. 1042 (1996); EEOC v. BJ Servs. Co., 921 F. Supp. 1509, 1514 (N.D. Tex. 1995) (employer unable to accommodate employee's religious belief because there were no other employees available to work, safety concerns regarding untrained substitute personnel, and significant costs in bringing employees from other locations, and this accommodation would deny other employees their day off); Cary v. Carmichael, 908 F. Supp. 1334, 1351, 72 FEP 1178 (E.D. Va. 1995) (accommodation would require a violation of bargaining agreement, a more than de minimis cost).

[21]Hover v. Florida Power & Light Co., 67 FEP 34, 36 (S.D. Fla. 1994) (employee objection to use of Social Security numbers), *aff'd,* 101 F.3d 708 (11th Cir. 1996).

[22]Genas v. New York Dep't of Correctional Servs., 67 FEP 27, 32 (S.D.N.Y. 1994) ("Employers are not required to make accommodations that violate existing labor agreements."), *rev'd on other grounds,* 75 F.3d 825, 70 FEP 16 (2d Cir. 1996); Cary v. Carmichael, 908 F. Supp. 1334, 1351, 72 FEP 1178 (E.D. Va. 1995) (same).

[23]Genas v. New York Dep't of Correctional Servs., 67 FEP at 32 (fact question defeated employer's motion for summary judgment where it was not clear that possible accommodations would have violated a collective bargaining agreement); New York City Transit Auth. v. New York Div. of Human Rights, 674 N.E.2d 305, 310 (N.Y. 1996) (state Human Rights Law prohibited employer from relying solely on seniority provisions of its union contract to deny Sabbath days off to a newly hired bus driver without negotiating with union over possible accommodation that would not violate agreement).

3. Specific Accommodations

a. Work Scheduling. For the second time, the Eleventh Circuit rejected the claim of a Seventh Day Adventist police officer who complained of his new employer's failure to accommodate his request not to work on the Sabbath.[24] This time, however, the court went further and held that the employer was not even required to allow the plaintiff to swap shifts with other employees.[25] The court concluded that anything beyond a neutral rotating shift would create an undue hardship for an employer whose "business involves the protection of lives and property."[26] Involuntary scheduling of other employees to accommodate weekend Sabbath observance is often rejected as a reasonable accommodation,[27] as is substitution of less efficient or untrained workers.[28] Courts also require that employees make good faith attempts to utilize accommodations offered by their employers rather than requiring employers to continuously monitor their employees' use of accommodations put in place.[29]

Not all courts have interpreted the "more than a de minimis" burden in the same way. In *Opuku-Boateng v. California,*[30] the Ninth

---

[24]Beadle v. City of Tampa, 42 F.3d 633, 636–37, 66 FEP 1540 (11th Cir.), *cert. denied,* 115 S. Ct. 2600 (1995).

[25]*Compare id. with* Beadle v. Hillsborough County Sheriff's Dep't, 29 F.3d 589, 593, 65 FEP 1069 (11th Cir. 1994) (discussed in note 118 in Main Edition), *cert. denied,* 115 S. Ct. 2001 (1995).

[26]Beadle v. City of Tampa, 42 F.3d at 637. *See also* Beadle v. Hillsborough County Sheriff's Dep't, 29 F.3d at 593 ("[O]ur reading of *Hardison* suggests that the Court was concerned primarily with the neutrality of the [scheduling] system utilized [rather than only seniority systems].").

[27]Lee v. ABF Freight Sys., Inc., 22 F.3d 1019, 1022–24, 64 FEP 896 (10th Cir. 1994) (employer not required to assign another employee to perform duties). *Cf.* New York City Transit Auth. v. New York Div. of Human Rights, 627 N.Y.S.2d 360, 362 (N.Y. App. Div. 1995) (violation of seniority rules in collective bargaining contract not a required accommodation), *rev'd in part,* 674 N.E.2d 305 (N.Y. 1996) (employer cannot rest solely on the collective bargaining agreement as a defense to the duty to make reasonable accommodations; employer failed to make genuine search for reasonable alternatives to the seniority provisions of the contract such as additional negotiating with the union, additional training for the employee to assume another position, or dispensing with employee's services during her Sabbath).

[28]EEOC v. BJ Servs. Co., 921 F. Supp. 1509, 1513–14 (N.D. Tex. 1995).

[29]Beadle v. Hillsborough County Sheriff's Dep't, 29 F.3d 589, 593, 65 FEP 1069 (11th Cir. 1994) (allowing employee to announce his need for shift swaps during meetings and on employer's bulletin board was sufficient accommodation), *cert. denied,* 115 S. Ct. 2001 (1995).

[30]95 F.3d 1461, 1470, 71 FEP 1849 (9th Cir. 1996), *cert. denied,* 65 U.S.L.W. 3764 (1997).

Circuit reversed a district court's judgment for the state and held that significant scheduling modifications should have been undertaken to accommodate a state agriculture inspector to allow an exemption from work even on a weekend day that was always busy. The court concluded that *Hardison* prohibited preferential treatment, not differential treatment. Cases finding unlawful denial of an accommodation often focus on the lack of undue hardship to the employer.[31]

b. Employment Testing and Preemployment Inquiries. Even though preemployment inquiries into an applicant's need for accommodation have come under scrutiny, employees and applicants are not entitled to accommodation unless they have informed the employer of a bona fide religious belief that conflicts with a preemployment testing requirement.[32]

c. Union Membership. In *EEOC v. American Federation of State, County & Municipal Employees,*[33] the court held that a union's policy of refunding the portion of an employee's shop fee that the union contributed to causes that the employee opposed did not reasonably accommodate an employee who objected on religious grounds not only to certain causes championed by the union, but also to supporting an organization that promoted such causes. The court ruled that the complainant was entitled to contribute an amount equal to his shop fee to an agreed-upon charitable organization.[34]

d. Personal Appearance. Courts continue to recognize that § 701(j) covers employee dress and grooming habits.[35]

---

[31]EEOC v. Ilona of Hungary, Inc., 108 F.3d 1569, 1576 (7th Cir. 1996) (other employees could have taken up slack or appointments could have been rearranged; fact that employer did not replace discharged employee evidenced lack of hardship); Genas v. New York Dep't of Correctional Servs., 67 FEP 27, 31–32 (S.D.N.Y. 1994) (union's support of employee's grievance creates doubt that requested accommodation would violate collective bargaining agreement); Shpargel v. Stage & Co., 914 F. Supp. 1468, 1475–76, 5 AD 1558 (E.D. Mich. 1996) (employer could have assigned duties to other staff at no cost).

[32]Cary v. Carmichael, 908 F. Supp. 1334, 1343, 72 FEP 1178 (E.D. Va. 1995) (employee failed to give employer proper notice so that it could attempt an accommodation of his religious objection to signing consent form for drug test).

[33]937 F. Supp. 166, 168, 71 FEP 1151 (N.D.N.Y. 1996).

[34]*Id.*

[35]EEOC v. United Parcel Serv., 94 F.3d 314, 71 FEP 1301 (7th Cir. 1996) (denying summary judgment to employer maintaining no-beard policy for certain positions, where material issue of fact remained regarding whether employer had informed employee he would have to wait two years to obtain a comparable job in which he would be permitted to wear a beard); Wilson v. U.S. West Communications, 58 F.3d

e. Other Common Employer Accommodation Issues. One court has held that an employer that required its employees to live within their respective sales territories violated Title VII by refusing to accommodate an employee's request that he be permitted to live in a town with a synagogue and an active Jewish community.[36] The employer's proposed accommodation, allowing the plaintiff to live outside his sales territory but still in a town that did not have an active synagogue, did not satisfy Title VII since it failed to resolve the plaintiff's religious conflict.[37] The court held that the employer would not suffer an undue hardship by allowing the plaintiff to live in the town that he had proposed (although it was further from his sales territory than the town chosen by his employer) since the plaintiff was willing to absorb any additional costs associated with his choice of residence, the employer did not demonstrate that its suggested accommodation was less burdensome than that favored by the plaintiff, and the employer had permitted other employees to live beyond their sales regions.[38]

Several recent cases address an employer's duty to accommodate employee religious expression *within* the workplace. In such cases, courts have required employers to provide religious accommodations to the extent that such accommodations will not have adverse effects upon employee morale or workplace productivity.[39]

1337, 1340, 68 FEP 341 (8th Cir. 1995) (employee's wearing graphic antiabortion button based on religious vow triggered employer's duty to attempt accommodation); Reid v. Kraft Gen. Foods, Inc., 67 FEP 1367, 1372 (E.D. Pa. 1995) (denying summary judgment to employer that waited four months to offer plaintiff an accommodation to its policy requiring women to wear pants in the workplace).

[36]Vetter v. Farmland Indus., Inc., 901 F. Supp. 1446 (N.D. Iowa 1995).
[37]*Id.* at 1456–57.
[38]*Id.* at 1455–57.
[39]Wilson v. U.S. West Communications, 58 F.3d 1337, 1341, 68 FEP 341 (8th Cir. 1995) (wearing graphic antiabortion button was protected religious activity, but employer need not accommodate employee's desire to wear button uncovered because it was offensive to other employees); Brown v. Polk County, 61 F.3d 650, 655–56, 68 FEP 648 (8th Cir. 1995) (public employer must accommodate supervisor's occasional workplace prayer because it was voluntary, infrequent, spontaneous, and work related, in the absence of evidence the employee's behavior was polarizing employees along religious lines, but employee has no right to direct a secretary to type Bible class notes in disregard of business-related work or to have such work reassigned, thereby imposing an undue hardship upon the employer), *cert. denied,* 116 S. Ct. 1042 (1996); Helland v. South Bend Community Sch. Corp., 93 F.3d 327, 330–31, 71 FEP 1621 (7th Cir. 1996) (school need not accommodate teacher's injection of personal religious beliefs into classroom

III. Disparate Treatment

Courts continue to apply the established disparate treatment allocation-of-proof principles to religious disparate treatment discrimination cases.[40] Some courts require, as part of the prima facie case, that the employee must have informed the employer of his or her religious beliefs.[41]

In *Shabat v. Blue Cross Blue Shield*,[42] an employee claimed that he had received several written disciplinary notices and had not been promoted as quickly as he should have been allegedly as a result of his supervisor's bias against those of the Jewish faith. The court held that the disciplinary notices and speed of promotion were insufficient to show any "adverse action" against the employee,[43] which prevented the plaintiff from establishing a prima facie case.

IV. Harassment

Courts continue to hold that religious-based harassment that creates a hostile work environment violates Title VII.[44] An employer may avoid liability for religious harassment by an employee's co-workers if it conducts a prompt investigation and takes adequate remedial measures to prohibit a recurrence.[45]

---

activities under either Title VII or the Religious Freedom Restoration Act), *cert. denied,* 117 S. Ct. 769 (1997).

[40]Chaudhuri v. Tennessee, 886 F. Supp. 1374, 1380–81 (M.D. Tenn. 1995) (applying the traditional shifting burden analysis to a "failure to promote" case based upon race and religious discrimination).

[41]Vetter v. Farmland Indus., Inc., 884 F. Supp. 1287, 1299–1302, 73 FEP 595 (N.D. Iowa 1995).

[42]925 F. Supp. 977 (W.D.N.Y. 1996), *aff'd,* 108 F.3d 1370 (2d Cir. 1997).

[43]*Id.* at 986–89.

[44]Amin v. Quad/Graphics, Inc., 929 F. Supp. 73, 81–82 (N.D.N.Y. 1996) (harassment based on racial and religious grounds). *Cf.* Kaplan v. Banque Nationale de Paris, 1995 WL 753900, at *5–6 (S.D.N.Y. Dec. 19, 1995) (four isolated antisemitic remarks by a supervisor were insufficient to establish a hostile environment, but were evidence supporting a claim of disparate treatment); Kantar v. Baldwin Cooke Co., 69 FEP 851, 854 (N.D. Ill. 1995) (needling comments by a supervisor to an employee about her ethnic/religious background were not so frequent or pervasive as to create a violation of Title VII).

[45]Sarin v. Raytheon Co., 905 F.Supp. 49, 53, 69 FEP 856 (D. Mass. 1995) (employer's remedial action was sufficient to avoid liability).

The EEOC Guidelines on national origin discrimination[46] have been relied upon, by analogy, in analyzing a religious-based hostile work environment claim.[47]

Harassment issues are discussed more extensively in Chapter 20 (Sexual and Other Forms of Harassment).

V. PERMISSIBLE RELIGIOUS DISCRIMINATION—SPECIAL EXEMPTIONS

A. Educational and Religious Institutions Under § 702

Courts continue to allow religious institutions to discriminate in employment decisions when the employee's conduct is inconsistent with the employer's religious precepts. For example, in *Boyd v. Harding Academy of Memphis, Inc.*,[48] the court determined the defendant could lawfully terminate an unmarried teacher after learning of her pregnancy because having sex outside of marriage violated defendant's code of conduct.[49] The defendant, a Christian school, had given each teacher a handbook stating: "Each teacher . . . is expected in all actions to be a Christian example for the students."[50]

Courts also continue to hold that § 702 provides an exemption only for religious discrimination. Religious and educational institutions are not exempt from claims based on other forms of discrimination.[51]

The Free Exercise Clause may, however, preclude courts from adjudicating gender discrimination claims by ministers against the religious institutions employing them. In *EEOC v. Catholic University of America*,[52] for example, the court refused to decide a

---

[46]29 C.F.R. § 1606.8.
[47]Sarin v. Raytheon Co., 905 F. Supp. at 52.
[48]88 F.3d 410, 71 FEP 300 (6th Cir. 1996).
[49]*Id.* at 414.
[50]*Id.* at 411.
[51]*Id.* at 413 (Title VII applies to a religious institution charged with sex discrimination); Shirkey v. Eastwind Community Dev. Corp., 941 F. Supp. 567, 576–77 (D. Md. 1996) (employment decisions of religious institutions subject to judicial scrutiny where the institution is not exercising its right to discriminate in favor of members of its religious community or doctrine) (§ 1981 case).
[52]83 F.3d 455, 461, 70 FEP 1230 (D.C. Cir. 1996).

claim that the school engaged in sex discrimination in not granting tenure to a nun in its employ.[53] It did not matter that the university did not assert any religious basis for denying tenure; the motives were irrelevant once the court determined the decision involved a pastoral appointment.[54] The court also held that the Religious Freedom Restoration Act prohibited Congress from burdening the university's free exercise of religion absent a compelling governmental interest and that Title VII's purpose of eliminating employment discrimination was not a sufficiently compelling interest to overcome a religious institution's interest in being able to employ ministers of its choice.[55]

B. Educational Institutions Under § 703(e)(2)

In *Killinger v. Samford University*,[56] the court broadly interpreted § 703(e)(2) when it determined that Samford University was a religious institution for purposes of § 703 because its purpose was to encourage Christianity with a Baptist emphasis. The court stated that because no trier of fact could conclude that Samford espoused secular beliefs, it was entitled to the exemption provided under §§ 702 and 703.[57] The court concluded that it "must indulge the presumption . . . in favor of what an institution says about itself when it claims status as a religious institution."[58]

VI. RECENT LEGISLATION

In *City of Boerne v. Flores*,[59] the Supreme Court held that Congress exceeded its powers in enacting the Religious Freedom Restoration Act, noting that the Fourteenth Amendment of the Constitution only permits Congress to enact remedial-type legislation directed at unconstitutional actions and not measures that substantively change the governing law. To the extent that the law was

---

[53] *Id.* at 460–66.
[54] *Id.* at 464–65.
[55] *Id.* at 467–68.
[56] 917 F. Supp. 773, 775–76, 70 FEP 421 (N.D. Ala. 1996), *aff'd*, 113 F.3d 196, 73 FEP 1533 (11th Cir. 1997).
[57] *Id.* at 777.
[58] *Id.*
[59] 1997 WL 345322 (U.S. June 25, 1997).

intended to be remedial, the Court noted that the law's scope was far too broad and intruded far too much into the states' general authority to regulate themselves.[60]

It is unclear what effect *Boerne* will have on the American Indian Religious Freedom Act Amendments of 1994,[61] which prohibit states from discriminating against American Indians for using peyote in bona fide traditional ceremonial purposes. Because that Act focuses on a specific practice, it may pass constitutional muster. On the other hand, since the Act specifically references the balancing test set forth in the Religious Freedom Restoration Act, which is now unconstitutional, it too may be unconstitutional.[62]

The Personal Responsibility and Work Opportunity Reconciliation Act of 1996 provides that any religious organization receiving funds under the Act will not lose its exemption regarding employment decisions under § 702 of the Civil Rights Act.[63]

The Violent Crime Control and Law Enforcement Act of 1996 provides that no employee of any state department of corrections, the U.S. Department of Justice, the Federal Bureau of Prisons, or the U.S. Marshals Service, and no employee providing services to any of the above entities, shall be required as a condition of employment to be in attendance or to participate in any prosecution or execution under the Act if such participation is contrary to the moral or religious convictions of the employee.[64]

---

[60]*Id.* at *15.

[61]Pub. L. No. 103-344, 1994 U.S.C.C.A.N. (108 Stat.) 3125 (codified as amended at 42 U.S.C. § 1996a).

[62]42 U.S.C. § 1996a(4) ("Any regulation promulgated pursuant to this section shall be subject to the balancing test set forth in section 3 of the Religious Freedom Restoration Act.").

[63]Pub. L. No. 104-193, § 104(f), 1996 U.S.C.C.A.N. (110 Stat.) 2105, 2163 (codified as 42 U.S.C. § 604a(f)).

[64]Pub. L. No. 103-322, § 60002, 1994 U.S.C.C.A.N. (108 Stat.) 1796, 1968 (codified as 18 U.S.C. § 3597(b)).

CHAPTER 9

DISABILITY

I. Overview of Disability Law

Courts continue to recognize that the Americans with Disabilities Act is broad in scope and remedial in design[1] and that, although generally modeled on and similar to the Rehabilitation Act of 1973,[2] the ADA was enacted, at least in part, to remedy the perceived inadequacies of the Rehabilitation Act.[3] Plaintiffs may contend that some courts have interpreted the ADA so narrowly

---

[1] *See* Anderson v. Gus Mayer Boston Store, 924 F. Supp. 763, 771, 5 AD 673 (E.D. Tex. 1996) ("The ADA was the culmination of the disability rights movement's efforts to effectuate civil rights protection for [people] with [d]isabilities [, and] . . . lawmakers made clear that the ADA was *norm-changing legislation,* akin to the legislative turning points in this country's struggle to overcome racial discrimination." (footnote omitted)); *accord* Webb v. Garelick Mfg. Co., 94 F.3d 484, 487, 6 AD 127 (8th Cir. 1996); Jacques v. Clean-Up Group, Inc., 96 F.3d 506, 510, 5 AD 1594 (1st Cir. 1996); Rauenhorst v. United States Dep't of Transp., 95 F.3d 715, 716, 5 AD 1621 (8th Cir. 1996); Katz v. City Metal Co., 87 F.3d 26, 30, 5 AD 1120 (1st Cir. 1996); Vande Zande v. Wisconsin Dep't of Admin., 44 F.3d 538, 541, 3 AD 1636 (7th Cir. 1995).
  In the signing ceremony on the White House lawn, President Bush called the ADA an " 'historic new civil rights Act' " and " 'the world's first comprehensive declaration of equality for people with disabilities.' " Remarks by the President during Ceremony for the Signing of the Americans with Disabilities Act of 1990, 2 (July 26, 1990), quoted in Robert L. Burgdorf, Jr., *The Americans with Disabilities Act: Analysis and Implications of Second-Generation Civil Rights Statute,* 26 Harv. C.R.-C.L. L. Rev. 413, 413–14 (1991).

[2] *See* Yin v. California, 95 F.3d 864, 867, 5 AD 1487 (9th Cir. 1996) ("The [ADA] drew heavily upon the language and structure of the Rehabilitation Act. . . ."), *cert. denied,* 116 S. Ct. 64 (1997).

[3] *See* Helen L. v. DiDario, 46 F.3d 325, 332, 3 AD 1775 (3d Cir.) (Title II case containing a thorough historical discussion of the reasons the ADA was enacted), *cert. denied,* 116 S. Ct. 64 (1995); Fink v. Kitzman, 881 F. Supp. 1347, 1368, 4 AD 644 (N.D. Iowa 1995); Heather K. v. City of Mallard, 887 F. Supp. 1249, 1263, 4 ADA 878 (N.D. Iowa 1995); Hutchinson v. United Parcel Serv., Inc., 883 F. Supp. 379, 387, 4 AD 536 (N.D. Iowa 1995). *See generally* Barbara A. Lee, *Reasonable Accommodation Under the Americans with Disabilities Act: The Limitations of Rehabilitation Act Precedent,* 14 Berkley J. Emp. & Lab. L. 201 (1993).

that its broad scope and remedial design have been frustrated.[4] Defendants may contend, however, that because the ADA requires an individualized inquiry into whether a particular person is a qualified individual with a disability, what may appear to be a narrow interpretation of the Act may be only a case-specific one.[5]

II. Coverage of the Major Statutes

B. The Rehabilitation Act

Sections 501 through 505 of the Rehabilitation Act[6] have been amended, but none of the amendments changed the substantive law of the Act. The most significant change was substituting the word "disabilities" for "handicaps" throughout the text of the Act.

1. Federal Government Employers—§ 501

A federal government employer is not required to provide an accommodation that imposes "undue financial and administrative burdens" or requires "a fundamental alteration in the nature of [the] program."[7]

The courts remain divided over whether § 501 is the exclusive remedy for federal employees with a claim for disability-based

---

[4]*See, e.g.,* Ostwalt v. Sara Lee Corp., 74 F.3d 91, 92, 5 AD 385 (5th Cir. 1996) (employee whose high blood pressure was controlled through medication is not disabled without evidence that one or more major life activities is affected); Vande Zande v. Wisconsin Dep't of Admin., 44 F.3d 538, 541, 3 AD 1636 (7th Cir. 1995) ("In the common case in which such an impairment [that limits a major human capability] interferes with the individual's ability to perform up to the standards of the workplace, or increases the cost of employing him, hiring and firing decisions based on the impairment are not 'discriminatory' in a sense closely analogous to employment discrimination on racial grounds."); Dutcher v. Ingalls Shipbuilding, 53 F.3d 723, 727, 4 AD 802 (5th Cir. 1995) (no substantial limitation of any major life activity of former employee whose permanently damaged arm prevents her from doing heavy lifting and repetitive arm movements); Roth v. Lutheran Gen. Hosp., 57 F.3d 1446, 1453–55, 4 AD 936 (7th Cir. 1995) (physician with strabismus (crossed-eyes) and other eye disorders was not disabled under the Rehabilitation Act or the ADA).

[5]*See, e.g.,* EEOC v. Union Carbide Chems. & Plastics Co., Inc., 4 AD 1409, 1410 (E.D. La. 1995) (whether employee with medication-controlled bipolar disorder was disabled was a fact-specific issue to be determined by the trier of fact).

[6]*See* 29 U.S.C. §§ 791–794a.

[7]Mazzarella v. United States Postal Serv., 849 F. Supp. 89, 94, 3 AD 232 (D. Mass. 1994) (not reasonable for Postal Service to juggle personnel to seclude an employee with a mental impairment that makes him aggressive (quoting School Bd. of Nassau Co. v. Arline, 480 U.S. 273 287 n.17 (1987))).

discrimination or whether a federal employee may also bring a claim under § 504.[8]

2. Federal Contractors—§ 503

In *Iacampo v. Hasbro, Inc.*,[9] the plaintiff claimed that her employer, a federal contractor, not only discriminated against her because of her multiple sclerosis but also breached an agreement in the employer's contracts with the federal government not to discriminate on the basis of disability. The district court stated that in determining whether § 503 preempts common-law contract claims, courts should analyze the contractual provisions at issue. If those provisions are "greater than, or different from, the 'boiler plate language' required by § 503," then, the court concluded, § 503 does not preempt the plaintiff's third-party beneficiary claims, and these claims may proceed.

> However, if the *only* source of [the plaintiff's] federal breach-of-contract claims is language detailing § 503 rights and remedies, then [the plaintiff] is attempting to masquerade a § 503 action as a suit in contract. In that case, ... § 503 of the Rehabilitation Act preempts [the state law claims], and [the plaintiff's] third-party beneficiary claims, rooted in alleged disability-based discrimination, must be dismissed.[10]

3. Recipients of Federal Financial Assistance and Federal Agencies—§ 504

Medicare and Medicaid reimbursements are considered to be federal financial assistance under the Rehabilitation Act.[11]

The courts continue to define when an employer receives federal financial assistance and therefore is covered by § 504. In

---

[8]*See* Leary v. Dalton, 58 F.3d 748, 752, 4 AD 1165 (1st Cir. 1995) (civilian employee of naval shipyard may bring an action under both §§ 501 and 504).

[9]929 F. Supp. 562, 5 AD 1075 (D.R.I. 1996).

[10]*Id.* at 579–80. In its analysis, the *Iacampo* court relied upon the First Circuit's holding in Ellenwood v. Exxon Shipping Co., 984 F.2d 1270, 1278, 2 AD 415 (1st Cir. 1993), that § 503 does not preempt state-law disability discrimination claims, based on either statutory or common law, against federal contractors. Nevertheless, the *Ellenwood* court acknowledged a narrow exception to this general rule, which the Eleventh Circuit articulated in Howard v. Uniroyal, Inc., 719 F.2d 1552, 1562, 1 AD 526 (11th Cir. 1983): if a state-law claim is brought solely to vindicate § 503 rights, then the claim is preempted. Ellenwood v. Exxon Shipping Co., 984 F.2d 1270, 1278, 2 AD 415 (1st Cir.), *cert. denied,* 508 U.S. 981 (1993).

[11]*See, e.g.,* People v. Mid Hudson Med. Group, 877 F. Supp. 143, 149–50 (S.D.N.Y. 1995).

Moreno v. Consolidated Rail Corp.,[12] the Sixth Circuit held that the indirect receipt of federal funds may qualify as federal financial assistance. There, the state of Michigan received federal highway repair funds, which it in turn gave to the defendant to repair railroad tracks. The court of appeals held that the defendant was covered by the Rehabilitation Act, even though it did not receive the funds directly from the federal government: "It makes no difference, in our view, that the federal funds of which [the defendant] is the recipient come to it through the State of Michigan rather than being paid to it by the United States directly."[13]

The same court of appeals reached a different conclusion, however, when considering the status of a bank handling student loans under federal student-loan legislation. In *Gallagher v. Croghan Colonial Bank*,[14] the Sixth Circuit held that a bank's disbursing federal student loans and its being paid for making those loans at below-market rates did not constitute federal financial assistance. The bank was not the intended recipient of the benefit of the federal funds, the court stated, and "[t]he coverage of the Rehabilitation Act does not follow federal aid 'past the intended recipient to those who merely derive a benefit from the aid or receive compensation for services rendered pursuant to a contractual arrangement.' "[15]

An unsettled issue is whether the states are immune from suits under the Rehabilitation Act after the Supreme Court's recent decision in *Seminole Tribe v. Florida*.[16] In *Seminole Tribe,* the Supreme Court restated the test for whether the states enjoy immunity under the Eleventh Amendment: Congress abrogates the states' traditional Eleventh Amendment immunity only if it passes the legislation pursuant to the Fourteenth Amendment.[17] The ADA was expressly enacted under the Fourteenth Amendment, and thus states are not immune from the ADA's requirements.[18] The Rehabilitation Act, however, is silent about the constitutional authority under which it was passed. One district court has held that Congress passed the Rehabilitation Act under both the Fourteenth Amendment and

---

[12] 99 F.3d 782, 6 AD 86 (6th Cir. 1996).
[13] *Id.* at 787.
[14] 89 F.3d 275, 278, 5 AD 1089 (6th Cir. 1996).
[15] *Id.* at 278 (emphasis added).
[16] 116 S. Ct. 1114 (1996).
[17] 116 S. Ct. at 1125.
[18] *See* 42 U.S.C. § 12101(b)(4).

the Spending Clause and therefore intended to abrogate the states' Eleventh Amendment immunity from Rehabilitation Act suits.[19]

C. State and Local Laws

State statutes and local ordinances remain beyond the scope of this text; however, an updated table of relevant state statutes has been provided as an appendix to this chapter. Alabama and Mississippi are the only remaining states that have not enacted some form of legislation prohibiting disability-based discrimination by private employers; the statutes of these two states apply only to public employment. The Virgin Islands also has a narrow disability-discrimination law, which prohibits discrimination against only those who are blind and only by employers that are supported by public funds.[20]

Courts have held that ERISA does not preempt state laws against disability-based discrimination if the particular state laws are compatible with the ADA.[21]

D. The Veterans' Readjustment Assistance Act

The Office of Federal Contract Compliance Programs has amended the regulations requiring government contractors to invite job applicants to identify themselves as disabled veterans or veterans of the Vietnam era under the contractor's affirmative action program.[22] The purpose of the amendment is to harmonize the regulations under the Vietnam Era Veterans' Readjustment Assistance Act, § 503 of the Rehabilitation Act, and the ADA.[23] The new rule requires contractors to invite job applicants to "self-identify,"

---

[19]*See* Armstrong v. Wilson, 942 F. Supp. 1252, 1262, 6 AD 1193 (N.D. Cal. 1996), *aff'd,* 124 F.3d 1019, 7 AD 323 (9th Cir. 1997), *petition for cert. filed,* 66 U.S.L.W. 3308 (U.S. Oct. 20, 1997) (No. 97-686).

[20]V.I. CODE ANN. tit. 10, § 154.

[21]*See, e.g.,* Esfahani v. Medical College, 919 F. Supp. 832, 837, 5 AD 761 (E.D. Pa. 1996) (the ADA, like Title VII, contains work-sharing arrangements between the federal and state governments; therefore, the federal government's ability to enforce its laws, and the ADA's own objectives, would be impaired if state provisions parallel to the ADA were subject to preemption by ERISA); Le v. Applied Biosystems, 886 F. Supp. 717, 720, 4 AD 617 (N.D. Cal. 1995).

[22]Affirmative Action Obligations of Contractors and Subcontractors for Disabled Veterans and Veterans of the Vietnam Era, 61 Fed. Reg. 19,366 (1996) (to be codified at 41 C.F.R. § 60-250).

[23]*Id.*

that is, state whether they are disabled veterans or veterans of the Vietnam era but only after the contractor has made the applicant an offer of employment.[24] Before an employment offer has been made, contractors may invite applicants to self-identify only under two circumstances:

> (1) if the invitation to self-identify is made when the contractor is actually undertaking affirmative action for disabled veterans or veterans of the Vietnam era at the pre-offer stage; or
> (2) if the invitation to self-identify is made under a Federal, state or local law requiring affirmative action for disabled veterans or veterans of the Vietnam era.[25]

The contractor must also keep separate files on all applicants and employees who identify themselves as covered disabled veterans or veterans of the Vietnam era,[26] a requirement that is similar to the separate-file requirements under § 503.[27]

E. Protection Under the Constitution

1. *Disability as a Suspect or Quasi-Suspect Class*

The federal courts continue to refuse to characterize disability as a suspect or quasi-suspect class. Consequently, to determine in a government employment case whether a particular classification based on disability violates the Equal Protection Clause, the courts apply only a rational-relationship test. For example, the Fourth Circuit has held that a hospital's restrictions on the activities of employees whose HIV-positive status was known to the hospital was rationally related to the hospital's legitimate interest in protecting the health of its patients and did not violate the Equal Protection Clause.[28]

---

[24]41 C.F.R. § 60-250.5(d).
[25]*Id.*
[26]41 C.F.R. § 60-250.5(d)(4).
[27]*See* 41 C.F.R. § 60-741.42(b).
[28]*See* Doe v. University of Md. Med. Sys. Corp., 50 F.3d 1261, 1267, 4 AD 379 (4th Cir. 1995) (although the plaintiff claimed he was treated differently than those whose HIV status was not known to the hospital, the court concluded that the hospital could not logically be expected to restrict the activities of persons whom they did not know were HIV-positive).

2. Due Process Protection

One district court has held that a state's policy of denying an armed security-guard license to all applicants who have only one hand violates the Due Process Clause of the Fourteenth Amendment.[29] There, the applicant had been denied a license after the issuing board determined that a person with only one hand could not perform fully all the duties required by the position and therefore would be more likely to use deadly force on another person than would an armed guard with two hands.[30] According to the court, "[p]resumptions that irrebuttably determine that an individual is unqualified for a particular job violate the Due Process clause."[31]

III. THE MAJOR SUBSTANTIVE PROTECTIONS OFFERED BY THE ADA AND THE REHABILITATION ACT

A. "Individuals With Disabilities"

1. Is the Condition an "Impairment"?

Most courts addressing claims that plaintiffs were "regarded as" disabled by their employers have found that the plaintiffs failed to prove they were so regarded.[32] Some courts, however, have found

---

[29]Stillwell v. Kansas City Bd. of Police Comm'rs, 872 F. Supp. 682, 688, 3 AD 1828 (W.D. Mo. 1995).

[30]*Id.* at 683 (the applicant was never given the opportunity to demonstrate his physical abilities because of the board's blanket prohibition against giving licenses to one-handed applicants).

[31]*Id.* at 688.

[32]*See* Runnebaum v. NationsBank, N.A., 7 AD 216, 227 (4th Cir. 1997) (although evidence showed that bank personnel twice inadvertently opened plaintiff's packages of AZT sent to the bank, that a supervisor felt "panicky" and "uncontrolled" after learning of plaintiff's HIV infection, and that plaintiff was fired, there was no genuine issue of material fact on whether the relevant decisionmakers regarded plaintiff as disabled because of his HIV infection); Foreman v. Babcock & Wilcox Co., 117 F.3d 800, 805–06, 7 AD 331 (5th Cir. 1997) (employer does not necessarily regard an employee as having a substantially limiting impairment if the employer believes that the employee is incapable of performing a particular job; reasonable jury could not find that employer regarded employee with bad heart and pacemaker as disabled where employee was medically restricted because of pacemaker from working within six feet of welding equipment or 50 feet of power lines); Christian v. St. Anthony Med. Ctr., Inc., 117 F.3d 1051, 1053, 6 AD 1665 (7th Cir. 1997) ("This is a subtle but important point and we wish to be as emphatic about it as we can. The [ADA] is

that there were genuine issues of material fact concerning whether the individual was regarded as impaired,[33] and still other courts have held that a plaintiff proved that he or she was regarded as impaired.[34] A plaintiff need not establish an actual impairment in order to make out a "regarded-as-impaired" claim.[35]

One district court has held that a 15-year-old Air Force report purporting to diagnose a Peace Corp volunteer as having a personality disorder creates a "record of an impairment" that may serve as the basis for a lawsuit stemming from the government's refusal to hire the volunteer.[36]

---

not a general protection of medically afflicted persons. It protects people who are discriminated against by their employer * * * either because they are in fact disabled or because their employer mistakenly believes them to be disabled. If the employer discriminates against them on account of their being (or being believed by him to be) ill, even permanently ill, but not disabled, there is no violation."); Kelly v. Drexel Univ., 94 F.3d 102, 109, 5 AD 1353 (3d Cir. 1996) (the employer's awareness that an employee walked with a limp could not form the basis for a claim that the employee was perceived as disabled, even though the limp was caused by degenerative hip disease); Stewart v. Brown County, 86 F.3d 107, 111, 5 AD 1018 (7th Cir. 1996) (even though a sheriff concluded that a deputy was temperamentally unfit for the job in question, this was not the same as regarding the deputy as having a mental illness that substantially limits a major life activity); MacDonald v. Presbyterian Hosp., 5 AD 314, 316 (S.D.N.Y. 1996) (billing manager failed to prove an employer's discomfort with his facial tic caused by Graves' disease was reason for termination).

[33]See Olson v. General Elec. Astrospace, 101 F.3d 947, 954–55, 6 AD 270 (3d Cir. 1996) (reversing summary judgment because, although plaintiff did not demonstrate disability under ADA, there was a material issue of fact as to whether the employee was perceived as impaired where a significant portion of the employee's evaluation interview dealt with his health, marital status, and hospitalization for depression); Holihan v. Lucky Stores, Inc., 87 F.3d 362, 366, 5 AD 1068 (9th Cir. 1996) (a reasonable jury could infer that the employer regarded a store manager as suffering from disabling mental conditions that substantially limited his ability to work because the employer called the employee into two meetings to discuss his aberrational behavior, asked if he was having any "problems," and encouraged him to seek counseling), cert. denied, 117 S. Ct. 1349 (1997); Katz v. City Metal Co., 87 F.3d 26, 32–33, 5 AD 1120 (1st Cir. 1996) (a heart attack victim whose employer had empirical evidence of the severity of the victim's symptoms was entitled to go to a jury on his "regarded as disabled" liability theory).

[34]See, e.g., EEOC v. Chrysler Corp., 917 F. Supp. 1164, 1169, 5 AD 517 (E.D. Mich. 1996) (an electrician proved that his employer regarded him as disabled by using a blanket rule precluding hiring all persons with diabetes).

[35]Johnson v. American Chamber of Commerce Publishers, Inc., 108 F.3d 818, 819–20, 6 AD 801 (7th Cir. 1997).

[36]Taylor v. Gearan, 1997 WL 595301, at **6–7 (D.D.C. Sept. 14, 1997); see Davidson v. Midelfort Clinic, Ltd., 1998 WL 3360, at **8–9 & nn.6, 8 (7th Cir. 1998) (reversing summary judgment on plaintiff's record-of-impairment claim because genuine issues of material fact exist; declining to address whether an employer "incur[s] a duty to accommodate an employee based on her history of a substantially limiting impairment, even if her current limitations are not substantial").

Only a few courts have addressed when a treatment for a condition or illness itself is disabling and therefore may trigger ADA protection.[37]

Consistent with the ADA's legislative history that environmental, cultural, or economic disadvantages are not to be considered impairments, the Eleventh Circuit has held that an individual who was never taught to read does not have an impairment as defined by the ADA.[38]

The Supreme Court has held that HIV infection is an impairment under the ADA from the moment of infection.[39]

It remains unsettled whether obesity[40] is an impairment under the ADA.

There are only a few reported cases addressing discrimination claims based on a claimant's relationship or association with an individual with a disability.[41]

---

[37]*See, e.g.,* Gordon v. E.L. Hamm & Assocs., 100 F.3d 907, 912, 6 AD 282 (11th Cir. 1996) (although side effects from chemotherapy for cancer may be a "physical impairment," to state a claim under the ADA the employee must show that the side effects "substantially limited" the employee's ability to work or engage in some other "major life activity"); Ellison v. Software Spectrum, Inc., 85 F.3d 187, 191, 5 AD 920 (5th Cir. 1996) (although an employee's cancer was an impairment and although she suffered serious side effects from her treatment, the employee was not substantially limited in any major life activities because she was physically and mentally able to perform her job).

[38]Morisky v. Broward County, 80 F.3d 445, 448, 5 AD 737 (11th Cir. 1996) ("While illiteracy is a serious problem, it does not always follow that someone who is illiterate is necessarily suffering from a physical or mental impairment.").

[39]Bragdon v. Abbott, 1998 WL 332958 (U.S. June 25, 1998). The Supreme Court's determination, in the same case, that reproduction is a major life activity may resolve the disagreement among the lower federal courts regarding whether infertility is an impairment under the ADA. *Compare* Krauel v. Iowa Methodist Med. Ctr., 915 F. Supp. 102, 108, 4 AD 1734 (S.D. Iowa 1995) (procreation and caring for others are not cognizable major life activities under the ADA), *aff'd,* 95 F.3d 674, 5 AD 1503 (8th Cir. 1996) *with* Erickson v. Board of Governors for Northeastern Ill. Univ., 911 F. Supp. 316, 323, 5 AD 1861 (N.D. Ill. 1995) (infertility is a physical impairment that substantially limits the major life activity of reproduction, and therefore the plaintiffs stated a claim under the ADA).

[40]*See* Andrews v. Ohio, 104 F.3d 803, 808–09, 6 AD 322 (6th Cir. 1997) (state police officers who failed a weight-limit test were not disabled or perceived as disabled because their weight was not so outside the normal range as to constitute a statutory disability, even though they did not meet the stricter standards for law enforcement officers); Torcasio v. Murray, 57 F.3d 1340, 1353, 4 AD 974 (4th Cir. 1995) ("[N]either the statutes, nor the caselaw, nor the applicable regulations clearly establish that the ADA or the Rehabilitation Act apply to the obese."), *cert. denied,* 116 S. Ct. 771 (1996).

[41]*See, e.g.,* Den Hartog v. Wasatch Academy, 129 F.3d 1076, 1077–78 (10th Cir. 1997) ("the ADA allows an employer to discipline or discharge a non-disabled

2. Does the Impairment "Substantially Limit" a Major Life Activity?

For an impairment to be a substantial limitation, courts hold that the impairment must result in at least a severe restriction upon a major life activity, not merely a partial limitation or some slight shortcoming.[42] Likewise, courts continue to hold that temporary or transitory conditions are not impairments under the ADA.[43]

---

employee whose relative or associate, because of such relative or associate's disability, poses a direct threat to the employer's workplace"; affirming summary judgment for employer where no genuine dispute of fact that discharged teacher's son, although disabled, posed a direct threat in the workplace); Ennis v. National Ass'n of Bus. & Educ. Radio, Inc., 53 F.3d 55, 62, 4 AD 589 (4th Cir. 1995) (employee did not prove connection between her son's HIV-positive status and her discharge because of evidence that she was terminated for poor performance).

[42]*See, e.g.,* Helfter v. United Parcel Serv., Inc., 115 F.3d 613, 617–18, 6 AD 1499 (8th Cir. 1997) (an employee with carpal tunnel syndrome who could not perform repetitive tasks or frequent lifting of more than 10 pounds was not disabled under the ADA; her impairment did not render her unable to perform a broad range of jobs within a geographical area to which she had reasonable access); Price v. Marathon Cheese Corp., 119 F.3d 330, 336, 7 AD 138 (5th Cir. 1997) (because a former employee with carpal tunnel syndrome was able to perform other jobs, she was not substantially limited in one or more major life activities); Williams v. Channel Master Satellite Sys., Inc., 101 F.3d 346, 349, 6 AD 131 (4th Cir. 1996) ("we hold, as a matter of law, that a twenty-five pound lifting limitation . . . does not constitute a significant restriction on one's ability to lift, work, or perform any other major life activity"), *cert. denied,* 117 S. Ct. 1844 (1997); Ray v. Glidden Co., 85 F.3d 227, 229, 5 AD 991 (5th Cir. 1996) (a lift-truck operator who was unable to lift 50-pound containers continuously all day was not substantially limited in his ability to perform a major life activity); Weiler v. Household Fin. Corp., 101 F.3d 519, 524, 6 AD 106 (7th Cir. 1996) (the major life activity of working was not substantially limited simply because the employee's stress rendered her unable to work under a specific supervisor). *Cf.* Doane v. City of Omaha, 115 F.3d 624, 628–29, 6 AD 1553 (8th Cir. 1997) (affirming jury verdict for former police officer who was partially blind and was not rehired for a position he had held for nine years).

[43]*See, e.g.,* Burch v. Coca-Cola Co., 119 F.3d 305, 317, 7 AD 241 (5th Cir. 1997) (the fact that the employee had to be hospitalized does not establish that his alcoholism substantially limited his major life activities), *cert. denied,* 66 U.S.L.W. 3364 (U.S. Jan. 20, 1998) (No. 97-791); Sanders v. Arneson Prods., Inc., 91 F.3d 1351, 1354, 5 AD 1292 (9th Cir. 1996) (a "temporary injury with minimal residual effects cannot be the basis for a sustainable claim under the ADA[]"; a temporary psychological impairment resulting from cancer that lasted approximately five months was not of sufficient duration to fall within the ADA's protections as a disability), *cert. denied,* 117 S. Ct. 1247 (1997); McDonald v. Department of Pub. Welfare, 62 F.3d 92, 97, 4 AD 1185 (3d Cir. 1995) (the plaintiff's inability to work after surgery was a transient, nonpermanent condition, and therefore the plaintiff was not entitled to protection under the ADA or the Rehabilitation Act).

Because of the individualized inquiry required by the ADA, courts continue to reach different conclusions where asthma is asserted to be a substantially limiting impairment under the Act.[44]

The circuit courts are divided over whether to consider the effect of mitigating remedies in determining whether an individual's major life activities are substantially limited.[45] Plaintiffs may argue that for courts to consider the effect of mitigating measures in determining whether an individual's major life activities are substantially limited by an impairment is contrary to the EEOC's interpretation of the ADA and to the Supreme Court's general admonition that an administering agency's interpretation of a statute should be given great weight in the absence of statutory language or legislative history to the contrary.[46]

---

[44] *Compare* Suttles v. United States Postal Serv., 927 F. Supp. 990, 1004–05 (S.D. Tex. 1996) (plaintiff's asthma did not constitute a disability under the Rehabilitation Act because he did not suffer substantial limitation of major life activities), *with* Parker v. Chestnut Hill Hosp., 1996 U.S. Dist. LEXIS 8283, at **2–3 (E.D. Pa. June 12, 1996) (plaintiff's claim that she suffered from bronchial asthma, which substantially limited her breathing capacity and entire respiratory system, was sufficient to withstand dismissal under Rule 12(b)(6)); Huber v. Howard County, 849 F. Supp. 407, 412–13, 3 AD 262 (D. Md. 1994) (although firefighter's asthma is a handicap under the Rehabilitation Act, he was not entitled to protection because he could not perform essential functions of a career firefighter), *aff'd mem.*, 56 F.3d 61 (4th Cir. 1995).

[45] *Compare* Doane v. City of Omaha, 115 F.2d 624, 627 (8th Cir. 1997) (stating "analysis of whether [the plaintiff] is disabled does not include consideration of mitigating measures"), *and* Harris v. H & W Contracting Co., 102 F.3d 516, 520–21, 6 AD 460 (11th Cir. 1996) (holding EEOC's interpretation is consistent with the ADA's legislative history; therefore, an individual's disability must be assessed without regard to mitigating measures), *and* Holihan v. Lucky Stores, Inc., 87 F.3d 362, 366, 5 AD 1068 (9th Cir. 1996) (mitigating measures are not considered in determining whether an individual is disabled under EEOC regulations), *cert. denied,* 117 S. Ct. 1349 (1997), *with* Gilday v. Mecosta County, 7 AD 348, 352 (6th Cir. 1997) (an employee with diabetes whose condition was kept in check through oral medication, diet, and exercise is nevertheless an individual with a disability under the ADA); Ellison v. Software Spectrum, Inc., 85 F.3d 187, 191–92 n.3, 5 AD 920 (5th Cir. 1996) (recognizing legislative history providing that mitigating measures should not be considered in determining whether an individual is substantially limited in a major life activity, but noting that "had Congress intended that substantial limitation be determined without regard to mitigating measures, it would have provided for coverage under § 12102(2)(A) for impairments that have the potential to substantially limit a major life activity").

[46] *See, e.g.,* Anderson v. Gus Mayer Boston Store, 924 F. Supp. 763, 772, 5 AD 673 (E.D. Tex. 1996) ("Ever since the Supreme Court's decision in [Chevron, U.S.A., Inc. v. Natural Resources Defense Council, Inc., 467 U.S. 837, 843–44 (1984)], courts

3. What Qualifies as a "Major Life Activity"?

Courts continue to find that the inability to work at one particular job does not demonstrate a substantial limitation in the major life activity of working.[47]

The First Circuit has rejected the claim of a plaintiff who alleged that because of periodic episodes of depression, he lost his ability to get along with others, which he argued was a major life activity.[48]

In *Bragdon v. Abbott*,[49] a public accommodations case, the Supreme Court held that human reproduction is a major life activity for purposes of the ADA.

B. "Qualified" Individuals With Disabilities and "Essential Job Functions"

1. An Individualized Inquiry

The District of Columbia Circuit has followed the First Circuit's view that categorically excluding individuals with particular disabilities may be permissible if such individuals are demonstrably

---

have recognized that the agency responsible for administering a regulatory scheme is often in the best position to interpret the scheme. Economies of scale, collective expertise, and other factors weigh in favor of deferring to the agencies who are most familiar with specialized issues of regulation. Furthermore, the interpretive process often requires policy making. The courts are not chartered to engage in policy making, and a choice between competing interpretations often is predicated upon policy considerations.").

[47]*See, e.g.,* Siemon v. AT & T Corp., 117 F.3d 1173, 1176 (10th Cir. 1997) (employee whose severe depression and anxiety was allegedly caused by working under a certain supervisor was prevented from only working under a few supervisors, not from performing a class of jobs or broad range of jobs); Zirpel v. Toshiba Am. Info. Sys., 111 F.3d 80, 81, 6 AD 929 (8th Cir. 1997) (the plaintiff's panic disorder did not substantially limit a major life activity, even though she had difficulty breathing and speaking during panic attacks, where psychologist testified that with treatment disorder was manageable and where plaintiff had held three jobs since her discharge, one of which was nearly identical to her former position); McKay v. Toyota Motor Mfg., USA, Inc., 110 F.3d 369, 373, 6 AD 933 (6th Cir. 1997) (assembly-line worker with carpal tunnel syndrome who was fired for excessive absences has no claim under ADA because not substantially limited from performing either a class of jobs or a broad range of jobs, only from a narrow range of repetitive motion jobs).

[48]Soileau v. Guilford of Maine, Inc., 105 F.3d 12, 15, 6 AD 437 (1st Cir. 1997) ("To impose legally enforceable duties on an employer based on such an amorphous concept would be problematic.").

[49]1998 WL 332958, at *9.

unable to perform the job's essential functions with reasonable accommodation. In *Buck v. United States Department of Transportation*,[50] the District of Columbia Circuit held that because the Federal Highway Administration had reasonably determined that a driver must be able to hear to operate a motor vehicle, the DOT did not have to conduct individualized assessments of three deaf truck drivers. Rejecting the employees' claim as a "collateral attack upon the validity of the hearing requirement," the court noted that the proper forum for relief is the agency that promulgated the rule.[51]

2. *Delineating a Job's Essential Functions*

    a. Are Employees Actually Required to Perform the Functions at Issue? The Seventh Circuit has held that if a position requires an individual to perform multiple job duties, a disabled employee is not qualified unless he or she can carry out enough of those duties to warrant a judgment that he or she can perform the essential functions of the job.[52]

    b. Would Removing That Function Fundamentally Change the Job? Courts continue to hold that if altering or excusing performance of a job function would fundamentally change the job, then the function is an essential one.[53]

    c. Proof.

        (1) *The employer's judgment.* The Tenth Circuit has held that "the fact that the defendant made changes to its business

---

[50]56 F.3d 1406, 1408–09, 4 AD 833 (D.C. Cir. 1995).

[51]*Id.* at 1409.

[52]Miller v. Illinois Dep't of Corrections, 107 F.3d 483, 485, 6 AD 678 (7th Cir. 1997) (no violation in prison's failure to reemploy a blind correctional officer who could perform only the duties of switchboard officer and armory officer and who could not help in emergencies; "If it is reasonable for a farmer to require each of his farmhands to be able to drive a tractor, clean out the stables, bale the hay, and watch the sheep, a farmhand incapable of performing any of these tasks except the lightest one (watching the sheep) is not able to perform the essential duties of his position.").

[53]*See, e.g.,* Haysman v. Food Lion, 893 F. Supp. 1092, 1102, 4 AD 1297 (S.D. Ga. 1995) ("[T]he fact that a function [can] be delegated has minimal bearing on whether it is essential. In theory, any function may be delegated, so under [the plaintiff's] analysis, few functions would ever be essential. . . . The ADA specifically does not require an employer to reallocate essential functions."); Cheatwood v. Roanoke Indus., 891 F. Supp. 1528, 1537, 5 AD 141 (N.D. Ala. 1995) ("The ADA does not require employers to modify the actual duties of a job in order to make an accommodation for individuals who are not physically capable of performing them.").

in order to increase profit is not an impermissible action under the ADA."[54]

(2) *Job descriptions.* Job descriptions created after the onset of the employee's disability are not only given less weight, but may also be evidence in the employee's favor. One district court has held that the plaintiff raised an inference of discrimination by showing that the job description for his position had been created after he became paralyzed.[55]

(3) *The amount of time spent on the job performing the function.* Even a function performed infrequently may still be an essential function.[56] One district court has held that restraining juvenile inmates was an essential function for a remedial-teacher position at a state correctional facility even though performing this function had only been necessary once or twice in a three-year period.[57]

(4) *The consequences of not requiring the incumbent to perform the function.* Determining what would happen if an employee were unable to perform a particular function is relevant for determining if the function is an essential one.[58]

(5) *The terms of a collective bargaining agreement.* Courts continue to rule that collective bargaining agreement provisions are significant factors in identifying essential job functions.[59]

---

[54]Milton v. Scrivner, Inc., 53 F.3d 1118, 1124, 4 AD 432 (10th Cir. 1995) (the plaintiffs' inability to meet new speed and quality standards rendered them unable to perform an essential function of the job).

[55]Muller v. Hotsy Corp., 917 F. Supp. 1389, 1413, 6 AD 35 (N.D. Iowa 1996).

[56]Holbrook v. City of Alpharetta, 112 F.3d 1522, 1527, 6 AD 1409 (11th Cir. 1997) (although a police detective may spend small amounts of time on field work collecting certain types of evidence at a crime scene, this is an essential function which the visually impaired plaintiff could not perform).

[57]Barnfield v. New Hampshire, 5 AD 1819, 1823–24 (D.N.H. 1996) ("While infrequency is a fact to be considered, it must be considered in context and not in a vacuum." (citation omitted)).

[58]*See, e.g.,* Santos v. Port Auth., 4 AD 1245, 1247–48 (S.D.N.Y. 1995) (apprehending violators, directing traffic, and operating emergency equipment "strike at the heart of a police officer's job"); Champ v. Baltimore County, 884 F. Supp. 991, 997–98, 4 AD 808 (D. Md. 1995) (essential functions of police officer's job include ability to make forcible arrest, drive vehicle under emergency conditions, and qualify with a weapon), *aff'd mem.,* 91 F.3d 129, 5 AD 1184 (4th Cir. 1996).

[59]*See* Foreman v. Babcock & Wilcox Co., 117 F.3d 800, 810, 7 AD 331 (5th Cir. 1997) ("the ADA does not require an employer to take action inconsistent with the contractual rights of other workers under a collective bargaining agreement");

While some courts have continued to apply the judicial estoppel doctrine strictly,[60] the majority of courts have been reluctant to adopt a per se rule that a previous representation of total disability or the receipt of disability benefits is an absolute bar to bringing an ADA claim.[61] Nevertheless, most courts agree that a previous representation or a prior determination that an individual

---

Blankenship v. Martin Marietta Energy Sys., 83 F.3d 153, 155–56, 5 AD 789 (6th Cir. 1996) (employee, who was discharged after she lost security clearance because of her paranoid schizophrenia, cannot recover where collective bargaining agreement authorized immediate discharge if an employee lost security clearance and company had never retained an employee whose security clearance had been revoked). For a complete discussion, see Section IV.B.4 infra.

[60]See McNemar v. Disney Stores, Inc., 91 F.3d 610, 618, 5 AD 1227 (3d Cir. 1996) (employee with AIDS "effectively admitted" he was not qualified for the job when he certified that he was permanently disabled on disability benefits application and was therefore judicially estopped from asserting he was qualified under the ADA), cert. denied, 117 S. Ct. 958 (1997); Harris v. Marathon Oil Co., 948 F. Supp. 27, 29 (W.D. Tex. 1996) (former oil field laborer with back injury who asserted he was totally disabled before the long-term disability plan administrator and the Social Security Administration was estopped from claiming he was qualified under the ADA), aff'd mem., 108 F.3d 332 (5th Cir. 1997); Pegues v. Emerson Elec. Co., 913 F. Supp. 976, 980–81, 5 AD 376 (N.D. Miss. 1996) (since plaintiff with work-related carpal tunnel syndrome had asserted for purposes of Social Security disability and state workers' compensation that she could not work, she was not a "qualified individual with a disability").

[61]See Swanks v. Washington Metro. Area Transit Auth., 116 F.3d 582, 587, 6 AD 1544 (D.C. Cir. 1997) (because the ADA requires reasonable accommodation and the Social Security Act has no such requirement but awards benefits to persons whose disabilities keep them from performing "work which exists in the national economy," an employee who applied for and was receiving Social Security disability benefits is free to sue under the ADA; a ruling that receiving such disability benefits bars relief under the ADA would force persons with disabilities to choose between getting immediate subsistence benefits or pursuing legal rights, which would undermine the purposes of the ADA); Cleveland v. Policy Management Sys. Corp., 120 F.3d 513, 517–18 (5th Cir. 1997) (declining to adopt a per se rule that automatically estops an applicant for or recipient of Social Security disability benefits from asserting a claim of discrimination under the ADA but holding that the application for or receipt of Social Security benefits "creates a *rebuttable* presumption that the claimant or recipient of such benefits is judicially estopped from asserting that he is a 'qualified individual with a disability' "); Graboski v. Guiliani, 937 F. Supp. 258, 266, 6 AD 253 (S.D.N.Y. 1996) (firefighters who retired on disability have Title I ADA standing); Overton v. Reilly, 977 F.2d 1190, 1196, 2 AD 254 (7th Cir. 1992) (Social Security disability application is not inconsistent with employee's claim that he could perform his job because Social Security Administration does not look at the range of possible jobs or at every possible job available). *Cf.* Dush v. Appleton Elec. Co., 7 AD 183, 187–88 & n.8 (8th Cir. 1997) (unnecessary to decide judicial estoppel issue where plaintiff failed to present "strong, countervailing evidence" that she was "qualified" to perform the essential functions of her position); Kennedy v.

is disabled is evidence of lack of qualified status upon which an employer may rely and which the plaintiff has the burden to refute with additional evidence:

> When employees (and/or their physicians) represent that they are "totally disabled," "wholly unable to work," or some other variant to the same effect, employers and factfinders are entitled to take them at their word; and, such representations are relevant evidence of the extent of a plaintiff's disability, upon which an employer may rely in attempting to establish that an ADA plaintiff is not a "qualified individual with a disability." ... When a defendant in an ADA action relies on such representations as the basis for contending that a plaintiff is not a "qualified individual," the plaintiff is free to come forward with additional evidence that shows she could perform the essential duties of a desired position with or without accommodation notwithstanding the fact that she might have been deemed disabled under some other statutory or contractual framework. As a general matter ... absent some such affirmative showing of the plaintiff's ability to perform the essential functions of the position, there will be no genuine issue of material fact as to whether the plaintiff is a "qualified individual" and the employer will be entitled to judgment as a matter of law.[62]

Applause, Inc., 90 F.3d 1477, 1481 n.3 (9th Cir. 1996) (unnecessary to decide judicial estoppel question where no genuine issue of material fact existed on whether worker, who represented on a Social Security application that she was "completely disabled for all work-related purposes" and whose doctor testified that she was totally disabled when she applied for Social Security disability benefits, could perform the essential functions of her job with reasonable accommodation).

The Eighth Circuit has been less than clear on the issue. *Compare* Budd v. ADT Sec. Sys., Inc., 103 F.3d 699, 700, 6 AD 867 (8th Cir. 1996) (per curiam) (employee who admitted on his Social Security and disability insurance benefits forms that he was totally disabled for all work-related purposes was estopped from claiming that he was able to return to his former job where he was still drawing these benefits, and his evidence to the contrary did not present a genuine issue of material fact on whether he was a qualified individual with a disability) *with* Robinson v. Neodata Servs., Inc., 94 F.3d 499, 502 n.2, 5 AD 1441 (8th Cir. 1996) (rejecting plaintiff's claim that because she was "totally disabled" for purposes of Social Security benefits she was also "disabled" under the ADA; "At best, the Social Security determination was evidence for the trial court to consider in making its own independent determination [of whether the plaintiff was disabled under the ADA].").

[62]Weigel v. Target Stores, 122 F.3d 461, 468–69, 7 AD 358 (7th Cir. 1997) (affirming summary judgment for employer where plaintiff failed to show that a reasonable accommodation in the form of additional leave would have rendered her able to return to work and perform the essential functions of her job; therefore, plaintiff failed to establish that she was a "qualified individual with a disability"); *accord* Cleveland v. Policy Management Sys. Corp., 120 F.3d 513, 518 (5th Cir. 1997); Swanks v. Washington Metro. Area Transit Auth., 116 F.3d 582, 587, 6 AD 1544 (D.C. Cir. 1997); Dush v. Appleton Elec. Co., 7 AD 183, 188 (8th Cir. 1997).

In February 1997, the EEOC issued Enforcement Guidance[63] taking the position that representations of total disability made by a claimant when applying for Social Security, workers' compensation, disability insurance, and other disability benefits are not inconsistent with the claimant's later filing of an ADA charge. According to the EEOC, there may be "fundamental differences" in the definitions of disability under the ADA and under the disability benefit programs in question.[64]

Applicants or employees may try to preserve their rights to file a later action under the ADA by representing on disability benefits applications that they do not waive any claim to any reasonable accommodations that would allow them to perform the essential functions of their jobs.[65]

3. Special Issues

c. Attendance as an Essential Function. Courts continue to hold that attendance is an essential function and that an employee who cannot satisfy the employer's attendance requirement is not a qualified individual with a disability.[66]

---

[63]*See* EEOC, Enforcement Guidance on the Effect of Representations Made in Applications for Benefits on the Determination of Whether a Person Is a "Qualified Individual with a Disability" Under the Americans with Disabilities Act of 1990 (ADA), EEOC COMPL. MAN. (BNA) § 902, at N-915.002 (Feb. 12, 1997), *reprinted in* 3 EEOC COMPL. MAN. (BNA) N:2281 (1997), *and reprinted in* 1 AM. WITH DISABILITIES ACT MAN. (BNA) 70:1251 (1997).

[64]The EEOC advises agency investigators to consider a number of factors to determine if a party is a qualified individual with a disability including: whether the representations of total disability were in the charging party's own words; whether the employer had suggested that the person apply for benefits; whether the charging party asked for and was denied a reasonable accommodation; and the definitions of terms such as "disability," "permanent disability," and "inability to work" in the statute or contract under which the person applied for disability benefits. *Id.* at E-13.

[65]*See* Anzalone v. Allstate Ins. Co., 5 AD 455, 456–57 (E.D. La.) (plaintiff receiving long-term disability benefits is not barred from ADA coverage because he always had maintained that he could work as a claims adjuster with an accommodation), *aff'd mem.*, 74 F.3d 1236 (5th Cir. 1995); Ward v. Westvaco Corp., 859 F. Supp. 608, 613–14, 3 AD 739 (D. Mass. 1994) (when applying for Social Security and disability retirement benefits, employee indicated an ability to continue working if a reasonable accommodation had been made).

[66]*See, e.g.,* Kotlowski v. Eastman Kodak Co., 922 F. Supp. 790, 796–98, 6 AD 609 (W.D.N.Y. 1996) (an employee who cannot get to work does not satisfy the essential requirements of her employment); Aquinas v. Federal Express Corp., 940 F. Supp. 73, 78–79, 6 AD 485 (S.D.N.Y. 1996) (regular attendance was an essential function of plaintiff's job, and her request for a more flexible work schedule was

IV. Prohibited Conduct

A. Discrimination

1. Limiting, Segregating, or Classifying Candidates

Courts continue to hold that an employer may select the most qualified applicant.[67] Analytically, the employer should assess the disabled applicant's or employee's qualifications after considering the effect of any reasonable accommodation that would not be an undue hardship.[68]

Transferring or refusing to transfer a disabled employee to a different position may also be analyzed as possibly "limiting, segregating or classifying" the employee in a way that adversely affects the employee's opportunities and violates § 102(b)(1) of the ADA.[69] Likewise, changing an employee's work schedule or job duties may be challenged as violating § 102(b)(1).[70] In addition,

---

really a request to work only when her illness permitted and, thus, was not a reasonable accommodation because it would eliminate an essential function of the job); Johnson v. Children's Hosp., 4 AD 806, 807 (E.D. Pa. 1995), aff'd mem., 79 F.3d 1138 (3d Cir. 1996); Barfield v. Bell S. Telecomms., Inc., 886 F. Supp. 1321, 1327, 4 AD 1159 (S.D. Miss. 1995) (plaintiff whose disability (migraine headaches) caused her to miss more than 40 days in a nine-month period was not otherwise qualified because attendance was an essential function of the job that she could not perform).

[67]See, e.g., Antol v. Perry, 82 F.3d 1291, 1299–1300, 5 AD 769 (3d Cir. 1996) (issue of fact whether disabled veteran was not selected for promotion because other candidates were more qualified); Aka v. Washington Hosp. Ctr., 6 AD 1623, 1625–27 (D.D.C. 1996) (plaintiff must do more than offer his own conclusory opinions regarding the qualifications of those hired); Barnes v. Cochran, 944 F. Supp. 897, 905–06, 5 AD 1685 (S.D. Fla. 1996) (evidence established that employer's reasons for not hiring disabled applicant were legitimate and nondiscriminatory); Gower v. Wrenn Handling, Inc., 892 F. Supp. 724, 727–28, 4 AD 1154 (M.D.N.C. 1995) (issue of fact whether individual hired for position was more qualified than disabled applicant where disabled applicant was only given brief consideration); Pitts v. Carolinas Cement Co., 1995 WL 859603, at *3 (W.D. Va. Dec. 18, 1995) (evidence supporting motion for summary judgment clearly established that disabled employee's performance was substandard).

[68]See Barth v. Gelb, 2 F.3d 1180, 1186, 1189, 2 AD 1180 (D.C. Cir. 1993) ("[The employer] introduced sufficient evidence to support a claim of undue hardship by virtue of the loss of essential operational flexibility that would have resulted from an attempt to accommodate [Rehabilitation Act plaintiff's] medical needs.").

[69]See Kohnke v. Delta Air Lines, 5 AD 345, 350 (N.D. Ill. 1995) (transfer of a disabled employee to an unwanted position may violate § 102(b)(1)).

[70]See Rizzo v. Children's World Learning Ctr., 84 F.3d 758, 765, 5 AD 1155 (5th Cir. 1996) (issue of fact whether reducing disabled employee's hours, which required her to work a split shift and changed her duties from bus driver to cook, constitutes unlawful segregation or classification on the basis of disability).

courts continue to scrutinize closely policies that expressly exclude from employment all applicants or employees with a particular disability.[71]

2. Utilizing Discriminatory Tests, Standards, or Selection Criteria

In evaluating allegedly discriminatory tests, standards, or selection criteria under § 102(b)(6), courts continue to focus on whether the test, standard, or criteria is job related and consistent with business necessity.[72] Because § 102(b)(7) requires that employment tests be administered so that they will reflect the applicant's or employee's abilities, not his or her impairment, an employer may be required to provide a reader or other assistance to an impaired applicant or employee taking a test that is designed

---

[71] *See, e.g.,* Hammer v. Board of Educ., 955 F. Supp. 921, 927 (N.D. Ill. 1997) (question of fact whether employer's refusal to reinstate disabled employee until he was free from work restrictions constituted an unlawful discriminatory policy or merely a statement of the employer's position after assessing plaintiff's capabilities); EEOC v. Chrysler Corp., 917 F. Supp. 1164, 1172–73, 5 AD 517 (E.D. Mich. 1996) (policy excluding from employment all applicants with a blood sugar level over a designated amount violates the ADA); Stillwell v. Kansas City Bd. of Police Comm'rs, 872 F. Supp. 682, 686–88, 3 AD 1828 (W.D. Mo. 1995) (prohibiting all one-handed applicants from obtaining an armed security guard license violates Title II of the ADA).

[72] *See, e.g.,* Ellis v. United Airlines, Inc., 73 F.3d 999, 1010, 69 FEP 1167 (10th Cir.) (weight requirements for flight attendants are permissible job-related criteria), *cert. denied,* 116 S. Ct. 2500 (1996); Daugherty v. City of El Paso, 56 F.3d 695, 697–98, 4 AD 993 (5th Cir. 1995) (qualification standard that excludes insulin-dependent diabetics from position of bus driver does not violate ADA), *cert. denied,* 116 S. Ct. 1263 (1996); EEOC v. AIC Sec. Investigations, 55 F.3d 1276, 1283, 4 AD 693 (7th Cir. 1995) (a requirement that employees not pose a significant threat to the workplace is consistent with business necessity); McCoy v. Pennsylvania Power & Light Co., 933 F. Supp. 438, 443–44 (M.D. Pa. 1996) (qualification standard that caused alcoholic employee to lose his security clearance is job related and consistent with business necessity); Kohnke v. Delta Airlines, Inc., 932 F. Supp. 1110, 1113 (N.D. Ill. 1996) ("[T]he fact that a person with a certain disability would injure himself on the job could provide evidence that an employer's qualification standards or selection criteria are 'job-related and consistent with business necessity.' " (quoting 42 U.S.C. § 12113(a))); Turco v. Hoechst Celanese Chem. Group, 906 F. Supp. 1120, 1129–30, 6 AD 579 (S.D. Tex. 1995) (direct threat), *aff'd,* 101 F.3d 1090, 6 AD 278 (5th Cir. 1996); Ryan v. City of Highland Heights, 4 AD 1389, 1390–91 (N.D. Ohio 1995) (issue of fact whether fitness test is job related where the test is not mentioned in any procedure manual and not all police officers were required to take the test); Tafoya v. Bobroff, 865 F. Supp. 742, 750, 3 AD 1329 (D.N.M. 1994) (no evidence that the defendants required applicants to complete an endurance test with the intent to adversely affect disabled persons), *aff'd mem.,* 74 F.3d 1250 (10th Cir. 1996); Ethridge v. Alabama, 860 F. Supp. 808, 816–17, 3 AD 1013 (N.D. Ala. 1994) (police academy's handgun test, which required the use of two hands, is job related and consistent with business necessity).

to measure the individual's knowledge of a particular subject.[73] In other instances, there may be inadequate evidence to require a test-taking accommodation.[74] Some employment tests may measure skills that are themselves essential functions of the job in question; in that case, the test is job related and consistent with business necessity.[75] Applicants or employees must provide the employer with advance notice of a need for an accommodation in taking an employment test.[76]

Because "[t]he purpose of the ADA is to place those with disabilities on an equal footing and not to give them an unfair advantage," complying with § 102(b)(7) often requires employers to strike a "delicate balance" between the rights of disabled and nondisabled applicants or employees.[77]

3. Improperly Conducting Medical Examinations or Inquiries

a. Preemployment Medical Examinations and Inquiries. In October 1995, the EEOC issued its final Enforcement Guidance on

---

[73]*See* Fink v. New York City Dep't of Personnel, 53 F.3d 565, 567–68, 4 AD 641 (2d Cir. 1995) (defendant provided visually impaired civil service examinees with a tape recording of the examination, a tape recorder to record their answers, a reader-assistant, a private room, and double the time afforded to other test takers). *Cf.* Burke v. Virginia, 938 F. Supp. 320, 323, 5 AD 1747 (E.D. Va. 1996) (applicant for correctional officer position who suffers from developmental expressive and receptive language disorder is not entitled to accommodation where test is designed to measure whether applicant could read and comprehend written material), *aff'd mem.*, 114 F.3d 1175, 6 AD 1440 (4th Cir. 1997).

[74]Pazer v. New York State Bd. of Law Examiners, 849 F. Supp. 284, 287, 3 AD 360 (S.D.N.Y. 1994) (accommodations for taking state bar examination are not required where the evidence did not show that the applicant had a learning disability).

[75]*See* Ethridge v. Alabama, 860 F. Supp. 808, 816, 3 AD 1013 (N.D. Ala. 1994) (defendant is not required to accommodate disabled applicant for police officer position by allowing him to take the handgun test using only one hand because the ability to shoot using two hands was an essential function of the job).

[76]*See* Morisky v. Broward County, 80 F.3d 445, 447–48, 5 AD 737 (11th Cir. 1996) (vague or conclusory statements revealing an unspecified incapacity are not sufficient to put an employer on notice of its obligation to provide accommodations with respect to a preemployment written examination); Fussell v. Georgia Ports Auth., 906 F. Supp. 1561, 1569–70, 1574, 5 AD 1236 (S.D. Ga. 1995) (plaintiff failed to request any accommodations at the time that he took the firearm proficiency tests that led to his discharge), *aff'd mem.*, 106 F.3d 417 (11th Cir. 1997).

[77]D'Amico v. New York State Bd. of Law Examiners, 813 F. Supp. 217, 220–21, 2 AD 534 (W.D.N.Y. 1993) (granting visually impaired individual four days to take state bar examination but noting the "delicate balance" that must be made in determining the reasonableness of a requested accommodation).

preemployment disability-related questions and medical examinations[78] to which the federal courts have generally deferred.[79] According to the EEOC, "disability-related" questions include those that "are *likely to elicit* information about a disability" and those that are "*closely related* to disability."[80] Thus, an employer may ask an applicant whether he or she can perform the duties of the job " 'with or without reasonable accommodation.' "[81] Likewise, an employer may state its attendance requirements and ask applicants if they can meet them.[82]

b. Entrance Medical Examinations. The EEOC has taken the position that because disability-related questions and medical examinations are permitted only after an employment offer, an employer's offer must be a "*real*" one[83]; that is, the employer must have "evaluated all relevant non-medical information which it reasonably could have obtained and analyzed prior to giving the offer."[84]

The EEOC has defined a "medical" examination as a "procedure or test that seeks information about an individual's physical

---

[78]EEOC, Enforcement Guidance on Pre-Employment Disability-Related Inquiries and Medical Examinations Under the ADA, EEOC COMPL. MAN. (BNA) § 902, at N-915.002 (Oct. 10, 1995), *reprinted in* 3 EEOC COMPL. MAN. (BNA) N:2319 (1995), *and reprinted in* 1 AM. WITH DISABILITIES ACT MAN. (BNA) 70:1103 (1995).

[79]*See, e.g.,* Thompson v. Borg-Warner Protective Servs. Corp., 1996 WL 162990, at *4 (N.D. Cal. Mar. 11, 1996) (courts "must accord broad deference to the agency's construction"); *cf.* Grenier v. Cyanamid Plastics, 70 F.3d 667, 673, 5 AD 875 (1st Cir. 1995) (EEOC Enforcement Guidance "is not binding law, but as a detailed analysis of the relevant ADA provisions, it aids our interpretation of the statute").

[80]Enforcement Guidance on Pre-employment Inquiries, 3 EEOC COMPL. MAN. (BNA) at N:2320. Not all courts, however, have flatly prohibited preoffer disability-related inquiries. *See, e.g.,* EEOC v. Texas Bus Lines, 923 F. Supp. 965, 981, 5 AD 878 (S.D. Tex. 1996) (preoffer questions asking applicants to list "[p]hysical defects such as eyesight, hearing, limb impairment, diabetes, back or heart trouble, high blood pressure, fits, convulsions, fainting, etc." were permissible because they were "relevant job-related inquiries and . . . consistent with business necessity").

[81]Enforcement Guidance on Pre-employment Inquiries, 3 EEOC COMPL. MAN. (BNA) at N:2320.

[82]*Id.* at N:2321.

[83]*Id.*

[84]*Id.; see* Buchanan v. City of San Antonio, 85 F.3d 196, 199, 5 AD 987 (5th Cir. 1996) (conditional job offer had not yet been extended at the time a medical examination was given to the police officer applicant because "offer was not conditioned solely on a medical examination, but was instead conditioned on successful completion of 'the entire screening process,' which included 'physical and psychological examinations, a polygraph examination, a physical fitness test, an assessment board, and an extensive background investigation' ").

or mental impairments or health."[85] According to the agency, there are many relevant factors in determining whether an examination is medical, including whether the test is "administered by a health care professional or someone trained by a health care professional," whether the results are "interpreted by a health care professional or someone trained by a health professional," whether the test is "designed to reveal" impairments or health, whether the employer is "trying to determine" impairments or health, whether the test is "invasive," whether the test measures "physiological responses," whether it is given in a "medical setting," and whether medical equipment is used.[86] Under the EEOC definitions, both physical and psychological examinations are considered medical examinations.[87] If, however, a test is designed and used to measure only things such as honesty, tastes, and habits, it is not medical.[88]

c. *Medical Examinations and Inquiries for Existing Employees.* Courts continue to require that medical examinations and disability-related questions for existing employees be job related and consistent with business necessity.[89] This standard also applies to "fitness-for-duty" examinations if those examinations are medical.[90]

4. Discriminatory Contractual Arrangements

An employer cannot use its relationship with an examining physician to avoid liability under the ADA: "[I]f an employer's

---

[85]Enforcement Guidance on Pre-employment Inquiries, 3 EEOC COMPL. MAN. (BNA) at N:2322.
[86]*Id.*
[87]*Id.* at N:2322–23; *see* Barnes v. Cochran, 944 F. Supp. 897, 904–05, 5 AD 1685 (S.D. Fla. 1996) (ADA's prohibition concerning preoffer medical examinations "includes psychological examinations").
[88]Enforcement Guidance on Pre-employment Inquiries, 3 EEOC COMPL. MAN. (BNA) at N:2323; *see* Thompson v. Borg-Warner Protective Servs. Corp., 1996 WL 162990, at *7 (N.D. Cal. Mar. 11, 1996) (employer may ask about honesty, ability to get along with others, and organizational and time-management skills).
[89]*See, e.g.,* Roe v. Cheyenne Mountain Conference Resort, 920 F. Supp. 1153, 1154–55, 5 AD 258 (D. Colo. 1996) (requiring employees to disclose prescription drug use was illegal disability-related question because employer could not prove that it was job related and consistent with business necessity); Judice v. Hospital Serv. Dist. No. 1, 919 F. Supp. 978, 984 (E.D. La. 1996) (hospital could require alcoholic neurosurgeon to undergo specialized medical evaluation before reinstating his staff privileges because it had reasonable fears that he posed a direct threat as a result of his history of relapse and his safety-sensitive job duties).
[90]*See* Deckert v. City of Ulysses, 4 AD 1569, 1573 (D. Kan. 1995) (medical fitness-for-duty examination was "fair and appropriate" when police officer with good

relationship with a physician who conducts a medical examination results in the discriminatory rejection of applicants protected by the ADA, the employer is liable."[91] Nor can an employer avoid ADA liability by contracting with a group insurer that regularly refuses coverage to certain disabled employees or by referencing a policy prohibiting reassignment of employees.[92] Similarly, an employer cannot use a collective bargaining agreement to accomplish what it would be prohibited from doing otherwise under the ADA.[93]

5. Discriminatory Benefit Plans

Several sections of the ADA apply to the discriminatory provision of employee benefits. Title I prohibits covered entities from participating in contractual or other relationships with an "organization providing fringe benefits" if the contract or relationship has the effect of discriminating against the covered entity's employees[94] or if the organization uses "standards, criteria, or methods of administration" that discriminate on the basis of disability.[95] Title I also prohibits discrimination in the provision of equal benefits based on a person's known relationship or association with a disabled person.[96] Title III prohibits insurance companies from discriminating against persons with disabilities in providing services.[97] Finally,

---

record began violating safety procedures, left his vehicle unattended, and failed to make written reports), *aff'd mem.*, 105 F.3d 669 (10th Cir. 1996).

[91] EEOC v. Texas Bus Lines, 923 F. Supp. 965, 982, 5 AD 878 (S.D. Tex. 1996) (decision to reject disabled applicant was based on the results of a discriminatory medical examination).

[92] *See* Anderson v. Gus Mayer Boston Store, 924 F. Supp. 763, 769, 5 AD 673 (E.D. Tex. 1996) (employer violates the ADA when it contracts with a group insurer that makes a policy of refusing to extend coverage to employees with a disability); United States v. City of Denver, 943 F. Supp. 1304, 1311–13, 6 AD 245 (D. Colo. 1996) (provision in city charter prohibiting transfers from a classified to a career-services status is preempted by the ADA if a transfer would otherwise constitute a reasonable accommodation and waiver not shown to be an undue hardship).

[93] *See* Eckles v. Consolidated Rail Corp., 94 F.3d 1041, 1046, 5 AD 1367 (7th Cir. 1996) (no evidence that collectively bargained seniority system was a subterfuge to bypass the duty to accommodate under the ADA), *cert. denied*, 117 S. Ct. 1318 (1997); Aka v. Washington Hosp. Ctr., 6 AD 1623, 1628 (D.D.C. 1996) (an employer may not make a contract with a union that discriminates against disabled workers). For a discussion regarding the significance of collective bargaining agreements and the duty to provide reasonable accommodations, *see* Section IV.B.4 *infra*.

[94] 42 U.S.C. § 12112(b)(2).
[95] *Id.* § 12112(b)(3).
[96] *Id.* § 12112(b)(4).
[97] *Id.* §§ 12181(7), 12182.

although Title V makes clear that insurance plans must be *bona fide,* that they must comply with state insurance laws, and that they may limit coverage based on sound determinations of actuarial risk, it emphasizes that this risk analysis "shall not be used as a subterfuge to evade the purposes of subchapters I and III [of the ADA]."[98]

Generally, the discriminatory provision of benefits issue arises in three contexts: long-term disability insurance, health insurance, and retirement benefits. In the long-term disability insurance context, mentally disabled plaintiffs may allege benefits-based discrimination if physically disabled employees receive longer or better disability benefits.[99] Employers may rely on a Rehabilitation Act case, *Beauford v. Father Flanagan's Boys' Home,*[100] to argue that the ADA does not prohibit mentally disabled employees from receiving different disability benefits than physically disabled employees.

In the health insurance context, Congress has enacted the Mental Health Parity Act of 1996 (MHPA).[101] Among other things, this Act, which took effect on January 1, 1998, requires that health insurance policies with limited lifetime or annual medical or surgical benefits have the same limits for mental health benefits and that

---

[98]*Id.* § 12201(c).

[99]*See* Parker v. Metropolitan Life Ins. Co., 6 AD 1865, 1872–73 (6th Cir. 1997) (because a benefit plan offered by a private employer is not a "good" or "service" offered by a place of public accommodation, Title III does not govern long-term disability plans offered by employers; moreover, the ADA does not "mandate equality between individuals with different disabilities" but only "prohibits discrimination between the disabled and the non-disabled"), *cert. denied,* 66 U.S.L.W. 3338 (U.S. Jan. 20, 1998) (No. 97-747); EEOC v. CNA Ins. Cos., 96 F. 3d 1039, 1043–44, 5 AD 1769 (7th Cir. 1996) (a "benefit recipient" is not an employee and therefore has no ADA standing to object to payment difference in benefits between physical and mental illness in long-term disability plan); Esfahani v. Medical College, 919 F. Supp. 832, 835–36, 5 AD 761 (E.D. Pa. 1996) (professor with bipolar illness had standing to raise claim regarding difference in physical and mental health long-term disability benefits while he was capable of working; however, after he became totally disabled, he was no longer a "qualified individual with a disability"); Modderno v. King, 871 F. Supp. 40, 42–43, 5 AD 749 (D.D.C. 1994) (foreign service benefit plan with $75,000 maximum for mental health benefits does not violate § 504 of the Rehabilitation Act), *aff'd,* 82 F.3d 1059, 5 AD 749 (D.C. Cir. 1996), *cert. denied,* 117 S. Ct. 772 (1997).

[100]831 F.2d 768, 773, 1 AD 1153 (8th Cir. 1987) (although discrimination in the provision of disability benefits to mentally disabled employees is "undesirable," "protection from such discrimination is simply not contemplated under Section 504").

[101]29 U.S.C. § 1185a; 42 U.S.C. § 300gg-5. The MHPA has a sunset provision of September 30, 2001. 29 U.S.C. § 1185a; 42 U.S.C. § 300gg-5(f).

policies with no lifetime or annual limits on medical or surgical benefits have no such limits for mental health benefits.[102] The Health Insurance Portability Act, which the MHPA amends, however, exempts from its coverage "disability income insurance."[103] Therefore, while the Mental Health Parity Act applies to health insurance policies, it does not apply to disability insurance benefits.

Also in the health insurance context, the Eleventh Circuit held, in *Gonzales v. Garner Food Services, Inc.*,[104] that a former employee is not a "qualified individual with a disability" who may assert a claim for discrimination in the provision of health insurance benefits. In *Gonzales,* an employee with AIDS was discharged to reduce the employer's future health insurance costs, and the employee's COBRA benefits were deliberately capped for AIDS coverage. Holding that the employee could not bring an ADA claim for benefits discrimination because he was neither an applicant nor an employee, the court of appeals stated that the plaintiff was "a participant in the health benefit plan only by virtue of his status as a former employee."[105] Applying the reasoning of *Beauford,* the court held that because the employee was not a "qualified individual with a disability" at or after the time of the alleged discrimination, he was not covered by the ADA.[106]

The Eighth Circuit held in *Krauel v. Iowa Methodist Medical Center*[107] that an employee whose infertility treatments were excluded from coverage by her employer's health insurance plan was not discriminated against on the basis of her disability. According to the court, "[i]nsurance distinctions that apply equally to all insured employees, that is, to individuals with disabilities and to those who are not disabled, do not discriminate on the basis of disability."[108]

---

[102]*See id.*
[103]*See* 42 U.S.C. § 300gg-91(c)(1)(A).
[104]89 F.3d 1523, 1526–28, 5 AD 1202 (11th Cir. 1996), *cert. denied,* 117 S. Ct. 1822 (1997).
[105]*Id.* at 1526.
[106]*Id.* at 1530–31; *see* Pappas v. Bethesda Hosp. Ass'n, 861 F. Supp. 616, 619–20, 3 AD 590 (S.D. Ohio 1994) (nurse lost her ADA Title I claims against the administrator of employer's health insurance plan because health benefits administrator is not an agent of the employer or a "covered entity" of employer; she lost her Title III claim because Title III covers only physical access issues, not the sale of insurance products).
[107]95 F.3d 674, 677–78, 5 AD 1503 (8th Cir. 1996).
[108]*Id.* at 678.

Whether former employees are protected by Title I, which prohibits disability-based discrimination in the provision of fringe benefits,[109] also arises in the context of retirement benefits. Some courts have observed that denying former employees standing to bring benefits-based discrimination claims is contrary to the broad remedial purposes of the ADA, its legislative history, and the EEOC interpretative guidelines.[110] Plaintiffs may argue that the definition of "employee" under the ADA is the same as under Title VII,[111] that under Title VII the term "employee" has been broadly construed, and that under Title VII any discrimination related to or arising out of an employment relationship, whether or not the person discriminated against is an employee at the time of the discriminatory conduct, is actionable.[112] Again, following *Beauford,* employers may argue that a former employee cannot be a "qualified individual with a disability" unless he or she is employed at or immediately after the time of the alleged discrimination and therefore is not covered by the ADA.

Employers and health insurance plans may not restrict coverage for specific disabilities or treatments if the restrictions are motivated by a particular employee's disability or medical condition.[113] Also, plaintiffs may challenge the denial of benefits for

---

[109]42 U.S.C. § 12112(b); *see* 29 C.F.R. § 1630.4(f).

[110]*See* Graboski v. Guiliani, 937 F. Supp. 258, 265–66, 6 AD 253 (S.D.N.Y. 1996) (to deny disability retirees ADA coverage because they are no longer able to perform the essential functions of the job is "a crabbed view of the ADA's coverage [which] would undermine the statute's unambiguous remedial purpose"); *cf.* Gonzales v. Garner Food Servs., Inc., 89 F.3d 1523, 1532, 5 AD 1202 (11th Cir. 1996) ("It would be counter-intuitive, and quite surprising, to suppose . . . that Congress intended to protect current employees' fringe benefits, but intended to then abruptly terminate that protection upon retirement or termination, at precisely the time that those benefits are designed to materialize." (Anderson, J., dissenting)), *cert. denied,* 117 S. Ct. 1822 (1997).

[111]The EEOC's Interpretive Guidance on Title I of the ADA states that "[i]n general, the term 'employee' has the same meaning that it is given under [T]itle VII." 29 C.F.R. app. § 1630.2(a)–(f).

[112]*See* Northern v. City of Chicago, 841 F. Supp. 234, 236, 2 AD 1864 (N.D. Ill. 1993) (definition of "employee" under ADA should be interpreted like Title VII where being an employee is not the *sine qua non* for coverage but rather the existence of an employment relationship); *cf.* Robinson v. Shell Oil Co., 117 S. Ct. 843, 846, 72 FEP 1856 (1997) (postemployment retaliation case holding that "Title VII's definition of employee . . . lacks any temporal qualifier and is consistent with either current or past employment").

[113]*See* Hilliard v. BellSouth Medical Assistance Plan & Blue Cross Blue Shield, 918 F. Supp. 1016, 1026–27 (S.D. Miss. 1995) (employee's ADA claim dismissed

"experimental" treatments if those types of treatments are covered by the plan for related conditions.[114]

Most cases involving targeting certain disabilities for different benefits or insurance coverage arise in the context of applicants or employees with HIV or AIDS. The courts have held that an employer may not target employees known to have HIV or AIDS by selecting a group insurer that refuses to cover a specific disability but covers other disabilities.[115]

B. Failure to Make Reasonable Accommodation

1. General Guidelines

An employer's duty of reasonable accommodation is triggered only if the employee indicates that he or she is disabled and provides any necessary supporting medical information.[116] Because a reasonable accommodation is one that enables an employee to perform the essential functions of his or her job,[117] some courts have held that where an employee is able to perform the essential functions without accommodation, there is no duty to accommodate.[118]

---

because plan's restrictive coverage was instituted two years before the employee was diagnosed and the employer's actions were not motivated by the employee's disability).

[114] Henderson v. Bodine Aluminum, Inc., 70 F.3d 958, 961, 6 AD 99 (8th Cir. 1995) (*per curiam*) (remanding for trial on issue of whether high-dose chemotherapy was experimental treatment for breast cancer in light of its acceptance for other types of cancer).

[115] *See* Anderson v. Gus Mayer Boston Store, 924 F. Supp. 763, 778, 5 AD 673 (E.D. Tex. 1996) ("[W]hen an employer changes group health providers to an insurer that would never consider covering one of the employees in the group because of that employee's disability (in this case, AIDS) the employer violates the ADA (because it has not provided equal access to insurance)." (footnote omitted)).

[116] *See* McDonald v. Pennsylvania, 62 F.3d 92, 96, 4 AD 1185 (3d Cir. 1995) (the employer is not required to provide a reasonable accommodation unless the employee is disabled); Gonzalez v. Perfect Carton Corp., 6 AD 151, 154 (N.D. Ill. 1996) (the notion of accommodation does not come into play if the employee fails to show he or she is disabled).

[117] *See* Miranda v. Wisconsin Power & Light Co., 91 F.3d 1011, 1017, 5 AD 1856 (7th Cir. 1996) (a reasonable accommodation enables an employee to perform essential job functions); Garza v. Abbott Lab., 940 F. Supp. 1227, 1238–39, 6 AD 1507 (N.D. Ill. 1996) (accommodations provided by employer were not reasonable because they did not allow plaintiff to continue performing the essential functions of her job); Abbasi v. Herzfeld & Rubin, 4 AD 797, 799 (S.D.N.Y. 1995) (purpose of reasonable accommodation is to enable employee to perform the essential functions of job).

[118] *See, e.g.,* Kocsis v. Multi-Care Management, Inc., 97 F.3d 876, 883, 6 AD 442 (6th Cir. 1996) (employee not entitled to reasonable accommodation when she

2. Examples of Reasonable Accommodations

a. Readily Accessible Facilities. Courts have held that a reasonable accommodation may require changes to the work environment to make the employer's workplace readily accessible.[119] In *Lyons v. The Legal Aid Society*,[120] a staff attorney for the Legal Aid Society claimed that her employer should accommodate her disability by paying for a parking space near the building. The Second Circuit determined that the employer-provided parking could be a reasonable accommodation: "It is clear that an essential aspect of many jobs is the ability to appear at work regularly and on time and that Congress envisioned that employer assistance with transportation to get an employee to and from the job might be covered."[121]

b. Job Restructuring. An employer may be required to accommodate an employee by restructuring a job to remove marginal

---

could already perform her duties as a nursing supervisor and unit registered nurse); Patterson v. City of Seattle, 1996 WL 528267, at *3 (9th Cir. Sept. 17, 1996) (employer not required to accommodate plaintiff by moving plaintiff's former supervisor to a different building to alleviate plaintiff's stress where plaintiff could not show he had any working relationship with or was continuously exposed to former supervisor in his current position).

[119]*See, e.g.*, Wernick v. Federal Reserve Bank, 91 F.3d 379, 384–385, 5 AD 1345 (2d Cir. 1996) (employer reasonably accommodated plaintiff's back condition by providing ergonomic furniture); Stewart v. County of Brown, 86 F.3d 107, 112, 5 AD 1018 (7th Cir. 1996) (employer met its duty of accommodation by building a platform to change angle of plaintiff's chair, by putting up miniblinds, and by purchasing a more ergonomically correct chair); Pangalos v. Prudential Ins. Co. of Am., 5 AD 1825, 1827 (E.D. Pa. 1996) (employer met its reasonable accommodation obligation by offering to provide portable toilet to employee with ulcerative colitis), *aff'd mem.*, 118 F.3d 1577 (3d Cir. 1997); EEOC v. Newport News Shipbuilding & Drydock Co., 949 F. Supp. 403, 408–09, 6 AD 369 (E.D. Va. 1996) (employer met its duty to accommodate when it took measures to ensure that air quality of plaintiff's work environment was improved); Trotter v. B & S Parts & Accessories, Inc., 5 AD 1584, 1592 (D. Kan. 1996) (defendant reasonably accommodated plaintiff's bending restrictions by providing higher work table).

[120]68 F.3d 1512, 1516, 4 AD 1694 (2d Cir. 1995).

[121]*Id.; accord* Smallwood v. Witco Corp., No. 94 Civ. 7766 (LMM), 1995 U.S. Dist. LEXIS 18106, at **3–4 (S.D.N.Y. Dec. 4, 1995) (whether morbidly obese employee is entitled to transportation to employer's relocated facility cannot be decided on summary judgment). *But see* Schneider v. Continental Cas. Co., 1996 U.S. Dist. LEXIS 19631, at *25 (N.D. Ill. Dec. 16, 1996) (employer is not required to transfer employee to different facility to eliminate barriers outside the work environment, for example, employee's commute).

duties,[122] but an employer is not required to eliminate an essential function of a job.[123] Thus, although an employer may choose to

---

[122]*See* Burnett v. Western Resources, Inc., 929 F. Supp. 1349, 1358, 6 AD 711 (D. Kan. 1996) (ADA requires employers to make job-related adjustments or modifications enabling employees to do essential job functions); Rogers v. International Marine Terminal, 4 AD 304, 308 n.19 (E.D. La. 1995) (employer reasonably accommodated employee by allowing him to work on jobs that did not require going up and down stairs when employee was having problems with his legs), *aff'd,* 87 F.3d 755, 5 AD 1115 (5th Cir. 1996); Vazquez v. Bedsole, 888 F. Supp. 727, 731, 4 AD 970 (E.D.N.C. 1995) (reasonable accommodation may include job restructuring); Davis v. York Int'l, Inc., 2 AD 1810, 1816 (D. Md. 1993) (employer reasonably accommodated employee by modifying job duties as her condition deteriorated).

[123]*See* Smith v. Blue Cross Blue Shield, 102 F.3d 1075, 1076, 6 AD 367 (10th Cir. 1996) (employer need not remove telephone responsibilities from a correspondent position), *petition for cert. filed,* 65 U.S.L.W. 3783 (U.S. May 6, 1997) (No. 96-1832); Jacques v. Clean-Up Group, Inc., 96 F.3d 506, 512, 5 AD 1594 (1st Cir. 1996) (employer was not required to allow plaintiff to start work two hours late because starting earlier was necessary to complete work before building opened each day); Conklin v. Englewood, 1996 WL 560370, at *2 (6th Cir. Oct. 1, 1996) (municipality was not required to reallocate essential job duties of a police officer); Borkowski v. Valley Cent. Sch. Dist., 63 F.3d 131, 140, 4 AD 1264 (2d Cir. 1995) ("[A]n employer is not required to accommodate an individual with a disability by eliminating essential functions from the job."); Benson v. Northwest Airlines, Inc., 62 F.3d 1108, 1114, 4 AD 1234 (8th Cir. 1995) (employer does not have a duty to eliminate essential job functions); Daugherty v. City of El Paso, 56 F.3d 695, 700, 4 AD 993 (5th Cir. 1995) (ADA does not require employers to modify actual duties of a job as an accommodation), *cert. denied,* 116 S. Ct. 1263 (1996); Milton v. Scrivner, Inc., 53 F.3d 1118, 1124, 4 AD 432 (10th Cir. 1995) (employer is not required to reallocate job duties to change essential functions of a job); Myers v. Hose, 50 F.3d 278, 284, 4 AD 391 (4th Cir. 1995) (ADA does not require employers to modify the actual job duties to accommodate individuals who are not physically capable of performing them); White v. York Int'l Corp., 45 F.3d 357, 362, 3 AD 1746 (10th Cir. 1995) (ADA does not require eliminating essential functions of job as a reasonable accommodation); Carrozza v. Howard County, 4 AD 512, 512 (4th Cir. 1995) (employer need not honor plaintiff's request for unspecified job restructuring, alleviation of stress, and exemption from normal performance reviews because these accommodations would change essence of the clerk-typist position); Johnson v. Maryland, 940 F. Supp. 873, 878 (D. Md. 1996) (employer was not required to eliminate essential function of proficiency with firearms for corrections officers), *aff'd,* 113 F.3d 1232 (4th Cir. 1997); Miller v. Department of Corrections, 916 F. Supp. 863, 869, 6 AD 497 (C.D. Ill. 1996) (employer need not eliminate inmate supervision from duties of a correctional officer), *aff'd,* 107 F.3d 483 (7th Cir. 1997); Holbrook v. City of Alpharetta, 911 F. Supp. 1524, 1541, 6 AD 1394 (N.D. Ga. 1995) (employer was not required to eliminate function of collecting evidence in field investigations for police officer in small department), *aff'd,* 112 F.3d 1522, 6 AD 1409 (11th Cir. 1997); Fussell v. Georgia Ports Auth., 906 F. Supp. 1561, 1573, 5 AD 1236 (S.D. Ga. 1995) (employer was not required to eliminate essential function of being able to shoot a firearm to accommodate police officer applicants), *aff'd mem.,* 106 F.3d 417 (11th Cir. 1997); Palmer v. Circuit Court, 905 F. Supp. 499, 509, 6 AD 375 (N.D. Ill. 1995) (circuit court is not required to

eliminate essential functions to allow a disabled employee to perform "light duty," the employer is not required to do so.[124]

An employer may also be required to restructure a job by modifying work schedules or providing part-time employment.[125] The

---

eliminate employee's ability to get along with co-workers and supervisors as an essential job function), *aff'd,* 117 F.3d 351, 6 AD 1569 (7th Cir. 1997); Champ v. Baltimore County, 884 F. Supp. 991, 999 (D. Md. 1995) (an accommodation is unreasonable if it requires eliminating an essential duty), *aff'd mem.,* 91 F.3d 129 (4th Cir. 1996); Rucker v. City of Philadelphia, 4 AD 1443, 1445 (E.D. Pa. 1995) (employer was not required to eliminate physical duties of youth detention center counselor where physical contact with youth residents was essential function), *aff'd mem.,* 85 F.3d 612 (3d Cir. 1996); Wann v. American Airlines, 3 AD 1607, 1610 (S.D. Tex. 1994) (employer is not required to eliminate essential duties requiring exposure to fumes), *aff'd mem.,* 58 F.3d 636 (5th Cir. 1995).

[124]*See* Shiring v. Runyon, 90 F.3d 827, 831, 5 AD 1216 (3d Cir. 1996) (Postal Service was not required to create light-duty letter-sorting job for mail carrier who could no longer walk more than one hour a day); Smith v. Blue Cross Blue Shield, 894 F. Supp. 1463, 1469, 4 AD 1378 (D. Kan. 1995) (employer was not required to keep employee on light duty indefinitely), *aff'd,* 102 F.3d 1075, 6 AD 367 (10th Cir. 1996), *petition for cert. filed,* 65 U.S.L.W. 3783 (U.S. May 6, 1997) (No. 96-1832); Champ v. Baltimore County, 884 F. Supp. 991, 1000, 4 AD 808 (D. Md. 1995) (police officer was not entitled to remain on desk duty indefinitely where all officers were required to be able to perform all duties in an emergency), *aff'd mem.,* 91 F.3d 129, 5 AD 1184 (4th Cir. 1996); Nguyen v. IBP, Inc., 905 F. Supp. 1471, 1485–86, 5 AD 465 (D. Kan. 1995) (employer is not required to make temporary light-duty position permanent); McDonald v. Department of Corrections, 880 F. Supp. 1416, 1423, 4 AD 1258 (D. Kan. 1995) (employer could terminate plaintiff after 60 days in temporary light-duty position under its policy where plaintiff could not perform all essential job duties).

[125]*See* Wernick v. Federal Reserve Bank, 91 F.3d 379, 384–85, 5 AD 1345 (2d Cir. 1996) (employer reasonably accommodated plaintiff's back condition by allowing breaks so that plaintiff could move around or stretch); Hardy v. Sears, Roebuck & Co., 1996 U.S. Dist. LEXIS 19008, at *23 (N.D. Ga. Aug. 28, 1996) (defendant reasonably accommodated plaintiff by allowing extended lunch breaks to attend counseling sessions and time off for psychiatric care); Pattison v. Meijer, Inc., 897 F. Supp. 1002, 1007–08, 4 AD 997 (W.D. Mich. 1995) (putting plaintiff on part-time flexible schedule that enabled him to use public transportation when his seizure disorder prevented him from driving was reasonable accommodation); Heise v. Genuine Parts Co., 900 F. Supp. 1137, 1153–54, 4 AD 1551 (D. Minn. 1995) (employer was required to allow sales representative to work a flexible schedule to make up for absences caused by his illness where the ability to work flexible hours was part of the job description, other sales representatives had no set hours, and plaintiff had successfully performed his duties working on such a schedule in the past); Smith v. Kitterman, Inc., 897 F. Supp. 423, 430, 4 AD 1487 (W.D. Mo. 1995) (employer may be required to give employee with carpal tunnel syndrome breaks between repetitive tasks); Hall v. Center, 1995 U.S. Dist. LEXIS 5801, at *10 (N.D. Ill. Apr. 14, 1995) (while employer generally is not required to allow an employee to modify her work schedule, such an accommodation may be required if it will enable employee to perform essential functions of her job); Vande Zande v. Wisconsin Dep't

ADA does not require an employer to provide full-time compensation or benefits to an employee who has been reduced to a part-time schedule as an accommodation.[126]

Generally, an employer will not be required to restructure a job to allow an employee to work at home[127] though in certain circumstances this accommodation may be required.[128]

Courts continue to hold that an employer is not required to accommodate an employee by lowering its qualitative or quantitative

---

of Admin., 851 F. Supp. 353, 361, 2 AD 1846 (W.D. Wis. 1994) (employer reasonably accommodated plaintiff by allowing her to modify her work schedule to attend her doctor appointments), *aff'd,* 44 F.3d 538, 3 AD 1636 (7th Cir. 1995). *But see* Jacques v. Clean-Up Group, Inc., 96 F.3d 506, 512, 5 AD 1594 (1st Cir. 1996) (company was not required to modify employee's starting time where certain work had to be performed during particular hours).

[126]*See* Willett v. Kansas, 942 F. Supp. 1387, 1395 (D. Kan. 1996) (employer is not required to pay full-time wages to employee working a partial shift); Tenbrink v. Federal Home Loan Bank, 920 F. Supp. 1156, 1164 (D. Kan. 1996) (employer could provide part-time employment as an accommodation even if the company did not provide health insurance to part-time employees); Pattison v. Meijer, Inc., 897 F. Supp. 1002, 1008, 4 AD 997 (W.D. Mich. 1995) (employer could reduce pay and benefits for employee who was no longer working full time); Rhodes v. Bob Florence Contractor, 890 F. Supp. 960, 967, 4 AD 1201 (D. Kan. 1995) (employer was not required to give pay raise to employee whose hours had been reduced due to medical restrictions so that employee could continue to make the same amount of money per week). *But see* Vande Zande v. Wisconsin Dep't of Admin., 851 F. Supp. 353, 360–61, 2 AD 1846 (W.D. Wis. 1994) (defendant was required to maintain same pay and benefits for employee who was classified as part time where employee worked a 95% schedule), *aff'd,* 44 F.3d 538, 3 AD 1636 (7th Cir. 1995).

[127]*See* Patterson v. City of Seattle, 1996 WL 528267, at *3 (9th Cir. Sept. 17, 1996) (employer was not required to allow plaintiff to work at home to alleviate stress caused by working in the same building as a former supervisor); Schneider v. Continental Cas. Co., 1996 U.S. Dist. LEXIS 19631, at *25 (N.D. Ill. Dec. 16, 1996) (employer was not required to allow employee to work at home without supervision when employee's job required interactive teamwork); Whillock v. Delta Air Lines, 926 F. Supp. 1555, 1565–66, 5 AD 1027 (N.D. Ga. 1995) (employer did not need to allow reservations agent to work at home), *aff'd mem.,* 86 F.3d 1171 (11th Cir. 1996); Vande Zande v. Wisconsin Dep't of Admin., 851 F. Supp. 353, 360–61, 2 AD 1846 (W.D. Wis. 1994) (defendant did not violate its duty to accommodate by refusing to allow plaintiff to work at home when it did not have appropriate work available), *aff'd,* 44 F.3d 538, 3 AD 1636 (7th Cir. 1995).

[128]*See, e.g.,* Spath v. Berry Plastics Corp., 900 F. Supp. 893, 903–04, 4 AD 1811 (N.D. Ohio 1995) (disabled sales representative could have been accommodated if employer had allowed her to make planning and sales calls by phone from her home); Anzalone v. Allstate Ins. Co., 5 AD 455, 457–58 (E.D. La. 1995) (allowing plaintiff to work at home may be a reasonable accommodation where plaintiff was a claims adjuster who usually worked in the field, not in an office, and was allowed to conduct his business by telephone).

standards.[129] While the ADA requires employers to make job-related adjustments or modifications that enable an employee to perform a job's essential functions,[130] it does not require the employer to provide modifications that assist an individual throughout his or her daily activities on and off the job.[131]

Just because an employer restructured a job in the past does not make this accommodation reasonable under the ADA.[132]

c. Reassignment. Relying on the statutory language of the ADA, many courts continue to hold that an employer must reasonably accommodate an incumbent employee with a disability by reassigning the employee to an appropriate vacant position if one exists.[133] Other courts have held, however, that

---

[129]*See, e.g.,* Sutton v. United Airlines, Inc., 6 AD 116, 121 (D. Colo. 1996) (airline was not required to lower its vision requirement to accommodate plaintiffs); Milton v. Scrivner, Inc., 901 F. Supp. 1541, 1545 (W.D. Okla. 1994) (defendant was not required to reduce its production standards in violation of the collective bargaining agreement), *aff'd,* 53 F.3d 1118, 4 AD 432 (10th Cir. 1995); Massey v. Scrivner, Inc., 901 F. Supp. 1546, 1551 (W.D. Okla. 1994) (employer was not required to reduce a plaintiff's production requirements below the standards set by the collective bargaining agreement), *aff'd sub nom.* Milton v. Scrivner, Inc., 53 F.3d 1118, 4 AD 432 (10th Cir. 1995).

[130]*See* 29 C.F.R. app. § 1630.9.

[131]*See* Burnett v. Western Resources, Inc., 929 F. Supp. 1349, 1358, 6 AD 711 (D. Kan. 1996).

[132]*See* Holbrook v. City of Alpharetta, 112 F.3d 1522, 1528 & n.4, 6 AD 1409 (11th Cir. 1997) (that a police detective job was restructured for a four-year period to accommodate a highly competent employee does not indicate that the accommodation is required by the ADA, but only that the employer may have exceeded what the ADA requires).

[133]*See, e.g.,* Shiring v. Runyon, 90 F.3d 827, 831, 5 AD 1216 (3d Cir. 1996) (trial court erred in failing to consider whether reassignments were a reasonable accommodation); Gile v. United Airlines, Inc., 95 F.3d 492, 498, 5 AD 1466 (7th Cir. 1996) (ADA may require an employer to reassign an employee as a reasonable accommodation); Benson v. Northwest Airlines, Inc., 62 F.3d 1108, 1114, 4 AD 1234 (8th Cir. 1995) (reassignment to vacant position is a possible accommodation); Conklin v. City of Englewood, 1996 WL 560370, at *2 (6th Cir. Oct. 1, 1996) (reassignment may be a reasonable accommodation under the ADA); Taylor v. Gilbert & Bennett, 6 AD 201, 204–05 (N.D. Ill. 1996) (employer was required to determine whether plaintiff could physically perform the functions of any vacant position before denying reassignment request); McCoy v. Penn. Power & Light Co., 933 F. Supp. 438, 444 (M.D. Pa. 1996) (reassignment of employee who had lost security clearance to a loading dock position was reasonable accommodation); Garza v. Abbott Lab., 940 F. Supp. 1227, 1243–44, 6 AD 1507 (N.D. Ill. 1996) (employer was required to attempt to reassign plaintiff even though she had not filled out formal transfer request); Davoll v. Webb, 943 F. Supp. 1289, 1300–01 (D. Colo. 1996) (employer may be required to reassign police officers to vacant positions that do not require the ability to use firearms or make

employers are not required to locate other positions for employees who are not qualified for their present jobs.[134] Of

---

arrests, even though nondisabled employees would not be eligible for reassignment); Miller v. Department of Corrections, 916 F. Supp. 863, 870, 6 AD 497 (C.D. Ill. 1996) (if employee cannot perform the essential functions of his or her current position, then reassignment to a vacant position may be considered as a reasonable accommodation), aff'd, 107 F.3d 483, 6 AD 678 (7th Cir. 1997); Morton v. GTE N., Inc., 922 F. Supp. 1169, 1179, 5 AD 524 (N.D. Tex. 1996) (because there was no suitable vacant position available the company had no duty to grant plaintiff a transfer), aff'd mem., 114 F.3d 1132 (5th Cir. 1997); Rayha v. United Parcel Serv., Inc., 940 F. Supp. 1066, 1069 (S.D. Tex. 1996) (employer reasonably accommodated plaintiff by transferring him to a job that enjoyed the same union classification, hourly wage, minimum guaranteed hours, seniority, and other benefits of employee's previous position); Leslie v. St. Vincent New Hope, Inc., 916 F. Supp. 879, 887, 5 AD 1773 (S.D. Ind. 1996) (the plain language of the ADA may require reassignment even if the employer does not have a regular policy or practice of permitting nondisabled employees to transfer); Munoz v. H & M Wholesale, Inc., 926 F. Supp. 596, 608, 6 AD 355 (S.D. Tex. 1996) (reassignment to a vacant position may be considered a reasonable accommodation); Haysman v. Food Lion, 893 F. Supp. 1092, 1104–05, 4 AD 1297 (S.D. Ga. 1995) (employer must reassign employee to vacant position within his or her restrictions, but it is employee's burden to identify such a position); Hurley-Bardige v. Brown, 900 F. Supp. 567, 571, 4 AD 1744 (D. Mass. 1995) (transfer to alternative site may be a reasonable accommodation).

[134]See, e.g., Smith v. Midland Brake, Inc., 1998 WL 110011, at *6 (10th Cir. Mar. 13, 1998) (footnote omitted) (holding that "under the ADA, when a plaintiff is not qualified, even with reasonable accommodation, for the job which he currently holds (or, as here, from which he was terminated), the employing entity has no obligation to consider reassigning him to another position. Under the current EEOC guidelines, the employer's obligation to consider reassignment arises only if the employer can accommodate the employee in his current position, but would experience undue hardship in doing so."); Schmidt v. Methodist Hosp., 89 F.3d 342, 344, 5 AD 1340 (7th Cir. 1996) (employer was not required to find a new position for a nurse who could not successfully perform the position for which he had been hired); Gomez v. American Bldg. Maintenance, 940 F. Supp. 255, 259 (N.D. Cal. 1996) (plaintiff was not entitled to transfer because he could not physically perform the essential functions of his current job as janitor); Vaughn v. Harvard Indus., 926 F. Supp. 1340, 1348 (W.D. Tenn. 1996) (lead die cast set-up man with a back problem was not entitled to alternative employment if he could not meet the demands of his present position); Miller v. Department of Corrections, 916 F. Supp 863, 870, 6 AD 497 (C.D. Ill. 1996) (the ADA does not impose upon the employer the affirmative duty to find another job for an employee who is no longer qualified for the job he was doing), aff'd, 107 F.3d 483 (7th Cir. 1997); Pangalos v. Prudential Ins. Co. of Am., 5 AD 1825, 1826 (E.D. Pa. 1996) (employer not required to transfer plaintiff to another position), aff'd mem., 118 F.3d 1577 (3d Cir. 1997); Smith v. Blue Cross Blue Shield, 894 F. Supp. 1463, 1469, 4 AD 1378 (D. Kan. 1995) (even if plaintiff could have worked in some position, there was no duty to transfer him because he could not perform the essential functions of his existing job), aff'd, 102 F.3d 1075, 6 AD 367 (10th Cir. 1996), petition for cert. filed, 65 U.S.L.W. 3783 (U.S. May 6, 1997) (No. 96-1382); Champ v. Baltimore County, 884 F. Supp. 991, 1000, 4 AD 808 (D. Md. 1995) (plaintiff was not eligible for reassignment because he could not perform the essential functions of his existing

course, the employee who seeks reassignment must be able to perform the job sought.[135]

Some courts have required that the employer give the disabled employee only the same opportunities for transfer that other employees would enjoy.[136] As the Fifth Circuit stated in *Daugherty v. City*

---

position), *aff'd mem.*, 91 F.3d 129, 5 AD 1184 (4th Cir. 1996); Marschand v. Norfolk & W. Ry., 876 F. Supp. 1528, 1543–44, 4 AD 1099 (N.D. Ind. 1995) (employer has no affirmative duty to find another job for an employee who is no longer qualified for his or her existing position), *aff'd*, 81 F.3d 714, 5 AD 1184 (7th Cir. 1996); Kuehl v. Wal-Mart Stores, Inc., 909 F. Supp. 794, 803, 5 AD 91 (D. Colo. 1995) (employer does not have to provide employee with alternative employment); Dyer v. Jefferson County Sch. Dist. R-1., 905 F. Supp. 864, 869, 5 AD 109 (D. Colo. 1995) (employer not required to provide disabled employee with alternative employment when the employee is unable to meet the demands of his present position); Johnson v. City of Port Arthur, 892 F. Supp. 835, 842 (E.D. Tex. 1995) (reassignment to light duty is not a reasonable accommodation to assist in the performance of a job, but rather is an entirely different job, and therefore is not required); Cheatwood v. Roanoke Indus., 891 F. Supp. 1528, 1537, 5 AD 141 (N.D. Ala. 1995) (defendant was not required to provide plaintiff with alternative employment where plaintiff could not perform the essential functions of his existing job); F.F. v. City of Laredo, 912 F. Supp. 248, 254–55 (S.D. Tex. 1995) (reasonable accommodation does not require reassignment to another position); Henson v. City of Greensboro, 1995 U.S. Dist. LEXIS 19962, at *8 (M.D.N.C. Dec. 12, 1995) (the duty of reasonable accommodation does not encompass a responsibility to provide a disabled employee with alternative employment when the employee is unable to meet the demands of his or her present position), *aff'd mem.*, 107 F.3d 866 (4th Cir. 1997).

[135]*See* Gile v. United Airlines, Inc., 95 F.3d 492, 499, 5 AD 1466 (7th Cir. 1996) (an employer is only required to reassign a disabled employee to a position for which the employee is otherwise qualified); Champ v. Baltimore County, 5 AD 1184 (4th Cir. 1996) (employer is not required to transfer disabled police officer from patrol to a light-duty position where employee could not perform required emergency functions); DeWitt v. Carsten, 941 F. Supp. 1232, 1237, 6 AD 1255 (N.D. Ga. 1996) (employer is not required to transfer employee to position she cannot perform); Lawrence v. IBP, Inc., 4 AD 632, 637 (D. Kan. 1995) (defendant was not required to transfer plaintiff where there was no evidence, beyond plaintiff's speculation, that she could perform the alternative jobs), *aff'd mem.*, 96 F.3d 1453 (10th Cir. 1996); Riley v. Weyerhaeuser Paper Co., 898 F. Supp. 324, 327, 5 AD 325 (W.D.N.C. 1995) (employer is not required to reassign an employee unless employee is qualified for the vacant position, which means that he or she can perform the essential functions of the vacant position with or without reasonable accommodation), *aff'd in part and dismissed in part*, 77 F.3d 470 (4th Cir. 1996); Marschand v. Norfolk & W. Ry., 876 F. Supp. 1528, 1543, 4 AD 1099 (N.D. Ind. 1995) (employer is not required to reassign an employee to a position for which he or she is not qualified), *aff'd*, 81 F.3d 714 (7th Cir. 1996).

[136]*See* Wernick v. Federal Reserve Bank, 91 F.3d 379, 384–85, 5 AD 1345 (2d Cir. 1996) (company only had an obligation to treat plaintiff in the same manner that it treated similarly situated qualified candidates); Riel v. Electronic Data Sys. Corp., 99 F.3d 678, 683, 6 AD 26 (5th Cir. 1996) (plaintiff could overcome summary judgment

of El Paso,[137] "we do not read the ADA as requiring affirmative action in favor of individuals with disabilities, in the sense of requiring that disabled persons be given priority in hiring or reassignment over those who are not disabled."[138] Still other courts have held that reassignment must be considered but not necessarily given.[139]

---

by showing that the company often transferred employees and that he himself had been transferred repeatedly); Schmidt v. Methodist Hosp., Inc., 89 F.3d 342, 345, 5 AD 1340 (7th Cir. 1996) (employer cannot deny employee alternative employment opportunities available under existing policies, but is not required to find another job for an employee who is not qualified for the job he or she was doing); Braziel v. Loram Maintenance of Way, Inc., 943 F. Supp. 1083, 1100–01 (D. Minn. 1996) (employer was not required to transfer plaintiff to positions for which he did not apply); Amariglio v. National R.R. Passenger Corp., 941 F. Supp. 173, 179 (D.D.C. 1996) (employer reasonably accommodated plaintiff by advising him of procedure for requesting transfer); McCollough v. Atlanta Beverage Co., 929 F. Supp. 1489, 1504 (N.D. Ga. 1996) (employer must reassign employee only if the employer has a regular practice or policy of reassigning nondisabled employees); Rosamond v. Pennaco Hosiery, Inc., 942 F. Supp. 279, 284 n.4 (N.D. Miss. 1996) (employer is not required to give disabled employee priority in reassignment over applicants who are not disabled); Geuss v. Pfizer, Inc., 971 F. Supp. 164, 6 AD 1140, 1147 (E.D. Pa. 1996) (employer has an obligation to permit a transfer to another facility when there is a practice of the employer's doing so); Hoyt v. NYNEX Corp., 1996 U.S. Dist. LEXIS 14230, at *13 (N.D.N.Y. Sept. 25, 1996) (generally, an employer is not required to find another job for an employee, but cannot deny an employee alternative employment opportunities reasonably available under the employer's existing policies); Weiler v. Household Fin. Corp., 5 AD 550, 555–56 (N.D. Ill. 1995) (offering plaintiff an opportunity to apply for new positions and giving her a leave of absence in the interim was reasonable accommodation), *aff'd,* 101 F.3d 519, 6 AD 106 (7th Cir. 1996); Riley v. Weyerhaeuser Paper Co., 898 F. Supp. 324, 328–29, 5 AD 325 (W.D.N.C. 1995) (an employer has no duty to give transfer rights above and beyond what other employees get, which means that the employer had no duty to transfer an hourly employee to another facility); Lewis v. Zilog, Inc., 908 F. Supp. 931, 948, 4 AD 1787 (N.D. Ga. 1995) (employer is not required to give disabled employees preference over nondisabled employees in transfers and can assign personnel as company needs dictate), *aff'd mem.,* 87 F.3d 1331 (11th Cir. 1996).

[137]56 F.3d. 695, 4 AD 993 (5th Cir. 1995), *cert. denied,* 116 S. Ct. 1263 (1996).

[138]*Id.* at 700; *accord* Turco v. Hoechst Celanese Corp., 101 F.3d 1090, 1094, 6 AD 278 (5th Cir. 1996) ("The law does not require affirmative action in favor of individuals with disabilities."); Taylor v. Dover Elevator Sys., Inc., 917 F. Supp. 455, 463, 5 AD 616 (N.D. Miss. 1996) (the ADA is not designed to give disabled persons preferential treatment).

[139]*See, e.g.,* Gower v. Wrenn Handling, Inc., 892 F. Supp. 724, 728, 4 AD 1154 (M.D.N.C. 1995) (defendant was not required to transfer plaintiff to vacant position, but had a duty to consider plaintiff for the position before giving it to someone else). *See also* Williams v. Channel Master Satellite Sys., Inc., 101 F.3d 346, 350, 6 AD 131 (4th Cir. 1996) (district court erred in suggesting that a qualified ADA plaintiff can never rely on reassignment to a vacant position as a reasonable accommodation), *cert. denied,* 117 S. Ct. 1844 (1997).

The courts are split over whether the employer must provide training to the employee for the new position.[140]

Courts continue to hold that an employer is not required to create a new position for a disabled employee.[141] Similarly, an employer is not required to create a light-duty position as an accommodation.[142] But if an appropriate existing light-duty position is vacant, then assignment to the position may be a reasonable accommodation.[143]

Courts continue to hold that an employer is not required to accommodate a disabled employee by bumping another employee from his or her position.[144] Where an employer has a collective bargaining

---

[140]*Compare* Riley v. Weyerhaeuser Paper Co., 898 F. Supp. 324, 328, 5 AD 325 (W.D.N.C. 1995) (employer not required to retrain an employee who can no longer perform his existing duties) *and* Hoyt v. NYNEX Corp., 1996 U.S. Dist LEXIS 14230, at *14 (N.D.N.Y. Sept. 25, 1996) (employer not required to train plaintiff before testing him for alternative positions) *with* Marschand v. Norfolk & W. Ry., 876 F. Supp. 1528, 1544, 4 AD 1099 (N.D. Ind. 1995) (employer reasonably accommodated plaintiff by giving him typing lessons).

[141]*See, e.g.,* Weiler v. Household Fin. Corp., 101 F.3d 519, 526, 6 AD 106 (7th Cir. 1996) (employer not required to create an entirely new position for plaintiff); Gile v. United Airlines, Inc., 95 F.3d 492, 499, 5 AD 1466 (7th Cir. 1996) (employer is not obligated to create a new position for disabled employee); Lawrence v. IBP, Inc., 1996 WL 508423, at *2 (10th Cir. Sept. 9, 1996) (ADA does not require employer to create new position for disabled employee); Conklin v. Englewood, 1996 WL 560370, at *2 (6th Cir. Oct. 1, 1996) (ADA does not require the city to create a new position to accommodate a disabled police officer); Riley v. Weyerhaeuser Paper Co., 898 F. Supp. 324, 327, 5 AD 325 (W.D.N.C. 1995) (employer is not required to create a new position as a reasonable accommodation); Gov't Employees (AFGE) Council 33, Local 51 v. Bentsen, No. 92-15521, 1994 U.S. App. LEXIS 25260, at *8 (9th Cir. Sept. 7, 1994) (Rehabilitation Act does not require an employer to create a new position).

[142]*See* Turco v. Hoechst Celanese Corp., 101 F.3d 1090, 1094, 6 AD 278 (5th Cir. 1996) (employer need not create light-duty position); McCollough v. Atlanta Beverage Co., 929 F. Supp. 1489, 1503 (N.D. Ga. 1996) (employer need not create light-duty position); Simmerman v. Hardee's Food Sys., Inc., 1996 U.S. Dist. LEXIS 3437, at **30–31 (E.D. Va. Mar. 22, 1996) (employer need not create a "light duty position"); Rucker v. City of Philadelphia, 4 AD 1443, 1445 (E.D. Pa. 1995) (employer was not required to create a new permanent light-duty position), *aff'd mem.,* 85 F.3d 612 (3d Cir. 1996).

[143]*See* Nguyen v. IBP, Inc., 905 F. Supp. 1471, 1485–86, 5 AD 465 (D. Kan. 1995) (transferring an employee to a vacant light-duty position would be a reasonable accommodation). *Cf.* Lamury v. Boeing Co., 5 AD 39, 43–44 (D. Kan. 1995) (plaintiff has no cause of action for failure to reassign to light duty where vacant light-duty positions were given to other disabled employees).

[144]*See, e.g.,* Gile v. United Airlines, Inc., 95 F.3d 492, 499, 5 AD 1466 (7th Cir. 1996) (employer is not required to bump other employees to create vacancy for

agreement under which vacancies are filled by seniority or on some other nondiscriminatory basis, the employer is not required to pass over an employee who would have filled the vacancy in favor of a disabled employee.[145] As the Seventh Circuit stated in *Eckles v. Consolidated Rail Corp.*,[146] "[t]he ADA does not require disabled

---

disabled employee); Lawrence v. IBP, Inc., 1996 WL 508423, at *2 (10th Cir. Sept. 9, 1996) (employer not required to reassign plaintiff to a position occupied by another employee); Leslie v. St. Vincent New Hope, Inc., 916 F. Supp. 879, 887, 5 AD 1773 (S.D. Ind. 1996) (employer not required to reassign employee to an occupied position); Rayha v. United Parcel Serv., Inc., 940 F. Supp. 1066, 1069–70 (S.D. Tex. 1996) (employer not required to transfer disabled employee to occupied position); Munoz v. H & M Wholesale, Inc., 926 F. Supp. 596, 608, 6 AD 355 (S.D. Tex. 1996) (ADA does not require an employer to reassign the employee to an occupied position to accommodate the disabled worker); Duffy v. Al Packer Ford, Inc., 1996 U.S. Dist. LEXIS 7038, at *10 (D. Md. May 13, 1996) (an employer is not required to transfer another employee out of his job as an accommodation); Riley v. Weyerhaeuser Paper Co., 898 F. Supp. 324, 327, 5 AD 325 (W.D.N.C. 1995) (employer is not required to bump an employee as a reasonable accommodation); Marschand v. Norfolk & W. Ry., 876 F. Supp.1528, 1542, 4 AD 1099 (N.D. Ind. 1995) (employer is not required to reassign the employee to an occupied position as a reasonable accommodation), *aff'd,* 81 F.3d 714 (7th Cir. 1996); Weiler v. Household Fin. Corp., 5 AD 550, 556 (N.D. Ill. 1995) (employer is not required to reassign plaintiff to an occupied position), *aff'd,* 101 F.3d 519, 6 AD 106 (7th Cir. 1996); Kuehl v. Wal-Mart Stores, Inc., 909 F. Supp. 794, 802, 5 AD 91 (D. Colo. 1995) (employer not required to reassign employee to an occupied position).

[145]*See* Taylor v. Food World, Inc., 946 F. Supp. 937, 942 (N.D. Ala. 1996) (as a matter of law, an accommodation that forces an employer to violate a collective bargaining agreement is not reasonable); Koedding v. Brinckerhoff, 1996 U.S. Dist. LEXIS 545, at *24 (N.D. Cal. Jan. 16, 1996) (disabled employee not entitled to a vacant position for which another employee has hiring or transfer priority); Pattison v. Meijer, Inc., 897 F. Supp. 1002, 1007–08, 4 AD 997 (W.D. Mich. 1995) (there is no duty to violate other employees' rights under a collective bargaining agreement); Milton v. Scrivner, Inc., 901 F. Supp. 1541, 1545 (W.D. Okla. 1994) (defendant was not required to transfer plaintiff in violation of the collective bargaining agreement), *aff'd,* 53 F.3d 1118, 4 AD 432 (10th Cir. 1995); Massey v. Scrivner, Inc., 901 F. Supp. 1546, 1551 (W.D. Okla. 1994) (employer not required to transfer plaintiff in violation of the collective bargaining agreement), *aff'd sub nom.* Milton v. Scrivner, Inc., 53 F.3d 1118, 4 AD 432 (10th Cir. 1995). *But see* Lally v. Commonwealth Edison Co., 1996 U.S. Dist. LEXIS 19386, at *68 (N.D. Ill. Dec. 16, 1996) (provision in collective bargaining agreement stating that all other provisions shall not apply when attempting to accommodate a disabled employee may require an employer to transfer a disabled employee to a position otherwise not available to her because of seniority rights); Emrick v. Libbey-Owens-Ford Co., 875 F. Supp. 393, 396–97, 4 AD 1 (E.D. Tex. 1995) (employer might be required to reassign an employee notwithstanding seniority provisions of a collective bargaining agreement where another employee voluntarily gives up his or her rights to the position in order to accommodate the disabled employee).

[146]94 F.3d 1041, 5 AD 1367 (7th Cir. 1996), *cert. denied,* 117 S. Ct. 1318 (1997).

individuals to be accommodated by sacrificing the collectively bargained, bona fide seniority rights of other employees."[147]

Nor does the ADA require an employer to promote an employee as an accommodation.[148] If the employee can no longer perform the essential functions of a comparable position, however, reassignment to a lower position may be reasonable accommodation.[149]

d. Employment Tests. An employer is not prohibited from using employment tests that may screen out persons with disabilities if the test actually measures the employee's or applicant's ability to perform the essential functions of the position in question.[150]

---

[147]*Id.* at 1051.

[148]*See* Shiring v. Runyon, 90 F.3d 827, 832, 5 AD 1216 (3d Cir. 1996) (employer was not required to promote plaintiff to a higher level to accommodate her disability); White v. York Int'l Corp., 45 F.3d 357, 362, 3 AD 1746 (10th Cir. 1995) (the ADA does not require promotion as reasonable accommodation); Lawrence v. IBP, Inc., 1996 WL 508423, at *2 (10th Cir. Sept. 9, 1996) (employer not required to promote plaintiff as an accommodation); Gomez v. American Bldg. Maintenance, 940 F. Supp. 255, 259–60 (N.D. Cal. 1996) (an employer is not required to consider reassignment except to equivalent position); Burnett v. Western Resources, Inc., 929 F. Supp. 1349, 1358, 6 AD 711 (D. Kan. 1996) (employer not required to promote plaintiff to supervisory position at a higher rate of pay as an accommodation); Riley v. Weyerhaeuser Paper Co., 898 F. Supp. 324, 327, 5 AD 325 (W.D.N.C. 1995) (employer is not required to promote an employee as a reasonable accommodation); Ricks v. Xerox Corp., 877 F. Supp. 1468, 1477, 4 AD 233 (D. Kan. 1995) (defendant was not required to promote plaintiff who admitted that he could not perform the essential functions of his existing job), *aff'd mem.*, 96 F.3d 1453 (10th Cir. 1996); Marschand v. Norfolk & W. Ry., 876 F. Supp.1528, 1542, 4 AD 1099 (N.D. Ind. 1995) (employer not required to promote an employee as a reasonable accommodation), *aff'd*, 81 F.3d 714 (7th Cir. 1996).

[149]*See* Altman v. New York City Health & Hosps. Corp., 903 F. Supp. 503, 514, 4 AD 1665 (S.D.N.Y. 1995) (reassigning plaintiff to an attending physician position was reasonable accommodation where he could no longer perform the duties of chief of medicine), *aff'd*, 100 F.3d 1054, 6 AD 73 (2d Cir. 1996); Harden v. Delta Air Lines, 900 F. Supp. 493, 498, 4 AD 1241 (S.D. Ga. 1995) (employer reasonably accommodated customer service agent who could no longer perform physical duties by offering him a clerical position); Pattison v. Meijer, 897 F. Supp. 1002, 1007, 4 AD 997 (W.D. Mich. 1995) (if there is no vacancy in a comparable position, the employer may reassign an employee to a position with lower grade and pay); Graehling v. Village of Lombard, 4 AD 815, 819 (N.D. Ill. 1994) (the ADA does not prohibit an employer from keeping an employee in a lower capacity if the disabilities impede the employee's ability to perform the essential functions of the original job), *aff'd*, 58 F.3d 295, 4 AD 864 (7th Cir. 1995).

[150]*See, e.g.,* Schmidt v. Methodist Hosp., 89 F.3d 342, 344, 5 AD 1340 (7th Cir. 1996) (hospital reasonably accommodated plaintiff with performance problems by offering additional training); Burke v. Virginia, 938 F. Supp. 320, 323, 5 AD 1747 (E.D. Va. 1996) (corrections officer position required reading and writing and comprehending written materials so employer could test those abilities), *aff'd mem.*, 114 F.3d 1175, 6 AD 1440 (4th Cir. 1997); Fussell v. Georgia Ports Auth., 906 F. Supp. 1561, 1573, 5 AD 1236 (S.D. Ga. 1995) (employer could require firearms test for police officers despite impact on individual with arm impairment), *aff'd mem.*, 106

e. Policies and Training Materials. An employer may be required to modify its policies to permit an otherwise qualified disabled employee to perform the job.[151] Such a modification may include special training for employees with mental disabilities.[152]

Most courts continue to hold that an employer is not required to modify its attendance or leave policies to tolerate sporadic attendance.[153] As the district court stated in *Aquinas v. Federal Express*

F.3d 417 (11th Cir. 1997); Coffman v. Michigan, 914 F. Supp. 172, 175 (W.D. Mich. 1995) (the Army is not required to give officer troubled by ulcers a third opportunity to run two miles in the required time), *aff'd,* 120 F.3d 57 (6th Cir. 1997); Ethridge v. Alabama, 860 F. Supp. 808, 817, 3 AD 1013 (N.D. Ala. 1994) (employer was not required to modify shooting test to allow plaintiff to shoot one handed where the ability to shoot two handed was an essential function of the job).

[151]*See, e.g.,* Czopek v. General Elec. Co., 4 AD 1231, 1233 (N.D. Ill. 1995) (reasonable accommodation includes considering changes in work rules); Sarsycki v. United Parcel Serv., 862 F. Supp. 336, 342, 3 AD 1039 (W.D. Okla. 1994) (reasonable accommodation for employer to waive policy against driving smaller trucks by insulin-dependent diabetics, require that the employee have food within reach, and prohibit carrying of passengers or hazardous materials); Bombrys v. City of Toledo, 849 F. Supp. 1210, 1218, 3 AD 651 (N.D. Ohio 1993) (allowing insulin-dependent diabetic to use blood sugar monitoring equipment and to carry food or glucose tablets and insulin injection kit while working would be reasonable accommodation).

[152]*See* Fernbach v. Dominick's Finer Foods, 936 F. Supp. 467, 473, 5 AD 1543 (N.D. Ill. 1996) (employer might be required to specifically explain rules to mentally disabled employees).

[153]*See, e.g.,* Gore v. GTE S., Inc., 917 F. Supp. 1564, 1573 (M.D. Ala. 1996) (no way for employer to accommodate a telephone operator's unpredictable absences); Johnson v. Children's Hosp., 4 AD 806, 807 (E.D. Pa. 1995) (employer was not required to accommodate plaintiff's substantial and unpredictable absences), *aff'd mem.,* 79 F.3d 1138 (3d Cir. 1996); Hendry v. GTE N., Inc., 896 F. Supp. 816, 826–27, 6 AD 451 (N.D. Ind. 1995) (requiring other employees to substitute for frequent and unpredictable absences is not a reasonable accommodation, and employer is not required to allow plaintiff to use vacation time, which normally must be scheduled in advance, to cover for unscheduled absences); Haysman v. Food Lion, 893 F. Supp. 1092, 1103, 4 AD 1297 (S.D. Ga. 1995) (regular attendance is an essential function of the job, and an employer is not required to tolerate a manager's sporadic attendance); Barfield v. Bell S. Telecomms., Inc., 886 F. Supp. 1321, 1327, 4 AD 1159 (S.D. Miss. 1995) (allowing an employee to just work when able is not required as a reasonable accommodation); Kennedy v. Applause, Inc., 3 AD 1734, 1740 (C.D. Cal. 1994) (allowing a plaintiff to "work when able" is not required as a reasonable accommodation), *aff'd in part and dismissed in part,* 90 F.3d 1477, 5 AD 1249 (9th Cir. 1996); Larkins v. CIBA Vision Corp., 858 F. Supp. 1572, 1583–84 & n.5, 3 AD 715 (N.D. Ga. 1994) (employer was not required to accommodate plaintiff's unpredictable absences). *But see* Dutton v. Johnson County Bd. of County Comm'rs, 859 F. Supp. 498, 507–09, 3 AD 808 (D. Kan.) (employer may be required to modify policies to allow employee with migraines to use vacation time for unscheduled absences), *later proceeding,* 868 F. Supp. 1260, 1265, 3 AD 1614 (D. Kan. 1994) (court ordered that plaintiff be allowed to take sick leave and vacation time without advance notice otherwise required by policies to accommodate absences caused by migraines, but did not require employer to grant more total paid leave time than given to other employees). *See* Section III.B.3.c *supra.*

Corp.,[154] "[a] request for permission to work only when ... illness permits, necessarily undermines the policy of regular attendance that is essential to [the] job."[155]

The employer's duty to accommodate by modifying policies may be satisfied by allowing an employee a brief leave of absence.[156] This may include giving alcoholic employees time off to enter treatment programs[157] though such an accommodation is less likely to be required where the request comes in response to a disciplinary

---

[154]940 F. Supp. 73, 6 AD 485 (S.D.N.Y. 1996).

[155]*Id.* at 79.

[156]*See* Voytek v. University of Cal., 77 F.3d 491, 5 AD 1344 (9th Cir. 1996) (affirming grant of summary judgment to university, which reasonably accommodated associate director who claimed he could not carry out his duties due to the stress of management-level position by providing rehabilitation training counseling to him); Davis v. Jim Quinlan Ford, Lincoln-Mercury, Inc., 932 F. Supp. 1389, 1392 (M.D. Fla. 1996) (whether a heart attack patient's request for time to participate in a four-to-eight-week recovery program was a reasonable accommodation is a question of fact for the jury); Horton v. Board of Trustees, 1996 U.S. Dist. LEXIS 6879, at **14–15 (N.D. Ill. May 15, 1996) (board made the greatest possible accommodation in allowing plaintiff a five-year leave of absence); Hardy v. Sears, Roebuck & Co., 1996 U.S. Dist. LEXIS 19008, at *23 (N.D. Ga. Aug. 28, 1996) (defendant reasonably accommodated plaintiff by granting a short leave of absence for psychiatric care); Weiler v. Household Fin. Corp., 5 AD 550, 555 (N.D. Ill. 1995) (placing plaintiff on a temporary leave of absence while she applied for vacant positions within her restrictions was reasonable accommodation), *aff'd,* 101 F.3d 519, 6 AD 106 (5th Cir. 1995); Ferry v. Roosevelt Bank, 883 F. Supp. 435, 441–42, 4 AD 476 (E.D. Mo. 1995) (employer met its duty to accommodate by allowing plaintiff with performance problems following a cerebral hemorrhage an unpaid medical leave of absence to allow her to obtain treatment); Vializ v. New York City Bd. of Educ., 4 AD 345, 347 (S.D.N.Y. 1995) (court denied motion to dismiss when plaintiff was unable to return to work six months after a work-related injury, holding that a temporary leave of absence may be a reasonable accommodation); Vande Zande v. Wisconsin Dep't of Admin., 851 F. Supp. 353, 360–61, 2 AD 1846 (W.D. Wis. 1994) (employer reasonably accommodated by allowing employee to take paid sick leave when employer did not have work meeting her restrictions), *aff'd,* 44 F.3d 538, 3 AD 1636 (7th Cir. 1995); Kennedy v. Applause, Inc., 3 AD 1734, 1739–40 (C.D. Cal. 1994) (employer reasonably accommodated plaintiff by giving her a four-month leave of absence and was not required to extend the leave another month), *aff'd in part and dismissed in part,* 90 F.3d 1477, 5 AD 1249 (9th Cir. 1996).

[157]*See* Williams v. Widnall, 79 F.3d. 1003, 1006, 5 AD 663 (10th Cir. 1996) (reasonable accommodation requires that an alcoholic be given time off to participate in a treatment program); Office of Senate Sergeant at Arms v. Office of Senate Fair Employment Practices, 95 F.3d 1102, 1107, 6 AD 1237 (Fed. Cir. 1996) ("Treatment would seem to be essential to any accommodation for alcoholism."); Corbett v. National Prods. Co., 4 AD 987, 990–91 (E.D. Pa. 1995) (employer had a duty to accommodate plaintiff by giving him a 28-day leave of absence to complete an alcohol treatment program); Schmidt v. Safeway, Inc., 864 F. Supp. 991, 996, 3 AD 1141 (D. Or. 1994) (reasonable accommodation may require an employer to provide a leave of absence to an employee with an alcohol problem so that he can enter treatment).

action for alcohol-related conduct.[158] Generally, while some courts have required employers to give employees leave from work for rehabilitation, they have not required that the employer pay for that rehabilitation.[159] Some courts have held that an employer is not required to give an employee more leave time than otherwise provided under the employer's policies.[160]

Numerous courts have held that the ADA does not require employers to provide disabled employees with indefinite leave.[161] For example, in *Myers v. Hose*,[162] the court observed:

---

[158]*See* Labrucherie v. Regents of Univ. of Cal., 1995 U.S. Dist. LEXIS 12763, at *18 (N.D. Cal. Aug. 30, 1995) (employer was not required to grant plaintiff a leave of absence for alcohol treatment when the treatment would have been while plaintiff was in jail for the conduct for which he was being terminated), *aff'd mem.*, 119 F.3d 6 (9th Cir. 1997).

[159]*See, e.g.,* Burnett v. Western Resources, Inc., 929 F. Supp. 1349, 1358, 6 AD 711 (D. Kan. 1996).

[160]*See, e.g.,* Lewis v. Zilog, Inc., 908 F. Supp. 931, 952, 4 AD 1787 (N.D. Ga. 1995) (termination pursuant to the expiration of a medical leave under the company's policies is not unlawful), *aff'd mem.*, 87 F.3d 1331 (11th Cir. 1996); Dockery v. North Shore Med. Ctr., 909 F. Supp. 1550, 1560, 5 AD 1443 (S.D. Fla. 1995) (employer not required to grant a one-year leave of absence unless such leave is provided for other employees).

[161]*See, e.g.,* Rogers v. International Marine Terminals, Inc., 87 F.3d 755, 759, 5 AD 1115 (5th Cir. 1996) (employee not entitled to indefinite leave); Weiler v. Household Fin. Corp., 101 F.3d 519, 526, 6 AD 106 (7th Cir. 1996) (employer not required to wait indefinitely for an employee to return to work); Smith v. Blue Cross Blue Shield, 102 F.3d 1075, 1076, 6 AD 367 (10th Cir. 1996) (employer is not required to wait indefinitely for an employee's recovery), *petition for cert. filed,* 65 U.S.L.W. 3783 (U.S. May 6, 1997) (No. 96-1832); Hudson v. MCI Telecomms. Corp., 87 F.3d 1167, 1169, 5 AD 1099 (10th Cir. 1996) (unpaid leave of indefinite duration does not constitute reasonable accommodation); Hunt-Golliday v. Metropolitan Water Reclamation Dist., 6 AD 698, 703 (N.D. Ill. 1996) (no requirement to provide indefinite leave), *aff'd in part and rev'd in part on other grounds,* 104 F.3d 1004, 6 AD 725 (7th Cir. 1997); Munoz v. H & M Wholesale, Inc., 926 F. Supp. 596, 608, 6 AD 355 (S.D. Tex. 1996) (reasonable accommodation does not require the defendant to wait indefinitely for the plaintiff's medical condition to be corrected); Pegues v. Emerson Elec. Co., 913 F. Supp 976, 981, 5 AD 376 (N.D. Miss. 1996) (employer is not required to extend a year-long leave indefinitely); Murphy v. United Parcel Serv., Inc., 946 F. Supp. 872, 883, 6 AD 517 (D. Kan. 1996) (employer is not required to give an employee an indefinite amount of time to lower his blood pressure); Johnson v. Foulds, Inc., 5 AD 1635, 1639 (N.D. Ill. 1996) (indefinite leave of absence is not a reasonable accommodation); Robison-Fisher v. Township of Elgin, 1996 U.S. Dist. LEXIS 7645, at *5 (N.D. Ill. May 20, 1996) (indefinite leave not an accommodation that enables one to work); Horton v. Board of Trustees, 1996 U.S. Dist. LEXIS 6879, at **14–15 (N.D. Ill. May 15, 1996) (board made the greatest possible accommodation in allowing plaintiff a five-year leave of absence); Egan v. Blue Water Dev. Hous., Inc., 1996 U.S. Dist. LEXIS 15937, at *2 (E.D. Mich. Aug. 20, 1996) (company was allowed to terminate plaintiff after six-month leave of absence in accordance with company policy); Henson v. City of Greensboro, 1995 U.S. Dist. LEXIS 19962, at *8 (M.D.N.C. Dec. 12, 1995) (employer need not allow employee to miss work indefinitely).

[162]50 F.3d 278, 283, 4 AD 391 (4th Cir. 1995).

Significantly, these provisions [of the ADA] contain no reference to an individual's future ability to perform the essential functions of his position. To the contrary, they are formulated entirely in the present tense, framing the precise issue as whether an individual "can" (not "will be able to") perform the job with reasonable accommodation. Nothing in the text of the reasonable accommodation provision requires an employer to wait an indefinite period for an accommodation to achieve its intended effect. Rather, reasonable accommodation is by its terms most logically construed as that which presently, or in the immediate future, enables the employee to perform the essential functions of the job in question.

An employer may be required to modify its policies to provide equal benefits to a disabled employee who is disqualified from receiving those benefits through a third-party provider.[163]

f. Readers, Interpreters, and Other Helpers or Aids. Some courts have held that the duty to accommodate may include hiring an assistant for a disabled employee,[164] such as by providing a qualified interpreter for a deaf employee.[165] But an employer is not required to hire two individuals to perform one person's job; nor is the employer required to reassign essential functions of the job to an assistant.[166]

---

[163] *See* Holmes v. City of Aurora, 4 AD 1781, 1787 (N.D. Ill. 1995) (city was required to provide plaintiff with pension comparable to other employees even though pension fund, managed by a third party, excluded plaintiff because of his diabetes).

[164] *See* Borkowski v. Valley Cent. Sch. Dist., 63 F.3d 131, 142, 4 AD 1264 (2d Cir. 1995) (employer might be required to provide help to teacher who was unable to control her students); EEOC v. AIC Sec. Investigation, 820 F. Supp. 1060, 1066, 2 AD 561 (N.D. Ill. 1993) (plaintiff's inability to drive could be accommodated by hiring a driver).

[165] *See* Mohamed v. Marriott Int'l, Inc., 905 F. Supp. 141, 153, 5 AD 50 (S.D.N.Y. 1995) (employer could have provided an interpreter without undue hardship).

[166] *See* Cochrum v. Old Ben Coal Co., 102 F.3d 908, 912, 6 AD 219 (7th Cir. 1996) (employer not required to assign the essential overhead work of a roof bolter to an assistant); Altman v. New York City Health & Hosps. Corp., 903 F. Supp. 503, 511–12, 4 AD 1665 (S.D.N.Y. 1995) (hospital was not required to hire monitor for alcoholic chief of staff, holding that the assistant could not effectively monitor the doctor, who often made decisions outside working hours, without effectively taking over the chief's duties), *aff'd,* 100 F.3d 1054, 6 AD 73 (2d Cir. 1996); Krennerich v. Inhabitants of Bristol, 943 F. Supp. 1345, 1352 (D. Me. 1996) (employer not required to hire a substitute to perform some of plaintiff's essential duties or to delegate those duties to other employees); Murphy v. United Parcel Serv., Inc., 946 F. Supp. 872, 883, 6 AD 517 (D. Kan. 1996) (ADA does not require employers to transfer essential functions to another employee); Ricks v. Xerox Corp., 877 F. Supp. 1468, 1477, 4 AD 233 (D. Kan. 1995) (employer was not required to hire full-time helper to assist plaintiff with essential functions that he could not perform), *aff'd mem.,* 96

The courts have held that an employer may be required to provide technical aids or devices as an accommodation.[167] Thus, in *Garza v. Abbott Laboratories*,[168] the district court held that the employer might be required to provide an employee with a split keyboard or a voice-activated computer to accommodate the limited use of her arms.[169]

3. What Accommodations Are Not "Reasonable"?

A number of courts have held that evaluating whether an accommodation is reasonable or poses an undue hardship requires a cost-benefit analysis.[170] An accommodation, however, is not unreasonable merely because the accommodation costs the employer

---

F.3d 1453 (10th Cir. 1996); Mauro v. Borgess Med. Ctr., 886 F. Supp. 1349, 1354, 4 AD 737 (W.D. Mich. 1995) (hospital not required to add another person to the operating team to handle surgical incisions for surgical technician with HIV); Holbrook v. City of Alpharetta, 911 F. Supp. 1524, 1542, 6 AD 1394 (N.D. Ga. 1995) (defendant had no duty to hire an assistant to perform essential function of surveying crime scenes for evidence where plaintiff's visual impairment prohibited him from doing so), *aff'd,* 112 F.3d 1522, 6 AD 1409 (11th Cir. 1997); Hogue v. MQS Inspection, Inc., 875 F. Supp. 714, 722, 3 AD 1793 (D. Colo. 1995) (defendant might be required to hire a helper to assist plaintiff in nonessential physical functions, but would not be required to hire a helper to assume plaintiff's position).

[167]*See, e.g.,* Willett v. Kansas, 942 F. Supp. 1387, 1394 (D. Kan. 1996) (providing plaintiff with light-weight cart to carry supplies was reasonable accommodation); Bryant v. Better Bus. Bureau, 923 F. Supp. 720, 739, 5 AD 625 (D. Md. 1996) (TTY device may be reasonable accommodation for an individual with a hearing disability); Smith v. Kitterman, Inc., 897 F. Supp. 423, 430, 4 AD 1487 (W.D. Mo. 1995) (employer may be required to purchase larger handles for small hand tools to accommodate employee with carpal tunnel syndrome); Vande Zande v. Wisconsin Dep't of Admin., 851 F. Supp. 353, 361, 2 AD 1846 (W.D. Wis. 1994) (employer reasonably accommodated plaintiff by providing her with a laptop computer instead of a desktop computer with laser printer), *aff'd,* 44 F.3d 538, 3 AD 1636 (7th Cir. 1995) (employer was not required to install computer in employee's home so that she could avoid having to use accumulated sick leave time).

[168]940 F. Supp. 1227, 6 AD 1507 (N.D. Ill. 1996).

[169]*Id.* at 1240–43.

[170]*See, e.g.,* Jacques v. Clean-Up Group, Inc., 96 F.3d 506, 512, 5 AD 1594 (1st Cir. 1996) (employer was not required to hire another employee to drive plaintiff in light of profit margin); Borkowski v. Valley Cent. Sch. Dist., 63 F.3d 131, 142, 4 AD 1264 (2d Cir. 1995) (an accommodation is reasonable only if its costs do not outweigh the benefits); Garza v. Abbott Lab., 940 F. Supp. 1227, 1238–39, 6 AD 1507 (N.D. Ill. 1996) (a reasonable accommodation is cost effective where the costs to the employer do not greatly exceed the benefits to the employer and employee); Amariglio v. National R.R. Passenger Corp., 941 F. Supp. 173, 179 (D.D.C. 1996) (employer was not required to open separate office for single employee); Williams v. Avnet, Inc., 910 F. Supp. 1124, 1133–34, 5 AD 835 (E.D.N.C. 1995) (within the

more to obtain the same level of performance from the disabled employee than from nondisabled employees.[171]

Accommodations that pose a direct threat to those in the workplace are not reasonable,[172] but the employer bears the burden of proving that such a threat exists.[173]

An employer is not required to give a futile accommodation, that is, an accommodation that will not enable the employee to perform the essential functions of the job.[174] Therefore, the question of reasonable accommodation is not reached when an employee is totally and permanently disabled because no accommodation will

---

context of reasonable accommodation, the requirement of reason is a requirement of economic rationality; just because defendants can afford plaintiff's requests does not mean it is reasonable to grant them), *aff'd sub nom.* Williams v. Channel Master Satellite Sys., 101 F.3d 346 (4th Cir. 1996), *cert. denied,* 117 S. Ct. 1844 (1997); Fussell v. Georgia Ports Auth., 906 F. Supp. 1561, 1571, 5 AD 1236 (S.D. Ga. 1995) (an accommodation is reasonable only if its costs are not clearly disproportionate to the benefits that are produced), *aff'd mem.,* 106 F.3d 417 (11th Cir. 1997); Mohamed v. Marriott Int'l, Inc., 905 F. Supp. 141, 152, 5 AD 50 (S.D.N.Y. 1995) ("[A]n accommodation is reasonable only if its costs are not clearly disproportionate to the benefits it will produce."); Hutchinson v. United Parcel Serv., 883 F. Supp. 379, 392, 4 AD 536 (N.D. Iowa 1995) (a cost-benefit analysis is relevant to the determination of reasonable accommodation); Vande Zande v. Wisconsin Dep't of Admin., 851 F. Supp. 353, 362, 2 AD 1846 (W.D. Wis. 1994) (employer was not required to spend over $1,000 to modify a sink for an employee in a wheelchair when an accessible sink was nearby), *aff'd,* 44 F.3d 538, 3 AD 1636 (7th Cir. 1995).

[171]*See* Borkowski v. Valley Cent. Sch. Dist., 63 F.3d 131, 138 n.3, 4 AD 1264 (2d Cir. 1995) (reasonable accommodation may mean that an employer pays more to get the same performance from a disabled employee as it would get from a nondisabled employee); Lyons v. Legal Aid Soc'y, 68 F.3d. 1512, 1517, 4 AD 1694 (2d Cir. 1995) (employee's request for a parking space may be reasonable even though the employer does not normally provide parking for its employees); Hoyt v. NYNEX Corp., 1996 U.S. Dist. LEXIS 14230, at **11–12 (N.D.N.Y. Sept. 25, 1996) (reasonable accommodation includes paying more for disabled employee to get same results as nondisabled employee).

[172]*See* Guneratne v. St. Mary's Hosp., 943 F. Supp. 771, 775, 6 AD 476 (S.D. Tex. 1996) (eliminating heavy lifting required of nurse's job could pose a risk to the health and safety of hospital patients); Hardy v. Sears, Roebuck & Co., 1996 U.S. Dist. LEXIS 19008, at *24 (N.D. Ga. Aug. 28, 1996) (defendant was not required to place its other employees in jeopardy by employing plaintiff with bipolar disorder who refused to take his lithium).

[173]*See* Siefken v. Village of Arlington Heights, 3 AD 1281, 1282 (N.D. Ill. 1994) (defendant must prove that an accommodation is unreasonable and that plaintiff poses a direct threat to the safety or health of others that cannot be eliminated by an accommodation), *aff'd,* 65 F.3d 664, 4 AD 1441 (7th Cir. 1995).

[174]*See* Moses v. American Nonwovens, Inc., 97 F.3d 446, 448, 5 AD 1651 (11th Cir. 1996) (employer need not investigate reasonable accommodations when such an investigation would have been fruitless), *cert. denied,* 117 S. Ct. 964 (1997);

allow the employee to perform the essential functions of the job.[175] Moreover, an employer is not required to make accommodations that would violate the rights of other employees. For example, courts

---

Carrozza v. Howard County, 4 AD 512, 512 (4th Cir. 1995) (where county has already provided ample training, complying with request for more would be futile); Taylor v. Food World, Inc., 946 F. Supp. 937, 942 (N.D. Ala. 1996) ("[A]n employer need not investigate reasonable accommodations when such an investigation 'would have been fruitless.' "); Jackson v. Boise Cascade Corp., 941 F. Supp. 1122, 1128–29 (S.D. Ala. 1996) (employer not required to allow plaintiff naps when he still would not be able to perform essential functions of job); Sweet v. Electronic Data Sys., 5 AD 853, 860 (S.D.N.Y. 1996) (providing motivational audio tapes is not a reasonable accommodation for a visually impaired sales worker who could not make quota because there is no evidence that such tapes would bring the employee's performance to acceptable levels); Hoyt v. NYNEX Corp., 1996 U.S. Dist. LEXIS 14230, at **16–17 (N.D.N.Y. Sept. 25, 1996) (employer was not required to provide a bucket truck that would not obviate all heavy-lifting and pole-climbing requirements of plaintiff's position); Hendry v. GTE N., Inc., 896 F. Supp. 816, 827 (N.D. Ind. 1995) (noting that at the time the employer rejected plaintiff's request that she be allowed time off until she got her medication worked out, there was no evidence that the medication would ultimately solve plaintiff's attendance problem, even though that later turned out to be true); Riblett v. Boeing Co., 4 AD 1679, 1684 (D. Kan. 1995) (plaintiff's request for more time to learn the essential functions of the job was denied where an expert testified that he did not believe that plaintiff would ever be able to perform the essential functions).

[175]*See* Rogers v. International Marine Terminals, 87 F.3d 755, 759, 5 AD 1115 (5th Cir. 1996) (no reasonable accommodation could have allowed plaintiff to perform his job when he had been off work for three months); Kennedy v. Applause, Inc., 90 F.3d 1477, 1482, 5 AD 1249 (9th Cir. 1996) (rejecting plaintiff's claim that she should have been given part-time or restructured schedule where she claimed that she was totally disabled); Johnson v. U.S. Steel Corp., 943 F. Supp. 1108, 1114–15 (D. Minn. 1996) (plaintiff cannot claim that he could have worked with accommodation while receiving workers' compensation benefits); Trotter v. B & S Aircraft Parts & Accessories, Inc., 5 AD 1584, 1591 (D. Kan. 1996) (defendant was not required to accommodate plaintiff who claimed that he was totally disabled); Smith v. Blue Cross Blue Shield, 894 F. Supp. 1463, 1469, 4 AD 1378 (D. Kan. 1995) (no accommodation is necessary where plaintiff claims that she is totally disabled and unable to work), *aff'd,* 102 F.3d 1075, 6 AD 367 (10th Cir. 1996), *petition for cert. filed,* 65 U.S.L.W. 3783 (U.S. May 6, 1997) (No. 96-1382); Mears v. Aerospace Corp., 905 F. Supp. 1075, 1080, 5 AD 1295 (S.D. Ga. 1995) (employer had no duty to accommodate plaintiff where she was unable to work and indicated that she would not be able to work no matter where she was transferred with the employer), *aff'd mem.,* 87 F.3d 1331, 6 AD 1152 (11th Cir. 1996); Agster v. Furnival/State Mach. Co., 4 AD 1614, 1615 (E.D. Pa. 1995) (not reaching reasonable accommodation question because plaintiff was totally and permanently disabled and thus could not perform the essential functions of his job with or without accommodation). *But see* Johnson-Goeman v. Michigan Dep't of Commerce, 1995 U.S. Dist. LEXIS 1806, at *21 (W.D. Mich. Jan. 18, 1995) (if plaintiff's inability to work is due to stress caused by defendant's initial failure to accommodate, defendant may be liable).

have consistently held that an employer is not required to violate the terms of a collective bargaining agreement in order to accommodate a disabled employee.[176] Likewise, employers are not required to make accommodations that would result in longer, harder hours or an increased workload for other employees.[177]

Employers also are not required to make accommodations that adversely impact fellow employees in other ways. In *Kennedy v. Chemical Waste Management, Inc.*,[178] the Seventh Circuit held that the reasonable accommodation duty does not require granting disabled employees "super-seniority."

Most courts have held that an employer is not required to accommodate an employee by providing a different supervisor or a stress-free workplace.[179] Thus, in *Wernick v. Federal Reserve*

---

[176]*See, e.g.,* Wooten v. Farmland Foods, 58 F.3d 382, 386, 4 AD 920 (8th Cir. 1995) (an accommodation that violates the rights of other employees is not reasonable); Collins v. Yellow Freight Sys., Inc., 942 F. Supp. 449, 453, 6 AD 102 (W.D. Mo. 1996) (employer was not required to permit employee with permanent disability to enter modified work program designed for employees with temporary disabilities).

[177]*See* Turco v. Hoechst Celanese, 101 F.3d 1090, 1094, 6 AD 278 (5th Cir. 1996) (transferring operator from rotating shift to straight day shift was not required because of the heavier burden the move would place on other operators); Borkowski v. Valley Cent. Sch. Dist., 63 F.3d 131, 140, 4 AD 1264 (2d Cir. 1995) (employer need not transfer heavy-lifting responsibility to other units); Milton v. Scrivner, Inc., 53 F.3d 1118, 1125, 4 AD 432 (10th Cir. 1995) (reduction of production standards would impose a heavier workload on other employees and was not reasonable); Munoz v. H & M Wholesale, Inc., 926 F. Supp. 596, 607, 6 AD 355 (S.D. Tex. 1996) (ADA does not require an accommodation that would result in other employees having to work harder or longer hours); Tenbrink v. Federal Home Loan Bank, 920 F. Supp. 1156, 1164 (D. Kan. 1996) (same); Mears v. Gulfstream Aerospace Corp., 905 F. Supp. 1075, 1081, 5 AD 1295 (S.D. Ga. 1995) (employer was not required to have six different people from six different departments bring things to plaintiff rather than having her make her rounds because an accommodation that adversely impacted other employees would be an undue burden), *aff'd mem.,* 87 F.3d 1331, 6 AD 1152 (11th Cir. 1996).

[178]79 F.3d 49, 52, 5 AD 565 (7th Cir. 1996).

[179]*See, e.g.,* Weiler v. Household Fin. Corp., 101 F.3d 519, 526, 6 AD 106 (7th Cir. 1996) (ADA does not require an employer to give employee a different supervisor as a reasonable accommodation); Patterson v. City of Seattle, 1996 U.S. App. LEXIS 24667, at *3 (9th Cir. Sept. 17, 1996) (employer was not required to remove plaintiff from any possible contact with former supervisor as accommodation for Crohn's disease aggravated by stress); DeWitt v. Carsten, 941 F. Supp. 1232, 1235, 6 AD 1255 (N.D. Ga. 1996) (employer is not required to transfer employee due to stress); Mears v. Gulfstream Aerospace Corp., 905 F. Supp. 1075, 1080–81, 5 AD 1295 (S.D. Ga. 1995) (employer was not required to accommodate plaintiff by forbidding her supervisor from having any contact with her or by not requiring plaintiff to make her rounds so that she would not bump into former co-workers, which would cause her stress), *aff'd mem.,* 87 F.3d 1331, 6 AD 1152 (11th Cir. 1996);

Bank,[180] the Second Circuit rejected the employee's claim that she should have been reassigned to a less stressful supervisor: "[N]othing in the law leads us to conclude that in enacting the disability acts, Congress intended to interfere with personnel decisions within an organizational hierarchy."[181] Employers are also not required to make managers attend sensitivity training as an accommodation.[182]

Employers are not required to ignore a disabled employee's violation of workplace rules.[183]

Generally, employers are not required to provide accommodations that violate federal law or regulations.[184]

Carrozza v. Howard County, 847 F. Supp. 365, 368, 3 AD 197 (D. Md. 1994) (defendant was not required to strip a job of its inherent stressors by changing a work schedule to alleviate stressful periods or giving plaintiff a less stressful supervisor), *aff'd mem.*, 45 F.3d 425, 4 AD 512 (4th Cir. 1995).

[180]91 F.3d 379, 5 AD 1345 (2d Cir. 1996).

[181]*Id.* at 384.

[182]*See* Hunt-Golliday v. Metropolitan Water Reclamation Dist., 6 AD 698, 703 (N.D. Ill. 1996) (plaintiff's suggestion that supervisors be requested to attend sensitivity seminars on gender and cultural issues does not constitute a request for reasonable disability accommodation), *aff'd in part and rev'd in part on other grounds*, 104 F.3d 1004, 6 AD 725 (7th Cir. 1997).

[183]*See* Williams v. Widnall, 79 F.3d 1003, 1006, 5 AD 663 (10th Cir. 1996) (reasonable accommodation does not require employer to accept an alcoholic's threats against supervisors and co-workers when that same behavior exhibited by a nondisabled employee would result in termination); Leary v. Dalton, 58 F.3d 748, 753, 4 AD 1165 (1st Cir. 1995) (Rehabilitation Act does not prevent employers from holding persons suffering from alcoholism to reasonable rules of conduct); Siefken v. Village of Arlington Heights, 65 F.3d 664, 666, 4 AD 1441 (7th Cir. 1995) (police officer who had a diabetic reaction that produced his erratic driving of squad car at high speeds, and who failed to properly monitor his disease, was not entitled to a "second chance" as an accommodation for his alleged disability); Despears v. Milwaukee County, 63 F.3d 635, 637, 4 AD 1313 (7th Cir. 1995) (alcoholic employee who loses his driver's license after his fourth DUI cannot recover for his demotion to a job that did not require driving); Taylor v. Dover Elevator Sys., Inc., 917 F. Supp. 455, 463, 5 AD 616 (N.D. Miss. 1996) (ADA does not require employers to ignore a disabled employee's disregard of company rules); Larson v. Koch Ref. Co., 920 F. Supp. 1000, 1005, 5 AD 136 (D. Minn. 1995) (employer not required to ignore alcoholic's regular failures to report to work). *But cf.* Borkowski v. Valley Cent. Sch. Dist., 63 F.3d 131, 143, 4 AD 1264 (2d Cir. 1995) (if employer's failure to provide reasonable accommodation leads to inadequate performance and discipline, a resulting discharge amounts to a discharge on account of disability).

[184]*See* McCoy v. Pennsylvania Power & Light Co., 933 F. Supp. 438, 443–44 (M.D. Pa. 1996); McDaniel v. AlliedSignal, Inc., 896 F. Supp. 1482, 1489–91, 4 AD 1471 (W.D. Mo. 1995) (employer was not required to allow plaintiff to work without security clearance that was required for federal contractors). *But cf.* Dorris v. City of Kentwood, 4 AD 741, 744 (W.D. Mich. 1994) (employer had a duty to seek

Finally, the duty to accommodate applies only to a disabled applicant or employee and does not extend to an employee with a disabled child.[185]

4. Significance of Collective Bargaining and Other Agreements

The courts continue to be confronted with the relationship between the duty of reasonable accommodation and the provisions of negotiated labor agreements. Generally, courts are reluctant to require an accommodation that would contravene a co-worker's rights under a contractual seniority provision.[186]

---

a waiver of a federal requirement that police officers meet state and local physical requirements where employee was assigned to a teaching position).

[185]See Sawinski v. Bill Currie Ford, Inc., 881 F. Supp. 1571, 1574, 4 AD 462 (M.D. Fla. 1995) (employer had no duty to accommodate plaintiff by altering his work schedule to enable him to take care of disabled child).

[186]See Foreman v. Babcock & Wilcox Co., 117 F.3d 800, 810, 7 AD 331 (5th Cir. 1997) ("[t]he ADA does not require an employer to take action inconsistent with the contractual rights of other workers under a collective bargaining agreement."); Eckles v. Consolidated Rail Corp., 94 F.3d 1041, 1051, 5 AD 1367 (7th Cir. 1996) (despite a contractual provision allowing a union and an employer, on a case-by-case basis, to displace a more senior employee to accommodate a disabled employee's job limitations, duty of reasonable accommodation does not require an employer and a union to sacrifice the collectively negotiated, bona fide seniority rights of other employees; court rejected the EEOC's position that, while the ADA does not require "bumping" of more senior employees, an employer and a union have a duty to negotiate "a good faith" variance from collective bargaining rules where the only available accommodation would violate those rules but not impose an undue burden on the affected employees), *cert. denied,* 117 S. Ct. 1318 (1997); Kennedy v. Chemical Waste Management, Inc., 79 F.3d 49, 52 (7th Cir. 1996) (employee was not eligible for super-seniority and therefore protection from reduction in force); Cochrum v. Old Ben Coal Co., 102 F.3d 908, 913, 6 AD 219 (7th Cir. 1996) (the ADA does not require an employer to violate the provisions of a collective bargaining agreement to reassign a disabled employee); Benson v. Northwest Airlines, 62 F.3d 1108, 1114, 4 AD 1234 (8th Cir. 1995) (the ADA does not require an employer to undertake action that is inconsistent with the rights of other workers under a labor agreement); Wooten v. Farmland Foods, 58 F.3d 382, 386, 4 AD 920 (8th Cir. 1995) (employer has no duty to violate a labor contract in order to accommodate an employee with work restrictions); Milton v. Scrivner, Inc., 53 F.3d 1118, 1125, 4 AD 432 (10th Cir. 1995) (the duty of accommodation under the ADA does not require an employer to transfer an employee to a light-duty position for which the employee lacks seniority); Mason v. Frank, 32 F.3d 315, 319, 3 AD 835 (8th Cir. 1994) (transfer to light duty is not reasonable where injured employee neither possesses sufficient seniority nor is currently employed, as required by the collective bargaining agreement); Taylor v. Food World, Inc., 946 F. Supp. 937, 942, 6 AD 106 (N.D. Ala. 1996) (an accommodation that forces an employer to violate a contractual promotion process is not "reasonable" as a matter of law); Poindexter v. Atchison, T. & S.F. Ry., 914 F. Supp. 454, 458–59 (D. Kan. 1996) (an employer is not required to make an

5. *The Process of Determining Reasonable Accommodation*

Employers are required to make reasonable accommodations only for the "known" physical and mental impairments of qualified individuals with disabilities.[187] A number of courts have held that the applicant or employee must inform the employer of the need for an accommodation to trigger the employer's duty to reasonably accommodate.[188] Some courts have held that the applicant

---

accommodation involving shift preference that would violate rights of more senior employees); Kindle v. Mid-Central/Sysco Food Servs., Inc., 7 AD 147, 154 (D. Kan. 1996) (employee is not a "qualified individual with a disability" if he lacks the requisite seniority to take alternate positions). *But cf.* Emrick v. Libbey-Owens-Ford Co., 875 F. Supp. 393, 397, 4 AD 1 (E.D. Tex. 1995) (while the ADA does not require an employer to create a vacancy by "bumping" another employee, an offer by other employee to voluntarily vacate a position and be reassigned may be a valid means of accommodating a disabled employee). *See generally* NLRB Gen. Couns. Mem. 92-9 (Aug. 7, 1992), *reprinted in* 1 AM. WITH DISABILITIES ACT MAN. (BNA) 70:1021 (1992) (discussing interface between concept of reasonable accommodation and obligations under NLRA).

[187]*See, e.g.,* Morisky v. Broward County, 80 F.3d 445, 448, 5 AD 737 (11th Cir. 1996) ("Vague or conclusory statements revealing an unspecified incapacity are not sufficient to put an employer on notice of its obligations under the ADA."); Office of Senate Sergeant at Arms v. Office of Senate Fair Empl. Practices, 95 F.3d 1102, 1107–08, 6 AD 1237 (Fed. Cir. 1996) (employer has no duty to retroactively accommodate an employee by undoing discipline imposed before the employer was aware of the disability); Simpkins v. Specialty Envelope, Inc., 1996 U.S. App. LEXIS 22327, at *13 (6th Cir. Aug. 9, 1996) (employer is not expected to accommodate disabilities of which it is unaware); Huppenbauer v. May Dep't Stores Co., 1996 U.S. App. LEXIS 27480, at *17 (4th Cir. Oct. 23, 1996) (no accommodation obligation when the employer does not have actual or constructive knowledge of the disability or of an employee's need for accommodation); Miller v. National Cas. Co., 61 F.3d 627, 630, 4 AD 1089 (8th Cir. 1995) (ADA does not require clairvoyance; if employee needs accommodation, he or she must first tell the employer of the disability).

[188]*See, e.g.,* Derbis v. U.S. Shoe Corp., 1995 U.S. App. LEXIS 27636, at *6–7 (4th Cir. Sept. 29, 1995) (employer is under no duty to provide an accommodation to an employee who does not seek one); Jackson v. Boise Cascade Corp., 941 F. Supp. 1122, 1127 (S.D. Ala. 1996) (plaintiff's failure to accommodate claim was denied because he never made a request while employed); Fussell v. Georgia Ports Auth., 906 F. Supp. 1561, 1569–70, 5 AD 1236 (S.D. Ga. 1995) (burden is on the nonobviously disabled plaintiff to timely alert employer to his or her disability and to afford the employer an opportunity to make the accommodation; employee must request the accommodation at the time the disability presents a problem on the job and cannot wait until the filing of a lawsuit to assert a failure to accommodate), *aff'd mem.,* 106 F.3d 417 (11th Cir. 1997); Carlson v. Inacomp Corp., 885 F. Supp. 1314, 1322, 4 AD 600 (D. Neb. 1995) (although employer was aware that plaintiff occasionally had headaches, employer was not aware that plaintiff's absences were caused by migraines, and plaintiff never requested any accommodation, so the employer

or employee must specifically identify the desired accommodation.[189] Other courts, however, have rejected the argument that an employee must specifically request an accommodation.[190]

---

had no duty to accommodate); Ferry v. Roosevelt Bank, 883 F. Supp. 435, 440–41, 4 AD 476 (E.D. Mo. 1995) (holding that it is generally an employee's duty to request an accommodation, though an employer can initiate discussions when an employee with a known disability has performance problems).

[189]See, e.g., Shiring v. Runyon, 90 F.3d 827, 832, 5 AD 1216 (3d Cir. 1996) (plaintiff must show that he requested transfers to specific vacant positions that he could perform); Taylor v. Principal Fin. Group, Inc., 93 F.3d 155, 165, 5 AD 1653 (5th Cir.) ("When the nature of the disability, resulting limitations, and necessary accommodations are uniquely within the knowledge of the employee and his health-care provider, a disabled employee cannot remain silent and expect his employer to bear the initial burden of identifying the need for, and suggesting, an appropriate accommodation."), cert. denied, 117 S. Ct. 586 (1996); Moses v. American Nonwovens, Inc., 97 F.3d 446, 448, 5 AD 1651 (11th Cir. 1996) (employer's failure to investigate reasonable accommodation did not relieve the plaintiff of his burden of producing probative evidence that reasonable accommodations were available), cert. denied, 117 S. Ct. 964 (1997); Braziel v. Loram Maintenance of Way, Inc., 943 F. Supp. 1083, 1099 (D. Minn. 1996) (employee must specifically request the accommodation he seeks); Sieberns v. Wal-Mart Stores, Inc., 946 F. Supp. 664, 669, 6 AD 403 (N.D. Ind. 1996) ("[W]hatever the time frame may be for a disabled employee to 'describe' the reasonable accommodations sufficient to qualify him or her for a job, the court is confident that it is not so generous as to encompass suggestions made only in a resistance to summary judgment."); Valentine v. American Home Shield Corp., 939 F. Supp. 1376, 1400–01, 6 AD 163 (N.D. Iowa 1996) (employee who suggests possible accommodations only long after the fact is barred from creating a fact issue as to the viability of those accommodations); Roberts v. County of Fairfax, 937 F. Supp. 541, 549 (E.D. Va. 1996) (plaintiff's claim that he should have been given a leave of absence is barred by his failure to request such a leave while employed); Cheatwood v. Roanoke Indus., 891 F. Supp. 1528, 1538–39, 5 AD 141 (N.D. Ala. 1995) (burden is on the employee to inform the employer that an accommodation is needed and to request a specific accommodation); Ferry v. Roosevelt Bank, 883 F. Supp. 435, 441–42, 4 AD 476 (E.D. Mo. 1995) (employer cannot be required to guess what accommodation an employee wants; if an offered accommodation is unsatisfactory, employee has duty to identify alternate accommodations); Davis v. Cottage Hill Baptist Church, 6 AD 1173, 1178 (S.D. Ala. 1995) (plaintiff's argument that the poor performance for which he was terminated was caused by his physical ailments was rejected where the employer had given plaintiff time off in the past, but plaintiff had not made a specific request for time off in this instance).

[190]See, e.g., Burnett v. Western Resources, Inc., 929 F. Supp. 1349, 1357, 6 AD 711 (D. Kan. 1996) ("[E]ven if not specifically designated by plaintiff as a request for accommodation, knowledge by defendant of plaintiff's permanent medical restrictions and that they are preventing him from performing his job was sufficient to permit defendant to commence the reasonable accommodation process."); Corbett v. National Prods. Co., 4 AD 987, 990 (E.D. Pa. 1995) ("The statute does not require the plaintiff to speak any magic words before he is subject to its protections. The employee need not mention the ADA or even the term 'accommodation.' " (quoting Schmidt v. Safeway, Inc., 864 F. Supp. 991, 997, 3 AD 1141 (D. Or. 1994)));

After receiving the employee's request for accommodation, an employer should consult with the individual with a disability[191]; failure to do so may result in punitive damages.[192] If an employer has a defined procedure for handling accommodation requests, it should follow that procedure.[193] The determination of whether an accommodation is reasonable is based on the facts known to the employer at the time the accommodation decision is made[194] though the nature of the accommodation required may change over time.[195]

Schmidt v. Safeway, Inc., 864 F. Supp. 991, 997, 3 AD 1141 (D. Or. 1994) ("The employee need not mention the ADA or even the term 'accommodation.' The real issue is whether the employer had reason to believe the employee could . . . [do the job with accommodation].").

[191]29 C.F.R. § 1630.2(O)(3) ("To determine the appropriate reasonable accommodation it may be necessary for the covered entity to initiate an informal, interactive process with the qualified individual with a disability in need of the accommodation. This process should identify the precise limitations resulting from the disability and potential reasonable accommodations that could overcome those limitations.").

[192]See Katz v. City Metal Co., Inc., 87 F.3d 26, 33, 5 AD 1120 (1st Cir. 1996) (employee's requests for accommodation rejected "out of hand" with no attempt to consult with employee); Stopka v. Alliance of Am. Insurers, 1996 U.S. Dist. LEXIS 18329, at **22–23 (N.D. Ill. Dec. 6, 1996) (determining a reasonable accommodation is a cooperative process that requires an employer to discuss the employee's needs with her); Siefken v. Village of Arlington Heights, 3 AD 1281, 1282 (N.D. Ill. 1994) (employer must make an individualized assessment of the potential risks and potential accommodations in consultation with the individual to be accommodated), aff'd, 65 F.3d 664, 4 AD 1441 (7th Cir. 1995). But cf. Cheatwood v. Roanoke Indus., 891 F. Supp. 1528, 1539, 5 AD 141 (N.D. Ala. 1995) (employer had no duty to engage in interactive process where, based on employee's testimony in his workers' compensation action that he could not perform any job, even with accommodation, employer had no reason to believe that employee could be accommodated); Kerno v. Sandoz Pharm. Corp., 4 AD 1195, 1200 n.16 (N.D. Ill. 1994) (defendant met its burden by discussing possible accommodations with plaintiff's physicians, even though interaction with plaintiff was limited).

[193]See Heise v. Genuine Parts Co., 900 F. Supp. 1137, 1154, 4 AD 1551 (D. Minn. 1995) (employer's failure to follow its own procedures for determining accommodations, including using a checklist for the various steps of the accommodation process, may be evidence of a failure to make reasonable accommodation).

[194]See Kerno v. Sanchez Pharm. Corp., 4 AD 1195, 1201 (N.D. Ill. 1994) (reassignment to different position accommodating plaintiff's work restrictions was reasonable even though new position was subsequently eliminated, so long as defendant did not know of pending elimination at time accommodation was made).

[195]See Feliberty v. Kemper Corp., 98 F.3d 274, 279–80, 5 AD 1729 (7th Cir. 1996) (even if the employer acceded to an employee's requested form of accommodation, this does not eliminate the employer's responsibility to consider additional accommodations as circumstances change).

If the employee refuses a reasonable accommodation, then the employer may be relieved of its duty of reasonable accommodation,[196] and in some instances the employee may not be considered a qualified individual with a disability.[197]

Absent medical evidence to the contrary, the opinion of a treating physician is accorded great weight in determining what accommodation an individual needs.[198] If, upon request, an employee fails to provide the employer necessary medical information to support a requested accommodation, then the request may be denied.[199]

---

[196] See Gile v. United Airlines, Inc., 95 F.3d 492, 499, 5 AD 1466 (7th Cir. 1996) (employer cannot be held liable for denying employee's transfer request where employer offered other reasonable accommodations that employee refused); Ellis v. Ford Motor Co., 1996 U.S. App. LEXIS 8236, at *3 (6th Cir. Mar. 14, 1996) (employer offered employee numerous positions he could perform despite his medical conditions; employee continually refused but showed up years later demanding a job; given employee's earlier refusals employer had no obligation to provide a position); Hoyt v. NYNEX Corp., 1996 U.S. Dist. LEXIS 14230, at *18–19 (N.D.N.Y. Sept. 25, 1996) (defendant was not required to transfer plaintiff who refused to take qualifications examinations for new positions); Anzalone v. Allstate Ins. Co., 5 AD 455, 457 (N.D. La. 1995) (employee who rejects an accommodation that is reasonable can be precluded from claiming failure to accommodate), aff'd mem., 74 F.3d 1236 (5th Cir. 1995).

[197] See Willett v. Kansas, 942 F. Supp. 1387, 1395 (D. Kan. 1996) (if, as a result of refusing a reasonable accommodation, an employee cannot perform the essential functions of a job, the employee is not a qualified individual with a disability); Valentine v. American Home Shield Corp., 939 F. Supp. 1376, 1399, 6 AD 163 (N.D. Iowa 1996) (rejection of reasonable accommodation may establish that plaintiff is not qualified); Roberts v. County of Fairfax, 937 F. Supp. 541, 548–49 (E.D. Va. 1996) (because plaintiff refused suggestions to seek treatment for mental problems that affected his performance, he was not a qualified individual with a disability).

[198] See Gerdes v. Swift-Eckrich, Inc., 949 F. Supp. 1386, 1406 (N.D. Iowa 1996) ("The court does not believe that the ADA was intended to penalize an employer who reads work restrictions strictly or literally, in the absence of other clarification, because such an employer is simply not acting on 'myths' or 'stereotypes,' but upon a careful, if perhaps overly cautious, reading of actual restrictions imposed by a treating physician.").

[199] See McAlpin v. National Semiconductor Corp., 921 F. Supp. 1518, 1525, 5 AD 1047 (N.D. Tex. 1996) (employee's failure to provide required medical support for an accommodation request is cause to deny the requested accommodation); Czopek v. General Elec. Co., 4 AD 1231, 1233 (N.D. Ill. 1995) (plaintiff's claim was rejected because he refused to provide additional medical information after failing physical examination); Ballard v. Alabama, 1996 U.S. Dist. LEXIS 1822, at *54–55 (S.D. Ala. Jan. 25, 1996) (plaintiff's demand for an executive chair was properly denied when plaintiff failed to produce some medical or other professional evidence supporting the claim for need for this special equipment); Gerdes v. Swift-Eckrich, Inc., 949 F. Supp. 1386, 1405–06 (N.D. Iowa 1996) (a party's failure to provide information that is uniquely within that party's knowledge may be the cause of the breakdown of the interactive process); Derbis v. U.S. Shoe Corp., 3 AD 1029, 1033

In *Beck v. University of Wisconsin Board of Regents*,[200] the court of appeals focused on the party responsible for the breakdown in the interactive process:

> No hard and fast rule will suffice, because neither party should be able to cause a breakdown in the process for the purpose of either avoiding or inflicting liability. Rather, courts should look for signs of failure to participate in good faith or failure to help the other party determine what specific accommodations are necessary. A party that obstructs or delays the interactive process is not acting in good faith. A party that fails to communicate, by way of initiation or response, may also be acting in bad faith. In essence, courts should attempt to isolate the cause of the breakdown and then assign responsibility.[201]

Although employers should consider an employee's choice of accommodation, employers are not required to accept the employee's preferred accommodation or even to provide the "best" accommodation.[202]

(D. Md. 1994) (where employee provided a medical report indicating that she needed some sort of accommodation, but failed to provide any information regarding what sort of accommodation would be appropriate, employer was not required to permit employee to return to work to do "as much as she can take"), *aff'd in part,* 67 F.3d 294 (4th Cir. 1995).

[200]75 F.3d 1130, 1137, 5 AD 304 (7th Cir. 1996).

[201]*Id.* at 1135.

[202]*See* Weiler v. Household Fin. Corp., 101 F.3d 519, 526, 6 AD 106 (7th Cir. 1996) (employer acted reasonably to accommodate the plaintiff by providing her time off to attend therapy sessions, providing short-term disability benefits, applying for long-term disability benefits on her behalf, allowing her to post for a new position, searching for a similar position under a different supervisor, granting her extended leave, and offering her alternative available positions within her salary range); Gile v. United Airlines, Inc., 95 F.3d 492, 499, 5 AD 1466 (7th Cir. 1996) (employer is not obligated to provide employee the accommodation he requests or prefers); Schmidt v. Methodist Hosp., Inc., 89 F.3d 342, 344, 5 AD 1340 (7th Cir. 1996) ("Reasonable accommodation does not require an employer to provide literally everything the disabled employee requests."; employer not required to transfer nurse with a hearing disability); Conklin v. City of Englewood, 1996 U.S. App. LEXIS 26173, at *2 (6th Cir. Oct. 1, 1996) (ADA does not require employer to give employee the best accommodation or even the accommodation requested so long as the accommodation made is reasonable); Kemer v. Johnson, 900 F. Supp. 677, 686, 4 AD 1823 (S.D.N.Y. 1995) (employer did not have to adopt plaintiff's suggested accommodations), *aff'd mem.,* 101 F.3d 683 (2d Cir.), *cert. denied,* 117 S. Ct. 441 (1996); Marschand v. Norfolk & W. Ry., 876 F. Supp. 1528, 1543, 4 AD 1099 (N.D. Ind. 1995) (defendant was not required to offer plaintiff the reassignment of his choice), *aff'd,* 81 F.3d 714 (7th Cir. 1996); Vande Zande v. Wisconsin Dep't of Admin., 851 F. Supp. 353, 359, 2 AD 1846 (W.D. Wis. 1994) (defendant was not required to provide plaintiff with every accommodation she requested as long as the accommodations provided were reasonable), *aff'd,* 44 F.3d 538, 3 AD 1636 (7th Cir. 1995).

As the court stated in *Miranda v. Wisconsin Power & Light Co.*,[203] "[t]he ADA does not obligate an employer to provide a disabled employee every accommodation on his [or her] wish list."[204] Where the accommodation offered by the employer is reasonable, the fact that additional accommodations could have been made is irrelevant.[205] Indeed, an employer's accommodation may be reasonable even if the choice of accommodation was motivated by the employer's business interests and not the employee's request.[206]

Although an employer must act in good faith, there is no bright-line test for when an employer must actually provide an accommodation.[207]

An employer may not compel a qualified individual with a disability to accept an accommodation if the accommodation is neither requested nor needed.[208]

---

[203] 91 F.3d 1011, 5 AD 1856 (7th Cir. 1996).

[204] *Id.* at 1016; *see also* Kuehl v. Wal-Mart Stores, Inc., 909 F. Supp. 794, 803, 5 AD 91 (D. Colo. 1995) (the ADA does not require an employer to provide the best accommodation possible or to accommodate the employee in the exact way he or she requests; an employer has discretion to choose among effective accommodations and may choose the less expensive or more convenient accommodation).

[205] *See* Lewis v. Zilog, Inc., 908 F. Supp. 931, 947, 4 AD 1787 (N.D. Ga. 1995) (employer is not required to provide the maximum accommodation or every conceivable accommodation possible), *aff'd mem.,* 87 F.3d 1331 (11th Cir. 1996).

[206] *See* Rayha v. United Parcel Serv., Inc., 940 F. Supp. 1066, 1069 (S.D. Tex. 1996) (employer has wide latitude in selecting the accommodation that is easiest for it to provide); Williams v. Channel Master Satellite Sys., Inc., 101 F.3d 346, 350, 6 AD 131 (4th Cir. 1996) (whether an accommodation is reasonable is an objective analysis, not a subjective one dominated by the employer's business judgment), *cert. denied,* 117 S. Ct. 1844 (1997); Weiler v. Household Fin. Corp., 5 AD 550, 555 (N.D. Ill. 1995) (offering plaintiff an opportunity to apply for vacant positions and placing her on short-term disability while she applied were reasonable accommodations, despite the fact that they did not give plaintiff anything other than what the normal policies already provided), *aff'd,* 101 F.3d 519, 6 AD 106 (7th Cir. 1996).

[207] *See* Feliberty v. Kemper Corp., 98 F.3d 274, 279–80, 5 AD 1729 (7th Cir. 1996) (question of fact as to whether giving plaintiff accommodations within one month of request was reasonable); Vande Zande v. Wisconsin Dep't of Admin., 851 F. Supp. 353, 361–62, 2 AD 1846 (W.D. Wis. 1994) (some bureaucratic delay in providing an accommodation is reasonable; that it took three weeks to make a structural modification, when many other accommodations had already been provided, was not unreasonable), *aff'd,* 44 F.3d 538, 3 AD 1636 (7th Cir. 1995); Easley v. West, 4 AD 1323, 1329 (E.D. Pa. 1994) (employer is entitled to sufficient time to investigate and acquire an accommodation, but the reasonableness of the delay in a particular circumstance may be a question of fact), *aff'd mem.,* 85 F.3d 611, 5 AD 1343 (3d Cir. 1996); Davis v. York Int'l, Inc., 2 AD 1810, 1816 (D. Md. 1993) (three-month delay in installing special computer equipment was reasonable where employer had to authorize the purchase of the special equipment, inquire into its availability, order it, and install it).

[208] *See* Roberts v. County of Fairfax, 937 F. Supp. 541, 549 (E.D. Va. 1996) (employer is not required to force employee to seek treatment as accommodation);

Finally, courts generally hold that employers are not required to provide accommodations simply because the accommodations have been provided in the past.[209]

V. DEFENSES

A. Job Relatedness and Business Necessity

Courts continue to hold that covered employers may not use qualification standards that screen out disabled applicants or employees on the basis of their disabilities unless the challenged standard is consistent with business necessity.[210] Analyzing job

---

Burnett v. Western Resources, Inc., 929 F. Supp. 1349, 1359, 6 AD 711 (D. Kan. 1996) (employee is not required to accept accommodation).

[209]See Shiring v. Runyon, 90 F.3d 827, 831, 5 AD 1216 (3d Cir. 1996) (employer was not required to continue plaintiff in light-duty position it had created for him); Myers v. Hose, 50 F.3d 278, 284, 4 AD 391 (4th Cir. 1995) (an employer's having provided more than reasonable accommodations for some disabled employees did not require the employer to continue its previous practice: "If an employer undertook extraordinary treatment in one case, the same level of accommodation would be legally required of it in all subsequent cases; in other words, a good deed would effectively ratchet up liability, and thus not go unpunished."); Braziel v. Loram Maintenance of Way, Inc., 943 F. Supp. 1083, 1100 (D. Minn. 1996) (employer is not required to convert a temporary light-duty job into a permanent position); Vaughan v. Harvard Indus., Inc., 926 F. Supp. 1340, 1349 (W.D. Tenn. 1996) (defendant is not required to provide indefinitely a helper or newly created light-duty position); McCollough v. Atlanta Beverage Co., 929 F. Supp. 1489, 1502 (N.D. Ga. 1996) (the fact that employer has once allowed plaintiff to perform light duty does not mean it is forever bound to allow him to perform such functions); Cheatwood v. Roanoke Indus., 891 F. Supp. 1528, 1539, 5 AD 141 (N.D. Ala. 1995) (that other employees have been given light duty does not mean that every employee is entitled to this accommodation; otherwise, the employer's incentive would be to never provide accommodation); Simmerman v. Hardee's Food Sys., Inc., 1996 U.S. Dist. LEXIS 3437, at *31 (E.D. Va. Mar 22, 1996) (that employer offered certain accommodations to some employees as a matter of good faith does not mean that employer must extend same accommodations to all employees as a matter of law); Wisniewski v. Ameritech, 1996 U.S. Dist. LEXIS 12822, at *20 (N.D. Ill. Aug. 30, 1996) (defendant was not required to find individual tasks for plaintiff indefinitely while it attempted to locate a position for which plaintiff was qualified, and should not be penalized for finding such tasks for a short time rather than terminating plaintiff immediately when no vacancy was available). *But see* Stone v. City of Mt. Vernon, 118 F.3d 92, 101, 6 AD 1685 (2d Cir. 1997) (firefighter may be qualified for light-duty assignment, and fire department in past has assigned persons not capable of fighting fires to light duty and has never required them to engage in fire-suppression activity).

[210]See, e.g., EEOC v. AIC Sec. Investigations, 55 F.3d 1276, 1283, 4 AD 693 (7th Cir. 1995) ("[A]ny defense based on a qualification standard that adversely affects the disabled must be consistent with business necessity.").

relatedness and business necessity requires identifying essential job functions.[211]

Courts also continue to hold that qualification standards that are based on federal government regulations are job related and consistent with business necessity.[212] Disabled employees, however, may challenge the application of a particular regulation to their disability.[213] Similarly, a disabled employee's inability to attain other forms of certification can be a job-related basis for disqualification.[214] A medical fitness release or report also can be a job-related qualification.[215]

---

[211]*See* Martinson v. Kinney Shoe Corp., 104 F.3d 683, 687, 6 AD 434 (4th Cir. 1997) (proper to disqualify epileptic shoe salesman because providing store security at all times is a job-related essential function that could not be met during periods of unconsciousness); Grenier v. Cyanamid Plastics, Inc., 70 F.3d 667, 675, 5 AD 75 (1st Cir. 1995) (electrician known to be paranoid about plant manager properly disqualified because getting along with one's co-workers is job related and an essential function); Turco v. Hoechst Celanese Chem. Group, Inc., 906 F. Supp. 1120, 1132, 6 AD 579 (S.D. Tex. 1995) (standards of lifting, walking, and standing were job related and disqualify employee with neuropathy), *aff'd*, 101 F.3d 1090, 6 AD 278 (5th Cir. 1996).

[212]*See, e.g.,* Buck v. United States Dep't of Transp., 56 F.3d 1406, 1408, 4 AD 833 (D.C. Cir. 1995) (hearing-impaired driver applicant seeking waiver of FHA hearing requirements was not entitled to collaterally attack the validity of the requirements in a Rehabilitation Act action); Murphy v. United Parcel Serv., Inc., 946 F. Supp. 872, 883, 6 AD 517 (D. Kan. 1996) (mechanic with high blood pressure who is required to test-drive trucks was properly denied employment based on his inability to obtain DOT certification as such requirement is job related).

[213]*See* EEOC v. Texas Bus Lines, 923 F. Supp. 965, 973–74, 5 AD 878 (S.D. Tex. 1996) (ADA liability despite DOT requirement of general medical certification and examining physician's denial of certification to driver applicant based on obesity, where the examining physician had no special expertise regarding DOT regulations and there was no evidence to show why obesity would prevent driver from reacting in an emergency).

[214]*See* Kocsis v. Multi-care Management, Inc., 97 F.3d 876, 883, 6 AD 442 (6th Cir. 1996) (nursing home company justified in failing to promote nurse with multiple sclerosis where nurse lacked training certification that was a prerequisite to the job).

[215]*See* Grenier v. Cyanamid Plastics, Inc., 70 F.3d 667, 676, 5 AD 75 (1st Cir. 1995) (employer properly required treating psychiatrist to provide medical certification to electrician suffering from paranoia about plant manager); Ferguson v. Texasgulf, Inc., 5 AD 722, 730 (S.D. Tex. 1996) (mechanic who suffered serious heart attack was lawfully required to produce full medical release before returning to work), *aff'd mem.,* 106 F.3d 397 (5th Cir. 1997). *Cf.* EEOC v. Texas Bus Lines, 923 F. Supp. 965, 973, 5 AD 878 (S.D. Tex. 1996) (employer could not rely on physician's failure to provide medical certification where physician lacked the proper knowledge of regulation so that disqualification was not job related).

B. Undue Hardship

Courts continue to hold that employers bear the burden of proving that providing an accommodation would be an undue hardship.[216] Although discrete concepts, courts sometimes blur the distinctions between reasonable accommodation, undue hardship, and other defenses.[217] Other courts recognize that an accommodation could be reasonable and still cause undue hardship.[218] Courts continue to agree that application of the undue hardship defense is fact specific.[219]

The undue hardship factors found in the ADA and in the regulations are "relational"; that is, the analysis "looks not merely to the cost that the employer is asked to assume, but also to the benefits to others that will result" from the accommodation.[220] Therefore, employers raising the defense should undertake a detailed cost-benefit analysis "through the lens of the factors listed in the

---

[216]*See* Monette v. Electronic Data Sys. Corp., 90 F.3d 1173, 1186, 5 AD 1326 (6th Cir. 1996) (employer will bear the burden of proving that a proposed accommodation will impose an undue hardship); Vande Zande v. Wisconsin Dep't of Admin., 44 F.3d 538, 543, 3 AD 1636 (7th Cir. 1995) (once prima facie showing is made, employer has opportunity to prove costs are excessive in relation to benefits conferred or employer's financial survival); Borkowski v. Valley Cent. Sch. Dist., 63 F.3d 131, 138–39, 4 AD 1264 (2d Cir. 1995) (in a Rehabilitation Act case, defendant has the burden of persuading the factfinder that the proposed accommodation would cause it to suffer an undue hardship).

[217]*See, e.g.,* Williams v. Widnall, 79 F.3d 1003, 1007, 5 AD 663 (10th Cir. 1996) (court held that alcoholic in rehabilitation who threatened co-workers could not be accommodated without undue hardship in the form of potential harm to others so that reasonable accommodation could not be established); Borkowski v. Valley Cent. Sch. Dist., 63 F.3d 131, 138, 4 AD 1264 (2d Cir. 1995) (defendant's "meeting the burden of nonpersuasion on the reasonableness of the accommodation and demonstrating that the accommodation imposes an undue hardship amount to the same thing") (Rehabilitation Act case).

[218]*See, e.g.,* Vande Zande v. Wisconsin Dep't of Admin., 44 F.3d 538, 543, 3 AD 1636 (7th Cir. 1995) (even if prima facie showing is made, employer has opportunity to prove costs are excessive in relation either to the benefits of the accommodation or to the employer's financial survival or health); Bryant v. Better Bus. Bureau, Inc., 923 F. Supp 720, 736–37, 5 AD 625 (D. Md. 1996) (reasonable accommodation analysis asks whether the accommodation would be effective in addressing job-related difficulties and would allow the employee to attain an equal level of achievement and participation, while undue hardship focuses on the impact the accommodation would have on the specific employer in question at a particular time).

[219]*See, e.g., Bryant,* 923 F. Supp. at 737 (case-by-case analysis required).

[220]Borkowski v. Valley Cent. Sch. Dist., 63 F.3d 131, 138–39, 4 AD 1264 (2d Cir. 1995) (" 'Reasonable' is a relational term: it evaluates the desirability of a particular accommodation according to the consequences that the accommodation will produce."); *accord* Vande Zande v. Wisconsin Dep't of Admin., 44 F.3d 538, 543, 3

regulations"; while this analysis need not be mathematically precise, it must be imbued with common sense.[221]

Although financial cost is not the only consideration in the undue hardship analysis, it is the factor courts most often discuss. Undertaking fact-specific analysis, courts have found that an accommodation posed an economic undue hardship where plaintiffs requested establishment of an on-site medical department,[222] the hiring of a full-time assistant or extra staff,[223] special transportation,[224] or extra paid leave.[225] By contrast, the courts have found no undue hardship where the employer could not establish unreasonable cost in reassigning a disabled employee's nonessential duties to a nondisabled employee.[226]

Courts have found that the noneconomic, operational burden of an accommodation rose to the level of undue hardship where plaintiffs have sought the reassignment of essential functions to others,[227] a position where no vacancy existed,[228] indefinite leave,[229]

AD 1636 (7th Cir. 1995) (undue hardship and accommodation are "terms of relation" requiring an analysis of the benefits of the accommodation to the disabled worker as well as to the employer's resources).

[221] *Borkowski*, 63 F.3d at 139.

[222] *See, e.g.*, Huber v. Howard County, 849 F. Supp. 407, 414, 3 AD 262 (D. Md. 1994) (asthmatic firefighter need not be provided an on-site medical department), *aff'd mem.*, 56 F.3d 61 (4th Cir. 1995).

[223] *See, e.g.*, EEOC v. Amego, Inc., 110 F.3d 135, 148, 6 AD 997 (1st Cir. 1997) (small nonprofit agency cannot afford the expense of duplicate employees to relieve plaintiff of drug administration duties).

[224] *See, e.g.*, Jacques v. Clean-Up Group, Inc., 96 F.3d 506, 515, 5 AD 1594 (1st Cir. 1996) (undue burden to provide van transportation to work where vehicles were needed by other cleaning crews).

[225] *See, e.g.*, Myers v. Hose, 50 F.3d 278, 283, 4 AD 391 (4th Cir. 1995) (bus driver with heart condition not entitled to extra paid leave as accommodation as this would "upset the employer's settled budgetary expectations").

[226] *See, e.g.*, Hogue v. MQS Inspection, Inc., 875 F. Supp. 714, 722, 3 AD 1793 (D. Colo. 1995) (fact issue present where company with $30 million in sales claims undue hardship when employee requested exchange of duties).

[227] *See, e.g.*, Jones v. Alabama Power Co., 3 AD 1717 (N.D. Ala. 1995) (reassignment of heavy-lifting duties to others, which were essential job functions composing 40% of employee's tasks, would impose undue hardship on employer), *aff'd mem.*, 77 F.3d 498 (11th Cir. 1996).

[228] *Id.* at 1730 ("[F]ailure to secure another position for plaintiff, when one is not reasonably available, does not result in liability under § 504 . . . requiring an employer to secure another position for the employee would impose an undue hardship on the employer.").

[229] *See, e.g.*, Monette v. Electronic Data Sys. Corp., 90 F.3d 1173, 1187, 5 AD 1326 (6th Cir. 1996) ("employers simply are not required to keep an employee on

a position isolated from criticism and supervisory contact,[230] extended use of shared equipment,[231] special consideration for absenteeism,[232] or a complete ban on smoking.[233] Upon the specific facts presented, courts have found no undue hardship in permanently reassigning a disabled worker,[234] in providing TTY equipment,[235] or in providing a librarian with an aide or assistant.[236] Moreover, a requested accommodation that conflicts with the terms of a collective bargaining agreement often will be found to constitute an undue hardship[237]; however, not all provisions of a labor

---

staff indefinitely in the hope that some position may become available some time in the future"); Myers v. Hose, 50 F.3d 278, 283, 4 AD 391 (4th Cir. 1995) (undue hardship for county employer to hold position open indefinitely, especially in light of uncertainty of cure).

[230] *See, e.g.,* Mears v. Gulfstream Aerospace Corp., 905 F. Supp. 1075, 1080–81, 5 AD 1295 (S.D. Ga. 1995) (undue hardship to arrange plaintiff's work so that she would have no contact with certain departments or supervisors since "an accommodation that adversely impacts other employees' ability to do their jobs is an undue burden on the employer"), *aff'd mem.,* 87 F.3d 1331, 6 AD 1152 (11th Cir. 1996).

[231] *See, e.g.,* Jones v. Alabama Power Co., 3 AD 1717, 1729 (N.D. Ala. 1995) (providing plaintiff extended use of a forklift for performing heavy duties would preclude other workers from using the forklift).

[232] *See, e.g.,* Hendry v. GTE N., Inc., 896 F. Supp. 816, 826, 6 AD 451 (N.D. Ind. 1995) (company was not obligated to allow plaintiff unlimited, unpredictable absences, given her history of prior medication failure, which would cause an undue hardship).

[233] *See, e.g.,* Hall v. Hackley Hosp., 532 N.W.2d 893, 897, 4 AD 961 (Mich. Ct. App. 1995) (undue hardship to impose complete smoking ban in a psychiatric hospital because this would threaten the mental and physical health of the patients and takes precedence over plaintiff's asthmatic condition).

[234] *See, e.g.,* United States v. City of Denver, 943 F. Supp. 1304, 1312, 6 AD 245 (D. Colo. 1996) (city policy against transfers must give way to ADA where employer cannot demonstrate undue hardship caused by transfer of four police officers into nonpolice jobs among a large work force); Taylor v. Secretary of Navy, 852 F. Supp. 343, 353–54, 3 AD 497 (E.D. Pa. 1994) (Navy policy of reassignment of workers with permanent or indefinite medical restrictions precludes argument that permanent reassignment of plaintiff suffering from back injury is undue hardship), *aff'd mem.,* 61 F.3d 896 (3d Cir. 1995).

[235] *See, e.g.,* Bryant v. Better Bus. Bureau, 923 F. Supp. 720, 739–40, 5 AD 625 (D. Md. 1996) (no undue hardship caused by alleged delay to clients from having calls answered by text telephone system device).

[236] *See, e.g.,* Borkowski v. Valley Cent. Sch. Dist., 63 F.3d 131, 142, 4 AD 1264 (2d Cir. 1995) (court rejects argument that it is an undue hardship as a matter of law to provide a librarian with an assistant).

[237] *See* Cochrum v. Old Ben Coal Co., 102 F.3d 908, 912–13, 6 AD 219 (7th Cir. 1996) (employee with shoulder injury has no right to super-seniority, and employer is not required to violate the contract to reassign disabled employee); Eckles v. Consolidated Rail Corp., 94 F.3d 1041, 1051, 5 AD 1367 (7th Cir. 1996) ("[t]he ADA does not require disabled individuals to be accommodated by sacrificing the collectively

agreement are immune from the duty to provide reasonable accommodation.[238]

C. Direct Threat to Health and Safety

At least one district court has approved the ADA regulations' expansion of the direct-threat defense to include not only a threat to others but also to the individual with a disability.[239] Courts continue to hold that the evidence must be weighed objectively, without speculation; that an individual assessment of the employee's ability to safely perform is required[240]; and that the factors enumerated in the regulations must be applied on a case-by-case basis.[241]

Generally, the threat of harm must arise from performing an essential job function; if not, the duty of reasonable accommodation requires the employer to remove any nonessential duty that gives rise to the threat.[242] The courts disagree over whether the

---

bargained, bona fide seniority rights of other employees"), *cert. denied,* 117 S. Ct. 1318 (1997); Blankenship v. Martin Marietta Energy Sys., 83 F.3d 153, 155–56, 5 AD 789 (6th Cir. 1996) (employer acted properly where collective bargaining agreement allowed for termination of employee who lost Department of Energy clearance following diagnosis of mental illness); Wooten v. Farmland Foods, 58 F.3d 382, 386, 4 AD 920 (8th Cir. 1995) (employee is not entitled to insist that employer violate collective bargaining agreement in order to accommodate him); Milton v. Scrivner, Inc., 53 F.3d 1118, 1125, 4 AD 432 (10th Cir. 1995) (allowing injured employees to bid into light-duty jobs would violate seniority provisions of the contract); Collins v. Yellow Freight Sys., 942 F. Supp. 449, 453, 6 AD 102 (W.D. Mo. 1996) (trucker with back injury not entitled to light-duty work where collective bargaining agreement reserved such positions to the temporarily disabled only).

[238]*See Eckles,* 94 F.3d at 1051–52 (while confirming that the ADA does not require disabled employees to be accommodated by sacrificing collectively bargained seniority rights, that "conclusion is limited to individual seniority rights and should not be interpreted as a general finding that all provisions found in collective bargaining agreements are immune from limitation by the ADA duty to reasonably accommodate").

[239]*See* Kohnke v. Delta Air Lines, 5 AD 334, 343 (N.D. Ill. 1995). Although the ADA regulations include a risk of harm to "the individual" in the definition of "direct threat," the statute speaks only about a threat to others. *See* 42 U.S.C. § 12113(b); 29 C.F.R. § 1630.2(r).

[240]*See, e.g.,* EEOC v. Chrysler Corp., 917 F. Supp. 1164, 1173, 5 AD 517 (E.D. Mich. 1996) (revocation of job offer upon discovery that applicant is diabetic is unjustified where defendant failed to demonstrate that it performed an individualized assessment of plaintiff's condition).

[241]*See, e.g.,* Rizzo v. Children's World Learning Ctrs., Inc., 84 F.3d 758, 764, 5 AD 1155 (5th Cir. 1996) ("Whether one is a direct threat is a complicated, fact intensive determination, not a question of law.").

[242]*See* Moses v. American Nonwovens, Inc., 97 F.3d 446, 447, 5 AD 1651 (11th Cir. 1996) ("[t]here is no direct threat defense if the employer could have made

employer bears the burden of proving a direct threat as an affirmative defense or whether the ability to perform a job safely is part of the plaintiff's burden to establish that he or she is "qualified."[243]

Courts recognize that a severe potential harm can outweigh the low probability that the harm will occur.[244] The ability to function safely in rare or emergency situations may also be properly considered.[245] The inability of public safety employees to function without compromise often results in a finding of a direct threat,[246] and courts recognize that some vehicle drivers suffering

---

'reasonable accommodation[s]' "), *cert. denied,* 117 S. Ct. 964 (1997); EEOC v. AIC Sec. Investigations, 55 F.3d 1276, 1284, 4 AD 693 (7th Cir. 1995) (employer would "simply have to remove the non-essential functions from the employee's job, thereby eliminating the danger").

[243]*Compare* Rizzo v. Children's World Learning Ctrs., Inc., 84 F.3d 758, 764, 5 AD 1155 (5th Cir. 1996) ("As with all affirmative defenses, the employer bears the burden of proving that the employee is a direct threat.") *and* EEOC v. Chrysler Corp., 917 F. Supp. 1164, 1171, 5 AD 517 (E.D. Mich. 1996) ("[I]t is Defendant's burden to prove that [plaintiff] was in fact a 'direct threat.' ") *with* EEOC v. Amego, Inc., 110 F.3d 135, 144, 6 AD 997 (1st Cir. 1997) (holding that in cases where the essential job functions implicate the safety of others, plaintiff "must demonstrate that she can perform those functions in a way that does not endanger others," while recognizing that other cases may place the burden on defendants) *and Moses,* 97 F.3d at 447 ("The employee retains at all times the burden of persuading the jury either that he was not a direct threat or that reasonable accommodations were available.") *and* Ferguson v. Texasgulf, Inc., 5 AD 722, 730 (S.D. Tex. 1996) (holding that it was plaintiff's prima facie burden to show that mechanic recovering from heart attack could "perform the job of mechanic without risking his health or those of others"), *aff'd mem.,* 106 F.3d 397 (5th Cir. 1997).

[244]*See, e.g.,* Doe v. University of Md. Med. Sys. Corp., 50 F.3d 1261, 1266, 4 AD 379 (4th Cir. 1995) (HIV-infected surgeon not qualified under Rehabilitation Act even where risk of transmission of virus to patient is small because consequences of transmission are dire). *Cf.* EEOC v. Kinney Shoe Corp., 917 F. Supp. 419, 429, 5 AD 506 (W.D. Va. 1996) (no direct threat posed by shoe salesman with epilepsy who could suffer uncontrolled fall at any time because the nature and severity of harm was "not overwhelming"), *aff'd sub nom.* Martinson v. Kinney Shoe Corp., 104 F.3d 683, 6 AD 434 (4th Cir. 1997).

[245]*See* Guneratne v. St. Mary's Hosp., 943 F. Supp. 771, 775, 6 AD 476 (S.D. Tex. 1996) (nurse restricted from lifting posed threat because she could be required to lift in an emergency situation); Yodice v. Metropolitan Dade County, 4 AD 1384, 1388 (S.D. Fla. 1995) (police officer with wrist injury unfit for nonfield duty because in an emergency all forces could be mobilized).

[246]*See* Fussell v. Georgia Ports Auth., 906 F. Supp. 1561, 1574, 5 AD 1236 (S.D. Ga. 1995) (officer with tremor posed threat because he must be able to shoot accurately), *aff'd mem.,* 106 F.3d 417 (11th Cir. 1997); *Yodice,* 4 AD at 1388 (police officer who could not apply physical force due to wrist injury posed safety risk); Lassiter v. Reno, 885 F. Supp. 869, 874, 4 AD 609 (E.D. Va. 1995) (U.S. marshal with psychiatric condition cannot carry firearm without posing direct threat), *aff'd mem.,* 86 F.3d 1151, 5 AD 1343 (4th Cir. 1996), *cert. denied,* 117 S. Ct. 766 (1997).

from impairments that affect vision or consciousness pose special safety risks.[247] Drivers suffering from other impairments, however, may pose insignificant safety risks.[248]

Courts have held that healthcare workers with impairments that increase health risks to patients pose a direct threat if the risk posed cannot be controlled through a reasonable accommodation.[249] Courts often find that employees who have mental or emotional impairments that could lead to workplace violence pose a direct threat.[250] By contrast, HIV-positive employees generally do not pose a direct threat unless they are required to perform invasive medical procedures.[251] Essential job duties that require working with dangerous equipment or substances can pose a direct threat to

---

[247]*See, e.g.,* Daugherty v. City of El Paso, 56 F.3d 695, 698, 4 AD 993 (5th Cir. 1995) (holding that as a matter of law an insulin-dependent diabetic presents a substantial risk that he could injure himself or others), *cert. denied,* 116 S. Ct. 1263 (1996); Myers v. Hose, 50 F.3d 278, 282, 4 AD 391 (4th Cir. 1995) (bus driver with diabetes and heart condition poses threat of loss of consciousness and thereby poses threat to safety of passengers and others).

[248]*See* Rizzo v. Children's World Learning Ctrs., Inc., 84 F.3d 758, 764, 5 AD 1155 (5th Cir. 1996) (hearing-impaired school driver posed no risk); EEOC v. Texas Bus Lines, 923 F. Supp. 965, 974, 5 AD 878 (S.D. Tex. 1996) (morbidly obese driver applicant did not pose direct threat where no safety regulations addressed the issue).

[249]*See, e.g.,* Johnson v. New York Hosp., 96 F.3d 33, 34, 5 AD 1537 (2d Cir. 1996) (off-duty misconduct involving appearing drunk at hospital can disqualify alcoholic nurse); Altman v. New York City Health & Hosps. Corp., 100 F.3d 1054, 1060, 6 AD 73 (2d Cir. 1996) (alcoholic chief of medicine poses unacceptable risk due to possibility of relapse); Doe v. University of Md. Med. Sys. Corp., 50 F.3d 1261, 1266, 4 AD 379 (4th Cir. 1995) (HIV-positive neurosurgical resident can be barred from exposure-prone procedures); Guneratne v. St. Mary's Hosp., 943 F. Supp. 771, 775, 6 AD 476 (S.D. Tex. 1996) (back injury kept nurse from lifting patients, thereby exposing them to increased risk); Mauro v. Borgess Med. Ctr., 886 F. Supp. 1349, 1356, 4 AD 737 (W.D. Mich. 1995) (surgical technician can be laid off for refusing HIV test demanded upon reasonable suspicion).

[250]*See, e.g.,* Williams v. Widnall, 79 F.3d 1003, 1006, 5 AD 663 (10th Cir. 1996) (employee's continued threats against co-workers while in rehabilitation posed threat); Palmer v. Circuit Ct., 905 F. Supp. 499, 511, 6 AD 375 (N.D. Ill. 1995) (employee's continued expression of hostility to supervisor posed direct threat), *aff'd,* 117 F.3d 351, 6 AD 1569 (7th Cir. 1997); Lassiter v. Reno, 885 F. Supp. 869, 875, 4 AD 609 (E.D. Va. 1995) (paranoid U.S. marshal posed threat), *aff'd mem.,* 86 F.3d 1151, 5 AD 1343 (4th Cir. 1996), *cert. denied,* 117 S. Ct. 766 (1997).

[251]*See* EEOC v. Dolphin Cruise Line, 945 F. Supp. 1550, 1555, 6 AD 187 (S.D. Fla. 1996) (shipboard entertainer posed no direct threat to passengers or crew); EEOC v. Prevo's Family Mkt., Inc., 5 AD 1526, 1529 (W.D. Mich. 1996) (risk of transmission from produce clerk negligible); *cf.* Doe v. University of Md. Med. Sys. Corp., 50 F.3d. 1261, 1266, 4 AD 379 (4th Cir. 1995) (neurosurgical resident posed direct threat); Mauro v. Borgess Med. Ctr., 886 F. Supp. 1349, 1354, 4 AD 737 (W.D. Mich. 1995) (surgical technician who refused HIV test properly laid off).

individuals with certain impairments where the risk cannot be managed through accommodation.[252]

Courts continue to hold that employers may consider the individual-specific likelihood of imminent re-injury when evaluating an employee's ability to work safely.[253]

D. Special Issues

1. Contagious Diseases and AIDS

A sharply divided Supreme Court, in *Bragdon v. Abbott*,[254] resolved the question of whether asymptomatic HIV infection is a covered disability under the ADA. The plaintiff in *Bragdon* asserted that she had been denied dental treatment because of her HIV-infected status in violation of the public accommodations (Title III) section of the ADA. In a 5–4 decision, the Court held that HIV infection, even in the asymptomatic phase, is an impairment that substantially limits the major life activity of reproduction and, consequently, is a disability under the ADA.[255] The Court reasoned that HIV infection must be regarded as a physical impairment from the moment of infection because of its constant and detrimental effect on a person's hemic and lymphatic systems.[256] The majority also concluded that reproduction and the sexual dynamics surrounding it are central to the life process itself,[257] and

---

[252]*See* EEOC v. Amego, Inc., 110 F.3d 135, 144–47, 6 AD 997 (1st Cir. 1997) (recovering drug user could not be allowed access to therapeutic drugs without posing threat); Turco v. Hoechst Celanese Corp., 101 F.3d 1090, 1094, 6 AD 278 (5th Cir. 1996) (diabetic's job required him to work with complicated machinery and dangerous chemicals so that any diabetic episode or loss of concentration would endanger himself and others); Moses v. American Nonwovens, Inc., 97 F.3d 446, 448, 5 AD 1651 (11th Cir. 1996) (epileptic exposed to rollers, conveyors, and hot machinery faced danger that could not be eliminated by accommodation), *cert. denied*, 117 S. Ct. 964 (1997).

[253]*See, e.g.*, Jimeno v. Mobil Oil Corp., 66 F.3d 1514, 1521, 4 AD 1646 (9th Cir. 1995) (under state law an "employer cannot terminate an employee merely because of a physical impairment that might endanger the employee's health sometime in the future if the employee continues with the type of work that he or she is currently doing"); Collins v. Yellow Freight Sys., 942 F. Supp. 449, 453, 6 AD 102 (W.D. Mo. 1996) (employee with back condition cannot be returned to job as hostler without serious risk of injury).

[254]1998 WL 332958 (U.S. June 25, 1998).
[255]1998 WL 332958, at *15.
[256]1998 WL 332958, at *9.
[257]1998 WL 332958, at *9.

that HIV infection substantially limits the reproductive process due to the risk of transmission to the sexual partner and offspring.[258] The dissenting Justices would have applied a case-by-case approach to whether a particular individual was substantially limited in a major life activity by asymptomatic HIV infection and were of the further view that the reproductive process is not a major life activity as contemplated by the statute.[259]

The Ninth Circuit has withdrawn its opinion in *Doe v. Attorney General*,[260] which addressed what inquiries an employer may make about whether an employee has a contagious disease. In the superseding opinion, which was vacated on other grounds by the Supreme Court, the court of appeals determined that the FBI's questions about whether a medical facility director had AIDS were irrelevant to whether the director was "otherwise qualified" under the Rehabilitation Act.

2. Drug or Alcohol Impairment

Courts continue to define when an individual is "currently" engaged in the illegal use of drugs under the ADA and the Rehabilitation Act. Most hold that employees who enter a rehabilitation program for current drug use do not automatically become protected individuals with a disability under the ADA or the Rehabilitation Act.[261] If this were the case, then employees could escape an adverse employment action by enrolling in a drug treatment program before the employer learned of the employee's drug use.

The courts have been less clear about how recent an employee's drug use must be for the employee to be classified as a "current" user. Some courts look to whether the employee was using drugs at the time of the adverse action.[262] Others look to whether the

---

[258] 1998 WL 332958, at *10–11. The majority opinion also suggests that HIV infection may substantially limit other major life activities, but declines to address this issue. *Id.* *9.

[259] 1998 WL 332958, at *21–22, 25.

[260] 44 F.3d 715, 4 AD 52 (9th Cir.), *withdrawn,* 58 F.3d 490, 4 AD 992 (9th Cir.), *superseded by* 5 AD 1096 (9th Cir. 1995), *vacated on other grounds sub nom.* Reno v. Doe, 116 S. Ct. 2543, 5 AD 1152 (1996). This opinion was originally discussed in the Main Edition at note 383.

[261] *See, e.g.,* Baustian v. Louisiana, 910 F. Supp. 274, 276–77 (E.D. La. 1996); McDaniel v. Mississippi Baptist Med. Ctr., 877 F. Supp. 321, 327–28, 4 AD 241 (S.D. Miss.), *aff'd mem.,* 74 F.3d 1238, 6 AD 800 (5th Cir. 1995).

[262] *See, e.g.,* Grimes v. United States Postal Serv., 872 F. Supp. 668, 674–75, 3 AD 1764 (W.D. Mo. 1994) (defining current use as use of drugs at time of misconduct

employee used illegal drugs within weeks or months of the adverse action.[263] Still others focus on whether the employer had a reasonable belief that the employee's drug problem was real and ongoing rather than a past problem.[264] Whatever the approach, courts recognize that there is some threshold beyond which an addict will not be considered a current user.[265]

An employer may be required to accommodate an alcoholic employee by providing a leave of absence for rehabilitation.[266]

Courts continue to hold that employers may enforce policies prohibiting the use of drugs and alcohol in the workplace.[267] Courts distinguish between discharging an employee for alcoholism and discharging the employee for the misconduct that may have been caused by alcoholism. Generally, an employee's alcoholism will

---

that caused termination or at time of proposed termination), *aff'd mem.*, 74 F.3d 1243, 6 AD 800 (8th Cir. 1996).

[263]*See, e.g.,* Collings v. Longview Fibre Co., 63 F.3d 828, 833, 4 AD 1278 (9th Cir. 1995) (defining current use as use within weeks or months of adverse action), *cert. denied,* 116 S. Ct. 711 (1996); Baustian v. Louisiana, 910 F. Supp. 274, 276–77 (E.D. La. 1996) (seven-week period between being caught with drug and termination is not long enough to avoid classification as current user); McDaniel v. Mississippi Baptist Med. Ctr., 877 F. Supp. 321, 327–28, 4 AD 241 (S.D. Miss.) (six-week period between drug use and termination is not long enough to avoid classification as current user), *aff'd,* 74 F.3d 1238, 6 AD 800 (5th Cir. 1995).

[264]*See, e.g.,* Wormley v. Arkla, Inc., 871 F. Supp. 1079, 1084, 3 AD 1703 (E.D. Ark. 1994) (use of drugs one month before termination was sufficiently recent to justify employer's reasonable belief that the drug use was an ongoing problem rather than a problem that was in the past); Colorado State Bd. of Med. Examiners v. Davis, 893 P.2d 1365, 1369, 4 AD 316 (Colo. Ct. App. 1995) (an individual is a current user if evidence warrants a reasonable belief that illegal use of drugs was real and ongoing problem, and the individual need not use drugs at time of disciplinary hearing or other employment-related action).

[265]*See, e.g.,* Montegue v. City of New Orleans, 1996 U.S. Dist. LEXIS 13795, at *10 (E.D. La. Sept. 13, 1996) (no reason to believe that an addict who completed a certified substance-abuse program more than one year before his request for reinstatement is not a "stable" former addict).

[266]*See* Corbett v. National Prods. Co., 4 AD 987, 990–91 (E.D. Pa. 1995) (employer unlawfully terminated alcoholic after he admitted himself to a rehabilitation program; a 28-day leave of absence for rehabilitation is a reasonable accommodation).

[267]*See, e.g.,* Rodgers v. Federal Express Corp., 1996 U.S. App. LEXIS 8241, at *3 (6th Cir. Mar. 13, 1996) (under Ohio handicap discrimination law, drug addict was lawfully discharged for violating employer's no-drug policy); Altman v. New York City Health & Hosps. Corp., 100 F.3d 1054, 1060, 6 AD 73 (2d Cir. 1996) (hospital permitted to ask doctor to resign as chief of medicine after he committed improper acts, including being under the influence of alcohol in the workplace); Flynn v. Raytheon Co., 868 F. Supp. 383, 386–87, 3 AD 1495 (D. Mass. 1994) (pursuant to its policy, employer lawfully discharged alcoholic who came to work intoxicated), *aff'd mem.,* 94 F.3d 640 (1st Cir. 1996).

not immunize the employee from the consequences of his or her misconduct.[268] Similarly, an employer may hold an alcoholic employee to the same performance and attendance standards as other employees.[269]

Courts continue to find that alcoholics are not protected when their current use of alcohol directly threatens the health or safety of others.[270]

Although the rehabilitated drug user may be a "qualified individual with a disability," drug testing by an employer does not violate the ADA.[271]

---

[268]*See* Newland v. Dalton, 81 F.3d 904, 906, 5 AD 735 (9th Cir. 1996) (U.S. Navy properly discharged alcoholic who attempted to fire assault rifle at individuals in bar); Larson v. Koch Ref. Co., 920 F. Supp. 1000, 1004–05, 5 AD 136 (D. Minn. 1996) (employer lawfully discharged alcoholic for arrest for drunk driving and assault); Warren v. Runyon, 1995 U.S. Dist. LEXIS 5819, at *12 n.7 (N.D. Ill. Apr. 28, 1995) (court upheld termination of recovering alcoholic for obscene name calling where no demonstration that real reason for termination was status as recovering alcoholic).

[269]*See* Leary v. Dalton, 58 F.3d 748, 753, 4 AD 1165 (1st Cir. 1995) (in Rehabilitation Act case, employee incarcerated for drug and alcohol charges is not a qualified individual with a disability because of his excessive unauthorized absence); Labrucherie v. Regents of Univ. of Cal., 1995 U.S. Dist. LEXIS 12763, at **12–14 (N.D. Cal. Aug. 30, 1995) (employer properly discharged alcoholic police officer who was incarcerated after third drunk driving conviction and did not have permissible excuse for not reporting to work for five days), *aff'd mem.,* 119 F.3d 6 (9th Cir. 1996); Adamczyk v. Chief, Baltimore County Police Dep't, 952 F. Supp. 259, 266 (D. Md. 1997) (employer lawfully demoted alcoholic police lieutenant who was found guilty of seven counts of improper conduct, including giving away his badge); *accord* Teahan v. Metro-North Commuter R.R., 80 F.3d 50, 54, 5 AD 603 (2d Cir. 1996) (employee was not otherwise qualified where railroad had reasonable belief that he was likely to relapse into substance abuse and excessive absenteeism).

[270]*See, e.g.,* Williams v. Widnall, 79 F.3d 1003, 1006–07, 5 AD 663 (10th Cir. 1996) (discharge of alcoholic employee upheld where his continuing threats to supervisors and co-workers constituted direct threat to their safety); Altman v. New York City Health & Hosps. Corp., 903 F. Supp. 503, 513–14, 4 AD 1665 (S.D.N.Y. 1995) (hospital lawfully refused to reinstate alcoholic doctor as chief of medicine where risk of relapse created significant risk of substantial harm to the public), *aff'd,* 100 F.3d 1054 (2d Cir. 1996); Johnson v. New York Hosp., 96 F.3d 33, 34, 5 AD 1537 (2d Cir. 1996) (district court properly instructed jury to consider off-duty conduct when determining whether employee fit into the current alcohol abuse exception of the Rehabilitation Act); *cf.* Dimonda v. New York City Police Dep't, 1996 WL 194325, at *5 (S.D.N.Y. Apr. 22, 1996) (disputed issue of fact about whether alcoholic police officer who had discharged firearm into wall of building was otherwise qualified where he had entered a rehabilitation program two months before and had completed the program one month before his detective designation was removed).

[271]*See, e.g.,* Buckley v. Consolidated Edison Co., Inc., 934 F. Supp. 104, 106, 5 AD 1459 (S.D.N.Y. 1996) (drug testing only violates the ADA if it fails to reasonably

VI. PROOF

Courts agree that to establish a prima facie case of disability discrimination, a plaintiff must first prove that he or she is a qualified individual with a disability who has been subjected to an adverse employment action by a covered entity.[272] Once these prerequisites are established, the allocation of proof depends on the defense presented.

Where the defendant claims that the plaintiff's disability was not a motivating factor for the challenged employment action, traditional Title VII proof models are applied.[273] But where the defendant acknowledges that it relied, at least in part, on the plaintiff's disability, or where direct evidence establishes this, the courts have had a "difficult task" in developing an appropriate analytical framework.[274]

Some courts have criticized early decisions that applied a modified version of the traditional Title VII burden-shifting model where direct evidence is admitted or established. These courts reason that, where the defendant admits or where it is otherwise

---

accommodate a known physical or mental limitation of an otherwise qualified individual with a disability).

[272]*See, e.g.,* Jacques v. Clean-Up Group, 96 F.3d 506, 511, 5 AD 1594 (1st Cir. 1996); Williams v. Channel Master Satellite Sys., 101 F.3d 346, 348, 6 AD 131 (4th Cir. 1996), *cert. denied,* 117 S. Ct. 1844 (1997); Rizzo v. Children's World Learning Ctrs., Inc., 84 F.3d 758, 763, 5 AD 1155 (5th Cir. 1996); Monette v. Electronic Data Sys. Corp., 90 F.3d 1173, 1178, 5 AD 1326 (6th Cir. 1996); Benson v. Northwest Airlines, 62 F.3d 1108, 1112, 4 AD 1234 (8th Cir. 1995); Milton v. Scrivner, Inc., 53 F.3d 1118, 1123, 4 AD 432 (10th Cir. 1995). For claims brought under the Rehabilitation Act, the plaintiff must also prove that the entity receives federal funds. *See, e.g.,* Doherty v. Southern College of Optometry, 862 F.2d 570, 573 (6th Cir. 1988).

[273]*See Monette,* 90 F.3d at 1184; Ennis v. National Ass'n of Bus. & Educ. Radio, Inc., 53 F.3d 55, 57–58, 4 AD 589 (4th Cir. 1995) (*McDonnell-Douglas* paradigm applied "at least in those circumstances where the defendant disavows any reliance on discriminatory reasons for its adverse employment action"); Newman v. GHS Osteopathic, Inc., 60 F.3d 153, 157, 4 AD 1051 (3d Cir. 1995); Sackett v. WPNT, Inc., 4 AD 1597, 1599 (W.D. Pa. 1995), *aff'd mem.,* 91 F.3d 125 (3d Cir. 1996).

[274]*Monette,* 90 F.3d at 1178 ("Defining and applying an appropriate framework for analyzing claims of discrimination based on an individual's disability has proven to be a difficult task."); *see* Bryant v. Better Bus. Bureau, Inc., 923 F. Supp. 720, 733, 5 AD 625 (D. Md. 1996) (holding that while plaintiff bears the burden of proof on reasonable accommodation, "little else is entirely clear with respect to the allocation of the burden of production and the burden of proof generally . . . under the ADA or the Rehabilitation Act").

proved that the defendant relied on the plaintiff's disability in reaching its challenged employment decision, the burden-shifting analysis that is used to glean employer intent is inapposite.[275]

Different proof formulations also may apply depending upon whether the plaintiff claims or disavows the need for an accommodation. The Sixth Circuit has held that, where the plaintiff claims to be qualified for the job without accommodation, and the employer insists that the plaintiff's disability precludes satisfactory performance, the burden does not shift to the employer, and the plaintiff bears the traditional burden of objectively proving that he or she is able to perform the job in question.[276]

Where the plaintiff seeks an accommodation, however, the Eighth and Tenth Circuits have held that, if the plaintiff makes a facial showing that a reasonable accommodation is possible, then the employer bears a burden of production to show that it cannot reasonably accommodate the plaintiff.[277] The Tenth Circuit also has held that if the defendant meets its burden of production, then the plaintiff must rebut the employer's evidence.[278]

The Eighth Circuit has held that if the employer "shows that the employee cannot perform the essential functions of the job even with reasonable accommodation, the employee must rebut the showing with evidence of his [or her] individual capabilities. At that point, the employee's burden merges with [the] ultimate burden of persuading the trier of fact that he [or she] has suffered unlawful discrimination."[279]

---

[275]*See, e.g., Monette,* 90 F.3d at 1179–80 (criticizing *Pushkin v. Regents of Univ. of Col.,* 658 F.2d 1372, 1387, 2 AD 11 (10th Cir. 1981), which adopted a modified shifting burden analysis); Williams v. Channel Master Satellite Sys., 101 F.3d 346, 348 n.1, 6 AD 131 (4th Cir. 1996) ("The McDonnell Douglas 'inferential proof scheme' is not appropriate when, as here, the reason for discharge [back injury] is undisputed."), *cert. denied,* 117 S. Ct. 1844 (1997); Bultemeyer v. Fort Wayne Community Sch., 100 F.3d 1281, 1283, 6 AD 67 (7th Cir. 1996) (court erred in applying burden shifting where facts are alleged that would directly establish an ADA violation); White v. York Int'l Corp., 45 F.3d 357, 361 n.6, 3 AD 1746 (10th Cir. 1995) (acknowledging that traditional burden shifting is achieved from the outset where the employer readily acknowledges that the challenged decision was premised, at least in part, on the employee's disability).

[276]*Monette,* 90 F.3d at 1183.

[277]Benson v. Northwest Airlines, 62 F.3d 1108, 1112, 4 AD 1234 (8th Cir. 1995); Milton v. Scrivner, Inc., 53 F.3d 1118, 1124, 4 AD 432 (10th Cir. 1995).

[278]White v. York Int'l Corp., 45 F.3d 357, 361, 3 AD 1746 (10th Cir. 1995).

[279]*Benson,* 62 F.3d at 1112 (citation omitted).

In a failure-to-accommodate case, the Sixth Circuit held that the plaintiff bears the burden of showing both that the accommodation is objectively reasonable or possible and that the accommodation will enable the plaintiff to perform the job's essential functions.[280] If this burden is carried, then the employer bears the burden of persuasion to establish that the requested accommodation will impose an undue hardship.[281]

The Seventh Circuit has held that the "employee must show that the accommodation is reasonable in the sense both of efficacious and of proportional to cost."[282] The employer then has the "opportunity to prove that upon more careful consideration the costs are excessive in relation either to the benefits of the accommodation or to the employer's financial survival or health."[283]

As to the requirement that a requested accommodation be reasonable, the Second Circuit has held that "the plaintiff bears only a burden of production," and this burden "is not a heavy one."[284] Thus, it is enough for the plaintiff to show the existence of a plausible accommodation as long as the cost of the accommodation does not exceed its benefit. Thereafter, the employer has the burden of proving that the accommodation sought is unreasonable, which "merges, in effect, with its burden of showing, as an affirmative defense, that the proposed accommodation would cause it to suffer an undue hardship."[285]

The Eleventh Circuit has disagreed with the Second Circuit's approach. Combining the question of whether an accommodation is reasonable with the question of whether the accommodation will impose an undue hardship not only "confuses an element of the plaintiff's case (reasonable accommodation) with an affirmative defense (undue burden)" but also "effectively relieves the plaintiff of [the] obligation to prove [his or] her case."[286] "[T]he question

---

[280]*Monette*, 90 F.3d at 1183–84.
[281]*Id.*
[282]Vande Zande v. Wisconsin Dep't of Admin., 44 F.3d 538, 543, 3 AD 1636 (7th Cir. 1995).
[283]*Id.*
[284]Borkowski v. Valley Cent. Sch. Dist., 63 F.3d 131, 138, 4 AD 1264 (2d Cir. 1995).
[285]*Id.*
[286]Willis v. Conopco, Inc., 108 F.3d 282, 286 (11th Cir. 1997) (citing 42 U.S.C. § 12112(b)).

of whether an accommodation is reasonable (though it must be determined within a given set of specific facts) is more of a 'generalized' inquiry than the question of whether an accommodation causes a 'hardship' on the particular employer that is undue."[287]

Where the plaintiff alleges that a particular job requirement is nonessential, the Sixth Circuit has held that the employer bears the burden of proving that the challenged requirement is job related and consistent with business necessity.[288]

Where the essential functions of a job necessarily implicate the safety of others, the plaintiff may have to establish that he or she can perform the job safely to satisfy the burden of proving that he or she is a qualified individual with a disability.[289] Other courts view the ability of the plaintiff to perform without posing a safety threat as an affirmative defense borne by the employer.[290]

VII. Enforcement Issues

A. ADA

1. Agency Proceedings

In determining whether a plaintiff must exhaust administrative procedures, it is important to distinguish private from public employers. For example, in *Chatoff v. West Publishing Co.*,[291] the employee argued that he did not have to exhaust administrative remedies because his employer had " 'substantial contracts with the Federal Government' "[292] and was therefore a public entity under Title II of the ADA. Agreeing that if the employer was a

---

[287]*Id.* (citing Barth v. Gelb, 2 F.3d 1180, 1187 (D.C. Cir. 1993)).

[288]Monette v. Electronic Data Sys. Corp., 90 F.3d 1173, 1184, 5 AD 1326 (6th Cir. 1996).

[289]*See* EEOC v. Amego, Inc., 110 F.3d 135, 144, 6 AD 997 (1st Cir. 1997); Moses v. American Nonwovens, Inc., 97 F.3d 446, 447, 5 AD 1651 (11th Cir. 1996) (per curiam) ("The employee retains at all times the burden of persuading the jury either that he was not a direct threat or that reasonable accommodations were available."), *cert. denied,* 117 S. Ct. 964 (1997).

[290]*See, e.g.,* Rizzo v. Children's World Learning Ctrs., Inc., 84 F.3d 758, 764, 5 AD 1155 (5th Cir. 1996) ("[T]he employer bears the burden of proving that the employee is a direct threat.").

[291]948 F. Supp. 176, 6 AD 414 (E.D.N.Y. 1996).

[292]*Id.* at 179.

public entity, then there was no exhaustion requirement, the district court nevertheless found that federal contracts did not bring the particular employer within the ADA's definition of "public entity."[293] Thus, Title I of the ADA and the normal exhaustion requirements applied.

2. Private Suits

Punitive damages are not available under Title II of the ADA, which applies to public entities, or under § 504 of the Rehabilitation Act.[294]

A Title I plaintiff may survive summary judgment on the issue of punitive damages with a small showing that an employer showed "malice or reckless indifference" to the employee's rights under the ADA.[295]

With regard to damages caps, determining whether facially separate entities may be considered a single employer is a significant issue. Generally, courts follow the four-part test in Title VII cases, which examines the interrelation of operations, common management, centralized control of labor relations, and common ownership or financial control existing among the several entities.[296]

---

[293]*Id.*

[294]*See* Moreno v. Consolidated Rail Corp., 99 F.3d 782, 788–92, 6 AD 86 (6th Cir. 1996) (Rehabilitation Act); Winfrey v. Chicago, 957 F. Supp. 1014, 1024–25 (N.D. Ill. 1997) (Title II of the ADA).

[295]*See* Stone v. La Quinta Inn, Inc., 942 F. Supp. 261, 266, 6 AD 60 (E.D. La. 1966) (employer's motion for summary judgment denied where employee had received positive performance evaluations but, after seeking an accommodation of her disability, received negative evaluations); Wilson v. Gayfers Montgomery Fair Co., 953 F. Supp. 1415, 1422, 6 AD 1076 (M.D. Ala. 1996) (employee survived summary judgment because of witness's affidavit that one of the employer's agents had "mocked" the employee's hearing problem); Oswald v. Laroche Chems., 894 F. Supp. 988, 997–98, 5 AD 401 (E.D. La. 1995) (denying summary judgment based on evidence that the manager had reviewed the employee's medical file once; the manager did not consult other employees about accommodating the employee in a particular position after the medical review officer refused to allow the plaintiff to work in that position; the manager knew that the medical review officer had never visited the plant to consider possible positions for the plaintiff; and the medical review officer relied on the employer's representations for information about the physical requirements of the possible positions).

[296]*See, e.g.,* Greenway v. Buffalo Hilton Hotel, 951 F. Supp. 1039, 1055–57 (W.D.N.Y. 1997) (applying four factors and concluding that two facially separate entities were not a single employer; therefore, number of employees for each entity could not be combined to raise punitive damages limit to $300,000).

3. Alternative Dispute Resolution

One common technique used by many employers is to ask employees to sign arbitration agreements in which they agree to arbitrate employment disputes rather than litigate them in court. Courts have held that these agreements encompass ADA claims.[297]

The majority view of the federal circuits is that where a collective bargaining agreement contains a mandatory arbitration provision, an employee may still bring a lawsuit involving an ADA claim instead of submitting the claim to arbitration.[298]

4. Attorney's Fees

As in other civil rights and discrimination cases, the courts in ADA cases use two tests to determine whether a party is a "prevailing party" and therefore may recover attorney's fees. Under the first, parties "are considered to be prevailing parties 'if they succeed on any significant issue in litigation which achieves some of the benefit the parties sought in bringing the suit.' "[299] Thus,

---

[297]*See* Topf v. Warnaco, Inc., 942 F. Supp. 762, 770–71, 6 AD 1315 (D. Conn. 1996) (arbitration agreement that covered "any controversy arising out of the employment relationship" included ADA claims); *accord* Satario v. A.G. Edwards & Sons, 941 F. Supp. 609, 612–13 (N.D. Tex. 1996); Golenia v. Bob Baker Toyota, 915 F. Supp. 201, 204–05, 5 AD 482 (S.D. Cal. 1996); Connors v. AMISUB, 5 AD 961, 962 (S.D. Fla. 1996); McWilliams v. Logicon, Inc., 5 AD 1456, 1458 (D. Kan. 1996).

[298]*See* Brisentine v. Stone & Webster Eng'g Corp., 117 F.3d 519, 526–27, 6 AD 1878 (11th Cir. 1997) (a mandatory arbitration clause in a collective bargaining agreement does not bar litigation of a federal statutory claim under the ADA); Harrison v. Eddy Potash, Inc., 112 F.3d 1437, 1453, 73 FEP 1384 (10th Cir. 1997) (stating that " 'statutory employment claims are independent of a collective bargaining agreement's grievance and arbitration procedures' "), *petition for cert. filed*, 66 U.S.L.W. 3137 (U.S. Aug. 6, 1997) (No. 97-232); Pryner v. Tractor Supply Co., 109 F.3d 354, 363, 72 FEP 1235 (7th Cir. 1997) (holding that "the union cannot consent *for* the employee by signing a collective bargaining agreement that consigns the enforcement of statutory rights to the union-controlled grievance and arbitration machinery created by the agreement"), *aff'd*, 109 F.3d 354, 73 FEP 615 (7th Cir. 1997), *petition for cert. filed*, 65 U.S.L.W. 3783 (U.S. May 6, 1997) (No. 96-1830); Varner v. National Super Mkts., Inc., 94 F.3d 1209, 1213 (8th Cir. 1996) (exhaustion of grievance and administrative remedies under a collective bargaining agreement is not required in order to bring a Title VII claim in federal court), *cert. denied*, 117 S. Ct. 946 (1997). *Contra* Austin v. Owens-Brockway Glass Container, Inc., 78 F.3d 875, 886, 5 AD 488 (4th Cir.) (an employee's individual statutory claim is subject to compulsory arbitration pursuant to an arbitration clause in a collective bargaining agreement), *cert. denied*, 117 S. Ct. 432 (1996).

[299]*See* Special Educ. Servs. v. RREEF Performance Partnership-I, L.P., 1996 U.S. Dist. LEXIS 9698, at *6 (N.D. Ill. July 10, 1996) (quoting Hensley v. Eckerhart, 461 U.S. 424, 433 (1983)).

for example, one district court found an ADA plaintiff to be a prevailing party where, in a pretrial settlement, the defendant agreed to allow patrons dining at his restaurant to use service animals.[300]

Under the second test, parties are considered "prevailing" even if they "do not win on any significant issue in the litigation, 'but obtain what they seek anyway.' "[301]

One district court, however, declined to award attorney's fees because the plaintiff failed to meet both of the tests of a prevailing party.[302] The court stated that to be considered a prevailing party, the party must "succeed on any significant issue in litigation *and* obtain a result that affects the defendant's behavior toward the plaintiff."[303] Although he had succeeded on his reasonable accommodation claim, "the plaintiff did not change the legal relationship between the parties," and therefore the court declined to award attorney's fees.[304]

Courts in ADA cases use the "lodestar" method to determine the amount of attorney's fees to be awarded, multiplying the number of hours reasonably expended by a reasonable hourly rate.[305]

B. Rehabilitation Act

1. *Federal Government Employers—§ 501*

The courts remain divided over whether § 501 is the exclusive remedy for federal employees with a disability-based discrimination claim or whether a federal employee may bring a claim under § 504.[306]

---

[300]*See* Flores v. Villerose, Inc., 5 A.D. 1672, 1673 (E.D. Pa. 1996).

[301]*See Special Educ. Servs.*, 1996 U.S. Dist. LEXIS 9698, at *6 (quoting Coalition for Basic Human Needs v. King, 691 F.2d 597, 601 (1st Cir. 1982)).

[302]Frey v. Alldata Corp., 895 F. Supp. 221, 4 AD 1627 (E.D. Wis. 1995).

[303]*Id.* at 225 (emphasis added).

[304]*Id.* (plaintiff won a "hollow victory" when he prevailed on liability, but the jury awarded no compensatory damages and erroneously awarded $115 in punitive damages, which the court struck after the verdict, and where the court denied injunctive relief).

[305]*See, e.g.,* Greenway v. Buffalo Hilton Hotel, 951 F. Supp. 1039, 1068 (W.D.N.Y. 1997); Flores v. Villerose, Inc., 5 AD 1672, 1673 (E.D. Pa. 1996); Special Educ. Servs. v. RREEF Performance Partnership-I, LP, 1996 U.S. Dist. LEXIS 9698, at *14 (N.D. Ill. July 10, 1996).

[306]*See* Leary v. Dalton, 58 F.3d 748, 752, 4 AD 1165 (1st Cir. 1995) (civilian employee of naval shipyard may bring an action under both § 501 and § 504).

Punitive damages are not available under § 504.[307] Although one district court has allowed a Postal Service employee to seek punitive damages under § 501,[308] other courts have held that punitive damages are not available against federal employers under § 501.[309]

2. Federal Contractors—§ 503

Courts continue to hold that individuals have no private right of action under § 503.[310] Plaintiffs therefore are limited to administrative enforcement under this section.

3. Recipients of Federal Financial Assistance and Federal Agencies—§ 504

b. Private Enforcement. The Supreme Court held in *Lane v. Peña*[311] that a plaintiff cannot obtain monetary damages from federal agencies under § 504. In *Lane,* a Merchant Marine Academy cadet brought suit under the Rehabilitation Act against the Department of Transportation, alleging that his termination violated § 504, which prohibits disability-based discrimination "under any program or activity conducted by an Executive agency." The cadet claimed that the academy terminated his enrollment because

---

[307] *See* Moreno v. Consolidated Rail Corp., 99 F.3d 782, 790–91, 6 AD 86 (6th Cir. 1996).

[308] *See* Roy v. Runyon, 954 F. Supp. 368, 381 (D. Me. 1997). The district court's opinion in *Roy* was based on a Title VII case, which was reversed on appeal. *See* Baker v. Runyon, 922 F. Supp. 1296 (N.D. Ill. 1996), *rev'd,* 114 F.3d 668, 669 (7th Cir. 1997) (punitive damages are not available against governmental entities in Title VII action).

[309] *See, e.g.,* Tuers v. Runyon, 950 F. Supp. 284, 285–86 (E.D. Cal. 1996) (punitive damages are not available against the Postal Service under § 501 in Rehabilitation Act case); Suhr v. Runyon, 1995 WL 617478, at *3 (N.D. Ill. Oct. 12, 1995) (same) (Rehabilitation Act case); *see also* Montalvo v. United States Postal Serv., 887 F. Supp. 63, 66 (E.D.N.Y. 1995) (Title VII case), *aff'd mem.,* 1996 U.S. App. LEXIS 12262 (2d Cir. 1996); Ausfeldt v. Runyon, 950 F. Supp. 478, 487–88 (N.D.N.Y. 1997) (Title VII case); Miller v. Runyon, 932 F. Supp. 276, 277, 71 FEP 1024 (M.D. Ala. 1996) (Title VII case).

[310] *See, e.g.,* Csoka v. United States, 1996 U.S. App. LEXIS 20583, at *22 (7th Cir. Aug. 12, 1996) (employee had no private right of action against employer even assuming that a federal contract was involved); Clemmer v. Enron Corp., 882 F. Supp. 606, 611, 4 AD 437 (S.D. Tex. 1995) (employee had no private right of action against his employer, a federal contractor).

[311] 116 S. Ct. 2092, 2100, 5 AD 973 (1996).

he was diagnosed with diabetes mellitus, which rendered him ineligible to be commissioned for service.[312] Although recognizing that monetary damages are generally available under § 504, the Court held that the statute lacks an "unequivocal expression" of intent to waive the federal government's sovereign immunity.[313]

Private plaintiffs asserting a § 504 claim may have a claim under the Administrative Procedures Act (APA) as well as under the Rehabilitation Act.[314] As one district court has held, "[s]ection 504 and the APA provide overlapping rights of action for injunctive relief for plaintiffs alleging discrimination on the basis of a disability by a federal agency."[315]

---

[312]*Id.* at 2095.

[313]*Id.* at 2110.

[314]*See* Mendez v. Gearan, 947 F. Supp. 1364, 1367 (N.D. Cal. 1996) ("An individual adversely affected or aggrieved by the action of an agency is entitled to judicial review of the action under the APA.").

[315]*Id.* at 1367. Given the holding in *Lane,* the district court in *Mendez* held that the critical question was whether the claim is for "individualized discrimination" or "a request for systemic change." *Id.* at 1370. If the essence of a plaintiff's claim is that he or she is otherwise qualified for a particular position, was excluded from the position solely because of a disability, and seeks a reasonable accommodation, then the claim is for "individualized discrimination" and should be analyzed under § 504. On the other hand, if the essence of the claim is to effect a change in an agency's operating policies, then the claim seeks "systemic change" and should be analyzed under the APA. *Id.* The distinction is significant, in part, because of the exhaustion of administrative remedies requirement under the APA. *Id. See also* Jeremy H. v. Mount Lebanon Sch. Dist., 95 F.3d 272, 280 (3d Cir. 1996) (in a § 504 suit where child sued school district to require district to accommodate his visual disability, plaintiff need not exhaust administrative remedies). *But see* Spence v. Straw, 54 F.3d 196, 201, 4 AD 528 (3d Cir. 1995) (a plaintiff bringing an employment discrimination claim under § 504 must exhaust administrative procedures; otherwise, a plaintiff bringing an employment discrimination claim could circumvent the administrative procedures of § 501 by bringing a § 504 claim).

APPENDIX

State	Public Employment or Employment Supported by Public Funds*	Affirmative Action in Public Employment*	Private Employment*
Alabama	Ala. Code § 21-7-8		
Alaska			Alaska Stat. § 18.80.220
Arizona		Ariz. Exec. Order No. 89-7	Ariz. Rev. Stat. Ann. §§ 41-1461, 41-1463, 14-1464
Arkansas	Ark. Code Ann. § 20-14-301		Ark. Code Ann. §§ 16-123-101–16-123-108
California**	Cal. Gov't Code § 19702	Cal. Gov't Code § 19702	Cal. Gov't Code § 12940
Colorado	Col. Rev. Stat. § 24-34-801		Col. Rev. Stat. §§ 24-34-301–24-34-406
Connecticut	Conn. Gen. Stat. § 46a-70		Conn. Gen. Stat. § 46a-60
Delaware**	Del. Code Ann. tit. 16, § 9501		Del. Code Ann. tit. 19, § 724
District of Columbia	D.C. Code Ann. § 6-1705		D.C. Code Ann. §§ 1-2501–1-2557
Florida	Fla. Stat. Ann. § 413.08		Fla. Stat. Ann. § 760.10

State	Public Employment or Employment Supported by Public Funds*	Affirmative Action in Public Employment*	Private Employment*
Georgia	Ga. Code Ann. §§ 30-1-2, 45-19-29		Ga. Code Ann. § 34-6A-4
Guam			22 Guam Code Ann. § 5203
Hawaii	Haw. Rev. Stat. § 78-2		Haw. Rev. Stat. § 378-2
Idaho	Idaho Code §§ 56-701, 56-707		Idaho Code §§ 67-5901–67-5909
Illinois	Ill. Comp. Stat. ch. 775, para. 30/5	Ill. Comp. Stat. ch. 775, para. 5/2-105	Ill. Comp. Stat. ch. 775, para. 5/2-102
Indiana	Ind. Code § 16-32-3-5		Ind. Code § 22-9-5-19
Iowa		Iowa Code § 19B.2	Iowa Code § 216.6
Kansas	Kan. Stat. Ann. § 39-1105		Kan. Stat. Ann. §§ 44-1001 et seq.
Kentucky**	Ky. Rev. Stat. Ann. § 18A.138	Ky. Rev. Stat. Ann. § 18A.138	Ky. Rev. Stat. Ann. §§ 207.150, 344.040
Louisiana	La. Rev. Stat. Ann. § 46:1951		La. Rev. Stat. Ann. §§ 51:2232, 51:2242–51:2245
Maine**	Me. Rev. Stat. Ann. tit. 5, § 784	Me. Rev. Stat. Ann. tit. 5, §§ 781–791	Me. Rev. Stat. Ann. tit. 5, §§ 4551–4576

State	Public Employment or Employment Supported by Public Funds*	Affirmative Action in Public Employment*	Private Employment*
Maryland	Md. Ann. Code art. 49B, § 7		Md. Ann. Code art. 49B, § 16
Massachusetts**			Mass. Ann. Laws. ch. 151B, §§ 1 et seq.
Michigan			Mich. Comp. Laws §§ 37.1202-37.1206
Minnesota		Minn. Stat. Ann. § 473.143	Minn. Stat. Ann. § 363.03
Mississippi	Miss. Code Ann. §§ 25-9-149, 43-6-15		
Missouri			Mo. Rev. Stat. § 213.055
Montana	Mont. Code Ann. § 49-3-201	Mont. Code Ann. §§ 39-30-101 et seq.	Mont. Code Ann. §§ 49-2-303, 49-4-101
Nebraska**	Neb. Rev. Stat. § 20-131	Neb. Rev. Stat. § 81-1355	Neb. Rev. Stat. §§ 48-1101 et seq.
Nevada	Nev. Rev. Stat. § 284.012		Nev. Rev. Stat. § 613.330
New Hampshire	N.H. Rev. Stat. Ann. § 167-C:5		N.H. Rev. Stat. Ann. § 354-A:7
New Jersey			N.J. Stat. Ann. §§ 10:5-4.1, 10:5-29.1
New Mexico**	N.M. Stat. Ann. § 28-7-7		N.M. Stat. Ann. § 28-1-7

State	Public Employment or Employment Supported by Public Funds*	Affirmative Action in Public Employment*	Private Employment*
New York	N.Y. Exec. Law § 312	N.Y. Exec. Law § 312	N.Y. Civ. R. Law § 47-a N.Y. Exec. Laws §§ 292 et seq.
North Carolina**	N.C. Gen. Stat. §§ 126-16 et seq.	N.C. Gen. Stat. § 128-15.3	N.C. Gen. Stat. §§ 168A-1 et seq.
North Dakota	N.D. Cent. Code § 25-13-05		N.D. Cent. Code §§ 14-02.3, 14-02.4
Ohio	Ohio Rev. Code Ann. § 153.59		Ohio Rev. Code Ann. § 4112.02
Oklahoma	Okla. Stat. tit. 74, § 954		Okla. Stat. tit. 25, §§ 1301–1306
Oregon**		Ore. Rev. Stat. § 243.305	Ore. Rev. Stat. § 659.425
Pennsylvania			4 Pa. Stat. Ann. tit. 43, § 955
Puerto Rico			P.R. Laws Ann. tit. 1, § 505
Rhode Island**	R.I. Gen. Laws §§ 28-5.1-1 et seq.		R.I. Gen. Laws § 28-5-7
South Carolina	S.C. Code Ann. § 43-33-60		S.C. Code Ann. §§ 1-13-20 et seq.
South Dakota	S.D. Codified Laws Ann. § 3-6A-15		S.D. Codified Laws Ann. §§ 20-13-10–20-13-13
Tennessee	Tenn. Code Ann. § 71-4-202	Tenn. Code Ann. § 8-50-104	Tenn. Code Ann. § 8-50-103

State	Public Employment or Employment Supported by Public Funds*	Affirmative Action in Public Employment*	Private Employment*
Texas	Tex. Hum. Res. Code Ann. § 121.001		Tex. Lab. Code Ann. § 21.051
Utah	Utah Code Ann. §§ 26-30-3, 67-19-4		Utah Code Ann. §§ 34-35-6, 35A-5-106
Vermont**			Vt. Stat. Ann. tit. 21, §§ 495, 497
Virginia**			Va. Code Ann. § 51.5-41
Virgin Islands	V.I. Code Ann. tit. 10, § 154		
Washington**	Wash. Rev. Code §§ 70.84.010-70, 70.84.080	Wash. Rev. Code §§ 49.74.005–49.74.050	Wash. Rev. Code § 49.60.180
West Virginia**			W.Va. Code §§ 5-11-1 et seq.
Wisconsin**	Wis. Stat. Ann. §§ 230.01 et seq.	Wis. Stat. Ann. §§ 230.01 et seq.	Wis. Stat. Ann. §§ 111.31 et seq.
Wyoming			Wyo. Stat. § 27-9-105

*These statutes are only as of October 1, 1996. Current statutes should be consulted.
**These states also have specific statutes that prohibit an employer from discriminating against an employee or applicant for employment because the employee is HIV positive and that prohibit the employer from requiring an employee or applicant for employment to undergo an HIV test as a condition of employment.

Part 5

Specific Bases for Discrimination

Chapter 10

RACE AND COLOR

I. Discrimination Based on Race-Linked Characteristics

Adverse employment decisions based on language differences, such as a heavy foreign accent, that do not interfere with the ability to perform the duties of a position are unlawful.[1] Language difficulties that interfere with performance may be legitimately considered in employment decisions.[2]

V. Racial Harassment

One appeals court has held that an employer's liability under Title VII is not dependent upon the intent of the perpetrator of the harassment. Thus, where employees can reasonably perceive the conduct in question to be hostile or abusive, the actor's lack of specific discriminatory intent does not prevent his or her deliberate conduct from being actionable under Title VII.[3]

While an employer may be held liable under Title VII for failing to investigate or to prevent harassment from occurring, liability attaches only where harassment has actually occurred. A plaintiff must first prove a prima facie case of actual environmental harassment before the employer can be held liable for failure to take reasonable steps to prevent harassment from occurring in the workplace.[4] Courts continue to hold that isolated or minor incidents are not sufficient to create a racially hostile environment.[5]

---

[1] Arzate v. City of Topeka, 884 F. Supp. 1494, 1500, 72 FEP 681 (D. Kan. 1995) (citing Carino v. University of Okla. Bd. of Regents, 750 F.2d 815, 819, 36 FEP 826 (10th Cir. 1984)).
[2] *Id.* at 1501 (plaintiff failed to demonstrate, due to his subpar communication skills, that he was equally qualified as the person selected for the position).
[3] Newton v. Department of the Air Force, 85 F.3d 595, 599 (Fed. Cir. 1996).
[4] Karibian v. Columbia Univ., 930 F. Supp. 134, 146, 71 FEP 325 (S.D.N.Y. 1996).
[5] Arzate v. City of Topeka, 884 F. Supp. 1494, 1503, 72 FEP 681 (D. Kan. 1995) (plaintiff did not demonstrate that conduct in the workplace, which included the

VI. "Race Plus"

The Ninth Circuit affirmed the usage of the sex-plus category, holding that race and sex are not "distinct elements amenable to almost mathematical treatment."[6] The court held that "where two bases for discrimination exist, they cannot be neatly reduced to distinct components,"[7] as to do so "often distorts or ignores the particular nature of [the plaintiff's] experiences."[8]

VII. Defenses to Race and Color Discrimination

Courts have also rejected the argument that corrective action by an employer constitutes a concession that discrimination actually occurred. In *Dennis v. County of Fairfax*,[9] the Fourth Circuit reasoned that if corrective action implied liability, employers would have little or no incentive to investigate allegations of discrimination.[10]

---

mocking of his accent, permeated the workplace so as to create a hostile work environment); Shabat v. Blue Cross Blue Shield, 925 F. Supp. 977, 984, 16 AD 1021 (W.D.N.Y. 1996) (infrequent utterance of racial remarks is insufficient to show a hostile work environment; moreover, an objective standard—not plaintiff's perception—determines the existence vel non of a hostile environment); Bolden v. PRC, 43 F.3d 545, 67 FEP 1790 (10th Cir. 1994) (racial remarks made by two co-workers were not considered pervasive enough in an environment described as typically blue collar and joking), *cert. denied*, 116 S. Ct. 92 (1995).

[6]Lam v. University of Hawaii, 40 F.3d 1551, 1561–62, 66 FEP 74 (9th Cir. 1994) (reversing summary judgment entered in favor of university and against Asian female faculty member).

[7]*Id.* at 1562 (citing Jefferies v. Harris County Community Action Ass'n, 615 F.2d 1025, 1032–34), 22 FEP 974 (5th Cir. 1980)). *See* Section VI. C in Chapter 13 in the Main Edition.

[8]*Id.* The court, citing *Jefferies v. Harris County Community Action Ass'n* (which dealt with the discrimination claim of an African-American woman), explained that "[l]ike other subclasses under Title VII, Asian women are subject to a set of stereotypes and assumptions shared neither by Asian men nor by white women" *Id.* (615 F.2d at 1032).

[9]55 F.3d 151, 67 FEP 1681 (4th Cir. 1995).

[10]*Id.* at 154–55.

Chapter 11

NATIONAL ORIGIN AND CITIZENSHIP

I. Introduction

National origin discrimination claims continue to follow the model established in other discrimination cases. Cases are brought under theories of disparate treatment[1] and adverse impact.[2] National origin discrimination claims continue to arise from employment decisions affecting a wide variety of terms and conditions of employment including hiring,[3] academic tenure,[4]

---

[1] de la Cruz v. New York City Human Resources Admin. Dep't, 82 F.3d 16, 21–23, 70 FEP 893 (2d Cir. 1996) (in disparate treatment national origin discrimination claim, transfer of Puerto Rican plaintiff because of language difficulties found not pretextual); Roxas v. Presentation College, 90 F.3d 310, 316–18, 71 FEP 609 (8th Cir. 1996) (disparate treatment challenge to denial of sabbatical to Filipino priest unsuccessful due to plaintiff's failure to show college's proffered reasons were pretext for unlawful discrimination); Randle v. City of Aurora, 69 F.3d 441, 453–54, 69 FEP 489 (10th Cir. 1995) (genuine issues of material fact regarding whether Filipino plaintiff was qualified for promotion and whether city's proffered reason for not selecting plaintiff was pretextual warranted reversal of summary judgment).

[2] Vitug v. Multistate Tax Comm'n, 88 F.3d 506, 513–14, 71 FEP 1445 (7th Cir. 1996) (plaintiff failed to establish a prima facie case of disparate impact national origin discrimination because he failed to show that challenged hiring practices had an adverse impact on protected group).

[3] Sandhu v. Commonwealth of Va., 874 F. Supp. 122, 127 (E.D. Va.) (plaintiff failed to carry burden of showing employer's legitimate reason for not hiring plaintiff was pretext for national origin discrimination), aff'd, 68 F.3d 461 (4th Cir. 1995).

[4] Jimenez v. Mary Washington College, 57 F.3d 369, 383–84, 67 FEP 1867 (4th Cir.) (West Indian former professor failed to establish that college's decision to give him a terminal contract rather than keeping him in a tenure-track position was pretext for national origin discrimination), cert. denied, 116 S. Ct. 380 (1995); Javetz v. Board of Control, 903 F. Supp. 1181, 1188–90 (W.D. Mich. 1995) (Israeli professor failed to establish that university's denial of tenure was due to her national origin, religion, or sex).

medical staff privileges,[5] promotion,[6] discipline,[7] and discharge.[8]

II. Sources of Protection

A. Title VII

1. Defining "National Origin"

Courts continue to hold that discrimination on the basis of association with a person of a specific national origin violates Title VII's prohibition against national origin discrimination.[9]

2. National Origin Versus Citizenship

b. Title VII's Lack of Protection Against Citizenship Discrimination. Courts continue to hold that discrimination on the basis of citizenship does not violate Title VII.[10]

---

[5]Muzquiz v. W.A. Foote Mem'l Hosp., Inc., 70 F.3d 422, 427–28, 69 FEP 540 (6th Cir. 1995) (physician who sued hospital for national origin and age discrimination due to the denial of his application for invasive cardiology privileges unsuccessful in jury trial).

[6]Vitug v. Multistate Tax Comm'n, 88 F.3d 506, 515–16, 71 FEP 1445 (7th Cir. 1996) (Filipino employee failed to establish that he was intentionally passed over for promotion because of his national origin).

[7]Devera v. Adams, 874 F. Supp. 17, 22, 67 FEP 102 (D.D.C. 1995) (plaintiff's claim that he was disciplined because of his Filipino national origin rejected).

[8]Long v. Eastfield College, 88 F.3d 300, 308, 71 FEP 750 (5th Cir. 1996) (reversing district court order granting summary judgment to employer on plaintiff's discriminatory and retaliatory discharge claim, finding factual issues warranting trial); Park v. Washington Metro. Area Transit Auth., 892 F. Supp. 5, 10 (D.D.C. 1995) (Asian-American employee failed to prove discriminatory discharge claim because he could not show that superintendent who made decision did not reasonably believe that employee struck his supervisor).

[9]Chandler v. Fast Lane, Inc., 868 F. Supp. 1138, 1143–44, 66 FEP 675 (E.D. Ark. 1994) (white employee who alleged that she was discriminated against for refusing to enforce employer's discriminatory practices against African-Americans stated a cause of action under Title VII for interference with her right of association, as well as for retaliation).

[10]Weeks v. Samsung Heavy Indus. Co., 933 F. Supp. 711, 713, 71 FEP 920 (N.D. Ill. 1996) (treaty provision allowing Korea and United States to favor their own citizens when filling executive positions did not conflict with Title VII). *See also* Cheung v. Merrill Lynch, Pierce, Fenner & Smith, Inc., 913 F. Supp. 248, 251–52 (S.D.N.Y. 1996) (the New York Civil Rights law does not extend to claims of discrimination based on citizenship).

B. The Fourteenth Amendment and the 1871 Civil Rights Act

Courts continue to apply traditional rules of liability to suits against political subdivisions of states alleging national origin discrimination.[11]

C. The 1866 Civil Rights Act

While claims based on racial discrimination are actionable, courts continue to reject claims based solely on the plaintiff's place of birth.[12]

D. The Immigration Reform and Control Act of 1986 (IRCA)

2. *Administrative Enforcement of, and Exhaustion for, Charges of Discrimination Brought Under IRCA*

a. Subpoenas. The Eleventh Circuit has held that the Special Counsel of Immigration Related Unfair Employment Practices has the authority to issue an administrative subpoena to the employer for evidence in the course of an investigation.[13]

---

[11] *See, e.g.,* Randle v. City of Aurora, 69 F.3d 441, 69 FEP 489 (10th Cir. 1995) (court held that municipal employee alleging race and national origin discrimination failed to show that city maintained a custom of discriminatory employment practices, but found disputed issue as to whether city officials were "final policy makers" so as to impute potential liability to the city if plaintiff ultimately prevailed on discrimination claim).

[12] Bisciglia v. Kenosha Unified Sch. Dist., 45 F.3d 223, 229 (7th Cir. 1995) (Italian-American school superintendent should have been allowed leave to amend his complaint to include the assertion of a § 1981 claim based on ethnic discrimination); Yusuf v. Vassar College, 35 F.3d 709, 714 (2d Cir. 1994) (foreign student's § 1981 claim against private college alleging racial discrimination was too conclusory to withstand motion to dismiss); Al-Wardi v. Command Airways/American Eagle, 39 F.3d 1166 (1st Cir. 1994) (full text available at 1994 U.S. App. LEXIS 29944 (Oct. 25, 1994)) (commercial pilot did not allege discrimination based on his being Arab; rather his claim was based on his place of origin (Iraq), which is not covered by § 1981).

[13] United States v. Florida Azalea Specialists, 19 F.3d 620, 623, 64 FEP 769 (11th Cir. 1994) (Special Counsel's authority to obtain evidence in course of investigation and to compel production of such evidence by subpoena was clear from the face of the statute; information requested was specific and relevant to the investigation of charge alleging that employer discriminated against individual by refusing to hire her because of her national origin).

b. Sovereign Immunity. The United States has been held immune from an employer's claims for attorney's fees in a case where the employer prevailed in an unfair immigration-related employment practice claim initiated by the Special Counsel, rather than by an individual.[14]

Furthermore, the Tenth Circuit has held that the United States, when acting as an employer, is not subject to suit under IRCA.[15] The court held that a claim against a federal teaching hospital was barred because IRCA does not contain explicit and unambiguous language waiving sovereign immunity.[16] Likewise, the court held that a state university was immune from suit because the state had not waived its Eleventh Amendment immunity, and the statutory language of IRCA did not evince a clear intent by Congress to abrogate the Eleventh Amendment and permit suits against state governments.[17]

III. Language and Accent

A. Fluency Requirements

Job qualifications that require the ability to speak English fluently continue to be challenged. An emerging type of fluency requirement generating litigation involves requiring Spanish-speaking employees to utilize their language skill as an integral part of their employment.[18] Plaintiffs in these cases assert that they are required to do more work than their co-workers who speak only English.[19]

B. English-Only Rules

The controversial issue of whether an employer can require bilingual employees to speak only English while at work still faces

---

[14] General Dynamics Corp. v. U.S., 49 F.3d 1384, 1385 (9th Cir. 1995).
[15] Hensel v. Office of Chief Admin. Hearing Officer, 38 F.3d 505, 509, 66 FEP 58 (10th Cir. 1994).
[16] Id.
[17] Id. at 508.
[18] Morales v. Human Rights Div., 878 F. Supp. 653, 656, 67 FEP 531 (S.D.N.Y. 1995) (employer's practice of frequently utilizing the Spanish-speaking abilities of bilingual employees was not discriminatory).
[19] Id. at 656–57.

the courts. A recent Ninth Circuit case, *Yniguez v. Arizonans for Official English*,[20] dealt with the issue of whether a state government employer may impose an English-only requirement on employees. The decision has since been vacated on grounds of mootness by the Supreme Court, so it is not citable authority; however, the court's reasoning may still be instructive. In the *Yniguez* decision, the Ninth Circuit, sitting en banc, rejected an amendment to the Arizona Constitution making English the official language of the state that required government officials and employees to conduct government business only in English.[21] State employees who failed to obey the English-only provision were vulnerable to sanctions.[22] The plaintiff, a government employee at the time, initiated an action seeking a declaration that the amendment violated the First and Fourteenth Amendments, as well as civil rights laws.[23] The district court construed the plain language of the amendment as broadly prohibiting all government officials and employees from speaking languages other than English in performing their official duties, except as permitted pursuant to the provision's narrow exceptions.[24] Consequently, the district court ruled that the amendment was unconstitutionally overbroad on its face and invalid in its entirety.[25] The Ninth Circuit, following much of the reasoning

---

[20]Yniguez v. Arizonans for Official English, 69 F.3d 920 (9th Cir. 1995), *vacated, remanded*, 117 S. Ct. 1309 (1997).

[21]*Id.* at 924.

[22]*Id.* at 925.

[23]*Id.*

[24]*Id.* at 929. Employees in all political subdivisions of the state were permitted to speak in a language other than English under the following circumstances:
    (a) to assist students who are not proficient in the English language, to the extent necessary to comply with federal law, by giving educational instruction in a language other than English to provide as rapid as possible a transition into English.
    (b) to comply with other federal laws.
    (c) to teach a student a foreign language as part of a required or voluntary educational curriculum.
    (d) to protect public health or safety.
    (e) to protect the rights of criminal defendants or victims of crime.
A.R.S. CONST. Art. 28 § 3 (2)(a–e)(1996).

[25]*Id.* at 925. The court construed the provision as designed to achieve the specific result of prohibiting the use in all oral and written communications of all words and phrases in any language other than English by persons connected with the government. *Id* at 926. The court further stated there is no fair reading of the article that would permit some of its language to be divorced from this overriding objective. *Id.* at 929.

of the district court, likewise ruled that the amendment was not a valid regulation of the speech of public employees and was unconstitutionally overbroad.[26] The Supreme Court granted certiorari but declined to address the merits of the English-only rule since the plaintiff had by that time resigned from state government employment in order to accept a job in the private sector.[27]

English-only rules in the workplace are permissible, however, if an employer can establish a business necessity for the practice.[28] Frequently, employers request that employees refrain from speaking languages other than English in the workplace to promote productivity and efficiency.[29]

---

[26]*Id.* at 931, 942. The Ninth Circuit found that "the measure inhibits rather than advances the state's interest in the efficient and effective performance of its duties. . . . [The] direct effect of the provision is not only to restrict the rights of all state and local government servants in Arizona, but also to severely impair the free speech interests of a portion of the populace they serve." *Id.* at 946–47. The court also noted that the adverse impact of the amendment was especially egregious "because it is not uniformly spread over the population, but falls almost entirely upon Hispanics and other national origin minorities." *Id.* at 947. Consequently, the court stated that restrictions on speech must be examined with particular care when the effects concern groups in society differently. "Since language is a close and meaningful proxy for national origin, restrictions on the use of languages may mask discrimination against specific national origin groups or, more generally, conceal nativist sentiment." *Id.* at 947–48.

[27]117 S. Ct. 1055, 1997 U.S. LEXIS 1455 at *52. The Court ordered that both the district court and the Ninth Circuit decisions be vacated on the grounds of mootness because the lower federal courts should have deferred to the Arizona Supreme Court, through certification procedures, on the issue of the proper interpretation of the Arizona constitutional amendment, since it involved a novel and important issue of state law. *Id.* at *54–55, 58–66. In a state court case also dealing with the validity of the Arizona constitutional amendment, *Ruiz v. Hull,* 1998 Ariz. LEXIS 34, 268 Ariz. Adv. Rep. 3 (April 28, 1998), the Arizona Supreme Court (which had earlier stayed proceedings pending the outcome of the U.S. Supreme Court decision in *Yniquez,* also held that the English-only requirement violated both the First and Fourteenth Amendments by impermissibly burdening speech, since the provision was not narrowly tailored to serve the state interest in promoting English as a common language).

[28]Long v. First Union Corp. of Va., 894 F. Supp. 933, 940, 68 FEP 917 (E.D. Va. 1995) (holding that a legitimate business reason for an English-only policy provides a defense to a disparate impact claim and that denying bilingual employees the opportunity to speak Spanish on the job is not a violation of Title VII because nothing in Title VII protects or provides that employees have a right to speak their native tongue on the job).

[29]Hernandez v. Kansas, 1994 U.S. Dist. LEXIS 18967, 1994 WL 725092 *4, 66 FEP 1552 (D. Kan. 1994) (employer requested that employees not engage a fellow co-worker in extended conversations in Spanish as an attempt to keep the co-worker from wasting time and distracting other employees).

C. Accents

Courts have rejected discrimination claims based on accent where the employee's poor communication skills interfered with the performance of duties essential to the position.[30] Also, a plaintiff must prove that a nexus exists between the employer's alleged discriminatory actions and the plaintiff's accent.[31]

VI. EXCEPTIONS

B. Bona Fide Occupational Qualification

Some courts have held that U.S. incorporated subsidiaries of foreign companies have the burden of proving that national origin is a bona fide occupational qualification for the position in question in order to avoid liability under Title VII.[32]

C. Treaty Obligations

A friendship, commerce, and navigation (FCN) treaty generally allows a foreign company with operations in the United States to give preference to its own country's citizens for employment in executive positions (as well as other enumerated types of positions

---

[30]Arzate v. City of Topeka, 884 F. Supp. 1494, 1500–01, 72 FEP 681 (D. Kan. 1995) (employer had legitimate nondiscriminatory reason for not promoting Hispanic employee who had difficulty with English because he lacked the ability to communicate with fellow employees and the public).

[31]Liberman v. Brady, 926 F. Supp. 1197, 1211–12, 73 FEP 695 (E.D.N.Y 1996) (former IRS employee proved that his employer had a "mixed motive" when terminating him; however, employer established that it had valid, nondiscriminatory reasons for failing to promote the employee and for terminating him for reasons other than his accent); Cecilio v. Allstate Ins. Co., 908 F. Supp. 519, 531, 70 FEP 971 (E.D. Ill. 1995) (Filipino employee failed to prove requisite nexus between her supervisor's allegedly mimicking her accent and speaking slowly to her, so as to imply that she was "an Asian foreigner who could not understand or speak English," and her termination).

[32]Shane v. The Tokai Bank, Ltd., 1997 U.S. Dist. LEXIS 16000 (S.D.N.Y. 1997) (defendant employer not entitled to protection of FCN treaty because no evidence that Japanese national origin was a bona fide occupational qualification for the position in question); Robins v. Max Mara, USA, Inc., 923 F. Supp. 460, 471–72, 72 FEP 335 (S.D.N.Y. 1996) (explaining that defendant was not shielded by FCN treaty because he presented no evidence that Italian national origin was a bona fide occupational qualification for position that plaintiff held).

covered by the individual treaty). A foreign citizen who enters the United States with an E-1 visa is deemed an "executive" for purposes of an FCN treaty because such visas are "granted exclusively to foreign employees who perform duties of a supervisory or executive character."[33]

In *Papaila v. Uniden American Corp.*,[34] the Fifth Circuit followed *Fortino v. Quasar Co.*[35] and explained that the defendant employer's parent company dictated the discriminatory conduct because the Japanese citizens who were favored were hired in Japan by the parent company; their salaries, wages, benefits, and evaluations were controlled by the parent; and their job was to manage shareholder interests.[36] Therefore, the domestic subsidiary was permitted to assert the FCN treaty rights of its Japanese parent corporation and to favor Japanese citizens for executive positions without violating Title VII or other U.S. antidiscrimination laws.[37]

---

[33]Weeks v. Samsung Heavy Indus. Co., 933 F. Supp. 711, 713, 71 FEP 920 (N.D. Ill. 1996) (finding that Korean citizen who replaced plaintiff as national sales manager held an executive position), quoting MacNamara v. Korean Airlines, 863 F.2d 1135, 1141–42 , 48 FEP 980 (3d Cir. 1988), *cert. denied,* 493 U.S. 944, 51 FEP 112 (1989).
[34]51 F.3d 54, 67 FEP 993 (5th Cir.), *cert. denied,* 116 S. Ct. 187 (1995).
[35]950 F.2d 389, 57 FEP 712 (7th Cir. 1991).
[36]*Papaila,* 51 F.3d at 55 n.1.
[37]*Id.*

Chapter 12

NATIVE AMERICANS

III. Liability of Indian Tribes

A. Section 701(b) Exemption

In interpreting the exemption of Indian tribes from the term "employer" in § 701(b) of Title VII, courts have drawn a distinction between Native American tribes functioning as political entities, which are entitled to the exemption, and corporations owned by tribes, which generally are not entitled to the exemption.[1]

In *Barker v. Menominee Nation Casino*,[2] however, the court dismissed wrongful termination claims (not brought pursuant to Title VII) against the Menominee Nation Casino and the Menominee Tribal Gaming Commission on the ground that they, like the tribe, were immune from suit in federal court on the basis of sovereign immunity.[3] Unlike the employer in *Myrick v. Devils Lake Sioux Manufacturing Corp.*, 51 percent of which was owned by a Native American tribe and which was incorporated under the laws of the state of North Dakota,[4] "the [Menominee Nation] Casino is operated by the [Menominee Tribal Gaming] Commission; the

---

[1] *Compare* Dille v. Council of Energy Resource Tribes, 801 F.2d 373, 41 FEP 1345 (10th Cir. 1986) (council of 39 tribes formed for the purpose of managing tribes' energy resources was exempt from suit under § 701(b)) *with* Myrick v. Devils Lake Sioux Mfg. Corp., 718 F. Supp. 753, 50 FEP 517 (D.N.D. 1989) (manufacturing corporation that was 51% owned by Native American tribe was not exempt under § 701(b) from the definition of "employer" in Title VII).

[2] 897 F. Supp. 389 (E.D. Wis. 1995).

[3] *Id.* at 393–94. Sovereign immunity may be limited by a clear waiver on the part of the sovereign nation as to certain activities or transactions. *See, e.g.,* Altheimer & Gray v. Sioux Mfg. Corp., 983 F.2d 803, 812 (7th Cir.), *cert. denied*, 510 U.S. 1019 (1993), in which a corporation wholly owned by an Indian tribe entered into a written agreement expressly stating that the tribe would "waive all sovereign immunity in regards to all contractual disputes." The corporation's charter also contained a waiver of sovereign immunity with respect to written contracts.

[4] 718 F. Supp. 753, 50 FEP 517.

Commission is a wholly-owned, chartered business venture of the Menominee Indian Tribe, and was created pursuant to ordinance adopted by the Legislature under the provisions of the Constitution and By-Laws of the Menominee Indian Nation."[5] Therefore, the court held that the casino and the Tribal Gaming Commission were tribal enterprises subject to the same common law immunity as enjoyed by the tribe itself.[6]

B. Exemption From Other Antidiscrimination Statutes

In *Krempel v. Prairie Island Indian Community*,[7] a sexual harassment case brought against an Indian tribe under the Minnesota Human Rights Act,[8] the court granted a motion to dismiss where plaintiff had failed to exhaust his tribal court remedies by seeking relief in the newly established tribal court. The court stated:

> [T]he Court is inclined to stay its hand in favor of the fledgling Prairie Island tribal court. In this Court's view, ". . . the orderly administration of justice in the federal court will be served by allowing a full record to be developed in the Tribal Court before either the merits or any question concerning appropriate relief is addressed."[9]

---

[5] 897 F. Supp. at 391 n.1.

[6] Although § 701(b) was not at issue in *Barker* because the plaintiff's claim was not brought under Title VII, the court's reliance on the legal basis for the establishment of the casino and Tribal Gaming Commission is consistent with the rationale of Dille v. Council of Energy Resource Tribes, 801 F.2d 373, 41 FEP 1345 (10th Cir. 1986) and Myrick v. Devils Lake Sioux Mfg. Corp., 718 F. Supp. 753, 50 FEP 517 (D.N.D. 1989).

[7] 888 F. Supp. 106, 68 FEP 215 (D. Minn. 1995).

[8] MINN. STAT. § 363.03.

[9] 888 F. Supp at 108, 68 FEP at 217, quoting National Farmers Union Ins. Cos. v. Crow Tribe of Indians, 471 U.S. 845, 856 (1985).

CHAPTER 13

SEX

I. BONA FIDE OCCUPATIONAL QUALIFICATION (BFOQ)

B. Required Elements of the BFOQ Defense

1. Direct Relationship Between Sex and Ability to Perform the Job

The Third Circuit has held that an employer need not produce objective, empirical evidence to establish that sex is a necessary requirement for a particular job. The court in *Healey v. Southwood Psychiatric Hospital*[1] concluded that the employer may use "common sense and deference to experts in the field" to establish a "basis in fact" for its belief. In that case, a psychiatric hospital for emotionally disturbed and sexually abused adolescents and children of both sexes established through expert opinion that therapeutic concerns mandated the presence of both male and female health care specialists on all shifts.

3. No Reasonable Alternative

One federal circuit has relaxed the requirement that employers look for reasonable alternatives to gender exclusion in cases involving gender-specific prison job assignments that favor women. In *Tharp v. Iowa Department of Corrections*,[2] the Eighth Circuit eschewed BFOQ analysis altogether and applied a Title VII balancing test to a policy of assigning only female residential advisors to the women's unit of a mixed-gender minimum security prison: "a prison employer's reasonable gender-based job assignment policy, particularly a policy that is favorable to the protected class of women employees, will be upheld if it imposes only a

---

[1] 78 F.3d 128, 132, 70 FEP 439 (3d Cir. 1996).
[2] 68 F.3d 223, 69 FEP 42 (8th Cir. 1995), *cert. denied,* 116 S. Ct. 1420 (1996).

'minimal restriction' on other employees."[3] The court upheld the policy in that case because it had been implemented to further legitimate penological and privacy concerns and worked only a minimal restriction on the employment of the male plaintiffs, who had ample other opportunities for employment and promotion within the prison.

C. The Theories of BFOQ

2. Privacy

Privacy concerns sufficient to support a BFOQ may include, in the appropriate case, not only the prevention of observation or touching by members of the opposite sex, but the availability of same-sex specialists for necessary private conversation. The court in *Healey v. Southwood Psychiatric Hospital*[4] allowed a policy that required both male and female health care specialists on all shifts at a psychiatric hospital for emotionally disturbed and sexually abused adolescents and children in part because "adolescent patients have hygiene, menstrual, and sexuality concerns which are discussed more freely with a staff member of the same sex."

There is some indication that privacy concerns sufficient to support a BFOQ in a prison setting, where privacy is most often invoked as a justification for sex-based employment policies, need not rise to the level of a constitutional interest. The director of the Nevada Department of Prisons argued in *Carl v. Angelone*[5] that his policy of assigning only female officers to women's correctional facilities was a BFOQ because the alternative—allowing male officers to conduct body searches of female prisoners—would constitute cruel and unusual punishment. The district court rejected this BFOQ defense because it found no Eighth Amendment violation under the facts of the case, but the court explained that the policy might have been justified as a BFOQ on more general grounds of privacy or rehabilitation, which the defendant had not argued.[6]

---

[3]*Id.* at 226 (quoting Timm v. Gunter, 917 F.2d 1093, 1102 n.13 (8th Cir. 1990), *cert. denied,* 501 U.S. 1209 (1991)).
[4]78 F.3d 128, 133, 70 FEP 439 (3d Cir. 1996).
[5]883 F. Supp. 1433 (D. Nev. 1995).
[6]*Id.* at 1442 n.3.

4. Role Models

Role modeling may justify sex-based employment practices where the need for role models goes to the essence of the employer's business. Expert opinion in *Healey v. Southwood Psychiatric Hospital*[7] established that the presence of health care specialists of both sexes was necessary at all times at a psychiatric hospital for adolescents and children whose treatment required the presence of parental figures. Moreover, many of the children had been sexually abused and could be expected to disclose their problems more easily to a member of one sex or the other. This testimony was sufficient to establish a BFOQ.[8]

II. SENIORITY SYSTEMS AND LINES OF PROGRESSION

A. The Intentional Discrimination Requirement

Courts have continued to recognize that only intentionally discriminatory seniority systems violate Title VII.[9]

B. What Constitutes a "Seniority System"?

The Eleventh Circuit held in *Irby v. Bittick*,[10] an Equal Pay Act (EPA) case, that "a seniority system, like a merit system, should be uniformly enforced and written" and that in order to rely on the EPA's "seniority system" affirmative defense, an employer "must be able to identify standards for measuring seniority which are systematically observed and applied."[11] In that case, the employer claimed that under its system, pay for those of the same rank was based solely on year of hire, but the evidence showed that employees with the same year of hire and rank were paid differently.

---

[7]78 F.3d 128, 70 FEP 439 (3d Cir. 1996).
[8]*Id.* at 133.
[9]*See* Kennedy v. Chemical Waste Management, Inc., 79 F.3d 49, 51 (7th Cir. 1996) (only intentionally discriminatory seniority systems can be challenged under Title VII); *see also* Fontelroy v. Day & Zimmermann, Inc., 1995 WL 530666, *at 3 (D. Kan. Sept. 7, 1995) (whether employer's seniority system was fairest or best it could be is not the inquiry; critical question is whether employer enacted system with discriminatory intent), *aff'd,* 83 F.3d 431 (10th Cir. 1996).
[10]44 F.3d 949, 67 FEP 70 (11th Cir. 1995) (citations omitted).
[11]*Id.* at 954.

The court therefore held that the employer did not have " 'a seniority system' under the EPA justifying a variance in salary between employees of the opposite sex performing the same work."[12]

III. SEX DISCRIMINATION IN EXECUTIVE AND PROFESSIONAL EMPLOYMENT

A. The Glass Ceiling

The Glass Ceiling Commission issued its report in two parts in 1995. In March, the Commission issued the results of its fact finding.[13] That report concluded, not surprisingly, that a glass ceiling does exist at the highest levels of business. The most telling fact was that 95 to 97 percent of senior managers in Fortune 1000 industrial and Fortune 500 companies are male. While the data indicated that the situation is improving, and many of the women in corporate America to whom the Commission spoke were cautiously optimistic, the perception among these women was that the problem had not been solved. The Commission found numerous structural impediments to the advancement of women and minorities in business, including inadequate outreach and recruitment practices, lack of mentoring, and the placement of women in positions within corporations where they are less likely to gain the necessary experience and contacts for advancement.

The Commission issued its recommendations in November 1995.[14] These included a series of goals for both business and government. The Commission called for CEO commitment to diversity, the increased use of affirmative action, the preparation of minorities and women for senior positions, and family-friendly work policies. The Commission called on the government to strengthen enforcement of antidiscrimination laws, improve data collection, and increase disclosure of corporate diversity data, particularly regarding the most senior corporate positions.

---

[12]*Id.* at 954–55.

[13]THE FEDERAL GLASS CEILING COMMISSION, GOOD FOR BUSINESS: MAKING FULL USE OF THE NATION'S HUMAN CAPITAL (Mar. 1995).

[14]THE FEDERAL GLASS CEILING COMMISSION, A SOLID INVESTMENT: MAKING FULL USE OF THE NATION'S HUMAN CAPITAL (Nov. 1995).

Although the Commission's reports generally were well received, some groups questioned the Commission's methodology as well as its conclusion that a glass ceiling exists that prevents the advancement of women in executive and professional employment. Shortly after publication of the Commission's reports, the Pacific Research Institute and the Independent Women's Forum issued studies with nearly identical conclusions.[15] Both studies criticized the Commission for relying too heavily on a comparison between the number of women at the top levels of corporate America and their numbers in the general population. They argued that the Commission did not give adequate consideration to the qualified labor pool (which for senior management positions is typically an MBA and 25 years of work experience) and the effect of women's choices. As women have been working in significant numbers for only about 30 years, these critics would not expect many women to have reached the top corporate ranks. In fact, their number in these ranks has grown appreciably in recent years. These studies criticized the Commission also for focusing on the small portion of the economy represented by the Fortune 1000 companies and ignoring women's gains in starting their own businesses.

C. Second-Guessing the Employer

The district court in *Fisher v. Vassar College*[16] rejected the college's proffered tenure criteria as too vague, and proceeded to compare the plaintiff's qualifications under each of the alleged criteria to that of other academics not denied tenure, finding that the college's purported justification for denying tenure to Fisher was pretextual. On appeal, the college argued that the district court had paid insufficient deference to the college's authority to set its own academic standards. The Second Circuit disagreed, concluding that tenure standards are by their nature unquantifiable and therefore properly the subject of the type of comparative analysis

---

[15]PACIFIC RESEARCH INSTITUTE, FREE MARKETS, FREE CHOICES: WOMEN IN THE WORKFORCE (Dec. 1995); DIANA FURCHTGOTT-ROTH & CHRISTINE SOLBA, INDEPENDENT WOMEN'S FORUM, WOMEN'S FIGURES: THE ECONOMIC PROGRESS OF WOMEN IN AMERICA (1996).

[16]852 F. Supp. 1193, 1228, 64 FEP 1346 (S.D.N.Y. 1994).

undertaken by the district court.[17] The Second Circuit found no error in the district court's conclusion that the college's stated justification for its decision was pretextual, but nonetheless reversed the district court's finding of sex discrimination. The court held that the evidence would support only the conclusion that Fisher was denied tenure because she had taken off a considerable period of time to raise her children. There was no evidence that men who took comparable periods of time away from their careers were not treated similarly.[18]

IV. FRINGE BENEFITS

B. Retirement Plans

1. Contributions and Benefits

The district court in *Carter v. American Telephone & Telegraph Co.*[19] held that an employer violated Title VII in how it calculated service credits under an early retirement plan by giving employees credit for time spent on temporary disability leave but not crediting women for pregnancy leave taken prior to enactment of the PDA.

D. Insurance, Medical, and Disability Plans

One law review article has suggested that the exclusion of certain treatment for breast cancer from coverage under employer-provided health insurance plans may discriminate against women and therefore violate Title VII.[20] There does not appear to be any recent Title VII case law on this issue, although the issue has arisen in the ADA context.[21]

---

[17]Fisher v. Vassar College, 70 F.3d 1420, 1435, 70 FEP 1155 (2d Cir. 1995).
[18]*Id.* at 1448.
[19]870 F. Supp. 1438, 1444 (S.D. Ohio 1994).
[20]Laurie Dechery, *Preferential Treatment or Discriminatory Standards: Do Employer-provided Insurance Plans Violate Title VII When They Exclude Treatment for Breast Cancer?*, 80 MINN. L. REV. 945, 947 (1996).
[21]*See, e.g.,* Henderson v. Bodine Aluminum, Inc., 70 F.3d 958, 960 (8th Cir. 1995) (directing entry of preliminary injunction requiring health care provider to underwrite the cost of high-dose chemotherapy program for breast cancer).

V. Pregnancy, Childbirth, and Parenting

A. General Theory

2. The Pregnancy Discrimination Act

The PDA's prohibition of discrimination because of "pregnancy, childbirth or related medical conditions" has been held to cover abortion. In *Turic v. Holland Hospitality, Inc.*,[22] the Sixth Circuit affirmed the position of the EEOC, and a few courts, that the PDA prohibits an employer from discriminating against a female employee because she has exercised her right to have an abortion.

Courts have reached different conclusions on whether infertility is a medical condition related to pregnancy or childbirth, and thus covered by the PDA. The Eighth Circuit has held that the PDA's "other related conditions" provision does not include infertility. In *Krauel v. Iowa Methodist Medical Center*,[23] the court held that infertility was simply not analogous to "pregnancy" or "childbirth." The court noted further that infertility is not a gender-specific condition, while pregnancy and childbirth affect women only. On the other hand, one district court has taken exactly the opposite point of view.[24]

Courts continue to hold that the PDA, under a disparate treatment theory, does not prohibit employment decisions based on employee conduct caused by or related to pregnancy. In *Armstrong v. Flowers Hospital, Inc.*,[25] the Eleventh Circuit affirmed the trial court's ruling that the discharge of a pregnant home health care nurse was proper after she refused to treat a patient who was HIV-positive, thereby violating a hospital policy requiring nurses to treat *all* assigned patients.

---

[22]85 F.3d 1211, 1213–14, 71 FEP 28 (6th Cir. 1996) (the plain language of Title VII, the legislative history, and the EEOC guidelines preclude workplace discrimination against a female employee because she has considered having an abortion).

[23]95 F.3d 674, 679–80, 71 FEP 1326 (8th Cir. 1996).

[24]Pacourek v. Inland Steel Co., 858 F. Supp. 1393, 1402–03, 65 FEP 758 (N.D. Ill. 1994) (holding that Title VII covers infertility as a pregnancy-related medical condition).

[25]33 F.3d 1308, 1314–16, 65 FEP 1742 (11th Cir. 1994).

C. Right to Voluntary Leave

1. Title VII

   b. *Parenting Leave.* The district court in *Pearlstein v. Staten Island University Hospital*[26] held that a female employee on leave to adopt a child is not protected by the PDA. Title VII simply does not protect an employee who takes child-care leave unrelated to pregnancy disability.[27]

   c. *Reinstatement After Leave.* Courts continue to uphold the well-settled principle that an employee attempting to return to work following a pregnancy leave must be treated as any other employee returning from voluntary or disability leave.[28]

VI. SEX PLUS

B. Sex Plus Marriage and Family

Courts continue to hold that Title VII prohibits distinctions based on marital or family status only if the requirements are applied differently to males as compared to females. In *Fisher v. Vassar College,*[29] the Second Circuit held that a sex-plus-marriage claim may not rest solely on evidence that married women were treated

---

[26] 886 F. Supp. 260, 70 FEP 206, 209 n.5 (E.D.N.Y. 1995).

[27] *Id. See also* Mayorga v. Donnelley Marketing, 70 FEP 670 (N.D. Ill. 1996) (former employee did not make out a prima facie case of pregnancy discrimination where, among other performance deficiencies, she missed substantial hours because she could not arrange for child care). Note that leaves for child adoption are mandated by the Family and Medical Leave Act.

[28] *See* Piraino v. International Orientation Resources, Inc., 84 F.3d 270, 70 FEP 1739 (7th Cir. 1996) (female employee stated pregnancy discrimination claim when employer dismissed her after she took maternity leave, where employer applied ad hoc leave policy to disfavor her pregnancy leave); Quaratino v. Tiffany & Co., 71 F.3d 58, 64–65, 69 FEP 507 (2d Cir. 1995) (summary judgment improperly granted to employer who eliminated employee's position while she was on maternity leave); Farhat v. Sally Beauty Co., 65 FEP 1516 (E.D. Mo. 1994) (discharged employee was treated differently from similarly situated nonpregnant employee after returning from second maternity leave). *But see* Smith v. F.W. Morse & Co., 76 F.3d 413, 421–23, 69 FEP 1687 (1st Cir. 1996) (discharge of employee while on pregnancy leave was not discriminatory where employer acquiring company discovered that employee's job was expendable, and decision was made for legitimate business reasons).

[29] 70 F.3d 1420, 1446–48, 70 FEP 1155 (2d Cir. 1995).

less favorably than single women. The Second Circuit reversed the district court's finding of sex-plus-marriage discrimination, citing a lack of evidence that married women were disadvantaged when compared to married men. The court went on to hold that a tenure policy that discriminates against employees who had taken long periods of leave to raise their children does not give rise to a sex-plus-family claim under Title VII absent evidence that women who took extended leaves were treated less favorably than men who had also taken long leaves.

In *Panis v. Mission Hills Bank*,[30] the Tenth Circuit held that an employment decision based on the identity or behavior of an employee's spouse is not actionable as sex-plus-marriage discrimination under Title VII. The court rejected the plaintiff's challenge to the defendant bank's decision to terminate her based on its concern that publicity surrounding her husband's indictment for embezzlement would undermine customer confidence. The court required that the plaintiff show some difference in treatment between the sexes before upholding a marriage-based sex discrimination claim under Title VII; in this case, the bank's board of directors had indicated that it would have similarly discharged a male employee whose wife had been indicted for embezzlement.

C. Sex Plus Race

In *Lam v. University of Hawaii*,[31] the Ninth Circuit held that the district court had erred in analyzing separately the race and sex discrimination claims of an Asian-American woman:

> As other courts have recognized, where two bases for discrimination exist, they cannot be neatly reduced to distinct components. Rather than aiding the decisional process, the attempt to bisect a person's identity at the intersection of race and gender often distorts or ignores the particular nature of their experiences. Like other subclasses under Title VII, Asian women are subject to a set of stereotypes and assumptions shared neither by Asian men nor by white women.[32]

---

[30] 60 F.3d 1486, 1490–91, 70 FEP 625 (10th Cir. 1995), *cert. denied*, 116 S. Ct. 1045 (1996).

[31] 40 F.3d 1551, 66 FEP 74 (9th Cir. 1994).

[32] *Id.* at 1562 (citations and footnote omitted). *See also* Anthony v. County of Sacramento, 898 F. Supp. 1435, 1445, 68 FEP 1837 (E.D. Cal. 1995) ("Where a woman of color alleges that she has been subject to discrimination on the combined bases of

Thus the court held that Asian-American women may be the targets of unlawful sex-plus-race discrimination under Title VII even if Asian-American men and white women were not similarly disadvantaged.

D. Sex Plus Appearance and Grooming Standards

The Second Circuit continues to subscribe to the view, as do most of the circuits, that employer policies requiring male employees to wear short hair do not violate Title VII.[33]

E. Sex Plus Age [New Topic]

Some courts have applied the reasoning used in "sex plus race" cases to conclude that older women are a protected subclass under Title VII. For example, in *Arnett v. Aspin*,[34] the plaintiff offered evidence that every woman ever selected for the position in question was under 40 and every male selected was over 40. She brought a sex-plus claim, alleging that the defendants required more of her than of male candidates: they required that she be under 40. In denying the employer's motion for summary judgment, the *Arnett* court reasoned that the Fifth Circuit's analysis of sex-plus-race claims in *Jefferies v. Harris Community Action Association*[35] applied to sex-plus-age cases as well. The court thus ruled that the plaintiff could survive summary judgment even when the defendant had not discriminated against all women.[36]

---

her race and gender, it is error for the court to analyze sex and race separately."). *Contra* DeGraffenreid v. General Motors Assembly Div., 413 F. Supp. 142, 145, 12 FEP 1627 (E.D. Mo. 1976) (holding that African-American women cannot state an actionable claim under Title VII when the employer did not disadvantage white women and black men), *aff'd in part, rev'd in part on other grounds*, 558 F.2d 480 (8th Cir. 1977).

[33]Tavora v. New York Mercantile Exch., 101 F.3d 907, 908, 72 FEP 979 (2d Cir. 1996), *cert. denied*, 117 S. Ct. 1821 (1997).

[34]846 F. Supp. 1234, 69 FEP 966 (E.D. Pa. 1994).

[35]615 F.2d 1025, 1032–34, 22 FEP 974 (5th Cir. 1980). *See* Section VI.C in the Main Edition for a discussion of *Jefferies*.

[36]846 F. Supp. at 1238–39. *See also* Good v. U.S. West Communications, Inc., 1995 WL 67672 (D. Or. Feb. 16, 1995) (recognizing an age-plus-sex claim under the ADEA and allowing the plaintiff to argue that she had been discriminated against due to the combination of her age and sex). *Contra* Thompson v. Mississippi State Personnel Bd., 674 F. Supp. 198, 203–04, 45 FEP 530 (N.D. Miss. 1987) ("[N]either [Title VII nor the ADEA] recognizes the subset of women over 40 as being protected from adverse treatment as opposed to men over 40.").

VII. Transsexuality

No court has held that a plaintiff may state a claim under Title VII based upon discrimination on account of transsexuality, but at least one court has refused to dismiss such claims under a local antidiscrimination law.[37]

VIII. Height, Weight, and Physical Agility Requirements

In *Novack v. Northwest Airlines, Inc.*,[38] the court upheld an airline's 5'2" minimum height requirement for flight attendants. The court held that although the height requirement had an adverse impact on women, the employer had proved that it was "manifestly related" to the job and thereby defeated the female flight attendants' disparate impact claim under the Minnesota Human Rights Act.[39]

---

[37]*See* Maffei v. Kolaeton Indus., Inc., 626 N.Y.S.2d 391, 395–96, 68 FEP 1039 (N.Y. Sup. Ct. 1995) (interpreting § 8-107(1) of the New York City Administrative Code (NYCAC), finding the opinions of "all federal courts that have considered the issue . . . unduly restrictive" and denying the defendant's motion to dismiss the plaintiff's claim of discrimination based on sex).

[38]525 N.W.2d 592, 598 (Minn. Ct. App. 1995) (minimum height requirement satisfied both *Wards Cove* and *Griggs* standards and therefore rebutted disparate impact claim).

[39]*Id.* at 598–99.

CHAPTER 14

SEXUAL ORIENTATION

I. TITLE VII

Same-gender sexual harassment claims arising under Title VII are actionable, unlike sexual orientation discrimination claims. In *Oncale v. Sundowner Offshore Services, Inc.*,[1] the Supreme Court conclusively resolved the split among the courts and held that same-sex sexual harassment is actionable under Title VII if it occurs "because of sex."[2] The Court noted, however, that Title VII's prohibition of sexual harassment "does not reach genuine but innocuous differences in the ways men and women routinely interact with members of the same sex and of the opposite sex."[3] Finally, the Court emphasized that in a same-sex harassment case based on a hostile environment theory, the plaintiff still must prove that "the conduct at issue was not merely tinged with offensive sexual connotations, but actually constituted 'discrimination . . . because of . . . sex.'"[4]

II. STATE STATUTES AND INITIATIVES

Some states continue to add sexual orientation to their protected categories for the purpose of their employment discrimination statutes.[5]

---

[1] 118 S. Ct. 998, 76 FEP 221.

[2] *Id.* at 1002.

[3] *Id.* at 1002–03. Additionally, the Court emphasized that the objective severity of any harassment must be viewed "from the perspective of a reasonable person in the plaintiff's position, considering 'all the circumstances.'" *Id.* at 1003, quoting Harris v. Forklift Sys., Inc., 510 U.S. 17, 23 (1993).

[4] *Id. See also* the discussion of *Oncale* at Chapter 20, Sections III.B.4.a and IV.B.1 of this supplement.

[5] *See, e.g.,* N.H. REV. STAT ANN. § 354-A; R.I. GEN. LAWS tit. 28, ch. 5, § 7; and ME. REV. STAT. ANN. tit. 5, § 4552, repealed by referendum vote, February 10, 1998. The 1995 Maine antigay rights initiative, however, was defeated by the voters (in a vote of 52–48%). *See* Lois R. Shea, *Analysts Cautious on Gay-Rights Loss,* BOSTON GLOBE, Feb. 12, 1998, at B1, B17.

In *Romer v. Evans*,[6] the Supreme Court invalidated Colorado's Amendment 2, an amendment to the state constitution prohibiting all state, local, legislative, and judicial protections of gay men and lesbians from discrimination, applying rational basis scrutiny.[7] Notwithstanding the *Romer* holding, the Sixth Circuit upheld an amendment to the Cincinnati city charter, which prohibits the city of Cincinnati from enacting any measure designed to protect individuals due to their sexual orientation.[8] Despite a remand from the United States Supreme Court in the wake of its *Romer* decision,[9] the same Sixth Circuit panel that rejected initial challenges to the amendment's constitutionality reinstated its original decision.[10]

III. Constitutional Issues and Federal Statutes Applicable to Public Employment

B. Due Process and Equal Protection

As discussed in Section II *supra*, the Supreme Court in *Romer v. Evans*[11] applied a rational basis test in striking down Colorado's amendment barring measures protecting homosexuals from discrimination.[12] Another recent case preliminarily applying a rational basis

---

[6]517 U.S. 620, 70 FEP 1180 (1996).

[7]*Id.* at 631–33. "Amendment 2 fails, indeed defies, even this conventional inquiry. First, the amendment has the peculiar property of imposing a broad and undifferentiated disability on a single named group, an exceptional and, as we shall explain, invalid form of legislation. Second, its sheer breadth is so discontinuous with the reasons offered for it that the amendment seems inexplicable by anything but animus toward the class that it affects; it lacks a rational relationship to legitimate state interests." *Id.*

[8]Equality Found. v. City of Cincinnati, 128 F.3d 289, 75 FEP 115 (1997), *reh'g denied*, 75 FEP 1763 (1998), *petition for writ of cert. filed*, 66 U.S.L.W. 3749 (May 4, 1998) (No. 97-1795).

[9]518 U.S. 1001, 71 FEP 64 (1996), *granting petition for writ of certiorari, vacating judgment, and remanding for further consideration in light of Romer v. Evans* 517 U.S. 620 (1996) (6–3 decision).

[10]128 F.3d 289, 300, 75 FEP 115, 123–24 (1997). The court found the Cincinnati Charter Amendment survived rational basis review, in "contradistinction" with *Romer*, because the Cincinnati "voters had clear, actual, and direct individual and collective interests in that measure, and in the potential costs savings and other contingent benefits which could result from that local law." *Id.*

[11]517 U.S. 620, 70 FEP 1180 (1996).

[12]*Id.* at 651–53, 70 FEP at 1186.

standard of review was *Tester v. City of New York*,[13] in which the court held that a former New York City police officer could state claims under the Equal Protection and Due Process Clauses for his alleged constructive discharge stemming from harassment by his fellow officers due to his sexual orientation.

C. First Amendment

In *Shahar v. Bowers*,[14] the Eleventh Circuit, en banc, upheld the withdrawal of an offer of employment by the Georgia Department of Law to a female attorney who had "married" another woman.

The Fourth Circuit has also denied First Amendment protection to employees based on issues touching on sexual orientation. In *Boring v. Buncombe County Board of Education*,[15] the court held that a high school teacher who was transferred in part for selecting a play with lesbian themes for performance by students could not state a claim for violation of her First Amendment rights. The court noted that the play was a part of the school curriculum and did not involve the employee speaking out as a citizen upon a matter of public concern.[16] Therefore, the employee's First Amendment rights were not infringed by the school principal's actions in objecting to the play's content, editing the play, and ultimately transferring the plaintiff.

IV. SPECIAL ISSUES REGARDING SERVICE IN THE ARMED FORCES

On appeal in the *Cammermeyer* case, the Ninth Circuit ruled that the government's appeal of the district court decision ordering reinstatement of the plaintiff and expungement of the records containing reference to her sexual orientation was moot.[17] The panel noted that the plaintiff had been reinstated and that the 1993 change in policy (to the "don't ask, don't tell" policy) had rescinded the regulation under which she had been discharged.[18]

---

[13]1997 U.S. Dist. LEXIS 1937, at *19–20 (S.D.N.Y. 1997).
[14]114 F.3d 1097, 1103 (11th Cir. 1997), *cert. denied*, 118 S. Ct. 693 (1998).
[15]136 F.3d 364, 367–68 (4th Cir. 1998).
[16]*Id.*
[17]Cammermeyer v. Perry, 97 F.3d 1235, 1237–38, 72 FEP 93 (9th Cir. 1996).
[18]*Id.*

Challenges to the new "don't ask, don't tell" policy have been largely unsuccessful. The policy has been attacked through use of both the First and Fifth Amendments. Courts have generally determined that the policy is subject to rational basis review under equal protection analysis.[19] Under rational basis review, government policies are presumed constitutional and the burden is on the challenger to negate every conceivable basis that might support the legislation.[20] In *Holmes v. California Army National Guard*,[21] the Ninth Circuit upheld the discharges of two service members. The panel accepted the constitutionality of the policy under rational basis scrutiny, noting that review of military policy is "especially deferential."[22] The court determined that the military had a legitimate interest in preventing homosexual conduct from occurring by presuming that self-identified homosexuals have a propensity to engage in such conduct, and that such presumption was rational.[23] This conclusion was bolstered by several federal appellate decisions considering this issue.[24] Courts have also concluded that the "don't ask, don't tell" policy is also sustainable against due process and free speech challenges.[25]

---

[19] *See, e.g.*, Holmes v. California Army Nat'l Guard, 124 F.3d 1126, 1133 (9th Cir. 1997); Richenberg v. Perry, 97 F.3d 256, 260–61 (8th Cir. 1996), *cert. denied*, 118 S. Ct. 45 (1997); Thomasson v. Perry, 80 F.3d 915, 928 (4th Cir.), *cert. denied*, 117 S. Ct. 358 (1996).

[20] *See* Heller v. Doe, 509 U.S. 312, 320 (1993).

[21] 124 F.3d 1126 (9th Cir. 1997).

[22] *Id.* at 1133.

[23] *Id.* at 1136.

[24] *E.g.*, Philips v. Perry, 106 F.3d 1420, 1429 (9th Cir. 1997) (finding portion of the current policy that requires discharge for *actual* homosexual conduct was constitutional, even though homosexual conduct at issue was off base and with non-military personnel); *Richenberg*, 97 F.3d at 262 (presumption that openly gay people will engage in homosexual conduct is rational means for the military to avoid expected problems); *Thomasson*, 80 F.3d at 927 (written statement of service member that he was gay without any offer of evidence to rebut the presumption of homosexual conduct is grounds for discharge); Able v. United States, 88 F.3d 1280, 1296–97, 71 FEP 419 (2d Cir. 1996) (deciding that the "presumption" theory was rational if the ban on conduct was constitutional); Selland v. Perry, 100 F.3d 950, 1996 U.S. App. LEXIS 29054 (4th Cir.) (denying appeal by lieutenant from decision upholding naval discharge based on his statement that he is gay), *cert. denied*, 117 S. Ct. 1691 (1996).

[25] *See, e.g.*, *Holmes*, 124 F.3d at 1136 (upheld discharges because they were for conduct, not for speech); *Philips*, 106 F.3d at 1430 (discharge permissible as it was based on homosexual activity, not because service member had merely talked about it); *Thomasson*, 80 F.3d at 931 (statute targets homosexual acts or propensity to engage in same; speech is permissibly used as evidence).

In *Able v. United States*,[26] the Second Circuit remanded a case for consideration of whether it violated equal protection for the government to treat homosexual conduct differently from heterosexual conduct in its military personnel policies. Ruling on remand, the district court found the policy in violation of the equal protection requirement of the Fifth Amendment because it imposed different rules on homosexual and heterosexual service members.[27] The district court determined that the policy's broad definition of a "homosexual act" would enable "the Armed Forces to dismiss someone who, for example, kisses or holds hands off base and in private or has done so before entering the service."[28] Finding that "[n]o such sanction is imposed on a heterosexual who, with the same purpose, does the same thing with someone of a different sex," the court held the policy was unconstitutionally discriminatory. The court found that the three government justifications for the policy—(1) fostering unit cohesion, (2) promoting the privacy of heterosexual service members, and (3) reducing sexual tensions—boiled down to catering to the presumed antigay prejudices of heterosexual service members.[29] Ultimately, the district court declared that the policy violates both the First and Fifth Amendments and enjoined its enforcement against the plaintiffs (six class members, none of whom had admitted engaging in homosexual conduct).[30] The government has appealed the district court decision again to the Second Circuit.

---

[26] 88 F.3d 1280, 71 FEP 419 (2d Cir. 1996). The Second Circuit's decision reversed the original district court decision as discussed in the Main Edition, enjoining enforcement of the policy on First and Fifth Amendment grounds.
[27] Able v. United States, 968 F. Supp. 850 (E.D.N.Y. 1997).
[28] *Id.* at 857.
[29] *Id.* at 858–59.
[30] *Id.* at 865.

Chapter 15

EQUAL PAY

II. The Equal Pay Act's Coverage

A. The Parties

In determining who is an employee as opposed to an independent contractor under the FLSA (and therefore under the Equal Pay Act, which is a part of the FLSA), the Fifth Circuit examines "whether the [individual], as a matter of economic reality, is economically dependent upon the business to which she renders her services."[1] A court is to consider five factors in deciding this issue: (1) the degree of control exercised by the employer; (2) the extent of the relative investments of the worker and alleged employer; (3) the degree to which the workers' opportunity for profit and loss is determined by the alleged employer; (4) the skill and initiative required in performing the job; and (5) the permanence of the relationship.[2]

The Eleventh Circuit has held that the issue of whether a particular defendant is an "employer" under the Equal Pay Act depends upon "the total employment situation," including "whether or not [the] employment [took] place on the premises of the [alleged employer]; how much control [did] the [alleged employer] exert on the employees; and [did] the [alleged employer] have the power to fire, hire, or modify the employment condition of the employees."[3]

---

[1] Reich v. Circle C. Invs., Inc., 998 F.2d 324, 327 (5th Cir. 1993) (court disagreed with employer's contentions that topless dancers were not employees but "tenants" renting space and that it did not have to comply with FLSA's minimum wage, overtime, and recordkeeping requirements).

[2] Id.; see also Reed v. R.C. Johnson, 1995 WL 684882, at *1, 1995 U.S. Dist. LEXIS 17221, 2 Wage & Hour Cas.2d 1789 (E.D. La. 1995) (court applied five factors and concluded that plaintiff was an employee, not a "student learner," under the FLSA).

[3] Welch v. Laney, 57 F.3d 1004, 1010–11 (11th Cir. 1995) (alterations in original) (finding county commissioners in their official capacities and deputy sheriff in

Some courts continue to conclude that executives and employees may be personally liable for violations of the Equal Pay Act if they wielded supervisory control over claimants, since the EPA broadly defines an "employer" to include "any person acting directly or indirectly in the interest of an employer in relation to an employee."[4]

III. THE RELEVANT COMPARISON

A. "Wages"

The court in *Chisholm v. Foothill Capital Corp.* held that access to business opportunities, including networking, constitutes "wages" for EPA purposes.[5]

C. "Within Any Establishment"

Whether multiple locations constitute a single establishment for EPA purposes continues to hinge on whether the party advocating "single establishment" treatment can prove that the employer's operations are centralized.[6]

---

his official and individual capacity did not qualify as employers of plaintiff, who was a dispatcher at the sheriff's department, but allowing plaintiff to proceed against sheriff in his official capacity); *accord* Marshall v. Miller, 873 F. Supp. 628, 632 (M.D. Fla. 1995) (citing Aimable v. Long & Scott Farms, 20 F.3d 434, 439 (11th Cir.), *cert. denied,* 115 S. Ct. 351 (1994)).

[4]EEOC v. Home by Hemphill, Inc., 69 FEP 1198, 1200 (N.D. Ill. 1995) (holding that owner of company might be personally liable if plaintiff amended complaint to allege that owner had supervisory involvement and was directly responsible for alleged violations); *cf.* Witham v. Regency Sav. Bank, 1995 WL 680313, at *1, 1995 U.S. Dist. LEXIS 17021 (N.D. Ill. Nov. 13, 1995) (noting that Seventh Circuit has "signaled" that corporate executives may not be personally liable for EPA violations, but that earlier case law tends to impose such liability).

[5]940 F. Supp. 1273, 1282 (N.D. Ill. 1996) (plaintiff, a female credit underwriter, alleged that she was not assigned to "house accounts" and was excluded from networking opportunities like golf outings and business dinners, which were available to her male co-workers).

[6]Meeks v. Computer Assocs. Int'l, 15 F.3d 1013, 1017, 64 FEP 258 (11th Cir. 1994) (in limiting comparison to employees at same office location, rather than nationwide, court found that defendant had not shown the requisite degree of centralization, since hiring and salary decisions were made at local office); Spiers v. McNeil Real Estate Management, Inc., 65 FEP 1446, 1449 (D. Kan. 1994) (declining to find exception to general rule that an establishment is one physical location where plaintiff failed to prove that various locations had "uniform pay standards, applicable to all employees, regardless of geographic location").

IV. Determining the Equality of Jobs

A. The Applicable Standard

Although several courts and the EEOC[7] have concluded that plaintiffs can use opposite-sex predecessors and/or successors as EPA comparators as long as they performed substantially equal work, some courts have disagreed or limited this rule.[8]

B. Equal Skill, Effort, and Responsibility

In analyzing whether jobs involve "equal skill, effort, and responsibility," after a plaintiff establishes a common core of tasks, the issue becomes whether any additional tasks make the jobs substantially different.[9] Time spent on additional tasks will not justify a wage disparity if the tasks do not consume a significant portion of the comparator employee's time.[10]

Similarly, jobs may be substantially equal even if plaintiffs perform more duties than their comparators. To establish a case under

---

[7] 29 C.F.R. § 1620.13(b)(4) (1996).

[8] *Compare* Bielawski v. AMI, Inc., 870 F. Supp. 771, 775–76, 66 FEP 1160, 1163–64 (N.D. Ohio 1994) (holding that plaintiff may not rely on salary of successor employees in her position, due to inflation and the Equal Pay Act's language, which uses the present tense in discussing comparisons) *and* Brinkley-Obu v. Hughes Training, Inc., 36 F.3d 336, 349 & n.30, 65 FEP 1840, 1850–51 & n.30 (4th Cir. 1994) (allowing comparison to predecessors and successors as well as co-workers performing similar work, while noting Sixth Circuit case holding that claimant can only compare wages to predecessor or successor when no similarly situated employee of the opposite sex was working at the time of the alleged violation) *with* Dubowsky v. Stern, Lavinthal, Norgaard & Daly, 922 F. Supp. 985, 991 (D.N.J. 1996) (rejecting inflationary forces as a logical explanation for 20% salary differential and permitting establishment of prima facie case through comparison with successor who replaced plaintiff five months after her departure) *and* Dey v. Colt Constr. & Dev. Co., 28 F.3d 1446, 1461–62, 65 FEP 523 (7th Cir. 1994) (allowing comparison with successor, though accepting defense that higher salary was based on factors other than sex). *See* McNierney v. McGraw-Hill, Inc., 919 F. Supp. 853, 860, 70 FEP 935 (D. Md. 1995) (rejecting comparison to "successor" where male plaintiff never accepted position that was subsequently awarded to a female at a higher salary than that offered to plaintiff, since the EPA "does not appear to apply to potential employees").

[9] EEOC v. Grinnell Corp., 881 F. Supp. 406, 410 (S.D. Ind. 1995) (rejecting employer's contention that, as a matter of law, female workers did not perform equal work because male sales representatives were more skilled and performed extra duties).

[10] Weissman v. General Cable Co., 862 F. Supp. 731, 735 (D. Conn. 1994) (finding genuine issue of fact as to whether female plaintiff's duties as data processing manager were substantially equal to those of male comparators).

this "extra duties doctrine," "the jobs at issue must involve substantially equal responsibilities, the other sex must also perform 'extra duties of equal skill, effort and responsibility,' or the extra duties must 'take little time' and be of 'only peripheral importance.' "[11]

Courts continue to focus on overall job content, rather than individual criteria in isolation, in evaluating whether a plaintiff's job involves "equal skill, effort, and responsibility" as compared with another job. For example, in *Kellett v. Glaxo Enterprises, Inc.*,[12] the district court suggested that Congress could not have intended the EPA's "effort" prong to ensure that every worker receives the same compensation as her supervisor as long as she works equally hard. In *Atkinson v. Washington International Insurance Co.*,[13] the court rejected an account executive's claim that she was performing the work of a higher-level executive, concluding that the plaintiff's supervisory duties over other employees did not make her job substantially equal to that of the regional vice president, who, unlike plaintiff, had responsibility for revenue generation and sales as well as supervisory duties.

In *Welde v. Tetley, Inc.*,[14] the court found that the plaintiff's job did not require the same degree of "responsibility" as that of her comparator. The court found significant, among other things, the fact that the plaintiff had received an award for excellence, thus indicating that the plaintiff's performance went beyond the employer's expectations for that position.

V. Statutory Defenses

A. "Differences ... Pursuant to ... a Seniority System"

Whether an employer has a seniority system in place under the Equal Pay Act is a question of law.[15] Courts generally are reluctant

---

[11]Baumgardner v. ROA Gen., Inc., 864 F. Supp. 1107, 1110, 72 FEP 514 (D. Utah 1994) (dismissing Title VII and EPA claims, finding that plaintiffs failed to establish that job duties were substantially the same as, or even similar to, comparators' duties) (quoting EEOC v. Central Kan. Med. Ctr., 705 F.2d 1270, 1273, 31 FEP 1510, 1511 (10th Cir. 1983)).

[12]66 FEP 1071, 1075 (S.D.N.Y. 1994) (rejecting plaintiff's claim that her job was substantially equal to that of her supervisor, despite his greater responsibilities as fund manager).

[13]1995 WL 68756, at *13–*14, 1995 U.S. Dist. LEXIS 1865 (N.D. Ill. Feb. 14, 1995).

[14]864 F. Supp. 440, 456, 65 FEP 1423, 1436 (M.D. Penn. 1994).

[15]Irby v. Bittick, 44 F.3d 949, 954, 67 FEP 70 (11th Cir. 1995).

to second-guess employers' business judgments as to their use of seniority-based pay practices because "[e]mployers may prefer and reward experience, believing it makes a more valuable employee, for whatever reason."[16]

An employer that relies on a system of basing salaries on employees' longevity of service "must be able to identify standards for measuring seniority which are systematically applied and observed."[17] To utilize this affirmative defense, therefore, the seniority system must be applied to all employees unless there are "defined exceptions" that are communicated to and understood by the employees.[18]

B. "Differences ... Pursuant to ... a Merit System"

An employer's merit-system defense to a plaintiff's bonus claim was upheld where a greater number of employees—both male and female—did not receive bonuses, as compared to the four male employees who did receive them, and the employees who received the bonuses worked more hours than did plaintiff.[19]

D. "Differences ... Pursuant to ... a Differential Based on Any Other Factor Other Than Sex"

In *Deli v. University of Minnesota*,[20] the court held that the "factor other than sex" defense pertains to the gender of the claimant, not the gender of those supervised or served by the claimant. The plaintiff, a former head coach of the women's gymnastics team, filed suit under the EPA claiming that the university discriminatorily paid her less than the head coaches of several men's athletic teams. Plaintiff did not contend that the discrepancy in pay was based on

---

[16]Harker v. Utica College of Syracuse Univ., 885 F. Supp. 378, 390, 72 FEP 693 (N.D.N.Y. 1995) (defendants established a legitimate reason for wage difference between a male and female coach as the male coach had nine years of seniority over female coach); Blount v. Alabama Coop. Extension Serv., 869 F. Supp. 1543, 1554, 66 FEP 889 (M.D. Ala. 1994) (wage differentials were justified primarily by individual employees' length and history of service).

[17]*Irby*, 44 F.3d at 954 (rejecting a "seniority system" defense raised by county sheriff's department where two male sheriff's deputies were paid more than deputies who were hired in earlier years even though neither deputy had been promoted).

[18]*Id.* at 955.

[19]Sigmon v. Parker Chapin Flattau & Klimpl, 901 F. Supp. 667, 679, 69 FEP 69 (S.D.N.Y. 1995).

[20]863 F. Supp. 958, 65 FEP 1026 (D. Minn. 1994).

her gender but, instead, alleged it was based on the gender of the athletes she coached. Granting the university's motion for summary judgment, the court held that the "EPA prohibits discrimination based on the gender of the claimant only and does not reach compensation differentials based on the gender of student athletes coached by a claimant. Such compensation differentials are based on a 'factor other than sex' and thus are not proscribed by the EPA."[21]

2. Market Rate

Courts continue to question the role prior salary history should play in an employer's determination of wages. For instance, in *Dey v. Colt Construction & Development Co.*,[22] the employer attributed the salary differential between the plaintiff and her successor, in part, to the fact that the successor had negotiated a salary higher than originally offered, which was closer to his prior salary. The Seventh Circuit warned that "[s]uch evidence must be considered with some caution, of course, as undue reliance on salary history to explain an existing wage disparity may serve to perpetuate differentials that ultimately may be linked to sex."[23] The court concluded, however, that because additional factors supported the salary differential—i.e., the successor had a master's degree that related to his job and was hired almost a year after plaintiff's last pay raise—summary judgment for the employer was appropriate.

3. Other

Employers that assign salaries according to a gender-neutral determination of job grades or the relative importance or profitability of various positions have successfully invoked the "factor other than sex" defense.[24]

---

[21]*Id.* at 961.
[22]28 F.3d 1446, 65 FEP 523 (7th Cir. 1994).
[23]*Id.* at 1462 (citation omitted).
[24]*See* Galarraga v. Marriott Employees Fed. Credit Union, 70 FEP 1605, 1610 (D. Md. 1996) (employer's assignment of job grades and salary ranges through a program that considers a position's duties and responsibilities based on independent market analysis and surveys comparing the employer's positions with similar positions at other organizations was a "factor other than sex"); Byrd v. Ronayne, 61 F.3d 1026, 1033–34, 68 FEP 769 (1st Cir. 1995) (male employee's ability to bring in greater billable revenue to the employer than female employees substantiates his higher salary); Strag v. Board of Trustees of Craven Community College, 55 F.3d 943, 951, 68 FEP 163 (4th Cir. 1995) (factor other than sex established where college generally paid instructors "on scale" but allowed deviation from formula for exceptionally

VI. Enforcement Mechanisms

B. Judicial Enforcement

1. Relief Available

The Eleventh Circuit has determined that the "after-acquired evidence" doctrine set forth in *McKennon v. Nashville Banner Publishing Co.*,[25] a case involving an alleged violation of the Age Discrimination in Employment Act, applies to claims brought pursuant to Title VII and the Equal Pay Act.[26] As to a discharged employee's claim for lost wages under the EPA, the circuit court concluded that back pay would be calculated up to the date the employer discovered the plaintiff's resume fraud.[27]

The Seventh Circuit has held that compensatory and punitive damages may be available to persons retaliated against for asserting rights under the Equal Pay Act (as well as the FLSA and ADEA).[28]

2. Timeliness of Suit

The statute of limitations is an affirmative defense to an EPA claim that can be waived if not asserted in an answer or through a motion.[29] As a result, the defense may not be raised for the first time on appeal.[30]

---

qualified individuals, and where higher-paid male instructor was well known in the college community for his innovative teaching techniques, had more experience, had earned more in previous job, and was unwilling to take a pay cut, and where his presence would attract more students); Welde v. Tetley, Inc., 864 F. Supp. 440, 457, 65 FEP 1423 (M.D. Pa. 1994) (employer's use of "HAY System" to establish salary based upon relative importance of position using factors such as "know how," "problem-solving," and "accountability" without regard to the person filling the position "clearly is gender-neutral"). *But see* Tomka v. Seiler Corp., 66 F.3d 1295, 1312, 68 FEP 1508 (2d Cir. 1995) (reversing dismissal of plaintiff's EPA claim where employer failed to demonstrate that male's higher salary resulted from his previous experience *and* that this experience was a job-related qualification for the position).

[25] 513 U.S. 352, 66 FEP 1192 (1995).
[26] Wallace v. Dunn Constr. Co., 62 F.3d 374, 378, 68 FEP 990 (11th Cir. 1995).
[27] *Id.* at 379.
[28] Avitia v. Metropolitan Club of Chicago, Inc., 49 F.3d 1219, 1226, 2 Wage & Hour Cases 2d 993 (7th Cir. 1995) ("Ever since a 1977 amendment to the Fair Labor Standards Act, however, the jury has also been authorized to award, though only in retaliation cases . . . all appropriate legal and equitable relief."); Soto v. Adams Elevator Equip. Co., 941 F.2d 543, 551, 56 FEP 1270 (7th Cir. 1991) (victims of retaliation for asserting Equal Pay Act rights may recover compensatory and punitive damages for emotional distress).
[29] Fisher v. Vassar College, 70 F.3d 1420, 1452, 68 FEP 1537 (2d Cir. 1995).
[30] *Id.*

The Fourth and Sixth Circuits, adopting the continuing-violation principle in pay discrimination claims, have held that "each issuance of a paycheck to a female employee at a lower wage than that issued to her male counterpart constitutes a new discriminatory action for purposes of Equal Pay Act limitations accrual."[31] Each issuance of a discriminatorily low paycheck is an EPA violation, even if the opposite-sex comparator ceases to work for the employer.[32]

VII. "COMPARABLE WORTH"

B. The Prima Facie Case

Courts continue to reject Equal Pay Act claims founded upon the theory of comparable worth.[33] Even though plaintiffs, as a result, avoid using the phrase "comparable worth" in their lawsuits, courts may nevertheless infer its presence from the underlying allegations. In *Baumgardner v. ROA General, Inc.*,[34] two female employees sued their employer under the EPA, alleging that a former male employee's job responsibilities "were no more complicated" than theirs. The court held that this argument "contemplates a claim of comparable worth which is inadequate to support an Equal Pay Act claim."[35]

---

[31] Brinkley-Obu v. Hughes Training, Inc., 36 F.3d 336, 347, 65 FEP 1840 (4th Cir. 1994) (citation omitted). *Accord* Moten v. American Linen Supply Co., 67 FEP 1080, 1083 (D. Kan. 1995) (applying continuing violation doctrine to EPA claim); Gandy v. Sullivan County, Tenn., 24 F.3d 861, 864 (6th Cir. 1994) (noting that a separate cause of action accrues with each unequal payment, so that the continuing violation doctrine is technically not implicated in an EPA claim).

[32] *Id.* See discussion of continuing-violation doctrine in Chapter 15.VII.B.2 of the Main Edition.

[33] *See, e.g.,* Tomka v. Seiler Corp., 66 F.3d 1295, 1310, 68 FEP 1508 (2d Cir. 1995) (holding that jobs which are "merely comparable" are insufficient to satisfy a plaintiff's prima facie case); Bartges v. University of N.C., 908 F. Supp. 1312, 1324, 70 FEP 1643 (W.D.N.C. 1995) (holding that, under the EPA, the question is whether plaintiff "received equal pay for substantially equal work, not whether she should be paid more because the work she performed is of comparable worth"), *aff'd mem.*, 94 F.3d 641 (4th Cir. 1996).

[34] 864 F. Supp. 1107, 72 FEP 514 (D. Utah 1994).

[35] *Id.* at 1109.

CHAPTER 16

AGE

I. JURISDICTION

A. Protected Individuals

1. *Generally*

Section 4(h)(2) of the ADEA,[1] which states that the Act "does not apply where the employer is a foreign person not controlled by a United States employer" does not apply to the U.S. operations of a foreign corporation.[2] Where an individual applies for employment with a foreign corporation and the position sought is outside the United States, the ADEA does not apply unless the foreign corporation is controlled by its American affiliate.[3]

The ADEA's "foreign laws" exception, which excuses any employer from complying with the ADEA if to do so would violate the laws of a foreign country,[4] was held to allow an employer to observe the terms of a collective bargaining agreement covering overseas workers that required mandatory retirement at age 65.[5]

Section 321 of the Civil Rights Act of 1991,[6] which extended the same rights and remedies enjoyed by federal employees under the ADEA to the state and local employees listed in § 11(f) of the ADEA,[7] was held not to be retroactive.[8] In addition, several courts

---

[1] 29 U.S.C. § 623(h)(2).
[2] EEOC v. Kloster Cruise, Ltd., 888 F. Supp. 147, 151, 68 FEP 1 (S.D. Fla. 1995) (EEOC's interpretation of § 623(h)(2) as applying only to overseas operations is reasonable and consistent with the purposes and context of the statute).
[3] Denty v. SmithKline Beecham Corp., 907 F. Supp. 879, 884–85, 69 FEP 376 (E.D. Pa. 1995), *aff'd*, 109 F.3d 147 (3d Cir.), *cert. denied*, 118 S. Ct. 74 (1997).
[4] 29 U.S.C. § 623(f)(1).
[5] Mahoney v. RFE/RL, Inc., 47 F.3d 447, 450, 67 FEP 170 (D.C. Cir.), *cert. denied*, 516 U.S. 866 (1995).
[6] Pub. L. No. 102-166, § 321(a), 1991 U.S.C.C.A.N. (105 Stat.) 1071, 1097 (codified in relevant part at 2 U.S.C. § 1220).
[7] 29 U.S.C. § 630(f).
[8] Rutland v. Moore, 54 F.3d 226, 230, 67 FEP 1707 (5th Cir. 1995).

have continued to rule on the applicability of the § 11(f) exemptions despite the change by the Civil Rights Act of 1991.[9]

Retired employees may still be considered "employees" under the ADEA as long as the alleged discrimination is related to or arises out of the employment relationship.[10]

2. Exemptions for Certain Military Personnel and Executives

One court sanctioned an employer's increase in an employee's benefits in order to satisfy the minimum retirement benefit requirement of the "high policymaking" exemption.[11] In addition, the court interpreted the EEOC's regulations defining "high policymaker" to include those who "play a significant role in the development of corporate policy" even if they lack the authority to be "executives."[12]

In 1996, Congress enacted legislation that permanently reinstates the exemption giving state and local governments the option of setting mandatory retirement ages for public safety officers, including police and firefighters, regardless of whether or not such a policy previously existed.[13]

3. Exclusion of Independent Contractors and Partners in a Bona Fide Partnership

Courts continue to employ a "hybrid standard," which combines the common law "right to control test" and the "economic

---

[9]*See, e.g.*, Americanos v. Carter, 74 F.3d 138, 143–44, 69 FEP 1183 (7th Cir.) (deputy attorney general reporting directly to elected Attorney General not an "employee" under ADEA), *cert. denied*, 116 S. Ct. 1853 (1996); Gunaca v. Texas, 65 F.3d 467, 470 n.3, 68 FEP 1678 (5th Cir. 1995) (although § 321 of the Civil Rights Act of 1991 may have offered district attorney's investigator a way to circumvent § 630(f)'s personal staff exemption, neither party raised the issue); Mraz v. County of Lehigh, 862 F. Supp. 1344, 1350 (E.D. Pa. 1994) (plaintiff, who was terminated in 1992, raised genuine issue of fact as to whether or not he is an "employee" under ADEA).

[10]Milwaukee Prof'l Firefighters v. City of Milwaukee, 869 F. Supp. 633, 649, 72 FEP 121 (E.D. Wis. 1994) ("To interpret retirees as completely outside the scope of the ADEA could potentially eviscerate the protective scheme of the statute."); McKeever v. Ironworker's District Council, 73 FEP 1000 (E.D. Pa. 1997) (retired union members have standing under ADEA to sue union for excluding retirees at age 65 from health plan).

[11]Morrissey v. Boston Five Cents Sav. Bank, 54 F.3d 27, 34, 67 FEP 1338 (1st Cir. 1995) ("the high policymaker . . . need only be entitled to the statutory minimum amount in nonforfeitable annual pension benefits immediately upon retirement").

[12]*Id.* at 33.

[13]The temporary exemption enacted in 1986 only grandfathered retirement policies in effect as of March 3, 1983.

realities test" of the FLSA, to distinguish between employees and independent contractors.[14] To survive a motion to dismiss, however, plaintiffs need only allege that they were "employed" with the defendant. Application of the "hybrid test" is unnecessary at the pleadings stage.[15]

A court rejected an employer's argument that individuals who were terminated pursuant to its mandatory retirement policy, which required employees sitting on its board of directors to retire at the earlier of age 62 or age 60 with 15 years of service, were more like "partners" than "employees," when the individuals enjoyed both employee status and director status and lost both roles when forced to retire.[16]

B. Covered Employers

1. Private Employers

The "joint employer" doctrine continues to be the standard by which courts determine whether both a parent corporation and its subsidiary may be held liable for the discriminatory actions of the subsidiary.[17] Although this doctrine is also used to determine whether

---

[14]*See, e.g.,* Fronduti v. Trinity Indus., 928 F. Supp. 1107, 1113 (M.D. Ala. 1996) ("totality of circumstances" favored finding that plaintiff was independent contractor; employer's sole interest was in work product, not in how it was done); Mukhtar v. Castleton Serv. Corp., 920 F. Supp. 934, 944, 70 FEP 1128 (S.D. Ind. 1996) (district court found that "economic realities" demonstrated employment relationship existed between plaintiff and defendant notwithstanding fact that contract between parties was labeled a lease); Moore v. Ford Motor Co., 901 F. Supp. 1293, 1297 (N.D. Ill. 1995) (dealer/proprietor exercises too much independence to be considered employee of automobile manufacturer); Wilson v. United Farm Bureau Mut. Ins. Co., 68 FEP 631, 636 (S.D. Ind. 1995) (even though parties may have labeled their relationship one way, that label does not control if enough indicia of employment relationship are present).

[15]Strange v. Nationwide Mut. Ins. Co., 867 F. Supp. 1209, 1212 (E.D. Pa. 1994).

[16]EEOC v Johnson & Higgins, Inc., 887 F. Supp. 682, 687–88, 68 FEP 1481 (S.D.N.Y. 1995), *aff'd,* 91 F.3d 1529, 71 FEP 818 (2d Cir. 1996), *cert. denied,* 118 S. Ct. 47 (1997).

[17]EEOC v. Illinois, 69 F.3d 167, 171, 69 FEP 306 (7th Cir. 1995) (since local school district controlled "key powers" of hiring and firing, state may not be held liable for local school code requiring mandatory retirement at age 60); Regan v. In the Heat of the Nite, Inc., 68 FEP 1463, 1465 (S.D.N.Y. 1995) (plaintiff established genuine issue of fact as to whether defendants were sufficiently involved in each other's activities to constitute "integrated enterprise" where (1) employees rotated informally, and (2) employee records, payroll records, and bank deposits of each defendant were kept together); Rittmeyer v. Advance Bancorp, Inc., 868 F. Supp. 1017, 1023, 68 FEP 1283 (N.D. Ill. 1994) (most important factor in applying "single

the employees of the parent are counted in determining ADEA coverage of the subsidiary,[18] it may not be applied to count the employees of a foreign corporation not controlled by a U.S. employer.[19]

The Supreme Court held, in *Walters v. Metropolitan Educational Enterprises, Inc.*,[20] that the "payroll" method of counting employees[21] is the appropriate means for determining if an employer is covered by Title VII of the Civil Rights Act of 1964.[22] Since the definition of "employer" under the ADEA is virtually identical to the definition of employer under § 701(b) of Title VII, the *Walters* decision will most likely be used in interpreting § 630(b) of the ADEA.[23] However, other issues will likely continue to be litigated under this definition.[24]

---

employer doctrine" is whether there is centralized control of labor relations and personnel, which is determined by whether parent controls subsidiary's day-to-day employment decisions); Kellett v. Glaxo Enters., 66 FEP 1071, 1074–75 (S.D.N.Y. 1994) (use of common benefits package, parent corporation's control of decision to transfer certain functions to different subsidiary, and common board member were insufficient to establish that employer and its parent corporation are single employer).

[18]Dewey v. PTT Telecom Netherlands, 68 FEP 1112, 1115 (S.D.N.Y. 1995) (court refused to count employees of both parent and subsidiary toward jurisdictional minimum where plaintiff failed to demonstrate parent and subsidiary were sufficiently integrated), *aff'd mem.*, 101 F.3d 1392 (2d Cir. 1996); Astrowsky v. First Portland Mortgage Corp., 887 F. Supp. 332, 337, 70 FEP 195 (D. Me. 1995) ("In the absence of *any* control . . . no joint employer relationship existed" and consequently defendants did not meet jurisdictional requirements for "employer" under ADEA.).

[19]Robins v. Max Mara, U.S.A., Inc., 914 F. Supp. 1006, 1009, 72 FEP 331 (S.D.N.Y. 1996) ("If an integrated enterprise (comprising foreign and domestic components) is controlled by the foreign component, then . . . [o]nly those employees of the enterprise (whether on the payroll of the foreign or the domestic component) who work in the United States for twenty or more calendar weeks per year are to be counted for purposes of determining whether the enterprise is covered by the provisions of the ADA, ADEA and Title VII."); Feit v. Biosynth Int'l, Inc., 1996 WL 99726 (N.D. Ill. Mar. 4, 1996) ("Independent foreign corporations have been expressly exempted by the ADEA . . . under § 623(h)(2), and the court must not expand the judicially created single employer doctrine in a manner that might intrude upon the § 623(h)(2) exemption.").

[20]117 S. Ct. 660, 72 FEP 1211 (1997).

[21]Under the payroll method, "the test for when an employer 'has' an employee is no different from the test for when an individual *is* an employee: whether the employer has an employment relationship with the individual on the day in question." *Id.* at 663.

[22]*Id.* at 664.

[23]The Seventh Circuit currently employs the "workplace method" of counting only "those weeks where at least twenty employees are at the workplace or on paid leave for each of the seven days of the week." Elias v. Naperville Eye Assoc., Ltd., 928 F. Supp. 757, 759 (N.D. Ill. 1996).

[24]*See, e.g.,* Jones v. Midway Broad. Co., 69 FEP 789, 791 (N.D. Ill. 1995) (corporate officer is counted as 1 of 20 employees necessary to establish coverage under

There is no blanket exemption for religious institutions under the ADEA. Instead, the courts apply the test set out in *NLRB v. Catholic Bishop of Chicago*[25] on a case-by-case basis.[26]

Although there is still no consensus as to whether an individual employee, such as a supervisor or manager, may be held individually liable under the ADEA, most recent cases hold that they cannot.[27]

ADEA, "unless the officer's title was merely honorary for a shareholder or director who is unpaid as an employee and who does no meaningful work for the company"); Rao v. Kenya Airways, Ltd., 73 FEP 1633 (S.D.N.Y 1995) (employees of foreign corporations in foreign countries and independent contractors are not counted when determining ADEA's threshold minimum of 20 employees); Mooney v. Bayfield Constr. Co., 1995 WL 530656 (N.D. Ill. Aug. 23, 1995) ("[i]f a shareholder is also an employee, meaning that he is compensated as an employee and performs the work of an employee, he is an employee under the ADEA [for the purpose of satisfying the jurisdictional minimum], regardless of how much stock he owns"; presence of person on payroll, even if person performs little meaningful work, "has obvious tax, payroll, and other legal implications" and must be counted toward jurisdictional minimum).

[25]440 U.S. 490, 100 LRRM 2913 (1979).

[26]Weissman v. Congregation Shaare Emeth, 38 F.3d 1038, 1044–45, 66 FEP 113 (8th Cir. 1994) ("[A] court cannot focus solely on the character of the religious institution. It must consider the nature of the relationship between the employer and the employee."; since plaintiff's duties were overwhelmingly secular, his ADEA claim did not pose significant risk of First Amendment infringement); Powell v. Stafford, 859 F. Supp. 1343, 1349, 65 FEP 1275 (D. Colo. 1994) (application of ADEA to Roman Catholic theology teacher's termination from Catholic high school would result in "excessive entanglement" with religion and violate employer's First Amendment religious freedoms).

[27]*E.g.,* Stults v. Conoco, Inc., 76 F.3d 651, 655, 70 FEP 732 (5th Cir. 1996); Birkbeck v. Marvel Lighting Corp., 30 F.3d 507, 511, 65 FEP 669 (4th Cir.), *cert. denied,* 513 U.S. 1058 (1994); Kelleher v. Aerospace Community Credit Union, 927 F. Supp. 361, 363, 70 FEP 1279 (E.D. Mo. 1996); Gausmann v. City of Ashland, 926 F. Supp. 635, 640, 75 FEP 525 (N.D. Ohio 1996) (government worker in his individual capacity is not liable under ADEA); Wray v. Edward Blank Assocs., Inc., 924 F. Supp. 498, 504 (S.D.N.Y. 1996); Jungels v. State Univ. College of N.Y., 922 F. Supp. 779, 783 (W.D.N.Y. 1996), *aff'd,* 112 F.3d 504 (1997); Griswold v. New Madrid County Group Practice, Inc., 920 F. Supp. 1046, 1048, 73 FEP 151 (E.D. Mo. 1996) (individual board of directors of defendant cannot be personally liable under ADEA); Pouncy v. Vulcan Materials Co., 920 F. Supp. 1566, 1578 (N.D. Ala. 1996); Storr v. Anderson Sch. & William Doyle, 919 F. Supp. 144, 148, 72 FEP 107 (S.D.N.Y. 1996); Vakharia v. Little Co. of Mary Hosp. & Health Care Ctrs., 917 F. Supp. 1282, 1296 (N.D. Ill. 1996); Whitchurch v. Apache Prods. Co., 916 F. Supp. 809, 812, 6 AD 1589 (N.D. Ill. 1996); Pardasani v. Rack Room Shoes, Inc., 912 F. Supp. 187, 191 (M.D.N.C. 1996); Griswold v. Alabama Dep't of Indus. Relations, 903 F. Supp. 1492, 1497, 71 FEP 1336 (M.D. Ala. 1995) (supervisors of Alabama Department of Industrial Relations are not liable in either individual or official capacities under ADEA); Quiron v. L.N. Violette Co., 897 F. Supp. 18, 20, 4 AD 1852 (D. Me. 1995); Falbaum v. Pomerantz, 891 F. Supp. 986, 991, 72 FEP

2. The Federal Government

The only proper defendant in a federal employee's ADEA action is the head of the federal agency that employed the plaintiff.[28]

Congress has not provided an express waiver of sovereign immunity with respect to retaliation claims under the ADEA.[29] In addition, the United States did not waive sovereign immunity to allow ADEA suits by participants in the Senior Environmental Employment Program (SEE).[30]

The courts still have not reached consensus regarding the appropriate statute of limitations for ADEA suits against the federal government, although most courts borrow Title VII's limitations period.[31]

3. State and Local Governments

Prior to *Seminole Tribe v. Florida*,[32] in which the Supreme Court restated the test for congressional abrogations of Eleventh Amendment immunity,[33] most courts held that suits under the ADEA

---

141 (S.D.N.Y. 1995) (congressional intent to protect employers of fewer than 20 persons precludes idea of individual liability for agents); Rifkinson v. CBS, Inc., 69 FEP 8, 9 (S.D.N.Y. 1995) (ADEA liability is directed toward employers, not individual persons, unless there is separate, intentional misconduct alleged against the individual); Heinz v. Belcan Eng'g Corp., 68 FEP 1238, 1240 (W.D. Pa. 1995); Hrosik v. Latrobe Steel Co., 4 AD 555, 559 (W. D. Pa. 1995); Flamand v. American Int'l Group, Inc., 876 F. Supp. 356, 363, 69 FEP 675 (D.P.R. 1994); Straka v. Francis, 867 F. Supp. 767, 773 & n.3 (N.D. Ill. 1994); Brogdon v. Alabama Dep't of Econ. & Community Affairs, 864 F. Supp. 1161, 1164, 66 FEP 325 (M.D. Ala. 1994); Rogers v. Atwork Corp., 863 F. Supp. 242, 245, 66 FEP 391 (E.D. Pa. 1994); Pacourek v. Inland Steel Co., 858 F. Supp. 1393, 1405, 3 AD 726 (N.D. Ill. 1994), *partial summary judgment denied,* 916 F. Supp. 797, 5 AD 438 (N.D. Ill. 1996). *But see* Schallehn v. Central Trust & Sav. Bank, 877 F. Supp. 1315, 1331, 69 FEP 1292 (N.D. Iowa 1995) ("personal liability under the ADEA does lie against supervisory employees").

[28]Gregor v. Derwinski, 911 F. Supp. 643, 654, 75 FEP 797 (W.D.N.Y. 1996); Meyer v. Runyon, 869 F. Supp. 70, 76 (D. Mass. 1994).

[29]Tomasello v. Rubin, 920 F. Supp. 4, 6 (D.D.C. 1996).

[30]Daniels v. Browner, 63 F.3d 906, 908, 68 FEP 961 (9th Cir. 1995).

[31]*See, e.g.,* Edwards v. Shalala, 64 F.3d 601, 606, 68 FEP 1414 (11th Cir. 1995) (since ADEA does not specify statutory period for actions against federal government, court borrowed Title VII's 30-day statute of limitations); Jones v. Runyon, 32 F.3d 1454, 1456, 65 FEP 1066 (10th Cir. 1994) (Title VII limitations period applicable to federal employee Title VII claims applies to federal employee ADEA claims); Metsopulos v. Runyon, 918 F. Supp. 851, 859 (D.N.J. 1996) (court "borrowed" Title VII's new 90-day statute of limitations for federal employees).

[32]517 U.S. 44 (1996).

[33]In *Seminole,* the Court held that while congressional enactments pursuant to the Fourteenth Amendment may abrogate sovereign state immunity, enactments

brought by private litigants against state government entities are not barred by the Eleventh Amendment.[34] Since the *Seminole* and *City of Boerne* decisions, the district courts have been divided over whether states have Eleventh Amendment immunity from suits under the ADEA.[35] Only the Tenth Circuit has decided the issue post-*Seminole,* ruling that the ADEA's application to the states is constitutional.[36] In addition, one court held that Congress did not abrogate

---

pursuant to the Commerce Clause cannot. 517 U.S. at 59–74. In *City of Boerne v. Flores,* the Court held that a statute must be "responsive to, or designed to prevent, unconstitutional behavior" to be "appropriate legislation under the Fourteenth Amendment." 117 S. Ct. 2157, 2170 (1997). In *EEOC v. Wyoming,* the Court reserved the question of whether Congress acted pursuant to the Fourteenth Amendment in extending the ADEA's coverage to the states. 460 U.S. 226, 243 & n.18, 31 FEP 74 (1983).

[34]Hurd v. Pittsburgh State Univ., 29 F.3d 564, 565, 65 FEP 322 (10th Cir.), *cert. denied,* 513 U.S. 930 (1994); EEOC v. Newport Mesa Unified Sch. Dist., 893 F. Supp. 927, 929–30, 68 FEP 657 (C.D. Cal. 1995); Griswold v. Alabama Dep't of Indus. Relations, 903 F. Supp. 1492, 1496, 71 FEP 1336 (M.D. Ala. 1995); Van Pilsum v. Iowa State Univ. of Science, 863 F. Supp. 935, 940 n.5 (S.D. Iowa 1994); Brogdon v. Alabama Dep't of Econ. & Community Affairs, 864 F. Supp. 1161, 1165, 66 FEP 325 (M.D. Ala. 1994).

[35]*See, e.g.,* Young v. Pennsylvania House of Reps., 1998 WL 76249 (M.D. Pa. Feb. 18, 1998) (upholding abrogation); Carmen v. San Francisco Unified Sch. Dist., 982 F. Supp. 1396 (N.D. Cal. 1997) (upholding abrogation); Pietraszewski v. Buffalo State College, 1997 WL 436763 (W.D.N.Y. Aug. 1, 1997) (upholding abrogation); Simpson v. Texas Dep't of Criminal Justice, 975 F. Supp. 921 (W.D. Tex. 1997) (upholding abrogation); Gehrt v. University of Ill., 974 F. Supp. 1178, 74 FEP 961 (C.D. Ill. 1997) (upholding abrogation); Humenansky v. Board of Regents of the Univ. of Minn., 958 F. Supp. 439, 73 FEP 1004 (D. Minn. 1997) (invalidating abrogation), *appeal pending,* No. 97-2302 (8th Cir.); Migneault v. Peck, 973 F. Supp. 1295 (D.N.M. 1997) (upholding abrogation), *appeal pending,* No. 97-2099 (10th Cir.); Goshtasby v. University of Illinois-Chicago, 1997 WL 367362 (N.D. Ill. May 15, 1997) (upholding abrogation), *appeal pending,* No. 97-2297 (7th Cir.); Ullman v. Rector & Visitors of the Univ. of Va., 1997 WL 134557 (W.D. Va. Mar. 12, 1997) (upholding abrogation); Segall v. Megerson, Civ. No. A-96-CA-413 JN (W.D. Tex. Feb. 28, 1997) (invalidating abrogation); Young v. University of Kan. Med. Ctr., 1997 WL 150051 (D. Kan. Feb. 26, 1997) (upholding abrogation); Hodgson v. University of Tex. Med. Branch, 953 F. Supp. 168 (S.D. Tex. 1997) (upholding abrogation); Charney v. Gizzard, Civil 1997 U.S. Dist. LEXIS 2751 (E.D. Va. Jan. 31, 1997) (upholding abrogation); Coger v. State Bd. of Regents, 1997 U.S. Dist. LEXIS 5362 (W.D. Tenn. Jan. 2, 1997) (invalidating abrogation), *appeal pending,* No. 97-5134 (6th Cir.); Teichgraeber v. Memorial Union Corp., 946 F. Supp. 900, 72 FEP 1696 (D. Kan. 1996) (upholding abrogation); MacPherson v. University of Montevallo, 938 F. Supp. 785, 71 FEP 1318 (N.D. Ala. 1996) (invalidating abrogation), *appeal pending,* No. 96-6947 (11th Cir.); Kimel v. Florida Bd. of Regents, 1996 U.S. Dist. LEXIS 7995 (N.D. Fla. May 17, 1996) (upholding abrogation), *appeal pending,* No. 96-2788 (11th Cir.); Scott v. University of Miss. Law Sch., No. 1:94-CV-241 (N.D. Miss. May 16, 1996) (upholding abrogation), *appeal pending,* No. 96-60385 (5th Cir.).

[36]Hurd v. Pittsburgh State Univ., 109 F.3d 1540, 73 FEP 1448 (10th Cir. 1997).

the Eleventh Amendment's grant of constitutional immunity to the states when they are acting as "employment agencies" under the ADEA.[37]

A state does not violate the ADEA merely by failing to repeal a preempted law or by failing to notify its subdivisions of the change in the law.[38]

4. Labor Organizations and Employment Agencies

An international union and its subordinate unions ordinarily are not considered a single employer for purposes of determining whether or not they are covered by the ADEA.[39]

II. Prohibited Practices

An employment action short of discharge, such as reassignment, may be actionable under the ADEA.[40] However, a mere threat

---

[37]Blanciak v. Allegheny Ludlum Corp., 77 F.3d 690, 695–96, 70 FEP 27 (3d Cir. 1996) (when Congress explicitly expanded ADEA definition of "employer" to include states in 1974, it failed to similarly expand statutory definition of "employment agency").

[38]EEOC v. Illinois, 69 F.3d 167, 169–70, 69 FEP 306 (7th Cir. 1995) (state was not liable under ADEA for invalid mandatory retirement law it did not repeal, either as an "aider and abettor," or as an "indirect employer," where plaintiffs offered no evidence that state tried to enforce law or exercised hiring or firing power over plaintiffs). *See also* Quinones v. City of Evanston, 58 F.3d 275, 277, 69 FEP 791 (7th Cir. 1995) (discriminatory state law is not a defense to liability under federal law; state was not a necessary party even though city acted pursuant to state law).

[39]Herman v. Carpenters, 60 F.3d 1375, 1385, 4 AD 907 (9th Cir. 1995) (plaintiff sued local union in its capacity as employer, but failed to demonstrate that operations of local union are sufficiently intertwined with those of international union to warrant aggregating number of employees of two entities); Meredith v. Louisiana Fed'n of Teachers, 1996 WL 137632 (E.D. La. Mar. 26, 1996).

[40]Flaherty v. Gas Research Inst., 31 F.3d 451, 456, 65 FEP 941 (7th Cir. 1994) (plaintiff may establish prima facie case by showing that job transfer would cause personal inconvenience or altered job responsibilities); Whitchurch v. Apache Prods. Co., 916 F. Supp. 809, 814–15, 6 AD 1589 (N.D. Ill. 1996) (plaintiff established factual question regarding whether he sustained materially adverse employment action when new job he was offered had different responsibilities in different geographic area, even though pay was the same). *Contra* Caussade v. Brown, 924 F. Supp. 693, 701, 74 FEP 1027 (D. Md. 1996) (reassignments did not constitute adverse employment actions where plaintiff did not contend her duties were materially changed or that

that one's position may be downgraded does not amount to an adverse employment action.[41]

A majority of the circuits have concluded that former employees are protected from acts of retaliation under the ADEA.[42] The Supreme Court recently agreed with this result in a unanimous decision in a Title VII case.[43] Since the ADEA's retaliation provision is parallel to § 704(a) of Title VII, 42 U.S.C. § 2000e-(3)(a), the Supreme Court's decision in *Robinson* will most likely be relied upon in interpreting § 623(d) of the ADEA.[44]

III. PROCEDURE

B. Filing With the EEOC

1. The Charge

A letter filed with the EEOC in support of another's charge may not constitute an independent and proper filing of a charge where the employer did not have notice of the letter.[45] However, an intake questionnaire may meet the charge-filing requirements if it furnishes sufficient information and reasonable notice to the EEOC to initiate the administrative process.[46]

---

she was given more onerous duties or deprived of work; nor did she allege any "material loss of prestige or a reduced opportunity for future reassignments or salary/grade increases"), *aff'd,* 107 F.3d 865, 75 FEP 1887 (4th Cir. 1997).

[41]Egan v. Palos Community Hosp., 889 F. Supp. 331, 337, 68 FEP 509 (N.D. Ill. 1995).

[42]Veprinsky v. Fluor Daniel, Inc., 87 F.3d 881, 884–85, 71 FEP 170 (7th Cir. 1996) (listing circuit court cases that hold former employees are protected from retaliation).

[43]Robinson v. Shell Oil Co., 117 S. Ct. 843, 72 FEP 1856 (1997).

[44]Veprinsky v. Fluor Daniel, Inc., 87 F.3d 881, 884 n.1, 71 FEP 170 (7th Cir. 1996).

[45]Thomure v. Phillips Furniture Co., 30 F.3d 1020, 1026–27, 65 FEP 976 (8th Cir. 1994), *cert. denied,* 513 U.S. 1191 (1995). *Contra* Brook v. City of Montgomery, 916 F. Supp. 1193, 1202, 73 FEP 985 (M.D. Ala. 1996) (plaintiff's two-page typewritten letter to EEOC fulfilled charge-filing requirements).

[46]Downes v. Volkswagen of Am., Inc., 41 F.3d 1132, 1138–39, 69 FEP 11 (7th Cir. 1994) (information plaintiff provided on his intake questionnaire "manifested an intent to activate the Act's machinery").

Courts continue to allow a charge to serve as a basis for a lawsuit only if the subject of the suit is reasonably related to matters complained of in the charge.[47]

The filing of a charge is not a prerequisite to an investigation or litigation by the EEOC. When the ADEA has been violated, the EEOC may bring an action to eliminate the discrimination without the consent, and even against the wishes, of the aggrieved individuals.[48]

2. 180/300-Day Time Limit

The relevant filing period for an EEOC charge under the ADEA is governed by reference to the state in which the claim arose and not where the claim was filed or where the employer is located.[49]

Although the state claim need not be timely, a claim must still be filed with the appropriate state agency for a plaintiff to benefit from the 300-day extended filing period.[50]

One district court recently held that an employer's denial of the plaintiff's subsequent request for reinstatement did not constitute a new and separate discriminatory act so as to renew the 180-day charge-filing period. Instead, the plaintiff was "simply trying to redress his previous termination."[51]

3. Determining When Discrimination Has Occurred

There has been no change in the doctrine that the alleged discriminatory act occurs on the date the employee receives notice

---

[47]Caldwell v. Federal Express Corp., 908 F. Supp. 29, 35, 69 FEP 1055 (D. Me. 1995) (age discrimination claim is "related to [plaintiff's] sex discrimination claim articulated in [EEOC charge] and grows out of the same set of circumstances" because both claims are premised on same predicate facts, related to same conduct, and involve same individuals); Egan v. Palos Community Hosp., 889 F. Supp. 331, 338–39, 68 FEP 509 (N.D. Ill. 1995) (in assessing scope of charge, court may consider statements in sworn affidavit filed in support of charge; however, statements expressing desire to take on increased and new responsibilities are insufficient to suggest that one has unjustly been denied promotion opportunities).

[48]EEOC v. Johnson & Higgins, Inc., 887 F. Supp. 682, 688, 68 FEP 1481 (S.D.N.Y. 1995), aff'd, 91 F.3d 1529, 71 FEP 818 (2d Cir. 1996), cert. denied, 118 S. Ct. 47 (1997).

[49]Howlett v. Holiday Inns, Inc., 49 F.3d 189, 197, 67 FEP 289 (6th Cir.), cert. denied, 116 S. Ct. 379 (1995).

[50]Gorman v. Hughes Danbury Optical Sys., 908 F. Supp. 107, 114 (D. Conn. 1995).

[51]Fronduti v. Trinity Indus., 928 F. Supp. 1107, 1111 (M.D. Ala. 1996).

of the adverse action, rather than on the date the decision takes effect.[52] The courts also continue to hold that such notice must be "unequivocal."[53]

A deputy fire marshal who refused to retire pursuant to the state mandatory retirement statute had standing to maintain an ADEA action as a "person aggrieved," even though the statute will not be applied until its validity is determined in a separate proceeding, because his claim accrued on the date he was notified of the decision to terminate him.[54]

Because they are facially discriminatory, challenges to mandatory retirement policies may be made when the policy is applied as opposed to when it is adopted.[55]

---

[52]*See, e.g.,* Dring v. McDonnell Douglas Corp., 58 F.3d 1323, 1327–28, 70 FEP 481 (8th Cir. 1995) ("date of discrimination" was date plaintiff was informed he would be laid off, not date he received "formal notice" and was asked to train younger employee, and when he claimed he was "able to tie everything together and determine in his mind that his layoff was because of age discrimination"); Antos v. Bell & Howell Co., 891 F. Supp. 1281, 1286, 68 FEP 847 (N.D. Ill. 1995) ("date of discrimination" was when plaintiff received memorandum informing him he would be terminated, not date on which he was actually terminated); Ode v. Omtvedt, 883 F. Supp. 1308, 1317 (D. Neb. 1995) (filing time was triggered when plaintiff was told his contract would not be renewed, not when contract actually terminated), *aff'd mem.,* 81 F.3d 165 (8th Cir. 1996).

[53]Stone v. Georgia Power Co., 902 F. Supp. 1578, 1583–85, 69 FEP 25 (M.D. Ga. 1995) ("at risk" notices from employer informing employee that employer would terminate his position (not employment) and that unless he either found another position within company or participated in involuntary severance program, employer would likely terminate his employment, do not trigger limitations period for filing charge); Khair v. Campbell Soup Co., 893 F. Supp. 316, 328, 75 FEP 995 (D.N.J. 1995) (transfer prior to denial of promotion did not trigger limitations period where transfer was "a carefully concealed first step to deprive [the plaintiff] of the promotion"); Pacourek v. Inland Steel Co., 858 F. Supp. 1393, 1397–99, 3 AD 726 (N.D. Ill. 1994) (date of accrual is date plaintiff received written notice of termination rather than much earlier date when, according to her complaint, she was informed that she "was considered 'High Risk' and that it was inevitable that she would be terminated," where it was not clear that decision to terminate had been made at earlier date, and there was no evidence of apparent authority of person informing her that she was considered "High Risk").

[54]Horne v. Firemen's Retirement Sys., 69 F.3d 233, 236, 69 FEP 374 (8th Cir. 1995). *Contra* EEOC v. City of Chicago, 1994 WL 395068 (N.D. Ill. July 27, 1994) (statute of limitations on paramedic's claim challenging city's mandatory retirement policy did not begin to run until he retired, not when he received notice of his retirement).

[55]EEOC v. Kentucky State Police Dep't, 80 F.3d 1086, 1094, 71 FEP 1495 (6th Cir.), *cert. denied,* 117 S. Ct. 385 (1996); EEOC v. City of Chicago, 66 FEP 224, 225 (N.D. Ill. 1994).

The continuing violation theory continues to be applied in ADEA actions.[56]

4. Tolling of the Limitations Period

Courts are reluctant to equitably toll the charge-filing period[57] without some evidence of employer misconduct[58] or agency

---

[56]Caliendo v. Bentsen, 881 F. Supp. 44, 48 (D.D.C. 1995) (retaliation claims are particularly well suited to continuing violation theory); Moten v. American Linen Supply Co., 67 FEP 1080, 1084 (D. Kan. 1995) (plaintiff raised triable issue as to whether supervisor engaged in continuing course of discrimination). *But see* Egan v. Palos Community Hosp., 889 F. Supp. 331, 336, 68 FEP 509 (N.D. Ill. 1995) (isolated demotions over seven-year period were insufficient to constitute continuing violation).

[57]Bohac v. West, 85 F.3d 306, 312–13, 70 FEP 1734 (7th Cir. 1996) (plaintiff was not entitled to equitable estoppel where employer prominently displayed posters stating need to contact EEOC within 45 days of any alleged acts of discrimination by federal government); Dring v. McDonnell Douglas Corp., 58 F.3d 1323, 1330–31, 70 FEP 481 (8th Cir. 1995) (time period for filing charge was not "equitably tolled" where plaintiff failed to demonstrate that he was precluded from discovery of information to substantiate claim that he was terminated on basis of age); Hulsey v. Kmart, Inc., 43 F.3d 555, 557, 66 FEP 1327 (10th Cir. 1994) (alleged constructive discharge is not sufficient to invoke doctrine of equitable tolling because employee is not relieved of his duty to determine whether there was discriminatory motive for constructive discharge); Iglesias v. Mutual Life Ins. Co., 918 F. Supp. 31, 34 (D.P.R. 1996) (time for filing ADEA claim is not tolled while plaintiff is receiving disability insurance benefits); Young v. Easter Enters., Inc., 915 F. Supp. 58, 67 (S.D. Ind. 1995) ("[e]quitable tolling does not forestall a plaintiff's requirement to file indefinitely or until he is *certain* that discrimination has occurred . . . only until a 'reasonable person would believe he *may* have cause of action' " (quoting Thelen v. Marc's Big Boy Corp., 64 F.3d 264, 267 (7th Cir. 1995)); Crossman v. Crosson, 905 F. Supp. 90, 95 (E.D.N.Y. 1995) (equitable tolling inappropriate where plaintiffs chose to utilize employer's grievance procedure, which specifically provided that they gave up rights to pursue claims with state agency or EEOC), *aff'd*, 101 F.3d 684 (2d Cir. 1996); Parker v. Runyon, 888 F. Supp. 50, 52 (E.D.N.C.) (4½-year delay by employee in contacting EEO counselor is "patently unreasonable" and precludes application of doctrine of equitable estoppel to toll statute of limitations), *aff'd*, 61 F.3d 900 (4th Cir. 1995); Ode v. Omtvedt, 883 F. Supp. 1308, 1319 (D. Neb. 1995) (no equitable tolling where at the time his claim accrued, plaintiff possessed facts that alerted him to possibility that he had been discriminated against because of age), *aff'd mem.*, 81 F.3d 165 (8th Cir. 1996); Shapiro v. William Douglas McAdams, Inc., 68 FEP 199, 201 (E.D.N.Y. 1995) (Plaintiff's "lack of awareness [of sufficient facts to suggest that his termination was age-based] without more, does not toll the filing period."). *But see* Mirza v. Department of Treasury, 875 F. Supp. 513, 519 (N.D. Ill. 1995) (question whether administrative time limits should be tolled was factual dispute that could not be resolved on motion to dismiss).

[58]Bohac v. West, 85 F.3d 306, 312–13, 70 FEP 1734 (7th Cir. 1996) (mere silence by Army officials regarding ADEA time limits did not warrant equitable tolling where posters mentioning time limits were prominently displayed); EEOC v.

error.[59] The Seventh Circuit has held that the limitations period was not tolled by an employer giving erroneous information concerning a terminated plaintiff's replacement.[60]

C. Filing a Charge With the State FEP Agency

Unlike under Title VII, age discrimination charges may be filed simultaneously with the EEOC and a state agency.[61]

The filing of an ADEA charge with a state agency that has a work-sharing agreement with the EEOC is deemed to be received

---

Kentucky State Police Dep't, 80 F.3d 1086, 1095, 71 FEP 1495 (6th Cir.) (if employer fails to post required ADEA notices, charge-filing period will not begin to run until employee either retains attorney or acquires actual knowledge of his ADEA rights), *cert. denied,* 117 S. Ct. 385 (1996); Stafford v. Radford Community Hosp., Inc., 908 F. Supp. 1369, 1374 (W.D. Va. 1995) (where facts create issue regarding the possible concealment of relevant facts by defendant, equitable tolling principles apply), *aff'd without opinion,* 120 F.3d 262 (4th Cir. 1997); Chester v. American Tel. & Tel. Co., 907 F. Supp. 982, 986 (N.D. Tex. 1994) (equitable tolling not appropriate where employer gives employee time period to look for another job within company; rather, equitable tolling is only allowed where employer intentionally misleads employee or conceals facts from employee), *aff'd,* 68 F.3d 470 (5th Cir. 1995), *cert. denied,* 516 U.S. 1141 (1996); Denman v. Mississippi Power & Light Co., 906 F. Supp. 379, 383 (S.D. Miss. 1995) (defenses of equitable estoppel or equitable tolling must be supported by evidence that employer's conscious acts "lulled" employee into not timely filing charge); Whaley v. Sony Magnetic Prods., Inc., 894 F. Supp. 1517, 1523 (M.D. Ala. 1995) (no equitable tolling where plaintiff saw posted ADEA notice and was not misled by employer).

[59]Vernon v. Cassadaga Valley Cent. Sch. Dist., 49 F.3d 886, 891, 67 FEP 295 (2d Cir. 1995) (no tolling where EEOC's notice of right to sue did not contain erroneous information and was not intended to cause plaintiff to delay or forego filing suit); Anderson v. Unisys Corp., 47 F.3d 302, 307, 67 FEP 317 (8th Cir.) (letter sent to plaintiff from Minnesota Department of Human Rights discussing one-year statute of limitations could easily mislead unrepresented plaintiffs into believing time limits were identical for state and federal charges), *cert. denied,* 116 S. Ct. 299 (1995); Grinnell v. General Elec. Co., 907 F. Supp. 544, 547, 69 FEP 1005 (N.D.N.Y. 1995) (misinformation from EEOC, a nonparty, concerning statute of limitations insufficient to justify equitable tolling); Zellars v. Liberty Nat'l Life Ins. Co., 907 F. Supp. 355, 358–60, 69 FEP 1223 (M.D. Ala. 1995) (equity does not excuse plaintiff's untimely EEOC charge where plaintiff was aware of facts giving rise to his cause of action, EEOC did not mislead plaintiff concerning his rights under ADEA, and EEOC did not prevent plaintiff from filing his charge).

[60]Thelen v. Marc's Big Boy Corp., 64 F.3d 264, 267–68, 68 FEP 1090 (7th Cir. 1995).

[61]Brodsky v. City Univ. of N.Y., 56 F.3d 8, 9, 67 FEP 1505 (2d Cir. 1995); Jackson v. Lyons Falls Pulp & Paper, Inc., 865 F. Supp. 87, 93, 74 FEP 1667 (N.D.N.Y. 1994) (filing timely charge of discrimination with EEOC, which is later forwarded to state agency, is sufficient to commence state proceeding for purposes of ADEA).

by the EEOC on the date it was filed with the state agency for purposes of determining the timeliness of the charge.[62]

D. EEOC Conciliation

Cases filed prior to the expiration of the 60-day waiting period may be stayed to allow the statutory waiting period to expire.[63]

In cases where the EEOC is seeking an award of back pay, it must discuss the merits of the individual cases with the defendant during the conciliation process.[64]

An argument by a defendant that the EEOC failed to attempt conciliation will be undercut if the defendant takes an intransigent position regarding the alleged discrimination.[65]

E. Bringing Suit Under the ADEA

1. Right of Private Action

An individual may establish a violation of the ADEA by proving the existence of a hostile work environment.[66]

The courts are split on whether the ADEA recognizes "age-plus" theories of liability.[67] There is no cause of action under the ADEA for a complainant's dissatisfaction with the EEOC's handling of a charge.[68]

---

[62]Ford v. Bernard Fineson Dev. Ctr., 81 F.3d 304, 307–08, 70 FEP 825 (2d Cir. 1996).

[63]Strange v. Nationwide Mut. Ins. Co., 867 F. Supp. 1209, 1213 (E.D. Pa. 1994).

[64]EEOC v. Sara Lee Corp., 923 F. Supp. 994, 1000, 70 FEP 57 (W.D. Mich. 1995) (court declined to stay or dismiss action, but ordered EEOC to resume conciliation efforts by discussing merits of cases with defendant).

[65]EEOC v. Johnson & Higgins, Inc., 887 F. Supp. 682, 689, 68 FEP 1481 (S.D.N.Y. 1995), aff'd, 91 F.3d 1529, 71 FEP 818 (2d Cir. 1996), cert. denied, 118 S. Ct. 47 (1997).

[66]Dunn v. Medina Gen. Hosp., 917 F. Supp. 1185, 1193 (N.D. Ohio 1996) (plaintiff failed to establish prima facie case of hostile work environment where she did not complain about alleged instances to her supervisor).

[67]Arnett v. Aspin, 846 F. Supp. 1234, 69 FEP 966 (E.D. Pa. 1994) (recognizing sex-plus-age under Title VII); Godd v. West Communications, Inc., 1995 WL 67672 (D. Or. Feb. 16, 1995) (recognizing age-plus-sex under ADEA); contra Luce v. Dalton, 166 F.R.D. 457, 461 (S.D. Cal.) ("The rationale underlying 'sex-plus' theories of discrimination do not support the extension of the ADEA to subclass liability."), aff'd, 167 F.R.D. 88 (S.D. Cal. 1996).

[68]Forbes v. Reno, 893 F. Supp. 476, 483, 73 FEP 51 (W.D. Pa. 1995), aff'd, 91 F.3d 123 (3d Cir. 1996).

Spouses do not have standing to sue under the ADEA.[69]

The filing of a complaint by the EEOC on an individual's behalf terminates the right of the individual to bring his or her own suit.[70] An EEOC suit does not terminate the rights of opt-in plaintiffs who filed notices of their intent to opt in to a representative action prior to the date on which the EEOC filed its complaint. However, opt-in plaintiffs who filed opt-in notices after the EEOC filed its complaint are excluded from the previously filed representative action.[71]

2. Time for Filing Suit

The critical date for determining whether a suit is timely is the date the individual received notice from the EEOC that it has terminated its proceedings.[72] Although a court may presume that an EEOC letter of determination was received a reasonable time after it was mailed,[73] a plaintiff may rebut such a presumption with sworn testimony or other admissible evidence.[74]

Several courts have held that the 90-day statute of limitations adopted by the Civil Rights Act of 1991 applies when the complaint is filed after the effective date of the statute, even if the alleged act of discrimination occurred prior to its enactment.[75]

---

[69]Flamand v. American Int'l Group, Inc., 876 F. Supp. 356, 372, 69 FEP 675 (D.P.R. 1994).

[70]EEOC v. Louisiana Office of Community Servs., 47 F.3d 1438, 1442–43, 67 FEP 659 (5th Cir. 1995).

[71]Wilkerson v. Martin Marietta Corp., 875 F. Supp. 1456, 1464, 67 FEP 279 (D. Colo. 1995).

[72]Cheng v. Metropolitan Life Ins. Co., 1995 WL 37843 (S.D.N.Y. Jan. 31, 1995) (court rejected plaintiff's argument that filing suit within required time period would have been inconvenient because he was out of the country when the EEOC's determination was issued), aff'd mem., 71 F.3d 404 (2d Cir. 1995), cert. denied, 116 S. Ct. 2507 (1996).

[73]Hill v. Commercial Union Ins. Co., 4 AD 727, 730 (D. Kan. 1995), aff'd, 81 F.3d 172 (10th Cir. 1996).

[74]Sherlock v. Montefiore Med. Ctr., 84 F.3d 522, 526, 70 FEP 1377 (2d Cir. 1996).

[75]St. Louis v. Texas Worker's Compensation Comm'n, 65 F.3d 43, 47, 68 FEP 1631 (5th Cir. 1995), cert. denied, 116 S. Ct. 2563 (1996); Vernon v. Cassadaga Valley Cent. Sch. Dist., 49 F.3d 886, 889, 67 FEP 295 (2d Cir. 1995); Dunn v. Medina Gen. Hosp., 917 F. Supp. 1185, 1190 (N.D. Ohio 1996); Grinnell v. General Elec. Co., 907 F. Supp. 544, 546, 69 FEP 1005 (N.D.N.Y. 1995); Phuong v. National Academy of Sciences, 901 F. Supp. 12, 15 (D.D.C. 1995); Hesson v. Fireman's Fund Ins. Co., 897 F. Supp. 78, 80, 68 FEP 1747 (W.D.N.Y. 1995); Cloward v. Columbia Univ., 888 F. Supp. 21, 23, 67 FEP 905 (S.D.N.Y. 1995); Grady v. Bunzl Packaging Supply Co., 874 F. Supp. 387, 392 (N.D. Ga. 1994).

The filing of a request for reconsideration with the EEOC does not toll the 90-day period for filing an ADEA civil action.[76]

3. Scope of Suit

In some circumstances, courts will allow plaintiffs to challenge employer conduct that was not specifically mentioned in the EEOC charge[77] and/or bring suit against parties who were not named in the charge.[78]

---

[76]McCray v. Corry Mfg. Co., 872 F. Supp. 209, 212, 68 FEP 1685 (W.D. Pa. 1994), aff'd, 61 F.3d 224, 68 FEP 821 (3d Cir. 1995).

[77]Philipp v. ANR Freight Sys., Inc., 61 F.3d 669, 676, 70 FEP 1347 (8th Cir. 1995) (plaintiff's EEOC charge allegations that defendant's retaliation was of "continuing nature" sufficiently articulated cause of action for retaliatory refusal to rehire); Peterson v. Insurance Co. of N. Am., 884 F. Supp. 107, 111, 67 FEP 1390 (S.D.N.Y. 1995) (denying defendant's motion to dismiss claims for denial of promotion and two salary increases for lack of subject matter jurisdiction; scope of discrimination litigation is generally not limited to words of EEOC charge but to scope of EEOC's investigation of charge); Ellzey v. Espy, 66 FEP 1547 (E.D. La. 1995) (lawsuit may encompass constructive discharge if such claim "could reasonably be expected to grow out of the [prior] charge of discrimination"). *Contra* Evans v. Technologies Applications & Serv. Co., 80 F.3d 954, 963, 72 FEP 1222 (4th Cir. 1996) (plaintiff's claim of age discrimination did not necessarily arise from same facts and circumstances as her sex discrimination charge); Chester v. American Tel. & Tel. Co., 907 F. Supp. 982, 987 (N.D. Tex. 1994) (failure to transfer or hire charge is beyond scope of EEOC charge that alleges only discriminatory discharge, because employer will have responded to EEOC investigation with information related only to events surrounding employee's discharge, and not to employee's attempt to find another position), *aff'd*, 68 F.3d 470 (5th Cir. 1995), *cert. denied*, 516 U.S. 1141 (1996); Wishnoff v. Rubin, 1995 WL 591143 (W.D.N.Y. Sept. 11, 1995) ("constructive discharge claim is not like or reasonably related to a charge of discrimination in promotion").

[78]Sharkey v. Lasmo (Aul Ltd.), 906 F. Supp. 949, 954, 70 FEP 1673 (S.D.N.Y. 1995) (where identity of interest exists between corporation, which was not named in EEOC charge, and entity, which was named in charge, ADEA claim may proceed against unnamed corporation); Hrosik v. Latrobe Steel Co., 4 AD 555, 557 (W.D. Pa. 1995) (although plaintiffs failed to name employer's agents in their EEOC charge, court found no reason to preclude suit against agents where they held key positions with company, likely had notice of original EEOC charge, and were likely involved in initial voluntary conciliation process); Brogdon v. Alabama Dep't of Econ. & Community Affairs, 864 F. Supp. 1161, 1165, 66 FEP 325 (M.D. Ala. 1994) (director of state agency is not entitled to be dropped as defendant just because plaintiff failed to name him in EEOC charge, where charge named the agency as party, director is executive officer of agency, and director is sued in his official capacity). *Contra* Secrist v. Burns Int'l Sec. Servs., 926 F. Supp. 823, 826, 71 FEP 162 (E.D. Wis. 1996) (failure to name defendant in EEOC charge was basis for court's granting defendant's motion to dismiss plaintiff's ADEA and Title VII claims); Vakharia v. Little Co. of Mary Hosp. & Health Care Ctrs., 917 F. Supp. 1282 (N.D. Ill. 1996) (only those individuals named in EEOC charge can be sued for age discrimination);

F. Representative Actions

1. Standards for Determining Representativeness

Although ADEA representative actions are not controlled by Rule 23, one court considered Rule 23's requirements because it was not convinced that the FLSA's opt-in provisions were adequate for case management purposes and for ensuring that the class representatives fully and adequately protected the rights of opt ins.[79]

The Fifth Circuit upheld the decertification of a class where the district court had found that the "opt-in" employees were not similarly situated because they had widely disparate employment and discharge histories, and the employer had a variety of defenses to their claims.[80]

2. Notice to Potential Opt-In Plaintiffs

For a court to authorize notice, plaintiffs must describe the potential class within reasonable limits and provide some factual basis from which the court can determine if similarly situated potential plaintiffs exist.[81]

Stafford v. Radford Community Hosp., Inc., 908 F. Supp. 1369, 1373 (W.D. Va. 1995) (plaintiff failed to establish that named defendant had same substantial identity as unnamed defendant), *aff'd without opinion*, 120 F.3d 262 (4th Cir. 1997); Gerzog v. London Fog Corp., 907 F. Supp. 590, 72 FEP 371 (E.D.N.Y. 1995) (ADEA claims alleging liability of majority shareholder, not named in charged filed with state agency, dismissed, where there are no factual allegations to infer alter-ego or joint employer relationship); Catanzaro v. Supervalu, Inc., 67 FEP 10, 13 (E.D. Mo. 1994) (identity-of-interests doctrine did not subject corporation to liability for alleged age discrimination by its distant subsidiary that occurred prior to acquisition, where only evidence was list of pending claims presented during corporate buyout).

[79]Wilkerson v. Martin Marietta Corp., 875 F. Supp. 1456, 1461, 67 FEP 279 (D. Colo. 1995).

[80]Mooney v. Aramco Servs. Co., 54 F.3d 1207, 1215–16, 68 FEP 421 (5th Cir. 1995).

[81]Grayson v. KMart Corp., 79 F.3d 1086, 1099, 70 FEP 770 (11th Cir.) (plaintiffs met "similarly situated" requirement through substantial allegations and evidence of classwide discrimination), *cert. denied sub nom.* KMart Corp. v. Helton, 117 S. Ct. 447 (1996); Jackson v. New York Tel. Co., 163 F.R.D. 429, 432 (S.D.N.Y. 1995) (court held that plaintiffs seeking notice authorization were only required to demonstrate factual nexus that supported finding that potential plaintiffs were subject to common discriminatory scheme); Krueger v. New York Tel. Co., 163 F.R.D. 433, 445–46 (S.D.N.Y. 1995) (court approved notice where plaintiffs were similarly situated and alleged companywide discriminatory treatment); Schwed v. General Elec. Co., 159 F.R.D. 373, 376 (N.D.N.Y. 1995) (plaintiffs' request for discovery and notice

Class certification was denied in a case involving Title VII, ADEA, and FLSA claims in part because it would be difficult for the court to reconcile the conflicting "opt-out" procedure to which Title VII cases are subject with the "opt-in" procedure of the ADEA and the FLSA, and sending notice to the class would be extremely difficult.[82]

3. The Original EEOC Charge May Be Sufficient for Opt Ins

Courts continue to permit ADEA opt-in plaintiffs to rely on a co-plaintiff's EEOC charge, without having to file their own charge,[83] so long as the co-plaintiff's charge was timely filed and asserted classwide allegations.[84] However, there continues to be a split among the circuits as to whether the "single filing rule" should

---

reasonable where potential class was limited to salaried, exempt employees at specific geographic location who all had received notice of adverse employment action on specific date). *Cf.* Brooks v. Bellsouth Telecomms., Inc., 164 F.R.D. 561, 567 (N.D. Ala. 1995) (plaintiff's motion for class certification denied where plaintiff did not properly demonstrate sufficient factual basis for claim that defendants discriminated against their management employees on basis of age), *aff'd*, 114 F.3d 1202 (11th Cir. 1997); Oberg v. Allied Van Lines, 1994 WL 419679 (N.D. Ill. Aug. 5, 1994) (plaintiffs' motion to send class notices denied where charges only referred to their individual situations and did not contain allegations of classwide discrimination).

[82]Gorence v. Eagle Food Ctrs., Inc., 1994 WL 445149 (N.D. Ill. Aug. 16, 1994).

[83]Courts have also held that the fact that the individual filed his own untimely charge does not preclude him from relying on the timely charge of another class member. *See* Howlett v. Holiday Inns, Inc., 49 F.3d 189, 196–97, 67 FEP 289 (6th Cir.) (the purpose of the "single filing rule"—"to prevent a wooden application of the administrative charge requirement where the ends of the requirement have already been satisfied"—"is no less well served in application to a potential plaintiff who has untimely filed EEOC charge than to one who has never filed an administrative charge"), *cert. denied*, 116 S. Ct. 379 (1995); Bryson v. Fluor Corp., 914 F. Supp. 1292, 1297, 70 FEP 304 (D.S.C. 1995); Starr v. Westinghouse Elec. Corp., 1995 WL 817882 (D. Md. May 31, 1995). *Contra* Shapiro v. William Douglas McAdams, Inc., 68 FEP 199, 200 (E.D.N.Y. 1995) (plaintiff can "piggyback" onto another claimant's EEOC charge only if he could have filed his own timely charge on the date the named plaintiff filed his charge).

[84]Grayson v. KMart Corp., 79 F.3d 1086, 1101–02, 70 FEP 770 (11th Cir.), *cert. denied sub nom.* KMart Corp. v. Helton, 117 S. Ct. 447 (1996); Anderson v. Unisys Corp., 47 F.3d 302, 307, 67 FEP 317 (8th Cir.), *cert. denied,* 116 S. Ct. 299 (1995); EEOC v. Sara Lee Corp., 923 F. Supp. 994, 998–99, 70 FEP 57 (W.D. Mich. 1995); Bryson v. Fluor Corp., 914 F. Supp. 1292, 1294–96, 70 FEP 304 (D.S.C. 1995) (charge that is later amended to contain language asserting classwide allegations relates back to original filing date of charge). *Contra* Thomure v. Phillips Furniture Co., 30 F.3d 1020, 1027, 65 FEP 976 (8th Cir.) ("[i]n the absence of a properly filed discrimination charge, a party cannot be permitted to proceed with his discrimination lawsuit if he is attempting to piggyback on another's meritless charge . . ."), *cert. denied,* 513 U.S. 1191 (1995).

apply outside the class action setting in ADEA cases.[85] The Fifth Circuit has held that the "single filing rule" may not be used by an individual who filed his own EEOC charge to append an additional claim and avoid the statute of limitations on that claim.[86]

The Eleventh Circuit recently joined the Eighth Circuit in holding, for pre-1991 CRA cases, that only a written consent to opt in will toll the statute of limitations on an opt-in plaintiff's cause of action. Consequently, an opt-in plaintiff must file his or her written consent prior to the expiration of the statute of limitations on his or her ADEA claim.[87]

4. ADEA Trial Structure for Representative Actions

In *Flavel v. Svedala Industries, Inc.*,[88] the trial court, employing procedures similar to those used under Title VII, bifurcated ADEA pattern and practice claims into a liability phase, where the plaintiffs were required to prove discrimination by a preponderance of the evidence, and a remedial phase, where the scope of relief for each class member was to be determined.[89]

G. Jury Trial

The Seventh Circuit rejected an employer's argument that "a stricter scrutiny of jury verdicts is appropriate in age-discrimination than in other cases because juries tend . . . to be especially sympathetic to the plaintiffs in those cases."[90]

---

[85]*Compare* Whalen v. W.R. Grace & Co., 56 F.3d 504, 507, 67 FEP 1633 (3d Cir. 1995) (where plaintiffs choose to bring suit individually, they must first satisfy prerequisite of filing timely EEOC charges) *with* Howlett v. Holiday Inns, Inc., 49 F.3d 189, 194, 67 FEP 289 (6th Cir.) ("single filing rule" is not limited to class actions but also can permit plaintiff to join individual ADEA actions if named plaintiff filed timely administrative charge sufficient to permit "piggybacking" by joining plaintiff), *cert. denied,* 116 S. Ct. 379 (1995).

[86]Mooney v. Aramco Servs. Co., 54 F.3d 1207, 1223–24, 68 FEP 421 (5th Cir. 1995).

[87]Grayson v. KMart Corp., 79 F.3d 1086, 1106–07, 70 FEP 770 (11th Cir.) (ADEA opt-in plaintiffs commence their civil action only when they file their written consent to opt into class action), *cert. denied sub nom.* KMart Corp. v. Helton, 117 S. Ct. 447 (1996). *Contra* Sperling v. Hoffmann-LaRoche, Inc., 24 F.3d 463, 472–73, 64 FEP 910 (3d Cir. 1994) (statute of limitations for ADEA opt-in plaintiffs should be tolled by filing of original class complaint).

[88]868 F. Supp. 1422, 1460, 70 FEP 1088 (E.D. Wis. 1994).

[89]*Id.*

[90]EEOC v. G-K-G, Inc., 39 F.3d 740, 745, 66 FEP 344 (7th Cir. 1994).

A district court held that a plaintiff is not entitled to a jury trial concerning liquidated damages "since it appears that an award of liquidated damages is discretionary with the Court . . . ."[91]

IV. PROOF

A. Disparate Treatment

In *O'Connor v. Consolidated Coin Caterers Corp.*,[92] the Supreme Court sidestepped the issue of whether applying the *McDonnell Douglas*[93] evidentiary framework—a Title VII concept—to the ADEA context is appropriate. The Court "assume[d]," because "the parties do not contest the point," that the "application of the Title VII rule to the ADEA context is correct."[94]

1. The Prima Facie Case

Courts continue to display flexibility in applying the criteria for establishing a prima facie case,[95] particularly in reduction-in-force cases.[96] A plaintiff is not limited to the *McDonnell Douglas* frame-

---

[91]Johnston v. Metropolitan Life Ins. Co., 1995 WL 860757 (E.D. Mo. Mar. 23, 1995).
[92]517 U.S. 308, 70 FEP 486 (1996).
[93]McDonnell Douglas Corp. v. Green, 411 U.S. 792 (1973).
[94]517 U.S. at 311–13.
[95]Isenbergh v. Knight-Ridder Newspaper Sales, Inc., 97 F.3d 436, 440, 72 FEP 735 (11th Cir. 1996) (because employment discrimination cases are not easily categorized, any prima facie case test must be flexible), *cert. denied,* 117 S. Ct. 2511 (1997); Sanchez v. Puerto Rico Oil Co., 37 F.3d 712, 719, 66 FEP 148 (1st Cir. 1994) ("The prima facie case requirement embodies a concept, not a mechanical exercise."); Gould v. Kemper Nat'l Ins. Cos., 880 F. Supp. 527, 534 n. 3 (N.D. Ill. 1995) ("The Seventh Circuit has adopted an array of 'fourth elements,' each tailored for differing types of employment actions—hiring, nonpromotion, demotion, discharge."), *aff'd mem.*, 78 F.3d 586 (7th Cir. 1996); Wanamaker v. Columbian Rope Co., 907 F. Supp. 522, 530, 69 FEP 972 (N.D.N.Y. 1995) (in Second Circuit, to establish fourth element of prima facie case plaintiff need only show that discharge occurred under circumstances giving rise to inference of discrimination), *aff'd,* 108 F.3d 462, 73 FEP 321 (2d Cir. 1997); Dittmann v. Ireco, Inc., 883 F. Supp. 807, 811, 73 FEP 435 (N.D.N.Y.) ("Constructive discharge . . . may establish the third element of the prima facie case."), *partial summary judgment granted,* 903 F. Supp. 347, 73 FEP 441 (N.D.N.Y. 1995).
[96]*See, e.g.,* Collier v. Budd Co., 66 F.3d 886, 890–91, 68 FEP 1435 (7th Cir. 1995) (in RIF cases, fourth element of prima facie case is not that employee was replaced by younger employee, but instead that younger employees were treated more

work, but may establish a prima facie case with different types of proof.[97]

The transfer or shifting of an employee's duties and responsibilities to other persons who are already employed by the defendant does not constitute "replacement" for purposes of establishing a prima facie case under the ADEA.[98]

a. Plaintiff's Qualifications. Most courts require only a basic showing of qualifications at the prima facie stage.[99] Most courts

---

favorably); Jones v. Unisys Corp., 54 F.3d 624, 630, 67 FEP 1065 (10th Cir. 1995) (in RIF cases, plaintiff may fulfill fourth element by producing direct or circumstantial evidence that his employer intended to discriminate against him based on his age; this may be shown by introducing evidence that plaintiff was treated less favorably than younger workers); Woodman v. Haemonetics Corp., 51 F.3d 1087, 1091, 67 FEP 838 (1st Cir. 1995) (in RIF cases, plaintiff may fulfill fourth element by showing that employer did not treat age neutrally *or* it retained younger persons in same position); McCreless v. Moore Business Forms, Inc., 1996 WL 243378 (S.D. Tex. May 2, 1996) (prima facie case in RIF case requires evidence that employer did not treat employee's age neutrally in employment decision rather than evidence that employee was replaced by someone significantly younger); Fink v. Kitzman, 881 F. Supp. 1347, 1364, 4 AD 644 (N.D. Iowa 1995); Greyson v. McKenna & Cuneo, 879 F. Supp. 1065, 1067, 67 FEP 792 (D. Colo. 1995).

[97]Isenbergh v. Knight-Ridder Newspaper Sales, Inc., 97 F.3d 436, 439, 72 FEP 735 (11th Cir. 1996), *cert. denied,* 117 S. Ct. 2511 (1997).

[98]Kern v. Kollsman, 885 F. Supp. 335, 344 (D.N.H. 1995) (discharged employee is not replaced when another employee is assigned to perform plaintiff's duties in addition to other duties, or when work is redistributed among other existing employees already performing related work; replacement occurs only when another employee is hired or reassigned to perform plaintiff's duties); Campbell v. Fasco Indus., Inc., 861 F. Supp. 1385, 1391, 72 FEP 33 (N.D. Ill. 1994) (title is not determinative in establishing replacement; "replacement's" position must be substantially the same as plaintiff's former position), *aff'd mem.,* 67 F.3d 301, 72 FEP 96 (7th Cir. 1995); Nappi v. Meridian Leasing Corp., 859 F. Supp. 1177, 1181 (N.D. Ill. 1994) (fact that another employee was trained to do job similar to plaintiff's does not constitute replacement); Richardson v. William Powell Co., 3 AD 1751 (S.D. Ohio 1994).

[99]Kotas v. Waterman Broad., 927 F. Supp. 1547, 1552 (M.D. Fla. 1996) (fact that plaintiff continued to work as engineer one day per week after his demotion established his qualification for position); Saeli v. Motorola, Inc., 917 F. Supp. 589, 594 (N.D. Ill. 1996) ("A determination that an individual is performing a job well enough to satisfy the performance element of the test can be established solely by the plaintiff's own testimony about the quality of his work."); Mulqueen v. Daka, Inc., 909 F. Supp. 86, 90, 73 FEP 31 (N.D.N.Y. 1995) (plaintiff must produce sufficient evidence that he was qualified, but need not show that employer was satisfied with his performance), *aff'd,* 104 F.3d 351, 73 FEP 192 (2d Cir. 1996); Nakai v. Wickes Lumber Co., 906 F. Supp. 698, 704, 71 FEP 13 (D. Me. 1995) (where an employee has a long history of satisfactory performance, "he clears the low prima facie hurdle . . ."); Chastain v. USF&G Corp., 5 AD 310, 312 (W.D. Okla. 1996) (plaintiff is qualified where he presented evidence of prior performance appraisals indicating his performance was acceptable for seven years prior to termination); Mayo v. Dillard's

defer the issue of disputed qualifications to the pretext stage of the case.[100]

b. Someone "Younger." Some courts have held that proof that the plaintiff was replaced by someone younger, without further evidence that age bias prompted the adverse employment action, does not establish a prima facie case under the ADEA.[101]

Dep't Stores, Inc., 884 F. Supp. 417, 422–23 (D. Kan. 1995) (plaintiff was able to establish prima facie case based on her personal assessment that her performance was satisfactory, despite fact that her employer produced evidence that she did not meet her sales quota); Jones v. Alabama Power Co., 3 AD 1717 (N.D. Ala. 1995) (plaintiff's own conclusory assertions regarding her qualifications for job may be sufficient to establish qualification element of prima facie case), *aff'd mem.*, 77 F.3d 498, 7 AD 1536 (11th Cir. 1996); Brewer v. Quaker State Oil Ref. Corp., 874 F. Supp. 672, 682, 69 FEP 743 (W.D. Pa.) (employee's long-term experience as sales representative and receipt of bonus for exceeding sales requirements in past years is sufficient to demonstrate his basic qualifications as sales representative and thus satisfy prima facie case requirement that he was qualified for position), *rev'd and remanded on other grounds*, 72 F.3d 326, 69 FEP 753 (3d Cir. 1995); Barton v. Forbes, Inc., 67 FEP 138, 140 (S.D.N.Y. 1995) (bonuses and raises paid to plaintiff provide sufficient evidence that she was performing satisfactorily); Elguindy v. Commonwealth Edison Co., 903 F. Supp. 1260 (N.D. Ill. 1995) (in denial of promotion case, "qualification for promotion sought" element of the prima facie case can be met solely through plaintiff's own testimony concerning quality of her work); Jackson v. Lyons Falls Pulp & Paper, Inc., 865 F. Supp. 87, 96, 74 FEP 1667 (N.D.N.Y. 1994) ("Plaintiff's years of relevant work experience alone are sufficient to demonstrate that he had the minimum basic skills necessary to perform his job."); Schutz v. Finkelstein, Bruckman, Wohl, Most & Rothman, 66 FEP 1094, 1096 (S.D.N.Y. 1994) (jury could find that plaintiff was qualified because defendant hired him, kept him in their employ for four years, gave him significant annual raises, and never indicated that his work was substandard); Campbell v. Fasco Indus., Inc., 861 F. Supp. 1385, 1398, 72 FEP 33 (N.D. Ill. 1994) ("[A] plaintiff can establish the second element of the prima facie case through his own testimony that his performance was satisfactory."), *aff'd mem.*, 67 F.3d 301, 72 FEP 96 (7th Cir. 1995); Derbis v. U.S. Shoe Corp., 3 AD 1029, 1034 (D. Md. 1994) (plaintiff created genuine factual issue as to whether she met employer's legitimate expectations by submitting evidence that she received numerous awards and commendations for her job performance in months before she was discharged), *aff'd in part and remanded*, 67 F.3d 294 (4th Cir. 1995). *Cf.* Kennedy v. GN Danavox, 928 F. Supp. 866, 873 (D. Minn. 1996) (plaintiff's receipt of bonus based on companywide sales figures, as opposed to personal performance, was not sufficient evidence from which reasonable jury could conclude his performance was satisfactory).

[100]Hartsel v. Keys, 87 F.3d 795, 801, 72 FEP 951 (6th Cir. 1996), *cert. denied*, 117 S. Ct. 683 (1997); Whitchurch v. Apache Prods. Co., 916 F. Supp. 809, 815, 6 AD 1589 (N.D. Ill. 1996) (qualification "element of the prima facie case is intertwined with the issue of whether [the defendant's] legitimate nondiscriminatory reason . . . was in fact pretextual . . ."); Taylor v. Canteen Corp., 69 F.3d 773, 780–81, 69 FEP 310 (7th Cir. 1995).

[101]Bialas v. Greyhound Lines, Inc., 59 F.3d 759, 763, 68 FEP 552 (8th Cir. 1995) (during reduction in force, fact that plaintiff's duties are assumed by younger per-

The Supreme Court's decision in *O'Connor v. Consolidated Coin Caterers Corp.*[102] confirmed that the plaintiff's replacement need not be outside the protected group.[103] However, there will likely continue to be disagreement over what constitutes "substantially younger."[104]

2. Defendant's Articulation of a Legitimate, Nondiscriminatory Reason

Courts continue to require the defendant to produce evidence of a legitimate, nondiscriminatory reason for its employment decision, once the plaintiff has established a prima facie case.[105]

---

son is not in itself enough to establish prima facie case); Arroyo v. New York State Ins. Dep't, 4 AD 1830, 1834 (S.D.N.Y. 1995), *aff'd,* 104 F.3d 349 (2d Cir. 1996); Campbell v. Fasco Indus., Inc., 861 F. Supp. 1385, 1392, 72 FEP 33 (N.D. Ill. 1994) ("[a]n employer does not violate the ADEA merely by discharging an employee whose age falls within the protected category and replacing him with a younger worker"; such facts merely place the plaintiff within the protected class and establish injury).

[102]517 U.S. 308, 70 FEP 486 (1996).

[103]*O'Connor* held that the replacement need only be "substantially younger," 517 U.S. at 313. *See* Roper v. Peabody Coal Co., 47 F.3d 925, 927, 67 FEP 670 (7th Cir. 1995) ("The disparity in age within the protected class must be sufficient to create a reasonable inference of age discrimination.").

[104]*Compare* Barber v. CSX Distrib. Servs., 68 F.3d 694, 699, 69 FEP 81 (3d Cir. 1995) (eight-year age difference between plaintiff and successful candidate, who was also in protected age class, is sufficiently "younger" to establish prima facie case of age discrimination); Moody v. Department of Educ., 883 F. Supp. 624, 630 (M.D. Ala. 1995) (19- and 17-year age discrepancies are "substantial enough"), *aff'd mem.,* 77 F.3d 498 (11th Cir.), *cert. denied,* 117 S. Ct. 175 (1996), Kotas v. Waterman Broad., 927 F. Supp. 1547, 1551 (M.D. Fla. 1996) (58-year-old's replacement by 47-year-old was sufficient to establish prima facie case), *and* Nembhard v. Memorial Sloan-Kettering Cancer Ctr., 918 F. Supp. 784, 790 (S.D.N.Y. 1996) (given other significant evidence of discriminatory intent, one-year differential does not preclude finding of age discrimination), *aff'd,* 104 F.3d 353 (2d Cir. 1996) *with* Wilson v. International Bus. Mach. Corp., 62 F.3d 237, 241, 68 FEP 1019 (8th Cir. 1995) (inference of age discrimination cannot be drawn where three of eight persons who took over 52-year-old plaintiff's duties were age 50 or over), Mintzmyer v. Babbitt, 66 FEP 1804, 1815 (D.D.C.) (plaintiff cannot make out prima facie case because she was replaced by individual only three years younger), *aff'd mem.,* 72 F.3d 920 (D.C. Cir. 1995), Zambelli v. Historic Landmarks, Inc., 4 AD 308, 313 (E.D. Pa. 1995) (replacing plaintiff with new employee who is age 52 and only 11 months younger than plaintiff does not rise to inference of age discrimination), *and* Lubkeman v. Commonwealth Edison Co., 877 F. Supp. 1180, 1187, 67 FEP 514 (N.D. Ill. 1995) ("The simple fact that the age differences between the men and [the plaintiff] (four years, two years, four years, and six years respectively) were 'fairly marginal' weakens [the plaintiff's] claim.").

[105]Manzer v. Diamond Shamrock Chems. Co., 29 F.3d 1078, 1082, 65 FEP 585 (6th Cir. 1994).

However, most courts are reluctant to review the propriety of employers' business decisions.[106]

The need to reduce the workforce or reorganize is one of the most frequent reasons offered by defendants for termination decisions. In these cases, courts often defer to the employer's decision without necessarily requiring proof of profitability or the validity of the decision.[107] Other common legitimate business reasons for employment actions have included market conditions for establishment of salaries,[108] physical inability to perform,[109] and qualifications.[110] Legitimate, nondiscriminatory reasons can be based upon subjective reasons.[111]

3. Plaintiff's Proof of Pretext

Pretext continues to be a significant hurdle for the age discrimination plaintiff, including at the pretrial stage. To show pretext, the plaintiff must discredit the employer's proffered "legitimate nondiscriminatory reason" by showing that it is a post hoc

---

[106]Anderson v. Queen Carpet Corp., 68 FEP 83, 85 (N.D. Ga. 1995) ("Regardless of whether the court or the plaintiffs agree with the wisdom or logic of [defendant's] decision, it is not for the court to review the propriety of a business decision on the part of [defendant].").

[107]Birkbeck v. Marvel Lighting Corp., 30 F.3d 507, 511, 65 FEP 669 (4th Cir.) (deferring to defendant's business judgment in closing department), cert. denied, 513 U.S. 1058 (1994); Lewis v. Aerospace Community Credit Union, 934 F. Supp. 314, 320, 74 FEP 1339 (E.D. Mo. 1996) (refusing to require employer to provide evidence of financial distress to legitimize reduction in force), aff'd, 114 F.3d 745, 74 FEP 1443, petition for cert. filed (1997). See Philipp v. ANR Freight Sys., Inc., 61 F.3d 669, 672–73, 70 FEP 1347 (8th Cir. 1995) (defendant articulated legitimate nondiscriminatory reason where it submitted evidence of adverse economic conditions resulting in massive reduction in force).

[108]Rosen v. Columbia Univ., 68 FEP 1190, 1194–95 (S.D.N.Y. 1995) (market factors, e.g., current salaries of prospective employees, offers of competitors, are legitimate factors in establishing salary), aff'd mem., 101 F.3d 108 (2d Cir. 1996); Shannon v. Saks & Co., 66 EPD ¶ 43,591 at 82,907, 82,908 (N.D. Ill. 1995) (market-dictated higher salaries for recruited applicants are legitimate).

[109]Jones v. Alabama Power Co., 3 AD 1717, 1732 (N.D. Ala. 1995) (reliance upon medical evidence legitimate), aff'd, 77 F.3d 498, 7 AD 1536 (11th Cir. 1996); Derbis v. U.S. Shoe Corp., 65 FEP 1322, 1334 (D. Md. 1994) (failure to provide medical release legitimizes action).

[110]Lamb v. Runyon, 915 F. Supp. 300, 305 (M.D. Ala. 1995) (qualification ratings under defendant's selection criteria legitimate).

[111]Manzer v. Diamond Shamrock Chems. Co., 29 F.3d 1078, 1082, 65 FEP 585 (6th Cir. 1994) (legitimate reason was employee's argumentative, confrontational, "obnoxious and unreliable" behavior). Cf. Carlson v. WPLG/TV, 70 FEP 1596, 1601–02 (S.D. Fla. 1996) (customer preferences for younger anchors is not legitimate).

fabrication or otherwise unworthy of credence.[112] Attacks on collateral issues[113] and rebuttal of less than all of the employer's proffered reasons[114] are legally insufficient. On the other hand, evidence that directly challenges the factual basis for the employer's ultimate justification will generally suffice.[115]

---

[112]Isenbergh v. Knight-Ridder Newspaper Sales, Inc., 97 F.3d 436, 444, 72 FEP 735 (11th Cir. 1996) (plaintiff must introduce " 'significantly probative' " evidence directed at the veracity of the employer's ultimate justification (quoting Young v. General Foods Corp., 840 F.2d 825, 829 (11th Cir. 1988)), *cert. denied,* 117 S. Ct. 2511 (1997); Brewer v. Quaker State Oil Ref. Corp., 72 F.3d 326, 331, 69 FEP 753 (3d Cir. 1995) (plaintiff must demonstrate such "weaknesses, implausibilities, inconsistencies, incoherences, or contradictions" that a reasonable factfinder could find the employer's reason unworthy of credence (quoting Fuentes v. Perskie, 32 F.3d 759, 765 (3d Cir. 1994))).

[113]Isenbergh v. Knight-Ridder Newspaper Sales, Inc., 97 F.3d 436, 444, 72 FEP 735 (11th Cir. 1996) (affirming summary judgment for employer where evidence of plaintiff's superior sales abilities did not refute employer's determination that his managerial skills were inferior); Manzer v. Diamond Shamrock Chems. Co., 29 F.3d 1078, 1084–85, 65 FEP 585 (6th Cir. 1994) (directed verdict for employer affirmed where standard salary increases and invitation to participate in profit sharing did not refute employer's assertion that plaintiff was argumentative, confrontational, and inaccurate); Crumm v. Oce'-Bruning, Inc., 892 F. Supp. 1236, 1243–45 (E.D. Mo. 1995) (evidence that plaintiff was replaced by younger employee, that other employees in the protected age group were terminated, and that employer allegedly showed preference for younger employees by holding "disco dances" at sales meetings did not show that plaintiff's termination for poor performance was pretextual); Hiatt v. Union Pac. R.R., 859 F. Supp. 1416, 1421, 1429–30, 67 FEP 351 (D. Wyo. 1994) (evidence of employer's awareness that mandatory promotion policy would adversely impact older workers did not refute employer's assertion that policy was required by federal statute), *aff'd,* 65 F.3d 838, 68 FEP 1160 (10th Cir. 1995), *cert. denied,* 516 U.S. 1115 (1996); Adams v. DuPont Merck Pharm. Co., 67 FEP 1072, 1075 (E.D. Pa. 1994) (fact that plaintiff's negative performance evaluations coincided with announcement of retirement incentives did not show pretext where there was no evidence plaintiff was eligible for incentives), *aff'd mem.,* 70 F.3d 1254, 71 FEP 1408 (3d Cir. 1995).

[114]Wolf v. Buss (Am.), Inc., 77 F.3d 914, 923, 70 FEP 130 (7th Cir.) (affirming summary judgment for employer where plaintiff challenged only four of six proffered reasons), *cert. denied,* 117 S. Ct. 175 (1996); Tipsword v. Ogilvy & Mather, Inc., 918 F. Supp. 217, 223, 70 FEP 1514 (N.D. Ill. 1996) (plaintiff challenged only two of employer's three reasons), *aff'd,* 106 F.3d 403, 72 FEP 1279 (7th Cir. 1997).

[115]Rhodes v. Guiberson Oil Tools, 75 F.3d 989, 995–96, 69 FEP 1720 (5th Cir. 1996) (en banc) (jury verdict upheld where plaintiff successfully rebutted allegations of poor performance with customer testimony regarding his skills); Collier v. Budd Co., 66 F.3d 886, 892, 68 FEP 1435 (7th Cir. 1995) (summary judgment for employer reversed where laid-off plaintiff produced evidence that his qualifications may have been superior to those of younger employees who were retained); Waldron v. SL Indus., Inc., 56 F.3d 491, 496–98, 500–01, 67 FEP 1577 (3d Cir. 1995) (summary judgment for employer reversed where plaintiff produced evidence that his duties were divided after RIF but later reconsolidated and given to younger employee and that younger

Courts differ as to what evidence of intent the plaintiff must produce to survive a motion for summary judgment or for directed verdict. The Third, Sixth, and Seventh Circuits have held that an age discrimination plaintiff need only show that the employer's proffered reason is unworthy of credence to survive a motion for summary judgment.[116] District courts in the First and Tenth Circuits have reached an opposite conclusion—that age plaintiffs must produce evidence that the employer's proffered reason is false *and* additional evidence that the real reason is intentional discrimination.[117] A third group of courts—the Fifth, Eighth, and Eleventh Circuits—has applied traditional sufficiency-of-the-evidence principles to conclude that a showing of pretext alone will create a triable fact issue only if the evidence will also support a reasonable inference of intentional discrimination.[118]

---

employee lacked any experience in area in which plaintiff was primarily criticized); Khair v. Campbell Soup Co., 893 F. Supp. 316, 333, 339, 75 FEP 995 (D.N.J. 1995) (summary judgment denied in failure to promote case where employer did not raise alleged deficiencies in plaintiff's managerial skills until plaintiff applied for position); Schwarz v. Northwest Iowa Community College, 881 F. Supp. 1323, 1341, 4 AD 490 (N.D. Iowa 1995) (employer's motion for summary judgment denied where employer abandoned one of two conflicting reasons for adverse decision and plaintiff offered evidence rebutting second reason); Finch v. Hercules, Inc., 865 F. Supp. 1104, 1127, 74 FEP 1571 (D. Del. 1994) (fact issue existed as to whether performance-based layoff was pretextual where plaintiff produced evidence that he was strong decisionmaker and hard worker and that he had received greater than average salary increases).

[116]Collier v. Budd Co., 66 F.3d 886, 892–93, 68 FEP 1435 (7th Cir. 1995) (plaintiff may avoid summary judgment by showing employer's proffered reason has no basis in fact, did not actually motivate employer, or was insufficient to motivate employer); Brewer v. Quaker State Oil Ref. Corp., 72 F.3d 326, 331, 69 FEP 753 (3d Cir. 1995) (to avoid summary judgment, plaintiff need only "discredit" employer's proffered reason); Manzer v. Diamond Shamrock Chems. Co., 29 F.3d 1078, 1083, 65 FEP 585 (6th Cir. 1994) (plaintiff "must produce sufficient evidence from which the jury may reasonably reject the employer's explanation"); *accord* Stone v. Georgia Power Co., 902 F. Supp. 1578, 1585–86, 69 FEP 25 (M.D. Ga. 1995) (plaintiff may avoid summary judgment by showing that discrimination more likely than not motivated employer or that employer's reason is unworthy of credence).

[117]Kern v. Kollsman, 885 F. Supp. 335, 342–43 (D.N.H. 1995) and Braverman v. Penobscot Shoe Co., 859 F. Supp. 596, 601, 3 AD 847 (D. Me. 1994) (plaintiff must come forward with "minimally sufficient" evidence of pretext *and* evidence of discriminatory animus); Hiatt v. Union Pac. R.R., 859 F. Supp. 1416, 1429, 67 FEP 351 (D. Wyo. 1994) (holding that *St. Mary's Honor Ctr.* that plaintiff carries ultimate burden of proving pretext for intentional discrimination applies with full force at the summary judgment stage), *aff'd,* 65 F.3d 838, 68 FEP 1160 (10th Cir. 1995), *cert. denied,* 516 U.S. 1115 (1996).

[118]Isenbergh v. Knight-Ridder Newspaper Sales, Inc., 97 F.3d 436, 440–41, 72 FEP 735 (11th Cir. 1996) (showing of pretext alone is sufficient, at least in some

Most pretext arguments involve recurring themes or combinations thereof, including evidence of age-related comments in the workplace, evidence of the plaintiff's good performance, and evidence that younger comparables were treated differently. In addition, plaintiffs often challenge employers' business decisions, even though most courts continue to hold that attacks on employers' business decisions are insufficient to show pretext.[119] In the reduction-in-force context, courts are especially hesitant to second-guess an employer's business decisions, including the employer's RIF selection criteria and post-RIF hiring decisions.[120]

---

cases, to defeat motion for summary judgment), *cert. denied,* 117 S. Ct. 2511 (1997); Rothmeier v. Investment Advisers, Inc., 85 F.3d 1328, 1336, 71 FEP 1458 (8th Cir. 1996) (plaintiff may rely on same evidence to prove both pretext and intentional discrimination, provided overall strength of evidence is sufficient for a reasonable factfinder to infer that employer was motivated by intent to discriminate); Rhodes v. Guiberson Oil Tools, 75 F.3d 989, 994, 69 FEP 1720 (5th Cir. 1996) (en banc) (evidence of pretext, in combination with prima facie case, is legally sufficient only if it reasonably supports an inference of intentional discrimination).

[119]Isenbergh v. Knight-Ridder Newspaper Sales, Inc., 97 F.3d 436, 444, 72 FEP 735 (11th Cir. 1996) (employer's implementation of new performance ranking system was business decision not subject to court's review), *cert. denied,* 117 S. Ct. 2511 (1997); Slathar v. Sather Trucking Corp., 78 F.3d 415, 419, 70 FEP 574 (8th Cir.) (court found no error in business decision instruction, noting that employer has a right to make business decisions that should not be reviewed by judge or jury), *cert denied,* 117 S. Ct. 179 (1996); Krenik v. County of Le Sueur, 47 F.3d 953, 960, 67 FEP 312 (8th Cir. 1995) (affirming summary judgment where plaintiff merely attacked employer's determination of which skills were most important for position); Hill v. St. Louis Univ., 923 F. Supp. 1199, 1212, 71 FEP 43 (E.D. Mo. 1996) (failure to confront plaintiff with complaints or conduct thorough investigation before issuing reprimand was business decision), *aff'd,* 123 F.3d 1114 (8th Cir. 1997). *Cf.* Collier v. Budd Co., 66 F.3d 886, 892, 68 FEP 1435 (7th Cir. 1995) (fact issue existed as to relative importance of qualifications where employer insisted that sales ability was not most important skill for salesperson).

[120]Furr v. Seagate Tech., Inc., 82 F.3d 980, 986–87, 70 FEP 1325 (10th Cir. 1996) and Doan v. Seagate Tech., Inc., 82 F.3d 974, 977–79, 70 FEP 1202 (10th Cir. 1996) (noting that the wisdom and manner of RIF is not for a court or jury to decide, court reversed jury verdict for plaintiff, finding insufficient evidence of pretext even though the criteria for selection were subjective, the company was financially profitable at the time of the RIF, and the company hired employees shortly before and after the RIF), *cert. denied,* 117 S. Ct. 684 (1997); Langenfeld v. Stoelting, Inc., 902 F. Supp. 847, 857–58 (E.D. Wis. 1995) (finding no pretext even though employer hired a younger woman as a regional sales manager at the same time it eliminated plaintiff's regional sales manager position); Richardson v. William Powell Co., 3 AD 1751, 1754–55 (S.D. Ohio 1994) (rejecting argument that pretext could be inferred from evidence that company had more employees one year after plaintiff's discharge than it did at time of plaintiff's discharge); Smith v. Cook County, 869 F. Supp. 547, 551, 72 FEP 155 (N.D. Ill. 1994) (summary judgment granted for employer even though plaintiff

Increasingly, courts are rejecting age-related remarks by nondecisionmakers as probative evidence of pretext, even when the remarks are made by company officials.[121] Courts continue to discount "stray" or isolated age-related remarks in the absence of other evidence of pretext.[122] However, ageist comments by a decisionmaker made contemporaneously with the alleged discriminatory employment decision may be sufficient to prevent summary judgment for the employer.[123]

---

presented evidence that department from which plaintiff was laid off was allocated five additional positions at time of RIF), *aff'd*, 74 F.3d 829, 72 FEP 158 (7th Cir. 1996). *Cf.* Phillips v. Manufacturers Hanover Trust Co., 67 FEP 1737, 1738–39 (S.D.N.Y. 1995) (fact that new employees were hired post-RIF and given similar job duties as plaintiff was sufficient evidence of pretext to withstand summary judgment).

[121]Jones v. Unisys Corp., 54 F.3d 624, 632, 67 FEP 1065 (10th Cir. 1995) (stray remark by human resources employee responsible for job postings who was not involved in the decisionmaking process does not establish intent to discriminate); Courtney v. Biosound, Inc., 42 F.3d 414, 419, 66 FEP 971 (7th Cir. 1994) (executive's age-related comments not relevant because his possible discriminatory intent could not be attributed to primary decisionmaker); Tucker v. Kingsbury Corp., 929 F. Supp. 50, 55, 75 FEP 1316 (D.N.H. 1996) (age-related comments by executive vice president not probative evidence of pretext because he was not involved in decision to lay off plaintiff); *cf.* Finch v. Hercules, Inc., 865 F. Supp. 1104, 1123–24, 74 FEP 1571 (D. Del. 1994) (when major company executive makes age-related stray remarks, it does not matter whether he was a decisionmaker in adverse employment action).

[122]Birkbeck v. Marvel Lighting Corp., 30 F.3d 507, 511–12, 65 FEP 669 (4th Cir.) (ageist remark by decisionmaker made over two years before plaintiff's discharge did not constitute evidence of age discrimination nor did it create inference of age bias), *cert. denied,* 513 U.S. 1058 (1994). *Cf.* Ryther v. KARE 11, 84 F.3d 1074, 1084, 70 FEP 1709 (8th Cir. 1996) (stray ageist remarks can support inference of age discrimination if other evidence of pretext exists), *aff'd*, 108 F.3d 832 (8th Cir.) (en banc), *cert. denied,* 117 S. Ct. 2510 (1997).

[123]Woodman v. Haemonetics Corp., 51 F.3d 1087, 1093, 67 FEP 838 (1st Cir. 1995) (court reversed summary judgment for employer, concluding that decisionmaker's comment following meeting with upper management ("These damn people—they want younger people here. They will be the one[s] that will be successful here.") was probative evidence of pretext and age animus); Futrell v. J.I. Case, 38 F.3d 342, 347, 66 FEP 238 (7th Cir. 1994) (derogatory comments about older workers by persons who made decision to terminate plaintiff were sufficient to defeat employer's summary judgment motion); Armbruster v. Unisys Corp., 32 F.3d 768, 783, 65 FEP 828 (3d Cir. 1994) (contemporaneous comments by decisionmakers coupled with documents containing age notations were sufficient inferences of pretext to defeat summary judgment); Corbin v. Southland Int'l Trucks, 25 F.3d 1545, 1549, 65 FEP 552 (11th Cir. 1994) (single age-related remark by decisionmaker was circumstantial evidence from which discriminatory intent could be inferred). *See also* Tibbitts v. Van Den Bergh Foods Co., 859 F. Supp. 1168, 1173, 66 FEP 560 (N.D. Ill. 1994) (decisionmaker's comment almost two years before plaintiff's termination ("We've got to get rid of these old gals and get some young gals in here.") was sufficient

The mere fact that an employer solicits age information from the plaintiff or otherwise maintains age information is insufficient to establish pretext.[124]

Typically, courts will not consider an employee's good performance as probative evidence of pretext, except when the employer's reason for the adverse action against the employee is inadequate performance.[125] Perhaps the most effective method of establishing pretext is evidence that younger employees in similar positions were treated differently in similar circumstances.[126]

The "same actor" defense—that the same decisionmaker hired and fired the plaintiff, thus negating any inference of discriminatory intent or pretext—continues to gain acceptance with some courts.[127]

---

evidence of pretext to defeat employer's summary judgment motion even though it was not made contemporaneous with decision to terminate plaintiff because it related directly to termination decision).

[124]Duffy v. State Farm Mut. Auto. Ins. Co., 927 F. Supp. 587, 595 (E.D.N.Y. 1996) (employer's mere solicitation of age information regarding plaintiff was insufficient to support rational finding that employer's explanation for plaintiff's termination was false and true reason was her age).

[125]Hopper v. Hallmark Cards, Inc., 87 F.3d 983, 989, 5 AD 1531 (8th Cir. 1996) (evidence of good performance can serve as evidence of pretext when employee is discharged for poor performance but, standing alone, may be insufficient to establish pretext); Sirvidas v. Commonwealth Edison Co., 60 F.3d 375, 378, 68 FEP 602 (7th Cir. 1995) (adequate performance by plaintiff is ordinarily insufficient to create genuine issue of material fact regarding pretext).

[126]Corbin v. Southland Int'l Trucks, 25 F.3d 1545, 1550, 65 FEP 552 (11th Cir. 1994) (evidence that younger co-worker who exhibited negative attitude similar to plaintiff's was not terminated was sufficient to establish pretext); Nembhard v. Memorial Sloan-Kettering Cancer Ctr., 918 F. Supp. 784, 788–89 (S.D.N.Y.) (pretext established by showing that other employees were not disciplined under similar circumstances), aff'd, 104 F.3d 353 (2d Cir. 1996); Kraiman v. Georgia-Pacific Corp., 68 FEP 526, 530 (E.D. Pa. 1995) (evidence that plaintiff was terminated because of poor performance of paper mill he managed, but younger managers were not terminated even though paper mill's performance was equally poor under their management was sufficient evidence of pretext); cf. Cox v. Kentucky Dep't of Transp., 53 F.3d 146, 151, 67 FEP 1134 (6th Cir. 1995) (to prove pretext, plaintiff cannot rely solely upon evidence that younger individuals were consistently favored over him; rather plaintiff must present evidence beyond history of favoritism).

[127]Rothmeier v. Investment Advisers, Inc., 85 F.3d 1328, 1337, 71 FEP 1458 (8th Cir. 1996) (evidence that decisionmaker was older than plaintiff and was responsible for plaintiff's hiring and firing negated "any reasonable inference of discrimination based on age"). Cf. Haun v. Ideal Indus., Inc., 81 F.3d 541, 546, 70 FEP 923 (5th Cir. 1996) (while evidence that hirer and firer are same individual is relevant in determining whether discrimination occurred, court declined to establish rule that no inference of discrimination can ever arise under this circumstance).

While courts have continued to recognize the use of statistical evidence in disparate treatment cases,[128] they have also continued their close scrutiny, holding that the utility of such statistical evidence depends upon the surrounding facts and whether sufficient information is provided to permit meaningful conclusions to be drawn.[129] For statistics to be persuasive they must be reliable,[130] presented in a framework that is relevant,[131] and based upon a sample that is sufficiently large.[132] Statistical evidence must also compare similarly situated individuals,[133] eliminate all

---

[128]Roemer v. Public Serv. Co., 911 F. Supp. 464, 467, 69 FEP 1582 (D. Colo. 1996) ("Statistical data showing employer's pattern of conduct toward protected class can create inference that an employer discriminated against individual members of the class."); see Stratton v. Department for the Aging of N.Y., 922 F. Supp. 857, 864 (S.D.N.Y. 1996) (charts showing average age of highest-ranking officials in agency both before and 14 months after new commissioner assumed post were admissible even though no expert testified with regard to significance where jury was properly instructed on relevance). Cf. Jones v. Unisys Corp., 54 F.3d 624, 632, 67 FEP 1065 (10th Cir. 1995) ("Statistics taken in isolation are generally not probative of age discrimination.").

[129]Batch v. Russ Berrie & Co., 1994 WL 634052, at *4 (N.D. Cal. Oct. 20, 1994).

[130]Hopper v. Hallmark Cards, Inc., 87 F.3d 983, 989, 5 AD 1531 (8th Cir. 1996) (statistics based on plaintiff's own subjective interpretation of employer's records fail to create reasonable inference of age discrimination); EEOC v. Regency Windsor Management Co., 862 F. Supp. 189, 195, 65 FEP 1777 (W.D. Mich. 1994) (statistical evidence showing that only 3 of defendant's 42 leasing agents were over age 40 was of limited probative value where there was no evidence of (1) ages of leasing agents hired and fired during relevant time period, (2) composition of pool of qualified applicants for open positions, and (3) composition of same segment of employees prior to involvement of manager who allegedly favored filling positions with younger people).

[131]Rawlins v. Diamond M-Odeco Co., 1995 WL 110631, at *4 (E.D. La. Mar. 13, 1995) (statistical evidence supports inference of discrimination only if it reflects disparity between number of protected class persons employed by defendant in comparison with those in relevant labor market).

[132]Birkbeck v. Marvel Lighting Corp., 30 F.3d 507, 511, 65 FEP 669 (4th Cir.) (class of four persons too small to have any probative value), cert. denied, 513 U.S. 1058 (1994). Cf. Stratton v. Department for the Aging of N.Y., 922 F. Supp. 857, 863 n.5 (S.D.N.Y. 1996) (where evidence of 11 hires or promotions does not constitute "a sample," but rather universe of employment decisions undertaken by single person over four-year period, it may be properly admitted as circumstantial evidence of improper motive).

[133]Hopper v. Hallmark Cards, Inc., 87 F.3d 983, 989, 5 AD 1531 (8th Cir. 1996) (statistical evidence flawed because of failure to show discharged managerial employees were similarly situated); Furr v. Seagate Tech., Inc., 82 F.3d 980, 986–87, 70 FEP 1325 (10th Cir. 1996) (statistical evidence flawed because of grouping of employees without regard to specialty or skill, and failure to take into account nondiscriminatory reasons for numerical disparities), cert. denied sub nom. Doan v. Seagate, 117 S. Ct. 684 (1997); Doan v. Seagate Tech., Inc., 82 F.3d 974, 979, 70 FEP 1202 (10th Cir. 1996) (statistical evidence that compared age of persons selected for RIF with age of persons hired afterwards was flawed because of failure

non-discriminatory reasons for numerical disparities,[134] and show a significant disparity.[135]

4. Cases of Mixed Motives

The issue of whether a case is a pretext case or a mixed-motives case is a question for the court once all the evidence has been presented; thus, the plaintiff need not elect a pretext or mixed-motives framework prior to trial.[136]

To establish entitlement to the mixed-motives analysis in pre-1991 Civil Rights Act cases, courts have continued to require the plaintiff to introduce evidence directly reflecting discriminatory or retaliatory animus on the part of a person involved in the decision-making process.[137]

B. Adverse Impact

The Supreme Court has yet to decide whether an adverse impact theory of liability is available under the ADEA. While some courts continue to apply adverse impact theory under the ADEA,[138]

---

to compare similarly situated individuals and failure to eliminate nondiscriminatory reasons for numerical discrepancies).

[134]*Furr*, 82 F.3d at 986–87; *Doan*, 82 F.3d at 979.

[135]Roemer v. Public Serv. Co., 911 F. Supp. 464, 467, 69 FEP 1582 (D. Colo. 1996).

[136]Starceski v. Westinghouse Elec. Corp., 54 F.3d 1089, 1098, 67 FEP 1184 (3d Cir. 1995) (citing Armbruster v. Unisys Corp., 32 F.3d 768, 782 n.17 (3d Cir. 1994)).

[137]Philipp v. ANR Freight Sys., Inc., 61 F.3d 669, 674, 70 FEP 1347 (8th Cir. 1995) (numerous age-related statements made by individuals who were not involved in challenged employment decision and evidence that decisionmaker referred to plaintiff on occasion as "the old man" were insufficient to establish threshold showing for mixed-motives analysis); Mooney v. Aramco Servs. Co., 54 F.3d 1207, 1217–18 & n.12, 68 FEP 421 (5th Cir. 1995) (age-related statements by plaintiff's supervisor did not satisfy *Price Waterhouse* standard because they were primarily indicative of desire to save money by employing persons at lower pay); Armbruster v. Unisys Corp., 32 F.3d 768, 779, 65 FEP 828 (3d Cir. 1994) (comment that company could not afford to retain "people over 50 and 50" (meaning those over 50 years of age who earned over $50,000 annually) and evidence of documents containing information about age and date of birth of retained employees did not satisfy *Price Waterhouse* standard). *But see* Finch v. Hercules, Inc., 865 F. Supp. 1104, 1123–24, 74 FEP 1571 (D. Del. 1994) (when "major company executive" makes age-related remarks, it does not matter that he was not decisionmaker in challenged employment action).

[138]Mangold v. California Pub. Util. Comm'n, 67 F.3d 1470, 1474, 69 FEP 48 (9th Cir. 1995) ("existing Ninth Circuit precedent approves of a disparate impact theory under the ADEA) (citations omitted); Lewis v. Aerospace Community Credit

others have rejected or questioned the applicability of the adverse impact analysis to age discrimination claims.[139]

Workforce reductions continue to be the subject of adverse impact analysis.[140] Courts disagree on the appropriateness of the use of age subgroups to prove adverse impact.[141]

C. Reductions in Force

The courts continue to refuse to question the legitimacy of an employer's decision to reduce its workforce.[142] However, evidence

---

Union, 934 F. Supp. 314, 321–22, 74 FEP 1339 (E.D. Mo. 1996) (assuming adverse impact claim to be cognizable under ADEA), *aff'd,* 114 F.3d 745, 74 FEP 1443 (8th Cir. 1997); Tucker v. Kingsbury Corp., 929 F. Supp. 50, 57–58, 75 FEP 1316 (D.N.H. 1996) (assuming adverse impact theory applies to ADEA claims); EEOC v. Newport Mesa Unified Sch. Dist., 893 F. Supp. 927, 930, 68 FEP 657 (C.D. Cal. 1995) (ADEA plaintiff may proceed under either disparate treatment or adverse impact theory); Brothers v. NCR Corp., 885 F. Supp. 1043, 1049, 68 FEP 6 (N.D. Ohio 1995) (plaintiff may establish ADEA violation through adverse impact theory); Maidenbaum v. Bally's Park Place, Inc., 870 F. Supp. 1254, 1258–59, 68 FEP 1245 (D.N.J. 1994) (adverse impact analysis is applicable under ADEA), *aff'd,* 67 F.3d 291, 69 FEP 320 (3d Cir. 1995); Graffam v. Scott Paper Co., 870 F. Supp. 389, 395, 66 FEP 1007 (D. Me. 1994) (assuming, without discussion, that adverse impact theory applied to ADEA claim), *aff'd mem.,* 60 F.3d 809, 71 FEP 736 (1st Cir. 1995); Finch v. Hercules, Inc., 865 F. Supp. 1104, 1128, 74 FEP 1571 (D. Del. 1994) (assuming ADEA permits adverse impact claims).

[139]*See, e.g.,* Furr v. Seagate Tech., Inc., 82 F.3d 980, 987, 70 FEP 1325 (10th Cir. 1996) (adverse impact claims are not cognizable under ADEA), *cert. denied sub nom.* Doan v. Seagate, 117 S. Ct. 684 (1997); Ellis v. United Airlines, Inc., 73 F.3d 999, 1008–09, 69 FEP 1167 (10th Cir.) (ADEA does not permit adverse impact cause of action), *cert. denied,* 116 S. Ct. 2500 (1996); DiBiase v. SmithKline Beecham Corp., 48 F.3d 719, 732–34, 67 FEP 58 (3d Cir.) (noting that "it is doubtful that traditional disparate impact theory is a viable theory of liability under the ADEA," but declining to hold that adverse impact theory is "never available" under ADEA), *cert. denied,* 116 S. Ct. 306 (1995); EEOC v. Sears, Roebuck & Co., 883 F. Supp. 211, 214–15, 70 FEP 175 (N.D. Ill. 1995) (rejecting EEOC's argument for adverse impact claim under ADEA).

[140]*See, e.g.,* Finch v. Hercules, Inc., 865 F. Supp. 1104, 1128 n.26, 74 FEP 1571 (D. Del. 1994) (plaintiff challenged employer's forced ranking process as facially neutral policy producing adverse impact).

[141]*Cf. id.* at 1129–30 (plaintiff may seek to prove employer's forced ranking process for implementing RIF had adverse impact on age subgroup of which plaintiff is a member) *with* Lewis v. Aerospace Community Credit Union, 934 F. Supp. 314, 321–22, 74 FEP 1339 (E.D. Mo. 1996) (plaintiff's comparison of employees over 50 to employees under 50 was misplaced inasmuch as ADEA confers protected status on employees 40 years of age and older), *aff'd,* 114 F.3d 745, 74 FEP 1443 (8th Cir. 1997), *petition for cert. filed* (Nov. 29, 1997).

[142]Furr v. Seagate Tech., Inc., 82 F.3d 980, 986, 70 FEP 1325 (10th Cir. 1996) (wisdom of RIF is not for court or jury to decide; RIF is business decision and ADEA

of the legitimacy of the decision to downsize the workforce may be relevant to the employer's burden of establishing a legitimate, nondiscriminatory reason for its actions or in overcoming the plaintiff's claim of pretext.[143] The key issue continues to be the propriety of the employer's selection of particular employees for discharge.[144]

In *Thomure v. Phillips Furniture Co.*,[145] the Eighth Circuit held that employee wage reductions, which an employer implemented because of financial hardship, would be treated as a RIF.[146] The court reversed the lower court's finding of age discrimination as second-guessing the employer's business judgment in deciding, for financial reasons, to cut the wages of its highest-paid employees to a greater degree than its lower-paid employees.[147]

Courts continue to hold that the redistribution of work and the reassignment of the plaintiff's duties to younger retained employees

---

is not vehicle for reviewing propriety of business decisions), *cert. denied sub nom.* Doan v. Seagate, 117 S. Ct. 684 (1997); Lewis v. Aerospace Community Credit Union, 934 F. Supp. 314, 320, 74 FEP 1339 (E.D. Mo. 1996) (company's business decision to reduce its workforce is legitimate reason to discharge qualified employees; company need not provide evidence of financial distress or objective criteria for determining who should be discharged to show that its RIF was legitimate), *aff'd*, 114 F.3d 745, 74 FEP 1443 (8th Cir. 1997), *petition for cert. filed* (Nov. 29, 1997); Tucker v. Kingsbury Corp., 929 F. Supp. 50, 56, 75 FEP 1316 (D.N.H. 1996) (although "an employer who selectively cleans house cannot hide behind convenient euphemisms such as 'downsizing' or 'streamlining,' " "nondiscriminatory business decisions are beyond the legitimate purview of the courts" (citation omitted) (quoting Smith v. F.W. Morse, Inc., 76 F.3d 413, 422 (1st Cir. 1996))); Fink v. Kitzman, 881 F. Supp. 1347, 1364, 4 AD 644 (N.D. Iowa 1995) (when company's decision to reduce its workforce is due to exercise of its business judgment, it need not provide evidence of financial distress to make it a "legitimate" RIF).

[143]*See* Woroski v. Nashua Corp., 31 F.3d 105, 109, 65 FEP 824 (2d Cir. 1994) (summary judgment for employer affirmed where employer demonstrated that dismissals of plaintiffs occurred as part of legitimate business-motivated downsizing in which 298 employees were dismissed); Runyon v. Massachusetts Inst. of Tech., 871 F. Supp. 1502, 1510, 6 AD 233 (D. Mass. 1994) (by presenting evidence of need for reduction in force, employer adequately articulated legitimate, nondiscriminatory reason for its decision to terminate plaintiff).

[144]Cronin v. Aetna Life Ins. Co., 46 F.3d 196, 204, 66 FEP 1727 (2d Cir. 1995) (if plaintiff presents evidence that discharge in fact resulted from discriminatory treatment during process of eliminating positions and relocating employees, employer's statistical data showing nondiscriminatory overall impact, though perhaps relevant, is not dispositive as matter of law).

[145]30 F.3d 1020, 65 FEP 976 (8th Cir. 1994), *cert. denied*, 513 U.S. 1191 (1995).
[146]*Id.* at 1023.
[147]*Id.* at 1025.

do not constitute "replacement" for purposes of establishing a prima facie case.[148]

Some courts appear to place a higher burden on plaintiffs in RIF cases to establish a prima facie case. For example, the Eleventh Circuit utilizes a prima facie case standard that was articulated by the Fifth Circuit in *Williams v. General Motors Corp.*,[149] by requiring the plaintiff to produce evidence that the employer intended to discriminate.[150] The Eighth Circuit requires employees to " 'provide some additional showing that age was a factor in the termination.' "[151] However, most courts allow plaintiffs to meet

---

[148]Collier v. Budd Co., 66 F.3d 886, 890 n.5, 68 FEP 1435 (7th Cir. 1995) ("[s]hifting and/or consolidating work does not constitute replacement"); Bialas v. Greyhound Lines, Inc., 59 F.3d 759, 763, 68 FEP 552 (8th Cir. 1995) (during reduction in force, fact that plaintiff's duties were assumed by younger person is not in itself enough to establish prima facie case); Shenker v. Lockheed Sanders, Inc., 919 F. Supp. 55, 60 (D. Mass. 1996) (in context of RIF, redelegation of duties must involve more than decision to discontinue certain functions, assignment of another employee to perform plaintiff's duties in addition to prior duties or redistribution among other existing employees already performing related work); Phillips v. Manufacturers Hanover Trust Co., 67 FEP 1737, 1739 (S.D.N.Y. 1995) (positions held by employees terminated in RIF are presumed to be eliminated or left unfilled and job duties redistributed among remaining employees; however, plaintiff's assertion that new employees were hired and given similar job duties is sufficient to cast doubt on proffered reason for plaintiff's termination); Kern v. Kollsman, 885 F. Supp. 335, 344 (D.N.H. 1995) (" 'A discharged employee is not replaced when another employee is assigned to perform the plaintiff's duties in addition to other duties, or when the work is redistributed among other existing employees already performing related work.' " (quoting LeBlanc v. Great Am. Ins. Co., 6 F.3d 836, 846, 62 FEP 1668, 63 FEP 288 (1st Cir. 1993), *cert. denied,* 511 U.S. 1018 (1994) (internal quotes omitted))). *Contra* Raia v. Village of Skokie, 1995 WL 642828, at *7 (N.D. Ill. Oct. 31, 1995) (plaintiff established prima facie case by showing that younger person who was retained performed at least some of plaintiff's former duties).

[149]656 F.2d 120, 26 FEP 1381 (5th Cir. 1981), *cert. denied,* 455 U.S. 943 (1982).

[150]Jameson v. Arrow Co., 75 F.3d 1528, 1531–32, 70 FEP 153 (11th Cir. 1996). *See also* Meinecke v. H & R Block, 66 F.3d 77, 83, 70 FEP 311 (5th Cir. 1995) (in RIF case, plaintiff may establish fourth element of prima facie case by showing she was either replaced by someone outside protected class, replaced by someone younger, or otherwise discharged because of her age); Armendariz v. Pinkerton Tobacco Co., 58 F.3d 144, 150, 68 FEP 361 (5th Cir. 1995) (plaintiff failed to establish prima facie case of age discrimination in "job elimination" case because he failed to present evidence that employer "did not treat age as a neutral factor in its decision as to whether to retain or relocate" plaintiff), *cert. denied,* 116 S. Ct. 709 (1996).

[151]Aucutt v. Six Flags Over Mid-America, Inc., 85 F.3d 1311, 1316, 5 AD 902 (8th Cir. 1996) (quoting Nitschke v. McDonnell Douglas Corp., 68 F.3d 249, 251, 71 FEP 99 (8th Cir. 1995)); *accord* Allen v. Ethicon, Inc., 919 F. Supp. 1093, 1098 (S.D. Ohio 1996) (where plaintiff is discharged as result of reduction in force or corporate reorganization, she must come forward with " 'additional direct, circumstantial, or

their prima facie burden in RIF cases by producing evidence that younger employees were treated more favorably.[152] The Second Circuit merely requires a plaintiff in a RIF case to show that (1) he or she was within the protected age group, (2) he or she was qualified for the position, (3) he or she was discharged, and (4) the discharge " 'occurred under circumstances giving rise to an inference of age discrimination.' "[153] In establishing a prima facie case in a RIF situation, plaintiffs must show that the younger employees to whom the plaintiffs are comparing themselves are similarly situated.[154]

---

statistical evidence tending to indicate that the employer singled out the plaintiff for discharge for impermissible reasons' " (quoting Barnes v. GenCorp, Inc., 896 F.2d 1457, 1465 (6th Cir. 1990))).

[152] Smith v. Cook County, 74 F.3d 829, 831, 72 FEP 158 (7th Cir. 1996) (RIF plaintiff may establish prima facie case by showing as fourth element that others not in protected class were treated more favorably); Jones v. Unisys Corp., 54 F.3d 624, 630, 67 FEP 1065 (10th Cir. 1995) (RIF plaintiff may establish prima facie case by showing as fourth element that employer intended to discriminate in reaching decision at issue or that plaintiff was treated less favorably than younger employees); Woodman v. Haemonetics Corp., 51 F.3d 1087, 1091, 67 FEP 838 (1st Cir. 1995) (in RIF situation, plaintiff may establish fourth element of prima facie case by showing that company did not treat age neutrally or it retained younger employees in same position); DiBiase v. SmithKline Beecham Corp., 48 F.3d 719, 723 n.2, 67 FEP 58 (3d Cir.) (ordinarily, RIF plaintiff need not prove that she was replaced by younger worker; rather plaintiff can establish prima facie case by showing he or she was laid off and younger workers were retained), *cert. denied,* 116 S. Ct. 306 (1995).

[153] Cronin v. Aetna Life Ins. Co., 46 F.3d 196, 204, 66 FEP 1727 (2d Cir. 1995) (quoting Woroski v. Nashua Corp., 31 F.3d 105, 108 (2d Cir. 1994)).

[154] Brown v. CSC Logic, Inc., 82 F.3d 651, 654, 70 FEP 1273 (5th Cir. 1996) (holding that one plaintiff failed to establish prima facie case of age discrimination because, although employer did retain number of younger employees after terminating plaintiffs, "these individuals were not in management positions similar to the plaintiffs"); Gadsby v. Norwalk Furniture Corp., 71 F.3d 1324, 1331, 69 FEP 715 (7th Cir. 1995) ("In an RIF case, the inference of discrimination raised by the more favorable treatment of younger employees (typically the act of not firing them) is premised on some degree of fungibility between the plaintiff's job and the younger employee's job."); Gehring v. Case Corp., 43 F.3d 340, 342, 66 FEP 1373 (7th Cir. 1994) (where plaintiff attempts to establish discrimination by showing that younger employees were treated more favorably, plaintiff must show that employees selected for comparison are similarly situated to plaintiff), *cert. denied,* 515 U.S. 1159 (1995); Brothers v. NCR Corp., 885 F. Supp. 1043, 1048, 68 FEP 6 (N.D. Ohio 1995) (to establish prima facie case, RIF plaintiff must show he was similarly situated in all respects to employees outside protected class with whom he seeks to compare his treatment; this means younger employees must have dealt with same supervisor, been subject to same standards, and engaged in same conduct without such differentiating or mitigating circumstances that would distinguish their conduct or employer's treatment of them for it).

Comparative evidence[155] and probative[156] statistical[157] evidence continue to be effective weapons for both plaintiffs and defendants.

Courts continue to uphold an employer's use of performance, skill, and future job potential as selection criteria for layoffs.[158] In

---

[155]Woroski v. Nashua Corp., 31 F.3d 105, 109, 65 FEP 824 (2d Cir. 1994) (employer showed that, based on plaintiffs' age and seniority relative to their department colleagues and based on which employees were capable of doing which jobs in their departments, its reasons for terminating plaintiffs in RIF were legitimate); Brown v. Oscar Mayer Foods Corp., 1996 WL 99412, at *3 (N.D. Ill. Mar. 5, 1996) (employer terminated entire workforce, including employees over and under age 40); Kelley v. Unisys Corp., 66 FEP 387, 390 (N.D. W.Va. 1994) (evidence that no employees outside protected class were retained in same position as plaintiff precluded him from establishing prima facie case).

[156]Hutson v. McDonnell Douglas Corp., 63 F.3d 771, 777, 68 FEP 1209 (8th Cir. 1995) (plaintiff's statistical evidence not probative of pretext because it failed to analyze treatment of comparable employees); Jones v. Unisys Corp., 54 F.3d 624, 632, 67 FEP 1065 (10th Cir. 1995) (plaintiff's introduction of statistics regarding number of employees in protected class who were terminated was insufficient proof of discrimination; "[s]tatistics taken in isolation are generally not probative of age discrimination"); Shenker v. Lockheed Sanders, Inc., 919 F. Supp. 55, 59 (D. Mass. 1996) (even assuming plaintiff had personal knowledge that 7 of 14 workers laid off were over 40, his effort to use the "50%" figure to infer age discrimination was inadequate; in order to utilize statistics to demonstrate discrimination, there must be comparison between number of protected employees in (1) set of terminated employees, and (2) pool of employees from which terminated employees were drawn); Thurman v. Robertshaw Control Co., 869 F. Supp. 934, 941, 65 FEP 1652 (N.D. Ga. 1994) (unrelated series of incidents that plaintiff alleged constituted statistical evidence of age discrimination fell far short of "gross statistical disparities" necessary to establish disparate treatment case). *Cf.* Cronin v. Aetna Life Ins. Co., 46 F.3d 196, 205–06, 66 FEP 1727 (2d Cir. 1995) (evidence that reduction in force in general did not have discriminatory impact on protected class as whole did not eliminate possibility that plaintiff individually suffered disparate treatment).

[157]Lewis v. Aerospace Community Credit Union, 934 F. Supp. 314, 319, 74 FEP 1339 (E.D. Mo. 1996) (statistical evidence showed that RIF increased percentage of protected employees and increased average age of employees, and thus cannot be viewed as discriminatory), *aff'd*, 114 F.3d 745, 74 FEP 1443 (8th Cir. 1997), *petition for cert. filed* (Nov. 29, 1997); Allen v. Ethicon, Inc., 919 F. Supp. 1093, 1099 (S.D. Ohio 1996) (plaintiff failed to contradict results of company's adverse impact study, which indicated that higher percentage of employees under 40 were laid off than employees in protected class); Rogic v. Mallinckrodt Med., Inc., 917 F. Supp. 671, 678 (E.D. Mo. 1996) (after RIF completed, percentage of defendant's employees in protected age group increased by over 1%); Dickson v. Amoco Performance Prods., Inc., 910 F. Supp. 629, 636, 69 FEP 228 (N.D. Ga. 1994) (statistical evidence showing that RIF had disproportionate impact on protected employees can be used to establish nexus between age discrimination and adverse employment action).

[158]Furr v. Seagate Tech., Inc., 82 F.3d 980, 987, 70 FEP 1325 (10th Cir. 1996) (future job potential may be used as legitimate factor in making RIF decision), *cert. denied sub nom.* Doan v. Seagate, 117 S. Ct. 684 (1997); Tucker v. Kingsbury Corp.,

addition, RIF selection decisions based on business or economic considerations will be upheld.[159]

Although factors such as compensation remain controversial, replacement of older, higher-paid employees by younger, lower-paid employees does not necessarily violate the ADEA.[160]

During a RIF, an employer is not required to establish an internal transfer program.[161] In addition, courts continue to find that employers are not required to implement a new program of bumping rights.[162]

Should an employer undertake an obligation to relocate younger employees, however, it must make similar efforts on behalf of older employees.[163]

---

929 F. Supp. 50, 57, 75 FEP 1316 (D.N.H. 1996) (court granted summary judgment for employer without assessing merits or rationality of employer's business decision to lay off employee based on lower department ratings and conclusion that another employee possessed greater level of expertise); Campbell v. Fasco Indus., Inc., 861 F. Supp. 1385, 1402, 72 FEP 33 (N.D. Ill.) (summary judgment for employer where employee fired because of prior performance deficiencies; court " 'does not sit as a super-personnel department that reexamines an entity's business decisions' " (quoting Dale v. Chicago Tribune Co., 797 F.2d 458, 464 (7th Cir. 1986), *cert. denied*, 479 U.S. 1066 (1987)), *aff'd mem.*, 67 F.3d 301, 72 FEP 96 (7th Cir. 1994). *But see* Sperling v. Hoffmann-La Roche, Inc., 924 F. Supp. 1396, 1408–09, 76 FEP 267 (D.N.J. 1996) (employees alleging they were laid off based on perceptions that they were less productive or had limited skills stated cause of action under ADEA).

[159]Gould v. Kemper Nat'l Ins. Cos., 880 F. Supp. 527, 535 (N.D. Ill. 1995) (eliminating corporate function, which required discharging employees associated with that function, as part of the RIF "budgetary guillotine" was legitimate nondiscriminatory reason for firing employee), *aff'd*, 78 F.3d 586 (7th Cir. 1996); Kelley v. Unisys Corp., 66 FEP 387, 390 (N.D. W.Va. 1994) (employer may select employee whose layoff will have least impact on employer's business operations).

[160]*See* Bialas v. Greyhound Lines, Inc., 59 F.3d 759, 763, 68 FEP 552 (8th Cir. 1995) (terminating employees because of their status as higher-paid employees during RIF does not support inference of age discrimination).

[161]Taylor v. Canteen Corp., 69 F.3d 773, 780, 69 FEP 310 (7th Cir. 1995) (ADEA does not mandate that employer transfer employee to another position); *see* Pages-Cahue v. Iberia Lineas Aereas de Espana, 82 F.3d 533, 537–38, 70 FEP 1030 (1st Cir. 1996) (employers conducting RIF have no obligation to offer lower-paying jobs in restructured company to older employees).

[162]Jones v. Unisys Corp., 54 F.3d 624, 630–31 n.6, 67 FEP 1065 (10th Cir. 1995) (employer's refusal to allow plaintiffs to bump less senior employees was not evidence of age discrimination because employer has no duty to allow displaced senior employees to bump less senior employees).

[163]*Taylor v. Canteen Corp.*, 69 F.3d at 780 (employer cannot favor younger employees over older ones in relocation efforts; if so, employer must show why older employee is not similarly situated to younger employee).

In developing layoff procedures, at least one court has noted that uncontrolled subjective decisions from a variety of decisionmakers under uniform guidelines during a RIF, which resulted in the termination of a disproportionate number of older workers, did not support an inference of age discrimination.[164]

D. Summary Judgment

1. Stray Remarks

Courts continue to consider an employer's ageist remarks as direct or circumstantial evidence of discrimination.[165] Employers continue, however, to obtain summary judgment where courts view

---

[164]Sperling v. Hoffmann-La Roche, Inc., 924 F. Supp. 1346, 1360–61, 72 FEP 1401 (D.N.J. 1996) (discrimination allegations arising from employer's one-time use of procedure giving managers discretion in determining who would be terminated in mass layoff did not state claim for pattern or practice age discrimination); *accord* Doan v. Seagate Tech., Inc., 82 F.3d 974, 978, 70 FEP 1202 (10th Cir. 1996) (employer's use of subjective criteria in conducting RIF, such as employee's job potential, is insufficient to prove intentional discrimination), *cert. denied,* 117 S. Ct. 684 (1997).

[165]Ryther v. KARE 11, 84 F.3d 1074, 1084–86, 70 FEP 1709 (8th Cir. 1996) (co-worker's comments referring to plaintiff as "old fart," an "old man," "too old to be on the air," and having "no business being in the industry any more for his age" may support inference of age discrimination if decisionmaker is responsive to co-worker's ideas and demands and there is other evidence of pretext), *aff'd,* 108 F.3d 831 (8th Cir.) (en banc), *cert. denied,* 117 S. Ct. 2510 (1997); Schnidrig v. Columbia Mach., Inc., 80 F.3d 1406, 1411, 71 FEP 1763 (9th Cir.) (plaintiff's allegation that he was told on three separate occasions that the board wanted somebody younger for job precluded summary judgment), *cert. denied,* 117 S. Ct. 295 (1996); Brewer v. Quaker State Oil Ref. Corp., 72 F.3d 326, 333, 69 FEP 753 (3d Cir. 1995) (CEO's statements in newsletter that new executives were "two of our star young men in their mid-40s[; t]hat age group is our future," relevant to show culture in which employment decision made); Mangold v. California Pub. Utils. Comm'n, 67 F.3d 1470, 1476–77, 69 FEP 48 (9th Cir. 1995) (decisionmaker's remarks that "we want fresh young blood," "[w]e're going into a bright new future in which we have an excellent staff of young professional people," and "older employees, unfortunately, don't take advantage of all the opportunities," and other substantial evidence create strong inference of intentional discrimination); Hardin v. Hussmann Corp., 45 F.3d 262, 266, 66 FEP 1369 (8th Cir. 1995) (comment after hiring plaintiff that company does not generally hire persons over age 40 and later comment that plaintiff should keep antiquated textbook hidden sufficient to create fact issue); Armbruster v. Unisys Corp., 32 F.3d 768, 776, 783, 65 FEP 828 (3d Cir. 1994) (comments by one decisionmaker that transferees should be moved out of their offices quickly and that transferees "should have seen the writing on the

wall" and comment by another decisionmaker that he had been told to select "senior people," made contemporaneously with transfer or within a few weeks of RIF, preclude summary judgment); EEOC v. Manville Sales Corp., 27 F.3d 1089, 1093–94, 65 FEP 804 (5th Cir. 1994) (age-related comments by nondecisionmaker that "[plaintiff] was incapable; that he was old and inflexible," that he had "jumped that old man about smoking his pipe," and pulled down plaintiff's hat and said "old man hat," support finding of discrimination), *cert. denied,* 513 U.S. 1190 (1995); Barrett v. Tomkins Indus., Inc., 930 F. Supp. 508, 511–12 (D. Kan. 1996) (summary judgment denied in promotion case based in part upon retired employee's affidavit testimony that president commented that employees were "overaged and overpaid"); Nembhard v. Memorial Sloan-Kettering Cancer Ctr., 918 F. Supp. 784, 787, 789 (S.D.N.Y.) (supervisor's ageist comments were not stray remarks because they were made within months of plaintiff's termination and specifically mentioned desire to hire younger employees), *aff'd,* 104 F.3d 353 (2d Cir. 1996); Eymer v. Ground Round, Inc., 913 F. Supp 693, 701–02 (N.D.N.Y. 1996) (decisionmaker's statement "that all the employees were too old, that they couldn't change" standing alone insufficient to defeat summary judgment but creates fact issue when combined with evidence establishing pattern and practice of terminating older workers who are replaced with younger workers); Kunzman v. Enron Corp., 902 F. Supp. 882, 900–01, 73 FEP 803 (N.D. Iowa 1995) (decisionmaker's statement that older workers had to change to "get with these younger guys" creates fact issue regarding discriminatory animus); Schallehn v. Central Trust & Sav. Bank, 877 F. Supp. 1315, 1327–28, 69 FEP 1292 (N.D. Iowa 1995) (decisionmaker's statement that he preferred to hire younger workers, made after replacing plaintiff with younger employee, and reference to employee as "old man" create fact issue); Moten v. American Linen Supply Co., 67 FEP 1080, 1082, 1085 n.1 (D. Kan. 1995) (decisionmaker's deposition testimony that he "[was] looking for somebody young and aggressive" and subsequent attempt to correct himself by saying he was looking for "somebody aggressive" created fact issue regarding decisionmaker's motivation); Barton v. Forbes, Inc., 67 FEP 138, 140–41 (S.D.N.Y. 1995) (company vice president's statement to plaintiff that it "might be a good time for you to think about making a change . . . . We are none of us as young as we used to be and we all of us have a lot more gray hairs than we used to . . . . Have you thought about retirement?" and statement to job applicant that "she would be replacing 'an older person [who] didn't fit in' " sufficient to create fact issue); Dickson v. Amoco Performance Prods., Inc., 910 F. Supp. 629, 635–37, 69 FEP 228 (N.D. Ga. 1994) (supervisor's comments about plaintiff's age, whether intended as joke or not, may raise inference of age discrimination and establish pretext where supervisor provided negative input during reduction in force); Bragalone v. Kona Coast Resort Joint Venture, 866 F. Supp. 1285, 1293, 66 FEP 65 (D. Haw. 1994) (supervisor's comments about "young blood" and "at our age, maybe we don't want the stress" in response to question regarding failure to promote create fact issue as to pretext); Finch v. Hercules, Inc., 865 F. Supp. 1104, 1123–24, 74 FEP 1571 (D. Del. 1994) (age bias remarks by "major company executive" are not stray remarks even if he was not decisionmaker); Tibbitts v. Van Den Bergh Foods Co., 859 F. Supp. 1168, 1172–73, 66 FEP 560 (N.D. Ill. 1994) (comment that we've got to "get rid of these old gals and get some young gals in here" made year or two before discharge reflects age-based animus); Ward v. Westvaco Corp., 859 F. Supp. 608, 618–19, 3 AD 739 (D. Mass. 1994) (supervisor's remarks critical of older employees and frequently disparaging older person's methods of operation precluded summary judgment).

comments as merely "stray" ageist remarks by decisionmakers[166] or nondecisionmakers[167] alike.

---

[166]Brown v. CSC Logic, Inc., 82 F.3d 651, 655–58, 70 FEP 1273 (5th Cir. 1996) (decisionmaker's comments to one plaintiff that staff was "getting long in the tooth," that "you can't hire an ugly one and make them pretty," and that another plaintiff "was old" insufficient to show discrimination; remarks to one plaintiff that "you can't even get it up," "old goat," "you're getting too old," and "senility was setting in" establish prima facie case, but insufficient to establish pretext in RIF case where decisionmaker also hired plaintiff); Gadsby v. Norwalk Furniture Corp., 71 F.3d 1324, 1330, 69 FEP 715 (7th Cir. 1995) (manager's statement, made five years before plaintiff's termination, regarding another employee that "if he didn't retire this time, he would probably be let go" is ambiguous and too remote in time to support inference of discrimination); Carpenter v. Western Credit Union, 62 F.3d 143, 144–45, 68 FEP 545 (6th Cir. 1995) (company president's statement justifying terminations of plaintiff and another employee during reduction in force as "purely economical, they were the two oldest employees," does not create fact issue); Henson v. Liggett Group, Inc., 61 F.3d 270, 273, 276, 68 FEP 826 (4th Cir. 1995) (management's general discussion about being aware of possible age discrimination claims during RIF not evidence of discrimination where no link to decisions affecting plaintiff); Woroski v. Nashua Corp., 31 F.3d 105, 108, 109–10, 65 FEP 824 (2d Cir. 1994) (decisionmaker's statements that workforce was "older, had been around too long, made too much money and enjoyed too many benefits" and that company needed "new younger people," although providing some evidence of age bias, not sufficient to create fact issue); Thomure v. Phillips Furniture Co., 30 F.3d 1020, 1024–25, 65 FEP 976 (8th Cir. 1994) (where company reduced wages and older plaintiff making higher wages was subject to higher wage cut, comment about "getting rid" of plaintiff and comment made after wage cut that plaintiff should consider retirement not evidence of discrimination), *cert. denied,* 513 U.S. 1191 (1995); Birkbeck v. Marvel Lighting Corp., 30 F.3d 507, 511–12, 65 FEP 669 (4th Cir.) (affirming judgment as a matter of law for employer where decisionmaker's statement made two years before discharge that "there comes a time when we have to make way for younger people" reflects truism regarding generational passage and does not establish discrimination, judgment as a matter of law for employer), *cert. denied,* 513 U.S. 1058 (1994); Hill v. St. Louis Univ., 923 F. Supp. 1199, 1214–15, 71 FEP 43 (E.D. Mo. 1996) (decisionmaker's remarks about needing "fresh or new blood" made after plaintiff's termination does not give rise to inference of discrimination), *aff'd,* 123 F.3d 1114 (8th Cir. 1997); Shenker v. Lockheed Sanders, Inc., 919 F. Supp. 55, 60–61 (D. Mass. 1996) (supervisor's remark made three months before termination that plaintiff was older and better able to handle layoff and unauthenticated written statement that company might be letting "good young people go" and they should not stay with "older less qualified people because of emotional attachments" do not infer discrimination); Lamb v. Runyon, 915 F. Supp. 300, 306–07 (M.D. Ala. 1995) (no discriminatory intent inferred from manager's statement that "I asked [plaintiff] why he wanted to be a supervisor and he told me he was going to retire. This was the first thing out of his mouth and it cooked his goose"; manager testified that plaintiff's desire to be promoted to increase his retirement benefits indicated poor motivation); Nakai v. Wickes Lumber Co., 906 F. Supp. 698, 705, 71 FEP 13 (D. Me. 1995) (supervisor's statement that employee's career was at a "crossroads" does not create fact issue); Adams v. DuPont Merck Pharm. Co., 67 FEP 1072, 1075 (E.D. Pa. 1994) (supervisor's written comment that "retiring" was one of plaintiff's "5–10 year goals" did not create

fact issue where plaintiff "jokingly" expressed hope of receiving a "golden parachute," and announcement of termination incentive to all employees does not create fact issue), *aff'd mem.,* 70 F.3d 1254, 71 FEP 1408 (3d Cir. 1995); Duart v. FMC Wyoming Corp., 859 F. Supp. 1447, 1457–58, 65 FEP 999 (D. Wyo. 1994) (decisionmaker's remark that "[a]ll you old bastards ought to be retired and let us young people run the company the right way" does not create fact issue), *aff'd,* 72 F.3d 117, 69 FEP 1036 (10th Cir. 1995).

[167]Aucutt v. Six Flags Over Mid-Am., Inc., 85 F.3d 1311, 1315–16, 5 AD 902 (8th Cir. 1996) (affirming summary judgment for employer where nondecisionmaker's statements made 14 months before termination do not show discriminatory animus); Fuka v. Thomson Consumer Elecs., 82 F.3d 1397, 1403–04, 71 FEP 1417 (7th Cir. 1996) (nondecisionmaker's comments about hiring "young people fresh out of college" that could be molded were not evidence of discriminatory intent to terminate plaintiff; statements only revealed intent regarding hiring decisions); Slathar v. Sather Trucking Corp., 78 F.3d 415, 419–20, 70 FEP 574 (8th Cir.) (nondecisionmaker's comment, made after termination, that terminating plaintiff was risky because of his age held inadmissible; personnel director's response that company would "take care of it" not evidence of discrimination), *cert. denied,* 117 S. Ct. 179 (1996); Nitschke v. McDonnell Douglas Corp., 68 F.3d 249, 251–52, 71 FEP 99 (8th Cir. 1995) (document prepared by company's president in 1986 about hiring and retaining the "best young people" insufficient to show discrimination; president not involved in decision to terminate); Bialas v. Greyhound Lines, Inc., 59 F.3d 759, 763–64, 68 FEP 552 (8th Cir. 1995) (company president's statement in memorandum that "people over 45 years of age . . . generally have serious difficulty adjusting to change" and manager's statement referring to plaintiff's replacement as "a young man" did not create fact issue regarding elimination of plaintiff's position during reduction in force); Jones v. Unisys Corp., 54 F.3d 624, 632, 67 FEP 1065 (10th Cir. 1995) (comment by nondecisionmaker employee responsible for job posting that "its [sic] about time we unloaded some of this old driftwood" does not establish discriminatory intent); Armbruster v. Unisys Corp., 32 F.3d 768, 775, 779, 65 FEP 828 (3d Cir. 1994) (nondecisionmaker's comment that employer could not "afford to keep people over 50 and 50, meaning those over 50 years of age who were earning over $50,000.00 annually" not overt evidence of discrimination); Kotlowski v. Eastman Kodak Co., 922 F. Supp. 790, 801, 6 AD 609 (W.D.N.Y. 1996) (remark by supervisor, who did not participate in layoff decision, that plaintiff wore her skirts too short for her age insufficient to establish pretext); Galdauckas v. Interstate Hotels Corp., 901 F. Supp. 454, 460, 463–64 (D. Mass. 1995) (nondecisionmaker's comments that plaintiff was "a member of the Geritol Generation" and "served the Last Supper" insufficient to create fact issue); Crumm v. Oce'-Bruning, Inc., 892 F. Supp. 1236, 1241–42 (E.D. Mo. 1995) (former supervisor's written comments on sales report ("Not bad for an old man . . . . Keep young.") not evidence of discrimination where former supervisor was nondecisionmaker); Pina v. Texas Commerce Bank, 70 FEP 680, 682 (W.D. Tex. 1995) (interviewer's written statement that job candidate who received promotion sought by plaintiff was "professional young banker who is just what is needed" insufficient to create fact issue); Brothers v. NCR Corp., 885 F. Supp. 1043, 1049, 68 FEP 6 (N.D. Ohio 1995) (former supervisor's remarks that sales group was bunch of "old farts" too vague, too remote in time, and "too removed from the employment decision at issue" to infer discrimination); EEOC v. Regency Windsor Management Co., 862 F. Supp 189, 192–93, 65 FEP 1777 (W.D. Mich. 1994) (nondecisionmaker's statement that younger people should be working to attract yuppie clients is too abstract and ambiguous to constitute direct evidence that plaintiff's termination was motivated by age discrimination).

2. Older Decisionmaker

Where the decisionmaker is the same age as, or older than, the plaintiff, some courts are disinclined to find age discrimination, under the theory that a member of the protected class "is more likely to be the victim of age discrimination than its perpetrator."[168]

3. Same Decisionmaker

Several courts have found evidence of nondiscrimination where the same decisionmaker both hired and terminated the plaintiff,[169] particularly where the termination occurred within a relatively short time after the hiring.[170] However, one court has cautioned that the "same actor" inference does not preclude the plaintiff's proof of discrimination, but is simply a rebuttable inference that discrimination did not occur.[171]

---

[168]Waldemar v. American Cancer Soc'y, 70 FEP 1411, 1418 (N.D. Ga. 1996) (citing Elrod v. Sears, Roebuck & Co., 939 F.2d 1466, 1471, 56 FEP 1246 (11th Cir. 1991)); *accord* Brown v. CSC Logic, Inc., 82 F.3d 651, 658, 70 FEP 1273 (5th Cir. 1996) (affirming summary judgment for defendant, and holding that where same decisionmaker who made both hiring and firing decisions is also member of protected class, inference that age discrimination was not motive behind plaintiff's termination is further enhanced).

[169]Brown v. CSC Logic, Inc., 82 F.3d 651, 658, 70 FEP 1273 (5th Cir. 1996) (inference that age discrimination was not motive behind plaintiff's termination where plaintiff was hired and fired by same actor); Rand v. CF Indus., Inc., 42 F.3d 1139, 1147, 66 FEP 1114 (7th Cir. 1994) (strong inference that discrimination was not determining factor where same individual hired, and then fired, plaintiff within space of two years); Waldemar v. American Cancer Soc'y, 70 FEP 1411, 1418 (N.D. Ga. 1996) (fact that plaintiff's supervisor had hired her supports conclusion that supervisor's failure to select plaintiff for reorganized position was not discriminatory); *cf.* Caussade v. Brown, 924 F. Supp. 693, 703, 74 FEP 1027 (D. Md. 1996) (strong inference of nonpretext where, among other circumstances, same supervisor who reassigned plaintiff had earlier recommended her for promotion), *aff'd*, 107 F.3d 865, 75 FEP 1887 (4th Cir. 1997).

[170]Rothmeier v. Investment Advisers, Inc., 85 F.3d 1328, 1337, 71 FEP 1458 (8th Cir. 1996) (strong inference against age discrimination where hirer and firer were same individual and termination of employment occurred within three years following hiring); *Brown v. CSC Logic, Inc.*, 82 F.3d at 658 (inference against age discrimination where plaintiff hired and terminated by same individual four years after hiring); *cf.* Serben v. Inter-City Mfg. Co., 36 F.3d 765, 766, 65 FEP 1706 (8th Cir. 1994) (where employee was terminated less than one year after hiring, no basis on which to infer age discrimination), *cert. denied*, 514 U.S. 1037 (1995).

[171]*Brown v. CSC Logic, Inc.*, 82 F.3d at 658; *cf.* Abbasi v. Herzfeld & Rubin, 4 AD 797, 800 (S.D.N.Y. 1995) (although inference of nondiscriminatory intent may be made where plaintiff was hired while already member of protected class, such hiring does not refute other indicia of discrimination).

4. "Before and After" Age Statistics

Courts continue to find statistics regarding workforce composition before and after a RIF significant in determining if age discrimination was a factor in an employer's RIF decisionmaking process.[172] However, several courts have emphasized that statistics alone will not support a case of age discrimination, but must be viewed in light of other information.[173]

5. The Prima Facie Case in RIF Cases

Although a plaintiff in a RIF case bears no heavier a burden of proof than other ADEA plaintiffs,[174] the proof required to make out a prima facie case differs due to the context of the employment decision. Most significantly, because an individual affected

---

[172]Jones v. Unisys Corp., 54 F.3d 624, 632, 67 FEP 1065 (10th Cir. 1995) (no direct evidence of age discrimination where percentage of workforce aged 40 and above remained relatively stable before and after RIF); Lewis v. Aerospace Community Credit Union, 934 F. Supp. 314, 320, 74 FEP 1339 (E.D. Mo. 1996) (no age discrimination against managerial employee discharged in RIF where statistics showed post-RIF increase in managerial employees aged 40 and over and increase in average age of workforce), *aff'd*, 114 F.3d 745, 74 FEP 1443 (8th Cir.), *petition for cert. filed* (Nov. 29, 1997); Kotlowski v. Eastman Kodak Co., 922 F. Supp. 790, 801, 6 AD 609 (W.D.N.Y. 1996) (statistics showing hiring patterns that are consistent with applicant pool age ratio do not suggest age discrimination); Dickson v. Amoco Performance Prods., Inc., 910 F. Supp. 629, 635–36, 69 FEP 228 (N.D. Ga. 1994) (prima facie case established where statistical evidence showed that RIF had disproportionate impact on employees aged 40 and over). *But cf.* Henson v. Liggett Group, Inc., 61 F.3d 270, 276, 68 FEP 826 (4th Cir. 1995) (no inference of age discrimination, even where 59% of employees terminated in two-year period were over 40 and approximately 71% of new hires in one year were under 40); Allen v. Diebold, Inc., 33 F.3d 674, 678, 65 FEP 1202 (6th Cir. 1994) (statistics showing percentage of combined workforce that was age 40 or above decreased from 80% to 17% following plant closing and relocation insufficient to permit inference of age discrimination where no evidence offered to show that figure was disproportionate to hiring pool in new area or that age played any role in defendant's hiring process at new plants).

[173]Kern v. Kollsman, 885 F. Supp. 335, 345 n.11 (D.N.H. 1995) (statistical evidence alone rarely suffices to rebut employer's legitimate reason for employment action; there must be a connection between statistics, practices of employer, and plaintiff's case (citing Gadson v. Concord Hosp., 966 F.2d 32, 35 (1st Cir. 1992) (per curiam), *cert. denied,* 114 S. Ct. 1398 (1994))); Thurman v. Robertshaw Control Co., 869 F. Supp. 934, 940, 65 FEP 1652 (N.D. Ga. 1994) (as general proposition, "'statistics alone cannot make a case of individual disparate treatment'") (quoting Carmichael v. Birmingham Saw Works, 738 F.2d 1126, 1131, 35 FEP 791 (11th Cir. 1984)).

[174]*See* Section IV.C *infra;* Taylor v. Canteen Corp., 69 F.3d 773, 779, 69 FEP 310 (7th Cir. 1995).

by a RIF is, in most cases, not "replaced" directly, most courts modify the prima facie scheme to require the plaintiff to show instead that younger individuals were more favorably treated or that age was a factor in the plaintiff's termination.[175]

In applying the RIF scheme, courts continue to define what types of evidence will satisfy this modified fourth element so that the plaintiff's case can survive summary judgment.[176]

Additionally, where a plaintiff's qualifications are compared to those of other employees, establishing that he or she is "qualified" for the position formerly held can be more difficult.[177]

---

[175]*See* Section IV.C *infra*.

[176]*See, e.g.,* Jameson v. Arrow Co., 75 F.3d 1528, 1532–33, 70 FEP 153 (11th Cir. 1996) (plaintiff established prima facie RIF case where job for which plaintiff was qualified and applied was available at time of her termination; plaintiff was told position would not be filled, but position was filled by younger woman); Taylor v. Canteen Corp., 69 F.3d 773, 780 n.2, 782, 69 FEP 310 (7th Cir. 1995) (plaintiff in RIF case unable to show more favorable treatment of younger employees: plaintiff was unable to perform tasks required for other positions, and younger co-worker comparator not similarly situated where younger employee's position had been eliminated one year prior to plaintiff's and clerical position created for younger employee was justified by business necessity); Collier v. Budd Co., 66 F.3d 886, 891, 68 FEP 1435 (7th Cir. 1995) (retention of two youngest members of small sales/service force and expansion of duties of the youngest member, and termination of two of three oldest members is sufficient to establish more favorable treatment of younger employees); Armendariz v. Pinkerton Tobacco Co., 58 F.3d 144, 150, 68 FEP 381 (5th Cir. 1995) (plaintiff failed to show age was factor in termination where plaintiff did not allege there were other positions open at time of his termination, and defendant produced evidence of policy against relocation in plaintiff's position), *cert. denied,* 116 S. Ct. 709 (1996); Hardin v. Hussmann Corp., 45 F.3d 262, 265–66, 66 FEP 1369 (8th Cir. 1995) (plaintiff created fact issue where decision to include plaintiff in RIF was reached in cursory meeting, no personnel records were reviewed, and plaintiff's supervisor was not consulted); Bright v. Standard Register Co., 66 F.3d 171, 173, 68 FEP 1694 (8th Cir. 1995) (plaintiffs could not show age was factor in termination where younger workers were retained based on seniority); Ward v. Gulfstream Aerospace Corp., Inc., 894 F. Supp. 1573, 1580 (S.D. Ga. 1995) (no prima facie case where plaintiff failed to offer evidence that employer's modification of RIF selection criteria was motivated by discriminatory intent); EEOC v. Kloster Cruise, Ltd., 897 F. Supp. 1422, 1426, 68 FEP 1316 (S.D. Fla. 1995) (prima facie case established where territories of over-40 district sales managers terminated in RIF were divided among younger employees); Ryder v. Westinghouse Elec. Corp., 879 F. Supp. 534, 537 (W.D. Pa. 1995) (fact issue existed regarding prima facie case where it was unclear whether position was eliminated or if plaintiff was replaced by worker 16 years his junior); Kreimeyer v. Hercules, Inc., 892 F. Supp. 1369, 1373 (D. Utah 1994) (no prima facie case where plaintiff admitted in deposition that her termination was not due to "chronological age as much as length of service and the amount of money that I was making," and plaintiff's duties were absorbed by older workers).

[177]O'Connor v. Consolidated Coin Caterers Corp., 84 F.3d 718, 719–20, 70 FEP 1628 (4th Cir.) (on remand from Supreme Court, court held that RIF plaintiff failed to satisfy "qualification" element of prima facie case because he performed at the

6. Decisions Tied to Salary

Consistent with the analysis in *Hazen Paper Co. v. Biggins*,[178] courts continue to hold that the fact that an adverse employment decision was motivated solely by the plaintiff's high salary is not disparate treatment violative of the ADEA.[179]

7. Other Undisputed Reasons

Courts have held summary judgment is appropriate where the plaintiff fails to offer probative evidence disputing the defendant's legitimate nondiscriminatory explanation.[180]

When a plaintiff admits that the reason for the adverse action was something other than age, courts grant summary judgment even when that motivation is illegal under a different statute or based on poor judgment.[181]

---

lowest level of group of retained employees), *cert. denied,* 117 S. Ct. 608 (1996); *cf.* Stone v. Georgia Power Co., 902 F. Supp. 1578, 1585, 69 FEP 25 (M.D. Ga. 1995) (plaintiff established he was qualified for position open at time of termination where he alleged "that he felt very qualified for that position; that he applied for the position; and that he was not accepted, *i.e.,* the position was closed").

[178]507 U.S. 604, 612–13, 61 FEP 793 (1993).

[179]*E.g.,* Bialas v. Greyhound Lines, Inc., 59 F.3d 759, 763, 68 FEP 552 (8th Cir. 1995) (holding that summary judgment was proper because even if assertion that defendant terminated plaintiffs because of their high salaries was true, it did not in itself support inference of age discrimination); Mooney v. Aramco Servs. Co., 54 F.3d 1207, 1218, 68 FEP 421 (5th Cir. 1995) (concluding that statements indicative of a desire to save money by employing persons at lower pay does not support age discrimination claim); Bolton v. Scrivner, Inc., 36 F.3d 939, 944–45, 3 AD 1089 (10th Cir. 1994) (fact that defendant saved money by replacing plaintiff with casual worker is not evidence of pretext that will defeat summary judgment), *cert. denied,* 513 U.S. 1152 (1995); Serben v. Inter-City Mfg. Co., 36 F.3d 765, 766, 65 FEP 1706 (8th Cir. 1994) (observing that plaintiff's status as experienced and thus higher-paid employee did not in itself permit inference of age discrimination), *cert. denied,* 514 U.S. 1037 (1995); Woroski v. Nashua Corp., 31 F.3d 105, 109 n.2, 65 FEP 824 (2d Cir. 1994) (ADEA does not prohibit employer from acting out of concern for excessive costs, even if they arise from age-related facts—such as the fact that employees with longer seniority command higher salaries than new hires).

[180]*E.g.,* Hartsel v. Keys, 87 F.3d 795, 800–01, 72 FEP 951 (6th Cir. 1996) (concluding that summary judgment was appropriate because plaintiff failed to offer evidence disputing truthfulness of defendant's legitimate nondiscriminatory explanation), *cert. denied,* 117 S. Ct. 683 (1997); Douglass v. United Servs. Auto. Ass'n, 79 F.3d 1415, 1429–30, 70 FEP 701 (5th Cir. 1996) (holding that summary judgment was appropriate where plaintiff offered nothing to rebut evidence in support of the defendant's proffered reason for removing plaintiff from his position).

[181]*E.g.,* Rothmeier v. Investment Advisers, Inc., 85 F.3d 1328, 1337–38, 71 FEP 1458 (8th Cir. 1996) (holding that summary judgment was proper when plaintiff failed to offer probative evidence of age discrimination and admitted that he was discharged

V. AFFIRMATIVE DEFENSES

B. Reasonable Factors Other Than Age and Good Cause

Employment decisions based upon reasonable factors other than age are valid and will be upheld.[182] However, to qualify for the RFOA defense, an employment practice or policy must be "age neutral."[183]

D. Bona Fide Employee Benefit Plan

1. Early Retirement Incentives

Courts have continued to review the legality of early retirement programs in various contexts and have generally found them to be lawful.[184] Although the mere offer of early retirement does

---

because company wanted to cover up SEC violations); Marx v. Schnuck Mkts., Inc., 76 F.3d 324, 328, 73 FEP 21 (10th Cir.) (affirming summary judgment based on concession by plaintiff that sole reason for discharge was motive prohibited by law but not age discrimination), *cert. denied,* 116 S. Ct. 2552 (1996).

[182]Ellis v. United Airlines, Inc., 73 F.3d 999, 1005–06, 69 FEP 1167 (10th Cir.) (use of facially neutral weight requirement for flight attendants is a reasonable factor other than age), *cert. denied,* 116 S. Ct. 2500 (1996). *See also* Slathar v. Sather Trucking Corp., 78 F.3d 415, 418–19, 70 FEP 574 (8th Cir.) (termination based solely on salary or length of service does not violate ADEA), *cert. denied,* 117 S. Ct. 179 (1996); EEOC v. Insurance Co. of N. Am., 49 F.3d 1418, 1420, 67 FEP 411 (9th Cir. 1995) (refusal to hire based on "overqualification" does not necessarily violate ADEA even though " 'overqualification' might be strongly correlated with advanced age"); Thomure v. Phillips Furniture Co., 30 F.3d 1020, 1024, 65 FEP 976 (8th Cir. 1994) (no violation of ADEA where employer cut wages at different rates based on level of compensation, with higher-paid employees receiving larger pay reduction than lesser-paid employees), *cert. denied,* 513 U.S. 1191 (1995).

[183]EEOC v. Johnson & Higgins, Inc., 887 F. Supp. 682, 685–86, 68 FEP 1481 (S.D.N.Y. 1995) (court rejected RFOA defense and granted summary judgment for EEOC where employer's policy required employees who sit on company's board of directors to retire at age 60 or 62; court also rejected company's argument that termination of employee-directors was not due to age but rather to their "dual status"), *aff'd,* 91 F.3d 1529, 71 FEP 818 (2d Cir. 1996), *cert. denied,* 118 S. Ct. 47 (1997).

[184]Blistein v. St. John's College, 74 F.3d 1459, 1472, 69 FEP 1310 (4th Cir. 1996) (although fact that employee "was only eligible for the early retirement incentive because of his age might be evidence that age was not treated neutrally, it cannot be 'other evidence' [t]hat would give rise to an inference of an ADEA violation"); Lyon v. Ohio Educ. Ass'n & Prof'l Staff Union, 53 F.3d 135, 139–40, 67 FEP 1088 (6th Cir. 1995) (ADEA not violated where early retirement plan gave employees imputed service in order to equalize benefits and gave younger employees, with longer years of service, higher pension payments than older employees with equal years of service); Serben v. Inter-City Mfg. Co., 36 F.3d 765, 766, 65 FEP 1706 (8th Cir.

not establish a constructive discharge,[185] a constructive discharge occurs when the employee's choice is essentially between early retirement or continuing to work under intolerable conditions.[186]

2. Pensions

In *Lockheed Corp. v. Spink*,[187] the Supreme Court held that the provisions in the Omnibus Budget Reconciliation Act of 1986 (OBRA),[188] which amended the ADEA to prohibit age-based cessations of benefit accruals and age-based reductions in benefit accrual rates, do not apply retroactively.[189] Spink was reemployed by Lockheed in 1979 at the age of 61 and was lawfully excluded from participating in Lockheed's retirement plan. When the OBRA amendments were passed, Spink was permitted to participate in the plan, but did not receive credit for pre-OBRA service years. The Supreme Court held that the OBRA did not apply retroactively to require Lockheed to use pre-OBRA service years in calculating the plaintiff's benefits.[190] In another case, the Seventh Circuit held that the ADEA's toleration of an age cutoff for hiring firefighters did not justify a city's refusal, pursuant to state statute, to make pension contributions for firefighters who were 35 years of age or older when they were hired.[191] The court held that "a lower pension is equivalent to a lower salary for the same work" and ruled that the plaintiff was entitled to a full pension under the ADEA.[192]

1994) (per curiam) (offer of early retirement to protected employees does not violate ADEA and "does not support an inference of age discrimination"), *cert. denied*, 514 U.S. 1037 (1995).

[185]Smith v. World Ins. Co., 38 F.3d 1456, 1461, 66 FEP 13 (8th Cir. 1994). *But see* EEOC v. Sears, Roebuck & Co., 857 F. Supp. 1233, 1240–41, 65 FEP 479 (N.D. Ill. 1994), *modified*, 883 F. Supp. 211, 70 FEP 175 (N.D. Ill. 1995) (policy of giving employee five days to decide whether to resign or remain employed at reduced compensation may give only "an illusory right to choose" because "[w]hat appears to be voluntary early retirement is really an involuntary discharge").

[186]*Smith v. World Ins. Co.*, 38 F.3d at 1460–61 (employee was constructively discharged where he was told he could take early retirement or continue to work but if he elected to stay, company vice-president "would start to turn the screws and build a file" against him).

[187]116 S. Ct. 1783, 70 FEP 1633 (1996).

[188]29 U.S.C. § 623(i)(1).

[189]Lockheed Corp. v. Spink, 116 S. Ct. 1783, 1792, 70 FEP 1633 (1996).

[190]*Id.* at 1792–93.

[191]Quinones v. City of Evanston, 58 F.3d 275, 278–80, 69 FEP 791 (7th Cir. 1995).

[192]*Id.* at 278, 280.

3. Severance Benefits

A severance pay program may violate the ADEA if participation in the program is not knowing and voluntary.[193]

4. Disability Benefits

While the OWBPA permits employers to offset disability benefits by pension benefits to prevent double dipping, the OWBPA prohibits employers from taking an offset if the employee is not actually receiving the pension benefit or the offset would essentially force the employee to retire.[194]

Employees who began receiving disability retirement benefits payments prior to the effective date of the OWBPA and continue receiving such payments after the date of the OWBPA may not challenge their disability retirement scheme if such benefits constitute a single "series" of benefits payments.[195]

E. Bona Fide Seniority System

Courts continue to uphold bona fide seniority systems under the ADEA.[196]

---

[193]Griffin v. Kraft Gen. Foods, Inc., 62 F.3d 368, 370, 373–74, 68 FEP 1072 (11th Cir. 1995) (per curiam) (summary judgment for employer reversed where eligibility for severance package during plant closure was conditioned on employee signing release of ADEA rights that may not have been knowing and voluntary); EEOC v. Sears, Roebuck & Co., 857 F. Supp. 1233, 1239, 1240, 65 FEP 479 (N.D. Ill. 1994) (although "conditioning severance benefits on an invalid release is not actionable under ADEA section 4(d)," giving employees only five days to decide whether to resign and receive severance pay may be an involuntary discharge), *modified,* 883 F. Supp. 211, 70 FEP 175 (N.D. Ill. 1995).

[194]Kalvinskas v. California Inst. of Tech., 96 F.3d 1305, 71 FEP 1647 (9th Cir. 1996) (employer violated ADEA by essentially forcing involuntarily retirement by offsetting employee's long-term disability benefits by the amount of pension benefits employee could have received).

[195]Riva v. Massachusetts, 61 F.3d 1003, 1007–09, 68 FEP 688 (1st Cir. 1995) (plaintiffs claiming that their disability retirement scheme violated OWBPA could not challenge their retirement scheme because payments to plaintiffs constituted single "series" of payments).

[196]Hiatt v. Union Pac. R.R., 65 F.3d 838, 842–43, 68 FEP 1160 (10th Cir. 1995) (claim that bona fide seniority system had adverse impact on older employees dismissed), *cert. denied,* 516 U.S. 1115 (1996); EEOC v. Newport Mesa Unified Sch. Dist., 893 F. Supp. 927, 934, 68 FEP 657 (C.D. Cal. 1995) (salary table that determines teachers' salaries according to their qualifications and experience qualifies as seniority system and initial placement of workers on salary table is part of seniority system).

F. Settlement and Release

Courts have consistently held that ADEA releases must comply with the basic requirements of the OWBPA to be deemed knowing and voluntary.[197] Some courts also have applied additional criteria.[198]

In *Oubre v. Entergy Operations, Inc.*,[199] the Supreme Court ruled that a plaintiff who executes a release that does not comply with the OWBPA requirements[200] may sue under the ADEA without first tendering back the moneys or other benefits he or she received in return for the release.[201] However, two concurring and three dissenting justices believed noncompliance with the OWBPA made the release voidable, not void, and the concurrence suggested that once suit is commenced, nothing in the statute prevents the employer from petitioning for return of its reciprocal payment or relief from any ongoing reciprocal obligation.[202]

---

[197]EEOC v. Sara Lee Corp., 923 F. Supp. 994, 997, 70 FEP 57 (W.D. Mich. 1995) (waivers contained in severance agreements were not knowingly and voluntarily made because they did not contain OWBPA-required provisions in connection with employment termination program); EEOC v. Sears, Roebuck & Co., 857 F. Supp. 1233, 1237, 65 FEP 479 (N.D. Ill. 1994) (severance plan that gave employees five days to decide whether to stay on job and 45 days to accept or reject severance benefits if resigning, did not comply with OWBPA), *modified,* 883 F. Supp. 211, 70 FEP 175 (N.D. Ill. 1995); Raczak v. Ameritech Corp., 1994 WL 780899, at *7 (E.D. Mich. Aug. 1, 1994) (releases signed in connection with exit incentive program were not knowingly and voluntarily executed because employer provided employees with salary grades in lieu of job titles as required by statute), *rev'd,* 103 F.3d 1257, 72 FEP 1357 (6th Cir. 1997), *cert. denied,* 118 S. Ct. 1033 (1998).

[198]Adams v. Philip Morris, Inc., 67 F.3d 580, 583, 71 FEP 1025 (6th Cir. 1995) (to evaluate whether release has been knowingly and voluntarily executed, courts consider many factors including totality of circumstances); Griffin v. Kraft Gen. Foods, Inc., 62 F.3d 368, 373–74, 68 FEP 1072 (11th Cir. 1995) (per curiam) (nonstatutory circumstances, such as fraud, duress, or coercion in connection with execution of waiver, may render release not knowing and voluntary); Anderson v. Lifeco Servs. Corp., 881 F. Supp. 1500, 1503–04, 67 FEP 1047 (D. Colo. 1995) (in addition to criteria set forth in § 626(f), Tenth Circuit requires a subjective analysis of employee's understanding of consequences of release); Martinez v. National Broad. Co., 877 F. Supp. 219, 227, 73 FEP 1701 (D.N.J. 1994) (to determine whether employee has executed release knowingly and willfully, Third Circuit has adopted totality of circumstances test; general principles of contract construction, specifically absence of fraud or undue influence, are also applicable).

[199]118 S. Ct. 838, 75 FEP 1255 (1998).

[200]29 USC. § 626(f)(1).

[201]118 S. Ct. at 842.

[202]*Id.* at 844–46. *See* Soliman v. Digital Equip. Corp., 869 F. Supp. 65, 69, 67 FEP 1259 (D. Mass. 1994) (waiver that did not comply with OWBPA was void, and

Courts have held that employers need not pay employees additional consideration for waiver of ADEA claims.[203]

An employee may not prospectively waive his or her rights under the ADEA.[204] However, agreements to arbitrate future disputes have been upheld.[205]

At least two courts have held that a release that is deemed invalid because it does not comply with the OWBPA does not create a separate cause of action under the ADEA.[206]

VI. REMEDIES

B. Equitable Relief

1. Injunctions

Actions for declaratory relief may proceed against a ripeness challenge where the plaintiff can demonstrate hardship if review were postponed.[207] Equitable relief may include requiring an

---

plaintiff was not required to return consideration to proceed with age claims; rather, should plaintiff prevail, defendant would be entitled to determination of what portion, if any, was to be deducted from award plaintiff received).

[203]Griffin v. Kraft Gen. Foods, Inc., 62 F.3d 368, 374, 68 FEP 1072 (11th Cir. 1995) (employer need not pay additional consideration for waiver of ADEA claim); DiBiase v. SmithKline Beecham Corp., 48 F.3d 719, 730, 67 FEP 58 (3d Cir.) (declining to find disparate treatment of older employees where employer conditioned right to expanded severance benefits during RIF on each employee's blanket waiver of all accrued claims, including those under ADEA, because under such circumstances, "it is impossible to tell whose package of potential claims is more valuable"), *cert. denied*, 116 S. Ct. 306 (1995).

[204]Adams v. Philip Morris, Inc., 67 F.3d 580, 584, 71 FEP 1025 (6th Cir. 1995) (employee may not prospectively waive ADEA rights but not every settlement agreement that refers to postsettlement conduct necessarily results in prospective waiver, i.e., when it incorporates "continuing effects" of past discrimination).

[205]Williams v. Cigna Fin. Advisors, Inc., 56 F.3d 656, 660–61, 68 FEP 65 (5th Cir. 1995) (OWBPA not applicable to preemployment agreement to arbitrate employment disputes).

[206]EEOC v. Sears, Roebuck & Co., 883 F. Supp. 211, 215, 70 FEP 175 (N.D. Ill. 1995) (invalid release does not create a separate cause of action under the ADEA); Williams v. General Motors Corp., 901 F. Supp. 252, 255, 69 FEP 445 (E.D. Mich. 1995) (court did not accept plaintiff's contention "that a violation of [the OWBPA's waiver provisions] may be extrapolated into a holding that a substantive cause of action for age discrimination exists").

[207]Riva v. Massachusetts, 61 F.3d 1003, 1011–12, 68 FEP 688 (1st Cir. 1995) (56-year-old disabled employee's suit for violation of ADEA seeking declaration that Massachusetts statute, which would have likely prospective effect of reducing his

employer's managers to sign a statement regarding the substantive provisions of the ADEA.[208]

2. Reinstatement and Instatement

It is well settled that reinstatement is the preferred remedy over front pay, and the Fifth Circuit has held that the district court should articulate its reasons for awarding front pay rather than reinstatement.[209] Whether a successful plaintiff is ordered reinstated[210] or awarded front pay[211] continues to depend on the circumstances of each case.

C. Back Pay

Courts continue to make back-pay awards that include various forms of compensation lost as a result of age discrimination.[212] An

---

retirement benefits at age 65, allowed to proceed because plaintiff suffered immediate harm of not being able to plan for retirement and likely future harm of losing retirement benefits).

[208]Padilla v. Metro-North Commuter R.R., 1995 WL 4269, at *3 (S.D.N.Y. Jan. 5, 1995), aff'd, 92 F.3d 117, 72 FEP 1748 (2d Cir. 1996), cert. denied, 117 S. Ct. 2453 (1997).

[209]Weaver v. Amoco Prod. Co., 66 F.3d 85, 88–89, 70 FEP 931 (5th Cir. 1995).

[210]Philipp v. ANR Freight Sys., Inc., 61 F.3d 669, 674, 70 FEP 1347 (8th Cir. 1995) (no abuse of discretion in trial court ordering reinstatement where plaintiff failed to demonstrate that reinstatement was "impracticable or impossible" and supervisors who allegedly discriminated against plaintiff no longer worked for company); Shea v. Icelandair, 925 F. Supp. 1014, 1030–34, 70 FEP 1544 (S.D.N.Y. 1996) (balance of equities supported reinstatement where plaintiff was exemplary 30-year employee notwithstanding fact that former position had been restructured, innocent third party would be required to take new position in same department, and employer would have to accommodate health problems of plaintiff; friction between parties was normal byproduct of any litigation and did not rise to level of acrimony preventing reinstatement).

[211]Ray v. Iuka Special Mun. Separate Sch. Dist., 51 F.3d 1246, 1254–55, 67 FEP 1348 (5th Cir. 1995) (district court did not abuse discretion in awarding front pay rather than reinstatement because no comparable position existed for school principal after reorganization, plaintiff obtained substantially similar employment almost immediately, and reinstatement would require displacement of current employee); Mitchell v. Sisters of Charity of Incarnate Word, 924 F. Supp. 793, 803 (S.D. Tex. 1996) (although reinstatement generally preferred, front pay appropriate where antagonism exists between victim of discrimination and employer and reinstatement would result in displacement of innocent employees, making reinstatement unfeasible); Stratton v. Department for the Aging of N.Y., 922 F. Supp. 857, 866–67 (S.D.N.Y. 1996) (front pay appropriate where 66-year-old plaintiff had no reasonable prospect of obtaining similar employment).

[212]Rhodes v. Guiberson Oil Tools, 82 F.3d 615, 620, 71 FEP 83 (5th Cir. 1996) (pension plan benefits recoverable and should be calculated based on present value

employer's unconditional offer of reinstatement normally cuts off a plaintiff's right to back pay[213] (and front pay) unless the plaintiff acted reasonably in refusing the offer.[214] Back-pay (and front-pay) awards may also be cut off by discovery of "after-acquired evidence" if the employer can prove that such information would have otherwise led to the plaintiff's termination.[215] One district court has held that an employee's representation in a claim for disability benefits that he was disabled does not preclude a claim for back pay.[216]

---

of plaintiff's interest in pension plan); EEOC v. Kentucky State Police Dep't, 80 F.3d 1086, 1100, 71 FEP 1495 (6th Cir.) (back-pay awards may include overtime, sick leave, vacation pay, pension benefits, and other fringe benefits claimant would have received but for age discrimination (citing Rasimas v. Michigan Dep't of Mental Health, 714 F.2d 614, 626, 32 FEP 688 (6th Cir. 1983), *cert. denied,* 466 U.S. 950 (1984)), *cert. denied,* 117 S. Ct. 385 (1996); Smith v. World Ins. Co., 38 F.3d 1456, 1465–66, 66 FEP 13 (8th Cir. 1994) (pension benefits should not be deducted from back-pay award unless payment would result in double recovery).

[213]*See, e.g.,* Bragalone v. Kona Coast Resort Joint Venture, 866 F. Supp. 1285, 1295–97, 66 FEP 65 (D. Haw. 1994) (unconditional offer of reinstatement tolled back-pay liability because offer included assurances of no retaliation and plaintiff presented no medical evidence that returning to work environment would be too stressful).

[214]Smith v. World Ins. Co., 38 F.3d 1456, 1463–64, 66 FEP 13 (8th Cir. 1994) (jury could have found plaintiff acted reasonably in rejecting offer of reinstatement where offer made three years after separation, poor performance references would not be expunged from his record, and plaintiff felt employer had not changed); Gerardi v. Hofstra Univ., 897 F. Supp. 50, 55 (E.D.N.Y. 1995) (applicant complaining of age discrimination in hiring was not required to accept offer of reinstatement to position with materially different job duties and different working hours from position for which she originally applied); Miano v. AC & R Adver., Inc., 875 F. Supp. 204, 223–24, 66 FEP 1603 (S.D.N.Y. 1995) (court determined that reasonable person in plaintiffs' shoes would have refused offer of reinstatement because plaintiffs were high-level executives in positions requiring trust and confidence and evidence demonstrated long history of hostility and egregious acts of harassment).

[215]*See, e.g.,* McKennon v. Nashville Banner Publ'g Co., 513 U.S. 352, 361–63, 66 FEP 1192 (1995) (after-acquired evidence of employee's copying and removal of confidential documents before her discriminatory layoff, which would have been independent and sufficient grounds to terminate plaintiff had employer known of the conduct at time, precluded remedies of front pay and reinstatement; as general rule, back pay may be limited from date of discharge until date wrongdoing is discovered by employer); Ricky v. Mapco, Inc., 50 F.3d 874, 876, 68 FEP 1745 (10th Cir. 1995) (back pay limited to date of discovery of employee's wrongdoing if employer can prove (1) that employer was unaware of behavior at time of termination; and (2) that behavior was egregious enough to warrant termination). *Contra* Ryder v. Westinghouse Elec. Corp., 879 F. Supp. 534, 537–38 (W.D. Pa. 1995) (after-acquired evidence doctrine does not apply to alleged misconduct that occurs after the employee has been terminated). For a more extensive discussion of the after-acquired evidence doctrine, *see* Chapter 41, Section I.B.2.b.(iii) in this Supplement.

[216]EEOC v. Learonal, Inc., 66 FEP 697, 700, 702 (N.D. Ill. 1994) (it is employee's "*actual* ability to perform the duties of the job in question" and not the employee's representations that determine entitlement to back pay).

Certain items should be deducted from the back-pay award, including severance pay and interim earnings.[217] The courts remain split regarding whether amounts paid in Social Security taxes and unemployment compensation should be deducted.[218] Where a jury's back-pay award is supported by the evidence and mathematically correct, it should not be disturbed,[219] and any lack of certainty regarding the proper measure of back pay should be borne by the wrongdoer and not by the victim of discrimination.[220]

D. Front Pay

Front pay is an equitable remedy for the court's determination and not for the jury.[221] While it is well settled that front-pay awards should not be speculative, recent court decisions are split regarding the appropriate number of years on which to calculate front pay.[222] Although awards should be discounted to present value,

---

[217]Rhodes v. Guiberson Oil Tools, 82 F.3d 615, 620, 71 FEP 83 (5th Cir. 1996) (severance pay); Inks v. Healthcare Distribs., Inc., 901 F. Supp. 1403, 1409–10 (N.D. Ind. 1995) (severance pay); *see* EEOC v. Kentucky State Police Dep't, 80 F.3d 1086, 1100, 71 FEP 1495 (6th Cir.), *cert. denied,* 117 S. Ct. 385 (1996) (interim earnings).

[218]*Compare* EEOC v. Kentucky State Police Dep't, 80 F.3d 1086, 1100, 71 FEP 1495 (6th Cir.) (back-pay award should not be reduced by amount of unemployment compensation received and income and Social Security taxes that would have been deducted from claimant's wages absent discrimination), *cert. denied,* 117 S. Ct. 385 (1996) *with* Stratton v. Department for the Aging of N.Y., 922 F. Supp. 857, 865–66 (S.D.N.Y. 1996) (pension and unemployment compensation benefits should be set off against back-pay award). *See* Inks v. Healthcare Distribs., Inc., 901 F. Supp. 1403, 1410 & n.2, 73 FEP 643 (N.D. Ind. 1995) (jury not obligated to reduce back-pay award by amount of unemployment compensation received).

[219]Young v. Lukens Steel Co., 881 F. Supp. 962, 976–77, 71 FEP 739 (E.D. Pa. 1994) (beyond court's discretion to guess at how jury arrived at damage award figure as long as award supported by the evidence).

[220]Starceski v. Westinghouse Elec. Corp., 54 F.3d 1089, 1101, 67 FEP 1184 (3d Cir. 1995); Young v. Lukens Steel Co., 881 F. Supp. 962, 976–77, 71 FEP 739 (E.D. Pa. 1994).

[221]Wells v. New Cherokee Corp., 58 F.3d 233, 238–39, 68 FEP 284 (6th Cir. 1995) (trial court erred in allowing jury to decide whether award of front pay was proper, but error was harmless because jury was instructed on factors to consider and employer did not object to instruction); Downes v. Volkswagen of Am., Inc., 41 F.3d 1132, 1141, 69 FEP 11 (7th Cir. 1994) (jury's award of back pay did not preclude court from awarding front pay as equitable relief; court may consider factors such as hostility between parties, availability of vacant position, plaintiff's prospects of obtaining comparable employment, plaintiff's physical condition, and whether liquidated damages have been awarded).

[222]*Compare Downes v. Volkswagen of Am., Inc.,* 41 F.3d at 1143 (decision limiting front-pay award to three years was reasonable because employer's deteriorating financial condition made it unlikely plaintiff would have remained on job

it is appropriate to calculate front pay simply by multiplying the yearly loss by the expected number of years to be worked in the future, without any other calculations because it is reasonable to assume that the value of future pay increases would totally offset the discount rate.[223] Just like back-pay awards, awards of front pay may be limited or cut off by the plaintiff's failure to mitigate damages[224] or by evidence that termination would have occurred for a legitimate reason prior to trial.[225] The Fifth Circuit[226] has joined the First, Seventh, and Ninth Circuits[227] in holding that front pay should be limited or precluded where there is a substantial award of liquidated damages.

E. Liquidated Damages

In *Ryther v. KARE 11*,[228] the Eighth Circuit suggested, in upholding a jury finding of a willful ADEA violation, that the relevant inquiry under *Biggins*[229] for determining whether an ADEA

---

for longer period), Mitchell v. Sisters of Charity of the Incarnate Word, 924 F. Supp. 793, 804 (S.D. Tex. 1996) (limiting front-pay award to one year), *and* Rose v. Ireco, Inc., 872 F. Supp. 1127, 1135, 73 FEP 429 (N.D.N.Y. 1994) (front pay granted for approximately one year until age 60 because evidence showed that was age when most of defendant's employees elected to retire) *with* Jackson v. City of Cookeville, 31 F.3d 1354, 1358–61, 65 FEP 870 (6th Cir. 1994) (no error in awarding front pay for 11 years based on plaintiff's testimony that he expected to retire at age 65), *and* Newhouse v. McCormick & Co., 910 F. Supp. 1451, 1456–59 (D. Neb. 1996) (calculating front pay of 6.3 years based on yearly gross wage loss minus yearly amount plaintiff would have earned elsewhere multiplied by number of years remaining to age 70), *aff'd in part, rev'd in part,* 110 F.3d 635, 73 FEP 1496 (8th Cir. 1997).

[223]*Jackson,* 31 F.3d at 1358–61; *Newhouse,* 910 F. Supp. at 1457.

[224]Jackson v. City of Cookeville, 31 F.3d 1354, 1359, 65 FEP 870 (6th Cir. 1994) (employer has burden of establishing that damages were not mitigated).

[225]Dalal v. Alliant Techsystems, Inc., 927 F. Supp. 1374, 1377–78 (D. Colo. 1996) (denying any front-pay award because evidence showed plaintiff would have been laid off for legitimate reasons before trial).

[226]Weaver v. Amoco Prod. Co., 66 F.3d 85, 89, 70 FEP 931 (5th Cir. 1995); Shattuck v. Kinetic Concepts, Inc., 49 F.3d 1106, 1110, 67 FEP 798 (5th Cir. 1995). *But see* Newhouse v. McCormick & Co., 910 F. Supp. 1451, 1459 (D. Neb. 1996) (refusing to strike front-pay award because "I am aware of no law in [the Eighth Circuit] which holds that an award of liquidated damages precludes an award of front pay"), *aff'd in part, rev'd in part,* 110 F.3d 635, 73 FEP 1496 (8th Cir. 1997).

[227]*See* note 546 in the Main Edition.

[228]84 F.3d 1074, 70 FEP 1709 (8th Cir. 1996), *aff'd,* 108 F.3d 832 (8th Cir.) (en banc), *cert. denied,* 117 S. Ct. 2510 (1997).

[229]Hazen Paper Co. v. Biggins, 507 U.S. 604 (1993).

violation is willful is whether the employer "more likely [knew] its conduct to be illegal."[230]

A plaintiff successful in proving that the employer intentionally violated the ADEA will be entitled to liquidated damages if the employer fails to offer evidence that its conduct was nonreckless and in good faith.[231] For example, evidence that the employer was told by the plaintiff's legal counsel that plaintiff's termination would be a violation of the ADEA was sufficient to support a jury finding of reckless disregard with respect to the employer's actions.[232]

Courts continue to hold that liquidated damages are not available to federal government employees.[233]

A damage award resulting from an ADEA lawsuit initiated prior to the plaintiff's bankruptcy proceedings are part of the bankruptcy estate and are not considered exempt property for bankruptcy purposes.[234]

G. Punitive Damages

At least one district court has construed a plaintiff's request for punitive damages under the ADEA to be a de facto request for liquidated damages, noting that liquidated damages are punitive in nature.[235]

---

[230]*Ryther,* 84 F.3d at 1089.

[231]Dittmann v. Ireco, Inc., 903 F. Supp. 347, 352–53, 73 FEP 441 (N.D.N.Y. 1995) (plaintiff, who had prevailed on motion for partial summary judgment finding employer liable for intentionally violating ADEA, was entitled to liquidated damages since employer did not offer evidence that it acted nonwillfully or in good faith). One court has held that a plaintiff awarded punitive damages under Title VII is not entitled to liquidated damages under the ADEA, since liquidated damages are punitive in nature and awarding them in addition to punitive damages under Title VII would have the effect of punishing the defendant twice for the same conduct. Reynolds v. Octel Communications, 924 F. Supp. 743, 747, 69 FEP 1178, 71 FEP 1053 (N.D. Tex. 1995).

[232]Stratton v. Department for the Aging of N.Y., 922 F. Supp. 857, 863 n.4 (S.D.N.Y. 1996).

[233]Moore v. Stone, 1994 WL 549733, at *3 (D.D.C. Sept. 30, 1994) (citing Smith v. Office of Personnel Management, 778 F.2d 258, 262, 39 FEP 1851 (5th Cir. 1985) (holding that federal employees cannot recover either compensatory or liquidated damages), *cert. denied,* 476 U.S. 1105 (1986)).

[234]In re Williams, 197 B.R. 398, 402–03 (Bankr. M.D. Ga. 1996) (absent an exemption under federal or state bankruptcy law, ADEA damage award is property of the debtor's bankruptcy estate).

[235]Stafford v. Radford Community Hosp., Inc., 908 F. Supp. 1369, 1376 (W.D. Va. 1995), *aff'd without opinion,* 120 F.3d 262 (4th Cir. 1997); *see* Sanchez v. Puerto Rico Oil Co., 37 F.3d 712, 725, 66 FEP 148 (1st Cir. 1994) ("[T]he considerations

H. Attorney's Fees

A plaintiff may be entitled to an award of attorney's fees for time spent on claims arising from a common factual core or based on related legal theories even though not successful on each theory raised.[236] However, if the plaintiff has only limited success, the court may reduce attorney's fees to account for this.[237] Several courts have held that the ADEA allows a plaintiff to recover attorney's fees related to representation in prelawsuit administrative proceedings.[238]

An award of attorney's fees and litigation expenses for a suit filed before plaintiff initiates bankruptcy proceedings become part of the bankruptcy estate.[239]

I. Prejudgment Interest

In *Downes v. Volkswagen of America, Inc.*,[240] the Seventh Circuit held that where a plaintiff receives severance pay, the interest

---

that operate to bar multiple recoveries are conceptually and legally inapplicable to punitive damages."). *Contra* Clark v. Sun Elec. Corp., 1995 WL 708567, at *1–*2 (N.D. Ill. Nov. 30, 1995) (district court struck plaintiff's prayer for punitive damages and damages for pain and suffering as improper since those damages are unavailable under the ADEA; court nevertheless noted that jury could award liquidated damages as part of plaintiff's prayer for "any and all relief [ ] which he is entitled to"). One court has held that a plaintiff may not recover both liquidated damages under the ADEA and punitive damages under a state claim. Moses v. KMart Corp., 905 F. Supp. 1054, 1059, 70 FEP 1048 (S.D. Fla. 1995) (holding that since Trans World Airlines, Inc. v. Thurston, 469 U.S. 111, 36 FEP 977 (1985), held that liquidated damages are punitive in nature, to allow plaintiff to recover punitive damages under Florida Human Rights Act as well as liquidated damages under ADEA amounts to double recovery), *aff'd*, 119 F.3d 10 (11th Cir. 1997).

[236]Inks v. Healthcare Distribs. of Ind., Inc., 901 F. Supp. 1403, 1412–14, 73 FEP 643 (N.D. Ind. 1995) (attorney's fees award not reduced by court for ADEA plaintiff who was successful in obtaining back pay and liquidated damages but not front pay; front-pay claim was factually related to remainder of plaintiff's successful ADEA claims); Spradley v. Notami Hosps., Inc., 892 F. Supp. 1459, 1462–63 (M.D. Fla. 1995) (attorney's fees award not reduced for successful ADEA plaintiff who was unsuccessful on sex discrimination claim; plaintiff's claims arose from the same set of operative facts).

[237]Dalal v. Alliant Techsystems, Inc., 927 F. Supp. 1374, 1381–82 (D. Colo. 1996) (3% reduction of plaintiff's attorney's fees warranted in light of limited success with claims); Marinne v. Nabisco Brands, Inc., 1994 WL 533906, at *4 (E.D. Pa. Sept. 29, 1994) (20% reduction of fees warranted because results were not "excellent").

[238]Spradley v. Notami Hosps., Inc., 892 F. Supp. 1459, 1463 (M.D. Fla. 1995) (holding that ADEA allows fee award for time spent before state human rights commission (citing Reichman v. Bonsignore, Brignati & Mazzotta, P.C., 818 F.2d 278, 283, 43 FEP 1384 (2d Cir. 1987))).

[239]In re Williams, 197 B.R. 398, 404 (Bankr. M.D. Ga. 1996).

[240]41 F.3d 1132, 69 FEP 11 (7th Cir. 1994).

period for prejudgment interest on an award of back pay begins at the time severance pay ceases. In *Downes,* the plaintiff had received one year of severance pay after his termination was effective. The court, upholding the principle that the purpose of prejudgment interest is to compensate plaintiffs for the loss of use of money, held that the plaintiff's monetary injury was triggered when his severance pay ceased.[241] The Sixth Circuit has held that prejudgment interest should apply to each year an employee lost the use of his wages.[242]

In addition to having the discretion to award prejudgment interest, a district court has the discretion to determine the applicable prejudgment interest rate.[243] Courts differ on whether it is ordinarily an abuse of discretion not to include prejudgment interest in an award of back pay.[244]

In *Starceski v. Westinghouse Elec. Corp.,*[245] the Third Circuit joined the Second, Ninth, and Eleventh Circuits in holding that an ADEA plaintiff could recover both prejudgment interest and liquidated damages.

---

[241]*Id.* at 1144.

[242]EEOC v. Kentucky State Police Dep't, 80 F.3d 1086, 1099, 71 FEP 1495 (6th Cir.), *cert. denied,* 117 S. Ct. 385 (1996).

[243]Young v. Lukens Steel Co., 881 F. Supp. 962, 977–78, 71 FEP 739 (E.D. Pa. 1994) (court determined applicable prejudgment interest rate by looking toward interest-rate standard set out for postjudgment interest rates under 28 U.S.C. § 1961; however, contrary to § 1961, court applied interest rate on compounded basis instead of awarding interest on entire award annually).

[244]*Compare* EEOC v. Kentucky State Police Dep't, 80 F.3d 1086, 1098, 71 FEP 1495 (6th Cir.) (holding that it is ordinarily an abuse of discretion not to award prejudgment interest), *cert. denied,* 117 S. Ct. 385 (1996) *with* Rhodes v. Guiberson Oil Tools, 82 F.3d 615, 624, 71 FEP 83 (5th Cir. 1996) (holding that it was not an abuse of discretion for district court to deny prejudgment interest).

[245]54 F.3d 1089, 1102, 67 FEP 1184 (3d Cir. 1995).

Chapter 17

RETALIATION

I. An Overview of the Two Clauses of § 704(a)

Resolving a dispute among the circuits, the Supreme Court in *Robinson v. Shell Oil Co.*[1] held that § 704(a)'s protections applied to former employees. Robinson claimed that his former employer had given him a negative reference in retaliation for his filing a charge with the EEOC after he had been fired. It is not clear what effect *Robinson* might have on the Seventh Circuit's view that former employees may sue their former employers for postemployment acts of retaliation only "insofar as they are complaining of retaliation that impinges on their future employment prospects or otherwise has a nexus to employment."[2]

On the procedural front, courts remain polarized over whether a plaintiff must exhaust administrative remedies by asserting retaliation in a separate EEOC charge before filing suit.[3]

---

[1] 117 S. Ct. 843, 72 FEP 1856 (1997).

[2] Veprinsky v. Fluor Daniel, Inc., 87 F.3d 881, 891, 71 FEP 170 (7th Cir. 1996) (nonemployment-related retaliatory acts, such as posttermination assault or threats, are not actionable under § 704(a)); *accord* Nelson v. Upsala College, 51 F.3d 383, 389, 67 FEP 525 (3d Cir. 1995) (the college's requirement that the former employee obtain permission to enter its campus was not actionable retaliation under § 704(a), "as the requirement had no impact on any employment relationship Nelson had, or might have in the future").

[3] *Compare* Borase v. M/A-Com., Inc., 906 F. Supp. 65, 66–67, 73 FEP 1355 (D. Mass. 1995) (if the retaliation arises from the filing of an administrative charge, no separate charge is necessary); Hayes v. Shalala, 902 F. Supp. 259, 266, 73 FEP 3 (D.D.C. 1995) (an employee may raise a retaliation claim for the first time in federal court); *and* Boyd v. Brookstone Corp., 857 F. Supp. 1568, 1570 n.1, 71 FEP 3 (S.D. Fla. 1994) (employee need not exhaust administrative remedies before asserting retaliation claim in federal court) *with* Williams v. Perry, 907 F. Supp. 838, 845–46, 70 FEP 713 (M.D. Pa.) (while conceding that dismissal of retaliation claim was waste of judicial resources, court lacked subject matter jurisdiction over retaliation claim that employee had not asserted in EEOC charge), *aff'd mem.*, 72 F.3d 125 (3d Cir. 1995).

II. THE PARTICIPATION CLAUSE

The participation clause continues to be construed as providing protection from retaliation even for the filing of factually baseless charges.[4] Nevertheless, there remains a key distinction between factually baseless charges of, e.g., race or sex discrimination, and charges alleging conduct outside the realm of Title VII. Title VII does not protect employees from retaliation for filing *any* charge alleging *any* misconduct; to gain protection, the charge—factually supported or not—must allege conduct within the scope of the statute.[5]

Courts continue to allow derivative protection to the allies[6] of employees who assert their rights under Title VII. In *McDonnell v. Cisneros*,[7] the Seventh Circuit extended protection even to the "passive" participation of an ally. The participation clause forbids, the court held, an employer from taking adverse action against a

---

[4] "As for the participation clause, there is nothing in its wording requiring that the charges be valid, nor even that they be reasonable." Wyatt v. City of Boston, 35 F.3d 13, 15, 65 FEP 1441 (1st Cir. 1994); *accord* Steinle v. Boeing Co., 884 F. Supp. 424, 429, 68 FEP 69 (D. Kan. 1995) (even where ultimately unsuccessful, the underlying claim of discrimination may represent protected activity for purposes of proving retaliation); Volberg v. Pataki, 917 F. Supp. 909, 914 (N.D.N.Y.) ("It is well-settled that a finding of unlawful retaliation generally does not depend on the merits of the underlying discrimination complaint."), *aff'd mem.*, 112 F.3d 507 (2d Cir. 1996), *cert. denied*, 117 S. Ct. 1252 (1997). *But see* Amos v. Housing Auth., 927 F. Supp. 416, 421–22, 70 FEP 1590 (N.D. Ala. 1996) (ADEA retaliation case; an employer lawfully may discipline an employee who in bad faith files a knowingly baseless charge; in such cases, the filing of a charge "[is] itself an act of retaliation"; rejecting the notion that "a disgruntled current employee can, with impunity, even acting with malice, file an EEOC claim with a smirk, knowing that her employer is a helpless, squirming victim").

[5] *See* Balazs v. Liebenthal, 32 F.3d 151, 159, 65 FEP 993 (4th Cir. 1994) (the participation clause does not protect an employee from retaliation for filing a charge alleging that he was unjustly accused of sexual harassment, because being unjustly accused of sexual harassment "ha[s] nothing to do with [the employee's] race, color, religion, sex, or national origin"; "The EEOC had no more jurisdiction over this claim than it would have had of a charge that defendant had falsely accused him of reckless driving in the company parking lot.").

[6] *E.g.*, Robertson v. Alabama Dep't of Econ. & Community Affairs, 902 F. Supp. 1473, 1481 (M.D. Ala. 1995) (wearing buttons in support of a co-worker's Title VII lawsuit constitutes protected activity), *appeal dismissed mem.*, 89 F.3d 855 (11th Cir. 1996).

[7] 84 F.3d 256, 70 FEP 1459 (7th Cir. 1996).

supervisor for allowing a subordinate to file a charge.[8] Recent decisions are split on whether spouses and relatives who suffer adverse action merely because of their *relationship* to the employee who engaged in protected activity, and not because of anything the spouse or relative personally did, are protected under § 704(a).[9]

III. THE OPPOSITION CLAUSE

A. The Requirement That the Employment Practice Opposed Be "Made an Unlawful Employment Practice by [Title VII]"

Courts continue to construe the statute liberally, extending protection under the opposition clause even where the practice opposed ultimately is shown to be legal. However, an employee seeking protection under the opposition clause still must show a reasonable and good faith belief that the employer's conduct violated Title VII.[10]

---

[8]*Id.* at 262.

[9]*Compare* McKenzie v. Atlantic Richfield Co., 906 F. Supp. 572, 575, 70 FEP 547 (D. Colo. 1995) (spouse may seek derivative protection) *and* Thurman v. Robertshaw Control Co., 869 F. Supp. 934, 941, 65 FEP 1652 (N.D. Ga. 1994) (same) *with* Holt v. JTM Indus., Inc., 89 F.3d 1224, 71 FEP 809 (5th Cir. 1996) (ADEA retaliation case, construing Title VII authority; if the relative or spouse does not participate in any manner in the employee's charge of discrimination, the relative or spouse does not have standing to sue for statutory retaliation), *cert. denied,* 117 S. Ct. 1821 (1997).

[10]*See* Moyo v. Gomez, 40 F.3d 982, 984, 68 FEP 1419 (9th Cir. 1994) (a former prison guard stated a claim of retaliation under Title VII even though the practice he opposed may not have violated Title VII; his actions were protected if he shows a reasonable and good faith belief in a violation), *cert. denied,* 513 U.S. 1081 (1995); Dey v. Colt Constr. & Dev. Co., 28 F.3d 1446, 1457–58, 65 FEP 523 (7th Cir. 1994) (an employee's reasonable and sincere belief that her supervisor's offensive utterance constituted sexual harassment may establish the prima facie element of protected activity); Benekritis v. Johnson, 882 F. Supp. 521, 526, 67 FEP 1449 (D.S.C. 1995) (an employee may pursue a retaliation claim by showing "a reasonable, although mistaken, belief that such conduct violated the statute"); Hargens v. United States Dep't of Agric., 865 F. Supp. 1314, 1329, 66 FEP 245 (N.D. Iowa 1994) (denying summary judgment where a genuine issue of fact remained as to whether the plaintiff reasonably and in good faith believed that the conduct he complained of constituted sexual harassment); Trent v. Valley Elec. Ass'n, 41 F.3d 524, 527, 66 FEP 769 (9th Cir. 1994) (female employee could reasonably believe that her report of sexually offensive remarks was protected); Alexander v. Gerhardt Enters., 40 F.3d 187, 195, 68 FEP 595 (7th Cir. 1994) (employee could reasonably believe that the utterance of a single racial slur violated Title VII).

A belief that is either unreasonable[11] or held in bad faith[12] will not support a claim of retaliation.

Further, the practice opposed must be employment related in order to gain protection under the opposition clause. The Eighth Circuit held in *Evans v. Kansas City School District*,[13] for example, that a teacher did not oppose an unlawful employment practice when he disagreed with a school desegregation order. The teacher was concerned with student welfare, not an unlawful employment practice; thus, the court held, the teacher failed to state a cognizable retaliation claim under Title VII.[14]

B. Whether Ambiguous Protests Constitute Protected Opposition

In addition to qualifying as "passive" participation, the Seventh Circuit in *McDonnell v. Cisneros*[15] held that a supervisor's failure to prevent subordinates from filing complaints of discrimination is a form of opposition, protected by the opposition clause.[16]

C. Weighing the Disruption and Protection of Various Forms of Opposition

4. Intra-Office Disruption

Even if an employee establishes a prima facie case of retaliation, the employer may justifiably discharge the employee when the form or manner of opposition was extreme or disruptive—e.g., when the employee engages in workplace violence,[17]

---

[11]*E.g.*, Mayo v. Kiwest Corp., 898 F. Supp. 335, 337–38, 68 FEP 1761 (E.D. Va. 1995) (the employee could not reasonably believe that Title VII was intended to protect against same-sex harassment), *aff'd mem.*, 94 F.3d 641 (4th Cir. 1996). *But see* Oncale v. Sundowner Offshore Servs., Inc., 118 S. Ct. 998, 76 FEP 221 (1998).

[12]*E.g.*, Volberg v. Pataki, 917 F. Supp. 909, 914–15 (N.D.N.Y.) (the employee's belief could not have been held in good faith, where he knew that his layoff had resulted from the employer's bona fide seniority system), *aff'd mem.*, 112 F.3d 507 (2d Cir. 1996), *cert. denied*, 117 S. Ct. 1252 (1997).

[13]65 F.3d 98, 101, 68 FEP 1203 (8th Cir. 1995), *cert. denied*, 116 S. Ct. 1319 (1996).

[14]*Id.*

[15]84 F.3d 256, 70 FEP 1459 (7th Cir. 1996).

[16]*Id.* at 262.

[17]Armfield v. Runyon, 902 F. Supp. 823, 827 (N.D. Ill. 1995) (granting the employer's summary judgment motion; termination was justified because the postal

violates corporate rules and regulations,[18] or refuses to follow directives from superiors.[19]

D. The Special Role of Management and EEO Officers

A college's affirmative action officer should not receive special protection under Title VII merely because she works on matters of affirmative action.[20] Nor should a company's personnel manager receive special protection from retaliation merely because she "does her job" and brings to the employer's attention possible statutory violations.[21]

IV. Type of Adverse Treatment Cognizable Under § 704(a)

The following treatment has been found to constitute cognizable adverse action: intimidating and threatening comments,[22]

employee assaulted his supervisor when the supervisor told him that he was suspended for not following instructions and cursing at his supervisor).

[18]Dranchak v. Akzo Nobel, Inc., 88 F.3d 457, 460, 71 FEP 284 (7th Cir. 1996) (discharge was appropriate, where the employee's claimed act of opposition to age discrimination was entering into a covert "I'll scratch your back if you scratch mine" agreement with the company's departing president, in which each approved a generous severance package for the other).

[19]Knickerbocker v. City of Stockton, 81 F.3d 907, 912, 3 WH2d 453 (9th Cir. 1996) (transfer of a police sergeant due to his "seemingly willful disobedience of orders and willingness to create dissent among the rank and file officers during a time when a 'team' mentality was sorely needed" did not constitute unlawful retaliation under the FLSA, even though the sergeant was protesting what he perceived as unlawful overtime practices).

[20]Nelson v. Pima Community College, 83 F.3d 1075, 1082 (9th Cir. 1996).

[21]McKenzie v. Renberg's, Inc., 94 F.3d 1478, 1486, 3 WH2d 769 (10th Cir. 1996) (FLSA retaliation case; affirming j.n.o.v. for the employer, where the plaintiff was simply doing her job, not engaging in protected activity, when she communicated good faith concerns regarding possible wage-law violations; "[The plaintiff] never crossed the line from being an employee merely performing her job as personnel director to an employee lodging a personal complaint about the . . . practices of her employer and asserting a right adverse to the company.") (emphasis deleted), cert. denied, 117 S. Ct. 1468 (1997).

[22]Harrison v. Metropolitan Gov't, 80 F.3d 1107, 1119, 73 FEP 109 (6th Cir.) (supervisor's threatening comments and excessive scrutiny of performance), cert. denied, 117 S. Ct. 169 (1996); Sink v. Knox County Hosp., 900 F. Supp. 1065, 1076–77, 70 FEP 1560 (S.D. Ind. 1995) (decisionmaker's threats of discharge and admonishment); Weeks v. Maine, 866 F. Supp. 601, 604, 69 FEP 871 (D. Me. 1994) (supervisor calling plaintiff a troublemaker); Munday v. Waste Management, Inc., 858

transfer,[23] placement on involuntary maternity leave,[24] refusing to discipline a harassing supervisor,[25] termination of grievance procedures,[26] negative statements about the employee's participation that might affect his or her reputation,[27] conduct amounting to a constructive discharge,[28] filing criminal charges,[29] and refusal to rehire.[30] Courts are split on whether unfairly evaluating performance, alone, can trigger a retaliation claim.[31]

F. Supp. 1364, 1374, 72 FEP 471 (D. Md. 1994) (supervisor's yelling at and ordering co-workers to spy on and ignore the charging party).

[23]Wyatt v. City of Boston, 35 F.3d 13, 16, 65 FEP 1441 (1st Cir. 1994).

[24]Dunning v. Simmons Airlines, Inc., 62 F.3d 863, 869, 68 FEP 785 (7th Cir. 1995) (unpaid leave).

[25]Humphreys v. Medical Towers, Ltd., 893 F. Supp. 672, 687 (S.D. Tex. 1995), aff'd, 100 F.3d 952 (5th Cir. 1996).

[26]Wedding v. University of Toledo, 884 F. Supp. 253, 255, 71 FEP 514 (N.D. Ohio 1995) (employer's suspension of processing grievance under terms of collective bargaining agreement), rev'd in part on other grounds, 89 F.3d 316, 71 FEP 509 (6th Cir. 1996). But cf. United States v. New York City Transit Auth., 97 F.3d 672, 677, 72 FEP 114 (2d Cir. 1996) (the employer may take reasonable defensive measures in response to discrimination charges, "even though such steps are adverse to the charging employee and result in different treatment"; the employer lawfully segregated internal grievances based on whether they were filed internally or with outside agencies, the internal ones going to the EEO division and the outside ones going to the legal department).

[27]Howze v. Virginia Polytechnic Univ., 901 F. Supp. 1091, 1097–98, 69 FEP 1013 (W.D. Va. 1995) (negative report placed in professor's personnel records; adverse treatment includes "actions that would adversely affect one's professional reputation or ability to gain future employment"). The issue of whether § 704(a) protects former employees from retaliation, e.g., blacklisting, is discussed supra, Section I.

[28]West v. Marion Merrell Dow, Inc., 54 F.3d 493, 497, 67 FEP 1209 (8th Cir. 1995); Rupp v. Purolator Courier Corp., 45 F.3d 440 (unpublished opinion), 1994 WL 730892, at *1 (10th Cir. 1994).

[29]Berry v. Stevinson Chevrolet, 74 F.3d 980, 986, 69 FEP 1320 (10th Cir. 1996).

[30]Birch v. West, 870 F. Supp. 310, 315 (D. Colo. 1994).

[31]Compare Smart v. Ball State Univ., 89 F.3d 437, 442, 71 FEP 495 (7th Cir. 1996) ("There is little support for the argument that negative performance evaluations alone can constitute an adverse employment action"; affirming summary judgment for the employer) with Ruffino v. State St. Bank & Trust Co., 908 F. Supp. 1019, 1045, 71 FEP 109 (D. Mass. 1995) (ridicule and an unfair performance review constituted adverse action), Dortz v. City of New York, 904 F. Supp. 127, 156, 72 FEP 205 (S.D.N.Y. 1995), Hayes v. Shalala, 902 F. Supp. 259, 266, 73 FEP 3 (D.D.C. 1995) (reprimands and poor performance ratings established adverse action) and Boyd v. Brookstone Corp., 857 F. Supp. 1568, 1571, 71 FEP 3 (S.D. Fla. 1994) (false performance evaluations constituted sufficient adverse action). Cf. Nakai v. Wickes Lumber Co., 906 F. Supp. 698, 706, 71 FEP 13 (D. Me. 1995) (establishing a performance plan for the employee was sufficient adverse action).

The following treatment has not been considered cognizable retaliatory adverse action: a denial of tenure that was later granted after internal appeal,[32] vague or isolated remarks about protected activity,[33] a justifiable pattern of poor performance evaluations that began before the protected activity,[34] instructing other employees not to provide affidavits to assist the plaintiff,[35] changing the reason for an employment decision,[36] and contesting unemployment compensation.[37] The Fifth Circuit recently held that allegations of "harassment," denial of attendance at a training conference, and being given false information do not amount to cognizable adverse action.[38] According to that court, at least, "Title VII was designed to address ultimate employment decisions, not to address every decision made by employers that arguably might have some tangential effect upon those ultimate decisions."[39]

---

[32]*Howze*, 901 F. Supp. at 1096–97 (to hold otherwise would discourage employers from affirmatively responding to discrimination concerns).

[33]DeAngelis v. El Paso Mun. Police Officers Ass'n, 51 F.3d 591, 597, 67 FEP 1250 (5th Cir.) (remark that plaintiff had filed an E-I-E-I-O complaint), *cert. denied,* 116 S. Ct. 473 (1995); Nelson v. Upsala College, 51 F.3d 383, 389, 67 FEP 525 (3d Cir. 1995) (vague remark about unethical conduct, which had no adverse effect on the plaintiff's future employment).

[34]Zenni v. Hard Rock Cafe Int'l, Inc., 903 F. Supp. 644, 655 (S.D.N.Y. 1995) (although one poor performance review was issued shortly after filing the EEOC charge, two others predated the charge).

[35]McKenzie v. Illinois Dep't of Transp., 92 F.3d 473, 486, 71 FEP 1549 (7th Cir. 1996) (the threat to other employees pertained to plaintiff's *litigation,* not her *job,* and thus was more appropriately dealt with by court rules, not Title VII; of course, if the employer carried out its threat against other employees, those other employees—not the plaintiff—could sue for retaliation under Title VII for participating in the plaintiff's EEO lawsuit).

[36]Cole v. Ruidoso Mun. Schs., 43 F.3d 1373, 1382, 68 FEP 561 (10th Cir. 1994) (a change of reason for nonrenewal of a teacher's contract by itself cannot adversely affect employment).

[37]Baker v. Summit Unlimited, Inc., 855 F. Supp. 375, 376–77, 65 FEP 176 (N.D. Ga. 1994); *cf.* DeGuiseppe v. Village of Bellwood, 68 F.3d 187, 191 (7th Cir. 1995) (First Amendment retaliation claim; denial of a request for light-duty assignment was not an "adverse employment action," given that the employee was deemed unfit to return to work and was fully compensated for lost wages by his pension).

Under ERISA's antiretaliation provision, the Fourth Circuit held that an employer does not violate § 510 when it retaliatorily revokes *gratuitous* posttermination benefits, such as health insurance continuation. Stiltner v. Beretta U.S.A. Corp., 74 F.3d 1473, 1479–80 (4th Cir.), *cert. denied,* 117 S. Ct. 54 (1996).

[38]Dollis v. Rubin, 77 F.3d 777, 782, 70 FEP 517 (5th Cir. 1995).

[39]*Id.* at 781–82.

V. Proof

A. "False Motives" ("Pretext") Cases

Of the prima facie elements, causation continues to be the most often disputed. Courts often determine causation by evaluating whether temporal proximity[40] exists between protected activity known[41] by the employer and the adverse action. Where temporal proximity does not exist, a claimant may still make a prima facie showing of causation by direct evidence linking the protected activity with the adverse action. In *Chavez v. City of Arvada*,[42] however, the Tenth Circuit held that a supervisor's comment, "Oh, no, you're not going to pull that one again on me," was insuffi-

---

[40]The facts of a particular case seem to control the determination of whether temporal causation exists. *Compare* Harrison v. Metropolitan Gov't, 80 F.3d 1107, 1119, 73 FEP 109 (6th Cir.) (a 15-month interval may support causation), *cert. denied*, 117 S. Ct. 169 (1996), Wyatt v. City of Boston, 35 F.3d 13, 16, 65 FEP 1441 (1st Cir. 1994) (almost simultaneous adverse action supports an inference of causation), Devera v. Adams, 874 F. Supp. 17, 21, 67 FEP 102 (D.D.C. 1995) (eight months may be sufficient) *and* Strickland v. Hillsborough County, 65 FEP 255, 260 (M.D. Fla. 1994) (two months supports causation) *with* Balletti v. Sun Sentinel Co., 909 F. Supp. 1539, 1549, 73 FEP 1341 (S.D. Fla. 1995) (six months is too long), Eldred v. Consolidated Freightways Corp., 898 F. Supp. 928, 940, 71 FEP 33 (D. Mass. 1995) (18 months is too long) *and* EEOC v. Regency Architectural Metals Corp., 896 F. Supp. 260, 271–72 (D. Conn. 1995) (one year is too long). *Cf.* Candelaria v. EG & G Energy Measurements, Inc., 33 F.3d 1259, 1262, 72 FEP 1005 (10th Cir. 1994) (three years is too long to infer causation; applying Title VII authority by analogy in a breach-of-conciliation-agreement case).

As a matter of pleading, allegations of knowledge and temporal proximity will survive a motion to dismiss. Ortez v. Washington County, 88 F.3d 804, 809, 71 FEP 584 (9th Cir. 1996).

[41]Johnson v. United States Dep't of Health & Human Servs. 30 F.3d 45, 47, 65 FEP 702 (6th Cir. 1994) (where the plaintiffs failed to show at trial that the decisionmakers knew of the plaintiffs' EEOC complaints 10 years earlier, judgment for the employer was appropriate); Quansah v. IBM Corp., 70 FEP 1531, 1534 (N.D. Cal. 1996) (granting the employer summary judgment on the plaintiff's retaliation claim where the plaintiff offered no evidence at all that might establish that the decisionmakers knew he had filed an EEOC charge); Armfield v. Runyon, 902 F. Supp. 823, 826 (N.D. Ill. 1995) (the employer must know of the protected activity to prove causation). *But cf.* McKenzie v. Atlantic Richfield Co., 906 F. Supp. 572, 577, 70 FEP 547 (D. Colo. 1995) (knowledge can be inferred from circumstantial evidence; denying summary judgment even though the decisionmakers denied knowledge).

[42]88 F.3d 861, 866, 71 FEP 320 (10th Cir. 1996), *cert. denied*, 117 S. Ct. 684 (1997).

cient to link present-day adverse action to the plaintiff's claim filed 10 years previously.

Once a prima facie case is established[43] and the employer asserts a legitimate nondiscriminatory reason for adverse treatment, the plaintiff must prove that the employer acted with a false motive or pretext. Courts remain hotly divided on how much evidence of pretext a plaintiff must provide to get past summary judgment and proceed to trial.[44] Some district courts have suggested, in denying summary judgment, that once a prima facie case of retaliation is established, issues of intent ought to proceed to the trier of fact.[45] Other courts, however, reject that view, finding that temporal proximity of the adverse action and the protected activity is not enough, alone, to create a triable issue of fact as to pretext.[46]

---

[43] According to some courts, "establishing a prima facie case of retaliation is a burden easily carried." Terry v. Gallegos, 926 F. Supp. 679, 692 (W.D. Tenn. 1996); see Meeks v. Computer Assocs. Int'l, 15 F.3d 1013, 1021, 64 FEP 258 (11th Cir. 1994) (causation may be proven by showing that protected activity and adverse treatment "are not completely unrelated") (citation omitted).

[44] The debate arises primarily from varying constructions courts have placed upon certain oblique language in *St. Mary's Honor Ctr. v. Hicks,* 509 U.S. 502, 62 FEP 96 (1993). The issue is common to all disparate treatment cases, retaliation and discrimination alike. *See generally* Chapter 2 (Disparate Treatment).

[45] *E.g.,* Salas v. Richardson Elecs. Ltd., 70 FEP 459, 463 (N.D. Ill. 1996) (the close proximity between the protected activity and the adverse action is enough to raise a triable issue as to pretext); *see* Ruffino v. State St. Bank & Trust Co., 908 F. Supp. 1019, 1045, 1047, 71 FEP 109 (D. Mass. 1995) (saying, in dictum, that once the employer meets its burden of producing evidence of a legitimate nonretaliatory motive, the "ultimate determination of the employer's motive presents a 'pure question of fact' "; denying summary judgment where, in addition to temporal proximity, the plaintiff showed that she was described as "whacko," "off-her-rocker," and "unbalanced" in connection with discussions about how to handle her concerns); Nakai v. Wickes Lumber Co., 906 F. Supp. 698, 705, 71 FEP 13 (D. Me. 1995) (temporal proximity is evidence of both causation and motive); McKenzie v. Atlantic Richfield Co., 906 F. Supp. 572, 575–77, 70 FEP 547 (D. Colo. 1995) (denying summary judgment even though the plaintiff's only evidence of pretext was that the decisionmakers had the opportunity to know of the protected activity and that the employer never before disciplined an employee of plaintiff's level for like conduct).

[46] *E.g.,* Johnson v. University of Wis., 70 F.3d 469, 480–81, 69 FEP 644 (7th Cir. 1995) (timing alone cannot create a genuine issue of material fact); Hoeppner v. Crotched Mountain Rehabilitation Ctr., 31 F.3d 9, 17, 65 FEP 841 (1st Cir. 1994) (affirming summary judgment even though the plaintiff established a prima facie case of retaliation; the plaintiff's speculation along with merely a scintilla of evidence of pretext is insufficient); *see* Nelson v. J.C. Penney Co., Inc., 75 F.3d 343, 346, 69 FEP 1328 (8th Cir.) (mere coincidence in timing does not establish a submissible case of retaliatory discharge; reversing judgment for the plaintiff after

Once a case proceeds to trial, liability will be determined on the facts.[47]

B. "Mixed Motive" Cases

In proving retaliation, the plaintiff need not show that a retaliatory motive was the sole motive for the adverse treatment.[48] In the first published appellate decision to address the issue, however, the First Circuit held in *Tanca v. Nordberg*[49] that, if the employer proves that it would have taken the same action (e.g., terminated the plaintiff) anyway, for legitimate reasons, then the plaintiff is entitled to no recovery. The First Circuit thus concluded that the provisions of the Civil Rights Act of 1991, which allow *discrimination* plaintiffs some injunctive relief and attorney's fees under similar circumstances, do not apply in *retaliation* cases.[50]

---

trial, where the evidence showed only that the adverse action occurred one month after the plaintiff engaged in protected activity), *cert. denied,* 117 S. Ct. 61 (1996); *see also* Knickerbocker v. City of Stockton, 81 F.3d 907, 912, 3 WH2d 453 (9th Cir. 1996) (FLSA retaliation case; close timing is not enough to show pretext); Garcia v. Fulbright & Jaworski L.L.P., 3 WH2d 742 (S.D. Tex. 1996) (FMLA retaliation case; "Discriminatory intent cannot be inferred merely from the time an employee is terminated after returning from the FMLA leave.").

In addition to employer knowledge and timing, a plaintiff—under this general view—must provide probative evidence of pretext. *See, e.g.,* Ray v. Tandem Computers, Inc., 63 F.3d 429, 435–36, 68 FEP 1338 (5th Cir. 1995) (a supervisor's vague and remote remarks are insufficient evidence of pretext, as a matter of law; affirming summary judgment for the employer).

[47]*Compare, e.g.,* Alexander v. Gerhardt Enters., 40 F.3d 187, 196–97, 68 FEP 595 (7th Cir. 1994) (affirming judgment for the plaintiff after trial, where the plaintiff rebutted the employer's reasons for its decision by showing that she indeed was performing satisfactorily, that her performance never was criticized prior to her termination, and that she was terminated *immediately* after engaging in protected activity) *with* Steinle v. Boeing Co., 884 F. Supp. 424, 430–31, 68 FEP 69 (D. Kan. 1995) (finding for the employer after trial; the plaintiff's pretext case was based primarily on her own testimony that she believed that she had been retaliated against; finding the employer's witnesses more credible).

[48]*See* Jensvold v. Shalala, 925 F. Supp. 1109, 1113, 70 FEP 788 (D. Md. 1996) (entering judgment for the employer after trial because the plaintiff failed to prove *any* retaliatory motivation); Burrell v. City Univ., 894 F. Supp. 750, 760, 68 FEP 1398 (S.D.N.Y. 1995) (denying summary judgment for the employer).

[49]98 F.3d 680, 682–84, 72 FEP 166 (1st Cir. 1996), *cert. denied,* 117 S. Ct. 1253 (1997).

[50]*Id.* (the 1991 Act applies to mixed-motive discrimination claims based on race, color, religion, sex, or national origin, but not to retaliation).

VI. Special Issues Pertaining to Relief in Retaliation Cases

A. Reinstatement

One court has held that granting reinstatement to an employee who has been made whole by monetary relief would result in an unjustified windfall to the employee.[51] Another has held that reinstatement is improper where evidence of employee misconduct justified termination.[52]

VII. Alternative Causes of Action

A. Private Employers

1. *The Civil Rights Act of 1866—42 U.S.C. § 1981*

Although § 1981 does not specifically mention retaliation as within its realm of covered unlawful activity, most,[53] but not

---

[51]McIntosh v. Irving Trust Co., 873 F. Supp. 872, 878, 67 FEP 176 (S.D.N.Y. 1995).

[52]*E.g.,* Carlson v. American Meter Co., 896 F. Supp. 952, 954, 68 FEP 193 (D. Neb. 1995) (the employer discovered that the employee had taken confidential documents). In *Carlson,* discovery of misconduct *preceded* the termination decision. Had discovery been made later, the after-acquired evidence doctrine still likely would have precluded reinstatement. *See generally* Chapter 41 (Monetary Relief).

[53]*E.g.,* Lightner v. Town of Ariton, Ala., 902 F. Supp. 1489, 1496, 69 FEP 219 (M.D. Ala. 1995); Williams v. Carrier Corp., 889 F. Supp. 1528, 1530 (M.D. Ga. 1995); Wilborn v. Primary Care Specialists, Ltd., 866 F. Supp. 364, 369, 73 FEP 341 (N.D. Ill. 1994); *cf.* Barge v. Anheuser-Busch, Inc., 87 F.3d 256, 259, 72 FEP 426 (8th Cir. 1996) (affirming summary judgment for the employer on the plaintiff's § 1981 retaliation claim, *not* because such claim is not cognizable, but rather because the plaintiff failed to rebut the employer's legitimate nonretaliatory reason for the adverse employment action; not discussing whether § 1981 even allows for retaliation claims); Wixson v. Dowagiac Nursing Home, 87 F.3d 164, 167, 71 FEP 186 (6th Cir. 1996) (same); Evans v. Kansas City Mo. Sch. Dist., 65 F.3d 98, 101, 68 FEP 1203 (8th Cir. 1995) (citing a pre-*Patterson* decision, without analysis of *Patterson* or the 1991 Act, that § 1981 "does encompass 'allegations of retaliatory conduct' in a racial discrimination context"; ordering dismissal of the complaint because the plaintiff failed to establish that he had engaged in activity protected under the Act) (citation omitted), *cert. denied,* 116 S. Ct. 1319 (1996); Daulo v. Commonwealth Edison, 892 F. Supp. 1088, 1092, 72 FEP 1566 (N.D. Ill. 1995) ("All parties assume that there exists a retaliation cause of action under Section 1981.").

See also Suzanne E. Riley, Comment, *Employees' Retaliation Claims Under 42 U.S.C. § 1981: Ramifications of the Civil Rights Act of 1991,* 79 Marq. L. Rev. 579,

all,[54] courts construing the statute since enactment of the Civil Rights Act of 1991 have held that it does cover retaliation.

3. National Labor Relations Act—29 U.S.C. §§ 157 and 158(a)(1)

Developments in the law of retaliation for engaging in concerted activity under the NLRA are beyond the scope of this supplement.[55]

B. State and Local Government Employers

1. Section 1983

Developments under the Civil Rights Act of 1871 are discussed generally in Chapter 24 (The Civil Rights Acts of 1866 and 1871). By far the most prevalent § 1983 claim in the employment context remains one alleging unlawful retaliation for engaging in free speech.

2. First Amendment Right of Free Speech

Courts have held that the following speech pertains to matters of public concern: displaying religious items in the workplace,[56] attempting to organize co-employees for collective bargaining,[57]

592–601 (1996). As noted in that article, one reason for the relatively few decisions construing the 1991 Act's amendments to § 1981 is that the 1991 Act is not applied retroactively. See Rivers v. Roadway Express, Inc., 511 U.S. 298, 308–09, 64 FEP 842 (1994).

[54]See, e.g., Gorman v. Roberts, 909 F. Supp. 1479, 1484 (M.D. Ala. 1995).

[55]See generally ABA, SECTION OF LABOR & EMPLOYMENT LAW, THE DEVELOPING LABOR LAW ch. 6 (Patrick Hardin, ed., 3d ed. BNA Books 1992, and Supps.).

[56]Tucker v. California Dep't of Educ., 97 F.3d 1204, 1210, 71 FEP 1863 (9th Cir. 1996) (rejecting the state's suggestion that an employee's speech about religion is not a matter of public concern).

[57]Gregorich v. Lund, 54 F.3d 410, 416, 149 LRRM 2278 (7th Cir. 1995) (the judge who dismissed the attorney, however, is entitled to qualified immunity because his belief that the employee's interest in union organizing was outweighed by his own belief that unionization would threaten the "delicate working relationship" between judges and research attorneys was reasonable). An employee's alternative remedy under the NLRA when retaliated against for union organizing is discussed elsewhere. See Section VII.A.3 supra; see also Chapter 25 (National Labor Relations Act).

reporting that the school principal misrepresented test scores,[58] discussing with a newspaper reporter difficulties the employee perceived in operating an employee assistance program without a written policy,[59] and appearing pursuant to a subpoena at the supervisor's divorce proceeding (even though no testimony was given).[60] According to the Ninth Circuit, even recklessly false speech on matters of public concern can, but is less likely to, be protected.[61]

On the other hand, filing grievances regarding "internal departmental affairs and [matters] of personal interest"[62] are not matters of public concern. In the university setting, basketball coaches unsuccessfully argued that advising players of their right to financial aid[63] or using a racial epithet to motivate players during a lockerroom speech[64] were matters of public concern. The Seventh Circuit in *Smith v. Fruin*[65] held that a police officer's complaints to police officials that the department failed to enforce a smoke-free workplace were personal in nature, even though generally dealing with a matter of public concern. The officer spoke only of his own sensitivity to smoke, not that of others, and he brought his complaints in private; therefore, the court held, the complaints were not protected by the First Amendment.[66]

---

[58]Bernheim v. Litt, 79 F.3d 318, 325 (2d Cir. 1996) (reversing dismissal of the public school teacher's § 1983 free speech claim).

[59]Watters v. City of Philadelphia, 55 F.3d 886, 893 (3d Cir. 1995) (reversing judgment granted to the defendant as a matter of law; the speech generally touched on matters of public concern, even though the speech specifically involved administrative matters particular to the plaintiff's job).

[60]Pro v. Donatucci, 81 F.3d 1283, 1290 (3d Cir. 1996) (affirming denial of summary judgment for the supervisor/defendant).

[61]Johnson v. Multnomah County, 48 F.3d 420, 424 (9th Cir.) (such statements "are not per se unprotected by the First Amendment"; "Instead, the recklessness of the employee and the falseness of the statements should be considered in light of the public employer's showing of actual injury to its legitimate interests, as part of the *Pickering* balancing test."), *cert. denied,* 115 S. Ct. 2616 (1995).

[62]Hom v. Squire, 81 F.3d 969, 974 (10th Cir. 1996) (affirming summary judgment for the state department of supervisors).

[63]Wallace v. Texas Tech. Univ., 80 F.3d 1042, 1050, 70 FEP 1521 (5th Cir. 1996).

[64]Dambrot v. Central Mich. Univ., 55 F.3d 1177, 1187 (6th Cir. 1995) (affirming summary judgment for the university).

[65]28 F.3d 646, 651 (7th Cir. 1994), *cert. denied,* 513 U.S. 1083 (1995).

[66]*Id.*

If the threshold of public concern is met, courts apply the *Pickering*[67] balancing test to determine whether the employer's retaliatory[68] action violated the First Amendment. The outcome of such balancing will depend on a variety of factors, including the disruption caused by the speech, the business needs of the particular employer, and the plaintiff's position and job responsibilities.[69]

---

[67] Pickering v. Board of Educ., 391 U.S. 563, 568, 1 IER 8 (1968).

[68] Of course, as with any retaliation case, the employee must establish a causal connection between the adverse employment action and the protected speech. *Compare* Nelson v. Pima Community College, 83 F.3d 1075, 1080 (9th Cir. 1996) (affirming summary judgment for the defendant/college; while the employee's criticism of the college's affirmative action program was protected speech, she adduced no evidence that she was terminated *because* of such speech; the evidence showed, rather, that she was terminated for refusing to follow rules, including issuing unauthorized orders (which is not protected speech)) *and* Hom v. Squire, 81 F.3d 969, 974–75 (10th Cir. 1996) (mere declaration by a former employee alleging retaliatory intent is not sufficient to overcome summary judgment) *with* Beckwith v. City of Daytona Beach Shores, 58 F.3d 1554, 1565 (11th Cir. 1995) (the district court erred by granting judgment as a matter of law to the city; while the former fire chief's speech—opposing paramedic cuts and other city programs—occurred more than one year prior to his termination, the question of the city's motivation for terminating him should go to the jury).

[69] *Compare* Tucker v. California Dep't of Educ., 97 F.3d 1204, 1211, 71 FEP 1863 (9th Cir. 1996) (extensively analyzing, and rejecting, each of the state's asserted interests in forbidding the display of religious items outside an employee's immediate work space; none of the asserted interests are sufficiently substantial to outweigh the free expression interest of the employees), Cromer v. Brown, 88 F.3d 1315, 1327, 71 FEP 530 (4th Cir. 1996) (a letter to the sheriff from a group of African-American officers expressing concern about racial problems in the department involved a matter of public concern, and the *Pickering* balancing test tipped heavily in favor of the officers; reversing summary judgment for the defendant/sheriff), Feldman v. Philadelphia Hous. Auth., 43 F.3d 823, 830 (3d Cir. 1994) (the plaintiff's reports of misconduct were entitled to constitutional protection because, while the reports may potentially have caused disruption, the plaintiff's job with the internal audit department was designed to report misconduct and, to that extent, to cause the type of disruption defendants complained of; affirming judgment for the plaintiff) *and* Ramirez v. Oklahoma Dep't of Mental Health, 41 F.3d 584, 595 (10th Cir. 1994) (plaintiffs stated a viable free speech retaliation claim based on allegations that they were suspended without pay in retaliation for filing a complaint on behalf of a patient; reversing in relevant part dismissal of the complaint) *with* Caruso v. De Luca, 81 F.3d 666, 671 (7th Cir. 1996) (although the plaintiff's opposition to the new city clerk during elections was protected speech, the new clerk justifiably declined to reappoint the plaintiff as deputy clerk based on her legitimate concern that they could not work together in the small office because of the plaintiff's campaign tactics; affirming summary judgment for the employer/clerk), Tyler v. City of Mountain Home, 72 F.3d 568, 570 (8th Cir. 1995) (while the officer had spoken on a matter of public concern in a letter to a neighboring county sheriff's department, the city's interests in maintaining its chain of command and a good working relationship with the neighboring county were sufficient to outweigh the officer's

In *United States v. National Treasury Employees Union,*[70] the Supreme Court, applying *Pickering,* struck down a statute that prohibited federal government employees from accepting honoraria for speaking or writing. The Court held that the government's interest in regulating actual and perceived misuses of power does not outweigh the significant disincentive the honoraria ban would have on public speaking and writing by public officials and the resulting burden on dissemination of information to the public.[71]

Settling a split among the circuits, the Supreme Court has held that independent contractors are entitled to the same First Amendment protection from retaliation for free speech as public employees.[72]

---

interests in free speech; affirming summary judgment to the city), Voigt v. Savell, 70 F.3d 1552, 1557 (9th Cir. 1995) (while the court clerk's complaints regarding the judge arguably touched on matters of public concern, the judge's interests in not disrupting the workplace and not undermining his authority were sufficient to overcome the plaintiff's interests in speaking out; affirming summary judgment for the judge), *cert. denied,* 116 S. Ct. 1826 (1996) *and* Barnard v. Jackson County, 43 F.3d 1218, 1224 (8th Cir.) (the *Pickering* test weighed in favor of the county because the plaintiff/legislative auditor's "leaks" to the press regarding audit information prior to release of the information to the legislators had an adverse impact on legislators' ability efficiently to perform their jobs; affirming in relevant part summary judgment for the defendants), *cert. denied,* 116 S. Ct. 53 (1995).

[70]513 U.S. 454, 470–71 (1995).

[71]*Id.* at 466–71.

[72]*See* Board of County Comm'rs v. Umbehr, 116 S. Ct. 2342, 2349 (1996) (affirming reversal of summary judgment for the board of county commissioners and holding that independent contractors are entitled to the same First Amendment protections as public employees; the *Pickering* test applies to independent contractors as well as to employees); O'Hare Truck Serv., Inc. v. City of Northlake, 116 S. Ct. 2353, 2359 (1996) (reversing dismissal of claims by a private towing service that it was removed from the police department's list of towing services after it supported a challenger for the position of city mayor; independent contractors are entitled to similar First Amendment protections as public employees; termination based on political affiliation is proper only when the decisionmaker can demonstrate that party affiliation is an appropriate requirement for the effective performance of the job involved).

Courts apply traditional First Amendment analysis to claims of persons or entities not analogous to employees or independent contractors. *Compare, e.g.,* Blackburn v. City of Marshall, 42 F.3d 925, 932 (5th Cir. 1995) (claims by the owner of a towing and wrecking service based on revocation of his permission to use a police radio frequency should not be analyzed under *Pickering* because the owner was neither an employee of the city nor in a relationship analogous to that of an employee; his claims should be analyzed under traditional First Amendment principles applicable to any citizen) *with* Copsey v. Swearingen, 36 F.3d 1336, 1344–45 (5th Cir. 1994) (the claim of a blind vendor operator in the state capital building, alleging that he was terminated for publicly complaining about a state program, should be analyzed under *Pickering* because the vendor was sufficiently analogous to a public employee).

3. First Amendment Rights to Petition for Redress of Grievances and Assembly

Following the *Elrod/Branti/Rutan* line of cases, courts continue to hold that only policymaking and confidential employees may be terminated for their political views.[73]

---

[73]*E.g.*, Warzon v. Drew, 60 F.3d 1234, 1240 (7th Cir. 1995) (affirming judgment on the pleadings for the county defendants; the position of county controller was a policymaking position, so her termination for advocating position(s) in conflict with stated policies did not violate the First Amendment).

Part 6

Specific Employment Issues

Chapter 18

HIRING

II. Creating the Applicant Pool

B. Nepotism

While hiring policies that favor family members do not violate antidiscrimination laws per se, they may be evidence of intentional discrimination if they work to the detriment of a protected class.[1] In *EEOC v. Steamship Clerks Local 1066*,[2] the court held that the union's membership sponsorship policy, which required that applicants be sponsored by an existing member, had an unlawful disparate impact on minorities. The court rejected the union's argument that causation was lacking because no minority applicants had sought membership, noting that causation could be inferred despite the dearth of actual applicants because the policy itself discouraged potential minority candidates. The court also rejected the union's contention that the challenged practice was job related and consistent with business necessity because it represented an important vehicle for continuing "family traditions."[3]

Antinepotism policies continue to withstand judicial scrutiny under both federal and state law.[4]

---

[1] Howard v. BP Oil Co., 32 F.3d 520 (11th Cir. 1994) (discussing unwritten company policy that favored awarding gas stations to relations of successful dealers). *See also* Foster v. Dalton, 71 F.3d 52, 69 FEP 1402 (1st Cir. 1995) (job description rewritten to parallel qualifications of friend of hospital director; court held cronyism does not violate Title VII so long as it is not a pretext for unlawful bias).
[2] 48 F.3d 594, 67 FEP 629 (1st Cir.), *cert. denied*, 116 S. Ct. 65 (1995).
[3] 48 F.3d at 606.
[4] Blackwell v. Danbury Hosp., 1996 WL 409370 (Conn. Super. Ct. Jun. 26, 1996) (state statute prohibiting discrimination based on marital status was not violated by antinepotism policy because marital status refers only to the condition of being single or married and not the identity of the job applicant's spouse).

C. Recruitment Sources

An employer's even-handed use of a recruitment source is not discriminatory. For example, an employer's refusal to hire workers for permanent positions during the first 30 days of their temporary employment was justified when such hiring would have required the employer to pay a placement fee to the temporary employment agency.[5]

D. Walk-In Applications

When an employer is not soliciting applications, a plaintiff claiming discrimination must show that he or she realistically would have been in the running for the job absent the alleged discrimination.[6]

F. Chilling

Courts have continued to find that hiring practices that deter protected class members from seeking employment are actionable.[7]

III. SELECTING FROM THE APPLICANT POOL

A. Selection Criteria

Courts continue to decline to require employers to adopt optimal hiring practices; thus, an employer may base its employment decisions on any criteria that are not discriminatory.[8]

---

[5]Nesbit v. Louisiana-Pacific Corp., 39 F.3d 1184 (8th Cir. 1994).

[6]Balele v. Klauser, 74 F.3d 1242 (7th Cir. 1996) (claim dismissed where plaintiff failed to show his qualifications were equal to or better than the selectees and also failed to offer any direct or indirect evidence of discrimination), *cert. denied,* 116 S. Ct. 1577 (1996).

[7]EEOC v. Steamship Clerks Local 1066, 48 F.3d 594, 67 FEP 629 (1st Cir.) (union's membership policy requiring that prospective member be sponsored by current member—all of whom were white—discouraged minority candidates from seeking membership), *cert. denied,* 116 S. Ct. 65 (1995). *But cf.* Baker v. Ogden Servs. Corp., 74 F.3d 1248 (10th Cir. 1996) (perception of decisionmaker is relevant rather than employee's perception of himself, and plaintiff's claim that he did not apply because he did not believe that his supervisor would recommend him played no part in whether he was qualified for position).

[8]Ellis v. United Airlines, Inc., 73 F.3d 999, 69 FEP 1167 (10th Cir.) (employer's exercise of erroneous or even illogical business judgment does not, by itself, constitute

B. Proof of Hiring Discrimination

The *McDonnell Douglas-Burdine-Hicks* paradigm continues to be the principal analytical model employed in discriminatory hiring cases. A rigid application of this model, however, is not required.[9] The central inquiry is whether there is sufficient evidence to create an inference that the basis for the challenged employment decision was an illegal criterion.[10] After the employer

---

pretext for illegal discrimination in violation of ADEA), *cert. denied,* 116 S. Ct. 2500 (1996); Lewis-Webb v. Qualico Steel Co., 929 F. Supp. 385 (M.D. Ala. 1996), *aff'd,* 113 F.3d 1251 (11th Cir. 1997); Harrison v. Larue D. Carter Mem'l Hosp., 883 F. Supp. 328 (S.D. Ind. 1994).

[9]Birch v. West, 870 F. Supp. 310 (D. Colo. 1994).

[10]Collins v. Milwaukee Hous. Assistance Corp., 927 F. Supp. 1152 (E.D. Wis. 1996) (plaintiff must prove by probative evidence that he was qualified for position employer had available to establish a prima facie case); Arnold v. Boatmen's Nat'l Bank, 1996 U.S. App. LEXIS 15669 (7th Cir. Jun. 25, 1996) (plaintiff's unsolicited application failed to reveal his qualifications for job openings), *cert. denied,* 117 S. Ct. 586 (1996); EEOC v. Wiltel, Inc., 81 F.3d 1508 (10th Cir. 1996) (no evidence decisionmaker was aware of her partner's objection to plaintiff's expression of her religious beliefs); Baker v. Ogden Servs. Corp., 74 F.3d 1248 (10th Cir. 1996) (plaintiff did not establish a prima facie case where he failed to apply for position with a newly formed subsidiary of his former employer's parent); Jameson v. Arrow Co., 75 F.3d 1528, 70 FEP 153 (11th Cir. 1996) (in reduction-in-force context, inference of intentional age bias in hiring exists where plaintiff is qualified and applies for job at the time of separation but employer offers job to person outside protected group; employer may then rebut inference through nondiscriminatory reasons for its decision); Lewis-Webb v. Qualico Steel Co., 929 F. Supp. 385 (M.D. Ala. 1996) (no prima facie case where plaintiff lacked minimal qualifications for position); Grooms v. Wiregrass Elec. Co-op., Inc., 883 F. Supp. 643, 67 FEP 1663 (M.D. Ala. 1995) (plaintiff failed to establish prima facie case where he showed that he had seniority but not required qualifications); Pelli v. Stone Savannah River Pulp & Paper Corp., 878 F. Supp. 1559 (S.D. Ga. 1995) (sex discrimination case dismissed where plaintiff admitted male selectee had more experience than she despite her suggestion that he was over-qualified for job); Thomas v. Hoyt, Brumm & Link, Inc., 910 F. Supp. 1280 (E.D. Mich. 1994) (summary judgment granted where plaintiff failed to establish his qualifications were similar to those of nonprotected class employees); Kapossy v. McGraw-Hill, Inc., 921 F. Supp. 234, 70 FEP 752 (D.N.J. 1996) (no prima facie case where plaintiff failed to show others received "preferential training" or otherwise benefitted from training not offered to him); Darnell v. Northern Can Sys., 937 F. Supp. 668, 67 FEP 419 (N.D. Ohio 1995) (female plaintiff failed to make out prima facie case after conceding she was not qualified for job notwithstanding claim selectee also was not qualified), *clarified by* 1996 WL 343448 (N.D. Ohio 1996); Zolotarevsky v. General Elec. Co., 862 F. Supp. 659 (D. Mass. 1994) (summary judgment granted where submitted affidavits demonstrated plaintiff lacked necessary qualifications for open positions); Green v. Clarendon County Sch. Dist. 3, 923 F. Supp. 829 (D.S.C. 1996) (in a reverse discrimination case plaintiff must show factual circumstances that support position defendant discriminates against the majority, instead of proving that plaintiff is a member of protected class).

rebuts the inference of discrimination, plaintiff must still create a genuine issue of material fact as to whether the proffered reason for hiring someone else was pretextual.[11]

C. Preemployment Inquiries

Imprudent interview questions, while not per se violations of antidiscrimination laws, may raise questions that can defeat a summary

---

[11]Griffin v. Lockheed, 69 F.3d 544 (9th Cir. 1995) (plaintiff's affidavits from African-American former employees regarding racial harassment by other employees at the plant did not create triable issue of fact because none alleged discrimination in hiring process); Fuentes v. Perskie, 32 F.3d 759, 65 FEP 890 (3d Cir. 1994) (neither disagreement among supervisors about employee's job performance nor supervisor's failure to use Puerto Rican pronunciation of name evidenced discrimination); Lewis-Webb v. Qualico Steel Co., 929 F. Supp. 385 (M.D. Ala. 1996) (plaintiff's interpretation and speculation about interviewer's motives insufficient to establish pretext), *aff'd,* 113 F.3d 1251 (11th Cir. 1997); Pelli v. Stone Savannah River Pulp & Paper Corp., 878 F. Supp. 1559 (S.D. Ga. 1995) (statement by a nonmanagerial employee that "management is not the only one who does not want women in the electrical department" not evidence of discriminatory intent); Harrison v. Larue D. Carter Mem'l Hosp., 883 F. Supp. 328 (S.D. Ind. 1994) (plaintiff failed to present evidence from which rational factfinder could infer defendant lied in stating it did not promote her because she lacked expertise), *aff'd,* 61 F.3d 905, 69 FEP 768 (7th Cir. 1995); Thomas v. Hoyt, Brumm & Link, Inc., 910 F. Supp. 1280 (E.D. Mich. 1994) (plaintiff cannot create issue of fact as to whether he was qualified for particular job by challenging judgment of his superiors or questioning soundness of employer's business decision); Castner v. U.S. Dep't of Energy, 897 F. Supp. 481, 68 FEP 1642 (D. Or. 1995) (plaintiff, who challenged defendant's assertion that it did not hire him because of a new hire job freeze, must present some minimal evidence that freeze was a pretext to survive summary judgment); Wechsler v. R D Management Corp., 861 F. Supp. 1153, 73 FEP 195 (E.D.N.Y. 1994) (plaintiff's claim interviewer abruptly ended interview once plaintiff disclosed he was an Orthodox Jew was inadequate to show proffered explanation—that plaintiff performed poorly during interview—was pretextual); Blong v. Secretary of the Army, 886 F. Supp. 1576, 68 FEP 503 (D. Kan. 1995) (plaintiff's evidence of alleged sexism by interviewer was not proof of pretext, because (1) no evidence interviewer was sole decisionmaker; (2) plaintiff's evidence that interviewer had stereotypical attitudes toward women was counterbalanced by evidence interviewer treated women he worked with well; and (3) plaintiff's allegations that the male who held job before she applied for it was treated differently than her were irrelevant because remote in time and she and comparator not in same applicant pool), *aff'd,* 86 F.3d 1166, 72 FEP 1280 (10th Cir. 1996); Sandhu v. Commonwealth of Va., Dep't of Conserv & Rec., 874 F. Supp. 122 (E.D. Va.) (plaintiff must show both that the employer's proffered reason is false and that discrimination was real reason), *aff'd,* 68 F.3d 461 (4th Cir. 1995); Shore v. A.W. Hargrove Ins. Agency, Inc., 873 F. Supp. 992 (E.D. Va. 1995) (plaintiff must produce evidence showing that but for employer's motive to discriminate against her because of age bias, she would have been hired in place of selectee; speculative statements are insufficient to create triable issue of fact); Martinez v. National Broadcasting Co.,

judgment motion.[12] On the other hand, an employer does not violate the ADA when it requires a former employee with a recent known disability applying for reemployment to provide medical certification as to his or her ability to return to employment with or without reasonable accommodation as long as the inquiries are relevant to assessment of the applicant's ability to perform the essential job functions.[13]

D. Issues of Standing

A white manager who had sought to hire and promote African-American employees could state a claim under Title VII against her former employer where she alleged that her minority hiring efforts had been thwarted and that her employment had became so intolerable that she had to resign.[14]

IV. INITIAL JOB ASSIGNMENTS

In *EEOC v. Turtle Creek Mansion Corp.*,[15] a defendant that operated a luxury hotel with three restaurants—a "fine dining restaurant," a "casual restaurant," and a "private dining room" or catering service—was charged with discriminatorily relegating women employees to the "casual restaurant." The court found, however, that plaintiff's statistical analyses, which showed significant disparities, were flawed because plaintiff relied on statistics based on all women employed as waitresses, without accounting for those who actually held the qualifications listed on the job descriptions for the fine dining restaurant.[16]

---

877 F. Supp. 219, 73 FEP 1701 (D.N.J. 1994) (plaintiff need not show that illegitimate reason was sole reason for adverse employment decision, only that it was the determinative factor in deciding not to hire her).

[12]*E.g.,* Pressman v. Brigham Med. Group Found., Inc., 919 F. Supp. 516, 5 AD 609 (D. Mass. 1996) (employee asked whether in light of his age, he would get tired in mid-day and want to leave due to his history of cardiac problems).

[13]Grenier v. Cyanamid Plastics, Inc., 70 F.3d 667, 5 AD 75 (1st Cir. 1995) (affirming summary judgment where plaintiff, a former employee who went on medical leave, eventually was terminated and then reapplied for his old job; plaintiff claimed in his application to be disabled but capable of performing job, but failed to describe how he would do so and refused to provide medical documentation and, as a result, was not rehired).

[14]Chandler v. Fast Lane, Inc., 868 F. Supp. 1138, 66 FEP 675 (E.D. Ark. 1994).

[15]70 FEP 899 (N.D. Tex. 1995), *aff'd,* 82 F.3d 414, 71 FEP 1408 (5th Cir. 1996).

[16]*Id.*

Chapter 19

PROMOTION

I. Publicizing the Opening

In determining whether a desired position would have constituted a promotion, courts have looked to a number of factors including whether the new job would have involved changes in compensation, responsibilities, and advancement potential.[1] However, a job change may be considered a promotion even when the new position brings no increase in pay, benefits, or advancement opportunities.[2]

The existence of an actual promotion opportunity is an essential element of a claim.[3] Moreover, an employee's failure to apply for a position pursuant to established procedures will normally serve as a bar.[4] However, the failure to apply is frequently excused where

---

[1]Odima v. Westin Tucson Hotel, 53 F.3d 1484, 67 FEP 1222 (9th Cir. 1995) (no promotion in § 1981 case where no change in form of compensation and new position would not have provided plaintiff with supervisory duties); Minetos v. City Univ. of N.Y., 875 F. Supp. 1046, 68 FEP 355 (S.D.N.Y. 1995) (position change that would have involved increase in supervisory and administrative responsibilities was promotion); Grant v. Bullock County Bd. of Educ., 895 F. Supp. 1506, 1513 (M.D. Ala. 1995) (pay increase not only factor in determining if there has been a promotion; differences in job descriptions and responsibilities should be considered); Addy v. Bliss & Glennon, 44 Cal. App. 4th 205, 70 FEP 965 (Cal. App. 1996) (disputed position not really promotion since it had the same advancement potential as job plaintiff currently occupied and paid less).
[2]Dudley v. Wal-Mart Stores, 931 F. Supp. 773 (N.D. Ala. 1996) (new job was less physically demanding).
[3]Metsopulos v. Runyon, 918 F. Supp. 851 (D.N.J. 1996) (promotion claim dismissed where vacant position abolished prior to filling it).
[4]Zenni v. Hard Rock Cafe Int'l, 903 F. Supp. 644 (S.D.N.Y. 1995) (court rejects claim because, in part, plaintiff never applied for promotion); Jones v. J.C. Penney Co., 889 F. Supp. 432 (D. Kan. 1995) (failure to inquire about promotion opportunities undermines promotion claim). *Cf.* Smith v. Douglas Cable Communications, 881 F. Supp. 1510 (D. Kan. 1995) (no prima facie case where formal system of job posting exists and plaintiff fails to submit application, but rule not applied where unclear if there was formal system being operated and it was alleged one selectee had not submitted application for position); Lloyd v. WABC-TV, 879 F. Supp. 394,

the employer has no formal application process[5] or where the employee is unaware of the opportunity.[6] Courts also waive the application requirement where an application would have been futile because of the employer's perceived discriminatory practices.[7] There is, however, no legal obligation to disclose promotion opportunities and the mistaken failure to follow internal procedures requiring the posting of job opportunities will not, by itself, suggest unlawful motivation or pretext,[8] although courts may scrutinize how employers disseminate information about promotions.[9]

401, 73 FEP 1603 (S.D.N.Y. 1995) (fact issue whether plaintiff "applied" for job by putting in application prior to posting of job availability).

[5]Dudley v. Wal-Mart Stores, Inc., 931 F. Supp. 773 (N.D. Ala. 1996) (formal application not needed where evidence indicates employer used informal methods for filling vacancies and generally sought out employees for vacant position, especially where supervisor raised possibility management knew plaintiff was interested in position); Terry v. Gallegos, 926 F. Supp. 679, 704 (W.D. Tenn. 1996) (failure to apply is excused where employer promotes without advertising or publicizing openings); White v. Wells Fargo Guard Servs., 908 F. Supp. 1570 (M.D. Ala. 1995) (where employer required no formal application, plaintiff need not prove that application was actually submitted); Eldred v. Consolidated Freightways Corp. of Del., 898 F. Supp. 928, 938, 71 FEP 33 (D. Mass. 1995) (where employer has no formal application process for promotions and relies on employees "extending themsel[ves] . . . and . . . being 'aggressive,' " failure to formally apply for opening does not preclude establishing prima facie case as long as plaintiff makes reasonable attempt to convey interest in job to employer); Khair v. Campbell Soup Co., 893 F. Supp. 316, 331 (D.N.J. 1995) (requirement of application waived where employer had no formal application process).

[6]Elguindy v. Commonwealth Edison Co., 903 F. Supp. 1260, 1267 (N.D. Ill. 1995) (plaintiff need not actually apply for position to establish prima facie case where unaware of opening; only required to show if she had known she would have applied for and accepted it).

[7]Winbush v. Iowa, 66 F.3d 1471, 1481, 69 FEP 1348 (8th Cir. 1995); Codrington v. Virgin Islands Port Auth., 911 F. Supp. 907, 70 FEP 213 (D.V.I. 1996) (plaintiff's failure to apply for promotion is no defense under circumstances in retaliation case); Alford v. City of Montgomery, 879 F. Supp. 1143, 1152 (M.D. Ala. 1995) (application for position normally element of plaintiff's case but not inexorable bar if can prove that but for defendant's discriminatory practices plaintiff would have applied), aff'd, 79 F.3d 1160 (11th Cir. 1996).

[8]Randle v. City of Aurora, 69 F.3d 441, 69 FEP 489 (10th Cir. 1995) (failure to follow internal procedures regarding posting of job opportunities does not necessarily suggest employer bias or that reasons were pretextual); Evans v. Technologies Applications & Servs. Co., 875 F. Supp. 1115, 72 FEP 1215 (D. Md. 1995) (fact new position not posted as required by company policy not indicative of unlawful bias), aff'd, 80 F.3d 954, 72 FEP 1222 (4th Cir. 1996).

[9]Rush v. Scott Specialty Gases, Inc., 914 F. Supp. 104, 70 FEP 34 (E.D. Pa. 1996) (noting suspicious factors including employer's failure to disclose that course was prerequisite for a job), rev'd in part, 113 F.3d 476 (3d Cir. 1997).

II. Plaintiff's Qualifications

Unless there is direct evidence of a discriminatory motive,[10] a plaintiff must prove that he or she is qualified for the position sought in order to establish a prima facie case.[11] Some courts go further and require, as part of the prima facie case, that the plaintiff also show that the selectee does not have equal or better qualifications.[12]

---

[10]Schnidrig v. Columbian Mach., Inc., 80 F.3d 1406, 1410, 71 FEP 1763 (9th Cir.), *cert. denied,* 117 S. Ct. 295 (1996).

[11]Randle v. City of Aurora, 69 F.3d 441, 69 FEP 489 (10th Cir. 1995) (summary judgment affirmed because plaintiff did not have requisite experience qualifications notwithstanding fact defendant failed to follow its own internal promotion procedures); Douglas v. Evans, 916 F. Supp. 1539 (M.D. Ala. 1996) (plaintiff not qualified for position since she was not an attorney even though she had previously performed many of the functions), *aff'd,* 116 F.3d 492 (11th Cir. 1997); Evans v. Technologies Applications & Servs Co., 875 F. Supp. 1115, 72 FEP 1215 (D. Md. 1995) (plaintiff failed to establish prima facie case of sex discrimination because she failed to show she had required computer software skills needed for merged position and her moodiness and squabbles with other employees created problems), *aff'd,* 80 F.3d 954, 72 FEP 1222 (4th Cir. 1996); Lewis v. Zilog, Inc., 908 F. Supp. 931, 4 AD 1787 (N.D. Ga. 1995) (plaintiff could not establish prima facie case since she was not qualified as a result of not having required electrical engineering degree or equivalent experience and, in any event, selectee had required experience), *aff'd,* 87 F.3d 1331(11th Cir. 1996); Zenni v. Hard Rock Cafe Int'l, Inc., 903 F. Supp. 644 (S.D.N.Y. 1995) (plaintiff was not qualified for waiter position because he had no prior server experience and undisputed record of poor customer relations); Williams v. Port Auth. of N.Y. & N.J., 880 F. Supp. 980 (E.D.N.Y. 1995) (plaintiff's case dismissed because of lack of prima facie case based on his failure to pass both oral and written portions of required exam that was not administered in discriminatory manner); Alford v. City of Montgomery, 879 F. Supp. 1143 (M.D. Ala. 1995) (plaintiff failed to show she was qualified for position so as to establish prima facie case where minimum requirement was that plaintiff had held certain positions with employer), *aff'd,* 79 F.3d 1160 (11th Cir. 1996); Morales v. Human Rights Div., 878 F. Supp. 653, 67 FEP 531 (S.D.N.Y. 1995) (denial of supervisory promotion lawful where plaintiff did not show she was qualified since she lacked any supervisory experience); Young v. State Farm Mut. Auto Ins. Co., 868 F. Supp. 937, 69 FEP 1227 (W.D. Tenn. 1994) (promotion claim dismissed where plaintiff did not show she was qualified for position and company had legitimate nondiscriminatory reason based on greater experience of selectee); Webb v. Derwinski, 868 F. Supp. 1184, 69 FEP 419 (E.D. Mo. 1994) (plaintiff failed to establish prima facie case by showing he was qualified since he lacked the specialized experience or substitute experience necessary to qualify for promotion), *aff'd,* 68 F.3d 479, 69 FEP 768 (8th Cir. 1995); Dickinson v. McCarty, 65 FEP 1508 (S.D. Fla. 1994) (case dismissed because plaintiff did not have five years of teaching typically required and had not completed research papers during relevant time, thus prohibiting her from advancing as quickly as she would have liked).

[12]Brook v. City of Montgomery, 916 F. Supp. 1193, 73 FEP 985 (M.D. Ala. 1996) (no prima facie case established since credible evidence showed, notwithstanding

Even when a prima facie case is established, cases are often dismissed where the factfinder concludes that the selectee was the most qualified.[13] In some cases courts have dismissed claims absent

plaintiff's assessment of his own qualifications, that selectees were more qualified although court stressed it made no determination as to whether the employer exercised sound business judgment); Smith v. Douglas Cable Communications, 881 F. Supp. 1510 (D. Kan. 1995) (several of plaintiff's promotion claims dismissed because of failure to establish prima facie case since his qualifications and experience were markedly inferior to that of selectee and plaintiff produced no evidence suggesting employer's reasons were not legitimate; however, one claim involving supervisor position not dismissed because selectee's qualifications did not appear markedly superior to plaintiff's and there were material questions as to sales performance and age-based hostility toward him by other decisionmakers); Torre v. Federated Mut. Ins. Co., 897 F. Supp. 1332, 68 FEP 1850 (D. Kan. 1995) (promotion claim dismissed because plaintiff failed to establish prima facie case since she could not prove she was at least as objectively qualified as selectees), aff'd, 124 F.3d 218 (10th Cir. 1997).

[13]Kuhn v. Ball State Univ., 78 F.3d 330, 332, 70 FEP 449 (7th Cir. 1996) (university's denial of tenure not unlawful where plaintiff's achievement was competent but not superior since satisfactory performance does not entitle anyone to promotion because "the ADEA is not a merit-selection program"); Amirmokri v. Baltimore Gas & Elec. Co., 60 F.3d 1126, 68 FEP 809 (4th Cir. 1995) (court finds plaintiff qualified for position but dismisses case based on unrebutted evidence that selectee was better qualified based on more hands-on experience as engineer and outstanding performance ratings over a number of years; noting same decisionmaker hired and then shortly thereafter denied promotion to plaintiff, thus making it unlikely that denial was based on national origin); Lidge-Myrtil v. Deere & Co., 49 F.3d 1308, 70 FEP 521 (8th Cir. 1995) (selectee had better qualifications, interpersonal skills, and discretion for higher level secretary job; moreover, mere existence of comparable qualifications between two applicants does not raise bias inference and employer could legitimately consider plaintiff's unpleasant personality when making personnel decisions, which court is not going to second-guess); Carter v. Ball, 33 F.3d 450, 65 FEP 1414 (4th Cir. 1994) (plaintiff was not qualified for position since she was ranked well below the selectee and there was no evidence that rejection was based on circumstances giving rise to an inference of unlawful discrimination); Johnson v. United States Dep't of Health & Human Servs., 30 F.3d 45, 65 FEP 702 (6th Cir. 1994) (plaintiff's overall job performance and technical, analytical, writing, and communication skills were deficient as compared with selectee and no credible evidence indicating pretext apart from plaintiff's subjective testimony that she was more qualified than person selected); Causey v. Balog, 929 F. Supp. 900, 71 FEP 643 (D. Md. 1996) (plaintiff was not more qualified than person selected who had more administrative experience within the department); Taylor v. Brown, 928 F. Supp. 568 (D. Md. 1995) (even though plaintiff qualified, selectee more qualified based on broader experience defendant was seeking), aff'd, 86 F.3d 1152 (4th Cir. 1996); Williams v. Perry, 907 F. Supp. 838, 70 FEP 713 (M.D. Pa.) (evidence established selectee had volunteered for two 45-day shifts in promoted position while plaintiff had declined that opportunity and selectee also considered highly qualified for job and had received higher evaluations than plaintiff), aff'd, 72 F.3d 125 (3d Cir. 1995); Johnson v. Indopco, Inc., 887 F. Supp. 1092, 1097–98 (N.D. Ill. 1995) (plaintiff could not show she was more qualified than selectee who

a showing of pretext, even when the plaintiff was better qualified.[14] This extends to situations where the selectee is chosen for arbitrary or unfair reasons that are not discriminatory, such as nepotism, romance, or friendship.[15] Courts continue to stress that they are not super-personnel review boards and that their job is not to second-guess an employer's business judgment or to substitute their views for those of the employer when it comes to selection criteria, the promotion process, or the eventual decision.[16] Courts are willing, however, to discard their deference to an employer's business

---

had more experience and had almost completed all college courses while plaintiff had completed none; fact selectee was unfamiliar with two word processing functions not controlling because "[o]ne person's ability to perform one or more specific tasks does not automatically demonstrate that he is superior to another who has not mastered those tasks when the overall job performance is measured by the person's ability to perform many different functions"), *aff'd,* 79 F.3d 1150 (7th Cir. 1996); Arzate v. City of Topeka, 884 F. Supp. 1494, 72 FEP 681 (D. Kan. 1995) (court rejected plaintiff's argument that his poor communication skills were irrelevant to newly created management position; language difficulties that interfere with performance of duties are legitimate considerations); Hicks v. Arthur, 878 F. Supp. 737, 740 (E.D. Pa.) (selectee was more qualified), *aff'd,* 72 F.3d 122 (3d Cir. 1995); Shinholster v. Georgia Farm Bureau Mut. Ins. Co., 898 F. Supp. 913, 69 FEP 91 (M.D. Ga. 1995) (evidence established plaintiff was not as well qualified in terms of public relation skills as selectee and plaintiff produced no substantial evidence questioning defendant's legitimate nondiscriminatory reason); Russell v. Acme-Evans Co., 881 F. Supp. 378 (S.D. Ind. 1994) (undisputed evidence plaintiff was not selected because other candidate had shown mechanical aptitude), *aff'd,* 51 F.3d 64, 67 FEP 589 (7th Cir. 1995); Grauer v. Federal Express Corp., 894 F. Supp. 330, 68 FEP 218 (W.D. Tenn. 1994) (selectee had more management experience and possessed college degree while plaintiff did not; plaintiff's unsupported subjective belief or disagreement with employer's business judgment does not create issue of fact), *aff'd,* 73 F.3d 361 (6th Cir. 1996).

[14]Fishbach v. District of Columbia Dep't of Corrections, 86 F.3d 1180, 71 FEP 316, 71 FEP 448 (D.C. Cir. 1996) (fact employer misjudged plaintiff's performance or qualifications, while relevant, does not establish pretext); Harrison v. LaRue D. Carter Mem'l Hosp., 882 F. Supp. 128, 67 FEP 1639 (S.D. Ind. 1994) (even if plaintiff was the most qualified, that alone would not establish defendant's reason was a pretext for impermissible bias), *aff'd,* 61 F.3d 905, 69 FEP 768 (7th Cir. 1995).

[15]Cherry v. American Tel. & Tel. Co., 47 F.3d 225, 67 FEP 113 (7th Cir. 1995) (plaintiff not denied promotion because of sex since disputed opportunity was geared to company lobbyists and not attorneys, male or female); Spiers v. McNeil Real Estate Management, Inc., 65 FEP 1446 (D. Kan. 1994) (law does not prevent decisionmaker from promoting person because she is his girlfriend or because he wants to go to bars with selectee); East v. Dixie Yarns, Inc., 1994 WL 872892 (M.D.N.C. Dec. 9, 1994) (fact plaintiff denied promotion because selectee was having affair with decisionmaker not unlawful because preferential treatment based on consensual romantic relationship is not sex discrimination).

[16]Hartsel v. Keys, 87 F.3d 795, 72 FEP 951 (6th Cir. 1996) (court rejects inference of age bias based on plaintiff's belief it was unfair to require older workers

judgment and review promotion decisions if there is evidence that indicates the process or decision was the product of bias[17] or manipulation.[18]

---

who did not work on graphic computers to compete with younger employees, observing it had no desire to evaluate a "business judgment"), *cert. denied,* 117 S. Ct. 683 (1997); Jiminez v. Mary Washington College, 57 F.3d 369, 67 FEP 1867 (4th Cir.) (academic institutions have a long-recognized prerogative to determine who may teach and courts, absent showing of a discriminatory motive, should not question the wisdom or folly of those judgments), *cert. denied,* 116 S. Ct. 380 (1995); EEOC v. Louisiana Office of Community Servs., 47 F.3d 1438, 1445–46, 67 FEP 659 (5th Cir. 1995) (courts are not well suited by training or experience to evaluate qualifications for high-level promotions and, absent disparities, are reluctant to substitute their judgment for persons charged with making those decisions); Reynolds v. School Dist. No. 1, Denver, Colo., 69 F.3d 1523, 72 FEP 485 (10th Cir. 1995) (plaintiff's numerous denial of promotion claims rejected, noting budget constraints resulted in elimination of position and plaintiff could not show this reason was in any way pretextual even if it might have been erroneous or an illogical business decision); Fishbach v. Dist. of Columbia Dep't of Corrections, 86 F.3d 1180, 71 FEP 316, 71 FEP 448 (D.C. Cir. 1996) (court should not second-guess personnel decision absent demonstrated discriminatory intent even if court would conclude employer misjudged relative qualifications of candidates and failed to follow its own personnel policies where evidence showed that procedure followed was reasonable and consistent with prior selections even though not the prescribed procedure); Rooks v. Girl Scouts of Chicago, 69 FEP 329 (N.D. Ill. 1995) (court will not entertain plaintiff's suggestion that it reevaluate the observations, independent judgment, and business decisions of defendant).

[17]Glass v. Philadelphia Elec. Co., 34 F.3d 188, 65 FEP 1280, 65 FEP 1450 (3d Cir. 1994) (case reversed and remanded where plaintiff was barred at trial from introducing evidence about hostile work environment and how it related to his performance, which, according to defendant, was reason he had not been selected); Green v. Clarendon County Sch. Dist. No. 3, 923 F. Supp. 829 (D.S.C. 1996) (summary judgment denied where plaintiff was qualified for school principal position but African-American member of school board, concerned about statistical parity of students to principals, stated he would not vote for another white principal); Emmel v. Coca-Cola Bottling Co. of Chicago, Inc., 904 F. Supp. 723 (N.D. Ill. 1995) (defendant's posttrial motion to set aside verdict denied given manager's statement that plaintiff was just as qualified as men who were promoted but top management wanted men in those positions, along with several other sexist statements and fact upper management positions were held only by men), *aff'd,* 95 F.3d 627, 72 FEP 1811 (7th Cir. 1996).

[18]Stewart v. Rutgers, 120 F.3d 426, 74 FEP 545 (3d Cir. 1997) (summary judgment reversed where grievance committee had noted decision to deny tenure was "arbitrary and capricious"); Rush v. Scott Specialty Gases, Inc., 914 F. Supp. 104, 70 FEP 34 (E.D. Pa. 1996) (employer had manipulated selectee's duties before and after selection), *rev'd in part,* 113 F.3d 476 (3d Cir. 1997); Kolstad v. American Dental Ass'n, 912 F. Supp. 13, 69 FEP 1376 (D.D.C. 1996) (male applicant had been preselected), *aff'd in part, remanded in part,* 108 F.3d 1431, 73 FEP 625 (D.C. Cir. 1997); Nayar v. Howard Univ., 881 F. Supp. 15 (D.D.C. 1995) (court found triable issues regarding university's motive based on procedural irregularities in review of her application as well as defendant's departure from its normal hiring procedures); Weeks v. State, 866

Absent a showing that a specific practice has an adverse impact, or absent any statistical proof, courts continue to dismiss disparate impact claims.[19]

III. EXPERIENCE REQUIREMENTS AND SENIORITY

Experience and tenure requirements continue to be accepted as legitimate preselection criteria.[20] Rigid and inflexible requirements

---

F. Supp. 601, 69 FEP 871 (D. Me. 1994) (summary judgment denied where position given to allegedly less qualified person and defendant appeared to manipulate promotion process and requirements so as to deprive plaintiff of position); Chaudhuri v. State, 886 F. Supp. 1374 (M.D. Tenn. 1995) (summary judgment denied on Asian professor's claim of bias in selecting head of department because criteria for job changed after he applied and selectee given undue advantages). *Cf.* Taylor v. Brown, 928 F. Supp. 568 (D. Md. 1995) (summary judgment granted even though defendant used factors that went above and beyond minimum requirements necessary to move to final stage of evaluation process, noting that a personal interview is often a determinative factor in hiring/promotion decisions), *aff'd*, 86 F.3d 1152 (4th Cir. 1996).

[19]Khan v. State, 903 F. Supp. 881 (D. Md. 1995) (no evidence that specific elements of selection standards had an adverse impact on African-American candidates); Grauer v. Federal Express Corp., 894 F. Supp. 330, 68 FEP 218 (W.D. Tenn. 1994) (plaintiff offered no evidence that test had tendency to exclude women), *aff'd*, 73 F.3d 361 (6th Cir. 1996).

[20]Metsopulos v. Runyon, 918 F. Supp. 851 (D.N.J. 1996) (postal worker lawfully denied promotion to postmaster since, unlike applicants who had been selected, plaintiff had not had prior experience as a postmaster); Alford v. City of Montgomery, 879 F. Supp. 1143 (M.D. Ala. 1995) (plaintiff lawfully denied promotion to recreation supervisor because candidate required to have held position of Community Center Director III, a position plaintiff had not previously held nor applied for even though she knew it was prerequisite for other position), *aff'd*, 79 F.3d 1160 (11th Cir. 1996); Campbell v. Pennsylvania College of Optometry, 68 FEP 1488 (E.D. Pa. 1995) (summary judgment granted because plaintiff, apart from own assessment of her abilities, was not qualified for human resources director position where she had neither experience nor knowledge to perform majority of duties); Rabinovitz v. Pena, 905 F. Supp. 522, 73 FEP 400 (N.D. Ill. 1995) (plaintiff had significant experience in his field but lacked experience as supervisor and manager, which was fatal to application for a managerial position), *aff'd*, 89 F.3d 482, 73 FEP 410 (7th Cir. 1996); Webb v. Derwinski, 868 F. Supp. 1184, 69 FEP 419 (E.D. Mo. 1994) (race and age promotion claim dismissed where plaintiff did not have at least one year of experience at next lower grade level and also lacked education, which could be substituted for prior experience requirement), *aff'd*, 68 F.3d 479, 69 FEP 768 (8th Cir. 1995); Dickinson v. McCarty, 65 FEP 1508 (S.D. Fla. 1994) (tenure denial case dismissed in part because plaintiff sought tenure without having first taught for five years, which was typically required, and had not completed research papers during relevant time); Addy v. Bliss & Glennon, 44 Cal.App.4th 205, 70 FEP 965 (Cal. App. 1996) (plaintiff not qualified for disputed position since defendant was seeking person with four-year college degree for management trainee position and plaintiff only had two-year degree).

that bar otherwise qualified employees may, however, raise concerns.[21]

IV. SUBJECTIVE CRITERIA

The courts continue to reject the argument that the use of subjective criteria is per se unlawful or an indicia of bias.[22] Instead, courts recognize that subjective criteria should be closely scrutinized,[23]

---

[21]Walker v. New York State Office of Mental Health, 865 F. Supp. 124 (S.D.N.Y. 1994).

[22]Fishbach v. District of Columbia Dep't of Corrections, 86 F.3d 1180, 71 FEP 316, 71 FEP 448 (D.C. Cir. 1996) (there is nothing unusual or unreasonable in selecting a pool of qualified candidates based on written credentials and then making final decision based on personal interviews in hiring of professional and evidence did not establish selection process relied unduly on highly subjective criteria such as interpersonal skills); Lidge-Myrtil v. Deere & Co., 49 F.3d 1308, 70 FEP 521 (8th Cir. 1995) (employer's reliance on belief selectee was better qualified because it was concerned about plaintiff's abrasive demeanor and ability to be good team player not unlawful even though somewhat subjective); Amirmokri v. Baltimore Gas & Elec. Co., 60 F.3d 1126, 68 FEP 809 (4th Cir. 1995) (court observes that even if plaintiff's education and outside experience are objectively superior to selectee's, employer can properly consider other legitimate criteria including subjective factors like interpersonal skills and ability to lead); Johnson v. Runyon, 928 F. Supp. 575 (D. Md. 1996) (use of subjective criteria is neither improper nor indicative of unlawful discrimination); Brook v. City of Montgomery, 916 F. Supp. 1193, 73 FEP 985 (M.D. Ala. 1996) (denial of promotion claim dismissed where city was seeking supervisor who, apart from objective electronics experience, had personality traits that demonstrated management capabilities and ability to work well with subordinates); Taylor v. Brown, 928 F. Supp. 568 (D. Md. 1995) (multistep selection process leading to interview did not result in discrimination even though a personal interview is often determinative factor in many hiring decisions notwithstanding its subjective nature), *aff'd*, 86 F.3d 1152 (4th Cir. 1996); Csicseri v. Bowsher, 862 F. Supp. 547 (D.D.C. 1994) (court dismissed promotion claim even though selection process was, to considerable extent, subjective, because there were flexible guidelines, statistical analysis did not support disparate impact argument, and plaintiff failed to isolate any specific subjectively applied criteria and establish a manifestation of discrimination), *aff'd*, 67 F.3d 972 (D.C. Cir. 1995); *cf.* Fisher v. Vassar College, 70 F.3d 1420, 70 FEP 1155 (2d Cir. 1995) (courts must review, no matter how intuitive, decisions based on tenure standards that by their very nature are not objective and quantifiable in order to determine if they were used as pretext), *aff'd en banc*, 114 F.3d 1332, 74 FEP 109 (2d Cir. 1997).

[23]Warren v. City of Carlsbad, 58 F.3d 439 (9th Cir. 1995) (employer's reliance on subjective evaluation of plaintiff's communication skills in denying him a promotion should be closely scrutinized), *cert. denied*, 116 S. Ct. 1261 (1996); Terry v. Gallegos, 926 F. Supp. 679 (W.D. Tenn. 1996) (when a promotion decision is subjective, the legitimacy of the articulated reasons for the decision is subject to particularly close scrutiny).

especially where there are other indicia of bias.[24] The degree of attention varies based on the nature of the position, with greater scrutiny given to blue-collar as opposed to professional, artistic, supervisory, administrative, or executive opportunities.[25]

V. STATISTICAL PROOF:
THE QUALIFIED POTENTIAL APPLICANT POOL

Courts continue to reject statistical evidence in promotion cases where the sample is too small[26] or where the plaintiff has failed to compare similarly situated persons or take into account the qualifications of the applicants.[27]

---

[24]Eldred v. Consolidated Freightways Corp. of Del., 898 F. Supp. 928, 71 FEP 33 (D. Mass. 1995) (employer did not have objective criteria regarding promotion requirements; argument that plaintiff was hampered by her lack of aggressiveness found to be "smoke screen" where selection was based totally on supervisory discretion and "quite incapable of uniform administration and readily susceptible to bias" and "the personal taste, whim or fancy of the evaluator").

[25]Rosado v. Virginia Commonwealth Univ., 927 F. Supp. 917 (E.D. Va. 1996) (second-guessing tenure committee's finding there was not a "clear pattern of academic accomplishment" would be an unreasonable intrusion into the tenure and promotion process); Mendoza v. SSC & B Lintas, 913 F. Supp. 295 (S.D.N.Y. 1996) (plaintiff's denial of promotion claim to art director dismissed where advertising agency based decision on its belief that he lacked required creative ability); Brook v. City of Montgomery, 916 F. Supp. 1193, 73 FEP 985 (M.D. Ala. 1996) (denial of promotion claim dismissed where city was seeking supervisor who, apart from objective electronics experience, had personality traits that demonstrated management capabilities and ability to work well with his subordinates).

[26]Kuhn v. Ball State Univ., 78 F.3d 330, 332, 70 FEP 449 (7th Cir. 1996) (court refused to infer discrimination from employer's treatment of similarly situated individuals in tenure denial case absent a larger sample); Fisher v. Vassar College, 70 F.3d 1420, 70 FEP 1155 (2d Cir. 1995) (lower court finding reversed because plaintiff's statistics based on small sample), *aff'd en banc*, 114 F.3d 1332, 74 FEP 109 (2d Cir. 1997); Causey v. Balog, 929 F. Supp. 900, 71 FEP 643 (D. Md. 1996) (sample too small to have any statistical meaning); Nash v. Consolidated City of Jacksonville, 895 F. Supp. 1536, 1542 (M.D. Fla. 1995) (same), *aff'd*, 85 F.3d 643 (11th Cir. 1996); Csicseri v. Bowsher, 862 F. Supp. 547 (D.D.C. 1994) (same), *aff'd*, 67 F.3d 972 (D.C. Cir. 1995). *Cf.* Sims v. Montgomery County Comm'n, 873 F. Supp. 585, 601–02 (M.D. Ala. 1994) (limited size of population does not preclude finding of discrimination where a decisive historical pattern emerges).

[27]Shannon v. Ford Motor Co., 72 F.3d 678, 683, 69 FEP 1339 (8th Cir. 1996) (African-American plaintiff failed to demonstrate that promoted white applicants were similarly situated); Simon v. City of Youngstown, 73 F.3d 68, 72 (6th Cir. 1995) (statistics irrelevant when they failed to take into account the qualifications of the applicants); Carter v. Ball, 33 F.3d 450, 65 FEP 1414 (4th Cir. 1994) (relevant comparison is between percentage of minority employees and percentage of potential minority

VI. REMEDIES

Relief awarded in promotion cases continues to include one or more of the following: the sought-after promotion, back pay, front pay, compensatory damages, and punitive damages.[28]

---

applicants in qualified labor pool); Rosado v. Virginia Commonwealth Univ., 927 F. Supp. 917 (E.D. Va. 1996) (statistical evidence failed to address the qualifications of minority applicant pool).

[28]Odima v. Westin Tucson Hotel, 53 F.3d 1484, 67 FEP 1222 (9th Cir. 1995) (employer ordered to hire plaintiff for first available position and plaintiff awarded front pay, back pay, and compensatory damages); Terry v. Gallegos, 926 F. Supp. 679 (W.D. Tenn. 1996) (plaintiff entitled to previously denied position, back pay, front pay, and compensatory damages); Williams v. Pharmacia Ophthalmics, Inc., 926 F. Supp. 791, 794–98, 71 FEP 628 (N.D. Ind. 1996) (plaintiff awarded front pay, back pay, compensatory damages, and punitive damages); Luciano v. Olsten Corp., 912 F. Supp. 663, 73 FEP 221 (E.D.N.Y. 1996) (plaintiff awarded back pay, damages for emotional distress, and punitive damages), *aff'd*, 110 F.3d 210, 73 FEP 722 (2d Cir. 1997); Schaefer v. Tannian, 902 F. Supp. 746, 749 (E.D. Mich 1995) (back pay awarded to class of women discriminated against in promotion process). *Cf.* Edwards v. Lujan, 40 F.3d 1152, 68 FEP 32 (10th Cir. 1994) (even though plaintiff proved discrimination, court rejected request to reopen vacancies because there was no evidence that plaintiff would have secured positions given his weak credentials), *cert. denied,* 116 S. Ct. 417 (1995); Kolstad v. American Dental Ass'n, 912 F. Supp. 13, 69 FEP 1376 (D.D.C. 1996) (although court affirmed jury award of over $52,000, it denied plaintiff the sought-after position because plaintiff failed to prove case to court's satisfaction), *aff'd in part, remanded in part,* 108 F.3d 1431, 73 FEP 625 (D.C. Cir. 1997).

Chapter 20

SEXUAL AND OTHER FORMS OF HARASSMENT

II. Harassment on Bases Other Than Sex

A. Introduction

Claims of harassment based on characteristics other than sex continue to be evaluated under the same legal standard as applied to sexual harassment claims.[1]

B. Race, Color, and National Origin

Courts continue to find racially discriminatory statements to be compelling, if not always determinative, evidence of racial harassment.[2] Of course, these types of statements, as with other race-based conduct, must be sufficiently severe and pervasive to establish the existence of a racially hostile work environment.[3]

C. Religion

2. *Membership*

Religious harassment claims continue to be evaluated under the same analytical framework applied to other types of harassment

---

[1]Harrison v. Metropolitan Gov't, 80 F.3d 1107, 1118, 73 FEP 109 (6th Cir.) ("the elements and burden of proof that a Title VII plaintiff must meet are the same for racially charged harassment as for sexually charged harassment"), *cert. denied,* 117 S. Ct. 169 (1996).
[2]Aman v. Cort Furniture Rental Corp., 85 F.3d 1074, 1083–84, 70 FEP 1614 (3d Cir. 1996) (although acts of racial harassment do not have to be accompanied by racially discriminatory statements to prove intentional discrimination on a regular and pervasive basis, such statements make a plaintiff's racial discrimination claim "all the more compelling").
[3]Little v. United Tech., 103 F.3d 956, 960, 72 FEP 1560 (11th Cir. 1997) (an employee's objection to a single racist comment made by one co-worker to another is not opposition to an unlawful employment practice protected by Title VII).

claims.[4] Thus, to be actionable, conduct must be unwelcome, pervasive,[5] and because of the plaintiff's religious beliefs. In addition, the employer must have failed to take effective remedial action after obtaining actual or constructive knowledge of the harassment.[6]

D. Age

Courts are increasingly analyzing age-based harassment claims under the same framework applied to sexual and racial harassment claims. For example, in *Crawford v. Medina General Hospital*,[7] the court noted that while no circuit court had applied the hostile environment doctrine in an ADEA context, it was "a relatively uncontroversial proposition that such a theory is viable under the ADEA."[8] The court held that a plaintiff must establish the following elements to set forth a prima facie case for hostile environment age discrimination:

> (1) The employee is 40 years old or older; (2) The employee was subjected to harassment, either through words or actions, based on

---

[4]*E.g.,* Sarin v. Raytheon Co., 905 F. Supp. 49, 69 FEP 856 (D. Mass. 1995); Peck v. Sony Music Corp., 68 FEP 1025 (S.D.N.Y. 1995).

[5]*See* Kantar v. Baldwin Cooke Co., 69 FEP 851, 855 (N.D. Ill. 1995) (holding that the following conduct did not establish harassment sufficiently pervasive to be actionable under Title VII: several references to the plaintiff as a "princess" or "JAP"; inquiries into the plaintiff's religious faith; needling of the plaintiff in reference to her leaving early on Fridays to attend religious services; and a reference to the plaintiff's co-worker as "Jewish speaking"); Peck v. Sony Music Corp., 68 FEP 1025 (S.D.N.Y. 1995) (denying employer's motion for summary judgment on a religious harassment claim based on allegations that the plaintiff's colleague regularly made comments to plaintiff regarding her religion, called plaintiff a sinner, told her she would go to hell, and held a prayer session in plaintiff's work area).

[6]*E.g.,* Sarin v. Raytheon Co., 905 F. Supp. 49, 69 FEP 856 (D. Mass. 1995) (holding that employer's immediate response to complaints of religious harassment, consisting of apologies by harassing employee, transfer of harassing employee to another station, and discontinuation of offensive conduct, shielded employer from liability).

[7]96 F.3d 830 (6th Cir. 1996).

[8]*Id.* at 834. Likewise, several district courts have concluded that a claim for age-based harassment is cognizable under the ADEA. *See* O'Shea v. Yellow Tech. Servs., Inc., 979 F. Supp. 1390, 1396 (D. Kan. 1997) (holding that hostile-environment claims under the ADEA are equally as viable as those brought under Title VII); McKeown v. Dartmouth Bookstore, Inc., 975 F. Supp. 403, 405 (D.N.H. 1997) (assuming, without analysis, that age-harassment claims are actionable and applying the same analysis as applied to Title VII sexual harassment claims); Monica v. New York City Off-Track Betting Corp., 67 FEP 704 (S.D.N.Y. 1995) (same), *aff'd,* 100 F.3d 941 (2d Cir. 1996).

age; (3) The harassment had the effect of unreasonably interfering with the employee's work performance and creating an objectively intimidating, hostile, or offensive work environment; and (4) There exists some basis for liability on the part of the employer.[9]

E. Disability

Courts continue to find disability harassment actionable under the ADA.[10]

III. QUID PRO QUO HARASSMENT

B. The Prima Facie Case

Henson v. City of Dundee[11] remains the leading case addressing the elements of a prima facie case of quid pro quo sexual harassment.[12]

3. The Issue: The Adverse Employment Action

The Supreme Court, in *Burlington Industries, Inc. v. Ellerth*,[13] held that an employee who has been subjected to a demand for sexual favors, coupled with an implicit or explicit threat of an adverse job consequence that was not carried out, could still state a claim for sexual harassment. Following the Second Circuit's decision in *Karibian v. Columbia University*,[14] but prior to the Supreme Court's *Ellerth* decision, several district courts had held that "some adverse job consequence must actually have resulted

---

[9]Crawford v. Medina Gen. Hosp., 96 F.3d 830, 834–35 (6th Cir. 1996).

[10]*E.g.*, Butler v. City of Prairie Village, 974 F. Supp. 1386, 1401 (D. Kan. 1997) (holding that the elements of a claim of disability harassment are (1) that the plaintiff is a qualified individual with a disability; (2) that she was subjected to unwelcome harassment; (3) that the harassment was based on disability or on a request for accommodation; and (4) that the harassment altered a term, condition, or privilege of employment).

[11]682 F.2d 897, 903–04, 29 FEP 787 (11th Cir. 1982).

[12]*See also* Pfau v. Reed, 125 F.3d 927, 934, 75 FEP 1237 (5th Cir. 1997); Cram v. Lamson & Sessions Co., 49 F.3d 466, 473, 67 FEP 449 (8th Cir. 1995); Schrader v. E.G. & G., Inc., 953 F. Supp. 1160, 1166 (D. Colo. 1997); Webb v. Hyman, 861 F. Supp. 1094, 1103, 67 FEP 1425 (D.D.C. 1994).

[13]1998 U.S. LEXIS 4217 (June 26, 1998).

[14]14 F.3d 773, 63 FEP 1038 (2d Cir.), *cert. denied*, 512 U.S. 1213 (1994).

from the employee's refusal to submit to the requested conduct."[15] The *Ellerth* decision made clear that the lack of any adverse job action based on the employee's refusal to submit to a supervisor's request for sexual favors is not necessarily fatal to the employee's claim. The Court noted, however, that in the absence of an actual tangible job detriment, a claim involving unfulfilled threats "should be categorized as a hostile work environment claim that requires a showing of severe or pervasive conduct."[16] The Court accepted the district court's finding that the supervisor's numerous alleged threats directed at Ms. Ellerth were severe and pervasive and expressly reserved judgment on whether a single unlawful threat could be sufficient to constitute sexual harassment.[17]

In contrast, the majority of courts deciding the issue appear to follow the analysis of the D.C. Circuit articulated in *Gary v. Long*[18] in which the court held that the conduct of an employee who lacks the *authority* to follow through on his threats cannot be the basis for a quid pro quo harassment claim.[19] However, where an alleged harasser was not officially the plaintiff's supervisor, the

---

[15] Rushing v. United Airlines, 919 F. Supp. 1101, 1109, 70 FEP 815 (N.D. Ill. 1996).

[16] *Ellerth*, 1998 U.S. LEXIS 4217, at *23. The Court also observed that the terms quid pro quo and hostile environment had taken on "their own significance," and that traditionally an employer was subject to strict vicarious liability for quid pro quo cases. *Id.* at *21–22. The opinion went on to hold that in a hostile environment case involving a supervisor's unfulfilled threats to alter the terms or conditions of employment based on sex, the employer could be held vicariously liable, subject to an affirmative defense that the employer took steps to prevent and correct sexual harassment and that the employee failed to take advantage of the employer's preventive or corrective opportunities. *Id.* at *41–42. *See* discussion at Section III.B.5 *infra.*

[17] *Id.* at *23.

[18] 59 F.3d 1391, 68 FEP 581 (D.C. Cir.), *cert. denied*, 116 S. Ct. 569 (1995).

[19] *E.g.*, Hartleip v. McNeilab, Inc., 83 F.3d 767, 71 FEP 1636 (6th Cir. 1996) (plaintiff failed to raise a genuine fact issue regarding whether her rejection of a nonsupervisor's advances was a factor in a decision affecting her employment); Bonenberger v. Plymouth Township, 72 FEP 1241 (E.D. Pa. 1996) (no quid pro quo harassment established where it was undisputed that the alleged harasser lacked the authority to carry through on his threats and, in fact, never did carry through on his threats), *aff'd in part, rev'd in part on other grounds*, 132 F.2d 20 (3d Cir. 1997); Wenner v. C.G. Bretting Mfg. Co., 917 F. Supp. 640, 69 FEP 774 (W.D. Wis. 1995) (a customer's alleged harassment was not quid pro quo harassment because the customer was in no position to condition job benefits on submission to sexual conduct); Johnson v. Merry-Go-Round Enters., Inc., 67 FEP 1456 (N.D. Ill. 1995) (employee failed to state a quid pro quo harassment claim based on threats of an investigator who lacked the power to hire, fire, or recommend such decisions).

employer may still be held liable if the harasser in fact held the power to control the plaintiff's work environment.[20] As one court observed, "Surely it would be unfair if an employer could shield himself from liability for quid pro quo harassment merely by attributing a title to a supervisor that was misleading with respect to the actual authority wielded by him or her."[21]

In *Bryson v. Chicago State University*,[22] the Seventh Circuit held that the threatened adverse employment action need only be a tangible detriment, and not an economic one. The court concluded that there was a genuine issue of material fact as to whether a tenured university professor had shown a loss of tangible employment benefits arising out of loss of her title and her banishment from university committee work. The court rejected the employer's argument that there had been no adverse action because there had been no economic detriment and observed:

> Universities have few "carrots" to dangle in front of tenured faculty members who reach full professorhood. The subtle indicia of job status and reward thus may, in a particular institution, take on an importance that may be far greater in context than would appear on the outside—indicia like honorary or in-house titles (that may have no budgetary effect, unlike their administrative counterparts) and committee assignments.[23]

The court further reasoned, "committee assignments and titles may play a part in preparing for an administrative academic career. The [district court] erred in assuming that nothing adverse had happened to Bryson because she had not yet applied for a deanship. Depriving someone of the building blocks for such a promotion . . . is just as serious as depriving her of the job itself."[24]

4. The Causal Connection

a. On the Basis of Sex. In *Oncale v. Sundowner Offshore Services, Inc.*,[25] the Supreme Court unanimously held that same-sex harassment is actionable under Title VII if it occurs "because of

---

[20] Gostanian v. Bendel, 1997 WL 214966 (S.D.N.Y Apr. 25, 1997).
[21] *Id.* at *6.
[22] 96 F.3d 912, 71 FEP 1577 (7th Cir. 1996).
[23] *Id.* at 916–17.
[24] *Id.* at 917.
[25] 1998 WL 88039, at *3, 76 FEP 221 (U.S. Mar. 4, 1998).

sex." Although *Oncale* involved a hostile environment claim, the Court's analysis clearly applies to quid pro quo claims as well. The critical issue, the Court opined, is whether members of one sex are exposed to disadvantageous terms or conditions of employment to which members of the other sex are not exposed.

The majority of courts that faced the issue before *Oncale* also have held that same-sex quid pro quo harassment is actionable under Title VII where the unlawful threat or request would not have occurred "but for" the plaintiff's gender. Many, but not all, of these cases were based on the assumption that the alleged harasser was homosexual. For example, in *Yeary v. Goodwill Industries–Knoxville, Inc.,*[26] the court noted that "when a male sexually propositions another male because of sexual attraction, there can be little question that the behavior is a form of harassment that occurs because the propositioned male is a male—that is, because of sex."[27] The Supreme Court, in *Oncale,* also noted that the homosexuality of the alleged harasser in a same-sex harassment case could give rise to an inference that the conduct was "because of sex."[28] The Court, at the same time, however, also observed that the harassing conduct need not be motivated by sexual desire, but would be just as unlawful if it was motivated by a general hostility to the presence of men or women in the workplace because of their gender.[29]

The question of the even-handed harasser or the "bisexual defense" becomes more problematic in light of the viability of same-sex harassment claims. In *Ray v. Tandem Computers, Inc.,*[30] the Fifth Circuit affirmed summary judgment in favor of the employer in light of evidence that the alleged harasser treated all of his employees poorly, regardless of gender.[31] The court reasoned, "Title VII

---

[26]107 F.3d 443, 448, 73 FEP 146 (6th Cir. 1997).

[27]*See also* Fredette v. BVP Management Assocs., 112 F.3d 1503, 73 FEP 1519 (11th Cir. 1997) ("the reasonably inferred motives of the homosexual harasser are identical to those of the heterosexual harasser—*i.e.,* the harasser makes advances toward the victim because the victim is a member of the gender the harasser prefers"), *cert. denied,* 118 S. Ct. 1184 (1998); Wrightson v. Pizza Hut of Am., Inc., 99 F.3d 138, 72 FEP 186 (4th Cir. 1996) (male employee stated a viable Title VII claim for sex discrimination against his employer based on his homosexual male supervisor's sexual advances).

[28]Oncale v. Sundowner Offshore Servs., Inc., 1998 WL 88039, at *3, 76 FEP 221 (U.S. Mar. 4, 1998).

[29]*Id.*

[30]63 F.3d 429, 435, 68 FEP 1338 (5th Cir. 1995).

[31]*Id.* at 435 n.19.

does not exist to punish poor management skills; rather it exists to eliminate certain types of bias in the workplace."[32] In contrast, the Ninth Circuit has held that a harasser cannot "cure" his conduct towards women by treating males in the environment in an equally offensive and degrading manner.[33] Although the court recognized that men may have a different subjective reaction to certain conduct than women, the court stated that it did not "rule out the possibility that *both* men and women working at Showboat have viable claims against [the alleged harasser] for sexual harassment."[34]

b. *The Link Between Harassment and the Adverse Employment Action.* (i.) *Lapse of time.* In *Hott v. VDO Yazaki Corp.*,[35] the court held that whether the plaintiff's termination was causally connected to her refusal of her supervisor's sexual advances, the last of which was 15 months prior, was a fact question for the jury to decide.[36] In contrast, summary judgment was appropriate on an employee's quid pro quo claim where there was no evidence that the plaintiff's refusal to consent to sexual requests of a supervisor who had ceased to supervise her 30 months earlier was causally related to her discharge.[37] Of course, the lapse of mere days between the unlawful request and the adverse employment action will usually be sufficient to establish a fact issue as to causation.[38]

(ii.) *Comparative evidence.* Courts continue to permit the use of comparative evidence in a variety of contexts to establish a causal connection between an adverse employment action and an unlawful sexual advance.[39]

---

[32]*Id.*
[33]Steiner v. Showboat Operating Co., 25 F.3d 1459, 1464, 65 FEP 58 (9th Cir. 1994), *cert. denied,* 513 U.S. 1082 (1995).
[34]*Id.*
[35]922 F. Supp. 1114, 70 FEP 1008 (W.D. Va. 1996).
[36]*Id.* at 1123.
[37]Schuster v. New York State Unified Court Sys., 67 FEP 1758 (S.D.N.Y. 1995).
[38]*E.g.,* EEOC v. Domino's Pizza, Inc., 909 F. Supp. 1529, 69 FEP 570 (M.D. Fla. 1995) (holding that the EEOC had established a prima facie case of quid pro quo harassment where, six days before the employee's discharge, his supervisor came to his store and expressed her love for him and, after he rejected her advances, she threatened to get even), *aff'd,* 113 F.3d 1249 (11th Cir. 1997), *cert. denied,* 118 S. Ct. 687 (1998).
[39]*E.g.,* Heyne v. Caruso, 69 F.3d 1475, 69 FEP 408 (9th Cir. 1995) (permitting evidence of the employer's sexual harassment of other female employees as probative of intent in the context of quid pro quo sexual harassment); Valadez v. Uncle Julio's of Ill., Inc., 895 F. Supp. 1008, 70 FEP 451 (N.D. Ill. 1995) (holding that

(iii.) The alleged harasser's involvement in the adverse employment decision. Evidence that the alleged harasser participated in or influenced the adverse employment decision at issue continues to be a significant factor tending to establish a causal link between the employment detriment and the sexual request.[40]

5. Employer Responsibility

In its two recent sexual harassment opinions, issued on the same day, the Supreme Court reaffirmed that employers are strictly liable for quid pro quo harassment perpetrated by supervisors with authority over the plaintiff employee, at least where the threat of adverse employment action was actually carried out (or where the plaintiff submitted to the supervisor's unwelcome advances).[41] However, where no tangible employment action has been taken (in which case, the Court opined, the claim should properly be characterized as a hostile environment claim, rather than a quid pro quo), the employer may raise an affirmative defense, subject to proof by a preponderance of the evidence.[42] The affirmative

---

the plaintiff established a fact issue with regard to her quid pro quo harassment claim based on evidence that male employees who violated the same work rule that plaintiff was accused of violating were not disciplined in the same manner); Zveiter v. Brazilian Nat'l Superintendency, 833 F. Supp. 1089, 68 FEP 1429 (allowing evidence that new employees with allegedly inferior job skills were hired soon after the plaintiff's termination), *opinion supplemented on reconsideration,* 841 F. Supp. 111 (S.D.N.Y. 1993).

[40]Bryson v. Chicago St. Univ., 96 F.3d 912, 917, 71 FEP 1577 (7th Cir. 1996) (sufficient evidence of causation existed where alleged harasser was in a position to effect adverse employment actions); Valadez v. Uncle Julio's of Ill., Inc., 895 F. Supp. 1008, 70 FEP 451 (N.D. Ill. 1995) (holding that plaintiff established a prima facie case of quid pro quo harassment based, in part, on evidence that the alleged harasser influenced the decision to terminate the plaintiff).

[41]Burlington Indus., Inc. v. Ellerth, 1998 U.S. LEXIS 4217 (June 26, 1998); Faragher v. City of Boca Raton, 1998 U.S. LEXIS 4216 (June 26, 1998). *Accord* Pierce v. Commonwealth Life Ins. Co., 40 F.3d 796, 803, 66 FEP 600 (6th Cir. 1994); Nichols v. Frank, 42 F.3d 503, 513, 66 FEP 614 (9th Cir. 1994). *Contra* Sims v. Brown & Root Indus. Servs., Inc., 889 F. Supp. 920, 923, 70 FEP 501 (W.D. La. 1995), *aff'd without opinion,* 78 F.3d 581 (5th Cir.), *cert. denied,* 117 S. Ct. 68 (1996) (in case predating Supreme Court's *Ellerth* and *Faragher* decisions, 5th Circuit affirmed district court's holding that "whether making out a claim for hostile work environment or quid pro quo type sexual harassment, the plaintiff must prove that the employer knew or should have known of the harassment in question and failed to take prompt remedial action," 70 FEP at 504); Indest v. Freeman Decorating, Inc., 70 FEP 192 (E.D. La. 1996) (holding that employer's knowledge of the alleged harassment is a necessary element of both types of harassment claims).

[42]*Ellerth,* 1998 U.S. LEXIS 4217, at *41; *Faragher,* 1998 U.S. LEXIS 4216, at *59.

defense requires proof that: (1) the employer exercised reasonable care to prevent and to correct promptly any sexually harassing behavior; and (2) the plaintiff employee unreasonably failed to take advantage of any preventive or corrective opportunities or to avoid harm otherwise.[43] The requirements for the affirmative defense may be satisfied by a showing that the employer had promulgated and disseminated an antiharassment policy with a clear complaint procedure and that the employee failed to use the complaint procedure.[44] The employer's complaint policy should also include some sort of assurance that in cases of harassment by a supervisor, the employee could bypass the supervisor and register a complaint with another designated person, or with someone higher in the chain of command.[45]

C. The Employer's Rebuttal

2. Articulating a Legitimate Nondiscriminatory Reason

Employers continue to assert conduct such as insubordination and violation of company policy as legitimate, nondiscriminatory reasons for adverse employment actions.[46]

D. The Complainant's Proof of Pretext

To establish pretext, complainants generally rely on much of the same evidence used to establish a prima facie case of quid pro quo sexual harassment.[47]

---

[43]*Ellerth* at *41–42; *Faragher* at *59–60.
[44]*Id.*
[45]*Faragher* at *61–62.
[46]Heyne v. Caruso, 69 F.3d 1475, 69 FEP 408 (9th Cir. 1995) (plaintiff's failure to open the restaurant on time on two consecutive mornings constituted a legitimate, nondiscriminatory reason for her discharge); Cram v. Lamson & Sessions Co., 49 F.3d 466, 67 FEP 449 (8th Cir. 1995) (discharge occurred because of plaintiff's insubordination including leaving a meeting and work early); EEOC v. Domino's Pizza, Inc., 909 F. Supp. 1529, 69 FEP 570 (M.D. Fla. 1995) (employer stated legitimate reason for termination based on employee's violation of company policy in paying another employee out of the mileage account instead of the labor account and for hiding certain documentation in order to improve the financial appearance of the store), *aff'd,* 113 F.3d 1249 (11th Cir. 1997), *cert. denied,* 118 S. Ct. 687 (1998).
[47]Heyne v. Caruso, 69 F.3d 1475, 69 FEP 408 (9th Cir. 1995) (holding that testimony concerning employer's alleged harassment of other female employees was relevant to the issue of whether the plaintiff was discharged for an impermissible

IV. HOSTILE ENVIRONMENT HARASSMENT

B. The Prima Facie Case

The prima facie case of hostile work environment harassment adopted by most courts remains patterned on the formulation first set forth by the Eleventh Circuit.[48] For example, the Fifth Circuit articulated the elements of the plaintiff's prima facie case as follows: (1) the plaintiff is a member of a protected class; (2) he or she was subjected to unwelcome sexual harassment; (3) the harassment was based on sex; (4) the harassment affected "a term, condition, or privilege of employment"; and (5) the employer knew or should have known of the harassment and failed to take prompt and effective remedial action.[49]

1. The Basis: Membership in a Protected Group

The first element of an environment harassment claim, membership in a protected group, is rarely an issue and can be satisfied simply by a stipulation as to gender.[50]

Claims by male employees asserting hostile work environment harassment continue to be brought.[51]

---

reason and that exclusion of such evidence was reversible error); Valadez v. Uncle Julio's of Ill., Inc., 895 F. Supp. 1008, 70 FEP 451 (N.D. Ill. 1995) (evidence that employees had violated certain work rules without being terminated was sufficient evidence that the plaintiff's termination for similar violations was pretextual); Webb v. Hyman, 861 F. Supp. 1094, 67 FEP 1425 (D.D.C. 1994) (evidence that upon rejection of her supervisor's advances, the supervisor changed the plaintiff's days off against her wishes, slowed the processing of her disability papers, unfairly singled her out for a theft investigation, and denied her leave was sufficient to show pretext).

[48]Henson v. City of Dundee, 682 F.2d 897, 903–04, 29 FEP 787 (11th Cir. 1982).

[49]DeAngelis v. El Paso Mun. Police Officers Ass'n, 51 F.3d 591, 593, 67 FEP 1250 (5th Cir.), *cert. denied,* 116 S. Ct. 473 (1995). *Accord* Ecklund v. Fuisz Tech., Ltd., 905 F. Supp. 335, 339, 69 FEP 701 (E.D. Va. 1995); Ascolese v. Southeastern Pa. Transp. Auth., 902 F. Supp. 533, 542, 70 FEP 325 (E.D. Pa. 1995), *on reconsideration,* 925 F. Supp. 351, 72 FEP 1027 (E.D. Pa. 1996); Griffith v. Keystone Steel & Wire, 887 F. Supp. 1133, 1137, 68 FEP 841 (C.D. Ill. 1995).

[50]Prescott v. Independent Life & Accident Ins. Co., 878 F. Supp. 1545, 67 FEP 876 (M.D. Ala. 1995) (holding that this element of a harassment claim might be impossible not to establish since it appears that, to be in a protected group, one must be either male or female).

[51]*See, e.g.,* Tietgen v. Brown's Westminister Motors, Inc., 921 F. Supp. 1495, 1496, 70 FEP 1020 (E.D. Va. 1996) (male former employee brought Title VII action against employer alleging discrimination by supervisor); Tanner v. Prima Donna Resorts, Inc., 919 F. Supp. 351, 353, 72 FEP 435 (D. Nev. 1996) (male employee

The Supreme Court, in *Oncale v. Sundowner Offshore Services, Inc.*,[52] held that Title VII prohibits same-sex hostile environment harassment when that harassment occurs "because of sex." Thus, the viability of same-sex environmental harassment claims depends on whether the complained-about conduct was because of the target's gender rather than whether the target is within a protected group.[53]

2. The Activity: Unwelcome Conduct

Courts continue to hold that sex harassment is not limited only to "sexual" conduct. The courts have treated the concept much more broadly to include any unwelcome conduct inflicted due to the victim's gender that creates a hostile work environment.[54] In evaluating whether conduct is unwelcome or whether the plaintiff was a willing participant in that conduct, courts have considered, with varying outcomes, such factors as the plaintiff's wearing of provocative dress,[55] use of foul language,[56] apparent friendliness with

---

brought Title VII action against former employer); Blozis v. Mike Raisor Ford, Inc., 896 F. Supp. 805, 806, 68 FEP 711 (N.D. Ind. 1995) (male employees brought sexual harassment suit against employer and male co-employee); Raney v. District of Columbia, 892 F. Supp. 283, 286, 68 FEP 1620 (D.D.C. 1995) (male employee brought sexual harassment claim against employer); Griffith v. Keystone Steel & Wire, 887 F. Supp. 1133, 1135–36, 68 FEP 841 (C.D. Ill. 1995) (male employee brought sexual harassment suit against supervisor).

[52]1998 WL 88039, at *3, 76 FEP 221 (U.S. Mar. 4, 1998). *See* discussion *supra* at Section III.B.4.

[53]*See* Section III.B.4 *supra*.

[54]Curde v. Xytel Corp., 912 F. Supp. 335, 340, 71 FEP 843 (N.D. Ill. 1995) (hostile environment claims not limited solely to situations involving conduct of a sexual nature; actionable harassment encompasses all forms of conduct that unreasonably interfere with individual's work performance or create an intimidating, hostile, or offensive work environment); Easton v. Crossland Mortgage Corp., 905 F. Supp. 1368, 1378, 70 FEP 597 (C.D. Cal. 1995) (plaintiff can maintain hostile environment claim even though conduct complained of was not sexual in nature but was directed at victim because of her gender), *rev'd on other grounds*, 114 F.3d 979, 73 FEP 1885 (9th Cir. 1997); Hatley v. Store Kraft Mfg. Co., 859 F. Supp. 1257, 70 FEP 1361 (D. Neb. 1994) (same).

[55]Fowler v. Sunrise Carpet Indus., Inc., 911 F. Supp. 1560, 1579, 75 FEP 201 (N.D. Ga. 1996) (that female employee dressed in revealing manner did not establish that she welcomed supervisor's sexual advances).

[56]Galloway v. General Motors Serv. Parts Operations, 78 F.3d 1164, 1167, 70 FEP 341 (7th Cir. 1996) (plaintiff's use of bad language does not automatically demonstrate plaintiff's insensitivity to, or lack of harm from, co-workers' language); Fowler v. Sunrise Carpet Indus., Inc., 911 F. Supp. 1560, 1580, 75 FEP 201 (N.D. Ga. 1996) (female employee's cursing did not establish that she welcomed supervisor's

the harasser,[57] failure to report harassment,[58] and participation in sexual horseplay.[59]

3. *The Issue: Affecting a Term or Condition of Employment*

   a. *The Effect on Conditions of Employment Must Be "Severe or Pervasive."* While courts have had little difficulty identifying extreme behavior as actionable under Title VII, and identifying sporadic and only marginally offensive conduct as not actionable, drawing a precise and consistent line has been difficult.[60] Sporadic verbal utterances and casual touching usually are not sufficient to establish a hostile and pervasive work environment.[61] When there

---

sexual advances); Balletti v. Sun-Sentinel Co., 909 F. Supp. 1539, 1548, 73 FEP 1341 (S.D. Fla. 1995) (female employee who used vulgar language including open discussion of her use of vibrator not victim of hostile work environment).

[57]Dey v. Colt Constr. & Dev. Co., 28 F.3d 1446, 1454, 65 FEP 523 (7th Cir. 1994) (plaintiff established hostile work environment even though she considered buying automobile and asked for legal advice and help from employee who harassed her); Fowler v. Sunrise Carpet Indus., Inc., 911 F. Supp. 1560, 1576, 75 FEP 201 (N.D. Ga. 1996) (female employee's having lunch with supervisor on regular basis and giving supervisor Christmas gifts did not establish that employee welcomed supervisor's sexual advances).

[58]Fowler v. Sunrise Carpet Indus., Inc., 911 F. Supp. 1560, 1579, 75 FEP 201 (N.D. Ga. 1996) (that female employee did not scream for help when supervisor was allegedly raping her and remained in supervisor's hotel room after alleged rape did not establish that employee welcomed supervisor's sexual advances); Balletti v. Sun-Sentinel Co., 909 F. Supp. 1539, 1547, 73 FEP 1341 (S.D. Fla. 1995) (female employee who expressed reluctance to be involved in an investigation of sexual harassment and requested that the company not proceed with investigation not victim of hostile work environment); Stoeckel v. Environmental Management Sys., Inc., 882 F. Supp. 1106, 1114–15, 67 FEP 1716 (D.D.C. 1995) (no hostile work environment where plaintiff did not complain to anyone until four months after incidents commenced).

[59]Balletti v. Sun-Sentinel Co., 909 F. Supp. 1539, 1548, 73 FEP 1341 (S.D. Fla. 1995) (female employee who physically assaulted a male co-worker by ripping and then attempting to pull down his pants not victim of sexually hostile environment).

[60]Sanfelice v. Dominick's Finer Foods, Inc., 899 F. Supp. 372, 376, 69 FEP 170 (N.D. Ill. 1995) (noting that "[o]n one side lie sexual assaults; other physical contact, whether amorous or hostile, for which there is no consent express or implied; uninvited sexual solicitations; intimidating words or acts; obscene language or gestures; pornographic pictures. . . . and [o]n the other side lies the occasional vulgar banter, tinged with sexual innuendo, of coarse or boorish workers").

[61]*See, e.g.,* Galloway v. General Motors Serv. Parts Operations, 78 F.3d 1164, 1168, 70 FEP 341 (7th Cir. 1996) (male co-worker's calling female employee "sick bitch" a number of times over period of four years in context of failed sexual relationship did not create hostile environment in violation of Title VII); DeAngelis v. El Paso Mun. Police Officers Ass'n, 51 F.3d 591, 595–96, 67 FEP 1250 (5th Cir.), *cert. denied,* 116 S. Ct. 473 (1995) (anonymous comments in police association newsletter directed toward female police officer not so severe or pervasive as to create hostile environment); Sink v. Knox County Hosp., 900 F. Supp. 1065, 1076, 70 FEP

is physical contact, however, a court is more likely to find harassment hostile and pervasive.[62] Courts are less likely to find the existence of a hostile environment where the complaining party was unaware of the offensive conduct at the time it was occurring. As one court stated, "incidents not known to an individual . . . [cannot] contribut[e] to the individual's subjective view of a hostile environment."[63] However, in certain situations, evidence of such incidents may be admissible.[64]

b. The Standard and Perspective for Evaluating the Conduct. One issue that continues to plague the courts has been the proper perspective from which to evaluate whether a work environment, objectively viewed, is hostile or abusive. Some courts have applied a reasonable woman standard.[65] Still others have applied a gender neutral reasonable person standard.[66] Many courts, however, have adopted a compromise test, focusing on the perspective

---

1560 (S.D. Ind. 1995) (three incidents of conduct of sexual nature—one joke and two personal questions—do not rise to level of severe or pervasive conduct); Gearhart v. Eye Care Ctrs. of Am., Inc., 888 F. Supp. 814, 825 (S.D. Tex. 1995) (allegations of inappropriate comments and single touching of employee's breast do not rise to level of actionable claim for hostile work environment).

[62]*See, e.g.,* Curde v. Xytel Corp., 912 F. Supp. 335, 341 n.8, 71 FEP 843 (N.D. Ill. 1995) (existence of physical contact between co-workers as well as threatening nature of co-workers' remarks may establish hostile work environment); Sanfelice v. Dominick's Finer Foods, Inc., 899 F. Supp. 372, 376, 69 FEP 170 (N.D. Ill. 1995) (plaintiff's allegations that supervisor touched her on numerous occasions, even after it was made known to him that this was unwelcome, sufficient to support claim of sexual harassment); Shaw v. Mellon Bank, N.A., 69 FEP 550, 553 (W.D. Pa. 1995) (allegations that supervisor touched plaintiff on many occasions go beyond mere isolated incidents of vulgarity and crude banter and are sufficient to create genuine issue of material fact).

[63]Liberti v. Walt Disney World Co., 912 F. Supp. 1494, 1504–05 (M.D. Fla. 1995) (employees claimed that employer had failed to warn them about, or asked them to stop, peeping at and videotaping employees in dressing room and restroom).

[64]*Id.* (employees who learned after the fact of employee who had been peeping and videotaping them could use this knowledge as basis for feelings that hostile work environment existed, when it was clear that employee was not only individual engaging in these activities).

[65]*See, e.g.,* Fred v. Wackenhut Corp., 860 F. Supp. 1401, 1404, 73 FEP 1721 (D. Neb. 1994) (appropriate standard when evaluating evidence in hostile environment litigation is that of reasonable woman under similar circumstances), *aff'd,* 53 F.3d 335 (8th Cir.), *cert. denied,* 116 S. Ct. 190 (1995).

[66]*See, e.g.,* DeAngelis v. El Paso Mun. Police Officers Ass'n, 51 F.3d 591, 594, 67 FEP 1250 (5th Cir.), *cert. denied,* 116 S. Ct. 473 (1995) (standard is objective one, not "reasonable woman"); Simon v. Morehouse Sch. of Med., 908 F. Supp. 959, 969 n.11 (N.D. Ga. 1995) (court infers from Supreme Court's use of term "reasonable person" that standard does not take into account unique attributes and perspectives of women in workplace); Easton v. Crossland Mortgage Corp., 905 F. Supp.

of a reasonable person in the plaintiff's position, to determine if a work environment is hostile or abusive.[67] The Supreme Court has recently emphasized that the inquiry requires careful consideration of the social context of the workplace, including the constellation of surrounding circumstances, expectations, and relationships.[68]

It remains the case that whatever the perspective, courts regularly are called upon, in the context of summary judgment motions, to determine whether the plaintiff's allegations are sufficient, as a matter of law, to raise a fact issue as to the existence of a hostile environment.[69]

1368, 1377, 70 FEP 597 (C.D. Cal. 1995) (inquiry is whether "reasonable person" would find circumstances pervasive), *rev'd on other grounds,* 114 F.3d 979, 73 FEP 1885 (9th Cir. 1997); Fernot v. Crafts Inn, Inc., 895 F. Supp. 668, 677 (D. Vt. 1995) (requisite standard is what reasonable person would find hostile or abusive).

[67]*E.g.,* King v. Frazier, 77 F.3d 1361, 1363, 73 FEP 875 (Fed. Cir.) (sexual harassment must be judged from perspective of one being harassed), *cert. denied,* 117 S. Ct. 62 (1996); Fuller v. City of Oakland, 47 F.3d 1522, 1527, 67 FEP 153 (9th Cir. 1995) (whether workplace is objectively hostile to be determined from perspective of reasonable person with same fundamental characteristics); Ellerth v. Burlington Indus., Inc., 912 F. Supp. 1101, 1110–11, 70 FEP 229 (N.D. Ill. 1996) (objective viewpoint test examines likely impact on reasonable person in plaintiff's position), *aff'd in part, rev'd in part on other grounds,* 123 F.3d 490, 74 FEP 1138 (7th Cir. 1997), *rev'd on other grounds,* 1998 U.S. LEXIS 4217 (June 26, 1998); Zorn v. Helene Curtis, Inc., 903 F. Supp. 1226, 1240, 70 FEP 371 (N.D. Ill. 1995) (under objective test, court must consider effect similar conduct would have had on reasonable person in plaintiff's position); Sink v. Knox County Hosp., 900 F. Supp. 1065, 1076, 70 FEP 1560 (S.D. Ind. 1995) (examining whether environment perceived as abusive by a reasonable person in plaintiff's position); Anthony v. County of Sacramento, 898 F. Supp. 1435, 1447, 68 FEP 1837 (E.D. Cal. 1995) (objective hostility determined from perspective of reasonable person with same fundamental characteristics as plaintiff); Bottomly v. Leucadia Nat'l, 163 F.R.D. 617, 620 (D. Utah 1995) (conduct constituting sexual harassment must meet objective reasonable woman or man standard and be considered from the perspective of a reasonable person in plaintiff's position).

[68]Oncale v. Sundowner Offshore Servs., Inc., 1998 WL 88039, at *4, 76 FEP 221 (U.S. Mar. 4, 1998).

[69]Summary judgment granted: Gross v. Burggraf Constr. Co., 53 F.3d 1531, 1539, 68 FEP 88 (10th Cir. 1995) (single statement insufficient to establish gender discrimination); DeAngelis v. El Paso Mun. Police Officers Ass'n, 51 F.3d 591, 596, 67 FEP 1250 (5th Cir.), *cert. denied,* 116 S. Ct. 473 (1995) (anonymous comments in police association newspaper directed toward female officers not sufficient to create hostile environment); Callanan v. Runyun, 903 F. Supp. 1285, 1297–98 (D. Minn. 1994) (threatening phone call, critical poster, posting of pornographic photographs, and calling employee names not so serious and pervasive for reasonable person to conclude that workplace was hostile), *aff'd,* 75 F.3d 1293 (8th Cir. 1996); Ascolese v. Southeastern Pa. Transp. Auth., 902 F. Supp. 533, 544 (single conversation with supervisor and delay of weeks in receiving light duty not sufficient to satisfy standard for hostile or abusive environment), *on reconsideration,* 925 F. Supp. 351, 72

FEP 1027 (E.D. Pa. 1996); Sink v. Knox County Hosp., 900 F. Supp. 1065, 1075, 70 FEP 1560 (S.D. Ind. 1995) (three incidents of sexual nature—one joke and two personal questions during ride home—do not rise to necessary level of severity or pervasiveness); Keenan v. Allan, 889 F. Supp. 1320, 1375 (E.D. Wash. 1995) (infrequent comments that did not include profanity, threats, sexual references, or body part descriptions cannot make pervasive environment of sexual hostility or abuse), *aff'd,* 91 F.3d 1275 (9th Cir. 1996); Gearhart v. Eye Care Ctrs. of Am., Inc., 888 F. Supp. 814, 825 (S.D. Tex. 1995) (conduct that included numerous sexual comments and one inappropriate touching did not rise to level of actionable claim for hostile work environment sexual harassment); Fred v. Wackenhut Corp., 860 F. Supp. 1401, 1405, 73 FEP 1721 (D. Neb. 1994) (employee could not establish severe or pervasive harassment when only incident alleged was that employee was exposed to styrofoam cup containing sexually explicit language and illustrations), *aff'd,* 53 F.3d 335 (8th Cir.), *cert. denied,* 116 S. Ct. 190 (1995).

Summary judgment denied: Winsor v. Hinckley Dodge, Inc., 79 F.3d 996, 1000, 70 FEP 611 (10th Cir. 1996) (employee was victim of sexual harassment when co-workers called her sexually derogatory names and subjected her to other abuse); Fuller v. City of Oakland, 47 F.3d 1522, 1527–28, 67 FEP 992 (9th Cir. 1995) (female police officer subject to hostile work environment when ex-boyfriend who was also officer ran her off road, forcibly extracted unlisted phone number from her, and called her on numerous occasions); Hutchison v. Amateur Elec. Supply, Inc., 42 F.3d 1037, 1043, 66 FEP 1275 (7th Cir. 1994) (actionable hostile environment sexual harassment claim existed when male employer engaged in sexually explicit phone conversations with door open, regularly commented on female employee's appearance, and attempted physical contact with such employee); Dey v. Colt Constr. & Dev. Co., 28 F.3d 1446, 1454, 65 FEP 523 (7th Cir. 1994) (denying summary judgment in case in which plaintiff subjected to daily sexual comments and incident in elevator in which co-employee unzipped his pants); Hott v. VDO Yazaki Corp., 922 F. Supp. 1114, 1120, 70 FEP 1008 (W.D. Va. 1996) (plaintiff could prove case of sexual harassment when she had array of evidence both of unwelcome touching or fondling and of workplace pervaded with sexual slurs); Curde v. Xytel Corp., 912 F. Supp. 335, 340–41, 71 FEP 843 (N.D. Ill. 1995) (reasonable jury could conclude plaintiff suffered hostile environment when co-worker touched her in sexually offensive manner and made series of verbal attacks on her); Simon v. Morehouse Sch. of Med., 908 F. Supp. 959, 969–70 (N.D. Ga. 1995) (allegation of rape in workplace sufficiently severe to meet standard for establishing hostile environment sexual harassment); Ripberger v. Western Ohio Pizza, Inc., 908 F. Supp. 614, 619-20 (S.D. Ind. 1995) (isolated incident in which supervisor called female employee "whore" and "bitch," grabbed her, and shoved her did not constitute sexual harassment; however, conduct that included fondling of breasts, putting hands on employee's buttocks, putting dough down her blouse and pants, and making lewd comments met objective test for hostile environment); Fernot v. Crafts Inn, Inc., 895 F. Supp. 668, 677-78, 73 FEP 1635 (D. Vt. 1995) (persistent sexual advances and unwanted touching constitute hostile and abusive workplace); Redman v. Lima City Sch. Dist. Bd. of Educ., 889 F. Supp. 288, 293, 67 FEP 806 (N.D. Ohio 1995) (plaintiff can succeed on hostile environment claim when she was sexually assaulted, subject to sexual comments, and followed at work); Shaw v. Mellon Bank, 69 FEP 550, 553 (W.D. Pa. 1995) (allegations that supervisor touched plaintiff on many occasions sufficient to create genuine issue of material fact); Ulrich v. KMart Corp., 858 F. Supp. 1087, 1091, 74 FEP 565 (D. Kan. 1994) (conduct sufficiently severe to be hostile work environment when employee grabbed and fondled co-worker on more than one occasion), *aff'd,* 70 F.3d 1282 (10th Cir. 1995).

4. The Causal Connection: On the Basis of Sex

While most cases assume that gender-based epithets are motivated because of the plaintiff's sex, some courts have recently indicated a willingness to examine the speaker's purpose in employing such terms rather than assuming that the motivation is gender-based animus.[70]

Courts continue to struggle with the proper approach to analyzing the "even-handed harasser." The Seventh Circuit has recently had occasion to discuss this issue in *McDowell v. Cisneros*.[71] The court rejected the proposition that, because sexual harassment was directed against both a male and a female, there could be no discrimination based on sex.[72] The court concluded that such an argument interprets sex discrimination in too literal a fashion and fails to recognize that, although there is some homosexual harassment in the workplace and some women do harass men, sexual harassment is primarily a problem of men harassing women.[73] The court noted that it would be "exceedingly perverse" if a male worker could immunize his employer from liability by occasionally harassing a male co-worker, although his preferred targets were female.[74] Despite this, the same court later stated in *Pasqua v. Metropolitan Life Insurance Co.*[75] that harassment inflicted upon both males and females equally may not be actionable.[76] The court, quoting the Eleventh Circuit in *Henson v. City of Dundee*,[77] stated that a supervisor's sexual overtures to both men and women workers may not be actionable because the harassment is not based upon sex, since both men and women are "accorded like treatment."[78]

---

[70]*E.g.*, Galloway v. General Motors Serv. Parts Operations, 78 F.3d 1164, 1167–68, 70 FEP 341 (7th Cir. 1996) (use of the word "bitch" not necessarily motivated by gender; several possible motives explained speaker's reference to plaintiff as a "sick bitch"); Winsor v. Hinckley Dodge, Inc., 79 F.3d 996, 1000–01, 70 FEP 611 (10th Cir. 1996) (the term "floor whore" is sexually derogatory on its face; but "[t]he words 'honey' and 'baby,' although not overtly sexual, may be sexual in nature if their use occurs based only on the recipient's gender").

[71]84 F.3d 256, 70 FEP 1459 (7th Cir. 1996).

[72]*Id.* at 260.

[73]*Id.*

[74]*Id.*

[75]101 F.3d 514, 72 FEP 1158 (7th Cir. 1996).

[76]*Id.* at 517.

[77]682 F.2d 897, 904, 29 FEP 787 (11th Cir. 1982).

[78]Pasqua v. Metropolitan Life Ins. Co., 101 F.3d 514, 517, 72 FEP 1158 (7th Cir. 1996).

These two decisions suggest that the Seventh Circuit, at least, will look to the underlying harassment and determine whether it is truly gender motivated.[79]

Even where the motivation behind the harassment is gender neutral, sexual harassment may lie if the means by which the harassment is carried out is motivated by the recipient's sex[80] or exposes members of one sex to disadvantageous terms and conditions of employment when compared with members of the opposite sex.[81]

The Supreme Court recently resolved one of the most vexing issues concerning the causal connection between harassment and the victim's gender: the question of same-sex sexual harassment. In *Oncale v. Sundowner Offshore Services, Inc.*,[82] the Court held that Title VII prohibits hostile environment sexual harassment regardless of whether the harasser and victim are of the opposite or same gender. The Court opined that the proper inquiry is whether the harassment occurs "because of sex."[83]

5. Employer Responsibility

a. Employer Liability for Hostile Environment Harassment by Supervisors. Two recent Supreme Court decisions have cleared up much of the confusion created by lower court decisions on the issue of employer liability for hostile environment sexual harassment. In *Burlington Industries, Inc. v. Ellerth*[84] and *Faragher v.*

---

[79]*See also* Ray v. Tandem Computer Corp., 63 F.3d 429, 435 n.19, 68 FEP 1338 (5th Cir. 1995) (noting that the plaintiff's claims of sex discrimination were "undermined by her statement that [the alleged harasser] was an even-handed harasser, treating all of his employees poorly").

[80]Winsor v. Hinckley Dodge, Inc., 79 F.3d 996, 1000, 70 FEP 611 (10th Cir. 1996) ("[E]ven if the motivation behind plaintiff's mistreatment was gender neutral . . . the manner in which her co-workers expressed their anger and jealously was not. Rather, plaintiff's co-workers often chose sexually harassing behavior [calling her a 'fucking bitch' and directing sexually crude depictions of a woman at plaintiff] to express their dislike of plaintiff, which would not have occurred if she were not a woman.").

[81]Gillming v. Simmons Indus., 91 F.3d 1168, 1171–72, 71 FEP 1016 (8th Cir. 1996) (affirming judgment in favor of employer, court stated that the acts supporting a hostile environment claim "need not be explicitly sexual in nature" if " 'members of one sex are exposed to disadvantageous terms or conditions of employment to which members of the other sex are not exposed' ") (citations omitted).

[82]1998 WL 88039, 76 FEP 221 (U.S. Mar. 4, 1998).

[83]*Id.* at *2.

[84]1998 U.S. LEXIS 4217 (June 26, 1998).

City of Boca Raton,[85] the Court definitively stated that a different standard of liability applies when a hostile environment is created by a supervisor with immediate (or successively higher) authority over the plaintiff, and that the employer is vicariously liable for such harassment, subject to the availability of an affirmative defense.[86] In detailed discussions of the agency principles applicable to employer liability for sexual harassment by supervisors, the Court rejected the theories of respondeat superior and apparent authority as potential bases for vicarious liability of the employer but adopted the theory that the employer may be liable when an supervisor is "aided in accomplishing the tort by the existence of the agency relation."[87] The Court relied upon the principle set forth in the *Restatement (Second) of Agency,* § 219(2)(d), which provides:

> (2) A master is not subject to liability for the torts of his servants acting outside the scope of their employment, unless . . . (d) the servant purported to act or to speak on behalf of the principal and there was reliance upon apparent authority, or he was aided in accomplishing the tort by the existence of the agency relation.[88]

The Supreme Court tempered the operation of this principle, which in theory could apply to make the employer liable for almost all instances of supervisory harassment,[89] by allowing employers an affirmative defense in cases of harassment by supervisors that do not result in any tangible adverse employment action.[90] Accordingly, the Court held:

---

[85]1998 U.S. LEXIS 4216 (June 26, 1998).

[86]Prior to the Supreme Court decisions, the majority of courts had continued to apply a negligence standard in evaluating an employer's liability for hostile environment sexual harassment, even when a supervisor's conduct was at issue. *See, e.g.,* Stacy v. Shoney's, Inc., 955 F. Supp. 751, 756 (E.D. Ky. 1997) (rejecting theory of respondeat superior as means of imputing liability to the employer and relying instead on a negligence theory); Andrade v. Mayfair Mgmt., Inc., 88 F.3d 258, 261–62, 71 FEP 192 (4th Cir. 1996) (holding that supervisor's conduct may be imputed to employer only if supervisor is proprietor, partner, or corporate officer; otherwise, employer liable only if it knew or should have known of harassment and failed to take prompt remedial action).

[87]*Ellerth,* 1998 U.S. LEXIS 4217, at *26–40; *Faragher,* 1998 U.S. LEXIS 4216, at *42–56.

[88]*Ellerth* at *30; *Faragher* at *49.

[89]In *Ellerth,* the Court noted that because "a supervisor's power and authority invests his or her harassing conduct with a particular threatening character," a supervisor is always aided in the harassment by the agency relationship, to some extent. *Ellerth* at *38.

[90]In adopting the affirmative defense, the Court relied upon its own holding in *Meritor Savings Bank, FSB v. Vinson,* 477 U.S. 57, 72 (1986) that agency principles

> An employer is subject to vicarious liability to a victimized employee for an actionable hostile environment created by a supervisor with immediate (or successively higher) authority over the employee. When no tangible employment action is taken, a defending employer may raise an affirmative defense to liability or damages, subject to proof by a preponderance of the evidence. . . . The defense comprises two necessary elements: (a) that the employer exercised reasonable care to prevent and correct promptly any sexually harassing behavior, and (b) that the plaintiff employee unreasonably failed to take advantage of any preventive or corrective opportunities provided by the employer or to avoid harm otherwise.[91]

The Court then went on to explain that an employer could satisfy the requirements of the affirmative defense by showing that it had disseminated an antiharassment policy with a complaint procedure and that the plaintiff employee unreasonably failed to utilize the complaint procedure.[92] The *Faragher* opinion also made clear that to be an effective shield against liability, the employer's complaint procedure must provide for bypassing the offending supervisor in instances where the supervisor himself (or herself) is the alleged harasser.[93] Finally, the Court emphasized that the affirmative defense is not available in cases where the supervisor's harassment culminates in a tangible employment action, such as discharge, demotion, or undesirable reassignment.[94]

The measure of adequate timeliness in an employer's response to a complaint of sexual harassment can vary depending upon the need for extensive investigation or the complexity of the employer's

---

constrain the imposition of vicarious liability in cases of supervisory harassment. *Ellerth* at *39; *Faragher* at *54 (noting that the definition of "employer" in Title VII includes any "agent" of an employer, and that such language places some limits on the acts of employees for which employers are responsible). The Court also invoked the policy considerations behind Title VII, which is "designed to encourage the creation of antiharassment policies and effective grievance mechanisms" and "to promote conciliation rather than litigation." *Ellerth* at *40; *accord Faragher* at *57.

[91]*Ellerth* at *41–42; *Faragher* at *59–60.
[92]*Ellerth* at *42; *Faragher* at *60.
[93]*Faragher* at *61–62. *See also* the discussion at Section IV.B.5.a.iii in the Main Edition. In the *Faragher* case itself, the Court ruled that although the defendant city would normally have had the opportunity to raise the affirmative defense, the facts in the record established that the city could not possibly prove the elements of the affirmative defense. The plaintiff, employed as a lifeguard by the city, had been sexually harassed by her supervisors. The city had an antiharassment policy in place, yet it never disseminated the policy to the lifeguards or made any effort to keep track of the conduct of supervisors. Moreover, the city's complaint procedure contained in the policy had no assurance that supervisors could be bypassed. *Faragher* at *61–62.
[94]*Ellerth* at *42; *Faragher* at 60.

organization. In *Smith v. St. Louis University*,[95] the Eighth Circuit held that the university's response to a sexual harassment complaint, having taken four months, was not immediate.[96] Therefore, a question of fact existed as to whether the university had sufficient justification for the delay. The court then noted that the need for multiple interviews or the fact that pertinent investigators were on vacation could provide sufficient justification for such a delay.[97] In *Waymire v. Harris County*,[98] the Fifth Circuit held that a three-month investigation did not preclude a finding that the response was prompt.[99] The court stated that the investigation was initiated immediately and, taking into consideration the employer's organizational structure, it proceeded in accordance with the organization's "lines of command."[100]

b. Employer Liability for Hostile Environment Harassment by Co-Workers. (i.) Notice to the employer. The Tenth Circuit has held that an employer may be on notice of an employee's harassment of a co-worker where the employer is aware of prior instances of harassment by the same individual of others, even if the plaintiff herself did not complain.[101] The extent and seriousness of the earlier harassment, as well as the similarity and temporal proximity to the later harassment, are factors in determining whether evidence of harassment of others may be received to prove notice. It has been held that where previous incidents of harassment were never brought to management's attention, however, the employer lacks notice even if the alleged perpetrator was regarded as a harasser by co-workers.[102] But the employer may be deemed to have knowledge of harassing conduct where the conduct is reported to

---

[95]109 F.3d 1261, 74 FEP 459 (8th Cir. 1997) (reversing and remanding the district court's grant of summary judgment in favor of the employer).

[96]*Id.* at 1265.

[97]*Id.*

[98]86 F.3d 424, 72 FEP 637 (5th Cir. 1996) (affirming the district court's grant of summary judgment in favor of the employer).

[99]*Id.* at 429.

[100]*Id.*

[101]Hirase-Doi v. U.S. West Communications, Inc., 61 F.3d 777, 783–84, 69 FEP 1745 (10th Cir. 1995).

[102]*Compare* Garcia v. ANR Freight Sys., Inc., 942 F. Supp. 351, 358 (N.D. Ohio 1996) (unreported internal sentiment did not provide employer with notice of misconduct) *with* Zimmerman v. Cook County Sheriff's Dep't, 96 F.3d 1017, 1018–19, 71 FEP 1537 (7th Cir. 1996) (sheer pervasiveness of harassment might support inference that employer must have known of it). Where the harassment is known only to the harasser and the victim, the victim herself must provide the employer with sufficient information to conclude that harassment has occurred. *Id.* (informing supervisor

supervisory personnel other than those specified in the employer's sexual harassment policy.[103]

(ii.) *The employer's remedial response.* Although what constitutes an adequate response to sexual harassment is a fact-specific inquiry, it has been held that the more severe and frequent the harassment, the less likely that a nonpunitive remedy will be deemed adequate.[104] Where the employer's prompt remedial response to complaints of harassment effectively ends the complained-of conduct, however, the response may protect the employer from liability even if a different response might have been more effective or more satisfactory to the victim.[105]

c. *Employer Liability for Hostile Environment Harassment by Nonemployees.* Several courts, following the EEOC Guidelines, have held employers liable for sexual harassment committed by

---

of unspecified personality conflict and requesting change in work assignment insufficient notice; employer not required to institute an "Orwellian program of continuous surveillance").

[103]Varner v. National Super Markets, Inc., 94 F.3d 1209, 1213–14, 71 FEP 1367 (8th Cir. 1996) (employer had knowledge of alleged sexual harassment of plaintiff by co-worker in light of her boyfriend's reporting of incidents to store manager, even though employer's sexual harassment policy provided that such incidents were to be reported to human resources department; employer's policy "in effect required [plaintiff's] supervisor to remain silent notwithstanding his knowledge of the incidents"), *cert. denied,* 117 S. Ct. 946 (1997).

[104]*E.g.,* Knabe v. Boury Corp., 114 F.3d 407, 413, 73 FEP 1877 (3d Cir. 1997) (warning to harasser that violations of sexual harassment policy could result in termination deemed adequate response where plaintiff failed to present evidence that it was not reasonably calculated to end the harassment); Mart v. Dr. Pepper Co., 923 F. Supp. 1380, 1388, 71 FEP 478 (D. Kan. 1996) (what is reasonable in terms of remedial action depends on the gravity of the alleged harassment).

[105]Spicer v. Virginia, 66 F.3d 705, 711, 69 FEP 1255 (4th Cir. 1995) (employer not required to make the most effective response possible; where employer's prompt response resulted in cessation of complained-of conduct, liability ceased); Knabe v. Boury Corp., 114 F.3d 407, 414, 73 FEP 1877 (3d Cir. 1997) (if remedial action selected by employer is adequate, aggrieved employee cannot object); Fleenor v. Hewitt Soap Co., 81 F.3d 48, 51, 70 FEP 737 (6th Cir.) (employer's response in reprimanding harassing co-worker insulated employer from liability where harassing conduct stopped), *cert. denied,* 117 S. Ct. 170 (1996); Hallberg v. Eat'n Park, 70 FEP 361 (W.D. Pa. 1996) (employer's warning to restaurant patron that further offensive behavior towards waitresses would not be tolerated was adequate response; employer not required immediately to ban patron from restaurant). Where the identify of the harasser is unknown, however, an employer may still avoid liability as long as it takes prompt remedial action, even if the harassment does not stop. *E.g.,* Hirras v. National R.R. Passenger Corp., 95 F.3d 396, 399–400, 72 FEP 454 (5th Cir. 1996) (per curium) (employer not liable for conduct of unidentified sexual harasser(s) who over a three-year period left threatening written messages and telephone calls and spray-painted graffiti on the employer's door; employer notified police, independently investigated incidents, and assured plaintiff that harasser would be fired if discovered).

nonemployees where the employer "knows or should have known of the [harassment by the nonemployee] and fails to take immediate and appropriate corrective action."[106]

V. CLAIMS BY THIRD PARTIES AND "REVERSE" CLAIMS BY THE HARASSER

B. Third-Party Claims Based on Implicit Quid Pro Quo Harassment

The prevailing rule regarding implicit quid pro quo harassment continues to be that preferential treatment of a single employee based on a consensual sexual relationship will not state a cause of action under Title VII.[107] However, where the employer

---

[106] *E.g.,* Folkerson v. Circus Circus Enters., Inc., 107 F.3d 754, 756, 73 FEP 219 (9th Cir. 1997) (employer may be liable for sexual harassment by private individual where employer ratifies or acquiesces in harassment by not taking immediate corrective action when it knew or should have known of conduct); Jarman v. City of Northlake, 950 F. Supp. 1375, 1378–79 (N.D. Ill. 1997) (city could be liable for elected official's harassment of city employee; city's five-month delay in acting after it learned of harassment prevented it from characterizing its response as "immediate"); Mart v. Dr. Pepper Co., 923 F. Supp. 1380, 1387–88, 71 FEP 478 (D. Kan. 1996) (soft drink manufacturer could be liable for conduct of employee of bottling company if it failed to end harassment after being made aware of it; granting soft drink manufacturer summary judgment where, upon learning of alleged harassment, it took prompt and effective remedial action); Hallberg v. Eat'n Park, 70 FEP 361 (W.D. Pa. 1996) (restaurant not liable for patron's harassment of waitress where it took prompt and appropriate remedial action); Menchaca v. Rose Records, Inc., 67 FEP 1334 (N.D. Ill. 1995) (holding that an employer may be held liable under Title VII for the acts of customers).

[107] *E.g.,* Becerra v. Dalton, 94 F.3d 145, 71 FEP 1236 (4th Cir. 1996) (adopting the holding set forth in *DeCintio v. Westchester County Med. Ctr.,* 807 F.2d 304, 42 FEP 921 (2d Cir. 1986), *cert. denied,* 484 U.S. 825 (1987) (in finding that preferential treatment of a lover does not constitute sexual harassment of other employees treated less favorably)), *cert. denied,* 117 S. Ct. 1087 (1997); O'Patka v. Menasha Corp., 878 F. Supp. 1202, 70 FEP 11 (E.D. Wis. 1995) (holding that a male employee failed to state a claim under Title VII where he alleged having been treated less favorably than a female who entered into a consensual sexual relationship with their supervisor and where the plaintiff did not contend that the employer was guilty of widespread favoritism for those who accept sexual advances); Thompson v. Olson, 866 F. Supp. 1267, 1272, 72 FEP 24 (D.N.D. 1994) (disparate treatment of male employee arising from a romantic relationship between a supervisory employee and a female employee preferentially treated is not a cognizable Title VII claim), *aff'd,* 56 F.3d 69, 72 FEP 96 (8th Cir. 1995). *See also* Taken v. Oklahoma Corp. Comm'n, 934 F. Supp. 1294, 1301, 75 FEP 475 (W.D. Okla. 1996) (African-American supervisor's promotion of African-American woman with whom he had had consensual relationship over white females was not actionable under Title VII as either race discrimination or quid pro quo sexual harassment), *aff'd,* 125 F.3d 1366, 75 FEP 480 (10th Cir. 1997).

follows a policy of promoting or otherwise treating favorably only those employees who submit to sexual advances, a claim for sexual harassment will lie.[108]

C. Third-Party Hostile Environment Claims

2. Third-Party Hostile Environment Claims Based on Underlying Consensual Conduct

As with quid pro quo claims, the general rule remains that consensual sexual relationships between employees are generally insufficient to create a hostile work environment.[109]

D. "Reverse" Harassment Claims

Claims made by alleged harassers have included sexual harassment,[110] discrimination,[111] ERISA,[112] intentional and negligent

---

[108]Hott v. VDO Yazaki Corp., 922 F. Supp. 1114, 1122–25, 70 FEP 1008 (W.D. Va. 1996) (denying summary judgment for employer on plaintiff's quid pro quo claim where plaintiff alleged that she was denied a promotion, vacation, and emergency leave after refusing to go out on a date with a supervisor, while other female employees received promotions after they dated or had sexual relationships with supervisors); Bonner v. Guccione, 68 FEP 47 (S.D.N.Y. 1995) (holding that plaintiff stated a quid pro quo claim based on allegations that employer followed a policy of promoting only those employees who provided sexual favors).

[109]*E.g.*, Becerra v. Dalton, 94 F.3d 145, 71 FEP 1236 (4th Cir. 1996) (hostile environment sexual harassment claim fails where based solely on fact that the plaintiff's supervisor was accepting sexual favors from another employee for preferential treatment), *cert. denied,* 117 S. Ct. 1087 (1997); Mathews v. City of La Verne, 73 FEP 908 (C.D. Cal. 1997) (dismissing plaintiff's hostile environment claim that was based on plaintiff being subjected to jokes and insults resulting from his wife's affairs with the plaintiff's supervisors); Keenan v. Allan, 889 F. Supp. 1320 (E.D. Wash. 1995) (granting summary judgment against plaintiff whose hostile environment claims were based primarily on the existence of a consensual affair between her supervisor and a co-worker and where the manifestations of the affair were too insignificant to create a hostile environment), *aff'd,* 91 F.3d 1275 (9th Cir. 1996).

[110]Duffy v. Leading Edge Prods., Inc., 44 F.3d 308, 67 FEP 97 (5th Cir. 1995); O'Patka v. Menasha Corp., 878 F. Supp. 1202, 70 FEP 11 (E.D. Wis. 1995).

[111]Haley v. Virginia Commonwealth Univ., 948 F. Supp. 573, 72 FEP 1518 (E.D. Va. 1996) (no viable sex discrimination claim by male sexual harasser who could not show that women accused of similar conduct were treated more favorably); Sanjurjo v. New York Univ. Med. Ctr., 72 FEP 1 (S.D.N.Y. 1996) (religious discrimination), *aff'd,* 122 F.3d 1057 (2d Cir. 1997); Williams v. General Mills, Inc., 926 F. Supp. 1367, 71 FEP 272 (N.D. Ill. 1996) (race discrimination); Godby v. Electrolux Corp., 66 FEP 1704 (N.D. Ga. 1994) (age discrimination), *aff'd,* 58 F.3d 641 (11th Cir. 1995), *cert. denied,* 116 S. Ct. 1352 (1996).

[112]Chalmers v. Quaker Oats Co., 61 F.3d 1340, 68 FEP 865 (7th Cir. 1995) (employer did not violate ERISA by refusing to pay severance benefits to terminated accused harasser).

infliction of emotional distress,[113] and defamation.[114] The general experience continues to be that judges and juries are less than sympathetic toward discharged harassers.[115]

---

[113]Freeman v. Bechtel Constr. Co., 87 F.3d 1029, 71 FEP 353 (8th Cir. 1996) (even if employer was suspicious of complainant's truthfulness, suspension of supervisors was not sufficiently outrageous to give rise to claim of intentional infliction of emotional distress); Tischmann v. ITT/Sheraton Corp., 882 F. Supp. 1358, 68 FEP 1665 (S.D.N.Y. 1995) (defendant granted summary judgment on negligent and intentional infliction of emotional distress claims).

[114]Tischmann v. ITT/Sheraton Corp., 882 F. Supp. 1358, 68 FEP 1665 (S.D.N.Y. 1995).

[115]Tischmann v. ITT/Sheraton Corp., 882 F. Supp. 1358, 68 FEP 1665 (S.D.N.Y. 1995) (employer granted summary judgment on discharged male's wrongful discharge in violation of public policy, breach of contract, and violation of the implied covenant of good faith and fair dealing claims); Evans v. Bally's Health & Tennis, Inc., 64 FEP 33 (D. Md. 1994) (falsely accused employee has no wrongful discharge in violation of public policy claim); Nadeau v. Imtec, Inc., 670 A.2d 841, 69 FEP 812 (Vt. 1995) (no wrongful discharge in breach of an implied contract claim because employer had just cause to terminate alleged harasser).

Chapter 21

DISCHARGE

II. Constructive Discharge

The courts continue to apply an objective, reasonable person test, i.e., whether working conditions are so intolerable that a reasonable person in the employee's position would have felt compelled to resign under the circumstances.[1] Some courts continue to require that the employee also prove the employer *deliberately* made working conditions intolerable with the intent to force the employee to resign.[2] Some of those courts, however, have held that "deliberateness"

---

[1]*E.g.,* Burks v. Oklahoma Publ'g Co., 81 F.3d 975, 978, 70 FEP 945 (10th Cir.) (requirement that employee show employer, by its illegal discriminatory acts, made working conditions so difficult that a reasonable person would feel compelled to resign also constitutes paradigmatic jury instruction in constructive discharge case; district court did not err in refusing employee's request for jury instruction that an employee is constructively discharged if employer's actions reasonably led employee to conclude she would be discharged if she did not resign), *cert. denied,* 117 S. Ct. 302 (1996); Humphreys v. Medical Towers, Ltd., 893 F. Supp. 672, 687 (S.D. Tex. 1995) (working conditions must be viewed objectively by examining employer-imposed conditions, not employee's state of mind, but employee need not show employer imposed intolerable conditions with specific intent to force employee to resign), *aff'd,* 100 F.3d 952 (5th Cir. 1996); Turner v. Anheuser-Busch, Inc., 876 P.2d 1022, 1027, 9 IER 1185 (Cal. 1994) (essence of test for "intolerable" or "aggravated" conditions is whether reasonable employee would feel compelled to resign; employee is protected from unreasonably harsh conditions but may not be unreasonably sensitive to work environment) (citing Goldsmith v. Mayor & City Council of Baltimore, 987 F.2d 1064, 1072 (4th Cir. 1993)).

[2]*E.g.,* Andrade v. Mayfair Management, Inc., 88 F.3d 258, 262, 71 FEP 192 (4th Cir. 1996) (constructive discharge requires hostile work environment plus showing of deliberateness of employer's actions and intolerability of working conditions; sexually harassed employee's claim properly dismissed on basis of undisputed evidence she did not think harassing supervisor wanted her to quit and she wanted her job held open but did not return to work because she did not have a babysitter); Swain v. Roadway Express, 71 FEP 71, 75 (D. Md. 1996) (because plaintiff did not show actions were intended to force her to quit, court did not address whether working conditions were intolerable); Bartges v. University of N.C. at Charlotte, 908 F. Supp. 1312, 1331, 70 FEP 1643 (W.D.N.C. 1995) (no constructive discharge where plaintiff made no showing her working conditions were intolerable or that university

may be proved so long as the employee's resignation was a "reasonably foreseeable consequence" of the employer's actions.[3]

Virtually all courts require that the employer have *notice* of the ostensibly intolerable conditions before a constructive discharge can occur.[4] The California Supreme Court rejected a "constructive knowledge" standard and required proof the employer had *actual notice* of the intolerable conditions.[5] Other courts have held knowledge of the intolerable conditions may be inferred if the problem was sufficiently pervasive.[6] The employee must give the employer the opportunity to take remedial action and may not quit once such action is commenced,[7] absent evidence it is

"deliberately created working conditions that were designed to force her out of the job"), *aff'd,* 94 F.3d 641 (4th Cir. 1996).

[3]Martin v. Cavalier Hotel Corp., 48 F.3d 1343, 1355, 67 FEP 300 (4th Cir. 1995) (even where supervisor would have preferred employee to remain so he could continue harassing her, reasonably foreseeable consequence that she would quit constitutes intent that she quit); Jenkins v. Wal-Mart Stores, Inc., 910 F. Supp. 1399, 1422 n.9, 71 FEP 387 (N.D. Iowa 1995) (demoted employee raised material fact questions whether a reasonable person would find conditions intolerable and whether employer either consciously meant to force employee to quit or could at least reasonably foresee his termination as a consequence of its actions).

[4]*E.g.,* Piantanida v. Wyman Ctr., Inc., 927 F. Supp. 1226, 1245 (E.D. Mo. 1996) (no constructive discharge of plaintiff who rejected entry-level position at reduced salary on her return from maternity leave for purely economic reasons after she investigated child care costs; she did not make employer aware lower salary would be insufficient to meet her expenses, and there was no evidence salary was offered with intent to force her to quit), *aff'd,* 116 F.3d 340, 74 FEP 97 (8th Cir. 1997); Easton v. Crossland Mortgage Corp., 905 F. Supp. 1368, 70 FEP 597 (C.D. Cal. 1995), *rev'd on other grounds,* 114 F.3d 979, 73 FEP 1885 (9th Cir. 1997) (no constructive discharge where employees never complained).

[5]Turner v. Anheuser-Busch, Inc., 876 P.2d. 1022, 1028, 9 IER 1185 (Cal. 1994) (constructive knowledge test does not further goal of ensuring corrective measures will be attempted before a lawsuit is required; employer must either deliberately create the conditions or know about them and fail to remedy the situation to force employee to resign).

[6]*See, e.g.,* Hirase-Doi v. U.S. West Communications, Inc., 61 F.3d 777, 784, 69 FEP 1745 (10th Cir. 1995) (adopting view that plaintiff may prove employer has knowledge of sexually hostile work environment by proving harassment was so pervasive that awareness may be inferred; employer's knowledge could be inferred where supervisor sexually harassed 8 to 10 different women during his three-month tenure); Turner v. Anheuser-Busch, Inc., 876 P.2d 1022, 1028, 9 IER 1185 (Cal. 1994) (actual knowledge of and failure to remedy intolerable conditions may constitute circumstantial evidence that employer deliberately forced employee to resign).

[7]*See, e.g.,* Andrade v. Mayfair Management, Inc., 88 F.3d 258, 261, 71 FEP 192 (4th Cir. 1996) (employer is liable for hostile work environment only if the employer

merely a "token" action and not intended to remedy the problem.[8]

Discrimination, even where it is proven, will not rise to the level of intolerable conditions required for a constructive discharge absent aggravating factors.[9] Moreover, an employee cannot simply

---

knew or should have known of the conduct and failed to take adequate remedial action); Buchanan v. Sherrill, 51 F.3d 227, 229, 67 FEP 713 (10th Cir. 1995) (plaintiff who complained of sexual harassment and discrimination based on workers' compensation claim was not constructively discharged when she quit after employer arranged to transfer her to another restaurant); Maher v. Associated Servs. for the Blind, 929 F. Supp. 809, 814, 70 FEP 1730 (E.D. Pa. 1996) (employee who alleged manager sexually harassed her, including hugging and kissing her on several occasions, was not constructively discharged where employer acted promptly to stop harassment when it became aware of manager's conduct), aff'd, 107 F.3d 862 (3d Cir. 1997); Alvey v. Rayovac Corp., 922 F. Supp. 1315, 1333, 70 FEP 1331 (W.D. Wis. 1996) (plaintiff had obligation to seek legal redress while remaining on the job) (citing Bailey v. Binyon, 583 F. Supp. 923, 929, 36 FEP 1236 (N.D. Ill. 1984)); Larkin v. Town of W. Hartford, 891 F. Supp. 719, 728–29 (D. Conn. 1995) (a reasonable employee will thoroughly explore alternative avenues before concluding resignation is the only option; alternatives include filing a grievance or threatening to quit if changes are not made), aff'd, 101 F.3d 109 (2d Cir. 1996); Stewart v. Weis Mkts., Inc., 890 F. Supp. 382, 394, 72 FEP 259 (M.D. Pa. 1995) (although formal notice to employer of harassment is not required to maintain a case of constructive discharge under Title VII, where sexually related conduct ceased after plaintiff complained to harasser's supervisor, and plaintiff gave employer no opportunity to address perceived retaliation by former harasser and rejected proposed transfer, plaintiff did not establish requisite elements of constructive discharge); Bivins v. Jeffers Vet Supply, 873 F. Supp. 1500, 1509, 75 FEP 776 (M.D. Ala. 1994) (Title VII does not create a cause of action for constructive discharge where "employee assumes the worst and resigns before management is given a chance to rectify the situation"), aff'd, 58 F.3d 640 (11th Cir. 1995). But cf. Virgo v. Riviera Beach Assocs., Ltd., 30 F.3d 1350, 1363, 65 FEP 1317 (11th Cir. 1994) (filing of written complaint before resigning not required where no formal resolution procedure existed); Hart v. University Sys. of N.H., 938 F. Supp. 104, 108–09, 71 FEP 503 (D.N.H. 1996) (unnecessary for plaintiff to pursue legal redress while remaining in her job where supervisor suggested she resign and reduced her pay and work hours following her complaint about gender discrimination).

[8]Amirmokri v. Baltimore Gas & Elec. Co., 60 F.3d 1126, 1133, 68 FEP 809 (4th Cir. 1995) (employer's response must be reasonably calculated to end the intolerable environment); accord Curde v. Xytel Corp., 912 F. Supp. 335, 71 FEP 843, 848 (N.D. Ill. 1995) (plaintiff presented sufficient evidence to raise genuine dispute whether conditions and proposed remedial action forced her to resign, where employer offered to move her to new location in the office away from co-worker, who touched her in sexually offensive manner and was disciplined, but still in close proximity to him, and president told plaintiff if she could not work with co-worker she should resign).

[9]E.g., Davis v. Sheraton Soc'y Hill Hotel, 907 F. Supp. 896, 904, 71 FEP 1087 (E.D. Pa. 1995) (although male employee's sex discrimination claim survived summary judgment, constructive discharge claim did not; no reasonable jury could find

speculate as to an intolerable environment or an impending termination.[10] A plaintiff must establish a causal link between the alleged intolerable conditions and some illegal discrimination.[11]

---

conditions were so intolerable a reasonable person would have felt compelled to resign); Cargile v. Star Enter., 872 F. Supp. 1514, 1516 (M.D. La. 1994) (aggravating factors are required to show constructive discharge); Manos v. Bunzl-Papercraft, Inc., 69 FEP 1189, 1191–93 (N.D. Ill. 1995) (employee's allegations of aggravating circumstances were sufficient to create issues of fact for jury).

[10]*E.g.*, Burks v. Oklahoma Publ'g Co., 81 F.3d 975, 978, 70 FEP 945 (10th Cir.) (employee's evidence she got no answer when she asked supervisor about her future in the department and supervisor refused to authorize new business cards for her was insufficient to show she would be fired if she did not resign), *cert. denied*, 117 S. Ct. 302 (1996); Bradford v. Norfolk S. Corp., 54 F.3d 1412, 1420, 71 FEP 259 (8th Cir. 1995) (speculative considerations about working conditions employees expected to encounter if they accepted a transfer offer did not constitute evidence of constructive discharge where other employees did accept the transfer and there was no evidence employer intended to force the employees to quit); Cargile v. Star Enter., 872 F. Supp. 1514, 1517 (M.D. La. 1994) (not reasonable for an employee to resign before he even knows the duties of his new job; unsupported speculation employee would eventually be forced to retire was insufficient); Towle v. Flexel Corp., 867 F. Supp. 954, 959 (D. Kan. 1994) (employee who retired believing he was about to be terminated failed to establish constructive discharge, which would require that his decision be the product of an intolerable set of circumstances created by the employer), *aff'd*, 68 F.3d 484 (10th Cir. 1995); Dobson v. Unigraphic Color Corp., 71 FEP 1343, 1346 (M.D. Pa. 1994) (African-American employee who resigned when told she would be removed from switchboard and offered a position "in the back," which she inferred as demeaning, should have first determined whether new position would be satisfactory; reasonable employee will thoroughly explore alternatives before concluding resignation is only option), *aff'd*, 66 F.3d 310 (3d Cir. 1995).

[11]*See, e.g.*, Winsor v. Hinckley Dodge, Inc., 79 F.3d 996, 1002, 70 FEP 611 (10th Cir. 1996) (employee who was subjected to hostile environment sexual harassment was not constructively discharged where she left employment because of her personal relationship with former manager rather than the harassment); Bolden v. PRC, Inc., 43 F.3d 545, 552, 67 FEP 1790 (10th Cir. 1994) (employee who failed to show that taunting in workplace was caused by racial animus or that employee was singled out for abuse could not establish constructive discharge under Title VII), *cert. denied*, 116 S. Ct. 92, 70 FEP 578 (1995); Mayorga v. Donnelley Mktg., Inc., 70 FEP 670, 672 (N.D. Ill. 1996) (employee who resigned following maternity leave because employer denied her request to work at home, pursuant to internal guidelines, did not show she was compelled to resign for discriminatory reasons); Jenkins v. Wal-Mart Stores, Inc., 910 F. Supp. 1399, 1422 n.9, 71 FEP 387 (N.D. Iowa 1995) (seven-year African-American employee demoted from and then repeatedly passed over for promotion back to department manager in favor of white candidates, some of whom had serious performance problems, presented sufficient, albeit indirect, evidence of race discrimination to survive summary judgment); Eichenwald v. Krigel's, Inc., 908 F. Supp. 1531, 1540, 75 FEP 76 (D. Kan.

A work environment discriminatorily hostile to others can form the basis of a constructive discharge under some circumstances.[12]

Constructive discharge claims arising under the Americans with Disabilities Act may allege failure or inadequate efforts to accommodate disabilities; such claims fail, however, where the employee is held not "otherwise qualified" to perform essential functions of the job under the ADA.[13]

Sexual harassment, especially of the hostile environment variety, continues to be a leading area for constructive discharge claims.[14]

1995) (intolerable conditions must be the result of employer's illegal discriminatory acts, and plaintiff must show causal connection between her leaving and employer's Title VII violation); Long v. First Union Corp., 894 F. Supp. 933, 943–44, 68 FEP 917 (E.D. Va. 1995) (supervisor's refusal to adjust plaintiff's work schedule to accommodate her school schedule was not conclusively an adverse employment action in violation of Title VII, where plaintiff failed to establish connection to filing of discrimination charges), aff'd, 86 F.3d 1151, 71 FEP 736 (4th Cir. 1996); Medearis v. Old Cowtown Museum, 67 FEP 1694, 1699–1700 (D. Kan. 1995) (70-year-old employee who alleged he received unfair evaluation, excessive workload, undue criticism, and was threatened with being fired if he did not resign could present as evidence of causal nexus with age discrimination only "rumors" that employer intended to get rid of older workers and thus failed to prove a prima facie case).

[12]Chandler v. Fast Lane, Inc., 868 F. Supp. 1138, 1143–45, 66 FEP 675 (E.D. Ark. 1994) (white employee whose efforts to hire and promote African-American employees were thwarted by employer had standing under Title VII; it was "plainly foreseeable" an employee might choose to resign rather than acquiesce in or enforce employer's discriminatory and illegal practices).

[13]E.g., Suttles v. U.S. Postal Serv., 927 F. Supp. 990, 1011, 153 LRRM 2042 (S.D. Tex. 1996) (mail carrier with asthma and history of repeated hospitalizations, who was under doctor's orders to avoid exposure to dust, fumes, smoke, or pollen, was unable to perform essential functions of job even after Postal Service's efforts at accommodation; his own perception of aggravated, intolerable conditions did not support constructive discharge claim); Holbrook v. City of Alpharetta, 911 F. Supp. 1524, 1542, 6 AD 1394 (N.D. Ga. 1995) (police detective with severe visual impairment who could no longer perform essential functions of job but was retained at former salary was not a qualified individual with a disability under the Americans with Disabilities Act; city's failure to allow him to conduct field investigations would not have made a reasonable person feel compelled to resign), aff'd, 112 F.3d 1522, 6 AD 1409 (11th Cir. 1997).

[14]See, e.g., Virgo v. Riviera Beach Assocs., Ltd., 30 F.3d 1350, 1363, 65 FEP 1317 (11th Cir. 1994) (employee who was subjected to sexual advances did not need to file a written complaint before resigning after notifying several individuals by telephone, where no formal resolution procedure existed); Waag v. Thomas Pontiac, Buick, GMC, Inc., 930 F. Supp. 393, 406, 74 FEP 12 (D. Minn. 1996) (male car salesperson who was sexually harassed by male general sales manager over a period of two

Once the employer has effectively remedied the harassment, the reasonable person standard makes constructive discharge much more difficult to establish.[15]

Often whether the employer's actions constitute constructive discharge is a matter of degree. A mere demotion, especially without an accompanying reduction in salary, is unlikely to constitute constructive discharge[16]; however, a substantial demotion may suffice.[17] Likewise, although isolated acts of discrimination are insufficient,

---

months and complained to a vice president about manager's conduct alleged sufficient facts to show he was constructively discharged); Farris v. Board of County Comm'rs, 924 F. Supp. 1041, 1047 (D. Kan. 1996) (material fact issue whether reasonable person would have continued to work after reporting relationship with supervisor who subjected plaintiff to sexual harassment, where employer refused to place plaintiff in a position where she would have no contact with that supervisor); Simon v. Morehouse Sch. of Med., 908 F. Supp. 959, 971 (N.D. Ga. 1995) (clerical worker's allegations of sexual harassment by director and co-worker, including sexual assault by co-worker, created disputed issue of material fact whether her working conditions were so intolerable as to compel her to go on sick leave and resign); Hirase-Doi v. U.S. West Communications, Inc., 61 F.3d 777, 784, 69 FEP 1745 (10th Cir. 1995) (employer's knowledge of sexually hostile work environment could be inferred where supervisor sexually harassed 8 to 10 different women during his three-month tenure); Eichenwald v. Krigel's, Inc., 908 F. Supp. 1531, 1540, 75 FEP 76 (D. Kan. 1995) (three female plaintiffs were constructively discharged as a result of hostile work environment caused by pervasive sexual harassment by three different male supervisors).

[15]See, e.g., Clark v. Johnson Controls World Servs., Inc., 939 F. Supp. 884, 891, 74 FEP 814 (S.D. Ga. 1996) (following employer's investigation of sexual harassment complaint and discipline and eventual termination of harasser, female firefighter who resigned because she was afraid of co-workers and embarrassed that they knew about her complaint failed to establish constructive discharge), aff'd, 124 F.3d 222, 74 FEP 1792 (11th Cir. 1997); Mart v. Dr. Pepper Co., 923 F. Supp. 1380, 1390, 71 FEP 478 (D. Kan. 1996) (even assuming manager's language created hostile work environment, employer took prompt, adequate, and effective action upon learning of the alleged harassment, which had ceased when plaintiff resigned).

[16]E.g., Patton v. United Parcel Serv., Inc., 910 F. Supp. 1250, 1265, 69 FEP 1665 (S.D. Tex. 1995) (plaintiff's demotion of one level without change in salary did not create working conditions so difficult or unpleasant that he had no choice but to resign, where there was no evidence he was treated disrespectfully or asked to perform demeaning duties).

[17]E.g., Humphreys v. Medical Towers, Ltd., 893 F. Supp. 672, 687 (S.D. Tex. 1995) (employee's demotion, coupled with purported abusive behavior, including sexually oriented name-calling, directed against her by two male co-workers, raised issues of material fact precluding summary judgment on constructive discharge claim), aff'd, 100 F.3d 952 (5th Cir. 1996); Manos v. Bunzl-Papercraft, Inc., 69 FEP 1189, 1191–93 (N.D. Ill. 1995) (although plaintiff alleged only demotion as incident of discrimination, allegations of aggravating circumstances comprising loss of salary and responsibility and the fact she would be supervised by someone she trained and

evidence of continuous or pervasive discrimination can support a claim of constructive discharge.[18] The employer may not avoid a constructive discharge by offering choices between intolerable options,[19] nor by making misrepresentations as to benefits of early retirement or disadvantages of remaining employed[20] to persuade the employee to retire. A mere offer of early retirement, however, will not support a constructive discharge claim.[21]

---

supervised previously were sufficient to create issues of fact for jury); Flamand v. American Int'l Group, 876 F. Supp. 356, 369, 69 FEP 675 (D.P.R. 1994) (allegations of hostile actions such as deprivation of transfer or promotion, misrepresentations that no vacant positions were available, progressive reduction in responsibilities and functions, pressure to accept a position at lower pay, and denial of managerial flexibility raised genuine issue of material fact as to whether conditions had become so intolerable a reasonable person would feel compelled to resign rather than submit to "looming indignities").

[18]*E.g.,* Aman v. Cort Furniture Rental Corp., 85 F.3d 1074,1084, 70 FEP 1614 (3d Cir. 1996) (continuous discrimination during employment could support conclusion employee "simply had had enough"); Carr v. Allison Gas Turbine Div., General Motors Corp., 32 F.3d 1007, 1011–12, 65 FEP 688 (7th Cir. 1994) (to obtain remedy for constructive discharge, plaintiff only had to show sex discrimination was sufficiently serious to cause a reasonable person to quit; it need not rise to the level of "suffering"); Griswold v. Alabama Dep't of Indus. Relations, 903 F. Supp. 1492, 1496, 71 FEP 1336 (M.D. Ala. 1995) (supervisors falsely lowered employee's performance appraisals and ridiculed her in front of peers because of age-based animus); Flavel v. Svedala Indus., 868 F. Supp. 1422, 70 FEP 1088 (E.D. Wis. 1994) (where new general manager decided to replace plaintiff before ever giving him a performance review, demoted him, suggested he consider retirement, and forced him to report to known abusive manager, reasonable jury could conclude he was forced out on the basis of age).

[19]*See, e.g.,* Rollison v. Gwinnett County, 865 F. Supp. 1564, 1570, 7 AD 1355 (N.D. Ga. 1994) (material issue of fact existed as to whether alcoholic police officer was constructively discharged when he was offered choice between recommendation for termination and voluntary resignation).

[20]Maez v. Mountain States Tel. & Tel., Inc., 54 F.3d 1488, 1502–03, 19 EBC 1283 (10th Cir. 1995) (plaintiffs sufficiently pled constructive discharge under ERISA by alleging employer fraudulently induced them into quitting by deceiving them about the costs and benefits of accepting early retirement to prevent them from attaining additional pension rights).

[21]*See, e.g.,* Parker v. Chrysler Corp., 929 F. Supp. 162, 166–67 (S.D.N.Y. 1996) (African-American employee who voluntarily signed early retirement plan document after discussing it with family members and other employees and being "aggressively encouraged" to sign it by his supervisors did not establish duress or coercion required to prevail on claim of constructive discharge); *cf.* Smith v. World Ins. Co., 38 F.3d 1456, 1461, 66 FEP 13 (8th Cir. 1994) (employer's offer of early retirement constituted a constructive discharge when the choice presented to the employee was essentially either early retirement or continuing to work under intolerable conditions, consisting of employer's threats of termination without benefits).

Generally, a failure to promote will not constitute constructive discharge,[22] nor will a change in job duties,[23] a transfer,[24] a

---

[22] *E.g.,* Tidwell v. Meyer's Bakeries, Inc., 93 F.3d 490, 71 FEP 1284 (8th Cir. 1996) (alleged denial of promotion insufficient to establish constructive discharge); Hartsel v. Keys, 87 F.3d 795, 800, 72 FEP 951 (6th Cir. 1996) (failure to promote city employee to what she perceived as her rightful position did not constitute constructive discharge where no other evidence was offered to show she was driven out of prior position), *cert. denied,* 117 S. Ct. 683, 72 FEP 1504 (1997); Schnidrig v. Columbia Mach., Inc., 80 F.3d 1406, 1412, 71 FEP 1763 (9th Cir. 1996) (employee who was passed over for presidency of closely held company in favor of younger applicant failed to establish claim for constructive discharge where he was not demoted, did not receive a cut in pay, was not encouraged to resign or retire, and was not disciplined), *cert. denied,* 117 S. Ct. 295, 71 FEP 1888 (1996); Riley v. Technical & Management Servs. Corp., 872 F. Supp. 1454, 1461, 66 FEP 1643 (D. Md. 1995) (employee's own view of her qualifications irrelevant where employer promoted a male employee to position for which plaintiff believed herself better qualified), *aff'd,* 79 F.3d 1141, 70 FEP 832 (4th Cir. 1996); Bartges v. University of N.C. at Charlotte, 908 F. Supp. 1312, 1331, 70 FEP 1643 (W.D.N.C. 1995) (part-time basketball coach not subjected to constructive discharge when university made the position full time and placed her in another part-time coaching position), *aff'd,* 94 F.3d 641 (4th Cir. 1996); Doyle v. Sentry Ins., 877 F. Supp. 1002, 1007, 67 FEP 484 (E.D. Va. 1995) (employee who resigned after filing EEOC charge alleging only failure to promote could not claim discriminatory discharge; general allegations to EEOC of discrimination were "wholly insufficient to support a Title VII constructive discharge complaint"); *cf.* Minetos v. City Univ. of N.Y., 875 F. Supp. 1046, 1052, 68 FEP 355 (S.D.N.Y. 1995) (Hispanic secretary who was denied promotion in spite of her seniority and college's customary promotion of most senior office assistant to head secretary presented issue of fact as to constructive discharge by evidence that two music professors used racial slurs in her presence and told her she was too old for the job).

[23] *E.g.,* Greenberg v. Union Camp Corp., 48 F.3d 22, 27, 67 FEP 120 (1st Cir. 1995) (employee who was required to spend two additional days a week (total of five) making sales calls, in territory he originally voluntarily accepted was not constructively discharged); Mayberry v. Endocrinology-Diabetes Assoc., 926 F. Supp. 1315, 1325 (M.D. Tenn. 1996) (half-hour change in work shift that interfered with plaintiff's family commitments constituted neither pregnancy discrimination nor constructive discharge); Cargile v. Star Enter., 872 F. Supp. 1514, 1516 (M.D. La. 1994) (mere change of position, without more, will not support claim of constructive discharge, even if change in job assignments are based on discriminatory action); *but cf.* Schwarz v. Northwest Iowa Community College, 881 F. Supp. 1323, 1338, 4 AD 490 (N.D. Iowa 1995) (college not entitled to summary judgment against library employee with "night blindness" who resigned after she was reassigned to evening hours, where reasons for the change were in dispute as were the nature and extent of plaintiff's vision problems and the level of hardship on the college to accommodate her restrictions and plaintiff alleged employer "knew of and intentionally exploited" her vision problems to force her to quit).

[24] *E.g.,* Tidwell v. Meyer's Bakers, Inc., 93 F.3d 490, 71 FEP 1284 (8th Cir. 1996) (transfer to second shift did not support constructive discharge claim); Mintzmyer v. Department of the Interior, 84 F.3d 419, 424 (D.C. Cir. 1996) (national park service regional director who was transferred from Denver to Philadelphia could not

change in compensation or benefits,[25] criticism,[26] or pressure from a supervisor.[27] Quitting to accept another job strongly militates against a finding of constructive discharge.[28]

---

show subsequent retirement was constructive discharge based on age and sex discrimination); Rivers v. Northwest Airlines, Inc., 71 FEP 1217, 1218–19 (E.D. Mo.) (offer of job in Chicago office at same salary as alternative to severance upon closure of St. Louis office would not constitute intolerable conditions to reasonable person), aff'd, 72 F.3d 133, 72 FEP 1280 (8th Cir. 1995).

[25]E.g., Allen v. Bridgestone/Firestone, Inc., 81 F.3d 793, 797, 70 FEP 942 (8th Cir. 1996) (reduction in pay was not constructive discharge where employer simply eliminated employee's overtime workload and other objectionable actions by employer pertained not only to plaintiff but to other employees as well); Blistein v. St. John's College, 74 F.3d 1459, 1469, 69 FEP 1310 (4th Cir. 1996) (withdrawal of gratuitous postretirement health benefits cannot make continued employment so intolerable that employee would be compelled to resign); West v. Marion Merrell Dow, Inc., 54 F.3d 493, 497, 67 FEP 1209 (8th Cir. 1995) (employee's unreasonable refusal to accept employer's offer to accommodate her request to relocate, after promised position with employer in another city was revoked, precluded a claim of constructive discharge where employer made efforts to place employee in lower-level jobs at same compensation and she declined all alternatives); King v. AC & R Adver., 65 F.3d 764, 768, 68 FEP 1234 (9th Cir. 1995) (employee's decision to resign was unreasonable as matter of law where his status changed to "at will," his managerial duties were reduced, his compensation was restructured, reduced from $235,000 to $175,000, and bonus program was reduced); Ulrich v. KMart Corp., 858 F. Supp. 1087, 1093, 74 FEP 565 (D. Kan. 1994) (employee who returned to lay-away position following leave of absence during which her harasser was terminated, and who was given occasional duties as door greeter with no reduction in pay, was not constructively discharged), aff'd, 70 F.3d 1282, 74 FEP 1792 (10th Cir. 1995).

[26]E.g., Weeks v. Samsung Heavy Indus. Co., 933 F. Supp. 711, 71 FEP 920 (N.D. Ill. 1996) (two reprimands were insufficient to show retaliatory constructive discharge, where plaintiff admitted the conduct leading to one reprimand), aff'd, 126 F.3d 926, 74 FEP 1776 (7th Cir. 1997); Riley v. Technical & Management Servs. Corp., 872 F. Supp. 1454, 1462, 66 FEP 1643 (D. Md. 1995) (employee failed to show intolerable working conditions, where supervisors unfairly criticized her attire and work habits), aff'd, 79 F.3d 1411, 70 FEP 832 (4th Cir. 1996).

[27]Aikens v. Banana Republic, Inc., 877 F. Supp. 1031, 1039, 4 AD 283 (S.D. Tex. 1995) ("pressure" and "nitpicking" from supervisor did not establish intolerable working conditions).

[28]See, e.g., Galarraga v. Marriott Employees FCU, 70 FEP 1605, 1614 (D. Md. 1996) (where plaintiff began work at another credit union three days after leaving, court was "led to the inescapable conclusion that Plaintiff did not leave because his working conditions were intolerable"); Jimoh v. Ernst & Young, 908 F. Supp. 220, 226–27 (S.D.N.Y. 1995) (employee who resigned to take a "better opportunity" after employer's failure to promote him and issuance of disciplinary warnings did not raise a triable issue of fact where alleged instances were business decisions that did not rise to level of "aggravating factors" under the law); Sims v. Brown & Root Indus. Servs., Inc., 889 F. Supp. 920, 931, 70 FEP 501 (W.D. La. 1995) (no constructive discharge of employee who resigned 70 days after harassing supervisor was terminated, never complained of further problems, had secured other employment, and

III. Disparate Treatment Discharge Cases

A. The Allocation of Proof

This topic is covered for disparate treatment cases generally in Chapter 2 (Disparate Treatment) of the Main Edition and this supplement.

B. The Plaintiff's Prima Facie Case

In order for a plaintiff to establish that he or she is qualified for the position from which he or she was discharged, the plaintiff need not show that his or her performance was superior.[29]

In reduction-in-force cases, courts continue to hold that a plaintiff may establish a prima facie case without showing that he or she was replaced by someone outside the protected group.[30]

After *O'Connor v. Consolidated Coin Caterers Corp.*,[31] ADEA plaintiffs must show they were replaced by a person "substantially younger," regardless of whether the replacement is outside the protected age group.

---

presented no credible evidence conditions were so intolerable she was forced to resign), *aff'd,* 78 F.3d 581 (5th Cir.), *cert. denied,* 117 S. Ct. 68 (1996); Hogue v. MQS Inspection, Inc., 875 F. Supp. 714, 723–24, 3 AD 1793 (D. Colo. 1995) (no constructive discharge where employee returned to work after he was fired in retaliation for filing EEOC complaint based on failure to accommodate his disabilities, then worked five months before leaving to take a new job but alleged no discriminatory acts following return to work, testified he was "treated fairly" during that time, and thought about new job offer for a week and a half before resigning).

[29]de la Cruz v. New York City Human Resources Admin. Dep't of Social Servs., 82 F.3d 16, 20, 70 FEP 893 (2d Cir. 1996) (in order to establish prima facie case plaintiff did not need to show that his performance was superior; proof needed to establish prima facie case is "low").

[30]Brown v. CSC Logic, Inc., 82 F.3d 651, 654, 70 FED 1273 (5th Cir. 1996) (in age cases, prima facie case can be established if plaintiff shows that he "was otherwise discharged because of his age").

[31]517 U.S. 308, 70 FEP 486 (1996).

Part 7

Union and Employment Agency Respondents

Chapter 22

UNIONS

I. A Union's Liability for Its Own Discrimination

A. Liability of a Union in Its Role as Employer

To be held liable under Title VII or the ADEA for discrimination in its role as an employer, a union must have the minimum number of employees necessary to meet the statutory definition of an employer.[1] Nonofficer members of a union's board who perform no traditional employee duties are not employees under Title VII.[2]

In an action brought under the ADEA, the Ninth Circuit rejected the argument that a local union and its international be treated as a single entity for determining the requisite number of employees.[3] In doing so, the court applied a four-part test used to determine whether two employing entities constitute a single employer for purposes of Title VII.[4] Similarly, a federal district court concluded that persons employed by an apprentice training fund and a local union's parent international could not be counted for the purpose of determining whether the local had a sufficient number of employees to be a covered employer under Title VII.[5]

In what it called a case of first impression, the Ninth Circuit held that a union is not subject to suit by one of its employees for

---

[1]Yerdon v. Henry, 91 F.3d 370, 375–77, 71 FEP 1733, 1735–37 (2d Cir. 1996) (union sued as an employer under Title VII must meet statutory definition of employer and have 15 or more employees); Herman v. Carpenters Local 971, 60 F.3d 1375, 1384, 68 FEP 181, 186–87 (9th Cir. 1995) (union sued as an employer under ADEA must have 20 or more employees).
[2]Kern v. City of Rochester, 93 F.3d 38, 47, 71 FEP 1391, 1398 (2d Cir. 1996), cert. denied, 117 S. Ct. 1335 (1997).
[3]Herman v. Carpenters Local 971, 60 F.3d 1375, 68 FEP 181 (9th Cir. 1995).
[4]Id. at 1383 (four factors to be considered are: (1) interrelation of operations; (2) common management; (3) centralized control of labor relations; and, (4) common ownership or financial control).
[5]Shepherdson v. Local 401, 823 F. Supp. 1245, 1252–57, 66 FEP 476, 482–86 (E.D. Pa. 1993).

alleged disability discrimination under the Rehabilitation Act of 1973,[6] even though it benefitted from federal involvement in its certification as an exclusive bargaining agent, federally sponsored union apprenticeship programs, federal wage regulation protection, and its access to the services of the Federal Mediation and Conciliation Service.[7] The court would not equate these benefits to the federal financial assistance required to trigger Rehabilitation Act coverage.[8]

B. Liability of a Union in Its Role as Union

1. Membership

A union is subject to injunctions and remedial orders when it fails to file Form EEO-3 containing statistics on the race, color, national origin, and sex of members, persons referred, and apprentices.[9]

A union has been found to violate Title VII where its requirement that new union members be sponsored by present members operated to exclude minority members.[10]

2. Referrals

In individual disparate treatment cases, the *McDonnell Douglas-Burdine-Hicks* tripartite allocation of proof continues to apply.[11]

---

[6] 29 U.S.C. § 794.

[7] Herman v. Carpenters Local 971, 60 F.3d 1375, 1381–83, 68 FEP 181, 184–86 (9th Cir. 1995) (allowing the case to proceed, however, on the claim that her union-employer breached a collective bargaining agreement).

[8] *Id.*

[9] EEOC v. Laborers' Local 100, 49 F.3d 304, 307, 67 FEP 205, 207–08 (7th Cir. 1995) (affirming a remedial order requiring more than the minimum regulatory requirements).

[10] EEOC v. Steamship Clerks Local 1066, 48 F.3d 594, 607, 67 FEP 629, 631–33 (1st Cir.) (union had no African-American or Hispanic members when it adopted the sponsorship policy; court employed disparate impact approach), *cert. denied*, 116 S. Ct. 65 (1995).

[11] Dimitropoulos v. Painters Union Dist. Council 9, 893 F. Supp. 297, 299–300, 68 FEP 1070, 1071–72 (S.D.N.Y. 1995) (union's failure to refer protected-age member for work following his termination from employer and later expelling him from union for fighting does not rise to bias, despite his allegation that younger workers were referred on jobs, where he did not sign the "out-of-work" book to register his availability for work; elements of a prima facie case of alleged ADEA discrimination in referral are: (1) plaintiff is a member of a protected class; (2) plaintiff is qualified

4. Apprenticeship Programs

Courts have also applied the *McDonnell Douglas-Burdine-Hicks* allocation of proof in cases where an individual plaintiff claims to be the victim of disparate treatment in an apprenticeship program.[12]

Court-ordered affirmative action is permissible in the face of persistent or egregious discrimination, or where necessary to dissipate the lingering effects of pervasive discrimination.[13]

An apprenticeship program is not liable for the discriminatory conduct of a local union unless the plaintiff proves that the two entities have an actual agency relationship or constitute an "integrated enterprise."[14]

5. Duty of Fair Representation

a. Handling of Grievances. Union members who allege that their union fails to provide them with assistance and support in

---

for the jobs being referred, which includes being qualified under union's legitimate rules governing referrals; and (3) plaintiff was not referred for jobs consistent with union's legitimate rules or other younger members were referred inconsistent with those rules); Stair v. Lehigh Valley Carpenters Local 600, 66 FEP 1473, 1486–88 (E.D. Pa. 1993) (To establish a prima facie case of sex discrimination in the operation of a local union job referral system, female apprentice must show that: (1) she is female; (2) she was qualified for work referrals from the local; (3) despite her qualifications, the local did not refer her to work, or referred her to nonlocal contractors, or referred her to short-term jobs; and (4) following its failure to refer her to work, the local continued to refer other apprentices with her qualifications, or referred other apprentices to local contractors or to long-term jobs. Though female apprentice established a prima facie case, the local articulated legitimate nondiscriminatory reasons to rebut that case, and plaintiff failed to prove referral discrimination by a preponderance of the evidence.), *aff'd,* 43 F.3d 1463 (3d Cir. 1994).

[12]*Stair v. Lehigh Valley Carpenters,* 66 FEP at 1492 (joint apprenticeship committee did not discriminate against female apprentice when it disciplined her for accumulating more than three unexcused absences, where apprentice succeeded in establishing prima facie case but ultimately failed to prove that committee disciplined her more harshly than male apprentices with more than three unexcused absences); Smith v. Local 28, Sheet Metal Workers, 877 F. Supp. 165, 170–72, 148 LRRM 2856, 2858–60 (S.D.N.Y. 1995) (plaintiff failed to establish prima facie case that he had been prevented from advancing in the apprenticeship program, that he had not been paid correct amount of wages as an apprentice, and that defendants had appropriated certain annuity contributions during his apprenticeship), *aff'd,* 100 F.3d 943, 152 LRRM 2384 (2d Cir.), *cert. denied,* 117 S. Ct. 101 (1996).

[13]*See* Eldredge v. Carpenters 46 N. Cal. Counties JATC, 94 F.3d 1366, 1370, 71 FEP 1385, 1390 (9th Cir. 1996) (court ordered committee to refer one woman for every five referrals until 20% of apprentices were women), *cert. denied,* 117 S. Ct. 1470 (1997).

[14]*Stair v. Lehigh Valley Carpenters,* 66 FEP at 1490.

prosecuting grievances must set forth facts demonstrating that an impermissible discriminatory factor played a role in the manner in which the union prosecuted the grievance to prevail under Title VII. Dissatisfaction alone does not raise an inference of discrimination.[15]

The six-month statute of limitations for a claim against a labor union for breach of its duty of fair representation begins to accrue at the time that plaintiff knew or should have known that the union was withdrawing its grievance.[16]

b. Grievance Settlements. A settlement between the union and the employer of an individual's grievance based on claims

---

[15]Dimitropoulos v. Painters Union Dist. Council 9, 893 F. Supp. 297, 299–300, 68 FEP 1070, 1071–72 (S.D.N.Y. 1995) (union member alleging that union violated ADEA when, because of his age, it did not provide him with assistance and support and unlawfully sided with employer must set forth facts indicating that age played a role in the manner in which the union prosecuted his grievance; bald assertions will not withstand summary judgment); Sanders v. Bethlehem Steel Corp., 68 FEP 695, 700–01 (D. Md. 1995) (union granted summary judgment on female employee's claim that union steward discriminatorily refused to file a grievance on her behalf, despite a nexus between his statement that "there won't be a broad over top of me," and his refusal to file the grievance, where she did not refute the union's showing that it would have made the same decision not to process her grievance regardless of her sex), *aff'd,* 91 F.3d 133 (4th Cir. 1996); President v. Illinois Bell Tel. Co., 865 F. Supp. 1279, 1291, 3 AD 1218, 1227 (N.D. Ill. 1994) (union entitled to summary judgment where plaintiff "offered no evidence whatever" that union's handling of his grievances was tainted by discriminatory animus); Thomas v. Rite Aid Corp., 147 LRRM 2886, 2890 (E.D. Pa. 1994) (court observed that "to establish a prima facie case of discrimination in the grievance process, plaintiff must produce evidence that: (1) she was a member of a protected class; (2) she was qualified to have the union represent her in a grievance process; (3) a grievance process was in place; and (4) similarly situated non-protected grievance filers were treated differently"; union granted summary judgment because plaintiff "failed to produce any evidence that similarly situated white grievance filers were treated differently"; nor did plaintiff provide any evidence for claim that local acquiesced in the employer's discrimination; record did not establish that employer actually engaged in discrimination or that union had a policy of rejecting grievances based on racial discrimination), *aff'd,* 68 F.3d 457, 150 LRRM 2575 (3d Cir. 1995); Edwards v. Nestle Beverage Co., 147 LRRM 2935, 2939 (E.D. La. 1993) (union granted summary judgment on claim that it violated its duty of fair representation in handling grievance/arbitration proceeding in which plaintiff charged employer with race and sex discrimination; court noted that "[p]laintiff's dissatisfaction with the outcome of the arbitration does not imply that Plaintiff was treated in an arbitrary, discriminatory or unfair manner. It is idle speculation to assume the result would have been different when Plaintiff fails to establish what he could have added to the case if he had been represented differently."), *aff'd,* 43 F.3d 669 (5th Cir. 1994).

[16]Frank v. New York State Elec. & Gas, 871 F. Supp. 167, 173, 69 FEP 711, 715 (W.D.N.Y. 1994).

of handicap discrimination did not preclude plaintiff's suit under Michigan's Handicapper's Civil Rights Act.[17] A union's duty of fair representation does not include pursuit of civil rights claims of its members that arise independent of the collective bargaining agreement.[18]

6. Failure to Accommodate

b. Disabilities. Notwithstanding the EEOC's view that it is not a defense under the ADA that a requested accommodation would violate a collective bargaining agreement, the Seventh Circuit held that the ADA does not require an employer and its union to make a "reasonable accommodation" that would violate a "bona fide" seniority system at the expense of other employees' rights under a collective bargaining agreement.[19] Thus, a union and employer were not *required* to transfer a plaintiff suffering from epilepsy to a position and shift assignment in violation of the seniority rights of other employees under the collective bargaining agreement, notwithstanding the fact that the collective bargaining agreement contained a provision allowing the union and the employer to agree to accommodations for disabled employees on a case-by-case basis.[20] Other circuits have reached the same result.[21]

---

[17]Florence v. Department of Social Servs., 544 N.W.2d 723, 725, 151 LRRM 2823, 2825 (Mich. Ct. App. 1996).
[18]*Id.*
[19]Eckles v. Consolidated Rail Corp., 94 F.3d 1041, 1051, 5 AD 1367, 1374–75 (7th Cir. 1996) (rejecting the EEOC's argument (as *amicus curiae*) that employers and unions have a duty to negotiate in good faith for variances from collectively bargained seniority rules where the only available effective accommodation contravenes these rules and the proposed accommodation will not unduly burden other employees), *cert. denied,* 117 S. Ct. 1318 (1997). *See* EEOC Technical Assistance Manual at III-25; 29 C.F.R. 1630.15(d); and ADA legislative history at H.R. REP. NO. 101-485 (II) at 63 (1990), saying "[t]he Committee also wishes to make clear the reassignment need only be to a vacant position—as 'bumping' another employee out of a position to create a vacancy is not required."
[20]*Id.*
[21]*See* Benson v. Northwest Airlines, Inc., 62 F.3d 1108, 1114, 4 AD 1234, 1238 (8th Cir. 1995) ("The ADA does not require that Northwest take action inconsistent with the contractual rights of other workers under a collective bargaining agreement."); Wooten v. Farmland Foods, 58 F.3d 382, 386, 4 AD 920, 923 (8th Cir. 1995) ("An employer is not required to make accommodations that would violate the rights of other employees."); Milton v. Scrivner, Inc., 53 F.3d 1118, 1125, 4 AD 432, 437 (10th Cir. 1995) ("Additionally, plaintiffs' collective bargaining agreement prohibits their transfer to any other job because plaintiffs lack the requisite seniority.");

7. Liability for the Acts of Union Agents

The courts continue to hold that a union is responsible for any discriminatory actions taken by its agents and officials, such as business agents.[22]

8. Liability of Regional and International Unions

It has been held that an international does not bear agency liability for the alleged discrimination of an affiliated local merely because the union constitution vests the international with certain broad regulatory powers over local unions, such as the power to revoke or suspend charters.[23]

II. JOINT UNION-EMPLOYER LIABILITY

A. Joint Liability for Discrimination Caused by the Provisions of a Collective Bargaining Agreement

Both an employer and a union may be sued where the plaintiff alleges that an early retirement provision in the collective bargaining agreement between the defendants violates the ADEA.[24]

Daugherty v. City of El Paso, 56 F.3d 695, 700, 4 AD 993, 997 (5th Cir. 1995) ("[W]e do not read the ADA as requiring affirmative action in favor of individuals with disabilities, in the sense of requiring that disabled persons be given priority in hiring or reassignment over those who are not disabled."), *cert. denied,* 116 S. Ct. 1263 (1996).

[22]Johnson v. Teamsters Local 559, 67 FEP 1150, 1154 (D. Mass. 1995) (Applying agency principles, a union is responsible for the harassing acts of its agents and supervisory employees, even if the acts were not authorized by the union, where the union knew, or in the exercise of reasonable care should have known, of the alleged harassment. However, defendant union was granted summary judgment because it took prompt and sufficient remedial action.), *aff'd,* 102 F.3d 21, 153 LRRM 3031 (1st Cir. 1996); Stair v. Lehigh Valley Carpenters, 66 FEP at 1488–90 (E.D. Pa. 1993) (union liable under respondeat superior for an intimidating, offensive, and hostile work environment created when the local's officers and business agents purchased and distributed calendars featuring photos of nude and partially nude women), *aff'd,* 43 F.3d 1463 (3d Cir. 1994).

[23]Shepherdson v. Local 401, 823 F. Supp. 1245, 1256, 66 FEP 476, 484–85 (E.D. Pa. 1993).

[24]Lyon v. Ohio Educ. Ass'n & Professional Staff Union, 53 F.3d 135, 140, 67 FEP 1088, 1090–92 (6th Cir. 1995) (holding, however, that the district court properly entered summary judgment on behalf of both defendants because plaintiffs failed to establish a prima facie case that the provision violated the ADEA).

E. Procedural Issues in Cases of Joint Liability

1. Contribution

At least two district courts have held that the rationale in *Northwest Airlines, Inc. v. Transport Workers*,[25] precluding a losing party in a Title VII case from seeking contribution against an entity not properly part of the original action, applies equally to the ADA.[26]

2. Joinder of Unions as Co-Defendants in Suits Against Employers

Courts continue to hold that unions are not "necessary parties" in discrimination claims brought against the employer.[27]

An employer sued by an employee for alleged sexual harassment under Title VII was not allowed to pursue a third-party claim against the union on the theory that the union breached the labor contract's nondiscrimination provisions by permitting alleged harassment to continue.[28]

In *Gilmore v. Local 295, Teamsters*,[29] a federal district court dismissed Title VII claims against the defendant union where the plaintiff's underlying EEOC charge named only his employer as respondent. The court noted that: (1) the union was not included in the EEOC charge; (2) the union did not have an identity of interest or an agency relationship with the named employer, and, thus, a charge against the employer could not properly be considered a charge against the union; and (3) absent any reference to the union in the EEOC charge, the EEOC could not infer any collusion between the union and the employer. In these circumstances, the court concluded, "[to] require the Union to defend

---

[25] 451 U.S. 77, 96–97, 25 FEP 737, 744–45 (1981).
[26] Lane v. United States Steel, 871 F. Supp. 1434, 1436, 3 AD 1605, 1607 (N.D. Ala. 1994) (dismissing employer's third-party complaint against union in a case brought under both Title VII and ADA); Pattison v. Meijer, Inc., 897 F. Supp. 1002, 1009, 4 AD 997, 1001 (W.D. Mich. 1995) (rejecting claim of employer that union is a necessary party where the plaintiff-employee asserts no claim against union).
[27] Pattison v. Meijer, Inc., 897 F. Supp. at 1009, 4 AD at 1001 (case brought under ADA).
[28] Cole v. Appalachian Power Co., 67 FEP 1729, 1730–31 (S.D. W. Va. 1995) (no proof that the union directed, induced, authorized, or ratified any acts of harassment; creation of proper work environment is management responsibility).
[29] 798 F. Supp. 1030, 1038, 64 FEP 1187, 1192 (S.D.N.Y 1992), *aff'd*, 23 F.3d 396, 67 FEP 96 (2d Cir.), *cert. denied*, 513 U.S. 936, 72 FEP 320 (1994).

against plaintiff's claim would violate Title VII's scheme for providing notice to respondents."[30]

III. OTHER PROCEDURAL PROBLEMS INVOLVING THE ROLE OF UNIONS IN EMPLOYMENT DISCRIMINATION CASES

C. A Union as Intervenor

Intervention remains an important procedural device that may permit unions a voice in employment discrimination litigation affecting the interests of union members.[31]

---

[30]*Id.*
[31]*See* Vanguards of Cleveland v. City of Cleveland, 23 F.3d 1013, 64 FEP 1611 (6th Cir. 1994) (firefighters union sought unsuccessfully to overturn district court's approval of modification to consent decree).

Chapter 23

EMPLOYMENT AGENCIES

II. Definition of an Employment Agency

As stated in the Main Edition, Title VII does not require an employment agency to be of any particular size before subject matter jurisdiction attaches with respect to its activities as an employment agency.[1] However, when an employment agency is charged or sued with respect to its activities as an employer, subject matter jurisdiction only attaches if the employment agency satisfies the Title VII definition of employer,[2] including having the requisite number of employees.[3] If the employment agency is not a covered employer, dismissal for lack of subject matter jurisdiction is appropriate.[4]

---

[1] To be a covered employment agency, a person or entity must regularly undertake specified employment procurement activities with respect to a covered employer. 42 U.S.C. § 2000e(c). A person or entity that does not "regularly undertake" such activity is not a covered employment agency. *See, e.g.,* Moore v. Ford Motor Co., 901 F. Supp. 1293, 1297 (N.D. Ill. 1995) (dismissing plaintiff's ADEA claim premised on Ford's acting as an "employment agency" in connection with its failure to accept plaintiff, a nonemployee, into its Minority Dealer Training Program: "Even if such placements were considered acts of an employment agency (an unlikely conclusion), plaintiff has failed to produce any evidence that Ford 'regularly undertakes' such actions. There is no evidence that even one person was accepted into the Training Program during the relevant period alleged in the complaint.").

[2] 42 U.S.C. § 2000e(b).

[3] The workers assigned by a temporary employment agency count as employees of the agency for purposes of the statutory definition of employer only where appropriate under common-law agency principles. Kellam v. Snelling Personnel Servs., 866 F. Supp. 812, 814–16, 68 FEP 195 (D. Del. 1994) (court found that employment agency's roster of temporary workers were not to be counted as employees of the agency, stating that where a federal statute does not define "employee," the "Supreme Court has directed that the common-law principles of agency shall apply in determining who is an employee") (citing Nationwide Mut. Ins. Co. v. Darden, 503 U.S. 318, 322–25 (1992)), *aff'd without opinion,* 65 F.3d 162 (3d Cir. 1995). The hiring party's right to control the manner and means by which the work is accomplished is normally the most important of the factors to be considered. *Id.* at 815–16.

[4] Greenlees v. Eidenmuller Enters., 32 F.3d 197, 198–99, 66 FEP 457, 458–59 (5th Cir. 1994) (upholding dismissal of Title VII claim brought by employment

The statutory definitions of employment agency are broad. For example, a private association may be a statutory employment agency where it places association members into employment positions with employers.[5] On the other hand, the courts have recognized limits even where the person or entity is engaging in "employment agency" types of activities.[6]

III. UNLAWFUL PRACTICES

A. Initial Processing of Applicants

While it is unlawful for an employment agency to segregate or classify on the basis of protected characteristics, it is lawful to segregate or classify on the basis of characteristics that are not protected under the law. For example, in *McBride v. Lawstaf, Inc.*,[7] the court held that an employment agency's refusal to place applicants

---

agency's former placement specialist because agency employed fewer than 15 employees and rejecting the EEOC's position that an employment agency is covered by Title VII when acting in its capacity as an employer even if it does not meet the statutory definition of employer).

[5]Jones v. Southeast Alabama Baseball Umpires Ass'n, 864 F. Supp. 1135, 1137–38 (M.D. Ala. 1994) (factual issue exists as to whether baseball umpires' association is an employment agency under the ADA since it is unclear from the record whether the umpires whom the association procures for public high schools are employees of the association or are procured to be employees of the high schools; association would be an employment agency only if the latter were true).

[6]Blanciak v. Allegheny Ludlum Corp., 77 F.3d 690, 694–96, 70 FEP 27, 29–31 (3d Cir. 1996) (affirming dismissal of ADEA claim against Commonwealth of Pennsylvania because the ADEA's language "simply does not evince an unmistakably clear intention to abrogate the states' Eleventh Amendment immunity from suit while acting in their capacity as employment agencies under that act," whereas Congress did explicitly say that states, and political subdivisions and agencies thereof, could be liable for violations of the ADEA when acting as employers). *Cf.* § 502 of the ADA, 42 U.S.C. § 12202 ("A State shall not be immune under the eleventh amendment to the Constitution of the United States from an action in Federal or State court of competent jurisdiction for a violation of this chapter," indicating clear, broad waiver of states' sovereign immunity.); Title VII at 42 U.S.C. §§ 2000e(a), (c) (defining employment agencies to include "any person . . ." and specifically defining "person" to include "governments, governmental agencies . . .", waiving sovereign immunity of states when acting as employment agencies).

[7]1996 U.S. Dist. LEXIS 16190, at *6–7 (N.D. Ga. 1996), *magistrate's recommendation adopted,* 71 FEP 1758 (N.D. Ga. 1996).

having braided hair does not constitute an unlawful employment practice. "An all-braided hair style is an 'easily changed characteristic' and, even if socioculturally associated with a particular race or nationality, is not an impermissible basis for distinction in the application of employment practices by the employer." Rather, it is a policy that applies equally to members of all races, unlike "a policy prohibiting an 'Afro/bush' style, as the later [sic] is the 'product of natural hair growth,' and would more likely be considered violative of Title VII."[8]

B. Accepting Discriminatory Job Orders

Title VII's prohibition against employment agencies accepting job orders that discriminate on the basis of protected characteristics includes job orders that discriminate in favor of minorities.[9]

C. Discriminatory Referrals

A discriminatory referral will be unlawful only where the characteristic upon which the referral decision is based is a protected characteristic.[10]

---

[8]*Id.* at *7 n.2 (citing Rogers v. American Airlines, 527 F. Supp. 229, 231–33 (S.D.N.Y. 1981)).

[9]*See, e.g.,* EEOC v. David Gomez & Assocs., 1997 U.S. Dist. LEXIS 3269, at *2, 6 (N.D. Ill. 1997) (denying summary judgment where the EEOC presented evidence supporting claim that defendant informed a white male applicant he should not apply for a specific position, despite being "a more-than-qualified" applicant, because the customer-client "looked to fill the opening with a black or Hispanic female"). *See also* EEOC v. Superior Temporary Servs., 56 F.3d 441, 446–47, 67 FEP 1700 (2d Cir. 1995) (enforcing administrative subpoena duces tecum issued by EEOC to investigate charge that the agency accepted job orders that discriminated on the basis of gender).

[10]*Compare* EEOC v. David Gomez & Assocs., 1997 U.S. Dist. LEXIS 3269, at *2, 6 (N.D. Ill. 1997) (alleged referral of minority candidates and refusal to refer white male candidates states discrimination claim that withstands summary judgment motion), *and* EEOC v. Superior Temporary Servs., 56 F.3d 441, 446–47, 67 FEP 1700, 1704–05 (2d Cir. 1995) (administrative subpoena duces tecum enforced to permit EEOC investigation of allegedly gender-based referrals), *with* McBride v. Lawstaf, Inc., 1996 U.S. Dist. LEXIS 16190, at *6–7 (N.D. Ga. 1996) (holding that as a matter of law an employer's grooming policy prohibiting a braided hair style is not an impermissible basis for distinction), *magistrate's recommendation adopted,* 71 FEP 1758 (N.D. Ga. 1996).

D. Agency Employee Complaints

Courts continue to hold that an employee of an employment agency may file charges against the employment agency in its capacity as an employment agency[11] or as an employer.[12]

E. EEOC Investigations of Alleged Unlawful Practices

Pursuant to § 707(c)[13] of Title VII, the EEOC has the "authority to investigate and act on a charge of a pattern or practice of discrimination, whether filed by or on behalf of a person claiming to be aggrieved or by a member of the Commission." Further, pursuant to § 709(a),[14] the EEOC investigatory authority includes the right to inspect and copy relevant documents. In *EEOC v. Superior Temporary Services*,[15] the court upheld an order enforcing an administrative subpoena duces tecum issued by the EEOC in connection with its investigation of a Commissioner's charge. The charge alleged that the employment agency unlawfully discriminated on the basis of gender in its acceptance of customer-client job orders and in its referrals of workers for temporary positions. Superior opposed the subpoena, arguing that the charge failed to disclose adequately the specifics of the alleged discrimination. The court enforced the subpoena, holding that the charge sufficiently identified the groups of alleged discriminatees (male and female temporary workers),[16] the jobs involved (clerical and light industrial), the

---

[11]McBride v. Lawstaf, Inc., 1996 U.S. Dist. LEXIS 16190, at *6–7 (N.D. Ga. 1996) (dismissing plaintiff's claim of wrongful discharge in retaliation for her expressed opposition to the agency's lawful practice of referring only applicants with nonbraided hair styles because plaintiff did not engage in a statutorily protected activity), *magistrate's recommendation adopted,* 71 FEP 1758 (N.D. Ga. 1996).

[12]*But see* Kellam v. Snelling Personnel Servs., 866 F. Supp. 812, 816–17, 68 FEP 195, 196–97 (D. Del. 1994) (holding that employment agencies with fewer than 15 employees may not be sued under Title VII in their capacities as employers), *aff'd without opinion,* 65 F.3d 162 (3d Cir. 1995), *and* Greenlees v. Eidenmuller Enters., 32 F.3d 197, 198–99, 66 FEP 457, 458–59 (5th Cir. 1994) (same).

[13]42 U.S.C. § 2000e-6.

[14]42 U.S.C. § 2000e-8.

[15]56 F.3d 441, 446–47, 67 FEP 1700 (2d Cir. 1995).

[16]The court stated: "As to the groups affected, the Charge refers to 'persons,' 'employees,' 'applicants,' and 'individuals.' Given that the allegation is discrimination on the basis of gender, we do not regard the use of these broad categories as necessarily imprecise, since both men and women are susceptible to discrimination on the basis of gender." *Id.* at 446.

methods of alleged discrimination (acceptance of job orders and referrals), and the relevant periods of time.[17]

---

[17]*Id.* at 446–47. In dissent, Judge Owens disagreed with the conclusion that the EEOC provided adequate notice of the charges, describing the charges as "but a mere tracking of the statute" that "tells Superior virtually nothing" regarding the charges. He would "reverse and remand with instructions that the EEOC be directed to articulate an adequate charge, if it can, and thereafter provide Superior Temporary Services, Inc. with a meaningful and adequate notice of circumstances of the allegedly unlawful employment pattern-and-practice discrimination. Then, if a remedy or resolution cannot be negotiated there is time enough to come to the Courts for enforcement of an administrative subpoena." *Id.* at 448–49 (citation omitted).

Part 8

Other Sources of Protection and Problems of Affirmative Action

Chapter 24

THE CIVIL RIGHTS ACTS OF 1866 AND 1871

II. Scope and Coverage of the Civil Rights Act of 1866, 42 U.S.C. § 1981

A. Statutory Authority

Based on the Supreme Court's decision in *Rivers v. Roadway Express, Inc.*,[1] the amendments to § 1981 in the Civil Rights Act of 1991[2] do not apply to claims that arose before November 1991.[3]

B. Cognizable Defendants Under § 1981

1. Private Entities

A private employer may be liable under § 1981 for acts of intentional discrimination committed by its employees even when they are not supervisors.[4]

---

[1] 511 U.S. 298, 311–13, 64 FEP 842 (1994).
[2] Pub. L. No. 102-166, § 101, 1991 U.S.C.C.A.N. (105 Stat.) 1071, 1072.
[3] Winbush v. Iowa, 66 F.3d 1471, 1476, 69 FEP 1348 (8th Cir. 1995) (Civil Rights Act of 1991 does not apply retroactively); Boone v. Federal Express Corp., 59 F.3d 84, 86, 68 FEP 353 (8th Cir. 1995) (same); Odima v. Westin Tucson Hotel, 53 F.3d 1484, 1494, 67 FEP 1222 (9th Cir. 1995) (same); Theard v. Glaxo, Inc., 47 F.3d 676, 679, 67 FEP 348 (4th Cir. 1995) ("[A]bsent a clear congressional statement to the contrary, a new statutory provision should not be applied retroactively if in so doing it would impose new legal consequences for events completed before the statute's enactment."); Jeffries v. Metro-Mark, Inc., 45 F.3d 258, 66 FEP 1316 (8th Cir.), *cert. denied*, 516 U.S. 830 (1995) (same); Nickeo v. Virgin Islands Tel. Corp., 42 F.3d 804, 806, 66 FEP 1020 (3d Cir. 1994) (same); Harlston v. McDonnell Douglas Corp., 37 F.3d 379, 67 FEP 762 (8th Cir. 1994) (same); Hopkins v. Seagate, 30 F.3d 104, 105–06 (10th Cir. 1994) (same); Smith v. New York City Bd. of Educ., 918 F. Supp. 120, 122 (S.D.N.Y. 1996); Humphrey v. Council of Jewish Fed'ns, 901 F. Supp. 703, 710, 69 FEP 201 (S.D.N.Y. 1995); Sciarrino v. Municipal Credit Union, 894 F. Supp. 102, 106, 73 FEP 661 (E.D.N.Y. 1995).
[4] Fitzgerald v. Mountain States Tel. & Tel. Co., 68 F.3d 1257, 1262–63, 69 FEP 163 (10th Cir. 1995) (although employee was not a supervisor she played a role in the selection of trainers). A private employer is also liable under § 1981 where the

A district court has held that a claim under § 1981 can be maintained against a medical board that administers examinations and awards certifications.[5] Additionally, individual employees, such as supervisors who make or recommend employment decisions, are subject to liability under § 1981.[6] However, no personal liability may be imposed on a corporate official when the official is not alleged to have participated in the actual discrimination.[7]

2. The Federal Government

As noted in the Main Edition, § 1981 protects federal employees only where discrimination in federal employment is not covered by Title VII.[8]

3. State and Local Governments

Courts continue to hold that the Eleventh Amendment prohibits any suit for damages under § 1981 against state governmental entities.[9] The Eleventh Amendment also bars actions under § 1981

---

supervisor's actions violate company policy if he or she had the authority to hire, fire, and supervise the aggrieved individual. *Id.* at 1263. *But see* Collin v. Rector & Bd. of Visitors of Univ. of Va., 873 F. Supp. 1008, 1014 (W.D. Va. 1995) (there is no *respondeat superior* liability under § 1981 and § 1983 in cases involving public entities).

[5]Morrison v. American Bd. of Psychiatry & Neurology, Inc., 908 F. Supp. 582, 588, 69 FEP 1217 (N.D. Ill. 1996) (motion to dismiss denied where physician alleged that, without certification, she would not be able to contract with medical facilities that require board certification). The discrimination prohibited by § 1981 includes both nongovernmental discrimination and discrimination under color of state law. Grimes v. Superior Home Health Care of Middle Tenn., Inc., 929 F. Supp. 1088, 1094, 74 FEP 1539 (M.D. Tenn. 1996).

[6]Vakharia v. Little Co. of Mary Hosp. & Health Care Ctrs., 917 F. Supp. 1282, 1293 (N.D. Ill. 1996); Leige v. Capitol Chevrolet, Inc., 895 F. Supp. 289, 293 (M.D. Ala. 1995); Clark v. City of Macon, 860 F. Supp. 1545, 1553 (M.D. Ga. 1994).

[7]Daulo v. Commonwealth Edison, 892 F. Supp. 1088, 1091, 72 FEP 1566 (N.D. Ill. 1995).

[8]Haynes v. Department of Health & Human Servs., 879 F. Supp. 127, 129 (D.D.C. 1995), *aff'd,* 1997 WL 362503 (D.C. Cir. 1997) (federal employee may not assert §§ 1981, 1985, or 1986 claims if covered by Title VII); Carlton v. Ryan, 916 F. Supp. 832, 838 (N.D. Ill. 1996) (citing Espinueva v. Garrett, 895 F.2d 1164, 1165, 58 FEP 1225 (7th Cir.), *cert. denied,* 497 U.S. 1005 (1990)).

[9]Dennis v. County of Fairfax, 55 F.3d 151, 156, 67 FEP 1681 (4th Cir. 1995) (when a suit is brought against a state actor, § 1983 is the exclusive federal remedy for violation of rights guaranteed under § 1981); Blankenship v. Warren County, 931 F. Supp. 447, 449, 74 FEP 1459 (W.D. Va. 1996) (Eleventh Amendment bars only a claim for monetary recovery against state actors; injunctive relief is permissible);

against governmental employees in their official capacity,[10] although it does not bar suits for damages against state and local officials in their individual capacity.[11]

C. Bases of Discrimination Prohibited by § 1981

Testers do not have a cause of action under § 1981.[12] Likewise, § 1981 does not confer a cause of action on organizations whose injuries derive only from the violation of others' civil rights.[13]

1. Race Discrimination

Courts continue to permit individuals of differing ethnic backgrounds to proceed under § 1981 if they allege discrimination based on their race or color.[14] Section 1981 may also be a vehicle

---

Gorman v. Roberts, 909 F. Supp. 1479, 1489 (M.D. Ala. 1995) (Eleventh Amendment applies in § 1981 litigation); Ebrahimi v. City of Huntsville Bd. of Educ., 905 F. Supp. 993, 994–95 (N.D. Ala. 1995) (§ 1983 is the exclusive means by which a plaintiff may pursue a federal damages remedy for violation of rights guaranteed by § 1981 when the claim is pursued against a state actor) (citing Jett v. Dallas Indep. Sch. Dist., 491 U.S. 701, 731, 50 FEP 27 (1989)); Johnson v. City of Fort Lauderdale, 903 F. Supp. 1520, 1523, 74 FEP 571 (S.D. Fla. 1995) (the only means for a plaintiff to seek redress from a municipality for violation of § 1981 is to maintain an action under § 1983), *aff'd,* 114 F.3d 1089, 74 FEP 578 (11th Cir. 1997); Khan v. Maryland, 903 F. Supp. 881, 888 (D. Md. 1995) (§ 1981 claim against state agency is prohibited by the Eleventh Amendment); Minetos v. City Univ. of N.Y., 875 F. Supp. 1046, 1053, 68 FEP 355 (S.D. N.Y. 1995) (Eleventh Amendment bars claims against state university under § 1981 or § 1983).

[10]Gorman v. Roberts, 909 F. Supp. 1479, 1489 (N.D. Ala. 1995); Roberson v. Bowie State Univ., 899 F. Supp. 235, 237, 72 FEP 899 (D. Md. 1995); Philippeaux v. North Cent. Bronx Hosp., 871 F. Supp. 640, 656, 68 FEP 223 (S.D.N.Y. 1994), *aff'd,* 104 F.3d 353 (2d Cir. 1996), *cert. denied,* 117 S. Ct. 1110 (1997); McAdoo v. Toll, 591 F. Supp. 1399, 1402, 35 FEP 833 (D. Md. 1984).

[11]*Gorman,* 909 F. Supp. at 1489.

[12]Fair Employment Council v. BMC Mktg. Corp., 28 F.3d 1268, 1271, 65 FEP 512 (D.C. Cir. 1994) ("The loss of the opportunity to enter into a *void* contract— i.e., a contract that *neither* party can enforce—is not an injury cognizable under § 1981, for a void contract is a legal nullity.").

[13]*Id.* at 1279 (fair employment organization that sent testers to employer cannot maintain a claim under § 1981).

[14]Bisciglia v. Kenosha Unified Sch. Dist. No. 1, 45 F.3d 223, 229–30 (7th Cir. 1995) ("Congress intended to protect from discrimination identifiable classes of persons who are subjected to intentional discrimination solely because of their ancestry or ethnic characteristics"; court held that historical research suggested that Italians may be considered an identifiable race and, thus, reversed district court's dismissal of § 1981 claim); Donaire v. NME Hosp., Inc., 27 F.3d 507, 509, 65 FEP 674 (11th Cir. 1994) (Filipino who alleged discrimination because of "ancestry or

for bringing "hostile environment" racial harassment claims.[15] Race-based claims of constructive discharge are also actionable under § 1981.[16]

Section 1981 prohibits race discrimination in private employment against white persons as well as persons of color.[17] However, in the reverse discrimination context, at least one court of appeals has required the plaintiff to identify background circumstances that would justify applying to a majority plaintiff the same presumption of discrimination afforded to minority plaintiffs.[18]

2. Retaliation

Several courts have held that the 1991 amendments to § 1981 expanded the scope of the statute to cover retaliatory discharge claims based on race.[19]

---

ethnic characteristics" satisfied the pleading requirement of § 1981); Lovell v. Brinker Int'l, Inc., 71 FEP 417 (W.D. Mo. 1996) (Chinese who alleged discrimination based on her national origin could state race discrimination claim under § 1981); Thankachen v. Cardone Indus., 70 FEP 1391 (E.D. Pa. 1996) (Asian-Indian employee properly brought action for race discrimination under § 1981); Mandala v. Coughlin, 920 F. Supp. 342, 351 (E.D.N.Y. 1996) (§ 1981 covers race and alienage discrimination).

[15]Humphrey v. Council of Jewish Fed'ns, 901 F. Supp. 703, 710–11, 69 FEP 201 (S.D.N.Y. 1995) (African-American employee who was not properly paid under employment contract for appearance at arbitration, given negative performance evaluations, required to perform jobs outside of his job description, and given shorter notice of his termination stated harassment claim under § 1981). *But cf.* Harley v. McCoach, 928 F. Supp. 533, 541, 72 FEP 1725 (E.D. Pa. 1996) ("[H]ostile environment claims must demonstrate a continuous period of harassment, and [three] comments do not create an atmosphere.") (quoting Drinkwater v. Union Carbide Corp., 904 F.2d 853, 863, 56 FEP 483 (3d Cir. 1990)).

[16]Reynolds v. School Dist. No. 1, Denver, Colo., 69 F.3d 1523, 1534, 72 FEP 485 (10th Cir. 1995).

[17]Bellairs v. Coors Brewing Co., 907 F. Supp. 1448, 1455 (D. Colo. 1995), *aff'd*, 107 F.3d 880 (10th Cir. 1997).

[18]Reynolds v. School Dist. No. 1, Denver, Colo., 69 F.3d 1523, 1534, 72 FEP 485 (10th Cir. 1995) (white plaintiff must show that the defendant discriminates against the majority).

[19]Evans v. Kansas City, Mo. Sch. Dist., 65 F.3d 98, 101, 68 FEP 1203 (8th Cir. 1995) (§ 1981 encompasses allegations of retaliatory conduct in a racial discrimination context), *cert. denied*, 517 U.S. 1104 (1996); Lightner v. Town of Ariton, 902 F. Supp. 1489, 1496, 69 FEP 219 (M.D. Ala. 1995); Humphrey v. Council of Jewish Fed'ns, 901 F. Supp. 703, 711, 69 FEP 201 (S.D.N.Y. 1995) (retaliatory termination unlawful under § 1981); Williams v. Carrier Corp., 889 F. Supp. 1528, 1529, 74 FEP 1475 (M.D. Ga. 1995) (a retaliatory discharge claim is cognizable under § 1981), *aff'd*, 130 F.3d 444 (11th Cir. 1997); Wilborn v. Primary Care Specialists, Ltd., 866 F. Supp. 364, 369, 73 FEP 341 (N.D. Ill. 1994) (plaintiff's claim of retaliatory discharge under

3. Other Bases of Discrimination

a. National Origin and Religion. A § 1981 claim based on allegations of national origin or religion discrimination cannot be maintained.[20]

c. Sex. The courts continue to hold that § 1981 is not applicable to gender discrimination, including claims of sexual harassment.[21]

d. Disability. [New Topic] Section 1981 does not apply to claims of disability discrimination.[22]

e. Age. [New Topic] Section 1981 does not apply to claims of age discrimination.[23]

III. SCOPE AND COVERAGE OF CIVIL RIGHTS ACT OF 1871, 42 U.S.C. § 1983

B. Cognizable Defendants Under § 1983

1. The State Action Requirement and Private Discrimination

In *Richardson v. McKnight*,[24] the Supreme Court held that employees of a private prison management firm were not entitled to qualified immunity under § 1983. The Court noted, however, that it had not been asked to decide the question of whether the

---

§ 1981 may proceed under the mixed-motive analysis announced in *Price Waterhouse* or the approach set forth in *McDonnell Douglas*).

[20]Betkerur v. Aultman Hosp. Ass'n, 78 F.3d 1079, 1095 n.11 (6th Cir. 1996); Gorman v. Roberts, 909 F. Supp. 1479, 1484 (M.D. Ala. 1995).

[21]Sherlock v. Montefiore Med. Ctr., 84 F.3d 522, 527, 70 FEP 1377 (2d Cir. 1996); Bratton v. Roadway Package Sys., Inc., 77 F.3d 168, 177, 70 FEP 178 (7th Cir. 1996); Moore v. Allstate Ins. Co., 928 F. Supp. 744, 752, 75 FEP 983 (N.D. Ill. 1996) ("Section 1981 does not address claims for sex discrimination; it only prohibits discrimination based on race or alienage."); Gorman v. Roberts, 909 F. Supp. 1479, 1484 (M.D. Ala. 1995); Hartman v. Smith & Davis Mfg. Co., 904 F. Supp. 983, 986 n.3, 73 FEP 99 (E.D. Mo. 1995); McCoy v. Johnson Controls World Servs., Inc., 878 F. Supp. 229, 232–33, 67 FEP 1763 (S.D. Ga. 1995) (sexual harassment is not actionable under § 1981).

[22]Tafoya v. Bobroff, 865 F. Supp. 742, 752, 3 AD 1329 (D.N.M. 1994), *aff'd*, 74 F.3d 1250, 6 AD 1888 (10th Cir. 1996).

[23]Sherlock v. Montefiore Med. Ctr., 84 F.3d 522, 527, 70 FEP 1377 (2d Cir. 1996).

[24]117 S. Ct. 2100 (1997).

employees could be held liable under § 1983 because they were employed by a private firm.[25] Lower courts have held that government subsidies and regulation will not convert private entities into state actors.[26]

3. State and Local Governments

a. Local Governments. Generally, a municipality can only be held liable for acts that it officially sanctioned or ordered[27] or where the constitutional deprivation occurred as a result of a custom or policy of the municipality.[28] Thus, the Supreme Court found that a municipality could not be held liable under § 1983 for a nonpolicy maker's wrongful conduct unless the plaintiff could demonstrate

---

[25]*Id.* at 2108 ("it is for the district court to determine whether under this Court's decision in *Lugar v. Edmonds Oil Co.,* 457 U.S. 922 (1982), defendants actually acted under color of state law").

[26]Henderson v. Center for Community Alternatives, 911 F. Supp. 689, 707 (S.D.N.Y. 1996). *See also* Sherlock v. Montefiore Med. Ctr., 84 F.3d 522, 527, 70 FEP 1377 (2d Cir. 1996) (the fact that a municipality is responsible for providing medical attention to persons held in its custody does not make an independent contractor rendering services for the municipality a state actor with respect to its employment decisions).

[27]Board of County Comm'rs of Bryan County v. Brown, 117 S. Ct. 1382, 12 IER 1217 (1997) (municipalities not liable under theory of respondeat superior); Randle v. City of Aurora, 69 F.3d 441, 447, 69 FEP 489 (10th Cir. 1995) (only those officials with "final policymaking authority" can subject a municipality to liability; question of whether an official has "final policymaking authority" is a question of state law).

[28]*Randle,* 69 F.3d at 447 (the challenged conduct must have been taken pursuant to a policy adopted by the official or officials responsible under state law for making policy in that area; the failure to allege the existence of similar discrimination as to others undermines claim that the city maintained a custom of discriminatory employment practices); Gierlinger v. New York State Police, 15 F.3d 32, 34, 65 FEP 1667 (2d Cir. 1994) (responsible supervisors and employers can be exposed to § 1983 liability for failing to "investigate and address allegations of sexual harassment when through this failure, the conduct becomes an accepted custom or practice of the employer"). Under certain circumstances, however, a supervisory or authoritative policy maker's actions, even if contrary to the municipality's published policies, may give rise to § 1983 liability if the plaintiff can prove that the alleged misconduct was so pervasive among the employees of the municipality as to constitute a custom or usage with the force of law. Greensboro Prof'l Fire Fighters Ass'n Local 3157 v. City of Greensboro, 64 F.3d 962, 966, 150 LRRM 2261 (4th Cir. 1995); McGautha v. Jackson County, 36 F.3d 53, 56 (8th Cir. 1994), *cert. denied,* 515 U.S. 1133 (1995); Williams v. District of Columbia, 916 F. Supp. 1, 6, 70 FEP 294 (D.D.C. 1996).

the "need for action by the policymaker [was] so obvious that the failure to act [rose] to deliberate indifference."[29]

b. State Governments. A state is not divested of Eleventh Amendment immunity even when it is being indemnified by the federal government for costs of litigation as well as the costs of an adverse judgment.[30]

4. State and Local Governmental Officials in Their Individual Capacities

In *Bogan v. Scott-Harris*,[31] the Supreme Court held that a mayor and city council member were absolutely immune from civil liability for their legislative action of eliminating the job of an African-American who had complained about race discrimination.

A court in its analysis of whether an individual defendant is entitled to qualified immunity may not consider developments in the law that occur after the alleged violation of protected rights.[32] A government employee with supervisory responsibilities may be held liable where the supervisor fails to respond to complaints of sexual harassment.[33]

---

[29]Board of County Comm'rs of Bryan County v. Brown, 117 S. Ct. 1382 (1997).
[30]Regents of the Univ. of Cal. v. Doe, 117 S. Ct. 900 (1997).
[31]118 S. Ct. 966, 76 FEP 146 (1998).
[32]Hansen v. Soldenwager, 19 F.3d 573, 575, 9 IER 712 (11th Cir. 1994). The *Hansen* case emphasized that the qualified immunity analysis is fact-specific:

When considering whether the law applicable to certain facts is clearly established, the facts of cases relied upon as precedent are important. The facts need not be the same as the facts of the immediate case. But they do need to be materially similar. Public officials are not obligated to be creative or imaginative in drawing analogies from previously decided cases.

Id. at 575 (quoting Adams v. St. Lucie County Sheriff's Dep't, 962 F.2d 1563, 1575 (11th Cir. 1992), *modified,* 998 F.2d 923 (11th Cir. 1993) (en banc)). "If case law, in factual terms, has not staked out a bright line, qualified immunity almost always protects the defendant." Rodgers v. Horsley, 39 F.3d 308, 311 (11th Cir. 1994) (quoting Post v. City of Lauderdale, 7 F.3d 1552, 1557 (11th Cir. 1993), *modified,* 14 F.3d 583 (11th Cir. 1994)).

[33]Cross v. Alabama, 49 F.3d 1490,1503, 67 FEP 844 (11th Cir. 1995) (reasonable person in the governmental supervisor's position would have taken some remedial action "in light of the clearly established law that sexual harassment and discrimination was an infringement of legal rights"); Bator v. Hawaii, 39 F.3d 1021, 1029, 66 FEP 290 (9th Cir. 1994) ("A supervisor who has been apprised of unlawful harassment, however, should know that her [complete] failure to investigate and

C. Bases of Discrimination Prohibited by § 1983

Section 1983 does not create federal rights but is used to enforce federal rights established by other sources of federal law.[34]

1. Equal Protection

To establish a cause of action under § 1983 for a violation of equal protection, plaintiffs are required to demonstrate intentional discrimination; mere disparate impact will not suffice.[35] The right to be free from sexual harassment, gender discrimination, and racial discrimination is clearly established under the Equal Protection Clause, the violation of which will result in liability under § 1983.[36]

A white plaintiff generally does not have standing under § 1983 solely for the purpose of vindicating the rights of minorities who have suffered from racial discrimination.[37] An exception exists,

---

stop the harassment is itself unlawful . . . even if the contours of a supervisor's responsibility are uncertain."); Andrews v. City of Philadelphia, 895 F.2d 1469, 1479, 54 FEP 184 (3d Cir. 1990) (condoning or failing to investigate allegations of sexual harassment violates the Equal Protection Clause).

[34]Albright v. Oliver, 114 S. Ct. 807, 811 (1994).

[35]National Ass'n of Gov't Employees v. City Pub. Serv. Bd. of San Antonio, 40 F.3d 698, 714–15, 67 FEP 1013 (5th Cir. 1994); Lewellen v. Metropolitan Gov't of Nashville, 34 F.3d 345, 348–51 (6th Cir. 1994), *cert. denied*, 513 U.S. 1112 (1995) (§ 1983 action can only be based on an intentional deprivation of a protected constitutional right; negligent or grossly negligent conduct on the state actor's part will not trigger § 1983 liability); Ascolese v. Southeastern Pa. Transp. Auth., 925 F. Supp. 351, 358, 72 FEP 1027 (E.D. Pa. 1996) (only intentional sexual harassment can give rise to a § 1983 claim).

[36]Lankford v. City of Hobart, 73 F.3d 283, 286, 69 FEP 1149 (10th Cir. 1996) ("Sexual harassment can violate the Fourteenth Amendment right to equal protection of the laws."); Cross v. Alabama, 49 F.3d 1490, 1507, 67 FEP 844 (11th Cir. 1995) (employees have a constitutional right to be free from unlawful sex discrimination and sexual harassment in public employment); Smith v. Lomax, 45 F.3d 402, 407, 67 FEP 1005 (11th Cir. 1995) (intentional discrimination in the workplace based on an employee's race is patently and obviously illegal and gives rise to § 1983 liability); Bator v. Hawaii, 39 F.3d 1021, 1027, 66 FEP 290 (9th Cir. 1994) (sexual harassment is "impermissible sex discrimination in violation of the Equal Protection Clause"); Annis v. County of Westchester, 36 F.3d 251, 254, 65 FEP 1657 (2d Cir. 1994); Beardsley v. Webb, 30 F.3d 524, 530, 65 FEP 696 (4th Cir. 1994) (sexual harassment has long been recognized as a type of gender discrimination in contravention of the Equal Protection Clause); Yeldell v. Cooper Green Hosp., 956 F.2d 1056, 1064, 66 FEP 607 (11th Cir. 1992) (race discrimination in public employment violates the Fourteenth Amendment).

[37]Maynard v. City of San Jose, 37 F.3d 1396, 1402, 66 FEP 123 (9th Cir. 1994).

however, where the employer retaliates against a nonminority employee for assisting or interacting with minorities.[38]

Courts have been divided over whether Title VII provides the exclusive remedy for plaintiffs who allege that they have been subjected to unlawful discrimination in employment in violation of § 1983.[39]

---

[38]*Maynard,* 37 F.3d at 1403 (white plaintiff has standing under § 1983 where plaintiff asserts own right to be free from retaliation, alleges injuries that are personal to him, and is the only effective plaintiff who can bring the suit).

[39]*Compare* Jackson v. City of Atlanta, 73 F.3d 60, 63, 69 FEP 1505 (5th Cir.) ("Congress intended for Title VII—with its own substantive requirements, procedural rules, and remedies—to be the exclusive means by which an employee may pursue a discrimination claim. Allowing a plaintiff to state a discrimination claim under § 1983 as well would enable him to sidestep the detailed and specific provisions of Title VII."), *cert. denied,* 117 S. Ct. 70 (1996) *and* Lakoski v. James, 66 F.3d 751, 753 (5th Cir. 1995) (Title VII is the exclusive remedy for victims of discrimination who seek money damages, but possibly not the exclusive remedy for plaintiffs who seek only declaratory or injunctive relief), *cert. denied,* 117 S. Ct. 357 (1996) *with* Annis v. County of Westchester, 36 F.3d 251, 254, 65 FEP 1657 (2d Cir. 1994) ("Congress did not intend to make Title VII the exclusive remedy for employment discrimination claims, at least not those claims cognizable under the Constitution."), Beardsley v. Webb, 30 F.3d 524, 527, 65 FEP 696 (4th Cir. 1994) (Title VII and § 1983 co-exist to afford relief for employment discrimination), Saulpaugh v. Monroe Community Hosp., 4 F.3d 134, 143, 62 FEP 1315 (2d Cir. 1993) (§ 1983 claim not barred by concurrent Title VII claim if former is based on substantive rights different from Title VII), *cert. denied,* 510 U.S. 1164 (1994), Houck v. City of Prairie Village, 912 F. Supp. 1438, 1443 (D. Kan.) (§ 1983 harassment claims are not precluded by Title VII), *modified,* 924 F. Supp. 120 (D. Kan. 1996) *and* Philippeaux v. North Cent. Bronx Hosp., 871 F. Supp. 640, 652, 68 FEP 223 (S.D.N.Y. 1994) ("Although a Title VII claim cannot form the basis of a Section 1983 action, plaintiff may assert a claim under Section 1983 based on a violation of the Fourteenth Amendment that arises out of the same nucleus of facts. In such a case, the Fourteenth Amendment violation is analyzed under the same *McDonnell-Burdine* test used in Title VII actions." (citations omitted)), *aff'd,* 104 F.3d 353 (2d Cir. 1996), *cert. denied,* 117 S. Ct. 1110 (1997). Several district court decisions have also addressed the issue of whether the Age Discrimination in Employment Act (ADEA) bars § 1983 claims brought on the basis of age. *See* Gregor v. Derwinski, 911 F. Supp. 643, 75 FEP 797 (W.D.N.Y. 1996) (actions under § 1983 based on age are foreclosed by ADEA); Tranello v. Frey, 758 F. Supp. 841, 850–51 n.3, 55 FEP 699 (W.D.N.Y. 1991) (ADEA provides exclusive remedy for age discrimination), *aff'd,* 962 F.2d 244, 58 FEP 1334 (2d Cir.), *cert. denied,* 506 U.S. 1034 (1992). *But see* Jungels v. State Univ. College of N.Y., 922 F. Supp. 779, 785 (W.D.N.Y. 1996) (cognizable claims distinct from rights exclusively protected by Title VII and ADEA may be brought under § 1983), *aff'd,* 112 F.3d 504 (2d Cir. 1997); Mummelthie v. City of Mason City, 873 F. Supp. 1293, 1312–29, 66 FEP 1393 (N.D. Iowa 1995) (facts giving rise to ADEA claim and constitutional violation may be prosecuted under § 1983), *aff'd,* 78 F.3d 589, 70 FEP 928 (8th Cir. 1996).

Favoritism to family members is not unlawful discrimination under § 1983.[40] A violation of the Veterans' Preference Act likewise cannot form the basis of a § 1983 claim.[41]

2. Speech

A claim that a public sector employee was retaliated against because of his or her advocacy of minority issues may give rise to a claim under § 1983.[42] An action also may lie where the employee is denied a promotion in retaliation for the employee's activities on behalf of a union.[43]

IV. Scope and Coverage of Civil Rights Act of 1871, 42 U.S.C. §§ 1985 and 1986

B. Cognizable Defendants

1. The Applicability of § 1985 to Private Discrimination

Section 1985(3) does not apply to claims of discrimination based on political association.[44]

2. The Conspiracy Requirement

Lower courts continue to hold that intracorporate discussions and actions cannot form the basis of a conspiracy within the meaning of § 1985(3).[45] Because a corporation cannot conspire with itself,

---

[40]Backlund v. Hessen, 104 F.3d 1031, 1033, 12 IER 753 (8th Cir. 1997).

[41]Philippeaux v. North Cent. Bronx Hosp., 871 F. Supp. 640, 647, 68 FEP 223 (S.D.N.Y. 1994), aff'd, 104 F.3d 353 (2d Cir. 1996), cert. denied, 117 S. Ct. 1110 (1997).

[42]Collin v. Rector & Bd. of Visitors of the Univ. of Va., 873 F. Supp. 1008, 1016 (W.D. Va. 1995) (employee must show that retaliation was the result of speech on a matter of public concern).

[43]Greensboro Prof'l Fire Fighters Ass'n Local 3157 v. City of Greensboro, 64 F.3d 962, 964, 150 LRRM 2261 (4th Cir. 1995) (to prevail against the city under § 1983, plaintiff must prove existence of officially adopted policy of disfavoring union employees).

[44]Pierce v. Montgomery County Opportunity Bd., Inc., 884 F. Supp. 965, 978 (E.D. Pa. 1995).

[45]Wright v. Illinois Dep't of Children & Family Servs., 40 F.3d 1492, 1508–09, 10 IER 87 (7th Cir. 1994) (except in egregious circumstances, intraentity discussions that result in discriminatory or retaliatory actions lie outside the scope of § 1985; a corporation's consultation with outside counsel prior to the termination of the plaintiff did not generate a conspiracy); Vakharia v. Little Co. of Mary Hosp. & Health

employees generally cannot be liable for a conspiracy under § 1985(3).[46] In this regard, one court has held that a university cannot conspire with its own employees in violation of § 1985(3).[47] An exception to the general rule involving intracorporate discussions arises when the challenged activity takes place outside the course of employment.[48]

3. Federal and State Governments

Sections 1985 and 1986 do not apply to federal employees whose claims are covered by Title VII.[49] The Eleventh Amendment also precludes actions against state governments and their employees in their official capacity.[50]

C. Bases of Discrimination Prohibited by §§ 1985 and 1986

Plaintiffs have standing under § 1985 only if they can show that they are members of a class that the government has determined "require[s] and warrant[s] special federal assistance in protecting their civil rights."[51] At least one court has held that a white plaintiff has standing under § 1985 where the employee alleges that he or she was subjected to retaliation for assisting minorities.[52]

While violations of federal rights secured by § 1981 may support a § 1985 claim, an action under § 1985 may not be used to obtain relief for Title VII or ADEA violations.[53]

Care Ctrs., 917 F. Supp. 1282, 1299 (N.D. Ill. 1996) (citing Travis v. Gary Community Mental Health Ctr., Inc., 921 F.2d 108, 110, 30 WH 122 (7th Cir. 1990), *cert. denied*, 502 U.S. 812 (1991)); Baker v. American Juice, Inc., 870 F. Supp. 878, 883, 68 FEP 52 (N.D. Ind. 1994).

[46]Johnson v. Hills & Dales Gen. Hosp., 40 F.3d 837, 838, 66 FEP 504 (6th Cir. 1994), *cert. denied*, 514 U.S. 1060 (1995).

[47]Roberson v. Bowie State Univ., 899 F. Supp. 235, 72 FEP 899 (D. Md. 1995).

[48]*Johnson*, 40 F.3d at 838, 841.

[49]Haynes v. Department of Health & Human Servs., 879 F. Supp. 127, 129 (D.D.C. 1995), *aff'd*, 1997 WL 362503 (D.C. Cir. 1997).

[50]Gorman v. Roberts, 909 F. Supp. 1479, 1489 (M.D. Ala. 1995). *But see* Johnson v. City of Fort Lauderdale, 126 F.3d 1372, 75 FEP 519 (11th Cir. 1997) (qualified immunity is not available to governmental employees sued in their individual capacities as a defense to a § 1985(3) claim).

[51]Maynard v. City of San Jose, 37 F.3d 1396, 1403, 66 FEP 123 (9th Cir. 1994) (quoting Sever v. Alaska Pulp Corp., 978 F.2d 1529, 1536–37, 141 LRRM 2678 (9th Cir. 1992)).

[52]*Maynard*, 37 F.3d at 1403.

[53]Sherlock v. Montefiore Med. Ctr., 84 F.3d 522, 527, 70 FEP 1377 (2d Cir. 1996); *Maynard*, 37 F.3d at 1403 n.4; Causey v. Balog, 929 F. Supp. 900, 913, 71 FEP 643

V. Litigation, Proof, Procedure, and Remedies

B. Timeliness

It is now well established that courts should look at the analogous state personal injury statute of limitations to determine the limitations period for claims arising under the Civil Rights Acts of 1866 and 1871.[54]

At least one court has held that the continuing violation theory applies to § 1981 actions.[55]

D. Proof

The *McDonnell Douglas* burden-shifting analysis developed in Title VII disparate treatment cases continues to be applied to claims under § 1981.[56] If the plaintiff can present sufficiently direct evidence of discrimination, the mixed-motive standard applies.[57] A plaintiff may prove discriminatory intent through the failure to follow established policies.[58]

Despite the fact that Title VII's standard of proof is applied to § 1981 claims, there are also significant differences between the

---

(D. Md. 1996); Johnson v. City of Fort Lauderdale, Fla., 903 F. Supp. 1520, 1529, 74 FEP 571 (S.D. Fla. 1995), *aff'd,* 114 F.3d 1089, 74 FEP 578 (11th Cir. 1997); Johnson v. Greater Southeast Community Hosp. Corp., 903 F. Supp. 140, 153–54, 69 FEP 280 (D.D.C. 1995), *vacated in part,* 1996 WL 377147 (D.D.C. June 24, 1996).

[54]Rozar v. Mullis, 85 F.3d 556, 561 (11th Cir. 1996) (limitations period for §§ 1983 and 1985 is measured by the personal injury limitations period of the state); Jones v. Merchants Nat'l Bank & Trust Co., 42 F.3d 1054, 66 FEP 865 (7th Cir. 1994) (Indiana's two-year statute of limitations for personal injury actions applied to § 1981 claims).

[55]Moore v. Allstate Ins. Co., 928 F. Supp. 744, 753, 75 FEP 983 (N.D. Ill. 1996).

[56]*See, e.g.,* Betkerur v. Aultman Hosp. Ass'n, 78 F.3d 1079, 1093 (6th Cir. 1996); Bratton v. Roadway Package Sys., Inc., 77 F.3d 168, 175–76, 70 FEP 178 (7th Cir. 1996); Singh v. Shoney's, Inc., 64 F.3d 217, 219, 68 FEP 1288 (5th Cir. 1995); Barbour v. Merrill, 48 F.3d 1270, 1276, 67 FEP 369 (D.C. Cir. 1995) ("A plaintiff may establish a violation of this section using the same three-step framework of proof used to establish racial discrimination under Title VII."), *cert. granted,* 516 U.S. 1086, *cert. dismissed,* 516 U.S. 1155 (1996); Turnes v. AmSouth, N.A., 36 F.3d 1057, 1060, 66 FEP 340 (11th Cir. 1994). The *McDonnell Douglas* analysis also applies to § 1983 claims. Richardson v. Leeds Police Dep't, 71 F.3d 801, 805, 69 FEP 795 (11th Cir. 1995); Cross v. Alabama, 49 F.3d 1490, 1508, 67 FEP 844 (11th Cir. 1995).

[57]Fuller v. Phipps, 67 F.3d 1137, 1141, 69 FEP 111 (4th Cir. 1995).

[58]Landon v. Northwest Airlines, Inc., 72 F.3d 620, 625, 72 FEP 675 (8th Cir. 1995) (supervisor's failure to follow drug testing policy created genuine issue of material fact as to whether decision to administer drug test was racially motivated).

two statutes.[59] However, to the extent that a plaintiff has articulated a valid cause of action under Title VII, courts have found that the plaintiff has sufficiently alleged a violation of § 1981.[60]

E. Remedies

While under §§ 1981 and 1983 a court has wide discretion to award equitable relief,[61] compensatory damages such as for emotional distress caused by the deprivation of civil rights may be awarded only when the claimants submit proof of actual injury.[62]

In §§ 1981 and 1983 cases, punitive damages are proper only on a showing of "evil motive or intent or reckless or callous indifference to the federally protected rights of others."[63] In order to impose punitive damages upon the employer, it must have knowledge of malicious or reckless conduct, or authorize, ratify, or approve an employee's malicious or reckless conduct.[64] Any award

---

[59]Grimes v. Superior Home Health Care of Middle Tenn., Inc., 929 F. Supp. 1088, 1095, 74 FEP 1539 (M.D. Tenn. 1996) (proof of discriminatory intent is required under § 1981, whereas it is not required under Title VII, and individual defendants may be held liable under § 1981 while there is no individual liability under Title VII) (citing Johnson v. Railway Express Agency, Inc., 421 U.S. 454, 461, 10 FEP 817 (1975)).

[60]Humphrey v. Council of Jewish Fed'ns, 901 F. Supp. 703, 710, 69 FEP 201 (S.D.N.Y. 1995); Philippeaux v. North Cent. Bronx Hosp., 871 F. Supp. 640, 654, 68 FEP 223 (S.D.N.Y. 1994), aff'd, 104 F.3d 353 (2d Cir. 1996), cert. denied, 117 S. Ct. 1110 (1997).

[61]Barbour v. Merrill, 48 F.3d 1270, 1278, 67 FEP 369 (D.C. Cir. 1995).

[62]Patterson v. P.H.P. Healthcare Corp., 90 F.3d 927, 938–40, 72 FEP 613 (5th Cir. 1996), cert. denied, 117 S. Ct. 767 (1997) (vacating damage award of $40,000 as testimony of mental distress insufficient to support anything more than nominal damages; no corroborating testimony or expert medical or psychological evidence of damages); Fitzgerald v. Mountain States Tel. & Tel. Co., 68 F.3d 1257, 1263, 69 FEP 163 (10th Cir. 1995) (remanding an emotional distress damage award of $250,000 per plaintiff as clearly excessive when the award was based solely on the plaintiffs' testimony; no medical or psychological evidence and plaintiffs' continued to work in their chosen field); Jimoh v. Ernst & Young, 908 F. Supp. 220, 226 (S.D.N.Y. 1995) (no compensatory damages under § 1981 because no alleged emotional distress arising from defendant's actions and no evidence that plaintiff sought professional help).

[63]Patterson, 90 F.3d at 941 ("The general rule in this circuit permits a punitive damage award against a § 1981 defendant when the defendant acts willfully or with gross disregard for the plaintiff's rights."); Fitzgerald, 68 F.3d at 1263 (punitive damages in civil rights cases require that the discrimination must have been malicious, willful, and in gross disregard of the plaintiff's rights; claim for punitive damages dismissed where no evidence existed that employer authorized employee's actions); Barbour v. Merrill, 48 F.3d 1270, 1277, 67 FEP 369 (D.C. Cir. 1995).

[64]Patterson, 90 F.3d at 944 (employer is not liable for punitive damages where it took no part in malicious or reckless conduct); Fitzgerald, 68 F.3d at 1263 (same).

of punitive damages must comply with the criteria established by the Supreme Court to determine the reasonableness of a punitive damage award.[65] Although the Civil Rights Act of 1991 does not permit the recovery of punitive damages in a Title VII action against "a government, government agency or political subdivision,"[66] one district court has held that punitive damages can be assessed against a political subdivision under § 1981.[67]

The prevailing party in a § 1981 case may be entitled to an award of reasonable attorney's fees.[68]

A plaintiff has a duty under § 1981 to use reasonable diligence to attain substantially similar employment and mitigate any claimed damages.[69]

G. Res Judicata

If an employee has agreed to arbitrate all grievances he or she has with the employer, including discrimination claims, any suit filed by the plaintiff pursuant to § 1981 may be stayed pending arbitration.[70] However, an adverse arbitration award under a collective bargaining agreement will not preclude a plaintiff from bringing an action under § 1981 involving the identical set of facts and issues.[71]

---

[65]*Patterson,* 90 F.3d at 943. *See* BMW of N. Am., Inc. v. Gore, 517 U.S. 559 (1996) (the factors to be considered in determining whether a punitive damage award was reasonable are (1) the degree of reprehensibility of the defendant's conduct; (2) the disparity between the harm suffered and the damage award; and (3) the difference between the damages awarded in this case and comparable cases).

[66]42 U.S.C. § 1981a(b)(1).

[67]Johnson v. Metropolitan Sewer Dist., 926 F. Supp. 874, 875–76, 74 FEP 683 (E.D. Mo. 1996) (motion to strike prayer for punitive damages under § 1981 denied).

[68]Schofield v. Trustees of Univ. of Penn., 919 F. Supp. 821, 825 (E.D. Pa. 1996) ("The Civil Rights Attorney's Fees Awards Act of 1976, 42 U.S.C. § 1988, confers upon the court the discretion to award to the prevailing party 'a reasonable attorney's fee as part of the costs.' ").

[69]Patterson v. P.H.P. Healthcare Corp., 90 F.3d 927, 935, 72 FEP 613 (5th Cir.1996), *cert. denied,* 117 S. Ct. 767 (1997).

[70]Pitter v. Prudential Life Ins. Co. of Am., 906 F. Supp. 130, 131, 138 (E.D.N.Y. 1995) (citing Gilmer v. Interstate/Johnson Lane Corp., 500 U.S. 20, 26–27, 55 FEP 1116 (1991)).

[71]Humphrey v. Council of Jewish Fed'ns, 901 F. Supp. 703, 710, 69 FEP 201 (S.D.N.Y. 1995).

Chapter 25

NATIONAL LABOR RELATIONS ACT

II. Remedies Against Unions

C. Challenges to Certification

The NLRB and federal appellate courts continue to struggle with the issue of whether a union's references to race, ethnicity, national origin, or religion during a representation election constitute election interference.[1]

III. Employer Discrimination

B. Concerted Activity Protesting Alleged Discrimination

Employee complaints concerning discrimination continue to be deemed protected concerted activity under the National Labor Relations Act.[2]

---

[1]*Compare* KI (U.S.A.) Corp. v. NLRB, 35 F.3d 256, 258–60, 147 LRRM 2275, 2277–79 (6th Cir. 1994) (Applying standard established by the NLRB in *Sewell Mfg. Co.*, 138 NLRB 66, 51 LRRM 1611 (1962), the Sixth Circuit sustained the objection of the employer, a wholly owned subsidiary of a Japanese corporation, based on the union's distribution of literature on the day before the election in which a Japanese businessman with no connection to the employer expressed "very negative views regarding American workers.") *and* Zartic, Inc., 315 NLRB 495, 497–98, 147 LRRM 1201, 1203–04 (1994) (NLRB set aside election based on the union's sustained and inflammatory appeal to the ethnic sensibilities of the employer's Hispanic employees) *with* Catherine's, Inc., 316 NLRB 186, 189–90, 148 LRRM 1181 (1995) (NLRB ruled that union did not interfere with election when its representative told employees that employer's law firm was a Jewish firm, that certain white employees were "no" votes, and that Jews "would fight you hard, but when you beat them, they would sit down and negotiate a contract with you"; Board stated that "while [representative's] gratuitous comments in this case clearly were not germane to the Union's organizing campaign and we certainly do not condone the introduction of irrelevant religious and racial issues, we find them insufficient to warrant setting aside the election as they were isolated and lacked inflammatory appeal").

[2]Franklin Iron & Metal Corp., 315 NLRB 819, 822–26, 148 LRRM 1246 (1994) (NLRB ruled that employer violated § 8(a)(1) of the Act by retaliating against

Yet another court has held that Title VII and the National Labor Relations Act offer overlapping remedies for retaliation claims. In *Pelech v. Klaff-Joss, LP*,[3] the court held that plaintiff's Title VII claim of retaliatory discharge and on-going retaliation was not preempted by §§ 7 and 8 of the National Labor Relations Act. The court observed that the preemption doctrine articulated in *San Diego Building Trades Council v. Garmon*[4] has been used to guard against the very specific danger of conflict between state and federal systems for regulating labor activity. "Not only is [this] danger not presented by Title VII claims," the court observed,

> but *Garmon* has never been applied to preempt the hearing of a federal, as opposed to a state, claim. Moreover, while courts have set about protecting the NLRB's jurisdiction over labor disputes, Congress has clearly mandated that federal courts have jurisdiction to decide cases of employment discrimination. For these reasons, it is not surprising that the scant references made to the interplay of Title VII and the NLRA suggest that the statutes offer concurrent remedies.[5]

C. Employer's Duty to Bargain and Furnish Union With Information on Composition of Workforce

In *NLRB v. U.S. Postal Service*,[6] the Third Circuit reviewed the NLRB's findings regarding an employer's refusal to supply information or bargain over the elimination of two new hiring procedures that were alleged to be unlawfully discriminatory. As to the duty to bargain, the court noted that an employer's obligation to bargain is not triggered until the union adduces sufficient evidence in support of its allegations of discrimination. The union must first make a demand and communicate information to the employer indicating that it has an objective basis for alleging discrimination. The court noted, however, that a separate analysis is required with respect to the duty to provide information. When

---

African-American employees because of their protected concerted activity, which included protesting alleged payment of higher wage rate to white employees who had less seniority and then filing complaints with state civil rights commission), *enforcement granted*, 83 F.3d 156, 152 LRRM 2383 (6th Cir. 1996).

[3] 828 F. Supp. 525, 65 FEP 1011 (N.D. Ill. 1993).
[4] 359 U.S. 236 (1959).
[5] 828 F. Supp. at 530, 65 FEP at 1014.
[6] 18 F.3d 1089, 64 FEP 305 (3d Cir. 1994).

seeking information concerning persons it does not represent, a union has the burden of showing that the information is necessary to the performance of representational responsibilities. The union meets this burden whenever it has a rational basis for believing that the hiring practice *may* discriminate, i.e., "information sufficiently probative of discrimination to support a belief that further inquiry is justified."[7] The employer is obligated to respond to the information request once that burden is satisfied.

---

[7] *Id.* at 1101.

CHAPTER 26

RELATED CAUSES OF ACTION

II. PROCEDURAL ISSUES IN COMBINING COMMON LAW AND FEDERAL STATUTORY CLAIMS

B. Preemption

As noted in the Main Edition, federal EEO laws generally are held not to preempt state law claims, and may even be relied upon in a state common law claim for termination in violation of public policy.[1]

Whether a state law claim is preempted by § 301 of the Labor Management Relations Act (LMRA) continues to turn upon a comparison of language of the collective bargaining agreement and the specific facts and legal theory alleged.[2]

---

[1] *E.g.*, Rains v. Criterion Sys., Inc., 80 F.3d 339, 345, 70 FEP 635 (9th Cir. 1996) (Title VII does not preempt California state law claim of wrongful discharge in violation of public policy against religious discrimination, even though complaint cites Title VII as one source of public policy); Anderson v. Martin Brower Co., 1994 U.S. Dist. LEXIS 10682, *6–7, 3 AD 829 (D. Kan. 1994) (Americans with Disabilities Act did not preempt state law fraud claim); Smuck v. National Management Corp., 540 N.W.2d 669, 672, 11 IER 33 (Iowa Ct. App. 1995) (state law claim for wrongful termination may be based on public policy embodied in federal law); Garavaglia v. Centra, Inc., 536 N.W.2d 805, 808, 11 IER 308 (Mich. Ct. App. 1995) (same).

[2] Preempted: Baker v. Farmers Elec. Co-op, Inc., 34 F.3d 274, 282, 10 IER 1556 (5th Cir. 1994) (intentional infliction of emotional distress claim preempted by LMRA); DeCoe v. General Motors Corp., 32 F.3d 212, 217, 9 IER 1255 (6th Cir. 1994) (defamation claim involving allegation of sexual harassment preempted by LMRA); Jobes v. Tokheim Corp., 657 N.E.2d 145, 149, 11 IER 1453 (Ind. Ct. App. 1995) (defamation and invasion of privacy based on drug testing preempted by LMRA because claims inextricably intertwined with analysis of collective bargaining agreement).

Not Preempted: Sanford v. MeadowGold Dairies, Inc., 534 N.W.2d 410, 414, 11 IER 249 (Iowa 1995) (employee's claim that he was discharged for seeking workers' compensation benefits not preempted where court not required to consider terms or effect of collective bargaining agreement).

Other federal statutes,[3] including ERISA,[4] may preempt state common law claims.

III. CONTRACT AND TORT CAUSES OF ACTION THAT LIMIT THE "EMPLOYMENT-AT-WILL" DOCTRINE

A. Contract Theory

2. Employment Policies/Oral Representations as the Basis for a Contract

Employer policies or statements continue to be a common basis for alleging the existence of a restriction on an employer's right to terminate employment without cause. Employee handbooks often serve as the basis for implied contract claims.[5] An employer's other

---

[3]*E.g.,* Keaveney v. Town of Brookline, 937 F. Supp. 975, 982–83, 11 IER 1838, 1842 (D. Mass. 1996) (Omnibus Transportation Employee Testing Act preempted state law claim for invasion of privacy based on drug testing required by OTETA); *cf.* Ditto v. American Airlines, Inc., 1995 U.S. Dist. LEXIS 4425, 10 IER 1628, 1631 (N.D. Ill. 1995) (Airline Deregulation Act did not preempt state law wrongful discharge claim based on allegation that plaintiff was discharged for voicing safety concerns); Walt's Drive-A-Way Serv., Inc. v. Powell, 638 N.E.2d 857, 859, 10 IER 789 (Ind. Ct. App. 1994) (federal Surface Transportation Assistance Act did not preempt state law claim that truck driver was discharged for refusing to violate federal safety regulations); Wenners v. Great State Beverages, Inc., 663 A.2d 623, 626, 10 IER 1649 (N.H. 1995) (Bankruptcy Code did not preempt state law claim that employee was fired for filing bankruptcy), *cert. denied,* 516 U.S. 1119, 11 IER 736 (1996).

[4]*E.g.,* Wilcott v. Matlack, Inc., 64 F.3d 1458, 1462–63, 11 IER 311 (10th Cir. 1995) (ERISA preempted misrepresentation claim based on alleged promise that plaintiff could use disability leave benefits without jeopardizing his job, but did not preempt related wrongful termination claims); Fairneny v. Savogran Co., 664 N.E.2d 5, 8-10, 11 IER 1132 (Mass. 1996) (ERISA preempted wrongful discharge, breach of implied covenant of good faith, promissory estoppel, and defamation claims by employee-trustees of stock ownership plan allegedly terminated for carrying out fiduciary responsibilities).

[5]*See, e.g.,* Amoco Fabrics & Fibers Co. v. Hilson, 669 So. 2d 832, 835, 10 IER 1651 (Ala. 1995) (employees of plant that had been sold were entitled to vacation pay as outlined in handbook and consistent with past practice); Taggart v. Drake Univ., 549 N.W.2d 796, 801, 11 IER 1450 (Iowa 1996) (procedural standards for nonrenewal of faculty appointments in faculty handbook created enforceable contract); Anderson v. Douglas & Lomason Co., 540 N.W.2d 277, 285, 11 IER 263 (Iowa 1995) (handbook containing progressive discipline procedures may have contractual effect, even though employee never read procedures); O'Brien v. New England Tel. & Tel. Co., 422 Mass. 686, 664 N.E.2d 843, 849, 11 IER 1221 (Mass. 1996) (personnel manual's progressive discipline and grievance procedure created enforceable contractual obligations;

written policy statements can also constitute a contractual obligation binding on the employer.[6] Whether oral promises of secure employment are enforceable is another issue that arises frequently.[7]

In *Scott v. Pacific Gas & Electric Co.*,[8] the California Supreme Court held that the principles underlying an implied contract not to terminate without good cause are equally applicable in wrongful demotion or discipline cases. The court recognized a presumption that an employee may be demoted at will, but concluded that the employer's written progressive discipline policy gave rise to an implied contract restricting the employer's right to demote employees.[9]

Some courts refuse to give contractual effect to handbooks, policy manuals, or oral statements where there was no employer intent to be bound,[10] the statements were too vague to

---

action barred because plaintiff failed to pursue manual's grievance procedures); King v. PYA/Monarch, Inc., 453 S.E.2d 885, 888, 10 IER 337 (S.C. 1995) (personnel manual's progressive discipline policy created implied contract); Farnum v. Brattleboro Retreat, Inc., 671 A.2d 1249, 1254–55, 11 IER 713 (Vt. 1995) (contractual effect given to handbook's progressive discipline policy, despite at-will disclaimer elsewhere in handbook).

[6]*E.g.,* Hodgkins v. New England Tel. Co., 82 F.3d 1226, 1231, 11 IER 1159 (1st Cir. 1996) (under Maine law, employer's written suggestion program constituted enforceable contract, despite clause granting employer "sole, exclusive and complete discretion" over program's operation); *cf.* DePetris v. Union Settlement Assoc., 657 N.E.2d 269, 271, 11 IER 119 (N.Y. 1995) (personnel policy manual's provisions regarding pretermination warnings and written reasons for warning not given contractual effect, where no manual provision limited employer's right to terminate or obligated employer to follow manual procedures).

[7]*See, e.g.,* Rinck v. Association of Reserve City Bankers, 676 A.2d 12, 17–18, 11 IER 1285 (D.C. Ct. App. 1996) (additional consideration beyond continued employment is required to make employer's oral promise of job security enforceable as to existing employee; triable issue of fact whether employee's foregoing seeking other employment and remaining with employer after merger was sufficient consideration); Ross v. Times Mirror, Inc., 665 A.2d 580, 583, 68 FEP 1756 (Vt. 1995) (oral representations of continuous employment insufficient to overcome at-will status).

[8]11 Cal. 4th 454, 904 P.2d 834 (1995).

[9]*Id.* at 465.

[10]*See, e.g.,* St. Peters v. Shell Oil Co., 77 F.3d 184, 188, 11 IER 804 (7th Cir. 1996) (under Illinois law, handbook language regarding progressive discipline was not binding because it used permissive "may" and provided that employer could skip levels of progressive discipline); Heurtebise v. Reliable Bus. Computers, Inc., 550 N.W.2d 243, 247, 11 IER 1665 (Mich. 1996) (handbook stating that employer reserved right to modify handbook policies at its sole discretion indicated intent not to be bound, therefore employee was not bound by handbook's arbitration provision); Trader v. People Working Cooperatively, Inc., 663 N.E.2d 335, 337–38, 11

be enforceable,[11] or the handbook or policy contained a statement disclaiming contractual effect.[12] A valid disclaimer should be clear and conspicuous; vague or hidden contractual disclaimers may prove ineffective.[13]

3. Employment Policies/Oral Representations in Conjunction With Other Factors as the Basis for a Contract

Courts in some states continue to recognize implied contracts limiting an employer's right to terminate employees, based on a

---

IER 1350 (Ohio Ct. App. 1994) (handbook policy that employees could not be terminated unless they accumulated excessive disciplinary points did not modify terms of written at-will contract, where handbook was unilaterally distributed without consideration or mutual assent), *appeal dismissed,* 660 N.E.2d 737 (1995).

[11]*E.g.,* Pulla v. Amoco Oil Co., 72 F.3d 648, 657, 11 IER 432 (8th Cir. 1995) (under Iowa law, progressive discipline and merit policies that said they "should" be followed and that workplace should be friendly and cooperative, when viewed collectively, were not sufficiently definite to be enforceable); Gould v. Maryland Sound Indus., Inc., 31 Cal. App. 4th 1137, 10 IER 405 (Cal. Ct. App. 1995) (statements that employees would become "members" of company upon completion of probation and that employer was looking for "long term" employees were too vague to support implied contract); Simonelli v. Anderson Concrete Co., 650 N.E.2d 488, 495, 11 IER 236 (Ohio Ct. App. 1994) (executive's statement that he hoped employee would work there "a lot more years" was too indefinite to enforce); Hayes v. Eateries, Inc., 905 P.2d 778, 784, 11 IER 110 (Okla. 1995) (vague oral assurances of continued employment lacked specificity necessary to transform at-will employment into that requiring good cause for termination).

[12]*E.g.,* Coatney v. Enterprise Rent-a-Car, 897 F. Supp. 1205, 1211, 11 IER 628 (W.D. Ark. 1995) (valid disclaimer in employee handbook precluded breach of contract claim based on handbook); Comer v. ENSR Operations, 10 IER 672 (S.D. W.Va. 1994) (under Ohio law, discharged employee had no claim for breach of implied contract in view of a contract disclaimer in handbook), *aff'd,* 10 IER 960 (4th Cir. 1995); Hanna v. Marshall Field & Co., 665 N.E.2d 343, 348, 11 IER 1045 (Ill. App. Ct. 1996) (employer's personnel handbook and policies did not form enforceable employment contract, where handbook contained specific disclaimer stating that termination could occur at any time without notice); Anderson v. Douglas & Lomason Co., 540 N.W.2d 277, 288–89, 11 IER 263 (Iowa 1995) (disclaimer stating that handbook was not intended to create contractual rights defeated implied covenant claim).

[13]*See, e.g.,* Southwest Gas Corp. v. Vargas, 901 P.2d 693, 697–98, 11 IER 228 (Nev. 1995) (ambiguous disclaimers, stating that employment could be terminated according to applicable policies in effect from time to time, did not bar implied contract claim); Farnum v. Brattleboro Retreat, Inc., 671 A.2d 1249, 1254, 11 IER 713 (Vt. 1995) (contractual effect given to handbook's progressive discipline policy, despite disclaimer elsewhere in handbook saying all employment was at will); Payne v. Sunnyside Community Hosp., 894 P.2d 1379, 1384, 10 IER 1344 (Wash. Ct. App. 1995) (issue of fact existed whether hospital's employment practices negated contractual disclaimer in handbook); Dent v. Fruth, 453 S.E.2d 340, 344, 10 IER 351 (W. Va. 1994) (vague disclaimer in handbook did not preclude breach of implied contract action).

combination of factors such as length of employment, promotions, assurances of continued employment, employer policies, and past practices.[14]

Implied contract claims may be defeated by express agreements that the employment relationship is at will.[15] In some states, the statute of frauds may bar an implied contract claim.[16] There continues to be disagreement regarding whether an employer may unilaterally modify implied contractual obligations for incumbent employees.[17]

---

[14]*E.g.,* Huey v. Honeywell, Inc., 82 F.3d 327, 332–33, 11 IER 1098 (9th Cir. 1996) (under Arizona law, issue of fact existed whether employer's course of conduct and representations modified at-will nature of employment because employer had written, but not distributed, progressive discipline policy and other employees had been progressively disciplined, but not terminated, for policy violations); Fair v. Red Lion Inn, 920 P.2d 820, 826, 11 IER 146 (Colo. Ct. App. 1995) (written medical leave of absence form, combined with oral assurances by human resources director, created implied contract governing return from medical leave, despite employee's initial at-will agreement and handbook statement that employment was at will); Southwest Gas Corp. v. Vargas, 901 P.2d 693, 697–98, 11 IER 228 (Nev. 1995) (statement in employee manual that employees could be terminated only for good cause and oral assurances of long-term employment created implied contract); de la Rosa v. Southwest Community Health Servs., 10 IER 1564 (N.M. 1994) (16 years of employment, combined with assurances of long-term employment, created implied contract requiring good cause for termination); Wright v. Honda of Am. Mfg., 653 N.E.2d 381, 384–85, 11 IER 27 (Ohio 1995) (handbooks, progress reports, promotion letters, oral representations of management, and past practice created triable issue of fact concerning implied contract).

[15]*See, e.g.,* McDermott v. Chilton Co., 938 F. Supp. 240, 245–46, 11 IER 1460 (D.N.J. 1995) (under New Jersey law, fact that employee signed at-will documents at hire defeated claim based on policy manual's discharge provisions); Bonastia v. Berman Bros., Inc., 914 F. Supp. 1533, 1538–39, 11 IER 725 (W.D. Tenn. 1995) (under Tennessee law, at-will agreement precluded breach of contract claim based on letter saying employee would get specified salary for two years); Smuck v. National Management Corp., 540 N.W.2d 669, 672, 11 IER 33 (Iowa Ct. App. 1995) (policy manual that explicitly stated that employment was at will precluded breach of contract action); Trader v. People Working Cooperatively, Inc., 663 N.E.2d 335, 337, 11 IER 1350 (Ohio Ct. App. 1994) (handbook policies on progressive discipline and termination did not override written at-will employment contract), *appeal dismissed,* 660 N.E.2d 737 (1995).

[16]*E.g.,* Wilcott v. Matlack, Inc., 64 F.3d 1458, 1465, 11 IER 311 (10th Cir. 1995) (under Colorado law, enforcement of promise of job "for as long as you wish" barred by statute of frauds and for lack of consideration when plaintiff totally disabled and unable to perform); Wior v. Anchor Indus., Inc., 669 N.E.2d 172, 175, 11 IER 1742 (Ind. 1996) (oral promise to employ for "twenty plus" years until retirement barred by statute of frauds); Jarboe v. Landmark Community Newspapers, 644 N.E.2d 118, 121, 10 IER 172 (Ind. 1994) (alleged oral employment contract unenforceable under statute of frauds).

[17]*See, e.g.,* Torosyan v. Boehringer Ingelheim, 662 A.2d 89, 99, 10 IER 1313 (Conn. 1995) (employer's issuance of amended handbook, removing "for cause" requirement for discharge, was not conclusively binding on employee); Lytle v.

4. Promissory Estoppel

Most courts continue to be wary of promissory estoppel claims.[18] Courts remain more receptive to such claims in situations involving relocation or giving up employment in reliance upon employer promises.[19]

5. Breach of Implied Covenant of Good Faith and Fair Dealing

Numerous states do not recognize a cause of action for breach of implied covenant of good faith and fair dealing in the employment context.[20] In most states that do recognize the cause of action,

---

Malady, 566 N.W.2d 582, 591–92 (Mich.) (disclaimer of at-will employment, inserted in handbook after employee started working, held ineffective where employee received no notice that disclaimer applied to her and was told by supervisor that it applied only to new employees), *reh'g granted,* 570 N.W.2d 785 (1997); King v. PYA/Monarch, Inc., 453 S.E.2d 885, 889, 10 IER 337 (S.C. 1995) (handbook's progressive discipline policy not overridden by later at-will agreement); *cf.* Alston v. City of Camden, 471 S.E.2d 174, 179, 11 IER 1337 (S.C. 1996) (employer could replace handbook with new handbook providing for reduced benefits).

[18]*See, e.g.,* Fox v. T-H Continental Ltd. Partnership, 78 F.3d 409, 413–14, 11 IER 988 (8th Cir. 1996) (under Minnesota law, no promissory estoppel where employee failed to show clear and definite promise of continued employment terminable only for cause); Nguyen v. CNA Corp., 44 F.3d 234, 241, 10 IER 329 (4th Cir. 1995) (under Virginia law, no promissory estoppel absent express promise that could reasonably be interpreted as altering at-will status); Friedman v. BRW, Inc., 40 F.3d 293, 297, 10 IER 538 (8th Cir. 1994) (under Minnesota law, no promissory estoppel claim because employee could not reasonably rely on alleged promise of permanent employment in light of at-will statement in handbook); Simonelli v. Anderson Concrete Co., 650 N.E.2d 488, 495, 11 IER 236 (Ohio Ct. App. 1994) (no promissory estoppel absent specific promise and reasonable reliance); Madden v. Omega Optical, Inc., 683 A.2d 386, 11 IER 1606 (Vt. 1996) (no promissory estoppel absent reasonable reliance); Garcia v. Uniwyo Fed. Credit Union, 920 P.2d 642, 646–47, 11 IER 1550 (Wyo. 1996) (no promissory estoppel because employee could not reasonably rely on promises made by persons without authority to make binding promises).

[19]*E.g.,* Gorham v. Benson Optical, 539 N.W.2d 798, 800–02, 11 IER 187 (Minn. Ct. App. 1995) (employee terminated on first day of work could recover reliance damages when he quit previous job in good faith reliance on promises of new employment); Baldwin v. National College, 537 N.W.2d 14, 18, 11 IER 297 (S.D. 1995) (employee who voluntarily quit entitled to bonus, despite contract saying no bonus if she quit, where employee reasonably relied on executive's assurance that bonus would be paid).

[20]*See, e.g.,* Mudlitz v. Mutual Serv. Ins. Co., 75 F.3d 391, 394, 11 IER 620 (8th Cir. 1996) (under Minnesota law, no implied covenant of good faith and fair dealing in employment contracts); Coatney v. Enterprise Rent-a-Car, 897 F. Supp. 1205, 1211–12, 11 IER 628 (W.D. Ark. 1995) (Arkansas law does not recognize the implied covenant of good faith and fair dealing in the employment context).

it sounds in contract, not tort.[21] The distinction between causes of action for breach of implied contract and for breach of the implied covenant is not always clear, though some courts continue to require something over and above a breach of contract in order to state a cause of action for breach of the implied covenant.[22]

B. Tort Theories

3. Public Policy

As noted in the Main Edition, many states recognize a tort cause of action for termination in violation of public policy, although the parameters of the tort vary widely from state to state. Courts generally require the plaintiff to show an identifiable public policy that inures to the benefit of the public at large, rather than only to the parties in the lawsuit.[23] Thus, plaintiffs continue

---

[21]*See, e.g.,* E.I. Dupont de Nemours & Co. v. Pressman, 679 A.2d 436, 444–45, 11 IER 1643 (Del. 1996) (cause of action for breach of implied covenant of good faith and fair dealing sounds in contract).

[22]*See, e.g., id.* at 444, 11 IER 1643 (Del. 1996) (intentionally fabricating basis for termination could constitute breach of implied covenant of good faith and fair dealing); Shoen v. Amerco, Inc., 896 P.2d 469, 476, 10 IER 1082 (Nev. 1995) (discharged founder of company sufficiently alleged elements of reliance, trust and dependency, and fraudulent and malicious termination to establish claim for breach of implied covenant of good faith and fair dealing); Garcia v. Uniwyo Fed. Credit Union, 920 P.2d 642, 646, 11 IER 1550 (Wyo. 1996) (only when employee and employer have special relationship arising from long-term employment and discharge is calculated to avoid some employer responsibility to employee).

[23]Public Policy Recognized: Rocky Mountain Hosp. & Med. Serv. v. Mariani, 916 P.2d 519, 526, 11 IER 1153 (Colo. 1996) (state board of accountancy rules of professional conduct constituted public policy); Barratt v. Cushman & Wakefield of N.J., 675 A.2d 1094, 1100, 11 IER 1172 (N.J. 1996) (real estate broker fired for disclosing that competing broker may have participated in commercial bribery scheme could state public policy claim because promoting honesty of brokers benefits public as a whole); MacDougall v. Weichert, 677 A.2d 162, 173, 11 IER 1411 (N.J. 1996) (employee discharged for voting as legislator in way adverse to employer's interests could state claim for violation of public policy); Simonelli v. Anderson Concrete Co., 650 N.E.2d 488, 492, 11 IER 236 (Ohio Ct. App. 1994) (employee fired for consulting with attorney about employment dispute could state public policy claim); Gardner v. Loomis Armored, Inc., 913 P.2d 377, 384–85, 11 IER 993 (Wash. 1996) (employee terminated for leaving truck unattended, in violation of work rule, to come to assistance of hostages stated claim for termination in violation of Washington's policy of saving lives).

Public Policy Not Recognized: Roberts v. Hit or Miss, Inc., 11 IER 54 (N.D. Cal. 1995) (employer violated no fundamental public policy when it terminated at-will employee who took vacation after being denied time off); E.I. Dupont de

to allege public policy claims based on retaliation for exercising a statutory right,[24] satisfying a legal obligation,[25] refusing to violate a statute,[26] and reporting a statutory violation.[27]

Nemours & Co. v. Pressman, 679 A.2d 436, 442, 11 IER 1643 (Del. 1996) (concerns about conflicts of interest and propriety of internal business practices do not rise to level of public policy); Leweling v. Schnadig Corp., 657 N.E.2d 1107, 1111, 11 IER 178 (Ill. Ct. App. 1995) (carrier tariff rates did not constitute public policy because they only affect relations between carriers and shippers); Hayes v. Eateries, Inc., 905 P.2d 778, 789, 11 IER 110 (Okla. 1995) (employee allegedly terminated for reporting that supervisor had embezzled from employer fails to state public policy claim because only private interests of employer involved); Madden v. Omega Optical, Inc., 683 A.2d 386, 391, 11 IER 1606 (Vt. 1996) (employee discharged for refusal to sign allegedly unenforceable noncompetition agreement failed to state public policy claim).

[24]*E.g.,* Heil Co. v. Crowley, 659 So. 2d 105, 107, 11 IER 1212 (Ala. 1995) (filing workers' compensation claim); Badih v. Myers, 36 Cal. App. 4th 1289, 1296, 68 FEP 592 (Cal. Ct. App. 1995) (plaintiff could state common law public policy claim based on pregnancy discrimination); Adolphsen v. Hallmark Cards, Inc., 907 S.W.2d 333, 338–39, 11 IER 133 (Mo. Ct. App. 1995) (reporting violations of FAA safety regulations); Schultz v. Stillwater Mining Co., 920 P.2d 486, 488, 11 IER 1726 (Mont. 1996) (reporting safety concerns); Smith v. Troy Moose Lodge, 645 N.E.2d 1352, 1353–54, 10 IER 845 (Ohio Ct. App. 1994) (employee who alleges she was discharged for exercising her statutory right to apply for temporary unemployment benefits may have claim for discharge in violation of public policy); Simonelli v. Anderson Concrete Co., 650 N.E.2d 488, 492, 11 IER 236 (Ohio Ct. App. 1994) (consulting with attorney about employment dispute); Groce v. Foster, 880 P.2d 902, 908, 9 IER 1768 (Okla. 1994) (Oklahoma constitution's open-access-to-courts provision supported discharge in violation of public policy claim by employee fired for suing employer's customer); *cf.* Wior v. Anchor Indus., Inc., 669 N.E.2d 172, 177, 11 IER 1742 (Ind. 1996) (manager fired for refusing to fire employee who had filed workers' compensation claim has no cause of action because public interest adequately protected by permitting subordinate to sue).

[25]*E.g.,* Reynolds v. Ozark Motor Lines, Inc., 887 S.W.2d 822, 824–25, 10 IER 100 (Tenn. 1994) (discharge of drivers for refusing to violate state statute by driving truck without sufficient inspection violated public policy).

[26]*E.g.,* Ebasco Constructors, Inc. v. Rex, 923 S.W.2d 694, 699, 11 IER 1030 (Tex. Ct. App. 1996) (refusing to falsify reports in violation of Nuclear Regulatory Commission regulations); *cf.* Devoid v. Clair Buick Cadillac, Inc., 669 A.2d 749, 751, 11 IER 525 (Me. 1996) (employee fired for refusing to issue check he believed was illegal did not state claim under Maine Whistleblower's Protection Act, which only prohibits termination for refusing to carry out directive involving dangerous conditions or reporting in good faith what is reasonably believed to be violation of law).

[27]*E.g.,* Gould v. Maryland Sound Indus., 31 Cal. App. 4th 1137, 1148–49, 10 IER 405 (Calif. Ct. App. 1995) (employee allegedly discharged for reporting to management that co-workers were not being paid for overtime stated claim for discharge in violation of public policy); Lynch v. Blanke Baer & Bowey Krimko, Inc., 901 S.W.2d 147, 150–51, 11 IER 808 (Mo. Ct. App. 1995) (public policy exception to at-will doctrine does not require that report of statutory or regulatory violation be made to outside agency); Trader v. People Working Cooperatively, Inc., 663 N.E.2d 335, 339, 11 IER 1350 (Ohio Ct. App. 1994) (employee discharged for reporting marijuana use by co-employees could state claim for termination in violation of public

Courts usually require the plaintiff to allege a public policy embodied in a statute, regulation, or constitutional provision.[28] Some courts, however, have recognized public policies not derived from one of these sources.[29]

The issue of whether an employee must be right about his or her belief concerning a reported violation of law in order to be protected remains controversial. Some, but not all, courts have held that the employee is protected if he or she has a reasonable and/or good faith belief in the report of a legal violation.[30]

If the statute upon which a public policy claim is founded itself provides a remedy, some courts hold that remedy to be exclusive,[31]

---

policy), *appeal dismissed,* 660 N.E.2d 737 (1995); *cf.* Chandler v. Dowell Schlumberger, Inc., 542 N.W.2d 310, 315, 11 IER 707 (Mich. Ct. App. 1995) (under Michigan law, only employees who actually report, or are about to report, violation of law are protected; employee discharged because of employer's erroneous belief that he reported violation was not protected).

[28]*See, e.g.,* Lawrence Chrysler Plymouth Corp. v. Brooks, 465 S.E.2d 806, 809, 11 IER 523 (Va. 1996) (public policy must be based on statute, regulation, or constitutional provision).

[29]*E.g.,* Thompto v. Coborn's, Inc., 871 F. Supp. 1097, 1116–17, 10 IER 263 (N.D. Iowa 1994) (under Iowa law, judicial decisions could be used as source of public policy prohibiting termination for threatening to retain attorney, in absence of clear expression of such policy in state statute or constitution); General Dynamics Corp. v. Superior Court, 7 Cal. 4th 1164, 1181–82, 876 P.2d 487, 498, 9 IER 1089 (Cal. 1994) (attorney rules of professional conduct can serve as source of public policy); Painter v. Graley, 639 N.E.2d 51, 56, 9 IER 1741 (Ohio 1994) (public policy may be based on common law, in addition to constitution, legislation, administrative rule, or regulation).

[30]*See, e.g.,* Frederick v. Justice Dep't, 73 F.3d 349, 352, 11 IER 507 (Fed. Cir. 1996) (under federal Whistleblower Protection Act, there must be a reasonable belief that conduct violates law); Crandon v. Kansas, 897 P.2d 92, 104, 10 IER 1156 (Kan. 1995) (report of suspected violation made with reckless disregard of truth or falsity not protected under Kansas whistleblowing statute), *cert. denied,* 116 S. Ct. 913 (1996); Devoid v. Clair Buick Cadillac, Inc., 669 A.2d 749, 751, 11 IER 525 (Me. 1996) (good faith reasonable belief required); *cf.* Bordell v. General Elec., 667 N.E.2d 923, 11 IER 1183 (N.Y. Ct. App. 1996) (New York whistleblower statute requires proof of actual violation of law, rule, or regulation).

[31]*E.g.,* Hamros v. Bethany Homes & Methodist Hosp. of Chicago, 894 F. Supp. 1176, 1179, 10 IER 1750 (N.D. Ill. 1995) (under Illinois law, federal Family and Medical Leave Act cannot be basis of state public policy claim because FMLA provides its own protection against retaliation); Talley v. Washington Inventory Serv., 37 F.3d 310, 313, 65 FEP 1665 (7th Cir. 1994) (Illinois Human Rights Act was exclusive remedy for marital status discrimination, precluding common law retaliatory discharge claim); Johnson v. Kraft Gen. Foods, Inc., 885 S.W.2d 334, 336, 9 IER 1804 (Mo. 1994) (Missouri statute prohibiting retaliation for court order to withhold delinquent child support provided exclusive remedy); Fandrich v. Capital Ford Lincoln Mercury, 901 P.2d 112, 115, 11 IER 194 (Mont. 1995) (employee cannot allege common law tort claims based on sex harassment; state Human Rights Act is exclusive remedy).

while others hold that a common law public policy claim exists in addition to the statutory remedy.[32]

IV. OTHER COMMON LAW TORT THEORIES

A. Intentional Infliction of Emotional Distress

Intentional infliction of emotional distress remains a frequently alleged cause of action in the employment context. In many cases, intentional infliction claims have been rejected on the basis that the complained-of conduct was not sufficiently "outrageous."[33] A claim for intentional infliction of emotional distress remains more likely to succeed when based on an allegation of prolonged harassment or discrimination.[34]

---

[32]*E.g.,* Legard v. Winn-Dixie La., Inc., 1995 U.S. Dist. LEXIS 12429, 10 IER 1647, 1649 (E.D. La. 1995) (Louisiana drug testing statute did not provide exclusive remedy; therefore plaintiff could sue for defamation); Molesworth v. Brandon, 672 A.2d 608, 613–14, 70 FEP 524 (Md. Ct. App. 1996) (small employer not covered by Maryland's Fair Employment Practices Act could be sued for termination in violation of the public policy against sex discrimination contained in Act); Trader v. People Working Cooperatively, 663 N.E.2d 335, 339–40, 11 IER 1350 (Ohio Ct. App. 1994) (Ohio whistleblower statute not exclusive remedy, where claim seeks damages, such as emotional distress, not covered by statute), *appeal dismissed,* 660 N.E.2d 737 (1995).

[33]Mathis v. Pacific Gas & Elec., 75 F.3d 498, 505, 11 IER 564 (9th Cir. 1996) (under California law, excluding contractor employees from nuclear power plant based on suspected drug use was not outrageous); Wright v. Metro Health Med. Ctr., 58 F.3d 1130, 1140, 10 IER 1418 (6th Cir. 1995) (under Ohio law, enforcement of antinepotism policy not outrageous), *cert. denied,* 116 S. Ct. 1041 (1996); Wilcott v. Matlack, Inc., 64 F.3d 1458, 1465, 11 IER 311 (10th Cir. 1995) (under Colorado law, termination while on medical leave and denial of disability insurance benefits not outrageous); King v. AC & R Adver., 65 F.3d 764, 770, 10 IER 1731 (9th Cir. 1995) (under California law, changing to at-will employment, restructuring compensation, terminating after refusal to accept lower salary, and making generally offensive age-related comments were not outrageous); Barber v. Whirlpool Corp., 34 F.3d 1268, 1276, 9 IER 1492 (4th Cir. 1994) (under South Carolina law, verbal abuse and accusation of theft during 40-minute meeting not outrageous); Taggart v. Drake Univ., 549 N.W.2d 796, 802, 11 IER 1450 (Iowa 1996) (yelling at employee in sexist and condescending manner was not outrageous); Simonelli v. Anderson Concrete Co., 650 N.E.2d 488, 493, 11 IER 236 (Ohio Ct. App. 1994) (manner in which at-will employee terminated was not outrageous); Farnum v. Brattleboro Retreat, Inc., 671 A.2d 1249, 1256–57, 11 IER 713 (Vt. 1995) (summoning employee into office on day off, firing without warning and without opportunity to rebut charges not outrageous conduct).

[34]Harris v. Proctor & Gamble Cellulose Co., 73 F.3d 321, 324, 11 IER 605 (11th Cir. 1996) (under Georgia law, allegations of continued harassment, combined with retaliatory motive for reporting toxic chemical exposure, sufficient to state a claim); Lightning v. Roadway Express, Inc., 60 F.3d 1551, 1558, 10 IER 1592 (11th Cir.

The defense that the workers' compensation laws provide the exclusive remedy for intentional infliction claims is one that continues to arise, with mixed results.[35]

B. Defamation

The four most commonly litigated issues in employment-related defamation cases continue to be: (1) was there a defamatory statement of fact? (2) was it published? (3) was it privileged? and (4) was it true?

On the first issue, courts have considered whether the statements were defamatory per se,[36] were nonactionable statements of opinion,[37] or were too ambiguous to be actionable.[38]

On the issue of publication, two common subissues continue to be whether statements directed only to co-workers are published for purposes of a cause of action for defamation[39] and whether a

---

1995) (two-year pattern of verbal and physical abuse supported claim for intentional infliction of emotional distress under Georgia law); Elson v. Consolidated Edison Co. of N.Y., 641 N.Y.S.2d 294, 294–95, 226 AD.2d 288 (N.Y. App. Div. 1996) (employee with psychological problems, known to employer, states claim by alleging that interrogated for eight hours, shown gun, denied lunch, and intimidated into taking lie detector test).

[35]Tacket v. General Motors, 93 F.3d 332, 335, 11 IER 1729 (7th Cir. 1996) (no workers' compensation preemption because only emotional distress alleged, but not physical injury resulting in disability covered by Indiana Workers' Compensation Act); Kroger Co. v. Willgruber, 920 S.W.2d 61, 64, 11 IER 1087 (Ky. 1996) (workers' compensation exclusivity did not cover posttermination conduct, including lying to employee about possible future job and delaying disability insurance payments to get him to sign release); Birklid v. Boeing Co., 904 P.2d 278, 287, 11 IER 97 (Wash. 1995) (intentional or reckless exposure of employees to toxic chemicals not barred because workers' compensation exclusivity does not apply to deliberate attempts to injure).

[36]Swick v. Liautaud, 662 N.E.2d 1238, 1245, 11 IER 646 (Ill. 1996) (accusation of being industrial spy and stealing were defamatory per se).

[37]Quinn v. Jewel Food Stores, 658 N.E.2d 1225, 1231, 11 IER 380 (Ill. Ct. App. 1995) ("cocky," "conartist," "bullshit" are nonactionable opinion).

[38]Anderson v. Vanden Dorpel, 667 N.E.2d 1296, 1301, 11 IER 1103 (Ill. 1996) (statement that plaintiff could not get along with co-workers and did not follow up on assignments was nonactionable).

[39]Torosyan v. Boehringer Ingelheim Pharmaceuticals, Inc., 662 A.2d 89, 103, 10 IER 1313 (Conn. 1995) (communication to plaintiff's supervisors and inclusion in personnel file of false accusations constituted publication); Schrader v. Eli Lilly & Co., 639 N.E.2d 258, 261–62, 9 IER 1830 (Ind. 1994) (intracompany communication of reason for discharge constituted publication); Huegerich v. IBP, Inc., 547 N.W.2d 216, 221, 11 IER 1092 (Iowa 1996) (intracompany communication of accusation of drug abuse was publication); Wallulis v. Dymowski, 918 P.2d 755, 760 (Or. 1996) (intracompany communications were "published").

cause of action for defamation exists based on "self-publication," where the plaintiff repeats to third parties the reasons for termination given by the employer.[40]

In *Bolton v. Department of Human Services*,[41] the Minnesota Supreme Court refused to recognize a "defamation by action" claim based on escorting an employee from the building immediately after termination.

The third issue involves the application of either an absolute privilege or a qualified privilege.[42] A qualified privilege can be overcome if the defendant acted maliciously or otherwise improperly.[43]

Truth is, of course, a defense to a defamation claim.[44]

---

[40]Coatney v. Enterprise Rent-a-Car, 897 F. Supp. 1205, 1212, 11 IER 628 (W.D. Ark. 1995) (applying Arkansas law, denying motion to dismiss cause of action based on self-publication); Strange v. Nationwide Mutual Ins. Co., 867 F. Supp. 1209, 1222, 10 IER 1257 (E.D. Pa. 1994) (self-publication in employment context not recognized under Pennsylvania law); de la Rosa v. Southwest Community Health Servs., 10 IER 1564 (N.M. 1994) (self-publication not recognized under New Mexico law).

[41]540 N.W.2d 523, 526, 11 IER 369 (Minn. 1995).

[42]Columbia First Bank v. Ferguson, 665 A.2d 650, 656, 11 IER 43 (D.C. Ct. App. 1995) (qualified privilege for report by bank employee to OTS and police); Quinn v. Jewel Food Stores, 658 N.E.2d 1225, 1234, 11 IER 380 (Ill. Ct. App. 1995) (qualified privilege applied to references about former employee); Schrader v. Eli Lilly & Co., 639 N.E.2d 258, 262, 9 IER 1830 (Ind. 1994) (qualified privilege applied to intracompany communications of reasons for plaintiff's discharge); Taggart v. Drake Univ., 549 N.W.2d 796, 803, 11 IER 1450 (Iowa 1996) (qualified privilege in university peer review); Wallulis v. Dymowski, 918 P.2d 755, 762–63 (Or. 1996) (qualified but not absolute privilege for union steward's statement that supervisor was drug abuser); Petersen v. Dacy, 550 N.W.2d 91, 94 (S.D. 1996) (statements by management to other employees regarding reason for plaintiff's discharge were qualifiedly privileged); Flugge v. Wagner, 532 N.W.2d 419, 422, 11 IER 1783 (S.D. 1995) (absolute privilege for statements made to state board of accounting).

[43]Duffy v. Leading Edge Prods., 44 F.3d 308, 314, 67 FEP 97 (5th Cir. 1995) (actual knowledge or reckless disregard for truth required to overcome qualified privilege under Texas law); Lyons v. National Car Rental Sys., Inc., 30 F.3d 240, 244, 9 IER 1302 (1st Cir. 1994) (under Massachusetts law, qualified privilege overcome by malice and recklessness); Wallulis v. Dymowski, 918 P.2d 755, 762 (Or. 1996) (reversing summary judgment because malice was question of fact, where defendant was angry when statement was made and defendant accused plaintiff of having "substance abuse problem," but defendant only believed plaintiff had drinking problem); Petersen v. Dacy, 550 N.W.2d 91, 94 (S.D. 1996) (qualified privilege not overcome because plaintiff offered no proof that defendant did not believe statements to be true).

[44]Strange v. Nationwide Mut. Ins. Co., 867 F. Supp. 1209, 1222, 10 IER 1257 (E.D. Pa. 1994) (under Pennsylvania law, "the literal accuracy of individual statements will not insulate a defendant from liability where the overall impression left by those statements is false"); Randall's Food Markets, Inc. v. Johnson, 891 S.W.2d

Another potential defense is that the plaintiff consented to or authorized the defamatory statements.[45]

C. Misrepresentation or Fraud

Courts continue to carefully scrutinize claims of misrepresentation or fraud in the employment context.[46]

A misrepresentation or fraud claim remains more likely to succeed if the plaintiff has relocated or relinquished other employment based on an employer's representation.[47]

Employers continue to defend fraud and misrepresentation claims by asserting, among other things, that the statements were nonactionable predictions of future events,[48] that the statements were believed to be true by the maker,[49] or that the fraud claim is merely an attempt to circumvent the at-will doctrine or a limitation on recoverable damages.[50]

640, 646, 10 IER 427 (Tex. 1995) (employer's statement that employee left store without paying for item was nonactionable because true).

[45]Cox v. Nasche, 70 F.3d 1030, 1031–32, 11 IER 281 (9th Cir. 1995) (release form authorizing government agency to contact plaintiff's former employers gave former employer absolute privilege under Alaska law).

[46]Hodgkins v. New England Tel. Co., 82 F.3d 1226, 1234, 11 IER 1159 (1st Cir. 1996) (fraud claim failed under Maine law because plaintiff could not show reasonable reliance); Mudlitz v. Mut. Serv. Ins. Co., 75 F.3d 391, 395, 11 IER 620 (8th Cir. 1996) (failure to show reliance damages fatal under Minnesota law); Fatland v. Quaker State Corp., 62 F.3d 1070, 1073, 10 IER 1569 (8th Cir. 1995) (under North Dakota law, reliance on co-worker statements regarding contents and interpretation of employer policies was unreasonable); Johnson & Johnson Med., Inc. v. Sanchez, 924 S.W.2d 925, 930, (Tex. 1996) (plaintiff presented no evidence of reasonable reliance necessary for fraud claim).

[47]Lazar v. Superior Court, 909 P.2d 981, 11 IER 545 (Cal. 1996) (terminated employee who allegedly had been induced by the defendant's knowingly false promises of job security to give up secure employment in another state and move his family across country to accept defendant's employment offer stated valid cause of action for promissory fraud).

[48]Krisak v. Gourmet Coffees of Am., 10 IER 433, 437 (D. Md. 1995) (promises regarding future equity participation were nonactionable); Kary v. Prudential Ins. Co. of N. Am., 541 N.W.2d 703, 705, 11 IER 530 (N.D. 1996) (predictions of future earnings are not statements of fact; therefore not actionable).

[49]Roberts v. Hit or Miss, Inc., 11 IER 54 (N.D. Cal. 1995) (granting summary judgment for employer on false promise claim because no evidence of requisite intent presented).

[50]Dewachter v. Scott, 657 So. 2d 962, 962–63, 11 IER 95 (Fla. Dist. Ct. App. 1995) (claim that plaintiff was fraudulently induced to leave job and accept employment by

An employer may be able to sue a former employee for fraud in proper cases.[51]

D. Interference With Contractual Relations

In cases involving claims for interference with contractual relations, the three most commonly litigated issues continue to be: (1) whether the contractual relationship or prospective business advantage was sufficiently definite[52]; (2) whether a co-employee or supervisor is legally distinct from the employer, so that the co-employee or supervisor can be sued for interfering with a contract between the plaintiff and the employer[53]; and (3) whether the "interference" was legally privileged.[54]

---

promise of lifetime employment rejected as attempt to circumvent Florida's at-will rules); Sanford v. MeadowGold Dairies, Inc., 534 N.W.2d 410, 413, 11 IER 249 (Iowa 1995) (fraud claim rejected where no showing of damages beyond those available under plaintiff's claim for retaliatory discharge).

[51]Rash v. Hilb, Rogal & Hamilton Co. of Richmond, 467 S.E.2d 791, 795, 11 IER 789 (Va. 1996) (imposing constructive trust based on successful claim by employer against former employees who, by improper means, diverted firm's contracts to competing business).

[52]Hamros v. Bethany Homes & Methodist Hosp. of Chicago, 894 F. Supp. 1176, 1181, 10 IER 1750 (N.D. Ill. 1995) (under Illinois law, intentionally causing termination of at-will contract is actionable); Anderson v. Vanden Dorpel, 667 N.E.2d 1296, 1299, 11 IER 1103 (Ill. 1996) (prospective job too indefinite); Keith v. Mendus, 661 N.E.2d 26, 33, 11 IER 671 (Ind. Ct. App. 1996) (can state claim for interference with at-will employment relationship); Hoschler v. Kozlik, 529 N.W.2d 822, 826, 10 IER 896 (Neb. Ct. App. 1995) (at-will employment protected against third party's unjustified interference).

[53]McDermott v. Chilton Co., 938 F. Supp. 240, 11 IER 1460 (D.N.J. 1995) (under New Jersey law, supervisor, as employer's agent, cannot tortiously interfere with employment contract between employer and other employee); Keith v. Mendus, 661 N.E.2d 26, 36, 11 IER 671 (Ind. Ct. App. 1996) (co-employees acting outside course and scope of employment can be liable for interference); Lytle v. Malady, 530 N.W.2d 135, 146, 69 FEP 1070 (Mich. Ct. App. 1995) (employer's agent may not be held liable when acting on employer's behalf rather than for personal benefit), *aff'd in part and rev'd in part on other grounds,* 566 N.W.2d 582, *reh'g granted,* 570 N.W.2d 785 (1997); McGanty v. Staudenraus, 901 P.2d 841, 846, 10 IER 1793 (Or. 1995) (supervisor acting within scope of employment cannot be liable for intentional interference with other employee's economic relations with employer).

[54]Wardlaw v. Inland Container Corp., 76 F.3d 1372, 1380, 11 IER 873 (5th Cir. 1996) (under Texas law, employer's client was privileged in notifying employer that employee had written letter to competition disclosing volume of client's business with employer; privilege to prevent dissemination of confidential information); Chandler v. Bombardier Capital, Inc., 44 F.3d 80, 82–83, 10 IER 212 (2d Cir. 1994) (under Vermont law, "honest advice" given in good faith is nonactionable); Willey v.

E. Negligence

Negligence claims by employees against their employers continue to meet with mixed results.[55]

F. Invasion of Privacy

Plaintiffs continue to assert causes of action for invasion of privacy arising from various factual settings.[56]

V. APPLICABILITY OF WORKERS' COMPENSATION LAWS

Employers often assert the doctrine of workers' compensation exclusivity as a defense, particularly to tort claims. The success of

---

Riley, 541 N.W.2d 521, 526–27, 11 IER 445 (Iowa 1995) (to be actionable, interference must be for predominate purpose of financially injuring plaintiff); O'Brien v. New England Tel. & Tel Co., 664 N.E.2d 843, 845, 11 IER 1221 (Mass. 1996) (malicious conduct unrelated to employer's legitimate business interests was not privileged); Pratt v. Prodata, Inc., 885 P.2d 786, 789, 9 IER 1509 (Utah 1994) (former employer committed intentional interference with economic relations by causing employee's discharge from subsequent employment based on noncompetition agreement).

[55]McDermott v. Chilton Co., 938 F. Supp. 240, 11 IER 1460 (D.N.J. 1995) (no cause of action for negligent supervision under New Jersey law); Doe v. Western Restaurants Corp., 674 So. 2d 561, 564, 11 IER 542 (Ala. Civ. App. 1995) (employer not vicariously liable under negligence theory for off-the-job sexual conduct by manager); Maguire v. Hilton Hotels Corp., 79 Haw. 10, 899 P.2d 393, 398, 10 IER 1326 (1995) (employee of hotel contractor could state negligence claim against hotel for on-the-job assault); Terrell v. Rowsey, 647 N.E.2d 662, 666, 10 IER 650 (Ind. 1995) (Indiana does not recognize claim for negligent performance of employment contract); Huegerich v. IBP, Inc., 547 N.W.2d 216, 220, 11 IER 1092 (Iowa 1996) (Iowa does not recognize negligent discharge as exception to at-will employment); Shoen v. Amerco, Inc., 896 P.2d 469, 477, 10 IER 1082 (Nev. 1995) (recognizing cause of action for negligent infliction of emotional distress in the employment context).

[56]Green v. Bryant, 887 F. Supp. 798, 801, 10 IER 1179 (E.D. Pa. 1995) (under Pennsylvania law, discharge of at-will employee after discovering she had been victim of spousal abuse did not violate right to privacy); Porter v. City of Royal Oak, 542 N.W.2d 905, 910, 11 IER 798 (Mich. Ct. App. 1995) (public disclosure of private facts); Greenwood v. Taft, Stettinius & Hollister, 663 N.E.2d 1030, 10 IER 1744 (Ohio Ct. App. 1995) (employer that allegedly disseminated fact that homosexual employee's male partner was listed as insurance and pension beneficiary could be sued for invasion of privacy); Morrow v. II Morrow, Inc., 911 P.2d 964, 968, 11 IER 780 (Or. Ct. App. 1996) (false light invasion of privacy).

this defense may depend on employer intent,[57] the type of injury allegedly suffered,[58] or other issues.[59]

---

[57]McGowan v. Our Savior's Lutheran Church, 527 N.W.2d 830, 834, 10 IER 909 (Minn. 1995) (negligence action based on rape by client barred by workers' compensation exclusivity); Birklid v. Boeing Co., 904 P.2d 278, 287, 11 IER 97 (Wash. 1995) (claim by employee injured by exposure to dangerous materials was not barred by workers' compensation, where employer conduct constituted "deliberate intent to injure").

[58]Tacket v. General Motors, 93 F.3d 332, 335, 11 IER 1729 (7th Cir. 1996) (under Indiana law, workers' compensation exclusivity does not bar breach of contract and intentional infliction of emotional distress claims, where plaintiff has not alleged physical injury compensable under workers' compensation law); Wolf v. F & M Banks, 534 N.W.2d 877, 883, 10 IER 827 (Wis. Ct. App. 1995) (defamation claims preempted by Wisconsin workers' compensation law).

[59]Goins v. Mercy Ctr., 667 N.E.2d 652, 655, 11 IER 1760 (Ill. App. Ct. 1996) (workers' compensation exclusivity does not bar privacy action by hospital employee arising from hospital's disclosure of HIV-test results, since hospital was acting in role of medical provider, not employer); Kroger Co. v. Willgruber, 920 S.W.2d 61, 67, 11 IER 1087 (Ky. 1996) (workers' compensation exclusivity did not bar intentional infliction of emotional distress claim based largely on posttermination conduct); Li v. C.N. Brown Co., 645 A.2d 606, 609, 9 IER 1404 (Me. 1994) (wrongful death action against employer of convenience store clerk fatally stabbed during robbery was barred by workers' compensation exclusivity).

Chapter 27

REVERSE DISCRIMINATION AND AFFIRMATIVE ACTION

I. Introduction

Issues surrounding the area known as "reverse discrimination" have been the focus of much recent legal, political, and social attention. Unfortunately, this increased attention has not clarified many of the questions raised in the debates regarding reverse discrimination.

The concern over the "unfairness" of reverse discrimination in selecting, preferring, or enabling minorities to the detriment of the majority was highlighted in the recent passage of the state "California Civil Rights Initiative," Proposition 209.[1] Proposition 209, which amended the California Constitution to read, "[t]he state shall not discriminate against, or grant preferential treatment to, any individual or group on the basis of race, sex, color, ethnicity or national origin in the operation of public employment, public education, or public contracting,"[2] was passed on November 5, 1996, by a vote of 54 to 46 percent.[3] The future effect and impact of Proposition 209 remains to be seen. On the day after its controversial passage, opponents and proponents of the proposition filed lawsuits, one seeking to enjoin its enforcement, the other seeking to enforce it. In ruling on these cases, the Ninth Circuit has held that Proposition 209 does not violate the Equal Protection Clause of the U.S. Constitution and that it is not preempted by Title VII.[4]

---

[1] CAL. CONST. of 1849, art. I, § 31(a) (1996).
[2] *Id.*
[3] *See* Robert Pear, *In California, Foes of Affirmative Action See a New Day,* N.Y. TIMES, Nov. 7, 1996, at B7. Proponents of the proposition have heralded it as a way to prevent discrimination by the government, which is precluded from awarding a job, an admission to a university, or a contract on the basis of one's race or sex. Opponents fear that it will eliminate all affirmative action programs, including those that help to ensure equal opportunity for women and minorities. *Id.*
[4] Coalition for Economic Equity v. Wilson, 122 F.3d 692 (9th Cir. 1997) (lifting preliminary injunction granted by district court, which had barred implementation of Proposition 209).

Some commentators have suggested economic-based affirmative action as an alternative and less controversial means of reaching some of the traditional goals of affirmative action.[5] The goal of this type of affirmative action is to identify and foster existing talents that might otherwise remain unnoticed due to the many disadvantages associated with poverty.[6] Proponents argue that economic-based affirmative action does not offend the principles enumerated in Title VII, California's Proposition 209, or other anti-discrimination laws, because it does not make classifications based on race, sex, color, ethnicity, or national origin.

II. Reverse Discrimination Outside the Context of Affirmative Action Programs

A. Prohibited Bases for Discrimination

1. Race

White employees have stated valid claims of reverse discrimination based on race in hiring,[7] termination,[8] promotion,[9] demo-

---

[5]For a detailed discussion of the pros and cons of affirmative action based on economic disadvantage, *see* Richard M. Fallon, *Affirmative Action Based on Economic Disadvantage*, 43 UCLA L. Rev. 1913 (1996).

[6]*Id.* at 1950.

[7]*See, e.g.,* Fairbairn v. Board of Educ. of S. Country Cent., 876 F. Supp. 432, 437 (E.D.N.Y. 1995) (white school employee who sought position of assistant principal established prima facie case by showing that she was qualified for position and was passed over in favor of African-American male).

[8]*See, e.g.,* Lisek v. Norfolk & W. Ry., 918 F. Supp. 1202, 1209 (N.D. Ill. 1996) (white employee terminated for sleeping on job established prima facie case where nonwhite employees were not terminated for same offense); Bush v. Barnett Bank of Pinellas County, 916 F. Supp. 1244, 1254 (M.D. Fla. 1996) (white employee survived summary judgment by alleging that employer targeted and trained African-American for plaintiff's position, offering her opportunities not offered to plaintiff, frequently meeting with her privately, and placing her in plaintiff's position without first posting vacancy); *cf.* Brown v. Westinghouse Savannah River Corp., 928 F. Supp. 1168, 1171–73, 71 FEP 516 (S.D. Ga. 1996) (white employee terminated from nuclear weapons facility for cheating on safety exam unable to establish prima facie case by alleging that other nonwhite employees committed violations of company policy without being terminated because he could not show others committed same violation).

[9]*See, e.g.,* Reynolds v. School Dist. No. 1, Denver, Colo., 69 F.3d 1523, 1534–35, 72 FEP 485 (10th Cir. 1995) (white employee who was denied promotion established prima facie case by showing that she was only white employee in her

tion,[10] and transfer.[11] Some recent cases have acknowledged the significance of the racial makeup of the plaintiff's workplace or department and the race of the person who allegedly discriminated against the plaintiff. In *Reynolds v. School District No. 1, Denver, Colorado,*[12] for example, the Tenth Circuit held that the plaintiff, a white bilingual education teacher, established a prima facie case of reverse discrimination against a public school district for failing to promote her. Plaintiff created an inference of discrimination by showing that she was the only white employee in the otherwise all-Hispanic department and that the supervisors who denied her the promotions were also Hispanic.[13] Conversely, a district court in Pennsylvania found no prima facie case where the majority of plaintiff's supervisors were white and the decisions to place the white plaintiff on probation, and then to terminate him, were made by white executives.[14]

White employees have also been successful in bringing reverse discrimination claims based on disparate treatment by their employers in comparison to similarly situated co-workers. In *Lisek v. Norfolk*

---

department and supervisors who denied her promotions were Hispanic); Causey v. Balog, 929 F. Supp. 900, 910, 71 FEP 643 (D. Md. 1996) (white employee established prima facie case based on failure to promote where African-American official named as head of transportation department).

[10]*See, e.g.,* Hall v. City of Brawley, 887 F. Supp. 1333, 1342, 68 FEP 1343 (S.D. Cal. 1995) (white former employee established prima facie case by showing he was qualified for position, demoted from that position, and replaced by Hispanic).

[11]*See, e.g.,* Douglas v. Evans, 888 F. Supp. 1536, 1546, 68 FEP 472, 478 (M.D. Ala. 1995) (white employee established prima facie case of discriminatory transfer by showing that she routinely received above-average evaluations and that an African-American ultimately replaced her).

[12]69 F.3d at 1534–35.

[13]*Id.* at 1535 (finding plaintiff to have been qualified for position for which she was seeking promotion). *But see* Taken v. Oklahoma Corp. Comm'n, 934 F. Supp. 1294, 1298, 75 FEP 475 (W.D. Okla. 1996) (stating that single fact that official who allegedly discriminated against two white females on basis of race was African-American was insufficient to establish prima facie case), *aff'd,* 125 F.3d 1366 (10th Cir. 1997).

[14]Daly v. Unicare Corp.—Township Manor Nursing Ctr., 1995 U.S. Dist. LEXIS 5426, at *20, 68 FEP 208 (E.D. Pa. 1995); *accord* Patton v. United Parcel Serv., Inc., 910 F. Supp. 1250, 1264, 69 FEP 1665 (S.D. Tex. 1995) (white manager could not establish a prima facie case of discriminatory demotion because white employees held the majority of management positions in plaintiff's district); *cf.* Sciarrino v. Municipal Credit Union, 894 F. Supp. 102, 106–07, 73 FEP 661 (E.D.N.Y. 1995) (Italian-American employee failed to establish prima facie case against defendants, credit union, and African-American CEO, as plaintiff's work deficiencies had been brought to CEO's attention by plaintiff's Italian-American supervisor, and CEO had previously protected and promoted plaintiff).

& *Western Ry.*,[15] a white former employee of a railway company who was dismissed for sleeping on duty brought an action under Title VII for race discrimination. The district court found that the plaintiff established a prima facie case by showing that several nonwhite employees who were also caught sleeping on the job were not dismissed, thereby creating the inference that plaintiff was "treated less favorably than similarly-situated, nonwhite employees."[16]

Courts also have considered the relative qualifications of the plaintiff and co-workers in determining whether a white employee has been discriminated against on the basis of race.[17]

The Seventh Circuit, in *Carson v. Bethlehem Steel Corp.*,[18] was the first federal court of appeals to hold that a white employee can establish a prima facie case of reverse race discrimination even though the employee was replaced by another white employee. The Seventh Circuit relied on the recent Supreme Court decision, *O'Connor v. Consolidated Coin Caterers*,[19] which held that the

---

[15]918 F. Supp. 1202, 1209 (N.D. Ill. 1996). *Cf.* Brown v. Westinghouse Savannah River Corp., 928 F. Supp. 1168, 1172–73, 71 FEP 516 (S.D. Ga. 1996) (white employee terminated from nuclear weapons facility for cheating on safety exam could not establish prima facie case by alleging that nonwhite employees committed different violations of company policy without being terminated); Vore v. Indiana Bell Tel. Co., 32 F.3d 1161, 1164, 65 FEP 897 (7th Cir. 1994) (white employees did not state a claim of hostile work environment harassment by black employee by alleging that employer would have dealt more harshly with a white employee who harassed a group of African-American employees).

[16]*Lisek v. Norfolk & W. Ry.*, 918 F. Supp. at 1209. However, plaintiff's dismissal was ultimately upheld because his overall disciplinary record was poorer than those of the similarly situated employees who were not dismissed. *Id.* at 1210–11.

[17]*E.g.*, Terry v. Gallegos, 926 F. Supp. 679, 706–07 (W.D. Tenn. 1996) (white plaintiff's superior qualifications were factor in holding that employer discriminated against plaintiff when employer hired two African-Americans).

[18]82 F.3d 157, 158–59, 70 FEP 921 (7th Cir. 1996) (stating that plaintiff's replacement by another race is neither sufficient nor necessary to bring reverse discrimination claim; finding, however, that plaintiff's claim failed for lack of any evidence of discrimination). *But see* Reynolds v. School Dist. No. 1, Denver, Colo., 69 F.3d 1523, 1534 (10th Cir. 1995) (white employee could not satisfy essential element of prima facie case of race discrimination because another white woman was promoted to position for which plaintiff applied); Singh v. Shoney's, Inc., 64 F.3d 217, 219, 68 FEP 1288 (5th Cir. 1995) (terminated white employee could not establish prima facie case when replaced by white employee); Ellison v. Chilton County Bd. of Educ., 894 F. Supp. 415, 419 (M.D. Ala. 1995) (white plaintiffs precluded from establishing prima facie case of discriminatory hiring because they failed to claim that position was filled by minority).

[19]116 S. Ct. 1307, 1310 (1996) (noting that laws against discrimination protect persons, not classes).

plaintiff in an age discrimination suit does not have to show that he or she was replaced by a person outside the protected class.[20]

An employer's efforts to prevent a white employee from hiring and promoting African-Americans, and that employer's effective insistence that the white employee discriminate against African-Americans, continue to be actionable under Title VII.[21] Such employment practices impinge upon the rights of a white person to associate with African-Americans and to be free from discrimination based on opposition to an unlawful employment practice.[22]

2. Other Bases

Employees continue to pursue reverse discrimination claims based not only on race, but also on national origin and sex.

In *Stern v. Trustees of Columbia University*,[23] for example, an employee brought an action under Title VII alleging that the university failed to appoint him as the director of the Spanish language program and instead appointed an American of Hispanic national origin to that position.[24] The Second Circuit reversed the district court's grant of summary judgment in favor of the employer, holding that evidence of plaintiff's superior qualifications, experience, and recommendations, the existence of an affirmative action plan, a pool of other serious candidates that was limited to females and/or Hispanics, and other factors showed discrimination sufficient to send the case to a jury.[25]

Male employees claiming discrimination based on sex have brought a number of recent cases. One male employee proved discriminatory hiring by showing an outright admission by the employer that it considered gender in its decision to offer a position

---

[20]*Carson*, 82 F.3d at 158.

[21]*E.g.*, Chandler v. Fast Lane, Inc., 868 F. Supp. 1138, 1143–44, 66 FEP 675 (E.D. Ark. 1994) (white former employee's claim that she was forced to resign because defendants thwarted her from hiring and promoting African-Americans and insisted that she enforce anti-African-American practices, if proven, states cause of action under Title VII). *Cf.* Woods v. Bentsen, 889 F. Supp. 179, 187, 72 FEP 1554 (E.D. Pa. 1995) (supervisor's comment that white employee's husband is African-American was not sufficient to establish prima facie case of reverse racial harassment under Title VII).

[22]*Chandler*, 868 F. Supp. at 1144.

[23]131 F.3d 305, 306–07, 75 FEP 1423 (2d Cir. 1997).

[24]*Id.* at 312.

[25]*Id.* at 312–13.

to a female instead of a male.[26] Male employees have also brought discrimination claims challenging demotions or terminations based on allegations that similarly situated females were disciplined less severely for the same improper conduct[27] or that the male employee's supervisors as well as other employees in the same position were primarily women.[28]

---

[26]Hannon v. Chater, 887 F. Supp. 1303, 1314–16, 72 FEP 1379 (N.D. Cal. 1995) (male proved that he was passed over for the position of administrative law judge in the Social Security Administration due to reverse gender discrimination; deputy chief administrative law judge who made hiring decision stated that gender played a role in offering position to lower-rated female). *See also* Fairbairn v. Board of Educ. of S. Country Cent., 876 F. Supp. 432, 437–38 (E.D.N.Y. 1995) (defendants' admitted reliance on fact that African-American male would be an "excellent male role model" in hiring him over white female raises material issue as to whether defendants' hiring was discriminatory and, therefore, court denied defendants' motion for summary judgment).

[27]*E.g.*, Pierce v. Commonwealth Life Ins. Co., 40 F.3d 796, 801, 66 FEP 600 (6th Cir. 1994) (male employee demoted for violating sexual harassment policy claimed discrimination because female employee allegedly engaged in similar conduct and was not disciplined); Brown v. Westinghouse Savannah River Corp., 928 F. Supp. 1168, 1172–73, 71 FEP 516 (S.D. Ga. 1996) (male employee terminated from nuclear weapons facility for cheating on safety exam brought action alleging that female employees committed violations of other company policies without being terminated); Castleberry v. Boeing Co., 880 F. Supp. 1435, 1440 (D. Kan. 1995) (male former managerial employees terminated for unacceptable conduct pointed to allegedly similarly situated female employee who was treated more leniently); *see also* O'Patka v. Menasha Corp., 878 F. Supp. 1202, 1206–07, 70 FEP 11 (E.D. Wis. 1995) (male employee claimed supervisor discriminated against him because he was male, pointing to preferential treatment of female co-worker with whom supervisor had a romantic relationship); *cf.* James v. Ranch Mart Hardware, Inc., 881 F. Supp. 478, 481, 67 FEP 862 (D. Kan. 1995) (anatomically male transsexual brought Title VII action alleging that his employer would not have terminated a similarly situated female, living and working full time as a male); EEOC v. Walden Book Co., 885 F. Supp. 1100, 1103, 67 FEP 1446 (M.D. Tenn. 1995) (finding that same-sex sexual harassment is actionable under Title VII, court stated, "[i]t would be untenable to allow reverse discrimination cases but not same-sex sexual harassment cases to proceed under Title VII").

[28]*E.g.*, Davis v. Sheraton Soc'y Hill Hotel, 907 F. Supp. 896, 902, 71 FEP 1087 (E.D. Pa. 1995) (establishing prima facie case by showing that female employees outnumbered males in plaintiff's position, all of his supervisors were women, he had to wait several months longer for pay raise, and female employee received tuition reimbursement denied to plaintiff); Roemer v. Public Serv. Co. of Colo., 911 F. Supp. 464, 468–69, 69 FEP 1582 (D. Colo. 1996) (white male former employee pointed to historical makeup of workforce and statistical results of defendant's terminations and demotions).

B. Proof of Reverse Discrimination

The Supreme Court has yet to address how the *McDonnell Douglas*[29] prima facie case standard should be applied or modified in reverse discrimination cases. Courts remain split[30] as to whether to apply the *McDonnell Douglas* standard[31] or the modified standard set forth in *Parker v. Baltimore & Ohio R.R.*,[32] which requires some showing of "background circumstances [that] support the suspicion that the defendant is that unusual employer who discriminates against the majority."[33] While some courts consider

---

[29] McDonnell Douglas Corp. v. Green, 411 U.S. 792, 802, 5 FEP 965 (1973).

[30] *See* Bush v. Barnett Bank of Pinellas County, 916 F. Supp. 1244, 1253 (M.D. Fla. 1996) (discussing the split in courts regarding prima facie case standard to be applied in reverse discrimination cases).

[31] *See, e.g.,* Hill v. Burrell Communications Group, Inc., 67 F.3d 665, 668 n.2, 69 FEP 207 (7th Cir. 1995) (applying *McDonnell Douglas* test and explicitly rejecting idea that there should be two separate formulas, "since the rationale for the *McDonnell Douglas* formula is the difficulty of proving discrimination in general"); Lisek v. Norfolk & W. Ry., 918 F. Supp. 1202, 1209 (N.D. Ill. 1996) (applying *McDonnell Douglas* test in dismissal case); Bush v. Barnett Bank of Pinellas County, 916 F. Supp. 1244, 1253 (M.D. Fla. 1996) (applying *McDonnell Douglas* elements in termination case); Sciarrino v. Municipal Credit Union, 894 F. Supp. 102, 106, 73 FEP 661 (E.D.N.Y. 1995) (plaintiff alleging racial discrimination with respect to discharge can establish prima facie case by showing that: (1) he belongs to a protected class; (2) his job performance was satisfactory; (3) he was discharged; and (4) his discharge occurred in circumstances giving rise to an inference of racial discrimination); Hall v. City of Brawley, 887 F. Supp. 1333, 1341–42, 68 FEP 1343 (S.D. Cal. 1995) (*McDonnell Douglas* standard applied in white former employee's claim of discriminatory demotion against municipal employer; white former employee established prima facie case of race discrimination by showing that he was qualified for position, demoted from that position, and replaced by a Hispanic); Fairbairn v. Board of Educ. of S. Country Cent., 876 F. Supp. 432, 437 (E.D.N.Y. 1995) (applying *McDonnell Douglas* model in promotion case; white female school employee, who sought position of assistant principal, established prima facie case of race discrimination, as she was qualified for the position and was passed over in favor of a African-American male); Douglas v. Evans, 888 F. Supp. 1536, 1546, 68 FEP 472, 478 (M.D. Ala. 1995) (applying *McDonnell Douglas* in case where white employee alleged she was transferred due to her race); Ellison v. Chilton County Bd. of Educ., 894 F. Supp. 415, 419 (M.D. Ala. 1995) (applying *McDonnell Douglas* in hiring case brought under § 1981).

[32] 652 F.2d 1012, 1017, 25 FEP 889 (D.C. Cir. 1981).

[33] *Id.* at 1017. *See, e.g.,* Reynolds v. School Dist. No. 1, Denver, Colo., 69 F.3d 1523, 1534, 72 FEP 485 (10th Cir. 1995) (*Parker* standard applied to § 1981 claim of discriminatory demotion and constructive discharge); Pierce v. Commonwealth Life Ins Co., 40 F.3d 796, 801–02, 66 FEP 600 (6th Cir. 1994) (applying *Parker* test in male employee's claim that he was demoted on basis of his sex); Gilbert v.

the *Parker* standard to be a stricter standard than that set forth in *McDonnell Douglas*,[34] at least one court has held that the *Parker* standard "is not intended to be rigidly applied or difficult to show."[35]

In *Patton v. United Parcel Services, Inc.*,[36] a district court in Texas offered a more specific modification of the *McDonnell Douglas* test for a reverse discrimination case. The court held that to satisfy the first element of the prima facie case, a white employee must belong to a racial minority within the company.[37] In *Patton*, a white manager who had been demoted was precluded from establishing a prima facie case of race discrimination because white employees held the majority of management positions in plaintiff's district.[38]

The *Parker* and *Patton* standards are similar in application in that courts have found a sufficient showing of "background circumstances" where the white or male employee is the minority in the group in which that employee works.[39] Sufficient background

---

Penn-Wheeling Closure Corp., 917 F. Supp. 1119, 1126–27 (N.D. W. Va. 1996) (applying *Parker* standard, court found that failure to show that employer "has a history of terminating white males" precluded finding of prima facie case of race discrimination); Olenick v. New York Tel./A Nynex Co., 881 F. Supp. 113, 114–15 (S.D.N.Y. 1995) (court granted employer summary judgment because white applicant presented no evidence supporting suspicion that defendant is that unusual employer who discriminates against the majority); Plummer v. Safeway, Inc., 1995 U.S. Dist. LEXIS 3428, at *6–7 (D.D.C. 1995) (applying *Parker* standard, court found that white plaintiff presented insufficient evidence of background circumstances); O'Patka v. Menasha Corp., 878 F. Supp. 1202, 1206–07 (E.D. Wis. 1995) (male employee claiming reverse discrimination required to show "background circumstances").

[34] *See* Reynolds v. School Dist. No. 1, Denver, Colo., 69 F.3d at 1534 (plaintiff "does not necessarily deserve the presumption of discrimination afforded to a member of an ostensibly disfavored minority class"); Roemer v. Public Serv. Co. of Colo., 911 F. Supp. 464, 468, 69 FEP 1582 (D. Colo. 1996) (stricter standard applied to white male former employee's claim that termination was due to reverse gender discrimination).

[35] Davis v. Sheraton Soc'y Hill Hotel, 907 F. Supp. 896, 900, 71 FEP 1087 (E.D. Pa. 1995).

[36] 910 F. Supp. 1250 (S.D. Tex. 1994) (citing Flanagan v. Aaron E. Henry Community Health Serv. Ctr., 876 F.2d 1231, 1233, 51 FEP 1483 (5th Cir. 1989)).

[37] *Patton*, 910 F. Supp. at 1262–64.

[38] *Id.* at 1263–64.

[39] *See, e.g.*, Reynolds v. School Dist. No. 1, Denver, Colo., 69 F.3d at 1534–35 (white bilingual education teacher identified background circumstances that would justify presumption of discrimination; she was the only white employee in the otherwise all-Hispanic bilingual department and Hispanic supervisors made most of the employment decisions); Davis v. Sheraton Soc'y Hill Hotel, 907 F. Supp. at 902 (terminated male employee alleged sufficient background circumstances; there were

circumstances were also found when a defendant admitted reliance on a discriminatory factor in making employment decisions.[40]

III. Reverse Discrimination Pursuant to Affirmative Action Programs

A. Affirmative Action Under the Equal Protection Clause

1. Voluntary State and Local Government Plans

a. Race-Based Plans. As the Supreme Court held in *City of Richmond v. J.A. Croson Co.*,[41] evidence of identified racial discrimination in a particular industry may justify voluntary adoption of an affirmative action program based on race even if there is no direct evidence of actual discrimination. Adoption of such a plan is a voluntary measure, however, and is not constitutionally mandated.[42]

In a recent decision in the academic context, *Hopwood v. Texas*,[43] the Fifth Circuit concluded that the University of Texas School of Law's affirmative action admissions program was unconstitutional because the stated reasons for the program did not

---

more female employees than males in plaintiff's position, all of plaintiff's supervisors were women, plaintiff had to wait longer for pay raise than female co-worker, and female employee received tuition reimbursement denied to plaintiff). *Cf.* Daly v. Unicare Corp.—Township Manor Nursing Ctr., 1995 U.S. Dist. LEXIS 5426, at *20, 68 FEP 208 (E.D. Pa. 1995) (white employee did not present "background circumstances" where the majority of those he worked for were white and white executives fired him); Taken v. Oklahoma Corp. Comm'n, 934 F. Supp. 1294, 1298 (W.D. Okl. 1996) (single fact that official who allegedly discriminated against two white females on basis of race was African-American held insufficient to establish necessary background circumstances), *aff'd,* 125 F.3d 1366 (10th Cir. 1997).

[40]*E.g.,* Hannon v. Chater, 887 F. Supp. 1303, 1314–16 (N.D. Cal. 1995) (male applicant for position of administrative law judge met higher standard of prima facie case by showing that deputy chief administrative law judge, who offered position to lower-rated female, stated that "the fact that she was a woman was a factor in her favor").

[41]488 U.S. 469, 509–11, 53 FEP 197 (1989).

[42]*See* Austin Black Contractors v. City of Austin, 78 F.3d 185, 186 (5th Cir. 1996) (court dismissed contractors association's requests for a 10% set aside for African-American contractors based on historical study by city that found minorities statistically "under-utilized" in city construction work).

[43]78 F.3d 932 (5th Cir.), *cert. denied sub nom.* Texas v. Hopwood, 518 U.S. 1033 (1996).

satisfy the compelling interest prong of the strict scrutiny analysis commanded by *Wygant v. Jackson Board of Education*.[44] The admissions program at issue in *Hopwood* included lowered admission requirements for Mexican-American and African-American applicants, color-coded applications according to race, separate discussions of each minority candidate in meetings of a minority subcommittee (candidates who were not African-American or Mexican-American were not discussed individually), and segregated waiting lists.[45] The district court had found two of the stated reasons to be compelling justifications for the practice: (1) "obtaining the educational benefits that flow from a racially and ethnically diverse student body" and (2) "the present effects at the law school of past discrimination in both the University of Texas system and the Texas educational system as a whole."[46] The Fifth Circuit determined that "any consideration of race or ethnicity by the law school for the purpose of achieving a diverse student body is not a compelling interest,"[47] and the use of race as a factor in admissions to further diversity actually contradicts the goals of equal protection.[48] Instead, the appeals court stated, the appropriate method to foster diversity in higher education is to individually scrutinize applicants, without reference to race.[49] The Fifth Circuit also found that the second asserted justification failed to show a compelling state interest sufficient to justify using race in the admission process.[50] The court held that in order for the law school's admissions program to function as a remedy for any present effects of

---

[44] 476 U.S. 267, 40 FEP 1321 (1986).
[45] 78 F.3d at 936–38.
[46] *Id.* at 941.
[47] *Id.* at 944, 948. *See also* Back v. Carter, 933 F. Supp 738, 756 (N.D. Ind. 1996) (in employment situation, desire for diversity does not justify governmental race-based actions). *But cf.* Wittmer v. Peters, 87 F.3d 916, 919, 71 FEP 312 (7th Cir. 1996) (in employment case, Seventh Circuit rejected argument that only form of racial discrimination that can withstand strict scrutiny is remedial discrimination to cure the adverse effects of past discrimination and upheld the preference given to an African-American applicant for the position of lieutenant in a prison boot camp), *cert. denied,* 117 S. Ct. 949, 74 FEP 768 (1997); McLaughlin v. Boston Sch. Comm., 938 F. Supp. 1001, 1014–15 (D. Mass. 1996) (in equal protection challenge to 35% set-aside for African-American and Hispanic students at public school, court noted that whether diversity is a compelling interest justifying racial classifications is a big question yet to be decided by the Supreme Court).
[48] *Hopwood v. Texas,* 78 F.3d at 945.
[49] *Id.* at 947.
[50] *Id.* at 955.

past discrimination, the law school must be identified as the relevant past discriminator,[51] and that general past discrimination in education did not justify the consideration of race in the law school's admissions system.[52] In other words, there must be a proven connection between the present effects of past discrimination and the program at issue.[53]

With respect to the "compelling interest" prong of the *Wygant* strict scrutiny standard, several recent cases indicate that mere evidence of general "societal discrimination" is insufficient as the sole justification for race-based preferential treatment.[54] Instead, to justify this preferential treatment, there must be evidence of the effects of discrimination in the industry that is addressed by the plan.[55] In addition, an identification of a link between the plan and the discrimination would further support the given program's factual predicate.[56]

---

[51]*Id.* at 952.

[52]*Id.* at 954.

[53]*Id.* at 952. Judge Wiener's concurring opinion found the admissions program did not withstand strict scrutiny because it was not narrowly tailored. *Id.* at 962. He specifically declined to concur in the majority's compelling interest analysis, finding their conclusion that *"any consideration of race or ethnicity by the law school for the purposes of achieving a diverse student body is not a compelling interest under the Fourteenth Amendment,"* to be an extension of the Supreme Court's position and unnecessary to the resolution of the case. *Id.* at 963.

[54]*See, e.g.,* Associated Gen. Contractors of Am. v. City of Columbus, 936 F. Supp. 1363, 1378 (S.D. Ohio 1996) (societal discrimination alone cannot justify a racial or gender classification); Back v. Carter, 933 F. Supp. 738, 755 (N.D. Ind. 1996) (need more than a showing of general societal discrimination to justify imposition of race and gender quotas in judicial nominating commission); McLaughlin v. Boston Sch. Comm., 938 F. Supp. 1001, 1014 (D. Mass. 1996) (societal discrimination is not enough to solely justify a racial classification but it does not follow that societal discrimination is therefore irrelevant); North State Law Enforcement Officers Ass'n v. Charlotte-Mecklenburg Police Dep't, 862 F. Supp. 1445, 1457–58, 65 FEP 1537 (W.D.N.C. 1994) (remedying general societal discrimination is not a compelling interest that justifies the consent decree). *See* Wittmer v. Peters, 87 F.3d 916, 919 (7th Cir. 1996) ("common sense" that there should be correspondence between the racial composition of the prison population and that of the staff is not enough, but permitting preference for African-American lieutenant in special situation of prison boot camp), *cert. denied,* 117 S. Ct. 949, 74 FEP 768 (1997).

[55]*See* Associated Gen. Contractors v. City of New Haven, 41 F.3d 62, 66 (2d Cir. 1994) ("[A]n amorphous claim that there has been past discrimination in a particular industry cannot justify the use of an unyielding racial quota." (citation omitted)).

[56]*See, e.g.,* Concrete Works v. City & County of Denver, 36 F.3d 1513, 1520–22 (10th Cir. 1994) (denying defendant's motion for summary judgment but holding that anecdotal evidence and postenactment evidence may be admissible to

As to the "narrowly tailored" prong of the strict scrutiny analysis, recent cases continue to hold that any quotas implemented as part of an affirmative action plan must be tailored to a defensible purpose because it is unrealistic to assume that the relevant reference pool of minority applicants or candidates for a given trade or industry will mirror the percentage of minorities in the general population.[57] In *Back v. Carter*,[58] the district court discussed the irrelevance of a showing of the percentage of the protected class in the general population when the position at issue required the specific qualifications and skills of an attorney in the designated county.[59]

Plans that satisfy both prongs of the strict scrutiny analysis continue to be upheld as constitutional. In *Wittmer v. Peters*,[60] the Seventh Circuit upheld the preference for an African-American lieutenant in the prison boot camp because it believed the expert's analysis that there was a need for an African-American lieutenant or African-American authority figure in order to encourage the African-American inmates to participate in the "correctional game

---

show past or present race or gender discrimination; additionally, court stated that identification of a linkage between the award of public contracts and private discrimination would enhance the program's factual predicate), *cert. denied*, 514 U.S. 1004 (1995).

[57] *See, e.g.*, Contractors Ass'n of E. Penn., Inc. v. City of Philadelphia, 91 F.3d 586, 606-07 (3d Cir. 1996) (set-aside for minority subcontractors focused solely on percentage of women and minorities in general population and not the percentage in the applicable labor pool), *cert. denied*, 117 S. Ct. 953 (1997); Middleton v. City of Flint, 92 F.3d 396, 406, 71 FEP 962 (6th Cir. 1996) (when particular position requires special qualifications, relevant labor pool is not general population), *cert. denied*, 117 S. Ct. 1552 (1997); Dallas Fire Fighters Ass'n v. City of Dallas, 885 F. Supp. 915, 923 (N.D. Tex. 1995) (as percentage of qualified candidates in lower ranks fluctuates, no one percentage goal for each rank can be sufficiently related to the number of qualified candidates in the appropriate reference pool); Mallory v. Harkness, 895 F. Supp. 1556, 1560 (S.D. Fla. 1995) (statute requiring one third of all appointees to judicial nominating commission to be women or minorities is unconstitutional because there is no correlation between the 33% quota and the relevant population or the unknown percentage of women and minority members of the Florida bar; percentage of women and minorities in Florida's general population is not relevant pool), *aff'd without opinion*, 109 F.3d 771 (11th Cir. 1997).

[58] 933 F. Supp. 738 (N.D. Ind. 1996).

[59] *Id.* at 756. The 1990 census statistics showing 52% of the general population in the county were women and 30% were minorities were not determinative when only 20% of the attorneys in the county were women and only 10% were minorities. *Id.* at 747, 756, 758.

[60] 87 F.3d 916, 920, 71 FEP 312 (7th Cir. 1996), *cert. denied*, 117 S. Ct. 949, 74 FEP 768 (1997).

of brutal drill sergeant and brutalized recruit."[61] The *Wittmer* court, distinguishing its rationale from the "role model" theory that has been rejected by the Supreme Court, noted that boot camp inmates do not aspire to become correctional officers.[62] The Seventh Circuit further noted that government officials could legally take race into account when making decisions under certain circumstances and that this consideration was not narrowly limited to situations that seek to rectify past discrimination.[63]

In the context of desegregation of schools, the court in *Stanley v. Darlington County School District*[64] upheld a court-fashioned consent order to implement a magnet school program with a temporary 10 percent set-aside for neighborhood students and a requirement of a 50/50 (African-American/white) racial composition.[65] The district court found that these measures survived strict scrutiny even in the wake of *Adarand Constructors, Inc. v. Peña*,[66] by reasoning that *Adarand* applied only to racial classifications that subjected a person to unequal treatment, and the requirements for admissions to the magnet school did not subject any person to unequal treatment.[67] The court determined that the 50/50 requirement was a "race-conscious" provision that impacts all races equally, rather than a "race-based" provision to which *Adarand*'s strict scrutiny test applies.[68] The court further found that the magnet school program's admissions requirements survived strict scrutiny by meeting both the compelling interest and narrowly tailored prongs of the analysis.[69]

Another example of a plan satisfying strict scrutiny requirements is *Sims v. Montgomery County Comm'n*,[70] where the district court upheld the sheriff department's affirmative action promotion plan.[71] The court found a compelling interest because the department had

---

[61]*Id.*
[62]*Id.*
[63]*Id.* at 919.
[64]915 F. Supp. 764, 776, 67 FEP 1828 (D.S.C. 1996).
[65]*Id.*
[66]115 S. Ct. 2097 (1995).
[67]915 F. Supp. at 774–75.
[68]*Id.* at 775.
[69]*Id.* at 776.
[70]890 F. Supp. 1520 (M.D. Ala. 1995), *aff'd without opinion*, 119 F.3d 9 (11th Cir. 1997).
[71]*Id.* at 1532–33.

intentionally discriminated against African-Americans in promotion and the present effects of this past discrimination had continued.[72] The court also found that the plan was narrowly tailored in light of its short duration and its limited application only to equally qualified candidates.[73]

Plans that fail to establish that there is any prior discrimination to be remedied, or that there is any current discrimination that must be prevented, do not withstand the strict scrutiny analysis and are, therefore, unconstitutional.[74] In *Middleton v. City of Flint*,[75] the Sixth Circuit reiterated that evidence of prior discrimination, remote in time, which the government subsequently has taken measures to reverse, does not support a claim of compelling interest.[76] Nor does evidence of a disparity between the percentage of the minority group employed in a given occupation and the percentage of that minority group in the regional labor pool constitute a compelling interest.[77] The *Middleton* court therefore found that the "Flint Plan," which required that 50 percent of all police officers promoted to sergeant be members of specific minorities, satisfied neither the compelling interest prong nor the narrowly tailored prong of the strict scrutiny analysis.[78]

Likewise, in *Contractors Ass'n of Eastern Pennsylvania v. City of Philadelphia*,[79] the Third Circuit held that the Philadelphia ordinance that created a set-aside for "participation goals" for minority subcontractors on city public works contracts was not narrowly tailored.[80] The court determined that the race-based preferential set-aside was not justified by prior discrimination and

---

[72]*Id.* at 1532.

[73]*Id.* at 1532–33.

[74]*See, e.g.,* Mallory v. Harkness, 895 F. Supp. 1556, 1559 (S.D. Fla. 1995) (past discrimination neither asserted nor proven).

[75]92 F.3d 396, 71 FEP 962 (6th Cir. 1996), *cert. denied,* 117 S. Ct. 1552 (1997).

[76]*Id.* at 409.

[77]*Id.* at 406, 408.

[78]*Id.* at 412–13 (while denial of promotional opportunities for almost a decade equals a significant, legally cognizable, and adverse impact on the rights of third parties, challenged plan was unable to meet narrowly tailored requirements). *See also* Back v. Carter, 933 F. Supp. 738, 757 (N.D. Ind. 1996) (race and gender quotas struck down where no showing of compelling interest or narrowly tailored plan).

[79]91 F.3d 586 (3d Cir. 1996), *cert. denied,* 117 S. Ct. 953 (1997).

[80]*Id.* at 591. *See* Associated Gen. Contractors of Am. v. City of Columbus, 936 F. Supp. 1363, 1433–39 (S.D. Ohio 1996) (equal business opportunity code, which included race- and gender-based subcontracting goals of 10% for MBEs and 7%

that the set-aside failed to include either race-neutral or less burdensome remedies to encourage participation of minority subcontractors in the market for city contracts.[81]

Recent cases illustrate that affirmative action plans do not satisfy the narrowly tailored requirement of the equal protection analysis when the adverse impact on the rights of nonbeneficiaries of the plan is unnecessary. In *Dallas Fire Fighters Ass'n v. City of Dallas*,[82] for example, the district court determined that a "skip promotion" affirmative action plan violated equal protection by its unnecessary adverse impact on the rights of nonminorities.[83] The "skip promotion" policy trumped the seniority policy, and the court stated that "the City's interest in race-conscious promotion policies is not as strong as the rights and expectations surrounding seniority."[84] In *Alexander v. Estepp*,[85] the Fourth Circuit held that the fire department's program was unconstitutional as it was not narrowly tailored to meet its goals.[86] The Fourth Circuit found that the fire department's affirmative action program gave a preference to all minority groups even though the only evidence presented was of discrimination against African-Americans.[87] Courts have also overturned affirmative action plans as not narrowly tailored when the plans implement a rigid quota that adversely impacts the nonbeneficiaries of the plan.[88]

---

for FBEs was not narrowly tailored, as the city did not try any of the race- or gender-neutral programs recommended before resorting to race- and gender-conscious legislation, the participation goals were not sufficiently flexible, and the city did not demonstrate any relationship between the availability of MBEs and FBEs and the participation goals).

[81]91 F.3d at 609–10.

[82]885 F. Supp. 915 (N.D. Tex. 1995).

[83]*Id.* at 923.

[84]*Id. See* Michael Delikat, *Rightsizing: Legal and Practical Problems of Reductions in Force*, 542 PLI/Lit 665, 690–93 (1996).

[85]95 F.3d 312 (4th Cir. 1996), *cert. denied sub nom.* Prince George's County v. Alexander, 117 S. Ct. 1425 (1997).

[86]*Id.* at 316.

[87]*Id.* Additionally, the court determined that there were less drastic means available than the outright racial classifications used. *Id.*

[88]*See, e.g.,* Mallory v. Harkness, 895 F. Supp. 1556, 1562 (S.D. Fla. 1995) (rigid quota imposes significant burden on white men), *aff'd without opinion,* 109 F.3d 771 (11th Cir. 1997); North State Law Enforcement Officer's Ass'n v. Charlotte-Mecklenburg Police Dep't, 862 F. Supp. 1445, 1459, 65 FEP 1537 (W.D.N.C. 1994) (decree not narrowly tailored where rigid quotas absolutely prohibit non-African-Americans from ever holding more than 80% of all available positions).

b. *Sex-Based Plans.* Despite the strict scrutiny test for race-based affirmative action plans promulgated by the Supreme Court in *Adarand Constructors, Inc. v. Peña*,[89] recent cases continue to apply only intermediate scrutiny to evaluate gender-based classifications.[90]

In *Shuford v. Alabama State Board of Education*,[91] an Alabama district court took a novel approach to affirmative action analysis when it considered whether the plan at issue was inclusive or exclusive.[92] The court explained that inclusive techniques include a larger number of qualified candidates in the selection process, while exclusive methods focus on selection of certain candidates over others from the relevant pool.[93] Inclusive affirmative action methods, the court noted, do not even require traditional Title VII or equal protection analyses because the inclusion of more qualified candidates in the relevant pool is both desirable and proper.[94] The *Shuford* court applied this analysis to a court-approved consent decree aimed at increasing the numbers of women and African-Americans in professional positions in Alabama's postsecondary education system and determined that the decree was one of inclusion that withstood equal protection scrutiny.[95] The decree's sex-conscious provisions withstood the test of intermediate scrutiny, which requires "substantial evidence" of past discrimination, either by the individual defendants or by general societal discrimination.[96]

---

[89]115 S. Ct. 2097, 67 FEP 1828 (1995).

[90]*See, e.g.,* Concrete Works of Colo. v. City & County of Denver, 36 F.3d 1513, 1519 (10th Cir. 1994) (evaluating gender-based classifications under intermediate scrutiny standard), *cert. denied,* 514 U.S. 1004 (1995); Back v. Carter, 933 F. Supp. 738, 755 (N.D. Ind. 1996) (gender classifications reviewed under intermediate scrutiny test); Shuford v. Alabama State Bd. of Educ., 897 F. Supp. 1535, 1556–57 (M.D. Ala. 1995) (courts examine sex-conscious provisions using intermediate scrutiny). For a discussion of gender-based affirmative action and the applicable level of scrutiny, *see* Rebecca L. Berkeley, *Gender Based Affirmative Action: A Journey That Has Only Just Begun,* 50 WASH. U.J. URB. & CONTEMP. L. 353 (1996); Deborah L. Brake, *Sex as a Suspect Class: An Argument for Applying Strict Scrutiny to Gender Discrimination,* 6 SETON HALL CONST. L.J. 953 (1996).

[91]897 F. Supp. 1535 (M.D. Ala. 1995).

[92]*Id.* at 1551–56. (consent decree established numerical goals for percentages of women and African-Americans to be employed in positions within the Alabama postsecondary school system).

[93]*Id.* at 1551–52.

[94]*Id.* at 1552.

[95]*Id.* at 1570.

[96]*Id.* at 1557–59, 1566. The court considered historical, anecdotal, and statistical evidence in making this determination. *Id. See also* Back v. Carter, 933 F. Supp. 738, 757 (N.D. Ind. 1996) (government can show important interest by showing

In determining that the remedy was "substantially related" to the goal of eliminating sex discrimination within the professional positions in the postsecondary system of education, the court found that the decree was substantially related to its goal and that the remedy was both necessary and "mild."[97]

B. Voluntary Affirmative Action Plans Under Title VII

2. Requirements for a Valid Plan

b. The Necessary Factual Predicate. Several recent cases have further defined the factual predicate necessary for affirmative action under Title VII.

In *Taxman v. Board of Education of Township of Piscataway*,[98] the Third Circuit rejected a voluntary affirmative action plan that did not satisfy the requirements of *Steelworkers v. Weber*[99] and *Johnson v. Transportation Agency, Santa Clara County*.[100] The *Taxman* court noted that the board of education of the township of Piscataway had not adopted its affirmative action plan in order to address a manifest imbalance in its employment practices.[101] Indeed, the parties stipulated that the plan was not "intended to remedy the results of any prior discrimination or identified underrepresentation" of minority candidates within the applicable workforce.[102] Instead, the board had invoked its existing, discretionary affirmative action plan as an anticipatory measure, designed to ensure that its business department was not staffed by an all-white faculty when deciding which of two equally qualified teachers to lay off.[103] According to the Third Circuit, although the board's stated interest in ensuring a "racially diverse faculty" was perhaps laudatory, it was not sufficient to meet the requirements of *Weber* and *Johnson*.[104]

---

government unit engaged in discrimination itself or by showing societal discrimination in the field).

[97] 897 F. Supp. at 1566–67.
[98] 91 F.3d 1547, 71 FEP 848 (3d Cir. 1996), *cert. granted,* 117 S. Ct. 2506 (1997), *cert. dismissed,* 118 S. Ct. 595 (1997).
[99] 443 U.S. 193, 20 FEP 1 (1979).
[100] 480 U.S. 616, 43 FEP 411 (1987).
[101] *Taxman,* 91 F.3d at 1563.
[102] *Id.* The board conceded that "[b]lacks are not underrepresented in its teaching workforce as a whole or even in the Piscataway High School" and did not "contend that its action here was directed at remedying any *de jure* or *de facto* segregation." *Id.*
[103] *Id.*
[104] *Id.* at 1563–65.

In *Smith v. Virginia Commonwealth University*,[105] the Fourth Circuit considered, at the summary judgment stage, a university's use of "multiple regression analysis" to demonstrate the existence of a manifest imbalance in the salaries of male versus female employees.[106] The court found that the Supreme Court's decision in *Bazemore v. Friday*,[107] although allowing for the use of multiple regression analysis, required that such analysis be evaluated in "light of all the evidence in the record."[108] The *Smith* court concluded that the lower court's grant of summary judgment was improper as there was a dispute of material fact regarding whether the multiple regression analysis could establish manifest imbalance.[109]

In *Dallas Fire Fighters Ass'n v. City of Dallas*,[110] the district court considered whether the city's statistical analysis demonstrated a manifest imbalance in the rate of promotion of minorities. The city had examined the number of employees, the number of minority employees, the percentage and number of minority employees available for promotion, and the actual number and percentage promoted.[111] The court, while accepting that the city's statistics did reflect a manifest imbalance, questioned whether the statistical evidence addressed the issue of whether unlawful discrimination was the *cause* of the manifest imbalance.[112] The court concluded, however, that the city merely needed to show that an imbalance existed and did not need to explain the imbalance.[113] The court did not consider what effect proof that the imbalance was not due to discrimination would have had on this analysis.

In *McNamara v. City of Chicago*,[114] relying on *Johnson v. Transportation Agency, Santa Clara County*,[115] the district court upheld

---

[105] 84 F.3d 672, 70 FEP 1248 (4th Cir. 1996).
[106] *Id.* at 676.
[107] 478 U.S. 385, 41 FEP 92 (1986).
[108] *Smith*, 84 F.3d at 676. The court also noted that the particular multiple regression analysis under consideration failed to account for "performance factors" and that "*Bazemore* and common sense require that any multiple regression analysis used to determine pay disparity must include all the *major* factors on which pay is determined." *Id.* (emphasis in original).
[109] *Id.* at 676–77.
[110] 885 F. Supp. 915 (N.D. Tex. 1995).
[111] *Id.* at 924.
[112] *Id.*
[113] *Id.* at 925.
[114] 867 F. Supp. 739 (N.D. Ill. 1994), *aff'd*, 138 F.3d 1219 (7th Cir. 1998).
[115] 480 U.S. 616, 43 FEP 411 (1987).

an affirmative action plan adopted by the Chicago fire department. The court first noted that "[a] 'manifest imbalance' is less than a disparity needed to make out a prima facie Title VII violation."[116] The court then reviewed the statistical evidence introduced to support the adoption of the affirmative action plan and found that the evidence did demonstrate a manifest imbalance.[117] The *McNamara* court explicitly noted that "[w]hether the cause of the disparity is past discrimination is not relevant to Title VII analysis."[118] On appeal, the Seventh Circuit affirmed the district court decision, noting that there was evidence that the disparity in the representation of African-Americans and Hispanics in the fire department "was due, at least in part, to discrimination by the City."[119]

In *Shuford v. Alabama State Board of Education*,[120] the district court held that statistical evidence was not necessary to demonstrate a manifest imbalance in the subject workforce. The court concluded that "it is impossible in this case to develop qualified labor pools because the defendants have not adhered to any objective measure of qualifications."[121] The court noted that it had previously decided that the strict scrutiny standard does not require statistical analysis where sufficient historical and anecdotal evidence demonstrate a case of discrimination.[122] Under Title VII, therefore, historical and anecdotal evidence could substitute for statistical proof of a manifest imbalance.[123]

c. Permissible Scope of a Voluntary Plan. (i.) Considering the rights of nonminority employees. In *Taxman v. Board of Education of Township of Piscataway*,[124] the Third Circuit rejected an affirmative action plan because it impermissibly interfered with the rights

---

[116]*McNamara*, 867 F. Supp. at 750.

[117]*Id.* at 750–51 ("The difference between the expected percentage of blacks and Hispanics in the captain rank and the observed percentage was 3.96 standard deviations, a significant and suspicious disparity.").

[118]*Id.* at 750–51 n.10.

[119]McNamara v. City of Chicago, 138 F.3d 1219, 1998 U.S. App. LEXIS 5052, at *13–14 (7th Cir. 1998).

[120]897 F. Supp. 1535 (M.D. Ala. 1995).

[121]*Id.* at 1557.

[122]*Id.*

[123]*Id.* ("Any other holding would make Title VII more restrictive than strict scrutiny, which is inappropriate.").

[124]91 F.3d 1547, 71 FEP 848 (3d Cir. 1996), *cert. granted,* 117 S. Ct. 2506 (1997), *cert. dismissed,* 118 S. Ct. 595 (1997).

of nonminority employees. The court found that the plan contained an "utter lack of definition and structure" and that it did not define what "racial diversity" the plan was aiming to create.[125] The plan, therefore, lacked the necessary objectives and indicators against which its success could be measured.[126] These objectives and indicators serve to ensure that "only those minority preferences necessary to further the plans' purpose" are included.[127] Moreover, the plan directly harmed the interests of nonminority employees because it favored the retention of minority employees during layoff considerations. Relying upon *Steelworkers v. Weber*[128] and *Johnson v. Transportation Agency, Santa Clara County*,[129] the court concluded that the loss of employment was too great a harm to justify the plan.[130]

The district court in *Dallas Fire Fighters Ass'n v. City of Dallas*[131] also considered and rejected an affirmative action plan as it applied to the grant of promotions because it impeded the rights of nonminorities.[132] The court found that the promotion policy at issue was "starkly different" from the promotion policy under consideration in *Johnson*.[133] There was no evidence that the employer had utilized interviews or individual or comparative evaluations in considering the promotions.[134] Furthermore, the promotional goals adopted by the employer were unrelated to the relevant pools of qualified employees for the various job classifications affected by the promotion policy.[135] In essence, the employer had allowed race and gender "to become *the* factor in making promotional decisions

---

[125]*Id.* at 1564. The court noted that it did not intend to suggest that specific numerical goals must be set for an affirmative action plan to be acceptable. Rather, "[t]he absence of goals, while it may not have been fatal alone, is a factor contributing to the overall vagueness of the plan." *Id.* at 1564 n.15.

[126]*Id.* at 1564.

[127]*Id.* ("[T]he Board's policy, devoid of goals and standards, is governed entirely by the Board's whim. . . . Such a policy unnecessarily trammels the interests of nonminority employees.").

[128]443 U.S. 193, 20 FEP 1 (1979).

[129]480 U.S. 616, 43 FEP 411 (1987).

[130]*Taxman*, 91 F.3d at 1564 (the "loss of his or her job is so substantial and the cost so severe that the Board's goal of racial diversity, even if legitimate under Title VII, may not be pursued in this particular fashion").

[131]885 F. Supp. 915 (N.D. Tex. 1995).

[132]*Id.* at 927.

[133]*Id.* at 925.

[134]*Id.* ("there is no evidence of an evaluation of the applicants based upon their past job performance, experience or personal attributes. All of these factors are present in *Johnson*").

[135]*Id.* at 926.

instead of but one factor among many,"[136] and thus the promotional policy as implemented unduly trammeled the rights of nonminority employees.[137]

The Ninth Circuit in *Gilligan v. Department of Labor*[138] found that an affirmative action plan was not deficient where gender was only a factor, but not the exclusive factor, considered by the employer.[139] Any affirmative action plan that relies exclusively on one factor would result in illegal discrimination.[140]

In *McNamara v. City of Chicago*,[141] the district court followed *Johnson v. Transportation Agency, Santa Clara County*[142] in upholding an affirmative action plan that was originally developed with the knowledge of available employment information concerning the applicable pool of employees. The hiring objectives as detailed in the affirmative action plan were only developed after consideration of the qualifications of the applicable set of employees.[143] In these circumstances, the plan's promotion goals did not unnecessarily affect the rights of nonminority employees, as preferences in promotion do not affect an employee's rights in the same manner as preferences in hiring or layoff.[144] The court also concluded that the policy did not prevent, but only postponed, nonminority employees' opportunities for promotion.[145] There was, therefore, no permanent bar to promotion for nonminority employees, and all of the plaintiffs remained eligible for promotion in the future.[146]

---

[136]*Id.* (emphasis in original).

[137]*Id.* at 927 ("[T]he City's policy of skip promotions fails under Title VII because the single, arbitrary percentage goal for every rank coupled with the City's failure to consider race or gender as one of several factors . . . unnecessarily trammels the rights of nonminority firefighters.").

[138]81 F.3d 835, 70 FEP 856 (9th Cir. 1996). The Ninth Circuit focused on whether an action that is consistent with, but not taken in reliance on or pursuant to, the relevant affirmative action policy may be defended by reference to the affirmative action policy. The court concluded that "in an institutional setting, it is not necessarily determinative whether the hiring officials actually relied upon the plan as long as they acted consistently with it." *Id.* at 839.

[139]*Id.* at 839.

[140]*Id.* ("any affirmative action program which specifically provides for such discrimination or in practice results in such discrimination is illegal").

[141]867 F. Supp. 739, 750 (N.D. Ill. 1994), *aff'd*, 138 F.3d 1219 (7th Cir. 1998).

[142]480 U.S. 616, 43 FEP 411 (1987).

[143]*McNamara*, 867 F. Supp. at 750.

[144]*Id.* at 751 ("denial of a future employment opportunity is not as intrusive as loss of an existing job") (quoting United States v. Paradise, 480 U.S. 149 (1987)).

[145]*Id.*

[146]*Id.* at 751–52.

Similarly, in *Hannon v. Chater*,[147] the court upheld an "outreach" affirmative action plan that did not set aside positions for minority or female employees or establish fixed quotas that would have the result of permanently excluding nonminority or male employees. Relying upon the Supreme Court's rationale in *Johnson,* the *Hannon* court found that the white male applicants did not maintain any legitimate expectation in obtaining employment.[148]

(ii.) Attaining, not maintaining, balanced workforces. In *Taxman v. Board of Education of Township of Piscataway*,[149] the Third Circuit rejected an affirmative action plan because it did not seek to attain, but to maintain, a racial balance.[150] The court noted that the plan was originally enacted in 1975, did not provide for a termination date, and, therefore, could not be described as the type of "temporary" affirmative action plan endorsed by the Court in *Johnson.*[151] Instead, the plan was "an established fixture of unlimited duration, to be resurrected from time to time whenever the Board believes that the ratio between Blacks and Whites in any Piscataway School is skewed."[152] The plan, therefore, did not seek to attain but instead to maintain racial balance and thus it failed to meet the *Steelworkers v. Weber*[153] requirements.[154]

Conversely, in *McNamara v. City of Chicago*[155] the district court approved a plan to evaluate candidates for promotion that did contain a self-defined termination date. The employer maintained lists of employees eligible for promotion, and those lists were viable only for a period of years.[156] The court found that the plan was a temporary measure that specifically designed to attain, rather than maintain, a racial balance.[157]

---

[147]887 F. Supp. 1303, 1316–18 (N.D. Cal. 1995).

[148]*Id.* at 1318 ("Moreover, Hannon did not have an 'absolute entitlement' to or 'legitimate firmly rooted expectation' of obtaining a position.").

[149]91 F.3d 1547, 71 FEP 848 (3d Cir. 1996), *cert. granted,* 117 S. Ct. 2506 (1997), *cert. dismissed,* 118 S. Ct. 595 (1997).

[150]*Id.* at 1564.

[151]*Id.*

[152]*Id.*

[153]443 U.S. 193, 20 FEP 1 (1979).

[154]*Taxman,* 91 F.3d at 1564.

[155]867 F. Supp. 739 (N.D. Ill. 1994), *aff'd,* 138 F.3d 1219 (7th Cir. 1998).

[156]*Id.* at 752.

[157]*Id.*

d. Consent Decrees. In *Plott v. General Motors Corp., Packard Electrical Division,*[158] the Sixth Circuit considered and rejected an employee's objection to General Motor's adherence to a "Conciliation Agreement" entered into in 1983 between General Motors and the EEOC. The employee alleged that he was not admitted into a skilled trade apprentice program because General Motors adhered to percentages for the representation of minorities and women established in the Conciliation Agreement, and had actually exceeded the percentages with regard to the number of women admitted into the program.[159] Because General Motors argued that it acted in reliance upon a letter from the EEOC concerning the effect of its good faith compliance under the Conciliation Agreement, the court examined whether General Motors had in fact acted in good faith.[160] First, the court noted that General Motors had limited its affirmative action efforts to those individuals who had or were likely to develop the applicable skill levels.[161] Second, the court found that the percentages contained in the Conciliation Agreement were not quotas or fixed set-asides.[162] Finally, as mandated by *Johnson v. Transportation Agency, Santa Clara County,*[163] and *Steelworkers v. Weber,*[164] the Conciliation Agreement did not displace any seniority rights of nonminority or male employees and did not require the replacement of such workers or mandate their ineligibility from participation in the apprenticeship program.[165] The court concluded that General Motors had acted properly under the Conciliation Agreement.

In contrast, the Eleventh Circuit has rejected the use of affirmative action goals as established in a consent decree. In *Ensley Branch, NAACP v. Seibels,*[166] the court held that to withstand challenge, affirmative action must be flexible, reasonably related to the applicable pool of qualified candidates, and not unduly burdensome to nonminorities.[167] The plan at issue in *Seibels* detailed

---

[158]71 F.3d 1190, 69 FEP 826 (6th Cir.1995), *cert. denied,* 517 U.S. 1157 (1996).
[159]*Id.* at 1192–93.
[160]*Id.* at 1194.
[161]*Id.* at 1194–95.
[162]*Id.* at 1195.
[163]480 U.S. 616, 43 FEP 411 (1987).
[164]443 U.S. 193, 20 FEP 1 (1979).
[165]*Plott,* 71 F.3d at 1195.
[166]31 F.3d 1548 (11th Cir. 1994).
[167]*Id.* at 1576.

certain percentages for the hiring and promotion of minority employees, and the employer's practice was to rigidly adhere to the established percentages as fixed and immutable requirements.[168] The court held that, while the inclusion of percentages for minority employment and promotion itself does not condemn an affirmative action plan as illegal, the decree at issue was impermissible because of the employer's practice of rigid adherence to the specified percentages and the lack of clearly flexible language in the decree.[169]

3. The Effect of the Civil Rights Act of 1991

a. Martin v. Wilks. Recent cases hold that § 108 of the Civil Rights Act of 1991 does not apply retroactively and, therefore, does not bar a nonparty's challenge to a consent decree that was entered into before § 108's effective date, regardless of the nonparty's opportunity to object.[170]

When the provisions of § 108 have been followed, courts have precluded later challenges to a consent decree. In *Sims v. Montgomery County Commission*,[171] the court determined that notices to white officers regarding the proposed consent decree and invitations to respond to the decree either in writing and/or at two fairness hearings were sufficient under § 108 of the 1991 Act to preclude later challenges to the decree.[172]

The Fifth Circuit, in *Edwards v. City of Houston*,[173] distinguished the situation where nonparties sought to intervene in the same litigation that produced the challenged consent decree, from

---

[168]*Id.* at 1576–77.

[169]*Id.*

[170]*See, e.g.,* Rafferty v. City of Youngstown, 54 F.3d 278, 281–82 n.2, 67 FEP 1564 (6th Cir.) (§ 108 is not applied retroactively), *cert. denied,* 516 U.S. 931 (1995); Maitland v. University of Minnesota, 43 F.3d 357, 363, 66 FEP 796 (8th Cir. 1994) (same). *But see* Aiken v. City of Memphis, 37 F.3d 1155, 1176–77, 65 FEP 1757 (6th Cir. 1994) (Jones, J., dissenting) (supporting retroactive application of § 108 while recognizing that court can only make such a determination after the issue has been raised; if § 108 were applied retroactively in this case, white police officers and fire department employees would have been precluded from challenging race-based promotion goals of consent decree entered into in early 1980s).

[171]890 F. Supp. 1520 (M.D. Ala. 1995), *aff'd without opinion,* 119 F.3d 9 (11th Cir. 1997).

[172]*Id.* at 1530.

[173]78 F.3d 983 (5th Cir. 1996).

the situation where nonparties brought a separate reverse discrimination suit after being provided with notice of the decree and an opportunity to object in accordance with § 108.[174] The nonparties were not precluded by § 108 from intervening in the litigation that produced the challenged consent decree.[175]

b. Burden of Proof. A recent case discussing § 107 of the Civil Rights Act of 1991,[176] *Hannon v. Chater,*[177] reiterates the proposition that by considering gender in an employment decision, an employer violates Title VII, even if the employer would have made the same decision solely on the basis of a completely legitimate criteria.[178] The court further stated that § 107's mixed-motive analysis is "arguably a direct anti-affirmative action provision."[179] On the other hand, where the consideration of gender is consistent with an existing affirmative action plan, § 107's mixed-motive analysis is inapplicable. In *Gilligan v. Department of Labor,*[180] the Ninth Circuit determined that an employer's consideration of gender, as contemplated by an affirmative action plan, constituted a legal consideration of gender.[181]

The legislative history of § 116 of the Civil Rights Act of 1991[182] has been cited as protective of consent decrees. In *Aiken v. City of Memphis,*[183] the dissenting opinion interpreted § 116 as providing protection for consent decrees, stating that it is "prudent . . . to remain mindful of the quagmire that we create when we use laws which are intended to *remedy* past racial discrimination *against* the very people who have historically been made to bear the burden of legal and extra-legal racial discrimination."[184]

---

[174]*Id.* at 997–98.
[175]*Id.* at 998.
[176]Civil Rights Act of 1991 § 107, 42 U.S.C. § 2000e-2(m).
[177]887 F. Supp. 1303 (N.D. Cal. 1995).
[178]*Id.* at 1314–16.
[179]*Id.* at 1315 n.48 (quoting Note, *The Continuing Evolution of Affirmative Action Under Title VII: New Directions After the Civil Rights Act of 1991,* 81 VA. L. REV. 565, 596 (1995)).
[180]81 F.3d 835, 70 FEP 856 (9th Cir. 1996).
[181]*Id.* at 840. Additionally, the court noted that in this situation it is not necessarily determinative whether the employer actually relied on the affirmative action plan in making the employment decision, as long as the decision was consistent with the plan. *Id.* at 839.
[182]Civil Rights Act of 1991 § 116, 42 U.S.C. § 1981 note (Supp. IV 1992).
[183]37 F.3d 1155, 65 FEP 1757 (6th Cir. 1994).
[184]*Id.* at 1177 n.5 (Jones, J., dissenting) (emphasis in original).

c. Race-Norming. In *Fioriglio v. New Jersey, Department of Personnel*,[185] the court interpreted § 106, the "race-norming" provision of the Civil Rights Act of 1991,[186] and determined that the white male plaintiff did not state a claim under § 106 because the employer rescored an examination pursuant to a consent decree and applied new criteria "evenhandedly to each and every score, not just to the scores of minority candidates."[187]

d. Enhanced Damages. A recent case illustrating an employer's successful defense to a charge of reverse discrimination using § 713(b)(1) of the Civil Rights Act of 1991[188] is *Plott v. General Motors Corp., Packard Electrical Division.*[189] In *Plott,* § 713(b) insulated the employer from liability in a reverse discrimination suit because the employer's affirmative action plan was a good faith attempt to comply with the employer's agreement with the EEOC, instituted in reliance on the previously issued EEOC opinion.[190]

---

[185] 1996 U.S. Dist. LEXIS 15399 (D.N.J. Oct. 15, 1996).

[186] Civil Rights Act of 1991 § 106, 42 U.S.C. § 2000e-2(1). *See also* Koski v. Gainer, 1995 U.S. Dist. LEXIS 14604 (N.D. Ill. Oct. 5, 1995) (where white males brought claim under Title VII objecting to employer's practice of race-norming implemented pursuant to a settlement agreement with the EEOC).

[187] *Fioriglio,* 1996 U.S. Dist. LEXIS, at *17.

[188] Civil Rights Act of 1991 § 713(b)(1), 42 U.S.C. § 2000e-12(b)(1).

[189] 71 F.3d 1190, 69 FEP 826 (6th Cir. 1995), *cert. denied,* 517 U.S. 1157 (1996).

[190] *Id.* at 1194. Based on the successful § 713(b) defense, the district court properly granted summary judgment to the employer. *Id.* at 1194–95.

CHAPTER 28

FEDERAL CONTRACTOR AFFIRMATIVE ACTION COMPLIANCE

Since publication of the Main Edition, the Office of Federal Contract Compliance Programs (OFCCP) has revised portions of the regulations governing Executive Order 11246 (the Executive Order)[1] and § 503 of the Rehabilitation Act of 1973 (Rehabilitation Act),[2] corrected certain regulations governing § 403 of the Vietnam Era Veterans' Readjustment Act of 1972 (Veterans Act),[3] and issued an interim rule to the regulations governing the Veterans Act.[4]

On August 19, 1997, the OFCCP published the final rule that contains the revised regulations governing the Executive Order. The OFCCP revised the regulations relating to record retention, compliance monitoring, maintenance of nonsegregated facilities, and other aspects of enforcement.[5] Generally, the revised regulations became effective on September 18, 1997. However, the record retention regulations became effective on December 22, 1997.[6]

---

[1]Government Contractors, Affirmative Action Requirements, Executive Order 11246; Final Rule, 62 Fed. Reg. 44,174 (1997); 41 C.F.R. pts. 60-1 & -60.

[2]Affirmative Action and Nondiscrimination Obligations of Contractors and Subcontractors Regarding Individuals With Disabilities, Disabled Veterans and Veterans of the Vietnam Era; Invitation to Self Identify; Final Rules, 61 Fed. Reg. 19,335 (1996); 41 C.F.R. pt. 60-741.

[3]Affirmative Action Obligations of Contractors and Subcontractors for Disabled Veterans and Veterans of the Vietnam Era; Correction, 61 Fed. Reg. 6,116 (1996); 41 C.F.R. pt. 60-250. The OFCCP was considering revising the regulations governing the Veterans Act to conform to the regulations governing the Rehabilitation Act at the time of the deadline for this supplement. See Unified Agenda, 62 Fed. Reg. 57,725 (1997).

[4]Affirmative Action Obligations of Contractors and Subcontractors for Disabled Veterans and Veterans of the Vietnam Era; Invitation to Self-Identify, 61 Fed. Reg. 19,366 (1996).

[5]62 Fed. Reg. at 44,174.

[6]Government Contractors, Affirmative Action Requirements, Executive Order 11246; Approval of Information Collection Requirements and OMB Control Numbers; Correction, 62 Fed. Reg. 66,970 (1997); 41 C.F.R. pts. 60-1 & -999.

On May 1, 1996, the OFCCP published the final rule that contains the revised regulations governing the Rehabilitation Act. The OFCCP revised the nondiscrimination provisions of the regulations to conform with regulations published by the Equal Employment Opportunity Commission (EEOC) governing Title I of the Americans with Disabilities Act of 1990[7] (ADA).[8] The revised regulations also incorporate recent amendments to the Rehabilitation Act and strengthen and clarify the regulations relating to affirmative action, record keeping, enforcement, and other issues.[9] These revised regulations were effective on August 29, 1996.[10]

On February 16, 1996, the OFCCP published its corrections to the final regulations governing the Veterans Act published on January 5, 1995. The OFCCP corrected the affirmative action regulations contained in 41 C.F.R. § 60-250.4.[11] On May 1, 1996, the OFCCP published an interim rule relating to invitations to self-identify under the Veterans Act.[12]

---

[7] 42 U.S.C. § 12101 et seq.
[8] The regulations issued by the EEOC are contained in 29 C.F.R. pt. 1630.
[9] 61 Fed. Reg. at 19,336.
[10] Id.
[11] 61 Fed. Reg. at 6,116–17. The OFCCP corrected 41 C.F.R. § 60-250.4(b) by including the following two sentences, which were inadvertently left out of the regulations, at the end of the paragraph:

> The contractor further agrees to provide such reports to such local office regarding employment openings and hires as may be required. State and local government agencies holding Federal contracts of $10,000 or more shall also list all their employment openings with the appropriate office of the State employment service, but are not required to provide those reports set forth in paragraphs (d) and (e).

Id. at 6,117. The OFCCP corrected 41 C.F.R. § 60-250.4(g) as follows to delete reference to exemptions for employer-union arrangements:

> The provisions of paragraphs (b), (c), (d), and (e) of this clause do not apply to openings which the contractor proposes to fill from within his own organization. This exclusion does not apply to a particular opening once an employer decides to consider applicants outside his own organization for that opening.

Id. at 6,117–18.

[12] 61 Fed. Reg. at 19,366. This interim rule conforms to the regulation relating to self-identification under the Rehabilitation Act. Id.

I. Coverage and Exemptions

A. Contracts[13] and Covered Subcontracts

1. Prime Contracts

The revised regulations changed the definition of "government contract" to clarify that contracts covered by the affirmative action requirements include contracts under which the government is a seller of goods or services, as well as contracts under which the government is a purchaser.[14] The term "government contract" is defined by the revised regulations[15] as

> any agreement or modification thereof between any contracting agency and any person for the purchase, sale or use of personal property[16] or nonpersonal services.[17]

This change may merely be technical because courts and administrative law judges have applied the requirements of the Executive Order, the Rehabilitation Act, and the Veterans Act to contracts in which the government was the seller.[18]

2. Subcontracts

A "subcontract" subject to the requirements of the Executive Order, Rehabilitation Act, and Veterans Act is defined by the revised regulations[19] as

---

[13] The term "contract" includes any government contract or subcontract. 62 Fed. Reg. at 44,175, 44,188; 61 Fed. Reg. at 19530–31; 41 C.F.R. § 60-1.3 & -741.2(h). The addition of "subcontract" to this definition avoids the need to make separate reference to a subcontract when the term "contract" is used. 62 Fed. Reg. at 44,175.

[14] Id.

[15] Id. at 44,188; 61 Fed. Reg. at 19,530–31; 41 C.F.R. § 60-1.3 & -741.2(i).

[16] The term "personal property" includes "supplies, and contracts for the use of real property (such as lease arrangements), unless the contract for the use of real property itself constitutes real property (such as easements)." 62 Fed. Reg. at 44,188; 41 C.F.R. § 60-1.3.

[17] The term "nonpersonal services" "includes, but is not limited to, the following services: Utilities, construction, transportation, research, insurance, and fund depository." 62 Fed. Reg. at 44,188; 41 C.F.R. § 60-1.3.

[18] See footnote 21 in Main Edition and accompanying text.

[19] 62 Fed. Reg. at 44,188; 61 Fed. Reg. at 19,351; 41 C.F.R. § 60-1.3 & -741.2(l).

any agreement or arrangement between a contractor and any person (in which the parties do not stand in the relationship of an employer and an employee):
(1) For the purchase, sale or use of personal property or nonpersonal services which, in whole or in part, is necessary to the performance of any one or more contracts; or
(2) Under which any portion of the contractor's obligation under any one of [sic] more contracts is performed, undertaken or assumed.

This revision was made in order to conform the definition of "subcontract" with the new definition of "government contract."[20]

B. Coverage Thresholds

1. Basic Threshold

The former regulations governing the Rehabilitation Act were applicable to work performed abroad by employees who were recruited within the United States.[21] The revised regulations apply only to employment activities within the United States.[22] Therefore, the OFCCP narrowed the scope of coverage and clarified that the regulations cover employment within the United States and decisions regarding employment made within the United States, pertaining to applicants and employees who are within the United States, regarding opportunities abroad.[23]

The regulations governing the Rehabilitation Act have also been revised with regard to which employees are covered by them. For all decisions made and employment practices occurring before October 29, 1992, the regulations apply only to employees who were employed in, and applicants for, positions that were engaged in carrying out a government contract.[24] For all decisions made

---

[20] 62 Fed. Reg. at 44,176.
[21] 61 Fed. Reg. at 19,342.
[22] *Id.* at 19,342, 19,354; 41 C.F.R. § 60-741.4(a)(4).
[23] 61 Fed. Reg. at 19,342, 19,354; 41 C.F.R. § 60-741.4(a)(4).
[24] 61 Fed. Reg. at 19,341–42, 19,353; 41 C.F.R. § 60-741.4(a)(2). The revised regulations state:
A position shall be considered to have been engaged in carrying out a contract if: (A) The duties of the position included work that fulfilled a contractual obligation, or work that was necessary to, or that facilitated, performance of the contract or a provision of the contract; or (B) The cost or a portion of the cost of the position was allowable as a cost of the contract under the principles set forth in the Federal Acquisition Regulations at 48 C.F.R. Ch. 1, part 31: Provided, That a position shall not be considered to have been covered by this part

and employment practices occurring after October 29, 1992, the regulations apply to all positions in a contractor's workforce irrespective of whether the employees are or were engaged in carrying out a government contract.[25]

III. SECTION 503 OF THE REHABILITATION ACT OF 1973

In the revised regulations governing the Rehabilitation Act, the OFCCP changed the definitions of "substantially limits," "reasonable accommodation," and "direct threat" to be consistent with the EEOC regulations adopted under the ADA.[26] The term "substantially limits" is defined by the revised regulations[27] as

> (i) Unable to perform a major life activity that the average person in the general population can perform[28]; or (ii) Significantly restricted as to the condition, manner or duration under which an individual can perform a particular major life activity as compared to the condition, manner, or duration under which the average person in the general population can perform that same major life activity.

The term "reasonable accommodation" is defined by the revised regulations[29] as

> (i) Modifications or adjustments to a job application process that enable a qualified applicant with a disability to be considered for the position such applicant desires[30]; or (ii) Modifications or adjustments to the work environment, or to the manner or circumstances under which the position held or desired is customarily

---

by virtue of this provision if the cost of the position was not allocable in whole or in part as a direct cost to any Government contract, and only a de minimis (less than 2%) portion of the cost of the position was allocable as an indirect cost to Government contracts, considered as a group.
41 C.F.R. § 60-741.4(a)(2).
[25]Id.; 61 Fed. Reg. at 19,341–42, 19,353.
[26]61 Fed. Reg. at 19,340–41.
[27]Id. at 19,351; 41 C.F.R. § 60-741.2(q).
[28]People have a range of abilities with regard to many major life activities such as walking, lifting, and bending, and a range of such abilities may be considered average. Thus, the term "average" person in the general population does not indicate a need to determine a precise average ability, but rather reflects that a range of abilities may be considered average.
(This quote is footnote 1 in 41 C.F.R. § 60-741.2.(q)).
[29]61 Fed. Reg. at 19,352; 41 C.F.R. § 60-741.2(v).
[30]A contractor's duty to provide a reasonable accommodation with respect to applicants with disabilities is not limited to those who ultimately demonstrate

performed, that enable a qualified individual with a disability to perform the essential functions of that position; or (iii) Modifications or adjustments that enable the contractor's employee with a disability to enjoy equal benefits and privileges of employment as are enjoyed by the contractor's other similarly situated employees without disabilities.

The term "direct threat" is defined by the revised regulations[31] as

a significant risk of substantial harm to the health or safety of the individual or others that cannot be eliminated or reduced by reasonable accommodation.

V. Affirmative Action Programs for Veterans and Individuals With Disabilities

The regulations relating to invitations to self-identify were revised in 1996 in order to conform with the ADA's provisions regarding preemployment inquiries.[32] The revised regulations require each contractor to invite all special disabled veterans, veterans of the Vietnam era, and individuals with a disability to identify themselves in order to benefit under the contractor's affirmative action plan (AAP) after making an offer of employment and before the applicant begins his or her employment.[33] Under the revised regulations, a contractor may only invite an individual to self-identify before an offer of employment if the invitation is made when the contractor actually is undertaking affirmative action at the preoffer stage or if the invitation is made pursuant to federal, state, or local law requiring affirmative action for individuals with disabilities.[34]

In addition to the items identified in the Main Edition, the invitation to self-identify must contain a statement informing the individual that the request for benefit under the contractor's AAP can be made immediately upon receipt of the invitation and/or at any time in the future.[35]

---

that they are qualified to perform the job in issue. Applicants with disabilities must be provided a reasonable accommodation with respect to the application process if they are qualified with respect to that process (e.g., if they present themselves at the correct location and time to fill out an application).

(This quote is footnote 2 in 41 C.F.R. § 60-741.2.(v)).

[31] 61 Fed. Reg. at 19,351; 41 C.F.R. § 60-741.2(y).
[32] 61 Fed. Reg. at 19,344–45; 61 Fed. Reg. at 19,367.
[33] 61 Fed. Reg. at 19,344–45, 19,357; 61 Fed. Reg. at 19,367, 19,369; 41 C.F.R. § 60-250.5 & -741.42.
[34] Id.
[35] Id.

In addition to the items discussed in the Main Edition, the revised regulations[36] governing the Rehabilitation Act require that AAPs include the following:
- an equal employment opportunity statement[37];
- reasonable accommodation to the known physical or mental limitations of an otherwise qualified individual with a disability[38]; and
- procedures to ensure that employees with disabilities are not harassed because of their disability.[39]

VI. COMPLIANCE REVIEW AND COMPLAINT INVESTIGATION PROCESS: DESK AUDIT LETTER THROUGH EXIT CONFERENCE

The regulations governing the Executive Order have been revised to provide for a "compliance evaluation"[40] instead of a compliance review. A compliance evaluation may consist of any one or a combination of the following: (1) a compliance review, (2) an off-site review of records, (3) a compliance check, and (4) a focused review.[41]

---

[36]These regulations are codified at 41 C.F.R. § 60-741.44 and generally parallel the content requirements for AAPs required by the Executive Order and governing regulations. 61 Fed. Reg. at 19,345.

[37]61 Fed. Reg. at 19,345, 19,357–58; 41 C.F.R. § 60-741.44. The revised regulation provides that this equal employment opportunity statement should (1) indicate the chief executive officer's attitude on affirmative action; (2) provide for an audit and reporting system; (3) assign overall responsibility for implementation of affirmative action; and (4) contain a statement that the contractor will recruit, hire, train, and promote persons in all job titles and ensure that all employment decisions are based on valid job requirements. The revised regulation requires that the policy state that employees and applicants will not be subject to harassment, intimidation, threats, coercion, or discrimination because they have engaged in activities protected by the Rehabilitation Act or any other federal, state, or local law requiring equal employment opportunity for disabled persons. 41 C.F.R. § 60-741.44.

[38]61 Fed. Reg. at 19,345, 19,358; 41 C.F.R. § 60-741.44. Under the revised regulations, if the employee has a known disability that could lead to the reasonable conclusion that a significant performance problem is related to the disability, a contractor must confidentially notify the employee of the performance problem and inquire whether it is related to the employee's disability. If the employee indicates that the problem is related to his or her disability, the contractor is required to confidentially ask the employee if he or she needs a reasonable accommodation. 41 C.F.R. § 60-741.44.

[39]61 Fed. Reg. at 19,358; 41 C.F.R. § 60-741.44.

[40]The term "compliance evaluation" has been defined by the revised regulations as any one or combination of actions OFCCP may take to examine a Federal contractor or subcontractor's compliance with one or more of the requirements of Executive Order 11246. 62 Fed. Reg. at 44,188; 41 C.F.R. § 60-1.3.

[41]62 Fed. Reg. at 44,179–80, 44,189–90; 41 C.F.R. § 60-1.20.

A compliance review is the same comprehensive examination of a contractor's employment practices that was provided for in the regulations prior to their revision.[42] The compliance review still consists of a desk audit, on-site review, and when necessary, an off-site analysis of information.[43]

An off-site review of records consists of

[a]n analysis and evaluation of the AAP (or any part thereof) and supporting documentation, and other documents related to the contractor's personnel policies and employment actions that may be relevant to a determination of whether the contractor has complied with the requirements of the Executive Order and regulations.[44]

The scope of the off-site review of records is similar to the scope of the desk audit.[45]

A compliance check is

[a] visit to the establishment to ascertain whether data and other information previously submitted by the contractor are complete and accurate; whether the contractor has maintained records consistent with Sec. 60-1.12[46]; and/or whether the contractor has developed an AAP consistent with Sec. 60-1.40.[47]

---

[42] 62 Fed. Reg. at 44,180, 44,189. For a more thorough discussion of a compliance review, see Chapter 28, Section VI in the Main Edition.

[43] 62 Fed. Reg. at 44,180, 44,189; 41 C.F.R. § 60-1.20(a)(1).

[44] 62 Fed. Reg. at 44,180, 44,189–90; 41 C.F.R. § 60-1.20(a)(2). The off-site review of records has caused concern among the contractor community that this new regulation does not ensure protection of confidential or proprietary information. 62 Fed. Reg. at 44,180. Contractors must remember to label all confidential and proprietary information before providing it to the OFCCP for an off-site review. See Chapter 28, Section II.B.1.(a)(iii) in the Main Edition.

[45] 62 Fed. Reg. at 44,180. For a more thorough discussion of the desk audit, see Chapter 28, Section VI.C in the Main Edition.

[46] 41 C.F.R. § 60-1.12 adds a record retention provision. This provision requires contractors to retain personnel or employment records for two years if the contractor has more than 150 employees or has a government contract of at least $150,000. If the contractor has fewer than 150 employees or does not have a government contract of at least $150,000, the contractor is required to retain the records for one year. This provision also specifies that failure to retain the required records constitutes noncompliance with the contractor's obligations under the Executive Order and regulations and that destruction or failure to retain the records may lead to the presumption that the information would have been unfavorable to the contractor. This presumption will not apply if the contractor demonstrates that the destruction or failure to retain records results from circumstances beyond the contractor's control. 62 Fed. Reg. at 44,177–79, 44,189; 41 C.F.R. § 60-1.12. This provision became effective on December 22, 1997. 62 Fed. Reg. at 66,970.

[47] 62 Fed. Reg. at 44,179–80, 44,190; 41 C.F.R. § 60-1.20(a)(3).

A focused review is

> [a]n on-site review restricted to one or more components of the contractor's organization or one or more aspects of the contractor's employment practices.[48]

When it published the final rule governing the Executive Order, the OFCCP stated that it intended to follow the standards already established for the frequency and duration of the compliance review and that it would establish similar standards for the off-site review of records, compliance check, and focused review to ensure that they are not overly intrusive. The OFCCP also stated that it would not use any new methods of evaluation until after the Compliance Manual is updated to include policy and procedural guidance and is made public.[49]

A. Selection for Review

2. *Pre-Award Review*

The revised regulations governing the Executive Order raised the trigger for a pre-award compliance evaluation to $10 million or more.[50] The revised regulations also provide that a contractor will not be subject to a pre-award review if the OFCCP has issued a finding of compliance within the previous 24 months, instead of the previous 12 months.[51]

Furthermore, the revised regulations establish time frames for the OFCCP to inform the awarding agency of the necessity for conducting a pre-award evaluation and for the OFCCP to provide its conclusions about the contractor's compliance status.[52] Specifically, 41 C.F.R. § 1.20(d) provides that the OFCCP must inform the awarding agency, within 15 days of the awarding agency's notice to OFCCP of its intent to award a contract, of its intention to conduct a pre-award compliance evaluation. If the OFCCP fails to do so, the awarding agency can presume clearance and proceed with the award.[53] If the OFCCP notifies an awarding agency of its

---
[48] 62 Fed. Reg. at 44,179–80, 44,190; 41 C.F.R. § 60-1.20(a)(4).
[49] 62 Fed. Reg. at 44,180.
[50] 62 Fed. Reg. at 44,181, 44,190; 41 C.F.R. § 60-1.20(d).
[51] *Id.*
[52] *Id.*
[53] *Id.*

intention to conduct a pre-award compliance evaluation, it must inform the awarding agency of its conclusions within 20 days.[54] If the OFCCP fails to provide the awarding agency with its conclusions within 20 days, the awarding agency can presume clearance and proceed with the award.[55]

3. Discrimination Complaint

The revised regulations governing the Rehabilitation Act have enlarged the time period in which an employee can file an administrative complaint from 180 days to 300 days, unless the time for filing is extended for good cause shown.[56] Moreover, the revised regulations allow a third party to file a complaint on behalf of an aggrieved person. The third party must provide the name of the aggrieved person to the investigator so that the investigator can confirm that the aggrieved person authorized the filing of the complaint. However, the OFCCP will attempt to keep the aggrieved person's name confidential if possible.[57] Finally, the revised regulations eliminated the provision that previously allowed contractors with an applicable internal review procedure 60 days to review and internally resolve Rehabilitation Act complaints before the OFCCP begins an independent investigation.[58]

D. The On-Site Review

3. Components of the On-Site Review

h. *Document Review.* In addition to the records identified in the Main Edition at Section VI.D.3.(h), the revised regulation governing the Executive Order requires that a contractor permit access to computerized records.[59] The regulation does not require a contractor to reprogram its computers in order to generate responsive data to an OFCCP request; rather, it simply requires access to existing records and data in computerized forms.[60]

---

[54] *Id.*
[55] *Id.*
[56] 61 Fed. Reg. at 19,346, 19,360; 41 C.F.R. § 60-741.61(b). The OFCCP enlarged the deadline to 300 days in order to establish a uniform national standard of at least as long as the complaint filing period under the ADA. 61 Fed. Reg. at 19,346.
[57] 61 Fed. Reg. at 19,346, 19,360; 41 C.F.R. § 60-741.61(c).
[58] *See* 61 Fed. Reg. at 19,335.
[59] 62 Fed. Reg. at 44,186, 44,192; 41 C.F.R. § 60-1.43 & -741.81.
[60] 62 Fed. Reg. at 44,186.

CH. 28   FEDERAL CONTRACTOR AFFIRMATIVE ACTION COMPLIANCE   407

6. Notice of Violations, Contractor Responses, Conciliation Agreements, and Letters of Commitment

The revised regulations governing the Executive Order provide that in a proceeding involving the alleged violation of a conciliation agreement, the OFCCP does not have to present proof of the underlying violation resolved by the agreement when seeking enforcement of the agreement.[61]

VII. ENFORCEMENT PROCEDURES AND SANCTIONS FOR NONCOMPLIANCE

A. Administrative Enforcement

The regulations governing the Rehabilitation Act have been revised to give the Deputy Assistant Secretary[62] the discretion to issue a show cause notice, requiring the contractor to show cause within 30 days why monitoring, enforcement, or other action should not be instituted to ensure compliance.[63]

The regulations governing the Executive Order and the Rehabilitation Act have also been revised to require that interest on back pay be compounded quarterly, instead of allowing simple interest.[64]

B. Cancellation, Debarment, and Other Sanctions Following Administrative Hearing

The regulations governing the Executive Order and the Rehabilitation Act have been revised to allow debarment for a fixed period of at least six months.[65] The revised regulations governing the Rehabilitation Act impose a maximum period of three years for a fixed debarment.[66] The length of a fixed term debarment will be decided on a case-by-case basis and will depend upon such

---

[61]*Id.* at 44,185–86, 44,192; 41 C.F.R. § 60-1.34.
[62]The phrase "Deputy Assistant Secretary" replaces the word "Director" throughout the revised regulations governing the Executive Order and Rehabilitation Act. 62 Fed. Reg. at 44,175; 61 Fed. Reg. at 19,339.
[63]61 Fed. Reg. at 19,360–61; 41 C.F.R. § 60-741.64.
[64]62 Fed. Reg. at 44,184, 44,190; 61 Fed. Reg. at 19,361; 41 C.F.R. § 60-1.26(a)(2) & -741.65(a)(1).
[65]62 Fed. Reg. at 44,184–85, 44,191; 61 Fed. Reg. at 19,346–47, 19,361; 41 C.F.R. § 60-1.27 & -741.66.
[66]61 Fed. Reg. at 19,346–47, 19,361; 41 C.F.R. § 60-741.66.

factors as the nature and severity of the violations, the contractor's compliance history, and whether the violations can be fully remedied in the absence of a fixed term debarment.[67]

The regulations governing the Executive Order and Rehabilitation Act have been revised to require the Deputy Assistant Secretary to ensure that the heads of agencies are notified of debarments.[68]

IX. VALIDITY OF THE EXECUTIVE ORDER AND RESULTING ACTIONS

B. Validity of the Back-Pay Remedy

In *American Airlines v. Hermann*,[69] a federal district court held that OFCCP had no authority under the Rehabilitation Act to seek back pay or other remedies on behalf of alleged victims of disability discrimination for acts occurring prior to the 1992 amendments to that statute.

---

[67] 62 Fed. Reg. at 44,184–85; 61 Fed. Reg. at 19,346–47.
[68] 62 Fed. Reg. at 44,185, 44,191; 41 C.F.R. § 60-1.30 & -741.67.
[69] 971 F. Supp. 1096, 1097–98 (N.D. Tex. 1997).

Part 9

Procedure

Chapter 29

EEOC ADMINISTRATIVE PROCESS

III. The EEOC Enforcement Process

C. The Intake and Initial Investigation of a Charge

Since April 1995, the EEOC has followed new procedures elaborating on the three categories for classifying new charges.[1] The first category, in addition to including charges that fall within the national or local enforcement plan and charges where further investigation will probably result in a finding of discrimination, includes charges where "irreparable harm will result unless processing is expedited."[2] The second category is reserved for cases where additional information is needed to determine whether the cases should be assigned to either the first or third categories.[3] A charge may be placed in the third category and dismissed when the office has sufficient information from which to conclude that it is not likely that further investigation will result in a cause finding.[4] Examples of cases falling into the third category are cases where the Commission lacks jurisdiction, cases where the charges are unsupported by any evidence and the complaining party was in a position to have such evidence, cases where the complaining party is not credible, cases where the charging party has a history of filing repetitive charges and is not credible, cases filed beyond the limitations period, and cases where the complaining party has failed to cooperate with the Commission.[5]

The EEOC adopted its National Enforcement Plan on February 8, 1996, in which the Commission identified three major categories

---

[1] Priority Charge Handling Procedures, *reprinted in* 1 FEP Man. (BNA) 405:7311 (June 20, 1995).
[2] *Id.* at 7313.
[3] *Id.*
[4] *Id.* at 7313–14.
[5] *Id.*

of priorities: (1) cases that by their nature could have a potential significant impact beyond the parties to the particular dispute; (2) cases having the potential of promoting the development of law supporting the purposes of the statutes enforced by the Commission; and (3) cases "involving the integrity or effectiveness of the Commission's enforcement process."[6]

H. Negotiated Settlement Prior to Determination

The EEOC will no longer facilitate settlements of cases that fall into the third category, i.e., the dismissal category, although the Commission will not stand in the way of parties who are interested in settling their dispute.[7] Charges under investigation that fall into the first two categories but do not fall within the national or local enforcement plans may be settled at any time by the enforcement staff, without the consultation of legal staff.[8]

I. Investigations and Determinations

2. Requests for Information (RFIs) and On-Site Reviews

The new Priority Charge Handling Procedures again reiterate the Commission's position that RFIs be tailored to the particular charge and that boilerplate requests for information should be avoided.[9]

6. Determination Counseling and the Investigative Memorandum

In light of the elimination of "no cause" determinations, the EEOC's new procedures emphasize the importance of explaining its determinations to complaining parties.[10]

7. EEOC Letters of Determination and EEOC Decisions

"No cause" determinations are no longer used.[11] Instead, the EEOC provides the following uniform language:

---

[6]National Enforcement Plan (Feb. 8, 1996), *reprinted in* DAILY LAB. REP. (BNA) at D-20 (Feb. 9, 1996).
[7]Priority Charge Handling Procedures, *reprinted in* 1 FEP MAN. (BNA) 405:7311, 7317.
[8]*Id.* at 7317.
[9]*Id.*
[10]*Id.* at 7318.
[11]*Id.* at 7317.

Based upon the Commission's investigation, the Commission is unable to conclude that the information obtained establishes violations of the statutes. This does not certify that the respondent is in compliance with the statutes. No finding is made as to any other issue that might be construed as having been raised by this charge.[12]

8. Reconsideration

The new procedures advocate reconsideration only if one of the following circumstances exists: (1) there is evidence of misconduct by an agency official that may have affected the outcome; (2) there is substantial new and material evidence; (3) there was an error in the interpretation of the law that may have affected the outcome.[13]

IV. EEOC INVESTIGATION AND SUBPOENA POWERS

A. Statutory Authority Under Title VII and the ADA

1. Title VII and the ADA

Courts continue to hold that a respondent who fails to exhaust available administrative remedies may not challenge subsequent judicial enforcement of a subpoena.[14]

B. The "Valid Charge" Requirement Under Title VII and the ADA

Courts continue to exercise deference and to enforce most EEOC subpoenas, even where the underlying charge does not literally satisfy each of the four factors set forth in *EEOC v. Shell Oil Co.*[15] In *EEOC v. Quad/Graphics, Inc.*,[16] the Seventh Circuit upheld enforcement of an EEOC subpoena that had been issued in

---

[12]*Id.* at 7317–18.
[13]*Id.* at 7318.
[14]EEOC v. City of Milwaukee, 919 F. Supp. 1247, 1254–55 (E.D. Wis. 1996) (subpoena should be enforced where city did not petition to revoke or modify within five days, notwithstanding the fact that the city failed to petition only because it was involved in ongoing negotiations with the EEOC regarding the scope of the subpoena).
[15]466 U.S. 54, 73, 34 FEP 709 (1984).
[16]63 F.3d 642, 68 FEP 1085 (7th Cir. 1995).

connection with a charge alleging violation of Title VII and the ADEA for failure to recruit or hire Asians, Hispanics, and individuals over age 40 based on their national origin and/or age, despite the fact that the underlying charge failed to state the categories of employment positions from which affected individuals allegedly were excluded. The court explained that the *Shell Oil* test was not meant to be a rigid formula for scrutinizing an EEOC charge.[17] Instead, the four factors listed by the Supreme Court should be applied pragmatically, and "the key inquiry must be whether the allegations in the charge, when assessed against these four factors, fulfill the legislative and regulatory command that the charging Commissioner identify as precisely as possible the appropriate area of inquiry to determine whether there is a violation of the Act."[18] Applying this reasoning, the court concluded that the charge was not deficient for failing to state the categories of positions from which affected individuals allegedly were excluded, since the omission did not leave the charge without "meaningful limitations."[19]

In *EEOC v. Superior Temporary Services, Inc.*,[20] the Second Circuit held that the charge's identification of the groups and positions affected was sufficient to satisfy the *Shell Oil* test, where, all in all, the respondent was given fair notice of the allegedly discriminatory nature of its conduct.[21]

A bare allegation that the charge underlying an EEOC subpoena was issued in bad faith continues to be insufficient to prevent judicial enforcement of the subpoena.[22] Courts have enforced EEOC subpoenas that may lead to the discovery of records that would support EEOC jurisdiction.[23] As in the past, courts have

---

[17]*Id.* at 646–47.
[18]*Id.* at 647.
[19]*Id.* at 648.
[20]56 F.3d 441, 67 FEP 1700 (2d Cir. 1995).
[21]*Id.* at 447.
[22]EEOC v. Quad/Graphics, Inc., 63 F.3d 642, 649, 68 FEP 1085 (7th Cir. 1995) (affirming district court's holding that the EEOC did not issue subpoena in bad faith in retaliation for respondent's failure to cooperate fully with a Department of Labor investigator during a routine audit).
[23]EEOC v. Superior Temporary Servs., Inc., 56 F.3d 441, 447, 67 FEP 1700 (2d Cir. 1995) (enforcing subpoena and indicating that the underlying charge was not substantially flawed since, without access to employer records, the EEOC may not have had enough information to specify categories of jobs from which individuals have been discriminatorily excluded).

continued to enforce subpoenas despite ambiguity as to their timeliness.[24]

The Eleventh Circuit has followed other circuits in holding that the EEOC has jurisdiction to investigate suspected violations of the ADEA in the absence of a valid underlying charge.[25]

C. Permissible Scope of Inquiry

Courts continue to allow the EEOC broad subpoena power.[26] As in the past, courts enforce most EEOC subpoenas, including those that appear to be broad or that seek marginally relevant information.[27] In addition, courts continue to allow the EEOC broad access to information where the EEOC alleges classwide discrimination in the charge.[28] Courts may even be willing to enforce an EEOC subpoena that requests information pertaining to types of discrimination that are not raised in the charge if the information is arguably relevant to the investigation.[29]

---

[24]EEOC v. City of Norfolk Police Dep't, 45 F.3d 80, 85, 66 FEP 1425 (4th Cir. 1995) (EEOC has jurisdiction to investigate charge where untimeliness of individual charge is not "readily apparent").

[25]EEOC v. Tire Kingdom, Inc., 80 F.3d 449, 70 FEP 744 (11th Cir. 1996).

[26]Courts have continued to hold that a district court's role in reviewing EEOC subpoenas is deferential and limited to an inquiry of: (1) whether the administrative investigation is within the agency's authority, (2) whether the agency's demand is too indefinite, and (3) whether the information sought is reasonably relevant. EEOC v. Tire Kingdom, Inc., 80 F.3d 449, 450, 70 FEP 744 (11th Cir. 1996); EEOC v. Quad/Graphics, Inc., 63 F.3d 642, 645, 68 FEP 1085 (7th Cir. 1995); United States v. Florida Azalea Specialists, 19 F.3d 620, 623, 64 FEP 769 (11th Cir. 1994).

[27]EEOC v. City of Milwaukee, 919 F. Supp. 1247, 1259 (E.D. Wis. 1996) (enforcing in large part subpoena that requested, among other things, applicant background investigation files for 1991–95, all personnel files for employees who served probation from 1991 to the present, internal affairs files created since 1989, all reports prepared on various topics, information regarding officers who underwent drug testing, and numerous other documents relating to individual claimants in connection with a charge of pattern and practice of race discrimination).

[28]EEOC v. Quad/Graphics, 63 F.3d 642, 68 FEP 1085 (7th Cir. 1995) (subpoena enforced where charge alleged pattern and practice of discrimination in failing to recruit or hire protected individuals). *See also* note 16.

[29]EEOC v. City of Milwaukee, 919 F. Supp. 1247 (E.D. Wis. 1996) (portion of subpoena requesting all information regarding sexual harassment complaints made during a specified period deemed reasonably relevant in a race discrimination investigation where it was alleged that sexual harassment complaints lodged against African-American officers were treated more seriously than those lodged against white officers).

Courts continue to reject most undue burden challenges to EEOC subpoenas.[30] A detailed description of the burden involved in complying with a subpoena will not defeat enforcement of the subpoena where the estimate appears to be an exaggeration or fails to account for an EEOC offer to limit the scope of the subpoena.[31]

However, as in the past, courts will on occasion limit the scope of grossly overbroad subpoenas or subpoenas that the court concludes seek wholly irrelevant information.[32] Indeed, the Sixth Circuit has stated that the EEOC's broad subpoena power has limits and that the EEOC is not entitled to "any material which it deems relevant in its discretion."[33]

An objection that the state discrimination agency has exclusive jurisdiction over investigating claims of discrimination is insufficient to challenge an EEOC subpoena where the state agency has a work-sharing agreement with the EEOC.[34]

---

[30]EEOC v. Lockheed Martin Corp., 70 FEP 1457 (D. Md. 1996) (enforcing EEOC subpoena that required respondent to generate and provide the EEOC with a detailed description of its personnel computer files despite the burden of such a task where the EEOC demonstrated that the request ultimately would result in administrative convenience for the respondent and that the information would contribute to the efficiency and accuracy of the EEOC's investigation), aff'd, 116 F.3d 110, 74 FEP 202 (4th Cir. 1997); EEOC v. City of Milwaukee, 919 F. Supp. at 1259 (rejecting respondent's contention that the EEOC's subpoena was unreasonably burdensome).

[31]EEOC v. Quad/Graphics, 63 F.3d 642, 648–49, 68 FEP 1085 (7th Cir. 1995) (respondent failed to meet its burden of establishing that compliance with the subpoena would threaten its normal business operations and was therefore unduly burdensome where respondent's detailed affidavit setting forth the precise burden it would undergo in complying with the subpoena was an exaggeration and failed to account for the EEOC's offer to mitigate the burden).

[32]EEOC v. Ford Motor Credit Co., 26 F.3d 44, 47–48, 65 FEP 65 (6th Cir. 1994) (limiting scope of subpoena and permitting discovery of personnel information relating to people other than claimant for only a specific time period on the ground that the "extremely tenuous" relevance of such information is outweighed by the burden to Ford of producing it); EEOC v. City of Milwaukee, 919 F. Supp. 1247, 1259–60 (E.D. Wis. 1996) (refusing to enforce portions of subpoena that sought information regarding an individual that was too indefinite and ambiguous, and portion that sought medical records of third parties).

[33]26 F.3d at 47.

[34]EEOC v. Superior Temporary Servs., Inc., 56 F.3d 441, 447, 67 FEP 1700 (2d Cir. 1995) (EEOC had complied with Title VII provision requiring deferral to state agencies where EEOC and New York are parties to a work-sharing agreement, which provided that New York waived the exclusive processing rights granted it under Title VII).

Challenges to subpoenas rooted in state-law arguments such as confidentiality have been rejected.[35] In *EEOC v. City of Milwaukee*,[36] the EEOC subpoenaed, among other things, the police department's ongoing internal affairs investigatory files.[37] The city refused to produce them, arguing that disclosure of these files could compromise ongoing investigations and thereby "threaten the normal operations" of the police force by rendering its promises of confidentiality a "sham."[38] Relying on *University of Pennsylvania v. EEOC*,[39] *EEOC v. Illinois Department of Employment Security*,[40] and *EEOC v. County of San Benito*,[41] the court explained that it was the clear intent of Congress that EEOC mandates preempt state restrictions and concluded that since the information requested was within the agency's authority, reasonably relevant to the inquiry, and not too indefinite or unreasonably broad or burdensome, the enforcement of the subpoena should be ordered.[42]

V. ACCESS TO EEOC FILES AND ADMISSIBILITY OF THE EEOC DETERMINATION

A. Access to EEOC Files

1. Statutory Framework

b. The Freedom of Information Act. The FOIA includes nine, rather than seven, exemptions.[43] With respect to the fourth exemption for trade secrets and commercial or financial information, one court has held that confidential and privileged adverse impact

---

[35]EEOC v. City of Orange, 905 F. Supp. 381, 382 (E.D. Tex. 1995) (enforcing EEOC subpoena for all tapes and transcripts of city council meetings held in closed executive sessions on nine specific dates from October 1992 through April 1994, notwithstanding a state law requiring confidentiality of such sessions, on the ground that federal discrimination law preempted any state law).
[36]919 F. Supp. 1247 (E.D. Wis. 1996).
[37]*Id.* at 1255.
[38]*Id.* at 1256.
[39]493 U.S. 182, 51 FEP 1118 (1990).
[40]995 F.2d 106, 61 FEP 1385 (7th Cir. 1993).
[41]818 F. Supp. 289, 61 FEP 946 (N.D. Cal. 1993).
[42]EEOC v. City of Milwaukee, 919 F. Supp. 1247, 1256–57 (E.D. Wis. 1996).
[43]5 U.S.C. § 552(b).

analyses voluntarily provided to the EEOC during an investigation are exempt from subsequent disclosure to a third party.[44]

4. Federal Employees' Procedures

The EEOC's regulations pertaining to federal sector equal employment opportunity were updated in 1992.[45] The new regulations continue to protect the identity of an aggrieved federal employee before the filing of a formal complaint.[46]

B. Admissibility Into Evidence of EEOC Findings

Whether or not an EEOC determination will be admitted into evidence continues to depend on a number of factors, including the facts and circumstances unique to a given case and whether the case involves a bench trial or a jury trial.[47] As to the admissibility of the EEOC investigative files underlying a determination, the Third Circuit has stated that admissibility of both an EEOC probable cause decision and its file is entrusted to the discretion of the trial court.[48]

---

[44]McDonnell Douglas Corp. v. EEOC, 922 F. Supp. 235, 70 FEP 980 (E.D. Mo. 1996).
[45]Codified at 29 C.F.R. § 1614.
[46]29 C.F.R. § 1614.105(g) (1996).
[47]Walker v. NationsBank, 53 F.3d 1548, 1554–55, 68 FEP 314 (11th Cir. 1995) (approving trial court ruling excluding determination issued by EEOC's Washington, D.C. office, which conflicted with determination issued by EEOC's Miami office, on the ground of potential confusion to the jury); EEOC v. Manville Sales Corp., 27 F.3d 1089, 1095, 65 FEP 804 (5th Cir. 1994) (contrasting EEOC letters of violation with EEOC determinations in letting stand a ruling excluding the former from evidence), cert. denied, 513 U.S. 1190 (1995); EEOC v. Regency Architectural Metals Corp., 896 F. Supp. 260, 263 (D. Conn. 1995) (admissibility of EEOC reasonable cause determinations is within the discretion of the trial court; determination excluded because it consisted largely of "brief factual assertions which were the subject of testimony at trial, and legal reasoning, which is the province of the court"); Strauss v. Microsoft Corp., 68 FEP 1576, 1578–79 (S.D.N.Y. 1995) (concluding that probative value of EEOC determination outweighed danger of unfair prejudice under Fed. R. Evid. 403, but requiring limiting instruction); see also Heyne v. Caruso, 69 F.3d 1475, 1482–84, 69 FEP 408 (9th Cir. 1995) (reversing trial court's decision to exclude state administrative agency's probable cause finding from evidence).
[48]Starceski v. Westinghouse Elec. Corp., 54 F.3d 1089, 1100 n.12, 67 FEP 1184 (3d Cir. 1995) (rejecting contention that admitting document in EEOC file but excluding EEOC determination was improper).

Chapter 30

TITLE VII COVERAGE

I. Overview

Substantial litigation continues to surround issues of Title VII coverage. Two cases dealing with these issues, *Robinson v. Shell Oil Co.*[1] and *Walters v. Metropolitan Educational Enterprises, Inc.*,[2] have been decided by the Supreme Court in the short time since publication of the Main Edition.

II. The Substantive and Formal Elements of a Charge of Discrimination

B. Formal Requirements

As a general rule, Title VII requires a plaintiff to file a verified charge of discrimination with the EEOC before bringing a Title VII action in federal court.[3] The courts continue to recognize alternative means of meeting Title VII's requirement of filing a charge, provided they satisfy the purposes underlying the requirement, which include providing adequate notice to the employer of the conduct complained of and supplying the EEOC with information specific enough to investigate and attempt conciliation.[4] Thus, courts have found satisfaction of the charge-filing requirement where a plaintiff has completed an EEOC intake questionnaire that identifies the parties and the alleged discriminatory acts with the required specificity.[5] While the EEOC's regulations permit a charging party to

---

[1] 117 S. Ct. 843, 72 FEP 1856 (1997).
[2] 117 S. Ct. 660, 72 FEP 1211 (1997).
[3] 42 U.S.C. § 2000e-5(f)(1).
[4] Downes v. Volkswagen of Am., Inc., 41 F.3d 1132, 1138, 69 FEP 11 (7th Cir. 1994) (citing Steffen v. Meridian Life Ins. Co., 859 F.2d 534, 542–44, 48 FEP 173 (7th Cir. 1988), *cert. denied,* 491 U.S. 907 (1989)).
[5] Howze v. Virginia Polytechnic & State Univ., 901 F. Supp. 1091, 69 FEP 1013 (W.D. Va. 1995) (plaintiff's filing of affidavit and intake questionnaire with EEOC

correct technical defects in a charge, such as lack of verification, by subsequent amendment, the Fourth Circuit has held that a charging party may not do so where a right-to-sue letter has been issued and litigation has commenced.[6]

Courts continue to recognize that, where the EEOC has a work-sharing agreement in place with a state fair employment agency, charges filed with the EEOC are deemed filed with the state agency.[7] Conversely, in "deferral" states, charges filed with the state agency are deemed filed with the EEOC.[8]

The Fifth Circuit has limited the EEOC's investigative authority by refusing to enforce an EEOC subpoena issued after the charging party filed suit, holding that the EEOC may not continue an administrative investigation based upon an individual's charge once the charging party has been issued a notice of right to sue and initiated litigation.[9]

III. CHARGING PARTIES

B. Charges Filed by Persons Who Are Members of the Protected Group in Question and Who Are Affected by an Adverse Employment Decision or Practice

1. Is the Complainant Personally Aggrieved?

Courts have continued to find the inquiry regarding who may sue under Title VII to be co-extensive with Article III standing.[10]

---

held sufficient). *See also* EEOC v. Quad/Graphics, Inc., 63 F.3d 642, 68 FEP 1085 (7th Cir. 1995) (EEOC Commissioner's charge described offending conduct with necessary specificity despite omission of categories of employment positions from which affected individuals allegedly were excluded).

[6]Balazs v. Liebenthal, 32 F.3d 151, 157, 65 FEP 993 (4th Cir. 1994) (employee could not perfect charge of retaliation by amending charge to include required verification after EEOC had issued right-to-sue letter and terminated processing of charge, federal court action had been instituted, and employer had filed motion to dismiss).

[7]Hill v. St. Louis Univ., 920 F. Supp. 124, 127 (E.D. Mo. 1996) (where work-sharing agreement was in place, complaint filed with EEOC was deemed filed with Missouri Commission on Human Rights on same day).

[8]Reed v. A.W. Lawrence & Co., 95 F.3d 1170, 1176, 72 FEP 1345 (2d Cir. 1996) (because New York is a "deferral" state, complaint filed with New York State Division of Human Rights was deemed concurrently filed with EEOC).

[9]EEOC v. Hearst Corp., 103 F.3d 462, 72 FEP 1541 (5th Cir. 1997).

[10]*See* Foote v. Folks, Inc., 864 F. Supp. 1327, 1328, 3 AD 1342 (N.D. Ga. 1994) (stating that inquiries under Title VII and Article III are "coextensive"); NAACP v.

In an ADEA case, the court found that the wife of a former company vice president had no standing to assert ADEA claims against the company for age discrimination allegedly suffered by her husband because the wife was never an employee of the employer.[11]

2. Is the Complainant Protected by Title VII?

b. Independent Contractors and Other Nonemployees. In light of the Supreme Court's decision in *Nationwide Mutual Insurance Co. v. Darden*,[12] some courts are now applying a common-law agency test to Title VII cases to determine whether a plaintiff is an employee for Title VII purposes.[13] In *Darden,* the Court held

---

Town of East Haven, 892 F. Supp. 46, 67 FEP 1055, 1056 (D. Conn. 1995) ("Congress in enacting Title VII intended to confer standing to the full extent authorized by Article III of the Constitution."); Loomis v. General Motors Corp., 70 FEP 691, 695 (E.D. Mich. 1994) (holding that plaintiff cannot assert violation under Title VII because he did not meet the requirements for constitutional standing).

[11]Flamand v. American Int'l Group, Inc., 876 F. Supp. 356, 69 FEP 675 (D.P.R. 1994).

[12]503 U.S. 318 (1992) ("employee" as used in ERISA incorporates traditional agency criteria).

[13]*See, e.g.,* Walker v. Correctional Medical Sys., 886 F. Supp. 515, 520, 68 FEP 42 (W.D. Pa. 1995) (rejecting the hybrid test in favor of common-law agency test in light of *Darden*); Frankel v. Bally, Inc., 987 F.2d 86, 61 FEP 218 (2d Cir. 1993) (holding that after *Darden* the question of whether an individual is an employee under the ADEA or an independent contractor must be determined in accordance with common-law agency principles); EEOC v. Catholic Knights Ins. Soc'y, 915 F. Supp. 25, 29–30, 70 FEP 281 (N.D. Ill. 1996) (insurance agents were not Title VII "employees" of insurance society under *Darden,* where agents' contracts specified they were independent contractors, the agents determined their own days and hours of work, paid their own taxes, and received no benefits; the facts that society monitored agents' sales activity, provided them with optional marketing materials, and required them to submit sales reports did not establish requisite degree of control); Oshiver v. Levin, Fishbein, Sedran & Berman, 910 F. Supp. 225, 69 FEP 1288 (E.D. Pa.) (attorney who performed indexing of discovery documents for law firm when work was available was not an employee for purposes of Title VII because the firm lacked control over her work and she was considered by the firm to be self-employed for tax purposes), *aff'd,* 96 F.3d 1434 (3d Cir. 1996); Kellam v. Snelling Personnel Servs., 866 F. Supp. 812, 814–15, 68 FEP 195 (D. Del. 1994) (applying *Darden*'s common-law agency test to determine that temporary workers were not employees of personnel services agency), *aff'd,* 65 F.3d 162, 69 FEP 768 (3d Cir. 1995); McFadden-Peel v. Staten Island Cable, 873 F. Supp. 757, 760, 67 FEP 147 (E.D.N.Y. 1994) (director of administration and marketing under Title VII was employee under common-law agency principles even though she was not paid a salary but submitted bills for her work, taxes were not withheld from her checks, and she listed her occupation as "consultant," where plaintiff's duties were not of the kind normally turned over to an independent contractor); Stetka v. Hunt Real Estate Corp., 859 F. Supp. 661, 65 FEP 1311 (W.D.N.Y. 1994) (real estate agent was not employee

that where Congress does not helpfully define the term "employee," courts should use the common-law agency test to determine employee status,[14] and consider several nonexclusive factors: (1) skill required, (2) source of the instrumentalities and tools, (3) location of work, (4) duration of the relationship between the parties, (5) whether the hiring party has the right to assign additional projects to the hired party, (6) the extent of the hired party's discretion over when and how long to work, (7) the method of payment, (8) the hired party's role in hiring and paying assistants, (9) whether the work is part of the regular business of the hiring party, (10) whether the hiring party is in business, (11) the provision of employee benefits, and (12) the tax treatment of the hired party.[15] The "hybrid test" is still favored by other courts.[16]

---

under Title VII where she worked her own hours, was paid by commission, and worked autonomously); Breen v. Hunt Real Estate Corp., 65 FEP 1392 (W.D.N.Y. 1994) (same). *But see* Wilde v. County of Kandiyohi, 15 F.3d 103, 105–06, 63 FEP 1167 (8th Cir. 1994) (following *Darden* to require rejection of economic realities test in favor of common law of agency; upholding reliance on hybrid test because of "no significant difference" between hybrid test and common law test favored by the Court in *Darden*); Wilson v. United Farm Bureau Mut. Ins. Co., 68 FEP 631, 635 (S.D. Ind. 1995) (applying factors in *Darden* for common law agency to decide the employee issue under Title VII and the ADEA, but considering related factors as well).

[14]503 U.S. at 322–25 ("where a statute containing the term 'employee' does not helpfully define it, the common law agency test should be applied").

[15]*Id.* at 323.

[16]Nowlin v. Resolution Trust Corp., 33 F.3d 498, 505–07, 65 FEP 1870 (5th Cir. 1994) (citing Mares v. Marsh, 777 F.2d 1066, 1067, 40 FEP 858 (5th Cir. 1985), for the proposition that the hybrid test controls and requires consideration of the business's right to control the worker, the kind of occupation, whether the work is usually performed under the direction of a supervisor, the skill required, the place where the work is to be performed, whether the worker furnishes the equipment used, the duration of the work, the method of payment, the manner in which the work relationship is terminated, whether annual leave is afforded, whether the work is an integral part of the business of the "employer," whether the worker accumulates retirement benefits, whether the business pays Social Security taxes, and the intention of the parties); St. Germain v. Simmons Airline, 930 F. Supp. 1144 (N.D. Tex. 1996) (applying hybrid test to find that trainee in flight attendant training program was not an employee because trainee received no compensation, did not accrue vacation time or retirement benefits, did not perform any services for the "employer," and the "employer" did not intend for trainees to be considered employees; however, "employer" did furnish the equipment used and the place of work); Vick v. Foote, Inc., 898 F. Supp. 330, 333, 68 FEP 1628 (E.D. Va. 1995) (Fourth Circuit requires the court to analyze the facts under a standard that incorporates both the common law test derived from principles of agency and the so-called economic realities test, and concluding that vice president who was 60% shareholder was an independent contractor and not an employee under Title VII because he did not

Although the various tests purport to focus on different aspects of the employment relationship, in actuality, the courts generally evaluate the same factors[17] and place the greatest emphasis on the business's right to control the manner and means by which the work is accomplished.[18]

---

receive compensation in exchange for services, and no one tells him when to work, what to do, "or anything else about the services he performs"), *aff'd*, 82 F.3d 411 (4th Cir.), *cert. denied*, 117 S. Ct. 311 (1996); Lane v. David P. Jacobson & Co., 880 F. Supp. 1091, 70 FEP 391 (E.D. Va. 1995) (determining that sales representative was independent contractor by analyzing facts of employment relationship under standard incorporating principles of agency and economic realities); Goudeau v. Dental Health Servs., Inc., 901 F. Supp. 1139, 69 FEP 629 (M.D. La. 1995) (applying hybrid test to determine that accountant and dentists-stockholders were not employees of a professional dental corporation).

[17]Walker v. Correctional Medical Sys., 886 F. Supp. 515, 521, 68 FEP 42 (W.D. Pa. 1995) (stating that there is very little difference between the hybrid test and the *Darden* common-law agency test); Frankel v. Bally, Inc., 987 F.2d 86, 90, 61 FEP 218 (2d Cir. 1993) (stating that "in practice there is little discernable difference" between the hybrid test and the common-law agency test); Stouch v. Brothers of the Order of Hermits of St. Augustine, 836 F. Supp. 1134, 1140 n.5, 63 FEP 1107 (E.D. Pa. 1993) ("there appears to be little difference between the tests").

[18]*See* Alexander v. Rush N. Shore Med. Ctr., 101 F.3d 487, 72 FEP 742 (7th Cir. 1996) (while the common-law agency test applies, control is the most important factor), *cert. denied*, 118 S. Ct. 54 (1997); Ost v. West Suburban Travelers Limousine, Inc., 88 F.3d 435, 71 FEP 304 (7th Cir. 1996) (right to control is the most important factor of five relevant factors in finding that limousine driver was not employee of airport dispatch service where the driver worked when he chose, could refuse any assignment, and provided and serviced his own vehicle; other factors include the kind of occupation and nature of skill required, responsibility for the costs of operation, methods and form of payment and benefits, and length of job commitment); Poff v. Prudential Ins. Co., 882 F. Supp. 1534, 4 AD 596 (E.D. Pa. 1995) (degree of control is most important factor under ADA, but other factors to consider include means of employment, skill required, source of tools, location of work, duration of the relationship between the parties, business's right to assign additional duties, individual's discretion over hours, method of payment, individual's role in hiring and paying assistants, provisions for employee benefits, and the individual's tax treatment); Johnson v. Greater Southeast Community Hosp. Corp., 903 F. Supp. 140, 155, 69 FEP 280 (D.D.C. 1995) ("[t]he lack of control over a contracted worker is the distinguishing feature of an independent contractor"); Kellam v. Snelling Personnel Servs., 866 F. Supp. 812, 815, 68 FEP 195 (D. Del. 1994) (under the hybrid test "the greatest emphasis is placed on the hiring party's right to control the manner and means by which work is accomplished"), *aff'd*, 65 F.3d 162, 69 FEP 768 (3d Cir. 1995); Walker v. Correctional Med. Sys., 886 F. Supp. 515, 520–21, 68 FEP 42 (W.D. Pa. 1995) (among the *Darden* factors, "the greatest emphasis is placed on the hiring party's right to control the manner and means by which the work is accomplished;" "[b]oth tests place their greatest emphasis on the hiring party's right to control the manner and means by which the work is accomplished and consider a nonexhaustive list of factors as part of a flexible test of the totality of the circumstances").

Courts continue to apply a case-by-case approach to determine whether a business "partner" is, in fact, an employee protected by Title VII.[19] There also continues to be disagreement about the scope of the holding in *Sibley Memorial Hospital v. Wilson*,[20] which interpreted Title VII to protect individuals from interference with their employment opportunities by third parties.[21]

c. *"Personal Staff" Exemption.* Courts continue to rely on the six-factor test established in *Teneyuca v. Bexar County*.[22] However,

---

[19] *See* Simpson v. Ernst & Young, 100 F.3d 436, 72 FEP 343 (6th Cir. 1996) (a "partner" in an accounting firm was an employee protected by ADEA because he could not participate in personnel determinations or vote on the firm management committee, and he did not participate in profits), *cert. denied*, 117 S. Ct. 1862 (1997); Strother v. Southern Cal. Permanente Med. Group, 79 F.3d 859, 72 FEP 905 (9th Cir. 1996) (factual hearing should be held to consider whether "partner" in medical group was employee for Title VII purposes; relevant factors include setting of compensation and discipline rights).

[20] 488 F.2d 1338, 1342–43, 6 FEP 1029 (D.C. Cir. 1973).

[21] *Compare* Hudson v. Radnor Valley Country Club, 70 FEP 1207, 1210 (E.D. Pa. 1996) (stating that a "Title VII plaintiff may sue a defendant with whom he had no actual or prospective employment relationship if that defendant controlled the plaintiff's access to employment and then foreclosed such employment by unlawfully discriminating against the plaintiff"), *with* Alexander v. Rush N. Shore Med. Ctr., 101 F.3d 487, 72 FEP 742 (7th Cir. 1996) (nonemployee physician whose staff privileges were revoked has no protection under Title VII), *cert. denied*, 118 S. Ct. 54 (1997); EEOC v. Illinois, 69 F.3d 167, 169, 69 FEP 306 (7th Cir. 1995) (stating that it is "implausible to impute to Congress an intention to create, by language not at all suggestive of any such intention, aider and abetter liability of one employer to the employees of another employer"); *and* Vakharia v. Swedish Covenant Hosp., 765 F. Supp. 461, 464 n.1, 61 FEP 533 (N.D. Ill. 1991) (stating that Seventh Circuit precedent "cast some doubt on the proposition that a defendant could be liable under Title VII for interference with an individual's employment opportunities with third parties").

[22] 767 F.2d 148, 38 FEP 989 (5th Cir. 1985). *E.g.,* Montgomery v. Brookshire, 34 F.3d 291, 65 FEP 1866 (5th Cir. 1994) (*Teneyuca* factors precluded granting defendant sheriff's motion for summary judgment on whether deputy sheriff in department of 113 law enforcement employees fell within personal staff exemption, because sheriff rarely controlled deputy sheriff's daily activities, deputy sheriff was on lowest rung in chain of command, and sheriff and deputy sheriff discussed business once a month at most); Johnson v. Board of County Comm'rs, 859 F. Supp. 438, 443, 65 FEP 1073 (D. Colo. 1994) (applying *Teneyuca* factors to deny defendant sheriff's motion for summary judgment on claims of former dispatchers and deputy sheriff, because the mere fact that the sheriff had the power to hire and fire plaintiffs did not establish the level of intimacy required); Dubisar-Dewberry v. Folmar, 883 F. Supp. 648, 67 FEP 1660 (M.D. Ala. 1995) (applying *Teneyuca* factors to decide whether former child support coordinator for district attorney's office fell within personal staff exemption). *Cf.* Americanos v. Carter, 74 F.3d 138, 69 FEP 1183 (7th Cir.) (test to determine whether Constitution permits state official to be fired for lack

§ 321 of the Civil Rights Act effectively protects many of these same individuals from discrimination, albeit with modified procedures.[23]

d. Former Employees. In *Robinson v. Shell Oil Co.*,[24] the Supreme Court resolved a split among the circuits by holding that the term "employees," as used in the retaliation provision of Title VII,[25] includes former employees. Thus, an individual may bring suit against his or her former employer for postemployment actions allegedly taken in retaliation for the individual's having filed a charge with the EEOC.[26]

D. Charges Filed by Persons Who Are Not Members of the Protected Group in Question, But Who Still Claim to Be Aggrieved

1. Charges Alleging an Independent Violation

A number of cases have held that a white employee has standing to complain that he or she suffered from illegal retaliation for acting to protect the rights of minority groups.[27] This has been

---

of political loyalty is appropriate for whether Indiana deputy attorney general fell within personal staff exemption), *cert. denied,* 116 S. Ct. 1853 (1996); Cromer v. Brown, 88 F.3d 1315, 1322–23, 71 FEP 530 (4th Cir. 1996) (former sheriff's department employee was exempt from Title VII as "personal staff" while serving as captain in sheriff's "command staff," but not while serving as lieutenant; as captain, he met with sheriff every week, determined operations and policies with five other members of "command staff," and spoke on sheriff's behalf with members of the public). *But see* Rutland v. Moore, 54 F.3d 226, 231, 67 FEP 1707 (5th Cir. 1995) (special assistant attorney general of Mississippi not protected by ADEA where "immediate legal advisor" exemption applied; attorney general expected and received advice from such individuals with respect to exercise of constitutional or legal powers of office; *Teneyuca* factors not considered).

[23]2 U.S.C. § 1220(a).
[24]117 S. Ct. 843, 72 FEP 1856 (1997).
[25]42 U.S.C. § 2000e-3(a).
[26]Former employees who do not have a continued interest in reemployment may not be able to obtain certain injunctive relief for themselves or remaining workers. In *Ward v. Johns Hopkins Univ.,* 861 F. Supp. 367, 66 FEP 872 (D. Md. 1994), for example, former employees who had alleged sexual harassment during their employment with defendant did not have standing to obtain reinstatement and implementation of sexual harassment complaint procedures, where they had not asserted a constructive discharge claim and had not applied for reemployment.
[27]Chandler v. Fast Lane, Inc., 868 F. Supp. 1138, 1144, 66 FEP 675 (E.D. Ark. 1994) (white plaintiff can establish unlawful retaliation under Title VII by demonstrating that employer insisted, over the plaintiff's opposition, that plaintiff exercise her supervisory authority to deprive African-Americans of employment opportunities).

extended in some cases to include claims by white employees disciplined for refusing to discriminate against African-Americans.[28] Other cases have held that Title VII grants protection to whites who are denied association with members of other groups because of an employer's discriminatory practices.[29]

2. Charges "on Behalf of" a Person Aggrieved

Courts continue to find that a plaintiff does not have standing to *sue* to remedy violations of the Title VII rights of other persons.[30]

E. Charges Filed by an Organization Itself Claiming to Be an Aggrieved Person

An association may have standing to assert a Title VII claim absent injury to itself if it can establish that (1) one of its members would have standing; (2) the interest it seeks to protect is

---

[28]*See* Moyo v. Gomez, 32 F.3d 1382, 1385, 65 FEP 821 (white plaintiff stated a claim for unlawful retaliation under Title VII where he alleged that he was discriminated against for refusing to carry out or otherwise protesting the employer's alleged policy of discrimination against African-Americans), *amended*, 40 F.3d 982, 68 FEP 1419 (9th Cir. 1994), *cert. denied*, 513 U.S. 1081 (1995).

[29]Maynard v. City of San Jose, 37 F.3d 1396, 1398, 66 FEP 123 (9th Cir. 1994) ("Section 706 of Title VII, 42 U.S.C. § 2000e-5, grants special protection to whites who are denied association with members of other groups because of an employer's discriminatory practices.") (dictum); Chandler v. Fast Lane, Inc., 868 F. Supp. at 1140, 66 FEP 675 (Title VII protects white person's right to associate with African-Americans); Childress v. City of Richmond, 120 F.3d 476, 74 FEP 749 (4th Cir. 1997) (white male employees could bring Title VII claim for disparaging comments supervisor made to women and African-Americans). *But see* Holt v. JTM Indus., Inc., 89 F.3d 1224, 71 FEP 809 (5th Cir. 1996) (no ADEA cause of action where employer engaged in adverse action against plaintiff in retaliation for his wife's filing a claim under the ADEA, absent any showing that plaintiff participated in conduct protected by the ADEA), *cert. denied*, 117 S. Ct. 1821 (1997).

[30]*See* Miller v. Aristech Chem. Corp., 67 FEP 216, 217 (W.D. Pa. 1995) (plaintiff does not have standing to assert that her *husband* was denied promotion in retaliation for *her* protected activities); Ventura County Ry. v. Hadley Auto Transp., 45 Cal. Rptr.2d 362, 4 AD 1523 (Cal. Ct. App. 1995) (railroad had no standing under ADA to press cross-claim against employer of victim of railroad accident on theory that employer's failure to accommodate the victim's injuries prevented accident victim from mitigating damages); Evans v. Kansas City Sch. Dist., 65 F.3d 98, 68 FEP 1203 (8th Cir. 1995) (school teacher failed to state claim for retaliation under Title VII, Missouri Human Rights Act, and § 1981 based on his opposition to school principal's plans to implement desegregation order at school; students and their parents would be proper plaintiffs), *cert. denied*, 116 S. Ct. 1319 (1996).

germane to its purposes; and (3) neither the claim nor the relief sought requires participation of individual members in the lawsuit.[31]

F. Testers

The EEOC continues to take the position that testers have standing to file charges of employment discrimination.[32]

In *Molovinsky v. Fair Employment Council of Greater Washington, Inc.*,[33] the court determined that two testers, who posed as job seekers and suffered harassment as a result, had standing to assert discrimination claims against the owner of an employment agency under the District of Columbia Human Rights Act.

G. Commissioner Charges

One court dismissed an EEOC discrimination action under Rule 12(b)(6) of the Federal Rules of Civil Procedure, holding that the EEOC lacked standing to pursue a claim under the ADEA because its complaint had failed to identify a single employee who had a colorable claim of age discrimination.[34]

IV. RESPONDENTS

A. Employer

In certain circumstances, courts will entertain employment discrimination claims against entities that are not the direct employers of the individual Title VII plaintiff. In many such instances, an entity's liability as an "employer" depends on whether the entity is in a position to control the employment relationship between the plaintiff and a third party.[35] For example, one court sustained a

---

[31] NAACP v. Town of East Haven, 892 F. Supp. 46, 67 FEP 1005, 1056 (D. Conn. 1995).

[32] *See* EEOC Notice No. 915.002 (May 22, 1996) (superseding "testers" policy cited in *Policy Guidance* at N:3943, n.18). *See generally* 2 EEOC COMP. MAN. (BNA) at § 631.8 regarding EEOC investigatory procedures.

[33] 683 F.2d 142, 72 FEP 79 (D.C. Cir. 1996).

[34] EEOC v. Sears, Roebuck & Co., 883 F. Supp. 211, 214, 70 FEP 175 (N.D. Ill. 1995).

[35] *Compare* Johnson v. Board of County Comm'rs, 859 F. Supp. 438, 65 FEP 1073 (D. Colo. 1994) (board of county commissioners was an "employer" of sheriff's

psychiatrist's race discrimination claims against the private board that denied her professional certification, even though the board was not her direct employer.[36] Observing that "total foreclosure from future employment opportunities is not necessary," the court allowed the action to proceed because the plaintiff had alleged that the lack of board certification would "significantly inhibit her future employment prospects."[37] Another court ruled that a valet parking company, its president, and its manager could not press Title VII claims against a country club for canceling its contract, allegedly because the company refused to discharge its African-American employees, because the valet company, its president, and its manager were not "employees" of the country club.[38] However, the court held that the African-American employees of the valet company could maintain a Title VII action against the country club if they could show that the club controlled their access to employment and then foreclosed such employment through discrimination.[39]

1. Definition

a. Who May Be Counted as "Employees."[40] Employers are not liable for discrimination under Title VII unless they employ the statutorily required 15 employees for each day during 20 calendar weeks in the year.[41] Officers and board members are not counted

---

dispatchers, because the board was responsible for allocating funds to the sheriff's department and thus had some degree of control over the dispatchers' working conditions) *with* Lambertsen v. Utah Dep't of Corrections, 922 F. Supp. 533, 70 FEP 1387 (D. Utah 1995) (a state corrections department was not an "employer"of an educational aide assigned to work at a prison school because the school district had ultimate control over the aide and the school in which she taught), *aff'd*, 70 F.3d 1024, 70 FEP 631 (10th Cir. 1996).

[36]Morrison v. American Bd. of Psychiatry & Neurology, Inc., 908 F. Supp. 582, 69 FEP 1217 (N.D. Ill. 1996).

[37]*Id.* at 587.

[38]Hudson v. Radnor Valley Country Club, 70 FEP 1207 (E.D. Pa. 1996).

[39]*Id.* at 1210.

[40]*See* Section III.B.2.b *supra.*

[41]*E.g.*, Greenlees v. Eidenmuller Enters., Inc., 32 F.3d 197, 66 FEP 457 (5th Cir. 1994) (employment agency that had fewer than 15 employees could not be sued under Title VII in its capacity as an employer); Lightner v. City of Ariton, 884 F. Supp. 468, 69 FEP 215 (M.D. Ala. 1995) (former police chief could not maintain claim of discrimination under Title VII against either city or mayor where city employed fewer than 15 people).

where they do not perform traditional employee duties.[42] Relying on common law principles, one court has held that a majority shareholder is not an "employee" for Title VII purposes where the plaintiff could not establish that compensation was in return for any service he performed, and there was no proof that anyone else supervised his work.[43] However, courts are divided over whether shareholders of a professional association or professional corporation are employees for purposes of Title VII coverage.[44] Independent contractors are not counted for purposes of the 15-employee minimum.[45] In determining whether an individual is an employee or an independent contractor, some courts rely on the hybrid economic

---

[42]Kern v. City of Rochester, 93 F.3d 38, 71 FEP 1391 (2d Cir. 1996) (plaintiff failed to show nonofficer board members of local union were employees where there was no proof that the board members performed traditional employee duties or reported to anyone but themselves), *cert. denied,* 117 S. Ct. 1335 (1997); Edwards v. Esau Invs., Inc., 66 FEP 711, 713 (D. Kan. 1994) (corporate officers could not be counted as employees where plaintiff failed to establish that they performed traditional employee duties).

[43]Vick v. Foote, Inc., 898 F. Supp. 330, 334–35, 68 FEP 1628 (E.D. Va. 1995) (vice president and 60% shareholder was not an employee for Title VII's 15-employee minimum, where services were provided as an owner with no nexus between benefits received and services performed), *aff'd,* 82 F.3d 411 (4th Cir.), *cert. denied,* 117 S. Ct. 311 (1996).

[44]*Compare* Goudeau v. Dental Health Servs., Inc., 901 F. Supp. 1139, 1147, 69 FEP 629 (M.D. La. 1995) (dentist shareholders in professional dental corporation were not "employees" under Title VII) *and* Devine v. Stone, Leyton & Gershman, 100 F.3d 78, 72 FEP 394 (8th Cir. 1996) (partners in law firm do not count toward 15-employee minimum where they have meaningful voice in policy), *cert. denied,* 117 S. Ct. 1694 (1997) *with* Johnson v. Cooper, Deans & Cargill, P.A., 884 F. Supp. 43, 45, 71 FEP 931 (D.N.H. 1994) (shareholder-employees of law firm, a professional association, count toward 15-employee minimum) *and* Strother v. Southern Cal. Permanente Med. Group, 79 F.3d 859, 72 FEP 905 (9th Cir. 1996) (court must look behind wording of partnership agreement to actual relationship; physician in large medical group held to be employee).

[45]Clifton v. Mars Telecom, Inc., 70 FEP 1315, 1317–18 (D. Kan. 1996) (sales representatives were independent contractors and not employees for purposes of 15-employee minimum where employer did not control their work, provide benefits, services, or training; and paid them on commission basis); Powell-Ross v. All Star Radio, Inc., 68 FEP 1148 (E.D. Pa. 1995) (finding that radio station disc jockey, chief engineer, and program director were all independent contractors and therefore did not count toward 15-employee requisite for Title VII coverage); Kellam v. Snelling Personnel Servs., 866 F. Supp. 812, 68 FEP 195 (D. Del. 1994) (1,000 temporary workers referred by employment agency were independent contractors who could not be counted to provide subject matter jurisdiction over agency that employed maximum of eight staff employees), *aff'd,* 65 F.3d 162, 69 FEP 768 (3d Cir. 1995).

realities/common-law control test,[46] while others employ the standard common-law agency test[47] approved by the Supreme Court in *Nationwide Mutual Insurance Co. v. Darden.*[48]

   b. *How the Counting Is Done.* In *Walters v. Metropolitan Educational Enterprises, Inc.,*[49] the Supreme Court resolved a circuit split over which employees should be counted for purposes of Title VII's requirement that a statutory employer have at least 15 employees for each working day for at least 20 calendar weeks in the year, by adopting the "payroll approach," under which employees may be counted if they are on the payroll during the required 20 weeks. "The ultimate touchstone," the Court ruled, "is whether an employer has employment relationships with 15 or more individuals for each working day in 20 or more weeks during the year in question."[50] Under the payroll method, hourly part-time employees can be counted even though they do not actually work every day.[51]

   Courts continue to recognize that the "current" calendar year in which employees are counted is the year in which the alleged discrimination occurred.[52]

3. Determining Who Is the "Employer"

   Courts continue to apply different theories in analyzing the question of who "employs" a given individual for purposes of enforcing the various laws dealing with employment discrimination.

---

[46]*Clifton v. Mars Telecom,* 70 FEP at 1317–18 (applying hybrid test); Goudeau v. Dental Health Servs., Inc., 901 F. Supp. at 1142, 69 FEP 629 (applying hybrid test to find accountant who performed payroll services was independent contractor, where accountant worked for other companies and was called only when needed); Vick v. Foote, Inc., 898 F. Supp. at 332 (applying common-law agency test and economic realities test to hold that vice president and 60% shareholder was not an employee).

[47]Powell-Ross v. All Star Radio, Inc., 68 FEP 1148, 1153 (E.D. Pa. 1995); Kellam v. Snelling Personnel Servs., Inc., 866 F. Supp. 812, 814–15, 68 FEP 195 (D. Del. 1994).

[48]503 U.S. 318 (1992).

[49]117 S. Ct. 660, 72 FEP 1211 (1997).

[50]*Id.* at 666.

[51]Vera-Lozano v. International Broadcasting, 50 F.3d 67, 69–70, 67 FEP 667 (1st Cir. 1995).

[52]Villasenor v. Industrial Wire & Cable, Inc., 929 F. Supp. 310, 313 n.5, 5 AD 1160 (N.D. Ill. 1996); Vick v. Foote, Inc., 898 F. Supp. 330, 332, 68 FEP 1628 (E.D. Va. 1995), *aff'd,* 82 F.3d 411 (4th Cir.), *cert. denied,* 117 S. Ct. 311 (1996).

a. "Single Employer" Theory. In assessing whether separate business entities constitute an integrated enterprise and are therefore to be treated as a single employer, the focus remains upon four factors: degree of interrelationship; common ownership and control; common management; and centralization of labor relations and personnel functions.[53]

The single employer theory is asserted most frequently in the context of a parent-subsidiary relationship.[54] Not all claims of single employer, however, involve parent-subsidiary issues,[55] and

---

[53]Garcia v. Elf Atochem N. Am., 28 F.3d 446, 450, 66 FEP 1700 (5th Cir. 1994) ("Although the term 'employer' under Title VII was meant to be liberally construed," an integrated enterprise may not be found in the absence of proof of all four factors.). *But see* Burdi v. Uniglobe Cihak Travel, Inc., 932 F. Supp. 1044, 1048, 71 FEP 925 (N.D. Ill. 1996) (common control of labor relations is the most important factor, but "the presence or absence of any one factor is not controlling") (citing Rogers v. Sugar Tree Prods., 7 F.3d 577, 582, 63 FEP 60 (7th Cir. 1993)); Bielawski v. AMI, Inc., 870 F. Supp. 771, 66 FEP 1160 (N.D. Ohio 1994) (courts are to construe Title VII definition of employer broadly; it is not necessary for all four indicia of integration to be present so long as the facts and circumstances indicate the entities are highly integrated).

[54]*See, e.g.,* Howry v. NISUS, Inc., 910 F. Supp. 576, 69 FEP 471 (M.D. Fla. 1995); Alie v. NYNEX Corp., 158 F.R.D. 239, 246, 66 FEP 812 (E.D.N.Y. 1994); Kellett v. Glaxo Enters., Inc., 66 FEP 1071 (S.D.N.Y. 1994).

[55]Zarnoski v. Hearst Business Communications, Inc., 69 FEP 1514 (E.D. Pa. 1996) (advertising agency and its sole client were not a single employer where their transactions were at arm's length, and they did not share office space or supplies, aggregate accounts or have common payrolls or labor relations policies, and agency was not foreclosed from seeking other clients); Switalski v. Iron Workers Local No. 3, 881 F. Supp. 205, 4 AD 417 (W.D. Pa. 1995) (international and local union were not a single employer where local maintains its own bylaws, elects its own officers, and negotiates its own contracts, and there is no evidence of commonality with respect to personnel and labor relations issues); Barbero v. Catawba Valley Legal Servs., Inc., 69 FEP 460 (W.D.N.C. 1995) (former employee of private, nonprofit legal services corporation that receives federal funds has not shown that a federally funded Legal Services Corporation (LSC) and employer are single entity where LSC owns part of the employer's office building, sets criteria for eligibility for services, establishes general salary and benefits guidelines, and oversees general mission, but does not set individual salaries, have hiring and firing authority, and does not dominate operation of private organization); Walker v. City of Elba, 874 F. Supp. 361, 67 FEP 212 (M.D. Ala. 1994) (city did not constitute single employer with local water board where board was separately incorporated and city not involved in hiring, firing, work hours, or payroll for board employees); Jackson v. National Football League, 65 FEP 358 (S.D.N.Y. 1994) (National Football League and World League of American Football were not a single employer even though they used the same counsel and accountants, shared office space in Germany, and the NFL provided insurance for the WLAF where they had separate payrolls, lines of credit, bank accounts); Regan v. In the Heat of the Nite, Inc., 68 FEP 1463 (S.D.N.Y. 1995) (genuine issue of fact existed as to whether group of commonly owned restaurants was integrated enterprise where staff

not all parent-subsidiary relationships are integrated enterprises.[56] In general, the standard of proof required to demonstrate integration is high.[57]

b. "Joint Employer" Theory. There is disagreement about whether the workforces of joint employers may be aggregated to meet the jurisdictional minimums.[58]

In general, courts look to three factors in assessing whether a joint employer relationship exists: authority to hire and fire the employee, promulgate work rules and assignments, and set conditions of employment; day-to-day supervision, including discipline; and control of employee records, including payroll and taxes.[59]

---

at one restaurant was subject to emergency call by others; records, payroll, and bank documents were maintained at common site; and common owner hired managers for all restaurants).

[56]Marzano v. Computer Science Corp., 91 F.3d 497, 71 FEP 1120 (3d Cir. 1996) (female former employee challenging layoff under New Jersey Law Against Discrimination may not proceed against the parent of her employer where her only connection to parent at the time of her layoff was participation in its pension plan—all other aspects of employment relationship were governed by the subsidiary); Dewey v. PTT Telecom Netherlands, U.S., Inc., 68 FEP 1112 (S.D.N.Y. 1995) (former employee of 13-employee subsidiary failed to show that subsidiary and its parent were single employer where there is no evidence of common offices, records, or bank accounts and, although nearly all the subsidiary's directors were employees of the parent, none were simultaneously officers of both entities), *aff'd,* 101 F.3d 1392 (2d Cir. 1996); Corragio v. Time, Inc. Magazine Co., 67 FEP 1880 (S.D.N.Y. 1995) (claim against parent company based solely upon fact of ownership of the subsidiary dismissed where there was no evidence of interrelated operations, common management, or centralized labor and personnel policies); Brennan v. National Tel. Directory Corp., 881 F. Supp. 986, 67 FEP 922 (E.D. Pa. 1995) (former employee may not include in Title VII action company that she alleges was "interrelated" with her employer where she has produced no evidence that the interrelationship rose to the level of an integrated enterprise).

[57]*Compare* Kellett v. Glaxo Enters., Inc., 66 FEP 1071 (S.D.N.Y. 1994) (absent evidence of extraordinary relationship between hiring entity and its parent, or evidence that parent-subsidiary relationship is a sham, the two companies are not a single employer), *with* Alie v. NYNEX Corp., 158 F.R.D. 239, 246, 66 FEP 812 (E.D.N.Y. 1994) (contrasting the liberal construction afforded to the term "employer" under Title VII with New York state and city human rights laws that require actual control by the parent in order to establish a single employer relationship).

[58]Virgo v. Riviera Beach Assocs. Ltd., 30 F.3d 1350, 65 FEP 1317 (11th Cir. 1994) (Title VII jurisdiction found by aggregating employees of hotel owner and employees of company hired to manage hotel, where evidence supported joint employer relationship between owner and management company, and they jointly employed minimum of 15 people). *Contra:* Burdi v. Uniglobe Cihak Travel, Inc., 932 F. Supp. 1044, 1048, 71 FEP 925 (N.D. Ill. 1996); Astrowsky v. First Portland Mortgage Corp., Inc., 887 F. Supp. 332, 70 FEP 195 (D. Me. 1995).

[59]*Id.;* Zarnoski v. Hearst Business Communications, 69 FEP 1514 (E.D. Pa. 1996).

However, the relationship is viewed in its totality; no single factor is dispositive.[60]

c. *The "Agent" Theory.* There continues to be disagreement among the courts concerning whether individual supervisors and managers may be held liable as agents where they possess authority to act for the employer.[61]

---

[60]Lambertsen v. Utah Dep't of Corrections, 922 F. Supp. 533, 70 FEP 1387 (D. Utah 1995) (teacher in prison school was not joint employee of school district and Department of Corrections where it was school district alone that hired and could fire her, paid her salary and benefits, and established her work hours), *aff'd,* 79 F.3d 1024, 70 FEP 631 (10th Cir. 1996); Astrowsky v. First Portland Mortgage Corp., 881 F. Supp 332, 70 FEP 195 (D. Me. 1995) (employee leasing agency that managed commissions and handled tax withholding of leased employee but exercised no other control over his work is not joint employer); Virgo v. Riviera Beach Assocs., 30 F.3d 1350, 1359–61, 65 FEP 1317 (11th Cir. 1994) (company that contracted out running of hotel, but retained responsibility for compensation, tax withholding, insurance, and labor negotiations was joint employer); Auslander v. Collier & Tiku Assocs., 68 FEP 702 (D. Mass. 1995) (receptionist who was hired and paid by owner of office space, but who performed set duties for tenant companies who contributed to her salary and benefits was employed only by owner who had exclusive authority to hire and fire, not jointly by owner and tenants); Hover v. Florida Power & Light Co., 67 FEP 34 (S.D. Fla. 1994) (power company that allegedly set work schedules and other conditions, made job assignments, did performance assessments, and provided protective clothing to service company employee who worked at one of its nuclear power plants was not a joint employer under Title VII).

[61]Individuals could not be sued as agents: Sheridan v. E.I. DuPont de Nemours & Co., 100 F.3d 1061, 1077, 72 FEP 518 (3d Cir. 1996) (supervisors are not individually liable under Title VII), *cert. denied,* 117 S. Ct. 2532 (1997); Haynes v. Williams, 88 F.3d 898, 71 FEP 414 (10th Cir. 1996) (psychiatrist in correctional unit was not liable for damage award occasioned by his discriminatory conduct even though that conduct was so egregious that his medical license was revoked); Tyson v. CIGNA Corp., 918 F. Supp. 836, 70 FEP 908 (D.N.J. 1996) (employees may not be held personally liable under Title VII); Miller v. CBC Cos., 908 F. Supp. 1054, 5 AD 1187 (D.N.H. 1995) ("virtual consensus" that there is no individual liability for supervisors under ADA); Hrosik v. Latrobe Steel, 4 AD 555 (W.D. Pa. 1995) (company president was not individually liable as "agent" under statutory language of ADA); Verde v. City of Philadelphia, 862 F. Supp. 1329, 67 FEP 1711 (E.D. Pa. 1994) (although supervisor who controls plaintiff's terms and conditions of employment is an "agent" of the employer, government officials may not be held liable for damages under Title VII in their individual capacities).

Individuals could be sued as agents: Coleman v. Kaye, 87 F.3d 1491, 71 FEP 236 (3d Cir. 1996) (county prosecutor acted as "agent" of the county when making personnel decisions), *cert. denied,* 117 S. Ct. 754 (1997); Iacampo v. Hasbro, Inc., 929 F. Supp. 562, 5 AD 1075 (D.R.I. 1996) (individuals may be held liable under ADA); Matherne v. St. Charles Parish Sch. Bd., 71 FEP 1183 (E.D. La. 1996) (associate superintendent of school system who had control over decisionmaking process may be sued in his official capacity); Ruffino v. State St. Bank & Trust Co., 908 F. Supp. 1019, 71 FEP 109 (D. Mass. 1995) (individuals may be held liable under Title VII; any other construction would deprive statutory language concerning agents

B. Unions and Apprenticeship Programs

When a union is sued under Title VII as an "employer," the union must satisfy the statutory definition of employer and not some other coverage provision of Title VII.[62]

C. Employment Agencies

While there is no size requirement for an action against an employment agency sued for discriminatory referral practices, a court will not have jurisdiction over an employment agency sued in its capacity as an employer unless the agency employs 15 or more employees.[63]

V. CERTAIN EXEMPTIONS AND EXCLUSIONS

A. Bona Fide Private Membership Clubs

In *EEOC v. Chicago Club*,[64] the Seventh Circuit Court of Appeals confirmed the continuing vitality of the private membership

---

of meaning); Domm v. Jersey Printing Co., 871 F. Supp. 732, 70 FEP 99 (D.N.J. 1994) (supervisor who has sexually harassed employee may be held personally liable under Title VII); Braverman v. Penobscot Shoe Co., 859 F. Supp. 596, 603, 65 FEP 882 (D. Me. 1994) (company president individually liable as "agent" under statutory language of ADA and ADEA); Jendusa v. Cancer Treatment Ctrs. of Am., Inc., 868 F. Supp. 1006, 3 AD 1819 (N.D. Ill. 1994) (ADA's use of term "agent" within its definition of "employer" demonstrates statutory intent to impose individual liability); Douglas v. Coca-Cola Bottling Co., 855 F. Supp. 518, 71 FEP 355 (D.N.H. 1994) (supervisor who had authority to hire and fire may be held individually liable under Title VII as agent of employer).

[62]*See* Herman v. Carpenters Local No. 971, 60 F.3d 1375, 68 FEP 181 (9th Cir. 1995) (union did not have the requisite number of employees to qualify under Title VII's definition of "employer" even though it fell within the statutory classification of "labor organization"); Kern v. City of Rochester, 93 F.3d 38, 71 FEP 1391 (2d Cir. 1996) (rejecting argument that there was no minimum number of employees required to maintain a Title VII action for discrimination against union in its role as an "employer"), *cert. denied,* 117 S. Ct. 1335 (1997).

[63]Greenlees v. Eidenmuller Enters., 32 F.3d 197, 66 FEP 457 (5th Cir. 1994) (employment agency that employs fewer than 15 employees does not fall within the statutory definition of employer); Kellam v. Snelling Personnel Servs., 866 F. Supp. 812, 68 FEP 195 (D. Del. 1994) (employment agency with fewer than 15 employees is not "employer" under Title VII; practices prohibited by "employment agencies" do not encompass the practices prohibited by "employers"), *aff'd,* 65 F.3d 162, 69 FEP 768 (3d Cir. 1995).

[64]86 F.3d 1423, 70 FEP 1749 (7th Cir. 1996).

club exception to Title VII. The court, relying upon the EEOC's policy statement,[65] found that the defendant was outside the purview of Title VII because it was owned and controlled by its membership, did not advertise that its facilities were open to the general public, limited its facilities and services to club members and their guests, and employed meaningful conditions of limited membership.

B. Exemption of Elected Officials, Policymaking Appointees, and Their Advisors

While continuing to emphasize the highly factual nature of the inquiry, recent cases have tended to find sheriff's office dispatchers protected by Title VII,[66] but deputy attorney generals not protected.[67]

E. Coverage of Foreign Employers

1. Foreign Employers Operating in the United States

In *Papaila v. Uniden America Corp.*,[68] the Fifth Circuit affirmed the dismissal of a Title VII action asserting national origin discrimination, holding that a wholly owned American subsidiary of a Japanese company may invoke its parent's rights under the Japanese-American Friendship, Commerce and Navigation (FCN) Treaty with respect to the subsidiary's employment decisions dictated by the parent.

---

[65]The court stated that EEOC Policy Statement at N:3173 "accurately reflects 'the state of the law.' " The policy statement instructs that a club's privacy is to be evaluated according to three factors:
  (1) the extent to which it limits its facilities and services to club members and their guests;
  (2) the extent to which and/or the manner in which it is controlled or owned by the membership;
  (3) whether, and, if so, to what extent and to what manner it publicly advertises to solicit members or to promote the use of its facilities or services by the general public.

[66]Johnson v. Board of County Comm'rs, 859 F. Supp. 438, 65 FEP 1073 (D. Colo. 1994) (exemption not applicable to sheriff's office dispatchers because no "immediate and personal relationship" between the elected sheriff and the dispatchers).

[67]Americanos v. Carter, 74 F.3d 138, 69 FEP 1183 (7th Cir.) (deputy attorney general is position of political patronage on staff of elected attorney general and powers inherent in position include meaningful input into governmental decisionmaking), *cert. denied,* 116 S. Ct. 1853 (1996).

[68]51 F.3d 54, 67 FEP 993 (5th Cir.), *cert. denied,* 116 S. Ct. 187 (1995).

2. Extraterritorial Activities of Foreign Employers

A federal district court dismissed an ADEA action by an American citizen employed in the United States by a foreign-controlled employer where the plaintiff was seeking promotion into a position outside the United States. The court held that the relevant work site for the purpose of determining Title VII coverage was the location of the position for which the plaintiff applied.[69]

---

[69]Denty v. SmithKline Beecham Corp., 907 F. Supp. 879, 69 FEP 376 (E.D. Pa. 1995), *aff'd*, 109 F.3d 147, 73 FEP 423 (3d Cir.), *cert. denied*, 118 S. Ct. 74 (1997).

CHAPTER 31

TIMELINESS

II. TIMELINESS OF FILING THE EEOC CHARGE

A. The 180/300-Day Limitations Periods

4. Availability of the 300-Day Filing Period

The Second and Fifth Circuits have joined the Third, Fourth, Seventh, Eighth, Ninth, and Eleventh Circuits in holding that a state or local agency's waiver of exclusive jurisdiction is self-executing, thus effecting the instantaneous termination of its proceedings, permitting the EEOC to commence its own proceedings when the charge is filed and making the charge timely filed with the EEOC.[1]

Even in those jurisdictions with work-sharing agreements, a plaintiff may still be required to prove before the district court that the provisions of the particular state's work-sharing agreement ultimately provide him or her with the benefit of the 300-day limitations period.[2]

B. When Has Discrimination Occurred?

1. Individual Acts

Courts have continued to rely upon *Delaware State College v. Ricks*[3] and *Chardon v. Fernandez*[4] in holding that the accrual date

---

[1]Ford v. Bernard Fineson Dev. Ctr., 81 F.3d 304, 311, 70 FEP 825 (2d Cir. 1996) ("This holding is consistent with the rulings of the seven other circuits that have considered this issue, and with the reasoning of the district courts in our Circuit that have unanimously reached the same conclusion."); Griffin v. City of Dallas, 26 F.3d 610, 613–14, 65 FEP 784 (5th Cir. 1994); *cf.* EEOC v. Green, 76 F.3d 19 nn.5–6, 70 FEP 88 (1st Cir. 1996) (citing case law from other circuits and advising the EEOC and Massachusetts Commission Against Discrimination to clarify the intent of the ambiguous language in their work-sharing agreement).

[2]Russell v. Delco Remy Div. of Gen. Motors Corp., 51 F.3d 746, 750–51, 67 FEP 673 (7th Cir. 1995) (because "[w]orksharing agreements are to some degree particularized . . . [and] each embodies a particular state's intent regarding its relationship with the EEOC . . . some fact-finding is necessary to determine the intended effect of Indiana's worksharing agreement with the EEOC").

[3]449 U.S. 250, 24 FEP 827 (1980).

[4]454 U.S. 6, 27 FEP 57 (1981).

of the cause of action for limitations purposes is the date on which the adverse employment action is communicated to the plaintiff, although almost all courts now recognize (or at least consider) that the limitations period may be subject to equitable tolling.[5]

2. Application of Policies

Finding the Supreme Court's decision in *Lorance v. AT & T Technologies*[6] controlling, at least one district court has held that a state statute pertaining to accidental disability retirement benefits for public employees was facially discriminatory under the ADEA, and thus discriminated each time it was applied.[7] As such, the plaintiffs' complaints, which were filed within 300 days of the first application of the statute to their benefit payments, were held timely.[8]

---

[5]Dring v. McDonnell Douglas Corp., 58 F.3d 1323, 1327–28, 70 FEP 481 (8th Cir. 1995) (accrual date of charge-filing period is the date on which the adverse employment action is communicated to the plaintiff); Thelen v. Marc's Big Boy Corp., 64 F.3d 264, 267, 68 FEP 1090 (7th Cir. 1995) (discovery rule refers to plaintiff's discovery that he or she has been injured, not to plaintiff's discovery of facts indicating a possible claim, but can be stopped because of equitable estoppel or equitable tolling); Hargett v. Valley Fed. Sav. Bank, 60 F.3d 754, 760–61, 68 FEP 852 (11th Cir. 1995) (ADEA claim is barred if claimant knew or reasonably should have known of the challenged acts more than 180 days prior to filing his EEOC claim; plaintiff who is aware that he is being replaced in a position, which he believes he is able to perform, by a person outside the protected age group, knows enough to support filing a claim); Oshiver v. Levin, Fishbein, Sedran & Berman, 38 F.3d 1380, 1386, 66 FEP 429 (3d Cir. 1994) (the discovery rule functions to delay the initial running of the limitations period, but only until the plaintiff has discovered or, by exercising reasonable diligence, should have discovered (1) that he or she has been injured and (2) that this injury has been caused by another party's conduct; held that the discovery rule is limited to discovery of the actual fact of injury, not the discovery of information showing that the injury was a legal wrong); Teumer v. General Motors Corp., 34 F.3d 542, 550 (7th Cir. 1994) (plaintiff is required to bring charge within a "reasonable time" after he or she obtained, or could have obtained by due diligence, information regarding the alleged wrongdoing); Hulsey v. KMart, Inc., 43 F.3d 555, 557–58, 66 FEP 1327 (10th Cir. 1994) (cause of action accrued as of date of discharge; rejecting plaintiffs' argument for equitable tolling based on their claim that they were constructively discharged by demotion and transfer as a pretext for age discrimination, and holding that plaintiffs had duty to determine whether there was discriminatory motive for alleged constructive discharge).

[6]490 U.S. 900, 49 FEP 1656 (1989).

[7]Riva v. Massachusetts, 871 F. Supp. 1511, 1516, 66 FEP 1142 (D. Mass. 1994), *aff'd in part, rev'd in part on other grounds*, 61 F.3d 1003, 68 FEP 688 (1st Cir. 1995). The statute in question mandated a change in benefits at age 65 for employees with less than 10 years of creditable service who were *over* age 55 when they received an accidental disability retirement, while employees who received such retirement when they were under age 55 would not have their benefits reduced.

[8]*Id.* at 1517. The court distinguished the case from one involving a facially neutral statute or policy, which under the *Lorance* rationale would have to be challenged for ADEA purposes within 300 days of its enactment or adoption. *Id.*

3. Continuing Violations

Although courts continue to struggle with the continuing violation theory and its applications, at least some measure of consistency has emerged with regard to the initial analysis. The first question is whether an actual violation of Title VII occurred during the statutory period.[9] The next question is whether this discriminatory act either was part of a series of related discriminatory acts or was caused by a discriminatory system in effect both before and during the limitations period.[10] This latter inquiry will turn largely upon the specific facts of the case.[11]

---

[9]West v. Philadelphia Elec. Co., 45 F.3d 744, 754–55, 66 FEP 1524 (3d Cir. 1995) ("The crucial question is whether any *present* violation exists" [emphasis added], quoting United Airlines, Inc. v. Evans, 431 U.S. 553, 558 (1977)). Courts continue to dismiss charges in which the plaintiff has failed to allege at least one discriminatory act within the limitations period that may serve as an anchor for the earlier conduct. Doe v. R.R. Donnelly & Sons, 42 F.3d 439, 446, 66 FEP 981 (7th Cir. 1994); Mascheroni v. Board of Regents of Univ. of Cal., 28 F.3d 1554, 1561–62, 65 FEP 632 (10th Cir. 1994) (no continuing violation where plaintiff failed to identify a discriminatory act that occurred within the statutory period and that was part of a continuing violation); Palmer v. Kelly, 17 F.3d 1490, 1496, 64 FEP 377 (D.C. Cir. 1994). As the *Mascheroni* court made clear, however, "[t]he discriminatory act occurring within the time period need not constitute a legally sufficient Title VII claim in itself." 28 F.3d at 1561.

[10]*Palmer*, 17 F.3d at 1496; *West*, 45 F.3d at 755 (plaintiff must establish that the harassment is "more than the occurrence of isolated or sporadic acts of intentional discrimination" [citation omitted]). When a plaintiff has alleged sufficient facts to support the application of the continuing violation doctrine, courts have appeared more willing to allow the plaintiff to litigate all conduct that was part of that violation, even conduct that occurred outside the limitations period. *West*, 45 F.3d at 755. *See also, e.g., Palmer*, 17 F.3d at 1496; Cornwell v. Robinson, 23 F.3d 694, 704, 64 FEP 1254 (2d Cir. 1995) ("Where a continuing violation can be shown, the plaintiff is entitled to bring suit challenging all conduct that was a part of that violation, even conduct that occurred outside the limitations period."); Greenlaw v. Garrett, 59 F.3d 994, 1000, 68 FEP 531 (9th Cir. 1995) (continuing violations doctrine "draws within the ambit of a Title VII claim all conduct occurring before and after the filing of the EEO charge, providing the conduct is 'like or reasonably related to' the events charged").

[11]*See, e.g.,* Van Zant v. KLM Royal Dutch Airlines, 80 F.3d 708, 713, 70 FEP 562 (2d Cir. 1996) (no continuing violation, where evidence failed to show any connection between KLM's treatment of plaintiff and any company policy or practice, nor that KLM allowed related incidents of discrimination to go unremedied for so long as to amount to a discriminatory policy or practice); Koelsch v. Beltone Elecs. Corp., 46 F.3d 705, 707–08, 66 FEP 1697 (7th Cir. 1995) (sexual harassment plaintiff failed to show that two instances of president's touching of her, which occurred outside of the limitations period, and two subsequent incidents of sexually suggestive and derogatory jokes by other employees, which occurred within the limitations period but did not implicate the president in any way, were "related closely enough" to be considered one ongoing violation); Cornwell v. Robinson, 23 F.3d 694, 704, 64 FEP 1254 (2d Cir. 1995) (plaintiff established continuing violation, based on substantial evidence of race and gender-based harassment and discrimination that occurred over several

The Third Circuit in *West v. Philadelphia Electrical Co.*[12] expressly declined to adopt a per se rule that a properly alleged hostile work environment claim also constitutes a continuing violation, although it went on to find that the race harassment plaintiff had alleged sufficient facts to support application of the continuing violation doctrine. The Seventh Circuit, meanwhile, has reiterated the three continuing violation theories recognized by that court.[13]

Compensation cases continue to be interpreted more liberally as continuing violations. For example, denials of pay increases are typically continuing violations for limitations purposes, because each paycheck at a discriminatory rate is a basis for a separate claim.[14] In addition, courts have held pay discrimination claims

---

years by the same people, and which supervisory personnel permitted to continue); Palmer v. Kelly, 17 F.3d 1490, 1496, 64 FEP 377 (D.C. Cir. 1994) (failure to communicate promotion offer to plaintiff was violation of Title VII within the charge-filing period, making the earlier pattern of conduct actionable as a continuing violation).

[12] 45 F.3d 744, 755–56, 66 FEP 1254 (3d Cir. 1995) (all of the alleged incidents involved racial harassment, occurred consistently over a four-year period with increased frequency and without respite, and did not cause a discrete event such that the plaintiff did not have a duty to assert his rights arising from such a deprivation); *cf.* Rush v. Scott Specialty Gases, Inc., 113 F.3d 476, 481, 74 FEP 1745 (3d Cir. 1997) (holding that plaintiff's failure-to-promote-and-train claim was time-barred, but that her hostile environment sexual harassment claim was viable as to all conduct at issue, based on the continuing violation doctrine). The *West* court also noted that since a plaintiff is not required to show that each co-worker's individual participation was pervasive and ongoing, the district court erred in requiring proof of a continuing violation by the same individual. *Id.* at 756.

[13] Jones v. Merchants Nat'l Bank & Trust Co., 42 F.3d 1054, 1058, 66 FEP 865 (7th Cir. 1994) ("The first theory encompasses decisions, usually relating to hiring and promotions, where the employer's decision-making process takes place over a period of time, making it difficult to determine the actual date of the allegedly discriminatory act . . . . The second continuing violation theory involves an employer's express, openly espoused policy that is alleged to be discriminatory. . . . Finally, a plaintiff can show a continuing violation where an employer covertly follows a practice of discrimination over a period of time."). The court found no continuing violation in that case under the third theory (or any other), given that the race harassment and discrimination plaintiff admitted that she felt that the refusals to promote were discriminatory at the time they occurred, and thus she was required to sue within the relevant statute of limitations. *Id.*

[14] Chambers v. American Trans Air, Inc., 17 F.3d 998, 1003, 64 FEP 213 (7th Cir.), *cert. denied,* 115 S. Ct. 512 (1994) (citing Bazemore v. Friday, 478 U.S. 385, 395–96, 41 FEP 92 (1986), for main proposition, but holding that alleged discriminatory denial of wage increases had no continuing effect inside limitations period, where Title VII employee was briefly promoted without pay increase, and then demoted back to her previous position); Gandy v. Sullivan County, 24 F.3d 861, 864–65, 64 FEP 1607 (6th Cir. 1994) (holding that "a plaintiff's action will not be time-barred as long as at least one forbidden discriminatory act occurs within the relevant limitations

timely even when the plaintiff's comparators ceased to be employed or ceased to hold equivalent positions before the limitations period, relying upon the EEOC's Equal Pay Act regulations.[15] Some courts have attempted to strike a balance by finding that each paycheck issued within the limitations period constitutes an independent wrongful action and allowing relief only for those paychecks issued within the limitations period.[16]

The Third, Tenth, and Eleventh Circuits, as well as several district courts, have adopted the Fifth Circuit's three-factor inquiry of subject matter, frequency, and permanency in seeking to determine whether a continuing violation has occurred.[17]

C. Tolling of the Charge-Filing Period

1. A Jurisdictional Prerequisite, or a Statute of Limitations That May Be Tolled for Equitable Reasons?

In *Girard v. Rubin*,[18] the Ninth Circuit rejected the argument of the IRS that it had not waived any challenge to the timeliness of

---

period" and that plaintiff's rights were violated with every check she received; categorizing case as one of "continuing wrongs," because the discriminatory acts of unequal paychecks were committed within the limitations period); Swartzbaugh v. State Farm Ins. Co., 924 F. Supp. 932, 934, 73 FEP 211 (E.D. Mo. 1995) (unlawful discrimination in pay occurs "not only when the employer sets pay levels, but as long as the discriminatory differential occurs"; held that employer's pay discrimination was continuing and plaintiff's claim filed outside of the 300-day period was timely).

[15]Brinkley-Obu v. Hughes Training, Inc., 36 F.3d 336, 345–46, 65 FEP 1840 (4th Cir. 1994) ("the statute of limitations does not operate to limit the evidence [a plaintiff] may introduce regarding her co-workers [and] . . . does not dictate which co-workers the plaintiff may submit as comparators").

[16]Ashley v. Boyle's Famous Corned Beef Co., 66 F.3d 164, 167–68, 68 FEP 1261 (8th Cir. 1995) ("Relief back to the beginning of the limitations period strikes a reasonable balance between permitting redress of an ongoing wrong and imposing liability for conduct long past.").

[17]West v. Philadelphia Elec. Co., 45 F.3d 744, 755 n.9, 64 FEP 1524 (3d Cir. 1995) (inquiry into the existence of a continuing violation should consider the subject matter, frequency, and permanence of the alleged violations); Mascheroni v. Board of Regents of Univ. of Cal., 28 F.3d 1554, 1561, 65 FEP 632 (10th Cir. 1994) (same); Lewis v. Board of Trustees of Ala. State Univ., 874 F. Supp. 1299, 1304 (M.D. Ala. 1995) (same) (citing Roberts v. Gadsden Mem'l Hosp., 835 F.2d 793, 800–01, 45 FEP 1246 (11th Cir. 1988)); Egan v. Palos Community Hosp., 889 F. Supp. 331, 335–36, 68 FEP 509 (N.D. Ill. 1995) (same); Clark v. City of Macon, 860 F. Supp. 1545, 1550 (M.D. Ga. 1994) (same); Cabiness v. YKK (USA), Inc., 859 F. Supp. 582, 586, 72 FEP 355 (M.D. Ga. 1994) (same).

[18]62 F.3d 1244, 68 FEP 1002 (9th Cir. 1995).

a Title VII and ADEA complaint filed by an employee three years after the alleged incidents, even though the IRS had alleged the limitations bar from the beginning. The court based its decision on the fact that the IRS neither appealed nor refused to proceed after a binding decision by the EEOC that the complaint was timely.[19]

3. Tolling Because of Resort to Another Forum

Courts continue to hold that the filing of a union grievance pursuant to a collective bargaining agreement does not toll the charge-filing limitations period, because the employee's statutory rights are independent of any contractual rights under a private agreement.[20] The same holds true for a complaint filed with the Department of Transportation, which is not deemed a filing with the EEOC and does not toll the limitations period.[21]

4. Other Grounds for Estoppel or Tolling

The various circuit courts persist in articulating in different ways the test for the type of conduct by the employer that will be sufficient to toll the limitations period. The First Circuit and its district courts continue to adhere to the most narrow view of equitable exceptions to the limitations period.[22] The Third and Eighth Circuits have reiterated their various tests.[23] The Tenth Circuit

---

[19]Id. at 1246–47. The court noted, however, that in a private sector case (unlike the case at bar against the IRS), the EEOC does not have the power to issue final decisions that are binding on the employer. Id. at 1247.

[20]Frank v. New York State Elec. & Gas, 871 F. Supp. 167, 172, 69 FEP 711 (W.D.N.Y. 1994); Yoonessi v. State Univ. of N.Y., 862 F. Supp. 1005, 1014 (W.D.N.Y. 1994), cert. denied, 516 U.S. 1075, 69 FEP 1504 (1996) ("In instituting an action under Title VII, the employee is not seeking review of the arbitrator's decision. Rather, he is asserting a statutory right independent of the arbitration process.").

[21]Ryan v. New York State Thruway Auth., 889 F. Supp. 70, 78–79, 73 FEP 1525 (N.D.N.Y. 1995) (holding that, in the absence of any equitable considerations, the filing with a federal agency other than the Office of Federal Contract Compliance does not constitute filing with the EEOC and cannot toll the limitations period).

[22]Lawton v. State Mut. Life Assurance Co. of Am., 924 F. Supp. 331, 339, 75 FEP 783 (D. Mass. 1996) ("To qualify for an exception, a complaining party must allege and prove not only that she had no reason to be aware of the employer's improper motivation when the alleged violation occurred, but also that the employer actively misled her and that she relied on that misconduct to her detriment.").

[23]Garfield v. J.C. Nichols Real Estate, 57 F.3d 662, 666, 68 FEP 188 (8th Cir.), cert. denied, 116 S. Ct. 380 (1995) (no tolling on equitable estoppel grounds unless the failure to file is due to deliberate design by the employer or to actions that the

appears to have adopted the test articulated by the Third Circuit.[24] Meanwhile, although the Fourth Circuit appeared to follow the Eighth Circuit test in the past,[25] a district court decision in that circuit raises some question as to that test's current application.[26]

Courts also continue to distinguish between equitable tolling and equitable estoppel in ADEA cases. Relying upon *Cada v. Baxter Healthcare Corp.*[27] in clarifying the distinction between those doctrines in the ADEA context, the Seventh and Eighth Circuits have set forth an objective test of when excusable ignorance may provide the basis for invocation of equitable tolling: when a reasonable person in the plaintiff's position would not be expected to know of the existence of a possible ADEA violation.[28] Recent

---

employer should unmistakably have understood would cause the employee to delay filing a charge); Oshiver v. Levin, Fishbein, Sedran & Berman, 38 F.3d 1380, 1387, 66 FEP 429 (3d Cir. 1994) (equitable tolling may be appropriate where the defendant has actively misled the plaintiff regarding the plaintiff's cause of action, where the plaintiff in some extraordinary way has been prevented from asserting his or her rights, or where the plaintiff has timely asserted his or her rights mistakenly in the wrong forum).

[24]Davis v. Wesley Retirement Communities, Inc., 913 F. Supp. 1437, 1442, 70 FEP 430 (D. Kan. 1995) (citing Hulsey v. KMart, Inc., 43 F.3d 555, 557, 66 FEP 1327 (10th Cir. 1994)) ("Equitable tolling under Title VII is appropriate only when the circumstances of the case rise to the level of active deception, or when the plaintiff has been lulled into inaction by their [sic] past employer, state or federal agencies, or the courts, or when the plaintiff has in some extraordinary way been prevented from asserting his or her rights in a timely manner."); Mascheroni v. Board of Regents of Univ. of Cal., 28 F.3d 1554, 1562–63, 65 FEP 632 (10th Cir. 1994) (same; finding no equitable tolling because plaintiff did not allege active deception by employer, just business reasons and a corporate culture that discouraged him from suing).

[25]English v. Pabst Brewing Co., 828 F.2d 1047, 1049, 44 FEP 1385 (4th Cir. 1987), *cert. denied,* 486 U.S. 1044 (1988) (no tolling on equitable estoppel grounds unless failure to file is due to employer's deliberate design or actions that employer unmistakably should have understood would cause delay in filing); Stafford v. Radford Community Hosp., Inc., 908 F. Supp. 1369, 1374 (W.D. Va. 1995) ("To invoke equitable tolling, the plaintiff must . . . show that the defendant attempted to mislead him and that the plaintiff reasonably relied on the misrepresentation by neglecting to file a timely charge," quoting *English,* 828 F.2d at 1049.).

[26]Lockett v. West, 914 F. Supp. 1229, 1234 (D. Md. 1995) (suggesting equitable tolling is available if plaintiff makes an affirmative showing of government misconduct or can successfully persuade the court that she was unaware of the time limitation, but declining to allow tolling because plaintiff could make neither such showing).

[27]920 F.2d 446, 54 FEP 961 (7th Cir. 1990), *cert. denied,* 501 U.S. 1261, 56 FEP 576 (1991).

[28]Dring v. McDonnell Douglas Corp., 58 F.3d 1323, 1328–29, 70 FEP 481 (8th Cir. 1995) (quoting *Cada* regarding the significance of the qualifying word "possible": "if a plaintiff were entitled to have all the time he needed to be certain his

decisions in these circuits also indicate that something more than an employer's silence or a mere misunderstanding is required to show affirmative misconduct such that equitable estoppel may be applied.[29]

The Seventh Circuit broke with the Third Circuit in holding that an employer's misrepresentation to the plaintiff (regarding who would take over his duties) should not result in equitable estoppel of his time to file an ADEA charge, because

> [i]t is the view of this court that such a position would eviscerate the concept of a limitations period because "[i]t implies that a defendant is guilty of fraudulent concealment unless it tells the plaintiff, 'We're firing you because of your age.'"[30]

The Sixth Circuit has joined others in holding that when the employer fails to post the required ADEA notices, the tolling continues until the employee either retains an attorney or acquires actual knowledge of his or her rights under the ADEA.[31]

---

rights had been violated, the statute of limitations would never run," and denying plaintiff's argument for equitable tolling); Chakonas v. City of Chicago, 42 F.3d 1132, 1135–36, 66 FEP 1164 (7th Cir. 1994) (same). The *Chakonas* court did make clear, however, that if a reasonable person would have been aware of a possible ADEA violation, but the plaintiff was not, then "resort to equitable tolling is inappropriate." *Id.* at 1135. These cases also reiterate that equitable tolling does not require any misconduct on the part of the defendant. *Dring,* 58 F.3d at 1328; *Chakonas,* 42 F.3d at 1136.

[29]Garfield v. J.C. Nichols Real Estate, 57 F.3d 662, 666, 68 FEP 188 (8th Cir. 1995) ("Silence . . . is generally not affirmative conduct that gives rise to a finding of equitable estoppel."); United States v. French, 46 F.3d 710, 714–15 (8th Cir. 1995) (same); Thelen v. Marc's Big Boy Corp., 64 F.3d 264, 268, 68 FEP 1090 (7th Cir. 1995) (employee was not sufficiently affirmatively misled to invoke equitable estoppel where the employer told him that one person was replacing employee when in fact another younger person actually replaced him); Miller v. Runyon, 32 F.3d 386, 390, 65 FEP 1063 (8th Cir. 1994) (mere misunderstanding as to the filing deadline deemed not affirmative misconduct for equitable estoppel); *cf.* EEOC v. Kentucky State Police Dep't, 80 F.3d 1086, 1095, 71 FEP 1495 (6th Cir. 1996) (finding that employer's leaving age out of its affirmative action policy, even though not malicious, combined with its failure to post the required ADEA notices, was sufficient wrongful conduct to toll the limitations period by equitable estoppel).

[30]Thelen v. Marc's Big Boy Corp., 64 F.3d 264, 267–68 (7th Cir. 1995) (citing *Cada,* 920 F.2d at 451); *cf.* Oshiver v. Levin, Fishbein, Sedran & Berman, 38 F.3d 1380, 1386 (3d Cir. 1994).

[31]EEOC v. Kentucky State Police Dep't, 80 F.3d 1086, 1096, 71 FEP 1495 (6th Cir. 1996) (rejecting employer's attempt to introduce document to show that plaintiffs had constructive knowledge of their rights under the ADEA); *see* Thelen v. Marc's Big Boy Corp., 64 F.3d 264, 268 (7th Cir. 1995); Mirza v. Department of Treasury, 875 F. Supp. 513, 519 (N.D. Ill. 1995).

The issue of mental illness as the basis for equitable tolling continues to confront the courts. The Seventh Circuit rejected the contention that mental illness per se tolls statutes of limitations in all cases in which discrimination based on that mental illness is the basis of the suit.[32] The court saw no reason "to depart from the traditional rule that mental illness tolls a statute of limitations only if the illness *in fact* prevents the sufferer from managing his affairs and thus from understanding his rights and acting upon them."[33]

Meanwhile, the Sixth Circuit, in *Cantrell v. Knoxville Community Development Corp.*,[34] recognized that the mental illness of a claimant's attorney may be available as a basis for equitable tolling of the charge-filing period, if the claimant pursued his claim diligently but was abandoned by his attorney because of the attorney's mental illness.[35]

Finally, even a plaintiff who fails to file a timely charge and cannot justify tolling the limitations period on equitable grounds may still not be out of luck. The Sixth and Eleventh Circuits recently joined the majority of circuit courts in finding that the "piggybacking" or "single filing" rule, under which a grievant who does not file an EEOC charge may opt into a class action by "piggybacking" onto a timely charge filed by one of the named plaintiffs in the class action, applies both to Title VII and ADEA cases.[36] Moreover, the "single filing" rule is not strictly limited to class actions;

---

[32]Miller v. Runyon, 77 F.3d 189, 191 (7th Cir.), *cert. denied,* 117 S. Ct. 316 (1996).

[33]*Id.* at 191–92 ("Any other conclusion would perpetuate the stereotype of the insane as raving maniacs or gibbering idiots and impair their employment opportunities, thus stigmatizing [the plaintiff's] own class.").

[34]60 F.3d 1177, 68 FEP 536 (6th Cir. 1995).

[35]*Id.* at 1179–80. The court remanded the case for a factual determination of whether the attorney was actually mentally incapacitated during the charge-filing period (which should not have been taken on judicial notice) and, if so, whether upon his abandonment of the case the claimant acted with due diligence.

[36]Howlett v. Holiday Inns, Inc., 49 F.3d 189, 194, 67 FEP 289 (6th Cir.), *cert. denied sub nom.* Holiday Inns, Inc. v. McNeely, 116 S. Ct. 379, 69 FEP 96 (1995); Grayson v. KMart Corp., 79 F.3d 1086, 1101–02, 70 FEP 770 (11th Cir.), *cert. denied sub nom.* Helton v. KMart Corp., 117 S. Ct. 435 (1996); Mooney v. Aramco Serv. Co., 54 F.3d 1207, 1223, 68 FEP 421 (5th Cir. 1995). A similar rule has been applied, with more limited effects, when an employee fails to file suit within the requisite 90-day period. *See* Winbush v. Iowa, 66 F.3d 1471, 1485–86, 69 FEP 1348 (8th Cir. 1995) (employee who filed his own charge but failed to file suit after receiving right-to-sue letter barred from recovering under Title VII for any injuries he suffered prior to expiration of his right-to-sue period; however, he could still piggyback on filings of other employees for his Title VII claims that might have

it can also permit a plaintiff to join an individual action filed by another person who is similarly situated, as long as the timely filed charge provided notice of the collective nature of the charge.[37]

III. TIMELINESS OF FILING SUIT

B. Time of Issuing Notice of Right to Sue

3. Premature Issuance of Right-to-Sue Notices and Premature Filing of Suit

The Eleventh Circuit held that employees who filed charges of discrimination with the EEOC after filing their lawsuit did not fail to meet the conditions precedent for filing suit under Title VII, given that the employees filed an amendment to their complaint after the EEOC issued notices of right to sue and prior to the expiration of the 90-day period.[38]

C. Timely Court Filing

2. What Triggers Commencement of the 90-Day Period

In *Sherlock v. Montefiore Medical Center*,[39] the Second Circuit emphasized that the initial presumptions surrounding the triggering of the 90-day period (a mailed document is received three days after its mailing, and notice provided by a government agency has been mailed on the date shown on the notice) are not dispositive, particularly if a claimant can present sworn testimony or other admissible evidence from which it could reasonably be inferred

---

accrued after expiration of his right-to-sue period); *cf.* Anderson v. Unisys Corp., 47 F.3d 302, 309, 67 FEP 317 (8th Cir.), *cert. denied,* 516 U.S. 913 (1995) (plaintiff who filed separate administrative charge but failed to timely file suit barred by statute of limitations and cannot "piggyback" on another employee's timely charge or lawsuit).

[37]*Mooney,* 54 F.3d at 1223; *Howlett,* 49 F.3d at 195. The "piggybacking" rule may only be applied where (1) the relied upon charge is not invalid, and (2) the individual claims of the filing and nonfiling plaintiff arise out of similar discriminatory treatment in the same time frame. *Grayson,* 79 F.3d at 1101–02 (citing Calloway v. Partners Nat'l Health Plans, 986 F.2d 446, 61 FEP 550 (11th Cir. 1993)).

[38]Cross v. State of Ala., State Dep't of Mental Health & Mental Retardation, 49 F.3d 1490, 1504, 67 FEP 844 (11th Cir. 1995).

[39]84 F.3d 522, 525–26, 70 FEP 1377 (2d Cir. 1996).

either that the notice was mailed later than its typewritten date or that it took longer than three days to reach her by mail.

The Tenth Circuit joined the approach adopted by the Fourth, Fifth, Ninth, and Eleventh Circuits in holding that the 90-day period begins to run when there has been receipt by a member of plaintiff's household at plaintiff's address, unless the plaintiff establishes equitable considerations that would justify tolling.[40]

Courts have held that certain events are sufficient to start the running of the 90-day suit-filing period, including the EEOC's sending a right-to-sue letter to a plaintiff's old address when the plaintiff failed to provide the EEOC with a current address.[41] Meanwhile, certain events have been held *insufficient* to start the running of the 90-day suit-filing period: receipt of a defective right-to-sue notice that fails to apprise a plaintiff of the correct limitations period[42]; the Postal Service's placing notice in a lay plaintiff's post office box that a certified letter addressed to her had been received[43]; and receipt of the right-to-sue letter by a claimant's former attorney.[44]

---

[40]Million v. Frank, 47 F.3d 385, 387–88, 67 FEP 254 (10th Cir. 1995) ("If the rule were otherwise, a plaintiff would be permitted to 'enjoy a manipulable, open-ended time extension which could render the statutory limitation meaningless. . . .' " [citation omitted]); *see also, e.g.,* Roberson v. Bowie State Univ., 899 F. Supp. 235, 238, 72 FEP 899 (D. Md. 1995) (plaintiff's daughter signed for letter, which plaintiff first saw 17 days later; 90-day period began to run upon receipt by daughter).

[41]Harding v. Fort Wayne Foundry/Pontiac Div., Inc., 919 F. Supp. 1223, 1231–32, 70 FEP 1074 (N.D. Ind. 1996) (dismissing plaintiff's claim even though he had provided change of address to local agency, because agency had no duty under work-sharing agreement to transmit information to EEOC, and rejecting plaintiff's claim that apparent authority agency relationship existed).

[42]Wilson v. Pena, 79 F.3d 154, 163–64, 72 FEP 67 (D.C. Cir. 1996) (the court held, "[w]hen an agency or department has taken final action but has failed to issue a proper notice, an employee can bring an action in the district court within a reasonable time," where the EEOC notice erroneously apprised plaintiff that he had only 30 days to file suit, instead of 90).

[43]Holmes v. World Wildlife Fund, Inc., 908 F. Supp. 19, 21, 69 FEP 1181 (D.D.C. 1995) (in refusing to dismiss complaint filed 94 days after delivery of such notice to plaintiff's post office box, court relied on fact that plaintiff actually received right-to-sue letter 87 days before filing, and letter stated that suit could be filed "within 90 days of . . . receipt of this letter"); *cf.* Biester v. Midwest Health Servs., Inc., 77 F.3d 1264, 1266, 70 FEP 397 (10th Cir. 1996) (impliedly holding that plaintiff's suit-filing period started running when he picked up his right-to-sue letter at the post office, after receiving two or three notices that he had a certified letter).

[44]Coates v. Shalala, 914 F. Supp. 110, 112, 72 FEP 644 (D. Md. 1996) (focusing on attorney's lack of authority to accept service for or act as representative of plaintiff).

3. What Constitutes a "Filing"

Courts continue to provide greater leeway to pro se plaintiffs in terms of what constitutes a "filing." The Fifth Circuit, for example, held that a pro se complaint was timely filed, even though it was devoid of the essential elements of a complaint, because it was submitted to the clerk for filing within the 90-day period and because the court gave the plaintiff free leave to amend the defective allegations in that pleading.[45]

Similarly, an amended Title VII complaint filed after the 90-day limitations period will be allowed if it "relates back" to an earlier complaint filed within the requisite time period under the standard set forth in Rule 15(c) of the Federal Rules of Civil Procedure.[46] Courts continue to apply the rules of relation back restrictively, particularly where a plaintiff seeks to add additional parties or new claims.[47]

The filing of a praecipe for writ of summons in state court within the 90-day period has been held sufficient to constitute a filing.[48] This holding, however, was based largely upon the fact that Pennsylvania courts expressly permit the commencement of a civil action by filing such a praecipe and that Pennsylvania courts have concurrent jurisdiction over ADA claims.[49]

---

[45]McClellon v. Lone Star Gas Co., 66 F.3d 98, 101–02, 69 FEP 36 (5th Cir. 1995).

[46]Kaup v. First Bank Sys., Inc., 926 F. Supp. 155, 158 (D. Colo. 1996).

[47]Anderson v. Unisys Corp., 47 F.3d 302, 307–09, 67 FEP 317 (8th Cir.), cert. denied, 116 S. Ct. 299, 68 FEP 1888 (1995) (claims of additional plaintiffs under amended complaint were held not to relate back to filing of original complaint, because they filed their own ADEA charges with the EEOC, received their own right-to-sue letters, and deliberately decided not to file suit within the limitations period); Sanders v. Venture Stores, Inc., 56 F.3d 771, 774–75, 75 FEP 637 (7th Cir. 1995) (district court did not abuse discretion in denying plaintiffs' motion for leave to amend time-barred Title VII complaint, where summary judgment motion was pending, discovery cutoff had passed, plaintiffs offered no reason for their delay in asserting proposed new claims, and allowing such amendment would result in additional discovery costs for the employer, undue delay, and prejudice to the parties and the court); Cornwell v. Robinson, 23 F.3d 694, 705, 64 FEP 1254 (2d Cir. 1994) (held that amended complaint that adds new individual defendants outside the limitations period does not relate back to original timely complaint, unless the individuals knew or should have known that such an action would be brought against them but for a mistake in the identity of the proper party).

[48]Krouse v. American Sterilizer Co., 872 F. Supp. 203, 208–09 (W.D. Pa. 1994).

[49]Id. at 209. The court noted that Title VII and the ADA specify only that "a civil action may be brought" within 90 days; the statute does not explicitly require the filing of a complaint. Id. at 205.

4. Tolling

Equitable tolling continues to be applied to the suit-filing period in some situations, such as where the plaintiff's failure to receive the right-to-sue letter was the EEOC's fault,[50] and until the denial of a plaintiff's motion to proceed *in forma pauperis* (filed within the 90-day period).[51] The 90-day limitations period will not be tolled, however, by the filing of a written request with the EEOC seeking reconsideration of its no-cause determination.[52]

Courts have continued to reject most efforts to argue that a plaintiff's mental incapacity tolls the 90-day limitations period, where there are no exceptional circumstances, where there is no evidence that the plaintiff was incapable of pursuing his or her own claim, and particularly where the plaintiff is represented by counsel during the 90-day period.[53]

5. Laches and Related Issues

Addressing the question of whether laches may bar a plaintiff for unreasonable delay when the EEOC charge and subsequent lawsuit were timely filed, the Eighth Circuit determined that separation of power principles dictate that federal courts not apply laches to bar a federal statutory claim that is timely filed under an express federal statute of limitations.[54] The court went on to note,

---

[50]Ryczek v. Guest Servs., Inc., 877 F. Supp. 754, 758, 67 FEP 461 (D.D.C. 1995) (limitations period may be tolled where plaintiff can demonstrate that she failed to receive the right-to-sue letter because of "fortuitous circumstances" or "events beyond [her] control" or "no fault" of her own, as where EEOC mistakenly sent notice to plaintiff at wrong address and failed to send copy to plaintiff's attorney, despite request by attorney).

[51]Madison v. BP Oil Co., 928 F. Supp. 1132, 1135–36 (S.D. Ala. 1996) (complaint was submitted within 90 days, with motion to proceed *in forma pauperis;* complaint not considered formally filed until filing fee paid, following denial of motion, but deemed constructively filed as of date of initial submission); Woods v. Bentsen, 889 F. Supp. 179, 184–85, 72 FEP 1554 (E.D. Pa. 1995) (same).

[52]McCray v. Corry Mfg. Co., 872 F. Supp. 209, 212–14, 68 FEP 1685 (W.D. Pa. 1994), *aff'd,* 61 F.3d 224, 227–28, 68 FEP 821 (3d Cir. 1995).

[53]Beister v. Midwest Health Servs., Inc., 77 F.3d 1264, 1268, 70 FEP 397 (10th Cir. 1996) (suit-filing period was not tolled by fact that plaintiff was suffering from major depression and attendant symptoms, given that the necessary exceptional circumstances were not present); Thornton v. South Cent. Bell Tel. Co., 906 F. Supp. 1110, 1118 (S.D. Miss. 1995) (plaintiff's mental breakdown held not to toll 90-day limitations period).

[54]Ashley v. Boyle's Famous Corned Beef Co., 66 F.3d 164, 169–70, 68 FEP 1261 (8th Cir. 1995) (rejecting defendant's argument that plaintiff should be barred from

however, that while only statutes of limitations are relevant in determining whether a plaintiff's claims are time-barred, "laches, like other equitable principles, may be relevant in determining the extent to which [a plaintiff] is entitled to equitable remedies."[55]

Cases concerning laches and the time for filing suit continue to turn on the specific facts involved.[56]

---

pursuing pay discrimination claims because she waited until her layoff, more than seven years after initial hiring, to challenge pay disparity; noting that equal pay claim still timely because each paycheck was potentially an actionable wrong).

[55]*Id.*

[56]In National Ass'n of Gov't Employees v. City Pub. Serv. Bd., 40 F.3d 698, 67 FEP 1013 (5th Cir. 1994), for example, the Fifth Circuit affirmed the district court's grant of summary judgment to the defendant on the Title VII claims on laches grounds, where there had been a delay of nine years in bringing suit on the EEOC charges filed by plaintiffs in 1977. *Id.* at 708–11. The court found that plaintiffs' delay was inexcusable, given their continuous representation by counsel since 1980, the active involvement of the plaintiff union, plaintiffs' failure to demand right-to-sue letters, and plaintiffs' failure to make inquiry with the Department of Justice or the EEOC, and that such delay unduly prejudiced the defendant, including by the substantial loss of witness testimony over time. *Id.*

CHAPTER 32

ELECTION AND EXHAUSTION OF REMEDIES

II. ELECTION OF REMEDIES

A. Preclusion Issues Resulting From Prior Resort to Another Forum

1. Preclusive Effect of Prior State Proceedings

a. State Court Judgments and Reviewed State Administrative Decisions. Federal courts have continued to give preclusive effect to a state court judgment in a subsequent action involving either the same claim or a claim that could have been raised in the prior action.[1]

b. Unreviewed State Administrative Decisions. The Ninth Circuit has held that a plaintiff must pursue a review of state administrative determinations, where such review is available, or forfeit any attempt at relitigation.[2]

---

[1]Sondel v. Northwest Airlines, Inc., 56 F.3d 934 (8th Cir. 1995) (certified class representatives in a federal Title VII class action also brought state court discrimination claims in their individual capacities; summary judgment against the individual plaintiffs in state court had binding res judicata effect against the entire class since all class members were in privity, based on fiduciary relationship, with the class representatives); Thomas v. St. Louis Bd. of Educ., 933 F. Supp. 817 (E.D. Mo. 1996) (school board entitled to summary judgment on plaintiff's Title VII racial discrimination claim because plaintiff could have raised the issue of discrimination in her prior state court suit against the board); Stone v. National Bank & Trust Co., 1996 WL 310351 (N.D.N.Y. June 6, 1996) (summary judgment granted to defendant in a federal ADEA claim because of the res judicata effect of plaintiff's prior state court action for age discrimination and retaliation, which state court dismissed based on a written release), *supplemented by* 1996 WL 341987 (N.D.N.Y. June 18, 1996).

[2]Misischia v. Pirie, 60 F.3d 626 (9th Cir. 1995) (dentist who repeatedly failed state dental qualifying examination was precluded from bringing a federal § 1983 action against the state board of dental examiners because he did not exhaust his state appeals of the board's decision upholding his failure); Miller v. County of Santa Cruz, 39 F.3d 1030 (9th Cir. 1994) (county sheriff employee who had been terminated was precluded from bringing a federal § 1983 action because he failed to seek state court review of civil service board's confirmation of his termination), *cert. denied,* 515 U.S. 1160 (1995).

In *Moodie v. Federal Reserve Bank*,[3] the Second Circuit held that a state law[4] that expressly deprives a state court of jurisdiction over a claim previously brought before the state FEP agency also served as a jurisdictional bar preventing the federal courts from entertaining the same state-based discrimination claim.

Decisions of state agencies involving claims under §§ 1981, 1983, or 1985 continue to preclude subsequent litigation, provided that the agency acted in a judicial capacity to resolve disputed fact issues before it and the parties were afforded an adequate opportunity to litigate their claims.[5]

2. Preclusive Effect of Prior Federal Proceedings

Federal courts may be required to give preclusive effect to federal agency determinations where the agency has acted in a judicial capacity[6] to resolve disputed issues of fact and the parties have had an adequate opportunity to litigate, or where the defendant has established a dispositive affirmative defense in the agency proceeding.[7] However, they may not give preclusive effect to EEOC

---

[3] 58 F.3d 879, 68 FEP 327 (2d Cir. 1995).

[4] N.Y. Exec. Law § 296(1)(e) (McKinney 1993).

[5] Misischia v. Pirie, 60 F. 3d 626 (9th Cir. 1995) (judicially unreviewed decision of state board of examiners denying dental license barred § 1983 suit in federal court); Odunmbaku v. New York Blood Ctr., 1996 WL 514867, 72 FEP 202 (S.D.N.Y. 1996) (§ 1981 claim barred based upon collateral estoppel effect due to no probable cause finding of state FEP agency applying state law principles since plaintiff was provided with full and fair hearing before agency), *decision adhered to on reconsideration,* 1996 WL 695748, 72 FEP 1564 (S.D.N.Y. 1996); Lindas v. Cady, 515 N.W.2d 458, 71 FEP 791 (Wis. 1994) (Wisconsin Personnel Commission's dismissal of discrimination-based complaint precluded relitigation of the issue of sex discrimination in her § 1983 state-commenced action since she was afforded adequate opportunity to litigate sex discrimination complaint before that state agency).

[6] Durko v. OI-NEG TV Prods., 870 F. Supp. 1278, 1281 (M.D. Pa. 1994) (defining elements required for acting in judicial capacity).

[7] Ali v. Jeng, 86 F.3d 1148, 1996 WL 293181 (4th Cir. June 4, 1996) (court dismissed plaintiffs' §§ 1983 and 1985 actions because the same claims were brought in their prior employment discrimination case, which was dismissed as untimely); Lee v. Kroger Co., 901 F. Supp.1218, 70 FEP 425 (S.D. Tex. 1995) (dismissing second Title VII action due to res judicata effect of dismissal of prior Title VII action for failure to timely commence that action). *Cf.* Criales v. American Airlines, Inc., 105 F.3d 93, 72 FEP 1690 (2d Cir.) (plaintiff's second Title VII action was not precluded by dismissal of prior Title VII action, which was based upon absence of right-to-sue notice from the EEOC; earlier dismissal was not on the merits but due to a procedural omission later corrected by plaintiff upon EEOC's issuance of notice to sue), *cert. denied,* 118 S. Ct. 264 (1997).

determinations.⁸ EEOC determinations may, however, be considered by the district courts as evidence.⁹

Although the EEOC may continue to seek injunctive relief against employers that have either settled claims against individuals or successfully had those claims dismissed,¹⁰ res judicata may prevent the individuals from joining or continuing as parties in the suit against the employer.¹¹

3. Preclusive Effect of Prior Arbitration Decisions

Where a state court has enforced an arbitration award without inquiring into the merits of the underlying dispute, principles of res judicata and collateral estoppel may not bar a plaintiff from relitigating a Title VII claim in federal court.¹²

4. Preclusive Effect of Jury Findings on Nonjury Claims

Courts continue to hold that jury findings have a preclusive effect on nonjury findings on common factual issues.¹³ However,

---

⁸*See, e.g.,* Castner v. Colorado Springs Cablevision, 979 F.2d 1417, 1422, 60 FEP 566 (10th Cir. 1992) ("When examining the merits, the district court may not give preclusive effect to an EEOC finding that the evidence does not support a finding of discrimination.").

⁹*See id.* (EEOC's administrative finding is a factor to be considered); Johnson v. City of Port Arthur, 892 F. Supp. 835, 840, 6 AD 547 (E.D. Tex. 1995) (determination reached by the EEOC should not be ignored, but the court should inquire as to the validity of the determination); Lee v. United States Postal Serv., 882 F. Supp. 589 (E.D. Tex. 1995) (same); Woods v. Trinity Mem'l Hosp., 1995 WL 55275 (E.D. Tex. Jan. 31, 1995) (same); Jason v. Baptist Hosp., 872 F. Supp. 1575 (E.D. Tex. 1994) (same); Tatum v. Community Bank, 866 F. Supp. 988 (E.D. Tex 1994) (same).

¹⁰EEOC v. Huttig Sash & Door Co., 511 F.2d 453, 10 FEP 529 (5th Cir. 1975) (termination of private party's Title VII suit does not estop EEOC from bringing suit on identical charges).

¹¹*See* EEOC v. Pasta House Co., 70 FEP 61 (E.D. Mo. 1996) (although the individual plaintiff whose suit was dismissed with prejudice may not join with EEOC as a party to a subsequent suit, she may still be called as a witness in EEOC's case) (dictum).

¹²Tang v. Rhode Island Dep't of Elderly Affairs, 904 F. Supp. 69, 69 FEP 577 (D.R.I. 1995) (prior arbitration of state civil rights claims does not preclude plaintiff from bringing Title VII claim in federal court even though the state court confirmed the arbitration award because in confirming, the state court did not inquire as to the merits).

¹³Dombeck v. Milwaukee Valve Co., 40 F.3d 230, 66 FEP 497 (7th Cir. 1994) (when nonjury and jury claims are simultaneously tried, court is bound by jury's finding on common factual issues); *cf.* Melendez v. Illinois Bell Tel. Co., 79 F.3d 661, 70 FEP 589 (7th Cir. 1996) (court is not bound by jury verdict regarding plaintiff's

a court's findings do not preclude a jury from hearing the same claims.[14]

6. Preclusion Issues in Class Actions

A finding that the defendant engaged in a pattern and practice of unlawful discrimination as to an identified class of persons may estop the defendant from denying such discrimination in subsequent litigation brought by individuals included in the class.[15]

In *Sondel v. Northwest Airlines*,[16] a class certified in a federal court disparate impact case under Title VII was found to be bound, on res judicata principles, by the outcome of a corollary state court suit initiated by the named class representatives. Subsequent to certification of the class in the federal court case, the named representatives brought a discrimination action in state court under state law in their individual capacities based on the alleged discriminatory policy. Summary judgment was granted to the employer in the state court action. The defendant then moved for summary judgment in the federal action on the grounds of res judicata. Affirming summary judgment in favor of the defendant, the Eighth Circuit held that the named class representatives had a fiduciary relationship with the unnamed class members that extended beyond "the four corners of the federal lawsuit"[17] and created privity among all class members for res judicata purposes, binding all class members to the actions of the named representatives.

7. Preclusive Effect of Prior Sworn Statements [New Topic]

There is a developing line of cases, arising under the Rehabilitation Act and the ADA, where employers have, in moving for

---

§ 1981 disparate treatment claim in resolving nonjury Title VII disparate impact case since the issues presented in the respective causes of action were not identical).

[14] Harvis v. Roadway Express, Inc., 973 F.2d 490, 61 FEP 91 (6th Cir. 1992) (court's nonjury findings on plaintiffs' Title VII claims do not preclude relitigation of same claims in front of a jury in a § 1981 claim).

[15] McKnight v. Circuit City Stores, Inc., 168 F.R.D. 550, 72 FEP 28 (E.D. Va. 1996) (holding defendant would be precluded from relitigating pattern-and-practice issue in subsequent cases, in event of adverse outcome on that issue, notwithstanding that class action was decertified).

[16] 56 F.3d 934 (8th Cir. 1995), *reh'g and suggestion for reh'g en banc denied* (Aug. 1, 1995) (unpublished decision).

[17] *Id.* at 939.

summary judgment, relied on prior inconsistent filings made by plaintiffs with workers' compensation and employment disability agencies indicating the employees' total disability. The courts disagree on the extent to which such prior statements will estop a plaintiff from subsequently claiming that he or she can perform the essential functions of the job.[18]

B. Contractual Election of Arbitration

Since its July 17, 1995, Policy Statement on the Use of Alternative Dispute Resolution, the EEOC has expressed its intent to utilize alternative dispute resolution techniques for certain discrimination charges, and has emphasized that one of the fundamental principles for ensuring a fair and equal process is that participation in the alternate process be voluntary. On July 10, 1997, the EEOC issued its Policy Statement on Mandatory Arbitration, in which it identified, in its view, the benefits of enforcing federal antidiscrimination laws in the public forum of judicial litigation, and the disadvantages of private arbitration proceedings.[19] The agency concluded that the use of unilaterally imposed mandatory arbitration agreements harms both the individual civil rights claimant and the public interest in eradicating discrimination.

---

[18]*Compare* Nixon v. Digital Equipment, 6 AD 353 (E.D.N.Y. 1996) (disability insurance claim found not to be identical or inconsistent with ADA suit), Smith v. Dovenmuhle Mortgage, Inc., 859 F. Supp. 1138, 4 AD 132 (N.D. Ill. 1994) (estoppel inapplicable based upon statements of complete disability on Social Security application), Ward v. Westvaco Corp., 859 F. Supp. 608, 3 AD 739 (D. Mass. 1994) (qualified statement of disability entered by plaintiff on disability application did not preclude ADA claim) *and* Overton v. Reilly, 977 F.2d 1190, 2 AD 254 (7th Cir. 1992) (while relevant to Rehabilitation Act suit, plaintiff's receipt of Social Security disability benefits did not constitute bar to disability discrimination claim) *with* McNemar v. Disney Stores, Inc., 91 F.3d. 610, 5 AD 1227 (3d Cir. 1996) (statements on Social Security application as to total and permanent disability operate as an estoppel on subsequent claim that plaintiff was qualified under ADA), *cert. denied,* 117 S. Ct. 958 (1997), Kennedy v. Applause, Inc., 90 F.3d 1477, 5 AD 1249 (9th Cir. 1996) (plaintiff's statements on disability applications that totally disabled coupled with expert testimony of same warranted summary judgment for employer), Garcia-Paz v. Swift Textiles, Inc., 873 F. Supp. 547, 3 AD 1844 (D. Kan. 1995) (plaintiff estopped based on statements that totally disabled on disability insurance and Social Security disability applications) and Reigel v. Kaiser Found. Health Plan, 859 F. Supp. 963, 3 AD 577 (E.D.N.C. 1994) (plaintiff's statements on disability income applications precluded her from showing she was able to perform essential duties of position).

[19]EEOC Policy Statement on Mandatory Arbitration, July 10, 1997.

Although arbitration continues to be the dominant method of resolving disputes arising under collective bargaining agreements, the Ninth Circuit has held that, unless the agreement expressly includes a commitment to arbitrate Title VII claims, no obligation exists to submit such claims to arbitration.[20]

Courts, nevertheless, have continued to apply *Gilmer* to cases involving a multitude of federal statutory rights.[21] In doing so, they have rejected the argument that the Federal Arbitration Act's exclusion of "contracts of employment" is meant to apply to all employees, rather than only to those who are actually involved in the transportation of people or goods.[22] Courts have disagreed, however, over whether Title VII or the ADA precludes enforcement of a collective bargaining agreement provision mandating arbitration of claims under those statutes.[23]

---

[20] Felt v. Atchison, Topeka & Santa Fe Ry., 60 F.3d 1416, 68 FEP 548 (9th Cir. 1995).

[21] Kuehner v. Dickinson & Co., 84 F.3d 316 (9th Cir. 1996) (applying FAA to Fair Labor Standards Act claim); Matthews v. Rollins Hudig Hall Co., 72 F.3d 50, 69 FEP 641 (7th Cir. 1995) (ADEA case); Williams v. Cigna Fin. Advisors, Inc., 56 F.3d 656, 68 FEP 65 (5th Cir. 1995) (applying *Gilmer* to the Older Workers Benefit Protection Act); Metz v. Merrill Lynch, Pierce, Fenner & Smith, Inc., 39 F.3d 1482, 66 FEP 439 (10th Cir. 1994) (applying *Gilmer* to Title VII actions); Pritzker v. Merrill Lynch, Pierce, Fenner & Smith, Inc., 7 F.3d 1110, 17 EBC 1719 (3d Cir. 1993) (applying *Gilmer* to an ERISA claim); Saari v. Smith Barney, Harris Upham & Co., 968 F.2d 877, 7 IER 929 (9th Cir.) (applying *Gilmer* to the Federal Employees Polygraph Protection Act), *cert. denied,* 506 U.S. 986 (1992); Willis v. Dean Witter Reynolds, Inc., 948 F.2d 305, 57 FEP 386 (6th Cir. 1991) (applying *Gilmer* to Title VII); Kahalnik v. John Hancock Funds, Inc., 1996 WL 145842 (N.D. Ill. Mar. 27, 1996) (applying *Gilmer* to Older Workers Benefit Protection Act); Pitter v. Prudential Life Ins. Co., 906 F. Supp. 130 (E.D.N.Y. 1995) (applying *Gilmer* to Title VII and § 1981); Moore v. Interacciones Global, Inc., 1995 U.S. Dist. LEXIS 971 (S.D.N.Y. Jan. 27, 1995) (applying *Gilmer* to Title VII); Kinnebrew v. Gulf Ins. Co., 67 FEP 189 (N.D. Tex. 1994) (applying *Gilmer* to the Equal Pay Act). *But see* Tran v. Tran, 54 F.3d 115, 149 LRRM 2350 (2d Cir. 1995) (holding that FLSA claims are not subject to mandatory arbitration), *cert. denied,* 116 S. Ct. 1417 (1996).

[22] Rojas v. TK Communications, Inc., 87 F.3d 745, 748, 71 FEP 664 (5th Cir. 1996) (FAA exclusion applies only to workers in the transportation industry); Asplundh Tree Expert Co. v. Bates, 71 F.3d 592, 11 IER 61 (6th Cir.1995) (same); Albert v. National Cash Register Co., 874 F. Supp. 1324, 66 FEP 567 (S.D. Fla. 1994) (same); Hull v. NCR Corp., 826 F. Supp. 303, 63 FEP 666 (E.D. Mo. 1993) (same).

[23] *Compare* Austin v. Owens-Brockway Glass Container, Inc., 78 F.3d 875, 70 FEP 272 (4th Cir.) (Civil Rights Act of 1991 does not render such a collective bargaining provision unenforceable), *cert. denied,* 117 S. Ct. 432 (1996) *with* Brisentine v. Stone & Webster Eng'g Corp., 117 F.3d 519, 6 AD 1878 (11th Cir. 1997) (refusing to enforce collective bargaining agreement provision requiring arbitration of federal statutory claims, unless the individual claimant, rather than the union, knowingly and expressly agreed to entrust such claims to an arbitrator).

C. Practical Considerations in Preparing and Negotiating Arbitration Agreements

1. FAA Coverage

The United States Supreme Court has recently held that the FAA's reference to interstate commerce reflects Congress' intent to extend the Act's coverage to the limits of federal power under the Commerce Clause.[24] The Court also recognized that the determination of whether a transaction or contract "involves" interstate commerce requires an expansive construction of the term in order to effectuate Congress' goal of encouraging alternative dispute resolution mechanisms.[25] Accordingly, the Court held that a matter "involves" commerce under the Act if it merely "affects" commerce—a standard commonly applied by the courts to situations in which it is clear that Congress intended to exercise its Commerce Clause powers to the fullest extent.[26]

3. Persons and Entities Covered

Disagreement continues to exist as to whether mandatory arbitration provisions in a collective bargaining agreement divests the judiciary of jurisdiction over an individual union member's discrimination actions.[27]

6. Punitive Damages

At least one court of appeals has held that an arbitrator may not award punitive damages in a proceeding under a collective

---

[24] Allied-Bruce Terminix Cos. v. Dobson, 115 S. Ct. 834 (1995).
[25] *Id.* at 834–38.
[26] *Id.* at 839–40.
[27] *Compare* Austin v. Owens-Brockway Glass, 78 F.3d 875, 70 FEP 272 (4th Cir. 1996) (dismissing complaint, without prejudice, upon finding that arbitration clause contained in labor agreement was mandatory remedy with respect to employee's Title VII and ADA claims) *with* Brisentine v. Stone & Webster Eng'g Corp., 117 F.3d 519, 6 AD 1878 (11th Cir. 1997) (refusing to enforce collective bargaining agreement provision to require arbitration of federal statutory claims unless the individual claimant (rather than the union), in entrusting such claims to an arbitrator, knowingly and expressly waived his or her federal rights—including the right to a jury trial). *See also* Pryner v. Tractor Supply Co., 927 F. Supp. 1140, 72 FEP 1235 (S.D. Ind. 1996) (arbitration remedy under labor contract does not foreclose employee from pursuing Title VII and § 1981 judicial remedies), *aff'd,* 109 F.3d 354, 73 FEP 615 (7th Cir. 1997); Griffith v. Keystone Steel & Wire Co., 858 F. Supp 802, 66 FEP 227 (C.D. Ill. 1994) (same).

bargaining agreement unless the agreement expressly permits such an award.[28] With respect to arbitration agreements that purport to prohibit or limit punitive damage awards, the courts have reached conflicting conclusions.[29]

7. Statute of Limitations

Jurisdictions that will enforce arbitration agreements that shorten applicable limitations periods may require that such agreements be clear and unambiguous. Parties should therefore make their intentions plain on the face of the contract.[30] Also, such provisions may be scrutinized by the courts and, if found to be onerous, invalidated.[31]

10. Adhesion-Contract Issues

Courts continue to apply state law adhesion-contract principles, such as those requiring that parties to a contract proceed knowingly and without duress, in determining whether a valid agreement to arbitrate exists.[32] The Supreme Court has made it

---

[28]Island Creek Coal Co. v. District 28, Mine Workers (UMW), 29 F.3d 126, 146 LRRM 2773 (4th Cir.) (the rule in the Fourth Circuit is that under a standard collective bargaining agreement, an arbitrator may not award punitive damages unless the agreement expressly permits such an award), *cert. denied,* 115 S. Ct. 583, 147 LRRM 2960 (1994).

[29]*Compare* Island Creek Coal Co. v. District 28, Mine Workers (UMW), *supra,* Kinnebrew v. Gulf Ins. Co., 67 FEP 189 (N.D. Tex. 1994) (enforcing contractual clause that precluded punitive damages, attorney's fees, and equitable relief); *and* DeGaetano v. Smith Barney, Inc., 70 FEP 401 (S.D.N.Y. 1996) (same) *with* Johnson v. Hubbard Broadcasting, Inc., 940 F. Supp. 1447 (D. Minn. 1996) (court would consider arbitration agreement unenforceable as unconscionable if arbitrator precluded compensatory and punitive damages in reliance upon contractual language barring such relief).

[30]*See* This Is Me, Inc. v. Taylor, 1996 WL 20745 (S.D.N.Y. Jan. 17, 1996) (holding that although parties may contract to shorten the statutory limitations period, such agreements are disfavored and are strictly construed against the party seeking to enforce them; any ambiguity as to the meaning of the contractually stipulated timeframe will therefore lengthen rather than shorten the limitations period).

[31]Salisbury v. Art Van Furniture, 938 F. Supp. 435 (W.D. Mich. 1996) (finding employment agreement that limited the statute of limitations on postemployment lawsuits to six months unreasonable, noting that on the ADA claim the EEOC was not required to issue its right-to-sue letter until six months after complaint was filed).

[32]*Compare* Prudential Ins. Co. of Am. v. Lai, 42 F.3d 1299, 1304–05, 66 FEP 933 (9th Cir. 1994) (since employee did not knowingly agree to arbitrate employment

clear, however, that, in evaluating whether an agreement to arbitrate exists and is valid, courts may not apply stricter standards to such agreements than applicable state law imposes on contracts in general.[33]

11. Manifestation of Intent to Arbitrate

The Ninth Circuit has held that an arbitration agreement may not be enforced to require an individual to submit federal statutory claims to binding arbitration unless that individual knowingly, willingly, and expressly waived his or her right to proceed in a judicial forum.[34] With respect to arbitration policies that are unilaterally formulated and implemented by employers, and which are deemed to have been accepted by employees who begin or continue their employment after receiving notice of those policies, these decisions require, first, that the employee receive clear notice that the waiver of the right to submit federal statutory claims to a judicial forum is a new term or condition of employment. Second, the employee must be informed of the means by which that term or condition can be accepted or rejected. Finally, the employee must accept the new term or condition.[35]

---

discrimination claims, arbitration would not be mandated; court finds that requirement of knowing agreement on part of employee is based in legislative history of CRA of 1991), *cert. denied,* 116 S. Ct. 61 (1995) *with* Beauchamp v. Great West Life Assurance Co., 918 F. Supp 1091, 73 FEP 361 (E.D. Mich. 1996) (contrary holding in reference to CRA of 1991). *See also* EEOC v. Rivers Oak Imaging, 67 FEP 1243 (S.D. Tex. 1995) (enjoining enforcement of ADR policy, which court finds to be retaliatory and contrary to principles of Title VII).

[33]Doctors' Assocs. v. Casarotto, 517 U.S. 681 (1996) (FAA preempts state contract laws that are specific to arbitration contracts and not generally applicable to other types of contracts. Applying this principle, the Court held that Montana's requirement that arbitration contracts have separate, explicit notices printed in large type on the face of the contract is preempted by the FAA.).

[34]Nelson v. Cyprus Bagdad Copper Corp., 119 F.3d 756, 761–62, 6 AD 1714 (9th Cir. 1997); Prudential Ins. Co. v. Lai, 42 F.3d 1299, 1304–05, 66 FEP 933 (9th Cir. 1994) (since employee did not knowingly agree to arbitrate employment discrimination claims, arbitration would not be mandated; court finds that requirement of knowing agreement on part of employee is based in legislative history of CRA of 1991), *cert. denied,* 116 S. Ct. 61 (1995); Nadeau v. Thomas, 1997 WL 542708 (N.D. Cal. 1997) (unpublished). *See also* Brisentine v. Stone & Webster Eng'g Corp., 117 F.3d 519, 6 AD 1878 (11th Cir. 1997). *But see* Beauchamp v. Great West Life Assurance Co., 918 F. Supp 1091, 73 FEP 361 (E.D. Mich. 1996) (for contrary holding in reference to CRA of 1991).

[35]*Nelson,* 119 F.3d at 761–62; *Lai,* 42 F.3d at 1305.

III. Exhaustion of Remedies

A. Duty of Nonfederal Employees to Exhaust State Administrative Remedies or Contractual Remedies Under a Collective Bargaining Agreement

ADA plaintiffs need not exhaust their state administrative remedies, but similar to Title VII, they must first file a charge with the EEOC.[36] Similarly, claimants under state workers' compensation or disability discrimination laws need not exhaust collective bargaining remedies under the Railway Labor Act.[37]

---

[36]*Compare* Dao v. Auchan Hypermarket, 96 F.3d 787, 5 AD 1633 (5th Cir. 1996) (in a case of first impression, the Fifth Circuit holds that the requirements for a claim under Title I of the ADA are similar to the procedural prerequisites of Title VII in that a charge must first be filed with the EEOC) *with* Davoll v. Webb, 943 F. Supp. 1289 (D. Colo. 1996) (claims brought under Title II of the ADA do not require the exhaustion of administrative remedies or a right-to-sue letter from the EEOC).

[37]Westbrook v. Sky Chefs, Inc., 35 F.3d 316, 147 LRRM 2491 (7th Cir. 1994) (state law protecting workers' compensation claimants from retaliation gives the plaintiff rights independent of and in addition to those contained in the collective bargaining agreement; her state law retaliation claims therefore are not preempted by the Railway Labor Act and can be heard by the federal court); Taggart v. Trans World Airlines, Inc., 40 F.3d 269, 3 AD 1441 (8th Cir. 1994) (same principle applies to state law protecting persons with handicaps; these "little ADA" laws are not preempted by the Railway Labor Act).

Chapter 33

LITIGATION PROCEDURE

I. Effect of Deficiencies in EEOC Administrative Process on Charging Party's Right to Sue

Federal courts continue to wrestle with the extent to which deficiencies in the EEOC administrative process will affect a subsequent Title VII lawsuit filed by the charging party. Most courts follow the general rule that a Title VII claim will be dismissed if the charging party did not cooperate in the administrative process[1] or caused the deficiency in the administrative process.[2] Of course, a litigant's unexcused failure to file any administrative charge with the EEOC also will result in dismissal of a subsequent Title VII suit.[3]

---

[1] *Compare* Francis v. Brown, 58 F.3d 191, 193, 68 FEP 555 (5th Cir. 1995) (Title VII lawsuit properly dismissed because rejection of settlement offer for full relief constituted a failure to exhaust his administrative remedies) *with* Greenlaw v. Garrett, 59 F.3d 994, 998–1000, 68 FEP 531 (9th Cir. 1995) (reversing dismissal of Title VII claim for failure to exhaust administrative remedies because requiring a pro se Title VII litigant to make the legal assessment of whether a settlement offer was one for "full relief" violates the policies and principles of Title VII).

[2] *E.g.,* Ryan v. New York State Thruway Auth., 889 F. Supp. 70, 78, 73 FEP 1525 (N.D.N.Y. 1995) (late filing of her Title VII charge will not be excused on grounds of equitable estoppel because notice from her employer, which stated that she could file a charge with the EEOC or the state agency, did not carry any implication about the time limitations for filing her charge); Guice-Mills v. Brown, 882 F. Supp. 1427, 1430, 5 AD 542 (S.D.N.Y. 1995) (pro se Title VII litigant's assertion of ignorance as to the time requirements in the EEOC regulations was "suspect, in light of her three prior Title VII actions" against the same federal agency, and her failure to timely comply with these requirements would not be equitably excused).

[3] *E.g.,* Hogan v. 50 Sutton Place S. Owners, Inc., 919 F. Supp. 738, 746, 71 FEP 1321 (S.D.N.Y. 1996) (Title VII claim dismissed because plaintiff neither filed a claim with the EEOC nor received a right-to-sue letter, and he did not claim or present facts excusing his failure); Tang v. Rhode Island, 904 F. Supp. 55, 58–59 (D.R.I. 1995) (Title VII claims dismissed without prejudice because "plaintiff's personal opinion that resort to the EEOC would have been a waste of time" based on her past experience with the same employer did not excuse her failure to file a charge or to obtain a right-to-sue letter from the EEOC).

An employer prejudiced by a delay in the filing of the lawsuit may argue that equitable considerations should result in dismissal of the lawsuit under the doctrine of laches.[4]

Recent cases reaffirm that a charging party does not have a civil cause of action against the EEOC over its allegedly improper handling of an administrative charge.[5]

A. EEOC Errors in Charge Filing

Whether charge-filing errors by the EEOC will toll time limitations or entirely excuse filing requirements appears largely to depend upon the particulars of the errors.[6] At least two federal courts have refused to equitably toll or excuse such failures when claimants' allegations were supported only by their oral representations.[7]

---

[4]National Ass'n of Gov't Employees v. City Pub. Serv. Bd., 40 F.3d 698, 708–11, 67 FEP 1013 (5th Cir. 1994) (doctrine of laches applied, resulting in dismissal of claim; nine-year delay was not excused because plaintiffs were represented by counsel continuously since conciliation efforts were terminated, and defendants were prejudiced by deaths and fading memories of a number of potential witnesses).

[5]*E.g.,* Forbes v. Reno, 893 F. Supp. 476, 482, 73 FEP 51 (W.D. Pa. 1995) (Title VII does not grant a plaintiff an express or implied right to bring suit against the EEOC for inadequate or improper investigation of a charge of discrimination), *aff'd without opinion,* 91 F.3d 123, 73 FEP 192 (3d Cir. 1996); Mitchell v. EEOC, 888 F. Supp. 710, 712–13, 68 FEP 397 (E.D. Pa. 1995) (neither Title VII nor the United States Constitution provides a cause of action against the EEOC for mishandling or otherwise improperly disposing of a discrimination charge).

[6]*E.g.,* Angotti v. Kenyon & Kenyon, 929 F. Supp. 651, 657–58, 70 FEP 316 (S.D.N.Y. 1996) (plaintiff's affidavit and documentary evidence, which supported her allegation that she told EEOC intake interviewer about her retaliation claims and was assured that these claims were encompassed by her charge of sex and disability discrimination, presented unresolved factual issues that could equitably excuse plaintiff's failure to include an explicit claim of retaliation in her EEOC charge; fact that the plaintiff was herself an attorney did not foreclose the availability of relief if it is shown that she was affirmatively misled by the EEOC interviewer). *Cf.* Anderson v. Unisys Corp., 47 F.3d 302, 307, 67 FEP 317 (8th Cir.) (EEOC's 300-day filing period tolled because pro se ADEA claimant received misleading letter from the state agency authorized to act on behalf of the EEOC; the ambiguous wording in the letter could have led the claimant to believe that he had one year in which to file his charge with the EEOC), *cert. denied,* 116 S. Ct. 299 (1995).

[7]Spira v. Ethical Culture Sch., 888 F. Supp. 601, 602, 68 FEP 202 (S.D.N.Y. 1995) (pro se plaintiff's "bare allegation" that his failure to timely file suit after receipt of a right-to-sue letter was due to an EEOC worker's oral representation to him that the 90-day limitations period was calculated in working days and not calendar days was "not credible" and was insufficient to invoke equitable tolling). *Cf.* Horne v. Cub Foods, 68 FEP 860, 863 (N.D. Ill. 1995) (plaintiff's "alleged oral representations [of her sexual harassment claims] to the EEOC did not fulfill her obligation to exhaust her administrative remedies").

B. EEOC Errors in Processing Charge/Failing to Defer Charge

Recent federal cases illustrate that work-sharing arrangements between the EEOC and state compliance agencies—in which the state agency designates the EEOC as its agent for the receipt of discrimination charges and waives its right to exclusive jurisdiction over these charges—can make it easier for the EEOC to meet its duty of deferral.[8] If work-sharing arrangements are present, the EEOC's acceptance of a charge constitutes a simultaneous filing with the state compliance agency, resulting in automatic application of the 300-day limitations period instead of the 180-day period.[9] If such a charge is filed after 180 days but before 300 days following the alleged discriminatory event, the state agency's waiver of exclusive jurisdiction is immediate, effectively terminating the state proceedings as soon as the EEOC receives the charge, thereby allowing the EEOC to initiate proceedings on the charge without having to wait for the state agency to first act.[10]

D. EEOC Failure to Investigate and/or Conciliate

Recent federal cases have addressed the importance of the employer's opportunity to engage in conciliation efforts.[11] In a case involving amendment of an unverified charge, the Fourth Circuit noted that an employer could be prejudiced by not having had the opportunity to participate in conciliation efforts.[12]

---

[8]*E.g.,* Griffin v. City of Dallas, 26 F.3d 610, 65 FEP 784 (5th Cir. 1994).

[9]*Id.* at 612–13.

[10]*Id.; accord* Brennan v. National Tel. Directory Corp., 881 F. Supp. 986, 993, 67 FEP 922 (E.D. Pa. 1995) (provided there is a work-sharing agreement, the aggrieved employee meets the statutory filing requirement as long as the claim is filed with the EEOC within 300 days of the allegedly discriminatory conduct).

[11]*Compare* Secrist v. Burns Int'l Sec. Servs., 926 F. Supp. 823, 825–26, 71 FEP 162 (E.D. Wis. 1996) (claims against defendant not named by pro se litigant in her EEOC charge will be dismissed because that defendant was not given notice of the EEOC charge and was not afforded an opportunity to participate in the EEOC proceedings) *and* Vakharia v. Little Co. of Mary Hosp. & Health Care Ctrs., 917 F. Supp. 1282, 1294 (N.D. Ill. 1996) ("Parties not named in a charge already filed with the EEOC may not be sued under Title VII or the ADEA unless that party had adequate notice of the charge and was given opportunity to participate in conciliation proceedings.") *with* Virgo v. Riviera Beach Assocs., 30 F.3d 1350, 1358–59, 65 FEP 1317 (11th Cir. 1994) (notice is imputed to defendant because it was a successor in interest to a company that had received notice).

[12]Balazs v. Liebenthal, 32 F.3d 151, 158, 65 FEP 993 (4th Cir. 1994) ("To say that an employer served with a lawsuit based on an unverified charge who has to

E. Charge Not Under Oath

An unverified document submitted to the EEOC, standing alone, does not suffice as a "charge" under Title VII.[13] Courts have continued to disagree, however, over the extent to which a Title VII claimant can later verify these documents by amendment in order to comply with Title VII's requirement that charges be made under oath or affirmation. Several courts have imposed a limitation upon the time for amendment, allowing amendment only while the charge remains open at the EEOC level, before the EEOC closes its file or issues a right-to-sue letter.[14]

---

employ counsel, file an answer and a motion to dismiss and appear in court to argue the motion has not been prejudiced is just plain wrong. Defendant here may well have welcomed the opportunity to respond to the charge and engage in efforts at conciliation as contemplated by the statutes, but it was never given this chance.").

[13]*E.g.,* Park v. Howard Univ., 71 F.3d 904, 908–09, 71 FEP 1838 (D.C. Cir. 1995) (plaintiff's precomplaint questionnaire completed for the state compliance agency is not the same as an EEOC charge; the questionnaire stated on its face that there was no guarantee the information provided therein would be part of the formal complaint, it was not verified, and there was no evidence that either the employer or the EEOC had access to the questionnaire), *cert. denied,* 117 S. Ct. 57 (1996); Vakharia v. Little Co. of Mary Hosp. & Health Care Ctrs., 917 F. Supp. 1282, 1294 (N.D. Ill. 1996) (plaintiff's EEOC intake questionnaire does not serve as a charge). *Cf.* Howze v. Virginia Polytechnic, 901 F. Supp. 1091, 1095, 69 FEP 1013 (W.D. Va. 1995) (plaintiff met Title VII's charge requirement by timely filing an affidavit and an intake questionnaire with the EEOC). Title VII's charge requirements should be contrasted with those in the Age Discrimination in Employment Act, which do not require that the charge be verified, making it easier for claimants to file ADEA charges. Some courts hold that intake questionnaires and other unverified documents received by the EEOC suffice as charges under the ADEA. *E.g.,* Downes v. Volkswagen of Am., Inc., 41 F.3d 1132, 1138–39, 69 FEP 11 (7th Cir. 1994) (intake questionnaire constituted a proper charge under the ADEA where claimant manifested an intent to activate the Act's machinery, notwithstanding that the EEOC itself did not treat the questionnaire as a charge); Brook v. City of Montgomery, 916 F. Supp. 1193, 1202 (M.D. Ala. 1996) (ADEA plaintiff's two-page handwritten letter sent to the EEOC and treated by the EEOC as a charge met the ADEA's liberal requirements for a charge). *Cf.* Diez v. Minnesota Min. & Mfg. Co., 88 F.3d 672, 675–77, 71 FEP 383 (8th Cir. 1996) (ADEA charges differ from those under Title VII because they need not be verified; however, the intake questionnaire submitted by the ADEA plaintiff to the state compliance agency did not constitute a valid charge because there was no evidence that the questionnaire was intended to "activate the machinery" of the ADEA).

[14]*E.g.,* Balazs v. Liebenthal, 32 F.3d 151, 157, 65 FEP 993 (4th Cir. 1994) (where a right-to-sue letter has issued, a suit has been instituted, and the EEOC has closed its file, there is no longer a charge pending before the EEOC that is capable of being amended); *accord* Danley v. Book-of-the-Month Club, Inc., 921 F. Supp. 1352, 1354, 70 FEP 1281 (M.D. Pa. 1996) (private litigant cannot maintain a Title VII claim where his or her EEOC charge was not verified prior to the EEOC's issuance of a right-to-sue letter), *aff'd,* 107 F.3d 861 (3d Cir. 1997).

F. EEOC Failure to Issue Notice of Right to Sue When Charging Party Is Entitled to It

Recent cases follow the line of authority that a right-to-sue letter from the EEOC is only a condition precedent to a Title VII lawsuit and not a jurisdictional requirement; thus, receipt of the right-to-sue letter even after institution of the lawsuit is sufficient.[15]

II. SUIT AGAINST PARTIES NOT NAMED IN EEOC CHARGE

A. Introduction

Many courts continue to allow plaintiffs to pursue claims against apparently unnamed parties by liberally construing what it means to be named in the charge.[16] Other courts have rejected dismissal for lack of jurisdiction by explicitly recognizing exceptions to the naming requirement. The Second, Eighth, and Eleventh Circuits have found exceptions to the naming requirement through the identity of interest test articulated by the Third Circuit in *Glus*.[17] Other courts continue to apply the reasonable scope of the investigation

---

[15]*Compare* Kounitz v. Slaatten, 901 F. Supp. 650, 655 (S.D.N.Y. 1995) (Title VII plaintiff's receipt of a right-to-sue letter after commencement of the civil action satisfies the statutory prerequisite that a plaintiff obtain notice of the right to sue before filing a civil action under Title VII) *with* Thomas v. St. Luke's Health Sys., Inc., 869 F. Supp. 1413, 1426 (N.D. Iowa 1994) (plaintiff failed to plead the procedural prerequisites for a Title VII lawsuit: he alleged that the state compliance agency referred his charge to the EEOC, but that he only received a right-to-sue letter from the state agency and not from the EEOC), *aff'd without opinion,* 61 F.3d 908 (8th Cir. 1995). The requirement of a right-to-sue letter apparently also is merely a condition precedent to a civil lawsuit under the Americans with Disabilities Act. *See* Gilday v. Mecosta County, 920 F. Supp. 792, 794 n.1, 5 AD 758 (W.D. Mich. 1996), *rev'd on other grounds,* 7 AD 348 (6th Cir. 1997).

[16]*See* Compton v. Chinn Enters., 936 F. Supp. 480, 487 (N.D. Ill. 1996) (corporate owner provided with adequate notice of retaliation charge where named as respondent in plaintiff's sexual harassment charge); Scales v. Sonic Indus., Inc., 887 F. Supp. 1435, 1437 (E.D. Okla. 1995) (informal reference to franchisor's trade name sufficiently linked charge to otherwise unnamed franchisor); Afande v. National Lutheran Home for the Aged, 868 F. Supp. 795, 800 (D. Md. 1994) (purposes of naming requirement met where supervisor had notice of charge and participated in conciliation process), *aff'd,* 69 F.3d 532 (4th Cir. 1995). *But see* Bishop v. Okidata, Inc., 864 F. Supp. 416, 425, 3 AD 1283 (D. N.J. 1994) (naming requirement not necessarily met where plaintiff names individuals in affidavit accompanying EEOC charge).

[17]Glus v. G.C. Murphy Co., 562 F.2d 880, 15 FEP 998 (3d Cir. 1977). *See* Cook v. Arrowsmith Shelburne, Inc., 69 F.3d 1235, 1241–42, 69 FEP 392 (2d Cir. 1995)

test suggested by the Ninth Circuit in *Kaplan*.[18] Whatever test is applied, however, the most important factor remains whether the unnamed party had actual or constructive notice of the charge and an opportunity to participate in conciliation efforts.[19]

While notice to the unnamed defendant remains of primary importance, some courts have also considered other equitable factors, such as whether the plaintiff was represented by counsel when EEOC charges were filed.[20] For example, one court stated that, as a threshold matter, the identity of interest exception will apply only

---

(finding identity of interest where unnamed parent corporation approved all of named subsidiary's personnel decisions); Winbush v. Iowa, 66 F.3d 1471, 1478 n.9, 69 FEP 1348 (8th Cir. 1995) (finding identity of interest where plaintiff failed to name individual school officials but named school); Virgo v. Riviera Beach Assoc., 30 F.3d 1350, 1358–59, 65 FEP 1317 (11th Cir. 1994) (finding identity of interest where plaintiff failed to name general partners of partnership but named business entity through which partnership operated).

[18]Kaplan v. Theatrical Stage Employees, 525 F.2d 1354, 11 FEP 872 (9th Cir. 1975). *See* Nogueras v. University of Puerto Rico, 890 F. Supp. 60, 63, 69 FEP 1007 (D.P.R. 1995) (allegations in charge sufficient to give notice to EEOC and unnamed parties that plaintiff considered unnamed parties to be culpable); Brogdon v. Alabama Dep't of Econ. & Community Affairs, 864 F. Supp. 1161, 1165, 66 FEP 325 (M.D. Ala. 1994) (conduct of head of state agency was within reasonable scope of investigation where agency itself was named in charge); Ajaz v. Continental Airlines, 156 F.R.D. 145, 147 (S.D. Tex. 1994) (unreasonable to conclude that EEOC investigation arising out of charge would focus upon unnamed immediate supervisor where only individual named in charge was the shift manager who notified plaintiff of discharge).

[19]*Compare* Chandler v. Fast Lane, Inc., 868 F. Supp. 1138, 1141, 66 FEP 675 (E.D. Ark. 1994) (unnamed owner and operator of named corporate defendant was given requisite notice and opportunity to be heard in administrative proceedings) *and* Johnson v. County of Cook, 864 F. Supp. 84, 86–87 (N.D. Ill. 1994) (unnamed sheriff's office had constructive notice because it initiated termination proceedings and was represented by same attorney as named department of corrections) *with* Banks v. Chicago Bd. of Educ., 895 F. Supp. 206, 210, 68 FEP 1333 (N.D. Ill. 1995) (plaintiff failed to allege that unnamed principals of elementary schools had notice of charge) *and* Smith v. Sheet Metal Workers Local 28, 877 F. Supp. 165, 172–73, 148 LRRM 2856 (S.D.N.Y. 1995) (unnamed union representatives not provided with constructive notice even though plaintiff named union in charge), *aff'd*, 100 F.3d 943, 152 LRRM 2384 (2d Cir.), *cert. denied*, 117 S. Ct. 101 (1996).

[20]*Compare* Dortz v. City of New York, 904 F. Supp. 127, 143, 72 FEP 205 (S.D.N.Y. 1995) (because plaintiff was proceeding pro se and was told by EEOC investigator not to change her charge, plaintiff permitted to pursue claims against unnamed employer of alleged harasser despite knowledge of employment relationship at time charges were filed) *and* Gilmore v. List & Clark Constr. Co., 862 F. Supp. 294, 297 (D. Kan. 1994) (explaining that since EEOC complaints are written by laypersons not versed in technicalities of pleading or jurisdictional requirements of Title VII, they must be construed liberally) *with* Crosten v. Kamauf, 932 F. Supp. 676, 682, 70 FEP 1144 (D. Md. 1996) (court aided in its conclusion that no exception to naming requirement was applicable by fact that plaintiff was represented by

if the plaintiff was not represented by counsel when charges were filed.[21] This threshold requirement reflects the fact that the identity of interest exception was created, in part, "because [Title VII] charges generally are filed by parties not versed in the vagaries of Title VII and its jurisdictional pleading requirements."[22]

B. Circumstances in Which Joinder of an Unnamed Party Has Been Permitted

1. Joinder Where Injustice Would Otherwise Result to Plaintiff and Defendant Named in EEOC Charge

Courts have continued to rely upon the *Glus*[23] factors in deciding whether to join a third party not originally named in the charge.[24] Although courts maintain that they consider all of the *Glus* factors before deciding whether to allow joinder, the first factor—whether the role of the unnamed party could have been ascertained through reasonable efforts by the plaintiff at the time the EEOC complaint was filed—often receives little weight.[25]

---

counsel during entire administrative process) *and* Bonner v. Guccione, 68 FEP 47, 50 (S.D.N.Y. 1995) (finding significant the fact that plaintiff was represented by counsel at time EEOC complaint was filed). *But see* Sanders v. Bethlehem Steel Corp., 68 FEP 695, 699 (D. Md. 1995) (plaintiff's argument that she was unrepresented by counsel when charges were filed and EEOC investigator drafted them failed to persuade court to allow plaintiff to bring claims against unnamed defendant), *aff'd,* 91 F.3d 133 (4th Cir. 1996).
   [21]Sharkey v. Lasmo (Aul Ltd.), 906 F. Supp. 949, 954, 70 FEP 1673 (S.D.N.Y. 1995).
   [22]Johnson v. Palma, 931 F.2d 203, 209, 55 FEP 1173 (2d Cir. 1991).
   [23]Glus v. G.C. Murphy Co., 562 F.2d 880, 15 FEP 998 (3d Cir. 1977).
   [24]*See* Cook v. Arrowsmith Shelburne, Inc., 69 F.3d 1235, 1241–42, 69 FEP 392 (2d Cir. 1995) (applying *Glus* factors to find substantial identity of interest and thus lack of prejudice to unnamed party by allowing joinder as defendant); Winbush v. Iowa, 66 F.3d 1471, 1478 n.9, 69 FEP 1348 (8th Cir. 1995) (applying *Glus* factors to find that purpose of Title VII's notice and conciliation requirements had been met); Virgo v. Riviera Beach Assoc., 30 F.3d 1350, 1358–59, 65 FEP 1317 (11th Cir. 1994) (same); Aguirre v. McCaw RCC Communications, Inc., 923 F. Supp. 1431, 1433–34 (D. Kan. 1996) (*Glus* factors supported allowing joinder of unnamed party); Minetos v. City Univ. of N.Y., 875 F. Supp. 1046, 1051–52, 68 FEP 355 (S.D.N.Y. 1995) (same); Stafford v. Radford Community Hosp., Inc., 908 F. Supp. 1369, 1373 (W.D. Va. 1995) (applying *Glus* factors to find that plaintiff failed to meet burden that unnamed and named parties had substantial identity of interest), *aff'd,* 120 F.3d 262 (4th Cir. 1997).
   [25]*See* Cook v. Arrowsmith Shelburne, Inc., 69 F.3d 1235, 1242, 69 FEP 392 (2d Cir. 1995) (although likely that plaintiff could easily have included unnamed party

One court abandoned the *Glus* identity of interest test in favor of a simpler, less expensive test: joinder of unnamed parties is allowed only if necessary to preserve the plaintiff's Title VII remedies.[26] The court suggested that this new test "follows the plain language and purpose of the statute by limiting the parties in a civil suit to those who were named in the charge," while still protecting "an unsophisticated plaintiff . . . from the loss of a claim due to technical procedural grounds."[27] Other courts have considered whether a plaintiff will be left without a Title VII remedy as one factor to be weighed.[28]

3. Joinder Where There Is an Agency Relationship or Substantial Identity Between the Named Party and the Unnamed Defendant

Under the "substantial identity" or "functional identity" doctrine, courts continue to allow joinder where the named and unnamed parties are so interrelated that they should be considered one entity.[29] This doctrine has been applied where unnamed individuals were sued in their official capacities as representatives of named entities,[30] where named and unnamed entities were alleged

---

in the EEOC charge, *Glus* factors weighed in plaintiff's favor); Dortz v. City of N.Y., 904 F. Supp. 127, 142–43, 72 FEP 205 (S.D.N.Y. 1995) (same); Tout v. Erie Community College, 923 F. Supp. 13, 15–16 (W.D.N.Y. 1995) (same). *But see* Panis v. Mission Hills Bank, N.A., 68 FEP 1813, 1822 (D. Kan. 1994) (plaintiff not allowed to bring claims against individual defendants in part because she had knowledge of their participation in alleged discrimination at time charges were filed but failed to name them), *aff'd*, 60 F.3d 1486, 70 FEP 625 (10th Cir. 1995), *cert. denied*, 116 S. Ct. 1045 (1996).

[26]Armstead v. Becton Dickinson Primary Care Diagnostics, Inc., 919 F. Supp. 188, 191 (D. Md. 1996) (applying new test and noting intra-district split over whether to apply new test or *Glus* test).

[27]*Id.* at 192.

[28]*See, e.g.,* Secrist v. Burns Int'l Sec. Servs., 926 F. Supp. 823, 825, 71 FEP 162 (E.D. Wis. 1996) (before rejecting joinder of unnamed party, court considered whether plaintiff would be deprived of Title VII remedy); Johnson v. County of Cook, 864 F. Supp. 84, 87 (N.D. Ill. 1994) (court considered fact that if claims were not permitted against unnamed defendant, plaintiff would be left with no Title VII remedy because named defendant was not a suable entity).

[29]*E.g.,* Virgo v. Riviera Beach Assoc., 30 F.3d 1350, 1359, 65 FEP 1317 (11th Cir. 1994) (general partners "functionally identical" to partnership and should not be protected by naming requirement); Tietgen v. Brown's Westminster Motors, Inc., 921 F. Supp. 1495, 1498, 70 FEP 1020 (E.D. Va. 1996) ("substantial identity" between two auto dealerships).

[30]Collin v. Rector & Bd. of Visitors of Univ. of Va., 873 F. Supp. 1008, 1012 (W.D. Va. 1995) (plaintiff could bring claim against unnamed university dean in his

to be under common control,³¹ and where named and unnamed entities hold themselves out as being closely related.³²

The related but distinct identity of interest doctrine, derived from the four-prong test articulated in *Glus,* continues to be invoked in a variety of circumstances.³³ The identity of interest doctrine is

---

official capacity because he was "substantially identified" with named department); Duffy v. Southeastern Penn. Transp. Co., 67 FEP 1797, 1799 (E.D. Pa. 1995) (plaintiff could bring claims against unnamed supervisors in their official capacities because of "substantial identity" with named employer).

³¹Tietgen v. Brown's Westminster Motors, Inc., 921 F. Supp. 1495, 1498–99, 70 FEP 1020 (E.D. Va. 1996) (finding "substantial identity" where plaintiff alleged common control of named and unnamed auto dealerships, noting that the same persons exercised control over employment decisions at both dealerships).

³²Johnson v. County of Cook, 864 F. Supp. 84, 85–86 (N.D. Ill. 1994) (reasonable for plaintiff to assume substantial identity between unnamed county and named department of corrections where employment-related correspondence from department to plaintiff bore county seal).

³³Lawsuit allowed against unnamed defendant based on identity of interest: Cook v. Arrowsmith Shelburne, Inc., 69 F.3d 1235, 1241–42, 69 FEP 392 (2d Cir. 1995) (identity of interest between unnamed parent company and subsidiary); Winbush v. Iowa, 66 F.3d 1471, 1478 n.9, 69 FEP 1348 (8th Cir. 1995) (identity of interest between unnamed individual school officials and school); Virgo v. Riviera Beach Assoc., 30 F.3d 1350, 1358–59, 65 FEP 1317 (11th Cir. 1994) (identity of interest between unnamed sole owner and named employer); Aguirre v. McCaw RCC Communications, Inc., 923 F. Supp. 1431, 1433–34 (D. Kan. 1996) (identity of interest between unnamed employer and named unincorporated association); Rivera v. Puerto Rican Home Attendants Servs., Inc., 922 F. Supp. 943, 946–48 (S.D.N.Y. 1996) (identity of interest between unnamed city and named agency that provided services on behalf of city); Sharkey v. Lasmo (Aul Ltd.), 906 F. Supp. 949, 954–57, 70 FEP 1673 (S.D.N.Y. 1995) (identity of interest between unnamed employer and named prospective employer); Tout v. Erie Community College, 923 F. Supp. 13 (W.D.N.Y. 1995) (identity of interest between unnamed individuals employed by county and named county); Dortz v. City of N.Y., 904 F. Supp. 127, 142–43, 72 FEP 205 (S.D.N.Y. 1995) (identity of interest between unnamed medical services provider and named city and hospital); Minetos v. City Univ. of N.Y., 875 F. Supp. 1046, 1051, 68 FEP 355 (S.D.N.Y. 1995) (identity of interest between unnamed city university and professor and named college within city university system); Genas v. New York Dep't of Correctional Servs., 67 FEP 27, 32–33 (S.D.N.Y. 1994) (identity of interest between unnamed individuals employed by department of corrections and named department of corrections), *rev'd on other grounds,* 75 F.3d 825 (2d Cir. 1996); Gilmore v. List & Clark Constr. Co., 862 F. Supp. 294, 297–98 (D. Kan. 1994) (identity of interest between two unnamed employers and one named employer where plaintiff alleged joint control of operations).

Lawsuit not allowed against unnamed defendant based on lack of identity of interest: Stafford v. Radford Community Hosp., Inc., 908 F. Supp. 1369, 1372–73 (W.D. Va. 1995) (no identity of interest between unnamed affiliate organization and named hospital); Smith v. Sheet Metal Workers Local 28, 877 F. Supp. 165, 172–73, 148 LRRM 2856 (S.D.N.Y. 1995) (no identity of interest between various unnamed union members and named union and contractor), *aff'd,* 100 F.3d 943, 152

intended to ensure that the naming requirement's twin purposes of notifying the charged party of the allegations and allowing the party an opportunity to participate in conciliation efforts are met.[34] Courts invoking the doctrine generally focus on the second and third factors from *Glus:* whether the interests of the named and unnamed party are so similar that the unnamed party's presence in EEOC proceedings was unnecessary to obtain voluntary conciliation and compliance, and whether the unnamed party's absence from the proceedings resulted in actual prejudice.[35]

III. SCOPE OF EEOC CHARGE AS LIMITING THE SCOPE OF A TITLE VII LAWSUIT

C. Application of the *Sanchez* Doctrine

1. Basic Rationale

Courts continue to view the EEOC charge as an impetus for an EEOC investigation rather than a blueprint for litigation.[36] In determining how broadly to construe the EEOC charge, courts consider whether the employer had adequate notice and an opportunity to participate in conciliation and whether a strict applica-

---

LRRM 2384 (2d Cir.), *cert. denied,* 117 S. Ct. 101 (1996); Catanzaro v. Supervalu, Inc., 67 FEP 10, 12–13 (E.D. Mo. 1994) (no identity of interest between unnamed corporation and named employer where former became parent to latter after plaintiff's discharge); Dreisbach v. Cummins Diesel Engines, Inc., 848 F. Supp. 593, 595–96, 64 FEP 926 (E.D. Pa. 1994) (no identity of interest between unnamed corporation and its executives and named employer).

[34]*See* Virgo v. Riviera Beach Assoc., 30 F.3d 1350, 1358–59, 65 FEP 1317 (11th Cir. 1994).

[35]*See, e.g.,* Cook v. Arrowsmith Shelburne, Inc., 69 F.3d 1235, 1241–42, 69 FEP 392 (2d Cir. 1995) (applying identity of interest exception to naming requirement where factors two and three from *Glus* test weighed strongly in favor of plaintiff, though court found it arguable that plaintiff could easily have included unnamed defendant in the charge).

[36]*See, e.g.,* Cheek v. Western & S. Life Ins. Co., 31 F.3d 497, 500, 65 FEP 727 (7th Cir. 1994) (dual purpose of charge is to put defendant on notice of charges and to trigger EEOC investigation); Ajaz v. Continental Airlines, 156 F.R.D. 145, 147 (S.D. Tex. 1994) (primary purpose of charge is to provide notice to defendant, to activate voluntary compliance and conciliation functions of EEOC, and to trigger investigation); Collins v. Executive Airlines, Inc., 934 F. Supp. 1378, 1380 (S.D. Fla. 1996) (charge gives EEOC opportunity to investigate and allows conciliation of dispute without need to resort to litigation).

tion of the filing requirements would deprive a plaintiff of redress for any legitimate grievance.[37]

2. Issues Rooted in the Same Basis of Discrimination

What issues courts consider sufficiently "like and related" or "of the same type and character" to those specified in the EEOC charge continues to vary greatly.[38]

3. Suit Alleging a Basis of Discrimination Different From That Specified in the Charge

Courts continue to reject plaintiffs' attempts to bring a suit on a basis different from that specified in their charge.[39]

4. Incidents Occurring Subsequent to the Filing of the EEOC Charge

Most courts continue to allow retaliation claims for conduct alleged to be in retaliation for filing the initial charge.[40]

---

[37]Secrist v. Burns Int'l Sec. Servs., 926 F. Supp. 823, 825, 71 FEP 162 (E.D. Wis. 1996) (court strictly applied filing requirements to EEOC charge filed by pro se applicant where employer had no notice and applicant could still receive full relief under Title VII).

[38]Clemmer v. Enron Corp., 882 F. Supp. 606, 4 AD 437 (S.D. Tex. 1995) (age discrimination plaintiff's failure to assert reverse discrimination and sexual harassment claims in her EEOC charge precluded her from amending complaint as these claims do not "relate to" or "grow out of" age discrimination claim); Duffy v. Southeastern Penn. Transp. Co., 67 FEP 1797, 1800 (E.D. Pa. 1995) (claim that plaintiff was removed from job after announcing pregnancy fell within scope of charge alleging that employer discriminated by refusing to assign her light duty because of pregnancy); Riley v. Technical & Management Servs. Corp., 872 F. Supp. 1454, 1459, 66 FEP 1643 (D. Md. 1995) (sexual harassment not like and related to sexual discrimination), *aff'd,* 79 F.3d 1141, 70 FEP 832 (4th Cir. 1996).

[39]Evans v. Technologies Applications & Servs. Co., 875 F. Supp. 1115, 1123, 72 FEP 1215 (D. Md. 1995) (age discrimination is not like or related to sex discrimination). *See also* Clemmer v. Enron Corp., 882 F. Supp. 606, 4 AD 437 (S.D. Tex. 1995) *and* Riley v. Technical & Management Servs. Corp., 872 F. Supp. 1454, 66 FEP 1643 (D. Md. 1995), *aff'd,* 79 F.3d 1141, 70 FEP 832 (4th Cir. 1996). *Cf.* Clements v. St. Vincent's Hosp. & Med. Ctr., 919 F. Supp. 161, 163 (S.D.N.Y. 1996) (where charge alleges race but not national origin discrimination, latter not barred because race and national origin discrimination claims are "of the same type and character").

[40]Saladin v. Turner, 936 F. Supp. 1571, 1580 (N.D. Okla. 1996) ("retaliatory acts occurring after filing of EEOC charge are reasonably related to the original charge obviating the need for a new or amended charge"); Rivera v. Puerto Rican Home Attendants Servs., Inc., 930 F. Supp. 124, 128–29 (S.D.N.Y. 1996) (if retaliation

5. The Suit Alleges Classwide Discrimination But the Charge Relates to Individual Treatment

Courts continue to hold that where the EEOC charge relates to individual treatment, but the ensuing lawsuit alleges classwide discrimination, the initial EEOC charge must put the employer on notice of the class-based nature of the allegations.[41] Litigants not parties to the EEOC charge normally may not expand the scope of the litigation beyond that properly presented by the charging party.[42] Where the EEOC itself seeks to litigate or intervene, some courts have not insisted on strict identity between the charge and the complaint.[43]

IV. MOOTNESS

Transferring a plaintiff to another work area does not moot his or her request for a permanent injunction.[44]

---

alleged for filing of initial EEOC charge, filing additional charge not necessary); Edwards v. Nederland Indep. Sch. Dist., 930 F. Supp. 272, 276 (E.D. Tex. 1996) (court has jurisdiction even where EEOC charge alleges discrimination but fails to allege retaliation); Daulo v. Commonwealth Edison, 892 F. Supp. 1088, 1093, 72 FEP 1566 (N.D. Ill. 1995) ("For retaliation for the filing of the base EEOC charge itself, no subsequent EEOC charge is required."); Webb v. District of Columbia, 864 F. Supp. 175, 184, 73 FEP 451 (D.D.C. 1994) (where charge alleges both discrimination and retaliation, similar acts occurring subsequent to charge are properly before court despite plaintiff's failure to amend or file new charge).

[41]Binion v. Metropolitan Pier & Exposition Auth., 163 F.R.D. 517, 528 (N.D. Ill. 1995) (although EEOC charge explicitly alleged only individual discrimination, class action upheld since facts in charge implied classwide discrimination); Mooney v. Aramco Serv. Co., 54 F.3d 1207, 1223 (5th Cir. 1995) (where plaintiff filed own individual EEOC charge, he has excluded himself from joining class because filing of individual charge failed to put defendant on notice of nature and scope of class).

[42]Brooks v. Bellsouth Telecommunications, Inc., 164 F.R.D. 561 (N.D. Ala. 1995) (opt-in plaintiffs may not piggyback claims on representative plaintiff's timely EEOC charge where opt-ins' claims do not arise out of the same discrimination), *aff'd*, 114 F.3d 1202 (11th Cir. 1997); Grayson v. KMart Corp., 79 F.3d 1086, 1104, 70 FEP 1086 (11th Cir.) (charge failed to put defendant on notice of scope of class alleging acts after filing of charge), *cert. denied*, 117 S. Ct. 435 *and* 117 S. Ct. 447 (1996).

[43]EEOC v. Air Line Employees, 885 F. Supp. 289, 293, 67 FEP 289 (D.D.C. 1995) ("EEOC has independent authority to file civil suit based on new claim arising from investigation of valid charge provided that the additional discrimination is included in the reasonable cause determination followed by compliance with proper conciliation procedures" to effectuate EEOC's broad remedial purpose).

[44]Dombeck v. Milwaukee Valve Co., 40 F.3d 230, 238, 66 FEP 497 (7th Cir. 1994) (plaintiff's request for permanent injunction in sexual harassment suit not mooted

V. VENUE

Courts continue to apply the specific venue provisions for Title VII.[45] If venue cannot be had in any of the districts specified by statute, the courts continue to look to the district where the employer's principal office is located.[46] Since the plaintiff has the burden of establishing proper venue, a mere allegation by plaintiff that the alleged unlawful employment decision was made in a particular state will be insufficient to establish venue where there is contradictory evidence.[47]

There is some authority that venue in ADA suits is governed by 42 U.S.C. § 2000e-5(f)(3), rather than by 28 U.S.C. § 1391.[48]

Where improper venue has been shown, courts have continued to transfer, rather than dismiss, actions to the proper district.[49]

---

by transfer to another work area because, unless injunction entered, employer could alter current work assignments).

[45]42 U.S.C. § 2000e-5(f)(3); Launer v. Buena Vista Winery, Inc., 916 F. Supp. 204, 212 (E.D.N.Y. 1996) (denying defendant's motion to dismiss Title VII claims for improper venue where a substantial part of the events giving rise to the discrimination claim occurred in New York); Wexler v. Runyon, 5 AD 896 (S.D.N.Y. 1996) (granting defendant's motion to transfer venue to New Jersey where plaintiff was hired by, worked for, and was fired by a New Jersey post office, and where all records and witnesses pertinent to the action were located in New Jersey); Blazy v. Woolsey, 64 FEP 724 (D.D.C. 1994) (granting defendant's motion to transfer venue to the Eastern District of Virginia notwithstanding a factual dispute as to whether any employment records were maintained in the District of Columbia where the relevant conduct occurred in Virginia and it appeared that, but for the alleged unlawful employment practices, plaintiff would have continued to work in Virginia).

[46]42 U.S.C. § 2000e-5(f)(3); Worthy v. Aspin, 64 FEP 65 (W.D. Pa.1994) (granting motion to transfer venue to the Eastern District of Virginia where the alleged discrimination occurred in Japan and Okinawa, plaintiff's employment records were maintained in Okinawa, plaintiff would have continued to work in Japan had he not been terminated, and defendant Les Aspin's principal office, the Pentagon, was located in the Eastern District of Virginia).

[47]Zughni v. Pena, 851 F. Supp. 300, 302–03 (N.D. Ill. 1994) (granting defendants' motion to transfer venue where plaintiff made only an unsupported assertion that the decision to terminate her was made in Illinois but defendants provided documentation supporting their contention that the disputed decision was made in Cleveland), *aff'd*, 56 F.3d 82 (Fed. Cir. 1995).

[48]Chubb v. Union Pacific R.R., 908 F. Supp. 853, 854–55, 5 AD 270 (D. Colo. 1995) (holding that § 2000e-5(f)(3) is applicable to actions brought under the ADA).

[49]Zughni v. Pena, 851 F. Supp. 300 (N.D. Ill. 1994) (granting defendant's motion to transfer and denying defendant's motion to dismiss for improper venue), *aff'd*, 56 F.3d 82 (Fed. Cir. 1995); Blazy v. Woolsey, 64 FEP 724 (D.D.C. 1994) (same); Worthy v. Aspin, 64 FEP 65 (W.D. Pa. 1994) (same).

VI. Summary Judgment

Most summary judgment motions in disparate treatment cases continue to be decided on the issue of pretext.[50] However, there are still disparate treatment cases in which defendants prevail because plaintiffs are simply unable to establish a prima facie case of discrimination.[51] Most courts have granted summary judgment

---

[50]*E.g.,* Long v. Eastfield College, 88 F.3d 300, 308, 71 FEP 750 (5th Cir. 1996) (reversing grant of summary judgment to employer as to Title VII retaliation claim where the employer alleged that plaintiffs were terminated for procedural violations but plaintiffs offered deposition and affidavit testimony that the procedure in question was inconsistently applied); Hartsel v. Keys, 87 F.3d 795, 800–02, 72 FEP 951 (6th Cir. 1996) (affirming summary judgment against plaintiff who claimed age and sex discrimination but failed to rebut her employer's claim that she was not promoted because she lacked the requisite computer skills), *cert. denied,* 117 S. Ct. 683 (1997); Tomsic v. State Farm Mut. Auto. Ins. Co., 85 F.3d 1472, 1478–79, 71 FEP 137 (10th Cir. 1996) (reversing grant of summary judgment to employer on former employees' claims of gender discrimination where employer claimed that the employees had been terminated for poor performance but supervisor had told one plaintiff that production was not the most important factor in succeeding, and he had told others, soon after he became another plaintiff's supervisor but months before her termination, that she would be fired); Rothmeier v. Investment Advisers, Inc., 85 F.3d 1328, 1335–37, 71 FEP 1458 (8th Cir. 1996) (trial judge may decide on a summary judgment motion that the evidence is insufficient for a reasonable trier of fact to infer age discrimination where plaintiff was hired at age 43 by supervisor, who was age 50 at the time; plaintiff was fired only three years later at age 46; and plaintiff's problems with his supervisor were unrelated to age); Wolf v. Buss (America), Inc., 77 F.3d 914, 920, 70 FEP 130 (7th Cir.) (affirming grant of summary judgment to employer where age discrimination plaintiff raised fact issues as to four of the employer's proffered reasons for plaintiff's termination but those reasons were neither so intertwined or "fishy" as to call into doubt the employer's two credible reasons for the termination), *cert. denied,* 117 S. Ct. 175 (1996); Cronin v. Aetna Life Ins. Co., 46 F.3d 196, 205–06, 66 FEP 1727 (2d Cir. 1995) (finding, in an age discrimination case arising out of a corporate reorganization, that material issues of fact as to whether the employer failed to consider plaintiff for positions for which he was best qualified precluded summary judgment); Fuentes v. Perskie, 32 F.3d 759, 764, 65 FEP 890 (3d Cir. 1994) (holding that, to avoid summary judgment under Title VII, plaintiff need not "cast doubt on each proffered [nondiscriminatory] reason [for the adverse employment action] in a vacuum.... If the defendant proffers a bagful of legitimate reasons, and the plaintiff manages to cast substantial doubt on a fair number of them, plaintiff may not need to discredit the remainder.").

[51]*E.g.,* Lowe v. Angelo's Italian Foods, Inc., 87 F.3d 1170, 1175–76, 5 AD 1064 (10th Cir. 1996) (Title VII plaintiff's claim of discriminatory discharge based upon her sex failed because she could not establish a prima facie case where she had not shown that her job remained available after her termination; retaliation claim failed because plaintiff could not establish a prima facie case where she produced no evidence of a causal connection between her termination and her protected activities); Mills v. First Fed. Sav. & Loan Ass'n, 83 F.3d 833, 843, 70 FEP 1263 (7th Cir. 1996)

in favor of defendants, regardless of whether or not the plaintiff could establish a prima facie case of discrimination, where the plaintiff was unable to produce evidence creating a genuine issue of material fact as to the defendant's legitimate, nondiscriminatory reason for its adverse employment action.[52] Some courts have cautioned, however, that summary judgment ought not to be granted too readily where a plaintiff claims intentional discrimination, since evidence of a defendant's intent or motive is uniquely available to the defendant.[53]

VII. JURY TRIAL

Following the Supreme Court's decision in *Landgraf v. USI Film Products*,[54] the courts are split on whether a plaintiff is entitled to a jury trial if he or she filed his or her Title VII lawsuit after the enactment date of the 1991 Civil Rights Act, or only if the alleged discriminatory conduct occurred after that date.[55] When

---

(ADEA plaintiff did not establish a prima facie case of discriminatory discharge where she failed to show that she was performing her job of quality control auditor well enough to meet her employer's legitimate expectations); Geraci v. Moody-Tottrup Int'l, Inc., 82 F.3d 578, 582, 70 FEP 1288 (3d Cir. 1996) (employee claiming she was terminated because of her pregnancy did not establish prima facie case where she had not been visibly pregnant, had not told her employer that she was pregnant, and produced no evidence that her employer in fact knew she was pregnant); McLaughlin v. Esselte Pendaflex Corp., 50 F.3d 507, 511–12, 67 FEP 474 (8th Cir. 1995) (plaintiff failed to establish a prima facie case of gender discrimination since she had not demonstrated that she was qualified for the position she desired or that her reassignment occurred under circumstances that would allow the court to infer that it was motivated by discrimination).

[52]*E.g.*, EEOC v. Our Lady of Resurrection Med. Ctr., 77 F.3d 145, 149–50, 70 FEP 104 (7th Cir. 1996) (summary judgment appropriate where the EEOC failed to demonstrate that the employer's legitimate, nondiscriminatory reason for terminating an employee—her failure to fulfill necessary licensing requirements—was pretextual, whether or not the EEOC could establish a prima facie case of discrimination).

[53]*E.g.*, Collier v. Budd Co., 66 F.3d 886, 892, 68 FEP 1435 (7th Cir. 1995) (summary judgment motions in employment discrimination cases must be approached with added rigor since credibility and intent are often central issues); Courtney v. Biosound, Inc., 42 F.3d 414, 418, 66 FEP 971 (7th Cir. 1994) (cautioning that evidence directly supporting claims of intentional discrimination is rare and that affidavits and depositions should be carefully scrutinized for circumstantial proof).

[54]511 U.S. 244, 64 FEP 820 (1994).

[55]*Compare* Craig v. O'Leary, 870 F. Supp. 1007, 1010, 69 FEP 452 (D. Colo. 1994) (although alleged discriminatory conduct occurred before enactment of the 1991 Civil Rights Act, jury trial right applies because lawsuit was filed after the

the Title VII plaintiff alleges discriminatory conduct occurring both before and after the enactment date, some courts have held that the right to compensatory and punitive damages, as well as to a jury trial, applies only to those claims arising from conduct occurring after the enactment date, requiring a bifurcated trial with preenactment claims decided by the court and postenactment claims decided by the jury.[56] However, at least one district court has declined to bifurcate when faced with this situation, instead holding that the plaintiffs could try both their pre and postenactment claims to the jury.[57]

---

enactment date) *with* Sena v. Denver Sch. Dist. No. 1, 902 F. Supp. 218, 220, 69 FEP 385 (D. Colo. 1995) (criticizing *Craig* and holding that under *Landgraf* the right to a jury trial applies only if the allegedly discriminatory conduct occurred after the enactment of the 1991 Civil Rights Act) *and* Hirschinger v. Allstate Ins. Co., 884 F. Supp. 317, 319, 69 FEP 997 (S.D. Ind. 1994) (noting that "*Landgraf* has made November 21, 1991, a day of utmost importance for civil rights litigants" and holding that the plaintiff had no right to a jury trial because no discriminatory conduct was alleged to have occurred after this date).

[56]*E.g.*, Amin v. Quad/Graphics, Inc., 929 F. Supp. 73, 79–80 (N.D.N.Y. 1996) (rejecting plaintiff's argument that the "continuing nature" of the discriminatory conduct creates a jury trial right for both pre and postenactment conduct and holding that the plaintiff was limited to equitable relief and a nonjury trial on the preenactment conduct); Hatley v. Store Kraft Mfg. Co., 859 F. Supp. 1257, 1259, 70 FEP 1361 (D. Neb. 1994) ("Since this case involved *both* pre-act and post-act conduct, it was necessary to bifurcate consideration of these issues [between the judge and the jury] in order to be faithful to *Landgraf*." (original emphasis)).

[57]Mills v. Amoco Performance Prods., 872 F. Supp. 975, 986, 74 FEP 835 (S.D. Ga. 1994) (declining to bifurcate trial; both the pre and postenactment claims shared common issues, and the court would be bound by the jury's determination of the postenactment claim as it affects disposition of the accompanying preenactment claim).

CHAPTER 34

EEOC LITIGATION

II. ADMINISTRATIVE PREREQUISITES TO SUIT

A. Administrative Prerequisites to Suit Under § 706 and the ADEA

1. *A Timely Charge*

The EEOC may bring suit on behalf of several aggrieved persons even if only one of them files a timely charge, as long as the charge contains "sufficient information to notify defendant of its potential liability . . . and to permit the EEOC to engage in conciliation of all . . . claims."[1] Where there is such a timely charge, the EEOC may sue on behalf of others whose claims it learns of through its investigation of that charge, even when the EEOC eventually decides not to pursue the charging party's claims.[2] However, the EEOC may not use a timely charge to "piggyback" untimely claims that are not part of a "continuous and ongoing course of discriminatory conduct."[3] Moreover, the EEOC is precluded from pursuing claims after it consents to the withdrawal of the filed charge.[4]

A timely filed charge is not a prerequisite to judicial enforcement of an EEOC subpoena or to the EEOC's jurisdiction to investigate allegations of discrimination unless it is apparent from the face of the charge, "otherwise apparent," or conceded that the charge is untimely.[5]

---

[1] EEOC v. Sara Lee Corp., 923 F. Supp. 994, 999, 70 FEP 57 (W.D. Mich. 1995) (four employees covered by one charge concerning single reduction in force).
[2] EEOC v. Air Line Pilots, 885 F. Supp. 289, 293, 67 FEP 1363 (D.D.C. 1995).
[3] EEOC v. Harvey L. Walner & Assocs., 1995 U.S. Dist. LEXIS 11239, at *15 (EEOC "cannot revive claims which are no longer viable") (N.D. Ill. Aug. 2, 1996), *aff'd,* 91 F.3d 963, 71 FEP 683 (7th Cir. 1996).
[4] *Id.* at **19–20.
[5] EEOC v. City of Norfolk Police Dep't, 45 F.3d 80, 83, 66 FEP 1425 (4th Cir. 1995).

3. Investigation

Generally, "the EEOC may not continue an administrative investigation ... once the charging party has been issued a right to sue letter."[6] As a result, courts will deny enforcement of an EEOC subpoena after issuance of right-to-sue letters.[7]

The courts continue to reject suits naming the EEOC as a defendant on claims alleging failure to properly process and investigate charges.[8] In addition, EEOC investigators' memoranda may be sheltered from disclosure under the Freedom of Information Act to the extent they are protected by the "deliberative process privilege."[9]

4. Reasonable Cause Determination

The admissibility of EEOC cause determinations was extensively examined by the Sixth Circuit in *EEOC v. Ford Motor Co.*[10] The court found that "district courts should be free to adopt a general rule that refuses to admit these cause determinations in any sort of trial, whether to the court or to a jury" because the courts' factfinding process should not be influenced by "what the EEOC thought the facts were when it brought the case before the district court."[11] The court concluded that an EEOC cause determination

---

[6] EEOC v. Hearst Corp., 103 F.3d 462, 469, 72 FEP 1541 (5th Cir. 1997) (also suggesting that the courts have been too lenient in failing to require EEOC to adhere to strict timetables in the processing of charges, with the consequence that cases often end up in "administrative limbo" for years).

[7] *Id.*

[8] Reed v. EEOC, 100 F.3d 957, *reported in full at* 1996 U.S. App. LEXIS 29032, *3–4 (6th Cir. 1996), *cert. denied,* 117 S. Ct. 1564 (1997); Garcia v. International Rehabilitation Assocs., 1994 U.S. App. LEXIS 19125, at *3 (9th Cir. July 25, 1994); Materson v. Stokes, 166 F.R.D. 368, 371, 70 FEP 1630 (E.D. Va. 1996); Adams v. EEOC, 932 F. Supp. 660, 663, 70 FEP 1357 (E.D. Pa. 1996); Dillon v. EEOC, 1996 U.S. Dist. LEXIS 68, at **2–3 (E.D. La. Jan. 3, 1996); Forbes v. Reno, 893 F. Supp. 476, 482, 73 FEP 51 (W.D. Pa. 1995), *aff'd,* 91 F.3d 123 (3d Cir. 1996); Baba v. Warren Management Consultants, Inc., 882 F. Supp. 339, 341, 74 FEP 707 (S.D.N.Y.), *aff'd,* 89 F.3d 826 (2d Cir. 1995); Kurian v. Social Serv. Employees Union Local 371, 1995 U.S. Dist. LEXIS 17951, at *5 (S.D.N.Y. Nov. 30, 1995).

[9] Greyson v. McKenna & Cuneo, 879 F. Supp. 1065, 1069, 67 FEP 792 (D. Colo. 1995) ("facts intertwined with the agency's policy and decision-making processes are protected" unless "adopted or incorporated by reference into the agency's final decision").

[10] 1996 WL 557800, at *5 (6th Cir. Sept. 30, 1996).

[11] *Id.* at *9–10.

"carries an evidentiary value of practically zero."[12] A concurring judge would have prohibited the EEOC from using cause determinations in its own litigation, but would have permitted their use in private litigation.[13]

Meanwhile, the Fifth Circuit has explained that while it considers EEOC determinations of reasonable cause to be presumptively admissible, district courts still retain discretion regarding the admissibility of such letters.[14] Moreover, the court found that an EEOC "letter of violation" is more likely to be excluded than a "letter of reasonable cause" because the former threatens greater prejudice by stating a "categorical legal conclusion," while the latter is "more tentative."[15]

Admissibility of no-cause determinations may soon be an issue of historical interest only since the EEOC's 1996 Enforcement Plan dispensed with the practice of issuing no-cause determinations.[16]

5. Conciliation

Generally, the courts continue to be lenient in construing the EEOC's obligation to engage in conciliation prior to litigation.[17] Even if there has been a failure of conciliation efforts by the EEOC, the courts continue to hold that the proper remedy for the EEOC's failure to conciliate is a stay of the proceedings to allow additional conciliation rather than dismissal of the EEOC's suit.[18]

---

[12]*Id.* at n.10.

[13]*Id.* at *13 (Wellford, J., concurring).

[14]EEOC v. Manville Sales Corp., 27 F.3d 1089, 1095, 65 FEP 804 (5th Cir. 1994), *cert. denied,* 513 U.S. 1190, 67 FEP 1632 (1995).

[15]*Id.*

[16]EEOC, *"National Enforcement Plan,"* Feb. 9, 1996 DAILY LAB. REP. (BNA) at E-1.

[17]EEOC v. Sara Lee Corp., 923 F. Supp. 994, 999–1000, 70 FEP 57 (W.D. Mich. 1995) (declining to dismiss or stay action where EEOC submitted no proof that it discussed the merits of individual claims for which relief was sought with defendant); *accord* EEOC v. Dolphin Cruise Line, 945 F. Supp. 1550, 1557, 6 AD 187 (S.D. Fla. 1996); EEOC v. Johnson & Higgins, Inc., 887 F. Supp. 682, 689, 68 FEP 1481 (S.D.N.Y. 1995), *aff'd,* 91 F.3d 1529, 71 FEP 818 (2d Cir. 1996), *cert. denied,* 118 S. Ct. 47, 74 FEP 1791 (1997); EEOC v. Acorn Niles Corp., 1995 U.S. Dist. LEXIS 12649, at *16 (N.D. Ill. Aug. 29, 1995); *but see* EEOC v. Warshawsky & Co., 1994 U.S. Dist. LEXIS 10058, at **7–8 (N.D. Ill. July 19, 1994) (EEOC may not receive relief for pre-1984 pregnant employees because it did not conciliate with the employer with respect to that group).

[18]EEOC v. City of Chicago, 66 FEP 224, 226 (N.D. Ill. 1994).

Failure of conciliation neither signals that the EEOC's administrative process has ended nor starts the clock for filing suit: "the EEOC has power to take administrative actions . . . until the matter is formally closed or referred to litigation."[19]

III. EEOC INTERNAL PROCESSES

B. Organization of the Office of General Counsel

2. Processing EEOC Suits Under § 706(f)(1)

The EEOC rescinded the "full investigation" policy, the "Policy Statement on Remedies and Relief for Individual Cases of Unlawful Discrimination," and the "Statement of Enforcement Policy" on April 19, 1995.[20] Simultaneously, the EEOC eliminated its practice of issuing a "no cause" finding when an investigation did not establish reasonable cause to believe discrimination had occurred and called for development of a National Enforcement Plan to "identify priority issues and set out a plan for administrative and litigation enforcement."[21] Additionally, the operations of the Office of General Counsel were altered in the following ways: (1) the General Counsel was requested to authorize regional attorneys to cease submitting recommendations against litigation and to stop submitting presentation memoranda concerning cases to be referred to the Department of Justice; (2) the General Counsel was authorized to make a final decision whether to litigate a case when the district director and regional attorney disagree; (3) the General Counsel was given final litigation authority over "individual claims of disparate treatment not rising to a pattern of discrimination" under Title VII and the ADEA; and (4) the General Counsel was requested to "develop further standards for delegation of litigation authority" to the regional attorneys.[22] Subsequently, the General Counsel did in fact delegate a certain amount of litigation authority to the regional attorneys.[23]

---

[19]EEOC v. CNA Ins. Cos., 96 F.3d 1039, 1042, 5 AD 1769 (7th Cir. 1996).
[20]"EEOC Adopts Charge-Priority Sys.; Gives General Counsel More Authority," Apr. 20, 1995 DAILY LAB. REP. (BNA) at AA-1, E-5.
[21]*Id.* at E-5.
[22]*Id.*
[23]"EEOC Sets Charge, Litigation Priorities; Delegates Authority to General Counsel," Feb. 9, 1996 DAILY LAB. REP. (BNA) at AA-1; "Commissioners Question

4. Processing Actions for Preliminary Relief

The EEOC's National Enforcement Plan establishes three areas of national priority: (1) "cases involving violations of established anti-discrimination principles," (2) cases with "the potential of promoting the development of [the] law," and (3) "cases involving the integrity or effectiveness of the Commission's enforcement process."[24] Presumably, the last category will continue to dominate the EEOC's attempts to obtain preliminary relief.

IV. EEOC Suits in the Nature of Class Actions

Courts continue to recognize the EEOC's authority to bring suits that could not be brought as class actions by private individuals.[25] For example, by incorporating the enforcement procedures of the FLSA, the ADEA authorizes the EEOC to intervene on behalf of multiple plaintiffs "whether or not they are similarly situated, common questions of law or fact predominate, or claims arise out of the same action or occurrence," as would be required for a class action under the FRCP.[26]

In an odd twist on the consequences of the breadth of the EEOC's authority to sue employers "on its own authority to vindicate the public interest," the EEOC is not necessarily "the aggrieved parties' *de facto* counsel."[27] One court, therefore, has concluded that an employer may communicate a settlement offer directly to "former employees who never filed a charge of discrimination and have not sought the EEOC's representation."[28] In contrast, another court held that where a charging party communicated with EEOC attorneys about matters relating to the lawsuit believing that an attorney-client relationship existed, but without formally seeking

---

General Counsel About Drop in Number of Cases Litigated," Oct. 23, 1996 DAILY LAB. REP. (BNA) at A-14.

[24]EEOC, "National Enforcement Plan," Feb. 9, 1996 DAILY LAB. REP. (BNA) at E-2, E-3.

[25]EEOC v. Air Line Pilots, 885 F. Supp. 289, 291–92, 67 FEP 1363 (D.D.C. 1995) (Title VII religion case).

[26]Flavel v. Svedala Indus., Inc., 875 F. Supp. 550, 553–54, 75 FEP 915 (E.D. Wis. 1994) (internal quotations omitted).

[27]EEOC v. McDonnell Douglas Corp., 948 F. Supp. 54, 55 (E.D. Mo. 1996).

[28]*Id.*

EEOC representation, such communications were shielded by the attorney-client privilege.[29]

V. STATUTES OF LIMITATIONS AND LACHES

A. Statutes of Limitations

1. Title VII and ADA

Courts continue to follow *Occidental Life Insurance Co. v. EEOC*[30] in permitting the EEOC to reach back more than 300 days prior to the charge in its litigation.[31]

The EEOC is barred from litigating claims of disability discrimination occurring prior to the effective date of the ADA.[32]

Statute of limitations issues also may arise when the EEOC attempts to add parties during litigation. Rule 15(c)(3) of the FRCP governs whether claims against a newly added party will "relate back" to the date of the original complaint. If the new claims do not relate back under Rule 15(c)(3), they may be barred.[33] In the Sixth Circuit, Rule 15(c)(3) is understood only to allow for "correction of misnomers"; thus, any amendment "which adds a new party creates a new cause of action and there is no relation back."[34]

2. ADEA and Equal Pay Act

Courts continue to hold that there is no statute of limitations for ADEA actions filed by the EEOC.[35]

---

[29]EEOC v. Chemtech Int'l Corp., 1995 U.S. Dist. LEXIS 21877, 4 AD 1465, 1466 (S.D. Tex. 1995) (communications between individual plaintiff and EEOC similar to "communications between a party and the attorney for a co-litigant").

[30]432 U.S. 355, 359, 14 FEP 1718 (1977).

[31]EEOC v. Warshawsky & Co., 1994 U.S. Dist. LEXIS 10058, at **4–5 (N.D. Ill. July 19, 1994) (allowing EEOC to bring suit on behalf of employees injured more than 300 days before first filed charge but cutting off certain claims as barred by laches).

[32]EEOC v. Knoll North Am., Inc., 1996 WL 544264, at *4 (W.D. Mich. May 2, 1996).

[33]EEOC v. Regency Windsor Management Co., 862 F. Supp. 189, 190, 65 FEP 1777 (W.D. Mich. 1994) (citing cases).

[34]*Id.*

[35]Wilkerson v. Martin-Marietta Corp., 875 F. Supp. 1456, 1459, 67 FEP 279 (D. Colo. 1995); EEOC v. Sara Lee Corp., 923 F. Supp. 994, 999, 70 FEP 57 (W.D. Mich. 1995).

B. Laches

The biggest stumbling block an employer faces in asserting the defense of laches is proving that it suffered material prejudice due to the EEOC's unreasonable delay; the accrual of additional back-pay liability, without more, does not amount to material prejudice.[36]

VI. Scope of the Litigation

B. Expansion of Basis and Issue

One district court concluded that under either the "like or related" standard or the "scope of investigation" standard a failure-to-accommodate religion charge by a current employee could properly serve as a vehicle for the EEOC to litigate possible religious discrimination in the employer's hiring practices.[37]

VII. The Relationship Between EEOC Suits and Private Suits

A. The EEOC's Right to File Suit in Addition to a Private Suit

Despite its criticism of the EEOC for "insisting on pressing on with its own duplicative suit," the Seventh Circuit held that the EEOC has "an unequivocal statutory right to sue to enforce the age-discrimination law."[38] The district court was, however, well within its authority to preclude the EEOC from redeposing previously deposed witnesses, examining or cross-examining trial witnesses, making lengthy opening and closing arguments, or otherwise duplicating the efforts of the employee's counsel.[39]

---

[36]EEOC v. Acorn Niles Corp., 1995 U.S. Dist. LEXIS 12649, at **14–15 (N.D. Ill. Aug. 29, 1995) (four-year delay by EEOC, including 21-month period where EEOC "did nothing at all," was unreasonable in a case against a small employer; however, mere showing that back-pay liability might extend for a longer period, absent witness unavailability or other factors, "will not suffice to demonstrate prejudice").

[37]EEOC v. Dillard Dep't Stores, 1994 WL 738971, *3. (E.D. Mo. 1994).

[38]EEOC v. G-K-G, Inc., 39 F.3d 740, 744, 66 FEP 344 (7th Cir. 1994).

[39]*Id.* at 745.

The traditional rule that an EEOC suit under the ADEA bars subsequent private actions does not prevent private parties from opting into a private collective action when their motion had not been acted upon at the time the EEOC filed suit.[40] On the other hand, plaintiffs who attempted to opt in after the EEOC filed its complaint were barred.[41]

B. Rights of Charging Parties When EEOC Has Filed Suit

While individuals may intervene as a matter of right following the filing of a Title VII suit by the EEOC,[42] intervention may be denied as untimely where late intervention would prejudice the existing parties by, for example, disturbing settlement negotiations,[43] adding tenuous state law claims or unrelated parties,[44] or interfering with efforts to terminate a consent decree that "has long outlived its original purpose."[45]

When a suit involves both the EEOC and private plaintiffs, questions sometimes arise concerning what attorney's fees are proper for the private plaintiffs' attorneys. While courts will not deny attorney's fees simply because the EEOC commenced or was involved in the litigation,[46] courts have often reduced fee requests by such plaintiffs to reflect the duplication of work done by the EEOC.[47]

---

[40]Wilkerson v. Martin Marietta Corp., 875 F. Supp. 1456, 1463–64, 67 FEP 279 (D. Colo. 1995) (option notices considered "functionally equivalent to bringing an action under the ADEA").

[41]*Id.*

[42]EEOC v. Federal Express Corp., 1995 WL 569446, at *4 (W.D. Wash. Aug. 8, 1995) (permitting intervention despite delay on ground that defendant had not been prejudiced).

[43]EEOC v. New York Times, 1995 U.S. Dist. LEXIS 3838, at **6–7 (S.D.N.Y. Mar. 24, 1995).

[44]EEOC v. Domino's Pizza, Inc., 870 F. Supp. 655, 657, 66 FEP 888 (D. Md. 1994). *See also* EEOC v. Dillard Dep't Stores, Inc., 1994 U.S. Dist. LEXIS 10358, at **5–6 (E.D. La. July 26, 1994) (dismissal of claims under state fair employment law).

[45]EEOC v. United Air Lines, 1995 U.S. Dist. LEXIS 2581, at *9 (N.D. Ill. Mar. 2, 1995).

[46]EEOC v. State, County & Municipal Employees, 1996 WL 663971, at *4 (N.D.N.Y. Nov. 12, 1996).

[47]EEOC v. Clear Lake Dodge, 60 F.3d 1146, 1154–55, 68 FEP 663 (5th Cir. 1995) (on remand, court should deduct for "redundant and unnecessary" work of private counsel); EEOC v. AIC Sec. Investigations, Ltd., 1994 U.S. Dist. LEXIS 10368, at *17 (N.D. Ill. July 27, 1994) (where three EEOC trial attorneys handled "the bulk of the trial and the preparation" for trial, attorney's fee reduction of 50% was appropriate).

VIII. Preliminary Relief

C. Standards for Relief

Standards for granting the EEOC preliminary relief remain unsettled. The threat of immediate and irreparable injury to an EEOC investigation has been found, not surprisingly, sufficient to justify a temporary restraining order to prevent the destruction of employee records.[48] Actions that "might constitute retaliation" for making complaints to the EEOC were found sufficient to justify a preliminary injunction prohibiting the employer from entering into "any ADR policy which would cause an employee to pay the costs of ADR proceedings" or "preclude or interfere with" an employee's right to file a complaint with the EEOC or subsequently sue under Title VII.[49]

IX. Discovery Against the EEOC

A defendant will not be allowed to depose an EEOC attorney unless the defendant can show that there is no other way to obtain relevant, nonprivileged information that is crucial to the defendant's preparation of the case.[50] Moreover, EEOC attorney work product will be protected from disclosure unless the underlying information is unobtainable by any other means.[51]

X. Settlement

Whether EEOC intervention will reduce or enhance private plaintiffs' chances of obtaining a satisfactory settlement will depend on the particular case and parties.[52] In the high-profile Texaco

---

[48]EEOC v. Cornwell Personnel Assocs., 1995 U.S. Dist. LEXIS 19930, at **1–2 (E.D. Wis. Aug. 15, 1995).

[49]EEOC v. River Oaks Imaging & Diagnostic, 67 FEP 1243, 1243–44 (S.D. Tex. 1995).

[50]EEOC v. HBE Corp., 157 F.R.D. 465, 466 (E.D. Mo. 1994).

[51]*Id.* (because the EEOC turned over investigation reports and identified witnesses, the EEOC's work product based on that information was protected from disclosure).

[52]*See* EEOC v. G-K-G, Inc., 39 F.3d 740, 744, 66 FEP 344 (7th Cir. 1994).

race discrimination class action, the EEOC initially indicated that it was not satisfied with a settlement that provided $176.1 million to class members because, in the EEOC's view, the equitable relief was insufficient.[53] The agency later joined in the settlement, which was modified slightly to meet the EEOC's objections.[54] In *EEOC v. McDonnell Douglas Corp.*,[55] a consent decree to which the EEOC had agreed was approved as fair, adequate, and reasonable despite objections from some individual class members, in part because the court found that the EEOC's support of the consent decree had "great weight in light of the agency's expertise in employment discrimination litigation."[56]

XI. DECREE ENFORCEMENT

Administration and termination of court orders and consent decrees have continued to present the courts with vastly divergent factual and legal situations. In one case, a district court rejected a union's defense of impossibility in connection with a 29.23 percent nonwhite membership goal, despite demographic changes in the 20 years after the court's order was entered.[57] A court may compel compliance with instructions from a special master who has broad powers to enforce recordkeeping obligations contained in an earlier court order.[58] When a consent decree expires, however, the court's authority to enforce the order ends.[59] In some cases, it may be unclear when or whether a consent decree has expired, especially if it contains a continuing jurisdiction clause and no clear termination clause.[60]

---

[53]Nov. 21, 1996 DAILY LAB. REP. (BNA) at *AA-1.
[54]Jan. 6, 1997 DAILY LAB. REP. (BNA) at *AA-1.
[55]894 F. Supp. 1329, 1335, 68 FEP 1115 (E.D. Mo. 1995).
[56]*Id.*
[57]EEOC v. Local 638 . . . Local 28 of Sheet Metal Workers, 889 F. Supp. 642, 658 (S.D.N.Y. 1995), *modified,* 921 F. Supp. 1126 (S.D.N.Y.), *aff'd in part and rev'd in part on other grounds,* 81 F.3d 1162 (2d Cir.), *cert. denied,* 117 S. Ct. 333 (1996) (noting the union's proof of impossibility was flawed).
[58]EEOC v. Local 638 . . . Local 28 of Sheet Metal Workers, 1995 U.S. Dist. LEXIS 7678, at **11–12 (S.D.N.Y. June 5, 1995).
[59]EEOC v. Local 40, Iron Workers, 76 F.3d 76, 79–80 (2d Cir. 1996).
[60]*Id.*

When the parties to a consent decree demonstrate "substantial attainment of the goals obtained therein," the consent decree should be terminated.[61]

XII. EEOC LIABILITY FOR ATTORNEY'S FEES AND COSTS

For the most part, the courts have rejected defendants' claims for attorney's fees against the EEOC.[62] On a few recent occasions, however, fees have been assessed against the agency.[63] The most significant judicial discussion of EEOC liability for attorney's fees concluded that the Equal Access to Justice Act (EAJA) applies in ADEA cases even though it is inapplicable in Title VII cases.[64] As a result, the EEOC is liable for attorney's fees in ADEA cases unless its position was "substantially justified," a standard far more onerous than the *Christianburg* standard, which only awards fees when a claim is demonstrably frivolous.

---

[61]EEOC v. United Air Lines, 1995 U.S. Dist. LEXIS 2604, at *1 (N.D. Ill. Mar. 2, 1995) (dissolving consent decree as recommended by the parties, who had demonstrated that an 18-year-old consent decree had been complied with in good faith and "no longer serve[d] any useful function").

[62]EEOC v. Hampton Mem'l Gardens, Inc., 1995 U.S. App. LEXIS 9015, at *8 (4th Cir. Apr. 20, 1995) (fee denial was not abuse of discretion where EEOC lost the case but did not act unreasonably or without foundation); EEOC v. Shoney's, Inc., 1994 U.S. App. LEXIS 16876, at *11 (6th Cir. July 5, 1994) (had EEOC brought only a national origin suit, court would have awarded fees because EEOC investigation was "grossly inadequate"; however, fees were denied because EEOC showed prima facie case of race discrimination); EEOC v. Turtle Creek Mansion Corp., 1995 U.S. Dist. LEXIS 12854, at *3 (N.D. Tex. June 30, 1995) (while EEOC's statistical theory was rejected in a pattern-or-practice case, the case was not "unreasonable, frivolous, meritless, or vexatious"); EEOC v. Northwest Structural Components, Inc., 897 F. Supp. 249, 252, 67 FEP 1761 (M.D.N.C. 1995) (though court was not convinced discrimination occurred, claim was not frivolous); EEOC v. Tandem Computers, Inc., 158 F.R.D. 224, 229 (D. Mass. 1994) (EEOC had initially found "no cause" and was ultimately unsuccessful, but had "a legally sufficient evidentiary basis upon which to put its ADEA claim to the jury" and therefore defendant's fee request was denied).

[63]EEOC v. Hendrix College, 53 F.3d 209, 211 (8th Cir. 1995) (EEOC's failure to investigate alleged recordkeeping violations before filing suit showed lawsuit initiated in bad faith); EEOC v. Kim & Ted, Inc., 69 FEP 1499, 1504 (N.D. Ill. 1995) (EEOC ordered to pay fees for defendant's motion for sanctions concerning failure to seek employee tax records).

[64]EEOC v. O & G Spring & Wire Forms Specialty Co., 38 F.3d 872, 880–81, 65 FEP 1823 (7th Cir. 1994), *cert. denied,* 513 U.S. 1198, 67 FEP 1632 (1995); *see also* EEOC v. Consolidated Serv. Sys., 30 F.3d 58, 59, 66 FEP 185 (7th Cir. 1994) (holding that EAJA is inapplicable to EEOC litigation under Title VII); *EEOC v. Northwest Structural Components, Inc.,* 897 F. Supp. at 251 (same).

CHAPTER 35

JUSTICE DEPARTMENT LITIGATION

There have been no significant changes or developments in the law since publication of the Main Edition.

Chapter 36

FEDERAL EMPLOYEE LITIGATION

I. Introduction and Historical Overview

In *Lane v. Pena*,[1] the Supreme Court reaffirmed the well-established rule that the United States has sovereign immunity to suit except where it has expressly consented to be sued.

With respect to federal employees claiming age discrimination under the ADEA, some courts have permitted an award of attorney's fees despite the fact that the ADEA does not authorize awarding attorney's fees against the U.S. government.[2] These courts have reasoned that the Equal Access to Justice Act,[3] which allows an award of fees against the United States "[u]nless expressly prohibited by statute," provides the basis for a discretionary award of fees to a prevailing plaintiff.[4]

Courts continue to hold that liquidated damages are not available in a federal employee's ADEA action.[5]

D. The Civil Rights Act of 1991: New Remedies, a Limitations Period, and Expanded Coverage of § 717

Courts have confirmed that although the 1991 Civil Rights Act gave federal employees the right to seek compensatory damages from

---

[1]518 U.S. 187 (1996) (finding no waiver of sovereign immunity from monetary damage awards in Rehabilitation Act case brought by plaintiff dismissed from Merchant Marine Academy due to diabetes).

[2]*See* Lewis v. Federal Prison Indus., Inc., 953 F.2d 1277, 1281, 58 FEP 127 (11th Cir. 1992) (rejecting plaintiff's claim for attorney's fees on ground of no express waiver in ADEA, but not addressing entitlement under Equal Access to Justice Act).

[3]28 U.S.C. § 2412.

[4]Nowd v. Rubin, 76 F.3d 25, 27–28, 69 FEP 1587 (1st Cir. 1996) (Equal Access to Justice Act permits attorney's fee award to prevailing federal employee); Craig v. O'Leary, 870 F. Supp. 1007, 1010, 69 FEP 452 (D. Colo. 1994) (rejecting *Lewis;* allowing federal employee to seek attorney's fees in ADEA action based partially upon Equal Access to Justice Act).

[5]Edwards v. Shalala, 846 F. Supp. 997, 1001 n.8, 68 FEP 1410 (N.D. Ga. 1994), *aff'd,* 64 F.3d 601, 68 FEP 1414 (11th Cir. 1995).

their government employers, they remain ineligible for awards of punitive damages (which are available against private employers).[6]

II. ADMINISTRATIVE ENFORCEMENT

A. Employees Covered by § 717

2. Individual Complaints

a. Individual Discrimination Complaints Not Appealable to the MSPB ("Pure EEO Cases"). The Fifth Circuit has joined the Second and Eighth Circuits in holding that a complainant's rejection of an agency's offer of full relief constitutes a failure to exhaust administrative remedies barring subsequent court action.[7] However, the Supreme Court has declined to accept review of *Greenlaw v. Garrett,*[8] which held that a plaintiff who rejected an offer of full relief at the administrative level still had access to the courts, thus preserving the circuit split.

It remains the case that a complaint filed in federal district court is time-barred unless filed within 90 days of receipt of the final agency decision or, if the agency decision was appealed to the EEOC, receipt of the EEOC decision in the appeal process.[9]

b. Individual Discrimination Complaints Appealable to the MSPB ("Mixed Cases"). Pursuant to a portion of the appropriations bill for the Federal Aviation Administration (FAA) effective

---

[6]*See, e.g.,* Erickson v. West, 876 F. Supp. 239, 244 (D. Haw. 1995) (punitive damages against federal government not allowed under Title VII either pre- or post-Civil Rights Act of 1991).

[7]Francis v. Brown, 58 F.3d 191, 193, 68 FEP 555 (5th Cir. 1995) (following *Wrenn v. Secretary, Dep't of Veterans Affairs* (citation omitted); holding that plaintiff who was docked 75 minutes of pay for taking excessive amount of time off for a blood donation, and who rejected employer's offer to restore pay and remove any reference to the unauthorized absence, was barred from pursuing claim in court).

[8]59 F.3d 994, 998–1000, 68 FEP 531 (9th Cir. 1995), *cert. denied,* 117 S. Ct. 110, 74 FEP 672 (1996).

[9]42 U.S.C. § 2000e-16(c); 29 C.F.R. §§ 1614.110 and .408; *see* Metsopulos v. Runyon, 918 F. Supp. 851, 861 (D. N.J. 1996) (complaints time-barred unless filed within 90 days of receiving EEOC's final decision). (Note that the case cited in the Main Edition, *Donaldson v. Tennessee Valley Auth.,* 759 F.2d 535, 538, 37 FEP 869 (6th Cir. 1985), referred to the old rule, which allowed only 30 days rather than 90.)

April 1, 1996, the MSPB no longer has jurisdiction of "mixed" case FAA employee complaints.[10]

Appeal of a final MSPB decision of a "mixed" case involving discrimination claims must be taken to the federal district court (in contrast to appeals of nondiscrimination MSPB cases, which are only appealable directly to the U.S. Court of Appeals for the Federal Circuit).[11] The complainant may choose to waive the discrimination portion of a case presented to the MSPB as a "mixed" case; if the complainant files an express waiver of the discrimination claim, the case may be appealed to the Federal Circuit rather than to district court.[12]

3. Class Complaints

The Fifth Circuit has held, in a class action case, that as long as the complainant participated in the administrative process for more than 180 days, exhaustion requires only that the complainant made a "[g]ood faith effort . . . to cooperate with the agency and EEOC and to provide all relevant, available information . . . ."[13]

4. Employees Covered by Collective Bargaining Agreements

Note that the requirement that most federal employees pursuing discrimination claims elect whether to pursue a remedy under an applicable collective bargaining agreement or through the EEOC's procedures represents a major distinction between the rights of federal employees and the rights of private sector employees. In the private sector, attempts to bar an employee's pursuit of a grievance under a collective bargaining agreement (or other employee entitlement) as well as an EEO claim run afoul of antiretaliation provisions because they impose a penalty on the employee's nonwaivable right to engage in protected activity.[14]

---

[10]Pub. L. No. 104-50 § 347(a), (b).

[11]Coffey v. United States, 939 F. Supp. 185, 192 (E.D.N.Y. 1996).

[12]Davidson v. U.S. Postal Serv., 24 F.3d 223, 224 (Fed. Cir. 1994) (waiver of discrimination claim will not be inferred from filing in Federal Circuit; rather, plaintiff must either explicitly waive discrimination claim or request transfer to appropriate district court).

[13]Munoz v. Aldridge, 894 F.2d 1489, 1493, 52 FEP 489 (5th Cir. 1990) (citation omitted) (rejecting argument by defendant Air Force that dismissal for failure to exhaust was warranted because plaintiff abandoned administrative process and filed suit in attempt to represent a larger class).

[14]*See, e.g.,* EEOC v. Board of Governors, 957 F.2d 424, 431, 58 FEP 292 (7th Cir.), *cert. denied,* 506 U.S. 906 (1992) (finding unlawful retaliation where collective

Whether a federal employee elects to pursue the grievance procedure under a collective bargaining agreement or an EEOC charge, he or she must pursue the chosen remedy to exhaustion as a prerequisite to filing suit.[15]

5. Retaliation

Some courts continue to require that a federal employee plaintiff seeking injunctive relief meet a heightened standard by showing that "extraordinary harm" would result if interim relief were denied.[16] In a noteworthy case, *Bonds v. Heyman*,[17] the court agreed that such a showing was required but found the federal employee, a 58-year-old woman who had worked for the Smithsonian Institution for nearly 40 years (and who had brought a previous discrimination claim that was settled), had met the standard by showing that she would suffer extraordinary harm if she were laid off in a pending reduction in force.[18]

6. Affirmative Action

Courts continue to hold that an employer's failure to comply with its own internal affirmative action program cannot form an independent basis for Title VII liability, yet may serve as evidence of discriminatory intent.[19]

---

bargaining agreement allowed termination of an administrative grievance proceeding upon filing a charge with EEOC).

[15]Macy v. Dalton, 853 F. Supp. 350, 353, 64 FEP 1718 (E.D. Cal. 1994) (plaintiffs who were in process of pursuing grievance procedure under collective bargaining agreement with respect to RIF, without expressly alleging discrimination, were barred from bringing claim in court as to same employment action).

[16]*E.g.,* Stromfield v. Smith, 557 F. Supp. 995, 998, 31 FEP 204 (S.D.N.Y. 1983) (requiring showing of "extraordinary harm," and finding that unwanted transfer of employee from Atlantic City to Miami was not enough).

[17]950 F. Supp. 1202, 1215, 72 FEP 1589 (D.D.C. 1997).

[18]*Id.* The court premised this finding in part on the assumption that the plaintiff would be unlikely to find comparable employment, if any employment, in the event of her layoff, notwithstanding the fact that she was eligible for retirement with full benefits and at 80% of her top three years' salary. *Id.*

[19]Antol v. Perry, 82 F.3d 1291, 1301, 70 FEP 997 (3d Cir. 1996) (evidence that employer failed to live up to its voluntary affirmative action plan is relevant to the question of discriminatory intent); Milburn v. West, 854 F. Supp. 1, 13 (D.D.C. 1994) (liability cannot be based on noncompliance with affirmative action plan, but noncompliance considered with other factors as evidence of discriminatory intent); *see also* Gonzales v. Police Dep't, San Jose, Cal., 901 F.2d 758, 761, 52 FEP 1132 (9th

III. Litigation Procedure

A. Administrative Exhaustion

Courts routinely continue to hold that federal employees must exhaust their administrative remedies before filing suit; failure to do so is grounds for dismissal or summary judgment in favor of the employer.[20]

Although a federal employee is required to name the agency or department head as the defendant in a suit brought under § 717 (rather than the agency or department itself), a court may, depending upon the circumstances, permit relation back to cure a failure to name and serve the head of the agency or department. Some courts have permitted a late amendment naming the correct defendant under the doctrine of equitable tolling, finding that the wording of the EEOC right-to-sue notice, which states "[y]ou must name the appropriate official agency or department head as the defendant" is ambiguous and misleading.[21]

B. Timeliness

Courts continue to dismiss actions based on the plaintiff's failure to initiate the administrative charge procedure within the required time period.[22] Whether a plaintiff can successfully invoke

---

Cir. 1990); Yatvin v. Madison Metro. Sch. Dist., 840 F.2d 412, 415–16, 45 FEP 1862 (7th Cir. 1988); Craik v. Minnesota State Univ. Bd., 731 F.2d 465, 472, 34 FEP 649 (8th Cir. 1984).

[20]*E.g.,* Francis v. Brown, 58 F.3d 191, 195, 68 FEP 555 (5th Cir. 1995) (summary judgment affirmed where federal employee failed to exhaust administrative remedies on Title VII claim by failing to accept agency's settlement offer of full relief in administrative process); Matos v. Hove, 940 F. Supp. 67 (S.D.N.Y. 1996) (summary judgment against FDIC employee who failed to exhaust administrative remedies by refusing to provide requested information on specific acts of alleged discrimination to enable agency to investigate complaint).

[21]*E.g.,* Brezovski v. U.S. Postal Serv., 905 F.2d 334, 336–37, 55 FEP 1717 (10th Cir. 1990) (noting that it is unclear whether "head" modifies only "department" or also "agency"); Warren v. Department of Army, 867 F.2d 1156, 1160, 49 FEP 141 (8th Cir. 1989) (same). *But see* Gardner v. Gartman, 880 F.2d 797, 799, 50 FEP 629 (4th Cir. 1989) (no relation back permitted; finding statutory language clear and unambiguous; no discussion of equitable tolling).

[22]*E.g.,* Cones v. Shalala, 945 F. Supp. 342, 348 (D.D.C. 1996) (failure to file administrative complaint within 45 days bars subsequent lawsuit); Kennedy v. Runyon, 933 F. Supp. 480, 485 (W.D. Pa. 1996) (same).

the continuing violation doctrine to bring otherwise time-barred incidents into a charge depends upon the individual circumstances of the case.[23]

Courts have continued to accept the EEOC's position that a federal employee who pursues administrative remedies must file an ADEA action within the same time period as under Title VII.[24]

The time periods for filing suit begin to run from the date the complainant's attorney receives a right-to-sue notice on behalf of the complainant (or the date the complainant himself or herself is deemed to have received notice, if earlier). The cases are in conflict as to whether notice may be imputed to the plaintiff if the attorney-client relationship has already been terminated when the right-to-sue notice is received by the plaintiff's former attorney, in the event the plaintiff has not notified the EEOC that he or she is no longer represented by the attorney.[25]

C. Trial de Novo

In *Hashimoto v. Dalton*,[26] the district court permitted the plaintiff to accept the favorable portion of the EEOC's finding while relitigating de novo the unfavorable portion.

---

[23]*Compare* Ciafrei v. Bentsen, 877 F. Supp. 788, 794 (D.R.I. 1995) (allowing plaintiff to invoke continuing violation theory as to allegations that she was harassed and discriminated against due to her gender, coupled with her appearance and size) *with* Janneh v. Runyon, 932 F. Supp. 412, 418 (N.D.N.Y. 1996) (employee's allegations that he was consistently denied reemployment were insufficient to constitute continuing violation so as to toll 45-day limitations period), *aff'd without opinion,* 108 F.3d 329 (2d Cir.), *cert. denied* 118 S. Ct. 150 (1997) *and* Cones v. Shalala, 945 F. Supp. at 347 (rejecting plaintiff's continuing violation argument; seven separate instances of denial of promotion or reassignment to different positions shared no common nexus).

[24]*E.g.*, Edwards v. Shalala, 64 F.3d 601, 606, 68 FEP 1414 (11th Cir. 1995) (holding that Title VII limitations period for private-sector actions, applied to ADEA by Civil Rights Act of 1991, is the appropriate analogous limitations period to apply to federal employee ADEA claims); Metsopulos v. Runyon, 918 F. Supp. 851, 860 (D.N.J. 1996) (same).

[25]*Compare* Mosley v. Pena, 100 F.3d 1515, 1518, 72 FEP 561 (10th Cir. 1996) (notice to former attorney properly imputed to plaintiff because plaintiff had not notified EEOC that she was no longer represented by counsel) *with* Coates v. Shalala, 914 F. Supp. 110, 112, 72 FEP 644 (D. Md. 1996) (notice to attorney not imputed to plaintiff where attorney-client relationship had been terminated prior to attorney's receipt of notice), *aff'd without opinion,* 133 F.3d 914 (4th Cir. 1997), *petition for cert. pending.*

[26]870 F. Supp. 1544, 1557 (D. Haw. 1994) (plaintiff allowed to accept EEOC finding that the defendant had acted with retaliatory animus while relitigating issue

D. Class Actions

Plaintiffs' failure to exhaust administrative class remedies continues to be fatal to maintaining a class action in court.[27]

F. Scope of Relief

Courts continue to hold that in order to afford full relief to a plaintiff injured by unlawful discrimination, it may be necessary to "bump" an incumbent employee.[28]

G. Attorney's Fees

Attorney's fees continue to be available to a federal employee who qualifies as a "prevailing party"[29] in a Title VII lawsuit, to the same extent as for a private employee.

H. Federal Officers as Defendants

The Supreme Court has held that the propriety of the Attorney General's "scope of employment" certification under § 2679(d) of the Westfall Act is not conclusively binding, for purposes of

---

of whether she would have been offered a job in absence of retaliatory, negative employment reference), *aff'd,* 118 F.3d 671 (9th Cir. 1997), *cert. denied,* 118 S. Ct. 1803 (1998).

[27]*E.g.,* Gulley v. Orr, 905 F.2d 1383, 1385, 53 FEP 97 (10th Cir. 1990) (class action barred since named plaintiff did not exhaust class administrative remedies; plaintiff exhausted individual administrative remedies but failed to assert class claims in administrative process); Murphy v. West, 945 F. Supp. 874, 877 (D. Md. 1996) (Title VII class claims dismissed due to failure to exhaust class or individual administrative remedies; rejecting plaintiff's argument that perceived futility of raising claims at administrative level should excuse exhaustion requirement). *See also* discussion at Section II.A.3 *supra.*

[28]*E.g.,* Doll v. Brown, 75 F.3d 1200, 1205 (7th Cir. 1996) ("No one has a right to occupy a position that he obtained as a result of unlawful discrimination, even if he himself was not complicit in the discrimination."); Hayes v. Shalala, 933 F. Supp. 21, 25, 71 FEP 1240 (D.D.C. 1996) (ordering reinstatement of federal employee even though incumbent had to be "bumped" as a result; hostility engendered by litigation could not be used as justification for denial of promotion).

[29]*See, e.g.,* Petite v. Reno, 822 F. Supp. 815, 816 (D.D.C. 1993) (former federal employee who received through settlement a significant portion of relief he sought in bringing Title VII action qualified as a "prevailing party" entitled to attorney's fees, even though there was no adjudication of his discrimination claim and no admission of liability by the employer).

substitution of parties, on the district court but is subject to judicial review.[30]

The Fifth Circuit has held that if certification is granted by the Attorney General but subsequently found improper by the district court, the court is nonetheless required to retain jurisdiction of the state law claims against the federal officer and may not remand the action to state court.[31] The Fifth Circuit based its holding on the language of the Westfall Act, which states that once the Attorney General certifies scope of employment, it is conclusively established "for purposes of removal."[32] The circuits remain split on this issue, with other courts holding that remand to state court is discretionary or even required.[33]

---

[30] Gutierrez de Martinez v. Lamagno, 515 U.S. 417 (1995).

[31] Garcia v. United States, 88 F.3d 318, 324 (5th Cir. 1996).

[32] *Id.*, citing 28 U.S.C. § 2679(d)(2). *See also Lamagno, supra,* which suggests that the statutory language makes the certification conclusive only for removal (and not for party substitution) purposes. 515 U.S. at 432.

[33] *See, e.g.,* Haddon v. United States, 68 F.3d 1420, 1426–27 (D.C. Cir. 1995) (requiring remand to state court following rejection of Attorney General's certification, based in part on concerns over district court's jurisdiction to decide state law claims); Nadler v. Mann, 951 F.2d 301, 306 n.9 (11th Cir. 1992) (holding that remand is discretionary); *see also* cases cited in Chapter 36, footnote 262 of the Main Edition.

CHAPTER 37

CLASS ACTIONS

I. THE APPLICATION OF RULE 23 TO TITLE VII CLASS ACTIONS

C. Across-the-Board Class Actions After *Falcon*

Courts continue to apply the *Falcon*[1] and *Rodriguez*[2] rule that "across-the-board" class actions should not be presumed.[3] Although some courts have certified this type of action when the plaintiff points to a general practice of discrimination[4] or shows that the

---

[1] General Tel. Co. v. Falcon, 457 U.S. 147, 28 FEP 1745 (1982).
[2] East Tex. Motor Freight Sys., Inc. v. Rodriguez, 431 U.S. 395, 14 FEP 1505 (1977).
[3] Zapata v. IBP, Inc., 167 F.R.D. 147, 158 (D. Kan. 1996) (citing *Falcon*, stating that "courts now require detailed allegations, affidavits and other evidence" of commonality and typicality, and that "[p]laintiffs cannot 'simply leap from the premise that they were the victims of discrimination to the position that others must also have been' "); McCree v. Sam's Club, 159 F.R.D. 572, 577, 67 FEP 1271 (M.D. Ala. 1995) (citing *Falcon*, concluding that Rule 23(a) was not satisfied because "Plaintiffs repeatedly emphasize that this suit is not just about the actions of the managers in [one] store, and yet, they offer no evidence of class members from other stores who were not promoted because of their race"); Hartman v. Duffy, 158 F.R.D. 525, 538 (D.D.C. 1994) (noting that the trial court narrowed the definition of a class of job applicants "such that it no longer resembled the 'across-the-board' class which the Supreme Court declined to affirm in *General Tel. Co. v. Falcon*"), *aff'd*, 88 F.3d 1232 (D.C. Cir. 1996).
[4] Binion v. Metropolitan Pier & Expo. Auth., 163 F.R.D. 517, 524 (N.D. Ill. 1995) (commonality and typicality prerequisites met by class of part-time and full-time employees who alleged that employer's centrally administered discipline policy, which applied to all employees, was discriminatory); Krueger v. New York Tel. Co., 163 F.R.D. 433, 441 (S.D.N.Y. 1995) (determining that Rule 23(a) requirements met because each class member raised the same fundamental legal and factual question of whether the defendant discriminated in the implementation of a companywide reduction in force); Hartman v. Duffy, 158 F.R.D. 525, 539 (D.D.C. 1994) (although plaintiffs challenged hiring practices in six separate job categories, commonality and typicality requirements met because "the Plaintiffs identif[ied] four major discriminatory practices that cut across all job categories"), *aff'd*, 88 F.3d 1232 (D.C. Cir. 1996); Latuga v. Hooters, Inc., 1996 U.S. Dist. LEXIS 4169, at *6–8 (N.D. Ill. Mar. 29, 1996) (although plaintiff sought to represent applicants for different positions, the allegations of discrimination centered on the legality of the defendants' policy of refusing to hire males for certain positions at Hooters restaurants).

alleged discriminatory actions were made through a subjective decisionmaking process,[5] other courts have found that such classes do not meet the Rule 23 requirements.[6]

In the context of a products liability case, the Seventh Circuit has expressed concern that certification of broad and diverse classes creates such enormous transaction costs and such a tremendously large risk of liability that defendants are unfairly coerced into settlement.[7] In the context of a putative employment discrimination class action, the potential for broad and diverse employee classes, as well as the availability of compensatory and punitive damages under Title VII,[8] makes this a ripe issue for future litigation.

D. Application of Rule 23 Requirements After the 1991 Amendments to Title VII [New Topic]

The 1991 amendments to Title VII created a fundamental change in the method and manner of proof for employment discrimination cases. Prior to 1991, Title VII claimants were limited to seeking equitable relief (including back pay), and it was well established that compensatory and punitive damages were not available.[9] The

---

[5]Butler v. Home Depot, 70 FEP 51, 53 (N.D. Cal. 1996) (finding Rule (23)(a) requirements met with respect to class of employees and applicants where plaintiff alleged employer maintained "a personnel system characterized by the use of subjective criteria by male management with hostile and stereotypical attitudes toward women").

[6]McKnight v. Circuit City Stores, 168 F.R.D. 550, 553–54, 72 FEP 28 (E.D. Va. 1996) (decertifying class of current and former employees alleging discrimination in promotion and transfer opportunities); Appleton v. Deloitte & Touche L.L.P., 168 F.R.D. 221, 229–32 (M.D. Tenn. 1996) (determining that the challenged employment practices involved varying elements of objective and subjective criteria, thus precluding a finding of commonality and typicality); Brooks v. Circuit City Stores, 71 FEP 102, 104 (D. Md. 1996) (managers' subjective decisionmaking did not provide commonality to claims because it merely "allow[ed] a situation to exist in which several different managers [were] able to discriminate intentionally . . . [t]he focus of the claim remain[ed] the individual employment decisions").

[7]In re Rhone-Poulenc Rorer, Inc., 51 F.3d 1293 (7th Cir. 1995), *cert. denied*, 115 S. Ct. 184 (1995) (issuing writ of mandamus reversing certification of a nationwide class of hemophiliacs purportedly infected with the AIDS virus as a consequence of using the defendants' blood products, reasoning that certification of such a broad class likely would have forced the defendants into a "blackmail settlement" given the tremendous amount of potential liability, and possible bankruptcy, they would have faced if the class were to prevail at trial).

[8]*See* Section I.D *infra*.

[9]Landgraf v. USI Film Prods., 511 U.S. 244, 256, 64 FEP 820 (1994) (noting that "[b]efore the enactment of the 1991 Act, Title VII afforded only 'equitable remedies,' " and that the 1991 amendments "significantly expand[ed] the monetary relief potentially

1991 amendments to Title VII, however, made both compensatory and punitive damages available to plaintiffs upon a showing of intentional discrimination.[10] In addition, those amendments gave the parties the right to a jury trial in the event that either compensatory or punitive damages were being sought.[11] Since enactment of the 1991 amendments, federal courts across the country have struggled with the interplay between the fundamental changes in employment discrimination actions and class certification under Rule 23.

Defendant employers commonly contend that the 1991 amendments rendered employment discrimination cases unsuitable for class action treatment. Asserting that compensatory and punitive damages sought under the amendments necessarily predominate the remedies at issue, employers argue that such actions cannot be certified under Rule 23(b)(2).[12] Employers further assert that individual claims for compensatory and punitive damages preclude class certification under Rule 23(b)(3) because individualized proof of damages predominate over common issues and render a potential class action wholly unmanageable.[13] Finally, employers argue that because the 1991 amendments expressly provide a right to jury trial, the Seventh Amendment requires that the same jury decide both liability and damages when individual compensatory and punitive damages are sought—an arrangement that cannot be practicably

---

available to plaintiffs" by providing for compensatory and punitive damages); Celestine v. Citgo Petroleum Corp., 165 F.R.D. 463, 468, 70 FEP 80 (W.D. La. 1995) ("Prior to the amendments to the Civil Rights Act of 1991, plaintiffs bringing a Title VII action could only seek injunctive relief and other equitable remedies such as back pay."); Taylor v. Central Pa. Drug & Alcohol Servs. Corp., 890 F. Supp. 360, 373, 72 FEP 1315 (M.D. Pa. 1995) (refusing to award compensatory damages to plaintiffs whose claims arose prior to effective date of 1991 amendments to Title VII).

[10]42 U.S.C. § 1981a(a) (as amended by § 102 of the 1991 Act, Pub. L. No. 102-166, 1991 U.S.C.C.A.N. (105 Stat.) 1071); *Celestine*, 165 F.R.D. at 467 ("[n]ow the Civil Rights Act of 1991 makes compensatory and punitive damages available to plaintiffs in cases involving intentional discrimination").

[11]42 U.S.C. § 1981a(c) (as amended by § 102 of the 1991 Act, Pub. L. No. 102-166, 1991 U.S.C.C.A.N. (105 Stat.) 1071); Dombeck v. Milwaukee Valve Co., 40 F.3d 230, 235, 66 FEP 497 (7th Cir. 1994) (noting that "[p]rior to the 1991 amendments, Title VII did not afford a right to a jury trial"); Oswald v. Laroche Chem., Inc., 162 F.R.D. 283, 284, 5 AD 409 (E.D. La. 1995) (1991 amendments to Title VII "change[d] the prior law and allow[ed] plaintiffs trials by jury" in discrimination cases); Jenkins v. Grenada, 813 F. Supp. 443, 448, 61 FEP 258 (N.D. Miss. 1993) ("[w]ith the passage of the 1991 Civil Rights Act, . . . discrimination claimants now enjoy the benefit of the right to a jury trial; whereas before, they did not").

[12]*See* Section V *infra*.

[13]*Id.*

accomplished.[14] The few courts that have addressed these issues are split, making this a likely topic for future discussion and development.[15]

II. THE "NEXUS" REQUIREMENTS OF RULE 23(a): COMMONALITY, TYPICALITY, AND ADEQUACY OF REPRESENTATION

A. Nexus Between Claims Asserted

2. Adverse Impact Claims

Courts routinely find the Rule 23(a) requirements are met in adverse impact cases when the plaintiffs identify a particular test or employment policy that created the allegedly discriminatory consequences.[16] Although at least one additional court has certified a class when the alleged discrimination arose from a policy that allowed managers to engage in significant subjective decisionmaking,[17] the commonality and typicality prerequisites of Rule 23(a) may be more difficult to establish under such a theory of liability. Courts continue to hold that decisionmaking processes that include subjective criteria are not *a priori* discriminatory.[18] Accordingly,

---

[14]*See* Sections X.A and B *infra.*
[15]*See* Sections V and X *infra.*
[16]*See, e.g.,* Celestine v. Citgo Petroleum Corp., 165 F.R.D. 463, 467, 71 FEP 1445 (W.D. La. 1995) (Rule 23(a) requirements met by employees alleging adverse impact in hiring and promotion because each plaintiff's claim was based upon "general hiring, training, and promotional policies which allegedly affect[ed] all persons seeking employment and those seeking advancement once employed"); Binion v. Metropolitan Pier & Expo. Auth., 163 F.R.D. 517, 524 (N.D. Ill. 1995) (commonality and typicality prerequisites met by employees alleging both disparate treatment and adverse impact based upon employer's centrally administered discipline policy, which applied to all employees); Krueger v. New York Tel. Co., 163 F.R.D. 433, 441 (S.D.N.Y. 1995) (determining that no distinction need be made between disparate treatment and adverse impact theories at class certification stage, finding Rule 23(a) requirements met because each claim focused on the defendant's implementation of a reduction-in-force plan); Hartman v. Duffy, 158 F.R.D. 525, 537 (D.D.C. 1994) (certifying class of female job applicants alleging that particular hiring tests and procedures created adverse impact), *aff'd*, 88 F.3d 1232 (D.C. Cir. 1996).
[17]Butler v. Home Depot, 70 FEP 51, 53 (N.D. Cal. 1996) (finding Rule (23)(a) requirements met in adverse impact and disparate treatment case where plaintiff alleged employer maintained a personnel system characterized by the use of subjective criteria that discriminated against women).
[18]Vitug v. Multistate Tax Comm'n, 88 F.3d 506, 514, 71 FEP 1445 (7th Cir. 1996) ("It is not enough for a plaintiff to demonstrate that an employment practice could

when such processes are the focus of the alleged discrimination, determining liability with respect to class members necessarily involves an individual assessment of each particular claim. This is especially true when the decisionmaking processes involved were not entirely subjective,[19] but included objective factors or defined "checks" on subjective decisions. In that respect, establishing liability in a subjective adverse impact case may require individualized proof similar to that generally offered in support of disparate treatment claims, which is likely to preclude a finding of commonality and typicality and, thus, class certification.[20]

3. *Disparate Treatment Claims*

While it is still generally recognized that "[t]he commonality requirement is more easily met in a disparate impact case rather than a disparate treatment case,"[21] courts will certify a class if the plaintiff can demonstrate that the discriminatory treatment was part of an overall pattern or practice.[22] A significant number of courts have

---

theoretically be used to discriminate—Title VII does not forbid subjective selection processes."); Furr v. Seagate Tech., Inc., 82 F.3d 980, 987, 70 FEP 1325 (10th Cir. 1996) ("the use of subjective criteria does not suffice to prove intentional age discrimination"), *cert. denied,* 117 S. Ct. 684 (1997); Hutson v. McDonnell Douglas Corp., 63 F.3d 771, 780, 68 FEP 1209 (8th Cir. 1995) ("the presence of subjectivity in employee evaluations is itself not a grounds for challenging those evaluations as discriminatory"); Johnson v. Runyon, 928 F. Supp. 575, 583 (D. Md. 1996) ("the use of subjective criteria is neither improper in the promotion process nor indicative of unlawful discrimination"); Keegan v. Dalton, 899 F. Supp. 1503, 1513 (E.D. Va. 1995) ("it is well-established that the use of subjective criteria alone is not evidence of pretext, especially where the employer is rating professional and managerial employees").

[19]General Tel. v. Falcon, 457 U.S. 147, 159 n.15, 28 FEP 1745 (1982) (noting that broad across-the-board class action may be appropriate if the discrimination manifested itself "in the same general fashion, such as through *entirely subjective* decisionmaking processes" [emphasis added]).

[20]*See, e.g.,* cases cited in note 4 *supra.*

[21]Brooks v. Circuit City Stores, 71 FEP 102, 104 (D. Md. 1996).

[22]*See, e.g.,* Butler v. Home Depot, 70 FEP 51, 53 (N.D. Cal. 1996) (Rule (23)(a) requirements met in adverse impact and disparate treatment case where plaintiff alleged employer maintained a personnel system characterized by the use of subjective criteria that discriminated against women); Bremiller v. Cleveland Psychiatric Inst., 898 F. Supp. 573, 579 (N.D. Ohio 1995) (certifying class under disparate treatment theory of discrimination where plaintiffs alleged pattern of ongoing and continuous sexual harassment); Wilkerson v. Martin Marietta Corp., 875 F. Supp. 1456, 1461–62, 67 FEP 279 (D. Colo. 1995) (finding Rule 23(a) requirements met in action under ADEA where plaintiffs alleged employer engaged in established pattern and practice of age discrimination against its employees); Binion v. Metropolitan

determined, however, that if individual issues relating to the alleged disparate treatment predominate, this precludes class certification.[23]

4. Reasonable Accommodation Claims

Although some courts have indicated that class certification may not be appropriate in employment cases under the Americans with Disabilities Act of 1990 (ADA) because of the many individual questions relating to the class members' varying disabilities and potential reasonable accommodations of each disability,[24]

Pier & Expo. Auth., 163 F.R.D. 517, 524 (N.D. Ill. 1995) (Rule 23(a) prerequisites met by employees alleging both disparate treatment and adverse impact based upon employer's centrally administered discipline policy); Johnson v. EEOC, 68 FEP 1712, 1722 (N.D. Ill. 1995) (although each class representative in age discrimination suit was female, and state laws vary regarding apprentice programs, typicality requirement met because claims based on particular age restrictions of particular apprenticeship program).

[23]See McKnight v. Circuit City Stores, 168 F.R.D. 550, 553 (E.D. Va. 1996) (decertifying class of employees suing for discrimination in promotion and transfer opportunities upon concluding that "the size of the class as well as the issues that must be hammered out" made class certification inefficient and unfair to defendants); Zapata v. IBP, Inc., 167 F.R.D. 147, 158–59 (D. Kan. 1996) (commonality and typicality lacking in hostile environment suit because plaintiffs' allegations "focus upon the individual actions taken by different individual supervisors, and not on a uniform policy or practice"); Brooks v. Circuit City Stores, 71 FEP 102, 104 (D. Md. 1996) (subjective decisionmaking processes did not provide commonality to claims because it merely "allow[ed] a situation to exist in which several different managers [were] able to discriminate intentionally . . . [t]he focus of the claim remain[ed] the individual employment decision"); Brooks v. BellSouth Telecomms., 164 F.R.D. 561, 566 (N.D. Ala. 1995) (class certification denied in ADEA action where plaintiff failed to show that the proposed class members were victims of a single decision, policy, or plan infected by discrimination); Lumpkin v. E.I. Du Pont de Nemours & Co., 161 F.R.D. 480, 482, 67 FEP 1263 (M.D. Ga. 1995) (commonality and typicality requirements of Rule 23(a) not met because plaintiffs were "employed in different departments, supervised by different people, work[ed] in different shifts and [were] at different levels within the company hierarchy"); McCree v. Sam's Club, 159 F.R.D. 572, 577, 67 FEP 1271 (M.D. Ala. 1995) (Rule 23(a) prerequisites not met in action alleging disparate treatment in promotion because "Plaintiffs offer[ed] no evidence from which the court could conclude that there exists a class of persons who have suffered the same injury allegedly suffered by [named plaintiffs]").

[24]See, e.g., Davoll v. Webb, 160 F.R.D. 142, 146, 4 AD 161 (D. Colo. 1995) (denying certification of class of disabled police officers who had been dismissed from force, determining Rule 23(a) factors could not be assessed because definition of proposed class was untenable: "The mere fact that each Plaintiff sustained work-related injuries resulting in physical impairments, being placed in a light duty position and later retiring would not mean he or she had a 'disability' as defined in the ADA.").

other courts have certified class actions under the ADA when a particular employment practice or policy is attacked. In *Hendricks-Robinson v. Excel Corp.*,[25] employees who had been terminated because of various medical restrictions brought suit under the ADA and sought to certify a class action. Focusing on "the highly individualized nature of claims and defenses inherent in litigation under the ADA," the court initially refused to certify the class.[26] Upon plaintiffs' motion for reconsideration, however, the court concluded that certification was proper because the plaintiffs attacked the employer's overall termination policy, not the individual actions taken with respect to each terminated employee.[27]

5. Claims for Compensatory Damages [New Topic]

Although the courts are split on whether a demand for compensatory and punitive damages under the 1991 Title VII amendments precludes class certification under Rule 23(b),[28] they uniformly hold that plaintiffs who seek such damages may still meet the Rule 23(a) commonality and typicality requirements.[29] Indeed, even in *Celestine v. Citgo Petroleum Corp.*, where the court refused to order (b)(2) certification in part because of the many questions relating to the plaintiffs' individual damages claims, it held that "the necessity for an individual calculation of damages is not a basis for defeating commonality" under Rule 23(a).[30]

---

[25] 164 F.R.D. 667 (C.D. Ill. 1996).

[26] *Id.* at 669.

[27] *Id.* at 670. *Accord* Wilson v. Pennsylvania State Police Dep't, 1995 U.S. Dist. LEXIS 9981, at *8 (E.D. Pa. July 17, 1995) (certifying class of plaintiffs who challenged the Pennsylvania State Police Department's employment policy against applicants with poor eyesight as violative of the ADA).

[28] *See* Section V *infra*.

[29] Shores v. Publix Super Mkts., Inc., 1996 U.S. Dist. LEXIS 3381, at *22 (M.D. Fla. Mar. 12, 1996) (noting that "[t]o the extent that Plaintiffs seek damages, they present unique issues.... However, the mere fact that questions peculiar to each individual member of the class remain after the common questions of the defendant's liability have been resolved does not dictate the conclusion that a class action is impermissible."); Bremiller v. Cleveland Psychiatric Inst., 898 F. Supp. 573, 579 (N.D. Ohio 1995) ("the existence of individual damages issues is not enough to defeat class certification on the commonality element"); Wilkerson v. Martin Marietta Corp., 875 F. Supp. 1456, 1462, 67 FEP 279 (D. Colo. 1995) (Rule 23(a) commonality and typicality requirements met in ADEA action "even in light of damages issues which are individual in character").

[30] 165 F.R.D. 463, 466, 70 FEP 80 (W.D. La. 1995).

B. Nexus Between Job Classifications

Courts continue to determine on a case-by-case basis whether certification is proper when the named plaintiff held a job different from those of the putative class members. When the plaintiff can show a common policy of discrimination that affected various job categories, courts are more apt to certify a class.[31]

C. Nexus Between Organizational Units or Geographical Facilities

Courts continue to find that, in the absence of a challenge to a centralized policy or practice, a plaintiff employed in a particular organizational unit or geographical facility cannot represent a class of employees working in other units or facilities.[32]

---

[31]*Compare* Hartman v. Duffy, 158 F.R.D. 525, 539 (D.D.C. 1994) (certifying class of employees challenging hiring practices in six separate job categories because "the Plaintiffs identif[ied] four major discriminatory practices that cut across all job categories"), *aff'd,* 88 F.3d 1232 (D.C. Cir. 1996) *with* Lumpkin v. E.I. Du Pont de Nemours & Co., 161 F.R.D. 480, 482, 67 FEP 1263 (M.D. Ga. 1995) (commonality requirements of Rule 23(a)(2) not met because plaintiffs "employed in different departments, supervised by different people, work in different shifts and are at different levels within the company hierarchy"), Alvarado v. Carnation Co., 1995 U.S. Dist. LEXIS 10084, at *13–14 (D. Idaho June 23, 1995) (named plaintiffs not typical of class of individuals who were denied promotion to "salaried supervisory or management position" because plaintiffs never applied for such positions; certifying narrowed class excluding such individuals) *and* Gorence v. Eagle Food Ctrs., 1994 U.S. Dist. LEXIS 11438, at *26–27 (N.D. Ill. Aug. 15, 1994) (determining that commonality and typicality not present where low-level employees sought to represent a class of "all present and future . . . employees at the level of assistant store manager and above").

[32]*See, e.g.,* Brooks v. Circuit City Stores, 71 FEP 102, 104 (D. Md. 1996) (commonality not present where plaintiffs' theory of discrimination "involve[d] widely different store locations rather than [a] centralized management"); McCree v. Sam's Club, 159 F.R.D. 572, 577, 67 FEP 1271 (M.D. Ala. 1995) (concluding that Rule 23(a) was not satisfied because "Plaintiffs repeatedly emphasize that this suit is not just about the actions of the managers in [one] store, and yet, they offer no evidence of class members from other stores who were not promoted because of their race"); Gorence v. Eagle Food Ctrs., 1994 U.S. Dist. LEXIS 11438, at *26–27 (N.D. Ill. Aug. 15, 1994) (determining that commonality and typicality not present where plaintiffs sought to represent class of "employees in all of [the employer's] organizational units, many of which are completely separate and distinct from one another").

III. Special Issues Pertaining to Adequacy of Representation

A. Adequacy of Plaintiff's Counsel

In the event of an attorney's conflict of interest, a court has the option of disqualifying the attorney rather than denying class certification outright based on inadequate representation.[33]

B. Adequacy of the Named Plaintiff

In *Amchem Products, Inc. v. Windsor*,[34] an asbestos litigation case, the Supreme Court reiterated that "[t]he adequacy inquiry under Rule 23(a)(4) serves to uncover conflicts of interest between named parties and the class they seek to represent."[35]

While a plaintiff seeking a remedy at odds with the interests of others in the class may give rise to a conflict of interest, the mere fact that there are not enough positions available with the defendant employer to accommodate every class member participating in the remedial phase of litigation (so that class members might be competing with each other for the same jobs) will not lead to a finding of inadequate representation.[36] Moreover, a named plaintiff's involvement, as an employee, in implementing the very practices challenged in the class action does not necessarily make his or her interests antagonistic to those of the class, precluding certification. If the plaintiff's authority was limited enough that he or she could not be considered an agent for the employer, the plaintiff may be deemed an adequate class representative.[37]

---

[33]*E.g.*, Palumbo v. Tele-Communications, Inc., 157 F.R.D. 129, 133 (D.D.C. 1994) (class counsel disqualified prior to certification decision because attorney held minority ownership interest in cable franchise affiliated with telecommunications defendant).

[34]117 S. Ct. 2231, 1997 U.S. LEXIS 4032 (1997).

[35]*Id.*, 1997 U.S. LEXIS 4032, at *61–62 (holding that class could not be certified because "named parties with diverse medical conditions sought to act on behalf of a single giant class" that encompassed currently injured plaintiffs as well as those who had been exposed to asbestos but as yet had no symptoms of injury, and that the interests within the class were not aligned in significant respects).

[36]Hartman v. Duffy, 158 F.R.D. 525, 546–47 (D.D.C. 1994), *aff'd*, 88 F.3d 1232 (D.C. Cir. 1996).

[37]*E.g.*, Wagner v. Nutrasweet Co., 170 F.R.D. 448, 451–52 (N.D. Ill. 1997) (named plaintiff in challenge to salary practices as discriminatory against women was a

More complex cases continue to generate disputes about the degree of knowledge of the case required by the class representative, and the named plaintiff's ability to finance litigation expenses. In *Buford v. H & R Block, Inc.*,[38] a nonemployment case, the court held that only a "minimal degree of participation and knowledge of the action" is required of the class representative in complex cases.[39] With respect to concerns about financing the litigation, courts have held it sufficient that plaintiffs have affirmed their willingness to pay the litigation expenses[40] or that class counsel has represented that counsel will underwrite the expenses of litigation.[41]

The Sixth Circuit has held that a plaintiff's suitability as a class representative may in some circumstances be called into question by a history of psychological problems.[42]

IV. NUMEROSITY

The number of class members sufficient to satisfy the numerosity requirement of Rule 23(a) continues to depend upon the specific facts and circumstances of each case.[43] Some courts

---

manager in the personnel office but had no salary-setting authority with respect to class members).

[38] 168 F.R.D. 340 (S.D. Ga. 1996), *aff'd*, 117 F.3d 1433 (11th Cir. 1997).

[39] *Id.* at 353–54 (named plaintiff demonstrated sufficient knowledge of underlying facts of case and familiarity with requirements of class representative status; court denied class certification on other grounds).

[40] Krueger v. New York Tel. Co., 163 F.R.D. 433, 443 n.6 (S.D.N.Y. 1995).

[41] *Buford*, 168 F.R.D. at 352–53.

[42] In re American Med. Sys., Inc., 75 F.3d 1069, 1083 (6th Cir. 1996) (in products liability case, plaintiff's history of psychological problems, creating concern about adequacy of representation, cited as one of many factors in court's decision to reverse district court's certification order).

[43] *E.g.*, Hum v. Dericks, 162 F.R.D. 628, 634 (D. Hawaii 1995) (denying certification of proposed class of 200 in medical malpractice case arising from use of specific medical procedure because proposed class members identifiable and joinder not impracticable; noting that courts have certified classes with as few as 13 members and denied certification of classes with over 300 members). *Compare* Rodger v. Electric Data Sys. Corp., 160 F.R.D. 532, 535–37 (E.D.N.C. 1995) (holding that class of 57 was sufficient, in wrongful discharge case, and noting that circuit precedent certified classes with as few as 18 members) *and* Hendricks-Robinson v. Excel Corp., 164 F.R.D. 667, 671 (C.D. Ill. 1996) (in ADA case challenging employer's "medical layoff program," 38 class members satisfied numerosity requirement) *with* Hernandez v. Alexander, 152 F.R.D. 192, 194 (D. Nev. 1993) (in fraud action by former students of vocational school, potential class of 52 was insufficient to meet numerosity requirements), McCree v. Sam's Club, 159 F.R.D. 572, 576–

CH. 37   CLASS ACTIONS   509

consider in the numerosity analysis future employees and individuals who were deterred from applying for positions.[44]

The burden of demonstrating numerosity remains on the plaintiff,[45] who may not rely on wholly conclusory allegations[46] yet need not specify the exact class size or identify all class members.[47] In making the numerosity determination, courts continue to consider such additional factors as geographic dispersion of class members, the size of the individual claims involved, and whether class members' fear of retaliation would prevent them from suing as individuals.[48]

---

77 (M.D. Ala. 1995) (in race discrimination case, class comprised of 15 members did not satisfy numerosity requirement) *and* National Ass'n of Gov't Employees v. City Pub. Serv. Bd., 40 F.3d 698, 715 (5th Cir. 1994) (potential class of 11 members, only two of whose claims concerned denial of promotion, insufficient under numerosity requirement).

[44]Bethesda Lutheran Homes & Servs. v. Leean, 165 F.R.D. 87, 88–89 (W.D. Wis. 1996) ("while potential future members of a class may be considered in the numerosity analysis this is only true to the extent that the court can reasonably approximate their number"); Johnson v. EEOC, 68 FEP 1712, 1721 (N.D. Ill. 1995) (numerosity requirement met in ADEA case when plaintiffs' evidence showed that individuals were deterred from applying to apprenticeship programs due to age restrictions); Adams v. Pinole Point Steel Co., 65 FEP 774, 779 (N.D. Cal. 1994) (court certified class of women that included those who were deterred from applying from employment at steel plant, stating "[a] class containing deterred and future applicants and employees supports a finding that joinder is impracticable since by their nature such actions involve class members who are difficult to identify").

[45]*E.g.,* Arenson v. Whitehall Convalescent & Nursing Home, Inc., 164 F.R.D. 659, 662 (N.D. Ill. 1996) (plaintiff in class action bears the burden of satisfying all four requirements of Rule 23(a), i.e., numerosity, commonality, typicality, and adequacy of representation).

[46]McCree v. Sam's Club, 159 F.R.D. 572, 576–77 (M.D. Ala. 1995).

[47]*E.g.,* Robidoux v. Celani, 987 F.2d 931, 935 (2d Cir. 1993) ("courts have not required evidence of exact class size or identity of class members to satisfy the numerosity requirement"); *Arenson,* 164 F.R.D. at 662–63 (N.D. Ill. 1996) (plaintiff is not required to specify exact number of class members so long as a good faith estimate is provided, although estimate cannot be purely speculative); *cf.* Bremiller v. Cleveland Psychiatric Inst., 898 F. Supp. 573, 576–77 (N.D. Ohio 1995) (in sexual harassment class action, defendants may not claim complete ignorance as to identities of class members or use plaintiffs' ignorance to defeat class certification when proposed class was composed of defendant's past and present employees and defendants could identify class members by reviewing own files). *But see* Davoll v. Webb, 160 F.R.D. 142, 144–46 (D. Colo. 1995) (court refused to find that class met numerosity requirement in discrimination case based on work-related disabilities because class not sufficiently defined and it was not feasible for court to determine if particular individuals had "disabilities" qualifying them as class members).

[48]Rodriguez v. Carlson, 166 F.R.D. 465, 471–72 (E.D. Wash. 1996) (under numerosity evaluation, court will examine not only the mere number of plaintiffs but

The issue of whether the manageability of a class action affects the class certification decision is still a controversial one. At least one court has held (in a nonemployment case) that manageability is not a relevant consideration and that the size of the proposed class should only be considered in the context of the numerosity requirement of Rule 23(a)(1).[49] Other courts have dealt with the manageability issue outside the context of Rule 23(a), in the course of determining under Rule 23(b)(3) whether a class action is "superior to other available methods" of litigating the case.[50] Courts continue to deal with manageability problems in employment cases through bifurcation of liability and damages issues[51] and other procedural means such as conditional certification.[52]

---

such factors as "geographical dispersion, degree of sophistication, and class members' reluctance to sue individually"). *See also, e.g.,* Gaspar v. Linvatec Corp., 167 F.R.D. 51, 56–57 (N.D. Ill. 1996) (in class action alleging ERISA violations, court found numerosity requirement met where 18 potential class members were geographically dispersed between three states); Arenson v. Whitehall Convalescent & Nursing Home, 164 F.R.D. 659, 663 (N.D. Ill. 1996) (in action against nursing home for overbilling patients, court concluded that relatively small size of individual claims supported certification of class action since individual class members might be hesitant to sue); Johnson v. EEOC, 68 FEP 1712, 1721 (N.D. Ill. 1995) (in ADEA case, court found that class of persons age 40 and older applying for apprenticeship programs satisfied numerosity requirement because class members were geographically dispersed); Ardrey v. Federal Kemper Ins. Co., 142 F.R.D. 105, 109–11 (E.D. Pa. 1992) (numerosity requirement met in class action brought by insurance agents and agencies against insurer, based in part on impracticability of joinder of all 200 class members, some of whom were reluctant to join action individually due to fears of retaliation).

[49]Marisol A. by Forbes v. Giuliani, 929 F. Supp. 662, 690 (S.D.N.Y. 1996) (class action by abused children against state child welfare agency).

[50]*E.g.,* Andrews v. American Tel. & Tel. Co., 95 F.3d 1014, 1023–25 (11th Cir. 1996) (in case against telephone companies relating to "900-number" telemarketing, stating that district court abused its discretion in certifying classes where manageability problems were insurmountable); Griffin v. Home Depot, Inc., 168 F.R.D. 187, 190 (E.D. La. 1996) (certifying class in sex discrimination case and holding that class certification under Rule 23(b)(3) involves consideration of manageability and judicial economy); Zapata v. IBP, Inc., 167 F.R.D. 147, 163 (D. Kan. 1996) (finding that manageability problems that existed with respect to calculating damages showed class action not superior to other available methods for fair and efficient adjudication); Buford v. H & R Block, Inc., 168 F.R.D. 340, 363–64 (S.D. Ga. 1996) (finding that class action would not be superior to other methods of adjudication because management of individual issues in class of approximately 10 million "would be impossible"). *See also* the discussion of manageability issues and Rule 23(b) requirements at Section V *infra,* and in the Main Edition.

[51]*See* the discussion of bifurcation at Section X.A *infra,* and in the Main Edition.

[52]*E.g.,* In re Aluminum Phosphide Antitrust Litig., 160 F.R.D. 609, 615 (D. Kan. 1995) (noting that court may modify certification order and decertify class as to damages if and when individual proof as to damages later proves unmanageable).

V. Rule 23(b) Requirements

The most controversial topic regarding Rule 23(b) in the employment discrimination arena is which type of class certification, if any, is appropriate when plaintiffs seek compensatory or punitive damages under the 1991 amendments to Title VII. Some courts have agreed with the district court in *Celestine v. Citgo Petroleum Corp.*[53] and held that actions seeking compensatory and punitive damages cannot be certified under Rule 23(b)(2) because monetary relief necessarily predominates the remedies sought.[54] Other courts, however, have followed the rationale of *Butler v. Home Depot*[55] and ordered (b)(2) certification notwithstanding the plaintiffs' request for such damages.[56]

The Supreme Court has twice passed up an opportunity to resolve the controversy over the constitutionality of class action

---

[53] 165 F.R.D. 463, 469, 70 FEP 80 (W.D. La. 1995) (refusing to certify (b)(2) class of employees alleging race discrimination because highly individualized proof would be necessary for purposes of determining compensatory damages and, therefore, such damages were not "integrally related to" and did not "flow from" injunctive relief).

[54] *E.g.,* Zapata v. IBP, Inc., 167 F.R.D. 147, 162 (D. Kan. 1996) (determining that putative class of Mexican-American employees alleging disparate treatment could not be certified under Rule 23(b)(2) because employees primarily sought compensatory damages); *Gorence,* 1994 U.S. Dist. LEXIS 11438, at *18 (denying (b)(2) certification where plaintiffs alleged their employer engaged in a practice of discrimination on the basis of age and sex, and sought "compensatory damages, including lost wages, retirement and other employment benefits, liquidated damages, punitive damages, prejudgment interest and attorneys' fees").

[55] 70 FEP 51, 55 (N.D. Cal. 1996) (certifying (b)(2) class of female employees alleging gender discrimination even though employees sought compensatory damages).

[56] *E.g.,* Shores v. Publix Super Mkts., Inc., 1996 U.S. Dist. LEXIS 3381, at *28 (M.D. Fla. Mar. 12, 1996) (certifying (b)(2) class of employees alleging gender discrimination notwithstanding the plaintiffs' claims for compensatory damages); Bremiller v. Cleveland Psychiatric Inst., 898 F. Supp. 573, 578–79 (N.D. Ohio 1995) (certifying (b)(2) class of employees alleging sexual harassment, rebuffing defendant's contention that individual claims for damages predominate). *Cf.* Stewart v. Rubin, 948 F. Supp. 1077, 1090–91 (D.D.C. 1996) (rejecting general premise advanced by *Celestine* court that "no class certification was appropriate in Title VII cases because of the new provisions of the Civil Rights Act of 1991," and approving settlement of case brought as (b)(2) class action as involving predominantly equitable relief, notwithstanding compensatory damages component); Arnold v. United Artists Theatre Circuit, 158 F.R.D. 439, 460–63 (N.D. Cal. 1994) (rejecting defendant's contention that 1991 amendments to Title VII necessarily result in monetary damages predominating plaintiffs' remedies, thereby precluding certification of (b)(2) classes).

Of course, courts continue to certify (b)(2) classes when the plaintiffs do not seek compensatory or punitive damages, but merely equitable relief. *See, e.g.,*

certifications under Rule 23(b)(2) in actions involving claims for compensatory and punitive damages. The argument against certification is that certification of a nationwide or multistate class action pursuant to Rule 23(b)(2) violates the Due Process Clause of the Fifth Amendment (or the Fourteenth Amendment, in the case of actions brought in state court) when the class members, who may not opt out of the (b)(2) class, allegedly suffered monetary damages.[57] In *Adams v. Robertson*,[58] the Supreme Court had initially granted certiorari but subsequently dismissed the writ as improvidently granted. The Court ruled that the petitioners, class members who had objected to a settlement of a class action certified under an Alabama state law analogous to federal Rule 23(b)(2),[59] had failed to preserve their federal due process claim by not raising it in the underlying Alabama Supreme Court proceeding.[60] The Supreme Court also refused to decide in *Ticor Title Insurance Co. v. Brown*[61] whether members of a (b)(2) class must be given the opportunity to opt out when the action includes claims for significant monetary damages. The Court has ruled in *Phillips Petroleum Co. v. Shutts*[62] that due process requires an opt-out right for out-of-state parties in class actions brought under state law "seeking to bind known plaintiffs concerning claims wholly or predominately for money judgments."

As with Rule 23(b)(2) certification, courts similarly remain split on the issue of whether Rule 23(b)(3) certification is appropriate when individual plaintiffs seek compensatory or punitive damages under the 1991 amendments. Under Rule 23(b)(3), the

---

Schaefer v. Tannian, 164 F.R.D. 630, 635 (E.D. Mich 1996) (court noted that requesting monetary relief in form of back pay does not preclude (b)(2) certification, but may present a situation where "the cohesiveness among individual members often will not be present"); Hendricks-Robinson v. Excel Corp., 164 F.R.D. 667, 672 (C.D. Ill. 1996) (certifying (b)(2) class of medically restricted employees laid off pursuant to employer's policy, which allegedly violated the ADA); Charles v. Dalton, 1996 U.S. Dist. LEXIS 1494, at *14 (N.D. Cal. Jan. 31, 1996) (certifying (b)(2) class in race discrimination case where plaintiffs sought promotions and back pay only).

[57]*See* Ticor Title Ins. Co. v. Brown, 511 U.S. 117, 114 S. Ct. 1359, 1361 (1994); Adams v. Robertson, 117 S. Ct. 1028 (1997).
[58]117 S. Ct. 1028, 1997 U.S. LEXIS 1490 (1997).
[59]Adams v. Robertson, 676 So. 2d 1265, 1270 (Ala. 1995), *cert. granted*, 117 S. Ct. 37 (1996), *cert. dismissed as improvidently granted*, 117 S. Ct. 1028 (1997).
[60]*Adams*, 117 S. Ct. 1028, 1997 U.S. LEXIS 1490, at *5.
[61]511 U.S. 117, 114 S. Ct. 1359, 1362 (1994).
[62]472 U.S. 797, 811 (1985).

putative class must show that common issues predominate and that a class action is the superior method of adjudicating the plaintiffs' claims. Courts refusing to certify a (b)(3) class of individuals seeking compensatory and punitive damages under Title VII have held that individualized claims for such damages predominate over common issues[63] and/or would make management of the class highly difficult.[64] Other courts have rejected those reasons and certified a (b)(3) class where the employees sought individual awards of compensatory damages pursuant to the 1991 amendments.[65]

The court in *Griffin v. Home Depot*[66] thoroughly examined both sides of the debate over class certification after the 1991 amendments to Title VII. The plaintiffs in *Griffin* alleged workplace sex discrimination and sought, *inter alia,* compensatory and punitive damages.[67] The court denied (b)(2) certification but found the allegations made by the plaintiffs sufficient to meet the requirements

---

[63]*See, e.g.,* Zapata v. IBP, Inc., 167 F.R.D. 147, 166 (D. Kan. 1996) ("Plaintiffs' claims are highly individualistic, inasmuch as the precise relief which this court would grant to each successful plaintiff depends upon a number of factors and characteristics specific to each particular plaintiff. [citation omitted] Consequently, the damages computation would require separate 'mini-trials,' where individual damages determinations would predominate over common issues."); *Gorence,* 1994 U.S. Dist. LEXIS 11438, at *34 (rejecting (b)(3) certification in light of "the personal nature of the claims" and the individual issues surrounding "whether each class member suffered discrimination, as well as individualized damages").

[64]*See Zapata,* 167 F.R.D. at 163 (rejecting (b)(3) certification based in part on "manageability problems . . . with respect to calculating the compensatory damages plaintiffs claim"); *Gorence,* 1994 U.S. Dist. LEXIS 11438, at *27–28 (denying (b)(3) certification in age and sex discrimination case, determining that class action treatment would not be "efficient or economical" because it was "foreseeable that the court would be forced to hold a series of mini-trials to determine whether each class member suffered discrimination, as well as individualized damages").

[65]*See, e.g.,* Griffin v. Home Depot, 168 F.R.D. 187, 191, 70 FEP 1678 (E.D. La. 1996) (concluding without significant analysis, in case where plaintiffs sought compensatory damages under 1991 amendments, that "the issues of manageability and judicial economy do not preclude a class action here under Rule 23(b)(3)" and that "one can postulate that there is sufficient commonality of facts to satisfy Rule 23(b)(3)"); Bremiller v. Cleveland Psychiatric Inst., 898 F. Supp. 573, 578–79 (N.D. Ohio 1995) (affirming certification of (b)(3) class of female employees and former employees alleging sexual harassment, rebuffing defendant's contention that individual claims for damages greatly complicate the management of the class action); Alvarado v. Carnation Co., 1995 U.S. Dist. LEXIS 10084, at *18–22 (D. Idaho June 23, 1995) (certifying (b)(3) class of employees alleging discrimination in promotion process notwithstanding that "the court will be required to make individual fact determinations on the issue of entitlement and extent of damages").

[66]168 F.R.D. 187, 70 FEP 1678 (E.D. La. 1996).

[67]*Id.* at 189.

of Rule 23(b)(3).[68] Until these issues are further developed and finally resolved, the interplay between Rule 23 and the 1991 amendments will continue to be litigated actively.

VI. ORGANIZATIONS AS CLASS REPRESENTATIVES

A few courts have granted class representative status to civil rights organizations, generally without extensive analysis of the Rule 23(a) requirements, where an individual class representative is also present,[69] or where the organization's primary function is to represent the interests of the class members.[70]

The Supreme Court has reaffirmed the concept of "associational standing," whereby an organization has limited standing to sue to redress its members' injuries.[71]

---

[68]*Id.* at 191. The court noted that "this aspect of class certification may be revisited . . . after the parties have pursued some discovery on these issues." *Id.*

[69]*E.g.,* Women's Comm. for Equal Employment Opportunity v. National Broad. Co., 77 F.R.D. 666, 668–71, 13 FEP 240 (S.D.N.Y. 1976) (unincorporated association certified, along with individuals, as class representative of female employees in sex discrimination case without comment on association's status as an organization).

[70]*E.g.,* Upper Valley Ass'n for Handicapped Citizens v. Mills, 168 F.R.D. 167, 171 (D. Vt. 1996) (in action by disabled children based on educational rights, court certified class represented by two individuals and civil rights organization, citing "the ability of associations . . . to act as class representatives . . . provided that the underlying purpose of the organization is to represent the interests of the class"); Webb v. Missouri Pac. R.R., 95 F.R.D. 357, 360–62 (E.D. Ark. 1982) (coalition of organizations from several states that existed to assist minorities and females in achieving equal employment opportunities was proper class representative); League of United Latin Am. Citizens v. Salinas Fire Dep't, 88 F.R.D. 533, 542–44, 28 FEP 470 (N.D. Cal. 1980) (organization devoted to achieving equal employment opportunities for Mexican-Americans permitted as class representative; court noted that such groups may be less prone to conflicts with class and more suited to class representation than labor unions); Percy v. Brennan, 384 F. Supp. 800, 809 (S.D.N.Y. 1974) (noting that representation of interests of minority members was primary reason for existence of two civil rights groups); *cf.* Harriss v. Pan Am. World Airways, Inc., 74 F.R.D. 24, 39 n.10, 15 FEP 1640 (N.D. Cal. 1977) (although organization cannot be member of class and therefore normally cannot be class representative, possible exception exists if organization's *raison d'être* is to represent the class).

[71]Food & Commercial Workers v. Brown Group, Inc., 517 U.S. 544 (1996) (reaffirming requirements for associational standing set forth in *Hunt v. Washington State Apple Adver. Comm'n,* 432 U.S. 333, 342–43 (1977), yet permitting union to sue for money damages on behalf of its members for violations of WARN Act, since Congress in enacting statute gave unions standing to assert such claims); *cf.* Sanner v. Board of Trade of City of Chicago, 62 F.3d 918, 923 (7th Cir. 1995) (because proof of damages ordinarily requires participation of association's members in lawsuit, "[w]e

VII. JURISDICTIONAL REQUIREMENTS

B. Intervention

The Eighth Circuit, in *Winbush v. Iowa*,[72] agreed with the courts holding that an intervenor need not independently satisfy the jurisdictional prerequisite of filing an EEOC charge if the intervenor's claims have a "similar and sufficient factual basis" to those of the original plaintiffs. In *Hartman v. Duffy*,[73] the district court permitted intervention to cure the defect that the original named plaintiffs could not represent all job categories sought to be included in the class definition. The court held that the intervenors could rely on the original EEOC charge, since the intervenors and the original plaintiffs shared a common complaint of discriminatory refusal to hire based on gender, albeit in different job categories.[74]

In some cases, intervention has been permitted when a class has been decertified[75] or to cure defects in the class certification.[76]

C. Tolling the Limitations Period

Two recent cases in the Third and Eleventh Circuits have made it clear that although the statute of limitations is tolled for members of the putative class while they are a part of a class action, the statute resumes running once class certification has been denied or a class has been certified that excludes the plaintiffs in question.[77] In those cases, plaintiffs argued that the statute of limitations continues

---

are unaware of any cases allowing associations to proceed on behalf of their members when claims for monetary as opposed to prospective relief are involved").

[72] 66 F.3d 1471, 1478, 69 FEP 1348 (8th Cir. 1995).

[73] 158 F.R.D. 525, 531–36 (D. D.C. 1994), *aff'd*, 88 F.3d 1232 (D.C. Cir. 1996).

[74] *Id.*

[75] *Winbush*, 66 F.3d at 1478–79 (putative class members permitted to intervene as plaintiffs following decertification of class).

[76] *Compare Hartman*, 158 F.R.D. at 531–32 (motion to intervene filed 25 days after appellate court remanded issue of class certification for reconsideration was timely, although 16 years after initiation of litigation) *with* Griffin v. Singletary, 64 FEP 516, 518–19 (11th Cir. 1994) (denying class action status to individuals who attempted to join suit to represent potential employees subjected to challenged testing requirement; across-the-board class had been decertified pursuant to *Falcon* and the EEOC charge upon which new plaintiffs relied was filed by employee without standing to challenge testing requirement), *cert. denied*, 513 U.S. 1077 (1995).

[77] Nelson v. County of Allegheny, 60 F.3d 1010, 1013 (3d Cir. 1995) (holding that tolling period ended upon denial of class certification and therefore affirming

to be tolled until the time for appeal has expired on the underlying class action, because the denial of class certification or exclusion of plaintiffs from the class does not become final until all opportunities for appeal of those issues have been exhausted.[78] Both the Third and Eleventh Circuits rejected that argument, holding that once certification has been denied or the class narrowed to exclude the plaintiffs, it is no longer reasonable for plaintiffs to rely on the class action to protect their interests.[79]

Whether a plaintiff's individual claims are sufficiently identified with the claims asserted in a class action to invoke the tolling rule continues to be decided on a case-by-case basis.[80]

D. The Employer in Bankruptcy

The Ninth Circuit has joined the Sixth, Seventh, and Eleventh Circuits in holding that an individual may file a proof of claim in bankruptcy court on behalf of a class.[81] Some courts have questioned the continuing validity of the Tenth Circuit's position that the Bankruptcy Code does not permit an individual to file a class proof of claim.[82]

---

lower court's dismissal of untimely claims and striking of untimely motions to intervene); Armstrong v. Martin Marietta Corp., 1998 U.S. App. LEXIS 7486 (11th Cir. 1998) (statute of limitations, which was tolled while plaintiffs were putative members of ADEA class action, resumed running when district court dismissed plaintiffs from class, even though district court's denial of certification in interlocutory order could still be reversed).

[78]*Nelson,* 60 F.3d at 1012–13; *Armstrong,* 1998 U.S. App. LEXIS 7486, at *10–12.

[79]*Nelson,* 60 F.3d at 1013 ("to permit the tolling of the statute of limitations until final resolution on appeal of all claims would disable the essential purpose of the statute and encourage plaintiffs to sleep on their rights"); *Armstrong,* at *51 (holding that if class certification has been denied in whole or in part, "no reasonable person would rely" on the pendency of the class action to protect his or her individual rights).

[80]*See, e.g.,* Grimes v. Housing Auth. of the City of New Haven, 242 Conn. 236, 698 A.2d 302, 310 (1998) (holding that *American Pipe* tolling rule applied to negligence claims brought by tenant and her daughter against housing agency when daughter was burned with water heated on stove for baths and class action had asserted claims for failure to provide heat and hot water; court held that class action, "construed broadly and realistically, rather than narrowly and technically ... provided the defendant with adequate notice that a potential class member could make damage claims for a serious personal injury resulting from the defendant's continuing failure to provide sufficient hot water").

[81]In re Birting Fisheries, 92 F.3d 939 (9th Cir. 1996) (Bankruptcy Code should be construed to permit proof of claims filed on behalf of a class).

[82]*See* In re Birting Fisheries, 178 B.R. 849, 851 (Bankr. W.D. Wash. 1995), *aff'd,* 92 F.3d 939, 940 (9th Cir. 1996); In re Amdura Corp., 170 B.R. 445, 447–49 (Bankr.

VIII. THE CLASS DETERMINATION HEARING

A. Setting and Timing of the Hearing

The tension between the requirement of Rule 23(c)(1) for a class determination "as soon as practicable" and the rigorous analysis required by *Falcon* into whether the plaintiff has satisfied the elements of Rule 23 continues to cause courts difficulty in deciding the timing of the class certification hearing and the degree of inquiry into the merits of the case. As noted in the Main Edition, some courts have dealt with this tension by using the express authority of Rule 23(c)(1) to enter a conditional certification order early in the case and treating class certification as a continuous process.[83] As the case and discovery proceed, it may be necessary to reexamine the conditional class certification in light of further factual developments.[84]

IX. RULE 23(d)—DISCRETIONARY ORDERS

Since the Civil Rights Act of 1991 authorizes nonequitable relief, including compensatory and punitive damages, there is a substantial question whether Title VII class actions will always be brought under Rule 23(b)(2). A Rule 23(b)(2) class is appropriate when injunctive and declaratory relief are the primary relief requested. Now, a plaintiff class may request compensatory and punitive damages, requiring the class to be brought under Rule 23(b)(1) or (3). If the class is brought under Rule 23(b)(3), then notice to class members is mandatory, not discretionary.[85]

The law is unclear whether Rule 23(e) applies prior to certification. The rule provides: "A class action shall not be dismissed or compromised without the approval of the court, and notice of the proposed dismissal or compromise shall be given to all members of the class in such manner as the court directs." The

---

D. Colo. 1994) (noting that case also distinguishable because class proof of claim filed *after* district court had certified class).

[83]*See, e.g.,* Medicare Beneficiaries' Defense Fund v. Empire Blue Cross Blue Shield, 938 F. Supp. 1131, 1149 (E.D.N.Y. 1996) (ordering that class be "conditionally certified" under Rule 23(b)(3)).

[84]*See* In re Newbridge Networks Sec. Litig., 926 F. Supp. 1163, 1178 (D.D.C. 1996).

[85]FED. R. CIV. P. 23(c)(2).

Seventh[86] and Ninth[87] Circuits have ruled that Rule 23(e) does apply prior to certification and that notice to putative class members is required. The Fourth Circuit has ruled that it does not.[88]

Courts also have discretion to limit or prevent communication between class members and defense counsel. In general, after class certification, it is not proper for defense counsel to communicate with members of a plaintiff class about the matters at issue in a lawsuit, and a trial court may prevent any such communication.[89] Prior to certification, a court has the discretion to limit communication between defense counsel and plaintiff class members but usually only in the case of actual or potential abuses.[90]

X. Procedural Devices for Resolving Class Monetary Claims

A. Bifurcation

Although courts continue to bifurcate employment discrimination class actions between liability and damages,[91] application

---

[86]Glidden v. Chromalloy Am. Corp., 808 F.2d 621, 625–28 (7th Cir. 1986) (case involving voluntary dismissal of class portion of lawsuit).

[87]Diaz v. Trust Territory of Pac. Islands, 876 F.2d 1401, 1406–11 (9th Cir. 1989) (Rule 23(e) applied where class allegations dismissed voluntarily, prior to class certification, based on risk of prejudice to putative class members who had relied on class action, foregoing filing of individual claims).

[88]Shelton v. Pargo, Inc., 582 F.2d 1298, 1304–14 (4th Cir. 1978) (notice not required where individual plaintiff voluntarily dismissed action pursuant to settlement, prior to any decision on class certification; noting, however, that court has discretionary power to decide class issue first, to deny dismissal, or to require notice, if appropriate, in event of collusive settlement or other abuse of the class action procedure).

[89]Kleiner v. First Nat'l Bank of Atlanta, 751 F.2d 1193, 1207 (11th Cir. 1985); Montgomery v. Aetna Plywood, Inc., 1996 U.S. Dist. LEXIS 9213, at *8–12 (N.D. Ill. 1996).

[90]*See, e.g.,* Kilgo v. Bowman Transp., Inc., 88 F.R.D. 592, 595 (N.D. Ga. 1980); Zarate v. Younglove, 86 F.R.D. 80, 105 (C.D. Cal. 1980).

[91]*See, e.g.,* Alvarado v. Carnation Co., 1995 U.S. Dist. LEXIS 10084, at *23 (D. Idaho June 23, 1995) (ordering bifurcation in disparate treatment and hostile environment class action); Flavel v. Svedala Indus., 875 F. Supp. 550, 555 (E.D. Wis. 1994) (preliminarily ordering bifurcation in ADEA class action); *cf.* Morgan v. United Parcel Serv. of Am., 169 F.R.D. 349, 358 (E.D. Mo. 1996) (in race discrimination case brought by African-American salaried employees, court severed issues of liability and injunctive relief from damages phase of trial and conditionally certified under Rule 23(b)(2) only liability and injunctive relief issues; court stated that it would consider certifying damages phase as Rule 23(b)(3) class action).

of that procedure is not automatic.[92] In addition, courts are beginning to recognize that the 1991 amendments to Title VII introduced constitutional concerns into the previously uncontroversial bifurcation analysis. Prior to 1991, the Seventh Amendment was not implicated by class action litigation involving claims of employment discrimination because the parties had no right to a jury trial under Title VII. The 1991 amendments to Title VII changed that by allowing plaintiffs to recover compensatory and punitive damages and by providing the right to a jury trial in cases in which such damages are sought.[93] The majority of courts addressing this issue have held that "the Seventh Amendment does not mandate that all phases of the litigation be heard by the same jury."[94] These courts have reasoned that a second phase of the trial, resolving only individual claims for compensatory damages, would not involve the "same issues" as the first phase addressing classwide liability issues and that the risk of inconsistent verdicts is minimal.[95]

---

[92]*See, e.g.,* Krueger v. New York Tel. Co., 163 F.R.D. 446, 448 (S.D.N.Y. 1995) (denying, as premature, plaintiffs' motion to bifurcate age discrimination class action due to the complexities raised but not addressed by their motion: "what issues will be tried in the first trial, what issues will be left to subsequent trials, and whether there should be individual trials of the claims of individual groups of plaintiffs").

[93]*See* Section I.D *supra.*

[94]Butler v. Home Depot, 70 FEP 51, 55–56 (N.D. Cal. 1996). *Accord* EEOC v. McDonnell Douglas Corp., 960 F. Supp. 203, 205, 72 FEP 769 (E.D. Mo. 1996) (rejecting defendant's argument that bifurcating ADEA claims into separate liability and damages trials would violate the Seventh Amendment, noting that "[a]lthough some of the evidence may overlap, the issues to be decided at the separate trials are wholly distinct"); *Griffin,* 168 F.R.D. at 191 (endorsing bifurcation analysis of *Butler* court); *cf.* Sperling v. Hoffman-La Roche, Inc., 924 F. Supp. 1346, 1353 (D.N.J. 1996) (quoting special master's decision rejecting defendant employer's Seventh Amendment arguments against bifurcation in class action under ADEA, reasoning that while bifurcation "certainly presents a risk of inconsistent verdicts, that risk is slight in pattern-or-practice case[s] . . . because . . . if plaintiffs do prove at a Stage I trial that a pattern of illegal discrimination existed, his chances are low that [defendant] could show, in a large number of later stage trials, that it did not discriminate against individual plaintiffs"; however, court vacated special master's bifurcation decision on other grounds).

Several courts in other types of class actions also have rejected the Seventh Amendment arguments. *See, e.g.,* Valentino v. Carter-Wallace, 97 F.3d 1227, 1232 (9th Cir. 1996) (products liability case against maker of epilepsy drug); In re Copley Pharm., Inc., 161 F.R.D. 456, 464 (D. Wyo. 1995) (products liability action against pharmaceutical company).

[95]*Butler,* 70 FEP at 55–56.

Other courts have disagreed, holding that Seventh Amendment rights are implicated when separate phases of a bifurcated trial are not heard by the same jury.[96]

The court in *McKnight v. Circuit City Stores*[97] considered the defendant's argument that bifurcation of that employment discrimination class action would violate its constitutional rights because "the Seventh Amendment of the United States Constitution forbids reexamination when the issues before the two juries are 'interwoven.'"[98] The court declined to adopt the Seventh Amendment arguments, stating that the "fairness concerns ... are not of unconstitutional proportions."[99] Instead, the court exercised its discretion under Rule 23(b) to decertify the class, due to the inherent "efficiency problems and unfairness issues involved in a complex bifurcated trial."[100] The court reasoned that the scenario proposed by the plaintiffs, whereby a Stage I jury would award punitive damages to the entire class based on limited evidence, was unfair to the defendants because "[t]he essential issues of motive and intent, reprehensibility, and relationship of a class-wide punitive damages claim to proven harm would not be fully developed or decided until the contemplated Stage II trials, and could not be resolved as to the class as a whole until all those trials were completed."[101] Finally, the *McKnight* court determined that because "[t]he same evidence would be relevant and admissible" at the

---

[96]Celestine v. Citgo Petroleum Corp., 165 F.R.D. 463, 470, 70 FEP 80 (W.D. La. 1995) (in denying certification, court presumed that Seventh Amendment required same jury to hear both liability and damages and emphasized the impracticability and unmanageability of having the same jury hear individual damages claims for many plaintiffs).

Several courts in other types of class actions also have embraced the Seventh Amendment arguments. *See, e.g.,* In re Castano v. American Tobacco Co., 84 F.3d 734, 750–51 (5th Cir. 1996) (ordering decertification of class in products liability action by cigarette smokers, based in part on "the risk that in order to make this class action manageable, the court will be forced to bifurcate issues in violation of the Seventh Amendment"); Rhone-Poulenc Rorer, Inc., 51 F.3d 1292, 1302–04 (7th Cir.) (products liability case brought by hemophiliacs allegedly infected with AIDS virus from using defendants' blood products), *cert. denied,* 116 S. Ct. 184 (1995).

[97]168 F.R.D. 550 (E.D. Va. 1996).

[98]*Id.* at 552 (quoting In re Rhone-Poulenc Rorer, Inc., 51 F.3d 1293, 1302–03 (7th Cir.), *cert. denied,* 116 S. Ct. 184 (1995)).

[99]*Id.* at 553.

[100]*Id.*

[101]*Id.*

various proposed trial stages, bifurcation would be inefficient and burdensome.[102]

At least one court has attempted to respond to the Seventh Amendment issue in an ADEA class action by refusing to conduct separate trials with different juries, and instead ordering a single trial in two stages, reasoning that such an arrangement would "address[] Plaintiffs' fear of repetitively presenting their pattern and practice evidence, and Defendants' concern of an unfair presumption resulting from evidence that a second jury has not had an opportunity to hear."[103]

B. Appointment of a Special Master

Defendant employers have also raised Seventh Amendment arguments in opposing the appointment of a special master to determine individual damages after liability has been decided, with some success. For example, in *Zapata v. IBP, Inc.*,[104] the court rejected the plaintiff's suggestion that a special master could be properly appointed to assess individual damages awards, finding such an appointment impermissible unless the defendant was willing to stipulate to it.[105] Other courts have continued to appoint special masters to determine various issues following a trial on liability.[106]

---

[102]*Id. Accord* Flavel v. Svedala Indus., 875 F. Supp. 550, 555 (E.D. Wis. 1994) (noting that when employment discrimination case is bifurcated, "efficiency is best enhanced if the same jury makes liability and remedial factual findings, as (1) the plaintiffs need not reintroduce in the remedies phase anecdotal evidence already presented in the liability phase, (2) the defendants need not reintroduce in the remedial phase defenses already presented in the liability phase, and (3) conflicting discrimination findings as to plaintiffs whose cases are litigated in the liability phase are avoided"); *cf. Celestine,* 165 F.R.D. at 470 (presuming that Seventh Amendment required same jury to hear both liability and damages, noting that such a trial might be impracticable and unmanageable due to the need to determine "individual damages for scores or even hundreds of plaintiffs").

[103]Rosen v. Reckitt & Colman, Inc., 1994 U.S. Dist. LEXIS 16511, at *15 (S.D.N.Y. Nov. 10, 1994).

[104]167 F.R.D. 147 (D. Kan. 1996).

[105]*Id.* at 164–65. *Accord* Neal v. Department of Corrections, 1995 U.S. Dist. LEXIS 11543, at *10 (D.D.C. Aug. 9, 1995) (determining that damages phase of Title VII sexual harassment class action could not be referred to special master because "defendants have not agreed to waive their Seventh Amendment right to a jury trial, [and] non-consensual referral to a special master would be constitutionally suspect").

[106]*See, e.g.,* Schaefer v. Tannian, 164 F.R.D. 630, 632 (E.D. Mich. 1996) (magistrate utilized as special master to equitably distribute monetary settlement amount as back pay to individual class members, in action predating 1991 Civil Rights Act,

C. Proof-of-Claim Forms

Courts continue to utilize proof-of-claim forms to determine class participation and individual damages claims.[107]

XI. SETTLEMENT

A. Precertification Settlements

The Supreme Court, in its decision in *Amchem Products, Inc. v. Windsor*,[108] ruled that a court may not certify for settlement purposes only a class that it could not certify through litigation. The Court held that while the settlement is relevant to the certification decision, the class still must independently meet all the requirements of Rule 23(a) and (b) in order to be certified.[109] Moreover, the plaintiffs' shared interest in receiving prompt compensation by settling is not in itself sufficient to satisfy Rule 23(b)(3)'s requirement that common questions of law or fact predominate.[110]

Prior to the Supreme Court's decision in *Amchem*, the Advisory Committee on Civil Rules proposed a new provision, Rule 23(b)(4),

---

alleging sex discrimination in police department's hiring, promotion, and compensation); Hartman v. Duffy, 158 F.R.D. 525, 530 (D.D.C. 1994) (special master appointed to conduct individual hearings to assess appropriate relief following court's determination that defendant had discriminated against female job applicants; no Seventh Amendment challenge raised, as both parties consented to appointment), aff'd, 88 F.3d 1232 (D.C. Cir. 1996).
    [107]*See, e.g., Schaefer*, 164 F.R.D. at 632 (using claim forms to calculate back pay in class action alleging sex discrimination in police department's hiring, promotion, and compensation); Neal v. Department of Corrections, 1995 U.S. Dist. LEXIS 11543, at *6 (D.D.C. Aug. 9, 1995) (utilizing claim forms to establish claimant's interest in class membership and award monetary damages in sexual harassment class action).
    [108]117 S. Ct. 2231, 1997 U.S. LEXIS 4032 (1997).
    [109]*Id.*, 1997 U.S. LEXIS 4032, at *50–54. *Cf.* Flanagan v. Ahearn (In re Asbestos Litig.), 90 F.3d 963, 975 (5th Cir. 1996) (holding that court is permitted to consider terms of proposed settlement when simultaneously deciding whether to certify a class, in accordance with Rule 23 requirements, and to approve the settlement), *vacated and remanded in light of* Amchem *decision*, 117 S. Ct. 2503 (1997), *aff'd on remand*, 134 F.3d 668 (5th Cir. 1998) (court affirmed its prior decision, concluding without much analysis that class did satisfy Rule 23 requirements); In re General Motors Corp. Pick-Up Truck Fuel Tank Prods. Liability Litig., 55 F.3d 768, 778 (3d Cir.), *cert. denied*, 116 S. Ct. 88 (1995) (holding that settlement class was not properly certified).
    [110]*Id.* at * 55–56.

which would permit certification for purposes of "settlement, even though the requirements of subdivision (b)(3) might not be met for purposes of trial."[111] If passed, this proposal would override the *Amchem* decision; however, the fate of the proposal is uncertain at this point.

B. Settlement Procedure and Court Approval

Developments in the law relating to affirmative action, and the provisions of the Civil Rights Act of 1991, have made the settlement procedure more complex in class action employment discrimination proceedings. In addition to the criteria set forth in the Main Edition,[112] courts must now consider whether any affirmative action contained in a proposed settlement is legal under the Fourteenth Amendment and Title VII. "Under the equal protection clause, the court must apply strict scrutiny to the race-conscious relief in the decree.... Sex-conscious relief, however, is subject to intermediate scrutiny."[113] To grant affirmative action relief, the court must determine that remedial action is justified based on the facts of the case and that the remedy proposed is narrowly tailored to the violation that exists. In the case of race-based affirmative action, there must be a compelling interest for the adoption of the remedy.[114] The courts have indicated that a remedy based on inclusion (e.g., attracting more qualified female or minority applicants through recruitment and other techniques) as opposed to one

---

[111]*See* Henry J. Reske, *Making Class Distinctions: Critics Say Class Action Proposals Encourage Collusion as Well as Settlements,* 83 A.B.A.J. 22 (1997), for a discussion of the proposed rule change.

[112]For an alternative statement of the criteria to be considered in approving settlements, *see* Shuford v. Alabama State Bd. of Educ., 897 F. Supp. 1535, 1548–49 (M.D. Ala. 1995), in which the district court identified the following factors: (1) views of class members; (2) views of class counsel; (3) substance and amount of opposition to the settlement; (4) possible existence of collusion; and (5) other factors, including (a) the stage of the proceedings; (b) the likelihood of success at trial; (c) the complexity, expense, and likely duration of the lawsuit; and (d) the range of possible recovery.

[113]*Id.* at 1550, citing Adarand Constructors, Inc. v. Pena, 115 S. Ct. 2097, 2113 (1995) and Ensley Branch, NAACP v. Seibels, 31 F.3d 1548, 1579–80 (11th Cir. 1994), among other cases.

[114]*See, e.g.,* In re Birmingham Reverse Discrimination Employment Litig., 20 F.3d 1525, 1544 (11th Cir. 1994), *cert. denied,* 514 U.S. 1065 (1995).

based on exclusion (i.e., selecting some candidates rather than others from a pool) is more likely to be acceptable.[115]

As discussed below, the Civil Rights Act of 1991 has provisions protecting consent decrees. Therefore, settling parties and courts are going to greater lengths to "ensure that all interested parties were informed of the settlement and had the opportunity to voice their objections."[116] Some courts are even going so far as to appoint a lawyer and/or a guardian *ad litem* for affected groups that are not parties to the action.

D. Collateral Attack on Consent Decrees

The law on the rights of affected nonclass members to challenge consent judgments has continued to develop.[117] Settling parties and courts are now careful to comply with the provisions of Title VII that protect against collateral attacks. "[T]he Civil Rights Act of 1991 precludes challenges to a consent judgment resolving employment discrimination claims from those non-class members who had actual notice of the proposed decree and a reasonable opportunity to present objections."[118]

XII. APPEALS

The Sixth and Seventh Circuits have recently used the writ of mandamus to review and reverse class certification orders, although those cases did not involve claims of employment discrimination.[119]

---

[115] *Shuford*, 897 F. Supp. at 1551 *et seq.*
[116] *Id.* at 1547.
[117] *See, e.g.*, In re Birmingham Reverse Discrimination Employment Litig., 20 F.3d 1525 (11th Cir. 1994) (holding that § 1981 consent decree mandating that city select employees for promotion based on race could not withstand scrutiny under Title VII or the Fourteenth Amendment), *cert. denied*, 514 U.S. 1065 (1995); Ensley Branch, NAACP v. Seibels, 31 F.3d 1548 (11th Cir. 1994) (remanding case to district court for further modification of a consent decree involving city employment practices to address changed circumstances).
[118] *Shuford*, 897 F. Supp. at 1547, citing 42 U.S.C.A. § 2000e-2(n)(1)(B) (West 1994).
[119] In re Rhone-Poulenc Rorer, Inc., 51 F.3d 1293 (7th Cir.), *cert. denied*, 116 S. Ct. 184 (1995) (products liability case brought by hemophiliacs allegedly infected with AIDS virus from blood products); In re American Med. Sys., Inc., 75 F.3d 1069 (6th Cir. 1996) (products liability case involving penile prostheses).

Courts have also continued to use the Interlocutory Appeals Act of 1958, 28 U.S.C. § 1292(b), to a limited extent to obtain review of class certification orders.[120]

The Advisory Committee on Civil Rules has proposed a new Rule 23(f) permitting discretionary appeals from an order granting or denying class action certification. The Notes to the Proposed Rule refer to the same standards applicable to 28 U.S.C. § 1292(b), but call for interlocutory appeals to be granted "with restraint."

If the named plaintiff settles a claim without reserving the right to appeal the adverse class certification ruling, then he or she may not appeal.[121]

---

[120]*See* Castano v. American Tobacco Co., 162 F.R.D. 112 (E.D. La. 1995), *class certification order rev'd,* 84 F.3d 734, 744 (5th Cir. 1996).

[121]Dugas v. Trans Union Corp., 99 F.3d 724 (5th Cir. 1996); Shores v. Sklar, 885 F.2d 760 (11th Cir. 1989), *cert. denied,* 493 U.S. 1045 (1990).

Part 10

Discovery and Proof

Chapter 38

DISCOVERY

I. Introduction

Courts continue to be guided by the principle that discovery under the federal rules is broad and that civil discovery rules are to be construed liberally in Title VII and ADEA cases.[1] For example, "[i]t is well settled that in a Title VII suit, an employer's general practices are relevant even when a plaintiff is asserting an individual claim for disparate treatment."[2] At the same time, courts recognize that discovery in discrimination cases is "not without limits."[3] Recent decisions have also required plaintiffs seeking "broad discovery" or discovery of confidential information to articulate the relevance of the information sought.[4] Courts have also

---

[1] *See, e.g.,* Sempier v. Johnson & Higgins, 45 F.3d 724, 734–35, 66 FEP 1214 (3d Cir.) (the court of appeals vacated the district court's discovery rulings after finding that they were an improper "wholesale substitution of court-engineered discovery"; the court of appeals stated that the district court had no authority to "rewrite a party's questions and in effect serve its own set of interrogatories"), *cert. denied,* 115 S. Ct. 2611, 68 FEP 64 (1995); Gomez v. Martin Marietta Corp., 50 F.3d 1511, 1520, 67 FEP 537 (10th Cir. 1995) (discovery in Title VII cases "should not be narrowly circumscribed"); Ladson v. Ulltra East Parking Corp., 164 F.R.D. 376, 378, 70 FEP 140 (S.D.N.Y. 1996) (explaining that "[a]ll that must be shown is that the discovery requested possibly might be relevant, . . . or is reasonably calculated to lead to the discovery of admissible evidence," court ordered defendant to produce personnel files of its current and former employees and supervisors); Peterson v. City College of the City Univ. of N.Y., 160 F.R.D. 22, 23–24, 70 FEP 259 (S.D.N.Y. 1994) (when plaintiff's complaint alleges a continuing pattern or practice of discrimination, plaintiff should be afforded a broad scope of discovery regarding defendant's employment policies and procedures); Rodger v. Electronic Data Sys., 155 F.R.D. 537, 539, 2 WH2d 1436 (E.D.N.C. 1994) ("Relevance is broadly construed . . . and 'encompass[es] any matter that bears on, or that reasonably could lead to any other matter that could bear on, any issue that is or that may be in the case.' [quotation omitted]. . . . This is especially the case with regard to discrimination claims, where the imposition of unnecessary discovery limitations is to be avoided.").

[2] Gomez v. Martin Marietta, 50 F.3d at 1520, 67 FEP at 543.

[3] *Id.;* Rodger v. Electronic Data Sys., 155 F.R.D. at 539, 2 WH2d 1436.

[4] *See* Hicks v. Arthur, 159 F.R.D. 468, 470 (E.D. Pa. 1995) (denying plaintiffs' motion to compel interrogatory responses that would have required defendant to conduct

shown a willingness to examine whether the discovery sought addresses the particular issues in the case.[5]

II. Strategy Considerations

A. Plaintiffs

Upon initiating litigation, plaintiffs should develop and adhere to a discovery plan.[6] Additionally, given that Fed. R. Civ. P. 33 limits the number of interrogatories a party can propound, plaintiffs should take care to formulate interrogatories that seek specific information not already contained in the employer's responses to other discovery requests.[7] Plaintiffs should utilize Rule 30(b)(6) depositions in conjunction with requests for production of documents to

---

a survey of all of its employees, past and present, over an eight-year period when defendant at the time of the request employed over 1,000 people, and plaintiffs "have not demonstrated the relevance of this expansive information"); Whittingham v. Amherst College, 164 F.R.D. 124, 127 (D. Mass. 1995) (rejecting plaintiff's request for personnel files of three other employees because plaintiff offered only a conclusory assertion that the files were relevant, and this assertion did not outweigh the three individuals' privacy interests).

[5]*Compare* Rodger v. Electronic Data Sys., 155 F.R.D. 537, 539–42, 2 WH2d 1436 (E.D.N.C. 1994) (limiting discovery in age discrimination action; distinguishing Hollander v. American Cyanamid Co., 895 F.2d 80, 51 FEP 1881 (2d Cir. 1990), on the grounds that, in the instant case, the facility in which the plaintiff worked exercised independent decisionmaking authority) *with* Kitchen v. Dial Page Co., 67 FEP 482, 484 (E.D. Tenn. 1995) (refusing to limit discovery to the employing unit because decision to terminate plaintiff's employment was not made locally). *See also* Gheesling v. Chater, 162 F.R.D. 649, 650, 68 FEP 965 (D. Kan. 1995) ("In employment discrimination cases, discovery is usually limited to information about employees in the same department or office absent a showing of a more particularized need for, and the likely relevance of, broader information"; court would examine plaintiffs' proof to determine whether earlier discovery "could possibly indicate a hiring practice applicable to all employing units.").

[6]*See* Ayala-Gerena v. Bristol Myers-Squibb Co., 95 F.3d 86, 91–92, 71 FEP 1398 (1st Cir. 1996) (affirming summary judgment for defendant, despite plaintiffs' request to conduct reasonable discovery pursuant to Fed. R. Evid. 56(f); because plaintiffs failed to exercise due diligence in obtaining discovery, plaintiffs filed their Rule 56(f) request after they filed their brief in opposition to defendant's motion for summary judgment, and plaintiffs' Rule 56(f) request failed to identify the specific outstanding items of discovery that would be dispositive to the issues raised).

[7]*See* Atkinson v. Denton Publ'g Co., 84 F.3d 144, 147, 70 FEP 1352 (5th Cir. 1996) (affirming district court's refusal to allow plaintiff to serve additional interrogatories, despite plaintiff's claim that he derived no benefit from defendant's responses to prior interrogatories that referenced defendant's mandatory disclosures).

obtain detailed information regarding defendant's employment practices, including hiring, promotion, transfer, termination, and compensation data.[8]

Plaintiffs should also utilize Rule 34 document requests and gather raw data necessary to create statistical analyses, which plaintiffs should use to (1) support pattern and practice allegations[9]; (2) rebut as pretextual defendant's purported nondiscriminatory reason for taking an adverse employment action[10]; and (3) support class certification motions.[11] In addition to payroll records, computerized or hard copy personnel files or employment histories are sources of such raw data.[12]

When conducting electronic media discovery, plaintiffs should also conduct Rule 30(b)(6) depositions or serve interrogatories to determine how the defendant has maintained, stored, and deleted relevant personnel and employment records.[13]

---

[8]*See* Coleman v. General Elec. Co., No. 94-CV-4740, 1995 U.S. Dist. LEXIS 8186, at *11–*16 (E.D. Pa. June 8, 1995) (permitting Rule 30(b)(6) deposition regarding defendant's hiring, promotion, and termination decisions affecting employees in defendant's 250-employee human resources department).

[9]*See* Lyoch v. Anheuser-Busch Cos., Inc., 164 F.R.D. 62, 65–68, 74 FEP 691 (E.D. Mo. 1995) (permitting companywide discovery regarding the hiring and promotion of employees similarly situated to plaintiffs, who alleged pattern or practice of gender discrimination).

[10]*Id.* at 66 (citing Hollander v. American Cyanamid Co., 895 F.2d 80, 84, 51 FEP 1881 (2d Cir. 1990) and Miles v. Boeing Co., 154 F.R.D. 117, 119–21 (E.D. Pa. 1994), which granted companywide discovery of employment practices with regard to particular position at issue).

[11]Orlowski v. Dominick's Finer Foods, Inc., No. 95 C 1666, 1995 U.S. Dist. LEXIS 12468, at *4–*7 (N.D. Ill. Aug. 22, 1995) (granting detailed companywide discovery of computer data base information and employment practices to determine the scope of the potential class), *clarified,* 1995 U.S. Dist. LEXIS 13197 (E.D. Ill. Sept. 11, 1995).

[12]Zapata v. IBP, Inc., No. 93-2366-EEO, 1994 U.S. Dist. LEXIS 16285, at *6–*12 (D. Kan. Nov. 10, 1994) (granting plaintiffs' request for companywide discovery of defendant's computerized work histories and dispensary records of all employees located at two of defendant's plants; such information was relevant to plaintiffs' motion for class certification), *review denied,* 1994 U.S. Dist. LEXIS 18660 (D. Kan. Dec. 12, 1994); Fed. R. Evid. 34(a) Advisory Committee's note (1970 amendment) ("Rule 34 applies to electronics data compilations from which information can be obtained only with the use of detection devices.").

[13]*See generally* Joseph L. Kashi, *Electronic Discovery Battleplan,* 6 LAW OFF. COMPUTING 54 (1997); Joseph L. Kashi, *How to Conduct Electronic Media Discovery,* 7 PRAC. LITIG. 75 (1996). For examples of computer-related interrogatories and document production requests in the context of Title VII class certification, *see* Orlowski v. Dominick's Finer Foods, Inc., No. 95 C 1666, 1995 U.S. Dist. LEXIS 12468 (N.D. Ill. Aug. 22, 1995) (information sought was relevant in determining scope

In appropriate circumstances, plaintiffs may consider requesting Rule 34(b) premises inspections to review the defendant's computer hard drive. In making such requests, plaintiffs should specify relevant materials that they are likely to find on the hard drive.[14] Plaintiffs should also work with computer experts to establish procedures by which they will have access to the relevant files yet minimize costs as well as intrusion into the defendant's operations and proprietary or otherwise confidential materials.[15]

Where the defendant has destroyed documents, plaintiffs may be entitled to an adverse inference, i.e., that the missing records would have supported their cases. However, courts will review the facts surrounding the defendant's failure to maintain documents, and courts do not always find the adverse inference supported nor impose sanctions on the defendant.[16]

In addition, courts now regularly order discovery of electronic communications, such as e-mail.[17]

---

of potential class and not overly burdensome), *reconsideration denied, clarified,* 1995 U.S. Dist. LEXIS 13197 (N.D. Ill. 1995); Zapata v. IBP, Inc., No. 93-2366-EEO, 1994 U.S. Dist. LEXIS 16285 (D. Kan. Nov. 10, 1994).

[14]*See* Fennell v. First Step Designs, Ltd., 83 F.3d 526, 532–34, 70 FEP 1305 (1st Cir. 1996) (affirming the district court's denial of plaintiff's request for access to defendant's hard drive because plaintiff failed to demonstrate a particularized likelihood of discovering that defendant had fabricated a document, and plaintiff made no effort to focus her request in a way that would minimize costs or risks of obtaining confidential information). *But see* Momah v. Albert Einstein Med. Ctr., 164 F.R.D. 412, 418 (E.D. Pa. 1996) (granting plaintiff's motion to compel requiring employer to produce copy of computer list-files screen listing date document created and last edited because such information could show if defendants backdated documents).

[15]Fennell v. First Step Designs, 83 F.3d at 532–34, 70 FEP at 1305.

[16]Gomez v. Martin Marietta, 50 F.3d 1511, 1519–20, 67 FEP 537 (10th Cir. 1995) (magistrate could refuse to impose sanctions on employer where employer destroyed files that were summaries of original files but had already provided original files to plaintiff); Hansen v. Dean Witter Reynolds, Inc., 887 F. Supp. 669, 675–76, 68 FEP 370 (S.D.N.Y. 1995) (denying plaintiff's motion for sanctions based on defendant's destruction of trading tickets processed by a unit in which plaintiff had worked; defendant destroyed tickets pursuant to internal document retention policy, neither complaint nor letters from EEOC created an independent duty to preserve tickets, and there was no evidence that plaintiff made initial request within period in which documents would have been retained).

[17]*In re* Brand Name Prescription Drugs Antitrust Litig., 1995 WL 360526 (N.D. Ill. June 15, 1995) (ordering production of e-mail including materials stored within computer system and refusing to require class plaintiffs to pay for the cost of retrieval of stored communications estimated at $50,000–70,000); *but see* Bass Public Ltd. Co. v. Promus Cos., 1994 WL 702052 (S.D.N.Y. Dec. 12, 1994) (ordering defendants to search system for e-mail to and from 10 individuals but denying more extensive search).

Courts vary in their decisions about which party should be assessed the expenses associated with generating computerized information that responds to plaintiffs' discovery requests. One court determined that an employer's expenditure of $1,500 for 30 hours of computer programming to respond to the plaintiff's interrogatory regarding persons terminated while on workers' compensation or injury leave was not unduly burdensome.[18]

B. Defendants

Strategy considerations for defendants described in the Main Edition remain valid and should be considered by defense counsel.

At the earliest opportunity, defendants should obtain a copy of the plaintiffs' EEOC files. However, before requesting copies of plaintiffs' EEOC files, defendants should consult EEOC guidelines.[19]

In an action in which a plaintiff is claiming disability discrimination under the ADA, the defendant should seek to obtain, through requests for production or subpoenas, all documents relating to the plaintiff's claims for benefits related to that disability, including records from insurance companies, the Social Security Administration, and any state agencies to which the plaintiff submitted a claim. Several courts have held that when an individual has represented himself or herself as totally disabled in order to receive disability benefits, the individual is estopped from claiming that he or she is a qualified individual with a disability under the ADA.[20] Other courts have considered such representations as factors to be weighed in determining whether the individual is protected by the ADA.[21] For a more complete discussion of the

---

[18]Mackey v. IBP, Inc., 167 F.R.D. 186, 199, 203 (D. Kan. 1996).

[19]*See* 29 C.F.R. pt. 1610 (EEOC's 1996 FOIA regulations); *Charge Processing Procedures Adopted by the EEOC and Task Force Recommendations To Be Implemented by the Chairman,* 3 EEOC COMPL. MAN. (BNA) at N:3067 (Apr. 9, 1995).

[20]*See, e.g.,* McNemar v. Disney Store, Inc., 91 F.3d 610, 618, 5 AD 1227 (3d Cir. 1996), *cert. denied,* 117 S. Ct. 958 (1997); Garcia-Paz v. Swift Textiles, Inc., 873 F. Supp. 547, 555, 3 AD 1844 (D. Kan. 1995); Nguyen v. IBP, Inc., 905 F. Supp. 1471, 1485, 5 AD 465 (D. Kan. 1995); Fussell v. Georgia Ports Auth., 906 F. Supp. 1561, 1575, 5 AD 1236 (S.D. Ga. 1995), *aff'd,* 106 F.3d 417 (11th Cir. 1997); Berry v. Norfolk S. Corp., 1995 WL 465819, at *2 (W.D. Va. June 23, 1995); Harden v. Delta Air Lines, Inc., 900 F. Supp. 493, 496–97, 4 AD 1241 (S.D. Ga. 1995).

[21]*See, e.g.,* Reigel v. Kaiser Found. Health Plan, 859 F. Supp. 963, 970, 3 AD 577 (E.D.N.C. 1994); Kennedy v. Applause, Inc., 1994 WL 740765, at *5 (C.D. Cal. Dec. 6, 1994), *aff'd,* 90 F.3d 1477, 5 AD 1249 (9th Cir. 1996).

courts' varying treatment of this issue, *see* Chapter 9, Section III.B.2.c, in this Supplement.

Defendants should also be aware that some courts hearing sexual harassment cases have held that Rule 412 of the Federal Rules of Evidence (the "rape shield rule") limits the discovery of plaintiffs' past sexual conduct.[22]

Answers to contention interrogatories may not cut off plaintiffs' right to assert additional theories.[23]

When taking a plaintiff's deposition, defendants should seek the evidentiary foundation for alleged discriminatory incidents or statements, i.e., including what statements were made, to whom they were made, and how and when the plaintiff became aware of them.[24]

III. LIMITATIONS ON DISCOVERY

A. Discovery Sought by Plaintiffs

1. Privileged Materials

Although *EEOC v. Associated Dry Goods Corp.*[25] is still the main authority on disclosure of information obtained during an EEOC investigation, the extent to which such information is discoverable is still being debated. It is clear that only parties to the agency proceeding are entitled to obtain information from the EEOC file.[26]

---

[22]*See* Barta v. City & County of Honolulu, 169 F.R.D. 132 (D. Haw. 1996); Sanchez v. Zabihi, 166 F.R.D. 500, 501–02, 71 FEP 835 (D.N.M. 1996); Alberts v. Wickes Lumber Co., 1995 WL 117886 (N.D. Ill. Mar. 15, 1995). *See also* Fed. R. Evid. 412 Advisory Committee's note ("[i]n order not to undermine the rationale of Rule 412 . . . court[s] should enter appropriate orders pursuant to Fed. R. Civ. P. 26(c) to protect the victim against unwarranted inquiries and to ensure confidentiality"). *See also, infra,* Section III.B.2.

[23]*See* Sperling v. Hoffman-La Roche, Inc., 924 F. Supp. 1396, 1411–12, 72 FEP 1401 (D.N.J. 1996) (plaintiffs not precluded from pursuing an additional theory of discrimination even though the theory was not stated in their answers to contention interrogatories).

[24]*See* Edwards v. Wallace Community College, 49 F.3d 1517, 1522, 67 FEP 949 (11th Cir. 1995) (refusing to consider on summary judgment alleged racial remarks that had no evidentiary foundation).

[25]449 U.S. 590, 24 FEP 1356 (1981) (holding that charging parties have the right to discover at least part of the EEOC's investigatory file).

[26]*See* J.J.C. v. Fridell, 165 F.R.D. 513, 518 (D. Minn. 1995) (EEOC materials are discoverable by parties to the agency proceeding since they could not logically be considered the "public"); Comas v. United Tel. Co., 70 FEP 159, 160 (D. Kan.

Even though charging parties have been given the right to discover portions of the EEOC's files concerning their charges, they have not been given the right to depose EEOC investigators about their investigation.[27]

Additionally, some courts have allowed the discovery of investigative files produced by other agencies or state departments.[28] However, courts have been reluctant to order discovery of information in defendants' investigative files when the investigation is performed by counsel.[29]

1995) (allowing plaintiff to discover internal investigation file prepared by the EEOC); EEOC v. Pasta House Co., 70 FEP 61, 63 (E.D. Mo. 1996) (limiting defendant's discovery of EEOC files to class members filing charges against defendant and denying access to any other files including class member charges against other employers, because defendant has no reason to know of class members' charges against other employers; therefore, defendant must be considered part of the "public" as to those other charges).

[27]Leyh v. Modicon, Inc., 881 F. Supp. 420, 424–25 (S.D. Ind. 1995) (in action where EEOC was not a party, plaintiff was not entitled to depose EEOC investigator about facts revealed during the EEOC's investigation of plaintiff's charge of discrimination).

[28]EEOC v. City of Milwaukee, 919 F. Supp. 1247, 1258–59 (E.D. Wis. 1996) (EEOC was entitled to enforcement of subpoena requiring city police department to produce investigatory files if subpoena related to investigation within agency's authority, information sought was relevant, and demand was not unreasonably burdensome).

[29]Motley v. Marathon Oil Co., 69 FEP 911, 914 (10th Cir. 1995) (documents prepared by employer's in-house attorney were protected by the attorney-client privilege even though the employer failed to show that the documents were prepared for the purpose of rendering legal advice), *cert. denied,* 116 S. Ct. 1678 (1996); McDonnell Douglas Corp. v. EEOC, 922 F. Supp. 235, 242–43, 70 FEP 980 (E.D. Mo. 1996) (analyses prepared by employer at the request of counsel for the purpose of rendering legal advice are protected from disclosure by the attorney-client privilege and the privilege is not waived by producing the analyses to the EEOC, which subpoenaed them for a limited purpose); United States *ex rel.* Falsetti v. Southern Bell Tel. & Tel. Co., 915 F. Supp. 308, 313 (N.D. Fla. 1996) (attorney-client and work-product privileges applied to company's internal investigation reports and were not mooted by the state court's rejection of these privileges); Harding v. Dana Transp., Inc., 914 F. Supp. 1084, 1091, 69 FEP 1603 (D.N.J. 1996) (attorney who investigated defendant's employees did so to further the defendant's representation; therefore, the investigation was covered by the attorney-client privilege); Curcio v. Chinn Enters., 70 FEP 9, 10–11 (N.D. Ill. 1996) (questionnaires completed by managerial employees at sexual harassment training seminar conducted by employer's attorneys, who reviewed and discussed questionnaires and provided legal advice, were protected by the attorney-client privilege); Burger v. Litton Indus., 68 FEP 737, 738 (S.D.N.Y. 1995) (documents prepared by employer's counsel for the purpose of providing legal advice regarding a proposed reduction in workforce were protected by the attorney-client privilege even though employer disclosed other related documents that were not privileged). *But see* Butta-Brinkman v. FCA Int'l, 164 F.R.D. 475, 476, 69 FEP 1276, 1277 (N.D. Ill. 1995) (employer cannot withhold information and documentation obtained

Courts continue to be split on the availability of the self-critical analysis privilege. A number of courts have declined to recognize the privilege altogether,[30] while other courts have refused to uphold the privilege under the specific circumstances of the cases before them.[31] On the other hand, a few courts have recognized the privilege and denied discovery of items within its scope.[32]

---

during investigation of other sexual harassment complaints, even though such discovery might undermine employer's policy of conducting confidential investigations into sexual harassment complaints; importance of allowing discovery of evidence that can support a sexual harassment claim outweighs interests served by confidentiality policy).

[30]*See, e.g.,* Holt v. KMI-Continental, Inc., 95 F.3d 123, 134, 73 FEP 1615 (2d Cir. 1996) (noting in Title VII case that there is no authority for the existence of the "self-evaluative" privilege under Connecticut law), *cert. denied,* 117 S. Ct. 1819, 74 FEP 192 (1997); Aramburu v. Boeing Co., 885 F. Supp. 1434, 1437–40 (D. Kan. 1995) (ordering production of defendant's affirmative action plan and documents related to the development of and compliance with the plan and declining to recognize the self-critical analysis privilege "where Congress itself has not seen fit to create [a privilege] after almost 30 years of implementation of the Civil Rights Act of 1964"); Zapata v. IBP, 1994 WL 649322, at *5–*6 (D. Kan. Nov. 10, 1994) (ordering production of defendant's affirmative action plans and reports under reasoning expressed in *Aramburu, supra*); *see also* Cloud v. Superior Court of Los Angeles County, 58 Cal. Rptr. 2d 365, 72 FEP 777 (Cal. Ct. App. 2d Dist. 1996) (self-critical analysis privilege is not among privileges contained in California Evidence Code and the court is not free to create new privileges as a matter of judicial policy; accordingly, in sex discrimination lawsuit, plaintiff may discover defendant's affirmative action plan and related self-critical analyses).

[31]*See, e.g.,* Harding v. Dana Trans., Inc., 914 F. Supp. 1084, 1099–101, 69 FEP 1603 (D.N.J. 1996) (self-critical analysis privilege does not protect defendant's investigation of sexual harassment allegations by two of its employees, notwithstanding defendant's contention that investigation was protected as frank self-criticism and evaluation in development of programs designed to eradicate sexual harassment, where investigation did not produce a generalized report that reviewed defendant's overall record, but was simply review of individual complaints); Whittingham v. Amherst College, 164 F.R.D. 124, 129–30 (D. Mass. 1995) (requiring production of memoranda prepared by affirmative action officer on the grounds that such documents were generated "as a result of Plaintiff's inquiry, not as part of an internal analysis of Defendant's employment and affirmative action policies"); Reilly v. Metro-North Commuter R.R., 1995 WL 105286, at *1 (S.D.N.Y. Mar. 13, 1995) (denying request to withhold from production a memorandum written by defendant's director of affirmative action concerning apparent problems in department and holding that self-critical analysis privilege is inapplicable because disclosure will not deter investigations into violations of Title VII); Reich v. Hercules, Inc., 857 F. Supp. 367, 371 (D.N.J. 1994) (in OSHA investigation, Secretary of Labor is entitled to subpoena explosives manufacturer's safety audit reports because self-critical analysis privilege is unavailable in light of (1) public interest in permitting the Secretary to proceed freely in investigations of potential OSHA violations, and (2) Congress' grant of extremely broad investigatory and subpoena power).

[32]Sheppard v. Consolidated Edison Co., 893 F. Supp. 6, 7–8 (E.D.N.Y. 1995) (upholding self-critical analysis privilege and prohibiting discovery of study performed

Plaintiffs' requests for discovery of other forms of "confidential" or "private" information pertaining to other employees have met with mixed results. Generally, absent a recognized privilege, such discovery has been compelled,[33] but in some instances it has been accompanied by an appropriate order to protect legitimate privacy and/or confidentiality interests.[34]

---

for defendant regarding equal employment opportunity and affirmative action and of survey of employee opinion to the extent such documents contain evaluative material, but permitting discovery on factual underpinnings of such studies); *cf.* Brem v. Decarlo, 162 F.R.D. 94, 101–02 (D. Md. 1995) (denying defendant's motion to compel discovery of information in possession of third-party witness relating to medical peer review committee proceedings on the grounds that (1) purpose of Maryland medical review committee statute would be thwarted if confidentiality not safeguarded; and (2) public interest in promoting quality health care outweighs the defendant's purported need for the information).

[33]*See, e.g.,* Kirkpatrick v. Raleigh County Bd. of Educ., 78 F.3d 579 (4th Cir. 1996) (published at 1996 WL 85122, at *1–*2) (holding that district court did not abuse its discretion in denying motion to compel production of personnel files of other teachers or in granting defendants a protective order as to those records); Ladson v. Ulltra East Parking Corp., 164 F.R.D. 376, 377–78, 70 FEP 140 (S.D.N.Y 1996) (requiring defendant to produce personnel files to plaintiff where files could provide information about defendant's hiring and promotion practices, notwithstanding defendant's contention that production would invade privacy rights of its employees and would be unnecessary in light of defendant's offer to provide certain information in files); Griffith v. Wal-Mart Stores, Inc., 163 F.R.D. 4, 5, 4 AD 1086 (E.D. Ky. 1995) (allowing plaintiff to discover personnel, appraisal, and discipline files of three managerial employees who were involved in plaintiff's termination; plaintiff does not have to allege a pattern or practice of discrimination to be entitled to personnel files); Soto v. City of Concord, 162 F.R.D. 603, 614 (N.D. Cal. 1995) (allowing discovery of officers' personnel files, including disciplinary records and any other files relating to officers' training, duties, and performance); Comas v. United Tel. Co., 70 FEP 159, 160 (D. Kan. 1995) (allowing discovery of redacted personnel files of four employees whose treatment was at issue); Peterson v. City College of Univ. of N.Y., 160 F.R.D. 22, 25, 70 FEP 259 (S.D.N.Y. 1994) (allowing discovery of personnel files of male and younger faculty members granted tenure where plaintiff alleged a cause of action for age and sex discrimination in tenure denial). *Cf.* Gehring v. Case Corp., 43 F.3d 340, 342, 66 FEP 1373 (7th Cir. 1994) (trial court has discretion to prevent discovery of employer's personnel files where other employees were not similarly situated to plaintiff claiming age discrimination and discovery of the files would invade the other employees' privacy interests), *cert. denied,* 115 S. Ct. 2612 (1995).

[34]*See, e.g.,* Black v. New York Univ. Med. Ctr., 1996 WL 294310, at *4 (S.D.N.Y. June 3, 1996) (requiring production of letters of outside evaluators and documents concerning deliberations of committees that considered plaintiff's request for promotion, but noting that such materials should be subject to a protective order and maintained as confidential); Butta-Brinkman v. FCA Int'l, 164 F.R.D. 475, 476–77, 69 FEP 1276 (N.D. Ill. 1995) (requiring defendant in sexual harassment case to produce documents relating to sexual harassment complaints in offices other than the location where plaintiff was employed and admonishing that defendant should

In sexual harassment cases, courts continue to find that evidence of an alleged harasser's prior habits and behavior in the workplace can be relevant to the defendant's knowledge of the harassment, the existence of a hostile work environment, and the supervisor's motive in quid pro quo cases.[35] However, defendants have successfully asserted that material remote in time or dissimilar

---

seek a protective order if it wishes to keep information confidential, but denying plaintiff's motion to compel production of confidential settlement agreements reached in other cases involving sexual harassment); Weinstock v. Columbia Univ., 1995 WL 567399, at *6–*8 (S.D.N.Y. Sept. 26, 1995) (requiring defendant to produce plaintiff's tenure dossier, the personnel files and tenure dossiers of faculty who were considered for tenure during relevant time period, and the names and job titles of members of committee that considered plaintiff's candidacy for tenure on the condition that parties enter into confidentiality agreement to protect privacy interests of faculty members whose files are produced); Ragge v. MCA/Universal Studios, 165 F.R.D. 601, 604–05 (C.D. Cal. 1995) (granting plaintiff's motion to compel production of individual job performance evaluations and reviews, promotion or demotion records, disciplinary actions, and complaints by other employees or customers in the personnel files of individual defendants on the grounds that (1) plaintiff has narrowed her request to specific documents relevant to issues in the case; and (2) any sensitive or personal materials that are discovered should be maintained as confidential under protective order).

[35]See Heyne v. Caruso, 69 F.3d 1475, 1480–81, 69 FEP 408 (9th Cir. 1995) (in a quid pro quo case, evidence of individual's harassment of others can be used to show motive in discharging claimant); Hirase-Doi v. U.S. West Communications, 61 F.3d 777, 783–84, 69 FEP 1745 (10th Cir. 1995) (employer's knowledge of individual's widespread harassment is relevant to issue of notice; however, court must evaluate extent and seriousness of earlier harassment as well as similarity and nearness in time to harassment at issue); Stalnaker v. KMart Corp., 71 FEP 705, 707 (D. Kan. 1996) (allowing discovery of individual's voluntary romantic and sexual activities with nonparty witnesses to extent inquiries showed harasser's conduct encouraged, solicited, or influenced any employee to engage in or continue such activities); EEOC v. National Cleaning Contractors, 71 FEP 159, 160 (S.D.N.Y. 1996) (allowing quid pro quo claimant to introduce co-worker's deposition statements that she too was harassed; such evidence is relevant to issues of motive or intent); Hurley v. Atlantic City Police Dep't, 933 F. Supp. 396, 411, 72 FEP 1828 (D.N.J. 1996) (admitting evidence of supervisor's harassment of others; such evidence is relevant to issues of motive, intent, adequacy of employer's response, and whether events were accidental rather than severe and pervasive); Wreath v. United States, 70 FEP 23, 25–26 (D. Kan. 1995) (co-worker's testimony regarding harasser's off-color jokes relevant to hostile environment claim); Butta-Brinkman v. FCA Int'l, 164 F.R.D. 475, 476, 69 FEP 1276 (N.D. Ill. 1995) (complaints of harassment in other offices probative of whether corporate policy was inadequate); Webb v. Hyman, 861 F. Supp. 1094, 1111–12, 67 FEP 1425 (D.D.C. 1994) (co-workers' testimony regarding harassment was admissible for purposes of showing motive, notice, and intent); *Ragge v. MCA/Universal Studios*, 165 F.R.D. at 604 (permitting discovery of portions of personnel files of harassers, distinguishing nondiscoverable information such as sexual, health, or financial matters).

in motive is intrusive and not reasonably calculated to lead to the discovery of admissible evidence.[36]

Courts continue to be divided on whether plaintiffs' counsel's ex parte contacts with former employees is permissible.[37] Some cases have also considered the relationship between the no ex parte contact rules and constraints based upon the attorney-client privilege.[38] Contact between plaintiffs' counsel and defendants' current lower-level employees is generally permitted.[39]

2. Burdensome or Irrelevant Discovery

Demands for voluminous information continue to be evaluated on a case-by-case basis, balancing the relevance of the request against the burden of producing the information.[40] Moreover, courts require a showing of a particularized need and relevance

---

[36]*See* Stahl v. Sun Microsystems, Inc., 19 F.3d 533, 539, 64 FEP 468 (10th Cir. 1994) (evidence that harasser engaged in consensual relationship with his assistant would be relevant to quid pro quo claim, but not a hostile environment claim); Biggs v. Nicewonger Co., 897 F. Supp. 483, 484–85, 68 FEP 1771 (D. Or. 1995) (evidence regarding harassment of a co-worker that was not witnessed by, or was not related to, the plaintiff was not relevant to prove a hostile work environment); *but cf.* Hurley v. Atlantic City Police Dep't, 933 F. Supp. 396, 410, 72 FEP 1828 (D.N.J. 1996) (evidence of supervisor's offensive remarks six years earlier than relevant time period nevertheless admitted at trial, over objection).

[37]*See* Terra Int'l, Inc. v. Mississippi Chem. Corp., 913 F. Supp. 1306, 1315, 1316–23 (N.D. Iowa 1996) (nonemployment case; opposing counsel's ex parte contacts with plaintiff's former employees not prohibited unless the former employees were in fact represented by plaintiff's counsel or other counsel; extensive analysis of case law regarding contacts with current employees and setting limits on such contacts); Aiken v. Business & Indus. Health Group, Inc., 885 F. Supp. 1474, 1476–78 (D. Kan. 1995) (rule prohibiting ex parte contacts does not apply to plaintiff's interviews of former employees of organization represented by defendant's counsel).

[38]*See* Camden v. Maryland, 910 F. Supp. 1115, 1120–23 (D. Md. 1996) (improper for plaintiff's counsel to have ex parte contact with defendant's former employee where plaintiff's counsel knew or should have known former employee had been extensively exposed to confidential client information; sanctions include striking evidence and disqualifying plaintiff's counsel).

[39]*See* Carter-Herman v. City of Philadelphia, 897 F. Supp. 899, 902–04, 68 FEP 1690, 1692–93 (E.D. Pa. 1996) (allowing ex parte interviews of nonmanagerial employees).

[40]*See* Burks v. Oklahoma Publ'g Co., 81 F.3d 975, 981, 70 FEP 945 (10th Cir.) (affirming lower court's determination that request for defendant to identify all persons over the age of 40 employed as managers or supervisors for last 10 years is overly burdensome and seeks irrelevant information; however, court declined to hold that such a request would never be warranted), *cert. denied*, 117 S. Ct. 302 (1996).

for discovery of information beyond the plaintiff's employing unit.[41] Whether information would be admissible at trial, however, does not control whether it is discoverable.[42]

As to the geographical scope of discovery, courts continue to take a case-by-case approach.[43]

The discovery rules in class actions have not been altered.[44]

B. Discovery Sought by Defendants

Defendants' discovery of private information regarding plaintiffs and nonparty witnesses remains an instructive area for examining the balancing process courts use when considering the burdensomeness versus the relevance of discovery requests.[45] The

---

[41]*See* Gheesling v. Chater, 162 F.R.D. 649, 650, 68 FEP 965 (D. Kan. 1995) (court ordered plaintiff to offer discovered materials that support contention of a companywide discriminatory hiring practice to decide whether it is reasonable to allow plaintiff to conduct discovery as to positions outside the employing unit).

[42]*See* EEOC v. Klockner H & K Machs., Inc., 168 F.R.D. 233, 235, 71 FEP 833 (E.D. Wis. 1996) (discoverable information governed by whether it is relevant, not whether it would be admissible at trial); Nelson v. Telecable of Overland Park, Inc., 70 FEP 859, 862 (D. Kan. 1996) ("Admissibility does not equate to discoverability."); Ladson v. Ulltra East Parking Corp., 164 F.R.D. 376, 377–78, 70 FEP 140 (S.D.N.Y. 1996) (defendant will not be allowed to determine what information is necessary to produce to plaintiff—standard for discovery is that requested information either be relevant or reasonably calculated to lead to the discovery of admissible evidence).

[43]*See* Gile v. United Airlines, Inc., 95 F.3d 492, 499, 5 AD 1466 (7th Cir. 1996) (district court committed reversible error in ADA reasonable accommodation case by limiting discovery to job vacancies for same position in same department in which plaintiff had worked and to positions to which she had requested a transfer; plaintiff requested discovery pertaining to all employer's job vacancies in metropolitan areas); Butta-Brinkman v. FCA Int'l, 164 F.R.D. 475, 476, 69 FEP 1276 (N.D. Ill. 1995) (plaintiff entitled to discover allegations or complaints of sexual harassment in other offices to show that employer failed to take action to remedy hostile work environment); Cisko v. Commonwealth Edison Co., 67 FEP 1630, 1631 (N.D. Ill. 1995) (rejecting plaintiff's request for nationwide discovery regarding all of defendant's facilities and limiting discovery to local office where plaintiff was employed).

[44]*See, e.g.,* Lumpkin v. E.I. DuPont de Nemours & Co., 67 FEP 1263, 1264 (M.D. Ga. 1995) (granting defendant's motion for protective order against further discovery where records revealed insufficient grounds for class certification and continuing discovery would "only cause needless delay and expenses").

[45]*See, e.g.,* Butler v. Burroughs Wellcome, Inc., 920 F. Supp. 90, 92 (E.D.N.C. 1996) (defendant's discovery request concerning plaintiff's sex life highly relevant where plaintiff built case upon a history of sexual abuse and a dysfunctional attitude toward members of the opposite sex); EEOC v. Kim & Ted, Inc., 1995 U.S. Dist. LEXIS 14510, at *11–12 (N.D. Ill. Oct. 3, 1995) (denying defendant's request

discovery of plaintiffs' medical records remains a frequently litigated issue with courts finding generally that such information is discoverable when plaintiffs have placed their particular mental states or physical conditions "in controversy."[46]

Courts are interpreting amended Fed. R. Evid. 412(b)(2) to limit the discoverability of sexual harassment plaintiffs' past sexual behavior. Although Rule 412 is intended to govern the admissibility of evidence at trial, the courts have applied it to discovery disputes arising under Fed. R. Civ. P. 26.[47] The courts have relied on

---

for tax and personnel information of nonclass members, finding the relevance of such information did not outweigh nonclass members' privacy interests); Burger v. Litton Indus., Inc., No. 91 Civ. 0918 (WK)(AJP), 1995 U.S. Dist. LEXIS 11373, at *5–6 (S.D.N.Y. Aug. 9, 1995) (finding that the probative value of nonparty witness' sexual conduct did not substantially outweigh the invasion of her privacy).

[46]*See Butler v. Burroughs Wellcome*, 920 F. Supp. at 92 (plaintiff's medical records discoverable in an ADA suit claiming that defendant failed to reasonably accommodate plaintiff's psychiatric disorder); Whitbeck v. Vital Signs, Inc., 163 F.R.D. 398, 399–400 (D.D.C. 1995) (plaintiff's allegation of failure to reasonably accommodate her disability put her medical condition into issue and prevented her from restricting access to her medical records), *motion granted in part, denied in part*, 933 F. Supp. 341 (S.D.N.Y. 1996); Bottomly v. Leucadia Nat'l, 163 F.R.D. 617, 620–21 (D. Utah 1995) (defendant entitled to discovery of plaintiff's medical records and information in suit claiming severe psychological and emotional distress caused by sexual harassment); Covell v. CNG Transmission Corp., 863 F. Supp. 202, 206, 70 FEP 914 (M.D. Pa. 1994) (performing balancing test with respect to reports concerning plaintiff's mental condition). *Cf.* O'Quinn v. New York Univ. Med. Ctr., 163 F.R.D. 226, 227–28, 68 FEP 1798 (S.D.N.Y. 1995) (denying defendant's request for psychiatric examination of plaintiff when plaintiff did not claim ongoing severe emotional injury but instead made a boilerplate damages claim for emotional distress and humiliation), *motion granted in part, denied in part*, 933 F. Supp. 341 (S.D.N.Y. 1996); J.J.C. v. Fridell, 165 F.R.D. 513, 517 (D. Minn. 1995) (denying defendant's motion to compel medical authorizations in sex harassment suit; plaintiff's attorney would be allowed to screen medical records to determine their confidential nature before producing them pursuant to previously signed release); Turner v. Imperial Stores, 161 F.R.D. 89, 98 (S.D. Cal. 1995) (court "unwilling to set a precedent requiring a party to undergo an independent psychiatric examination merely because the party claims damages for emotional distress in her complaint"); Curtis v. Express, Inc., 868 F. Supp. 467, 469, 66 FEP 449 (N.D.N.Y. 1994) (rejecting defendant's request for a mental examination where plaintiff brought only her past emotional condition into issue and did not pursue a separate tort claim for emotional distress).

[47]*See, e.g.*, Sanchez v. Zabihi, 166 F.R.D. 500, 502, 71 FEP 835 (D.N.M. 1996) (although Rule 412 addresses admissibility, it "is applicable and has significance in deciding" certain discovery motions); Barta v. City & County of Honolulu, 169 F.R.D. 132, 135 (D. Haw. 1996) (Rule 412 must inform the proper scope of discovery); Stalnaker v. KMart Corp., 71 FEP 705, 706 (D. Kan. 1996) (even when a motion "arises

Rule 412 to limit discovery when defendants seek information that relates to plaintiffs' sexual conduct (predisposition or behavior) outside the workplace.[48] When the discovery sought concerns plaintiffs' sexual conduct as it relates to the workplace, the courts are more likely to permit the discovery.[49] Likewise, when plaintiffs place an issue in controversy, the courts have allowed defendants broad discovery to rebut the plaintiffs' allegations.[50]

---

in the context of discovery under Rule 26 of the Federal Rules of Civil Procedure, the Court must remain mindful of Rule 412 and its implications"); Burger v. Litton Indus., Inc., 1995 WL 476712, at *2 (S.D.N.Y. Aug. 10, 1995) (Rule 412 does not apply directly to discovery but the court must consider it in order not to undermine the rationale of Rule 412). For an in-depth discussion of the 1994 amendments to Rule 412 as it pertains to sexual harassment cases, *see* Jacqueline H. Sloan, Comment, *Extending Rape Shield Protection to Sexual Harassment Actions: New Federal Rule of Evidence 412 Undermines* Meritor Savings Bank v. Vinson, 25 Sw. U.L. Rev. 363 (1996).

[48]*See, e.g.,* Barta v. City & County of Honolulu, 169 F.R.D. 132, 136 (D. Haw. 1996) (despite broad discovery permitted by Fed. R. Civ. P. 26(b)(1), discovery of plaintiff's sexual conduct outside the workplace is not permissible under Rule 412); Biggs v. Nicewonger Co., 897 F. Supp. 483, 484–85, 68 FEP 1771 (D. Or. 1995) (evidence related to alleged incidents of sexual harassment that were not witnessed by former employee or were not related to her while she was on the job was not relevant or admissible under Rule 412); Janopoulos v. Harvey L. Walner & Assoc., No. 93 C 5176, 1995 U.S. Dist. LEXIS 2751, at *3 (N.D. Ill Mar. 2, 1995) (Rule 412 does not give the court authority to exclude evidence of past marriages, only past sexual behavior), *summary judgment granted,* No. 93 C 5176, 1996 U.S. Dist. LEXIS 3157 (N.D. Ill. Mar. 14, 1996).

[49]*See, e.g.,* Sanchez v. Zabihi, 166 F.R.D. 500, 501–02, 71 FEP 835 (D.N.M. 1996) (using Rule 412 as a guide in resolving a discovery dispute under Fed. R. Civ. P. 26 and holding that plaintiff, whom defendant alleged was the actual sexual aggressor, must answer interrogatories about her history of making romantic or sexual advances toward other employees, but she need not disclose any information about her relationship with a co-worker who later became her spouse).

[50]Alberts v. Wickes Lumber Co., 1995 WL 117886, at *5 (N.D. Ill. Mar. 15, 1995) (permitting discovery of victim's sexual intimacy after alleged assault where plaintiff injected into her damage claim her inability to engage in postincident intimate sexual relationships; "To allow [plaintiff] to use these alleged experiences as evidence of her damages, but at the same time deny [defendant] the opportunity to prove that these claims are not true, would be to turn the rape 'shield' law into a sword solely for the plaintiff's benefit."); Ramirez v. Nabil's, Inc., 1995 WL 609415 (D. Kan. Oct. 5, 1995) (granting defendant's request for plaintiff's medical and psychiatric records, which could establish plaintiff's sexual propensity; plaintiff alleged she had suffered mental and emotional distress as a result of alleged sexual harassment by defendant); McCleland v. Montgomery Ward & Co., 1995 WL 571324, at *3 n.1 (N.D. Ill. Sept. 25, 1995) (because sexual harassment plaintiffs sought damages for humiliation and emotional suffering, Rule 412 would not per se prohibit admission of evidence that plaintiffs suffered childhood and adolescent sexual abuse).

Rule 412 may also be used to shield nonparties from discovery.[51] The nonparty should raise the Rule 412 objection and not rely on counsel for the parties to assert the objection.[52]

Defendants continue to seek discovery of "after-acquired evidence" in order to limit plaintiffs' entitlement to reinstatement, front pay, and back pay.[53] As long as the discovery sought reasonably constitutes "after-acquired evidence," defendants are entitled to such discovery.[54] However, courts will not permit defendants to abuse discovery under the guise of seeking "after-acquired evidence."[55]

Defendants' discovery as to the character or type of each named plaintiff's claim continues to be significant in challenging class certification.[56] Courts have allowed specific inquiries directed at the adequacy of class representatives, but are split on the issue of whether inquiring into the named plaintiffs' financial resources is appropriate.[57]

---

[51] *See* Fed. R. Evid. 412 Advisory Committee's note. *See also Burger v. Litton Indus.*, 1995 WL 476712 (questions at a deposition directed to a nonparty witness about the witness' consensual sexual conduct are prohibited by Rule 412 because the probative value of the witness' answers is substantially outweighed by the invasion of her privacy).

[52] *See Stalnaker v. KMart Corp.*, 71 FEP 705, 706–07 (D. Kan. 1996) (defendant filed a motion for protective order seeking to limit plaintiff's deposition questions to nonparty witnesses about their sexual activities; court granted defendant's motion in part but permitted plaintiff to discover sexual activities of a nonparty with the alleged harasser at work; court noted that Rule 412 applies to nonparty witnesses as well as parties, but held that Rule 412 was not controlling because nonparty witnesses sought no protection under the rule and raised no objection to the discovery).

[53] *See McKennon v. Nashville Banner Publ'g Co.*, 513 U.S. 352, 361–63, 66 FEP 1192 (1995), and its progeny. *See generally* Chapter 41 (Monetary Relief).

[54] *See Hankins v. City of Philadelphia*, 1996 WL 571755 (E.D. Pa. Oct. 4, 1996) (granting defendant's motion to compel production of plaintiff's fingerprints, which defendant alleged could link plaintiff to a letter containing derogatory remarks and that, defendant argued, would constitute "after-acquired evidence").

[55] *See McKennon* at 513 U.S. 360–61.

[56] *See* Chapter 37 (Class Actions).

[57] *See New Haven Temple SDA Church v. Consolidated Edison Corp.*, No. 94 Civ. 7128 (AGS)(BAL), 1995 U.S. Dist. LEXIS 8220 (S.D.N.Y. 1995) (finding class representative's financial resources relevant to the issue of adequacy of representation). *But see Zapata v. IBP, Inc.*, No. 93-2366-EEO, 1994 U.S. Dist. LEXIS 16285 (denying defendant's motion to compel discovery concerning financial information of class representatives); *Kaplan v. Pomerantz*, 131 F.R.D. 118, 125 (N.D. Ill. 1990) (cautioning that discovery into a class representative's financial resources should not be used as a means for discouraging class actions and noting "[t]he need to ensure that . . . the class action will be properly funded does not warrant wholesale discovery into the named plaintiff's personal affairs"); *see also* MANUAL FOR COMPLEX LITIGATION, THIRD, § 30.12 (1995) (precertification inquiries into the financial arrangements between class representatives and their counsel respecting the expenses of litigation are rarely appropriate).

CHAPTER 39

STATISTICAL PROOF

I. Introduction

Statistical proof can support disparate treatment or disparate impact claims, but generally is not determinative on the question of discriminatory intent. In *Grant v. News Group Boston, Inc.*,[1] a disparate treatment case, the employer admitted that word-of-mouth communication and nepotism were the primary methods of advertising available paperhandler positions. The plaintiff argued that these practices, which had resulted in the hiring of very few African-Americans, had been adopted by the employer as a method for effecting a discriminatory animus.[2] The First Circuit affirmed summary judgment for the defendant, holding that even if the statistical evidence tended to show that the employer was "insensitive to the need to provide fair and equal access" to employment, it was "inadequate to prove that [the employer] takes race into account" in making employment decisions.[3]

II. Types of Statistical Proof

Courts continue to focus on the composition of the pool of employees or applicants forming the basis for statistical analysis. The party offering statistical proof must compare groups of similarly situated individuals.[4] The pool of employees, or potential employees, used to make a statistical comparison varies in each

---
[1] 55 F.3d 1, 4, 67 FEP 1030 (1st Cir. 1995).
[2] *Id.*
[3] *Id.* at 8.
[4] *See* Furr v. Seagate Tech., Inc., 82 F.3d 980, 986–87, 70 FEP 1325 (10th Cir. 1996) (plaintiff's statistics did not account for differences in skill or specialty), *cert. denied,* 117 S. Ct. 684 (1997); Hutson v. McDonnell Douglas Corp., 63 F.3d 771, 777–78, 68 FEP 1209 (8th Cir. 1995) (finding statistics were not probative where they did not control for similar characteristics).

case.[5] "For statistical evidence to be probative, the statistical pool or sample used must logically be related to the employment decision at issue and the statistical method applied to the pool or sample must be meaningful and suitable under the facts and circumstances of the case."[6] Courts have rejected statistical evidence that is presented without expert testimony explaining its meaning.[7]

A. Selection Rate Comparisons

In *EEOC v. American Airlines, Inc.*,[8] the Fifth Circuit found that the selection rate comparison offered by the EEOC was not credible as an indicator of discrimination in pilot hiring because it made only a superficial attempt to account for the qualifications of the job. Specifically, the EEOC's analysis focused on just a few criteria assertedly relied upon by the airline such as experience, health, and failure to show up for an interview, but failed to account for other assertedly relevant criteria such as passing a flight simulator test.[9]

B. Potential Selection Rate Comparisons

In hiring and promotion cases, an appropriate statistical analysis generally will begin with a measure of the percentage of potential qualified applicants in the protected class.[10] In *Aiken v. City of Memphis*,[11] the city sought to justify its affirmative action program by demonstrating its own past discriminatory conduct and, toward that end, used potential selection rate comparisons. The

---

[5]Jones v. Pepsi-Cola Metro. Bottling Co., 871 F. Supp. 305, 310–11 (E.D. Mich. 1994) (finding that the proper pool for comparison for purposes of analyzing challenged examination process should be based on the pools of the relevant groups who took the exam).
[6]*Id.* at 310.
[7]Carter v. Ball, 33 F.3d 450, 457, 65 FEP 1414 (4th Cir. 1994) ("[I]f a plaintiff offers a statistical comparison without expert testimony as to methodology or relevance to plaintiff's claim, a judge may be justified in excluding the evidence."). *But see* Stratton v. Department for the Aging for the City of N.Y., 922 F. Supp. 857, 863–64 (S.D.N.Y. 1996) (expert testimony about raw statistical data in the form of charts was not "absolute prerequisite").
[8]48 F.3d 164, 172–73, 67 FEP 754 (5th Cir. 1995).
[9]*Id.* at 172.
[10]*Carter*, 33 F.3d at 457 (mere absence of minorities in upper-level positions is not sufficient to prove disparate treatment where plaintiff did not provide adequate comparison to the potential labor pool).
[11]37 F.3d 1155, 1163, 65 FEP 1757 (6th Cir. 1994).

city's statistical presentation showed that in 1971, 11 percent of patrol officers were African-American while only 5.9 percent of sergeants were African-American, and in 1978, 25 percent of patrol officers were African-American while only 7.5 percent of sergeants were African-American.[12] These statistics, the court held, were "probative enough to satisfy the City's burden of producing strong evidence that discrimination [had] occurred...."[13]

C. Population/Workforce Comparisons

Courts continue to recognize that where a job requires special skills or experience, the relevant labor pool for comparison is the segment of the local labor force possessing those qualifications.[14] In these circumstances, comparisons may not be based on general workforce classifications, but must account for the qualifications needed for the position in question.[15] Likewise, the data that is the basis for the analysis must not be overinclusive.[16]

D. Regression Analyses

In *Smith v. Virginia Commonwealth University*,[17] the defendant university used a regression analysis as a justification for an across-the-board pay increase for female, but not male, faculty members assertedly intended to address a perceived disparity in faculty compensation. The regression accounted for factors such as years of service and level of education. The analysis, however, did not account for a variety of factors relating to the quality of faculty performance such as teaching quality and publications. The analysis also failed to control for external factors that assertedly caused some faculty members to have higher salaries, such as prior service in the university's administration. In a fractured en banc decision, the Fourth Circuit held that these failings precluded summary judgment

---

[12]*Id.* at 1163.
[13]*Id.*
[14]*See* Section III.B *supra. See also* Sanchez v. City of Santa Ana, 928 F. Supp. 1494, 1503 (C.D. Cal. 1995) (limiting labor pool to those employed in lower-level positions with employer where promotion was limited to internal candidates).
[15]*See* Section III.B *supra.*
[16]Thomas v. IBM, 48 F.3d 478, 486, 67 FEP 270 (10th Cir. 1995) (plaintiff's study incorporated every possible group that may have been discriminated against, making it difficult for the court to focus on the specific age discrimination claim put forth).
[17]84 F.3d 672, 70 FEP 1248 (4th Cir. 1996) (en banc).

for the university on the sex discrimination claim of male faculty members.[18] At least one judge believed that the failings were even more serious, rendering the university's statistical analysis altogether meaningless.[19]

E. Other Kinds of Statistical Comparisons

In some circumstances, it may be appropriate for a party to compare an employer's workforce to comparable workforces that extend beyond the defendant employer's geographic locale. In *Vitug v. Multistate Tax Commission*,[20] for example, the Seventh Circuit refused to find that an employer's reliance on subjective criteria and word-of-mouth hiring had a disparate impact on minority applicants where the employer offered expert testimony that the percentage of minority auditors employed by the defendant exceeded the "total percentage of minorities among accountants and auditors in the national workforce."

F. The Bottom-Line Concept

As they have since *Connecticut v. Teal*,[21] courts generally continue to refuse to accept the bottom-line defense as applicable in employment discrimination claims.[22] At least one district court, however, originally adopted a bottom-line justification where the number of successful minorities far exceeded the expected number based on the qualified labor market.[23]

---

[18]*Id.* at 677.
[19]*Id.* at 684 (opinion of Luttig, concurring) (failure of study rendered it "inadmissible in a court of law"); *see also id.* at 677–78 (opinion of Wilkinson, C.J., concurring).
[20]88 F.3d 506, 514, 71 FEP 1445 (7th Cir. 1996).
[21]457 U.S. 440, 29 FEP 1 (1982).
[22]Woodman v. Haemonetics Corp., 51 F.3d 1087 n.3, 67 FEP 838 (1st Cir. 1995) (companywide statistics showing that workforce reduction process as a whole did not have a disproportionate impact on older employees did not refute a claim of disparate treatment of an individual employee); Anderson v. Douglas & Lomason Co., 26 F.3d 1277, 1291, 65 FEP 417, 69 FEP 131, 142 (5th Cir. 1994) (comparison of percentage of African-American supervisors at company to African-American supervisors countywide found insufficient as bottom-line defense), *cert. denied,* 513 U.S. 1149 (1995).
[23]Bailey v. DiMario, 925 F. Supp. 801, 69 FEP 233, 243 (D.D.C. 1995) (where hiring of African-Americans into disputed positions was 1½ to five times greater than the percentage in the qualified labor market, "[s]uch evidence demonstrates the absence of discrimination").

III. Sources of Statistics

Courts continue to follow the Supreme Court's cautionary words in *Teamsters v. United States*[24] that the "usefulness of statistics depends on the surrounding facts and circumstances."[25] "[S]tatistics, like any evidence, are not irrefutable; strong statistics may prove a case on their own, while shaky statistics may be insufficient unless accompanied by additional evidence."[26] Understanding the sources of statistical data is critical to comprehending its significance to the facts of a particular case.

A. Applicant Flow Data

Actual applicant flow figures are still considered the preferred method by which to measure an employer's hiring practices.[27] Where actual applicant flow data is incomplete or flawed, however, courts

---

[24] 431 U.S. 324, 340, 14 FEP 1514 (1977).

[25] *See, e.g.,* Carter v. Ball, 33 F.3d 450, 456, 65 FEP 1414 (4th Cir. 1994) (citing *Teamsters,* 431 U.S. at 340).

[26] EEOC v. O & G Spring & Wire Forms Specialty Co., 38 F.3d 872, 876, 65 FEP 1823 (7th Cir. 1994), *cert. denied,* 513 U.S. 1198 (1995). *See also* Fisher v. Vassar College, 70 F.3d 1420, 1443, 1447, 70 FEP 1155 (2d Cir. 1995) (where court found that plaintiff's statistics were "merely organized anecdotes" and that "[p]laintiff's statistical case is built on gerrymandered data and a series of statistical fallacies"), *aff'd on reh'g en banc,* 114 F.3d 1332 (2d Cir.), *petition for cert. filed,* 66 U.S.L.W. 3178 (Sept. 2, 1997) (No. 97-404).

[27] Courtney v. Biosound, Inc., 42 F.3d 414, 66 FEP 971 (7th Cir. 1994) (statistics unavailing where age plaintiff produced no evidence of applicant pool or any related evidence that substantial number of older workers actually applied for employment with the defendant); Anderson v. Douglas & Lomason Co., 26 F.3d 1277, 1286–87, 65 FEP 417, 69 FEP 131 (5th Cir. 1994) (appropriate labor market to use in statistical analysis of employer's hiring practices was composed of those persons who actually sought employment with the company), *cert. denied,* 513 U.S. 1149 (1995); Patterson v. U.S. Cold Storage, 1995 WL 871333, at * 3 (N.D. Cal. Mar. 28, 1995) (plaintiff's statistical evidence that defendant hired only one African-American out of 54 employees hired was ineffectual where statistics did not measure "the impact of defendant's practices on the protected class against the actual pool of employees affected by the practice"), *aff'd,* 87 F.3d 1321 (9th Cir. 1996); Jones v. Pepsi-Cola Metro. Bottling Co., 871 F. Supp. 305, 310 (E.D. Mich. 1994) (where employment practice at issue is a test taken by applicants, the actual examinees constitute the "most logical statistical pool"); Johnston v. City of Philadelphia, 863 F. Supp. 231, 235 (E.D. Pa. 1994) (relevant labor market was applicants for police officer recruit positions who had passed initial eligibility exam). *But see* Forehand v. Florida State Hosp. at Chattahoochee, 89 F.3d 1562, 1574, 71 FEP 905 (11th Cir. 1996) (declining to adopt "per se rule that applicant flow data are the best measure of the pool from which applicants are selected").

have declined to apply the resulting statistical analysis.[28] For instance, applicant flow data will not be credited where the employer did not keep accurate personnel records[29]; where the sample size is too small to provide meaningful statistical analysis[30]; or where the pool as defined omits applicants who were offered but declined the positions at issue.[31]

Courts have frequently rejected statistical analyses based upon overbroad labor pools.[32] In this regard, defendant employers frequently use actual applicant flow data to refute statistics offered by plaintiffs by focusing on particular job groups,[33] geographic

---

[28]*Id. But see* EEOC v. Regency Windsor Management Co., 862 F. Supp. 189, 195, 65 FEP 1777 (W.D. Mich. 1994) (court accepted plaintiff's statistics as supporting claim of age discrimination even though evidence did not include ages of comparators hired and fired and did not indicate composition of pool of qualified applicants for open positions during relevant periods).

[29]EEOC v. Turtle Creek Mansion Corp., 70 FEP 899 (N.D. Tex. 1995) (applicant flow data not used where employer did not maintain applicant flow log, and records did not indicate how long particular job was open, date job offer was made, who interviewed applicant, or for what position applicant applied), *aff'd,* 82 F.3d 414 (5th Cir. 1996). *See Anderson v. Douglas & Lomason Co.,* 26 F.3d at 1287 n.13 (affirming use of employer's applicant flow data even though employer failed to preserve employment applications for one year, contrary to the Uniform Guidelines on Employee Selection Procedures).

[30]*See* Section VI.B *supra;* Ward v. Gulfstream Aerospace Corp., Inc., 894 F. Supp. 1573, 1580 (S.D. Ga. 1995) (sample size of 11 candidates for departmental reduction in force not statistically compelling and of little relevance); Maidenbaum v. Bally's Park Place, Inc., 870 F. Supp. 1254, 1259, 68 FEP 1245 (D.N.J. 1994) (sample size of 16 terminated employees was insufficient to evidence disparate impact), *aff'd,* 67 F.3d 291 (3d Cir. 1995); Campbell v. Fasco Indus., 861 F. Supp. 1385, 1395, 72 FEP 33 (N.D. Ill. 1994) (group of nine too small), *aff'd,* 67 F.3d 301 (7th Cir. 1995).

[31]*See Anderson v. Douglas & Lomason Co.,* 26 F.3d at 1293 ("[T]he statistics submitted by the plaintiffs are fatally flawed because they overlook the black employees who turned down promotions later offered to white employees."). *But see* Mangold v. California Pub. Utils. Comm'n, 67 F.3d 1470, 1476, 69 FEP 48 (9th Cir. 1995) (plaintiff's statistics were admissible even though they did not factor out "repeaters" who failed but continued to take exam).

[32]*See, e.g.,* Smith v. Virginia Commonwealth Univ., 84 F.3d 672, 677, 70 FEP 1248 (4th Cir. 1996) (en banc) (pool of faculty that was subject of regression analysis to determine whether female faculty's salaries were lower than salaries of male faculty was inflated because it included male faculty members who also held positions with the university administration and consequently received higher salaries); Hutson v. McDonnell Douglas Corp., 63 F.3d 771, 777–78, 68 FEP 1209 (8th Cir. 1995) (plaintiff's companywide statistics on discharge failed to analyze treatment of comparable employees, i.e., those with low relative assessment score).

[33]*Anderson v. Douglas & Lomason Co.,* 26 F.3d at 1289 (discriminatory intent not established where percentage comparison of African-Americans and whites hired for each separate job was not statistically significant); *Forehand v. Florida State Hosp.,*

areas,[34] or on decisions by particular decisionmakers,[35] among other factors.

The relevant applicant pool should include only those candidates who are qualified. "Absent an analysis of either 'the qualified applicant pool or the flow of qualified candidates over a relevant period of time' the evidence . . . is not useful."[36] Of course, the qualifications required for each position must be assessed on a case-by-case basis.[37]

Courts have also refused to value statistical evidence that is underinclusive as to the appropriate labor pool.[38] For instance, courts

---

89 F.3d at 1572–73 (while concluding that defendant employer's statistical evidence understated racial disparities in promotions, court disapproved plaintiff's statistics as overstating discrimination by inflating number of minority candidates in applicant pool); Anderson v. Queen Carpet Corp., 68 FEP 83 (N.D. Ga. 1995) (although plaintiff alleged that out of 184 employees hired by defendant employer only two were over age 55, employer showed that a number were hired as college graduate sales trainees at significantly less salary than at-issue jobs, many other hires were in protected age group but under 55, and others were hired in territories different than plaintiff's previous work area); Graffam v. Scott Paper Co., 870 F. Supp. 389, 396–97, 66 FEP 1007 (D. Me. 1994) (court rejected employer's attempt to limit statistical analysis by job group; ultimate discharge decisions made by persons who had control over all employees), aff'd, 60 F.3d 809 (1st Cir. 1995).

[34]*United States v. North Carolina,* 914 F. Supp. 1257, 1268, 71 FEP 1347 (E.D.N.C. 1996) (court rejected government's statistical evidence comparing correctional facility job applicants and hires by gender on statewide basis, where state maintained 92 correctional facilities, each autonomous in its hiring practices); Anderson v. Queen Carpet Corp., 68 FEP 83 (N.D. Ga. 1995) (court omitted from plaintiff's statistics new hires at locations outside of plaintiff's work area).

[35]United States v. North Carolina, 914 F. Supp. at 1268, supra. But see Graffam v. Scott Paper, 870 F. Supp. at 396–97.

[36]Johnson v. Penske Truck Leasing Co., 949 F. Supp. 1153, 1177 (D.N.J. 1996) (plaintiff failed to present statistical evidence showing how many promotions were available, number of qualified female applicants, or how many qualified female applicants were denied the position), quoting Ezold v. Wolf, Block, Schorr & Solis-Cohen, 983 F.2d 509, 543, 60 FEP 849 (3d Cir. 1992), cert. denied, 510 U.S. 826 (1993).

[37]EEOC v. American Airlines, Inc., 48 F.3d 164, 172, 67 FEP 754 (5th Cir. 1995) (EEOC's statistics were rejected where EEOC did not produce comparison of pilots hired to those qualified to be hired; statistics simply compared pilots hired to those who had applied and were disqualified by certain "obvious criteria"); Aiken v. City of Memphis, 37 F.3d 1155, 1165, 1167, 65 FEP 1757 (6th Cir. 1994) (on remand, district court was required to consider whether racial makeup of qualified labor pool differed from general workforce); Anderson v. Queen Carpet Corp., 68 FEP 83 (N.D. Ga. 1995) (court rejected plaintiff's statistics where, among other inadequacies, plaintiff did not provide the court with the pool of available and qualified applicants and any applicable requirements or limitations with regard to the available positions).

[38]*See* Fisher v. Vassar College, 70 F.3d 1420, 1444–45, 70 FEP 1155 (2d Cir. 1995) (appeals court reversed district court for refusing to admit collegewide evidence of

have disregarded actual applicant pool data where the pool itself has been tainted by the employer's history of discrimination.[39] Likewise, courts will not use actual applicant flow data as a basis for statistical evidence where otherwise qualified applicants are discouraged from applying because of an employer's reputation for discrimination in the community.[40] Courts have also rejected employers' arguments that minority applicants self-select out of the applicant pool for reasons not attributable to discrimination.[41]

B. Population/Labor Market Data

1. Qualified Labor Market Data

Courts continue to require that statistical evidence control for the qualifications required for a particular position.[42] For example,

---

tenure decisions regarding married women faculty; review of statistics for "hard science" departments only was abuse of discretion where no such subcategory existed in the university decisionmaking process), *aff'd on reh'g en banc,* 114 F.3d 1332 (2d Cir.), *petition for cert. filed,* 66 U.S.L.W. 3178 (Sept. 2, 1997) (No. 97-404); Jones v. Pepsi-Cola Metro. Bottling Co., 871 F. Supp. 305, 311 (E.D. Mich. 1994) (plaintiffs used underinclusive applicant pool by only counting inside candidates who took test as opposed to all candidates, inside and outside, who took test); Maidenbaum v. Bally's Park Place, Inc., 870 F. Supp. 1254, 1259–60, 68 FEP 1245 (D.N.J. 1994) (larger sample size was appropriate for assessing layoff decisions in light of age discrimination claim), *aff'd,* 67 F.3d 291 (3d Cir. 1995).

[39]*See* Sims v. Montgomery County Comm'n, 873 F. Supp. 585, 602–03 (M.D. Ala. 1994) (statistical analysis of actual applicant pool alone would not accurately reflect adverse impact of past discrimination on minority applicants for promotion to police sergeant).

[40]EEOC v. Steamship Clerks Local 1066, 48 F.3d 594, 606, 67 FEP 629 (1st Cir.) (court below "could have inferred causation, despite the dearth of actual applicants," in part because union policy discouraged potential minority candidates from applying), *cert. denied,* 116 S. Ct. 65 (1995); EEOC v. Joe's Stone Crab, Inc., 969 F. Supp. 727, 736, 74 FEP 491 (S.D. Fla. 1997) (number of female applicants at annual "roll call" hiring event for wait staff at historic restaurant would not be used given the employer's reputation for not hiring waitresses); EEOC v. Rodriguez, 66 FEP 1649 (E.D. Cal. 1994) (court rejected defendant employer's argument that small number of African-Americans applying for positions as auto salesmen was appropriate labor pool based on evidence that potential applicants understood they would not be hired, so did not apply).

[41]*See, e.g.,* EEOC v. O & G Spring & Wire Forms Specialty Co., 38 F.3d 872, 877, 65 FEP 1823 (7th Cir. 1994) (court rejected employer's argument that African-Americans, who represented about 20% of the actual walk-in applicant pool, self-selected out of the pool because they preferred not to work with Polish and Spanish-speaking workers), *cert. denied,* 513 U.S. 1198 (1995).

[42]Hopper v. Hallmark Cards, Inc., 87 F.3d 983, 989, 71 FEP 1362 (8th Cir. 1996) (plaintiff failed to show that those discharged "were similarly situated, qualified

in *EEOC v. Turtle Creek Mansion Corp.*,[43] the court rejected the plaintiff's labor market statistics. The plaintiff tried to compare the percentage of women in the food service industry, based on census data, with the percentage in the defendant's luxury restaurant. The court found that the data was insufficient because it did not narrow the pool (which consisted of cocktail waitresses, room service waitresses, etc.) to the specific qualities that would make a waitress qualified to work in defendant's restaurant.[44]

3. *General Population Data*

Courts continue to recognize that general population data will only be an appropriate basis for statistical analysis where the positions at issue require no specialized skills.[45] In some circumstances,

---

individuals," and as such the court did not accept the statistical proof); Forehand v. Florida State Hosp. at Chattahoochee, 89 F.3d 1562, 1571–74, 71 FEP 905 (11th Cir. 1996) (plaintiff's statistics failed to control for competitive and noncompetitive promotions); Simon v. City of Youngstown, 73 F.3d 68, 72 (6th Cir. 1995) (court found that statistics, which assumed that all police officers in department rotated through assignments without regard to qualification, were invalid); EEOC v. American Airlines, Inc., 48 F.3d 164, 172–73, 67 FEP 754 (5th Cir. 1995) (court rejected EEOC's statistical comparisons, which omitted important qualification criteria such as a score on a flight simulator test); El Deeb v. University of Minn., 60 F.3d 423, 430–31, 68 FEP 1173, 1178 (8th Cir. 1995) (court found that doctor's statistical comparison of salaries was insufficient because it did not control for expertise); Aiken v. City of Memphis, 37 F.3d 1155, 1165, 1167, 65 FEP 1757 (6th Cir. 1994) (on remand, district court was required to consider whether racial makeup of qualified labor pool differed from general workforce); Carter v. Ball, 33 F.3d 450, 456, 65 FEP 1414 (4th Cir. 1994) ("In the case of discrimination in hiring or promoting, the relevant comparison is between the percentage of minority employees and the percentage of potential minority applicants in the qualified labor pool."); EEOC v. Turtle Creek Mansion Corp., 70 FEP 899, 905–06 (N.D. Tx. 1995) (census data that indicated percentage of female waitresses in general population was not probative in determining the percentage of waitresses with the requisite qualifications for a fine dining establishment), *aff'd*, 82 F.3d 414 (1996); Anderson v. Queen Carpet Corp., 68 FEP 83 (N.D. Ga. 1995) (court rejected plaintiff's statistics, among other things, because plaintiff did not provide the court with the pool of available and qualified applicants). In Middleton v. City of Flint, Mich., 92 F.3d 396, 71 FEP 962 (6th Cir. 1996), *cert. denied*, 117 S. Ct. 1552 (1997), the plaintiffs challenged a promotion plan that relied on racial quotas. The Sixth Circuit held that "raw" statistics based on a general labor pool cannot justify a hiring quota. *Id.* at 406.

[43]70 FEP 899, 904–06 (N.D. Tex. 1995).

[44]*Id.* at 906.

[45]*Middleton v. City of Flint, Mich.*, 92 F.3d at 406 (questioning the district court's acceptance of statistics that compared the number of minority-group members in the general labor pool and the number of minority-group members in the local police force).

however, use of general workforce statistics has been permitted because more refined data was simply unavailable. For example, in *Peightal v. Metropolitan Dade County*,[46] the Eleventh Circuit upheld the district court's reliance on general workforce data for individuals aged 18–55 in a case involving entry-level positions in the fire department. Although the employer allegedly had minimum education and language proficiency standards, the court found the lack of reliable raw data on these topics was a persuasive reason to rely on general population statistics instead.[47]

4. Employer's Workforce Data

Where a position is only available to current employees, a court will usually find that the qualified portion of the employer's workforce is the proper pool for comparison in any statistical analysis.[48]

IV. Proper Geographic Scope of Statistics

Courts continue to analyze the geographic scope of statistical data to ensure that the data is probative.[49] In *EEOC v. O & G Spring & Wire Forms Specialty Co.*,[50] the Seventh Circuit found that a series of statistical analyses, which used a variety of pools based on slightly different geographic areas, provided a "sufficiently accurate range against which the district court could evaluate [the employer's] hiring record."

In *Vitug v. Multistate Tax Commission*,[51] the Seventh Circuit accepted the defendant's statistical evidence, which compared the

---

[46]26 F.3d 1545, 1555, 71 FEP 1107 (11th Cir. 1994) (challenge to fire department's affirmative action program by white male who was passed over for hiring while minorities with lower scores were hired).

[47]*Id.*

[48]Aiken v. City of Memphis, 37 F.3d 1155, 1163, 65 FEP 1757 (6th Cir. 1994) (finding that the statistical make-up of the current fire department was more probative than general workforce statistics).

[49]*See, e.g.,* United States v. North Carolina, 914 F. Supp. 1257, 1268, 71 FEP 1347 (E.D.N.C. 1996) (court rejected government's statistical evidence where it compared job applicants at all 92 of defendant's correctional facilities, each of which was autonomous in its hiring practices); Anderson v. Queen Carpet Corp., 68 FEP 83 (N.D. Ga. 1995) (limiting statistics to new hires in plaintiff's work area).

[50]38 F.3d 872, 877, 65 FEP 1823 (7th Cir. 1994), *cert. denied,* 513 U.S. 1198 (1995).

[51]88 F.3d 506, 514, 71 FEP 1445 (7th Cir. 1996).

percentage of auditors employed at the defendant's firm and the percentage of auditors in the national workforce. The court found that this evidence directly contradicted the plaintiff's assertions that the employer's hiring criteria had an adverse impact on minorities.[52]

V. THE PROPER TIME FRAME FOR STATISTICS

In *Sims v. Montgomery County Commission*,[53] the district court held that in reviewing an adverse impact claim, it could consider a statistical analysis even where it omits historical data, if that data is absent because the employer failed to keep it. The decree in question had been in effect since 1973. However, the defendant could only produce the necessary data for the years 1981 through 1988. The court focused on the entire period of the decree from 1973 through 1988. The court found it "not without significance" that the defendant failed to keep the data that "would more than likely have been very incriminating."[54]

In *Pollis v. New School for Social Research*,[55] a sex discrimination case, the plaintiff challenged the exceptions made for certain individuals under the institution's mandatory retirement age of 70. The plaintiff limited her statistical evidence to a five-year time frame. The challenged policy, however, had been in effect much longer. The court held that the proper "universe" for analysis included all of those who were employed at the time of the challenged conduct and were affected by the mandatory retirement policy during the entire time frame that the policy was in force.[56]

VI. THE PROPER WEIGHT TO BE GIVEN STATISTICAL PROOF

The impact of a statistical presentation on the ultimate question of discrimination *vel non* will depend on the quality of the

---

[52]*Id.*
[53]873 F. Supp. 585, 601 (M.D. Ala. 1994) (finding that lack of data for prior period did not limit scope of court's consideration where defendant failed to keep such data).
[54]*Id.* at 601.
[55]913 F. Supp. 771, 780 (S.D.N.Y. 1996).
[56]*Id.* at 780.

analysis. "While statistical evidence may create an inference of discrimination, the evidence may be so flawed as to render it insufficient to raise a jury question."[57] The strength of the statistical evidence will dictate its effect on the outcome of the case,[58] and courts will exclude statistical evidence where it has "little or no probative value."[59] The trial courts continue to enjoy substantial discretion in determining the admissibility of statistical evidence, and the trial courts' evidentiary decisions are reviewed under a clearly erroneous standard.[60]

The party placing statistical analyses into evidence must provide adequate information about the pool of employees being analyzed before the analyses are admitted as evidence of discrimination.[61] For example, in *Allen v. Diebold*,[62] an age discrimination case, the court noted that prior layoffs had been administered on the basis of seniority. The prior reliance on seniority in layoffs had left a greater percentage of older workers employed at a plant than would

---

[57]Furr v. Seagate Tech., Inc., 82 F.3d 980, 986–87, 70 FEP 1325 (10th Cir. 1996), *cert. denied*, 117 S. Ct. 684 (1997).

[58]EEOC v. O & G Spring & Wire Forms Specialty Co., 38 F.3d 872, 876, 65 FEP 1823 (7th Cir. 1994), *cert denied*, 513 U.S. 1198 (1995).

[59]EEOC v. Texas Instruments, Inc., 100 F.3d 1173, 1184–86, 72 FEP 980 (5th Cir. 1996) (recognizing that where the employee pool selection is arbitrarily limited to a subgroup of the class in question, the statistics cannot be probative of pretext in a disparate treatment case; plaintiff used age 50, not 40, as cutoff in age discrimination suit with no justification); Carter v. Ball, 33 F.3d 450, 456–57, 65 FEP 1414 (4th Cir. 1994) (plaintiff's analysis properly excluded where it did not contain information on the race of those in high-level positions or of those in the potential pool of applicants); Anderson v. Douglas & Lomason Co., 26 F.3d 1277, 1293, 69 FEP 131, 143–44 (5th Cir. 1994) (the court criticized plaintiff's statistics because they ignored African-American employees who were offered but turned down promotions), *cert. denied*, 513 U.S. 1149 (1995).

[60]*Id.*

[61]Kuhn v. Ball State Univ., 78 F.3d 330, 332, 70 FEP 449 (7th Cir. 1996) ("[w]ithout knowing how many people, of what age, were not promoted, a court cannot decide" if there is discrimination); Henson v. Liggett Group, Inc., 61 F.3d 270, 68 FEP 826 (4th Cir. 1995) (in ADEA reduction-in-force suit, finding that information about both employees and the nature of the positions in question is necessary in order for the statistics to be probative of discrimination); Greenberg v. Union Camp Corp., 48 F.3d 22, 29, 67 FEP 120 (1st Cir. 1995) (court found that plaintiff's statistical evidence was not probative where it did not provide even basic demographic information about the available hiring pool such as the number of employees hired). Under a similar theory, in a suit brought by a doctor alleging discrimination in the allocation of clinical duties, the Eighth Circuit held that failing to control for patient preferences based on experience and qualifications may invalidate the statistical analysis. El Deeb v. University of Minn., 60 F.3d 423, 430–31, 68 FEP 1173 (8th Cir. 1995).

[62]33 F.3d 674, 678, 65 FEP 1202 (6th Cir. 1994).

have otherwise been the case. For this reason, the plaintiff's attempt to compare this plant to a second one, which did not have a similar history of seniority-based layoffs, was flawed.[63]

Courts generally insist that a statistical analysis that does not account for qualifications of those in the comparison group or other related factors is insufficient.[64] A party must factor nondiscriminatory explanations into its statistical analysis.[65] To accomplish this task, it is not sufficient for a litigant to support a claim with his or her own subjective interpretation of other employees' qualifications.[66]

Serious methodological flaws will typically render a statistical analysis inadmissible. There may be some peculiar circumstances, however, when courts will nonetheless admit a flawed analysis. In *Mangold v. California Public Utilities*,[67] a challenge to a promotion examination, the court considered an analysis that failed to differentiate between those above the age of 40 and those below the age of 40, and failed to factor out repeat test takers. The court stated that errors in the statistician's "assumptions and the composition of the promotion pools went towards the weight, not the admissibility of the statistical evidence."[68]

---

[63]*Id.*

[64]*See* Section III.B *supra*. *See also* Hutson v. McDonnell Douglas Corp., 63 F.3d 771, 775–76, 68 FEP 1209 (8th Cir. 1995) (plaintiff failed to compare treatment of employees with similar assessment scores). "Numbers selected in. . . an unreasoned fashion are not sufficient to support a reasoned inference of impermissible discrimination." Speen v. Crown Clothing Corp., 102 F.3d 625, 635, 73 FEP 347 (1st Cir. 1996) (court found statistics insufficient where the plaintiff randomly chose comparison employees without regard to factors such as sales territory and comparison with plaintiff's own sales performance), *cert. denied*, 117 S. Ct. 2457 (1997); Smith v. Virginia Commonwealth Univ., 84 F.3d 672, 677, 70 FEP 1248 (4th Cir. 1996) (en banc) (pool of faculty that was subject of regression analysis to determine whether female faculty's salaries were lower than salaries of male faculty was inflated because it included male faculty members who also held positions with the university administration and consequently received higher salaries); Hutson v. McDonnell Douglas Corp., 63 F.3d at 777–78 (plaintiff's companywide statistics on discharge failed to analyze treatment of comparable employees, i.e., those with low relative assessment score).

[65]Doan v. Seagate Tech., Inc., 82 F.3d 974, 979, 70 FEP 1202 (10th Cir. 1996) (analysis did not account for the difference in segments of the workforce, which tended to discount plaintiff's claim), *cert. denied*, 117 S. Ct. 684 (1997).

[66]Hopper v. Hallmark Cards, Inc., 87 F.3d 983, 989, 71 FEP 1362, 1365 (8th Cir. 1996) (plaintiff presented evidence only from his subjective interpretation of the employer's records).

[67]67 F.3d 1470, 69 FEP 48 (9th Cir. 1995).

[68]*Id.* at 1476.

The district court has the authority and responsibility for assuring that the jury is not misled by marginally probative statistics. In *Considine v. Newspaper Agency Corp.*,[69] the Tenth Circuit held that it was not error for the court to give a jury instruction informing the jury that the "usefulness or weight of statistical evidence depends on all the surrounding facts and circumstances" and "must not be accepted uncritically." The district court had also permissibly denied the plaintiff's request for an instruction stating that statistical evidence "alone may be sufficient for you to find that age was a determinative factor in denying plaintiff's employment. . . ."[70]

A. Degree of the Disparity

In *Watson v. Fort Worth Bank & Trust*,[71] the Supreme Court characterized the 80 percent rule as, at best, a rule of thumb. Some courts nonetheless continue to rely on the four-fifths or 80 percent rule to determine whether a challenged employment practice has an adverse impact.[72] The rule has been held not to apply where the sample is too small to provide adequate information.[73]

The rule has other limitations. In *Sanchez v. City of Santa Ana*,[74] for example, the defendant lowered the passing score on an employment test to ensure compliance with the 80 percent rule. However, the employer continued to rank employees based on their score. As a result, the employer's recalibration was only cosmetic; more minorities passed the exam, but they were still disadvantaged by

---

[69]43 F.3d 1349, 1367, 69 FEP 1732 (10th Cir. 1994).

[70]*Id.* Another circuit, however, held that "statistical evidence by no means diminishes the plaintiff's obligation to prove discriminatory intent—but in some cases, statistical disparities alone may prove intent." EEOC v. O & G Spring & Wire Forms Specialty Co., 38 F.3d 872, 876 (7th Cir. 1994) (employer used word-of-mouth and walk-in applications to fill positions to hire 87 employees, none of which were African-American), *cert. denied*, 513 U.S. 1198 (1995).

[71]487 U.S. 977 (1988).

[72]Sanchez v. City of Santa Ana, 928 F. Supp. 1494, 1500–01 (C.D. Cal. 1995) (finding an adverse impact where Hispanic candidates were selected at a rate of 10.8% of white candidates); Fickling v. New York State Dep't of Civil Serv., 909 F. Supp. 185, 188 (S.D.N.Y. 1995) (calling the four-fifths rule a "widely accepted benchmark").

[73]Nash v. Consolidated City of Jacksonville, 895 F. Supp. 1536, 1542–43 (M.D. Fla. 1995) (where only two African-American candidates were eligible for promotion, application of the 80% rule would not be statistically significant), *aff'd*, 85 F.3d 643 (11th Cir. 1996).

[74]*Sanchez*, 928 F. Supp. 1494.

their relative ranking, behind those who had scored better on the test. The district court found that allowing the employer to manipulate the rule was not consistent with Title VII's purpose of ensuring equal opportunity in employment.[75]

The courts continue to follow the rather uncertain standard described in *Hazelwood School District v. United States*,[76] which suggests the presence of a disparate impact where there are greater than "two or three" standard deviations between the expected number of the protected class in a given pool and the actual number in the pool.[77]

B. Size of the Statistical Sample

Courts will often discount the weight of statistics where the sample is too small to provide a reliable basis for statistical analysis.[78] In *EEOC v. Steamship Clerks Local 1066*,[79] however, the First Circuit held that a small sample size does not always invalidate statistical evidence. The plaintiff offered evidence that in a six-year period, 36 new union members were admitted; all were white and related to existing members. At the same time, the plaintiff demonstrated that between 8 and 20 percent of the relevant labor market was African-American. The defendant challenged these statistics based on the small sample size. The court stated that "[a] defendant who asserts that a plaintiff's prima facie case is insufficient must point out real deficiencies, not simply hurl epithets from

---

[75]*Id.* at 1501–02.

[76]433 U.S. 299, 308 n.13, 15 FEP 1 (1977).

[77]Peightal v. Metropolitan Dade County, 26 F.3d 1545, 1555–56, 71 FEP 1107 (11th Cir. 1994) (finding that there was strong evidence of discrimination where difference between expected and actual percentage of Hispanics in the fire department was 17.6 standard deviations); Sperling v. Hoffman-La Roche, Inc., 924 F. Supp. 1346, 1383, 72 FEP 1401 (D.N.J. 1996) (finding that a reasonable jury could find statistics persuasive where the standard deviation was in the 4 to 5 range).

[78]Birkbeck v. Marvel Lighting Corp., 30 F.3d 507, 511, 65 FEP 669 (4th Cir.), *cert. denied,* 513 U.S. 1058 (1994) (sample of four employees too small to be of any weight); Ward v. Gulfstream Aerospace Corp., 894 F. Supp. 1573, 1580 (S.D. Ga. 1995) (sample size of 11 candidates for departmental reduction in force not statistically compelling and of little relevance); Maidenbaum v. Bally's Park Place, Inc., 870 F. Supp. 1254, 1259, 68 FEP 1245 (D.N.J. 1994) (sample size of 16 terminated employees was insufficient to evidence disparate impact), *aff'd,* 67 F.3d 291 (3d Cir. 1995); Campbell v. Fasco Indus., Inc., 861 F. Supp. 1385, 1395, 72 FEP 33 (N.D. Ill. 1994) (group of nine too small), *aff'd,* 67 F.3d 301 (7th Cir. 1995).

[79]48 F.3d 594, 67 FEP 629 (1st Cir.), *cert. denied,* 116 S. Ct. 65 (1995).

behind gauzy generalizations."[80] The court considered the "unique factual mosaic" behind the case in analyzing the weight of the statistical evidence.[81]

In *Kuhn v. Ball State University*,[82] the Seventh Circuit characterized a statistical demonstration based on a small sample size as merely "anecdotal" and held that anecdotal evidence of this sort is not sufficient to prove discrimination.[83] "A plaintiff who wants a court to infer discrimination from the employer's treatment of comparable cases has to analyze a goodly sample. One is an anecdote, and several cases are several anecdotes. Judges do not find discrimination on such a thin basis."[84] The court required that the plaintiff subject the employer's decisions to more searching statistical analyses to find out whether the claim had any merit.

---

[80]*Id.* at 604.
[81]*Id.* at 604–05.
[82]78 F.3d 330, 332, 70 FEP 449 (7th Cir. 1996).
[83]*See also* Fisher v. Vassar College, 70 F.3d 1420, 1442–47, 70 FEP 1155 (2d Cir. 1995) (plaintiff presented evidence based on her perception of facts, not based on reliable sources), *aff'd on reh'g en banc*, 114 F.3d 1332 (2d Cir.), *petition for cert. filed*, 66 U.S.L.W. 3178 (Sept. 2, 1997) (No. 97-404).
[84]*Kuhn*, 78 F.3d at 332.

Part 11

Remedies

Chapter 40

INJUNCTIVE AND AFFIRMATIVE RELIEF

II. Enjoining Practices Found Unlawful

Courts continue to grant injunctive relief to curb specific, unlawful employment practices[1] as well as other discriminatory practices.[2] Courts additionally combat unlawful practices with various affirmative measures.[3] Most commonly, however, courts grant injunctions prohibiting defendants from future discrimination or retaliation against named plaintiffs[4] or others in the same protected class.[5]

---

[1] *E.g.,* EEOC v. Johnson & Higgins, Inc., 91 F.3d 1529, 1542, 71 FEP 818 (2d Cir. 1996) (affirming injunction against enforcing discriminatory policy requiring mandatory retirement of employee-directors at age 60 or 62 in violation of ADEA).

[2] Eldredge v. Carpenters 46 Northern Cal. Counties Joint Apprenticeship & Training Comm., 94 F.3d 1366, 1369–70, 71 FEP 1385 (9th Cir. 1996) (rejecting apprenticeship system that lists applicants by name, having a disparate impact on women who seek apprenticeships, and requiring the use of the numerical referral list and the implementation of a 20% affirmative action program); United States v. Board of Trustees of Ill. State Univ., 944 F. Supp. 714, 723, 72 FEP 382 (C.D. Ill. 1996) (granting injunctive relief to prevent university from using affirmative action program to circumvent lawful veterans' preference program, thereby wrongfully denying white male applicants positions at the university).

[3] EEOC v. Astra U.S.A., Inc., 94 F.3d 738, 745, 71 FEP 1267 (1st Cir. 1996) (affirming portion of injunction that prohibited defendant from entering into or enforcing settlement agreements that prohibited employees from aiding EEOC in its investigation of discrimination charges against employer); Hartman v. Duffey, 88 F.3d 1232, 1239 (D.C. Cir. 1996) (affirming order requiring government agency to set aside slots for foreign service positions for women, but remanding for reexamination of the number of slots that should be set aside).

[4] Hearn v. General Elec. Co., 927 F. Supp. 1486, 1501, 71 FEP 435 (M.D. Ala. 1996) (enjoining future discrimination against plaintiffs in layoffs and demotions after employer discharged plaintiffs on account of their gender); Stephenson v. Aluminum Co. of Am., 915 F. Supp. 39, 57 (S.D. Ind. 1995) (enjoining future acts of discrimination or retaliation against plaintiff who was reinstated after successful hostile environment and retaliation claims); Shepherd v. American Broadcasting Cos., 862 F. Supp. 486, 502 (D.D.C. 1994) (granting injunction ordering employer to desist from discriminatory conduct against plaintiff who still is employed at the company but denying similar relief as moot to plaintiff who is no longer employed at the company), *vacated on other grounds,* 62 F.3d 1469 (D.C. Cir. 1995); Fisher v. Vassar College, 852 F. Supp 1193, 1235, 64 FEP 1346 (S.D.N.Y. 1994) (enjoining retaliation against reinstated professor who was discriminated against in the denial of promotion and tenure in violation of Title VII, ADEA, and the Equal Pay Act), *aff'd in part, vacated in part,* 70 F.3d 1420 (2d Cir. 1995).

[5] Eldredge v. Carpenters 46 Northern Cal. Counties Joint Apprenticeship & Training Comm., 94 F.3d 1366, 1369–70, 71 FEP 1385 (9th Cir. 1996) (rejecting apprenticeship

Courts will decline to issue injunctions where injunctive relief would not be effective in retarding discriminatory employment practices. For example, injunctive relief will be denied in cases where the defendant proves that the perpetrator of the discriminatory behavior is no longer employed by the defendant[6] or where it is unnecessary to prevent future noncompliance.[7] In *EEOC v. Clayton Residential Home, Inc.*,[8] a sexual harassment case, the district court held that the EEOC was not entitled to injunctive relief where the last unlawful employment practice occurred 3¾

---

system that lists applicants by name, having a disparate impact on women who seek apprenticeships, and requiring the use of the numerical referral list and the implementation of a 20% affirmative action program); EEOC v. Ilona of Hungary, Inc., 108 F.3d 1569, 1578–79 (7th Cir. 1997) (injunction against future religious discrimination justified where employer violated Title VII in terminating employees for taking off Yom Kippur without permission, even where no pattern or practice of similar discrimination, based on possibility of future discrimination by same decisionmakers); United States v. Board of Trustees of Ill. State Univ., 944 F. Supp. 714, 723, 72 FEP 382 (C.D. Ill. 1996) (granting injunctive relief to prevent university from using affirmative action program to circumvent lawful veterans' preference program "to ensure that all individuals who have been denied the chance to compete for . . . positions may do so on equal footing in the future"); EEOC v. Accurate Mechanical Contractors, Inc., 863 F. Supp. 828, 838–40 (E.D. Wis. 1994) (granting injunction forbidding defendant from discriminating by failing or refusing to hire women where employer persisted in its denial of discrimination and the primary perpetrators of the discriminatory conduct remained at the company, suggesting a likelihood that discrimination could occur in the future).

[6]EEOC v. Clayton Residential Home, Inc., 874 F. Supp. 212, 215–16, 66 FEP 1745 (N.D. Ill. 1995) (denying injunctive relief where last unlawful employment practice occurred 3¾ years earlier, only one additional allegation of discrimination made in that time, perpetrators of the discriminatory behavior no longer employed at the company, and company has antidiscrimination policy); Amirmokri v. Baltimore Gas & Elec. Co., 60 F.3d 1126, 1132, 68 FEP 809 (4th Cir. 1995) (denying injunction against future harassment where plaintiff no longer employed at company; however, injunction would be appropriate if plaintiff were reinstated); Shepherd v. American Broadcasting Cos., 862 F. Supp. 486, 502 (D.D.C. 1994) (granting injunction ordering employer to desist from discriminatory conduct against plaintiff who still is employed at the company but denying similar relief as moot to plaintiff who is no longer employed at the company), *vacated on other grounds,* 62 F.3d 1469 (D.C. Cir. 1995).

[7]Griffith v. State of Col., Div. of Youth Servs., 17 F.3d 1323, 1330, 64 FEP 206 (10th Cir. 1994) (affirming that employee who alleged sexual and racial harassment was not entitled to injunction because employer had no pattern or practice of permitting such behavior, the alleged discrimination was isolated, and the employer acted promptly to eliminate hostile work environment when informed of the discriminatory conduct); Fisher v. Vassar College, 852 F. Supp. 1193, 1235, 64 FEP 1346 (S.D.N.Y. 1994) (denying injunctive relief as to a policy of discriminating against married women in hiring, promotion, and tenure because policy subsequently changed), *aff'd in part, vacated in part,* 70 F.3d 1420 (2d Cir. 1995).

[8]874 F. Supp. 212, 66 FEP 1745 (N.D. Ill. 1995).

years earlier; only one additional allegation of discrimination, not yet proven, had been made in that time; the perpetrators of the harassment were no longer employed at the company; and an antidiscrimination policy had been established at the company.[9] The court reasoned that there was little likelihood of recurrent violations and thus, "the purpose of Title VII will not be advanced further by enjoining [the defendant] from doing what it is already not doing, engaging in unlawful employment practices."[10]

Nevertheless, a court sometimes will insist on issuing an injunction even after the discontinuance of unlawful practices if it is skeptical about the recurrence of discriminatory behavior.[11] Specifically, some courts are suspicious of defendants who change their unlawful employment practices solely in response to being sued and accordingly grant injunctions.[12]

Because "injunctive relief should be no more burdensome than necessary to provide complete relief to the plaintiffs,"[13] appellate courts may narrow the scope of an injunction issued in a district court[14] or limit its application to benefit a particular victim of discrimination where there is no pattern or practice of discrimination

---

[9]*Id.* at 216.
[10]*Id.*
[11]*See* Dombeck v. Milwaukee Valve Co., 40 F.3d 230, 238, 66 FEP 497 (7th Cir. 1994) (approving injunctive relief in a hostile environment case because although plaintiff and alleged harasser were subsequently assigned to different work areas, employer could alter those assignments at any time absent injunctive relief); EEOC v. Ilona of Hungary, Inc., 108 F.3d 1569, 1578–79 (7th Cir. 1997) (affirming injunction prohibiting employer from engaging in future practices that discriminate on the basis of religion, where owners of business denied two employees' requests to take off work on Yom Kippur, then fired employees for their absence; court noted concern with possibility of future discrimination by same decisionmakers).
[12]EEOC v. Astra U.S.A., Inc., 94 F.3d 738, 745, 71 FEP 1267 (1st Cir. 1996) (affirming that injunction against entering or enforcing settlement agreements that prohibited employees from aiding EEOC in its investigation of discrimination charges against employer could not be defeated by defendant's "attempts to reinterpret the operative provisions of its agreements when under siege"); United States v. Board of Trustees of Ill. State Univ., 944 F. Supp. 714, 723, 72 FEP 382 (C.D. Ill. 1996) (granting injunctive relief to prevent university from using affirmative action program to circumvent lawful veterans' preference program because it appeared the affirmative action program was only abandoned after proceedings were initiated and therefore not voluntarily).
[13]EEOC v. Astra U.S.A., Inc., 94 F.3d at 746 (citing Califano v. Yamasaki, 442 U.S. 682 (1979)).
[14]*Id.* (vacating portion of injunction that prohibited defendant from entering into or enforcing nonfiling covenants in settlement agreements that prohibit employees from filing charges of discrimination).

at issue.[15] For example, in *United States v. Criminal Sheriff, Parish of Orleans*,[16] the Fifth Circuit narrowed an injunction that exceeded the scope of what was put "at issue" by stipulation of the parties. The parties had stipulated to adjudicate whether the sheriff's policy in assigning deputy sheriffs to duties on all-male-populated tiers of the jail discriminated against female deputy sheriffs.[17] Having found the policy discriminatory, the magistrate enjoined the sheriff from failing to hire females to the position of deputy sheriff according to the same criteria as males, from failing to promote female deputies on an equal basis to males, and from failing to implement a program to inform women of equal employment opportunities available at the prison and to attract qualified women to become deputies in proportion to their representation in the relevant labor market.[18] The court reasoned that such a broad injunction exceeded the scope of what was "at issue," and limited the scope of the injunction to correcting the disproportionate ratio of male to female deputy sheriffs assigned to duties on the all-male tiers of the prison.[19]

III. Relief for Identifiable Victims of Unlawful Employment Practices

Courts continue to tailor remedies to make victims whole for injuries suffered as a result of unlawful employment discrimination. Reinstatement or instatement, whereby a court orders that the plaintiff be placed in the same or a substantially comparable position that the plaintiff would have occupied in the absence of unlawful discrimination,[20] is the preferred make-whole

---

[15]Jones v. Washington Metro. Area Transit Auth., 946 F. Supp. 1023, 1033–34 (D.D.C. 1996) (limiting scope of injunction to future acts of retaliation against the named plaintiff only and not to similarly situated employees because case was pleaded and tried as a single disparate treatment claim).
[16]19 F.3d 238, 64 FEP 813 (5th Cir. 1994).
[17]*Id.* at 239.
[18]*Id.* at 240.
[19]*Id.*
[20]*See* Kraemer v. Franklin & Marshall College, 941 F. Supp. 479, 481–82 (E.D. Pa. 1996) (stating that the exact position that plaintiff was unlawfully denied need not be available, but substantially comparable position must be available for the court to order instatement); Shea v. Icelandair, 925 F. Supp. 1014, 1030, 70 FEP 1544

remedy[21]; however, it is not always required.[22] Reinstatement is an equitable remedy, therefore courts must consider whether reinstatement is appropriate in light of the surrounding circumstances. Such circumstances generally include whether a suitable position to which to reinstate plaintiff is available and the degree of hostility between the parties.[23] Courts generally hold that

---

(S.D.N.Y. 1996) (stating that "[a] court can grant reinstatement where a comparable job exists even if it bears a different title").

[21]Woodhouse v. Magnolia Hosp., 92 F.3d 248, 258, 71 FEP 1804 (5th Cir. 1996) (concluding that in light of recognition that reinstatement is preferred remedy, district court did not abuse its discretion in ordering plaintiff reinstated); Squires v. Bonser, 54 F.3d 168, 172–73 (3d Cir. 1995) (reinstatement is preferred remedy in the absence of special circumstances militating against it because it "advances the policy goals of make-whole relief and deterrence in a way which money damages cannot"); Weaver v. Amoco Prod. Co., 66 F.3d 85, 88, 70 FEP 931 (5th Cir. 1995) (stating that "[t]his Circuit continues to recognize the decided preference to award reinstatement instead of front pay for a discriminatory discharge in violation of the ADEA"); Stephenson v. Aluminum Co. of Am., 915 F. Supp. 39, 56 (S.D. Ind. 1995) (granting reinstatement, the preferred remedy, in Title VII action); *see also* Thurman v. Yellow Freight Sys., Inc., 90 F.3d 1160, 1171, 72 FEP 657 (6th Cir. 1996) (stating that "[v]ictims of discrimination are presumptively entitled to instatement or reinstatement in the usual case").

[22]Ray v. Iuka Special Mun. Separate Sch. Dist., 51 F.3d 1246, 1253, 67 FEP 1348 (5th Cir. 1995) (although reinstatement is the preferred equitable relief, front pay is appropriate where reinstatement not feasible); Feldman v. Philadelphia Hous. Auth., 43 F.3d 823, 831 (3d Cir. 1994) (reinstatement is preferred remedy to cover loss of future earnings; however, it is not the exclusive remedy, because it is not always feasible); Hutchison v. Amateur Elec. Supply, Inc., 42 F.3d 1037, 1045–46, 66 FEP 1275 (7th Cir. 1994) (reinstatement is preferred remedy, but is not always required); Downes v. Volkswagen of Am., Inc., 41 F.3d 1132, 1141, 69 FEP 11 (7th Cir. 1994) (although reinstatement is the preferred remedy, it is not always appropriate); *but see* Avitia v. Metropolitan Club of Chicago, Inc., 49 F.3d 1219, 1232 (7th Cir. 1995) (noting in dictum that front pay may be the socially preferable form of relief, as compared to reinstatement, because "it avoids the need for a tricky transaction").

[23]Doll v. Brown, 75 F.3d 1200, 1205, 5 AD 369 (7th Cir. 1996) (noting in dictum that reinstatement may not be appropriate remedy where there is friction in the workplace, changed circumstances, or incumbent employee currently occupying position to which plaintiff seeks reinstatement); Starceski v. Westinghouse Elec. Corp., 54 F.3d 1089, 1103, 67 FEP 1184 (3d Cir. 1995) (affirming district court's denial of reinstatement, reasoning that reinstatement not feasible because of lack of available positions and animosity between the parties); Downes v. Volkswagen of Am., Inc., 41 F.3d 1132, 1141, 69 FEP 11 (7th Cir. 1994) (noting that courts in exercising discretion to grant or deny reinstatement may consider hostility in employment relationship and lack of available position); Frank v. Relin, 851 F. Supp. 87, 91–93 (W.D.N.Y. 1994) (finding that reinstatement was not appropriate in § 1983 action where (1) it would require that the employee currently occupying plaintiff's position be fired; (2) plaintiff's former position had been modified; and (3) there is a

reinstatement is inappropriate where it would require "bumping" an innocent incumbent employee occupying the position to which plaintiff seeks reinstatement.[24] Moreover, whereas hostility developed during litigation cannot alone defeat reinstatement,[25] a finding of undue friction and controversy between the parties may render reinstatement infeasible.[26]

---

great potential for animosity if plaintiff were reinstated because plaintiff's former position was a sensitive one requiring that she work closely with the defendant); *cf.* Stephenson v. Aluminum Co. of Am., 915 F. Supp. 39, 56 (S.D. Ind. 1995) (ordering reinstatement where plaintiff's position still exists and employer failed to demonstrate exceptional circumstances militating against reinstatement).

[24]*See* Ray v. Iuka Special Mun. Separate Sch. Dist., 51 F.3d 1246, 1254–55, 67 FEP 1348 (5th Cir. 1995) (affirming that district court properly denied reinstatement upon concluding that (1) reinstatement infeasible where no existing vacancies; (2) ordering reinstatement would require bumping incumbent employee; (3) plaintiff secured substantially similar employment; and (4) due to consolidation, plaintiff's former position no longer exists); Frank v. Relin, 851 F. Supp. 87, 91–93 (W.D.N.Y. 1994) (finding that reinstatement was not appropriate in § 1983 action where (1) it would require that the employee currently occupying plaintiff's position be fired; (2) plaintiff's former position had been modified; and (3) there is a great potential for animosity if plaintiff were reinstated because plaintiff's former position was a sensitive one requiring that she work closely with the defendant); *accord* Doll v. Brown, 75 F.3d 1200, 1205 (7th Cir. 1996) (noting in dictum that reinstatement may not be appropriate remedy where there is friction in the workplace, changed circumstances, or incumbent employee currently occupying position to which plaintiff seeks reinstatement); *but see* Hayes v. Shalala, 933 F. Supp. 21, 25, 71 FEP 1240 (D.D.C. 1996) (ordering retroactive appointment of plaintiff despite fact that it will result in "bumping" of incumbent employee; stating that "the District of Columbia has indicated that bumping is authorized and appropriate in precisely the kind of situation presented by this case"); Shea v. Icelandair, 925 F. Supp. 1014, 1031, 70 FEP 1544 (S.D.N.Y. 1996) (ordering reinstatement despite potential displacement of another employee, stating that factors such as uniqueness of position denied plaintiff, the ability to minimize harm to "bumped" employee, and frequency of discriminatory acts may weigh in favor of reinstatement that results in the "bumping" of another employee).

[25]Philipp v. ANR Freight Sys., Inc., 61 F.3d 669, 674, 70 FEP 1347 (8th Cir. 1995) (friction arising from litigation is not alone sufficient to deny reinstatement since "a court might deny [employment] in virtually every case if it considered the hostility engendered from litigation as a bar to relief") (citation omitted); Squires v. Bonser, 54 F.3d 168, 175 (3d Cir. 1995) ("[i]n order to deny reinstatement, more than the ordinary tensions accompanying an unconstitutional discharge lawsuit must be present"); Hutchison v. Amateur Elec. Supply, Inc., 42 F.3d 1037, 1045–46, 66 FEP 1275 (7th Cir. 1994) (mere employer hostility developed during litigation cannot alone defeat reinstatement); Stephenson v. Aluminum Co. of Am., 915 F. Supp. 39, 56 (S.D. Ind. 1995) (hostility developed during litigation is insufficient in itself to defeat reinstatement).

[26]Simpson v. Ernst & Young, 100 F.3d 436, 445, 72 FEP 343 (6th Cir. 1996) (evidence in record indicated underlying hostility between the parties, making reinstatement highly impractical); Paperworkers Local 274 v. Champion Int'l Corp., 81

For example, in *Avitia v. Metropolitan Club of Chicago, Inc.*,[27] the Seventh Circuit upheld the district court's denial of an order of reinstatement where the court had determined that (1) the defendant would have to "bump" an innocent employee if the plaintiff were reinstated because there were no vacancies in the position plaintiff formerly held; and (2) the relationship between the parties "was so poisoned, and the poison so harmful to the [defendant's] legitimate concerns."[28]

At least one court has stated that plaintiff's expressed ambivalence regarding his or her desire for reinstatement may militate against such an award.[29] Moreover, an award of reinstatement or instatement may not be appropriate when the position sought

---

F.3d 798, 805 (8th Cir. 1996) (affirming denial of reinstatement where district court found that there was "[s]ubstantial hostility, above that normally incident to litigation"; noting, however, that the passage of time may soften such acrimonious relationship, therefore the reinstatement issue is not foreclosed on remand); Feldman v. Philadelphia Hous. Auth., 43 F.3d 823, 832 (3d Cir. 1994) (finding that district court's award of front pay, rather than reinstatement, was appropriate where there was ample evidence in record of irreparable hostility between the parties); Hutchison v. Amateur Elec. Supply, Inc., 42 F.3d 1037, 1046, 66 FEP 1275 (7th Cir. 1994) (friction legitimate reason for denying reinstatement where employer is a relatively small operation and district court would be faced with potentially difficult and expensive task of monitoring parties' future employment relationship); Thomas v. National Football League Players Ass'n, 941 F. Supp. 156, 163 (D.D.C. 1996) (denying reinstatement where relationship between the parties "is so hostile that there is no reason to believe that they would enjoy a productive and amiable working relationship"); *cf.* Philipp v. ANR Freight Sys., Inc., 61 F.3d 669, 674, 70 FEP 1347 (8th Cir. 1995) (district court did not abuse its discretion in ordering reinstatement where supervisors who allegedly discriminated against plaintiff were no longer with the company); Squires v. Bonser, 54 F.3d 168, 175–76 (3d Cir. 1995) (holding that district court's denial of reinstatement was not a proper exercise of its discretion because, inter alia, the court expressly found that animosity between the parties was not irreparable); Stephenson v. Aluminum Co. of Am., 915 F. Supp. 39, 56 (S.D. Ind. 1995) (ordering reinstatement where employer employs thousands of persons and therefore unlikely that friction will be of serious concern).

[27]49 F.3d 1219 (7th Cir. 1995).

[28]*Id.* at 1230–31 (action brought under the Fair Labor Standards Act).

[29]Hutchison v. Amateur Elec. Supply, Inc., 42 F.3d 1037, 1046, 66 FEP 1275 (7th Cir. 1994) (upholding denial of reinstatement despite reservations over district court's interpretation of plaintiff's testimony as demonstrating ambivalence with respect to her desire for reinstatement; stating that plaintiff's testimony that she is seeking reinstatement because "it is better to have a job when looking for another job" is not inconsistent with the make-whole nature of Title VII remedies); *cf.* Stephenson v. Aluminum Co. of Am., 915 F. Supp. 39, 56–57 (S.D. Ind. 1995) (distinguishing *Hutchison;* ordering reinstatement where plaintiff never expressed ambivalence as to her desire for reinstatement; rather, reinstatement is the point of her lawsuit).

by the plaintiff is soon to be eliminated[30] or when the plaintiff is not capable of performing the job in question.[31]

The after-acquired evidence doctrine, as articulated by the Supreme Court in *McKennon v. Nashville Banner Publishing Co.*,[32] also operates as a bar to reinstatement under certain circumstances. In *McKennon,* an action arising under the ADEA, the Court held that prospective relief, such as reinstatement and front pay, is inappropriate where there is after-acquired evidence of employee misconduct during employment "of such severity that the employee in fact would have been terminated on those grounds alone if the employer had known of it at the time of the discharge."[33] The Court

---

[30]Williams v. Pharmacia Opthalmics, Inc., 926 F. Supp. 791, 795, 71 FEP 628 (N.D. Ind. 1996) (declining to order reinstatement in light of pending merger and reorganization, which will result in the elimination of plaintiff's position).

[31]Thurman v. Yellow Freight Sys., Inc., 90 F.3d 1160, 1171–72, 72 FEP 657 (6th Cir. 1996) (finding that district court did not abuse its discretion in denying instatement where plaintiff injured himself and was unable to do heavy lifting required for position); *cf.* Shea v. Icelandair, 925 F. Supp. 1014, 1032–33, 70 FEP 1544 (S.D.N.Y. 1996) (ordering reinstatement upon concluding that plaintiff's health is not an impediment to his ability to perform former duties provided that defendant eliminate a particularly stressful duty that had been added to plaintiff's responsibilities after he was demoted); Legault v. aRusso, 842 F. Supp. 1479, 1491, 64 FEP 170 (D.N.H. 1994) (ordering instatement of plaintiff as firefighter upon concluding that defendants failed to establish that plaintiff lacked the physical abilities to be a safe and effective firefighter).

[32]115 S. Ct. 879, 66 FEP 1192 (1995).

[33]*Id.* at 886–87 (holding that employee's subsequently discovered misconduct in removing confidential documents from office precluded relief of reinstatement or front pay because "[i]t would be both inequitable and pointless to order the reinstatement of someone the employer would have terminated . . . upon lawful grounds"); *see* O'Day v. McDonnell Douglas Helicopter Co., 79 F.3d 756, 763–64, 70 FEP 615 (9th Cir. 1996) (concluding that ADEA plaintiff not entitled to remedies precluded under *McKennon* where defendant established that it would have discharged plaintiff for subsequently acquired evidence that plaintiff rifled through supervisor's office and copied confidential documents which plaintiff then showed to co-worker); Wallace v. Dunn Const. Co., 62 F.3d 374, 378–79, 68 FEP 990 (11th Cir. 1995) (concluding that after-acquired evidence doctrine advanced in *McKennon,* an ADEA action, is applicable to claims brought under Title VII and Equal Pay Act and holding that reasoning of *McKennon* applies with equal force when the after-acquired evidence concerns an employee's fraud in a job application or resume, rather than an employee's wrongful conduct during employment); *see also* Castle v. Rubin, 78 F.3d 654, 657–58, 72 FEP 1701 (D.C. Cir. 1996) (affirming district court's denial of reinstatement and front pay based on after-acquired evidence of plagiarism that would have resulted in plaintiff's termination; stating that the principles of *McKennon* clearly apply in Title VII actions); *cf.* Padilla v. Metro-North Commuter R.R., 92 F.3d 117, 124–25, 72 FEP 1748 (2d Cir. 1996) (holding that district court did not err in awarding plaintiff front pay despite after-acquired evidence of perjury because

noted, however, that after-acquired evidence of wrongdoing would not operate to bar all relief in every instance.[34]

After-acquired evidence of employee misconduct is a potential defense to the presumptive entitlement to reinstatement and other equitable remedies, with the burden of proof resting on the employer to establish not only that it *could* have fired plaintiff for the after-acquired evidence of misconduct, but that it *would* have done so.[35] The Supreme Court, in *McKennon,* however, left open the issue of the evidentiary standard applicable in the context of after-acquired evidence of misconduct.[36]

When reinstatement is not feasible, front pay is typically awarded in its place.[37] Front pay, like reinstatement, is an

---

evidence did not demonstrate that the wrongdoing was of such severity that plaintiff would have been demoted on that ground alone); *contra* Delli Santi v. CNA Ins. Cos., 88 F.3d 192, 204–05, 71 FEP 143 (3d Cir. 1996) (rejecting district court's determination that plaintiff's alleged theft rendered her ineligible for front pay under the after-acquired evidence rule; alleged theft was not after-acquired evidence because the employer knew of the alleged theft at the time plaintiff was terminated).

[34]*McKennon v. Nashville Banner Publ'g Co.,* 115 S. Ct. at 886 (holding that back pay should be calculated "from the date of the unlawful discharge to the date the new information was discovered" and in determining order for relief the court may take into further account "extraordinary equitable circumstances that affect the legitimate interests of either party"); *see also* Wallace v. Dunn Constr. Co., 62 F.3d 374, 380, 68 FEP 990 (11th Cir. 1995) (noting in dictum that: (1) after-acquired evidence is irrelevant to plaintiff's recovery of unpaid wages or liquidated damages because plaintiff does not recover such wages or damages after termination; and (2) back pay may be awarded from date of unlawful discharge to date after-acquired evidence is discovered).

[35]*McKennon v. Nashville Banner Publ'g Co.,* 115 S. Ct. at 886–87; *O'Day v. McDonnell Douglas Helicopter Co.,* 79 F.3d at 759 (stating that the burden, as set forth in *McKennon,* "comports with the well-established rule in mixed-motive cases, where the burden rests on the employer to prove by a preponderance of the evidence that it would have discharged the employee . . . regardless of its discriminatory motive"); *Wallace v. Dunn Constr. Co.,* 62 F.3d at 380–81 (holding that reinstatement, front pay, and injunctive relief unavailable to plaintiff because employer sufficiently demonstrated that plaintiff would have been fired when it learned that plaintiff lied on her job application about a prior conviction); *cf.* Thurman v. Yellow Freight Sys., Inc., 90 F.3d 1160, 1168, 72 FEP 657 (6th Cir. 1996) (holding that because employer failed to prove it could have and would have refused to hire plaintiff if it had known plaintiff made omissions and misrepresentations on employment application, the after-acquired evidence defense did not apply).

[36]*McKennon v. Nashville Banner Publ'g Co.,* 115 S. Ct. at 886; *but see O'Day v. McDonnell Douglas Helicopter Co.,* 79 F.3d at 760–61 (applying preponderance of evidence standard, rather than clear and convincing evidence standard).

[37]Reed v. A.W. Lawrence & Co., 95 F.3d 1170, 1182, 72 FEP 1345 (2d Cir. 1996) (upholding front pay award where antagonism between the parties made reinstatement inappropriate and plaintiff made a good faith effort to mitigate damages, but

equitable remedy intended to make the injured party whole.[38] While the determination of front pay is entrusted to the sound

---

[37] was unable to obtain comparable alternative employment); Paperworkers Local 274 v. Champion Int'l Corp., 81 F.3d 798, 805 (8th Cir. 1996) (stating that front pay is generally appropriate when reinstatement must be denied); Doll v. Brown, 75 F.3d 1200, 1205, 5 AD 369 (7th Cir. 1996) (noting in dictum that district court should have awarded front pay, an equitable substitute for reinstatement, if court had determined that reinstatement would be inequitable); Suggs v. Servicemaster Educ. Food Management, 72 F.3d 1228, 1234, 69 FEP 1270 (6th Cir. 1996) (front pay generally awarded when reinstatement is infeasible, "[t]hus, the remedies of reinstatement and front pay are alternative, rather than cumulative"); Weaver v. Amoco Prod. Co., 66 F.3d 85, 88, 70 FEP 931 (5th Cir. 1995) (stating that front pay is the appropriate award in ADEA action if reinstatement is not feasible; however, court should articulate the basis for its conclusion that reinstatement was not feasible); Scarfo v. Cabletron Sys., Inc., 54 F.3d 931, 954, 67 FEP 1474 (1st Cir. 1995) (district court has discretion to award front pay in Title VII case when reinstatement is "impracticable or impossible"); Avitia v. Metropolitan Club of Chicago, Inc., 49 F.3d 1219, 1232 (7th Cir. 1995) (noting in dictum that plaintiff may seek front pay in lieu of reinstatement when reinstatement infeasible); Hadley v. VAM P T S, 44 F.3d 372, 376, 67 FEP 186 (5th Cir. 1995) (equitable remedy of front pay appropriate when reinstatement not feasible); Feldman v. Philadelphia Hous. Auth., 43 F.3d 823, 832 (3d Cir. 1994) (front pay is alternative remedy when reinstatement not appropriate because of irreparable animosity between the parties); Smith v. World Ins. Co., 38 F.3d 1456, 1466, 66 FEP 13 (8th Cir. 1994) (stating that front pay may be awarded under ADEA "in lieu of, but not in addition to, reinstatement"); DiRussa v. Dean Witter Reynolds, Inc., 936 F. Supp. 104, 108, 71 FEP 1002 (S.D.N.Y. 1996) (confirming arbitrator's award of front pay to ADEA plaintiff where reinstatement is not feasible under the circumstances); Frank v. Relin, 851 F. Supp. 87, 93–94 (W.D.N.Y. 1994) (awarding plaintiff front pay to remedy a constitutional violation where reinstatement not practicable); cf. Squires v. Bonser, 54 F.3d 168, 176 (3d Cir. 1995) (concluding that fact that plaintiff was awarded front pay damages by jury does not preclude this court from remanding the case for entry of an order of reinstatement, rather, "it means that the issue of double recovery should be resolved by a new trial on compensatory damages"); Philipp v. ANR Freight Sys., Inc., 61 F.3d 669, 674, 70 FEP 1347 (8th Cir. 1995) (district court did not abuse its discretion in ordering reinstatement rather than front pay where no showing was made that reinstatement was impracticable or impossible); Ward v. Papa's Pizza To Go, Inc., 907 F. Supp. 1535, 1543 (S.D. Ga. 1995) (stating that front pay is to be awarded only when back pay does not fully redress plaintiff's injuries and reinstatement is not possible); but see EEOC v. Domino's Pizza, Inc., 909 F. Supp. 1529, 1537, 69 FEP 570 (M.D. Fla. 1995) (concluding that neither front pay nor reinstatement is necessary where back pay and other damages awarded are sufficient to fully compensate plaintiff for his damages) (citing Dillon v. Coles, 746 F.2d 998 (3d Cir. 1984)).

[38] Padilla v. Metro-North Commuter R.R., 92 F.3d 117, 125–26, 72 FEP 1748 (2d Cir. 1996) (stating that front pay award "serves a necessary role in making victims of discrimination whole in cases where the factfinder can reasonably predict that the plaintiff has no reasonable prospect of obtaining comparable alternative employment"); Suggs v. Servicemaster Educ. Food Management, 72 F.3d 1228, 1234, 69 FEP 1270 (6th Cir. 1996) (stating that "purpose of front pay in a Title VII case is to put an injured party in the same position the party would have occupied in the

CH. 40 INJUNCTIVE AND AFFIRMATIVE RELIEF 573

discretion of the trial court, the court may submit the issue to the jury.[39]

In deciding whether an award of front pay is appropriate, courts consider various factors, including "whether the plaintiff has a reasonable prospect of obtaining comparable employment, whether the time period for the award is relatively short, whether the plaintiff intended to work or was physically capable of working and whether liquidated damages have been awarded."[40] Some courts have held

---

absence of the discrimination, neither more nor less") (citation omitted); Avitia v. Metropolitan Club of Chicago, Inc., 49 F.3d 1219, 1231 (7th Cir. 1995) (noting in dictum that front pay is "designed to put [plaintiff] in the identical financial position that he would have occupied had he been reinstated" and may be awarded under the Fair Labor Standards Act); Barbour v. Merrill, 48 F.3d 1270, 1279, 68 FEP 126 (D.C. Cir. 1995) (stating that purpose of front pay award is "to make a victim of discrimination 'whole' and to restore him or her to the economic position he or she would have occupied but for the unlawful conduct of his or her employer") (citation omitted), *cert. granted in part,* 116 S. Ct. 805, *cert. dismissed,* 116 S. Ct. 1037 (1996); Schwartz v. Gregori, 45 F.3d 1017, 1023 (6th Cir. 1995) (front pay is an equitable remedy available under ERISA), *cert. denied,* 116 S. Ct. 77 (1995); Smith v. World Ins. Co., 38 F.3d 1456, 1466, 66 FEP 13 (8th Cir. 1994) (district court may award equitable remedy of front pay under ADEA to make party whole); Carter v. Sedgwick County, Kan., 36 F.3d 952, 957, 65 FEP 1585 (10th Cir. 1994) (stating that when fashioning a front pay award, the district court should determine the amount "required to compensate a victim for the continuing future effects of discrimination until the victim can be made whole"); Frank v. Relin, 851 F. Supp. 87, 94 (W.D.N.Y. 1994) (stating that "purpose of front pay is to make victims of employment discrimination whole and to compensate them for the continuing future effects of the unlawful discrimination"); *cf.* Thurman v. Yellow Freight Sys., Inc., 97 F.3d 833, 835 (6th Cir. 1996) (affirming district court's denial of front pay because award of back pay for a period of five years together with attorney's fees and costs made plaintiff whole); *but see* Squires v. Bonser, 54 F.3d 168, 176 (3d Cir. 1995) (noting that although circumstances of the case indicate that "front pay may come closer to providing make-whole relief than it otherwise might, they do not negate the additional psychological and deterrent benefits which reinstatement provides"); EEOC v. Domino's Pizza, Inc., 909 F. Supp. 1529, 1537, 69 FEP 570 (M.D. Fla. 1995) (stating that neither front pay nor reinstatement is necessary to complete the make-whole remedy; rather, front pay is only appropriate when back pay and other damages will not sufficiently compensate plaintiff).

[39]Simpson v. Ernst & Young, 100 F.3d 436, 444, 72 FEP 343 (6th Cir. 1996) (stating that it is within trial court's discretion to submit issue of front pay to the jury and such decision is reviewed on appeal for abuse of discretion); Downes v. Volkswagen of Am., Inc., 41 F.3d 1132, 1141–42, 69 FEP 11 (7th Cir. 1994) (stating that in ADEA cases, court may submit issue of front pay to jury for advice; however, court is not bound by jury's verdict).

[40]Downes v. Volkswagen of Am., Inc., 41 F.3d 1132, 1141–42, 69 FEP 11 (7th Cir. 1994); *see also* Suggs v. Servicemaster Educ. Food Management, 72 F.3d 1228, 1234, 69 FEP 1270 (6th Cir. 1996) (stating that the following factors are relevant in awarding front pay: (1) employee's future in position from which she was terminated;

that front pay is inappropriate where plaintiff had no reasonable expectation of continued employment[41] or where plaintiff failed to mitigate his or her damages.[42] Moreover, some courts have held

---

(2) her work and life expectancy; (3) her obligation to mitigate damages; (4) availability of comparable employment opportunities and the time reasonably required to find such employment; and (5) discount table to determine present value of future damages); Scarfo v. Cabletron Sys., Inc., 54 F.3d 931, 954–55, 67 FEP 1474 (1st Cir. 1995) (plaintiff's inability to return to former position or to find full employment at equivalent salary relevant in trial court's decision to award front pay and relevant in calculating amount of award); cf. Padilla v. Metro-North Commuter R.R., 92 F.3d 117, 125–26, 72 FEP 1748 (2d Cir. 1996) (holding that front pay award for a period of well over 20 years until plaintiff reaches the age of 67 was not excessive in view of the unique circumstance of this case in that plaintiff had "no reasonable prospect of obtaining comparable alternative employment").

[41]See Mungin v. Katten Muchin & Zavis, 941 F. Supp. 153, 156 (D.D.C. 1996) (plaintiff not entitled to front pay award because no reasonable expectation of continued employment where employer had closed down part of its practice and defections and terminations had substantially reduced the workforce); see also Inks v. Healthcare Distrib. of Ind., Inc., 901 F. Supp. 1403, 1408–09, 73 FEP 643 (N.D. Ind. 1995) (concluding that trial court's decision not to award front pay where court took into consideration, inter alia, that plaintiff's continued employment with defendant was uncertain, did not constitute manifest error of law); cf. Reed v. A.W. Lawrence & Co., 95 F.3d 1170, 1182, 72 FEP 1345 (2d Cir. 1996) (holding that district court's limitation of front pay to only seven weeks' salary was not abuse of discretion because plaintiff's job was scheduled to be eliminated in any case seven weeks after the jury verdict; therefore "an award of front pay beyond that date would have impermissibly placed her in a better position than she would have been in had she not been fired"); Williams v. Pharmacia Opthalmics, Inc., 926 F. Supp. 791, 797–98, 71 FEP 628 (N.D. Ind. 1996) (holding that uncertainty over continued employment of plaintiff in light of pending merger and deterioration in her pretermination performance affects duration of front pay award, not whether such an award should be granted).

[42]See Paperworkers Local 274 v. Champion Int'l Corp., 81 F.3d 798, 805 (8th Cir. 1996) (stating that plaintiff's relatively young age should improve his ability to mitigate damages through other employment opportunities, and therefore district court's front-pay award of 24 years until employee reaches retirement age was improper); Konstantopoulos v. Westvaco Corp., 893 F. Supp. 1263, 1279 (D. Del. 1994) (declining to award front pay where court rejected medical expert's testimony, which testimony plaintiff had asserted as a legitimate reason for not seeking other employment); see also Padilla v. Metro-North Commuter R.R., 92 F.3d 117, 125 (2d Cir. 1996) (defendant may challenge plaintiff's entitlement to front-pay award on the basis that plaintiff failed to mitigate his damages; however, defendant bears the burden of showing that comparable positions were available for plaintiff); Hutchison v. Amateur Elec. Supply, Inc., 42 F.3d 1037, 1045, 66 FEP 1675 (7th Cir. 1994) (stating that a reasonable jury could fail to award front pay where it found that plaintiff, "using reasonable diligence, should have found 'comparable' employment" at some date between termination and judgment); Mitchell v. Sisters of Charity of Incarnate Word, 924 F. Supp. 793, 803 (S.D. Tex. 1996) (stating that "front pay may be denied or reduced when the employee fails to mitigate damages by seeking other employment") (citations omitted).

that "a substantial liquidated damage award may indicate that an additional award of front pay is inappropriate or excessive."[43] So too, a large award of punitive damages may militate against an additional award of front pay.[44]

Courts also have held that front pay should not be awarded where plaintiff has rejected the employer's offer of reinstatement and it is determined that plaintiff's rejection of such offer was unreasonable.[45] In addition, in *McKennon v. Nashville Banner Publishing Co.*, the Supreme Court held that with respect to after-acquired evidence of misconduct during employment, if the employer can prove that it would have discharged plaintiff for such misconduct, both reinstatement and front pay are inappropriate.[46]

Front pay is usually awarded from the date of judgment forward.[47] The amount and duration of the award is left to the discretion of the courts[48]; however, courts generally refuse to award front

---

[43]Weaver v. Amoco Prod. Co., 66 F.3d 85, 89, 70 FEP 931 (5th Cir. 1995) (vacating front-pay award and remanding for a more thorough review of the issue where district court did not articulate a rational basis and calculation for the award, and where plaintiff already was awarded substantial liquidated damages) (quoting Walther v. Lone Star Gas Co., 952 F.2d 119 (5th Cir. 1992)); *see also* Inks v. Healthcare Distrib. of Ind., Inc., 901 F. Supp. 1403, 1409, 73 FEP 643 (N.D. Ind. 1995) (concluding that trial court's decision not to award front pay where court took into consideration, inter alia, that plaintiff was awarded liquidated damages, did not constitute manifest error of law).

[44]*See* Hadley v. VAM PTS, 44 F.3d 372, 376, 67 FEP 186 (5th Cir. 1995) (substantial punitive damages awarded in Title VII action may indicate that award of front pay is inappropriate); Reynolds v. Octel Communications Corp., 924 F. Supp. 743, 748, 64 FEP 886 (N.D. Tex. 1995) (holding that in light of large award of compensatory and punitive damages under Title VII, additional award of front pay is inappropriate).

[45]Smith v. World Ins. Co., 38 F.3d 1456, 1466, 66 FEP 13 (8th Cir. 1994) (unreasonably rejected offer of reinstatement bars front pay); James v. Sears, Roebuck & Co., 21 F.3d 989, 997, 64 FEP 886 (10th Cir. 1994) (ordering reinstatement instead of front pay was appropriate where plaintiff rejected employer's reinstatement offers); *cf.* Mungin v. Katten Muchin & Zavis, 941 F. Supp. 153, 156 (D.D.C. 1996) (noting that jury verdict in favor of plaintiff on constructive discharge claim precludes a finding that plaintiff's rejection of employer's transfer offer was unreasonable); Miano v. AC&R Advertising, Inc., 875 F. Supp. 204, 224–27, 66 FEP 1603 (S.D.N.Y. 1995) (holding that plaintiffs were eligible for front pay because their rejection of employer's offer of reinstatement was reasonable in light of exceptional circumstances of antagonism between the parties).

[46]115 S. Ct. 879, 886 (1995).

[47]Scarfo v. Cabletron Sys., Inc., 54 F.3d 931, 954, 67 FEP 1474 (1st Cir. 1995); Wilcox v. Stratton Lumber, Inc., 921 F. Supp. 837, 844 (D. Me. 1996); *see also* cases cited in note 48, *infra*.

[48]Reed v. A.W. Lawrence & Co., 95 F.3d 1170, 1182, 72 FEP 1375 (2d Cir. 1996) (holding that district court's limitation of front pay to only seven weeks' salary was

pay where calculation of the award involves undue speculation.[49]

not abuse of discretion because plaintiff's job was scheduled to be eliminated in any case seven weeks after the jury verdict; therefore "an award of front pay beyond that date would have impermissibly placed her in a better position than she would have been in had she not been fired"); Padilla v. Metro-North Commuter R.R., 92 F.3d 117, 125–26, 72 FEP 1748 (2d Cir. 1996) (concluding that front-pay award of the difference in salary paid to plaintiff in his current position and that paid to him prior to demotion, until plaintiff reaches the age of 67, a period of well over 20 years, was not an abuse of district court's discretion because plaintiff had "no reasonable prospect of obtaining comparable alternative employment"); Schwartz v. Gregori, 45 F.3d 1017, 1023 (6th Cir.) (affirming district court's award of front pay where amount of award was calculated based on difference between current income and income plaintiff would have received if she had not been discharged, for period of eight years until retirement, then amount was reduced by one-half to account for future uncertainties), *cert. denied,* 116 S. Ct. 77 (1995); Downes v. Volkswagen of Am., Inc., 41 F.3d 1132, 1141–43, 69 FEP 11 (7th Cir. 1994) (holding that district court's decision to limit front-pay award to three years, rather than the eight years calculated by plaintiff's expert, was not an abuse of discretion where plaintiff produced no evidence that he was willing or physically able to work for eight years and restructuring of defendant company made it speculative that plaintiff would have remained more than a few years absent the unlawful discrimination); Frank v. Relin, 851 F. Supp. 87, 95–96 (W.D.N.Y. 1994) (fashioning front-pay award to cover time it would take plaintiff to make up the difference in salary between former and current positions; refusing, however, to award front pay for duration of 20 years—plaintiff's remaining work expectancy—because an award of that duration is "speculative, unwarranted and excessive"); *cf.* Paperworkers Local 274 v. Champion Int'l Corp., 81 F.3d 798, 805 (8th Cir. 1996) (criticizing district court's award of 24 years of front pay until plaintiff reaches retirement age because district court improperly ignored plaintiff's duty to mitigate damages and award was improperly speculative); Barbour v. Merrill, 48 F.3d 1270, 1280, 68 FEP 126 (D.C. Cir. 1995) (recommending some factors for district court to consider in determining amount and duration of front-pay award: plaintiff's age, plaintiff's reasonable intention to work until retirement, length of time position generally held by defendants' employees as well as by persons in similar positions at other companies, and plaintiff's mitigation efforts), *cert. granted in part,* 116 S. Ct. 805, *cert. dismissed,* 116 S. Ct. 1037 (1996); Carter v. Sedgwick County, Kan., 36 F.3d 952, 957, 65 FEP 1585 (10th Cir. 1994) (remanding for recalculation of front-pay award upon concluding that district court abused its discretion in limiting the award to the difference between plaintiff's former and current salary for a six-month period; the court did not adequately remedy the effects of defendants' past discrimination).

[49]Sagendorf-Teal v. County of Rensselaer, 100 F.3d 270, 277 (2d Cir. 1996) (finding that it was within district court's discretion to deny plaintiff's motion for front pay on the ground that the proposed methods for calculating award were too speculative); Hutchison v. Amateur Elec. Supply, Inc., 42 F.3d 1037, 1045–46, 66 FEP 1275 (7th Cir. 1994) (Title VII plaintiff, who received above-market wage as a means of buying tolerance for employer's abusive behavior and who refused to mitigate her damages by seeking and accepting comparable jobs that paid market rate, was not entitled to front pay because of uncertainty in calculating present value of future discrepancy between market and above-market wage); *cf.* Ward v. Tipton County Sheriff Dep't, 937 F. Supp. 791, 797 (S.D. Ind. 1996) (stating that "[a]lthough front

Upon awarding plaintiff front-pay relief, courts may take into consideration not only future earnings, but also future benefits.[50]

The plaintiff bears the initial burden of supplying the district court with "the essential data necessary to calculate a reasonably certain front pay award, including 'the amount of the proposed award, the length of time the plaintiff expects to work for the defendant, and the applicable discount rate.' "[51] The defendant may then challenge the amount of the award, its duration, or interest rate.[52]

Other forms of affirmative relief for victims of unlawful employment practices may include retroactive seniority,[53] tenure,[54]

---

pay awards are by nature speculative, the longer the period of time for which an award is sought, the more speculative it becomes"); Frank v. Relin, 851 F. Supp. 87, 93 (W.D.N.Y. 1994) (awarding front pay where calculation of plaintiff's likely mitigated earnings and income she would have earned, but for unlawful termination, does not involve undue speculation); *contra* Barbour v. Merrill, 48 F.3d 1270, 1280, 67 FEP 369 (D.C. Cir. 1995) (stating that district court should not refuse to award front pay because it involves some speculation as to future earnings or because parties have introduced conflicting evidence), *cert. granted in part,* 116 S. Ct. 805, *cert. dismissed,* 116 S. Ct. 1037 (1996).

[50]*See* Cooley v. Carmike Cinemas, Inc., 25 F.3d 1325, 1334, 65 FEP 46 (6th Cir. 1994) (in calculating front-pay award, jury considered plaintiff's lost salary and benefits); Stratton v. Department for Aging, 922 F. Supp. 857, 867 (S.D.N.Y. 1996) (awarding plaintiff front pay and pension and Social Security benefits that she would have accrued but for the unlawful age discrimination in violation of ADEA); Mitchell v. Sisters of Charity of Incarnate Word, 924 F. Supp. 793, 804 (S.D. Tex. 1996) (awarding plaintiff front pay and lost retirement benefits); Raimondo v. AMAX, Inc., 843 F. Supp. 806, 810 (D. Conn. 1994) (awarding plaintiff in ADEA action lost savings plan contributions as part of front-pay award).

[51]Barbour v. Merrill, 48 F.3d 1270, 1279, 67 FEP 369 (D.C. Cir. 1995) (quoting McKnight v. General Motors Corp., 973 F.2d 1366, 1372 (7th Cir. 1992), *cert. denied,* 507 U.S. 915 (1993)); *see also* Wilcox v. Stratton Lumber, Inc., 921 F. Supp. 837, 844 (D. Me. 1996) (stating that plaintiff bears the burden of proving the amount of a front-pay award).

[52]*See* Barbour v. Merrill, 48 F.3d 1270, 1279–80, 67 FEP 369 (D.C. Cir. 1995), *cert. granted in part,* 116 S. Ct. 805, *cert. dismissed,* 116 S. Ct. 1037 (1996).

[53]Sands v. Runyon, 28 F.3d 1323, 1329, 3 AD 660 (2d Cir. 1994) (holding that district court clearly erred in denying plaintiff's claim for retroactive seniority because plaintiff met burden of demonstrating that but for defendant's discrimination he would be at an increased salary level; stating that "retroactive seniority is ordinarily considered to be a relatively fundamental form of relief where a plaintiff was subject to unlawful discrimination in the hiring process").

[54]Thornton v. Kaplan, 937 F. Supp. 1441, 1449 (D. Colo. 1996) (court reserved decision until trial on whether reinstatement of professor with tenure would be available to plaintiff, noting that such remedy should only be awarded in a most extraordinary case; judicial tenure award is an extremely intrusive remedy because it mandates a lifetime relationship between the university and the professor).

promotion,[55] letter of commendation by employer,[56] correction of plaintiff's personnel file,[57] and prospective relief in the value of stock options plaintiffs would have received but for the unlawful discrimination.[58] One court even considered awarding an increase in plaintiff's salary as a form of make-whole relief. In *Brinkley-Obu v. Hughes Training, Inc.*,[59] after a jury verdict was rendered in plaintiff's favor on her Equal Pay Act and Title VII claims, the district court ordered the defendant to increase plaintiff's salary by using the average male salary at her level. On reconsideration, however, the court struck the salary increase due to the lack of evidence in the record on which to calculate the requested relief.[60] The Fourth Circuit affirmed the denial, but noted that "[a] lack of prospective relief [ ] will leave the plaintiff with a series of new Equal Pay Act claims, accruing with each new paycheck subsequent to the date of this action, if [plaintiff] continues to be paid less than comparable male employees."[61]

---

[55]*Compare* Hayes v. Shalala, 933 F. Supp. 21, 25, 71 FEP 1240 (D. D.C. 1996) (ordering retroactive promotion following jury verdict in favor of plaintiff on his Title VII claim) *and* Milburn v. West, 854 F. Supp. 1, 14–15 (D.D.C. 1994) (ordering promotion of plaintiff who was found to have been unlawfully denied promotion in violation of Title VII) *with* Kemp v. Monge, 919 F. Supp. 404, 409 (M.D. Fla. 1996) (ordering reinstatement, but denying request for promotion as too speculative; to promote plaintiff without plaintiff having to take examination and go through screening process with other applicants would "be giving plaintiff a windfall").

[56]Sands v. Runyon, 28 F.3d 1323, 1330–31, 2 AD 660 (2d Cir. 1994) (holding that district court did not abuse its discretion in refusing plaintiff's request for defendant to prepare a letter of commendation for plaintiff's personnel file; noting that "[c]ircumstances are few in which a court can properly order an employer to sweeten a plaintiff's personnel file with praise of the employee's talents, abilities, and work habits—which affirmations might not even be true").

[57]*Compare* Hayes v. Shalala, 933 F. Supp. 21, 27, 71 FEP 1240 (D.D.C. 1996) (ordering correction of plaintiff's personnel folder and other relevant department records to reflect jury's verdict in favor of plaintiff and equitable relief provided by court) *with* Sands v. Runyon, 28 F.3d 1323, 1331–32, 3 AD 660 (2d Cir. 1994) (affirming district court's denial of plaintiff's request for order directing defendant to expunge negative information from his personnel file where there was lack of specific evidence of incidents of purposeful discrimination that caused plaintiff harm).

[58]Scarfo v. Cabletron Sys., Inc., 54 F.3d 931, 956, 959–60, 67 FEP 1474 (1st Cir. 1995).

[59]Brinkley-Obu v. Hughes Training, Inc., 1993 WL 747922 at *1 (E.D. Va. June 22, 1993).

[60]Brinkley-Obu v. Hughes Training, Inc., 36 F.3d 336, 356 65 FEP 1840 (4th Cir. 1994) (rejecting use of salaries of male employees to calculate plaintiff's prospective salary because males were demoted to a different department).

[61]*Id.* at 357.

IV. AFFIRMATIVE RELIEF BENEFITING PERSONS OTHER THAN IDENTIFIED VICTIMS OF DISCRIMINATION

B. Race- or Gender-Conscious Affirmative Relief

In its 1995 landmark decision, *Adarand Constructors, Inc. v. Pena*,[62] the Supreme Court held that a strict scrutiny standard should be used to review race-based voluntary affirmative action programs.[63] It is unclear how *Adarand* will be applied, if at all, to race-based court-ordered affirmative relief.[64] In his concurrence in *United States v. Paradise*,[65] Justice Stevens suggested that court-ordered affirmative decrees require greater deference since they result from a judicial determination that a party is guilty of racial discrimination and that remedial actions are warranted.[66]

The implication of the *Adarand* decision for gender-based court-ordered affirmative relief also is not clear. Generally, courts have analyzed gender-based programs under an intermediate level of scrutiny.[67]

---

[62]115 S. Ct. 2097, 67 FEP 1828 (1995).

[63]*See* Chapter 27 (Reverse Discrimination and Affirmative Action) for further discussion of voluntary affirmative action programs.

[64]Several commentators contend that *Adarand* supports extension of strict scrutiny to court-ordered affirmative relief. *See generally* C. Wayne K. Davis, *Raising the Standard: The Supreme Court Embarks on a New Era of Equal Protection Jurisprudence with the Institution of the Strict Scrutiny Paradigm in* Adarand Constructors, Inc. v. Pena, 40 ST. LOUIS U.L.J. 543 (Spring 1996) (analyzing decision and its effect on affirmative action policies); Michael Small, *Edited Comments on Affirmative Action in the Legal Context*, 95 ANN. SURV. AM. L. 445 (1995); David Zimmerman, *Five Supreme Court Constitutions: Race-Based Scrutiny Past, Present and Future*, 10 BYU J. PUB. L. 161 (1996).

[65]480 U.S. 149 (1987) (holding that a 50% promotion requirement for African-American state troopers was justified by a compelling government interest in eradicating discrimination).

[66]*Id.* at 193–94; *see* Middleton v. City of Flint, Mich., 92 F.2d 396, 401 (6th Cir. 1996) (differentiating a voluntarily adopted affirmative action plan, the court stated that "this plan differs from those that are crafted under the direction of a court order, resulting from a judicial fact-finding process . . . . Nor was this plan presented to a court by the participating parties as part of a motion for a judicially approved consent decree.").

[67]*See Adarand Constructors, Inc. v. Pena*, 115 S. Ct. at 2122 (Stevens J. dissenting) ("[A]s the law currently stands, the Court will apply 'intermediate scrutiny' to cases of invidious gender discrimination and 'strict scrutiny' to cases of invidious race discrimination . . . even though the primary purpose of the Equal Protection Clause was to end discrimination against the former slaves."); Ensley Branch, NAACP v. Seibels, 31 F.3d 1548, 1579–80 (11th Cir. 1994) (noting gender-based

V. Monitoring the Court Decree

Courts continue to retain jurisdiction to monitor compliance with their court decrees.[68] Some courts require recordkeeping and reporting to assess implementation of an affirmative remedy.[69] Refusal to implement a court-ordered affirmative plan can result in sanctions. In *EEOC v. Local 638, Sheet Metal Workers*,[70] the court held that the union's noncompliance with the court's recordkeeping order and its failure to achieve reasonable nonwhite membership goals warranted sanctions against it.[71] Statistical evidence demonstrated that the union's inability to achieve those goals was due to its discriminatory admission policy and job search practices.[72]

A court may modify a consent decree to either accommodate changed circumstances or extend the duration of the consent decree.[73]

---

affirmative action is subject to intermediate scrutiny after analysis of recent court decisions); Shuford v. Alabama State Bd. of Educ., 897 F. Supp. 1535, 1556 (M.D. Ala. 1995) (noting application of intermediate level scrutiny to gender-based affirmative remedies); *contra* Deborah L. Brake, *Sex As A Suspect Class: An Argument for Applying Strict Scrutiny to Gender Discrimination*, 6 SETON HALL CONST. L.J. 953 (1996).

[68]*See, e.g.,* Eldredge v. Carpenters 46 Northern Cal. Counties Joint Apprenticeship & Training Comm., 94 F.3d 1366, 1370–72, 71 FEP 1385 (9th Cir. 1996) (where court in ordering implementation of system for admitting women applicants to carpentry apprenticeship program asserted that it would continue to have jurisdiction over the case and supervise court-appointed monitor until 20% of apprentices were women).

[69]*See, e.g.,* EEOC v. Local 40, Bridge Workers, 76 F.3d 76, 81 (2d Cir. 1996) (noting that decree required union to keep permanent records of its hiring hall activities, to assign numbers to all job applicants, to keep a permanent register of people in the referral hall, and to name as stewards a number of minorities equal to the number of minority members in the union; in addition, union must provide EEOC access to a wide variety of other records for two years); Stewart v. Rubin, 948 F. Supp. 1077 (D.D.C. 1996) (to assist the parties in monitoring compliance with settlement agreement, defendant in class action racial discrimination suit would establish and maintain a computerized database containing relevant statistical data; also, expert who was mutually acceptable to parties would produce report analyzing the employment data to determine whether the employment practices had an adverse impact on African-American employees).

[70]889 F. Supp. 642 (S.D.N.Y. 1995).

[71]*Id.* at 685.

[72]*Id.* at 660–61.

[73]Vanguards v. City of Cleveland, 23 F.3d 1013, 64 FEP 1611 (6th Cir. 1994) (holding that district court properly extended consent decree between minority firefighters and city for two years based on its conclusion that lower than expected minority pass rates on promotion exams represented a significant change in circumstances that justified granting the city additional time to promote minority firefighters in order to fulfill decree's objectives).

However, in *EEOC v. Local 40, Bridge Workers*,[74] the Second Circuit overturned a district court opinion extending jurisdiction over an expired consent decree based on the court's "inherent power to enforce consent judgments."[75] The court explained that a court does not have such power, especially in the absence of a continuing jurisdiction clause, to enforce the decree 12 years after its expiration, because such an action would deprive the union of the "benefit of its bargain."[76] The fact that the union had agreed to take on some permanent responsibilities did not imply that the order had not expired.[77]

Section 108 of the Civil Rights Act of 1991[78] governs whether a party can challenge a consent judgment or order.[79] Courts also use § 108 to safeguard parties' interests when other motions for participation in the case are declined.[80] However, § 108 does not provide nonparties who fail to meet its requirements with a broader basis to intervene than those provided by the general intervention rule embodied in Federal Rule of Civil Procedure 24(b).[81] Nor does

---

[74]76 F.3d 76 (2d Cir. 1996).
[75]885 F. Supp. 488, 494 (S.D.N.Y. 1994), *rev'd*, 76 F.3d 76 (2d Cir. 1996).
[76]76 F.3d at 81.
[77]*Id.*
[78]Pub. L. No. 102-106, § 108, 1991 U.S.C.C.A.N. (105 Stat.) 1071, 1076 (codified at 42 U.S.C. § 2000e-2(n)(1)(A)).
[79]*See, e.g.*, Stewart v. Rubin, 948 F. Supp. 1077, 1097 (D.D.C. 1996) (noting that § 108 would not have preclusive effect on future claims by a class member that may develop as a result of the settlement agreement); United States v. City of Hialeah, 899 F. Supp. 603, 607 (S.D. Fla. 1994) (court complied with § 108 by publishing notice of hearing and proposed settlement, which allowed challenges to settlement agreement); Shuford v. Alabama State Bd. of Educ., 897 F. Supp. 1535, 1547 (M.D. Ala. 1995) (noting that § 108's notice requirement was met when court-approved notices were distributed individually to all present employees, both class and nonclass members of the institutions covered by the decree, and that notices were also posted in conspicuous places at each institution); Sims v. Montgomery, 890 F. Supp. 1520, 1528 (M.D. Ala. 1995) (holding that notices and fairness hearings were sufficient under § 108 with respect to nonclass plaintiff members where notices were sent to all employees not represented by plaintiffs, inviting all employees to respond in writing, and posting notices in conspicuous places).
[80]Adams v. City of Chicago, 1995 WL 491496, at *2 (N.D. Ill. Aug. 11, 1995) (denying nonminority Chicago police officers' request to intervene as amicus curiae in suit brought by minority police officers challenging city's promotional test; noting that § 108 already protected their interests should the parties enter into an order or judgment that resolves the lawsuit).
[81]*See* Edwards v. Houston, 78 F.3d 983, 996–98 (5th Cir. 1996) (holding that nonparty seeking to intervene to challenge consent decree cannot be denied intervention under § 108 simply because parties to the litigation provided him with notice and

this section provide nonparty nonintervenors a right to appeal.[82] In addition, those who are not parties to a consent decree lack standing to seek affirmative relief under the decree; they may only challenge the legality of the decree itself.[83]

In *Maitland v. University of Minnesota*,[84] the Eighth Circuit examined whether § 108 of the Civil Rights Act could apply retroactively to prevent a male university faculty member from bringing a sex discrimination claim against the university, challenging the implementation of a consent decree that granted salary increases to female faculty members but not to male faculty members. The court examined whether § 108 had "true retroactive effect," that is, whether it attached new legal consequences to events completed before its enactment.[85] The court concluded that retroactivity would prevent the male faculty member from pursuing his Title VII claim simply because of his limited participation in consent decree proceedings that took place well before enactment of the Civil Rights Act of 1991.[86] Thus, the court held that § 108 did not apply retroactively and the male faculty member was not estopped from pursuing his Title VII claims. However, at least one dissenting judge has argued that the retroactivity of § 108 remains unsettled.[87]

---

opportunity to voice his concerns at a fairness hearing prior to acceptance of the decree; right to intervene is established under Fed. R. Civ. P. 24); Reynolds v. Roberts, 846 F. Supp. 948, 956, 64 FEP 400 (M.D. Ala. 1994) (granting nonclass member employees the right to intervene under Rule 24 in a Title VII action brought against state transportation department).

[82]Johnson v. Reno, 1994 WL 189071 at *1 (D.D.C. Apr. 19, 1994).

[83]*See* Salter v. Douglas MacArthur State Technical College, 929 F. Supp. 1470, 1481 (M.D. Ala. 1996) (where due to mistaken reliance on draft version of decree, college hired an African-American faculty member who was significantly less qualified than white plaintiff bringing Title VII claim), *cert. denied,* 116 S. Ct. 338 (1995).

[84]43 F.3d 357, 66 FEP 796 (8th Cir. 1994).

[85]*Id.* at 361–62.

[86]Because the male faculty member had both actual notice of the proposed consent decree prior to its approval by the district court, and an opportunity to present objections to the consent decree, his later lawsuit challenging the terms and implementation of the consent decree would have been barred by § 108, unless he could show that he had not had a "reasonable" opportunity to present his objections. *See* Pub. L. No. 102-106, § 108, 1991 U.S.C.C.A.N. (105 Stat.) 1071, 1076 (codified at 42 U.S.C. § 20003-2(n)(1)(A)).

[87]*See* Aiken v. City of Memphis, 37 F.3d 1155, 175–78, 65 FEP 1757 (6th Cir. 1994) (Jones J., dissenting) (noting that the Sixth Circuit has yet to address whether § 108 can be retroactively applied, but favoring retroactive application to protect a longstanding remedial policy).

VI. Preliminary Injunctions

A. Rule 65 Preliminary Relief

Courts continue to affirm district courts' jurisdiction to grant preliminary injunctions under Title VII to maintain the status quo regardless of whether the plaintiff has exhausted available administrative remedies.[88] However, a request for injunctive relief becomes moot when the movant is no longer in harm's way, such as when the movant no longer works for that employer.[89]

The large majority of courts continue to apply some form of the traditional four-part test for preliminary injunctions.[90] One recent version of the test requires the moving party to prove: "(1) a substantial likelihood of success on the merits; (2) a significant risk of irreparable harm if the injunction is withheld; (3) a favorable balance of the hardships; and (4) a fit (or, at least, a lack of friction) between the injunction and the public interest."[91] However, the Ninth and Second Circuits continue to apply their own variations of the test.[92]

---

[88]Novellis v. Shalala, 947 F. Supp. 557, 559 (D. Mass. 1996) (failure to exhaust administrative remedies under ADEA does not preclude jurisdiction for preliminary injunctive relief designed to preserve the status quo pending exhaustion of those remedies); Olmeda v. Schneider, 889 F. Supp. 228, 230, 232 n.5 (D.V.I. 1995) ("plaintiff need not exhaust state remedies before initiating a § 1983 action in [district] court").

[89]Taylor v. Resolution Trust Corp., 56 F.3d 1497, 1504 (D.C. Cir. 1995) (stating that "[a]n employee who is mistreated on the job but who *voluntarily* chooses to leave the workplace permanently bears responsibility for the dispute becoming moot and must forego injunctive relief in favor of damages").

[90]Adam-Mellang v. Apartment Search, Inc., 96 F.3d 297, 299, 71 FEP 1633 (8th Cir. 1996) (traditional four-part test); Minnesota Ass'n of Nurse Anesthetists v. Unity Hosp., 59 F.3d 80, 82 (8th Cir. 1995) (same); Taylor v. Resolution Trust Corp., 56 F.3d 1497, 1505–06 (D.C. Cir. 1995) (same); Nedder v. Rivier College, 908 F. Supp. 66, 73, 4 AD 1530 (D.N.H. 1995) (same); Olmeda v. Schneider, 889 F. Supp. 228, 231 (D.V.I. 1995) (same); Maye v. City of Kannapolis, 872 F. Supp. 246, 247, 66 FEP 670 (M.D.N.C. 1994) (same); Gonzalez v. Trinity Marine Group, Inc., 1994 WL 623985, at *2, 66 FEP 667 (E.D. La. Nov. 7, 1994) (same); Brown v. City of Chicago, 917 F. Supp. 577, 584 (N.D. Ill. 1996) (movant must show at the threshold (1) some likelihood of succeeding on the merits and (2) that he or she has no adequate remedy at law and will suffer irreparable harm, and then court must balance that showing with the harm to the nonmovant and the public using a sliding scale approach).

[91]EEOC v. Astra U.S.A., Inc., 94 F.3d 738, 742, 71 FEP 1259 (1st Cir. 1996).

[92]Stanley v. University of S. Cal., 13 F.3d 1313, 1319, 63 FEP 1021 (9th Cir. 1994) (noting that courts should be more cautious where movant seeks mandatory preliminary relief that goes beyond a request to maintain the status quo); *see* Remlinger v. Nevada, 896 F. Supp. 1012, 1014 (D. Nev. 1995) (applying test in *Stanley*); Jayaraj v. Scappini, 66 F.3d 36, 38 (2d Cir. 1995).

Perhaps the most debated element of preliminary injunctions is defining irreparable injury. Generally, the loss of a job or job opportunity and accompanying harms such as financial hardship, humiliation, damaged reputation, and the inability to become reemployed continue to be treated as insufficient indicia of irreparable injury because they may be remedied by reinstatement or back pay.[93] Indeed, proof of irreparable harm is a substantial hurdle as evidenced in a recent Second Circuit decision, *Jayaraj v. Scappini*.[94] In *Jayaraj*, a municipal employee sought a preliminary injunction allowing him to continue his employment pending resolution of his claims against his employer, the city, for wrongful termination.[95] The Second Circuit vacated the district court's order for a preliminary injunction, finding that the following allegations were insufficient evidence of irreparable harm: (1) plaintiff was vulnerable to a low back-pay award because of his inability to find an interim job; (2) plaintiff's pension rights were not guaranteed should he later prevail on the merits; (3) plaintiff's ability

---

[93] Adam-Mellang v. Apartment Search, Inc., 96 F.3d 297, 300, 71 FEP 1633 (8th Cir. 1996) (removal from board of directors without accompanying "genuinely extraordinary situation" is not irreparable injury for which there is no adequate remedy at law); Minnesota Ass'n of Nurse Anesthetists v. Unity Hosp., 59 F.3d 80, 83 (8th Cir. 1995) (finding that "[t]he loss of a job is quintessentially reparable by money damages"); Brown v. City of Chicago, 917 F. Supp. 577, 584 (N.D. Ill. 1996) (African-Americans and Hispanics denied injunction preventing promotion of 18 sergeants to lieutenant based on results of promotional examination; no irreparable harm because 52 positions were open, any stigma from their being promoted as a result of a court order would result regardless of the 18 promotions, and back pay, pension benefits, and seniority were adequate remedies at law in the event they succeeded on the merits of the claim that the exam was discriminatory); Nedder v. Rivier College, 908 F. Supp. 66, 83–84, 4 AD 1530 (D.N.H. 1995) (denying preliminary injunction under ADA because no irreparable harm from alleged reputational injury and loss of income); Remlinger v. Nevada, 896 F. Supp 1012, 1015–16 (D. Nev. 1995) (loss of paycheck, health insurance, seniority, state contributions to retirement plan, and accrued sick leave and vacation time is not irreparable harm because legal remedies of back pay and reinstatement are available; rather, where the claimed injury is economic in nature, the employee must show: little chance of securing further employment; no personal or family resources at employee's disposal; lack of private unemployment insurance; inability to obtain a privately financed loan; ineligibility for any type of public support or relief; and any other compelling circumstances that weigh heavily in favor of granting interim equitable relief); Gonzalez v. Trinity Marine Group, Inc., 1994 WL 623985, at *2, 66 FEP 667 (E.D. La. Nov. 7, 1994) (stating that loss of income from termination is mere financial hardship that does not constitute irreparable injury; plaintiff's potential ineligibility for unemployment does not present an extraordinary situation).

[94] 66 F.3d 36 (2d Cir. 1995).

[95] *Id.* at 38.

to perform was compromised, leaving him susceptible to criticism; (4) plaintiff's absence created a work backlog; (5) it was possible that the employer would hire a replacement in the interim; and (6) plaintiff's work was sufficiently unique as to risk a significant impairment of his ability to obtain other employment.[96]

Where the movant's claimed injury is economic in nature, irreparability sometimes will be found where the employee shows extraordinary circumstances compelling interim relief.[97] Courts may also find irreparable harm warranting injunctive relief where retaliation interferes with the plaintiff's constitutional freedoms.[98]

Courts continue to deny injunctive relief where plaintiff fails to make an adequate showing under the relevant preliminary injunction standard.[99] But, where the standards are met, courts will grant injunctive relief either to maintain the status quo during the pendency of the litigation[100] or to restore the status quo where it has been upset by discriminatory practices.[101]

---

[96]*Id.* at 38–39.

[97]Novellis v. Shalala, 947 F. Supp. 557, 559 (D. Mass. 1996) (in retaliation case, choice among transferring to another office across the country, accepting a demotion, or retiring constitutes a sufficient showing of irreparable harm to merit preliminary injunctive relief); Remlinger v. Nevada, 896 F. Supp 1012 (D. Nev. 1995) (where the claimed injury is economic in nature, employee must show: little chance of securing further employment; no personal or family resources at employee's disposal; lack of private unemployment insurance; inability to obtain a privately financed loan; ineligibility for any type of public support or relief; and any other compelling circumstances that weigh heavily in favor of granting interim equitable relief); *cf.* Adam-Mellang v. Apartment Search, Inc., 96 F.3d 297, 300, 71 FEP 1633 (8th Cir. 1996) (removal from board of directors, without accompanying "genuinely extraordinary situation," is not irreparable injury for which there is no adequate remedy at law); Gonzalez v. Trinity Marine Group, Inc., 1994 WL 623985, at *2–3, 66 FEP 667 (E.D. La. Nov. 7, 1994) (stating that loss of income from termination is mere financial hardship that does not constitute irreparable injury; plaintiff's potential ineligibility for unemployment does not present an extraordinary situation).

[98]Olmeda v. Schneider, 889 F. Supp. 228, 233 (D.V.I. 1995) (loss of First Amendment freedoms for any amount of time constitutes irreparable injury); *cf.* Taylor v. Resolution Trust Corp., 56 F.3d 1497, 1508 (D.C. Cir. 1995) (suggesting that interference with First Amendment interests could constitute irreparable injury, but "none of the plaintiffs in this action has been so chilled" as to warrant injunctive relief).

[99]*See* notes 93–94 *supra.*

[100]Novellis v. Shalala, 947 F. Supp. 557, 559 (D. Mass. 1996) (in retaliation case, choice among transferring to another office across the country, accepting a demotion, or retiring constitutes sufficient showing of irreparable harm to merit preliminary injunctive relief to maintain the status quo during the pendency of a claim).

[101]Olmeda v. Schneider, 889 F. Supp. 228 (D.V.I. 1995) (territorial employees terminated by newly elected governor after occupying visible positions in opponent's

B. Section 706(f)(2) Preliminary Relief

The EEOC may prove irreparable harm sufficient for a grant of preliminary injunctive relief under § 706(f)(2) of Title VII by demonstrating that the unlawful employment practice at issue will have a chilling effect on the EEOC's ability to investigate claims. For example, in *EEOC v. Astra U.S.A., Inc.*,[102] proposed settlement agreements that prohibited communication with the EEOC had a chilling effect on the EEOC's ability to investigate sexual harassment claims, and constituted irreparable harm justifying injunctive relief against enforcement of the agreements.[103]

---

campaign sought preliminary injunction to reinstate them in their jobs; injunction granted because employees suffered irreparable injuries when they were deprived of First Amendment freedoms, showed a likelihood of success on the merits, and balance of hardships and public interest weighed in their favor).

[102] 94 F.3d 738 (1st Cir. 1996).
[103] *Id.* at 743.

Chapter 41

MONETARY RELIEF

I. Back Pay

A. A Discriminatee's Right to Back Pay in General

A defendant's lack of bad faith or evil motive does not operate to preclude or reduce an award of back pay.[1] A plaintiff's failure to mitigate damages may not preclude an award of back pay, although it may reduce or decrease the award.[2] However, a plaintiff is not entitled to receive back pay more than once for any one time period, regardless of how many of defendant's acts caused him or her to lose the back pay during that time period.[3]

An employer's discovery after termination that an employee engaged in pretermination wrongdoing that would have led to the employee's termination on lawful and legitimate grounds if that wrongdoing had been known is not a complete bar to back-pay recovery.[4] In *McKennon v. Nashville Banner Co.*, the Supreme Court held that in the case of such after-acquired evidence, the calculation of back pay should be from the date of the unlawful discharge to the date the new information was discovered.[5] However, where an employer learned of wrongdoing by a current employee in the course of discovery in a Title VII lawsuit for sex discrimination

---

[1]Dutton v. Johnson County Bd., 868 F. Supp. 1260, 1264, 3 AD 1614, 1617 (D. Kan. 1994).

[2]Booker v. Taylor Milk Co., 64 F.3d 860, 866, 71 FEP 525 (3d Cir. 1995).

[3]Emmel v. Coca-Cola Bottling Co., 904 F. Supp. 723, 750 (N.D. Ill. 1995), *aff'd*, 95 F.3d 627, 72 FEP 1811 (7th Cir. 1996).

[4]McKennon v. Nashville Banner Co., 115 S. Ct. 879, 883, 66 FEP 1192 (1995); O'Day v. McDonnell Douglas Helicopter Co., 79 F.3d 756, 761, 70 FEP 615 (9th Cir. 1996) (after-acquired evidence of former employee's misconduct would limit the extent of former employer's liability if former employer could prove by a preponderance of evidence that it would have fired the former employee for the misconduct); Ryder v. Westinghouse Elec. Corp., 879 F. Supp. 534, 537 (W.D. Pa. 1995) (plaintiff who established employer violated ADEA entitled to back pay from date of unlawful termination at least to date new information was discovered).

[5]115 S. Ct. at 886.

and retaliation and then terminated the employee-plaintiff based on such wrongdoing, the former employee was limited to recovery of back pay for the wage discrimination and denial of promotion that prompted the lawsuit only to the date of discovery of the wrongdoing and was denied reinstatement to employment.[6]

Some courts have held that "special factors" may prohibit the award of back pay.[7]

B. Calculation of the Back-Pay Award

1. Elements of a Back-Pay Award

a. Wages and Salary. The prevailing plaintiff bears the burden of establishing the value of the lost salary. Courts have limited the amount of a back-pay award where a plaintiff has been unable to establish an entitlement to a higher salary level.[8] However, a successful Title VII plaintiff can be awarded back pay even if the plaintiff's lost wages are not susceptible to exact dollar calculations.[9] Additionally, any uncertainties should be resolved against the discriminating employer.[10]

While the value of a promotion may be included in back pay, more than a mere possibility of promotion must be shown in order to include the promotion in a back-pay award.[11]

A back-pay award may include lost bonuses.[12]

---

[6]Carlson v. American Meter Co., 896 F. Supp. 952, 954, 68 FEP 193 (D. Neb. 1995).

[7]EEOC v. O & G Spring & Wire Forms Specialty Co., 38 F.3d 872, 880, 65 FEP 1823, 1829 (7th Cir. 1994) (court has discretion to alter back-pay award if full award would bankrupt defendant); EEOC v. Accurate Mech. Contractors, Inc., 863 F. Supp. 828, 835 (E.D. Wis. 1994) (special factors may include circumstances where state legislation is in conflict with Title VII).

[8]Barbour v. Merrill, 48 F.3d 1270, 1278, 67 FEP 369 (D.C. Cir. 1995) (calculation of back pay awarded on basis of $70,000 annual salary was not abuse of discretion where plaintiff was unable to establish that employer would have offered him the salary of $85,000 offered to successful applicant).

[9]Taylor v. Central Pa. Drug & Alcohol Servs. Corp., 890 F. Supp. 360, 370, 72 FEP 1315 (M.D. Pa. 1995).

[10]*Id.* at 370; Kahmann v. Reno, 928 F. Supp. 1209, 1217 (N.D.N.Y. 1996) (when determining proper placement of discriminatee, uncertainties must be resolved against discriminator).

[11]Felker v. Pepsi-Cola Co., 899 F. Supp. 882, 889, 68 FEP 1569 (D. Conn. 1995). *Cf.* EEOC v. Accurate Mech. Contractors, Inc., 863 F. Supp. 828, 837 (E.D. Wis. 1994) (possibility of callback work was too speculative to be included in back-pay award).

[12]EEOC v. Domino's Pizza, 909 F. Supp. 1529, 1537, 69 FEP 570 (M.D. Fla. 1995) (successful Title VII plaintiff could recover back pay for bonuses); Taylor v. Central Pa. Drug & Alcohol Servs., 890 F. Supp. 360, 372, 72 FEP 1315 (M.D. Pa. 1995) (plaintiffs entitled to have Christmas bonuses included in back-pay award where

b. Fringe Benefits. Back-pay awards may include unrealized fringe benefits,[13] including cafeteria benefits,[14] forfeited retirement benefits,[15] and savings plans benefits.[16]

However, the burden is on the plaintiff to show the value and the actual loss of the benefit.[17] One court held that the plaintiff was not entitled to recover projected employer contributions to a retirement plan because the employee did not elect to participate in the plan during employment.[18]

Health and life insurance also can be a component of back pay,[19] but again actual loss must be shown.[20]

c. Interest. While there continues to be a strong presumption that prejudgment interest on back-pay awards should be granted in employment discrimination actions,[21] appellate courts are hesitant

---

they would have received bonuses but for unlawful discrimination); Long v. Ringling Bros.–Barnum & Bailey Combined Shows, Inc., 882 F. Supp. 1553, 1561, 67 FEP 1685 (D. Md. 1995) (successful Title VII plaintiff received increase in annual salary of 10% to compensate plaintiff for increases in salary and bonuses).

[13]Dutton v. Johnson County Bd., 868 F. Supp. 1260, 1264, 3 AD 1614 (D. Kan. 1994).

[14]*Id.* at 1264.

[15]Carter v. American Tel. & Tel. Co., 870 F. Supp. 1438, 1449 (S.D. Ohio 1994) (successful Title VII plaintiff entitled to back pension benefits plus interest and future pension benefits in accordance with employer's pension plan).

[16]Kahmann v. Reno, 928 F. Supp. 1209 (N.D.N.Y. 1996) (successful Title VII plaintiff's back-pay award should have included benefits she would have received through participation in federal employee retirement system and thrift savings plan).

[17]Barbour v. Merrill, 48 F.3d 1270, 1278, 67 FEP 369 (D.C. Cir. 1995) (prevailing Title VII plaintiff not entitled to car allowance given to successful applicant where record contained no evidence that allowance was regular part of compensation package or that plaintiff would have received allowance).

[18]EEOC v. Domino's Pizza, Inc., 909 F. Supp. 1529, 1537, 69 FEP 570 (M.D. Fla. 1995).

[19]Kahmann v. Reno, 928 F. Supp. 1209, 1219 (N.D.N.Y. 1996); EEOC v. Domino's Pizza, 909 F. Supp. 1529, 1537, 69 FEP 570 (M.D. Fla. 1995) (plaintiff entitled to recover his out-of-pocket expenditures for health insurance).

[20]Kahmann v. Reno, 928 F. Supp. 1209, 1223 (N.D.N.Y. 1996) (court declined to make award for health and life insurance benefits where plaintiff failed to submit proof that lack of insurance left her in a different position than if she had obtained insurance); Eldred v. Consolidated Freightways Corp., 907 F. Supp. 26, 28 (D. Mass. 1995) (court declined to award compensation for lost health and life insurance and lost pension and stock plan benefits where plaintiff offered no evidence to indicate value of lost benefits); Taylor v. Central Pa. Drug & Alcohol Servs. Corp., 890 F. Supp. 360, 362, 72 FEP 1315 (M.D. Pa. 1995) (successful Title VII plaintiff not entitled to recover insurance premiums previously paid by employer where plaintiff did not introduce evidence of expenses incurred for substitute coverage or medical care).

[21]*See, e.g.,* Scarfo v. Cabletron Sys., Inc., 54 F.3d 931, 961, 67 FEP 1474 (1st Cir. 1995) ("A trial court has discretion whether to award prejudgment interest on a successful Title VII claim."); Hutchison v. Amateur Elec. Supply, Inc., 42 F.3d 1037,

to disturb the discretion of trial courts that have denied prejudgment interest awards.²² Also, many courts consider an award of punitive damages as a factor militating against the propriety of prejudgment interest.²³

1046, 66 FEP 1275 (7th Cir. 1994) ("Prejudgment interest is an element of complete compensation and a normal incident of relief under Title VII."); Kraemer v. Franklin & Marshall College, 941 F. Supp. 479, 487 (E.D. Pa. 1996) ("Because prejudgment interest reimburses the claimant for the loss of the use of his or her investment or funds from the time of the loss until judgment, the court concludes that an award of prejudgment interest is proper."); Lefevre v. Harrison Group, Inc., 71 FEP 449 (E.D. Pa. 1996) ("[U]nless the equities require otherwise, courts should award a plaintiff prejudgment interest on a backpay award under the ADEA."); Dailey v. Societe Generale, 889 F. Supp 108, 114, 68 FEP 345 (S.D.N.Y. 1995) ("The purposes of Title VII—to deter violations of the statute and to make the plaintiff whole—are both served by a prejudgment interest award on the back pay portion of the damage award.").

In addition to the "make whole" rationale, the Sixth Circuit has held that "an award of prejudgment interest is appropriate under circumstances where a party fails to negotiate a good faith settlement." Simpson v. Ernst & Young, 100 F.3d 436, 445, 72 FEP 343 (6th Cir. 1996).

²²*See, e.g.,* Rhodes v. Guiberson Oil Tools, 82 F.3d 615, 619, 623, 71 FEP 83 (5th Cir. 1996) (district court did not abuse its discretion in deciding not to award prejudgment interest in ADEA action where it determined that, in awarding damages for back pay, front pay, and pension benefits offset by interim earnings, projected future earnings, and pension benefits already paid, plaintiff was made whole without an award of prejudgment interest); Gloria v. Valley Grain Products, Inc., 72 F.3d 497, 500, 69 FEP 1163 (5th Cir. 1996) (district court's decision to refuse prejudgment interest award in Title VII action was not abuse of discretion where plaintiff's only argument to establish an abuse of discretion was that district court ignored the "make-whole" policies of Title VII; "[a] general rule that prejudgment interest on every backpay award must be granted would obliterate the discretion of the district court"); Hogan v. Bangor & Aroostook R.R. Co., 61 F.3d 1034, 1038, 4 AD 1251 (1st Cir. 1995) (district court did not abuse its discretion in not awarding ADA plaintiff prejudgment interest "where the award of damages is almost three times the size of the back pay award"); Philipp v. ANR Freight Sys., Inc., 61 F.3d 669, 675, 70 FEP 1347 (8th Cir. 1995) (it was within district court's discretion to deny age discrimination plaintiff prejudgment interest based on defendant company's " 'continued financial plight' and the fact that 'liability was far from clear in this case' "); Hadley v. VAM, 44 F.3d 372, 376, 67 FEP 186 (5th Cir. 1995) (because the circuit had adopted no per se rule requiring prejudgment interest to be included in back-pay awards, there was no abuse of the district court's discretion in failing to award prejudgment interest). *Contra* Thurman v. Yellow Freight Sys., Inc., 90 F.3d 1160, 1170, 72 FEP 657 (6th Cir.) (although prejudgment interest should be excluded for delays specifically attributable to the plaintiff, trial court abused its discretion by denying prejudgment interest altogether rather than reducing the interest award when plaintiff delayed case by requesting extensions to respond to summary judgment motion), *amended on other grounds,* 97 F.3d 833 (6th Cir. 1996).

²³*See, e.g.,* Hurley v. Atlantic City Police Dep't, 933 F. Supp. 396, 431, 72 FEP 1828 (D.N.J. 1996) (after sex discrimination plaintiff received "adequate compensation for her injuries" and $700,000 in punitive damages, which court characterized as "pure windfall," court declined to exercise its discretion "to increase the size of that windfall" and award prejudgment interest); Emmel v. Coca-Cola Bottling Co., 904

Most courts continue to hold that prejudgment interest may be awarded against state defendants[24]; however, one court has held that the waiver of sovereign immunity will not be applied retroactively.[25]

Courts continue to utilize a variety of sources for the applicable interest rate, such as the Treasury bill rate, statutory interest rates, and market rates. However, the trend seems to be in favor of the Treasury bill rate.[26] One court has allowed the plaintiff to choose between federal and state interest rates.[27]

F. Supp. 723, 736 (N.D. Ill. 1995) ("[P]rejudgment interest is disfavored in the Seventh Circuit when punitive damages have been awarded."), aff'd, 95 F.3d 627, 72 FEP 1811 (7th Cir. 1996). Contra Luciano v. Olsten Corp., 912 F. Supp. 663, 676, 73 FEP 221 (E.D.N.Y. 1996) ("In the Court's view, to award the plaintiff prejudgment interest, even where she has recovered punitive damages, will not overcompensate her.").

[24]See, e.g., Winbush v. Iowa, 66 F.3d 1471, 1483, 69 FEP 1348 (8th Cir. 1995) (holding as a matter of first impression "that under Title VII courts have the power to award prejudgment interest against state defendants"); Jones v. Washington Metropolitan Area Transit Auth., 946 F. Supp. 1023, 1032–33 (D.D.C. 1996) (public contractor enjoyed governmental immunity when dealing in a discretionary capacity with other contractors; however, it was "liable for, as opposed to immune from, discrimination against its employees on the basis of sex," and, therefore, plaintiff was entitled to prejudgment interest). Contra Coleman v. Kaye, 87 F.3d 1491, 1512, 71 FEP 236 (3d Cir. 1996) ("[T]he New Jersey Tort Claims Act 'specifically prohibits prejudgment interest against government tortfeasors.' "), cert. denied, 117 S. Ct. 754 (1997).

[25]Brown v. Secretary of Army, 78 F.3d 645, 647, 72 FEP 595 (D.C. Cir.) ("We hold that sovereign immunity bars application of the interest provision retroactively to this case."), cert. denied, 117 S. Ct. 607 (1996).

[26]Ward v. Tipton County Sheriff Dep't, 937 F. Supp. 791, 800 (S.D. Ind. 1996) (court followed lead of other district courts in the Seventh Circuit, which have used the federal postjudgment interest rate); Luciano v. Olsten Corp., 912 F. Supp. 663, 676, 73 FEP 221 (E.D.N.Y. 1996) (although plaintiff argued for New York statutory rate of 9%, the court agreed with other circuit courts that have rejected the 9% rate in favor of the 52-week U.S. Treasury bill rate); Rao v. New York City Health & Hosps. Corp., 882 F. Supp. 321, 327–28, 67 FEP 1234 (S.D.N.Y. 1995) ("Because there is no reason that a greater or lesser interest rate should be used to calculate prejudgment interest than to calculate post-judgment interest, the Treasury bill rate is a reasonable rate to use for an award of prejudgment interest."); McIntosh v. Irving Trust Co., 873 F. Supp. 872, 883, 67 FEP 176 (S.D.N.Y. 1995) (the Treasury bill rate "more adequately ensures that the plaintiff is sufficiently, but not overly, compensated"); Young v. Lukens Steel Co., 881 F. Supp. 962, 977–78, 71 FEP 739 (E.D. Pa. 1994) ("The Court finds persuasive the suggestion of the Third and Sixth Circuits that the district court look to the post-judgment interest rate contained in 28 U.S.C. § 1961 when determining the applicable prejudgment interest rate."). Contra Taxman v. Board of Educ., 91 F.3d 1547, 1566, 71 FEP 848 (3d Cir. 1996) (court did not abuse its discretion in using the IRS adjusted prime rate, codified in 26 U.S.C. § 6621, to calculate prejudgment interest rather than the postjudgment rate set forth in 28 U.S.C. § 1961); Stephenson v. Aluminum Co. of Am., 915 F. Supp. 39, 56 (S.D. Ind. 1995) (the proper rate "is the average prime market rate that prevailed during the pendency of the litigation").

[27]Mendoza v. Union St. Bus Co., 876 F. Supp. 8, 12, 67 FEP 365 (D. Mass. 1995) (where parallel claims were brought under federal and state laws, and damages were

There has been no significant change in the general split among the circuits over whether prejudgment interest is precluded by an award of liquidated damages. The tendency, however, is to deny prejudgment interest when liquidated damages are awarded.[28]

While plaintiffs must always comply with procedural rules to safeguard the possibility of recovering prejudgment interest, questionable situations are usually resolved in favor of the presumption supporting prejudgment interest.[29]

d. Mitigation Expenses. One district court recently held that the jury may award even more than the plaintiff seeks in other expenses associated with obtaining new employment if the amount is supported by the evidence.[30]

2. The Period of Recovery

a. Commencement of the Back-Pay Period. While an employer may be liable for acts occurring outside the limitations period if a continuing violation is shown, the continuing violation must be clearly demonstrated.[31]

---

not segregated into separate federal and state components, plaintiff was allowed to select the body of law prescribing payment of damages).

[28]Mitchell v. Sisters of Charity, 924 F. Supp. 793, 805 (S.D. Tex. 1996) (based on the court's finding that plaintiffs were entitled to both back pay and liquidated damages, court held that plaintiffs were not entitled to prejudgment interest); Ryther v. KARE 11, 864 F. Supp. 1525, 1532, 70 FEP 1701 (D. Minn. 1994) ("Because Congress intended that liquidated damages under the ADEA serve, at least in part, a compensatory function, the court adopts the majority rule that an award of liquidated damages under the ADEA precludes recovery of prejudgment interest on the back-pay award."); Braverman v. Penobscot Shoe Co., 859 F. Supp. 596, 601, 3 AD 847 (D. Me. 1994) ("The Court did not locate authority that bars Braverman from *demanding* both prejudgment interest and liquidated damages, but he is *not* entitled to a duplicative recovery."). *Contra* Starceski v. Westinghouse Elec. Corp., 54 F.3d 1089, 1102–03, 67 FEP 1184 (3d Cir. 1995) (acknowledging split among circuits over whether prejudgment interest may be awarded along with liquidated damages and following reasoning of those circuits that permit awards of both liquidated damages and prejudgment interest).

[29]*See, e.g.,* Woodson v. Scott Paper Co., 898 F. Supp. 298, 309, 68 FEP 947 (E.D. Pa. 1995) (where counsel stipulated to "a total backpay award of $150,000" and during closing plaintiff's counsel referred to the amount as " '$150,000 worth of past losses,' " prejudgment interest was nevertheless added to the verdict).

[30]Luciano v. Olsten Corp., 912 F. Supp. 663, 674, 73 FEP 221 (E.D.N.Y. 1996) (in addition to the $2,500 for job search expenses and $3,538 for early withdrawal tax penalty from her IRA account, which the plaintiff expressly sought, the court also allowed the jury to award other incidental monetary losses, such as the $11,675 that the plaintiff paid in taxes on the money she withdrew from the retirement account).

[31]In Cantrell v. Knoxville Community Dev. Corp., 60 F.3d 1177, 1181, 68 FEP 536 (6th Cir. 1995), the district court awarded back pay at the rate it felt the plaintiff

b. Termination of the Back-Pay Period. The general rule remains that back pay ceases when the plaintiff no longer suffers from the economic effects of discrimination; therefore, back pay usually terminates when judgment is rendered or the jury returns its verdict.[32] However, courts sometimes choose other particular events to trigger termination of the back-pay period.[33]

(ii.) Failure to mitigate. With respect to the question of what consequences flow from proof of a plaintiff's failure to mitigate, the Seventh Circuit has held that a jury's finding of partial failure

---

should have been receiving but for the employer's discriminatory conduct prior to the discharge. The appellate court opined that this approach "effectively affords Cantrell relief for a disparate pay claim that he failed to pursue." *Id.* Also, the court noted that whether a back-pay award includes the value of enhanced income has only been addressed in the context of a continuing violation and since "[t]here is no authority in support of or in opposition to basing a damages award for a discrete act of discriminatory discharge on non-actionable prior acts of discrimination . . .," the court remanded to allow the district court to recalculate the award based on the plaintiff's actual wages at the time of discharge. *Id.*

[32]*See, e.g.,* Suggs v. Servicemaster Educ. Food Mgmt., 72 F.3d 1228, 1233, 69 FEP 1270 (6th Cir. 1996) ("general rule is to award back pay through the date of judgment"); Daniel v. Loveridge, 32 F.3d 1472, 1476–78, 65 FEP 1052 (10th Cir. 1994) (defendant argued that plaintiff should receive back pay from the date of her firing to the date of her first subsequent employment; however, court awarded back pay through date of judgment).

[33]*See, e.g.,* Harper v. Godfrey Co., 45 F.3d 143, 149, 66 FEP 1258 (7th Cir. 1995) ("Regardless of whether the discrimination had occurred plaintiffs would have been fired in early 1987 for their misconduct. Accordingly, the district court correctly restricted their awards of back pay to the time preceding termination and disallowed their reinstatements."); Saladin v. Turner, 936 F. Supp. 1571, 1581–82 (N.D. Okla. 1996) (back pay cut off at expiration of employer's offer of reinstatement because plaintiff's rejection due to "mere recitation of hostility" was unreasonable); EEOC v. Domino's Pizza, Inc., 909 F. Supp. 1529, 1537, 69 FEP 570 (M.D. Fla. 1995) (although plaintiff is presumptively entitled to back pay from date of discharge to date of trial, less interim earnings, court found that plaintiff was "made whole" with an award of damages from the date of termination up to the date he enrolled in college to change careers); EEOC v. Regency Architectural Metals Corp., 896 F. Supp. 260, 271 (D. Conn. 1995) (cutoff point for recovering back pay is date when shop where plaintiff was working went out of business); Taylor v. Central Pa. Drug & Alcohol Servs. Corp., 890 F. Supp. 360, 371, 72 FEP 1315 (M.D. Pa. 1995) ("[T]he calculation period for back pay terminates if the former employer establishes that the plaintiff's position would have been eliminated at some point during the alleged entitlement period for business reasons or other unrelated factors."); Roberson v. Mullins, 876 F. Supp. 100, 104 (W.D. Va. 1995) (plaintiff only entitled to recover back pay accruing until date on which he had announced he was planning to retire). *See also* Odima v. Westin Tucson Hotel, 53 F.3d 1484, 1495–96, 67 FEP 1222 (9th Cir. 1995) (An employee who has been discriminatorily denied an opportunity for promotion typically may not collect back pay for periods beyond the employee's voluntary resignation unless the employee shows constructive discharge. This doctrine, however, does not apply when the employee was preparing to enter a completely different career

of a Title VII plaintiff to mitigate her damages does not defeat the presumption in favor of prejudgment interest.[34]

With regard to what the employer must prove in satisfying its burden of establishing as an affirmative defense that the plaintiff failed to reasonably mitigate, most courts continue to hold that the defendant must prove both that there were substantially equivalent positions available and that the plaintiff failed to use reasonable diligence in seeking such positions.[35] This burden, moreover, has been described as "extremely high."[36] However, while unreasonable rejection of an offer of reinstatement generally tolls the accrual of back pay,[37] plaintiffs are not obligated to

---

with the same employer. In this situation, the employer's refusal to offer the employee a new position would be considered a refusal to rehire rather than a refusal to promote and back pay should extend beyond the date the employee quit.).

[34]Hutchison v. Amateur Elec. Supply, Inc., 42 F.3d 1037, 66 FEP 1275 (7th Cir. 1994). The district court concluded that a reasonable jury could have believed defendants' expert's opinion that plaintiff did not act diligently in failing to utilize employment placement services. Also, given that plaintiff was being paid a "premium" above market rates to tolerate her supervisor's abuse, the district court did not abuse its discretion in determining that the jury acted within the law in concluding that the plaintiff had a duty to seek and accept compensation at the market rate. However, the district court did abuse its discretion in denying prejudgment interest altogether based on the jury's determination that the plaintiff abandoned the job market. "In any event, the amount of back pay on which interest is to be awarded in this case is not uncertain—the jury awarded $80,000. The fact that the jury had to make implicit calculations to reach that amount does not defeat the presumption in favor of prejudgment interest." *Id.* at 1047.

[35]*See, e.g.,* Booker v. Taylor Milk Co., 64 F.3d 860, 866, 71 FEP 525 (3d Cir. 1995) ("The duty of a successful Title VII claimant to mitigate damages is *not* met by using reasonable diligence to obtain *any* employment. Rather, the claimant must use reasonable diligence to obtain *substantially equivalent employment.*"); EEOC v. Farmer Bros. Co., 31 F.3d 891, 906, 65 FEP 857 (9th Cir. 1994) (to prevail on summary judgment motion, defendant had to prove that during the time in question there were substantially equivalent jobs available and that plaintiff failed to use reasonable diligence in pursuing them); Ali v. City of Clearwater, 915 F. Supp. 1231, 1242 (M.D. Fla. 1996) (while defendant city advanced evidence of plaintiff's failure to use reasonable diligence, defendant failed to point out any factual basis that there were suitable positions available; therefore, defendant failed to meet burden on its affirmative defense of failure to mitigate); Shpargel v. Stage & Co., 914 F. Supp. 1468, 1479, 5 AD 1558 (E.D. Mich. 1996) (since plaintiff demonstrated a prima facie case of discrimination and presented evidence on the issue of damages, "the burden is on the defendants to prove that there were substantially equivalent jobs available to the plaintiff but that he failed to exercise reasonable diligence in seeking such jobs").

[36]Brooks v. Fonda-Fultonville Cent. Sch. Dist., 938 F. Supp. 1094, 1109 (N.D.N.Y. 1996).

[37]Bahadirli v. Domino's Pizza, 873 F. Supp. 1528, 1535, 71 FEP 1615 (M.D. Ala. 1995) ("According to the Supreme Court, where a Title VII defendant unconditionally

accept unreasonable or conditional offers of reinstatement as part of their duty to mitigate.[38]

Furthermore, the Third Circuit has held that an examination of the plaintiff's reasonable diligence requires evaluation of the individual characteristics of the plaintiff and the job market and that failure to mitigate alone is insufficient to overcome the presumption in favor of prejudgment interest.[39]

A job search limited to review of want ads is generally insufficient to prove mitigation of damages.[40] Conversely, want ads alone may not provide sufficient evidence that substantially similar positions were available.[41] An employee who received an above-market salary has a duty to seek and obtain employment at the lower market rate.[42] Self-employment may be sufficient mitigation even where

---

offers the plaintiff the position she previously applied for, doing so immediately cuts off liability for back pay from the date of the offer.").

[38]*See, e.g.,* Smith v. World Ins. Co., 38 F.3d 1456, 1465, 66 FEP 13 (8th Cir. 1994) (district court erred in failing to provide a specific jury instruction on the effect of plaintiff's rejection of defendant's unconditional offer of reinstatement); Mertig v. Milliken & Michaels of Del., Inc., 923 F. Supp. 636, 648 (D. Del. 1996) ("an applicant or discharged employee is not required to accept a job by the employer on the condition that the employee's claims against the employer be compromised"); Wilcox v. Stratton Lumber Co., 921 F. Supp. 837, 843 (D. Me. 1996) (sexual harassment plaintiff who feared continued harassment reasonably declined offer of reinstatement; therefore, offer did not toll accrual of back-pay liability); Lesko v. Clark Publisher Servs., 904 F. Supp. 415, 421 (M.D. Pa. 1995) (defendants' letters to plaintiff offering her opportunity to apply and interview were not unconditional offers of employment that would toll back-pay liability); Talada v. International Serv. Sys., Inc., 899 F. Supp. 936, 958 (N.D.N.Y. 1995) (defendants' offer of reinstatement without back pay and with implicit understanding that plaintiff would drop sexual harassment charges was not unconditional and would not limit back-pay award).

[39]Booker v. Taylor Milk Co., 64 F.3d 860, 865, 869, 71 FEP 525 (3d Cir. 1995) (plaintiff's reduced back-pay award reflects his failure to mitigate his damages and even if plaintiff had satisfied his duty to mitigate, he would not have been made whole absent some award of back pay; therefore, he is entitled to prejudgment interest for the loss of use of the amount included in the back-pay award).

[40]*E.g.,* Booker v. Taylor Milk Co., 64 F.3d 860, 865–66, 71 FEP 525 (3d Cir. 1995) (plaintiff's "constant" and "continuous" review of want ads was insufficient where in three and one-half years following discharge plaintiff failed to submit any applications in response to want ads that advertised positions substantially similar to plaintiff's previous position).

[41]Shpargel v. Stage & Co., 914 F. Supp. 1468, 1480, 5 AD 1558 (E.D. Mich. 1996) (defendants' mere proffering of want ads at summary judgment did not provide court with information that positions were substantially similar to plaintiff's previous position).

[42]Hutchison v. Amateur Elec. Supply, Inc., 42 F.3d 1037, 1067, 66 FEP 1275 (7th Cir. 1994) (employee who received above-market "abuse premium" had duty to seek and accept comparable "nonabusive" employment at the market rate).

subsequent ventures ultimately fail.[43] Back-pay damages may be denied where the claimant planned to quit her job to pursue self-employment prior to the allegedly discriminatory discharge.[44]

Subsequent work in an unrelated field may satisfy the mitigation requirement.[45] In determining whether subsequent part-time employment satisfies the mitigation requirement, courts will look to the availability of comparable jobs and the plaintiff's diligence in seeking employment.[46] A former employee's termination for cause in subsequent employment will not constitute a failure to mitigate damages where the former employee did not act intentionally and did not commit "gross or egregious wrong."[47]

Courts continue to apply the Supreme Court's holding in *Ford Motor Co. v. EEOC*[48] that a claimant's rejection of an employer's

---

[43]*E.g.,* Taylor v. Central Pa. Drug & Alcohol Servs. Corp., 890 F. Supp. 360, 367, 72 FEP 1315 (M.D. Pa. 1995) (plaintiff twice attempted to start her own business, and both ventures failed; the court held that plaintiff's "attempt to mitigate her back pay damages by starting her own businesses when no offers of employment were forthcoming was a laudable effort and should not be used against her to cut off her right to receive back pay"); *see also* Teichgraeber v. Memorial Union Corp., 932 F. Supp. 1263, 1265–67 (D. Kan. 1996) (former employee's claim for back pay and assertion of self-employment as mitigation made relevant, and therefore discoverable, all documents reflecting compensation paid to any person who performed labor for former employee's business).

[44]EEOC v. Ilona of Hungary, Inc., 108 F.3d 1569, 1579 (7th Cir. 1997) (reversing district court's award of back pay where evidence showed that plaintiff planned to quit her job prior to discharge; plaintiff had acquired a site and applied for a zoning permit for a Subway sandwich shop franchise over one month before her discharge and planned to "be [her] own boss" and run the store herself).

[45]Suggs v. Servicemaster Educ. Food Mgmt., 72 F.3d 1228, 1234, 69 FEP 1270 (6th Cir. 1996) (plaintiff previously employed as director at corporate/institutional food catering service satisfied mitigation requirement by immediately securing alternative employment as substitute teacher for two years and then working at a Head Start program up to time of trial).

[46]*Compare* Meyer v. United Air Lines, 950 F. Supp. 874, 876, 73 FEP 202 (N.D. Ill. 1997) (attorney formerly employed in arbitration department of airline's legal department failed to satisfy mitigation requirement by accepting part-time position in county State's Attorney office "preparing appellate briefs and doing other related appellate work") *with* EEOC v. Northwestern Mem'l Hosp., 858 F. Supp. 759, 767, 73 FEP 742 (N.D. Ill. 1994) (plaintiff satisfied mitigation requirement by securing part-time work on an "as needed" basis from one hospital three months after termination and ultimately obtained a full-time position at another hospital less than two years later).

[47]Thurman v. Yellow Freight Sys., Inc., 90 F.3d 1160, 1169, 72 FEP 657 (6th Cir. 1996) (employee fired for cause from subsequent employment for driving a truck under an underpass that was too low and bending the exhaust pipe as a result did not fail to mitigate damages where plaintiff did not act willfully and did not commit a "gross or egregious wrong").

[48]458 U.S. 219, 238–39, 29 FEP 121 (1982).

unconditional offer of employment terminates the back-pay period. However, the employer must offer the claimant comparable employment[49]; merely offering the claimant the opportunity to interview for a position is insufficient to cut off the back-pay period.[50] In order for the employer's offer to be effective, it must be unconditional and may not require the claimant to compromise his or her claims against the employer.[51]

However, if the claimant rejects an unconditional offer of comparable employment or reinstatement, the rejection must be reasonable.[52] A frequently litigated issue is whether rejection premised on fear of hostility upon return to the workplace is reasonable.[53]

---

[49]EEOC v. Accurate Mech. Contractors, Inc., 863 F. Supp. 828, 835–36 (E.D. Wis. 1994) (offer of night-shift work was not an offer of comparable employment and therefore did not toll accrual of back-pay liability where night-shift pipefitters were required to do more work with less supervision and night shift was statistically more dangerous than day shift, even though pay was higher for night shift).

[50]*E.g.,* EEOC v. Manville Sales Corp., 27 F.3d 1089, 1097 n.7, 65 FEP 804 (5th Cir. 1994) ("an offer to interview is not tantamount to an unconditional job offer and therefore the plaintiff's refusal to interview does not automatically toll the plaintiff's accrual of damages"), *cert. denied,* 115 S. Ct. 1252 (1995); Lesko v. Clark Publisher Servs., 904 F. Supp. 415, 421 (M.D. Pa. 1995) (neither an employer's offer to employee to submit an application nor an employer's invitation to interview are offers of employment that end accrual of potential back-pay liability under Title VII); *cf.* Bahadirli v. Domino's Pizza, 873 F. Supp. 1528, 1535–36, 71 FEP 1615 (M.D. Ala. 1995) (employer's statement to EEOC that employer was "willing to employ [plaintiff] at the location with the next available driver position" was not a job offer that would warrant dismissal for failure to mitigate damages although it could limit back-pay recovery).

[51]*E.g.,* Odima v. Westin Tucson Hotel, 53 F.3d 1484, 1495–96, 67 FEP 1222 (9th Cir. 1995) (plaintiff's rejection of offer of employment conditioned on plaintiff relinquishing his discrimination claims against employer was not "unconditional offer" and did not constitute a failure to mitigate damages); Gerardi v. Hofstra Univ., 897 F. Supp. 50, 57–58 n.6 (E.D.N.Y. 1995) (university's settlement offer to job applicant made during administrative process could not be considered unconditional so as to limit university's back-pay liability under ADEA since offer specified that applicant would be required to provide a full and complete release of all claims).

[52]Bragalone v. Kona Coast Resort Joint Venture, 866 F. Supp. 1285, 1296, 66 FEP 65 (D. Hawaii 1994) (plaintiff's rejection of unconditional offer of reinstatement was unreasonable where the rejection was based on the belief that it "would require her to return to a stressful allegedly harassing work environment").

[53]*Compare* Saladin v. Turner, 936 F. Supp. 1571, 1581 (N.D. Okla. 1996) (mere recitation of hostility is not reasonable rejection of unconditional reinstatement offer because antagonism between parties is the natural byproduct of any litigation) *with* Naylor v. Georgia-Pacific Corp., 875 F. Supp. 564, 581 (N.D. Iowa 1995) (fear of continuing racial harassment created material issue of fact as to reasonableness of plaintiff's rejection of reinstatement offer precluding summary judgment) *and* Miano v. AC & R Advertising, Inc., 875 F. Supp. 204, 223–24, 66 FEP 1603 (S.D.N.Y.

(iii.) After-acquired evidence of employee misconduct or fraud. Courts continue to apply the Supreme Court's holding in *McKennon v. Nashville Banner Publishing Co.*[54] that back-pay liability ends when sufficient evidence of employee misconduct or application fraud preceding the discriminatory act is discovered. In the context of after-acquired evidence of employee misconduct, the employer must prove that it would have discharged the employee for such misconduct.[55] After-acquired evidence of employee misconduct limits back-pay liability to the period from the date of the unlawful discharge to the date the after-acquired evidence of misconduct was discovered and precludes front pay or reinstatement.[56] Such after-acquired evidence does not warrant summary judgment in favor of the employer; nor does it bar all damages to the former employee.[57] The after-acquired evidence doctrine does not apply to postemployment misconduct.[58]

Courts have determined that the reasoning underlying *McKennon* applies with equal force when the after-acquired evidence concerns an employee's fraud in the application process rather than

---

1995) (rejection of unconditional reinstatement offer reasonable where "exceptional circumstances existed whereby plaintiffs reasonably concluded their return to AC & R would be greeted by suspicion and antagonism, notwithstanding assurances to the contrary . . . the environment to which they were invited to return would have been one of serious discord and suspicion in a business where trust and open communication were essential").

[54] 115 S. Ct. 879, 886–87, 66 FEP 1192 (1995).

[55] *E.g.*, O'Day v. McDonnell Douglas Helicopter Co., 79 F.3d 756, 761, 70 FEP 615 (9th Cir. 1996) (employer must prove by a preponderance of the evidence that it would have fired the employee for that misconduct); *see* Castle v. Rubin, 78 F.3d 654, 659, 72 FEP 1701 (D.C. Cir. 1996) (court may not deny reinstatement based on after-acquired evidence of misconduct if the employer could not have lawfully fired the employee for that conduct).

[56] *O'Day*, 79 F.3d at 764 (under *McKennon*, if the plaintiff prevails on his discrimination claim, he would at the very least be entitled to back pay from the date of his wrongful termination to the date that his former employer learned of his misconduct, as well as to any other remedies not precluded by *McKennon*).

[57] *E.g.*, Schnidrig v. Columbia Mach., Inc., 80 F.3d 1406, 1412, 71 FEP 1763 (9th Cir.) (employer's discovery of after-acquired evidence of employee misconduct did not warrant summary judgment in favor of employer), *cert. denied,* 117 S. Ct. 295 (1996); Ryder v. Westinghouse Elec. Corp., 879 F. Supp. 534, 536 (W.D. Pa. 1995) (after-acquired evidence doctrine does not bar all damages to former employee).

[58] *E.g.*, Carr v. Woodbury County Juvenile Detention Ctr., 905 F. Supp. 619, 629, 69 FEP 1101 (N.D. Iowa 1995) (after-acquired evidence doctrine does not apply to former employee's postemployment marijuana use); *Ryder,* 879 F. Supp. at 537 (after-acquired evidence doctrine does not apply to former employee's alleged postemployment disclosure of confidential information).

wrongful conduct during employment.[59] The employer must prove that it would have fired the employee when it learned of the fraud in the application.[60] Reinstatement, front pay, and injunctive relief are not available where the employee has committed application fraud that would have led to his or her termination.[61] After-acquired evidence of application fraud will limit back pay to the period from the date of the unlawful discharge to the date the new information was discovered.[62] After-acquired evidence of application fraud does not bar all relief or warrant summary judgment for the employer, on the ground that the employer never would have hired the employee had it known of the application fraud at the time of hiring.[63]

(iv.) Other events terminating the back-pay period. There have been no significant changes relating to termination of the back-pay period. In termination cases, courts continue to hold that the back-pay period terminates on the day the plaintiff would have been laid off[64] or discharged for a nondiscriminatory reason,[65] including the

---

[59]*E.g.,* Russell v. Microdyne Corp., 65 F.3d 1229, 1240, 68 FEP 1602 (4th Cir. 1995) (applying *McKennon* to after-acquired evidence of misrepresentations in resume and application); Wallace v. Dunn Constr. Co., 62 F.3d 374, 379, 68 FEP 990 (11th Cir. 1995) (*McKennon* applies to after-acquired evidence of falsification of employment application regarding prior criminal convictions).

[60]*Wallace,* 62 F.3d at 379 n.8 (the pertinent inquiry is whether the employee would have been fired upon discovery of the wrongdoing, not whether he would have been hired in the first place).

[61]*Id.* at 380–81 (partial summary judgment in favor of employer was appropriate because reinstatement, front pay, and injunctive relief were unavailable in light of after-acquired evidence; summary judgment denied as to back pay because after-acquired evidence limits but does not bar back-pay liability).

[62]*Id.* at 380; Russell v. Microdyne Corp., 65 F.3d 1229, 1240, 68 FEP 1602 (4th Cir. 1995).

[63]*E.g.,* Shattuck v. Kinetic Concepts, Inc., 49 F.3d 1106, 1108, 67 FEP 798 (5th Cir. 1995) (rejecting argument that plaintiff should be barred from recovery because he never would have been hired if employer had known of fraud at time of application); DiPuccio v. United Parcel Serv., 890 F. Supp. 688, 693, 5 AD 561 (N.D. Ohio 1995); McCray v. DPC Indus., Inc., 875 F. Supp. 384, 387, 68 FEP 909 (E.D. Tex. 1995).

[64]*See, e.g.,* EEOC v. Cherry-Burrell Corp., 35 F.3d 356, 361–63, 66 FEP 1749 (8th Cir. 1994) (illustrating the practical difficulties associated with determining whether and when an employee would have been laid off absent discrimination).

[65]*See, e.g.,* Harper v. Godfrey Co., 45 F.3d 143, 149, 66 FEP 1258 (7th Cir. 1995) (ending back-pay liability at time that plaintiffs would have been terminated for misconduct); Cosgrove v. Sears, Roebuck & Co., 68 FEP 1006 (S.D.N.Y. 1995) (ending back-pay period at time plaintiff would have been terminated for poor performance under procedures in employer's management manual).

closure or sale of a business or a division thereof,[66] unless the plaintiff would have been retained by the purchaser.[67] Back pay also will cease on the date on which the plaintiff would have retired.[68]

3. Deductions and Offsets

a. Actual Interim Earnings. Some courts calculate back pay on a yearly basis.[69]

If a part-time "moonlighting" job could have (and likely would have) been worked while the plaintiff was also working for the defendant, arguably no deductions from the back-pay award should be made.[70]

It remains an open question whether amounts received in lieu of earnings, such as unemployment and workers' compensation benefits, should be treated as interim earnings and deducted from back pay or as payments from a collateral source and not deducted. Most of the recent cases have not allowed a deduction, and a number of courts have found that the issue is within the trial court's discretion.[71] The collateral source rule may be

---

[66]*See, e.g.,* Taylor v. Central Pa. Drug & Alcohol Servs. Corp., 890 F. Supp. 360, 375, 72 FEP 1315 (M.D. Pa. 1995) (back pay terminated at time defendant ceased operations).

[67]*Id.* (where plaintiff's employment would have continued with purchaser, plaintiff's back pay continues beyond time of sale).

[68]Roberson v. Mullins, 876 F. Supp. 100, 104 (W.D. Va. 1995) (back pay stopped at date on which plaintiff had stated he would retire).

[69]EEOC v. Domino's Pizza, Inc., 909 F. Supp. 1529, 1537–38, 69 FEP 570 (M.D. Fla. 1995); Brocklehurst v. PPG Indus., Inc., 865 F. Supp. 1253, 1264–66, 66 FEP 545 (E.D. Mich. 1994).

[70]*See, e.g.,* Selgas v. American Airlines, Inc., 858 F. Supp. 316, 323, 69 FEP 655 (D.P.R. 1994) (no deduction where defendant did not allow moonlighting but plaintiff presented evidence that other employees engaged in moonlighting), *aff'd in part, vacated in part,* 69 F.3d 1205, 69 FEP 944 (1st Cir. 1995).

[71]Deduction not allowed: EEOC v. Kentucky State Police Dep't, 80 F.3d 1086, 1100, 71 FEP 1495 (6th Cir. 1996) (following circuit precedent in declining to offset unemployment compensation but stating that not allowing such offset makes little sense where the state is both the employer and the party administering and financing the unemployment compensation, as the payments are not truly collateral); Daniel v. Loveridge, 32 F.3d 1472, 65 FEP 1052 (10th Cir. 1994) (offset of unemployment benefits is within the court's discretion, but will not be exercised in absence of evidence on manner in which defendant contributes to unemployment compensation fund); Talada v. International Serv. Sys., Inc., 899 F. Supp. 936, 960 (N.D.N.Y. 1995) (offset is within court's discretion but facts show no equitable basis for offset); Dailey v. Societe Generale, 889 F. Supp. 108, 112–13, 68 FEP 345 (S.D.N.Y. 1995) (denying offset of unemployment compensation because any windfall should go to injured plaintiff, not defendant that engaged in discrimination); Kohnke v.

inapplicable where the defendant is self-insured and thus paid the benefit directly.[72]

Courts continue to disagree on whether pension benefits should be deducted from back pay.[73] Since the value of pension benefits may be recovered as damages, pension benefits received prior to trial may be offset against this element of damages rather than against back pay.[74]

   b. Separation Payments. Courts continue to hold that separation payments, such as severance pay, normally are deductible from

---

Delta Airlines, Inc., 5 AD 334, 338–39 (N.D. Ill. 1995) (no offset, even for self-insured defendant, where workers' compensation benefits are for injuries unrelated to alleged discrimination); Taylor v. Central Pa. Drug & Alcohol Servs. Corp., 890 F. Supp. 360, 370, 72 FEP 1315 (M.D. Pa. 1995) (no offset of unemployment compensation); Neal v. Director, D.C. Dep't of Corrections, 1995 WL 517249, at *7 (D.D.C. 1995) (no offset because unemployment compensation is an obligation incurred by the defendant under a distinct and unrelated statutory scheme).

   Deduction allowed: Wilcox v. Stratton Lumber, Inc., 921 F. Supp. 837, 843 (D. Me. 1996) (court exercises its discretion to offset unemployment compensation, while noting that no circuit has determined that such benefits should be deducted as a general rule). In *Wheeler v. Catholic Archdiocese of Seattle,* 880 P.2d 29, 3 AD 1104 (Wash. 1994), the Washington Supreme Court, discussing this issue at length in connection with a workers' compensation award, concluded that the trial court erred in applying the collateral source rule to deny an offset, but held that an offset was appropriate only to the extent the award represented compensation for lost wages rather than for physical injury.

   [72]Goodman v. Boeing Co., 75 Wash. App. 60, 877 P.2d 703, 3 AD 983 (Wash. App. 1994) (since the employer is self-insured for workers' compensation, collateral source rule does not apply), *aff'd,* 127 Wash. 2d 1020, 890 P.2d 463 (Wash. 1995). See Stratton v. Department for the Aging, 922 F. Supp. 857, 865–66 (S.D.N.Y. 1996) (since the defendant city is the entity that effectively paid unemployment benefits, collateral source rule does not apply and thus offset is proper). *Contra* Kohnke v. Delta Airlines, Inc., 5 AD 334, 338–39 (N.D. Ill. 1995) (denying offset of workers' compensation disability payments made by self-insured defendant because payments were unrelated to charged discrimination).

   [73]Deduction allowed: Rhodes v. Guiberson Oil Tools, 82 F.3d 615, 620–21, 71 FEP 83 (5th Cir. 1996) (defendant allowed to offset lump-sum benefit paid at time of discriminatory termination against lump sum due at time plaintiff would have retired); Stratton v. Department for the Aging, 922 F. Supp. 857, 865 (S.D.N.Y. 1996) (deduction necessary to prevent defendant from paying wages and retirement benefits to plaintiff for same period of time).

   Deduction not allowed: Smith v. World Ins. Co., 38 F.3d 1456, 1465–66, 66 FEP 13 (8th Cir. 1994) (offset not allowed unless back-pay award includes pension contributions that plaintiff would have received if plaintiff had not been terminated); EEOC v. Illinois, 877 F. Supp. 1207, 66 FEP 1148 (C.D. Ill. 1994), *rev'd on other grounds,* 69 F.3d 167, 69 FEP 306 (7th Cir. 1995).

   [74]*See* Rhodes v. Guiberson Oil Tools, 82 F.3d 615, 620–21, 71 FEP 83 (5th Cir. 1996); Smith v. World Ins. Co., 38 F.3d 1456, 1465–66, 66 FEP 13 (8th Cir. 1994).

back pay because the employee would not have received them but for the discharge.[75]

c. Periods of Unavailability. Periods when the plaintiff was unavailable to work because he or she voluntarily left interim employment to care for an aged parent have been excluded from back pay.[76]

Courts continue to reach different conclusions as to the effect of the plaintiff's decision to attend college. The deciding factor is often whether the student continued to seek employment while attending school.[77]

d. Taxes. The IRS has issued guidance on the new rules regarding the taxability of damages for nonphysical personal injuries.[78] Specifically, the IRS has ruled that under current IRC § 104(a)(2), back pay and damages for emotional distress received in satisfaction of a Title VII employment discrimination claim must be included in gross income. However, to the extent that damages received under Title VII are for medical care attributable to the emotional distress, they are excludable.[79]

II. FRONT PAY

Reinstatement (or instatement) continues to be the generally preferred remedy for a discrimination victim.[80] However, courts readily acknowledge that reinstatement is not always feasible and

---

[75]Rhodes v. Guiberson Oil Tools, 82 F.3d 615, 620, 71 FEP 83 (5th Cir. 1996) (deduction proper because plaintiff would not have received severance benefits in absence of termination).

[76]Winbush v. Iowa, 66 F.3d 1471, 1486, 69 FEP 1348 (8th Cir. 1995).

[77]*Compare* EEOC v. Domino's Pizza, Inc., 909 F. Supp. 1529, 1537, 69 FEP 570 (M.D. Fla. 1995) (back pay terminated when plaintiff enrolled in college with goal of pursuing another career) *with* Taylor v. Central Pa. Drug & Alcohol Servs. Corp., 890 F. Supp. 360, 375, 72 FEP 1315 (M.D. Pa. 1995) (no reduction in back pay where plaintiff was available to work full-time and actually worked 30 to 35 hours per week while attending school).

[78]IRS Rev. Rul. 96-95 (Jan. 2, 1997).

[79]Before the August 21, 1996, amendments to § 104(a), all emotional distress damages were excludable from gross income.

[80]*See, e.g.,* Weaver v. Amoco Prod. Co., 66 F.3d 85, 88, 70 FEP 931 (5th Cir. 1995) ("This Circuit continues to recognize the decided preference to award reinstatement instead of front pay for a discriminatory discharge in violation of the

front pay may be more appropriate in certain situations.[81] For example, front pay would be more appropriate where there is no vacancy in which to place the plaintiff, or where reinstatement would necessitate the displacement of other employees.[82] Additionally, courts continue to consider feelings of animosity or hostility between the plaintiff and the employer as a factor militating against reinstatement.[83]

ADEA."); Squires v. Bonser, 54 F.3d 168, 172 (3d Cir. 1995) ("Reinstatement advances the policy goals of make-whole relief and deterrence in a way which money damages cannot."); Shea v. Icelandair, 925 F. Supp. 1014, 1030, 70 FEP 1544 (S.D.N.Y. 1996) ("Courts strongly favor reinstatement over alternative forms of relief."); Mitchell v. Sisters of Charity, 924 F. Supp. 793, 803 (S.D. Tex. 1996) (noting the Fifth Circuit's "preference to award reinstatement in lieu of front pay" in cases of discriminatory discharge); Rao v. New York City Health & Hosps. Corp., 882 F. Supp. 321, 329, 67 FEP 1234 (S.D.N.Y. 1995) ("Reinstatement is generally recognized to be an appropriate remedy for wrongful termination, because it serves the general purpose of making the plaintiff whole."); Miano v. AC & R Advertising, Inc., 875 F. Supp. 204, 224, 66 FEP 1603 (S.D.N.Y. 1995) ("The court recognizes the strong preference for reinstatement as the remedy for future lost earnings in discrimination cases.").

[81]Ward v. Tipton County Sheriff Dep't, 937 F. Supp. 791, 796 (S.D. Ind. 1996) (While "[a] victim of discrimination in violation of Title VII is presumptively entitled to complete relief [and] reinstatement is the preferred remedy, it is not always appropriate."); Shea v. Icelandair, 925 F. Supp. 1014, 1030, 70 FEP 1544 (S.D.N.Y. 1996) ("[R]einstatement does not always afford a practicable remedy for either the plaintiff or the defendant."); Reynolds v. Octel Communications Corp., 924 F. Supp. 743, 748, 69 FEP 1178 (N.D. Tex. 1995) ("When reinstatement is not feasible, the equitable remedy of front pay is available at the court's discretion.").

[82]Woodhouse v. Magnolia Hosp., 92 F.3d 248, 257, 71 FEP 1804 (5th Cir. 1996) (lower court erred in ordering plaintiff's reinstatement because her former position as director of admissions had been eliminated); Ray v. Iuka Special Mun. Separate Sch. Dist., 51 F.3d 1246, 1254, 67 FEP 1348 (5th Cir. 1995) (facts that there were no current openings in school district such that reinstatement would mandate displacement of an existing employee and that plaintiff almost immediately found substantially similar employment were properly relied upon by district court in denying reinstatement); Mitchell v. Sisters of Charity, 924 F. Supp. 793, 803 (S.D. Tex. 1996) (because "reinstatement is not preferred over front pay when there is no vacancy in the desired position," ADEA plaintiffs were awarded front pay when the positions they sought had been filled and reinstatement would have displaced innocent employees); Stephenson v. Aluminum Co. of Am., 915 F. Supp. 39, 56 (S.D. Ind. 1995) (because "reinstatement is warranted absent exceptional circumstances demonstrating that the position is no longer available or where a continued reduction in force occurs," court ordered reinstatement where Title VII plaintiff's position was still available despite employer's layoffs).

[83]*See, e.g.,* Hadley v. VAM, 44 F.3d 372, 376, 67 FEP 186 (5th Cir. 1995) (district court determined that reinstatement would not be feasible because of the animosity between the parties); Miano v. AC & R Advertising, Inc., 875 F. Supp. 204,

While front pay is calculated along the same lines as back pay, as essentially an augmentation of the back-pay award necessary to effectuate the make-whole purposes of antidiscrimination laws, it nevertheless will be denied if a calculation or accounting would be "hopelessly speculative."[84] However, provided that they are not too speculative, certain fringe benefits may be incorporated into the front-pay calculation.[85] Because of the inherent

---

224–25, 66 FEP 1603 (S.D.N.Y. 1995) ("[r]einstatement has been found to be unworkable in cases where antagonism between the parties was so great as to make alternative relief preferable"; court agreed with plaintiffs' prediction that returning to former positions would engender suspicion and antagonism, despite assurances to the contrary; therefore, plaintiffs' refusal of reinstatement offer was justified). *Contra* Philipp v. ANR Freight Sys., Inc., 61 F.3d 669, 674, 70 FEP 1347 (8th Cir. 1995) (given that new manager, who was not employed when plaintiff was terminated, agreed to work hard to make plaintiff part of management team and that plaintiff got along well with only other remaining supervisor, court found insufficient showing of animosity or friction to disturb lower court's award of reinstatement); Squires v. Bonser, 54 F.3d 168, 174–75 (3d Cir. 1995) (finding that factors considered by district court in denying reinstatement, such as incidents of poor performance by plaintiff, tension that would result from plaintiff resuming work with defendants, and plaintiff's ability to secure other employment, did not present special circumstances justifying denial of reinstatement).

[84]Suggs v. Servicemaster Educ. Food Mgmt., 72 F.3d 1228, 1235, 69 FEP 1270 (6th Cir. 1996) ("the court must make its award of front pay reasonably specific as to duration and amount"); Ward v. Papa's Pizza To Go, Inc., 907 F. Supp. 1535, 1543–44 (S.D. Ga. 1995) (where plaintiff sought monetary relief but not reinstatement, there was no definable terminating point for calculating front-pay award; therefore, court declined "to allow computation of an award spanning the rest of Plaintiff's working life"); Inks v. Healthcare Distribs., 901 F. Supp. 1403, 1408, 73 FEP 643 (N.D. Ind. 1995) (denying plaintiff's motion for reconsideration after lower court refused award of front pay based on consideration of lack of certainty that plaintiff would have remained at former employer and lack of evidence that plaintiff would suffer significant future damages). *Contra* Barbour v. Merrill, 48 F.3d 1270, 1280, 67 FEP 369 (D.C. Cir. 1995) ("[A] district court should not refuse to award front pay merely because some speculation about future earnings is necessary, or because the parties have introduced conflicting evidence."); Mitchell v. Sisters of Charity, 924 F. Supp. 793, 803 (S.D. Tex. 1996) ("Calculations of front pay cannot be totally accurate because they are prospective and necessarily speculative in nature."); Young v. Lukens Steel Co., 881 F. Supp. 962, 976–77, 71 FEP 739 (E.D. Pa. 1994) (employer not entitled to reduction of front-pay award despite argument that total economic loss figure from employee's termination date up to age 65 included back pay; it was beyond district court's discretion "to attempt to enter the jury deliberation room and guess how and why the jury used" the specific figure).

[85]*See, e.g.,* Lussier v. Runyon, 50 F.3d 1103, 1105, 4 AD 265 (1st Cir. 1995) (holding that it is within trial court's discretion to tailor a front-pay award to a Rehabilitation Act plaintiff to incorporate an increase in Veterans Administration benefits generated by the adverse employment action).

speculation involved in calculating front-pay awards, expert testimony is often utilized.[86]

Front pay may be denied in the following instances: the plaintiff obtains an equivalent position within a short time,[87] the court perceives that front pay would result in a windfall for the plaintiff,[88] and the employer discovers after the discriminatory act that the employee engaged in prehire fraud or other predischarge misconduct.[89]

Awarding front pay can be complicated by the fact that present dollar valuation differs from future dollar valuation. The process of calculating present versus future dollar valuations can be simplified by preverdict stipulations, which have been held to be enforceable.[90]

Courts continue to hold that a plaintiff's entitlement to front pay is for the court's determination, reasoning that as a substitute for reinstatement front pay is in effect equitable relief.[91] Moreover, if a court determines that reinstatement would be an inappropriate remedy whereas front pay would be proper, the court may consider continued court monitoring.[92]

---

[86]*See, e.g.,* Scarfo v. Cabletron Sys., Inc., 54 F.3d 931, 954, 67 FEP 1474 (1st Cir. 1995) (court awarded front pay based in part on testimony of plaintiff's expert that plaintiff only had a 10% chance of returning to full employment at an equivalent salary).

[87]Brocklehurst v. PPG Indus., Inc., 865 F. Supp. 1253, 1266, 66 FEP 545 (E.D. Mich. 1994) (within months of his termination plaintiff obtained a better-paying job, and while the benefits at subsequent job were not as great, this is not controlling on the issue of the propriety of front pay).

[88]Reynolds v. Octel Communications Corp., 924 F. Supp. 743, 748, 69 FEP 1178 (N.D. Tex. 1995) (front pay not appropriate where jury awarded plaintiff more than the statutory maximum amount of compensatory and punitive damages).

[89]Wallace v. Dunn Constr. Co., 62 F.3d 374, 380, 68 FEP 990 (11th Cir. 1995) (neither reinstatement nor front pay appropriate remedy for employee who was found to have lied on employment application). *Contra* Delli Santi v. CNA Ins. Cos., 88 F.3d 192, 205, 71 FEP 143 (3d Cir. 1996) (after-acquired evidence does not bar front pay to a discharged employee because it is not relevant to establish liability in a Title VII or ADEA case; sole question to be answered at this stage is whether the employer impermissibly discriminated against the employee).

[90]Woodson v. Scott Paper Co., 898 F. Supp. 298, 309, 68 FEP 947 (E.D. Pa. 1995).

[91]Wells v. New Cherokee Corp., 58 F.3d 233, 238, 68 FEP 284 (6th Cir. 1995) (district court erred in letting jury determine propriety of front-pay award).

[92]Suggs v. Servicemaster Educ. Food Mgmt., 72 F.3d 1228, 1235 n.4, 69 FEP 1270 (6th Cir. 1996) (if district court determines that reinstatement is inappropriate and front pay is warranted, the court may wish to consider a continued court-monitoring approach).

III. Compensatory and Punitive Damages

A. Statutory Bases for Compensatory and Punitive Damages

1. Title VII

Courts have begun to wrestle with the "cannot recover" language in § 1981a(a)(1), which allows for damages for intentional violations of Title VII "provided that the complaining party cannot recover" under § 1981.[93] In *Dunning v. General Electric Co.*,[94] the court noted that there are three ways to interpret "cannot recover." First, it can be interpreted simply to exclude compensatory and punitive damages for plaintiffs who are already covered by § 1981, irrespective of whether relief is actually available to them under § 1981 (i.e., to preclude such damages under Title VII for all claims of race and ethnic discrimination). Second, it can be interpreted to include compensatory and punitive damages for all plaintiffs, including those asserting claims of race and ethnic discrimination, unless compensatory and punitive damages are actually available to them under § 1981 (such that a plaintiff asserting such claims would be entitled to recover under Title VII if § 1981 damages are unavailable, as for example if the plaintiff's § 1981 claims are time-barred). Third, it can be interpreted to provide that a plaintiff who is covered by § 1981 because of race or ethnicity but also covered by Title VII because of sex or religion is not entitled to compensatory and punitive damages under Title VII even for the discrimination reached by Title VII (so that a plaintiff who alleged both race and sex discrimination would not be entitled to recover under Title VII, because he or she could recover under § 1981 for the race discrimination).[95] The court ultimately adopted the second interpretation, holding that the "cannot recover" language allows Title VII claims for compensatory and punitive damages when, at the time the Title VII claim is brought, relief under § 1981 is unavailable. In *Dunning,* this meant that the plaintiff was able to seek relief under Title VII because the statute of limitations had run on the plaintiff's § 1981 claim.[96]

---

[93]*See* discussion at note 246 in Main Edition.
[94]892 F. Supp. 1424, 1427–31 (M.D. Ala. 1995).
[95]*Id.* at 1428.
[96]*Cf.* Bradshaw v. University of Me. Sys., 870 F. Supp. 406, 408, 66 FEP 806 (D. Me. 1994) (plaintiff who could have pleaded race discrimination claim under

Section 1981a is a purely remedial provision that creates no additional bases for liability, but it does authorize recovery of compensatory and punitive damages as additional remedies to the equitable relief otherwise provided under Title VII.[97]

2. Civil Rights Acts of 1866 and 1871

b. Public Employers. Although punitive damages are not available against local (municipal) government agency employers under 42 U.S.C. §§ 1981 and 1983, punitive damages may be available against a local government agency or municipality pursuant to state law.[98]

B. The Entitlement to, and Calculation of, Compensatory Damages

Courts continue to contend with the proof necessary to support awards for intangible harm.[99]

Compensatory damages awarded by juries may be reviewed for both adequacy and excessiveness. Material deviation from

---

§ 1981 but did not do so is not barred from recovering Title VII race discrimination damages under § 1981a).

[97]West v. Boeing Co., 851 F. Supp. 395, 400–01, 66 FEP 836 (D. Kan. 1994).

[98]*See* Coleman v. Kaye, 87 F.3d 1491, 1506, 71 FEP 236 (3d Cir. 1996) (punitive damages against county for the county prosecutor's intentional discrimination against plaintiff were available for violation of New Jersey's Law Against Discrimination); Adams v. City of Chicago, 865 F. Supp. 445, 447, 73 FEP 547 (N.D. Ill. 1994) (immunity from punitive damages under § 1981 can be waived by federal or state law).

[99]*Compare* Patterson v. P.H.P. Healthcare Corp., 90 F.3d 927, 938–41, 72 FEP 613 (5th Cir. 1996) (compensatory damages award set aside where there was no corroborating testimony of emotional harm, no expert medical or psychological evidence of damage caused by the alleged distress, no evidence of physical manifestation, and one of the two plaintiffs had obtained a new job at higher pay), *cert. denied,* 117 S. Ct. 767 (1997) *and* Hetzel v. County of Prince William, 89 F.3d 169, 171–72, 71 FEP 520 (4th Cir. 1996) ($500,000 compensatory damage award for emotional distress based solely on plaintiff's own testimony concerning stress and headaches held excessive as a matter of law where there was no corroborating testimony and the plaintiff never saw a doctor, therapist, or counselor, and remained an employee in good standing) *with* Myers v. City of Cincinnati, 14 F.3d 1115, 1119 (6th Cir. 1994) ($25,000 award affirmed where plaintiff testified that he lost weight, had insomnia, and was under doctor's care for stomach problems). The EEOC favors testimony in addition to that by the plaintiff or evidence of physical manifestations to support compensatory awards. Office of Legal Counsel, EEOC, *Policy Guide on Compensatory and Punitive Damages Under 1991 Civil Rights Act,* 8 LABOR REL. REP. (BNA) 405:7091, 7097 (July 1992).

"reasonable compensation" guides courts in determining whether an award is excessive or inadequate,[100] with the extent of a plaintiff's emotional suffering providing a measure for the appropriateness of the award.[101]

Appellate courts declare their reluctance to disturb a jury award,[102] but where awards fall outside the acceptable range, courts

---

[100]*See, e.g.,* Shea v. Icelandair, 925 F. Supp. 1014, 1020–21, 70 FEP 1544 (S.D.N.Y. 1996) (applying New York law).

[101]*See, e.g.,* EEOC v. AIC Sec. Investigations, Ltd., 55 F.3d 1276, 1285–86, 4 AD 693 (7th Cir. 1995) (award of $50,000 for emotional distress was not "grossly excessive" in a discriminatory discharge case where, though the plaintiff did not undergo any formal psychological treatment, "the emotional burden on a person dying of cancer, perceiving himself as unable to adequately provide for his family, is considerably greater than that suffered by the ordinary victim of a wrongful discharge"); Luciano v. Olsten Corp., 912 F. Supp. 663, 673–74, 73 FEP 221 (E.D.N.Y. 1996) (upholding jury award of $11,400 for emotional distress where plaintiff testified that as a result of her termination she was "hurt, shocked, upset, overcome with sadness and depression, that she cried, worried about finances, had trouble sleeping and eating and felt purposeless"); Brockelhurst v. PPG Indus., Inc., 865 F. Supp. 1253, 1266, 66 FEP 545 (E.D. Mich. 1994) (upholding award of $500,000 for past emotional damages in age discrimination action where "jury had an opportunity to hear Plaintiff describe to them the frustration and humiliation he felt as a result of his discriminatory discharge, and to observe the callousness with which Defendant conducted itself at the time of the discharge"); Webb v. Hyman, 861 F. Supp. 1094, 1115–16, 67 FEP 1425 (D.D.C. 1994) (jury verdict awarding plaintiff $225,000 and $75,000 against the respective defendants was not "inordinately large or shocking to the conscience" given sexual harassment plaintiff's emotional trauma).

[102]*See, e.g.,* Hetzel v. County of Prince William, 89 F.3d 169, 171, 71 FEP 520 (4th Cir. 1996) ("A jury's award of compensatory damages will be set aside on the grounds of excessiveness only if 'the verdict is against the clear weight of evidence, or is based upon evidence which is false, or will result in a miscarriage of justice.' "), *cert. denied,* 117 S. Ct. 584 (1996); Delli Santi v. CNA Ins. Cos., 88 F.3d 192, 206, 71 FEP 143 (3d Cir. 1996) (declining to disturb the district court's discretion against the backdrop of the "severely limited" nature of appellate review and the additional deference mandated by the fact that the district court already granted a remittitur); McKinnon v. Kwong Wah Restaurant, 83 F.3d 498, 506, 70 FEP 1037 (1st Cir. 1996) (stating that court "will not override a damage determination unless the award is unsupported by the evidence, grossly excessive, or shocking to the conscience"); Fitzgerald v. Mountain States Tel. & Tel. Co., 68 F.3d 1257, 1261, 69 FEP 163 (10th Cir. 1995) (" '[A]bsent an award so excessive as to shock the judicial conscience and to raise an irresistible inference that passion, prejudice, corruption or other improper cause invaded the trial, the jury's determination of the damages is considered inviolate.' ") (citing Malandris v. Merrill Lynch, 703 F.2d 1152, 1168 (10th Cir. 1981) (en banc), *cert. denied,* 464 U.S. 824 (1983)); Hogan v. Bangor & Aroostock R.R., 61 F.3d 1034, 1037, 4 AD 1251 (1st Cir. 1995) (stating that the generousness of a jury's award alone does not justify an appellate court in setting it aside; rather an award of compensatory damages is excessive if it exceeds a rational appraisal of the damages actually incurred); EEOC v. AIC Sec. Investigations, Ltd., 55 F.3d 1276, 1285, 4 AD 693 (7th Cir. 1995) (stating that the court will inquire if the award is

will not hesitate to order remittitur or a new trial.[103] In performing their review, many courts consider awards in comparable cases.[104]

C. The Entitlement to, and Calculation of, Punitive Damages

The punitive damages standard of evil motive or intent or reckless indifference to the aggrieved individual's federally protected rights may be met by evidence that establishes an intentional violation of those rights.[105] Federal law governs the determination of punitive damages under the federal civil rights laws.[106]

"monstrously excessive," rationally connected to the evidence, and roughly comparable to awards made in similar cases).

[103]*See, e.g.,* Fitzgerald v. Mountain States Tel. & Tel. Co., 68 F.3d 1257, 1266, 69 FEP 163 (10th Cir. 1995) (jury verdict of $250,000 for emotional distress damages found to be clearly excessive in sex discrimination case); Hurley v. Atlantic City Police Dep't, 933 F. Supp. 396, 424–25, 72 FEP 1828 (D.N.J. 1996) (finding jury's award of compensatory damages of $595,000 so "excessive as to shock the judicial conscience" and remitting award to $175,000); Rush v. Scott Specialty Gases, Inc., 930 F. Supp. 194, 199 (E.D. Pa. 1996) (holding that evidence offered on plaintiff's emotional distress claim did not warrant $1,000,000 jury award; defendant's motion for a new trial on damages was denied on condition that plaintiff accept a remittitur of $900,000); Stratton v. Department for the Aging, 922 F. Supp. 857, 867 (S.D.N.Y. 1996) (denying defendant's motion for new trial on condition that plaintiff consent to reduction of a clearly excessive damage verdict); Newhouse v. McCormick & Co., 910 F. Supp. 1451, 1456–59 (D. Neb. 1996) (granting a remittitur for an excessive front-pay award); Brocklehurst v. PPG Indus., Inc., 865 F. Supp. 1253, 1265–66, 66 FEP 545 (E.D. Mich. 1994) (finding that jury verdict of back pay "was clearly unsupported by the evidence" and required remittitur where plaintiff earned more from severance payment and new job than he would have received had he not been discharged).

[104]*See, e.g.,* EEOC v. AIC Sec. Investigations, Ltd., 55 F.3d 1276, 1285–86, 4 AD 693 (7th Cir. 1995) (comparing other emotional damages awards in discriminatory discharge cases to determine if $50,000 jury verdict was "roughly comparable"); Hurley v. Atlantic City Police Dep't, 933 F. Supp. 396, 423–25, 72 FEP 1828 (D.N.J. 1996) (noting that awards in discrimination cases "in the realm of $500,000 have generally involved measurable economic damages," which were not present in this case, thus warranting remittitur); Luciano v. Olsten Corp., 912 F. Supp. 663, 674, 73 FEP 221 (E.D.N.Y. 1996) (noting that emotional damages award was not so excessive as to shock the court's conscience when there is case law to support a higher award); Lightfoot v. Union Carbide Corp., 901 F. Supp. 166, 169–70, 71 FEP 269 (S.D.N.Y. 1995) (reviewing New York cases to determine that damage verdict of $750,000 was a "material deviation from the norm" and remitting to $75,000); Brocklehurst v. PPG Indus., Inc., 865 F. Supp. 1253, 1266, 66 FEP 545 (E.D. Mich. 1994) (noting that emotional damage award of $500,000 was similar to other pain and suffering awards that had previously been upheld).

[105]Barbour v. Merrill, 48 F.3d 1270, 1277, 67 FEP 369 (D.C. Cir. 1995).

[106]McKinnon v. Kwong Wah Restaurant, 83 F.3d 498, 507, 70 FEP 1037 (1st Cir. 1996) ("Because plaintiffs' claims arise out of a federal statute designed to protect federal rights, federal rules of damages control.").

One court recently attempted to set forth a standard for review of punitive damages awards based upon the Supreme Court's decisions in *BMW of North America, Inc. v. Gore*,[107] and its predecessors, *TXO Production Corp. v. Alliance Resources Corp.*[108] and *Pacific Mutual Life Insurance Co. v. Haslip*.[109] In *Rush v. Scott Specialty Gases, Inc.*,[110] the court concluded that five factors could support a reasonable award: "These are (1) the reprehensibility of the wrongful conduct, (2) the difference between the actual or potential harm suffered and the punitive award, (3) the difference between the punitive award and any potential civil penalties, (4) the effectiveness of the award in meeting its goal of deterrence and (5) the amount of guidance given the jury."

Courts generally have reviewed punitive damages awards by measuring an award's anticipated effectiveness for retribution and deterrence[111] and have frequently reduced them.[112] Punitive damages

---

[107] 116 S. Ct. 1589 (1996).
[108] 509 U.S. 443 (1993).
[109] 499 U.S. 1 (1991).
[110] 930 F. Supp. 194, 201 (E.D. Pa. 1996).
[111] EEOC v. AIC Sec. Investigations, Ltd., 55 F.3d 1276, 1287, 4 AD 693 (7th Cir. 1995) (stating that $150,000 punitive damage award was suitable and necessary to punish and deter the defendant corporation); EEOC v. Farmer Bros. Co., 31 F.3d 891, 904, 65 FEP 857 (9th Cir. 1994) ("Punitive damages are intended to punish a defendant's past misconduct and deter future wrongful acts."); Luciano v. Olsten Corp., 912 F. Supp. 663, 672-73, 73 FEP 221 (E.D.N.Y. 1996) (stating that $300,000 punitive damage award was modest and necessary to deter the large corporate defendant where ratio of punitive damages to other damages awarded was less than two to one and the wealth of the defendant was deemphasized).
[112] Honda Motor Co. v. Oberg, 512 U.S. 415 (1994) (noting that "[j]udicial review of the size of punitive damage awards has been a safeguard against excessive verdicts for as long as punitive damages have been awarded"); Emmel v. Coca-Cola Bottling Co., 95 F.3d 627, 637, 72 FEP 1811 (7th Cir. 1996) (affirming award of punitive damages reduced to Title VII cap where "ample evidence" supported the jury's verdict); Hennessy v. Penril Datacomm Networks, Inc., 69 F.3d 1344, 1355, 69 FEP 398 (7th Cir. 1995) (affirming trial court's reduction of jury verdict for punitive damages from $300,000 to $100,000, stating that Title VII's statutory cap on punitive damages should be reserved for the most egregious cases); EEOC v. AIC Sec. Investigations, Ltd., 55 F.3d 1276, 1287, 4 AD 693 (7th Cir. 1995) (stating that court would not set aside jury's award of punitive damages unless it was "certain that it exceeds what is necessary to serve the objectives of deterrence and punishment"; $150,000 punitive damage award upheld); EEOC v. Farmer Bros. Co., 31 F.3d 891, 903, 65 FEP 857 (9th Cir. 1994) (court reviews a trial court's award of an unreasonable amount of punitive damages by applying an abuse of discretion standard); Rush v. Scott Specialty Gases, Inc., 930 F. Supp. 194, 202 (E.D. Pa. 1996) (award of $3 million in punitive damages was excessive; defendant's motion for new trial denied on condition that plaintiff accept a remittitur of her punitive damages award

can be awarded pursuant to the doctrines of agency and respondeat superior liability.[113]

IV. LIQUIDATED DAMAGES

Under the ADEA, liquidated damages are mandatory for willful violations in actions against private employers,[114] while under the EPA, liquidated damages are discretionary.[115] Liquidated damages are not available in ADEA actions against the federal government.[116]

---

to $300,000); Kimzey v. Wal-Mart Stores, Inc., 907 F. Supp. 1309, 1316, 69 FEP 664, 670 (W.D. Mo. 1995) (reducing $50 million punitive damages award to $5 million after finding that the previous award was excessive); Sassaman v. Heart City Toyota, 879 F. Supp. 901, 911, 66 FEP 1230, 1235 (N.D. Ind. 1994) ("The district court may alter a jury award if it is 'monstrously excessive, born of passion and prejudice, or not rationally connected to the evidence.' ") (citing Dresser Indus., Inc. v. Gradall Co., 965 F.2d 1442, 1446 (7th Cir. 1992)); cf. Lane v. Hughes Aircraft Co., 56 Cal. App. 4th 1038, 65 Cal. Rptr. 2d 889 (1997) (in case brought under California state law with no statutory cap on punitive damages, appellate court reversed trial court's grant of judgment notwithstanding the verdict but reduced award of $40 million in punitive damages to each of two plaintiffs claiming race discrimination and retaliation to an award of $5 million and $2,830,000, respectively).

[113]Patterson v. P.H.P. Healthcare Corp., 90 F.3d 927, 942, 72 FEP 613 (5th Cir. 1996) ("Although individuals may not be held liable under Title VII unless they meet § 2000e(b) definition of 'employer,' an individual employee's actions may subject the employer to liability under agency principles."), cert. denied, 117 S. Ct. 767 (1997).

[114]Weaver v. Amoco Prod. Co., 66 F.3d 85, 88, 70 FEP 931 (5th Cir. 1995) (upholding award of liquidated damages after review of record revealed evidence of taped conversation between employee and his supervisor illustrating knowing decision to force employee's retirement); Mitchell v. Sisters of Charity, 924 F. Supp. 793, 802 (S.D. Tex. 1996) (jury finding of willfulness mandates award of liquidated damages); Moses v. KMart Corp., 905 F. Supp. 1054, 1059 (S.D. Fla. 1995) (plaintiff cannot recover both liquidated damages under the ADEA and punitive damages under the Florida Civil Rights Act; therefore, since jury found that defendant willfully violated the ADEA, the award of liquidated damages became mandatory and punitive damages were fully remitted).

[115]See, e.g., Brinkley-Obu v. Hughes Training, Inc., 36 F.3d 336, 357, 65 FEP 1840 (4th Cir. 1994) ("[A]n employer in violation of the Equal Pay Act will be liable for liquidated damages, equal to and in addition to compensatory damages, unless the employer demonstrates to the satisfaction of the court that the act or omission giving rise to such action was in good faith and that he had reasonable grounds for believing that his act or omission was not violative of the Act. Under 29 U.S.C. § 260, the district court has the discretion to decline to award liquidated damages when good faith is established."); Cody v. Private Agencies Collaborating Together, Inc., 911 F. Supp. 1, 5 (D.D.C. 1995) (stating that courts have the flexibility to deny liquidated damages awards under the EPA if they would be unfair to the employer).

[116]See, e.g., Pendas v. Runyon, 933 F. Supp. 187, 189 (N.D.N.Y. 1996) (stating that plaintiff conceded in oral argument that liquidated damages are not available

Under the ADEA, "willful" conduct may be imputed.[117]

A split among the courts continues over whether an award of liquidated damages precludes the awarding of prejudgment interest.[118]

V. Right to Jury Trial

In Title VII, ADA, § 1981, and § 1983 cases, either party may demand a jury trial where the plaintiff seeks compensatory or punitive damages.[119]

The circuits are still split on whether the determination of the amount of front-pay awards in ADEA cases is a jury question.[120]

---

to federal employees suing the federal government under the ADEA); Edwards v. Shalala, 846 F. Supp. 997, 1001 n.8, 68 FEP 1410 (N.D. Ga. 1994) ("Though liquidated damages and attorney's fees are provided for in the private-action portion of the ADEA, such relief is not available when proceeding against the federal government under § 633a."), aff'd, 64 F.3d 601, 68 FEP 1414 (11th Cir. 1995).

[117]Tompulis v. Schwartz & Freeman, 66 FEP 1544, 1546 (N.D. Ill. 1994) (fact that defendant was a law firm "is a relevant factor [as to willfulness] since law firm administrators should be more apt to have knowledge of the various laws that apply to all employment decisions"). Cf. Wiehoff v. GTE Directories Corp., 61 F.3d 588, 593–94, 68 FEP 639 (8th Cir. 1995) (the difference between a willful violation and a basic ADEA violation is in the state of mind and in the remedy, not in the conduct).

[118]Mitchell v. Sisters of Charity, 924 F. Supp. 793, 805 (S.D. Tex. 1996) (where liquidated damages are awarded, a court may not award prejudgment interest on either the back-pay or liquidated damages award); Inks v. Health Care Distribs. of Ind., Inc., 901 F. Supp. 1403, 1407, 73 FEP 643 (N.D. Ind. 1995) ("prejudgment interest is not awardable when liquidated damages are awarded"); Braverman v. Penobscot Shoe Co., 859 F. Supp. 596, 601, 3 AD 847 (D. Me. 1994) (agreeing with defendants' assertion "that a plaintiff may not recover both liquidated damages on an ADEA claim and prejudgment interest on a backpay award"). Contra Starceski v. Westinghouse Elec. Corp., 54 F.3d 1089, 1102–03, 67 FEP 1184 (3d Cir. 1995) (prejudgment interest is not barred by an award of liquidated damages since liquidated damages are punitive in nature and prejudgment interest seeks to compensate the plaintiff).

[119]E.g., Del Monte Dunes v. City of Monterey, 95 F.3d 1422, 1423 (9th Cir. 1996) (jury trial under § 1983); Oswald v. LaRoche Chems., Inc., 162 F.R.D. 283, 284–85 (E.D. La. 1995) (plaintiff entitled to jury trial on claims for compensatory and punitive damages under ADA). Cf. Landgraf v. USI Film Prods., 114 S. Ct. 1483, 1488, 64 FEP 820 (1994) (Civil Rights Act of 1991 provisions for compensatory damages and jury trial do not apply retroactively to Title VII case pending when statute was enacted); accord Sena v. Denver Sch. Dist., 902 F. Supp. 218, 219–20, 69 FEP 385 (D. Colo. 1995) (CRA of 1991 provisions for compensatory damages and jury trial do not apply to Title VII case where events that give rise to the claim occurred prior to the effective date of the Act).

[120]E.g., Downes v. Volkswagen of Am., Inc., 41 F.3d 1132, 1141, 69 FEP 11 (7th Cir. 1994) (rejecting suggestion that jury plays role in determining amount of front pay). Contra Wells v. New Cherokee Corp., 58 F.3d 233, 237, 68 FEP 284 (6th Cir.

VI. Defenses to Monetary Relief

A. The Mixed-Motive Defense

In cases arising before the effective date of the Civil Rights Act of 1991, courts could not award damages, or any other relief, if an employer proved that it would have taken the same action regardless of its impermissible discriminatory motivation.[121] Under the Civil Rights Act of 1991, the employer can no longer avoid liability by proving that it would have made the same decision for nondiscriminatory reasons; however, such proof will limit plaintiff's remedies.[122]

One court has analyzed a retaliation claim in a mixed-motive case under the *Price Waterhouse* standard despite passage of the Civil Rights Act of 1991.[123] In *Tanca v. Nordberg*,[124] the First Circuit considered whether § 107 of the Civil Rights Act of 1991, "which explicitly appl[ies] only to discrimination claims (and which [was] meant to partially overrule *Price Waterhouse*), also appl[ies] to claims of retaliation."[125] The *Tanca* court held that it does not and that the *Price Waterhouse* rule applies to retaliation claims.

1995) (determination of the amount of front pay is a jury question, but determination of the propriety of front pay is a matter for the court that ordinarily must precede submission of the case to the jury).

[121]Smith v. F.W. Morse & Co., Inc., 76 F.3d 413, 419 n.3 & 420–22, 69 FEP 1687 (1st Cir. 1996) (*Price Waterhouse* framework applicable where events that formed the basis of plaintiff's claim occurred prior to the effective date of the Civil Rights Act of 1991); *accord* Bristow v. Drake St., Inc., 41 F.3d 345, 419 n.3 & 421, 66 FEP 739 (7th Cir. 1994); Chenault v. United States Postal Serv., 37 F.3d 535, 536, 3 AD 1185 (9th Cir. 1994); Preston v. Virginia ex rel. New River Community College, 31 F.3d 203, 207, 65 FEP 877 (4th Cir. 1994).

[122]*E.g.,* Fuller v. Phipps, 67 F.3d 1137, 1142, 69 FEP 111 (4th Cir. 1995) (Civil Rights Act of 1991 overruled *Price Waterhouse* to the extent that an employer can no longer avoid liability by proving that it would have made the same decision for nondiscriminatory reasons; such proof limits plaintiff's remedies); Russell v. Microdyne Corp., 65 F.3d 1229, 1237, 68 FEP 1602 (4th Cir. 1995) (same).

[123]Tanca v. Nordberg, 98 F.3d 680, 72 FEP 166 (1st Cir. 1996); *cf.* Veprinsky v. Fluor Daniel, Inc., 87 F.3d 881, 893, 71 FEP 170 (7th Cir. 1996) (applying *Price Waterhouse* to retaliation claim arising after effective date of the Civil Rights Act of 1991 without addressing the impact of § 107 of the 1991 CRA). *Contra* Woodson v. Scott Paper Co., 898 F. Supp. 298, 307, 68 FEP 947 (E.D. Pa. 1995) (applying 1991 CRA to Title VII retaliation claim: "The legislative intention to overturn *Price Waterhouse v. Hopkins* is clear . . . . [T]he amendment does not limit itself to a *Price Waterhouse*-type of mixed motives case.").

[124]98 F.3d 680, 72 FEP 166 (1st Cir. 1996).
[125]*Id.*

In *Tanca*, the plaintiff, a white male, was a long-term employee of defendant Massachusetts Department of Employment (DET). After several minority employees were promoted into positions for which Tanca had applied, Tanca complained to high-level DET managers. He believed that he was better qualified than the promoted employees and that their promotions were due to reverse discrimination. When a position became available in DET's Hyannis office, where Tanca worked, he applied. Instead of offering him the Hyannis position, however, DET offered him a similar position in New Bedford. Tanca sued DET, alleging that it had retaliated against him for making his complaints—a protected activity—by refusing him the Hyannis position and offering him the New Bedford one. Because of the distance between Hyannis, where Tanca lived, and New Bedford, he described the offered position as significantly less desirable. DET maintained that the decision was based solely on legitimate concerns regarding Tanca's management abilities and DET's ability to supervise Tanca in New Bedford.[126]

A jury found that Tanca had engaged in good faith activity protected under Title VII, that the activity was a motivating factor in DET's decision (and thus that DET had retaliated against Tanca), but that Tanca would not have received the Hyannis position even absent the illegitimate consideration. The court then granted defendant's motion for judgment as a matter of law, holding that *Price Waterhouse* governed the parties' dispute and that, under that case, because the jury found that DET would have reached the same decision absent any retaliatory motives, DET was not liable.[127] On appeal, the First Circuit focused on the statutory language:

> As always, we begin our analysis with the plain language of the statute. By doing so, we immediately encounter Tanca's fundamental problem: as a retaliation claim, his suit was brought under section 2000-e(3), and although section 107(b) specifically addresses section 107(a), it makes no mention of section 2000-e(3). Indeed, section 107(b) plainly states that it applies to "a claim in which an individual proves a violation under § 2000e-2(m) [107(a)]." Section 107(a), in turn, specifies that "an unlawful employment practice is established when the complaining party demonstrates that race, color, religion, sex, or national origin was a motivating

---

[126]*Id.* at 681.
[127]*Id.*

factor." There is no reference to section 2000-e(3) or retaliation claims in either provision. As the district court found, "nothing in the 1991 Act would appear to change any rule with respect to retaliation claims which existed prior to its enactment." . . . On its face, then, the statute seems to express an intent not to preclude application of *Price Waterhouse* in the context of mixed-motive retaliation cases.[128]

In so holding, the First Circuit in *Tanca* noted that "[w]e are conscious that our decision in this case goes against those of some federal courts that have looked at this issue."[129] However, the court concluded, an examination of these cases "reveals that, although all of them would apply § 107(b) to Title VII mixed-motive retaliation claims, and some of them examined the legislative history in drawing that conclusion, none of them weighed the plain language of the statute prior to borrowing the provision."[130]

B. Conformity With Government Rules and Regulations

In *Plott v. General Motors Corp.*,[131] the Sixth Circuit considered GM's defense to the plaintiff's reverse discrimination claim under Title VII based on GM's adoption of an EEOC conciliation agreement setting forth minority and female participation goals for apprenticeship openings.[132] In the year following adoption of the conciliation agreement, the EEOC sent GM a letter stating, in pertinent part, that

[i]t is the opinion of the Commission that any action or omission of General Motors Corporation . . ., or any of [its] officers, agents

---

[128]*Id.* at 682–83 (citations and footnotes omitted) (citing Riess v. Dalton, 845 F. Supp. 742, 744, 72 FEP 577 (S.D. Cal. 1993) (rejecting application of § 107(b) to Title VII mixed-motive retaliation claim as contrary to the plain meaning of the statute)).

[129]*Id.* at 684 (citing Beinlich v. Curry Dev., Inc., 54 F.3d 772 (4th Cir. 1995) (table)); Woodson v. Scott Paper Co., 898 F. Supp. 298, 304–06, 68 FEP 947 (E.D. Pa. 1995); Hall v. City of Brawley, 887 F. Supp. 1333, 1345, 68 FEP 1343 (S.D. Cal. 1995) (court ordered parties to brief issue of whether defendant's liability on plaintiff's retaliation claim was barred by *Price Waterhouse;* without analyzing statutory language, the court held that the 1991 Act does not preclude liability but limits damages).

[130]98 F.3d at 684. The *Tanca* court also observed that "the only case we found that examined the statute under traditional statutory interpretation methods supports our conclusions here." *Id.* (citing Riess v. Dalton, 845 F. Supp. 742, 744–45, 72 FEP 577 (S.D. Cal. 1993)).

[131]71 F.3d 1190, 69 FEP 826 (6th Cir. 1995), *cert. denied,* 116 S. Ct. 1546 (1996).

[132]*Id.* at 1193.

or employees, that is or shall be taken in a good faith attempt to comply with the affirmative action or other provisions of the Conciliation Agreement . . . will not constitute a violation of any of the provisions of Title VII.[133]

The court held "[t]he letter met all the requirements of 29 CFR § 1601.93 (1995) and therefore qualified as an EEOC opinion under section 713(b)."[134]

C. Equitable Defenses to Back-Pay and Front-Pay Relief

1. Laches

In one case a court applied laches to a preadministrative filing delay in order to bar the subsequent lawsuit but later vacated its opinion and held that laches could not be applied when the charge was timely under the express statute of limitations.[135]

2. Good Faith

Reliance on state law is not a defense to federal law liability when the state law conflicts with the federal law.[136]

---

[133]*Id.* at 1194.
[134]*Id.*
[135]Ashley v. Boyle's Famous Corned Beef Co., 48 F.3d 1051, 1054–55, 67 FEP 208 (8th Cir.) ("the same rationale supporting the laches defense for delays following administrative filing, applies equally as strong to delays prior to the administrative filing. The same potential prejudice to the defendant, e.g., loss of witnesses or evidence in support of a position, failing witness memory, etc., can occur regardless of whether the delay is before or after an administrative charge is made. In fact, we are inclined to agree with Boyle's that application of the laches doctrine may make more sense in pre-charge delay because once a charge has been filed with the EEOC, the company is at least put on notice that it is facing a claim. Without an administrative charge being filed, the defendant is wholly lacking in notice"; holding that although "no amount of time is per se unreasonable," here six-year delay between time that employer classified employee's position as nonunion and resisted allowing female workers to become union members and time that employee filed administrative charge with the EEOC was unreasonable and defendant was prejudiced by the delay, during which two key defense witnesses died), *opinion vacated on reh'g en banc,* 66 F.3d 164, 167–70, 68 FEP 1261 (1995) (rejecting laches defense where claim was timely filed under the continuing violation doctrine as a challenge to an ongoing practice, and holding that "separation of power principles dictate that federal courts not apply laches to bar a federal statutory claim that is timely filed under an express statutory federal statute of limitations").
[136]*E.g.,* Quinones v. City of Evanston, 58 F.3d 275, 280, 69 FEP 791 (7th Cir. 1995) (invalidating state law providing that local government employees are ineligible to receive pension benefits if hired at age 35 or older as in conflict with ADEA);

3. Unclean Hands

Unclean hands again was rejected as a defense to Title VII back-pay liability in *McKennon v. Nashville Banner Publishing Co.*[137]

VII. Individual Back-Pay Claims in Collective Proceedings

A. Determining Individual Back-Pay Damages

Uncertainty in the calculation of back-pay awards continues to be resolved against the employer.[138]

1. When Did the Period of Liability Commence?

The rationale behind the "single filing rule" is the belief that it would be wasteful for numerous employees with the same grievances to file identical complaints with the EEOC.[139]

2. How Many Available Positions Did Class Members Lose?

Class members may not receive back-pay relief for alleged discrimination in filling positions that were never open in the first place.[140]

United States v. Board of Trustees of Ill. State Univ., 944 F. Supp. 714, 722, 72 FEP 382 (C.D. Ill. 1996) (fact that voluntary affirmative action program was established pursuant to state law held no defense, since the program violated Title VII).

[137]115 S. Ct. 879, 885, 66 FEP 1192 (1995) ("Equity's maxim that a suitor who engaged in his own reprehensible conduct in the course of the transaction at issue must be denied equitable relief because of unclean hands, a rule which in conventional formulation operated *in limine* to bar the suitor from invoking the aid of the equity court, has not been applied where Congress authorizes broad equitable relief to serve important national policies. We have rejected the unclean hands defense 'where a private suit serves important public purposes.' ").

[138]*E.g.,* EEOC v. Accurate Mech. Contractors, Inc., 863 F. Supp. 828, 836 (E.D. Wis. 1994) ("There are a few uncertainties in the calculation of [plaintiff] Mrs. Johnson's backpay award, and they will be resolved against [defendant] employer Accurate.").

[139]EEOC v. Wilson Metal Casket Co., 24 F.3d 836, 840, 64 FEP 1402 (6th Cir. 1994) ("[W]here a substantially related non-filed claim arises out of the same time frame as a timely filed claim, the complainant need not satisfy Title VII's filing requirement to recover.").

[140]*E.g.,* Bishopp v. District of Columbia, 57 F.3d 1088, 1092–93 (D.C. Cir. 1995) (because a fire marshal position never opened, "plaintiffs did not, and indeed could not, allege illegal discrimination in the filling of that position").

3. Which Class Members Experienced Discrimination?

Plaintiff class members are not entitled to an award of damages if an employer can show that only one member of their class would have received a promotion absent discrimination.[141]

Courts continue to emphasize that the failure of class members to apply for job openings, promotions, or transfers may not be fatal to their claim for relief.[142]

Courts are still split on the level of burden (either by clear and convincing evidence or by a preponderance of evidence) that an employer must satisfy to demonstrate that a plaintiff would not have been hired even if the process had been fair.[143]

4. What Deductions Should Be Taken From Each Class Member's Damages?

In a Title VII action, rejecting an offer of reinstatement may toll accrual of back-pay liability.[144] Similarly, evidence of availability of

---

[141]*Id.* at 1093 ("Here, where only one position was filled in a discriminatory manner, and the district court was able to conclude that another member of the plaintiffs' class would have received the promotion absent discrimination," then the "remaining class members are entitled to nothing.").

[142]*E.g.,* Winbush v. Iowa, 66 F.3d 1471, 1481, 69 FEP 1348 (8th Cir. 1995) (court noted that the reason the class members did not apply for promotions was "either that they did not know how or when to apply or that they were led to believe that applying would do no good"); EEOC v. O & G Spring & Wire Forms Specialty Co., 38 F.3d 872, 880, 65 FEP 1823 (7th Cir. 1994) (back-pay award for hiring shortfall included lost wages and benefits for the number of positions that would have been filled by African-Americans absent the discriminatory word-of-mouth recruitment practice); Eldred v. Consolidated Freightways Corp., 898 F. Supp. 928, 938, 71 FEP 33 (D. Mass. 1995) ("failure to apply formally for a job opening when there is no formal application process will not preclude a Title VII plaintiff from establishing a prima facie case, as long as the plaintiff made a reasonable attempt to convey her interest in the job to the employer").

[143]*E.g.,* EEOC v. O & G Spring & Wire Forms Specialty Co., 38 F.3d 872, 878, 65 FEP 1823 (7th Cir. 1994) (employer may rebut prima facie case of discrimination by preponderance of evidence). *Cf.* Shipley v. Dugan, 874 F. Supp. 933, 942 (S.D. Ind. 1995) (employer must prove by clear and convincing evidence that a job applicant would not have been hired even in the absence of discrimination).

[144]EEOC v. Accurate Mech. Contractors, Inc., 863 F. Supp. 828, 835 (E.D. Wis. 1994) (accrual of back-pay liability is tolled when a Title VII claimant rejects an offer of the job that he originally sought; however, reinstatement offer must involve a job with virtually identical promotional opportunities, compensation, job responsibilities, working conditions, and status). *Cf.* Odima v. Westin Tucson Hotel, 53 F.3d 1484, 1496, 67 FEP 1222 (9th Cir. 1994) (back-pay award extended beyond the date of employee's voluntary resignation because the employee "was preparing to enter an entirely different career" with the same employer).

jobs in the area may support a finding that a plaintiff failed to mitigate his or her damages.[145]

In calculating a back-pay award, most courts hold that unemployment and workers' compensation benefits should not be deducted from the total award.[146]

B. Dividing a Classwide Award Among Class Members

Courts have broad discretion in determining how a classwide award will be divided among class members. For example, in *EEOC v. O & G Spring & Wire Forms Specialty Co.*,[147] the court awarded approximately $380,000 in back pay to be distributed pro rata to all 451 eligible class members. The eligible class members were those individuals who applied or would have applied for employment with O & G. The back-pay award was determined by multiplying the total wages and benefits of the employees hired by O & G (87 in total) times the percentage of the African-American hiring shortfall (17 out of 87) times the percentage of the African-American unemployment rate in the relevant market (22 percent). (This adjustment using the unemployment rate was made in order to approximate the proper offset to recovery for mitigation of damages, since all but 22 percent of the plaintiffs could be presumed to have found comparable entry-level jobs.)

---

[145] EEOC v. Farmers Bros. Co., 31 F.3d 891, 906, 65 FEP 857 (9th Cir. 1994) (employer surveyed 148 companies located near plaintiff's residence to demonstrate that there were substantially comparable jobs readily available and thus plaintiff failed to mitigate her damages when she stopped seeking employment).

[146] Thurman v. Yellow Freight Sys., Inc., 90 F.3d 1160, 1170–71, 72 FEP 657 (6th Cir. 1996) (unemployment and workers' compensation benefits are paid to carry out policies of the state and thus should not be deducted from back-pay award in an employment discrimination case). *See* discussion at Section I.B.3.a *supra*.

[147] 38 F.3d 872, 880, 65 FEP 1823 (7th Cir. 1994).

Chapter 42

ATTORNEY'S FEES

I. The Prevailing Plaintiff's Right to Attorney's Fees

B. The General Fee Rule for Prevailing Plaintiffs

1. Who Is a Prevailing Plaintiff?

a. The Relevance of Minimal Success. The standard for determining "prevailing party" status under the civil rights statutes continues to be whether the plaintiff has succeeded on any significant issue in the litigation achieving some of the benefit sought in bringing the suit, such that there has been a resolution of the dispute in a way that materially changes the legal relationship between the plaintiff and the defendant.[1] Courts generally find that this standard has been met where the plaintiff has obtained either an award of greater than "nominal" damages[2] or a judgment

---

[1] Farrar v. Hobby, 506 U.S. 103, 60 FEP 633 (1992); Texas State Teachers Ass'n v. Garland Indep. Sch. Dist., 489 U.S. 782, 49 FEP 465 (1989); *see also* Odima v. Westin Tucson Hotel, 53 F.3d 1484, 1499, 67 FEP 1222 (9th Cir. 1995) (plaintiff is prevailing party where he prevails on his claim that he was discriminated against in his employment because of his race and national origin and is awarded reinstatement, back pay, compensatory damages under § 1981, and prejudgment interest); Alexander v. Gerhardt Enters., Inc., 40 F.3d 187, 194, 68 FEP 595 (7th Cir. 1994) (plaintiff, who won a judgment that she had been discharged in retaliation for complaining about discriminatory workplace behavior and was awarded $10,000 in back wages, was a prevailing party who had obtained at least some relief on the merits); Dalal v. Alliant Techsystems, Inc., 927 F. Supp. 1374, 1381 (D. Colo. 1996) (plaintiff, who succeeded on ADEA claim and was awarded over $36,000 in damages, was a prevailing party because the legal relationship between the parties had changed following the judgment); Hannon v. Chater, 900 F. Supp. 1276, 1283 (N.D. Cal. 1995) (plaintiff, who succeeded on a significant issue through a declaratory judgment of liability for being disparately treated on the basis of gender and who materially altered the parties' relationship through an injunctive order forcing the defendant to consider his candidacy for the position sought, was a prevailing party).

[2] *E.g.,* Bridges v. Eastman Kodak Co., 102 F.3d 56, 72 FEP 948 (2d Cir. 1996) (prevailing Title VII plaintiff who was awarded no damages for failure to mitigate was nevertheless entitled to attorney's fees since she obtained damages under related state court action); Caban-Wheeler v. Elsea, 71 F.3d 837, 842, 69 FEP 1193

vindicating important personal or public constitutional or statutory rights.³

However, in *DiPietro v. Runyon*,⁴ the court found that a plaintiff who was *not* awarded *any* damages on his retaliation claim, but who obtained a jury finding that retaliation was a factor in but one of several instances of challenged conduct by the employer, had not surpassed the minimum prevailing party threshold established in *Farrar*.⁵ The court reasoned that the jury's refusal to award damages left the plaintiff with neither a judgment to enforce nor a mechanism through which to modify the defendant's behavior toward him.⁶

Similarly, in *Frey v. Alldata Corp.*,⁷ the court ruled that a plaintiff who obtained a jury verdict that his employer had failed to reasonably accommodate his disability under the ADA and an injunction requiring the defendant to create a procedure to deal with future accommodation requests, but who failed to recover any monetary damages, was not a prevailing party. The court acknowledged that the jury verdict of a failure to reasonably accommodate was

---

(11th Cir. 1996) (plaintiff who obtained a valid judgment on her national origin and race discrimination claims and was awarded $1 in nominal damages and $100,000 in punitive damages was a prevailing party under *Farrar*); Schofield v. Trustees of Univ. of Pa., 919 F. Supp. 821, 825–26 (E.D. Pa. 1996) (plaintiff met *Farrar* standard where she was awarded $40,000 in compensatory damages on her discrimination claims); *compare* Pino v. Locascio, 101 F.3d 235, 72 FEP 875 (2d Cir. 1996) (no attorney's fees or costs should have been awarded when plaintiff in sexual harassment case recovered only nominal damages of $1).

³*E.g.,* Koopman v. Water Dist. No. 1 of Johnson County, Kan., 41 F.3d 1417, 1420–21 (10th Cir. 1994) (plaintiff is a prevailing party in case raising a denial of due process claim, despite only a nominal award of damages, where the district court's judgment in her favor had significant implications by ensuring that other public employees would be guaranteed constitutionally adequate pretermination and post-termination hearings), *cert. denied*, 116 S. Ct. 420 (1995); Pederson v. Louisiana State Univ., 912 F. Supp. 892, 927–28 (M.D. La. 1996) (plaintiffs in Title IX action against university are prevailing parties, despite the denial of an award of monetary damages, where the awarded declaratory and injunctive relief requiring the university to immediately establish and accommodate a Division I women's fast pitch softball team vindicates important public rights); Johnson v. Lafayette Fire Fighters' Ass'n, 857 F. Supp. 1292, 1296–97 (N.D. Ind. 1994) (nonmember firefighters, who won a judgment that the union's procedures for the collection of agency fees from them violated their constitutional rights, achieved success on a significant issue serving a great public purpose and were thus prevailing parties), *aff'd*, 51 F.3d 726 (7th Cir. 1995).

⁴914 F. Supp. 714 (D. Mass. 1996).

⁵*Id.* at 716.

⁶*Id.*

⁷895 F. Supp. 221, 4 AD 1627 (E.D. Wis. 1995).

success on a significant issue in the litigation but nevertheless found that the jury's failure to award damages did not change the legal relationship of the parties as required under *Farrar*.[8] Moreover, because the plaintiff no longer worked for the defendant, the court found that the award of injunctive relief did not, as required under *Farrar*, accomplish the required change in the defendant's relationship to the plaintiff.[9]

Following the Supreme Court's directive in *Farrar*,[10] courts have also continued to construe most challenges based on the degree of relief actually obtained by the plaintiff as more properly directed to the *amount* of the attorney's fees award rather than to the plaintiff's *entitlement* to an award.[11]

"Mixed-motive" cases present an interesting dilemma in terms of awarding attorney's fees to a prevailing plaintiff. A "mixed-motive" case may involve a plaintiff who succeeds in proving that the defendant based an employment decision in part on an impermissible factor (such as race or sex), but who receives no monetary damages because the defendant demonstrates that it would have made the same decision absent the impermissible factor. Following the changes to Title VII accomplished by the Civil Rights Act of 1991,[12] courts have

---

[8]*Id.* at 225.

[9]*Id.*

[10]*See* 506 U.S. at 114.

[11]*E.g.,* Hetzel v. County of Prince William, 89 F.3d 169, 173–74, 71 FEP 520 (4th Cir.) (fact that the plaintiff received only an insignificant portion of the relief originally requested, failed to prevail on the most consequential claims, and will receive only a "pittance" of her original damages request goes to amount of fees properly awarded, not plaintiff's entitlement to an award of fees), *cert. denied,* 117 S. Ct. 584, 72 FEP 992 (1996); Koopman v. Water Dist. No. 1 of Johnson County, Kan., 41 F.3d 1417, 1421 (10th Cir. 1994) (where only nominal damages were obtained in conjunction with the vindication of a constitutional right, court will focus on reducing rather than denying the award of attorney's fees); Dalal v. Alliant Techsystems, Inc., 927 F. Supp. 1374, 1380 (D. Colo. 1996) (fact that the plaintiff recovered only $36,000 judgment following his rejection of $150,000 offer of judgment affects only amount of fee to be awarded, not the plaintiff's entitlement to a fee award); Pederson v. Louisiana State Univ., 912 F. Supp. 892, 928 (M.D. La. 1996) (court notes that the degree of change in the relationship between the plaintiff and the defendant following a judgment "does not control the *award* of attorney's fees, rather, impacts the *amount* of attorney's fees *awarded*") (emphasis in original).

[12]Section 107 of the Civil Rights Act of 1991 in part overruled the Supreme Court's decision in *Price Waterhouse v. Hopkins,* 490 U.S. 228, 49 FEP 954 (1989), and established that a violation of Title VII does in fact occur where an impermissible characteristic "was a motivating factor for any employment practice . . . ." *See* 42 U.S.C. § 2000e-2(m).

struggled to harmonize the *Farrar* Court's skepticism toward awarding attorney's fees where no actual damages were recovered with their post-1991 discretionary Title VII authority to award attorney's fees to the plaintiff who has prevailed on a "mixed-motive" claim even though monetary damages are not, by statute, available.[13] At least one court has stated that the more "restrictive" *Farrar* standards simply do not apply to these "mixed-motive" cases following the 1991 amendments to Title VII because "this statutory language prevails over the general case law set forth in *Farrar* for determining who is a prevailing party for purposes of an attorney fee award under 42 U.S.C. § 1988."[14] However, other courts, focusing on the permissive language in § 2000e-5(g)(2)(B), § 2000e-5(k),[15] and § 1988,[16] which states that the court "in its discretion *may* allow" prevailing parties to recover reasonable attorney's fees, have concluded that the *Farrar* standards also apply to a court's analysis of a successful plaintiff's prevailing party status in a "mixed-motive" case.[17] Explaining its conclusion that the *Farrar* standards are applicable to fee requests in "mixed-motive" cases under § 2000e-5(g)(2)(B), the Fourth Circuit, in *Sheppard v. Riverview Nursing Center, Inc.,* stated:

> In appropriate cases, for instance, courts should consider the reasons why injunctive relief was or was not granted, or the extent and nature of any declaratory relief. Moreover, *Farrar's* concern was not only with whether the extent of recovery accords with the amount of attorney's fees. The decision suggested a more general

---

[13]Under amended Title VII, the court "may grant . . . attorney's fees and costs demonstrated to be directly attributable only to the pursuit of a [mixed-motive] claim under section 2000e-2(m)." 42 U.S.C. § 20003-5(g)(2)(B).

[14]Hall v. City of Brawley, 887 F. Supp. 1333, 1346 n.5, 68 FEP 1343 (S.D. Cal. 1995).

[15]Section 2000e-5(k) provides, in pertinent part, that "the court, in its discretion, may allow the prevailing party . . . a reasonable attorney's fee as a part of the costs . . . ." 42 U.S.C. § 2000e-5(k).

[16]Section 1988 provides, in pertinent part, that: "the court, in its discretion, may allow the prevailing party . . . a reasonable attorney's fee as a part of the costs . . . ." 42 U.S.C. § 1988.

[17]Sheppard v. Riverview Nursing Ctr., Inc., 88 F.3d 1332, 1335–37, 71 FEP 218 (4th Cir.) (court remands case to district court to reconsider fee award where district court had erroneously concluded that fees were mandatory under § 2000e-5(g)(2)(B) and without regard to *Farrar*), *cert. denied,* 117 S. Ct. 483, 72 FEP 992 (1996); Snell v. Reno Hilton Resort, 930 F. Supp. 1428, 1431–32 (D. Nev. 1996) (court reduces requested attorney's fees by 50% to recognize policy objectives of § 2000e-5(g)(2)(B) and the degree of success considerations enunciated in *Farrar*); Hannon v. Chater, 900 F. Supp. 1276, 1282 n.19 (N.D. Cal. 1995) (court states that standards are the same for all three attorney's fees provisions: § 1988, § 2000e-5(k), and § 2000e-5(G)(2)(B)).

proportionality consideration as well: whether the public purposes served by resolving the dispute justifies the recovery of fees.

* * *

Such an analysis should apply here. By definition, an illicit factor will have played some role in cases subject to § 2000e-5(g)(2)(B). *See* 42 U.S.C. § 2000e-2(m). But within that category of cases, there are large differences. Some mixed-motive cases will evidence a widespread or intolerable animus on the part of a defendant; others will illustrate primarily the plaintiff's unacceptable conduct which, by definition, will have justified the action taken by the defendant. The statute allows the district court to distinguish among cases that in reality are quite different.[18]

Finally, courts have also applied the *Farrar* standards to interim claims for fees following the granting of temporary or preliminary injunctive relief, again basing the decision concerning the plaintiff's eligibility for an award of fees on the degree of relief obtained.[19]

b. The Attorney's Entitlement to Fees. Courts continue to find that a lawyer who represents himself or herself in a successful civil rights action may not recover attorney's fees, no matter what statutory authority is relied upon.[20]

c. The Forum. With respect to claims for attorney's fees incurred for work on administrative proceedings in connection with

---

[18]Sheppard v. Riverview Nursing Ctr., Inc., 88 F.3d 1332, 1336, 71 FEP 218 (4th Cir. 1996).

[19]*Compare* Scelsa v. City Univ. of N.Y., 827 F. Supp. 1073, 1075–76, 71 FEP 707 (S.D.N.Y. 1993) (plaintiff, who achieved a preliminary injunction keeping both the institute that he ran and his teaching position in place for the upcoming school year, as well as an order prohibiting discrimination against Italian-Americans pending trial, was a prevailing party under *Farrar* because he modified the defendant's behavior in a significant way to his benefit, even though that interim success was later negated by a loss on the merits at trial) *with* NAACP Detroit Branch v. DPOA, 46 F.3d 528, 531, 66 FEP 1569 (6th Cir. 1995) (plaintiffs, who obtained a preliminary injunction preventing the imminent lapse of contractual recall rights pending a full trial on the merits, were not prevailing parties simply by virtue of that order; plaintiffs ultimately lost their challenge to prevent the lapse of the contractual recall rights provision at issue and no officer was returned to work because of the temporary preservation of the contractual recall right in question). *See* Section I.H in the Main Edition for a fuller discussion of the permissibility of attorney's fees awards for the plaintiff's interim success.

[20]*E.g.,* Hannon v. Chater, 900 F. Supp. 1276, 1284 n.23 (N.D. Cal. 1995) (Title VII); Roepsch v. Bentsen, 846 F. Supp. 1363, 1370 (E.D. Wis. 1994) (ADEA).

court actions to enforce the civil rights laws covered by Title VII, the ADA, and § 1988, the key factor determining whether such fees may be awarded to the prevailing party continues to be whether the work on administrative proceedings was necessary to, or an integral part of, the civil rights action.[21] In a slightly different twist, the court, in *DiRussa v. Dean Witter Reynolds, Inc.,*[22] refused to vacate a security industry arbitrator's denial of an award of attorney's fees to a successful ADEA claimant as a "manifest disregard of the law," despite the clearly mandatory nature of the right to attorney's fees for a prevailing plaintiff under the ADEA. The court reasoned that the ADEA's statutory entitlement to attorney's fees for a prevailing plaintiff was not "capable of being readily and instantly perceived" by the average NASD securities industry arbitrator, and noted that the plaintiff's counsel had failed to make any mention to the arbitrator of the plaintiff's entitlement to fees under the statutory language of the ADEA.[23]

2. Discretion in Denying Attorney's Fees

Courts in civil rights suits continue to reject a wide variety of claims that "special circumstances" warrant a complete denial of attorney's fees to the prevailing plaintiff, including: (1) claims that the plaintiff failed to engage in meaningful settlement discussions[24]; (2) claims that the case was "simple" or could be "routinely handled"[25];

---

[21]*Compare* Spradley v. Notami Hosps. of Fla., Inc., 892 F. Supp. 1459, 1463 (M.D. Fla. 1995) (court approves award of fees for work before Florida Commission on Human Relations to prevailing plaintiff, where filing of complaint with state administrative agency is prerequisite to federal court suit under ADEA) and Stair v. Lehigh Valley Carpenters, 855 F. Supp. 90, 66 FEP 1502, 1504 (E.D. Pa.) (same—Title VII), *aff'd*, 43 F.3d 1463 (3d Cir. 1994) *with* Castle v. Bentsen, 872 F. Supp. 1062, 1067, 66 FEP 1498 (D.D.C. 1995) (time spent by the plaintiff's attorney to prepare for an administrative hearing that the plaintiff canceled and in an attempt to bar defense counsel during the administrative proceedings is not compensable; time was spent on matters unrelated to the issues in the litigation and did not in any way contribute to the litigation) and Williams v. Secretary of the Navy, 853 F. Supp. 66, 69, 64 FEP 1709 (E.D.N.Y. 1994) (court refused to award fees for time spent solely on internal Navy Adverse Action Appeal, as those administrative proceedings were not an integral part of the plaintiff's Title VII action).

[22]936 F. Supp. 104, 71 FEP 1002 (S.D.N.Y. 1996).

[23]*Id.* at 104–05.

[24]*E.g.,* Schofield v. Trustees of Univ. of Pa., 919 F. Supp. 821, 827 n.2 (E.D. Pa. 1996).

[25]*E.g.,* Jackson v. Philadelphia Hous. Auth., 858 F. Supp. 464, 471 (E.D. Pa. 1994).

(3) claims that the attorney's fees requested exceed the amount of damages awarded on the merits[26]; and (4) claims that the plaintiff failed to take into account his or her limited degree of success and made a "grossly excessive" fee request.[27]

However, courts do, on occasion, find sufficient "special circumstances" to warrant the complete denial of an award of attorney's fees to the prevailing plaintiff. For example, in *DiPietro v. Runyon*,[28] the court stated that the absence of an attorney's detailed, contemporaneous time records would, in egregious cases, warrant a complete disallowance of fees.[29] In addition, in *Mindler v. Clayton County, Georgia*,[30] the court found that the plaintiff's untimely request for an award of attorney's fees in the amount of $120,000, filed 45 days after the time had expired for the defendant to appeal the jury's $49,000 verdict for the plaintiff, was a "special circumstance" warranting the complete denial of an award of attorney's fees. The court reasoned that the untimely request for fees unduly prejudiced the defendant because, had the defendant been aware he was paying a judgment of $169,000 rather than $49,000, he might well have chosen to appeal that judgment.[31]

D. Awards to Prevailing Plaintiffs in Suits Against the Federal Government

Courts continue to split over the rationale for allowing prevailing plaintiffs to recover attorney's fees against the federal government

---

[26]*E.g.*, Dalal v. Alliant Techsystems, Inc., 927 F. Supp. 1374, 1382 (D. Colo. 1996) (fact that the plaintiff ultimately obtained judgment of only $36,000 was not sufficient to warrant a complete denial of a request for fees exceeding $134,000); Abrams v. Lightolier, Inc., 50 F.3d 1204, 1222, 67 FEP 543 (3d Cir. 1995) (fact that fee request of $546,000 exceeded damages award of $474,000 was not sufficient to warrant complete denial of fees to prevailing plaintiff).

[27]*E.g.*, St. Louis Fire Fighters Ass'n v. St. Louis, Missouri, 96 F.3d 323, 331–32, 71 FEP 1513 (8th Cir. 1996).

[28]914 F. Supp. 714 (D. Mass. 1996). The *DiPietro* court based its denial of attorney's fees primarily on the fact that plaintiff achieved only a bare minimum of success in the case. The plaintiff's claims of race and national origin discrimination were dismissed on summary judgment, and the jury found that retaliation was a motivating factor in only one of several challenged actions by the employer and awarded no damages. Because the plaintiff did not materially alter his legal relationship with the defendant, he was not considered a "prevailing party." *Id.* at 916–17.

[29]*Id.* at 717.

[30]864 F. Supp. 1329 (N.D. Ga. 1994), *aff'd*, 63 F.3d 1113 (11th Cir. 1995).

[31]*Id.* at 1331.

in ADEA actions. Some courts hold that such a prevailing plaintiff may recover attorney's fees under the ADEA on the ground that § 633a(c) of the ADEA contains an affirmative waiver of the government's sovereign immunity.[32] Other courts find that a prevailing plaintiff may not recover attorney's fees from a federal government defendant under the ADEA, yet nevertheless conclude that an award of attorney's fees is authorized under the Equal Access to Justice Act (EAJA).[33] These courts reason that, because the statutory language of the EAJA provides for attorney's fees awards against the United States where a private litigant would be amenable to a fee award under the statute establishing the particular right of action, attorney's fee awards are proper in ADEA cases against federal government defendants because the ADEA clearly authorizes an award of attorney's fees to prevailing plaintiffs against private defendants.[34]

I. Awards to Prevailing Plaintiffs for Services on Appeal

An appellate court has granted attorney's fees to a prevailing plaintiff for work defending an appeal even when the case is remanded for review of an original award for front pay.[35]

J. Awards to Prevailing Plaintiffs for Time Spent on the Fee Claim

Courts continue to award fees for time spent preparing an attorney's fee application.[36]

---

[32]*Compare* Nowd v. Rubin, 76 F.3d 25, 27–28, 69 FEP 1587 (1st Cir. 1996) (ADEA does not authorize award of attorney's fees against U.S. Department of Treasury) and Gregor v. Derwinski, 911 F. Supp. 643, 656 (W.D.N.Y. 1996) (ADEA does not authorize award of attorney's fees against federal Veterans Affairs medical center, so request for fees denied) *with* Craig v. O'Leary, 870 F. Supp. 1007, 1009, 69 FEP 452 (D. Colo. 1994) (reaching contrary result and citing cases).

[33]5 U.S.C. § 504. *See, e.g.,* Nowd v. Rubin, 76 F.3d 25, 28, 69 FEP 1587 (1st Cir. 1996); Craig v. O'Leary, 870 F. Supp. 1007, 1010, 69 FEP 452 (D. Colo. 1994).

[34]*Id.*

[35]*See* Weaver v. Amoco Prod. Co., 66 F.3d 85, 70 FEP 931, 934–35 (5th Cir. 1995), *aff'd after remand,* 95 F.3d 52 (5th Cir. 1996).

[36]*See* Luciano v. Olsten Corp., 925 F. Supp. 956, 964 (E.D.N.Y. 1996); Hatley v. Store Kraft Mfg. Co., 859 F. Supp. 1257, 70 FEP 1361, 1369–70 (D. Neb. 1994) ("The time it takes to prepare a fee application is appropriately included in a claim for attorney fees, and the time claimed . . . is well within the acceptable range for

One federal appellate court has allowed a contingency multiplier to be applied to a "fees-on-fees" award where both state and federal discrimination claims were decided by the jury in favor of the plaintiff and where the request for fees was made pursuant to a state statute. The court upheld use of the multiplier under state law even though such multipliers are unavailable under federal fee-shifting statutes.[37]

K. Awards of Costs

The Civil Rights Act of 1991 amended Title VII to provide that a court, in its discretion, may award the prevailing party a "reasonable attorney's fee (including expert fees) as part of the costs. . . ."[38] One court has held that the term "reasonable" in this provision applies to the expert's fees as well as the attorney's fees and that the court must examine the expert's fees for reasonableness.[39] The award of expert's fees is discretionary. A request for expert's fees has been denied in a case where a prevailing plaintiff achieved only a mixed-motive verdict and was not entitled to damages, back pay, or front pay, and the experts were retained to testify about damages issues.[40]

Courts continue to award out-of-pocket expenses as part of plaintiff's costs and attorney's fees.[41] A few courts have rejected

---

the tedious and time-consuming task of preparing such applications."); *accord* Dailey v. Societe Generale, 915 F. Supp. 1315, 1333 (S.D.N.Y. 1996) (time spent on posttrial motions, which included the fees request, is compensable), *aff'd in part, remanded in part,* 108 F.3d 451 (2d Cir. 1997) (remand was for additional consideration of fees award for posttrial motions and issue of unsuccessful claims asserted in motions).

[37]Mangold v. California Pub. Utils. Comm'n, 67 F.3d 1470, 1479, 69 FEP 48, 55 (9th Cir. 1995).

[38]42 U.S.C. § 2000e-5.

[39]Selgas v. American Airlines, Inc., 858 F. Supp. 316, 69 FEP 938, 943 (D.C. P.R. 1994).

[40]Snell v. Reno Hilton Resort, 930 F. Supp. 1428, 1434 (D. Nev. 1996).

[41]*See* Downes v. Volkswagen of Am., 41 F.3d 1132, 69 FEP 11, 19–20 (7th Cir. 1994) (expenses for postage, long-distance telephone calls, photocopying, attorney travel, paralegals, and expert witnesses are recoverable under the Civil Rights Attorneys Fees Awards Act); Dailey v. Societe Generale, 915 F. Supp. 1315 (S.D.N.Y. 1996) (reasonable costs for out-of-pocket expenses normally charged to a client); Ryther v. Kare 11, 864 F. Supp. 1525, 70 FEP 1701, 1707–08 (D.C. Minn. 1994) (prevailing party under ADEA can recover reasonable out-of-pocket expenses for duplicating, serving fees, long-distance charges, fax charges, and local travel expenses).

or cautioned against requests to award expenses incurred for computer-aided legal research.[42] One court has refused to award the costs of discovery depositions that "were investigatory in nature" and were not reasonably necessary for the litigation of the case.[43]

II. Computation of Attorney's Fees for Prevailing Plaintiffs

A. General Principles

4. The Primacy of the Lodestar

While the original 12 *Johnson* criteria retain vitality,[44] the analysis of these factors continues to be subsumed within the lodestar.[45]

B. Applying the General Criteria

1. Lodestar Components

a. Rates. Courts continue to select an appropriate hourly rate based on prevailing rates in the forum community for attorneys of

---

[42]*Compare* Jones v. Unisys Corp., 54 F.3d 624, 633, 67 FEP 1065 (10th Cir. 1995) (costs for computer research are not statutorily authorized and courts should "sparingly exercise its discretion with regard to expenses not specifically allowed by statute") and Ryther v. Kare 11, 864 F. Supp. 1525, 1534, 70 FEP 1701, 1707 (D.C. Minn. 1994) (computer-aided research, "like any form of legal research, is a component of attorneys' fees and cannot be taxed as an item of cost") *with* Snell v. Reno Hilton Resort, 930 F. Supp. 1428, 1434 (D. Nev. 1996) (LEXIS charges are recoverable where normally charged to a client) and Luciano v. Olsten Corp., 925 F. Supp. 956, 966–67 (E.D. N.Y. 1996) (Westlaw charges allowed).

[43]Ryther v. Kare 11, 864 F. Supp. 1525, 1534, 70 FEP 1701, 1708 (D.C. Minn. 1994).

[44]*See* Hadley v. Vam P T S, 44 F.3d 372, 375–76, 67 FEP 186 (5th Cir. 1995) ("Although the district judge's recitation of the reasons why he reduced the requested fee is not fulsome, it does evidence the required examination of the *Johnson* factors."); Hatley v. Store Kraft Mfg. Co., 859 F. Supp. 1257, 1267–69, 70 FEP 1361 (D. Neb. 1994) (court applied *Johnson* criteria to fee application of successful plaintiff in sex harassment case).

[45]Tabech v. Gunter, 869 F. Supp. 1446, 1457 (D. Neb. 1994) (court explained that *Johnson* factors are subsumed into the lodestar calculation); Spradley v. Notami Hosps., 892 F. Supp. 1459, 1461 (M.D. Fla. 1995) (court in ADEA case held that the 12 *Johnson* factors can be considered to determine a reasonable hourly rate); EEOC v. Accurate Mechanical Contractors, 863 F. Supp. 828, 838 (E.D. Wis. 1994) (court considered the *Johnson* factors in computing the lodestar).

similar experience in similar cases.[46] Similarly, different rates have been approved distinguishing between court appearances, noncourt appearances, and other legal work, in comparison to functions that may be performed by nonlawyers.[47] Finally, courts have awarded fees higher than prevailing market rates only where evidence establishes that competent local counsel was unavailable.[48]

b. Hours. In calculating the reasonableness of the hours expended, courts eliminate duplicative and unnecessary time.[49] However, the mere presence of more than one attorney will not automatically warrant a reduction of fees.[50] Claimed hours continue to be reduced where detailed, contemporaneous time records are not available.[51]

c. The Partially Prevailing Plaintiff. Following the Supreme Court's direction in *Hensley v. Eckerhart,*[52] plaintiffs who partially

---

[46]Wells v. New Cherokee Corp., 58 F.3d 233, 239–40, 68 FEP 284 (6th Cir. 1995) (in an ADEA case, district court chose plaintiff's theory that rate should be determined from affidavits of trial counsel and an experienced local practitioner over defendant's theory that rate should be the average awarded in four allegedly similar cases over four years); Andrade v. Jamestown Hous. Auth., 82 F.3d 1179, 1190 (1st Cir. 1996) (affirming reduction of hourly rate to that customary in forum community).

[47]*See* Reed v. Rhodes, 934 F. Supp. 1492, 1522 (N.D. Ohio 1996).

[48]*See* Hadix v. Johnson, 65 F.3d 532, 535–36 (6th Cir. 1995) (reversing award of fees based on hourly rate of nationally known, nonlocal counsel absent a showing that competent, local counsel was not available).

[49]*See* EEOC v. Clear Lake Dodge, 60 F.3d 1146, 1154, 68 FEP 663 (5th Cir. 1995) (attorney's fees must not be awarded for attorney hours that are excessive, redundant, or otherwise unnecessary); Thomlison v. City of Omaha, 63 F.3d 786, 791, 4 AD 1319 (8th Cir. 1995) (court affirmed district court's reduction in reasonable hourly rate, from $160 to $125, because the case did not present a "high level of difficulty").

[50]Altman v. Port Auth. of N.Y. & N.J., 879 F. Supp. 345, 354, 67 FEP 1355 (S.D.N.Y. 1995) (court refused to reduce fee award because two attorneys tried age discrimination and retaliation case); Wahad v. Coughlin, 870 F. Supp. 506, 507 (S.D.N.Y. 1994) (court in civil rights action permitted fees for conferences between attorneys, finding that the billing entries were sufficiently specific and detailed regarding such conferences).

[51]Walker v. U.S. Dep't of Hous. & Urban Dev., 99 F.3d 761, 773 (5th Cir. 1996) (rejecting fee request in its entirety because time records inadequately documented activities); Washington v. Philadelphia County Court of Common Pleas, 89 F.3d 1031, 1037–38 (3d Cir. 1996) (reversing and remanding district court's reduction of plaintiff's attorneys' hours because of improperly documented time, where appellate court found time records specifying the date of the work performed, the attorney performing the work, and the nature of the work to be sufficiently detailed).

[52]461 U.S. 424, 440, 31 FEP 1169 (1983).

prevail on interrelated theories may be entitled to recover attorney's fees for time spent litigating successful as well as unsuccessful claims.[53]

2. *Adjustments to the Lodestar*

a. Contingency. In *Park v. Howard University*,[54] the plaintiff and her attorney entered into a fee arrangement stating that plaintiff was obligated to compensate her attorney at the rate of $125 per hour or the amount of attorney's fees awarded by the court against the defendant. Following a trial on the merits in which the plaintiff was partially successful on her claims, the defendant opposed plaintiff's counsel's fee motion on the ground that, among other reasons, the $125 per hour figure in the agreement was the controlling rate.[55] The court rejected this argument and awarded plaintiff's counsel a standard lodestar figure.

b. Results Achieved. Courts continue to hold that fee awards in employment discrimination cases need not be proportional to the damages recovered.[56] However, the extent of a plaintiff's success is still a key factor in the calculation of any fee award.[57]

---

[53]*See* Dunning v. Simmons Airlines, 62 F.3d 863, 874, 68 FEP 785 (7th Cir. 1995) (district court did not abuse its discretion in awarding plaintiff attorney's fees because claims for retaliation [successful], sex harassment [unsuccessful], and gender discrimination [dismissed before trial] were interrelated); Altman v. Port Auth. of N.Y. & N.J., 879 F. Supp. 345, 354, 67 FEP 1355 (S.D.N.Y. 1995) (court held that fees did not have to be reduced where evidence regarding plaintiff's age discrimination claim, which was dropped at trial, was intertwined with evidence of plaintiff's retaliation claim).

[54]881 F. Supp. 653, 71 FEP 1830 (D.D.C. 1995).

[55]*Id.* at 654, 71 FEP at 1832.

[56]EEOC v. Accurate Mechanical Contractors, Inc., 863 F. Supp. 828, 839 (E.D Wis. 1994) ("Although the amount of damages a plaintiff recovers is relevant to an award of attorney's fees for that recovery, the size of the award does not dictate that the attorney's fee allowed must be proportional to the damage award.").

[57]Caruso v. Forslund, 47 F.3d 27, 31–32, 31 FEP 1455 (2d Cir. 1995) (court ruled that district court was within its discretion to award no fee where plaintiff recovered only nominal damages); McGinnis v. Kentucky Fried Chicken of Cal., 42 F.3d 1273, 1276–77, 3 AD 1813 (9th Cir. 1994) (court ruled that district court erred by not reducing fee award where plaintiff claimed fees of $138,672 on verdict of $34,000 in compensatory damages); Cragen v. Barnhill, 859 F. Supp 566, 574–75 (N.D. Fla. 1994) (plaintiff in pregnancy discrimination case had fees reduced 50% because of her limited success: she recovered no punitive damages, the compensatory damages recovered were only a small fraction of those requested, and the individual defendant was found not liable). *Cf.* Carter v. Sedgewick County, Kan., 36

c. Delay. In some circumstances, courts have enhanced fee awards due to delay in payment.[58]

C. Procedure

3. Hearing

Although hearings on motions for an award of attorney's fees are often unnecessary, the Seventh Circuit remanded a fee award to the district court on the ground that plaintiff's counsel should have been given an evidentiary hearing before the district court significantly reduced the fees sought.[59]

III. THE PREVAILING DEFENDANT'S RIGHT TO ATTORNEY'S FEES

In addressing motions for fees to prevailing defendants, courts continue to follow the standards enunciated in *Christiansburg Garment Co. v. EEOC*,[60] and award fees where a plaintiff's claims were "frivolous, unreasonable, or without foundation, even though not brought in subjective bad faith."[61] Although the question of whether plaintiff's claims are frivolous, unreasonable, or without foundation must be made on a case-by-case basis, the Eleventh Circuit has identified three factors that guide its inquiry: (1) whether the plaintiff established a prima facie case; (2) whether the defendant

---

F.3d 952, 957, 65 FEP 1585 (10th Cir. 1994) (court held that district court abused its discretion when it reduced the hourly rate and the number of compensable hours to account for duplication in services; the district court was found to have "corrected twice for a single problem").

[58]Walker v. U.S. Dep't of Hous. & Urban Dev., 99 F.3d 761, 773 (5th Cir. 1996) (awarding enhancement to compensate for delay in payment by adjusting fee upward based on historical rates); Tabech v. Gunter, 869 F. Supp. 1446, 1462 (D. Neb. 1994) (court addressed delay in payment of fees by increasing the reasonable rate for a case that was seven years old).

[59]Hutchinson v. Amateur Electronic Supply, Inc., 42 F.3d 1037, 1048, 66 FEP 1275, 1282 (7th Cir. 1994).

[60]434 U.S. 412, 16 FEP 502 (1978).

[61]*Id.* at 421; Walker v. Nationsbank of Fla., N.A., 53 F.3d 1548, 1558–59, 68 FEP 314 (11th Cir. 1995); EEOC v. Consolidated Serv. Sys., 30 F.3d 58, 59, 66 FEP 185 (7th Cir. 1994); Sayers v. Stewart Sleep Ctr., Inc., 932 F. Supp. 1415, 1417 (M.D. Fla. 1996).

offered to settle; and (3) whether the trial court dismissed the case prior to trial or held a full-blown trial on the merits.[62]

Courts have also adhered to the *Christiansburg Garment* standards when awarding fees to defendants when it became apparent during the pendency of the action that plaintiff's claims were not well taken,[63] including at least one case where the court awarded fees after a trial on the merits.[64]

---

[62] Walker v. Nationsbank of Fla., N.A., 53 F.3d 1548, 1559, 68 FEP 314 (11th Cir. 1995), citing Sullivan v. School Bd. of Pinellas County, 773 F.2d 1182, 1189, 39 FEP 53 (11th Cir. 1985).

[63] *See* Turner v. Sungard Business Sys., Inc., 91 F.3d 1418, 1423 (11th Cir. 1996) (the fact that plaintiff may have had a reasonable basis for suit when filed is insufficient to avoid a fee award where claims became frivolous during pendency of the case); Marquart v. Lodge 837, 26 F.3d 842, 849, 64 FEP 1789 (8th Cir. 1994) (prevailing defendant is entitled to fees if suit is frivolous when filed or if it becomes so during course of proceedings).

[64] Daramola v. Westinghouse Elec. Corp., 872 F. Supp. 1418, 1420 (W.D. Pa. 1995) (awarding fees to the defendant after a trial on the merits based on plaintiff's "willingness to lie and fabricate evidence so as to use this to punish Westinghouse").

Chapter 43

SETTLEMENT

I. Validity of Waivers of Discrimination Claims

A. Knowing and Voluntary Waivers of Past Claims Are Valid

2. *The Waiver Must Be Knowing and Voluntary*

The First, Seventh, and Eleventh Circuits have joined the Second, Third, Fifth, and Tenth Circuits in applying a "totality of the circumstances" standard in determining whether a release of discrimination claims was knowing and voluntary.[1] That the distinction between the "totality of the circumstances" test and the "ordinary contract principles" test may be more superficial than real is demonstrated by *Adams v. Philip Morris, Inc.*[2] There, the Sixth Circuit stated that it "applied ordinary contract principles in determining whether . . . a waiver is valid, remaining alert to ensure that employers do not defeat the policies of the ADEA or Title VII by taking advantage of their superior bargaining position or overreaching."[3] It then listed factors to be examined in evaluating whether

---

[1]Rivera-Flores v. Bristol-Myers Squibb Caribbean, 112 F.3d 9, 12 (1st Cir. 1997) (ADA case in which the court noted that it had earlier adopted the "totality of the circumstances" test in an ERISA case); Pierce v. Atchison, Topeka & Santa Fe Ry. Co., 65 F.3d 562, 571, 68 FEP 1270 (7th Cir. 1995) ("While we recognize the critical role that the plain language of the contract plays, our inquiry into knowledge and voluntariness cannot end there. . . . The totality of the circumstances approach is consistent with the strong congressional purpose underlying the ADEA to eradicate discrimination in employment [citations omitted]."); Beadle v. City of Tampa, 42 F.3d 633, 635, 66 FEP 1540 (11th Cir.) (factors to be considered include: "the plaintiff's education and business experience; the amount of time the plaintiff considered the agreement before signing it; the clarity of the agreement; the plaintiff's opportunity to consult with an attorney; the employer's encouragement or discouragement of consultation with an attorney; and the consideration given in exchange for the waiver when compared with the benefits to which the employee was already entitled"), *cert. denied,* 515 U.S. 1152 (1995).
[2]67 F.3d 580, 71 FEP 1025 (6th Cir. 1995).
[3]*Id.* at 583 (citation omitted).

a release is knowingly and voluntarily executed: "(1) plaintiff's experience, background and education; (2) the amount of time the plaintiff had to consider whether to sign the waiver, including whether the employee had an opportunity to consult with a lawyer; (3) the clarity of the waiver; (4) consideration for the waiver; as well as (5) the totality of the circumstances."[4] Not only did the court refer explicitly to consideration of the totality of the circumstances in applying "ordinary contract principles," the enumerated factors are those listed by the courts applying the "totality of the circumstances" test.[5]

The courts continue to examine, under either the "ordinary contract principles" or "totality of the circumstances" tests, the specific terms of releases to determine whether the waiver of claims was knowing and voluntary.[6]

---

[4] Id.

[5] Indeed, the court cited to *Bormann v. AT & T Communications, Inc.*, 875 F.2d 399, 49 FEP 1622 (2d Cir.), *cert. denied*, 493 U.S. 924 (1989) and *Riley v. American Family Mut. Ins. Co.*, 881 F.2d 368, 50 FEP 668 (7th Cir. 1989), cases that articulate the "totality of the circumstances" test.

[6] First Circuit: Rivera-Flores v. Bristol-Myers Squibb Caribbean, 112 F.3d 9, 12–13 (1st Cir. 1997) (court noted that heightened judicial scrutiny is warranted where person asserts that he was disabled at time release was signed, but cautioned that not all disabilities inherently involve a question about the capacity to act; release held valid where language was "clear and unmistakable" and where the ADA was specifically mentioned, even though there was little room for negotiation, and plaintiff lacked business sophistication).

Second Circuit: Nicholas v. Nynex, Inc., 929 F. Supp. 727, 731–32, 74 FEP 581 (S.D.N.Y. 1996) (release of race claims under Title VII upheld on summary judgment, where release was drafted in "clear, comprehensible and unambiguous language," explicitly referenced Title VII and race discrimination claims, and contained language in two places advising plaintiff of his right to consult an attorney; plaintiff was high school graduate with subsequent education in computer training, had held a management position, was given nearly two months to decide whether to sign the release, and consulted with an attorney before signing release; conclusory allegations of fraudulent concealment and alleged economic duress due to fears about obtaining another job and making mortgage payments failed to present question of fact); Baba v. Warren Management Consultants, Inc., 882 F. Supp. 339, 344, 74 FEP 707 (S.D.N.Y. 1995) (waiver of Title VII claim upheld even though release was a general release and plaintiff testified that she only intended to release state claims; plaintiff was represented by counsel, her claim that she had asked for agreement to be revised was not corroborated by documentary evidence, and she benefitted from employer's agreement not to appeal award in her favor for back wages and benefits).

Third Circuit: Martinez v. National Broadcasting Co., 877 F. Supp. 219, 227, 73 FEP 1701 (D.N.J. 1994) (in the Third Circuit the "totality of the circumstances" test is to be applied, but, in addition, general principles of contract construction, specifically an inquiry into the absence of fraud and undue influence, are applicable

B. Waivers of Future Claims Are Invalid

In *Wagner v. Nutrasweet Co.,*[7] the plaintiff, a human resources officer, signed an agreement that provided, in part, that her employment would continue for six months following the execution of the release. The agreement also provided that at the end of the retention period, the plaintiff would receive two months' "redeployment pay," outplacement assistance, and severance benefits worth more than $46,000. Shortly before its expiration, the plaintiff was presented with a second release covering the six-month retention period. She refused to sign, claiming she had been discriminated against in compensation during the retention period. The district court held her compensation claims were barred by the earlier release because the rate of pay she earned during the

---

in determining validity of waiver; because plaintiff testified that he understood he would be given a job if he signed the release, summary judgment was precluded).

Sixth Circuit: Adams v. Philip Morris, Inc., 67 F.3d 580, 583, 71 FEP 1025 (6th Cir. 1995) (release valid where waiver was plain, unambiguous, and easily understandable by someone of plaintiff's abilities, plaintiff was given five days to consider whether to sign and was advised to consult with an attorney, and plaintiff received approximately twice as much in benefits as he would otherwise have been entitled to receive).

Seventh Circuit: Pierce v. Atchison, Topeka & Santa Fe Ry. Co., 65 F.3d 562, 571, 68 FEP 1270 (7th Cir. 1995) (while an employee must specifically challenge a release as not "voluntary and knowing," the ultimate burden of proof that an employee has knowingly and voluntarily waived claims is properly placed on the employer); Pierce v. Atchison, Topeka & Santa Fe Ry. Co., 110 F.3d 431, 438, 73 FEP 1062 (7th Cir. 1997) (employee was given a short time to sign release, and the parties disagreed whether the employer's representative ever corrected initial statement to the employee that release did not include discrimination claims).

Eleventh Circuit: Puentes v. United Parcel Serv., 86 F.3d 196, 197–99, 71 FEP 106 (11th Cir. 1996) (although plaintiffs did not seriously contest that they had sufficient business experience to evaluate releases, that releases were clear, and that consideration exceeded benefits to which they were already entitled, summary judgment in favor of employer reversed due to question as to whether plaintiffs had only 24 hours to decide whether to sign releases; court collected cases concerning length of timeframe necessary for release to be considered valid and deemed 24 hours "insufficient"); Beadle v. City of Tampa, 42 F.3d 633, 635, 66 FEP 1540 (11th Cir.) (upholding magistrate's finding in religious discrimination case that there was no knowing and voluntary waiver where (1) employee reviewed agreement only for short time and was under financial pressure such that magistrate was unconvinced he had fair opportunity to consult with counsel, and (2) existence of consideration—city forbearing to exercise contract right to collect expenses when recruit secured other law enforcement employment within two years of completing field training and commencing full-time service—was questionable, because plaintiff had never completed field training), *cert. denied,* 515 U.S. 1152 (1995).

[7] 95 F.3d 527, 533–34, 72 FEP 284 (7th Cir. 1996).

retention period was based on the rate of pay earned prior to her execution of the first release, the time period as to which she had released all claims. Relying on a continuing violation theory, the appeals court reversed and stated that each paycheck received during the retention period was the basis for a separate claim. The court noted that even if it were possible to waive prospective claims, the fact that the company asked for a second release "speaks volumes" about whether the parties even intended the release to reach prospective claims.[8]

The *Wagner* case demonstrates the risk to an employer of permitting an employee to remain employed after the execution of a release supported by valuable consideration. If an employer wishes to obtain an immediate signed release from an employee who will continue to be employed for a period of time thereafter, thought should be given to constructing a plan that ensures that sufficient consideration is dependent on the employee's execution of the second release. A plaintiff-employee who remains employed during a transition period after signing a release, and who is discriminated against during the transition period, should be aware of the right to demand new and/or additional consideration in exchange for signing a second release.

In recent cases, courts have suggested that it is sometimes difficult to determine whether subsequent claims of discrimination are barred as the result of a prior settlement or consent decree or whether the claims are new ones that could not lawfully have been included within the scope of the prior consent decree/settlement.[9] In *Adams v. Philip Morris, Inc.*,[10] the plaintiff signed a settlement agreement waiving "any and all right to assert any claim or demand for reemployment or tenure with the company or for any benefits, etc., not specifically enunciated herein." The plaintiff applied for rehire, was rejected, and sued, contending that the provision in the settlement

---

[8] *Id.* at 533.

[9] *E.g.*, Huguley v. General Motors Corp., 52 F.3d 1364, 1366 (6th Cir. 1995) (*Huguley II*) ("The [consent] decree purported to settle all past claims of discrimination as well as all claims arising from the future effects of past discrimination. However, distinguishing between past acts of discrimination, the future effects of past discrimination and new acts of alleged discrimination has proved quite challenging."); Huguley v. General Motors Corp., 35 F.3d 1052 (6th Cir. 1994) (*Huguley I*) (failure to transfer following consent degree independently actionable).

[10] 67 F.3d 580, 582, 71 FEP 1025 (6th Cir. 1995).

agreement amounted to an unlawful waiver of a prospective claim. The district court granted summary judgment to the employer, but the court of appeals reversed. It noted that not every settlement agreement that refers to postsettlement conduct results in a prospective waiver and that a settlement agreement may lawfully release claims for the future effects of past discrimination.[11] The appeals court held, however, that the district court needed to determine whether the employer had discriminated anew or whether the refusal to consider the plaintiff's application related back or was a continuing effect of the alleged age discrimination that prompted the settlement agreement.[12]

In *Kendall v. Watkins*,[13] the Tenth Circuit considered the lawfulness of refusing to hire a former employee who had signed a settlement agreement providing that the employer had "no further obligation to [the former employee]." The court held that the employer's reason for not rehiring the plaintiff was the employer's reliance on the terms of the settlement agreement, a nondiscriminatory reason not prohibited by Title VII; accordingly, no prospective waiver of a Title VII claim was at issue.[14] The court noted, however, that a valid retaliation claim would have been stated if the reason for the failure to rehire had been simply the fact that the employee had earlier filed a Title VII claim, which the employer had to settle, as opposed to the employer's interpretation of the specific terms of the settlement agreement.[15]

II. Waiver of Age Discrimination Claims After the Older Workers Benefit Protection Act

The EEOC has issued proposed regulations concerning "Waiver of Rights and Claims Under the Age Discrimination in Employment Act."[16] The proposed waiver regulations answer in the negative the

---

[11]*Id.* at 584 (citing the court's holding in *Huguley II*).
[12]*Id.* at 584–85.
[13]998 F.2d 848, 62 FEP 681 (10th Cir. 1993), *cert. denied,* 510 U.S. 1120, 72 FEP 992 (1994).
[14]*Id.* at 851–52.
[15]*Id.*
[16]Notice of Proposed Rulemaking, 62 Fed. Reg. 10,787 (1997) (to be codified, if adopted, at 29 C.F.R. § 1625.22) (proposed Mar. 10, 1997).

issue of whether an employer is required to give a person age 40 or older a greater amount of consideration than one under the age of 40, solely because the person over 40 is a member of a protected class under ADEA.[17] The proposed waiver regulations thus are in accord with the Third Circuit's holding in *Dibiase v. SmithKline Beecham Corp.*[18] The Eleventh Circuit has followed the Third Circuit's reasoning as well.[19]

A. Waivers as Part of Settlement of EEOC Charge or Court Action

The proposed waiver regulations provide that the term "reasonable time within which to consider the settlement agreement"[20] means "reasonable under all the circumstances, including whether the individual is represented by counsel or has the assistance of counsel."[21] If the requirements for time periods specified in the OWBPA for prelitigation releases[22] are satisfied, the time will automatically be deemed reasonable, although compliance with these time periods is not mandatory outside of the prelitigation context.[23] Presumably, if the proposed waiver regulations are adopted, courts will look to the pre-OWBPA cases in determining "reasonableness under all the circumstances."

B. Prelitigation Releases

The proposed waiver regulations address a number of the issues that were left unresolved in the OWBPA itself. For example, with respect to time periods, it is specifically provided:

- The 21-day and 45-day consideration periods run from the date of the employer's final offer.[24]

---

[17]*Id.* at 10,790 (1997) (to be codified, if adopted, at 29 C.F.R. § 1625.22(d)(4)).
[18]48 F.3d 719, 721, 67 FEP 58 (3d Cir.), *cert. denied*, 516 U.S. 916 (1995).
[19]Griffin v. Kraft Gen. Foods, Inc., 62 F.3d 368, 374, 68 FEP 1072 (11th Cir. 1995) (no additional consideration needed).
[20]29 U.S.C. § 626(f)(2)(B).
[21]62 Fed. Reg. 10,793 (1997) (to be codified, if adopted, at 29 C.F.R. § 1625.22(g)(4)).
[22]29 U.S.C. § 626(f)(1).
[23]62 Fed. Reg. 10,793 (1997) (to be codified, if adopted, at 29 C.F.R. § 1625.22(g)(5)).
[24]*Id.* at 10,791 (to be codified, if adopted, at 29 C.F.R. § 1625.22(e)(4)).

- If material changes are made to the offer, the 21-day and 45-day periods begin to run anew, unless the parties agree to the contrary.[25]
- The 7-day revocation period cannot be shortened, even by agreement of the parties.[26]
- The 21-day and 45-day consideration periods are waivable, such that the employee may sign an agreement before the expiration of the applicable period, provided that the employee's acceptance of the shortened period is "knowing and voluntary."[27]

The proposed waiver regulations also address at length the informational requirements applicable to exit incentive and other group termination programs under OWBPA:[28]

- Generally, an "exit incentive program" is a voluntary program involving the offer of consideration in exchange for the decision to resign voluntarily and sign a waiver, whereas "other termination programs" involve involuntary terminations and the offer of consideration for the decision to sign a waiver.[29] A "program" exists when an employer offers consideration to two or more employees; the program need not constitute an employee benefit plan under ERISA.[30]
- Substantial guidance is provided concerning the "decisional unit" for purposes of the informational requirements. The terms "class," "unit," "group,"[31] and "job classification or organizational unit"[32] in the OWBPA are examples and are not exclusive listings.[33] The "decisional unit" must be determined in each case based upon an employer's structure and decisionmaking process.[34] It is "that portion of the

---

[25]*Id.*
[26]*Id.* at 10,791 (to be codified, if adopted, at 29 C.F.R. § 1625.22(e)(5)).
[27]*Id.* at 10,791 (to be codified, if adopted, at 29 C.F.R. § 1625.22(e)(6)).
[28]29 U.S.C. § 626(f)(1)(H).
[29]62 Fed. Reg. 10,791 (1997) (to be codified, if adopted, at 29 C.F.R. § 1625.22(f)(1)(iii)(A)).
[30]*Id.* at 10,791 (to be codified, if adopted, at 29 C.F.R. § 1625.22(f)(1)(iii)(B), (D)).
[31]29 U.S.C. § 626(f)(1)(H)(i).
[32]29 U.S.C. § 626(f)(1)(H)(ii).
[33]62 Fed. Reg. 10,791 (1997) (to be codified, if adopted, at 29 C.F.R. 1625.22(f)(3)).
[34]*Id.* (to be codified, if adopted, at 29 C.F.R. § 1625.22(f)(3)(i)(B)).

employer's organizational structure from which the employer chose the persons who would be offered consideration for the signing of a waiver."[35] Detailed examples are provided.[36]
- Age information cannot be presented in bands greater than one year.[37]
- If there are established grade levels or other established subcategories within a job category or title, information needs to be broken down by grade level or subcategory as well.[38]
- If information about voluntary and involuntary terminations is included, the information presented must distinguish between the two.[39]
- Information provided concerning involuntary termination programs that occur in increments over a period of time must be cumulative, but there is no obligation to supplement information given to earlier terminees.[40]
- A sample notification form is included for guidance.[41]

The courts have also begun to address the technical requirements of OWBPA in the context of exit incentive and group termination programs.

In *Griffin v. Kraft General Foods, Inc.*,[42] the court examined the sufficiency of the information provided to employees about a group termination program offered in connection with a plant closure. The court held that the OWBPA does not restrict the terms "job classification" and "organizational unit" to employees in the same plant. Because no facts were presented with respect to employees at other plants, summary judgment concerning compliance with OWBPA's notice requirements was inappropriate. Further, the court held that the statutory requirements of OWBPA that must be met for a release of age discrimination claims to be valid are not exclusive. It stated that the OWBPA sets forth *minimum* requirements and that

---

[35]*Id.*

[36]*Id.* at 10,792 (1997) (to be codified, if adopted, at 29 C.F.R. § 1625.22(f)(3)(iii) and (v)).

[37]*Id.* (to be codified, if adopted, at 29 C.F.R. § 1625.22(f)(4)(ii)).

[38]*Id.* (to be codified, if adopted, at 29 C.F.R. § 1625.22(f)(4)(iii)).

[39]*Id.* (to be codified, if adopted, at 29 C.F.R. § 1625.22(f)(4)(iv)).

[40]*Id.* (to be codified, if adopted, at 29 C.F.R. § 1625.22(f)(4)(vi)).

[41]*Id.* at 10,792–93 (1997) (to be codified, if adopted, at 29 C.F.R. § 1625.22(f)(4)(vii)).

[42]62 F.3d 368, 371–73, 68 FEP 1072 (11th Cir. 1995).

factors examined in pre-OWBPA cases to determine whether a waiver is knowing and voluntary (such as allegations of fraud, duress, or coercion) also must be considered. The case was remanded to the district court to consider whether the release was valid under the totality of the circumstances as well as under OWBPA.[43]

In *Raczak v. Ameritech Corp.*,[44] the court rejected the determination of the district court that, because the employer had provided required OWBPA information organized by salary grade instead of by job title, the OWBPA was violated. Instead the court held that "a rigid and mechanical interpretation" of [the OWBPA's disclosure requirements] is inappropriate."[45] It continued: "Holding an employer strictly accountable for what might be a technical violation of these imprecise terms, with no indication that this would facilitate the provision's purpose and might even hamper it, is untenable and would elevate form over substance."[46]

C. Unresolved Issues

As noted in the preceding section, the EEOC's proposed waiver regulations will, if adopted, provide clarification on many of the issues left unresolved under the terms of the OWBPA.

The issue of whether an employee must return the consideration received under a release of ADEA claims as a precondition to challenging the enforceability of the release for noncompliance with the OWBPA has been resolved by the Supreme Court. In *Oubre v. Entergy Operations, Inc.*,[47] the Court held that a release that did not comply with the OWBPA did not bar the plaintiff's ADEA lawsuit even though the plaintiff had not returned or promised to return the monies she received in return for signing the release. Five Justices, however, in one concurring and two dissenting opinions, intimated that once suit is filed, the employer may ask for return of its reciprocal payment or relief from any ongoing reciprocal obligation.[48]

---

[43]*Id.* at 373–74.
[44]103 F.3d 1257, 1259–60, 72 FEP 1357 (6th Cir. 1996), *cert. denied,* 1998 U.S. LEXIS 863 (1998).
[45]*Id.* at 1259.
[46]*Id.* at 1260.
[47]118 S. Ct. 838, 75 FEP 1255 (1998).
[48]*Id.* at 844–46.

III. Terms of the Settlement Agreement

A. The Defendant-Employer's Perspective

1. General and Special Releases

In *Wagner v. Nutrasweet Co.,*[49] the court held that a release that covered all claims, "known and unknown," including claims that an employee did not know about and that, the employee alleged, she could not have known about at the time of signing the release, was nevertheless valid and had been entered into knowingly and voluntarily.

3. Covenants Not to File Charges or to Assist in the Future Prosecution of Claims

In *EEOC v. Astra, Inc.,*[50] Astra challenged a preliminary injunction which barred it from entering into or enforcing any settlement agreements containing provisions that prohibited settling employees from filing charges with the EEOC and from assisting the EEOC in the investigation of EEOC charges. Astra had entered into at least 11 settlement agreements that contained provisions, among others, that the settling employees agreed not to file charges with the EEOC (the "nonfiling clause"), that the settling employees agreed not to assist others who filed EEOC charges (the "nonassistance clause"), and that the settling employees agreed not to discuss the incidents that gave rise to the claims (the "confidentiality clause"). The First Circuit held that the nonassistance covenants and the confidentiality clauses were void as against public policy, to the extent they prohibited communication with the EEOC, and upheld the preliminary injunction with respect to them.[51] Without determining the validity *vel non* of the nonfiling clause, the court found that the EEOC had not demonstrated that inclusion and enforcement of the clause would cause it to suffer irreparable injury absent a preliminary injunction. The court did note that it viewed the validity of the nonfiling covenants as a close question.[52]

---

[49] 95 F.3d 527, 533, 72 FEP 284 (7th Cir. 1996).
[50] 94 F.3d 738, 71 FEP 1267 (1st Cir. 1996).
[51] *Id.* at 744–45.
[52] *Id.* at 746.

On April 10, 1997, the EEOC published "Guidance on Waivers Under Civil Rights Laws,"[53] stating its position that employers may not limit individuals' rights to file charges or participate in EEOC proceedings by requiring employees to sign agreements relinquishing these rights. The EEOC contends that such agreements are void and that they may amount to separate and discrete violations of the antiretaliation provisions of the civil rights laws. The EEOC notes, however, that if an individual signs a valid waiver and then files an EEOC charge, the employer will be shielded against any further recovery by the employee.[54]

IV. Tax Considerations

On August 20, 1996, Congress passed the Small Business Job Protection Act of 1996,[55] significantly affecting the tax treatment of settlements in employment discrimination cases. The Internal Revenue Code now provides that punitive damages are taxable to the recipient, whether or not they are related to a physical injury or physical sickness.[56] The same result was reached by the Supreme Court in *O'Gilvie v. United States,* interpreting the tax law preamendment.[57] Further, even with respect to nonpunitive damages, the exclusion from gross income is now restricted to "personal *physical* injuries or sickness" [emphasis added].[58] This means that in the typical employment case, which involves only claims for back pay, front pay, and/or compensatory damages for emotional distress, but no actual physical injury to the plaintiff, the proceeds of a settlement will not be excludable from gross income and will be taxable.

For cases still governed by the pre-August 1996 law, the Supreme Court decision in *Commissioner of Internal Revenue v. Schleier*[59] governs the interpretation of the exclusion for damages

---

[53] *EEOC Policy Guidance on Waivers Under Civil Rights Laws,* reprinted in 8 FEP Man. (BNA) 405:7491.
[54] *Id.* at 405:7495.
[55] Pub. L. No. 104-188, 110 Stat. 1838 (1996).
[56] 26 U.S.C. § 104(a)(2).
[57] 117 S. Ct. 452, 455 (1996).
[58] 26 U.S.C. § 104(a)(2).
[59] 515 U.S. 323, 67 FEP 1745 (1995).

or settlement proceeds "on account of personal injuries or sickness," as § 104(a)(2) read prior to amendment. In *Schleier,* the Court found that a recovery under ADEA was taxable, holding that a recovery can be excluded only when it is both (1) received through prosecution or settlement of an action "based upon tort or tort type rights"; and (2) received "on account of personal injuries or sickness."[60]

V. RULE 68 OFFERS OF JUDGMENT

The courts continue to struggle with the issue of a plaintiff's entitlement to attorney's fees upon accepting a Rule 68 offer silent on the subject.[61] To avoid uncertainty, defendants making a Rule 68 offer should always explicitly specify whether or not the offer is inclusive or exclusive of attorney's fees.[62]

In *Sheppard v. Riverview Nursing Center, Inc.,*[63] the court considered the language added to Title VII by the Civil Rights Act of 1991, which provides that a court may award "attorney's fees and costs" in mixed-motive cases.[64] It held that, unlike the general remedy language found at § 2000e-5(k) of Title VII, which provides that attorney's fees may be awardable "as part of costs," attorney's

---

[60]*Id.* at 337.

[61]*E.g.,* Foster v. Kings Park Cent. Sch. Dist., 174 F.R.D. 19 (E.D.N.Y. 1997) (Rule 68 offer, which was accepted, was for "$14,000, together with costs accrued to date"; language in ADA provides for "reasonable attorney's fee, including litigation expenses, and costs" rather than including attorney's fees "as part of costs," in contrast to Title VII, the Rehabilitation Act, and other civil rights statutes; accordingly, court declined to award fees under the ADA, but did award them under the Rehabilitation Act); Nusom v. Comh Woodburn, Inc., 122 F.3d 830, 834 (9th Cir. 1997) (in Truth-in-Lending Act case, court held that by accepting Rule 68 offer, plaintiff had not waived entitlement to recover attorney's fees on top of Rule 68 judgment amount, noting that "while an offer to have judgment entered for a sum 'including costs and attorney fees' may shift attorney fees when the underlying statute makes attorney fees part of costs (as was the case in Marek), it does not follow that an offer to have judgment entered for a sum 'together with costs' has the same effect of being a lump-sum settlement, precluding the recovery of attorney fees, when the underlying statute does not make attorney's fees a part of costs").

[62]*See Nusom,* 122 F.3d at 834 (in holding that plaintiff could still seek recovery of attorney's fees, court noted that its ruling was not unfair because a defendant may explicitly state that Rule 68 offer, if accepted, does not permit plaintiff to recover attorney's fees).

[63]88 F.3d 1332, 71 FEP 218 (4th Cir.), *cert. denied,* 117 S. Ct. 483, 72 FEP 992 (1996).

[64]42 U.S.C. § 2000e-5(g)(2)(B).

fees are not includable as costs under 42 U.S.C. § 2000e-5(g)(2)(B).[65] Accordingly, the plaintiff, who had rejected a Rule 68 offer and who did not obtain a more favorable judgment than the Rule 68 offer, was still permitted to recover postoffer attorney's fees. The court, however, held that the rejection of the offer was a permissible factor to be considered by the district court in exercising its discretion in determining the amount of the fee award.[66]

VI. "BUSTED" SETTLEMENTS

The courts continue to grapple with the question whether agreements not reduced to a signed document are enforceable.[67] Counsel are well advised to prepare a draft settlement agreement (with blanks for matters such as dollar amounts) and to bring it to mediations, settlement conferences, and the like. The agreement can be revised as necessary and longhand changes initialed, or, if the agreement is on a laptop computer, revisions can be made and the revised document printed on-site for execution. The goal is to reduce any agreement to writing immediately and, if consistent with requirements that the agreement be entered into knowingly and voluntarily, executed immediately. (Of course, OWBPA requirements

---

[65]88 F.3d at 1337.
[66]*Id.*
[67]*E.g.*, Ciaramella v. Reader's Digest Ass'n, 131 F.3d 320, 323 (2d Cir. 1997) ("This court has articulated four factors to guide the inquiry regarding whether parties intended to be bound by a settlement agreement in the absence of a document executed by both sides. [citation omitted] We must consider (1) whether there has been an express reservation of the right not to be bound in the absence of a signed writing; (2) whether there has been partial performance of the contract; (3) whether all of the terms of the alleged contract have been agreed upon; and (4) whether the agreement at issue is the type of contract that is usually committed to writing. [citation omitted]."); Porter v. Chicago Bd. of Educ., 981 F. Supp. 1129, 1133–34 (N.D. Ill. 1997) (enforcing oral settlement reached at pretrial settlement conference conducted by magistrate, but refusing to incorporate into the settlement the "boilerplate terms" that were included in the draft written settlement agreement but that had not been discussed at the pretrial settlement conference); Lobeck v. City of Riviera Beach, 976 F. Supp. 1460, 1464 (S.D. Fla. 1997) (noting that the Eleventh and Fifth Circuits apply federal common law in determining the scope and validity of settlement agreements in Title VII cases and that oral agreements are enforceable; however, court will not infer the existence of an agreement by piecing together documents capable of differing interpretations, so summary judgment inappropriate as to existence of a settlement).

apply with respect to releases of age claims.) In any event, effort should be made to avoid a lengthy period of time during which "buyer's remorse" can set in and disputes can arise over "boilerplate" but often important terms.

The decision of the Supreme Court in *Oubre v. Entergy Operations, Inc.*,[68] that a plaintiff need not "tender back" funds received in exchange for signing a release as a precondition to bringing an ADEA action, obviously impacts all prior ADEA cases holding to the contrary or predicated upon the reasoning rejected in *Oubre*. (Note, however, that the decision does not have implications for non-ADEA cases, since the holding was predicated on the mandatory requirements for a valid waiver of ADEA claims found in the statutory language of the OWBPA.)

---

[68] 118 S. Ct. 838, 75 FEP 1255 (1998).

TABLE OF CASES

Cases are referenced to chapter and footnote number(s); e.g., *9:* 19, 32 indicates the case is cited in Chapter 9, at footnotes 19 and 32. Union locals and other subdivisions are included with the parent unions, which are sorted by popular name. Entries beginning with numerals are alphabetized as if spelled out. Alphabetization is letter-by-letter.

A

Abbasi v. Herzfeld & Rubin, 4 AD 797 (S.D.N.Y. 1995) *9:* 117; *16:* 171

Able v. United States, 88 F.3d 1280, 71 FEP 419 (2d Cir. 1996), *on remand,* 968 F. Supp. 850 (E.D.N.Y. 1997) *14:* 24, 27–30

Abrams v. Lightolier, Inc., 50 F.3d 1204, 67 FEP 543 (3d Cir. 1995) *42:* 26

Accurate Mech. Contractors, Inc.; EEOC v., 863 F. Supp. 828 (E.D. Wis. 1994) *40:* 5; *41:* 7, 11, 49, 138, 144; *42:* 45, 56

Acorn Niles Corp.; EEOC v., 1995 U.S. Dist. LEXIS 12649 (N.D. Ill. Aug. 29, 1995) *34:* 17, 36

Adamczyk v. Chief, Baltimore County Police Dep't, 952 F. Supp. 259 (D. Md. 1997) *9:* 269

Adam-Mellang v. Apartment Search, Inc., 96 F.3d 297, 71 FEP 1633 (8th Cir. 1996) *40:* 90, 93, 97

Adams
—v. City of Chicago
——865 F. Supp. 445, 73 FEP 547 (N.D. Ill. 1994) *41:* 98
——1995 WL 491496 (N.D. Ill. Aug. 11, 1995) *40:* 80
——1996 WL 137660 (N.D. Ill. Mar. 25, 1996) *5:* 1–2, 22, 30, 64
—v. DuPont Merck Pharm. Co., 67 FEP 1072 (E.D. Pa. 1994), *aff'd mem.,* 70 F.3d 1254, 71 FEP 1408 (3d Cir. 1995) *16:* 113, 166
—v. EEOC, 932 F. Supp. 660, 70 FEP 1357 (E.D. Pa. 1996) *34:* 8

—v. Philip Morris, Inc, 67 F.3d 580, 71 FEP 1025 (6th Cir. 1995) *16:* 198, 204; *43:* 2–4, 6, 10–12

—v. Pinole Point Steel Co., 65 FEP 774 (N.D. Cal. 1994) *37:* 44

—v. Robertson, 676 So. 2d 1265 (Ala. 1995), *cert. granted,* 117 S. Ct. 37 (1996), *cert. dismissed,* 117 S. Ct. 1028 (1997) *37:* 58–60

—v. St. Lucie County Sheriff's Dep't, 962 F.2d 1563 (11th Cir. 1992), *modified,* 998 F.2d 923 (11th Cir. 1993) *24:* 32

Adarand Constructors, Inc. v. Peña, 115 S. Ct. 2097, 67 FEP 1828 (1995) *27:* 66, 89; *37:* 11; *40:* 62, 67

Addy v. Bliss & Glennon, 44 Cal.App.4th 205, 70 FEP 965 (Cal. App. 1996) *19:* 1, 20

Adolphsen v. Hallmark Cards, Inc., 907 S.W.2d 333, 11 IER 133 (Mo. Ct. App. 1995) *26:* 24

Afande v. National Lutheran Home for the Aged, 868 F. Supp. 795 (D. Md. 1994), *aff'd,* 69 F.3d 532 (4th Cir. 1995) *33:* 16

Agster v. Furnival/State Mach. Co., 4 AD 1614 (E.D. Pa. 1995) *9:* 175

Aguirre v. McCaw RCC Communications, Inc., 923 F. Supp. 1431 (D. Kan. 1996) *33:* 24, 33

AIC Sec. Investigations; EEOC v.
—820 F. Supp. 1060, 2 AD 561 (N.D. Ill. 1993) *9:* 164
—1994 U.S. Dist. LEXIS 10368 (N.D. Ill. July 27, 1994) *34:* 47

AIC Sec. Investigations—*Contd.*
—55 F.3d 1276, 4 AD 693 (7th Cir. 1995) *9:* 72, 210, 242; *41:* 101–02, 104, 111–12
Aiken
—v. Business & Indus. Health Group, Inc., 885 F. Supp. 1474 (D. Kan. 1995) *38:* 37
—v. City of Memphis, 37 F.3d 1155, 65 FEP 1757 (6th Cir. 1994) *5:* 75–76; *27:* 170, 183–84; *39:* 11–13, 37, 42, 48; *40:* 87
Aikens v. Banana Republic, Inc., 877 F. Supp. 1031, 4 AD 283 (S.D. Tex. 1995) *21:* 27
Air Line Pilots; EEOC v., 885 F. Supp. 289, 67 FEP 1363 (D.D.C. 1995) *33:* 43; *34:* 2, 25
Ajaz v. Continental Airlines, 156 F.R.D. 145 (S.D. Tex. 1994) *33:* 18, 36
Aka v. Washington Hosp. Ctr., 6 AD 1623 (D.D.C. 1996) *9:* 67, 93
Albemarle Paper Co. v. Moody, 422 U.S. 405, 10 FEP 1181 (1975) *5:* 29
Albert v. National Cash Register Co., 874 F. Supp. 1324, 66 FEP 567 (S.D. Fla. 1994) *32:* 22
Alberts v. Wickes Lumber Co., 1995 WL 117886 (N.D. Ill. Mar. 15, 1995) *38:* 22, 50
Albright v. Oliver, 114 S. Ct. 807 (1994) *24:* 34
Alexander
—v. Estepp, 95 F.3d 312 (4th Cir. 1996), *cert. denied sub nom.* Prince Georges County v. Alexander, 117 S. Ct. 1425 (1997) *27:* 85–87
—v. Gerhardt Enters., 40 F.3d 187, 68 FEP 595 (7th Cir. 1994) *17:* 10, 47; *42:* 1
—v. Rush N. Shore Med. Ctr., 101 F.3d 487, 72 FEP 742 (7th Cir. 1996), *cert. denied,* 118 S. Ct. 54 (1998) *30:* 18, 21
Alford v. City of Montgomery, 879 F. Supp. 1143 (M.D. Ala. 1995), *aff'd mem.,* 79 F.3d 1160 (11th Cir. 1996) *4:* 10; *19:* 7, 11, 20
Ali
—v. City of Clearwater, 915 F. Supp. 1231 (M.D. Fla. 1996) *41:* 35

—v. Jeng, 86 F.3d 1148 (4th Cir. 1996) *32:* 7
Alie v. NYNEX Corp., 158 F.R.D. 239, 166 FEP 812 (E.D.N.Y. 1994) *30:* 54, 57
Allen
—v. Bridgestone/Firestone, Inc., 81 F.3d 793, 70 FEP 942 (8th Cir. 1996) *21:* 25
—v. Diebold, Inc., 33 F.3d 674, 65 FEP 1202 (6th Cir. 1994) *16:* 172; *39:* 62–63
—v. Ethicon, Inc., 919 F. Supp. 1093 (S.D. Ohio 1996) *16:* 151, 157
Allied-Bruce Terminix Cos. v. Dobson, 115 S. Ct. 834 (1995) *32:* 24–26
Alston v. City of Camden, 471 S.E.2d 174, 11 IER 1337 (S.C. 1996) *26:* 17
Altheimer & Gray v. Sioux Mfg. Corp., 983 F.2d 803 (7th Cir.), *cert. denied,* 510 U.S. 1019 (1995) *12:* 3
Altman
—v. New York City Health & Hosps. Corp., 903 F. Supp. 503, 4 AD 1665 (S.D.N.Y. 1995), *aff'd,* 100 F.3d 1054, 6 AD 73 (2d Cir. 1996) *9:* 149, 166, 249, 267, 270
—v. Port Authority of N.Y. & N.J., 879 F. Supp. 345, 67 FEP 1355 (S.D.N.Y. 1995) *42:* 50, 53
Aluminum Phosphide Antitrust Litig., In re, 160 F.R.D. 609 (D. Kan. 1995) *37:* 52
Alvarado v. Carnation Co., 1995 U.S. Dist. LEXIS 10084 (D. Idaho June 23, 1995) *37:* 31, 65, 91
Alvey v. Rayovac Corp., 922 F. Supp. 1315, 70 FEP 1331 (W.D. Wis. 1996) *21:* 7
Al-Wardi v. Command Airways/American Eagle, 39 F.3d 1166 (1st Cir. 1994) *11:* 12
Aman v. Cort Furniture Rental Corp., 85 F.3d 1074, 70 FEP 1614 (3d Cir. 1996) *20:* 2; *21:* 18
Amariglio v. National R.R. Passenger Corp., 941 F. Supp. 173 (D.D.C. 1996) *9:* 136, 170

Amchem Prods., Inc. v. Windsor, 117 S. Ct. 2231 (1997) *37:* 34–35, 108–10

Amdura Corp., In re, 170 B.R. 445 (Bankr. D. Colo. 1994) *37:* 82

Amego, Inc.; EEOC v., 110 F.3d 135, 6 AD 997 (1st Cir. 1997) *9:* 223, 243, 252, 289

American Airlines, Inc.
—v. Hermann, 971 F. Supp. 1096 (N.D. Tex. 1997) *28:* 69
—EEOC v., 48 F.3d 164, 67 FEP 754 (5th Cir. 1995) *39:* 8–9, 37, 42

American Med. Sys., Inc., In re, 75 F.3d 1069 (6th Cir. 1996) *37:* 42, 119

Americanos v. Carter, 74 F.3d 138, 69 FEP 1183 (7th Cir.), *cert. denied,* 116 S. Ct. 1853 (1996) *16:* 9; *30:* 22, 67

Amin v. Quad/Graphics, Inc., 929 F. Supp. 73 (N.D.N.Y. 1996) *8:* 44; *33:* 56

Amirmokri v. Baltimore Gas & Elec. Co., 60 F.3d 1126, 68 FEP 809 (4th Cir. 1995) *7:* 1; *19:* 13, 22; *21:* 8; *40:* 6

Amoco Fabrics & Fibers Co. v. Hilson, 669 So. 2d 832, 10 IER 1651 (Ala. 1995) *26:* 5

Amos v. Housing Auth., 927 F. Supp. 416, 70 FEP 1590 (N.D. Ala. 1996) *17:* 4

Anderson
—v. Douglas & Lomason Co.
——26 F.3d 1277, 65 FEP 417, 69 FEP 131 (5th Cir. 1994), *cert. denied,* 513 U.S. 1149 (1995) *4:* 28; *39:* 22, 27, 29, 31, 33, 59
——540 N.W.2d 277, 11 IER 263 (Iowa 1995) *26:* 5, 12
—v. Gus Mayer Boston Store, 924 F. Supp. 763, 5 AD 673 (E.D. Tex. 1996) *9:* 1, 46, 92, 115
—v. Lifeco Servs. Corp., 881 F. Supp. 1500, 67 FEP 1047 (D. Colo. 1995) *16:* 198
—v. Martin Brower Co., 1994 U.S. Dist. LEXIS 10682, 3 AD 829 (D. Kan. 1994) *26:* 1
—v. Queen Carpet Corp., 68 FEP 83 (N.D. Ga. 1995) *16:* 106; *39:* 33–34, 37, 42, 49
—v. Unisys Corp., 47 F.3d 302, 67 FEP 317 (8th Cir.), *cert. denied,* 516 U.S. 913, 68 FEP 1888 (1995) *16:* 59, 84; *31:* 36, 47; *33:* 6
—v. Vanden Dorpel, 667 N.E.2d 1296, 11 IER 1103 (Ill. 1996) *26:* 38, 52

Andrade
—v. Jamestown Hous. Auth., 82 F.3d 1179 (1st Cir. 1996) *42:* 46
—v. Mayfair Mgmt., Inc., 88 F.3d 258, 71 FEP 192 (4th Cir. 1996) *20:* 86; *21:* 2, 7

Andrews
—v. American Tel. & Tel. Co., 95 F.3d 1014 (11th Cir. 1996) *37:* 50
—v. City of Philadelphia, 895 F.2d 1469, 54 FEP 184 (3d Cir. 1990) *24:* 33
—v. Ohio, 104 F.3d 803, 6 AD 322 (6th Cir. 1997) *9:* 40

Angotti v. Kenyon & Kenyon, 929 F. Supp. 651, 70 FEP 316 (S.D.N.Y. 1996) *33:* 6

Annis v. County of Westchester, 36 F.3d 251, 65 FEP 1657 (2d Cir. 1994) *24:* 36, 39

Ansonia Bd. of Educ. v. Philbrook, 479 U.S. 60, 42 FEP 359 (1986) *8:* 9

Anthony v. County of Sacramento, 898 F. Supp. 1435, 68 FEP 1837 (E.D. Cal. 1995) *13:* 32; *20:* 67

Antol v. Perry, 82 F.3d 1291, 70 FEP 993 (3d Cir. 1996) *2:* 48, 50; *9:* 67; *36:* 19

Antos v. Bell & Howell Co., 891 F. Supp. 1281, 68 FEP 847 (N.D. Ill. 1995) *16:* 52

Anzalone v. Allstate Ins. Co., 5 AD 455 (E.D. La.), *aff'd mem.,* 74 F.3d 1236 (5th Cir. 1995) *9:* 65, 128, 196

Appleton v. Deloitte & Touche L.L.P., 168 F.R.D. 221 (M.D. Tenn. 1996) *37:* 6

Aquinas v. Federal Express Corp., 940 F. Supp. 73, 6 AD 485 (S.D.N.Y. 1996) *9:* 66, 154–55

Aramburu v. Boeing Co., 885 F. Supp. 1434 (D. Kan. 1995) *38:* 30

Ardrey v. Federal Kemper Ins. Co., 142 F.R.D. 105 (E.D. Pa. 1992) *37:* 48

Arenson v. Whitehall Convalescent & Nursing Home, Inc., 164 F.R.D. 659 (N.D. Ill. 1996) *37:* 45, 47–48

Armbruster v. Unisys Corp., 32 F.3d 768, 65 FEP 828 (3d Cir. 1994) *2:* 55–56; *16:* 123, 136–37, 165, 167

Armendariz v. Pinkerton Tobacco Co., 58 F.3d 144, 68 FEP 361 (5th Cir. 1995), *cert. denied,* 116 S. Ct. 709 (1996) *16:* 150, 176

Armfield v. Runyon, 902 F. Supp. 823 (N.D. Ill. 1995) *17:* 17, 41

Armstead v. Becton Dickinson Primary Care Diagnostics, Inc., 919 F. Supp. 188 (D. Md. 1996) *33:* 26–27

Armstrong
—v. Flowers Hosp., Inc., 33 F.3d 1308, 65 FEP 1742 (11th Cir. 1994) *13:* 25
—v. Martin Marietta Corp., 1998 U.S. App. LEXIS 7486 (11th Cir. 1998) *37:* 77–79
—v. Wilson, 942 F. Supp. 1252, 6 AD 1193 (N.D. Cal. 1996), *aff'd,* 124 F.3d 1019, 7 AD 323 (9th Cir. 1997), *petition for cert. filed,* 66 U.S.L.W. 3308 (U.S. Oct. 20, 1997) *9:* 19

Arnett v. Aspin, 846 F.Supp. 1234, 69 FEP 966 (E.D. Pa. 1994) *13:* 34, 36; *16:* 67

Arnold
—v. Boatmen's Nat'l Bank, 1996 U.S. App. LEXIS 15669 (7th Cir. Jun. 25, 1996), *cert. denied,* 117 S. Ct. 586 (1996) *18:* 10
—v. United Artists Theatre Circuit, 158 F.R.D. 439 (N.D. Cal. 1994) *37:* 56

Arroyo v. New York State Ins. Dep't, 4 AD 1830 (S.D.N.Y. 1995), *aff'd,* 104 F.3d 349 (2d Cir. 1996) *16:* 101

Arzate v. City of Topeka, 884 F. Supp. 1494, 72 FEP 681 (D. Kan. 1995) *10:* 1–2, 5; *11:* 30; *19:* 13

Ascolese v. Southeastern Pa. Transp. Auth., 902 F. Supp. 533, 70 FEP 325 (E.D. Pa. 1995), *on reconsideration,* 925 F. Supp. 351, 72 FEP 1027 (E.D. Pa. 1996) *20:* 49, 69; *24:* 35

Ashley v. Boyle's Famous Corned Beef Co., 48 F.3d 1051, 67 FEP 208 (8th Cir.), *opinion vacated on reh'g en banc,* 66 F.3d 164, 68 FEP 1261 (8th Cir. 1995) *31:* 16, 54–55; *41:* 135

Asplundh Tree Expert Co. v. Bates, 71 F.3d 592, 11 IER 61 (6th Cir. 1995) *32:* 22

Associated Dry Goods Corp.; EEOC v., 449 U.S. 590, 24 FEP 1356 (1981) *38:* 25

Associated Gen. Contractors of Am.
—v. City of Columbus, 936 F. Supp. 1363 (S.D. Ohio 1996) *27:* 54, 80
—v. City of New Haven, 41 F.3d 62 (2d Cir. 1994) *27:* 55

Association of Mexican-American Educators v. California
—836 F. Supp 1534, 62 FEP 1390 (N.D. Cal. 1993) *5:* 9
—937 F. Supp. 1397 (N.D. Cal. 1996) *5:* 16–18, 25, 30, 39, 51, 56–57, 59, 74

Astra U.S.A., Inc.; EEOC v., 94 F.3d 738, 71 FEP 1267 (1st Cir. 1996) *40:* 3, 12–14, 91, 102–03; *43:* 50–52

Astrowsky v. First Portland Mortgage Corp., 881 F. Supp 332, 70 FEP 195 (D. Me. 1995) *16:* 18; *30:* 59–60

Atkinson
—v. Denton Publ'g Co., 84 F.3d 144, 70 FEP 1352 (5th Cir. 1996) *38:* 7
—v. Washington Int'l Ins. Co., 1995 WL 68756, 1995 U.S. Dist. LEXIS 1865 (N.D. Ill. Feb. 14, 1995) *15:* 13

Aucutt v. Six Flags Over Mid-Am., Inc., 85 F.3d 1311, 5 AD 902 (8th Cir. 1996) *16:* 151, 167

Ausfeldt v. Runyon, 950 F. Supp. 478 (N.D.N.Y. 1997) *9:* 309

Auslander v. Collier & Tiku Assocs., 68 FEP 702 (D. Mass. 1995) *30:* 60

Austin v. Owens-Brockway Glass Container, Inc., 78 F.3d 875, 70 FEP 272 (4th Cir.), *cert. denied,* 117 S. Ct. 432 (1996) *9:* 298; *32:* 23, 27

Austin Black Contractors v. City of Austin, 78 F.3d 185 (5th Cir. 1996) *27:* 42

Avitia v. Metropolitan Club of Chicago, Inc., 49 F.3d 1219, 2 WH2d 993 (7th Cir. 1995) *15:* 28; *40:* 22, 27–28, 37–38

Ayala-Gerena v. Bristol Myers-Squibb Co., 95 F.3d 86, 71 FEP 1398 (1st Cir. 1996) *38:* 6

B

Baba v. Warren Management Consultants, Inc., 882 F. Supp. 339, 74 FEP 707 (S.D.N.Y.), aff'd, 89 F.3d 826 (2d Cir. 1995) **34:** 8; **43:** 6

Back v. Carter, 933 F. Supp 738 (N.D. Ind. 1996) **27:** 47, 54, 58–59, 78, 90, 96

Backlund v. Hessen, 104 F.3d 1031, 12 IER 753 (8th Cir. 1997) **24:** 40

Badih v. Myers, 36 Cal. App.4th 1289, 68 FEP 592 (Cal. Ct. App. 1995) **26:** 24

Bahadirli v. Domino's Pizza, 873 F. Supp. 1528, 71 FEP 1615 (M.D. Ala. 1995) **41:** 37, 50

Bailey v. DiMario, 925 F. Supp. 801, 69 FEP 233 (D.D.C. 1995) **39:** 23

Baker
—v. American Juice, Inc., 870 F. Supp. 878, 68 FEP 52 (N.D. Ind. 1994) **24:** 45
—v. Farmers Elec. Co-op, Inc., 34 F.3d 274, 10 IER 1556 (5th Cir. 1994) **26:** 2
—v. Ogden Servs. Corp., 74 F.3d 1248 (10th Cir. 1996) **18:** 7, 10
—v. Runyon, 922 F. Supp. 1296 (N.D. Ill. 1996), rev'd, 114 F.3d 668 (7th Cir. 1997) **9:** 308
—v. Summit Unlimited, Inc. 855 F. Supp. 375, 65 FEP 176 (N.D. Ga. 1994) **17:** 37

Balazs v. Liebenthal, 32 F.3d 151, 65 FEP 993 (4th Cir. 1994) **17:** 5; **30:** 6; **33:** 12, 14

Baldwin v. National College, 537 N.W.2d 14, 11 IER 297 (S.D. 1995) **26:** 19

Balele v. Klauser, 74 F.3d 1242 (7th Cir.), cert. denied, 116 S. Ct. 1577 (1996) **4:** 35; **18:** 6

Ballard v. Alabama, 1996 U.S. Dist. LEXIS 1822 (S.D. Ala. Jan. 25, 1996) **9:** 199

Balletti v. Sun-Sentinel Co., 909 F. Supp. 1539, 73 FEP 1341 (S.D. Fla. 1995) **17:** 40; **20:** 56, 58–59

Banks v. Chicago Bd. of Educ., 895 F. Supp. 206, 68 FEP 1333 (N.D. Ill. 1995) **33:** 19

Barber
—v. CSX Distrib. Servs., 68 F.3d 694, 69 FEP 81 (3d Cir. 1995) **16:** 104
—v. Whirlpool Corp., 34 F.3d 1268, 9 IER 1492 (4th Cir. 1994) **26:** 33

Barbero v. Catawba Valley Legal Servs., Inc., 69 FEP 460 (W.D.N.C. 1995) **30:** 55

Barbour
—v. Dynamics Research Corp., 63 F.3d 32 (1st Cir. 1995), cert. denied, 516 U.S. 1113 (1996) **2:** 38
—v. Merrill, 48 F.3d 1270, 67 FEP 369, reh'g denied en banc, 68 FEP 126 (D.C. Cir. 1995), cert. granted, 516 U.S. 1086, cert. dismissed, 516 U.S. 1155 (1996) **2:** 34; **24:** 56, 60, 62–63; **40:** 38, 48–49, 51–52, 84; **41:** 8, 17, 105

Barfield v. Bell S. Telecomms., Inc., 886 F. Supp. 1321, 4 AD 1159 (S.D. Miss. 1995) **9:** 66, 153

Barge v. Anheuser-Busch, Inc., 87 F.3d 256, 72 FEP 426 (8th Cir. 1996) **17:** 53

Barker v. Menominee Nation Casino, 897 F. Supp. 389 (E.D. Wis. 1995) **12:** 2–3, 5

Barnard v. Jackson County, 43 F.3d 1218 (8th Cir.), cert. denied, 116 S. Ct. 53 (1995) **17:** 69

Barnes
—v. Cochran, 944 F. Supp. 897, 5 AD 1685 (S.D. Fla. 1996) **9:** 67, 87
—v. GenCorp, Inc., 896 F.2d 1457 (6th Cir. 1990) **16:** 151

Barnfield v. New Hampshire, 5 AD 1819 (D.N.H. 1996) **9:** 57

Barratt v. Cushman & Wakefield of N.J., 675 A.2d 1094, 11 IER 1172 (N.J. 1996) **26:** 23

Barrett v. Tomkins Indus., Inc., 930 F. Supp. 508 (D. Kan. 1996) **16:** 165

Barta v. City & County of Honolulu, 169 F.R.D. 132 (D. Haw. 1996) **38:** 22, 47–48

Bartges v. University of N.C. at Charlotte, 908 F. Supp. 1312, 70 FEP 1643 (W.D.N.C. 1995), aff'd mem., 94 F.3d 641 (4th Cir. 1996) **15:** 33; **21:** 2, 22

Barth v. Gelb, 2 F.3d 1180, 2 AD 1180 (D.C. Cir. 1993)   *9:* 68, 287

Barton v. Forbes, Inc., 67 FEP 138 (S.D.N.Y. 1995)   *16:* 99, 165

Bass Pub. Ltd. v. Promus Cos., 1994 WL 702052 (S.D.N.Y. Dec. 12, 1994) *38:* 17

Batch v. Russ Berrie & Co., 1994 WL 634052 (N.D. Cal. Oct. 20, 1994)   *16:* 129

Bator v. Hawaii, 39 F.3d 1021, 66 FEP 290 (9th Cir. 1994)   *24:* 33, 36

Batson v. Powell, 912 F. Supp. 565 (D.D.C. 1996)   *2:* 13

Baumgardner v. ROA Gen., Inc., 864 F. Supp. 1107, 72 FEP 514 (D. Utah 1994)   *15:* 11, 34–35

Baustian v. Louisiana, 910 F. Supp. 274 (E.D. La. 1996)   *9:* 261, 263

Bazemore v. Friday, 478 U.S. 385, 41 FEP 92 (1986)   *27:* 107

Beadle
—v. City of Tampa, 42 F.3d 633, 66 FEP 1540 (11th Cir.), *cert. denied,* 515 U.S. 1152 (1995)   *8:* 20, 24–26; *43:* 1, 6
—v. Hillsborough County Sheriff's Dep't, 29 F.3d 589, 65 FEP 1069 (11th Cir. 1994), *cert. denied,* 115 S. Ct. 2001 (1995)   *8:* 18, 25–26, 29

Beardsley v. Webb, 30 F.3d 524, 65 FEP 696 (4th Cir. 1994)   *24:* 36, 39

Beauchamp v. Great W. Life Assur. Co., 918 F. Supp 1091, 73 FEP 361 (E.D. Mich. 1996)   *32:* 32, 34

Beauford v. Father Flanagan's Boys' Home, 831 F.2d 768, 1 AD 1153 (8th Cir. 1987)   *9:* 100

Becerra v. Dalton, 94 F.3d 145, 71 FEP 1236 (4th Cir. 1996), *cert. denied,* 117 S. Ct. 1087 (1997)   *20:* 107, 109

Beck v. University of Wis. Bd. of Regents, 75 F.3d 1130, 5 AD 304 (7th Cir. 1996)   *9:* 200–01

Beckwith v. City of Daytona Beach Shores, 58 F.3d 1554 (11th Cir. 1995)   *17:* 68

Beinlich v. Curry Dev., Inc., 54 F.3d 772 (4th Cir. 1995)   *41:* 129

Beister v. Midwest Health Servs., Inc., 77 F.3d 1264, 70 FEP 397 (10th Cir. 1996)   *31:* 53

Bellairs v. Coors Brewing Co., 907 F. Supp. 1448 (D. Colo. 1995), *aff'd,* 107 F.3d 880 (10th Cir. 1997)   *24:* 17

Benekritis v. Johnson, 882 F. Supp. 521, 67 FEP 1449 (D.S.C. 1995)   *17:* 10

Benson v. Northwest Airlines, Inc., 62 F.3d 1108, 4 AD 1234 (8th Cir. 1995)   *9:* 123, 133, 186, 272, 277, 279; *22:* 21

Bernheim v. Litt, 79 F.3d 318 (2d Cir. 1996)   *17:* 58

Berry
—v. Norfolk S. Corp., 1995 WL 465819 (W.D. Va. June 23, 1995)   *38:* 20
—v. Stevinson Chevrolet, 74 F.3d 980, 69 FEP 1320 (10th Cir. 1996)   *17:* 29

Bethesda Lutheran Homes & Servs. v. Leean, 165 F.R.D. 87 (W.D. Wis. 1996)   *37:* 44

Betkerur v. Aultman Hosp. Ass'n, 78 F.3d 1079 (6th Cir. 1996)   *24:* 20, 56

Bialas v. Greyhound Lines, Inc., 59 F.3d 759, 68 FEP 552 (8th Cir. 1995)   *2:* 56; *16:* 101, 148, 160, 167, 179

Bielawski v. AMI, Inc., 870 F. Supp. 771, 66 FEP 1160 (N.D. Ohio 1994)   *15:* 8; *30:* 53

Biester v. Midwest Health Servs., Inc., 77 F.3d 1264, 70 FEP 397 (10th Cir. 1996)   *31:* 43

Biggs v. Nicewonger Co., 897 F. Supp. 483, 68 FEP 1771 (D. Or. 1995)   *38:* 36, 48

Binder v. Long Island Lighting Co., 57 F.3d 193, 67 FEP 1783 (2d Cir. 1995)   *2:* 16, 24

Binion v. Metropolitan Pier & Expo. Auth., 163 F.R.D. 517 (N.D. Ill. 1995)   *37:* 4, 16, 22; *33:* 41

Birch v. West, 870 F. Supp. 310 (D. Colo. 1994)   *17:* 30; *18:* 9

Birkbeck v. Marvel Lighting Corp., 30 F.3d 507, 65 FEP 669 (4th Cir.), *cert. denied,* 513 U.S. 1058 (1994)   *16:* 27, 107, 122, 132, 166; *39:* 78

Birklid v. Boeing Co., 904 P.2d 278, 11 IER 97 (Wash. 1995)   *26:* 35, 57

Birmingham Reverse Discrimination Employment Litig., In re, 20 F.3d 1525 (11th Cir. 1994), *cert. denied,* 514 U.S. 1065 (1995)   *37:* 114, 117

Birting Fisheries, In re, 178 B.R. 849 (Bankr. W.D. Wash. 1995), aff'd, 92 F.3d 939 (9th Cir. 1996) *37:* 81–82

Bisciglia v. Kenosha Unified Sch. Dist. No. 1, 45 F.3d 223 (7th Cir. 1995) *11:* 12; *24:* 14

Bishop v. Okidata, Inc., 864 F. Supp. 416, 3 AD 1283 (D.N.J. 1994) *33:* 16

Bishopp v. District of Columbia, 57 F.3d 1088 (D.C. Cir. 1995) *41:* 140–41

Bivins v. Jeffers Vet Supply, 873 F. Supp. 1500, 75 FEP 776 (M.D. Ala. 1994), aff'd, 58 F.3d 640 (11th Cir. 1995) *21:* 7

BJ Servs. Co.; EEOC v., 921 F. Supp. 1509 (N.D. Tex. 1995) *8:* 5, 8, 20, 28

Black v. New York Univ. Med. Ctr., 1996 WL 294310 (S.D.N.Y. June 3, 1996) *38:* 34

Blackburn v. City of Marshall, 42 F.3d 925 (5th Cir. 1995) *17:* 72

Blackwell v. Danbury Hosp., 1996 WL 409370 (Conn. Super. Ct. Jun. 26, 1996) *18:* 4

Blanciak v. Allegheny Ludlum Corp., 77 F.3d 690, 70 FEP 27 (3d Cir. 1996) *16:* 37; *23:* 6

Blankenship
—v. Martin Marietta Energy Sys., 83 F.3d 153, 5 AD 789 (6th Cir. 1996) *9:* 59, 237
—v. Warren County, 931 F. Supp. 447, 74 FEP 1459 (W.D. Va. 1996) *24:* 9

Blazy v. Woolsey, 64 FEP 724 (D.D.C. 1994) *33:* 45, 49

Blistein v. St. John's College, 74 F.3d 1459, 69 FEP 1310 (4th Cir. 1996) *16:* 184; *21:* 25

Blong v. Secretary of the Army, 886 F. Supp. 1576, 68 FEP 503 (D. Kan. 1995), aff'd, 86 F.3d 1166, 72 FEP 1280 (10th Cir. 1996) *18:* 11

Blount v. Alabama Coop. Extension Serv., 869 F. Supp. 1543, 66 FEP 889 (M.D. Ala. 1994) *15:* 16

Blozis v. Mike Raisor Ford, Inc., 896 F. Supp. 805, 68 FEP 711 (N.D. Ind. 1995) *20:* 51

BMW of N. Am., Inc. v. Gore, 517 U.S. 559 (1996) *24:* 65; *41:* 107

Board of County Comm'rs v. Umbehr, 116 S. Ct. 2342 (1996) *17:* 72

Board of County Comm'rs of Bryan County v. Brown, 117 S. Ct. 1382, 12 IER 1217 (1997) *24:* 27, 29

Board of Governors; EEOC v., 957 F.2d 424, 58 FEP 292 (7th Cir.), cert. denied, 506 U.S. 906 (1992) *36:* 14

Board of Trustees of Ill. State Univ.; United States v., 944 F. Supp. 714, 72 FEP 382 (C.D. Ill. 1996) *40:* 2, 5, 12; *41:* 136

Boerne, City of, v. Flores, 117 S. Ct. 2157 (1997) *8:* 59–60; *16:* 33

Bogan v. Scott-Harris, 118 S. Ct. 966, 76 FEP 146 (1998) *24:* 31

Bohac v. West, 85 F.3d 306, 70 FEP 1734 (7th Cir. 1996) *16:* 57–58

Bolden v. PRC Inc., 43 F.3d 545, 67 FEP 1790 (10th Cir. 1994), cert. denied, 116 S. Ct. 92, 70 FEP 578 (1995) *10:* 5; *21:* 11

Bolton
—v. Department of Human Servs., 540 N.W.2d 523, 11 IER 369 (Minn. 1995) *26:* 41
—v. Scrivner, Inc., 36 F.3d 939, 3 AD 1089 (10th Cir. 1994), cert. denied, 513 U.S. 1152 (1995) *16:* 179

Bombrys v. City of Toledo, 849 F. Supp. 1210, 3 AD 651 (N.D. Ohio 1993) *9:* 151

Bonastia v. Berman Bros. Inc., 914 F. Supp. 1533, 11 IER 725 (W.D. Tenn. 1995) *26:* 15

Bonds v. Heyman, 950 F. Supp. 1202, 72 FEP 1589 (D.D.C. 1997) *36:* 17–18

Bonenberger v. Plymouth Township, 72 FEP 1241 (E.D. Pa. 1996), aff'd in part, rev'd in part, 132 F.2d 20 (3d Cir. 1997) *20:* 19

Bonner v. Guccione, 68 FEP 47 (S.D.N.Y. 1995) *20:* 108; *33:* 20

Booker v. Taylor Milk Co., 64 F.3d 860, 71 FEP 525 (3d Cir. 1995) *41:* 2, 35, 39–40

Boone v. Federal Express Corp., 59 F.3d 84, 68 FEP 353 (8th Cir. 1995) *24:* 3

Borase v. M/A-Com., Inc., 906 F. Supp. 65, 73 FEP 1355 (D. Mass. 1995) *17:* 3

Bordell v. General Elec., 667 N.E.2d 923, 11 IER 1183 (N.Y. Ct. App. 1996) *26:* 30

Boring v. Buncombe County Bd. of Educ., 136 F.3d 364 (4th Cir. 1998) *14:* 15–16

Borkowski v. Valley Cent. Sch. Dist., 63 F.3d 131, 4 AD 1264 (2d Cir. 1995) *9:* 123, 164, 170–71, 177, 183, 216–17, 220–21, 236, 284–85

Bormann v. AT&T Communications, Inc., 875 F.2d 399, 49 FEP 1622 (2d Cir.), *cert. denied,* 493 U.S. 924 (1989) *43:* 5

Bottomly v. Leucadia Nat'l, 163 F.R.D. 617 (D. Utah 1995) *20:* 67; *38:* 46

Boyd
—v. Brookstone Corp., 857 F. Supp. 1568, 71 FEP 3 (S.D. Fla. 1994) *17:* 3, 31
—v. Harding Academy of Memphis, Inc., 88 F.3d 410, 71 FEP 300 (6th Cir. 1996) *8:* 48–51

Bradford v. Norfolk S. Corp., 54 F.3d 1412, 71 FEP 259 (8th Cir. 1995) *21:* 10

Bradshaw v. University of Me. Sys., 870 F. Supp. 406, 66 FEP 806 (D. Me. 1994) *41:* 96

Bragalone v. Kona Coast Resort Joint Venture, 866 F. Supp. 1285, 66 FEP 65 (D. Haw. 1994) *16:* 165, 213; *41:* 52

Bragdon v. Abbott, 118 S. Ct. 2196, 8 AD 239 (1998) *1:* 3; *9:* 39, 49, 254–59

Brand Name Prescription Drugs Antitrust Litig., In re, 1995 WL 60526 (N.D. Ill. June 15, 1995) *38:* 17

Bratton v. Roadway Package Sys., Inc., 77 F.3d 168, 70 FEP 178 (7th Cir. 1996) *24:* 21, 56

Braverman v. Penobscot Shoe Co., 859 F. Supp. 596, 65 FEP 882 (D. Me. 1994) *16:* 117; *30:* 61; *41:* 28, 118

Braziel v. Loram Maintenance of Way, Inc., 943 F. Supp. 1083 (D. Minn. 1996) *9:* 136, 188, 209

Breen v. Hunt Real Estate Corp., 65 FEP 1392 (W.D.N.Y. 1994) *30:* 13

Brem v. Decarlo, 162 F.R.D. 94 (D. Md. 1995) *38:* 32

Bremiller v. Cleveland Psychiatric Inst., 898 F. Supp. 573 (N.D. Ohio 1995) *37:* 22, 29, 47, 56, 65

Brennan v. National Tel. Directory Corp., 881 F. Supp. 986, 67 FEP 922 (E.D. Pa. 1995) *2:* 13; *30:* 56; *33:* 10

Brewer v. Quaker State Oil Ref. Corp., 874 F. Supp. 672, 69 FEP 743 (W.D. Pa.), *rev'd and remanded,* 72 F.3d 326, 69 FEP 753 (3d Cir. 1995) *16:* 99, 112, 116, 165

Brezovski v. U.S. Postal Serv., 905 F.2d 334, 55 FEP 1717 (10th Cir. 1990) *36:* 21

Bridges v. Eastman Kodak Co., 102 F.3d 56, 72 FEP 948 (2d Cir. 1996) *42:* 2

Bright v. Standard Register Co., 66 F.3d 171, 68 FEP 1694 (8th Cir. 1995) *2:* 44; *16:* 176

Brinkley-Obu v. Hughes Training, Inc.
—1993 WL 747922 (E.D. Va. June 22, 1993) *40:* 59
—36 F.3d 336, 65 FEP 1840 (4th Cir. 1994) *2:* 45; *15:* 8, 31–32; *31:* 15; *40:* 60–61; *41:* 115

Briscoe v. Fred's Dollar Store, Inc., 24 F.3d 1026, 64 FEP 1185 (8th Cir. 1994) *2:* 50

Brisentine v. Stone & Webster Eng'g Corp., 117 F.3d 519, 6 AD 1878 (11th Cir. 1997) *9:* 298; *32:* 23, 27, 34

Bristow v. Drake St., Inc., 41 F.3d 345, 66 FEP 739 (7th Cir. 1994) *41:* 121

Brocklehurst v. PPG Indus., Inc., 865 F. Supp. 1253, 66 FEP 545 (E.D. Mich. 1994) *41:* 69, 87, 101, 103–04

Brodsky v. City Univ. of N.Y., 56 F.3d 8, 67 FEP 1505 (2d Cir. 1995) *16:* 61

Brogdon v. Alabama Dep't of Econ. & Community Affairs, 864 F. Supp. 1161, 66 FEP 325 (M.D. Ala. 1994) *16:* 27, 34, 78; *33:* 18

Brook v. City of Montgomery, 916 F. Supp. 1193, 73 FEP 985 (M.D. Ala. 1996) *16:* 45; *19:* 12, 22, 25; *33:* 13

Brooks
—v. Bellsouth Telecommunications, Inc., 164 F.R.D. 561 (N.D. Ala. 1995), *aff'd,* 114 F.3d 1202 (11th Cir. 1997) *16:* 81; *33:* 42; *37:* 23
—v. Circuit City Stores, 71 FEP 102 (D. Md. 1996) *37:* 6, 21, 23, 32
—v. Fonda-Fultonville Cent. Sch. Dist., 938 F. Supp. 1094 (N.D.N.Y. 1996) *41:* 36

Brothers v. NCR Corp., 885 F. Supp. 1043, 68 FEP 6 (N.D. Ohio 1995) *16:* 138, 154, 167

Brown
—v. City of Chicago, 917 F. Supp. 577 (N.D. Ill. 1996) *5:* 2, 30; *40:* 90, 93
—v. CSC Logic, Inc., 82 F.3d 651, 70 FEP 1273 (5th Cir. 1996) *16:* 154, 166, 168–71; *21:* 30
—v. Oscar Mayer Foods Corp., 1996 WL 99412 (N.D. Ill. Mar. 5, 1996) *16:* 155
—v. Polk County, 61 F.3d 650, 68 FEP 348 (8th Cir. 1995), *cert. denied,* 116 S. Ct. 1042 (1996) *8:* 6, 15–16, 20, 39
—v. Secretary of Army, 78 F.3d 645, 72 FEP 595 (D.C. Cir.), *cert. denied,* 117 S. Ct. 607 (1996) *41:* 25
—v. Westinghouse Savannah River Corp., 928 F. Supp. 1168, 71 FEP 516 (S.D. Ga. 1996) *27:* 8, 15, 27

Brunet
—v. City of Columbia
——1 F.3d 390, 64 FEP 1215 (6th Cir. 1993), *cert. denied sub nom.* Brunet v. Tucker, 510 U.S. 1164 (1994) *5:* 20, 31–32, 63
——58 F.3d 251, 68 FEP 518 (6th Cir. 1995) *5:* 64
—v. Tucker, *see* Brunet v. City of Columbia

Bryant v. Better Bus. Bureau, 923 F. Supp. 720, 5 AD 625 (D. Md. 1996) *9:* 167, 218–19, 235, 274

Bryson
—v. Chicago State Univ., 96 F.3d 912, 71 FEP 1577 (7th Cir. 1996) *20:* 22–24, 40
—v. Fluor Corp., 914 F. Supp. 1292, 70 FEP 304 (D.S.C. 1995) *16:* 83–84

Buchanan
—v. City of San Antonio, 85 F.3d 196, 5 AD 987 (5th Cir. 1996) *9:* 84
—v. Sherrill, 51 F.3d 227, 67 FEP 713 (10th Cir. 1995) *21:* 7

Buck v. United States Dep't of Transp., 56 F.3d 1406, 4 AD 833 (D.C. Cir. 1995) *9:* 50–51, 212

Buckley v. Consolidated Edison Co., 934 F. Supp. 104, 5 AD 1459 (S.D.N.Y. 1996) *9:* 271

Budd v. ADT Sec. Sys., Inc., 103 F.3d 699, 6 AD 867 (8th Cir. 1996) *9:* 61

Buford v. H&R Block, Inc., 168 F.R.D. 340 (S.D. Ga. 1996), *aff'd,* 117 F.3d 1433 (11th Cir. 1997) *37:* 38–39, 41, 50

Bultemeyer v. Fort Wayne Community Sch., 100 F.3d 1281, 6 AD 67 (7th Cir. 1996) *9:* 275

Burch v. Coca-Cola Co., 119 F.3d 305, 7 AD 241 (5th Cir. 1997), *cert. denied,* 66 U.S.L.W. 3364 (U.S. Jan. 20, 1998) *9:* 43

Burdi v. Uniglobe Cihak Travel, Inc., 932 F. Supp. 1044, 71 FEP 925 (N.D. Ill. 1996) *30:* 53, 59

Burger v. Litton Indus., 68 FEP 737 (S.D.N.Y. 1995) *38:* 29, 45, 47

Burke v. Virginia, 938 F. Supp. 320, 5 AD 1747 (E.D. Va. 1996), *aff'd mem.,* 114 F.3d 1175, 6 AD 1440 (4th Cir. 1997) *9:* 73, 150

Burks v. Oklahoma Publ'g Co., 81 F.3d 975, 70 FEP 945 (10th Cir.), *cert. denied,* 117 S. Ct. 302 (1996) *21:* 1, 10; *38:* 40

Burlington Indus., Inc. v. Ellerth, 118 S. Ct. 2257, 77 FEP 1 (1998) *1:* 1; *20:* 13, 16–17, 41–44, 84, 87–92, 94

Burnett v. Western Resources, Inc., 929 F. Supp. 1349, 6 AD 711 (D. Kan. 1996) *9:* 122, 131, 148, 159, 189, 208

Burrell v. City Univ., 894 F. Supp. 750, 68 FEP 1398 (S.D.N.Y. 1995) *17:* 48
Bush v. Barnett Bank of Pinellas County, 916 F. Supp. 1244 (M.D. Fla. 1996) *27:* 8, 30–31
Butler
—v. Burroughs Wellcome, Inc., 920 F. Supp. 90 (E.D.N.C. 1996) *38:* 45–46
—v. City of Prairie Village, 974 F. Supp. 1386 (D. Kan. 1997) *20:* 10
—v. Home Depot, 70 FEP 51 (N.D. Cal. 1996) *37:* 5, 17, 22, 55, 94–95
Butta-Brinkman v. FCA Int'l, 164 F.R.D. 475, 69 FEP 1276 (N.D. Ill. 1995) *38:* 29, 34–35, 43
Byrd v. Ronayne, 61 F.3d 1026, 68 FEP 769 (1st Cir. 1995) *2:* 46; *15:* 24

C

Caban-Wheeler v. Elsea, 71 F.3d 837, 69 FEP 1193 (11th Cir. 1996) *42:* 2
Cabiness v. YKK (USA), Inc., 859 F. Supp. 582, 72 FEP 355 (M.D. Ga. 1994) *31:* 17
Cada v. Baxter Healthcare Corp, 920 F.2d 446, 54 FEP 961 (7th Cir. 1990), *cert. denied*, 501 U.S. 1261, 56 FEP 576 (1991) *31:* 27
Calabritto v. Dillon, 920 F. Supp. 370, 73 FEP 675 (E.D.N.Y. 1996), *aff'd*, 107 F.3d 2 (2d Cir. 1997) *2:* 2
Caldwell v. Federal Express Corp., 908 F. Supp. 29, 69 FEP 1055 (D. Me. 1995) *16:* 47
Caliendo v. Bentsen, 881 F. Supp. 44 (D.D.C. 1995) *16:* 56
Callanan v. Runyun, 903 F. Supp. 1285 (D. Minn. 1994), *aff'd*, 75 F.3d 1293 (8th Cir. 1996) *20:* 69
Calloway v. Partners Nat'l Health Plans, 986 F.2d 446, 61 FEP 550 (11th Cir. 1993) *31:* 37
Camden v. Maryland, 910 F. Supp. 1115 (D. Md. 1996) *38:* 38
Cammermeyer v. Perry, 97 F.3d 1235, 72 FEP 93 (9th Cir. 1996) *14:* 17–18
Campbell
—v. Fasco Indus., Inc., 861 F. Supp. 1385, 72 FEP 33 (N.D. Ill. 1994), *aff'd mem.*, 67 F.3d 301, 72 FEP 96 (7th Cir. 1995) *16:* 98–99, 101, 158; *29:* 30; *39:* 78
—v. Pennsylvania College of Optometry, 68 FEP 1488 (E.D. Pa. 1995) *19:* 20
Candelaria v. EG & G Energy Measurements, Inc., 33 F.3d 1259, 72 FEP 1005 (10th Cir. 1994) *17:* 40
Cantrell v. Knoxville Community Dev. Corp., 60 F.3d 1177, 68 FEP 536 (6th Cir. 1995) *31:* 34–35; *41:* 31
Cargile v. Star Enter., 872 F. Supp. 1514 (M.D. La. 1994) *21:* 9–10, 23
Carl v. Angelone 883 F. Supp. 1433 (D. Nev. 1995) *13:* 5–6
Carlson
—v. American Meter Co., 896 F. Supp. 952, 68 FEP 193 (D. Neb. 1995) *17:* 52; *41:* 6
—v. Inacomp Corp., 885 F. Supp. 1314, 4 AD 600 (D. Neb. 1995) *9:* 187
—v. WPLG/TV, 70 FEP 1596 (S.D. Fla. 1996) *16:* 111
Carlton v. Ryan, 916 F. Supp. 832 (N.D. Ill. 1996) *24:* 8
Carmen v. San Francisco Unified Sch. Dist., 982 F. Supp. 1396 (N.D. Cal. 1997) *16:* 35
Carmichael v. Birmingham Saw Works, 738 F.2d 1126, 35 FEP 791 (11th Cir. 1984) *16:* 173
Carpenter v. Western Credit Union, 62 F.3d 143, 68 FEP 545 (6th Cir. 1995) *16:* 166
Carr
—v. Allison Gas Turbine Div., General Motors Corp., 32 F.3d 1007, 65 FEP 688 (7th Cir. 1994) *21:* 18
—v. Woodbury County Juvenile Detention Ctr., 905 F. Supp. 619, 69 FEP 1101 (N.D. Iowa 1995) *41:* 58
Carrozza v. Howard County, 847 F. Supp. 365, 3 AD 197 (D. Md. 1994), *aff'd mem.*, 45 F.3d 425, 4 AD 512 (4th Cir. 1995) *9:* 123, 174, 179
Carson v. Bethlehem Steel Corp., 82 F.3d 157, 70 FEP 921 (7th Cir. 1996) *2:* 9–10, 54; *27:* 18, 20

Carter
—v. American Tel. & Tel. Co., 870 F. Supp. 1438 (S.D. Ohio 1994) *13:* 19; *41:* 15
—v. Ball, 33 F.3d 450, 65 FEP 1414 (4th Cir. 1994) *19:* 13, 27; *29:* 7, 10, 25, 42, 59
—v. Sedgwick County, Kan., 36 F.3d 952, 65 FEP 1585 (10th Cir. 1994) *40:* 38, 48; *42:* 57
Carter-Herman v. City of Philadelphia, 897 F. Supp. 899, 68 FEP 1690 (E.D. Pa. 1996) *38:* 39
Caruso
—v. De Luca, 81 F.3d 666 (7th Cir. 1996) *17:* 69
—v. Forslund, 47 F.3d 27, 31 FEP 1455 (2d Cir. 1995) *42:* 57
Cary v. Carmichael, 908 F. Supp. 1334, 72 FEP 1178 (E.D. Va. 1995) *8:* 3, 8, 17–18, 20, 22, 32
Castano v. American Tobacco Co., 162 F.R.D. 112 (E.D. La. 1995), *class cert. order rev'd,* 84 F.3d 734 (5th Cir. 1996) *37:* 96, 120
Castle
—v. Bentsen, 872 F. Supp. 1062, 66 FEP 1498 (D.D.C. 1995) *42:* 21
—v. Rubin, 78 F.3d 654, 72 FEP 1701 (D.C. Cir. 1996) *40:* 33; *41:* 56
Castleberry v. Boeing Co., 880 F. Supp. 1435 (D. Kan. 1995) *27:* 27
Castner
—v. Colorado Springs Cablevision, 979 F.2d 1417, 60 FEP 566 (10th Cir. 1992) *32:* 8–9
—v. United States Dep't of Energy, 897 F. Supp. 481, 68 FEP 1642 (D. Or. 1995) *2:* 20; *18:* 11
Catanzaro v. Supervalu Inc., 67 FEP 10 (E.D. Mo. 1994) *16:* 78; *33:* 33
Catherine's Inc., 316 NLRB 186, 148 LRRM 1181 (1995) *25:* 1
Catholic Bishop of Chicago; NLRB v., 440 U.S. 490, 100 LRRM 2913 (1979) *16:* 25
Catholic Knights Ins. Soc'y; EEOC v., 915 F. Supp. 25, 70 FEP 281 (N.D. Ill. 1996) *30:* 13

Catholic Univ. of Am.; EEOC v., 83 F.3d 455, 70 FEP 1230 (D.C. Cir. 1996) *8:* 52–55
Causey v. Balog, 929 F. Supp. 900, 71 FEP 643 (D. Md. 1996) *19:* 13, 26; *24:* 53; *27:* 9
Caussade v. Brown, 924 F. Supp. 693, 74 FEP 1027 (D. Md. 1996), *aff'd,* 107 F.3d 865, 75 FEP 1887 (4th Cir. 1997) *16:* 40, 169
Cecilio v. Allstate Ins. Co., 908 F. Supp. 519, 70 FEP 971 (E.D. Ill. 1995) *11:* 31
Celestine v. Citgo Petroleum Corp., 165 F.R.D. 463, 70 FEP 80 (W.D. La. 1995) *37:* 9–10, 16, 53, 96, 102
Central Kan. Med. Ctr.; EEOC v., 705 F.2d 1270, 31 FEP 1510 (10th Cir. 1983) *15:* 11
Chakonas v. City of Chicago, 42 F.3d 1132, 66 FEP 1164 (7th Cir. 1994) *31:* 28
Chalmers v. Quaker Oats Co., 61 F.3d 1340, 68 FEP 865 (7th Cir. 1995) *20:* 112
Chambers v. American Trans Air, Inc., 17 F.3d 998, 64 FEP 213 (7th Cir.), *cert. denied,* 115 S. Ct. 512 (1994) *31:* 14
Champ v. Baltimore County, 884 F. Supp. 991, 4 AD 808 (D. Md. 1995), *aff'd mem.,* 91 F.3d 129, 5 AD 1184 (4th Cir. 1996) *9:* 58, 123–24, 134–35
Chandler
—v. Bombardier Capital Inc., 44 F.3d 80, 10 IER 212 (2d Cir. 1994) *26:* 54
—v. Dowell Schlumberger Inc., 542 N.W.2d 310, 11 IER 707 (Mich. Ct. App. 1995) *26:* 27
—v. Fast Lane, Inc., 868 F. Supp. 1138, 66 FEP 675 (E.D. Ark. 1994) *11:* 9; *18:* 14; *21:* 12; *27:* 21–22; *30:* 27, 29; *33:* 19
Chardon v. Fernandez, 454 U.S. 6, 27 FEP 57 (1981) *31:* 4
Charles v. Dalton, 1996 U.S. Dist. LEXIS 1494 (N.D. Cal. Jan. 31, 1996) *37:* 56
Charney v. Gizzard, 1997 U.S. Dist. LEXIS 2751 (E.D. Va. Jan. 31, 1997) *16:* 35

Chastain v. USF&G Corp., 5 AD 310 (W.D. Okla. 1996) *16:* 99

Chatoff v. West Publ'g Co., 948 F. Supp. 176, 6 AD 414 (E.D.N.Y. 1996) *9:* 291–93

Chaudhuri v. Tennessee, 886 F. Supp. 1374 (M.D. Tenn. 1995) *8:* 40; *19:* 18

Chavez v. City of Arvada, 88 F.3d 861, 71 FEP 320 (10th Cir. 1996), cert. denied, 117 S. Ct. 684 (1997) *17:* 42

Cheatwood v. Roanoke Indus., 891 F. Supp. 1528, 5 AD 141 (N.D. Ala. 1995) *9:* 53, 134, 188, 192, 209

Cheek
—v. Peabody Coal Co., 97 F.3d 200, 71 FEP 1775 (7th Cir. 1996) *2:* 12, 44
—v. Western & S. Life Ins. Co., 31 F.3d 497, 65 FEP 727 (7th Cir. 1994) *33:* 36

Chemtech Int'l Corp.; EEOC v., 1995 U.S. Dist. LEXIS 21877, 4 AD 1465 (S.D. Tex. 1995) *34:* 29

Chenault v. United States Postal Serv., 37 F.3d 535, 3 AD 1185 (9th Cir. 1994) *41:* 121

Cheng v. Metropolitan Life Ins. Co., 1995 WL 37843 (S.D.N.Y. Jan. 31, 1995), aff"d mem., 71 F.3d 404 (2d Cir. 1995), cert. denied, 116 S. Ct. 2507 (1996) *16:* 72

Cherry v. American Tel. & Tel. Co., 47 F.3d 225, 67 FEP 113 (7th Cir. 1995) *19:* 15

Cherry-Burrell Corp.; EEOC v., 35 F.3d 356, 66 FEP 1749 (8th Cir. 1994) *41:* 64

Chertkova v. Connecticut Gen. Life Ins. Co., 92 F.3d 81, 71 FEP 1006 (2d Cir. 1996) *2:* 7

Chester v. American Tel. & Tel. Co., 907 F. Supp. 982 (N.D. Tex. 1994), aff'd, 68 F.3d 470 (5th Cir. 1995), cert. denied, 516 U.S. 1141 (1996) *16:* 58, 77

Cheung v. Merrill Lynch, Pierce, Fenner & Smith, Inc., 913 F. Supp. 248 (S.D.N.Y. 1996) *11:* 10

Chevron, U.S.A., Inc. v. Natural Resources Defense Council, Inc., 467 U.S. 837 (1984) *9:* 46

Chicago, City of; EEOC v., 66 FEP 224 (N.D. Ill. 1994) *16:* 54–55; *34:* 18

Chicago Club; EEOC v., 86 F.3d 1423, 70 FEP 1749 (7th Cir. 1996) *30:* 64

Childress v. City of Richmond, 120 F.3d 476, 74 FEP 749 (4th Cir. 1997) *30:* 29

Chisolm v. Foothill Capital Corp., 940 F. Supp. 1273 (N.D. Ill. 1996) *15:* 5

Christian v. St. Anthony Med. Ctr., Inc., 117 F.3d 1051, 6 AD 1665 (7th Cir. 1997) *9:* 32

Christiansburg Garment Co. v. EEOC, 434 U.S. 412, 16 FEP 502 (1978) *42:* 60–61

Chrysler Corp.; EEOC v., 917 F. Supp. 1164, 5 AD 517 (E.D. Mich. 1996) *9:* 34, 71, 240, 243

Chubb v. Union Pac. R.R., 908 F. Supp. 853, 5 AD 270 (D. Colo. 1995) *33:* 48

Ciafrei v. Bentsen, 877 F. Supp. 788 (D.R.I. 1995) *36:* 23

Ciaramella v. Reader's Digest Ass'n, 131 F.3d 320 (2d Cir. 1997) *43:* 67

Cisko v. Commonwealth Edison Co., 67 FEP 1630 (N.D. Ill. 1995) *38:* 43

City of, see name of city

Civil Serv. Comm'n of City of New York v. Guardians Ass'n of New York City Police Dep't, see Guardians Ass'n of New York City Police Dep't, Inc. v. Civil Serv. Comm'n of New York

Clark
—v. City of Macon, 860 F. Supp. 1545 (M.D. Ga. 1994) *24:* 6; *31:* 17
—v. Hess Trucking Co., 879 F. Supp. 524, 69 FEP 195 (W.D. Pa. 1995) *2:* 56
—v. Johnson Controls World Servs., Inc., 939 F. Supp. 884, 74 FEP 814 (S.D. Ga. 1996), aff'd, 124 F.3d 222, 74 FEP 1792 (11th Cir. 1997) *21:* 15
—v. Pennsylvania, 885 F. Supp. 694, 69 FEP 1379 (E.D. Penn. 1995) *4:* 19; *5:* 26–27
—v. Sun Elec. Corp., 1995 WL 708567 (N.D. Ill. Nov. 30, 1995) *16:* 235

Clayton Residential Home, Inc.; EEOC v., 874 F. Supp. 212, 66 FEP 1745 (N.D. Ill. 1995) *40:* 6, 8–10

Clear Lake Dodge; EEOC v., 60 F.3d 1146, 68 FEP 663 (5th Cir. 1995) *34:* 47; *42:* 49

Clements v. St. Vincent's Hosp. & Med. Ctr., 919 F. Supp. 161 (S.D.N.Y. 1996) *33:* 39

Clemmer v. Enron Corp., 882 F. Supp. 606, 4 AD 437 (S.D. Tex. 1995) *9:* 310; *33:* 38–39

Cleveland v. Policy Management Sys. Corp., 120 F.3d 513 (5th Cir. 1997) *9:* 61–62

Clifton v. Mars Telecom, Inc., 70 FEP 1315 (D. Kan. 1996) *30:* 45–46

Cloud v. Superior Court of Los Angeles County, 58 Cal.Rptr.2d 365, 72 FEP 777 (Cal. Ct. App. 2d Dist. 1996) *38:* 30

Cloward v. Columbia Univ., 888 F. Supp. 21, 67 FEP 905 (S.D.N.Y. 1995) *16:* 75

CNA Ins. Cos.; EEOC v., 96 F. 3d 1039, 5 AD 1769 (7th Cir. 1996) *9:* 99; *34:* 19

Coalition for Basic Human Needs v. King, 691 F.2d 597, 601 (1st Cir. 1982) *9:* 301

Coalition for Economic Equity v. Wilson, 122 F.3d 692 (9th Cir. 1997) *27:* 4

Coates v. Shalala, 914 F. Supp. 110, 72 FEP 644 (D. Md. 1996), *aff'd without opinion,* 133 F.3d 914 (4th Cir. 1997) *31:* 44; *36:* 25

Coatney v. Enterprise Rent-a-Car, 897 F. Supp. 1205, 11 IER 628 (W.D. Ark. 1995) *26:* 12, 20, 40

Cochrum v. Old Ben Coal Co., 102 F.3d 908, 6 AD 219 (7th Cir. 1996) *9:* 166, 186, 237

Codrington v. Virgin Islands Port Auth., 911 F. Supp. 907, 70 FEP 213 (D.V.I. 1996) *19:* 7

Cody v. Private Agencies Collaborating Together, Inc., 911 F. Supp. 1 (D.D.C. 1995) *41:* 115

Coffey v. United States, 939 F. Supp. 185 (E.D.N.Y. 1996) *36:* 11

Coffman v. Michigan, 914 F. Supp. 172 (W.D. Mich. 1995), *aff'd,* 120 F.3d 57 (6th Cir. 1997) *9:* 150

Coger v. State Bd. of Regents, 1997 U.S. Dist. LEXIS 5362 (W.D. Tenn. Jan. 2, 1997), *appeal pending,* No. 97-5134 (6th Cir.) *16:* 35

Cole
—v. Appalachian Power Co., 67 FEP 1729 (S.D. W. Va. 1995) *22:* 28
—v. Ruidoso Mun. Schs., 43 F.3d 1373, 68 FEP 561 (10th Cir. 1994) *17:* 36

Coleman
—v. General Elec. Co., 1995 U.S. Dist. LEXIS 8186 (E.D. Pa. June 8, 1995) *38:* 8
—v. Kaye, 87 F.3d 1491, 71 FEP 236 (3d Cir. 1996), *cert. denied,* 117 S. Ct. 754 (1997) *30:* 61; *41:* 24, 98

Collier v. Budd Co., 66 F.3d 886, 68 FEP 1435 (7th Cir. 1995) *16:* 96, 115–16, 119, 148, 176; *33:* 53

Collin v. Rector & Bd. of Visitors of the Univ. of Va., 873 F. Supp. 1008 (W.D. Va. 1995) *24:* 4, 42; *33:* 30

Collings v. Longview Fibre Co., 63 F.3d 828, 4 AD 1278 (9th Cir. 1995), *cert. denied,* 116 S. Ct. 711 (1996) *9:* 263

Collins
—v. Executive Airlines, Inc., 934 F. Supp. 1378 (S.D. Fla. 1996) *33:* 36
—v. Milwaukee Hous. Assistance Corp., 927 F. Supp. 1152 (E.D. Wis. 1996) *18:* 10
—v. Yellow Freight Sys., Inc., 942 F. Supp. 449, 6 AD 102 (W.D. Mo. 1996) *9:* 176, 237, 253

Colorado State Bd. of Med. Examiners v. Davis, 893 P.2d 1365, 4 AD 316 (Colo. Ct. App. 1995) *9:* 264

Columbia First Bank v. Ferguson, 665 A.2d 650, 11 IER 43 (D.C. Ct. App. 1995) *26:* 42

Comas v. United Tel. Co., 70 FEP 159 (D. Kan. 1995) *38:* 26, 33

Combs v. Plantation Patterns, 106 F.3d 1519, 73 FEP 232 (11th Cir. 1997), *cert. denied,* 118 S. Ct. 685 (1998) *2:* 39, 41

Comer v. ENSR Operations, 10 IER 672 (S.D. W.Va. 1994), *aff'd,* 10 IER 960 (4th Cir. 1995) *26:* 12

Commissioner of Internal Revenue v. Schleier, 515 U.S. 323, 67 FEP 1745 (1995) *43:* 59–60

Compton v. Chinn Enters., 936 F. Supp. 480 (N.D. Ill. 1996) *33:* 16

Concrete Works of Colo. v. City & County of Denver, 36 F.3d 1513 (10th Cir. 1994), *cert. denied,* 514 U.S. 1004 (1995) *27:* 55, 90

Cones v. Shalala, 945 F. Supp. 342 (D.D.C. 1996) *36:* 22–23

Conklin v. Englewood, 1996 WL 560370, 1996 U.S. App. LEXIS 26173 (6th Cir. Oct. 1, 1996) *9:* 123, 133, 141, 202

Connecticut v. Teal, 457 U.S. 440, 29 FEP 1 (1982) *4:* 25; *39:* 21

Connors v. AMISUB, 5 AD 961 (S.D. Fla. 1996) *9:* 297

Considine v. Newspaper Agency Corp., 43 F.3d 1349, 69 FEP 1732 (10th Cir. 1994) *39:* 69–70

Consolidated Serv. Sys.; EEOC v., 30 F.3d 58, 66 FEP 185 (7th Cir. 1994) *34:* 64; *42:* 61

Contractors Ass'n of E. Pa., Inc. v. City of Philadelphia, 91 F.3d 586 (3d Cir. 1996), *cert. denied,* 117 S. Ct. 953 (1997) *27:* 57, 79–81

Cook v. Arrowsmith Shelburne, Inc., 69 F.3d 1235, 69 FEP 392 (2d Cir. 1995) *33:* 17, 24–25, 33, 35

Cooley v. Carmike Cinemas, Inc., 25 F.3d 1325, 65 FEP 46 (6th Cir. 1994) *40:* 50

Copley Pharm., Inc., In re, 161 F.R.D. 456 (D. Wyo. 1995) *37:* 94

Copsey v. Swearingen, 36 F.3d 1336 (5th Cir. 1994) *17:* 72

Corbett v. National Prods. Co., 4 AD 987 (E.D. Pa. 1995) *9:* 157, 189, 266

Corbin v. Southland Int'l Trucks, 25 F.3d 1545, 65 FEP 552 (11th Cir. 1994) *16:* 123, 126

Cornwell v. Robinson, 23 F.3d 694, 64 FEP 1254 (2d Cir. 1995) *31:* 10–11, 47

Cornwell Personnel Assocs.; EEOC v., 1995 U.S. Dist. LEXIS 19930 (E.D. Wis. Aug. 15, 1995) *34:* 48

Corragio v. Time Inc. Magazine Co., 67 FEP 1880 (S.D.N.Y. 1995) *30:* 56

Cosgrove v. Sears, Roebuck & Co., 68 FEP 1006 (S.D.N.Y. 1995) *41:* 65

Courtney v. Biosound, Inc., 42 F.3d 414, 66 FEP 971 (7th Cir. 1994) *16:* 121; *33:* 53; *39:* 27–28

Covell v. CNG Transmission Corp., 863 F. Supp. 202, 70 FEP 914 (M.D. Pa. 1994) *38:* 46

Cowan v. Gilless, 81 F.3d 160 (6th Cir. 1996) *8:* 9

Cox
—v. Kentucky Dep't of Transp., 53 F.3d 146, 67 FEP 1134 (6th Cir. 1995) *16:* 126
—v. Nasche, 70 F.3d 1030, 11 IER 281 (9th Cir. 1995) *26:* 45

Cragen v. Barnhill, 859 F. Supp 566 (N.D. Fla. 1994) *42:* 57

Craig v. O'Leary, 870 F. Supp. 1007, 69 FEP 452 (D. Colo. 1994) *33:* 55; *36:* 4; *42:* 32–33

Craik v. Minnesota State Univ. Bd., 731 F.2d 465, 34 FEP 649 (8th Cir. 1984) *36:* 19

Cram v. Lamson & Sessions Co., 49 F.3d 466, 67 FEP 449 (8th Cir. 1995) *2:* 55, 57; *20:* 12, 46

Crandon v. Kansas, 897 P.2d 92, 10 IER 1156 (Kan. 1995), *cert. denied,* 116 S. Ct. 913 (1996) *26:* 30

Crawford v. Medina Gen. Hosp., 96 F.3d 830 (6th Cir. 1996) *20:* 7–9

Criales v. American Airlines, Inc., 105 F.3d 93, 72 FEP 1690 (2d Cir.), *cert. denied,* 118 S. Ct. 264 (1997) *32:* 7

Criminal Sheriff, Parish of Orleans; United States v., 19 F.3d 238, 64 FEP 813 (5th Cir. 1994) *40:* 16–19

Cromer v. Brown, 88 F.3d 1315, 71 FEP 530 (4th Cir. 1996) *17:* 69; *30:* 22

Cronin v. Aetna Life Ins. Co., 46 F.3d 196, 66 FEP 1727 (2d Cir. 1995) *16:* 144, 153, 156; *33:* 50

Cross v. State of Alabama, State Dep't of Mental Health & Mental Retardation, 49 F.3d 1490, 67 FEP 844 (11th Cir. 1995) *24:* 33, 36, 56; *31:* 38

Crossman v. Crosson, 905 F. Supp. 90 (E.D.N.Y. 1995), *aff'd,* 101 F.3d 684 (2d Cir. 1996) **16:** 57

Crosten v. Kamauf, 932 F. Supp. 676, 70 FEP 1144 (D. Md. 1996) **33:** 20

Crumm v. Oce'-Bruning, Inc., 892 F. Supp. 1236 (E.D. Mo. 1995) **16:** 113, 167

Csicseri v. Bowsher, 862 F. Supp. 547 (D.D.C. 1994), *aff'd,* 67 F.3d 972 (D.C. Cir. 1995) **19:** 22, 26

Csoka v. United States, 1996 U.S. App. LEXIS 20583 (7th Cir. Aug. 12, 1996) **9:** 310

Curcio v. Chinn Enters., 70 FEP 9 (N.D. Ill. 1996) **38:** 29

Curde v. Xytel Corp., 912 F. Supp. 335, 71 FEP 843 (N.D. Ill. 1995) **20:** 54, 62, 69; **21:** 8

Curtis v. Express, Inc., 868 F. Supp. 467, 66 FEP 449 (N.D.N.Y. 1994) **38:** 46

Czopek v. General Elec. Co., 4 AD 1231 (N.D. Ill. 1995) **9:** 151, 199

D

Dailey v. Societe Generale
—889 F. Supp. 108, 68 FEP 345 (S.D.N.Y. 1995) **41:** 21, 71
—915 F. Supp. 1315 (S.D.N.Y. 1996), *aff'd in part, remanded in part,* 108 F.3d 451 (2d Cir. 1997) **42:** 36, 41

Dalal v. Alliant Techsystems, Inc, 927 F. Supp. 1374 (D. Colo. 1996) **16:** 225, 237; **42:** 1, 11, 26

Dale v. Chicago Tribune Co., 797 F.2d 458 (7th Cir. 1986), *cert. denied,* 479 U.S. 1066 (1987) **16:** 158

Dallas Fire Fighters Ass'n v. City of Dallas, 885 F. Supp. 915 (N.D. Tex. 1995) **5:** 65–67, 77–78; **27:** 57, 82–84, 110–13, 131–37

Daly v. Unicare Corp. Township Manor Nursing Ctr., 1995 U.S. Dist. LEXIS 5426, 68 FEP 208 (E.D. Pa. 1995) **27:** 14, 39

Dambrot v. Central Mich. Univ., 55 F.3d 1177 (6th Cir. 1995) **17:** 64

D'Amico v. New York State Bd. of Law Examiners, 813 F. Supp. 217, 2 AD 534 (W.D.N.Y. 1993) **9:** 77

Daniel v. Loveridge, 32 F.3d 1472, 65 FEP 1052 (10th Cir. 1994) **41:** 32, 71

Daniels v. Browner, 63 F.3d 906, 68 FEP 961 (9th Cir. 1995) **16:** 30

Danley v. Book-of-the-Month Club, Inc., 921 F. Supp. 1352, 70 FEP 1281 (M.D. Pa. 1996), *aff'd,* 107 F.3d 861 (3d Cir. 1997) **33:** 14

Dao v. Auchan Hypermarket, 96 F.3d 787, 5 AD 1633 (5th Cir. 1996) **32:** 36

Daramola v. Westinghouse Elec. Corp., 872 F. Supp. 1418 (W.D. Pa. 1995) **42:** 64

Darnell v. Northern Can Sys., Inc., 937 F. Supp. 668, 67 FEP 419 (N.D. Ohio 1995), *opinion clarified,* 1996 WL 343448 (N.D. Ohio 1996) **2:** 12; **18:** 10

Daugherty v. City of El Paso, 56 F.3d 695, 4 AD 993 (5th Cir. 1995), *cert. denied,* 116 S. Ct. 1263 (1996) **9:** 72, 123, 137–38, 247; **21:** 21

Daulo v. Commonwealth Edison, 892 F. Supp. 1088, 72 FEP 1566 (N.D. Ill. 1995) **17:** 53; **24:** 7; **33:** 40

David Gomez & Assocs.; EEOC v., 1997 U.S. Dist. LEXIS 3269 (N.D. Ill. 1997) **23:** 9–10

Davidson
—v. Midelfort Clinic, Ltd., 1998 WL 3360 (7th Cir. 1998) **9:** 36
—v. U.S. Postal Serv., 24 F.3d 223 (Fed. Cir. 1994) **36:** 12

Davis
—v. Cottage Hill Baptist Church, 6 AD 1173 (S.D. Ala. 1995) **9:** 188
—v. Jim Quinlan Ford, Lincoln-Mercury, Inc., 932 F. Supp. 1389 (M.D. Fla. 1996) **9:** 156
—v. Sheraton Soc'y Hill Hotel, 907 F. Supp. 896, 71 FEP 1087 (E.D. Pa. 1995) **21:** 9; **27:** 28, 35, 39
—v. Wesley Retirement Communities, Inc., 913 F. Supp. 1437, 70 FEP 430 (D. Kan. 1995) **31:** 24

Davis—*Contd.*
—v. York Int'l, Inc., 2 AD 1810 (D. Md. 1993) **9:** 122, 207
Davoll v. Webb
—160 F.R.D. 142, 4 AD 161 (D. Colo. 1995) **37:** 24, 47
—943 F. Supp. 1289 (D. Colo. 1996) **9:** 133; **32:** 36
DeAngelis v. El Paso Mun. Police Officers Ass'n, 51 F.3d 591, 67 FEP 1250 (5th Cir.), *cert. denied,* 116 S. Ct. 473 (1995) **17:** 33; **20:** 49, 61, 66, 69
DeCintio v. Westchester County Med. Ctr., 807 F.2d 304, 42 FEP 921 (2d Cir. 1986) **20:** 107
Deckert v. City of Ulysses, 4 AD 1569 (D. Kan. 1995), *aff'd mem.,* 105 F.3d 669 (10th Cir. 1996) **9:** 90
DeCoe v. General Motors Corp., 32 F.3d 212, 9 IER 1255 (6th Cir. 1994) **26:** 2
DeGaetano v. Smith Barney, Inc., 70 FEP 401 (S.D.N.Y. 1996) **32:** 29
DeGraffenreid v. General Motors Assembly Div., 413 F. Supp. 142, 12 FEP 1627 (E.D. Mo. 1976), *aff'd in part, rev'd in part,* 558 F.2d 480 (8th Cir. 1977) **13:** 32
DeGuiseppe v. Village of Bellwood, 68 F.3d 187 (7th Cir. 1995) **17:** 37
de la Cruz v. New York City Human Resources Admin. Dep't of Social Servs., 82 F.3d 16, 70 FEP 893 (2d Cir. 1996) **11:** 1; **21:** 29
de la Rosa v. Southwest Community Health Servs., 10 IER 1564 (N.M. 1994) **26:** 40
Delaware State College v. Ricks, 449 U.S. 250, 24 FEP 827 (1980) **31:** 3
Del Monte Dunes v. City of Monterey, 95 F.3d 1422 (9th Cir. 1996) **41:** 119
Deli v. University of Minn., 863 F. Supp. 958, 65 FEP 1026 (D. Minn. 1994) **15:** 20–21
Delli Santi v. CNA Ins. Cos., 88 F.3d 192, 71 FEP 143 (3d Cir. 1996) **40:** 33; **41:** 89, 102
DeNardo v. Clarence House Imports, Ltd., 870 F. Supp. 227, 70 FEP 1539 (N.D. Ill. 1994) **2:** 49
Den Hartog v. Wasatch Academy, 129 F.3d 1076 (10th Cir. 1997) **9:** 41

Denman v. Mississippi Power & Light Co., 906 F. Supp. 379 (S.D. Miss. 1995) **16:** 58
Dennis v. County of Fairfax, 55 F.3d 151, 67 FEP 1681 (4th Cir. 1995) **10:** 9–10; **24:** 8
Dent v. Fruth, 453 S.E.2d 340, 10 IER 351 (W. Va. 1994) **26:** 13
Denty v. SmithKline Beecham Corp., 907 F. Supp. 879, 69 FEP 376 (E.D. Pa. 1995), *aff'd,* 109 F.3d 147, 73 FEP 423 (3d Cir.), *cert. denied,* 118 S. Ct. 74 (1997) **16:** 3; **30:** 69
Denver, City of; United States v., 943 F. Supp. 1304, 6 AD 245 (D. Colo. 1996) **9:** 92, 234
DePetris v. Union Settlement Assoc., 657 N.E.2d 269, 11 IER 119 (N.Y. 1995) **26:** 6
Derbis v. U.S. Shoe Corp., 65 FEP 1322 (D. Md. 1994), *aff'd in part and remanded,* 67 F.3d 294 (4th Cir. 1995) **9:** 187, 199; **16:** 99, 109
Despears v. Milwaukee County, 63 F.3d 635, 4 AD 1313 (7th Cir. 1995) **9:** 183
Devera v. Adams, 874 F. Supp. 17, 67 FEP 102 (D.D.C. 1995) **11:** 7; **17:** 40
Devine v. Stone, Leyton & Gershman, 100 F.3d 78, 72 FEP 394 (8th Cir. 1996), *cert. denied,* 117 S. Ct. 1694 (1997) **30:** 44
Devoid v. Clair Buick Cadillac Inc., 669 A.2d 749, 11 IER 525 (Me. 1996) **26:** 26, 30
Dewachter v. Scott, 657 So. 2d 962, 11 IER 95 (Fla. Dist. Ct. App. 1995) **26:** 50
Dewey v. PTT Telecom Netherlands, U.S., Inc., 68 FEP 1112 (S.D.N.Y. 1995), *aff'd,* 101 F.3d 1392 (2d Cir. 1996) **16:** 18; **30:** 56
DeWitt v. Carsten, 941 F. Supp. 1232, 6 AD 1255 (N.D. Ga. 1996) **9:** 135, 179
Dey v. Colt Constr. & Dev. Co., 28 F.3d 1446, 65 FEP 523 (7th Cir. 1994) **15:** 8, 22–23; **17:** 10; **20:** 57, 69
Diaz v. Trust Territory of Pac. Islands, 876 F.2d 1401 (9th Cir. 1989) **37:** 87

DiBiase v. SmithKline Beecham Corp., 48 F.3d 719, 67 FEP 58 (3d Cir.), *cert. denied,* 516 U.S. 916 (1995) *16:* 139, 152, 203

Dickinson v. McCarty, 65 FEP 1508 (S.D. Fla. 1994) *19:* 11, 20

Dickson v. Amoco Performance Prods., Inc., 910 F. Supp. 629, 69 FEP 228 (N.D. Ga. 1994) *16:* 157, 165, 172

Diehl v. Xerox Corp., 933 F. Supp. 1157, 71 FEP 723 (W.D.N.Y. 1996) *4:* 28

Diez v. Minnesota Min. & Mfg. Co., 88 F.3d 672, 71 FEP 383 (8th Cir. 1996) *33:* 13

Dillard Dep't Stores, Inc.; EEOC v., 1994 WL 738971, 1994 U.S. Dist. LEXIS 10358 (E.D. La. July 26, 1994) *34:* 37, 44

Dille v. Council of Energy Resource Tribes, 801 F.2d 373, 41 FEP 1345 (10th Cir. 1986) *12:* 1, 6

Dillon
—v. Coles, 746 F.2d 998 (3d Cir. 1984) *40:* 37
—v. EEOC, 1996 U.S. Dist. LEXIS 68 (E.D. La. Jan. 3, 1996) *34:* 8

Dimitropoulos v. Painters Dist. Council 9, 893 F. Supp. 297, 68 FEP 1070 (S.D.N.Y. 1995) *22:* 11, 15

Dimonda v. New York City Police Dep't, 1996 WL 194325 (S.D.N.Y. Apr. 22, 1996) *9:* 270

DiPietro v. Runyon, 914 F. Supp. 714 (D. Mass. 1996) *42:* 4–6, 28–29

DiPuccio v. United Parcel Serv., 890 F. Supp. 688, 5 AD 561 (N.D. Ohio 1995) *41:* 63

DiRussa v. Dean Witter Reynolds, Inc., 936 F. Supp. 104, 71 FEP 1002 (S.D.N.Y. 1996) *40:* 37; *42:* 22–23

Dittmann v. Ireco, Inc., 883 F. Supp. 807, 73 FEP 435 (N.D.N.Y.), *partial summary judgment granted,* 903 F. Supp. 347, 73 FEP 441 (N.D.N.Y. 1995) *16:* 95, 231

Ditto v. American Airlines, Inc., 1995 U.S. Dist. LEXIS 4425, 10 IER 1628 (N.D. Ill. 1995) *26:* 3

Doan v. Seagate Tech., Inc., *see* Furr v. Seagate Tech., Inc.

Doane v. City of Omaha, 115 F.3d 624, 6 AD 1553 (8th Cir. 1997) *9:* 42, 45

Dobson v. Unigraphic Color Corp., 71 FEP 1343 (M.D. Pa. 1994), *aff'd,* 66 F.3d 310 (3d Cir. 1995) *21:* 10

Dockery v. North Shore Med. Ctr., 909 F. Supp. 1550, 5 AD 1443 (S.D. Fla. 1995) *9:* 160

Doctors' Assocs. v. Casarotto, 517 U.S. 681 (1996) *32:* 33

Doe
—v. Attorney Gen., 44 F.3d 715, 4 AD 52 (9th Cir.), *withdrawn,* 58 F.3d 490, 4 AD 992 (9th Cir.), *superseded by* 5 AD 1096 (9th Cir. 1995), *vacated sub nom.* Reno v. Doe, 116 S. Ct. 2543, 5 AD 1152 (1996) *9:* 260
—v. R.R. Donnelly & Sons, 42 F.3d 439, 66 FEP 981 (7th Cir. 1994) *31:* 9
—v. St. Joseph Hosp., 788 F.2d 411, 40 FEP 820 (7th Cir. 1986) *5:* 5
—v. Western Restaurants Corp., 674 So.2d 561, 11 IER 542 (Ala. Civ. App. 1995) *26:* 55

Doherty v. Southern College of Optometry, 862 F.2d 570 (6th Cir. 1988) *9:* 272

Doll v. Brown, 75 F.3d 1200, 5 AD 369 (7th Cir. 1996) *36:* 28; *40:* 23–24, 37

Dollis v. Rubin, 77 F.3d 777, 70 FEP 517 (5th Cir. 1995) *17:* 38–39

Dolphin Cruise Line; EEOC v., 945 F. Supp. 1550, 6 AD 187 (S.D. Fla. 1996) *9:* 251; *34:* 17

Dombeck v. Milwaukee Valve Co., 40 F.3d 230, 66 FEP 497 (7th Cir. 1994) *32:* 13; *33:* 44; *37:* 11; *40:* 11

Domino's Pizza, Inc.; EEOC v.
—870 F. Supp. 655, 66 FEP 888 (D. Md. 1994) *34:* 44
—909 F. Supp. 1529, 69 FEP 570 (M.D. Fla. 1995), *aff'd,* 113 F.3d 1249 (11th Cir. 1997), *cert. denied,* 118 S. Ct. 687 (1998) *20:* 38, 46; *40:* 37–38; *41:* 12, 18–19, 33, 69, 77

Domm v. Jersey Printing Co., Inc., 871 F. Supp. 732, 70 FEP 99 (D.N.J. 1994) *30:* 61

Donaire v. NME Hosp., Inc., 27 F.3d 507, 65 FEP 674 (11th Cir. 1994) *24:* 14

Donaldson v. Tennessee Valley Auth., 759 F.2d 535, 37 FEP 869 (6th Cir. 1985) *36:* 9

Donnelly v. Rhode Island Bd. of Governors for Higher Educ., 929 F. Supp. 583, 71 FEP 363 (D.R.I. 1996), *aff'd*, 110 F.3d 2, 73 FEP 972 (1st Cir. 1997) *4:* 28, 42–43, 47–48, 50–51; *5:* 35, 37

Dorris v. City of Kentwood, 4 AD 741 (W.D. Mich. 1994) *9:* 184

Dortz v. City of N.Y., 904 F. Supp. 127, 72 FEP 205 (S.D.N.Y. 1995) *17:* 31; *33:* 20, 25, 33

Douglas
—v. Coca-Cola Bottling Co., 855 F. Supp. 518, 71 FEP 355 (D.N.H. 1994) *30:* 61
—v. Evans
——888 F. Supp. 1536, 68 FEP 472 (M.D. Ala. 1995) *27:* 11, 31
——916 F. Supp. 1539 (M.D. Ala. 1996), *aff'd,* 116 F.3d 492 (11th Cir. 1997) *19:* 11

Douglass v. United Servs. Auto. Ass'n, 79 F.3d 1415, 70 FEP 701 (5th Cir. 1996) *16:* 180

Downes v. Volkswagen of Am., Inc., 41 F.3d 1132, 69 FEP 11 (7th Cir. 1994) *16:* 46, 221–22, 240–41; *30:* 4; *33:* 13; *40:* 22–23, 39–40, 48; *41:* 120; *42:* 41

Doyle v. Sentry Ins., 877 F. Supp. 1002, 67 FEP 484 (E.D. Va. 1995) *21:* 22

Dranchak v. Akzo Nobel Inc., 88 F.3d 457, 71 FEP 284 (7th Cir. 1996) *17:* 18

Drauel v. Iowa Methodist Med. Ctr., 915 F. Supp. 102, 4 AD 1734 (S.D. Iowa 1995), *aff'd,* 95 F.3d 674, 5 AD 1503 (8th Cir. 1996) *9:* 39

Dreisbach v. Cummins Diesel Engines, Inc., 848 F. Supp. 593, 64 FEP 926 (E.D. Pa. 1994) *33:* 33

Dring v. McDonnell Douglas Corp., 58 F.3d 1323, 70 FEP 481 (8th Cir. 1995) *16:* 52, 57; *31:* 5, 28

Drinkwater v. Union Carbide Corp., 904 F.2d 853, 56 FEP 483 (3d Cir. 1990) *24:* 15

Duart v. FMC Wyoming Corp., 859 F. Supp. 1447, 65 FEP 999 (D. Wyo. 1994), *aff'd,* 72 F.3d 117, 69 FEP 1036 (10th Cir. 1995) *16:* 166

Dubisar-Dewberry v. Folmar, 883 F. Supp. 648, 67 FEP 1660 (M.D. Ala. 1995) *30:* 22

Dubowsky v. Stern, Lavinthal, Norgaard & Daly, 922 F. Supp. 985 (D.N.J. 1996) *15:* 8

Dudley v. Wal-Mart Stores, Inc., 931 F. Supp. 773 (N.D. Ala. 1996) *19:* 2, 5

Duffy
—v. Al Packer Ford, Inc., 1996 U.S. Dist. LEXIS 7038 (D. Md. May 13, 1996) *9:* 144
—v. Leading Edge Prods., Inc., 44 F.3d 308, 67 FEP 97 (5th Cir. 1995) *20:* 110; *26:* 43
—v. Southeastern Pa. Transp. Co., 67 FEP 1797 (E.D. Pa. 1995) *33:* 30, 38
—v. State Farm Mut. Auto. Ins. Co., 927 F. Supp. 587 (E.D.N.Y. 1996) *16:* 124

Dugas v. Trans Union Corp., 99 F.3d 724 (5th Cir. 1996) *37:* 121

Dunn v. Medina Gen. Hosp., 917 F. Supp. 1185 (N.D. Ohio 1996) *16:* 66, 75

Dunning
—v. General Elec. Co, 892 F. Supp. 1424 (M.D. Ala. 1995) *41:* 94–95
—v. Simmons Airlines, Inc., 62 F.3d 863, 68 FEP 785 (7th Cir. 1995) *2:* 49; *17:* 24; *42:* 53

Durko v. OI-NEG TV Prods., 870 F. Supp. 1278 (M.D. Pa. 1994) *32:* 6

Dush v. Appleton Elec. Co., 7 AD 183 (8th Cir. 1997) *9:* 61–62

Dutcher v. Ingalls Shipbuilding, 53 F.3d 723, 4 AD 802 (5th Cir. 1995) *9:* 4

Dutton v. Johnson County Bd. of County Comm'rs, 859 F. Supp. 498, 3 AD 808 (D. Kan.), *later proceeding,* 868 F. Supp. 1260, 3 AD 1614 (D. Kan. 1994) *9:* 153; *41:* 1, 13–14

Dyer v. Jefferson County Sch. Dist. R-1, 905 F. Supp. 864, 5 AD 109 (D. Colo. 1995) *9:* 134

E

Easley v. West, 4 AD 1323 (E.D. Pa. 1994), aff'd mem., 85 F.3d 611, 5 AD 1343 (3d Cir. 1996) *9:* 207

East v. Dixie Yarns, Inc., 1994 WL 872892 (M.D.N.C. Dec. 9, 1994) *19:* 15

East Haven, Town of; EEOC v., 70 F.3d 219, 69 FEP 500 (2d Cir. 1995) *4:* 59

Easton v. Crossland Mortgage Corp., 905 F. Supp. 1368, 70 FEP 597 (C.D. Cal. 1995), rev'd, 114 F.3d 979, 73 FEP 1885 (9th Cir. 1997) *20:* 54, 66; *21:* 4

East Tex. Motor Freight Sys., Inc. v. Rodriguez, 431 U.S. 395, 14 FEP 1505 (1977) *37:* 2

Ebasco Constructors, Inc. v. Rex, 923 S.W.2d 694, 11 IER 1030 (Tex. Ct. App. 1996) *26:* 26

Ebrahimi v. City of Huntsville Bd. of Educ., 905 F. Supp. 993 (N.D. Ala. 1995) *24:* 9

Eckles v. Consolidated Rail Corp., 94 F.3d 1041, 5 AD 1367 (7th Cir. 1996), *cert. denied*, 117 S. Ct. 1318 (1997) *9:* 93, 146–57, 186, 237–38; *22:* 19–20

Ecklund v. Fuisz Tech., Ltd., 905 F. Supp. 335, 69 FEP 701 (E.D. Va. 1995) *20:* 49

Edwards
—v. City of Houston, 78 F.3d 983 (5th Cir. 1996) *27:* 173–75; *40:* 81
—v. Esau Invs., Inc., 66 FEP 711 (D. Kan. 1994) *30:* 42
—v. Lujan, 40 F.3d 1152, 68 FEP 32 (10th Cir. 1994), *cert. denied*, 116 S. Ct. 417 (1995) *19:* 28
—v. Nederland Indep. Sch. Dist., 930 F. Supp. 272 (E.D. Tex. 1996) *33:* 40
—v. Nestle Beverage Co., 147 LRRM 2935 (E.D. La. 1993), aff'd, 43 F.3d 669 (5th Cir. 1994) *22:* 15
—v. Shalala, 846 F. Supp. 997, 68 FEP 1410 (N.D. Ga. 1994), aff'd, 64 F.3d 601, 68 FEP 1414 (11th Cir. 1995) *16:* 31; *36:* 5, 24; *41:* 116
—v. U.S. Postal Serv., 909 F.3d 320 (8th Cir. 1990) *2:* 50

—v. Wallace Community College, 49 F.3d 1517, 67 FEP 949 (11th Cir. 1995) *4:* 24; *38:* 24

EEOC v., *see* name of opposing party

Egan
—v. Blue Water Dev. Hous., Inc., 1996 U.S. Dist. LEXIS 15937 (E.D. Mich. Aug. 20, 1996) *9:* 161
—v. Palos Community Hosp., 889 F. Supp. 331, 68 FEP 509 (N.D. Ill. 1995) *16:* 41, 47, 56; *31:* 17

Eichenwald v. Krigel's, Inc., 908 F. Supp. 1531, 75 FEP 76 (D. Kan. 1995) *21:* 11, 14

E.I. Dupont de Nemours & Co. v. Pressman, 679 A.2d 436, 11 IER 1643 (Del. 1996) *26:* 21–23

El Deeb v. University of Minn., 60 F.3d 423, 68 FEP 1173 (8th Cir. 1995) *39:* 42, 61

Eldred v. Consolidated Freightways Corp.
—898 F. Supp. 928, 71 FEP 33 (D. Mass. 1995) *2:* 49; *7:* 2; *17:* 40; *19:* 5, 24; *41:* 142
—907 F. Supp. 26 (D. Mass. 1995) *41:* 20

Eldredge v. Carpenters 46 Northern Cal. Counties Joint Apprenticeship & Training Comm., 94 F.3d 1366, 71 FEP 1385 (9th Cir. 1996), *cert. denied*, 117 S. Ct. 1470 (1997) *22:* 13; *40:* 2, 5, 55–56, 68

Elguindy v. Commonwealth Edison Co., 903 F. Supp. 1260 (N.D. Ill. 1995) *16:* 99; *19:* 6

Elias v. Naperville Eye Assoc., Ltd., 928 F. Supp. 757 (N.D. Ill. 1996) *16:* 23

Ellenwood v. Exxon Shipping Co., 984 F.2d 1270, 2 AD 415 (1st Cir.), *cert. denied*, 508 U.S. 981 (1993) *9:* 10

Ellerth v. Burlington Indus., Inc., 912 F. Supp. 1101, 70 FEP 229 (N.D. Ill. 1996), *aff'd in part, rev'd in part*, 123 F.3d 490, 74 FEP 1138 (7th Cir. 1997), *rev'd*, 1998 U.S. LEXIS 4217 (June 26, 1998) *20:* 67

Ellis
—v. Ford Motor Co., 1996 U.S. App. LEXIS 8236 (6th Cir. Mar. 14, 1996) *9:* 196

Ellis—*Contd.*
—v. United Airlines, Inc., 73 F.3d 999, 69 FEP 1167 (10th Cir.), *cert. denied,* 116 S. Ct. 2500 (1996) **9:** 72; **16:** 139, 182; **18:** 8
Ellison
—v. Chilton County Bd. of Educ., 894 F. Supp. 415 (M.D. Ala. 1995) **27:** 18, 31
—v. Software Spectrum, Inc., 85 F.3d 187, 5 AD 920 (5th Cir. 1996) **9:** 37, 45
Ellzey v. Espy, 66 FEP 1547 (E.D. La. 1995) **16:** 77
Elrod v. Sears, Roebuck & Co., 939 F.2d 1466, 56 FEP 1246 (11th Cir. 1991) **16:** 168
Elson v. Consolidated Edison Co. of N.Y., 641 N.Y.S.2d 294, 226 AD2d 288 (N.Y. App. Div. 1996) **26:** 34
Emmel v. Coca-Cola Bottling Co. of Chicago, Inc., 904 F. Supp. 723 (N.D. Ill. 1995), *aff'd,* 95 F.3d 627, 72 FEP 1811 (7th Cir. 1996) **19:** 17; **41:** 3, 23, 112
Emrick v. Libbey-Owens-Ford Co., 875 F. Supp. 393, 4 AD 1 (E.D. Tex. 1995) **9:** 145, 186
English v. Pabst Brewing Co., 828 F.2d 1047, 44 FEP 1385 (4th Cir. 1987), *cert. denied,* 486 U.S. 1044 (1988) **31:** 25
Ennis v. National Ass'n of Bus. & Educ. Radio, Inc., 53 F.3d 55, 4 AD 589 (4th Cir. 1995) **9:** 41, 273
Ensley Branch, NAACP v. Seibels, 31 F.3d 1548 (11th Cir. 1994) **5:** 76; **27:** 166–69; **27:** 113, 117; **40:** 67
Ensley-Gaines v. Runyon, 100 F.3d 1220, 72 FEP 602 (6th Cir. 1996) **2:** 13, 30
Equality Found. v. City of Cincinnati, 518 U.S. 1001, 71 FEP 64 (1996), *cert. granted, judgment vacated, and remanded,* 128 F.3d 289, 75 FEP 115 (1997), *reh'g denied,* 75 FEP 1763 (1998), *petition for writ of cert. filed,* 66 U.S.L.W. 3749 (May 4, 1998) **14:** 8–10
Erickson
—v. Board of Governors for Northeastern Ill. Univ., 911 F. Supp. 316, 5 AD 1861 (N.D. Ill. 1995) **9:** 39

—v. West, 876 F. Supp. 239 (D. Haw. 1995) **36:** 6
Erwin v. Daley, 92 F.3d 521 (7th Cir. 1996), *petition for cert. pending* **5:** 68
Esfahani v. Medical College, 919 F. Supp. 832, 5 AD 761 (E.D. Pa. 1996) **9:** 21, 99
Espinueva v. Garrett, 895 F.2d 1164, 58 FEP 1225 (7th Cir.), *cert. denied,* 497 U.S. 1005 (1990) **24:** 8
Ethridge v. Alabama, 860 F. Supp. 808, 3 AD 1013 (N.D. Ala. 1994) **9:** 72, 75, 150
Evans
—v. Bally's Health & Tennis, Inc., 64 FEP 33 (D. Md. 1994) **2:** 18; **20:** 115
—v. Connecticut, 935 F. Supp. 145, 73 FEP 131 (D. Conn. 1996), *opinion amended,* 967 F. Supp. 673 (D. Conn. 1997) **2:** 49
—v. Kansas City, Mo. Sch. Dist., 65 F.3d 98, 68 FEP 1203 (8th Cir. 1995), *cert. denied,* 517 U.S. 1104 (1996) **17:** 13–14, 53; **24:** 19; **30:** 30
—v. McClain of Ga., Inc., 934 F. Supp. 1383 (M.D. Ga. 1996), *rev'd,* 131 F.3d 957 (11th Cir. 1997) **2:** 25
—v. Technologies Applications & Servs Co., 875 F. Supp. 1115, 72 FEP 1215 (D. Md. 1995), *aff'd,* 80 F.3d 954, 72 FEP 1222 (4th Cir. 1996) **16:** 77; **19:** 8, 11; **33:** 39
Eymer v. Ground Round, Inc., 913 F. Supp 693 (N.D.N.Y. 1996) **16:** 165
Ezold v. Wolf, Block, Schorr & Solis-Cohen, 983 F.2d 509, 60 FEP 849 (3d Cir. 1992), *cert. denied,* 510 U.S. 826 (1993) **39:** 36

F

Fair v. Red Lion Inn, 920 P.2d 820, 11 IER 146 (Colo. Ct. App. 1995) **26:** 14
Fairbairn v. Board of Educ. of S. Country Cent., 876 F. Supp. 432 (E.D.N.Y. 1995) **27:** 7, 26, 31
Fair Employment Council v. BMC Mktg. Corp., 28 F.3d 1268, 65 FEP 512 (D.C. Cir. 1994) **24:** 12–13

Fairneny v. Savogran Co., 664 N.E.2d 5, 11 IER 1132 (Mass. 1996) *26:* 4

Falbaum v. Pomerantz, 891 F. Supp. 986, 72 FEP 141 (S.D.N.Y. 1995) *16:* 27

Falsetti, United States ex rel. v. Southern Bell Tel. & Tel. Co., 915 F. Supp. 308 (N.D. Fla. 1996) *38:* 29

Fandrich v. Capital Ford Lincoln Mercury, 901 P.2d 112, 11 IER 194 (Mont. 1995) *26:* 31

Faragher v. City Boca Raton, 118 S. Ct. 2275, 77 FEP 14 (1998) *1:* 1; *20:* 41, 45, 85, 87–88, 90–94

Farhat v. Sally Beauty Co., 65 FEP 1516 (E.D. Mo. 1994) *13:* 28

Farmer Bros. Co.; EEOC v., 31 F.3d 891, 65 FEP 857 (9th Cir. 1994) *41:* 35, 111–12, 145

Farnum v. Brattleboro Retreat Inc., 671 A.2d 1249, 11 IER 713 (Vt. 1995) *26:* 5, 13, 33

Farrar v. Hobby, 506 U.S. 103, 60 FEP 633 (1992) *42:* 1, 10

Farris v. Board of County Comm'rs, 924 F. Supp. 1041 (D. Kan. 1996) *21:* 14

Fatland v. Quaker State Corp., 62 F.3d 1070, 10 IER 1569 (8th Cir. 1995) *26:* 46

Federal Express Corp.; EEOC v., 1995 WL 569446 (W.D. Wash. Aug. 8, 1995) *34:* 42

Feit v. Biosynth Int'l, Inc., 1996 WL 99726 (N.D. Ill. Mar. 4, 1996) *16:* 19

Feldman v. Philadelphia Hous. Auth., 43 F.3d 823 (3d Cir. 1994) *17:* 69; *40:* 22, 26, 37

Feliberty v. Kemper Corp., 98 F.3d 274, 5 AD 1729 (7th Cir. 1996) *9:* 195, 207

Felker v. Pepsi-Cola Co., 899 F. Supp. 882, 68 FEP 1569 (D. Conn. 1995) *41:* 11

Felt v. Atchison, Topeka & Santa Fe Ry., 60 F.3d 1416, 68 FEP 548 (9th Cir. 1995) *32:* 20

Fennell v. First Step Designs, Ltd., 83 F.3d 526, 70 FEP 1305 (1st Cir. 1996) *38:* 14–15

Ferguson v. Texasgulf, Inc., 5 AD 722 (S.D. Tex. 1996), *aff'd mem.,* 106 F.3d 397 (5th Cir. 1997) *9:* 215, 243

Fernbach v. Dominick's Finer Foods, 936 F. Supp. 467, 5 AD 1543 (N.D. Ill. 1996) *9:* 152

Fernot v. Crafts Inn, Inc., 895 F. Supp. 668, 73 FEP 1635 (D. Vt. 1995) *20:* 66, 69

Ferry v. Roosevelt Bank, 883 F. Supp. 435, 4 AD 476 (E.D. Mo. 1995) *9:* 156, 187–88

F.F. v. City of Laredo, 912 F. Supp. 248 (S.D. Tex. 1995) *9:* 134

Fickling v. New York State Dep't of Civil Serv., 909 F. Supp. 185 (S.D.N.Y. 1995) *4:* 16; *5:* 16, 24, 49, 52–53; *5:* 40, 44–45, 81; *39:* 72

Finch v. Hercules, Inc., 865 F. Supp. 1104, 74 FEP 1571 (D. Del. 1994) *16:* 115, 121, 137–38, 140–41, 165

Fink
—v. Kitzman, 881 F. Supp. 1347, 4 AD 644 (N.D. Iowa 1995) *9:* 3; *16:* 96, 142
—v. New York City Dep't of Personnel, 53 F.3d 565, 4 AD 641 (2d Cir. 1995) *9:* 73

Fioriglio v. New Jersey, Dep't of Personnel, 1996 U.S. Dist. LEXIS 15399 (D.N.J. Oct. 15, 1996) *27:* 185, 187

Firefighters Inst. for Racial Equality v. City of St. Louis, 616 F.2d 350, 21 FEP 1140 (8th Cir. 1980), *cert. denied,* 452 U.S. 938 (1981) *5:* 54

Fischbach v. District of Columbia Dep't of Corrections, 86 F.3d 1180, 71 FEP 316 (D.C. Cir. 1996) *2:* 50; *19:* 14, 16, 22

Fisher v. Vassar College, 852 F. Supp. 1193, 64 FEP 1346 (S.D.N.Y. 1994), *aff'd in part, vacated in part,* 70 F.3d 1420, 70 FEP 1155 (2d Cir. 1995), *amended,* 1995 U.S. App. LEXIS 38412, *modified en banc,* 114 F.3d 1332 (2d Cir. 1997), *cert. denied,* 118 S. Ct. 851 (1998) *2:* 35–37, 47; *7:* 3; *13:* 16–18, 29; *15:* 29–30; *19:* 22, 26; *39:* 26, 38, 83; *40:* 4, 7

Fitzgerald v. Mountain States Tel. & Tel. Co., 68 F.3d 1257, 69 FEP 163 (10th Cir. 1995) **24:** 4, 62–64; **41:** 102–03

Flaherty v. Gas Research Inst., 31 F.3d 451, 65 FEP 941 (7th Cir. 1994) **16:** 40

Flamand v. American Int'l Group, Inc., 876 F. Supp. 356, 69 FEP 675 (D.P.R. 1994) **16:** 27, 69; **21:** 17; **30:** 11

Flanagan
—v. Aaron E. Henry Community Health Serv. Ctr., 876 F.2d 1231, 51 FEP 1483 (5th Cir. 1989) **27:** 36
—v. Ahearn (In re Asbestos Litig.), 90 F.3d 963 (5th Cir. 1996), *vacated and remanded,* 117 S. Ct. 2503 (1997), *aff'd on remand,* 134 F.3d 668 (5th Cir. 1998) **37:** 109

Flavel v. Svedala Indus., Inc.
—868 F. Supp. 1422, 70 FEP 1088 (E.D. Wis. 1994) **16:** 88–89 **21:** 18
—875 F. Supp. 550, 75 FEP 915 (E.D. Wis. 1994) **34:** 26; **37:** 91, 102

Fleenor v. Hewitt Soap Co., 81 F.3d 48, 70 FEP 737 (6th Cir.), *cert. denied,* 117 S. Ct. 170 (1996) **20:** 105

Florence v. Department of Social Servs., 544 N.W.2d 723, 151 LRRM 2823 (Mich. Ct. App. 1996) **22:** 17–18

Flores v. Villerose, Inc., 5 AD 1672 (E.D. Pa. 1996) **9:** 300, 305

Florida Azalea Specialists; United States v., 19 F.3d 620, 64 FEP 769 (11th Cir. 1994) **11:** 13; **29:** 26

Flugge v. Wagner, 532 N.W.2d 419, 11 IER 1783 (S.D. 1995) **26:** 42

Flynn v. Raytheon Co., 868 F. Supp. 383, 3 AD 1495 (D. Mass. 1994), *aff'd mem.,* 94 F.3d 640 (1st Cir. 1996) **9:** 267

Folkerson v. Circus Circus Enters., Inc., 107 F.3d 754, 73 FEP 219 (9th Cir. 1997) **20:** 106

Fontelroy v. Day & Zimmermann, Inc., 1995 WL 530666 (D. Kan. Sept. 7, 1995), *aff'd,* 83 F.3d 431 (10th Cir. 1996) **3:** 1; **13:** 9

Food & Commercial Workers v. Brown Group, Inc., 517 U.S. 544 (1996) **37:** 71

Foote v. Folks, Inc., 864 F. Supp. 1327, 3 AD 1342 (N.D. Ga. 1994) **30:** 10

Forbes v. Reno, 893 F. Supp. 476, 73 FEP 51 (W.D. Pa. 1995), *aff'd without opinion,* 91 F.3d 123, 73 FEP 192 (3d Cir. 1996) **16:** 68; **33:** 5; **34:** 8

Ford v. Bernard Fineson Dev. Ctr., 81 F.3d 304, 70 FEP 825 (2d Cir. 1996) **16:** 62; **31:** 1

Ford Motor Co.
—v. EEOC, 458 U.S. 219, 29 FEP 121 (1982) **41:** 48
—EEOC v., 1996 WL 557800 (6th Cir. Sept. 30, 1996) **34:** 10–13

Ford Motor Credit Co.; EEOC v., 26 F.3d 44, 65 FEP 65 (6th Cir. 1994) **29:** 32

Forehand v. Florida State Hosp. at Chattahoochee, 89 F.3d 1562, 71 FEP 905 (11th Cir. 1996) **4:** 24; **39:** 27, 33, 42

Foreman v. Babcock & Wilcox Co., 117 F.3d 800, 7 AD 331 (5th Cir. 1997) **9:** 32, 59, 186

Fortino v. Quasar Co, 950 F.2d 389, 57 FEP 712 (7th Cir. 1991) **11:** 35

Foster
—v. Dalton, 71 F.3d 52, 69 FEP 1402 (1st Cir. 1995) **2:** 1; **18:** 1
—v. Kings Park Cent. Sch. Dist., 174 F.R.D. 19 (E.D.N.Y. 1997) **43:** 61

Fowler v. Sunrise Carpet Indus., Inc., 911 F. Supp. 1560, 75 FEP 201 (N.D. Ga. 1996) **20:** 55–58

Fox v. T-H Continental Ltd. Partnership, 78 F.3d 409, 11 IER 988 (8th Cir. 1996) **26:** 18

Francis v. Brown, 58 F.3d 191, 68 FEP 555 (5th Cir. 1995) **33:** 1; **36:** 7, 20

Frank
—v. New York State Elec. & Gas, 871 F. Supp. 167, 69 FEP 711 (W.D.N.Y. 1994) **22:** 16; **31:** 20
—v. Relin, 851 F. Supp. 87 (W.D.N.Y. 1994) **40:** 23–24, 37–38, 48–49

Frankel v. Bally, Inc., 987 F.2d 86, 61 FEP 218 (2d Cir. 1993) **30:** 13, 17

Franklin Iron & Metal Corp., 315 NLRB 819, 148 LRRM 1246 (1994), *enforcement granted,* 83 F.3d 156, 152 LRRM 2383 (6th Cir. 1996) **25:** 2

Fred v. Wackenhut Corp., 860 F. Supp. 1401, 73 FEP 1721 (D. Neb. 1994), aff'd, 53 F.3d 335 (8th Cir.), cert. denied, 116 S. Ct. 190 (1995) **20:** 65, 69

Frederick v. Justice Dep't, 73 F.3d 349, 11 IER 507 (Fed. Cir. 1996) **26:** 30

Fredette v. BVP Management Assocs., 112 F.3d 1503, 73 FEP 1519 (11th Cir. 1997), cert. denied, 118 S. Ct. 1184 (1998) **20:** 27

Fredrick v. Goodyear Tire & Rubber Co., 71 FEP 1842 (S.D. Tex. 1996) **2:** 12

Freeman
—v. Bechtel Constr. Co., 87 F.3d 1029, 71 FEP 353 (8th Cir. 1996) **20:** 113
—v. Package Mach. Co., 865 F.2d 1331, 1342 n.5, 49 FEP 1139 (1st Cir. 1988) **4:** 38

French; United States v., 46 F.3d 710 (8th Cir. 1995) **31:** 29

Frey v. Alldata Corp., 895 F. Supp. 221, 4 AD 1627 (E.D. Wis. 1995) **9:** 302–04; **42:** 7–9

Friedman v. BRW Inc., 40 F.3d 293, 10 IER 538 (8th Cir. 1994) **26:** 18

Fronduti v. Trinity Indus., 928 F. Supp. 1107 (M.D. Ala. 1996) **16:** 14, 51

Fuentes v. Perskie, 32 F.3d 759, 65 FEP 890 (3d Cir. 1994) **16:** 112; **18:** 11; **33:** 50

Fuka v. Thomson Consumer Electronics, 82 F.3d 1397, 71 FEP 1417 (7th Cir. 1996) **2:** 54; **16:** 167

Fuller
—v. City of Oakland, 47 F.3d 1522, 67 FEP 992 (9th Cir. 1995) **20:** 67, 69
—v. Phipps, 67 F.3d 1137, 69 FEP 111 (4th Cir. 1995) **2:** 55–56; **24:** 57; **41:** 122

Furr v. Seagate Tech., Inc., 82 F.3d 974, 70 FEP 1201, 82 F.3d 980, 70 FEP 1325 (10th Cir. 1996), cert. denied sub nom. Doan v. Seagate, 117 S. Ct. 684 (1997) **2:** 47; **16:** 120, 133–34, 139, 142, 158, 164; **37:** 18; **39:** 4, 57, 65

Fussell v. Georgia Ports Auth., 906 F. Supp. 1561, 5 AD 1236 (S.D. Ga. 1995), aff'd mem., 106 F.3d 417 (11th Cir. 1997) **9:** 76, 123, 150, 170, 187, 246; **38:** 20

Futrell v. J.I. Case, 38 F.3d 342, 66 FEP 238 (7th Cir. 1994) **16:** 123

G

Gadsby v. Norwalk Furniture Corp., 71 F.3d 1324, 69 FEP 715 (7th Cir. 1995) **16:** 154, 166

Gadson v. Concord Hosp., 966 F.2d 32 (1st Cir. 1992), cert. denied, 114 S. Ct. 1398 (1994) **16:** 173

Galarraga v. Marriott Employees Fed. Credit Union, 70 FEP 1605 (D. Md. 1996) **15:** 24; **21:** 28

Galdauckas v. Interstate Hotels Corp., 901 F. Supp. 454 (D. Mass. 1995) **16:** 167

Gallaher v. Croghan Colonial Bank, 89 F.3d 275, 5 AD 1089 (6th Cir. 1996) **9:** 14–15

Galloway v. General Motors Serv. Parts Operations, 78 F.3d 1164, 70 FEP 341 (7th Cir. 1996) **20:** 56, 61, 70

Gandy v. Sullivan County, Tenn., 24 F.3d 861, 64 FEP 1607 (6th Cir. 1994) **15:** 31; **31:** 14

Garavaglia v. Centra Inc., 536 N.W.2d 805, 11 IER 308 (Mich. Ct. App. 1995) **26:** 1

Garcia
—v. ANR Freight Sys., Inc., 942 F. Supp. 351 (N.D. Ohio 1996) **20:** 102
—v. Elf Atochem N. Am., 28 F.3d 446, 66 FEP 1700 (5th Cir. 1994) **30:** 53
—v. Fulbright & Jaworski L.L.P., 3 WH2d 742 (S.D. Tex. 1996) **17:** 46
—v. International Rehabilitation Assocs., 1994 U.S. App. LEXIS 19125 (9th Cir. July 25, 1984) **34:** 8
—v. United States, 88 F.3d 318 (5th Cir. 1996) **36:** 31–32
—v. Uniwyo Fed. Credit Union, 920 P.2d 642, 11 IER 1550 (Wyo. 1996) **26:** 18, 22

Garcia-Paz v. Swift Textiles, Inc., 873 F. Supp. 547, 3 AD 1844 (D. Kan. 1995) **32:** 18; **38:** 20

Gardner
—v. Gartman, 880 F.2d 797, 50 FEP 629 (4th Cir. 1989) **36:** 21

Gardner—Contd.
—v. Loomis Armored Inc., 913 P.2d 377, 11 IER 993 (Wash. 1996) *26:* 23
Garfield v. J.C. Nichols Real Estate, 57 F.3d 662, 68 FEP 188 (8th Cir.), *cert. denied,* 116 S. Ct. 380 (1995) *31:* 23, 29
Gary v. Long, 59 F.3d 1391, 68 FEP 581 (D.C. Cir.), *cert. denied,* 116 S. Ct. 569 (1995) *20:* 18
Garza v. Abbott Lab., 940 F. Supp. 1227, 6 AD 1507 (N.D. Ill. 1996) *9:* 117, 133, 168–70
Gaspar v. Linvatec Corp., 167 F.R.D. 51 (N.D. Ill. 1996) *37:* 48
Gausmann v. City of Ashland, 926 F. Supp. 635, 75 FEP 525 (N.D. Ohio 1996) *16:* 27
Gaworski v. ITT Commercial Fin. Corp., 17 F.3d 1104, 64 FEP 382 (8th Cir.), *cert. denied,* 513 U.S. 946 (1994) *2:* 42
Gearhart v. Eye Care Ctrs. of Am., Inc., 888 F. Supp. 814 (S.D. Tex. 1995) *20:* 61, 69
Gehring v. Case Corp., 43 F.3d 340, 66 FEP 1373 (7th Cir. 1994), *cert. denied,* 515 U.S. 1159 (1995) *2:* 51–53; *16:* 154; *38:* 33
Gehrt v. University of Ill., 974 F. Supp. 1178, 74 FEP 961 (C.D. Ill. 1997) *16:* 35
Geir v. Medtronic, Inc., 99 F.3d 238, 72 FEP 249 (7th Cir. 1996) *2:* 44
Genas v. New York Dep't of Correctional Servs., 67 FEP 27 (S.D.N.Y. 1994), *rev'd,* 75 F.3d 825, 70 FEP 16 (2d Cir. 1996) *8:* 22–23, 31; *33:* 3
General Dynamics Corp.
—v. Superior Court, 7 Cal. 4th 1164, 876 P.2d 487, 9 IER 1089 (Cal. 1994) *26:* 29
—v. United States, 49 F.3d 1384 (9th Cir. 1995) *11:* 14
General Motors Corp. Pick-Up Truck Fuel Tank Prods. Liability Litig., In re, 55 F.3d 768 (3d Cir.), *cert. denied,* 116 S. Ct. 88 (1995) *37:* 109
General Tel. Co. v. Falcon, 457 U.S. 147, 28 FEP 1745 (1982) *37:* 1, 19

Geraci v. Moody-Tottrup, Int'l, Inc., 82 F.3d 578, 70 FEP 1288 (3d Cir. 1996) *33:* 51
Gerardi v. Hofstra Univ., 897 F. Supp. 50 (E.D.N.Y. 1995) *16:* 214; *41:* 51
Gerdes v. Swift-Eckrich, Inc., 949 F. Supp. 1386 (N.D. Iowa 1996) *9:* 198–99
Gerzog v. London Fog Corp., 907 F. Supp. 590, 72 FEP 371 (E.D.N.Y. 1995) *16:* 78
Geuss v. Pfizer, Inc., 971 F. Supp. 164, 6 AD 1140 (E.D. Pa. 1996) *9:* 136
Gheesling v. Chater, 162 F.R.D. 649, 68 FEP 965 (D. Kan. 1995) *38:* 5, 41
Gierlinger v. New York State Police, 15 F.3d 32, 65 FEP 1667 (2d Cir. 1994) *24:* 28
Gilbert v. Penn-Wheeling Closure Corp., 917 F. Supp. 1119 (N.D. W. Va. 1996) *27:* 33
Gilday v. Mecosta County, 920 F. Supp. 792, 5 AD 758 (W.D. Mich. 1996), *rev'd,* 7 AD 348 (6th Cir. 1997) *9:* 45; *33:* 15
Gile v. United Airlines, Inc., 95 F.3d 492, 5 AD 1466 (7th Cir. 1996) *9:* 133, 135, 141, 144, 196, 202; *38:* 43
Gilligan v. Department of Labor, 81 F.3d 835, 70 FEP 856 (9th Cir. 1996) *27:* 138–40, 180–81
Gillming v. Simmons Indus., 91 F.3d 1168, 71 FEP 1016 (8th Cir. 1996) *20:* 81
Gilmer v. Interstate/Johnson Lane Corp., 500 U.S. 20, 55 FEP 1116 (1991) *24:* 70
Gilmore
—v. List & Clark Constr. Co., 862 F. Supp. 294 (D. Kan. 1994) *33:* 20, 33
—v. Local 295, Teamsters, 798 F. Supp. 1030, 64 FEP 1187 (S.D.N.Y 1992), *aff'd,* 23 F.3d 396, 67 FEP 96 (2d Cir.), *cert. denied,* 513 U.S. 936, 72 FEP 320 (1994) *22:* 29–30
Girard v. Rubin, 62 F.3d 1244, 68 FEP 1002 (9th Cir. 1995) *31:* 18–19
G-K-G, Inc.; EEOC v., 39 F.3d 740, 66 FEP 344 (7th Cir. 1994) *16:* 90; *34:* 38–39, 52

Glass v. Philadelphia Elec. Co., 34 F.3d 188, 65 FEP 1280, 65 FEP 1450 (3d Cir. 1994) *19:* 17
Glidden v. Chromalloy Am. Corp., 808 F.2d 621 (7th Cir. 1986) *37:* 86
Gloria v. Valley Grain Prods., Inc., 72 F.3d 497, 69 FEP 1163 (5th Cir. 1996) *41:* 22
Glus v. G. C. Murphy Co., 562 F.2d 880, 15 FEP 998 (3d Cir. 1977) *33:* 17, 23
Godby v. Electrolux Corp., 66 FEP 1704 (N.D. Ga. 1994), *aff'd,* 58 F.3d 641 (11th Cir. 1995), *cert. denied,* 116 S. Ct. 1352 (1996) *10:* 111
Godd v. West Communications, Inc., 1995 WL 67672 (D. Or. Feb. 16, 1995) *16:* 67
Goins v. Mercy Ctr., 667 N.E.2d 652, 11 IER 1760 (Ill. App. Ct. 1996) *26:* 59
Goldsmith v. Mayor & City Council of Baltimore, 987 F.2d 1064 (4th Cir. 1993) *21:* 1
Golenia v. Bob Baker Toyota, 915 F. Supp. 201, 5 AD 482 (S.D. Cal. 1996) *9:* 297
Gomez
—v. Alexian Bros. Hosp., 698 F.2d 1019, 30 FEP 1705 (9th Cir. 1983) *5:* 5
—v. American Bldg. Maintenance, 940 F. Supp. 255 (N.D. Cal. 1996) *9:* 134, 148
—v. Martin Marietta Corp., 50 F.3d 1511, 67 FEP 537 (10th Cir. 1995) *38:* 1–3, 16
Gonzales
—v. Garner Food Servs., Inc. 89 F.3d 1523, 5 AD 1202 (11th Cir. 1996), *cert. denied,* 117 S. Ct. 1822 (1997) *9:* 104–06, 110
—v. Police Dep't, San Jose, Cal., 901 F.2d 758, 52 FEP 1132 (9th Cir. 1990) *36:* 19
Gonzalez
—v. Perfect Carton Corp., 6 AD 151 (N.D. Ill. 1996) *9:* 116
—v. Trinity Marine Group, Inc., 1994 WL 623985, 66 FEP 667 (E.D. La. Nov. 7, 1994) *40:* 90, 93, 97

Good v. U.S. West Communications, Inc., 1995 WL 67672 (D. Or. Feb. 16, 1995) *13:* 36
Goodman v. Boeing Co., 75 Wash. App. 60, 877 P.2d 703, 3 AD 983 (Wash. App. 1994), *aff'd,* 127 Wash. 2d 1020, 890 P.2d 463 (Wash. 1995) *41:* 72
Gordon v. E.L. Hamm & Assocs., 100 F.3d 907, 6 AD 282 (11th Cir. 1996) *9:* 37
Gore v. GTE S., Inc., 917 F. Supp. 1564 (M.D. Ala. 1996) *9:* 153
Gorence v. Eagle Food Ctrs., 1994 WL 445149, 1994 U.S. Dist. LEXIS 11438 (N.D. Ill. Aug. 15, 1994) *16:* 82; *37:* 31–32, 54, 63–64
Gorham v. Benson Optical, 539 N.W.2d 798, 11 IER 187 (Minn. Ct. App. 1995) *26:* 19
Gorman
—v. Hughes Danbury Optical Sys., 908 F. Supp. 107 (D. Conn. 1995) *16:* 50
—v. Roberts, 909 F. Supp. 1479 (M.D. Ala. 1995) *17:* 54; *24:* 9–11, 20–21, 50
Goshtasby v. University of Illinois-Chicago, 1997 WL 367362 (N.D. Ill., May 15, 1997), *appeal pending,* No. 97-2297 (7th Cir.) *16:* 35
Gostanian v. Bendel, 1997 WL 214966 (S.D.N.Y Apr. 25, 1997) *20:* 20–21
Goudeau v. Dental Health Servs., Inc., 901 F. Supp. 1139, 69 FEP 629 (M.D. La. 1995) *30:* 16, 44, 46
Gould
—v. Kemper Nat'l Ins. Cos., 880 F. Supp. 527 (N.D. Ill. 1995), *aff'd mem.,* 78 F.3d 586 (7th Cir. 1996) *16:* 95, 159
—v. Maryland Sound Indus., 31 Cal. App. 4th 1137, 10 IER 405 (Cal. Ct. App. 1995) *26:* 11, 27
Government Employees (AFGE) Council 33, Local 51 v. Bentsen, 1994 U.S. App. LEXIS 25260 (9th Cir. Sept. 7, 1994) *9:* 141
Gower v. Wrenn Handling, Inc., 892 F. Supp. 724, 4 AD 1154 (M.D.N.C. 1995) *9:* 67, 139
Graboski v. Guiliani, 937 F. Supp. 258, 6 AD 253 (S.D.N.Y. 1996) *9:* 61, 110

Grady v. Bunzl Packaging Supply Co., 874 F. Supp. 387 (N.D. Ga. 1994) *16:* 75

Graehling v. Village of Lombard, 4 AD 815 (N.D. Ill. 1994), *aff'd,* 58 F.3d 295, 4 AD 864 (7th Cir. 1995) *9:* 149

Graffam v. Scott Paper Co., 870 F. Supp. 389, 66 FEP 1007 (D.Me. 1994), *aff'd without opinion,* 60 F.3d 809, 71 FEP 736 (1st Cir. 1995) *4:* 30–34; *5:* 39, 42; *7:* 8; *16:* 138; *39:* 33, 35

Grant
—v. Bullock County Bd. of Educ., 895 F. Supp. 1506 (M.D. Ala. 1995) *19:* 1
—v. News Group Boston, Inc., 55 F.3d 1, 67 FEP 1030 (1st Cir. 1995) *39:* 1–3

Grauer v. Federal Express Corp., 894 F. Supp. 330, 68 FEP 218 (W.D. Tenn. 1994), *aff'd,* 73 F.3d 361 (6th Cir. 1996) *19:* 13, 19

Graves v. Nordstrom, Inc.
—1994 WL 721589 (N.D. Cal. 1994) *8:* 10–11
—1995 WL 55336 (N.D. Cal. 1995) *8:* 10, 12

Grayson v. KMart Corp., 79 F.3d 1086, 70 FEP 770 (11th Cir.), *cert. denied sub nom.* KMart Corp. v. Helton, 117 S. Ct. 447 (1996) *16:* 81, 84, 87; *31:* 36–37; *33:* 42

Green
—v. Bryant, 887 F. Supp. 798, 10 IER 1179 (E.D. Pa. 1995) *26:* 56
—v. Clarendon County Sch. Dist. No. 3, 923 F. Supp. 829 (D.S.C. 1996) *18:* 10; *19:* 17
—EEOC v., 76 F.3d 19, 70 FEP 88 (1st Cir. 1996) *31:* 1

Greenberg v. Union Camp Corp., 48 F.3d 22, 67 FEP 120 (1st Cir. 1995) *21:* 23; *39:* 61

Greenlaw v. Garrett, 59 F.3d 994, 68 FEP 531 (9th Cir. 1995), *cert. denied,* 117 S. Ct. 110, 74 FEP 672 (1996) *31:* 10; *33:* 1; *36:* 8

Greenlees v. Eidenmuller Enters., 32 F.3d 197, 66 FEP 457 (5th Cir. 1994) *23:* 4, 12; *30:* 41, 63

Greensboro Prof'l Fire Fighters Ass'n Local 3157 v. City of Greensboro, 64 F.3d 962, 150 LRRM 2261 (4th Cir. 1995) *24:* 28, 43

Greenway v. Buffalo Hilton Hotel, 951 F. Supp. 1039 (W.D.N.Y. 1997) *9:* 296, 305

Greenwood v. Taft, Stettinius & Hollister, 663 N.E.2d 1030, 10 IER 1744 (Ohio Ct. App. 1995) *26:* 56

Gregor v. Derwinski, 911 F. Supp. 643, 75 FEP 797 (W.D.N.Y. 1996) *16:* 28; *24:* 39; *42:* 32

Gregorich v. Lund, 54 F.3d 410, 149 LRRM 2278 (7th Cir. 1995) *17:* 57

Grenier v. Cyanamid Plastics, Inc., 70 F.3d 667, 5 AD 75 (1st Cir. 1995) *9:* 79, 211, 215; *18:* 13

Greyson v. McKenna & Cuneo, 879 F. Supp. 1065, 67 FEP 792 (D. Colo. 1995) *16:* 96; *34:* 9

Griffin
—v. City of Dallas, 26 F.3d 610, 65 FEP 784 (5th Cir. 1994) *31:* 1; *33:* 8–10
—v. Home Depot, Inc., 168 F.R.D. 187, 70 FEP 1678 (E.D. La. 1996) *37:* 50, 65–68
—v. Kraft Gen. Foods, Inc., 62 F.3d 368, 68 FEP 1072 (11th Cir. 1995) *16:* 193, 198, 203; *43:* 19, 42–43
—v. Lockheed, 69 F.3d 544 (9th Cir. 1995) *18:* 11
—v. Singletary, 64 FEP 516 (11th Cir. 1994), *cert. denied,* 513 U.S. 1077 (1995) *37:* 76, 94

Griffith
—v. Keystone Steel & Wire
——858 F. Supp 802, 66 FEP 227 (C.D. Ill. 1994) *32:* 27
——887 F. Supp. 1133, 68 FEP 841 (C.D. Ill. 1995) *20:* 49, 51
—v. State of Col., Div. of Youth Servs., 17 F.3d 1323, 64 FEP 206 (10th Cir. 1994) *40:* 7
—v. Wal-Mart Stores, Inc., 163 F.R.D. 4, 4 AD 1086 (E.D. Ky. 1995) *38:* 33

Griggs v. Duke Power Co., 401 U.S. 424, 3 FEP 175 (1971) *4:* 1; *5:* 28

Grimes
—v. Housing Auth. of the City of New Haven, 242 Conn. 236, 698 A.2d 302 (1998) *37:* 80
—v. Superior Home Health Care of Middle Tenn., Inc., 929 F. Supp. 1088, 74 FEP 1539 (M.D. Tenn. 1996) *24:* 5, 59
—v. United States Postal Serv., 872 F. Supp. 668, 3 AD 1764 (W.D. Mo. 1994), *aff'd mem.*, 74 F.3d 1243, 6 AD 800 (8th Cir. 1996) *9:* 262
Grinnell v. General Elec. Co., 907 F. Supp. 544, 69 FEP 1005 (N.D.N.Y. 1995) *16:* 59, 75
Grinnell Corp.; EEOC v., 881 F. Supp. 406 (S.D. Ind. 1995) *15:* 9
Griswold
—v. Alabama Dep't of Indus. Relations, 903 F. Supp. 1492, 71 FEP 1336 (M.D. Ala. 1995) *16:* 27, 34; *21:* 18
—v. New Madrid County Group Practice, Inc., 920 F. Supp. 1046, 73 FEP 151 (E.D. Mo. 1996) *16:* 27
Groce v. Foster, 880 P.2d 902, 9 IER 1768 (Okla. 1994) *26:* 24
Grooms v. Wiregrass Elec. Co-op., Inc., 883 F. Supp. 643, 67 FEP 1663 (M.D. Ala. 1995) *18:* 10
Gross v. Burggraf Constr. Co., 53 F.3d 1531, 68 FEP 88 (10th Cir. 1995) *20:* 69
Guardians Ass'n of New York City Police Dep't, Inc. v. Civil Serv. Comm'n of New York, 630 F.2d 79, 23 FEP 909 (2d Cir. 1980), *cert. denied sub nom.* Civil Serv. Comm'n of City of New York v. Guardians Ass'n of New York City Police Dep't, 452 U.S. 940, 25 FEP 1683 (1981) *5:* 47, 62; *7:* 11
Guice-Mills v. Brown, 882 F. Supp. 1427, 5 AD 542 (S.D.N.Y. 1995) *33:* 2
Gulley v. Orr, 905 F.2d 1383, 53 FEP 97 (10th Cir. 1990) *36:* 27
Gunaca v. Texas, 65 F.3d 467, 68 FEP 1678 (5th Cir. 1995) *16:* 9
Guneratne v. St. Mary's Hosp., 943 F. Supp. 771, 6 AD 476 (S.D. Tex. 1996) *9:* 172, 245, 249

Gutierrez de Martinez v. Lamagno, 515 S. Ct. 417 (1995) *36:* 30

H

Haddon v. United States, 68 F.3d 1420 (D.C. Cir. 1995) *36:* 33
Hadix v. Johnson, 65 F.3d 532 (6th Cir. 1995) *42:* 48
Hadley v. VAM, 44 F.3d 372, 67 FEP 186 (5th Cir. 1995) *40:* 37, 44; *41:* 22, 83; *42:* 44
Hairston v. Gainesville Sun Publ'g Co., 9 F.3d 913, 63 FEP 838 (11th Cir. 1993) *2:* 40
Haley v. Virginia Commw. Univ., 948 F. Supp. 573, 72 FEP 1518 (E.D. Va. 1996) *20:* 111
Hall
—v. Center, 1995 U.S. Dist. LEXIS 5801 (N.D. Ill. Apr. 14, 1995) *9:* 125
—v. City of Brawley, 887 F. Supp. 1333, 68 FEP 1343 (S.D. Cal. 1995) *27:* 10, 31; *41:* 129; *42:* 14
—v. Hackley Hosp., 532 N.W.2d 893, 4 AD 961 (Mich. Ct. App. 1995) *9:* 233
Hallberg v. Eat'n Park, 70 FEP 361 (W.D. Pa. 1996) *20:* 105–06
Hammer v. Board of Educ., 955 F. Supp. 921 (N.D. Ill. 1997) *9:* 71
Hammett v. Lankenau Hosp., 72 FEP 442 (E.D. Pa. 1996) *2:* 13
Hampton Mem'l Gardens, Inc.; EEOC v., 1995 U.S. App. LEXIS 9015 (4th Cir. Apr. 20, 1995) *34:* 62
Hamros v. Bethany Homes & Methodist Hosp. of Chicago, 894 F. Supp. 1176, 10 IER 1750 (N.D. Ill. 1995) *26:* 31, 52
Hankins v. City of Philadelphia, 1996 WL 571755 (E.D. Pa. Oct. 4, 1996) *38:* 54
Hanna v. Marshall Field & Co., 665 N.E.2d 343, 11 IER 1045 (Ill. App. Ct. 1996) *26:* 12
Hannon v. Chater
—887 F. Supp. 1303, 72 FEP 1379 (N.D. Cal. 1995) *27:* 26, 40, 147–48, 177–79

Hannon v. Chater—*Contd.*
—900 F. Supp. 1276 (N.D. Cal. 1995) *42:* 1, 17, 20
Hansen
—v. Dean Witter Reynolds, Inc., 887 F. Supp. 669, 68 FEP 370 (S.D.N.Y. 1995) *38:* 16
—v. Soldenwager, 19 F.3d 573, 9 IER 712 (11th Cir. 1994) *24:* 32
Harden v. Delta Air Lines, 900 F. Supp. 493, 4 AD 1241 (S.D. Ga. 1995) *9:* 149; *38:* 20
Hardin v. Hussmann Corp., 45 F.3d 262, 66 FEP 1369 (8th Cir. 1995) *16:* 165, 176
Harding
—v. Dana Trans., Inc., 914 F. Supp. 1084, 69 FEP 1603 (D.N.J. 1996) *38:* 29, 31
—v. Fort Wayne Foundry/Pontiac Div., Inc., 919 F. Supp. 1223, 70 FEP 1074 (N.D. Ind. 1996) *31:* 41
Hardy v. Sears, Roebuck & Co., 1996 U.S. Dist. LEXIS 19008 (N.D. Ga. Aug. 28, 1996) *9:* 125, 156, 172
Hargens v. United States Dep't of Agric., 865 F. Supp. 1314, 66 FEP 245 (N.D. Iowa 1994) *17:* 10
Hargett v. Valley Fed. Sav. Bank, 60 F.3d 754, 68 FEP 852 (11th Cir. 1995) *31:* 5
Harker v. Utica College of Syracuse Univ., 885 F. Supp. 378, 72 FEP 693 (N.D.N.Y. 1995) *15:* 16
Harley v. McCoach, 928 F. Supp. 533, 72 FEP 1725 (E.D. Pa. 1996) *24:* 15
Harlston v. McDonnell Douglas Corp., 37 F.3d 379, 67 FEP 762 (8th Cir. 1994) *24:* 3
Harper v. Godfrey Co., 45 F.3d 143, 66 FEP 1258 (7th Cir. 1995) *41:* 33, 65
Harris
—v. Forklift Sys., Inc., 510 U.S. 17 (1993) *14:* 3
—v. H & W Contracting Co., 102 F.3d 516, 6 AD 460 (11th Cir. 1996) *9:* 45
—v. Marathon Oil Co., 948 F. Supp. 27 (W.D. Tex. 1996), *aff'd mem.,* 108 F.3d 332 (5th Cir. 1997) *9:* 60
—v. Proctor & Gamble Cellulose Co., 73 F.3d 321, 11 IER 605 (11th Cir. 1996) *26:* 34
Harrison
—v. Eddy Potash, Inc., 112 F.3d 1437, 73 FEP 1384 (10th Cir. 1997), *petition for cert. filed,* 66 U.S.L.W. 3137 (U.S. Aug. 6, 1997) *9:* 298
—v. Larue D. Carter Mem'l Hosp., 883 F. Supp. 328, 67 FEP 1639 (S.D. Ind. 1994), *aff'd,* 61 F.3d 905, 69 FEP 768 (7th Cir. 1995) *18:* 8, 11; *19:* 14
—v. Metropolitan Gov't of Nashville, 80 F.3d 1107, 73 FEP 109 (6th Cir.), *cert. denied,* 117 S. Ct. 169 (1996) *2:* 13; *17:* 22, 40; *20:* 1
Harriss v. Pan Am. World Airways, Inc., 74 F.R.D. 24, 15 FEP 1640 (N.D. Cal. 1977) *37:* 70
Hart v. University Sys. of N.H., 938 F. Supp. 104, 71 FEP 503 (D.N.H. 1996) *21:* 7
Hartleip v. McNeilab, Inc., 83 F.3d 767, 71 FEP 1636 (6th Cir. 1996) *20:* 19
Hartman
—v. Duffy, 158 F.R.D. 525 (D.D.C. 1994), *aff'd,* 88 F.3d 1232 (D.C. Cir. 1996) *37:* 3–4, 16, 31, 36, 73–74, 76, 106; *40:* 3
—v. Smith & Davis Mfg. Co., 904 F. Supp. 983, 73 FEP 99 (E.D. Mo. 1995) *24:* 21
Hartsel v. Keys, 87 F.3d 795, 72 FEP 951 (6th Cir. 1996), *cert. denied,* 117 S. Ct. 683, 72 FEP 1504 (1997) *2:* 47; *16:* 100, 180; *19:* 16; *21:* 22; *33:* 50
Harvey L. Walner & Assocs.; EEOC v., 1195 U.S. Dist. LEXIS 11239, *aff'd,* 91 F.3d 963, 71 FEP 683 (7th Cir. 1996) *34:* 3–4
Harvis v. Roadway Express, Inc., 973 F.2d 490, 61 FEP 91 (6th Cir. 1992) *32:* 14
Hashimoto v. Dalton, 870 F. Supp. 1544 (D. Haw. 1994), *aff'd,* 118 F.3d 671 (9th Cir. 1997), *cert denied,* 118 S.Ct. 1803 (1998) *36:* 26
Hatley v. Store Kraft Mfg. Co., 859 F. Supp. 1257, 70 FEP 1361 (D. Neb. 1994) *20:* 54; *33:* 56; *42:* 36, 44

Haun v. Ideal Indus., Inc., 81 F.3d 541, 70 FEP 923 (5th Cir. 1996)   *16:* 127

Hayes

—v. Eateries Inc., 905 P.2d 778, 11 IER 110 (Okla. 1995)   *26:* 11, 23

—v. Shalala

——902 F. Supp. 259, 73 FEP 3 (D.D.C. 1995)   *17:* 3, 31

——933 F. Supp. 21, 71 FEP 1240 (D.D.C. 1996)   *36:* 28; *40:* 24, 55, 57

Haynes

—v. Department of Health & Human Servs., 879 F. Supp. 127 (D.D.C. 1995), *aff'd,* 1997 WL 362503 (D.C. Cir. 1997)   *24:* 8, 49

—v. W.C. Caye & Co., 52 F.3d 928, 67 FEP 1537 (11th Cir. 1995)   *2:* 45, 56

—v. Williams, 88 F.3d 898, 71 FEP 414 (10th Cir. 1996)   *30:* 61

Haysman v. Food Lion, 893 F. Supp. 1092, 4 AD 1297 (S.D. Ga. 1995)   *9:* 53, 133, 153

Hazelwood Sch. Dist. v. United States, 433 U.S. 299, 15 FEP 1 (1977)   *39:* 76

Hazen Paper Co. v. Biggins, 507 U.S. 604, 61 FEP 793 (1993)   *16:* 178, 229

HBE Corp.; EEOC v., 157 F.R.D. 465 (E.D. Mo. 1994)   *34:* 50–51

Healey v. Southwood Psychiatric Hosp., 78 F.3d 128, 70 FEP 439 (3d Cir. 1996)   *4:* 2–3; *13:* 1, 4, 7–8

Hearn v. General Elec. Co., 927 F. Supp. 1486, 71 FEP 435 (M.D. Ala. 1996)   *2:* 56; *40:* 4

Hearst Corp.; EEOC v., 103 F.3d 462, 72 FEP 1541 (5th Cir. 1997)   *30:* 9; *34:* 6–7

Heather K. v. City of Mallard, 887 F. Supp. 1249, 4 AD 878 (N.D. Iowa 1995)   *9:* 3

Heil Co. v. Crowley, 659 So. 2d 105, 11 IER 1212 (Ala. 1995)   *26:* 24

Heinz v. Belcan Eng'g Corp., 68 FEP 1238 (W.D. Pa. 1995)   *16:* 27

Heise v. Genuine Parts Co., 900 F. Supp. 1137, 4 AD 1551 (D. Minn. 1995)   *9:* 125, 193

Helen L. v. DiDario, 46 F.3d 325, 3 AD 1775 (3d Cir.), *cert. denied,* 116 S. Ct. 64 (1995)   *9:* 3

Helfter v. United Parcel Serv., Inc., 115 F.3d 613, 6 AD 1499 (8th Cir. 1997)   *9:* 42

Helland v. South Bend Community Sch. Corp., 93 F.3d 327, 71 FEP 1621 (7th Cir. 1996), *cert. denied,* 117 S. Ct. 769 (1997)   *8:* 39

Heller

—v. Doe, 509 U.S. 312 (1993)   *14:* 20

—v. EBB Auto Co., 8 F.3d 1433, 63 FEP 505 (9th Cir. 1993)   *8:* 6

Henderson

—v. Bodine Aluminum, Inc., 70 F.3d 958, 6 AD 99 (8th Cir. 1995)   *9:* 114; *13:* 21

—v. Center for Community Alternatives, 911 F. Supp. 689 (S.D.N.Y. 1996)   *24:* 26

—v. Corrections Corp. of Am., 918 F. Supp. 204, 71 FEP 1250 (E.D. Tenn. 1996)   *2:* 12

Hendricks-Robinson v. Excel Corp., 164 F.R.D. 667 (C.D. Ill. 1996)   *37:* 25–27, 43, 56

Hendrix College; EEOC v., 53 F.3d 209 (8th Cir. 1995)   *34:* 63

Hendry v. GTE N., Inc., 896 F. Supp. 816, 6 AD 451 (N.D. Ind. 1995)   *9:* 153, 174, 232

Hennessy v. Penril Datacomm Networks, Inc., 69 F.3d 1344, 69 FEP 398 (7th Cir. 1995)   *2:* 56; *41:* 112

Henry v. Gehl Corp., 867 F. Supp. 960, 68 FEP 175 (D. Kan. 1994)   *2:* 13

Hensel v. Office of Chief Admin. Hearing Officer, 38 F.3d 505, 66 FEP 58 (10th Cir. 1994)   *11:* 15–17

Hensley v. Eckerhart, 461 U.S. 424, 31 FEP 1169 (1983)   *42:* 52

Henson

—v. City of Dundee, 682 F.2d 897, 29 FEP 787 (11th Cir. 1982)   *20:* 11, 48, 77

—v. City of Greensboro, 1995 U.S. Dist. LEXIS 19962 (M.D.N.C. Dec. 12, 1995), *aff'd mem.,* 107 F.3d 866 (4th Cir. 1997)   *9:* 134, 161

Henson—*Contd.*
—v. Liggett Group, Inc., 61 F.3d 270, 68 FEP 826 (4th Cir. 1995) *16:* 166, 172; *39:* 61
Herman v. Carpenters Local 971, 60 F.3d 1375, 68 FEP 181, 4 AD 907 (9th Cir. 1995) *16:* 39; *22:* 1, 3–4, 7–8; *30:* 62
Hernandez
—v. Alexander, 152 F.R.D. 192 (D. Nev. 1993) *37:* 43
—v. Kansas, 1994 WL 725092, 66 FEP 1552 (D. Kan. 1994) *11:* 29
Hesson v. Fireman's Fund Ins. Co., 897 F. Supp. 78, 68 FEP 1747 (W.D.N.Y. 1995) *16:* 75
Hetzel v. County of Prince William, 89 F.3d 169, 71 FEP 520 (4th Cir.), *cert. denied,* 117 S. Ct. 584, 72 FEP 992 (1996) *41:* 99, 102; *42:* 11
Heurtebise v. Reliable Bus. Computers Inc., 550 N.W.2d 243, 11 IER 1665 (Mich. 1996) *26:* 10
Heyne v. Caruso, 69 F.3d 1475, 69 FEP 408 (9th Cir. 1995) *20:* 39, 46–47; *29:* 47; *38:* 35
Hialeah, City of; United States v., 899 F. Supp. 603 (S.D. Fla. 1994) *40:* 79
Hiatt v. Union Pac. R.R., 859 F. Supp. 1416, 67 FEP 351 (D. Wyo. 1994), *aff'd,* 65 F.3d 838, 68 FEP 1160 (10th Cir. 1995), *cert. denied,* 516 U.S. 1115 (1996) *3:* 3; *16:* 113, 117, 196
Hicks v. Arthur
—159 F.R.D. 468 (E.D. Pa. 1995) *38:* 4
—878 F. Supp. 737 (E.D. Pa.), *aff'd,* 72 F.3d 122 (3d Cir. 1995) *19:* 13
Hill
—v. Burrell Communications Group, Inc., 67 F.3d 665, 69 FEP 207 (7th Cir. 1995) *27:* 31
—v. Commercial Union Ins. Co., 4 AD 727 (D. Kan. 1995), *aff'd,* 81 F.3d 172 (10th Cir. 1996) *16:* 73
—v. St. Louis Univ.
——920 F. Supp. 124 (E.D. Mo. 1996) *30:* 7
——923 F. Supp. 1199, 71 FEP 43 (E.D. Mo. 1996), *aff'd,* 123 F.3d 1114 (8th Cir. 1997) *16:* 119, 166

Hilliard v. BellSouth Medical Assistance Plan & Blue Cross Blue Shield, 918 F. Supp. 1016 (S.D. Miss. 1995) *9:* 113
Hirase-Doi v. U.S. West Communications, Inc., 61 F.3d 777, 69 FEP 1745 (10th Cir. 1995) *20:* 101; *21:* 6, 14; *38:* 35
Hirras v. National R.R. Passenger Corp., 95 F.3d 396, 72 FEP 454 (5th Cir. 1996) *20:* 105
Hirschinger v. Allstate Ins. Co., 884 F. Supp. 317, 69 FEP 997 (S.D. Ind. 1994) *33:* 55
Hodgkins v. New England Tel. Co., 82 F.3d 1226, 11 IER 1159 (1st Cir. 1996) *26:* 6, 46
Hodgson v. University of Tex. Med. Branch, 953 F. Supp. 168 (S.D. Tex. 1997) *16:* 35
Hoeppner v. Crotched Mountain Rehabilitation Ctr., 31 F.3d 9, 65 FEP 841 (1st Cir. 1994) *17:* 46
Hogan
—v. Bangor & Aroostock R.R., 61 F.3d 1034, 4 AD 1251 (1st Cir. 1995) *41:* 22, 102
—v. 50 Sutton Place S. Owners, Inc., 919 F. Supp. 738, 71 FEP 1321 (S.D.N.Y. 1996) *33:* 3
Hogue v. MQS Inspection, Inc., 875 F. Supp. 714, 3 AD 1793 (D. Colo. 1995) *9:* 166, 226; *21:* 28
Holbrook v. City of Alpharetta, 911 F. Supp. 1524, 6 AD 1394 (N.D. Ga. 1995), *aff'd,* 112 F.3d 1522, 6 AD 1409 (11th Cir. 1997) *9:* 56, 123, 132, 166; *21:* 13
Holiday Inns, Inc. v. McNeely, *see* Howlett v. Holiday Inns, Inc.
Holihan v. Lucky Stores, Inc., 87 F.3d 362, 5 AD 1068 (9th Cir. 1996), *cert. denied,* 117 S. Ct. 1349 (1997) *9:* 33, 45
Hollander v. American Cyanamid Co., 895 F.2d 80, 84, 51 FEP 1881 (2d. Cir. 1990) *38:* 10
Holmes
—v. California Army Nat'l Guard, 124 F.3d 1126 (9th Cir. 1997) *14:* 19, 21–23, 25

—v. City of Aurora, 4 AD 1781 (N.D. Ill. 1995) *9:* 163
—v. World Wildlife Fund, Inc., 908 F. Supp. 19, 69 FEP 1181 (D.D.C. 1995) *31:* 43
Holt
—v. JTM Indus., Inc., 89 F.3d 1224, 71 FEP 809 (5th Cir. 1996), *cert. denied,* 117 S. Ct. 1821 (1997) *17:* 9; *30:* 29
—v. KMI-Continental, Inc., 95 F.3d 123, 73 FEP 1615 (2d Cir. 1996), *cert. denied,* 117 S. Ct. 1819, 74 FEP 192 (1997) *38:* 30
Hom v. Squire, 81 F.3d 969 (10th Cir. 1996) *17:* 62, 68
Home by Hemphill, Inc.; EEOC v., 69 FEP 1198 (N.D. Ill. 1995) *15:* 4
Honda Motor Co. v. Oberg, 512 U.S. 415 (1994) *41:* 112
Hopkins v. Seagate, 30 F.3d 104 (10th Cir. 1994) *24:* 3
Hopper v. Hallmark Cards, Inc., 87 F.3d 983, 71 FEP 1362, 5 AD 1531 (8th Cir. 1996) *16:* 125, 130, 133; *39:* 42, 66
Hopwood v. Texas, 78 F.3d 932 (5th Cir.), *cert. denied sub nom.* Texas v. Hopwood, 518 U.S. 1033 (1996) *27:* 43, 45–53
Horne
—v. Cub Foods, 68 FEP 860 (N.D. Ill. 1995) *33:* 7
—v. Firemen's Retirement Sys., 69 F.3d 233, 69 FEP 374 (8th Cir. 1995) *16:* 54
Horton v. Board of Trustees, 1996 U.S. Dist. LEXIS 6879 (N.D. Ill. May 15, 1996) *9:* 156, 161
Hoschler v. Kozlik, 529 N.W.2d 822, 10 IER 896 (Neb. Ct. App. 1995) *26;* 52
Hott v. VDO Yazaki Corp., 922 F. Supp. 1114, 70 FEP 1008 (W.D. Va. 1996) *20:* 35–36, 69, 108
Houck v. City of Prairie Village, 912 F. Supp. 1438, *modified,* 924 F. Supp. 120 (D. Kan. 1996) *24:* 39
Houghton v. SIPCO, Inc., 38 F.3d 953, 66 FEP 97 (8th Cir. 1994) *4:* 40–41

Hover v. Florida Power & Light Co., 67 FEP 34 (S.D. Fla. 1994), *aff'd,* 101 F.3d 708 (11th Cir. 1996) *8:* 3, 13–14, 21; *30:* 60
Howard
—v. BP Oil Inc., 32 F.3d 520 (11th Cir. 1994), *aff'd,* 102 F.3d 555 (11th Cir. 1996) *2:* 40; *7:* 9; *18:* 1
—v. Uniroyal, Inc., 719 F.2d 1552, 1 AD 526 (11th Cir. 1983) *9:* 10
—v. United States, 864 F. Supp. 1019 (D. Colo. 1994) *8:* 2
Howlett v. Holiday Inns, Inc., 49 F.3d 189, 67 FEP 289 (6th Cir.), *cert. denied sub nom.* Holiday Inns, Inc. v. McNeely, 116 S. Ct. 379, 69 FEP 96 (1995) *16:* 49, 83, 85; *31:* 36–37
Howry v. NISUS, Inc., 910 F. Supp. 576, 69 FEP 471 (M.D. Fla. 1995) *30:* 54
Howze v. Virginia Polytechnic & State Univ., 901 F. Supp. 1091, 69 FEP 1013 (W.D. Va. 1995) *17:* 27, 32; *30:* 5; *33:* 13
Hoyt v. NYNEX Corp., 1996 U.S. Dist. LEXIS 14230 (N.D.N.Y. Sept. 25, 1996) *9:* 136, 140, 171, 174, 196
Hrosik v. Latrobe Steel Co., 4 AD 555 (W. D. Pa. 1995) *16:* 27, 78; *30:* 61
Huber v. Howard County, 849 F. Supp. 407, 3 AD 262 (D. Md. 1994), *aff'd mem.,* 56 F.3d 61 (4th Cir. 1995) *9:* 44, 222
Hudson
—v. MCI Telecomms. Corp., 87 F.3d 1167, 5 AD 1099 (10th Cir. 1996) *9:* 161
—v. Radnor Valley Country Club, 70 FEP 1207 (E.D. Pa. 1996) *30:* 21, 38–39
Huegerich v. IBP, Inc., 547 N.W.2d 216, 11 IER 1092 (Iowa 1996) *26:* 39, 55
Huey v. Honeywell, Inc., 82 F.3d 327, 11 IER 1098 (9th Cir. 1996) *26:* 14
Huguley v. General Motors Corp.
—35 F.3d 1052 (6th Cir. 1994) *43:* 9
—52 F.3d 1364 (6th Cir. 1995) *43:* 9
Hull v. NCR Corp., 826 F. Supp. 303, 63 FEP 666 (E.D. Mo. 1993) *32:* 22
Hulsey v. KMart, Inc., 43 F.3d 555, 66 FEP 1327 (10th Cir. 1994) *16:* 57; *31:* 5, 24

Hum v. Dericks, 162 F.R.D. 628 (D. Haw. 1995) *37:* 43

Humenansky v. Board of Regents of the Univ. of Minn., 958 F. Supp. 439, 73 FEP 1004 (D. Minn. 1997), *appeal pending,* No. 97-2302 (8th Cir.) *16:* 35

Humphrey v. Council of Jewish Fed'ns, 901 F. Supp. 703, 69 FEP 201 (S.D.N.Y. 1995) *24:* 3, 15, 19, 60, 71

Humphreys v. Medical Towers, Ltd., 893 F. Supp. 672 (S.D. Tex. 1995), *aff'd,* 100 F.3d 952 (5th Cir. 1996) *17:* 25; *21:* 1, 17

Hunt v. Washington State Apple Adver. Comm'n, 432 U.S. 333 (1977) *37:* 71

Hunt-Golliday v. Metropolitan Water Reclamation Dist., 6 AD 698 (N.D. Ill. 1996), *aff'd in part and rev'd in part,* 104 F.3d 1004, 6 AD 725 (7th Cir. 1997) *9:* 161, 182

Huppenbauer v. May Dep't Stores Co., 1996 U.S. App. LEXIS 27480 (4th Cir. Oct. 23, 1996) *9:* 187

Hurd v. Pittsburgh State Univ.
—29 F.3d 564, 65 FEP 322 (10th Cir.), *cert. denied,* 513 U.S. 930 (1994) *16:* 34
—109 F.3d 1540, 73 FEP 1448 (10th Cir. 1997) *16:* 36

Hurley v. Atlantic City Police Dep't, 933 F. Supp. 396, 72 FEP 1828 (D.N.J. 1996) *38:* 35–36; *41:* 23, 103–04

Hurley-Bardige v. Brown, 900 F. Supp. 567, 4 AD 1744 (D. Mass. 1995) *9:* 133

Hutchinson
—v. Amateur Electronic Supply, Inc., 42 F.3d 1037, 66 FEP 1275 (7th Cir. 1994) *20:* 69; *40:* 22, 25–26, 29, 42, 49; *41:* 21, 34, 42; *42:* 59
—v. United Parcel Serv., Inc., 883 F. Supp. 379, 4 AD 536 (N.D. Iowa 1995) *9:* 3, 170

Hutson v. McDonnell Douglas Corp., 63 F.3d 771, 68 FEP 1209 (8th Cir. 1995) *2:* 42, 47, 55; *16:* 156; *37:* 18; *39:* 4, 32, 64

Huttig Sash & Door Co.; EEOC v., 511 F.2d 453, 10 FEP 529 (5th Cir. 1975) *32:* 10

I

Iacampo v. Hasbro, Inc., 929 F. Supp. 562, 5 AD 1075 (D.R.I. 1996) *9:* 9–10; *30:* 61

Iglesias v. Mutual Life Ins. Co., 918 F. Supp. 31 (D.P.R. 1996) *16:* 57

Illinois Dep't of Employment Sec.; EEOC v., 995 F.2d 106, 61 FEP 1385 (7th Cir. 1993) *29:* 40

Illinois, EEOC v., 877 F. Supp. 1207, 66 FEP 1148 (C.D. Ill. 1994), *rev'd,* 69 F.3d 167, 69 FEP 306 (7th Cir. 1995) *16:* 17, 38; *30:* 21; *41:* 73

Ilona of Hungary, Inc.; EEOC v., 885 F. Supp. 1111, 71 FEP 1874 (N.D. Ill. 1995), *aff'd in part and rev'd in part,* 108 F.3d 1569 (7th Cir. 1996) *8:* 20, 31; *40:* 5, 11; *41:* 44

Indest v. Freeman Decorating, Inc., 70 FEP 192 (E.D. La. 1996) *20:* 41

Inks v. Health Care Distribs. of Ind., Inc., 901 F. Supp. 1403, 73 FEP 643 (N.D. Ind. 1995) *16:* 217–18, 236; *41:* 41, 43, 84, 118

Insurance Co. of N. Am.; EEOC v., 49 F.3d 1418, 67 FEP 411 (9th Cir. 1995) *2:* 16, 24; *16:* 182

Irby v. Bittick, 44 F.3d 949, 67 FEP 70 (11th Cir. 1995) *13:* 10–12, 15, 17–18

Iron Workers Local 40; EEOC v., 885 F. Supp. 488 (S.D.N.Y. 1994), *rev'd,* 76 F.3d 76 (2d Cir. 1996) *34:* 59–60; *40:* 69, 74–77

Isenbergh v. Knight-Ridder Newspaper Sales, Inc., 97 F.3d 436, 72 FEP 735 (11th Cir. 1996), *cert. denied,* 117 S. Ct. 2511 (1997) *2:* 40; *16:* 95, 97, 112–13, 118–19

Island Creek Coal Co. v. District 28, Mine Workers (UMW), 29 F.3d 126, 146 LRRM 2773 (4th Cir.), *cert. denied,* 115 S. Ct. 583, 147 LRRM 2960 (1994) *32:* 28–29

J

Jackson
—v. Boise Cascade Corp., 941 F. Supp. 1122 (S.D. Ala. 1996) *9:* 174, 187
—v. City of Atlanta, 73 F.3d 60, 69 FEP 1505 (5th Cir. 1996), *cert. denied,* 117 S. Ct. 70 (1996) *24:* 39
—v. City of Cookeville, 31 F.3d 1354, 65 FEP 870 (6th Cir. 1994) *16:* 222–24
—v. Lyons Falls Pulp & Paper, Inc., 865 F. Supp. 87, 74 FEP 1667 (N.D.N.Y. 1994) *16:* 61, 99
—v. National Football League, 65 FEP 358 (S.D.N.Y. 1994) *30:* 55
—v. New York Tel. Co., 163 F.R.D. 429 (S.D.N.Y. 1995) *16:* 81
—v. Philadelphia Hous. Auth., 858 F. Supp. 464 (E.D. Pa. 1994) *42:* 25
Jacques v. Clean-Up Group, Inc., 96 F.3d 506, 5 AD 1594 (1st Cir. 1996) *9:* 1, 123, 125, 170, 224, 272
James
—v. Ranch Mart Hardware, Inc., 881 F. Supp. 478, 67 FEP 862 (D. Kan. 1995) *27:* 27
—v. Sears, Roebuck & Co., 21 F.3d 989, 64 FEP 886 (10th Cir. 1994) *40:* 45
Jameson v. Arrow Co., 75 F.3d 1528, 70 FEP 153 (11th Cir. 1996) *16:* 150, 176; *18:* 10
Janneh v. Runyon, 932 F. Supp. 412 (N.D.N.Y. 1996), *aff'd without opinion,* 108 F.3d 329 (2d Cir.), *cert. denied,* 118 S.Ct. 150 (1997) *36:* 23
Janopoulos v. Harvey L. Walner & Assoc., 1995 U.S. Dist. LEXIS 2751 (N.D. Ill Mar. 2, 1995), *summary judgment granted,* 1996 U.S. Dist. LEXIS 3157 (N.D. Ill. Mar. 14, 1996) *38:* 48
Jarboe v. Landmark Community Newspapers, 644 N.E.2d 118, 10 IER 172 (Ind. 1994) *26:* 16
Jarman v. City of Northlake, 950 F. Supp. 1375 (N.D. Ill. 1997) *20:* 106
Jason v. Baptist Hosp., 872 F. Supp. 1575 (E.D. Tex. 1994) *32:* 9
Javetz v. Board of Control, 903 F. Supp., 1181 (W.D. Mich. 1995) *11:* 4

Jayaraj v. Scappini, 66 F.3d 36 (2d Cir. 1995) *40:* 92, 94–96
Jefferies v. Harris County Community Action Ass'n, 615 F.2d 1025, 22 FEP 974 (5th Cir. 1980) *10:* 7–8; *13:* 35
Jeffries v. Metro-Mark, Inc., 45 F.3d 258, 66 FEP 1316 (8th Cir.), *cert. denied,* 516 U.S. 830 (1995) *24:* 3
Jendusa v. Cancer Treatment Ctrs. of Am., Inc., 868 F. Supp. 1006, 3 AD 1819 (N.D. Ill. 1994) *30:* 61
Jenkins
—v. Grenada, 813 F. Supp. 443, 61 FEP 258 (N.D. Miss. 1993) *37:* 11
—v. Wal-Mart Stores, Inc., 910 F. Supp. 1399, 71 FEP 387 (N.D. Iowa 1995) *21:* 3, 11
Jensvold v. Shalala, 925 F. Supp. 1109, 70 FEP 788 (D. Md. 1996) *17:* 48
Jeremy H. v. Mount Lebanon Sch. Dist., 95 F.3d 272 (3d Cir. 1996) *9:* 315
Jimenez v. Mary Washington College, 57 F.3d 369, 67 FEP 1867 (4th Cir.), *cert. denied,* 116 S. Ct. 380 (1995) *11:* 4; *19:* 16
Jimeno v. Mobil Oil Corp., 66 F.3d 1514, 4 AD 1646 (9th Cir. 1995) *9:* 253
Jimoh v. Ernst & Young, 908 F. Supp. 220 (S.D.N.Y. 1995) *21:* 28; *24:* 62
J.J.C. v. Fridell, 165 F.R.D. 513 (D. Minn. 1995) *38:* 26, 46
Jobes v. Tokheim Corp., 657 N.E.2d 145, 11 IER 1453 (Ind. Ct. App. 1995) *26:* 2
Joe's Stone Crab, Inc.; EEOC v., 969 F. Supp. 727, 74 FEP 491 (S.D. Fla. 1997) *39:* 40
Johnson
—v. American Chamber of Commerce Publishers, Inc., 108 F.3d 818, 6 AD 801 (7th Cir. 1997) *9:* 35
—v. Board of County Comm'rs, 859 F. Supp. 438, 65 FEP 1073 (D. Colo. 1994) *30:* 22, 35, 66
—v. Children's Hosp., 4 AD 806 (E.D. Pa. 1995), *aff'd mem.,* 79 F.3d 1138 (3d Cir. 1996) *9:* 66, 153
—v. City of Fort Lauderdale
——903 F. Supp. 1520, 74 FEP 571 (S.D. Fla. 1995), *aff'd,* 114 F.3d 1089, 74 FEP 578 (11th Cir. 1997) *24:* 9, 53

Johnson v. City of Fort Lauderdale—*Contd.*
——126 F.3d 1372, 75 FEP 519 (11th Cir. 1997) **24:** 50
—v. City of Port Arthur, 892 F. Supp. 835, 6 AD 547 (E.D. Tex. 1995) **9:** 134; **32:** 9
—v. Cooper, Deans & Cargill, P.A., 884 F. Supp. 43, 71 FEP 931 (D.N.H. 1994) **30:** 44
—v. County of Cook, 864 F. Supp. 84 (N.D. Ill. 1994) **33:** 19, 28, 32
—v. EEOC, 68 FEP 1712 (N.D. Ill. 1995) **37:** 22, 44, 48
—v. Foulds, Inc., 5 AD 1635 (N.D. Ill. 1996) **9:** 161
—v. Greater Southeast Community Hosp. Corp., 903 F. Supp. 140, 69 FEP 280 (D.D.C. 1995), *vacated in part,* 1996 WL 377147 (D.D.C. June 24, 1996) **24:** 53; **30:** 18
—v. Hills & Dales Gen. Hosp., 40 F.3d 837, 66 FEP 504 (6th Cir. 1994), *cert. denied,* 514 U.S. 1060 (1995) **24:** 46, 48
—v. Hubbard Broadcasting, Inc., 940 F. Supp. 1447 (D. Minn. 1996) **32:** 29
—v. Indopco, Inc., 887 F. Supp. 1092 (N.D. Ill. 1995), *aff'd,* 79 F.3d 1150 (7th Cir. 1996) **19:** 13
—v. J.C. Penney Co., 876 F. Supp. 135 (N.D. Tex. 1995) **2:** 15
—v. Kraft Gen. Foods Inc., 885 S.W.2d 334, 9 IER 1804 (Mo. 1994) **26:** 31
—v. Lafayette Fire Fighters' Ass'n, 857 F. Supp. 1292 (N.D. Ind. 1994), *aff'd,* 51 F.3d 726 (7th Cir. 1995) **42:** 3
—v. Maryland, 940 F. Supp. 873 (D. Md. 1996), *aff'd,* 113 F.3d 1232 (4th Cir. 1997) **9:** 123
—v. Merry-Go-Round Enters., Inc., 67 FEP 1456 (N.D. Ill. 1995) **20:** 19
—v. Metropolitan Sewer Dist., 926 F. Supp. 874, 74 FEP 683 (E.D. Mo. 1996) **24:** 67
—v. Multnomah County, 48 F.3d 420 (9th Cir.), *cert. denied,* 115 S. Ct. 2616 (1995) **17:** 61
—v. New York Hosp., 96 F.3d 33, 5 AD 1537 (2d Cir. 1996) **9:** 249, 270
—v. Palma, 931 F.2d 203, 55 FEP 1173 (2d Cir. 1991) **33:** 22
—v. Penske Truck Leasing Co., 949 F. Supp. 1153 (D.N.J. 1996) **39:** 36
—v. Railway Express Agency, Inc., 421 U.S. 454, 10 FEP 817 (1975) **24:** 59
—v. Reno, 1994 WL 189071 (D.D.C. Apr. 19, 1994) **40:** 82
—v. Runyon, 928 F. Supp. 575 (D. Md. 1996) **19:** 22; **37:** 18
—v. Teamsters Local 559, 67 FEP 1150 (D. Mass. 1995), *aff'd,* 102 F.3d 21, 153 LRRM 3031 (1st Cir. 1996) **22:** 22
—v. Transportation Agency, Santa Clara County, 480 U.S. 616, 43 FEP 411 (1987) **27:** 100, 115, 129, 142, 163
—v. United States Dep't of Health & Human Servs., 30 F.3d 45, 65 FEP 702 (6th Cir. 1994) **17:** 41; **19:** 13
—v. United States Steel Corp., 943 F. Supp. 1108 (D. Minn. 1996) **9:** 175
—v. University of Wis., 70 F.3d 469, 69 FEP 644 (7th Cir. 1995) **2:** 20; **17:** 46
Johnson-Goeman v. Michigan Dep't of Commerce, 1995 U.S. Dist. LEXIS 1806 (W.D. Mich. Jan. 18, 1995) **9:** 175
Johnson & Higgins, Inc.; EEOC v., 887 F. Supp. 682, 68 FEP 1481 (S.D.N.Y. 1995), *aff'd,* 91 F.3d 1529, 71 FEP 818 (2d Cir. 1996), *cert. denied,* 118 S. Ct. 47, 74 FEP 1791 (1997) **16:** 16, 48, 65, 183; **34:** 17; **40:** 1
Johnson & Johnson Med. Inc. v. Sanchez, 924 S.W.2d 925 (Tex. 1996) **26:** 46
Johnston
—v. City of Philadelphia, 863 F. Supp. 231 (E.D. Pa. 1994) **39:** 27
—v. Metropolitan Life Ins. Co., 1995 WL 860757 (E.D. Mo. Mar. 23, 1995) **16:** 91
Jones
—v. Alabama Power Co., 3 AD 1717 (N.D. Ala. 1995), *aff'd mem.,* 77 F.3d 498, 7 AD 1536 (11th Cir. 1996) **9:** 227–28, 231; **16:** 99, 109
—v. J.C. Penney Co., 889 F. Supp. 432 (D. Kan. 1995) **19:** 4

—v. Merchants Nat'l Bank & Trust Co., 42 F.3d 1054, 66 FEP 865 (7th Cir. 1994) *24:* 54; *31:* 13
—v. Midway Broad. Co., 69 FEP 789 (N.D. Ill. 1995) *16:* 24
—v. Pepsi-Cola Metro. Bottling Co., 871 F. Supp. 305 (E.D. Mich. 1994) *4:* 17; *39:* 5–6, 27, 38
—v. Runyon, 32 F.3d 1454, 65 FEP 1066 (10th Cir. 1994) *16:* 31
—v. Southeast Alabama Baseball Umpires Ass'n, 864 F. Supp. 1135 (M.D. Ala. 1994) *23:* 5
—v. Unisys Corp., 54 F.3d 624, 67 FEP 1065 (10th Cir. 1995) *16:* 96, 121, 128, 152, 156, 162, 167, 172; *42:* 42
—v. Washington Metro. Area Transit Auth., 946 F. Supp. 1023 (D.D.C. 1996) *40:* 15; *41:* 24
Judice v. Hospital Serv. Dist. No. 1, 919 F. Supp. 978 (E.D. La. 1996) *9:* 89
Jungels v. State Univ. College of N.Y., 922 F. Supp. 779 (W.D.N.Y. 1996), *aff'd,* 112 F.3d 504 (1997) *16:* 27; *24:* 39

K

Kahalnik v. John Hancock Funds, Inc., 1996 WL 145842 (N.D. Ill. Mar. 27, 1996) *32:* 21
Kahmann v. Reno, 928 F. Supp. 1209 (N.D.N.Y. 1996) *41:* 10, 16, 19–20
Kalvinskas v. California Inst. of Tech., 96 F.3d 1305, 71 FEP 1647 (9th Cir. 1996) *16:* 194
Kantar v. Baldwin Cooke Co., 69 FEP 851 (N.D. Ill. 1995) *8:* 44; *20:* 5
Kaplan
—v. Banque Nationale de Paris, 1995 WL 753900 (S.D.N.Y. Dec. 19, 1995) *8:* 44
—v. Pomerantz, 131 F.R.D. 118 (N.D. Ill. 1990) *38:* 57
—v. Theatrical Stage Employees, 525 F.2d 1354, 11 FEP 872 (9th Cir. 1975) *33:* 18
Kapossy v. McGraw-Hill, Inc., 921 F. Supp. 234, 70 FEP 752 (D.N.J. 1996) *18:* 10

Karibian v. Columbia Univ.
—14 F.3d 773, 63 FEP 1038 (2d Cir.), *cert. denied,* 512 U.S. 1213 (1994) *20:* 14
—930 F. Supp. 134, 71 FEP 325 (S.D.N.Y. 1996) *10:* 4
Kary v. Prudential Ins. Co. of N. Am., 541 N.W.2d 703, 11 IER 530 (N.D. 1996) *26:* 48
Kastel v. Winnetka Bd. of Educ., 946 F. Supp. 1329 (N.D. Ill. 1996) *2:* 11
Katz v. City Metal Co., 87 F.3d 26, 5 AD 1120 (1st Cir. 1996) *9:* 1, 33, 192
Kaup v. First Bank Sys., Inc., 926 F. Supp. 155 (D. Colo. 1996) *31:* 46
Keaveney v. Town of Brookline, 937 F. Supp. 975, 11 IER 1838 (D. Mass. 1996) *26:* 3
Keegan v. Dalton, 899 F. Supp. 1503 (E.D. Va. 1995) *37:* 18
Keenan v. Allan, 889 F. Supp. 1320 (E.D. Wash. 1995), *aff'd,* 91 F.3d 1275 (9th Cir. 1996) *20:* 69, 109
Keith v. Mendus, 661 N.E.2d 26, 11 IER 671 (Ind. Ct. App. 1996) *26:* 52–53
Kellam v. Snelling Personnel Servs., 866 F. Supp. 812, 68 FEP 195 (D. Del. 1994), *aff'd without opinion,* 65 F.3d 162, 69 FEP 768 (3d Cir. 1995) *23:* 3, 12; *30:* 13, 18, 45, 47, 63
Kelleher v. Aerospace Community Credit Union, 927 F. Supp. 361, 70 FEP 1279 (E.D. Mo. 1996) *16:* 27
Kellett v. Glaxo Enters., 66 FEP 1071 (S.D.N.Y. 1994) *15:* 12; *16:* 17; *30:* 54, 57
Kelley v. Unisys Corp., 66 FEP 387 (N.D. W.Va. 1994) *16:* 155, 159
Kelly
—v. Boeing Petroleum Servs., Inc., 61 F.3d 350, 4 AD 1284 (5th Cir. 1995) *2:* 44
—v. Drexel Univ., 94 F.3d 102, 5 AD 1353 (3d Cir. 1996) *9:* 32
Kemer v. Johnson, 900 F. Supp. 677, 4 AD 1823 (S.D.N.Y. 1995), *aff'd mem.,* 101 F.3d 683 (2d Cir.), *cert. denied,* 117 S. Ct. 441 (1996) *9:* 202

Kemp v. Monge, 919 F. Supp. 404 (M.D. Fla. 1996) **40:** 55

Kendall v. Watkins, 998 F.2d 848, 62 FEP 681 (10th Cir. 1993), *cert. denied,* 510 U.S. 1120, 72 FEP 992 (1994) **43:** 13–15

Kennedy
—v. Applause, Inc., 3 AD 1734 (C.D. Cal. 1994), *aff'd in part and dismissed in part,* 90 F.3d 1477, 5 AD 1249 (9th Cir. 1996) **9:** 61, 153, 156, 175; **32:** 18; **38:** 21
—v. Chemical Waste Management, Inc., 79 F.3d 49, 5 AD 565 (7th Cir. 1996) **9:** 178, 186; **13:** 9
—v. GN Danavox, 928 F. Supp. 866 (D. Minn. 1996) **16:** 99
—v. Runyon, 933 F. Supp. 480 (W.D. Pa. 1996) **36:** 22

Kentucky State Police Dep't; EEOC v., 80 F.3d 1086, 71 FEP 1495 (6th Cir.), *cert. denied,* 117 S. Ct. 385 (1996) **16:** 55, 58, 217–18, 242, 244; **31:** 29, 31; **41:** 71

Kern
—v. City of Rochester, 93 F.3d 38, 71 FEP 1391 (2d Cir. 1996), *cert. denied,* 117 S. Ct. 1335 (1997) **22:** 2; **30:** 42, 62
—v. Kollsman, 885 F. Supp. 335 (D.N.H. 1995) **16:** 98, 117, 148, 173

Kerno v. Sandoz Pharm. Corp., 4 AD 1195 (N.D. Ill. 1994) **9:** 192, 194

Khair v. Campbell Soup Co., 893 F. Supp. 316, 75 FEP 995 (D.N.J. 1995) **16:** 53, 115; **19:** 5

Khan v. Maryland, 903 F. Supp. 881 (D. Md. 1995) **19:** 19; **24:** 9

KI (U.S.A.) Corp. v. NLRB, 35 F.3d 256, 147 LRRM 2275 (6th Cir. 1994) **25:** 1

Kilgo v. Bowman Transp., Inc., 88 F.R.D. 592 (N.D. Ga. 1980) **37:** 90

Killinger v. Samford Univ., 917 F. Supp. 773, 70 FEP 421 (N.D. Ala. 1996), *aff'd,* 113 F.3d 196, 73 FEP 1533 (11th Cir. 1997) **8:** 56–58

Kimel v. Florida Bd. of Regents, 1996 U.S. Dist. LEXIS 7995 (N.D. Fla. May 17, 1996), *appeal pending,* No. 96-2788 (11th Cir.) **16:** 35

Kim & Ted, Inc.; EEOC v., 69 FEP 1499 (N.D. Ill. 1995) **34:** 64; **38:** 45

Kimzey v. Wal-Mart Stores, Inc., 907 F. Supp. 1309, 69 FEP 664 (W.D. Mo. 1995) **41:** 112

Kindle v. Mid-Central/Sysco Food Servs., Inc., 7 AD 147 (D. Kan 1996) **9:** 186

King
—v. AC & R Adver., 65 F.3d 764, 68 FEP 1234 (9th Cir. 1995) **21:** 25; **26:** 33
—v. Frazier, 77 F.3d 1361, 73 FEP 875 (Fed. Cir.), *cert. denied,* 117 S. Ct. 62 (1996) **20:** 67
—v. PYA/Monarch, Inc., 453 S.E.2d 885, 10 IER 337 (S.C. 1995) **26:** 5, 17

Kinnebrew v. Gulf Ins. Co., 67 FEP 189 (N.D. Tex. 1994) **32:** 21, 29

Kinney Shoe Corp.; EEOC v., 917 F. Supp. 419, 5 AD 506 (W.D. Va. 1996), *aff'd sub nom.* Martinson v. Kinney Shoe Corp., 104 F.3d 683, 6 AD 434 (4th Cir. 1997) **9:** 211, 244

Kirkpatrick v. Raleigh County Bd. of Educ., 78 F.3d 579 (4th Cir. 1996) **38:** 33

Kitchen v. Dial Page Co., 67 FEP 482 (E.D. Tenn. 1995) **38:** 5

Kleiner v. First Nat'l Bank of Atlanta, 751 F.2d 1193 (11th Cir. 1985) **37:** 89

Klockner H & K Machs., Inc.; EEOC v., 168 F.R.D. 233, 71 FEP 833 (E.D. Wis. 1996) **38:** 42

Kloster Cruise, Ltd.; EEOC v.
—888 F. Supp. 147, 68 FEP 1 (S.D. Fla. 1995) **16:** 2
—897 F. Supp. 1422, 68 FEP 1316 (S.D. Fla. 1995) **16:** 176

KMart Corp. v. Helton, *see* Grayson v. KMart Corp.

Knabe v. Boury Corp., 114 F.3d 407, 73 FEP 1877 (3d Cir. 1997) **20:** 104–05

Knickerbocker v. City of Stockton, 81 F.3d 907, 3 WH2d 453 (9th Cir. 1996) **17:** 19, 46

Knoll North Am., Inc.; EEOC v., 1996 WL 544264 (W.D. Mich. May 2, 1996) *34:* 32

Kobrin v. University of Minn., 34 F.3d 698, 65 FEP 1624 (8th Cir. 1994) *2:* 42, 50

Kocsis v. Multi-Care Management, Inc., 97 F.3d 876, 6 AD 442 (6th Cir. 1996) *9:* 118, 214

Koedding v. Brinckerhoff, 1996 U.S. Dist. LEXIS 545 (N.D. Cal. Jan. 16, 1996) *9:* 145

Koelsch v. Beltone Elecs. Corp., 46 F.3d 705, 66 FEP 1697 (7th Cir. 1995) *31:* 11

Kohnke v. Delta Airlines, Inc.
—5 AD 345 (N.D. Ill. 1995) *9:* 69, 239; *41:* 71–72
—932 F. Supp. 1110 (N.D. Ill. 1996) *9:* 72

Kolstad v. American Dental Ass'n, 912 F. Supp. 13, 69 FEP 1376 (D.D.C. 1996), *aff'd in part, remanded in part,* 108 F.3d 1431, 73 FEP 625 (D.C. Cir. 1997) *2:* 34; *19:* 18, 28

Konstantopoulos v. Westvaco Corp., 893 F. Supp. 1263 (D. Del. 1994) *40:* 42

Koopman v. Water Dist. No. 1 of Johnson County, Kan., 41 F.3d 1417 (10th Cir. 1994), *cert. denied,* 116 S. Ct. 420 (1995) *42:* 3, 11

Koski v. Gainer, 1995 U.S. Dist. LEXIS 14604 (N.D. Ill. Oct. 5, 1995) *5:* 76; *27:* 185

Kotas v. Waterman Broad., 927 F. Supp. 1547 (M.D. Fla. 1996) *16:* 99, 104

Kotlowski v. Eastman Kodak Co., 922 F. Supp. 790, 6 AD 609 (W.D.N.Y. 1996) *9:* 66; *16:* 167, 172

Kounitz v. Slaatten, 901 F. Supp. 650 (S.D.N.Y. 1995) *33:* 15

Kraemer v. Franklin & Marshall College, 941 F. Supp. 479 (E.D. Pa. 1996) *40:* 20–21

Kraiman v. Georgia-Pacific Corp., 68 FEP 526 (E.D. Pa. 1995) *16:* 126

Krauel v. Iowa Methodist Med. Ctr., 95 F.3d 674, 71 FEP 1326 (8th Cir. 1996) *9:* 107–08; *13:* 23

Kreimeyer v. Hercules, Inc., 892 F. Supp. 1369 (D. Utah 1994) *16:* 176

Krempel v. Prairie Island Indian Community, 888 F. Supp. 106, 68 FEP 215 (D. Minn. 1995) *12:* 7, 9

Krenik v. County of Le Sueur, 47 F.3d 953, 67 FEP 312 (8th Cir. 1995) *2:* 42; *16:* 119

Krennerich v. Inhabitants of Bristol, 943 F. Supp. 1345 (D. Me. 1996) *9:* 166

Krisak v. Gourmet Coffees of Am., 10 IER 433 (D. Md. 1995) *26:* 48

Kriss v. Sprint Communications Co., 58 F.3d 1276, 68 FEP 1382 (8th Cir. 1995) *2:* 56

Kroger Co. v. Willgruber, 920 S.W.2d 61, 11 IER 1087 (Ky. 1996) *26:* 35, 59

Krouse v. American Sterilizer Co., 872 F. Supp. 203 (W.D. Pa. 1994) *31:* 48–49

Krueger v. New York Tel. Co., 163 F.R.D. 433 (S.D.N.Y. 1995) *16:* 81; *37:* 4, 16, 40, 92

Kuehl v. Wal-Mart Stores, Inc., 909 F. Supp. 794, 5 AD 91 (D. Colo. 1995) *9:* 134, 144, 204

Kuehner v. Dickinson & Co., 84 F.3d 316 (9th Cir. 1996) *32:* 21

Kuhn v. Ball State Univ., 78 F.3d 330, 70 FEP 449 (7th Cir. 1996), *rev'd,* 124 F.3d 218, 74 FEP 545 (3d Cir. 1997) *2:* 46; *19:* 13, 26; *39:* 61, 82, 84

Kunzman v. Enron Corp., 902 F. Supp. 882, 73 FEP 803 (N.D. Iowa 1995) *2:* 19; *16:* 165

Kurian v. Social Serv. Employees Local 371, 1995 U.S. Dist. LEXIS 17951 (S.D.N.Y. Nov. 30, 1995) *34:* 8

L

Laborers' Local 100; EEOC v., 49 F.3d 304, 67 FEP 205 (7th Cir. 1995) *22:* 9

Labrucherie v. Regents of Univ. of Cal., 1995 U.S. Dist. LEXIS 12763 (N.D. Cal. Aug. 30, 1995), *aff'd mem.,* 119 F.3d 6 (9th Cir. 1997) *9:* 158, 269

La Cruz v. New York City Human Resources Admin., 82 F.3d 16, 70 FEP 893 (2d Cir. 1996), *cert. denied,* ___ U.S. ___ (1996) *2:* 56

Ladson v. Ulltra East Parking Corp., 164 F.R.D. 376, 70 FEP 140 (S.D.N.Y 1996) *38:* 1, 33, 42

Lakoski v. James, 66 F.3d 751 (5th Cir. 1995), *cert. denied,* 117 S. Ct. 357 (1996) *24:* 39

Lally v. Commonwealth Edison Co., 1996 U.S. Dist. LEXIS 19386 (N.D. Ill. Dec. 16, 1996) *9:* 145

Lam v. University of Haw., 40 F.3d 1551, 66 FEP 74 (9th Cir. 1994) *10:* 6–8; *13:* 31–32

Lamb v. Runyon, 915 F. Supp. 300 (M.D. Ala. 1995) *16:* 110, 166

Lambertsen v. Utah Dep't of Corrections, 922 F. Supp. 533, 70 FEP 1387 (D. Utah 1995), *aff'd,* 79 F.3d 1024, 70 FEP 631 (10th Cir. 1996) *30:* 35, 60

Lamury v. Boeing Co., 5 AD 39 (D. Kan. 1995) *9:* 143

Landgraf v. USI Film Prods., 511 U.S. 244, 64 FEP 820 (1994) *5:* 38; *33:* 54; *37:* 9; *41:* 119

Landon v. Northwest Airlines, Inc., 72 F.3d 620, 72 FEP 675 (8th Cir. 1995) *24:* 58

Lane
—v. David P. Jacobson & Co., 880 F. Supp. 1091, 70 FEP 391 (E.D. Va. 1995) *30:* 16
—v. Hughes Aircraft Co., 56 Cal. App. 4th 1038, 65 Cal. Rptr. 2d 889 (1997) *41:* 112
—v. Peña, 518 U.S. 187, 5 AD 973 (1996) *9:* 311–13; *36:* 1
—v. United States Steel, 871 F. Supp. 1434, 3 AD 1605 (N.D. Ala. 1994) *22:* 26

Langenfeld v. Stoelting, Inc., 902 F. Supp. 847 (E.D. Wis. 1995) *16:* 120

Lankford v. City of Hobart, 73 F.3d 283, 69 FEP 1149 (10th Cir. 1996) *24:* 36

Larkin v. Town of West Hartford, 891 F. Supp. 719 (D. Conn. 1995), *aff'd,* 101 F.3d 109 (2d Cir. 1996) *21:* 7

Larkins v. CIBA Vision Corp., 858 F. Supp. 1572, 3 AD 715 (N.D. Ga. 1994) *9:* 153

Larson v. Koch Ref. Co., 920 F. Supp. 1000, 5 AD 136 (D. Minn. 1996) *9:* 183, 268

Lassiter v. Reno, 885 F. Supp. 869, 4 AD 609 (E.D. Va. 1995), *aff'd mem.,* 86 F.3d 1151, 5 AD 1343 (4th Cir. 1996), *cert. denied,* 117 S. Ct. 766 (1997) *9:* 246, 250

Latuga v. Hooters, Inc., 1996 U.S. Dist. LEXIS 4169 (N.D. Ill. Mar. 29, 1996) *37:* 4

Launer v. Buena Vista Winery, Inc., 916 F. Supp. 204 (E.D.N.Y. 1996) *33:* 45

Lawrence v. IBP, Inc., 4 AD 632 (D. Kan. 1995), *aff'd mem.,* 96 F.3d 1453 (10th Cir. 1996) *9:* 135, 141, 144, 148

Lawrence Chrysler Plymouth Corp. v. Brooks, 465 S.E.2d 806, 11 IER 523 (Va. 1996) *26:* 28

Lawton v. State Mut. Life Assurance Co. of Am., 924 F. Supp. 331, 75 FEP 783 (D. Mass. 1996) *31:* 22

Lazar v. Superior Court, 909 P.2d 981, 11 IER 545 (Cal. 1996) *26:* 47

Le v. Applied Biosystems, 886 F. Supp. 717, 4 AD 617 (N.D. Cal. 1995) *9:* 21

League of United Latin Am. Citizens v. Salinas Fire Dep't, 88 F.R.D. 533, 28 FEP 470 (N.D. Cal. 1980) *37:* 70

Learonal Inc.; EEOC v., 66 FEP 697 (N.D. Ill. 1994) *16:* 216

Leary v. Dalton, 58 F.3d 748, 4 AD 1165 (1st Cir. 1995) *9:* 8, 183, 269, 306

LeBlanc v. Great Am. Ins. Co., 6 F.3d 836, 62 FEP 1668, 63 FEP 288 (1st Cir. 1993), *cert. denied,* 511 U.S. 1018 (1994) *16:* 148

Lee
—v. ABF Freight Sys., Inc., 22 F.3d 1019, 64 FEP 896 (10th Cir. 1994) *8:* 27
—v. Kroger Co., 901 F. Supp.1218, 70 FEP 425 (S.D. Tex. 1995) *32:* 7
—v. United States Postal Serv., 882 F. Supp. 589 (E.D. Tex. 1995) *32:* 9

Lefevre v. Harrison Group, Inc., 71 FEP 449 (E.D. Pa. 1996) *41:* 21

Legard v. Winn-Dixie La., Inc., 1995 US Dist. LEXIS 12429, 10 IER 1647 (E.D. La. 1995) *26:* 32

Legault v. aRusso, 842 F. Supp. 1479, 64 FEP 170 (D.N.H. 1994) *5:* 51, 81; *40:* 31

Leige v. Capitol Chevrolet, Inc., 895 F. Supp. 289 (M.D. Ala. 1995) *24:* 6

Lesko v. Clark Publisher Servs., 904 F. Supp. 415 (M.D. Pa. 1995) *41:* 38, 50

Leslie v. St. Vincent New Hope, Inc., 916 F. Supp. 879, 5 AD 1773 (S.D. Ind. 1996) *9:* 133, 144

Leweling v. Schnadig Corp., 657 N.E.2d 1107, 11 IER 178 (Ill. Ct. App. 1995) *26:* 23

Lewellen v. Metropolitan Gov't of Nashville, 34 F.3d 345 (6th Cir. 1994), *cert. denied,* 513 U.S. 1112 (1995) *24:* 35

Lewis
—v. Aerospace Community Credit Union, 934 F. Supp. 314, 74 FEP 1339 (E.D. Mo. 1996), *aff'd,* 114 F.3d 745, 74 FEP 1443 (8th Cir. 1997), *petition for cert. filed* (Nov. 29, 1997) *16:* 107, 138, 141–42, 157, 172

—v. Board of Trustees of Ala. State Univ., 874 F. Supp. 1299 (M.D. Ala. 1995) *31:* 17

—v. Federal Prison Indus., Inc., 953 F.2d 1277, 58 FEP 127 (11th Cir. 1992) *36:* 2

—v. Zilog, Inc., 908 F. Supp. 931, 4 AD 1787 (N.D. Ga. 1995), *aff'd mem.,* 87 F.3d 1331 (11th Cir. 1996) *2:* 12; *9:* 136, 160, 205; *19:* 11

Lewis-Webb v. Qualico Steel Co., 929 F. Supp. 385 (M.D. Ala. 1996), *aff'd,* 113 F.3d 1251 (11th Cir. 1997) *18:* 8, 10–11

Leyh v. Modicon, Inc., 881 F. Supp. 420 (S.D. Ind. 1995) *38:* 27

Li v. C.N. Brown Co., 645 A.2d 606, 9 IER 1404 (Me. 1994) *26:* 59

Liberman v. Brady, 926 F. Supp. 1197, 73 FEP 695 (E.D.N.Y 1996) *11:* 31

Liberti v. Walt Disney World Co., 912 F. Supp. 1494 (M.D. Fla. 1995) *20:* 63–64

Lidge-Myrtil v. Deere & Co., 49 F.3d 1308, 70 FEP 521 (8th Cir. 1995) *19:* 13, 22

Lightfoot v. Union Carbide Corp., 901 F. Supp. 166, 71 FEP 269 (S.D.N.Y. 1995) *41:* 104

Lightner v. City of Ariton, Ala.
—884 F. Supp. 468, 69 FEP 215 (M.D. Ala. 1995) *30:* 41
—902 F. Supp. 1489, 69 FEP 219 (M.D. Ala. 1995) *17:* 53; *24:* 19

Lightning v. Roadway Express Inc., 60 F.3d 1551, 10 IER 1592 (11th Cir. 1995) *26:*34

Lindas v. Cady, 515 N.W.2d 458, 71 FEP 791 (Wis. 1994) *32:* 5

Lisek v. Norfolk & W. Ry., 918 F. Supp. 1202 (N.D. Ill. 1996) *27:* 8, 15–16, 31

Little v. United Tech., 103 F.3d 956, 72 FEP 1560 (11th Cir. 1997) *20:* 3

Lloyd v. WABC-TV, 879 F. Supp. 394, 73 FEP 1603 (S.D.N.Y. 1995) *19:* 4

Lobeck v. City of Riviera Beach, 976 F. Supp. 1460 (S.D. Fla. 1997) *43:* 67

Lockett v. West, 914 F. Supp. 1229 (D. Md. 1995) *31:* 26

Lockheed Corp. v. Spink, 116 S. Ct. 1783, 70 FEP 1633 (1996) *16:* 187, 189–90

Lockheed Martin Corp.; EEOC v., 70 FEP 1457 (D. Md. 1996), *aff'd,* 116 F.3d 110, 74 FEP 202 (4th Cir. 1997) *29:* 30

Long
—v. Eastfield College, 88 F.3d 300, 71 FEP 750 (5th Cir. 1996) *11:* 8; *33:* 50
—v. First Union Corp. of Va., 894 F. Supp. 933, 68 FEP 917 (E.D. Va. 1995), *aff'd,* 86 F.3d 1151, 71 FEP 736 (4th Cir. 1996) *4:* 7, 9, 51; *11:* 28; *21:* 11
—v. Ringling Bros.-Barnum & Bailey Combined Shows, Inc., 882 F. Supp. 1553, 67 FEP 1685 (D. Md. 1995) *2:* 49; *41:* 12

Loomis v. General Motors Corp., 70 FEP 691 (E.D. Mich. 1994) *30:* 10

Lorance v. AT & T Technologies, 490 U.S. 900, 49 FEP 1656 (1989) *31:* 6

Louisiana Office of Community Servs.; EEOC v., 47 F.3d 1438, 67 FEP 659 (5th Cir. 1995) *16:* 70; *19:* 16
Lovell v. Brinker Int'l, Inc., 71 FEP 417 (W.D. Mo. 1996) *24:* 14
Lowe v. Angelo's Italian Foods, Inc., 87 F.3d 1170, 5 AD 1064 (10th Cir. 1996) *33:* 51
Lubkeman v. Commonwealth Edison Co., 877 F. Supp. 1180, 67 FEP 514 (N.D. Ill. 1995) *16:* 104
Luce v. Dalton, 166 F.R.D. 457 (S.D. Cal.), *aff'd,* 167 F.R.D. 88 (S.D. Cal. 1996) *16:* 67
Luciano v. Olsten Corp.
—912 F. Supp. 663, 73 FEP 221 (E.D.N.Y. 1996), *aff'd,* 110 F.3d 210, 73 FEP 722 (2d Cir. 1997) *19:* 28; *41:* 23, 26, 30, 101, 104, 111
—925 F. Supp. 956 (E.D.N.Y. 1996) *42:* 36, 42
Lugar v. Edmonds Oil Co., 457 U.S. 922 (1982) *24:* 25
Lumpkin v. E.I. du Pont De Nemours & Co., 161 F.R.D. 480, 67 FEP 1263 (M.D. Ga. 1995) *37:* 23, 31, 44
Lussier v. Runyon, 50 F.3d 1103, 4 AD 265 (1st Cir. 1995) *41:* 85
Lynch v. Blanke Baer & Bowey Krimko, Inc., 901 S.W.2d 147, 11 IER 808 (Mo. Ct. App. 1995) *26:* 27
Lyoch v. Anheuser-Busch Cos., 164 F.R.D. 62, 74 FEP 691 (E.D. Mo. 1995) *38:* 9–10
Lyon v. Ohio Educ. Ass'n & Prof'l Staff Union, 53 F.3d 135, 67 FEP 1088 (6th Cir. 1995) *16:* 184; *22:* 24
Lyons
—v. Legal Aid Soc'y, 68 F.3d 1512, 4 AD 1694 (2d Cir. 1995) *9:* 120–21, 171
—v. National Car Rental Sys., Inc., 30 F.3d 240, 9 IER 1302 (1st Cir. 1994) *26:* 43
Lytle v. Malady, 530 N.W.2d 135, 69 FEP 1070 (Mich. Ct. App. 1995), *aff'd in part and rev'd in part,* 566 N.W.2d 582 (Mich.), *reh'g granted,* 570 N.W.2d 785 (1997) *26:* 17, 53

M

MacDonald v. Presbyterian Hosp., 5 AD 314 (S.D.N.Y. 1996) *9:* 32
MacDougall v. Weichert, 677 A.2d 162, 11 IER 1411 (N.J. 1996) *26:* 23
Mackey v. IBP, Inc., 167 F.R.D. 186 (D. Kan. 1996) *38:* 18
MacNamara v. Korean Airlines, 863 F.2d 1135, 48 FEP 980 (3d Cir. 1988), *cert. denied,* 493 U.S. 944, 51 FEP 112 (1989) *11:* 33
MacPherson v. University of Montevallo, 938 F. Supp. 785, 71 FEP 1318 (N.D. Ala. 1996), *appeal pending,* No. 96-6947 (11th Cir.) *16:* 35
Macy v. Dalton, 853 F. Supp. 350, 64 FEP 1718 (E.D. Cal. 1994) *36:* 15
Madden v. Omega Optical Inc., 683 A.2d 386, 11 IER 1606 (Vt. 1996) *26:* 18, 23
Madison v. BP Oil Co., 928 F. Supp. 1132 (S.D. Ala. 1996) *31:* 51
Maez v. Mountain States Tel. & Tel., Inc., 54 F.3d 1488, 19 EBC 1283 (10th Cir. 1995) *21:* 20
Maffei v. Kolaeton Indus., Inc., 626 N.Y.S.2d 391, 68 FEP 1039 (N.Y. Sup. Ct. 1995) *13:* 37
Maguire v. Hilton Hotels Corp., 79 Haw. 10, 899 P.2d 393, 10 IER 1326 (1995) *26:* 55
Maher v. Associated Servs. for the Blind, 929 F. Supp. 809, 70 FEP 1730 (E.D. Pa. 1996), *aff'd,* 107 F.3d 862 (3d Cir. 1997) *21:* 7
Mahoney v. RFE/RL, Inc., 47 F.3d 447, 67 FEP 170 (D.C. Cir.), *cert. denied,* 516 U.S. 866 (1995) *16:* 5
Maidenbaum v. Bally's Park Place, Inc., 870 F. Supp. 1254, 68 FEP 1245 (D.N.J. 1994), *aff'd without opinion,* 67 F.3d 291, 69 FEP 320 (3d Cir. 1995) *2:* 56; *16:* 138; *39:* 30, 38, 78
Maitland v. University of Minn., 43 F.3d 357, 66 FEP 796 (8th Cir. 1994) *27:* 170; *40:* 84–85
Malandris v. Merrill Lynch, 703 F.2d 1152 (10th Cir. 1981), *cert. denied,* 464 U.S. 824 (1983) *41:* 102

Mallory v. Harkness, 895 F. Supp. 1556 (S.D. Fla. 1995), *affd without opinion,* 109 F.3d 771 (11th Cir. 1997)   *27:* 57, 74, 88

Mandala v. Coughlin, 920 F. Supp. 342 (E.D.N.Y. 1996)   *24:* 14

Mangold v. California Pub. Util. Comm'n, 67 F.3d 1470, 69 FEP 48 (9th Cir. 1995)   *16:* 138, 165; *30:* 31; *39:* 67–68; *42:* 37

Manos v. Bunzl-Papercraft, Inc., 69 FEP 1189 (N.D. Ill. 1995)   *21:* 9, 17

Manville Sales Corp.; EEOC v., 27 F.3d 1089, 65 FEP 804 (5th Cir. 1994), *cert. denied,* 513 U.S. 1190, 67 FEP 1632 (1995)   *16:* 165; *29:* 47; *34:* 14–15; *41:* 50

Manzer v. Diamond Shamrock Chems. Co., 29 F.3d 1078, 65 FEP 585 (6th Cir. 1994)   *1:* 113; *2:* 23, 55; *16:* 105, 111, 116

Marinne v. Nabisco Brands, Inc., 1994 WL 533906 (E.D. Pa. Sept. 29, 1994) *16:* 237

Marisol A. By Forbes v. Giuliani, 929 F. Supp. 662 (S.D.N.Y. 1996)   *37:* 49

Marquart v. Lodge 837, 26 F.3d 842, 64 FEP 1789 (8th Cir. 1994)   *42:* 63

Marschand v. Norfolk & W. Ry., 876 F. Supp. 1528, 4 AD 1099 (N.D. Ind. 1995), *aff'd,* 81 F.3d 714, 5 AD 1184 (7th Cir. 1996)   *9:* 134–35, 140, 144, 148, 202

Marshall v. Miller, 873 F. Supp. 628 (M.D. Fla. 1995)   *15:* 3

Mart v. Dr. Pepper Co., 923 F. Supp. 1380, 71 FEP 478 (D. Kan. 1996)   *20:* 104, 106; *21:* 15

Marthel v. Bridgestone/Firestone, Inc., 926 F. Supp. 1293 (M.D. Tenn. 1996) *2:* 12

Martin v. Cavalier Hotel Corp., 48 F.3d 1343, 67 FEP 300 (4th Cir. 1995)   *21:* 3

Martinez v. National Broad. Co., 877 F. Supp. 219, 73 FEP 1701 (D.N.J. 1994) *16:* 198; *18:* 11; *43:* 6

Martinson v. Kinney Shoe Corp., *see* Kinney Shoe Corp.; EEOC v.

Marx v. Schnuck Mkts., Inc., 76 F.3d 324, 73 FEP 21 (10th Cir.), *cert. denied,* 116 S. Ct. 2552 (1996)   *16:* 181

Marzano v. Computer Science Corp., 91 F.3d 497, 71 FEP 1120 (3d Cir. 1996) *30:* 56

Mascheroni v. Board of Regents of Univ. of Cal., 28 F.3d 1554, 65 FEP 632 (10th Cir. 1994)   *31:* 9, 17, 24

Mason v. Frank, 32 F.3d 315, 3 AD 835 (8th Cir. 1994)   *9:* 186

Massey v. Scrivner, Inc., 901 F. Supp. 1546 (W.D. Okla. 1994), *aff'd sub nom.* Milton v. Scrivner, Inc., 53 F.3d 1118, 4 AD 432 (10th Cir. 1995)   *9:* 54, 123, 129, 145, 177, 186, 237, 272, 277; *22:* 21

Materson v. Stokes, 166 F.R.D. 368, 70 FEP 1630 (E.D. Va. 1996)   *34:* 8

Matherne v. St. Charles Parish Sch. Bd., 71 FEP 1183 (E.D. La. 1996)   *30:* 61

Mathews v. City of La Verne, 73 FEP 908 (C.D. Cal. 1997)   *20:* 109

Mathis v. Pacific Gas & Elec., 75 F.3d 498, 11 IER 564 (9th Cir. 1996)   *26:* 33

Matos v. Hove, 940 F. Supp. 67 (S.D.N.Y. 1996)   *36:* 20

Matthews
—v. Rollins Hudig Hall Co., 72 F.3d 50, 69 FEP 641 (7th Cir. 1995)   *32:* 21
—v. Runyon, 860 F. Supp. 1347, 67 FEP 1515 (E.D. Wis. 1994)   *4:* 28

Mauro v. Borgess Med. Ctr., 886 F. Supp. 1349, 4 AD 737 (W.D. Mich. 1995)   *9:* 166, 249, 251

Mayberry
—v. Endocrinology-Diabetes Assoc., 926 F. Supp. 1315 (M.D. Tenn. 1996)   *21:* 23
—v. Vought Aircraft Co., 55 F.3d 1086, 68 FEP 401 (5th Cir. 1995)   *2:* 12

Maye v. City of Kannapolis, 872 F. Supp. 246, 66 FEP 670 (M.D.N.C. 1994) *40:* 90

Mayfield v. Patterson Pump Co., 101 F.3d 1371, 72 FEP 1153 (11th Cir. 1996) *2:* 40

Maynard v. City of San Jose, 37 F.3d 1396, 66 FEP 123 (9th Cir. 1994)   *24:* 29, 37–38, 51–53

Mayo
—v. Dillard's Dep't Stores, Inc., 884 F. Supp. 417 (D. Kan. 1995) **16:** 99
—v. Kiwest Corp., 898 F. Supp. 335, 68 FEP 1761 (E.D. Va. 1995), *aff"d mem.*, 94 F.3d 641 (4th Cir. 1996) **17:** 11
Mayorga v. Donnelley Marketing, 70 FEP 670 (N.D. Ill. 1996) **13:** 27; **21:** 11
Mazzarella v. United States Postal Serv., 849 F. Supp. 89, 3 AD 232 (D. Mass. 1994) **9:** 7
McAdoo v. Toll, 591 F. Supp. 1399, 35 FEP 833 (D. Md. 1984) **24:** 10
McAlpin v. National Semiconductor Corp., 921 F. Supp. 1518, 5 AD 1047 (N.D. Tex. 1996) **9:** 199
McBride v. Lawstaf, Inc., 1996 U.S. Dist. LEXIS 16190 (N.D. Ga.), *Magistrate's recommendation adopted*, 71 FEP 1758 (N.D. Ga. 1996) **23:** 7–8, 10–11
McCleland v. Montgomery Ward & Co., 1995 WL 571324 (N.D. Ill. Sept. 25, 1995) **38:** 50
McClellon v. Lone Star Gas Co., 66 F.3d 98, 69 FEP 36 (5th Cir. 1995) **31:** 45
McCollough v. Atlanta Beverage Co., 929 F. Supp. 1489 (N.D. Ga. 1996) **9:** 136, 142, 209
McCoy
—v. Johnson Controls World Servs., Inc., 878 F. Supp. 229, 67 FEP 1763 (S.D. Ga. 1995) **24:** 21
—v. Pennsylvania Power & Light Co., 933 F. Supp. 438 (M.D. Pa. 1996) **9:** 72, 133, 184
McCray
—v. Corry Mfg. Co., 872 F. Supp. 209, 68 FEP 1685 (W.D. Pa. 1994), *aff'd*, 61 F.3d 224, 68 FEP 821 (3d Cir. 1995) **16:** 76; **31:** 52
—v. DPC Indus., Inc., 875 F. Supp. 384, 68 FEP 909 (E.D. Tex. 1995) **41:** 63
McCree v. Sam's Club, 159 F.R.D. 572, 67 FEP 1271 (M.D. Ala. 1995) **37:** 3, 23, 32, 43, 46
McCreless v. Moore Business Forms, Inc., 1996 WL 243378 (S.D. Tex. May 2, 1996) **16:** 96

McDaniel
—v. AlliedSignal, Inc., 896 F. Supp. 1482, 4 AD 1471 (W.D. Mo. 1995) **9:** 184
—v. Mississippi Baptist Med. Ctr., 877 F. Supp. 321, 4 AD 241 (S.D. Miss.), *aff'd mem.*, 74 F.3d 1238, 6 AD 800 (5th Cir. 1995) **9:** 260, 263
McDermott v. Chilton Co., 938 F. Supp. 240, 11 IER 1460 (D.N.J. 1995) **26:** 15, 53, 55
McDonald
—v. Department of Corrections, 880 F. Supp. 1416, 4 AD 1258 (D. Kan. 1995) **9:** 124
—v. Department of Pub. Welfare, 62 F.3d 92, 4 AD 1185 (3d Cir. 1995) **9:** 43, 116
McDonnell Douglas Corp.
—v. EEOC, 922 F. Supp. 235, 70 FEP 980 (E.D. Mo. 1996) **29:** 44; **38:** 29
—v. Green, 411 U.S. 792, 5 FEP 965 (1973) **2:** 3; **16:** 93; **27:** 29
—EEOC v.
——894 F. Supp. 1329, 68 FEP 1115 (E.D. Mo. 1995) **34:** 55–56
——948 F. Supp. 54 (E.D. Mo. 1996) **34:** 17–28
——960 F. Supp. 203, 72 FEP 769 (E.D. Mo. 1996) **37:** 94
McDowell v. Cisneros, 84 F.3d 256, 70 FEP 1459 (7th Cir. 1996) **17:** 7–8, 15–16; **20:** 71–74
McFadden-Peel v. Staten Island Cable, 873 F. Supp. 757, 67 FEP 147 (E.D.N.Y. 1994) **30:** 13
McFarland v. Folsom, 854 F. Supp. 862 (M.D. Ala. 1994) **5:** 3, 11–12
McGanty v. Staudenraus, 901 P.2d 841, 10 IER 1793 (Or. 1995) **26:** 53
McGautha v. Jackson County, 36 F.3d 53 (8th Cir. 1994), *cert. denied*, 515 U.S. 1133 (1995) **24:** 28
McGinnis v. Kentucky Fried Chicken of Cal., 42 F.3d 1273, 3 AD 1813 (9th Cir. 1994) **42:** 57
McGowan v. Our Savior's Lutheran Church, 527 N.W.2d 830, 10 IER 909 (Minn. 1995) **26:** 57

McIntosh v. Irving Trust Co., 873 F. Supp. 872, 67 FEP 176 (S.D.N.Y. 1995) *17:* 51; *41:* 26

McKay v. Toyota Motor Mfg., USA, Inc., 110 F.3d 369, 6 AD 933 (6th Cir. 1997) *9:* 47

McKeever v. Ironworker's Dist. Council, 73 FEP 1000 (E.D. Pa. 1997) *16:* 10

McKennon v. Nashville Banner Publ'g Co., 513 U.S. 352, 66 FEP 1192 (1995) *15:* 25; *16:* 215; *38:* 53, 55; *40:* 32–36, 46; *41:* 4–5, 54, 137

McKenzie
—v. Atlantic Richfield Co., 906 F. Supp. 572, 70 FEP 547 (D. Colo. 1995) *17:* 9, 41, 45
—v. Illinois Dep't of Transp., 92 F.3d 473, 71 FEP 1549 (7th Cir. 1996) *17:* 35
—v. Renberg's Inc., 94 F.3d 1478, 3 WH2d 769 (10th Cir. 1996), *cert. denied,* 117 S. Ct. 1468 (1997) *17:* 21

McKeown v. Dartmouth Bookstore, Inc., 975 F. Supp. 403 (D.N.H. 1997) *20:* 8

McKinnon v. Kwong Wah Restaurant, 83 F.3d 498, 70 FEP 1037 (1st Cir. 1996) *41:* 102, 106

McKnight
—v. Circuit City Stores, 168 F.R.D. 550 (E.D. Va. 1996) *32:* 15; *37:* 6, 23, 97–101
—v. General Motors Corp., 973 F.2d 1366 (7th Cir. 1992), *cert. denied,* 507 U.S. 915 (1993) *40:* 51

McLaughlin
—v. Boston Sch. Comm., 938 F. Supp. 1001 (D. Mass. 1996) *27:* 47, 54
—v. Esselte Pendaflex Corp., 50 F.3d 507, 67 FEP 474 (8th Cir. 1995) *33:* 51

McNamara v. City of Chicago, 867 F. Supp. 739 (N.D. Ill. 1994), *aff'd,* 138 F.3d 1219 (7th Cir. 1998) *5:* 69; *27:* 114, 116–19, 141, 143–46, 155–57

McNemar v. Disney Stores, Inc., 91 F.3d 610, 5 AD 1227 (3d Cir. 1996), *cert. denied,* 117 S. Ct. 958 (1997) *9:* 60; *32:* 18; *38:* 20

McNierney v. McGraw-Hill, Inc., 919 F. Supp. 853, 70 FEP 935 (D. Md. 1995) *15:* 8

McWilliams v. Logicon, Inc., 5 AD 1456 (D. Kan. 1996) *9:* 297

Mears v. Gulfstream Aerospace Corp., 905 F. Supp. 1075, 5 AD 1295 (S.D. Ga. 1995), *aff'd mem.,* 87 F.3d 1331, 6 AD 1152 (11th Cir. 1996) *9:* 175, 177, 179, 230

Medearis v. Old Cowtown Museum, 67 FEP 1694 (D. Kan. 1995) *21:* 11

Medicare Beneficiaries' Defense Fund v. Empire Blue Cross Blue Shield, 938 F. Supp. 1131 (E.D.N.Y. 1996) *37:* 83

Meeks v. Computer Assocs. Int'l, 15 F.3d 1013, 64 FEP 258 (11th Cir. 1994) *15:* 6; *17:* 43

Meinecke v. H & R Block, 66 F.3d 77, 70 FEP 311 (5th Cir. 1995) *16:* 150

Melendez v. Illinois Bell Tel. Co., 79 F.3d 661, 70 FEP 589 (7th Cir. 1996) *4:* 41; *5:* 33, 39, 43, 79–80; *32:* 13

Menchaca v. Rose Records, Inc., 67 FEP 1334 (N.D. Ill. 1995) *20:* 106

Mendez v. Gearan, 947 F. Supp. 1364 (N.D. Cal. 1996) *9:* 314–15

Mendoza
—v. SSC & B Lintas, 913 F. Supp. 295 (S.D.N.Y. 1996) *19:* 25
—v. Union St. Bus Co., 876 F. Supp. 8, 67 FEP 365 (D. Mass. 1995) *41:* 27

Meredith v. Louisiana Fed'n of Teachers, 1996 WL 137632 (E.D. La. Mar. 26, 1996) *16:* 39

Meritor Savs. Bank, FSB v. Vinson, 477 U.S. 57 (1986) *20:* 90

Mertig v. Milliken & Michaels of Del., Inc., 923 F. Supp. 636 (D. Del. 1996) *41:* 38

Metsopulos v. Runyon, 918 F. Supp. 851 (D.N.J. 1996) *16:* 31; *19:* 3, 20; *36:* 9, 24

Metz v. Merrill Lynch, Pierce, Fenner & Smith, Inc., 39 F.3d 1482, 66 FEP 439 (l0th Cir. 1994) *32:* 21

Meyer
—v. Runyon, 869 F. Supp. 70 (D. Mass. 1994) *16:* 28

Meyer—Contd.
—v. United Air Lines, 950 F. Supp. 874, 73 FEP 202 (N.D. Ill. 1997) *41:* 46
Miano v. AC & R Adver., Inc., 875 F. Supp. 204, 66 FEP 1603 (S.D.N.Y. 1995) *16:* 214; *41:* 45, 53, 80, 83
Middleton v. City of Flint, Mich., 92 F.3d 396, 71 FEP 962 (6th Cir. 1996), *cert. denied,* 117 S. Ct. 1552 (1997) *27:* 57, 75–78; *39:* 42, 45; *40:* 66
Mid Hudson Med. Group; People v., 877 F. Supp. 143 (S.D.N.Y. 1995) *9:* 11
Migneault v. Peck, 973 F. Supp. 1295 (D.N.M. 1997), *appeal pending,* No. 97-2099 (10th Cir.) *16:* 35
Milburn v. West, 854 F. Supp. 1 (D.D.C. 1994) *36:* 19; *40:* 55
Miles v. Boeing Co., 154 F.R.D. 117 (E.D. Pa. 1994) *38:* 10
Miller
—v. Aristech Chem. Corp., 67 FEP 216 (W.D. Pa. 1995) *30:* 30
—v. CBC Cos., 908 F. Supp. 1054, 5 AD 1187 (D.N.H. 1995) *30:* 61
—v. County of Santa Cruz, 39 F.3d 1030 (9th Cir. 1994), *cert. denied,* 515 U.S. 1160 (1995) *32:* 2
—v. Department of Corrections, 916 F. Supp. 863, 6 AD 497 (C.D. Ill. 1996), *aff'd,* 107 F.3d 483 (7th Cir. 1997) *9:* 52, 123, 133–34
—v. Runyon
——32 F.3d 386, 65 FEP 1063 (8th Cir. 1994) *31:* 29
——932 F. Supp. 276, 71 FEP 1024 (M.D. Ala. 1996) *9:* 309
——77 F.3d 189 (7th Cir.), *cert. denied,* 117 S. Ct. 316 (1996) *31:* 32–33
Million v. Frank, 47 F.3d 385, 67 FEP 254 (10th Cir. 1995) *31:* 40
Mills
—v. Amoco Performance Prods., 872 F. Supp. 975, 74 FEP 835 (S.D. Ga. 1994) *33:* 57
—v. First Fed. Sav. & Loan Ass'n, 83 F.3d 833, 70 FEP 1263 (7th Cir. 1996) *33:* 51
Milton v. Scrivner, Inc., *see* Massey v. Scrivner, Inc.

Milwaukee, City of; EEOC v., 919 F. Supp. 1247 (E.D. Wis. 1996) *29:* 14, 27, 29–30, 32–33, 36–38, 42; *38:* 28
Milwaukee Prof'l Firefighters v. City of Milwaukee, 869 F. Supp. 633, 72 FEP 121 (E.D. Wis. 1994) *16:* 10
Mindler v. Clayton County, Ga., 864 F. Supp. 1329 (N.D. Ga. 1994), *aff'd,* 63 F.3d 1113 (11th Cir. 1995) *42:* 30–31
Minetos v. City Univ. of N.Y., 875 F. Supp. 1046, 68 FEP 355 (S.D.N.Y. 1995) *19:* 1; *21:* 22; *24:* 9; *33:* 24, 33
Minnesota Ass'n of Nurse Anesthetists v. Unity Hosp., 59 F.3d 80 (8th Cir. 1995) *40:* 90, 93
Mintzmyer
—v. Babbitt, 66 FEP 1804 (D.D.C.), *aff'd mem.,* 72 F.3d 920 (D.C. Cir. 1995) *16:* 104
—v. Department of the Interior, 84 F.3d 419 (D.C. Cir. 1996) *21:* 24
Miranda v. Wisconsin Power & Light Co., 91 F.3d 1011, 5 AD 1856 (7th Cir. 1996) *9:* 117, 203–04
Mirza v. Department of Treasury, 875 F. Supp. 513 (N.D. Ill. 1995) *16:* 57; *31:* 31
Misischia v. Pirie, 60 F. 3d 626 (9th Cir. 1995) *32:* 2, 5
Mitchell
—v. Data Gen. Corp., 12 F.3d 1310, 63 FEP 816 (4th Cir. 1993) *2:* 29
—v. EEOC, 888 F. Supp. 710, 68 FEP 397 (E.D. Pa. 1995) *33:* 5
—v. Sisters of Charity of the Incarnate Word, 924 F. Supp. 793 (S.D. Tex. 1996) *16:* 211, 222; *40:* 42, 50; *41:* 28, 80, 82, 84, 114, 118
Modderno v. King, 871 F. Supp. 40, 5 AD 749 (D.D.C. 1994), *aff'd,* 82 F.3d 1059, 5 AD 749 (D.C. Cir. 1996), *cert. denied,* 117 S. Ct. 772 (1997) *9:* 99
Mohamed v. Marriott Int'l, Inc., 905 F. Supp. 141, 5 AD 50 (S.D.N.Y. 1995) *9:* 165, 170
Molesworth v. Brandon, 672 A.2d 608, 70 FEP 524 (Md. Ct. App. 1996) *26:* 32

Molovinsky v. Fair Employment Council of Greater Washington, Inc., 683 F.2d 142, 72 FEP 79 (D.C. Cir. 1996) *30:* 33
Momah v. Albert Einstein Med. Ctr., 164 F.R.D. 412 (E.D. Pa. 1996) *38:* 14
Monette v. Electronic Data Sys. Corp., 90 F.3d 1173, 5 AD 1326 (6th Cir. 1996) *9:* 216, 229, 272–76, 280–81, 288
Monica v. New York City Off-Track Betting Corp., 67 FEP 704 (S.D.N.Y. 1995), *aff'd,* 100 F.3d 941 (2d Cir. 1996) *20:* 8
Montalvo v. United States Postal Serv., 887 F. Supp. 63 (E.D.N.Y. 1995), *aff'd mem.,* 1996 U.S. App. LEXIS 12262 (2d Cir. 1996) *9:* 309
Montegue v. City of New Orleans, 1996 U.S. Dist. LEXIS 13795 (E.D. La. Sept. 13, 1996) *9:* 265
Montgomery
—v. Aetna Plywood, Inc., 1996 U.S. Dist. LEXIS 9213 (N.D. Ill. 1996) *37:* 89
—v. Brookshire
——34 F.3d 291, 65 FEP 1866 (5th Cir. 1994) *30:* 22
——880 F. Supp. 483 (W.D. Tex. 1995) *2:* 14, 22
Moodie v. Federal Reserve Bank, 58 F.3d 879, 68 FEP 327 (2d Cir. 1995) *32:* 3
Moody v. Department of Educ., 883 F. Supp. 624 (M.D. Ala. 1995), *aff'd mem.,* 77 F.3d 498 (11th Cir.), *cert. denied,* 117 S. Ct. 175 (1996) *16:* 104
Mooney
—v. Aramco Serv. Co., 54 F.3d 1207, 68 FEP 421 (5th Cir. 1995) *2:* 55; *16:* 80, 86, 137, 179; *31:* 36–37; *33:* 41
—v. Bayfield Constr. Co., 1995 WL 530656 (N.D. Ill. Aug. 23, 1995) *16:* 24
Moore
—v. Allstate Ins. Co., 928 F. Supp. 744, 75 FEP 983 (N.D. Ill. 1996) *24:* 21, 55
—v. Ford Motor Co., 901 F. Supp. 1293 (N.D. Ill. 1995) *16:* 14; *23:* 1
—v. Interacciones Global, Inc., 1995 U.S. Dist. LEXIS 971 (S.D.N.Y. Jan. 27, 1995) *32:* 21

—v. Stone, 1994 WL 549733 (D.D.C. Sept. 30, 1994) *16:* 233
Morales v. Human Rights Div., 878 F. Supp. 653, 67 FEP 531 (S.D.N.Y. 1995) *11:* 18–19; *19:* 11
Moreno v. Consolidated Rail Corp., 99 F.3d 782, 6 AD 86 (6th Cir. 1996) *9:* 12–13, 294, 307
Morgan v. United Parcel Serv. of Am., 169 F.R.D. 349 (E.D. Mo. 1996) *37:* 91
Morisky v. Broward County, 80 F.3d 445, 5 AD 737 (11th Cir. 1996) *9:* 38, 76, 187
Morrison v. American Bd. of Psychiatry & Neurology, Inc., 908 F. Supp. 582, 69 FEP 1217 (N.D. Ill. 1996) *5:* 4, 7–8, 10, 13; *24:* 5; *30:* 36–37
Morrissey v. Boston Five Cents Sav. Bank, 54 F.3d 27, 67 FEP 1338 (1st Cir. 1995) *16:* 11–12
Morrow v. II Morrow, Inc., 911 P.2d 964, 11 IER 780 (Or. Ct. App. 1996) *26:* 56
Morton v. GTE N., Inc., 922 F. Supp. 1169, 5 AD 524 (N.D. Tex. 1996), *aff'd mem.,* 114 F.3d 1132 (5th Cir. 1997) *9:* 133
Moses
—v. American Nonwovens, Inc., 97 F.3d 446, 5 AD 1651 (11th Cir. 1996), *cert. denied,* 117 S. Ct. 964 (1997) *9:* 174, 188, 242–43, 252, 289
—v. KMart Corp., 905 F. Supp. 1054, 70 FEP 1048 (S.D. Fla. 1995), *aff'd,* 119 F.3d 10 (11th Cir. 1997) *16:* 235; *41:* 114
Mosley v. Peña, 100 F.3d 1515, 72 FEP 561 (10th Cir. 1996) *36:* 25
Moten v. American Linen Supply Co., 67 FEP 1080 (D. Kan. 1995) *15:* 31; *16:* 56, 165
Motley v. Marathon Oil Co., 69 FEP 911 (10th Cir. 1995), *cert. denied,* 116 S. Ct. 1678 (1996) *38:* 29
Moyo v. Gomez, 32 F.3d 1382, 65 FEP 821, *amended,* 40 F.3d 982, 68 FEP 1419 (9th Cir. 1994), *cert. denied,* 513 U.S. 1081 (1995) *17:* 10; *30:* 28

Mraz v. County of Lehigh, 862 F. Supp. 1344 (E.D. Pa. 1994) *16:* 9
Mudlitz v. Mutual Serv. Ins. Co., 75 F.3d 391, 11 IER 620 (8th Cir. 1996) *26:* 20, 46
Mukhtar v. Castleton Serv. Corp., 920 F. Supp. 934, 70 FEP 1128 (S.D. Ind. 1996) *16:* 14
Muller v. Hotsy Corp., 917 F. Supp. 1389, 6 AD 35 (N.D. Iowa 1996) *9:* 55
Mulqueen v. Daka, Inc., 909 F. Supp. 86, 73 FEP 31 (N.D.N.Y. 1995), *aff'd,* 104 F.3d 351, 73 FEP 192 (2d Cir. 1996) *16:* 99
Mummelthie v. City of Mason City, 873 F. Supp. 1293, 66 FEP 1393 (N.D. Iowa 1995), *aff'd,* 78 F.3d 589, 70 FEP 928 (8th Cir. 1996) *24:* 39
Munday v. Waste Management, Inc., 858 F. Supp. 1364, 72 FEP 471 (D. Md. 1994) *17:* 22
Mungin v. Katten Muchin & Zavis, 941 F. Supp. 153 (D.D.C. 1996) *40:* 41, 45
Munoz
—v. Aldridge, 894 F.2d 1489, 52 FEP 489 (5th Cir. 1990) *36:* 13
—v. H & M Wholesale, Inc., 926 F. Supp. 596, 6 AD 355 (S.D. Tex. 1996) *9:* 133, 144, 161, 177
Murphy
—v. United Parcel Serv., Inc., 946 F. Supp. 872, 6 AD 517 (D. Kan. 1996) *9:* 161, 166, 212
—v. West, 945 F. Supp. 874 (D. Md. 1996) *36:* 27
Muzquiz v. W.A. Foote Mem'l Hosp., Inc., 70 F.3d 422, 69 FEP 540 (6th Cir. 1995) *11:* 5
Myers
—v. City of Cincinnati, 14 F.3d 1115 (6th Cir. 1994) *41:* 99
—v. Hose, 50 F.3d 278, 4 AD 391 (4th Cir. 1995) *9:* 123, 162, 209, 225, 229, 247
Myrick v. Devils Lake Sioux Mfg. Corp., 718 F. Supp. 753, 50 FEP 517 (D. N.D. 1989) *12:* 1, 4, 6

N

NAACP v. Town of East Haven
—892 F. Supp. 46, 67 FEP 1055 (D. Conn. 1995) *30:* 10, 31
—70 F.3d 219, 69 FEP 500 (2d Cir. 1995) *4:* 19
NAACP Detroit Branch v. DPOA, 46 F.3d 528, 66 FEP 1569 (6th Cir. 1995) *42:* 19
Nadeau
—v. Imtec, Inc., 670 A.2d 841, 69 FEP 812 (Vt. 1995) *20:* 115
—v. Thomas, 1997 WL 542708 (N.D. Cal. 1997) *32:* 34
Nadler v. Mann, 951 F.2d 301 (11th Cir. 1992) *36:* 33
Nakai v. Wickes Lumber Co., 906 F. Supp. 698, 71 FEP 13 (D. Me. 1995) *16:* 99, 166; *17:* 31, 45
Nappi v. Meridian Leasing Corp., 859 F. Supp. 1177 (N.D. Ill. 1994) *16:* 98
Nash v. Consolidated City of Jacksonville, 895 F. Supp. 1536 (M.D. Fla. 1995), *aff'd without opinion,* 85 F.3d 643 (11th Cir. 1996) *5:* 16, 30, 48, 61–62, 80–81; *19:* 26; *39:* 73
National Ass'n of Gov't Employees v. City Pub. Serv. Bd. of San Antonio, 40 F.3d 698, 67 FEP 1013 (5th Cir. 1994) *24:* 35; *31:* 56; *33:* 4; *37:* 43
National Cleaning Contractors; EEOC v., 71 FEP 159 (S.D.N.Y. 1996) *38:* 35
National Farmers Union Ins. Cos. v. Crow Tribe of Indians, 471 U.S. 845 (1985) *12:* 9
National Treasury Employees Union; United States v., 513 U.S. 454 (1995) *17:* 70–71
Nationwide Mut. Ins. Co. v. Darden, 503 U.S. 318 (1992) *30:* 12, 14–15, 48
Nayar v. Howard Univ., 881 F. Supp. 15 (D.D.C. 1995) *19:* 18
Naylor v. Georgia-Pacific Corp., 875 F. Supp. 564 (N.D. Iowa 1995) *41:* 53
Neal v. Department of Corrections, 1995 U.S. Dist. LEXIS 11543 (D.D.C. Aug. 9, 1995) *37:* 105, 107; *41:* 71

Nedder v. Rivier College, 908 F. Supp. 66, 4 AD 1530 (D.N.H. 1995) **40:** 90, 93

Nelson
—v. Boatmen's Bancshares, Inc., 26 F.3d 796, 64 FEP 1799 (8th Cir. 1994) **2:** 42
—v. County of Allegheny, 60 F.3d 1010 (3d Cir. 1995) **37:** 77–79
—v. Cyprus Bagdad Copper Corp., 119 F.3d 756, 6 AD 1714 (9th Cir. 1997) **32:** 34–35
—v. J.C. Penney Co., 75 F.3d 343, 69 FEP 1328 (8th Cir.), *cert. denied,* 117 S. Ct. 61 (1996) **17:** 46
—v. Pima Community College, 83 F.3d 1075 (9th Cir. 1996) **17:** 20, 68
—v. Pulaski County Sheriff's Dep't, 859 F. Supp. 1228, 65 FEP 1563 (E.D. Ark. 1994) **2:** 16
—v. Telecable of Overland Park, Inc., 70 FEP 859 (D. Kan. 1996) **38:** 42
—v. Upsala College, 51 F.3d 383, 67 FEP 525 (3d Cir. 1995) **17:** 2, 33

Nembhard v. Memorial Sloan-Kettering Cancer Ctr., 918 F. Supp. 784 (S.D.N.Y.), *aff'd,* 104 F.3d 353 (2d Cir. 1996) **16:** 104, 126, 165

Nesbit v. Louisiana-Pacific Corp., 39 F.3d 1184 (8th Cir. 1994) **18:** 5

Newbridge Networks Secs. Litig., 926 F. Supp. 1163 (D.D.C. 1996) **37:** 84

New Haven Temple SDA Church v. Consolidated Edison Corp., 1995 U.S. Dist. LEXIS 8220 (S.D.N.Y. 1995) **38:** 57

Newhouse v. McCormick & Co., 910 F. Supp. 1451 (D. Neb. 1996), *aff'd in part, rev'd in part,* 110 F.3d 635, 73 FEP 1496 (8th Cir. 1997) **16:** 222–23, 226; **41:** 103

Newland v. Dalton, 81 F.3d 904, 5 AD 735 (9th Cir. 1996) **9:** 268

Newman v. GHS Osteopathic, Inc., 60 F.3d 153, 4 AD 1051 (3d Cir. 1995) **9:** 273

Newport Mesa Unified Sch. Dist.; EEOC v., 893 F. Supp. 927, 68 FEP 657 (C.D. Cal. 1995) **3:** 3; **16:** 34, 138, 196

Newport News Shipbuilding & Drydock Co.; EEOC v., 949 F. Supp. 403, 6 AD 369 (E.D. Va. 1996) **9:** 119

Newton v. Department of the Air Force, 85 F.3d 595 (Fed. Cir. 1996) **10:** 3

New York City Transit Auth.
—v. New York Div. of Human Rights, 627 N.Y.S.2d 360 (N.Y. App. Div. 1995), *rev'd in part,* 674 N.E.2d 305 (N.Y. 1996) **8:** 23, 27
—United States v., 97 F.3d 672, 72 FEP 114 (2d Cir. 1996) **17:** 26

New York Times; EEOC v., 1995 U.S. Dist. LEXIS 3838 (S.D.N.Y. Mar. 24, 1995) **34:** 43

Nguyen
—v. CNA Corp., 44 F.3d 234, 10 IER 329 (4th Cir. 1995) **26:** 18
—v. IBP, Inc., 905 F. Supp. 1471, 5 AD 465 (D. Kan. 1995) **9:** 124, 143; **38:** 20

Nicholas v. Nynex, Inc., 929 F. Supp. 727, 74 FEP 581 (S.D.N.Y. 1996) **43:** 6

Nichols v. Frank, 42 F.3d 503, 66 FEP 614 (9th Cir. 1994) **20:** 41

Nickeo v. Virgin Islands Tel. Corp., 42 F.3d 804, 66 FEP 1020 (3d Cir. 1994) **24:** 3

Nitschke v. McDonnell Douglas Corp., 68 F.3d 249, 71 FEP 99 (8th Cir. 1995) **2:** 55–56; **16:** 151, 167

Nixon v. Digital Equip., 6 AD 353 (E.D.N.Y. 1996) **32:** 18

NLRB v., *see* name of opposing party

Nogueras v. University of Puerto Rico, 890 F. Supp. 60, 69 FEP 1007 (D.P.R. 1995) **33:** 18

Norfolk Police Dep't, City of; EEOC v., 45 F.3d 80, 66 FEP 1425 (4th Cir. 1995) **29:** 24; **34:** 5

North Carolina; United States v., 914 F. Supp. 1257, 71 FEP 1347 (E.D.N.C. 1996) **39:** 34–35, 49

Northern v. City of Chicago, 841 F. Supp. 234, 2 AD 1864 (N.D. Ill. 1993) **9:** 112

North State Law Enforcement Officer's Ass'n v. Charlotte-Mecklenburg Police Dep't, 862 F. Supp. 1445, 65 FEP 1537 (W.D.N.C. 1994) **27:** 54, 88

Northwest Airlines, Inc. v. Transport Workers, 451 U.S. 77, 25 FEP 737 (1981) *22:* 25

Northwestern Mem'l Hosp.; EEOC v., 858 F. Supp. 759, 73 FEP 742 (N.D. Ill. 1994) *41:* 46

Northwest Structural Components, Inc.; EEOC v., 897 F. Supp. 249, 67 FEP 1761 (M.D.N.C. 1995) *34:* 62, 64

Novack v. Northwest Airlines, Inc., 525 N.W.2d 592 (Minn. Ct. App. 1995) *13:* 38–39

Novellis v. Shalala, 947 F. Supp. 557 (D. Mass. 1996) *40:* 88, 97, 100

Nowd v. Rubin, 76 F.3d 25, 69 FEP 1587 (1st Cir. 1996) *36:* 4; *42:* 32–33

Nowlin v. Resolution Trust Corp., 33 F.3d 498, 65 FEP 1870 (5th Cir. 1994) *30:* 16

Nusom v. Comh Woodburn, Inc., 122 F.3d 830 (9th Cir. 1997) *43:* 61–62

O

Oberg v. Allied Van Lines, 1994 WL 419679 (N.D. Ill. Aug. 5, 1994) *16:* 81

O'Brien v. New England Tel. & Tel. Co., 422 Mass. 686, 664 N.E.2d 843, 11 IER 1221 (1996) *26:* 5, 54

Occidental Life Ins. Co. v. EEOC, 432 U.S. 355, 14 FEP 1718 (1977) *34:* 30

O'Connor v. Consolidated Coin Caterers Corp, 84 F.3d 718, 70 FEP 1628 (4th Cir.), *cert. denied,* 517 U.S. 308, 70 FEP 486 (1996) *2:* 8; *16:* 92, 94, 102–03, 177; *21:* 31; *27:* 19

O'Day v. McDonnell Douglas Helicopter Co., 79 F.3d 756, 70 FEP 615 (9th Cir. 1996) *40:* 33, 35–36; *41:* 4, 44–56

Ode v. Omtvedt, 883 F. Supp. 1308 (D. Neb. 1995), *aff'd mem.,* 81 F.3d 165 (8th Cir. 1996) *16:* 52, 57

Odima v. Westin Tucson Hotel, 53 F.3d 1484, 67 FEP 1222 (9th Cir. 1995) *2:* 44; *19:* 1, 28; *24:* 3; *41:* 33, 51, 144; *42:* 1

Odunmbaku v. New York Blood Ctr., 1996 WL 514867, 72 FEP 202 (S.D.N.Y. 1996), *decision adhered to on reconsideration,* 1996 WL 695748, 72 FEP 1564 (S.D.N.Y. 1996) *32:* 5

Office of Senate Sergeant at Arms v. Office of Senate Fair Empl. Practices, 95 F.3d 1102, 6 AD 1237 (Fed. Cir. 1996) *9:* 157, 187

Officers for Justice v. Civil Serv. Comm'n, 979 F.2d 721, 62 FEP 868 (9th Cir. 1992) *5:* 32

O'Gilvie v. United States, 117 S. Ct. 452 (1996) *43:* 57

O & G Spring & Wire Forms Specialty Co.; EEOC v., 38 F.3d 872, 65 FEP 1823 (7th Cir. 1994), *cert. denied,* 513 U.S. 1198, 67 FEP 1632 (1995) *34:* 64; *39:* 26, 41, 50, 58, 70; *41:* 7, 142–43, 147

O'Hare Truck Serv., Inc. v. City of Northlake, 116 S. Ct. 2353 (1996) *17:* 72

Olenick v. New York Tel./A Nynex Co., 881 F. Supp. 113 (S.D.N.Y. 1995) *27:* 33

Olmeda v. Schneider, 889 F. Supp. 228 (D.V.I. 1995) *40:* 88, 90, 98, 101

Olson v. General Elec. Astrospace, 101 F.3d 947, 6 AD 270 (3d Cir. 1996) *9:* 33

Oncale v. Sundowner Offshore Servs., Inc., 118 S. Ct. 998, 76 FEP 221 (1998) *1:* 2; *14:* 1–4; *20:* 25, 28–29, 52, 68, 82–83

O'Patka v. Menasha Corp., 878 F. Supp. 1202, 70 FEP 11 (E.D. Wis. 1995) *20:* 107, 110; *27:* 27, 33

Opuku-Boateng v. California, 95 F.3d 1461, 71 FEP 1849 (9th Cir. 1996), *cert. denied,* 65 U.S.L.W. 3764 (1997) *8:* 20, 30

O'Quinn v. New York Univ. Med. Ctr., 163 F.R.D. 226, 68 FEP 1798 (S.D.N.Y. 1995), *motion granted in part, denied in part,* 933 F. Supp. 341 (S.D.N.Y. 1996) *38:* 46

Orange, City of; EEOC v., 905 F. Supp. 381 (E.D. Tex. 1995) *29:* 35

Orlowski v. Dominicks Finer Foods, Inc., 1995 U.S. Dist. LEXIS 12468 (N.D. Ill. Aug. 22, 1995), *clarified,* 1995 U.S. Dist. LEXIS 13197 (E.D. Ill. Sept.11, 1995) *38:* 11, 13

Ortez v. Washington County, 88 F.3d 804, 71 FEP 584 (9th Cir. 1996) *17:* 40

O'Shea v. Yellow Tech. Servs., Inc., 979 F. Supp. 1390 (D. Kan. 1997) *20:* 8

Oshiver v. Levin, Fishbein, Sedran & Berman
—38 F.3d 1380, 66 FEP 429 (3d Cir. 1994) *31:* 5, 23, 30
—910 F. Supp. 225, 69 FEP 1288 (E.D. Pa.), *aff'd,* 96 F.3d 1434 (3d Cir. 1996) *30:* 13

Ost v. West Suburban Travelers Limousine, Inc., 88 F.3d 435, 71 FEP 304 (7th Cir. 1996) *30:* 18

Ostwalt v. Sara Lee Corp., 74 F.3d 91, 5 AD 385 (5th Cir. 1996) *9:* 4

Oswald v. Laroche Chems., Inc.
—894 F. Supp. 988, 5 AD 401 (E.D. La. 1995) *9:* 295
—162 F.R.D. 283, 5 AD 409 (E.D. La. 1995) *37:* 11; *41:* 119

Oubre v. Entergy Operations, Inc., 118 S. Ct. 838, 75 FEP 1255 (1998) *1:* 4; *16:* 199, 201–02; *43:* 47–48, 68

Our Lady of the Resurrection Med. Ctr.; EEOC v., 77 F.3d 145, 70 FEP 104 (7th Cir. 1996) *2:* 46; *33:* 52

Overton v. Reilly, 977 F.2d 1190, 2 AD 254 (7th Cir. 1992) *9:* 61; *32:* 18

P

Pacific Mut. Life Ins. Co. v. Haslip, 499 U.S. 1 (1991) *41:* 109

Pacourek v. Inland Steel Co., 858 F. Supp. 1393, 3 AD 726, 65 FEP 758 (N.D. Ill. 1994), *partial summary judgment denied,* 916 F. Supp. 797, 5 AD 438 (N.D. Ill. 1996) *13:* 24; *16:* 27, 53

Padilla v. Metro-North Commuter R.R., 1995 WL 4269 (S.D.N.Y. Jan. 5, 1995), *aff'd,* 92 F.3d 117, 72 FEP 1748 (2d Cir. 1996), *cert. denied,* 117 S. Ct. 2453 (1997) *16:* 208; *40:* 33, 38, 40, 42, 48

Pages-Cahue v. Iberia Lineas Aereas de Espana, 82 F.3d 533, 70 FEP 1030 (1st Cir. 1996) *16:* 161

Painter v. Graley, 639 N.E.2d 51, 9 IER 1741 (Ohio 1994) *26:* 29

Palmer
—v. Circuit Court, 905 F. Supp. 499, 6 AD 375 (N.D. Ill. 1995), *aff'd,* 117 F.3d 351, 6 AD 1569 (7th Cir. 1997) *9:* 123, 250
—v. Kelly, 17 F.3d 1490, 64 FEP 377 (D.C. Cir. 1994) *31:* 9–11
—v. Kroger Co., 1994 U.S. Dist. LEXIS 8283 (E.D. Mich. Mar. 14, 1994) *4:* 16

Palumbo v. Tele-Communications, Inc., 157 F.R.D. 129 (D.D.C. 1994) *37:* 33

Pangalos v. Prudential Ins. Co. of Am., 5 AD 1825 (E.D. Pa. 1996), *aff'd mem.,* 118 F.3d 1577 (3d Cir. 1997) *9:* 119, 134

Panis v. Mission Hills Bank, N.A., 68 FEP 1813 (D. Kan. 1994), *aff'd,* 60 F.3d 1486, 70 FEP 625 (10th Cir. 1995), *cert. denied,* 116 S. Ct. 1045 (1996) *13:* 30; *33:* 25

Papaila v. Uniden Am. Corp., 51 F.3d 54, 67 FEP 993 (5th Cir.), *cert. denied,* 116 S. Ct. 187 (1995) *11:* 34, 36–37; *30:* 68

Paperworkers Local 274 v. Champion Int'l Corp., 81 F.3d 798 (8th Cir. 1996) *40:* 26, 37, 42, 48

Pappas v. Bethesda Hosp. Ass'n, 861 F. Supp. 616, 3 AD 590 (S.D. Ohio 1994) *9:* 106

Paradise; United States v., 480 U.S. 149 (1987) *27:* 144; *40:* 65–66

Pardasani v. Rack Room Shoes, Inc., 912 F. Supp. 187 (M.D.N.C. 1996) *16:* 27

Park
—v. Howard Univ.
——881 F. Supp. 653, 71 FEP 1830 (D.D.C. 1995) *42:* 54–55
——71 F.3d 904, 71 FEP 1838 (D.C. Cir. 1995), *cert. denied,* 117 S. Ct. 57 (1996) *33:* 13

Park—*Contd.*
—v. Washington Metro. Area Transit Auth., 892 F. Supp. 5 (D.D.C. 1995) *11:* 8
Parker
—v. Baltimore & Ohio R.R., 652 F.2d 1012, 25 FEP 889 (D.C. Cir. 1981) *27:* 32–33
—v. Chestnut Hill Hosp., 1996 U.S. Dist. LEXIS 8283 (E.D. Pa. June 12, 1996) *9:* 44
—v. Chrysler Corp., 929 F. Supp. 162 (S.D.N.Y. 1996) *21:* 21
—v. Metropolitan Life Ins. Co., 6 AD 1865 (6th Cir. 1997), *cert. denied,* 66 U.S.L.W. 3338 (U.S. Jan. 20, 1998) *9:* 99
—v. Runyon, 888 F. Supp. 50 (E.D.N.C.), *aff'd,* 61 F.3d 900 (4th Cir. 1995) *16:* 57
Partin v. Arkansas State Bd. of Law Examiners, 863 F. Supp. 924 (E.D. Ark. 1994), *aff'd,* 56 F.3d 69 (8th Cir.), *cert. denied,* 116 S. Ct. 308 (1995) *5:* 11
Pasqua v. Metropolitan Life Ins. Co., 101 F.3d 514, 72 FEP 1158 (7th Cir. 1996) *20:* 75–76, 78
Pasta House Co.; EEOC v., 70 FEP 61 (E.D. Mo. 1996) *32:* 11; *38:* 26
Patterson
—v. City of Seattle, 1996 WL 528267 (9th Cir. Sept. 17, 1996) *9:* 118, 127, 179
—v. P.H.P. Healthcare Corp., 90 F.3d 927, 72 FEP 613 (5th Cir. 1996), *cert. denied,* 117 S. Ct. 767 (1997) *24:* 62–65, 69; *41:* 99, 113
—v. U.S. Cold Storage, 1995 WL 871333 (N.D. Cal. Mar. 28, 1995), *aff'd,* 87 F.3d 1321 (9th Cir. 1996) *39:* 27
Pattison v. Meijer, Inc., 897 F. Supp. 1002, 4 AD 997 (W.D. Mich. 1995) *9:* 125–26, 145, 149; *22:* 26–27
Patton v. United Parcel Serv., Inc., 910 F. Supp. 1250, 69 FEP 1665 (S.D. Tex. 1995) *21:* 16; *26:* 36–38; *27:* 14
Payne v. Sunnyside Community Hosp., 894 P.2d 1379, 10 IER 1344 (Wash. Ct. App. 1995) *26:* 13

Pazer v. New York State Bd. of Law Examiners, 849 F. Supp. 284, 3 AD 360 (S.D.N.Y. 1994) *9:* 74
Pearlstein v. Staten Island Univ. Hosp., 886 F. Supp. 260, 70 FEP 206 (E.D. N.Y. 1995) *13:* 26–27
Peck v. Sony Music Corp., 68 FEP 1025 (S.D.N.Y. 1995) *20:* 4–5
Pederson v. Louisiana State Univ., 912 F. Supp. 892 (M.D. La. 1996) *42:* 3, 11
Pegues v. Emerson Elec. Co., 913 F. Supp. 976, 5 AD 376 (N.D. Miss. 1996) *9:* 60, 161
Peightal v. Metropolitan Dade County, 26 F.3d 1545, 71 FEP 1107 (11th Cir. 1994) *39:* 46–47, 77
Pelech v. Klaff-Joss, LP, 828 F. Supp. 525, 65 FEP 1011 (N.D. Ill. 1993) *25:* 3, 5
Pelli v. Stone Savannah River Pulp & Paper Corp., 878 F. Supp. 1559 (S.D. Ga. 1995) *18:* 10–11
Pendas v. Runyon, 933 F. Supp. 187 (N.D.N.Y. 1996) *41:* 116
People v., *see* name of opposing party
Percy v. Brennan, 384 F. Supp. 800 (S.D.N.Y. 1974) *37:* 70
Perdomo v. Browner, 67 F.3d 140, 68 FEP 1751 (7th Cir. 1995) *2:* 31; *6:* 4
Perkins v. Brigham & Women's Hosp., 78 F.3d 747, 70 FEP 568 (1st Cir. 1996) *2:* 46
Petersen v. Dacy, 550 N.W.2d 91 (S.D. 1996) *26:* 42–43
Peterson
—v. City College of Univ. of N.Y., 160 F.R.D. 22, 70 FEP 259 (S.D.N.Y. 1994) *38:* 1, 33
—v. Insurance Co. of N. Am., 884 F. Supp. 107, 67 FEP 1390 (S.D.N.Y. 1995) *16:* 77
Petite v. Reno, 822 F. Supp. 815 (D.D.C. 1993) *36:* 29
Petsch-Schmid v. Boston Edison Co., 914 F. Supp. 697, 6 AD 291 (D. Mass. 1996) *2:* 13
Pfau v. Reed, 125 F.3d 927, 75 FEP 1237 (5th Cir. 1997) *20:* 12

Philipp v. ANR Freight Sys., Inc., 61 F.3d 669, 70 FEP 1347 (8th Cir. 1995) *2:* 56; *16:* 77, 107, 137, 210; *40:* 25–26, 37; *41:* 22, 83

Philippeaux v. North Cent. Bronx Hosp., 871 F. Supp. 640, 68 FEP 223 (S.D.N.Y. 1994), *aff'd,* 104 F.3d 353 (2d Cir. 1996), *cert. denied,* 117 S. Ct. 1110 (1997) *24:* 10, 39, 41, 60

Philips v. Perry, 106 F.3d 1420 (9th Cir. 1997) *14:* 24–25

Phillips
—v. Holladay Prop. Servs., Inc., 937 F. Supp. 32, 75 FEP 375 (D.D.C. 1996), *aff'd,* 1997 WL 411695 (D.C. Cir., Jun. 19, 1997) *2:* 12
—v. Manufacturers Hanover Trust Co., 67 FEP 1737 (S.D.N.Y. 1995) *16:* 120, 148

Phillips Petroleum Co. v. Shutts, 472 U.S. 797 (1985) *37:* 62

Phuong v. National Academy of Sciences, 901 F. Supp. 12 (D.D.C. 1995) *16:* 75

Piantanida v. Wyman Ctr., Inc., 927 F. Supp. 1226 (E.D. Mo. 1996), *aff'd,* 116 F.3d 340, 74 FEP 97 (8th Cir. 1997) *21:* 4

Pickering v. Board of Educ., 391 U.S. 563, 1 IER 8 (1968) *17:* 67

Pierce
—v. Atchison, Topeka & Santa Fe Ry.
——65 F.3d 562, 68 FEP 1270 (7th Cir. 1995) *43:* 1, 6
——110 F.3d 431, 73 FEP 1062 (7th Cir. 1997) *43:* 6
—v. Commonwealth Life Ins Co., 40 F.3d 796, 66 FEP 600 (6th Cir. 1994) *2:* 12, 27, 46; *27:* 33; *20:* 41
—v. Montgomery County Opportunity Bd., Inc., 884 F. Supp. 965 (E.D. Pa. 1995) *24:* 44

Pietraszewski v. Buffalo State College, 1997 WL 436763 (W.D.N.Y. Aug. 1, 1997) *16:* 35

Pina v. Texas Commerce Bank, 70 FEP 680 (W.D. Tex. 1995) *16:* 167

Pino v. Locascio, 101 F.3d 235, 72 FEP 875 (2d Cir. 1996) *42:* 2

Piraino v. International Orientation Resources, Inc., 84 F.3d 270, 70 FEP 1739 (7th Cir. 1996) *13:* 28

Pitter v. Prudential Life Ins. Co. of Am., 906 F. Supp. 130 (E.D.N.Y. 1995) *24:* 70; *32:* 21

Pitts v. Carolinas Cement Co., 1995 WL 859603 (W.D. Va. Dec. 18, 1995) *9:* 67

Plott v. General Motors Corp., Packard Elec. Div., 71 F.3d 1190, 69 FEP 826 (6th Cir. 1995), *cert. denied,* 517 U.S. 1157 (1996) *27:* 158–62, 165, 189–90; *41:* 131–34

Plummer v. Safeway, Inc., 1995 U.S. Dist. LEXIS 3428 (D.D.C. 1995) *27:* 33

Poff v. Prudential Ins. Co., 882 F. Supp. 1534, 4 AD 596 (E.D. Pa. 1995) *30:* 18

Poindexter v. Atchison, Topeka & Santa Fe Ry., 914 F. Supp. 454 (D. Kan. 1996) *9:* 186

Pollis v. New Sch. for Social Research, 913 F. Supp. 771 (S.D.N.Y. 1996) *39:* 55–56

Porter
—v. Chicago Bd. of Educ., 981 F. Supp. 1129 (N.D. Ill. 1997) *43:* 67
—v. City of Royal Oak, 542 N.W.2d 905, 11 IER 798 (Mich. Ct. App. 1995) *26:* 56

Post v. City of Lauderdale, 7 F.3d 1552 (11th Cir. 1993), *modified,* 14 F.3d 583 (11th Cir. 1994) *24:* 32

Pouncy v. Vulcan Materials Co., 920 F. Supp. 1566 (N.D. Ala. 1996) *16:* 27

Powell v. Stafford, 859 F. Supp. 1343, 65 FEP 1275 (D. Colo. 1994) *16:* 26

Powell-Ross v. All Star Radio, Inc., 68 FEP 1148 (E.D. Pa. 1995) *30:* 45, 47

Pratt v. Prodata Inc., 885 P.2d 786, 9 IER 1509 (Utah 1994) *26:* 54

Prescott v. Independent Life & Accident Ins. Co., 878 F. Supp. 1545, 67 FEP 876 (M.D. Ala. 1995) *20:* 50

President v. Illinois Bell Tel. Co., 865 F. Supp. 1279, 3 AD 1218 (N.D. Ill. 1994) *22:* 15

Pressman v. Brigham Med. Group Found., Inc., 919 F. Supp. 516, 5 AD 609 (D. Mass. 1996) *18:* 12

Preston v. Virginia ex rel. New River Community College, 31 F.3d 203, 65 FEP 877 (4th Cir. 1994) *41:* 121

Prevo's Family Mkt., Inc.; EEOC v., 5 AD 1526 (W.D. Mich. 1996) *9:* 251

Price v. Marathon Cheese Corp., 119 F.3d 330, 7 AD 138 (5th Cir. 1997) *9:* 42

Price Waterhouse v. Hopkins, 490 U.S. 228, 49 FEP 954 (1989) *42:* 12

Prince Georges County v. Alexander, *see* Alexander v. Estepp

Pritzker v. Merrill Lynch, Pierce, Fenner & Smith, Inc., 7 F.3d 1110, 17 EBC 1719 (3d Cir. 1993) *32:* 21

Pro v. Donatucci, 81 F.3d 1283 (3d Cir. 1996) *17:* 60

Prudential Ins. Co. of Am. v. Lai, 42 F.3d 1299, 66 FEP 933 (9th Cir. 1994), *cert. denied,* 116 S. Ct. 61 (1995) *32:* 32, 34–35

Pryner v. Tractor Supply Co., 927 F. Supp. 1140, 72 FEP 1235 (S.D. Ind. 1996), *aff'd,* 109 F.3d 354, 72 FEP 1235 (7th Cir.), *aff'd,* 109 F.3d 354, 73 FEP 615 (7th Cir. 1997), *petition for cert. filed,* 65 U.S.L.W. 3783 (U.S. May 6, 1997) *9:* 298; *32:* 27

Puentes v. United Parcel Serv., 86 F.3d 196, 71 FEP 106 (11th Cir. 1996) *43:* 6

Pulla v. Amoco Oil Co., 72 F.3d 648, 11 IER 432 (8th Cir. 1995) *26:* 11

Q

Quad/Graphics, Inc.; EEOC v., 63 F.3d 642, 68 FEP 1085 (7th Cir. 1995) *29:* 16–19, 22, 27–28, 31; *30:* 5

Quansah v. IBM Corp., 70 FEP 1531 (N.D. Cal. 1996) *17:* 41

Quaratino v. Tiffany & Co., 71 F.3d 58, 69 FEP 507 (2d Cir. 1995) *13:* 28

Quinn v. Jewel Food Stores, 658 N.E.2d 1225, 11 IER 380 (Ill. Ct. App. 1995) *26:* 37, 42

Quinones v. City of Evanston, 58 F.3d 275, 69 FEP 791 (7th Cir. 1995) *16:* 38, 191–92; *41:* 136

Quiron v. L.N. Violette Co., 897 F. Supp. 18, 4 AD 1852 (D. Me. 1995) *16:* 27

R

Rabinovitz v. Pena, 905 F. Supp. 522, 73 FEP 400 (N.D. Ill. 1995), *aff'd,* 89 F.3d 482, 73 FEP 410 (7th Cir. 1996) *19:* 20

Raczak v. Ameritech Corp., 1994 WL 780899 (E.D. Mich. Aug. 1, 1994), *rev'd,* 103 F.3d 1257, 72 FEP 1357 (6th Cir. 1997), *cert. denied,* 118 S. Ct. 1033 (1998) *16:* 197; *43:* 44–46

Rafferty v. City of Youngstown, 54 F.3d 278, 67 FEP 1564 (6th Cir.), *cert. denied,* 516 U.S. 931 (1995) *27:* 170

Ragge v. MCA/Universal Studios, 165 F.R.D. 601 (C.D. Cal. 1995) *38:* 34–35

Raia v. Village of Skokie, 1995 WL 642828 (N.D. Ill. Oct. 31, 1995) *16:* 148

Raimondo v. AMAX, Inc., 843 F. Supp. 806 (D. Conn. 1994) *40:* 50

Rains v. Criterion Sys., Inc., 80 F.3d 339, 70 FEP 635 (9th Cir. 1996) *26:* 1

Ramirez v. Oklahoma Dep't of Mental Health, 41 F.3d 584 (10th Cir. 1994) *17:* 69

Rand v. CF Indus., Inc., 42 F.3d 1139, 66 FEP 1114 (7th Cir. 1994) *16:* 169

Randall's Food Mkts., Inc. v. Johnson, 891 S.W.2d 640, 10 IER 427 (Tex. 1995) *26:* 44

Randle v. City of Aurora, 69 F.3d 441, 69 FEP 489 (10th Cir. 1995) *2:* 33; *11:* 1, 11; *19:* 8, 11; *24:* 27–28

Raney v. District of Columbia, 892 F. Supp. 283, 68 FEP 1620 (D.D.C. 1995) *20:* 51

Rao
—v. Kenya Airways, Ltd., 73 FEP 1633 (S.D.N.Y 1995) *16:* 24
—v. New York City Health & Hosps. Corp., 882 F. Supp. 321, 67 FEP 1234 (S.D.N.Y. 1995) *41:* 26, 80

Rash v. Hilb, Rogal & Hamilton Co. of Richmond, 467 S.E.2d 791, 11 IER 789 (Va. 1996) *26:* 51

Rasimas v. Michigan Dep't of Mental Health, 714 F.2d 614, 32 FEP 688 (6th Cir. 1983), *cert. denied,* 466 U.S. 950 (1984) *16:* 212

Rauenhorst v. United States Dep't of Transp., 95 F.3d 715, 5 AD 1621 (8th Cir. 1996) *9:* 1

Rawlins v. Diamond M-Odeco Co., 1995 WL 110631 (E.D. La. Mar. 13, 1995) *16:* 131

Ray
—v. Glidden Co., 85 F.3d 227, 5 AD 991 (5th Cir. 1996) *9:* 42
—v. Iuka Special Mun. Separate Sch. Dist., 51 F.3d 1246, 67 FEP 1348 (5th Cir. 1995) *16:* 211; *40:* 22, 24; *41:* 82
—v. Tandem Computers, Inc., 63 F.3d 429, 68 FEP 1338 (5th Cir. 1995) *17:* 46; *20:* 30–32, 79

Rayha v. United Parcel Serv., Inc., 940 F. Supp. 1066 (S.D. Tex. 1996) *9:* 133, 144, 206

Redman v. Lima City Sch. Dist. Bd. of Educ., 889 F. Supp. 288, 67 FEP 806 (N.D. Ohio 1995) *20:* 69

Reed
—v. A.W. Lawrence & Co., 95 F.3d 1170, 72 FEP 1345 (2d Cir. 1996) *30:* 8; *40:* 37, 41, 48
—v. EEOC, 1996 U.S. App. LEXIS 29032 (6th Cir. 1996), *cert. denied,* 117 S. Ct. 1564 (1997) *34:* 8
—v. R.C. Johnson, 1995 WL 684882, 1995 U.S. Dist. LEXIS 17221, 2 WH2d 1789 (E.D. La. 1995) *15:* 2
—v. Rhodes, 934 F. Supp. 1492 (N.D. Ohio 1996) *42:* 47

Regan v. In the Heat of the Nite, Inc., 68 FEP 1463 (S.D.N.Y. 1995) *16:* 17; *30:* 55

Regency Architectural Metals Corp.; EEOC v., 896 F. Supp. 260 (D. Conn. 1995) *17:* 40; *29:* 47; *41:* 33

Regency Windsor Management Co.; EEOC v., 862 F. Supp 189, 65 FEP 1777 (W.D. Mich. 1994) *16:* 130, 167; *34:* 33–34; *39:* 28

Regents of the Univ. of Cal. v. Doe, 117 S. Ct. 900 (1997) *24:* 30

Reich
—v. Circle C. Invs., Inc., 998 F.2d 324 (5th Cir. 1993) *15:* 1–2
—v. Hercules, Inc., 857 F. Supp. 367 (D.N.J. 1994) *38:* 31

Reichman v. Bonsignore, Brignati & Mazzotta P.C., 818 F.2d 278, 43 FEP 1384 (2d Cir. 1987) *16:* 238

Reid v. Kraft Gen. Foods, Inc., 67 FEP 1367 (E.D. Pa. 1995) *8:* 15, 20, 35

Reiff v. Interim Personnel, Inc., 906 F. Supp. 1280, 5 AD 740 (D. Minn. 1995) *2:* 56

Reigel v. Kaiser Found. Health Plan, 859 F. Supp. 963, 3 AD 577 (E.D.N.C. 1994) *32:* 18; *38:* 21

Reilly v. Metro-North Commuter R.R., 1995 WL 105286 (S.D.N.Y. Mar. 13, 1995) *38:* 31

Remlinger v. Nevada, 896 F. Supp 1012 (D. Nev. 1995) *40:* 92–93, 97

Reno v. Doe, *see* Doe v. Attorney Gen.

Reynolds
—v. Octel Communications Corp., 924 F. Supp. 743, 71 FEP 1053 (N.D. Tex. 1995) *16:* 231; *40:* 44; *41:* 81, 88
—v. Ozark Motor Lines Inc., 887 S.W.2d 822, 10 IER 100 (Tenn. 1994) *26:* 25
—v. School Dist. No. 1, Denver, Colo., 69 F.3d 1523, 72 FEP 485 (10th Cir. 1995) *19:* 16; *24:* 16, 18; *27:* 9, 12–13, 18, 33–34, 39

Rhodes
—v. Bob Florence Contractor, 890 F. Supp. 960, 4 AD 1201 (D. Kan. 1995) *9:* 126
—v. Guiberson Oil Tools
——75 F.3d 989, 69 FEP 1720 (5th Cir. 1996) *2:* 39; *16:* 115, 118
——82 F.3d 615, 71 FEP 83 (5th Cir. 1996) *16:* 212, 217, 244; *41:* 22, 73–75

Rhone-Poulenc Rorer, Inc., In re, 51 F.3d 1292 (7th Cir.), *cert. denied,* 116 S. Ct. 184 (1995) *37:* 7, 96, 98, 119

Riblett v. Boeing Co., 4 AD 1679 (D. Kan. 1995) *9:* 174

Richardson
—v. Leeds Police Dep't, 71 F.3d 801, 69 FEP 795 (11th Cir. 1995) *24:* 56
—v. McKnight, 117 S. Ct. 2100 (1997) *24:* 24–25
—v. William Powell Co., 3 AD 1751 (S.D. Ohio 1994) *16:* 98, 120

Richenberg v. Perry, 97 F.3d 256 (8th Cir. 1996), *cert. denied,* 118 S. Ct. 45 (1997) *14:* 19, 24

Richmond, City of, v. J.A. Croson Co., 488 U.S. 469, 53 FEP 197 (1989) *27:* 41

Ricks v. Xerox Corp., 877 F. Supp. 1468, 4 AD 233 (D. Kan. 1995), *aff'd mem.,* 96 F.3d 1453 (10th Cir. 1996) *9:* 148, 166

Ricky v. Mapco, Inc., 50 F.3d 874, 68 FEP 1745 (10th Cir. 1995) *16:* 215

Riel v. Electronic Data Sys. Corp., 99 F.3d 678, 6 AD 26 (5th Cir. 1996) *9:* 136

Riess v. Dalton, 845 F. Supp. 742, 72 FEP 577 (S.D. Cal. 1993) *41:* 128, 130

Rifkinson v. CBS, Inc., 69 FEP 8 (S.D.N.Y. 1995) *16:* 27

Riley
—v. American Family Mut. Ins. Co., 881 F.2d 368, 50 FEP 668 (7th Cir. 1989) *43:* 5
—v. Technical & Management Servs. Corp., 872 F. Supp. 1454, 66 FEP 1643 (D. Md. 1995), *aff'd,* 79 F.3d 1411, 70 FEP 832 (4th Cir. 1996) *21:* 22, 26; *33:* 38–39
—v. Weyerhaeuser Paper Co., 898 F. Supp. 324, 5 AD 325 (W.D.N.C. 1995), *aff'd in part and dismissed in part,* 77 F.3d 470 (4th Cir. 1996) *9:* 135–36, 140–41, 144, 148

Rinck v. Association of Reserve City Bankers, 676 A.2d 12, 11 IER 1285 (D.C. Ct. App. 1996) *26:* 7

Ripberger v. Western Ohio Pizza, Inc., 908 F. Supp. 614 (S.D. Ind. 1995) *20:* 69

Rittmeyer v. Advance Bancorp, Inc., 868 F. Supp. 1017, 68 FEP 1283 (N.D. Ill. 1994) *16:* 17

Riva v. Commonwealth of Massachusetts, 871 F. Supp. 1511, 66 FEP 1142 (D. Mass. 1994), *aff'd in part, rev'd in part,* 61 F.3d 1003, 68 FEP 688 (1st Cir. 1995) *16:* 195, 207; *31:* 7–8

Rivera v. Puerto Rican Home Attendants Servs., Inc., 922 F. Supp. 943 (S.D.N.Y. 1996) *33:* 33, 40

Rivera-Flores v. Bristol-Myers Squibb Caribbean, 112 F.3d 9 (1st Cir. 1997) *43:* 1, 6

River Oaks Imaging & Diagnostic; EEOC v., 67 FEP 1243 (S.D. Tex. 1995) *32:* 32; *34:* 49

Rivers
—v. Northwest Airlines, Inc., 71 FEP 1217 (E.D. Mo.), *aff'd,* 72 F.3d 133, 72 FEP 1280 (8th Cir. 1995) *21:* 24
—v. Roadway Express, Inc., 511 U.S. 298, 64 FEP 842 (1994) *17:* 53; *24:* 1

Rizzo v. Children's World Learning Ctrs., Inc., 84 F.3d 758, 5 AD 1155 (5th Cir. 1996) *9:* 70, 241, 243, 248, 272, 290

Roberson
—v. Bowie State Univ., 899 F. Supp. 235, 72 FEP 899 (D. Md. 1995) *24:* 10, 47; *31:* 40
—v. Mullins, 876 F. Supp. 100 (W.D. Va. 1995) *41:* 33, 68

Roberts
—v. County of Fairfax, 937 F. Supp. 541 (E.D. Va. 1996) *9:* 188, 197, 208
—v. Hit or Miss Inc., 11 IER 54 (N.D. Cal. 1995) *26:* 23, 49

Robertson v. Alabama Dep't of Econ. & Community Affairs, 902 F. Supp. 1473 (M.D. Ala. 1995), *appeal dismissed mem.,* 89 F.3d 855 (11th Cir. 1996) *17:* 6

Robidoux v. Celani, 987 F.2d 931 (2d Cir. 1993) *37:* 47

Robins v. Max Mara, U.S.A., Inc.
—914 F. Supp. 1006, 72 FEP 331 (S.D.N.Y. 1996) *16:* 19
—923 F. Supp. 460, 72 FEP 335 (S.D.N.Y. 1996) *11:* 32

Robinson
—v. Neodata Servs., Inc., 94 F.3d 499, 5 AD 1441 (8th Cir. 1996) *9:* 61
—v. PPG Indus., Inc., 23 F.3d 1159, 64 FEP 1690 (7th Cir. 1994) *2:* 56
—v. Shell Oil Co., 117 S. Ct. 843, 72 FEP 1856 (1997) *9:* 112; *16:* 43; *17:* 1; *30:* 1, 24
Robison-Fisher v. Township of Elgin, 1996 U.S. Dist. LEXIS 7645 (N.D. Ill. May 20, 1996) *9:* 161
Roby v. United States Dep't of Navy, 76 F.3d 1052 (9th Cir. 1996) *8:* 1
Rocky Mountain Hosp. & Med. Serv. v. Mariani, 916 P.2d 519, 11 IER 1153 (Colo. 1996) *26:* 23
Rodger v. Electric Data Sys. Corp.
—155 F.R.D. 537, 2 WH2d 1436 (E.D.N.C. 1994) *38:* 1, 3, 5
—160 F.R.D. 532 (E.D.N.C. 1995) *37:* 43
Rodgers
—v. Federal Express Corp., 1996 U.S. App. LEXIS 8241 (6th Cir. Mar. 13, 1996) *9:* 267
—v. Horsley, 39 F.3d 308 (11th Cir. 1994) *24:* 32
Rodriguez
—v. Carlson, 166 F.R.D. 465 (E.D. Wash. 1996) *37:* 48
—v. City of Chicago, 69 FEP 993 (N.D. Ill. 1996) *8:* 7
—EEOC v., 66 FEP 1649 (E.D. Cal. 1994) *7:* 2; *39:* 40
Roe v. Cheyenne Mountain Conference Resort, 920 F. Supp. 1153, 5 AD 258 (D. Colo. 1996) *9:* 89
Roemer v. Public Serv. Co. of Colo., 911 F. Supp. 464, 69 FEP 1582 (D. Colo. 1996) *16:* 128, 135; *27:* 28, 34
Roepsch v. Bentsen, 846 F. Supp. 1363 (E.D. Wis. 1994) *42:* 20
Rogers
—v. American Airlines, 527 F. Supp. 229, 231-33 (S.D.N.Y. 1981) *23:* 8
—v. Atwork Corp., 863 F. Supp. 242, 66 FEP 391 (E.D. Pa. 1994) *16:* 27
—v. International Marine Terminal, 4 AD 304 (E.D. La. 1995), *aff'd*, 87 F.3d 755, 5 AD 1115 (5th Cir. 1996) *9:* 122, 161, 175
Rogic v. Mallinckrodt Med., Inc., 917 F. Supp. 671 (E.D. Mo. 1996) *16:* 157
Rojas v. TK Communications, Inc., 87 F.3d 745, 71 FEP 664 (5th Cir. 1996) *32:* 22
Rollison v. Gwinnett County, 865 F. Supp. 1564, 7 AD 1355 (N.D. Ga. 1994) *21:* 19
Romer v. Evans, 517 U.S. 620, 70 FEP 1180 (1996) *14:* 6-7, 11-12
Rooks v. Girl Scouts of Chicago, 69 FEP 329 (N.D. Ill. 1995) *19:* 16
Roper v. Peabody Coal Co., 47 F.3d 925, 67 FEP 670 (7th Cir. 1995) *16:* 103
Rosa v. Southwest Community Health Servs., 10 IER 1564 (N.M. 1994) *26:* 14
Rosado v. Virginia Commonwealth Univ., 927 F. Supp. 917 (E.D. Va. 1996) *19:* 25, 27
Rosamond v. Pennaco Hosiery, Inc., 942 F. Supp. 279 (N.D. Miss. 1996) *9:* 136
Rose v. Ireco, Inc., 872 F. Supp. 1127, 73 FEP 429 (N.D.N.Y. 1994) *16:* 222
Rosen
—v. Columbia Univ., 68 FEP 1190 (S.D.N.Y. 1995), *aff'd mem.*, 101 F.3d 108 (2d Cir. 1996) *16:* 108
—v. Reckitt & Colman, Inc., 1994 U.S. Dist. LEXIS 16511 (S.D.N.Y. Nov. 10, 1994) *37:* 103
Ross v. Times Mirror Inc., 665 A.2d 580, 68 FEP 1756 (Vt. 1995) *26:* 7
Roth v. Lutheran Gen. Hosp., 57 F.3d 1446, 4 AD 936 (7th Cir. 1995) *9:* 4
Rothmeier v. Investment Advisers, Inc., 85 F.3d 1328, 71 FEP 1458 (8th Cir. 1996) *2:* 42-43; *16:* 118, 127, 170, 181; *33:* 50
Roush v. KFC Nat'l Management Co., 10 F.3d 392, 63 FEP 609 (6th Cir. 1993), *cert. denied*, 513 U.S. 808 (1994) *2:* 21
Roxas v. Presentation College, 90 F.3d 310, 71 FEP 609 (8th Cir. 1996) *11:* 1

Roy v. Runyon, 954 F. Supp. 368 (D. Me. 1997) **9:** 308

Rozar v. Mullis, 85 F.3d 556 (11th Cir. 1996) ***24:*** 54

Rucker v. City of Philadelphia, 4 AD 1443 (E.D. Pa. 1995), *aff'd mem.,* 85 F.3d 612 (3d Cir. 1996) **9:** 123, 142

Rudder v. District of Columbia, 890 F. Supp. 23 (D.D.C. 1995), *aff'd without opinion,* 99 F.3d 448 (D.C. Cir. 1996) ***5:*** 1, 16, 21, 25, 30, 50, 55, 79, 81; ***7:*** 6–7, 12, 15

Ruffino v. State St. Bank & Trust Co., 908 F. Supp. 1019, 71 FEP 109 (D. Mass. 1995) ***17:*** 31, 45; ***30:*** 61

Ruiz v. Symington, 1998 Ariz. LEXIS 34, 268 Ariz. Adv. Rep. 3 (Apr. 18, 1998) ***11:*** 27

Runnebaum v. NationsBank of Md., N.A., 123 F.3d 156, 7 AD 216 (4th Cir. 1997) ***2:*** 29; **9:** 32

Runyon v. Massachusetts Inst. of Tech., 871 F. Supp. 1502, 6 AD 233 (D. Mass. 1994) ***16:*** 143

Rupp v. Purolator Courier Corp., 45 F.3d 440 (unpublished opinion), 1994 WL 730892 (10th Cir. 1994) ***17:*** 28

Rush v. Scott Specialty Gases, Inc.
—914 F. Supp. 104, 70 FEP 34 (E.D. Pa. 1996), *rev'd in part,* 113 F.3d 476, 74 FEP 1745 (3d Cir. 1997) ***19:*** 9, 18; ***31:*** 12
—930 F. Supp. 194 (E.D. Pa. 1996) ***41:*** 103, 110, 112

Rushing v. United Airlines, 919 F. Supp. 1101, 70 FEP 815 (N.D. Ill. 1996) ***20:*** 15

Russell
—v. Acme-Evans Co., 881 F. Supp. 378 (S.D. Ind. 1994), *aff'd,* 51 F.3d 64, 67 FEP 589 (7th Cir. 1995) ***2:*** 31; ***19:*** 13
—v. Delco Remy Div. of Gen. Motors Corp., 51 F.3d 746, 67 FEP 673 (7th Cir. 1995) ***31:*** 2
—v. Microdyne Corp., 65 F.3d 1229, 68 FEP 1602 (4th Cir. 1995) ***41:*** 59, 62, 122

Rutland v. Moore, 54 F.3d 226, 67 FEP 1707 (5th Cir. 1995) ***16:*** 8; ***30:*** 22

Ryan
—v. City of Highland Heights, 4 AD 1389 (N.D. Ohio 1995) **9:** 72
—v. New York State Thruway Auth., 889 F. Supp. 70, 73 FEP 1525 (N.D.N.Y. 1995) ***31:*** 21; ***33:*** 2

Ryczek v. Guest Servs., Inc., 877 F. Supp. 754, 67 FEP 461 (D.D.C. 1995) ***31:*** 50

Ryder v. Westinghouse Elec. Corp., 879 F. Supp. 534 (W.D. Pa. 1995) ***16:*** 176, 215; ***41:*** 4, 57–58

Ryther v. Kare 11
—864 F. Supp. 1525, 70 FEP 1701 (D.C. Minn. 1994) ***42:*** 28, 41–43
—84 F.3d 1074, 70 FEP 1709 (8th Cir. 1996), *aff'd,* 108 F.3d 832, 73 FEP 373 (8th Cir.), *cert. denied,* 117 S. Ct. 2510 (1997) ***2:*** 43; ***16:*** 122, 165, 228, 230

S

Saari v. Smith Barney, Harris Upham & Co., 968 F.2d 877, 7 IER 929 (9th Cir.), *cert. denied,* 506 U.S. 986 (1992) ***32:*** 21

Sackett v. WPNT, Inc., 4 AD 1597 (W.D. Pa. 1995), *aff'd mem.,* 91 F.3d 125 (3d Cir. 1996) **9:** 273

Saeli v. Motorola, Inc., 917 F. Supp. 589 (N.D. Ill. 1996) ***16:*** 99

Sagendorf-Teal v. County of Rensselaer, 100 F.3d 270 (2d Cir. 1996) ***40:*** 49

Saladin v. Turner, 936 F. Supp. 1571 (N.D. Okla. 1996) ***33:*** 40; ***41:*** 33, 53

Salas v. Richardson Elecs. Ltd., 70 FEP 459 (N.D. Ill. 1996) ***17:*** 45

Salisbury v. Art Van Furniture, 938 F. Supp. 435 (W.D. Mich. 1996) ***32:*** 31

Salter v. Douglas MacArthur State Technical College, 929 F. Supp. 1470 (M.D. Ala.), *cert. denied,* 116 S. Ct. 338 (1996) ***40:*** 83

Sample v. Aldi, 61 F.3d 544, 68 FEP 759 (7th Cir. 1995) ***2:*** 31

San Benito, County of; EEOC v., 818 F. Supp. 289, 61 FEP 946 (N.D. Cal. 1993) ***29:*** 41

Sanchez
—v. City of Santa Ana, 928 F. Supp. 1494 (C.D. Cal. 1995), *order issued,* 1996 WL 364765 (C.D. Cal. Jan. 23, 1996) *3:* 1; *4:* 16; *5:* 30, 46; *39:* 14, 72, 74–75
—v. Puerto Rico Oil Co., 37 F.3d 712, 66 FEP 148 (1st Cir. 1994) *16:* 95, 235
—v. Zabihi, 166 F.R.D. 500, 71 FEP 835 (D.N.M. 1996) *38:* 22, 47, 49
Sanders
—v. Arneson Prods., Inc., 91 F.3d 1351, 5 AD 1292 (9th Cir. 1996), *cert. denied,* 117 S. Ct. 1247 (1997) *9:* 43
—v. Bethlehem Steel Corp., 68 FEP 695 (D.Md.1995), *aff'd,* 91 F.3d 133 (4th Cir. 1996) *22:* 15; *33:* 20
—v. Venture Stores, Inc., 56 F.3d 771, 75 FEP 637 (7th Cir. 1995) *31:* 47
Sandhu v. Commonwealth of Va., Dep't of Conserv. & Rec., 874 F. Supp. 122 (E.D. Va.), *aff'd,* 68 F.3d 461 (4th Cir. 1995) *11:* 3; *18:* 11
San Diego Bldg. Trades Council v. Garmon, 359 U.S. 236 (1959) *25:* 4
Sands v. Runyon, 28 F.3d 1323, 2 AD 660 (2d Cir. 1994) *40:* 53, 56–57
Sanfelice v. Dominick's Finer Foods, Inc., 899 F. Supp. 372, 69 FEP 170 (N.D. Ill. 1995) *20:* 60, 62
Sanford v. MeadowGold Dairies, Inc., 534 N.W.2d 410, 11 IER 249 (Iowa 1995) *26:* 2, 50
Sanjurjo v. New York Univ. Med. Ctr., 72 FEP 1 (S.D.N.Y. 1996), *aff'd,* 122 F.3d 1057 (2d Cir. 1997) *20:* 111
Sanner v. Board of Trade of City of Chicago, 62 F.3d 918 (7th Cir. 1995) *37:* 71
Santos v. Port Auth., 4 AD 1245 (S.D.N.Y. 1995) *9:* 58
Sara Lee Corp.; EEOC v., 923 F. Supp. 994, 70 FEP 57 (W.D. Mich. 1995) *16:* 64, 84, 197; *34:* 1, 17, 35
Sarin v. Raytheon Co., 905 F. Supp. 49, 69 FEP 856 (D. Mass. 1995) *8:* 45, 47; *20:* 4, 6
Sarsycki v. United Parcel Serv., 862 F. Supp. 336, 3 AD 1039 (W.D. Okla. 1994) *9:* 151

Sassaman v. Heart City Toyota, 879 F. Supp. 901, 66 FEP 1230 (N.D. Ind. 1994) *41:* 112
Satario v. A.G. Edwards & Sons, 941 F. Supp. 609 (N.D. Tex. 1996) *9:* 297
Saulpaugh v. Monroe Community Hosp., 4 F.3d 134, 62 FEP 1315 (2d Cir. 1993), *cert. denied,* 510 U.S. 1164 (1994) *24:* 39
Sawinski v. Bill Currie Ford, Inc., 881 F. Supp. 1571, 4 AD 462 (M.D. Fla. 1995) *9:* 185
Sayers v. Stewart Sleep Ctr., Inc., 932 F. Supp. 1415 (M.D. Fla. 1996) *42:* 61
Scales v. Sonic Indus., Inc., 887 F. Supp. 1435 (E.D. Okla. 1995) *33:* 16
Scarfo v. Cabletron Sys., Inc., 54 F.3d 931, 67 FEP 1474 (1st Cir. 1995) *40:* 37, 40, 47, 58; *41:* 21, 86
Scelsa v. City Univ. of N.Y., 827 F. Supp. 1073, 71 FEP 707 (S.D.N.Y. 1993) *42:* 19
Schaefer v. Tannian
—902 F. Supp. 746 (E.D. Mich 1995) *19:* 28
—164 F.R.D. 630 (E.D. Mich 1996) *37:* 56, 106–07
Schallehn v. Central Trust & Sav. Bank, 877 F. Supp. 1315, 69 FEP 1292 (N.D. Iowa 1995) *16:* 27, 165
Schmidt
—v. Methodist Hosp., 89 F.3d 342, 5 AD 1340 (7th Cir. 1996) *9:* 134, 136, 150, 202
—v. Safeway, Inc., 864 F. Supp. 991, 3 AD 1141 (D. Or. 1994) *9:* 157, 189
Schneider v. Continental Cas. Co., 1996 U.S. Dist. LEXIS 19631 (N.D. Ill. Dec. 16, 1996) *9:* 121, 127
Schnidrig v. Columbia Mach., Inc., 80 F.3d 1406, 71 FEP 1763 (9th Cir.), *cert. denied,* 117 S. Ct. 295 (1996) *2:* 45; *16:* 165; *19:* 10; *21:* 22; *41:* 57
Schofield v. Trustees of Univ. of Pa., 919 F. Supp. 821 (E.D. Pa. 1996) *24:* 68; *42:* 2, 24
School Bd. of Nassau Co. v. Arline, 480 U.S. 273 (1987) *9:* 7

Schrader
—v. E.G. & G., Inc., 953 F. Supp. 1160 (D. Colo. 1997) *20:* 12
—v. Eli Lilly & Co., 639 N.E.2d 258, 9 IER 1830 (Ind. 1994) *26:* 39, 42
Schultz v. Stillwater Mining Co., 920 P.2d 486, 11 IER 1726 (Mont. 1996) *26:* 24
Schuster v. New York State Unified Court Sys., 67 FEP 1758 (S.D.N.Y. 1995) *20:* 37
Schutz v. Finkelstein, Bruckman, Wohl, Most & Rothman, 66 FEP 1094 (S.D.N.Y. 1994) *16:* 99
Schwartz v. Gregori, 45 F.3d 1017 (6th Cir.), *cert. denied,* 116 S. Ct. 77 (1995) *40:* 38, 48
Schwarz v. Northwest Iowa Community College, 881 F. Supp. 1323, 4 AD 490 (N.D. Iowa 1995) *16:* 115; *21:* 23
Schwed v. General Elec. Co., 159 F.R.D. 373 (N.D.N.Y. 1995) *16:* 81
Sciarrino v. Municipal Credit Union, 894 F. Supp. 102, 73 FEP 661 (E.D.N.Y. 1995) *24:* 3, 14, 31
Scott
—v. Pacific Gas & Elec. Co., 11 Cal. 4th 454, 904 P.2d 834 (1995) *26:* 8–9
—v. University of Miss. Law Sch., No. 1:94-CV-241 (N.D. Miss. May 16, 1996), *appeal pending,* No. 96-60385 (5th Cir.) *16:* 35
Sears, Roebuck & Co.; EEOC v., 857 F. Supp. 1233, 65 FEP 479 (N.D. Ill. 1994), *modified,* 883 F. Supp. 211, 70 FEP 175 (N.D. Ill. 1995) *16:* 139, 185, 193, 197, 206; *30:* 34
Secrist v. Burns Int'l Sec. Servs., 926 F. Supp. 823, 71 FEP 162 (E.D. Wis. 1996) *16:* 78; *33:* 11, 28, 37
Segall v. Megerson, Civ. No. A-96-CA-413-JN (W.D. Tex. Feb. 28, 1997) *16:* 35
Selgas v. American Airlines, Inc., 858 F. Supp. 316, 69 FEP 655 (D.P.R. 1994), *aff'd in part, vacated in part,* 69 F.3d 1205, 69 FEP 944 (1st Cir. 1995) *41:* 70; *42:* 39
Selland v. Perry, 100 F.3d 950 (4th Cir.), *cert. denied,* 117 S. Ct.1691 (1996) *14:* 24
Seminole Tribe v. Florida, 517 U.S. 44 (1996) *9:* 16–17; *16:* 32–33
Sempier v. Johnson & Higgins, 45 F.3d 724, 66 FEP 1214 (3d Cir.), *cert. denied,* 115 S. Ct. 2611, 68 FEP 64 (1995) *38:* 1
Sena v. Denver Sch. Dist. No. 1, 902 F. Supp. 218, 69 FEP 385 (D. Colo. 1995) *33:* 55; *41:* 119
Serben v. Inter-City Mfg. Co., 36 F.3d 765, 65 FEP 1706 (8th Cir. 1994), *cert. denied,* 514 U.S. 1037 (1995) *16:* 170, 179, 184
Sever v. Alaska Pulp Corp., 978 F.2d 1529, 141 LRRM 2678 (9th Cir. 1992) *24:* 52
Sewell Mfg. Co., 138 NLRB 66, 51 LRRM 1611 (1962) *25:* 1
Shabat v. Blue Cross Blue Shield, 925 F. Supp. 977, 76 FEP 363 (W.D.N.Y. 1996), *aff'd,* 108 F.3d 1370 (2d Cir. 1997) *8:* 42–43; *10:* 5
Shahar v. Bowers, 114 F.3d 1097 (11th Cir. 1997), *cert. denied,* 118 S. Ct. 693 (1998) *14:* 14
Shane v. The Tokai Bank, Ltd., 1997 U.S. Dist. LEXIS 16000 (S.D.N.Y. 1997) *11:* 32
Shannon
—v. Ford Motor Co., 72 F.3d 678, 69 FEP 1339 (8th Cir. 1996) *19:* 27
—v. Saks & Co., 66 EPD ¶ 43,591 (N.D. Ill. 1995) *16:* 108
Shapiro v. William Douglas McAdams, Inc., 68 FEP 199 (E.D.N.Y. 1995) *16:* 57, 83
Sharkey v. Lasmo (Aul Ltd.), 906 F. Supp. 949, 70 FEP 1673 (S.D.N.Y. 1995) *16:* 78; *33:* 21, 33
Shattuck v. Kinetic Concepts, Inc., 49 F.3d 1106, 67 FEP 798 (5th Cir. 1995) *16:* 226; *41:* 63
Shaw v. Mellon Bank, N.A., 69 FEP 550 (W.D. Pa. 1995) *20:* 62, 69
Shea v. Icelandair, 925 F. Supp. 1014, 70 FEP 1544 (S.D.N.Y. 1996) *16:* 210; *40:* 20, 24, 31; *41:* 80–81, 100

Table of Cases

Sheet Metal Workers Local 638...Local 28; EEOC v., 889 F. Supp. 642 (S.D.N.Y. 1995), *modified*, 921 F. Supp. 1126 (S.D.N.Y.), *aff'd in part and rev'd in part*, 81 F.3d 1162 (2d Cir.), *cert. denied*, 117 S. Ct. 333 (1996) *34:* 57–58; *40:* 70–72

Shell Oil Co.; EEOC v., 466 U.S. 54, 34 FEP 709 (1984) *29:* 15

Shelton v. Pargo, Inc., 582 F.2d 1298 (4th Cir. 1978) *37:* 88

Shenker v. Lockheed Sanders, Inc., 919 F. Supp. 55 (D. Mass. 1996) *16:* 148, 156, 166

Shepherd v. American Broad. Cos., 862 F. Supp. 486 (D.D.C. 1994), *vacated*, 62 F.3d 1469 (D.C. Cir. 1995) *40:* 4, 6

Shepherdson v. Local 401, 823 F. Supp. 1245, 66 FEP 476 (E.D. Pa. 1993) *22:* 5, 23

Sheppard
—v. Consolidated Edison Co., 893 F. Supp. 6 (E.D.N.Y. 1995) *38:* 32
—v. Riverview Nursing Ctr., Inc., 88 F.3d 1332, 71 FEP 218 (4th Cir.), *cert. denied*, 117 S. Ct. 483, 72 FEP 992 (1996) *42:* 17–18; *43:* 63, 65–66

Sheridan v. E.I. DuPont de Nemours & Co., 100 F.3d 1061, 72 FEP 518 (3d Cir. 1996), *cert. denied*, 117 S. Ct. 2532 (1997) *2:* 28; *30:* 61

Sherlock v. Montefiore Med. Ctr., 84 F.3d 522, 70 FEP 1377 (2d Cir. 1996) *16:* 74; *24:* 21, 23, 53, 67; *31:* 39

Shinholster v. Georgia Farm Bureau Mut. Ins. Co., 898 F. Supp. 913, 69 FEP 91 (M.D. Ga. 1995) *19:* 13

Shipley v. Dugan, 874 F. Supp. 933 (S.D. Ind. 1995) *41:* 143

Shiring v. Runyon, 90 F.3d 827, 5 AD 1216 (3d Cir. 1996) *9:* 124, 133, 148, 188, 209

Shirkey v. Eastwind Community Dev't Corp., 941 F. Supp. 567 (D. Md. 1996) *8:* 51

Shoen v. Amerco Inc., 896 P.2d 469, 10 IER 1082 (Nev. 1995) *26:* 22, 55

Shoney's, Inc.; EEOC v., 1994 U.S. App. LEXIS 16876 (6th Cir. July 5, 1994) *34:* 62

Shore v. A.W. Hargrove Ins. Agency, Inc., 873 F. Supp. 992 (E.D. Va. 1995) *18:* 11

Shores
—v. Publix Super Mkts., Inc., 1996 U.S. Dist. LEXIS 3381 (M.D. Fla. Mar. 12, 1996) *37:* 29, 56
—v. Sklar, 885 F.2d 760 (11th Cir. 1989), *cert. denied*, 493 U.S. 1045 (1990) *37:* 121

Shpargel v. Stage & Co., 914 F. Supp. 1468, 5 AD 1558 (E.D. Mich. 1996) *8:* 4–5, 20, 31; *41:* 35, 41

Shuford v. Alabama State Bd. of Educ., 897 F. Supp. 1535 (M.D. Ala. 1995) *27:* 90–97, 120–23; *37:* 112–13, 115–16, 118; *40:* 67, 79

Sibley Memorial Hosp. v. Wilson, 488 F.2d 1338, 6 FEP 1029 (D.C. Cir. 1973) *5:* 5; *30:* 20

Sieberns v. Wal-Mart Stores, Inc., 946 F. Supp. 664, 6 AD 403 (N.D. Ind. 1996) *9:* 188

Siefken v. Village of Arlington Heights, 3 AD 1281 (N.D. Ill. 1994), *aff'd*, 65 F.3d 664, 4 AD 1441 (7th Cir. 1995) *9:* 173, 183, 192

Siemon v. AT & T Corp., 117 F.3d 1173 (10th Cir. 1997) *9:* 47

Sigmon v. Parker Chapin Flattau & Klimpl, 901 F. Supp. 667, 69 FEP 69 (S.D.N.Y. 1995) *15:* 19

Simmerman v. Hardee's Food Sys., Inc., 1996 U.S. Dist. LEXIS 3437 (E.D. Va. Mar. 22, 1996) *9:* 142, 209

Simon
—v. City of Youngstown, 73 F.3d 68 (6th Cir. 1995) *19:* 27; *39:* 42
—v. Morehouse Sch. of Med., 908 F. Supp. 959 (N.D. Ga. 1995) *20:* 66, 69; *21:* 14

Simonelli v. Anderson Concrete Co., 650 N.E.2d 488, 11 IER 236 (Ohio Ct. App. 1994) *26:* 11, 18, 23–24, 33

Simpkins v. Specialty Envelope, Inc., 1996 U.S. App. LEXIS 22327 (6th Cir. Aug. 9, 1996) *9:* 187

Simpson
—v. Ernst & Young, 100 F.3d 436, 72 FEP 343 (6th Cir. 1996), *cert. denied*, 117 S. Ct. 1862 (1997) *30:* 19; *40:* 26, 39; *41:* 21
—v. Texas Dep't of Criminal Justice, 975 F. Supp. 921 (W.D. Tex. 1997) *16:* 35

Sims
—v. Brown & Root Indus. Servs., Inc., 889 F. Supp. 920, 70 FEP 501 (W.D. La. 1995), *aff'd without opinion*, 78 F.3d 581 (5th Cir.), *cert. denied*, 117 S. Ct. 68 (1996) *20:* 41; *21:* 28
—v. Montgomery County Comm'n
——873 F. Supp. 585 (M.D. Ala. 1994) *19:* 26; *39:* 39, 53–54
——890 F. Supp. 1520 (M.D. Ala. 1995), *aff'd without opinion*, 119 F.3d 9 (11th Cir. 1997) *5:* 16, 23, 70–71, 78; *27:* 70–73, 171–72; *40:* 79

Singh v. Shoney's, Inc., 64 F.3d 217, 68 FEP 1288 (5th Cir. 1995) *24:* 56; *27:* 18

Sink v. Knox County Hosp., 900 F. Supp. 1065, 70 FEP 1560 (S.D. Ind. 1995) *17:* 22; *20:* 61, 67, 69

Sirvidas v. Commonwealth Edison Co., 60 F.3d 375, 68 FEP 602 (7th Cir. 1995) *16:* 125

Slathar v. Sather Trucking Corp., 78 F.3d 415, 70 FEP 574 (8th Cir.), *cert denied*, 117 S. Ct. 179 (1996) *16:* 119, 167, 182

Smallwood v. Witco Corp., 1995 U.S. Dist. LEXIS 18106 (S.D.N.Y. Dec. 4, 1995) *9:* 121

Smart v. Ball State Univ., 89 F.3d 437, 71 FEP 495 (7th Cir. 1996) *17:* 31

Smith
—v. Blue Cross Blue Shield, 894 F. Supp. 1463, 4 AD 1378 (D. Kan. 1995), *aff'd*, 102 F.3d 1075, 6 AD 367 (10th Cir. 1996), *petition for cert. filed*, 65 U.S.L.W. 3783 (U.S. May 6, 1997) *9:* 123–24, 134, 161, 175
—v. City of Des Moines, 99 F.3d 1466, 6 AD 14 (8th Cir. 1996) *4:* 52–54
—v. Cook County, 869 F. Supp. 547, 72 FEP 155 (N.D. Ill. 1994), *aff'd*, 74 F.3d 829, 72 FEP 158 (7th Cir. 1996) *16:* 120, 152
—v. Douglas Cable Communications, 881 F. Supp. 1510 (D. Kan. 1995) *19:* 4, 12
—v. Dovenmuhle Mortgage, Inc., 859 F. Supp. 1138, 4 AD 132 (N.D. Ill. 1994) *32:* 18
—v. Fruin, 28 F.3d 646 (7th Cir. 1994), *cert. denied*, 513 U.S. 1083 (1995) *17:* 65–66
—v. F.W. Morse & Co., 76 F.3d 413, 69 FEP 1687 (1st Cir. 1996) *2:* 55; *13:* 28; *16:* 142; *41:* 121
— v. Kitterman, Inc., 897 F. Supp. 423, 4 AD 1487 (W.D. Mo. 1995) *9:* 125, 167
—v. Lomax, 45 F.3d 402, 67 FEP 1005 (11th Cir. 1995) *24:* 36
—v. Midland Brake, Inc., 1998 WL 110011 (10th Cir. Mar. 13, 1998) *9:* 134
—v. New York City Bd. of Educ., 918 F. Supp. 120 (S.D.N.Y. 1996) *24:* 3
—v. Office of Personnel Management, 778 F.2d 258, 39 FEP 1851 (5th Cir. 1985) *16:* 233
—v. Sheet Metal Workers Local 28, 877 F. Supp. 165, 148 LRRM 2856 (S.D.N.Y. 1995), *aff'd*, 100 F.3d 943, 152 LRRM 2384 (2d Cir.), *cert. denied*, 117 S. Ct. 101 (1996) *22:* 12; *33:* 19, 33
—v. St. Louis Univ., 109 F.3d 1261, 74 FEP 459 (8th Cir. 1997) *20:* 95–97
—v. Troy Moose Lodge, 645 N.E.2d 1352, 10 IER 845 (Ohio Ct. App. 1994) *26:* 24
—v. Virginia Commonwealth Univ., 84 F.3d 672, 70 FEP 1248 (4th Cir. 1996) *27:* 105–06, 108–09; *39:* 17–19, 32, 64
—v. World Ins. Co., 38 F.3d 1456, 66 FEP 13 (8th Cir. 1994) *16:* 185–86, 212, 214; *21:* 21; *40:* 37, 45; *41:* 38, 73–74

Smuck v. National Management Corp., 540 N.W.2d 669, 11 IER 33 (Iowa Ct. App. 1995) *26:* 1, 155

Snell v. Reno Hilton Resort, 930 F. Supp. 1428 (D. Nev. 1996) *42:* 17, 40, 42

Snyder v. Murray City Corp., 902 F. Supp. 1444, *amended by,* 902 F. Supp. 1455 (D. Utah 1995) *8:* 2

Soileau v. Guilford of Me., Inc., 105 F.3d 12, 6 AD 437 (1st Cir. 1997) *9:* 48

Soliman v. Digital Equip. Corp., 869 F. Supp. 65, 67 FEP 1259 (D. Mass. 1994) *16:* 202

Sondel v. Northwest Airlines, Inc., 56 F.3d 934 (8th Cir. 1995) *32:* 1, 16–17

Soto
—v. Adams Elevator Equip. Co., 941 F.2d 543, 56 FEP 1270 (7th Cir. 1991) *15:* 28
—v. City of Concord, 162 F.R.D. 603 (N.D. Cal. 1995) *38:* 33

Southwest Gas Corp. v. Vargas, 901 P.2d 693, 11 IER 228 (Nev. 1995) *26:* 13–14

Spath v. Berry Plastics Corp., 900 F. Supp. 893, 4 AD 1811 (N.D. Ohio 1995) *9:* 128

Special Educ. Servs. v. RREEF Performance Partnership-I, LP, 1996 U.S. Dist. LEXIS 9698 (N.D. Ill. July 10, 1996) *9:* 299, 301, 305

Speen v. Crown Clothing Corp., 102 F.3d 625, 73 FEP 347 (1st Cir. 1996), *cert. denied,* 117 S. Ct. 2457 (1997) *39:* 64

Spence v. Straw, 54 F.3d 196, 4 AD 528 (3d Cir. 1995) *9:* 315

Sperling v. Hoffman-La Roche, Inc.
—24 F.3d 463, 64 FEP 910 (3d Cir. 1994) *16:* 87
—924 F. Supp. 1346, 72 FEP 1401 (D.N.J. 1996) *16:* 158, 164; *37:* 94; *38:* 23; *39:* 77

Spicer v. Virginia, 66 F.3d 705, 69 FEP 1255 (4th Cir. 1995) *20:* 105

Spiers v. McNeil Real Estate Management, Inc., 65 FEP 1446 (D. Kan. 1994) *15:* 6; *19:* 15

Spira v. Ethical Culture Sch., 888 F. Supp. 601, 68 FEP 202 (S.D.N.Y. 1995) *33:* 7

Spradley v. Notami Hosps. of Fla., Inc., 892 F. Supp. 1459 (M.D. Fla. 1995) *16:* 236, 238; *42:* 21, 45

Squires v. Bonser, 54 F.3d 168 (3d Cir. 1995) *40:* 21, 25–26, 37–38; *41:* 80, 83

Stacks v. Southwestern Bell Yellow Pages, Inc., 27 F.3d 1316, 65 FEP 341 (8th Cir. 1994) *2:* 45

Stacy v. Shoney's, Inc., 955 F. Supp. 751 (E.D. Ky. 1997) *20:* 86

Stafford v. Radford Community Hosp., Inc., 908 F. Supp. 1369 (W.D. Va. 1995), *aff'd without opinion,* 120 F.3d 262 (4th Cir. 1997) *16:* 58, 78, 235; *31:* 25; *33:* 24, 33

Stahl v. Sun Microsystems, Inc., 19 F.3d 533, 64 FEP 468 (10th Cir. 1994) *38:* 36

Stair v. Lehigh Valley Carpenters, 855 F. Supp. 90, 66 FEP 1502 (E.D. Pa.), *aff'd,* 43 F.3d 1463 (3d Cir. 1994) *22:* 11–12, 14, 22; *42:* 21

Stalnaker v. KMart Corp., 71 FEP 705 (D. Kan. 1996) *38:* 35, 47, 52

Stanley
—v. Darlington County Sch. Dist, 915 F. Supp. 764, 67 FEP 1828 (D.S.C. 1996) *27:* 64–65, 67–69
—v. University of S. Cal., 13 F.3d 1313, 63 FEP 1021 (9th Cir. 1994) *40:* 92

Starceski v. Westinghouse Elec. Corp., 54 F.3d 1089, 67 FEP 1184 (3d Cir. 1995) *16:* 136, 220, 245; *29:* 48; *40:* 23, 28; *41:* 118

Starr v. Westinghouse Elec. Corp., 1995 WL 817882 (D. Md. May 31, 1995) *16:* 83

State, County, & Municipal Employees (AFSCME); EEOC v., 937 F. Supp. 166, 71 FEP 1151 (N.D.N.Y. 1996) *8:* 33–34; *34:* 46

Steamship Clerks Local 1066; EEOC v., 48 F.3d 594, 67 FEP 629 (1st Cir.), *cert. denied,* 116 S. Ct. 65 (1995) *4:* 4–6, 28, 36–38, 57–58; *5:* 39; *18:* 2–3, 7; *22:* 10; *39:* 40, 79–81

Steelworkers v. Weber, 443 U.S. 193, 20 FEP 1 (1979) *27:* 99, 128, 146, 153

Steffen v. Meridian Life Ins. Co., 859 F.2d 534, 48 FEP 173 (7th Cir. 1988), *cert. denied,* 491 U.S. 907 (1989) *30:* 4

Steiner v. Showboat Operating Co., 25 F.3d 1459, 65 FEP 58 (9th Cir. 1994), *cert. denied,* 513 U.S. 1082 (1995) *20:* 33–34

Steinle v. Boeing Co., 884 F. Supp. 424, 68 FEP 69 (D. Kan. 1995) *17:* 4, 47

Stemmons v. Missouri Dep't of Corrections, 82 F.3d 817, 70 FEP 1215 (8th Cir. 1996) *2:* 48

Stephenson v. Aluminum Co. of Am., 915 F. Supp. 39 (S.D. Ind. 1995) *40:* 4, 21, 23, 25–26, 29; *41:* 26, 82

Stern v. Trustees of Columbia Univ., 131 F.3d 305, 75 FEP 1423 (2d Cir. 1997) *27:* 23–25

Stetka v. Hunt Real Estate Corp., 859 F. Supp. 661, 65 FEP 1311 (W.D.N.Y. 1994) *30:* 13

Stewart
—v. Brown County, 86 F.3d 107, 5 AD 1018 (7th Cir. 1996) *9:* 32, 119
—v. Rubin, 948 F. Supp. 1077 (D.D.C. 1996) *37:* 56; *40:* 69, 79
—v. Rutgers, 120 F.3d 426, 74 FEP 545 (3d Cir. 1997) *19:* 18
—v. Weis Mkts., Inc., 890 F. Supp. 382, 72 FEP 259 (M.D. Pa. 1995) *21:* 7

St. Germain v. Simmons Airline, 930 F. Supp. 1144 (N.D. Tex. 1996) *30:* 16

Stillwell v. Kansas City Bd. of Police Comm'rs, 872 F. Supp. 682, 3 AD 1828 (W.D. Mo. 1995) *9:* 29–31, 71

Stiltner v. Beretta U.S.A. Corp., 74 F.3d 1473 (4th Cir.), *cert. denied,* 117 S. Ct. 54 (1996) *17:* 37

St. Louis v. Texas Worker's Compensation Comm'n, 65 F.3d 43, 68 FEP 1631 (5th Cir. 1995), *cert. denied,* 116 S. Ct. 2563 (1996) *16:* 75

St. Louis Fire Fighters Ass'n v. St. Louis, Missouri, 96 F.3d 323, 71 FEP 1513 (8th Cir. 1996) *42:* 27

St. Mary's Honor Ctr. v. Hicks, 509 U.S. 502, 62 FEP 96 (1993) *2:* 5, 26; *17:* 44

Stoeckel v. Environmental Management Sys., Inc., 882 F. Supp. 1106, 67 FEP 1716 (D.D.C. 1995) *20:* 58

Stone
—v. City of Mt. Vernon, 118 F.3d 92, 6 AD 1685 (2d Cir. 1997) *9:* 209
—v. Georgia Power Co., 902 F. Supp. 1578, 69 FEP 25 (M.D. Ga. 1995) *16:* 53, 116, 177
—v. La Quinta Inn, Inc., 942 F. Supp. 261, 6 AD 60 (E.D. La. 1966) *9:* 295
—v. National Bank & Trust Co., 1996 WL 310351 (N.D.N.Y. Jun. 6, 1996), *supplemented by* 1996 WL 341987 (N.D.N.Y. June 18, 1996) *32:* 1

Stopka v. Alliance of Am. Insurers, 1996 U.S. Dist. LEXIS 18329 (N.D. Ill. Dec. 6, 1996) *9:* 192

Storr v. Anderson Sch. & William Doyle, 919 F. Supp. 144, 72 FEP 107 (S.D.N.Y. 1996) *16:* 27

Stouch v. Brothers of the Order of Hermits of St. Augustine, 836 F. Supp. 1134, 63 FEP 1107 (E.D. Pa. 1993) *30:* 17

St. Peters v. Shell Oil Co., 77 F.3d 184, 11 IER 804 (7th Cir. 1996) *26:* 10

Strag v. Board of Trustees of Craven Community College, 55 F.3d 943, 68 FEP 163 (4th Cir. 1995) *15:* 24

Straka v. Francis, 867 F. Supp. 767 (N.D. Ill. 1994) *16:* 27

Strange v. Nationwide Mut. Ins. Co., 867 F. Supp. 1209, 10 IER 1257 (E.D. Pa. 1994) *16:* 15, 63; *26:* 40, 44

Stratton v. Department for the Aging for the City of N.Y., 922 F. Supp. 857 (S.D.N.Y. 1996) *16:* 128, 132, 211, 218, 232; *39:* 7; *40:* 50; *41:* 72–73, 103

Strauss v. Microsoft Corp., 68 FEP 1576 (S.D.N.Y. 1995) *29:* 47

Strickland v. Hillsborough County, 65 FEP 255 (M.D. Fla. 1994) *17:* 40

Stromfield v. Smith, 557 F. Supp. 995, 31 FEP 204 (S.D.N.Y. 1983) *36:* 16

Strother v. Southern Cal. Permanente Med. Group, 79 F.3d 859, 72 FEP 905 (9th Cir. 1996) *30:* 19, 44

Stults v. Conoco, Inc., 76 F.3d 651, 70 FEP 732 (5th Cir. 1996) *16:* 27

TABLE OF CASES 711

Suggs v. Servicemaster Educ. Food Management, 72 F.3d 1228, 69 FEP 1270 (6th Cir. 1996) *40:* 37–38, 40; *41:* 32, 45, 84, 92

Suhr v. Runyon, 1995 WL 617478 (N.D. Ill. Oct. 12, 1995) *9:* 309

Sullivan v. School Bd. of Pinellas County, 773 F.2d 1182, 39 FEP 53 (11th Cir. 1985) *42:* 62

Sunstrom v. Schering-Plough Corp., 856 F. Supp. 1265 (E.D. Tenn. 1994) *2:* 15, 18

Superior Temporary Servs., Inc.; EEOC v., 56 F.3d 441, 67 FEP 1700 (2d Cir. 1995) *23:* 9–10, 15–17 *29:* 20–21, 23, 34

Suttles v. U.S. Postal Serv., 927 F. Supp. 990, 153 LRRM 2042 (S.D. Tex. 1996) *9:* 44; *21:* 13

Sutton v. United Airlines, Inc., 6 AD 116 (D. Colo. 1996) *9:* 129

Swain v. Roadway Express, 71 FEP 71 (D. Md. 1996) *21:* 2

Swanks v. Washington Metro. Area Transit Auth., 116 F.3d 582, 6 AD 1544 (D.C. Cir. 1997) *9:* 61–62

Swartzbaugh v. State Farm Ins. Co., 924 F. Supp. 932, 73 FEP 211 (E.D. Mo. 1995) *31:* 14

Sweet v. Electronic Data Sys., 5 AD 853 (S.D.N.Y. 1996) *9:* 174

Swick v. Liautaud, 662 N.E.2d 1238, 11 IER 646 (Ill. 1996) *26:* 36

Switalski v. Iron Workers Local 3, 881 F. Supp. 205, 4 AD 417 (W.D. Pa. 1995) *30:* 55

T

Tabech v. Gunter, 869 F. Supp. 1446 (D. Neb. 1994) *42:* 45, 58

Tacket v. General Motors, 93 F.3d 332, 11 IER 1729 (7th Cir. 1996) *26:* 35, 58

Tafoya v. Bobroff, 865 F. Supp. 742, 3 AD 1329 (D.N.M. 1994), *aff'd mem.,* 74 F.3d 1250, 6 AD 1888 (10th Cir. 1996) *9:* 72; *24:* 22

Taggart
—v. Drake Univ., 549 N.W.2d 796, 11 IER 1450 (Iowa 1996) *26:* 5, 33, 42

—v. Trans World Airlines, Inc., 40 F.3d 269, 3 AD 1441 (8th Cir. 1994) *32:* 37

Taken v. Oklahoma Corp. Comm'n, 934 F. Supp. 1294, 75 FEP 475 (W.D. Okla. 1996), *aff'd,* 125 F.3d 1366, 75 FEP 480 (10th Cir. 1997) *20:* 107; *27:* 13, 39

Talada v. International Serv. Sys., Inc., 899 F. Supp. 936 (N.D.N.Y. 1995) *41:* 38, 71

Talley v. Washington Inventory Serv., 37 F.3d, 310, 65 FEP 1665 (7th Cir. 1994) *26:* 31

Tanca v. Nordberg, 98 F.3d 680, 72 FEP 166 (1st Cir. 1996), *cert. denied,* 117 S. Ct. 1253 (1997) *17:* 49–50; *41:* 123–30

Tandem Computers, Inc.; EEOC v., 158 F.R.D. 224 (D. Mass. 1994) *34:* 62

Tang v. Rhode Island Dep't of Elderly Affairs, 904 F. Supp. 69, 69 FEP 577 (D.R.I. 1995) *32:* 12; *33:* 3

Tanner v. Prima Donna Resorts, Inc., 919 F. Supp. 351, 72 FEP 435 (D. Nev. 1996) *20:* 51

Tatum v. Community Bank, 866 F. Supp. 988 (E.D. Tex 1994) *32:* 9

Tavora v. New York Mercantile Exch., 101 F.3d 907, 72 FEP 979 (2d Cir. 1996), *cert. denied,* 117 S. Ct. 1821 (1997) *13:* 33

Taxman v. Board of Educ. of Township of Piscataway, 91 F.3d 1547, 71 FEP 848 (3d Cir. 1996), *cert. granted,* 117 S. Ct. 2506, *cert.dismissed,* 118 S. Ct. 595 (1997) *27:* 98, 101–04, 124–27, 130, 149–52, 154; *41:* 26

Taylor
—v. Brown, 928 F. Supp. 568 (D. Md. 1995), *aff'd,* 86 F.3d 1152 (4th Cir. 1996) *19:* 13, 18, 22

—v. Canteen Corp., 69 F.3d 773, 69 FEP 310 (7th Cir. 1995) *16:* 100, 161, 163, 174, 176

—v. Central Pa. Drug & Alcohol Servs., 890 F. Supp. 360, 72 FEP 1315 (M.D. Pa. 1995) *37:* 9; *41:* 9–10, 12, 20, 33, 43, 66–67, 71, 77

Taylor—Contd.
—v. Dover Elevator Sys., Inc., 917 F. Supp. 455, 5 AD 616 (N.D. Miss. 1996) **9:** 138, 183
—v. Espy, 816 F. Supp. 1553, 61 FEP 785 (N.D. Ga. 1993) **36:** 24
—v. Food World, Inc., 946 F. Supp. 937, 6 AD 106 (N.D. Ala. 1996) **9:** 145, 174, 186
—v. Gearan, 1997 WL 595301 (D.D.C. Sept. 14, 1997) **9:** 36
—v. Gilbert & Bennett, 6 AD 201 (N.D. Ill. 1996) **9:** 133
—v. Principal Fin. Group, Inc., 93 F.3d 155, 5 AD 1653 (5th Cir.), *cert. denied,* 117 S. Ct. 586 (1996) **9:** 188
—v. Resolution Trust Corp., 56 F.3d 1497 (D.C. Cir. 1995) **40:** 89–90, 98
—v. Secretary of Navy, 852 F. Supp. 343, 3 AD 497 (E.D. Pa. 1994), *aff'd mem.,* 61 F.3d 896 (3d Cir. 1995) **9;** 234
Teahan v. Metro-North Commuter R.R., 80 F.3d 50, 5 AD 603 (2d Cir. 1996) **9:** 269
Teamsters v. United States, 431 U.S. 324, 14 FEP 1514 (1977) **39:** 24
Teichgraeber v. Memorial Union Corp.
—932 F. Supp. 1263 (D. Kan. 1996) **41:** 43
—946 F. Supp. 900, 72 FEP 1696 (D. Kan. 1996) **16:** 35
Tenbrink v. Federal Home Loan Bank, 920 F. Supp. 1156 (D. Kan. 1996) **9:** 126, 177
Teneyuca v. Bexar County, 767 F.2d 148, 38 FEP 989 (5th Cir. 1985) **30:** 22
Terra Int'l, Inc. v. Mississippi Chem. Corp., 913 F. Supp. 1306 (N.D. Iowa 1996) **38:** 37
Terrell v. Rowsey, 647 N.E.2d 662, 10 IER 650 (1995) **26:** 55
Terry v. Gallegos, 926 F. Supp. 679 (W.D. Tenn. 1996) **2:** 49; **17:** 43; **19:** 5, 23, 28; **27:** 17
Tester v. City of New York, 1997 U.S. Dist. LEXIS 1937 (S.D.N.Y. 1997) **14:** 13
Testerman v. EDS Tech. Prods. Corp., 98 F.3d 297, 72 FEP 959 (7th Cir. 1996) **2:** 31

Teumer v. General Motors Corp., 34 F.3d 542 (7th Cir. 1994) **31:** 5
Texas v. Hopwood, *see* Hopwood v. State of Texas
Texas Bus Lines; EEOC v., 923 F. Supp. 965, 5 AD 878 (S.D. Tex. 1996) **9:** 80, 91, 213, 215, 248
Texas Dep't of Community Affairs v. Burdine, 450 U.S. 248, 25 FEP 113 (1981) **2:** 4
Texas Instruments, Inc.; EEOC v., 100 F.3d 1173, 72 FEP 980 (5th Cir. 1996) **39:** 59–60
Texas State Teachers Ass'n v. Garland Indep. Sch. Dist., 489 U.S. 782, 49 FEP 465 (1989) **42:** 1
Thankachen v. Cardone Indus., 70 FEP 1391 (E.D. Pa. 1996) **24:** 14
Tharp v. Iowa Dep't of Corrections, 68 F.3d 223, 69 FEP 42 (8th Cir. 1995), *cert. denied,* 116 S.Ct. 1420 (1996) **13:** 2–3
Theard v. Glaxo, Inc., 47 F.3d 676, 67 FEP 348 (4th Cir. 1995) **24:** 3
Thelen v. Marc's Big Boy Corp., 64 F.3d 264, 68 FEP 1090 (7th Cir. 1995) **16:** 57, 60; **31:** 5, 29–31
This Is Me, Inc. v. Taylor, 1996 WL 20745 (S.D.N.Y. Jan. 17, 1996) **32:** 30
Thomas
—v. Hoyt, Brumm & Link, Inc., 910 F. Supp. 1280 (E.D. Mich. 1994) **18:** 10–11
—v. IBM, 48 F.3d 478, 67 FEP 270 (10th Cir. 1995) **39:** 16
—v. National Football League Players Ass'n, 941 F. Supp. 156 (D.D.C. 1996) **40:** 26
—v. Rite Aid Corp., 147 LRRM 2886 (E.D. Pa. 1994), *aff'd,* 68 F.3d 457, 150 LRRM 2575 (3d Cir. 1995) **22:** 15
—v. St. Louis Bd. of Educ., 933 F. Supp. 817 (E.D. Mo. 1996) **32:** 1
—v. St. Luke's Health Sys., Inc., 869 F. Supp. 1413 (N.D. Iowa 1994), *aff'd without opinion,* 61 F.3d 908 (8th Cir. 1995) **33:** 15
Thomasson v. Perry, 80 F.3d 915 (4th Cir.), *cert. denied,* 117 S. Ct. 358 (1996) **14:** 19, 24–25

Thomlison v. City of Omaha, 63 F.3d 786, 4 AD 1319 (8th Cir. 1995) *42:* 49
Thompson
—v. Borg-Warner Protective Servs. Corp., 1996 WL 162990 (N.D. Cal. Mar. 11, 1996) *9:* 79, 88
—v. Mississippi State Personnel Bd., 674 F. Supp. 198, 45 FEP 530 (N.D. Miss. 1987) *13:* 36
—v. Olson, 866 F. Supp. 1267, 72 FEP 24 (D.N.D. 1994), *aff'd,* 56 F.3d 69, 72 FEP 96 (8th Cir. 1995) *20:* 107
Thompto v. Coborn's Inc., 871 F. Supp. 1097, 10 IER 263 (N.D. Iowa 1994) *26:* 29
Thomure v. Phillips Furniture Co, 30 F.3d 1020, 65 FEP 976 (8th Cir. 1994), *cert. denied,* 513 U.S. 1191 (1995) *16:* 45, 84, 145–47, 166, 182
Thornton
—v. Kaplan, 937 F. Supp. 1441 (D. Colo. 1996) *40:* 54
—v. South Cent. Bell Tel. Co., 906 F. Supp. 1110 (S.D. Miss. 1995) *31:* 53
Thurman
—v. Robertshaw Control Co., 869 F. Supp. 934, 65 FEP 1652 (N.D. Ga. 1994) *16:* 156, 173; *17:* 9
—v. Yellow Freight Sys., Inc., 90 F.3d 1160, 72 FEP 657 (6th Cir.), *opinion amended,* 97 F.3d 833 (6th Cir. 1996) *2:* 50; *40:* 21, 31, 35, 38; *41:* 22, 47, 146
Tibbitts v. Van Den Bergh Foods Co., 859 F. Supp. 1168, 66 FEP 560 (N.D. Ill. 1994) *16:* 123, 165
Ticor Title Ins. Co. v. Brown, 511 U.S. 117, 114 S. Ct. 1359 (1994) *37:* 57, 61
Tidwell v. Meyer's Bakeries, Inc., 93 F.3d 490, 71 FEP 1284 (8th Cir. 1996) *21:* 22, 24
Tietgen v. Brown's Westminister Motors, Inc., 921 F. Supp. 1495, 70 FEP 1020 (E.D. Va. 1996) *20:* 51; *33:* 29, 31
Timm v. Gunter, 917 F.2d 1093 (8th Cir. 1990), *cert. denied,* 501 U.S. 1209 (1991) *13:* 3
Tipsword v. Ogilvy & Mather, Inc., 918 F. Supp. 217, 70 FEP 1514 (N.D. Ill. 1996), *aff'd,* 106 F.3d 403, 72 FEP 1279 (7th Cir. 1997) *16:* 114

Tire Kingdom, Inc.; EEOC v., 80 F.3d 449, 70 FEP 744 (11th Cir. 1996) *29:* 25–26
Tischmann v. ITT/Sheraton Corp., 882 F. Supp. 1358, 68 FEP 1665 (S.D.N.Y. 1995) *20:* 114–15
Tomasello v. Rubin, 920 F. Supp. 4 (D.D.C. 1996) *16:* 29
Tomka v. Seiler Corp., 66 F.3d 1295, 68 FEP 1508 (2d Cir. 1995) *2:* 49; *15:* 24, 33
Tompulis v. Schwartz & Freeman, 66 FEP 1544 (N.D. Ill. 1994) *41:* 117
Tomsic v. State Farm Mut. Auto. Ins. Co., 85 F.3d 1472, 71 FEP 137 (10th Cir. 1996) *2:* 55; *33:* 50
Topf v. Warnaco, Inc., 942 F. Supp. 762, 6 AD 1315 (D. Conn. 1996) *9:* 297
Torcasio v. Murray, 57 F.3d 1340, 4 AD 974 (4th Cir. 1995), *cert. denied,* 116 S. Ct. 771 (1996) *9:* 40
Torosyan v. Boehringer Ingelheim Pharms., Inc., 662 A.2d 89, 10 IER 1313 (Conn. 1995) *26:* 17, 39
Torre v. Federated Mut. Ins. Co., 897 F. Supp. 1332, 68 FEP 1850 (D. Kan. 1995), *aff'd,* 124 F.3d 218 (10th Cir. 1997) *2:* 17; *19:* 12
Tout v. Erie Community College, 923 F. Supp. 13 (W.D.N.Y. 1995) *33:* 25, 33
Towle v. Flexel Corp., 867 F. Supp. 954 (D. Kan. 1994), *aff'd,* 68 F.3d 484 (10th Cir. 1995) *21:* 10
Town of, *see* name of town
Trader v. People Working Cooperatively Inc., 663 N.E.2d 335, 11 IER 1350 (Ohio Ct. App. 1994), *appeal dismissed,* 660 N.E.2d 737 (1995) *26:* 10, 15, 27, 32
Tran v. Tran, 54 F.3d 115, 149 LRRM 2350 (2d Cir. 1995), *cert. denied,* 116 S. Ct. 1417 (1996) *32:* 21
Tranello v. Frey, 758 F. Supp. 841, 55 FEP 699 (W.D.N.Y. 1991), *aff'd,* 962 F.2d 244, 58 FEP 1334 (2d Cir.), *cert. denied,* 506 U.S. 1034 (1992) *24:* 39
Trans World Airlines, Inc.
—v. Hardison, 432 U.S. 63, 14 FEP 1697 (1977) *8:* 19
—v. Thurston, 469 U.S. 111, 36 FEP 977 (1985) *16:* 235

Travis v. Gary Community Mental Health Ctr., Inc., 921 F.2d 108, 30 WH 122 (7th Cir. 1990), *cert. denied*, 502 U.S. 812 (1991) *24:* 45

Trent v. Valley Elec. Ass'n, 41 F.3d 524, 66 FEP 769 (9th Cir. 1994) *18:* 10

Trotter
—v. Board of Trustees of Univ. of Ala., 91 F.3d 1449, 71 FEP 1175 (11th Cir. 1996) *2:* 44
—v. B & S Aircraft Parts & Accessories, Inc., 5 AD 1584 (D. Kan. 1996) *9:* 119, 175

Tucker
—v. California Dep't of Educ., 97 F.3d 1204, 71 FEP 1863 (9th Cir. 1996) *17:* 56, 69
—v. Kingsbury Corp., 929 F. Supp. 50, 75 FEP 1316 (D.N.H. 1996) *16:* 121, 138, 142, 158

Tuers v. Runyon, 950 F. Supp. 284 (E.D. Cal. 1996) *9:* 309

Turco v. Hoechst Celanese Chem. Group, Inc., 906 F. Supp. 1120, 6 AD 579 (S.D. Tex. 1995), *aff'd,* 101 F.3d 1090, 6 AD 278 (5th Cir. 1996) *9:* 72, 138, 142, 177, 211, 252

Turic v. Holland Hospitality, Inc., 85 F.3d 1211, 71 FEP 28 (6th Cir. 1996) *13:* 22

Turner
—v. Anheuser-Busch, Inc., 876 P.2d 1022, 9 IER 1185 (Cal. 1994) *21:* 1, 5–6
—v. Imperial Stores, 161 F.R.D. 89 (S.D. Cal. 1995) *38:* 46
—v. Sungard Business Sys., Inc., 91 F.3d 1418 (11th Cir. 1996) *42:* 63

Turnes v. AmSouth, N.A., 36 F.3d 1057, 66 FEP 340 (11th Cir. 1994) *24:* 56

Turtle Creek Mansion Corp.; EEOC v., 70 FEP 899 (N.D. Tex. 1995), *aff'd,* 82 F.3d 414, 71 FEP 1408 (5th Cir. 1996) *18:* 15–16; *34:* 62; *39:* 29, 42–44

TXO Prod. Corp. v. Alliance Resources Corp., 509 U.S. 443 (1993) *41:* 108

Tyler
—v. Bethlehem Steel Corp., 958 F.2d 1176, 59 FEP 875 (2d Cir.), *cert. denied,* 506 U.S. 826 (1992) *2:* 57
—v. City of Mountain Home, 72 F.3d 568 (8th Cir. 1995) *17:* 69

—v. Runyon, 70 F.3d 458, 5 AD 31 (7th Cir. 1995) *2:* 25

Tyson v. CIGNA Corp., 918 F. Supp. 836, 70 FEP 908 (D.N.J. 1996) *30:* 61

U

Ullman v. Rector & Visitors of the Univ. of Va., 1997 WL 134557 (W.D. Va. Mar. 12, 1997) *16:* 35

Ulrich v. KMart Corp., 858 F. Supp. 1087, 74 FEP 565 (D. Kan. 1994), *aff'd,* 70 F.3d 1282, 74 FEP 1792 (10th Cir. 1995) *20:* 69; *21:* 25

Umpleby v. Potter & Brumfield, Inc., 69 F.3d 209, 72 FEP 1047 (7th Cir. 1995) *2:* 54

Union Carbide Chems. & Plastics Co.; EEOC v., 4 AD 1409 (E.D. La. 1995) *9:* 5

United Air Lines; EEOC v., 1995 U.S. Dist. LEXIS 2581 (N.D. Ill. Mar. 2, 1995) *34:* 45, 61

United Black Firefighters Ass'n v. City of Akron, 66 FEP 1452 (N.D. Ohio 1994), *aff'd without opinion,* 81 F.3d 161 (6th Cir. 1996) *5:* 1

United Parcel Serv.; EEOC v., 94 F.3d 314, 71 FEP 1301 (7th Cir. 1996) *8:* 20, 35

United States v., *see* name of opposing party

University of Md. Med. Sys. Corp.; Doe v., 50 F.3d 1261, 4 AD 379 (4th Cir. 1995) *9:* 28, 244, 249, 251

University of Pa. v. EEOC, 493 U.S. 182, 51 FEP 1118 (1990) *29:* 39

Upper Valley Ass'n for Handicapped Citizens v. Mills, 168 F.R.D. 167 (D. Vt. 1996) *37:* 70

U.S. Postal Serv.; EEOC v., 18 F.3d 1089, 64 FEP 305 (3d Cir. 1994) *25:* 6–7

V

Vakharia
—v. Little Co. of Mary Hosp. & Health Care Ctrs., 917 F. Supp. 1282 (N.D. Ill. 1996) *16:* 27, 78; *24:* 6, 45; *33:* 11, 13

—v. Swedish Covenant Hosp., 765 F. Supp. 461, 61 FEP 533 (N.D. Ill. 1991) *30:* 21
Valadez v. Uncle Julio's of Ill., Inc., 895 F. Supp. 1008, 70 FEP 451 (N.D. Ill. 1995) *20:* 39–40, 47
Valentine v. American Home Shield Corp., 939 F. Supp. 1376, 6 AD 163 (N.D. Iowa 1996) *9:* 188, 197
Valentino v. Carter-Wallace, 97 F.3d 1227 (9th Cir. 1996) *37:* 94
Vande Zande v. Wisconsin Dep't of Admin., 851 F. Supp. 353, 2 AD 1846 (W.D. Wis. 1994), *aff'd,* 44 F.3d 538, 3 AD 1636 (7th Cir. 1995) *9:* 1, 4, 125–27, 156, 167, 170, 202, 207, 216, 218, 220, 282–83
Vanguards of Cleveland v. City of Cleveland, 23 F.3d 1013, 64 FEP 1611 (6th Cir. 1994) *22:* 31; *40:* 73
Van Pilsum v. Iowa State Univ. of Science, 863 F. Supp. 935 (S.D. Iowa 1994) *16:* 34
Van Zant v. KLM Royal Dutch Airlines, 80 F.3d 708, 70 FEP 562 (2d Cir. 1996) *31:* 11
Varner v. National Super Mkts., Inc., 94 F.3d 1209, 71 FEP 1367 (8th Cir. 1996), *cert. denied,* 117 S. Ct. 946 (1997) *9:* 298; *20:* 103
Vaughan v. Harvard Indus., Inc., 926 F. Supp. 1340 (W.D. Tenn. 1996) *9:* 134, 209
Vazquez v. Bedsole, 888 F. Supp. 727, 4 AD 970 (E.D.N.C. 1995) *9:* 122
Ventura County Ry. v. Hadley Auto Transp., 45 Cal. Rptr. 2d 362, 4 AD 1523 (Cal. Ct. App. 1995) *30:* 30
Veprinsky v. Fluor Daniel, Inc., 87 F.3d 881, 71 FEP 170 (7th Cir. 1996) *16:* 42, 44; *17:* 2; *41:* 123
Vera-Lozano v. International Broad., 50 F.3d 67, 67 FEP 667 (1st Cir. 1995) *30:* 51
Verde v. City of Philadelphia, 862 F. Supp. 1329, 67 FEP 1711 (E.D. Pa. 1994) *30:* 61
Vernon v. Cassadaga Valley Cent. Sch. Dist., 49 F.3d 886, 67 FEP 295 (2d Cir. 1995) *16:* 59, 75

Vetter v. Farmland Indus., Inc.
—884 F. Supp. 1287, 73 FEP 595 (N.D. Iowa 1995) *8:* 41
—901 F. Supp. 1446 (N.D. Iowa 1995) *8:* 20, 36–38
Vializ v. New York City Bd. of Educ., 4 AD 345 (S.D.N.Y. 1995) *9:* 156
Vick v. Foote, Inc., 898 F. Supp. 330, 68 FEP 1628 (E.D. Va. 1995), *aff'd,* 82 F.3d 411 (4th Cir.), *cert. denied,* 117 S. Ct. 311 (1996) *30:* 16, 43, 46, 52
Villasenor v. Industrial Wire & Cable, Inc., 929 F. Supp. 310, 5 AD 1160 (N.D. Ill. 1996) *30:* 52
Virgo v. Riviera Beach Assocs., Ltd., 30 F.3d 1350, 65 FEP 1317 (11th Cir. 1994) *33:* 11, 17, 24, 29, 33–34, 60; *21:* 7, 14; *30:* 58–59
Vitug v. Multistate Tax Comm'n, 88 F.3d 506, 71 FEP 1445 (7th Cir. 1995) *4:* 23, 35; *11:* 2, 6; *37:* 18; *39:* 20, 51–52
Voigt v. Savell, 70 F.3d 1552 (9th Cir. 1995), *cert. denied,* 116 S. Ct. 1826 (1996) *17:* 69
Volberg v. Pataki, 917 F. Supp. 909 (N.D.N.Y.), *aff'd mem.,* 112 F.3d 507 (2d Cir. 1996), *cert. denied,* 117 S. Ct. 1252 (1997) *17:* 4, 12
Vore v. Indiana Bell Tel. Co., 32 F.3d 1161, 65 FEP 897 (7th Cir. 1994) *27:* 15
Voytek v. University of Cal., 77 F.3d 491, 5 AD 1344 (9th Cir. 1996) *9:* 156

W

Waag v. Thomas Pontiac, Buick, GMC, Inc., 930 F. Supp. 393, 74 FEP 12 (D. Minn. 1996) *21:* 14
Wagner v. Nutrasweet Co.
—95 F.3d 527, 72 FEP 284 (7th Cir. 1996) *43:* 7–8, 49
—170 F.R.D. 448 (N.D. Ill. 1997) *37:* 37
Wahad v. Coughlin, 870 F. Supp. 506 (S.D.N.Y. 1994) *42:* 50
Waldemar v. American Cancer Soc'y, 70 FEP 1411 (N.D. Ga. 1996) *16:* 168–69

Walden Book Co.; EEOC v., 885 F. Supp. 1100, 67 FEP 1446 (M.D. Tenn. 1995) *27:* 27

Waldron v. SL Indus., Inc., 56 F.3d 491, 67 FEP 1577 (3d Cir. 1995) *16:* 115

Walker
—v. City of Elba, 874 F. Supp. 361, 67 FEP 212 (M.D. Ala. 1994) *30:* 55
—v. Correctional Med. Sys., 886 F. Supp. 515, 68 FEP 42 (W.D. Pa. 1995) *30:* 13, 17–18
—v. Nationsbank of Fla., N.A., 53 F.3d 1548, 68 FEP 314 (11th Cir. 1995) *2:* 40; *29:* 47; *42:* 61–62
—v. New York State Office of Mental Health, 865 F. Supp. 124 (S.D.N.Y. 1994) *19:* 21
—v. U.S. Dep't of Hous. & Urban Dev., 99 F.3d 761 (5th Cir. 1996) *42:* 51, 58

Wallace
—v. Dunn Constr. Co., 62 F.3d 374, 68 FEP 990 (11th Cir. 1995) *15:* 26–27; *40:* 33–35, 59–62, 89
—v. Texas Tech. Univ., 80 F.3d 1042, 70 FEP 1521 (5th Cir. 1996) *17:* 63

Wallulis v. Dymowski, 918 P.2d 755 (Or. 1996) *26:* 39, 42–43

Walters v. Metropolitan Educ. Enters., 117 S. Ct. 660, 72 FEP 1211 (1997) *16:* 20–22; *30:* 2, 49–50

Walther v. Lone Star Gas Co., 952 F.2d 119 (5th Cir. 1992) *40:* 43

Walt's Drive-A-Way Serv., Inc. v. Powell, 638 N.E.2d 857, 10 IER 789 (Ind. Ct. App. 1994) *26:* 3

Wanamaker v. Columbian Rope Co., 907 F. Supp. 522, 69 FEP 972 (N.D.N.Y. 1995), *aff'd,* 108 F.3d 462, 73 FEP 321 (2d Cir. 1997) *16:* 95

Wann v. American Airlines, 3 AD 1607 (S.D. Tex. 1994), *aff'd mem.,* 58 F.3d 636 (5th Cir. 1995) *9:* 123

Ward
—v. Gulfstream Aerospace Corp., 894 F. Supp. 1573 (S.D. Ga. 1995) *16:* 176; *39:* 30, 78
—v. Johns Hopkins Univ., 861 F. Supp. 367, 66 FEP 872 (D. Md. 1994) *30:* 26

—v. Papa's Pizza To Go, Inc., 907 F. Supp. 1535 (S.D. Ga. 1995) *40:* 37; *41:* 84
—v. Tipton County Sheriff Dep't, 937 F. Supp. 791 (S.D. Ind. 1996) *40:* 49; *41:* 26, 81
—v. Westvaco Corp., 859 F. Supp. 608, 3 AD 739 (D. Mass. 1994) *9:* 65; *16:* 165; *32:* 18

Wardlaw v. Inland Container Corp., 76 F.3d 1372, 11 IER 873 (5th Cir. 1996) *26:* 54

Wards Cove Packing Co. v. Atonio, 490 U.S. 642, 49 FEP 1519 (1989) *4:* 21–22, 27, 41, 45; *5:* 36

Warren
—v. City of Carlsbad, 58 F.3d 439 (9th Cir. 1995), *cert. denied,* 516 U.S. 1171 (1996) *2:* 32; *19:* 23
—v. Department of Army, 867 F.2d 1156, 49 FEP 141 (8th Cir. 1989) *36:* 21
—v. Runyon, 1995 U.S. Dist. LEXIS 5819 (N.D. Ill. Apr. 28, 1995) *9:* 268

Warshawsky & Co.; EEOC v., 1994 U.S. Dist. LEXIS 10058 (N.D. Ill. July 19, 1994) *34:* 17, 31

Warzon v. Drew, 60 F.3d 1234 (7th Cir. 1995) *17:* 73

Washington
—v. Garrett, 10 F.3d 1421, 63 FEP 540 (9th Cir. 1993) *2:* 32
—v. Philadelphia County Court of Common Pleas, 89 F.3d 1031 (3d Cir. 1996) *42:* 51

Watson v. Fort Worth Bank & Trust, 487 U.S. 977, 47 FEP 102 (1988) *4:* 13, 15; *7:* 6; *39:* 71

Watters v. City of Philadelphia, 55 F.3d 886 (3d Cir. 1995) *17:* 59

Waymire v. Harris County, 86 F.3d 424, 72 FEP 637 (5th Cir. 1996) *20:* 98–100

Weaver v. Amoco Prod.Co., 66 F.3d 85, 70 FEP 931 (5th Cir. 1995), *aff'd after remand,* 95 F.3d 52 (5th Cir. 1996) *16:* 209, 226; *40:* 21, 37, 43; *41:* 80, 114; *42:* 35

Webb
—v. Derwinski, 868 F. Supp. 1184, 69 FEP 419 (E.D. Mo. 1994), *aff'd,* 68

F.3d 479, 69 FEP 768 (8th Cir. 1995) *19:* 11, 20
—v. District of Columbia, 864 F. Supp. 175, 73 FEP 451 (D.D.C. 1994) *33:* 40
—v. Garelick Mfg. Co., 94 F.3d 484, 6 AD 127 (8th Cir. 1996) *9:* 1
—v. Hyman, 861 F. Supp. 1094, 67 FEP 1425 (D.D.C. 1994) *20:* 12, 47; *38:* 35; *41:* 101
—v. Missouri Pac. R.R., 95 F.R.D. 357 (E.D. Ark. 1982) *37:* 70
Wechsler v. R D Management Corp., 861 F. Supp. 1153, 73 FEP 195 (E.D.N.Y. 1994) *18:* 11
Wedding v. University of Toledo, 884 F. Supp. 253, 71 FEP 514 (N.D. Ohio 1995), *rev'd in part,* 89 F.3d 316, 71 FEP 509 (6th Cir. 1996) *17:* 26
Weeks
—v. Maine, 866 F. Supp. 601, 69 FEP 871 (D. Me. 1994) *17:* 22
—v. Samsung Heavy Indus. Co., 933 F. Supp. 711, 71 FEP 920 (N.D. Ill. 1996), *aff'd,* 126 F.3d 926, 74 FEP 1776 (7th Cir. 1997) *11:* 10, 33; *21:* 26
—v. State, 866 F. Supp. 601, 69 FEP 871 (D. Me. 1994) *19:* 18
Weigel v. Target Stores, 122 F.3d 461, 7 AD 358 (7th Cir. 1997) *9:* 62
Weiler v. Household Fin. Corp., 5 AD 550 (N.D. Ill. 1995), *aff'd,* 101 F.3d 519, 6 AD 106 (7th Cir. 1996) *9:* 42, 136, 141, 156, 161, 179, 202, 206
Weinstock v. Columbia Univ., 1995 WL 567399 (S.D.N.Y. Sept. 26, 1995) *38:* 34
Weissman
—v. Congregation Shaare Emeth, 38 F.3d 1038, 66 FEP 113 (8th Cir. 1994) *16:* 26
—v. General Cable Co., 862 F. Supp. 731 (D. Conn. 1994) *15:* 10
Welch v. Laney, 57 F.3d 1004 (11th Cir. 1995) *15:* 3
Welde v. Tetley, Inc., 864 F. Supp. 440, 65 FEP 1423 (M.D. Pa. 1994) *15:* 14, 24
Wells v. New Cherokee Corp., 58 F.3d 233, 68 FEP 284 (6th Cir. 1995) *2:* 44; *16:* 221; *41:* 46, 91, 120

Wenner
—v. C.G. Bretting Mfg. Co., 917 F. Supp. 640, 69 FEP 774 (W.D. Wis. 1995) *20:* 19
—v. Great State Beverages, Inc., 663 A.2d 623, 11 IER 1649 (N.H. 1995), *cert. denied,* 516 U.S. 1119 (1996) *26:* 3
Wernick v. Federal Reserve Bank, 91 F.3d 379, 5 AD 1345 (2d Cir. 1996) *9:* 119, 125, 136, 180–81
West
—v. Boeing Co., 851 F. Supp. 395, 66 FEP 836 (D. Kan. 1994) *41:* 97
—v. Marion Merrell Dow, Inc., 54 F.3d 493, 67 FEP 1209 (8th Cir. 1995) *17:* 28; *21:* 25
—v. Philadelphia Elec. Co., 45 F.3d 744, 64 FEP 1524 (3d Cir. 1995) *31:* 9–10, 12, 17
Westbrook v. Sky Chefs, Inc., 35 F.3d 316, 147 LRRM 2491 (7th Cir. 1994) *32:* 37
Wexler v. Runyon, 5 AD 896 (S.D.N.Y. 1996) *33:* 45
Whalen v. W.R. Grace & Co., 56 F.3d 504, 67 FEP 1633 (3d Cir. 1995) *16:* 85
Whaley v. Sony Magnetic Prods., Inc., 894 F. Supp. 1517 (M.D. Ala. 1995) *16:* 58
Wheeler v. Catholic Archdiocese of Seattle, 880 P.2d 29, 3 AD 1104 (Wash. 1994) *41:* 71
Whillock v. Delta Air Lines, 926 F. Supp. 1555, 5 AD 1027 (N.D. Ga. 1995), *aff'd mem.,* 86 F.3d 1171 (11th Cir. 1996) *9:* 127
Whitbeck v. Vital Signs, Inc., 163 F.R.D. 398 (D.D.C. 1995), *motion granted in part, denied in part,* 933 F. Supp. 341 (S.D.N.Y. 1996) *38:* 46
Whitchurch v. Apache Prods. Co., 916 F. Supp. 809, 6 AD 1589 (N.D. Ill. 1996) *16:* 27, 40, 100
White
—v. Wells Fargo Guard Servs., 908 F. Supp. 1570 (M.D. Ala. 1995) *19:* 5
—v. York Int'l Corp., 45 F.3d 357, 3 AD 1746 (10th Cir. 1995) *9:* 123, 148, 275, 278

Whittingham v. Amherst College, 164 F.R.D. 124 (D. Mass. 1995) *38:* 4, 31

Wiehoff v. GTE Directories Corp., 61 F.3d 588, 68 FEP 639 (8th Cir. 1995) *41:* 117

Wilborn v. Primary Care Specialists, Ltd., 866 F. Supp. 364, 73 FEP 341 (N.D. Ill. 1994) *17:* 53; *24:* 19

Wilcott v. Matlack, Inc., 64 F.3d 1458, 11 IER 311 (10th Cir. 1995) *26:* 4, 16, 33

Wilcox v. Stratton Lumber, Inc., 921 F. Supp. 837 (D. Me. 1996) *40:* 47, 51; *41:* 38, 71

Wilde v. County of Kandiyohi, 15 F.3d 103, 63 FEP 1167 (8th Cir. 1994) *30:* 13

Wilkerson v. Martin-Marietta Corp., 875 F. Supp. 1456, 67 FEP 279 (D. Colo. 1995) *16:* 71, 79; *34:* 35, 40–41; *37:* 22, 29

Willett v. Kansas, 942 F. Supp. 1387 (D. Kan. 1996) *9:* 126, 167, 197

Willey v. Riley, 541 N.W.2d 521, 11 IER 445 (Iowa 1995) *26:* 54

Williams
—In re, 197 B.R. 398 (Bankr. M.D. Ga. 1996) *16:* 234, 239
—v. Avnet, Inc., 910 F. Supp. 1124, 5 AD 835 (E.D.N.C. 1995), *aff'd sub nom.* Williams v. Channel Master Satellite Sys., 101 F.3d 346, 6 AD 131 (4th Cir. 1996), *cert. denied,* 117 S. Ct. 1844 (1997) *9:* 42, 139, 170, 206, 272, 275
—v. Bristol-Myers Squibb Co., 85 F.3d 270, 70 FEP 1639 (7th Cir. 1996) *2:* 49
—v. Carrier Corp., 889 F. Supp. 1528, 74 FEP 1475 (M.D. Ga. 1995), *aff'd,* 130 F.3d 444 (11th Cir. 1997) *17:* 53; *24:* 19
—v. Channel Master Satellite Sys., Inc., *see* Williams v. Avnet, Inc.
—v. Cigna Fin. Advisors, Inc., 56 F.3d 656, 68 FEP 65 (5th Cir. 1995) *16:* 205; *32:* 21
—v. District of Columbia, 916 F. Supp. 1, 70 FEP 294 (D.D.C. 1996) *24:* 29

—v. General Mills, Inc., 926 F. Supp. 1367, 71 FEP 272 (N.D. Ill. 1996) *20:* 111
—v. General Motors Corp.
——656 F.2d 120, 26 FEP 1381 (5th Cir. 1981), *cert. denied,* 455 U.S. 943 (1982) *16:* 149
——901 F. Supp. 252, 69 FEP 445 (E.D. Mich. 1995) *16:* 206
—v. Perry, 907 F. Supp. 838, 70 FEP 713 (M.D. Pa.), *aff'd mem.,* 72 F.3d 125 (3d Cir. 1995) *17:* 3; *19:* 3
—v. Pharmacia Ophthalmics, Inc., 926 F. Supp. 791, 71 FEP 628 (N.D. Ind. 1996) *19:* 28; *40:* 30, 41
—v. Port Auth. of N.Y. & N.J., 880 F. Supp. 980 (E.D.N.Y. 1995) *19:* 11
—v. Secretary of the Navy, 853 F. Supp. 66, 64 FEP 1709 (E.D.N.Y. 1994) *42:* 21
—v. Widnall, 79 F.3d 1003, 5 AD 663 (10th Cir. 1996) *9:* 157, 183, 217, 250, 270

Willis
—v. Conopco, Inc., 108 F.3d 282 (11th Cir. 1997) *9:* 286
—v. Dean Witter Reynolds, Inc., 948 F.2d 305, 57 FEP 386 (6th Cir. 1991) *32:* 21

Wilson
—v. Gayfers Montgomery Fair Co., 953 F. Supp. 1415, 6 AD 1076 (M.D. Ala. 1996) *9:* 295
—v. International Bus. Mach. Corp., 62 F.3d 237, 68 FEP 1019 (8th Cir. 1995) *16:* 104
—v. Peña, 79 F.3d 154, 72 FEP 67 (D.C. Cir. 1996) *31:* 42
—v. Pennsylvania State Police Dep't, 1995 U.S. Dist. LEXIS 9981 (E.D. Pa. July 17, 1995) *37:* 27
—v. Susquehanna Township Police Dep't, 55 F.3d 126, 67 FEP 1345 (3d Cir. 1995) *2:* 56
—v. United Farm Bureau Mut. Ins. Co., 68 FEP 631 (S.D. Ind. 1995) *16:* 14; *30:* 13
—v. U.S. West Communications, 58 F.3d 1337, 68 FEP 341 (8th Cir. 1995) *8:* 5, 9, 18, 20, 35, 39

Wilson Metal Casket Co.; EEOC v., 24 F.3d 836, 64 FEP 1402 (6th Cir. 1994) *41:* 139

Wiltel, Inc.; EEOC v., 81 F.3d 1508 (10th Cir. 1996) *18:* 10

Winbush v. Iowa, 66 F.3d 1471, 69 FEP 1348 (8th Cir. 1995) *19:* 7; *24:* 3; *31:* 36; *33:* 17, 24, 33; *37:* 72, 75; *41:* 24, 76, 142

Winfrey v. Chicago, 957 F. Supp. 1014 (N.D. Ill. 1997) *9:* 294

Winsor v. Hinckley Dodge, Inc., 79 F.3d 996, 70 FEP 611 (10th Cir. 1996) *20:* 69–70, 80; *21:* 11

Wior v. Anchor Indus. Inc., 669 N.E.2d 172, 11 IER 1742 (Ind. 1996) *26:* 16, 24

Wishnoff v. Rubin, 1995 WL 591143 (W.D.N.Y. Sept. 11, 1995) *16:* 77

Wisniewski v. Ameritech, 1996 U.S. Dist. LEXIS 12822 (N.D. Ill. Aug. 30, 1996) *9:* 209

Witham v. Regency Sav. Bank, 1995 WL 680313, 1995 U.S. Dist. LEXIS 17021 (N.D. Ill. Nov. 13, 1995) *15:* 4

Wittmer v. Peters, 87 F.3d 916, 71 FEP 312 (7th Cir. 1996), *cert. denied,* 117 S. Ct. 949, 74 FEP 768 (1997) *27:* 47, 54, 60–63

Wixson v. Dowagiac Nursing Home, 87 F.3d 164, 71 FEP 186 (6th Cir. 1996) *2:* 18; *17:* 53

Wohl v. Spectrum Mfg., Inc., 94 F.3d 353, 71 FEP 1081 (7th Cir. 1996) *2:* 31

Wolf
—v. Buss (Am.) Inc., 77 F.3d 914, 70 FEP 130 (7th Cir.), *cert. denied,* 117 S. Ct. 175 (1996) *16:* 114; *33:* 50
—v. F & M Banks, 534 N.W.2d 877, 10 IER 827 (Wis. Ct. App. 1995) *26:* 58

Women's Comm. for Equal Employment Opportunity v. National Broad. Co., 77 F.R.D. 666, 13 FEP 240 (S.D.N.Y. 1976) *37:* 69

Woodhouse v. Magnolia Hosp., 92 F.3d 248, 71 FEP 1804 (5th Cir. 1996) *40:* 21; *41:* 82

Woodman v. Haemonetics Corp., 51 F.3d 1087, 67 FEP 838 (1st Cir. 1995) *2:* 38; *16:* 96, 123, 152; *39:* 22

Woods
—v. Bentsen, 889 F. Supp. 179, 72 FEP 1554 (E.D. Pa. 1995) *27:* 21; *31:* 51
—v. Friction Materials, Inc., 30 F.3d 255, 65 FEP 1109 (1st Cir. 1994) *2:* 38
—v. Trinity Mem'l Hosp., 1995 WL 55275 (E.D. Tex. Jan. 31, 1995) *32:* 9

Woodson v. Scott Paper Co., 898 F. Supp. 298, 68 FEP 947 (E.D. Pa. 1995) *41:* 29, 90, 123, 129

Wooten v. Farmland Foods, 58 F.3d 382, 4 AD 920 (8th Cir. 1995) *9:* 176, 186, 237; *22:* 21

Wormley v. Arkla, Inc., 871 F. Supp. 1079, 3 AD 1703 (E.D. Ark. 1994) *9:* 264

Woroski v. Nashua Corp., 31 F.3d 105, 65 FEP 824 (2d Cir. 1994) *16:* 143, 155, 166, 179

Worthy v. Aspin, 64 FEP 65 (W.D. Pa. 1994) *33:* 46, 49

Wray v. Edward Blank Assocs., Inc., 924 F. Supp. 498 (S.D.N.Y. 1996) *16:* 27

Wreath v. United States, 70 FEP 23 (D. Kan. 1995) *38:* 35

Wright
—v. Honda of Am. Mfg., 653 N.E.2d 381, 11 IER 27 (Ohio 1995) *26:* 14
—v. Illinois Dep't of Children & Family Servs., 40 F.3d 1492, 10 IER 87 (7th Cir. 1994) *24:* 45
—v. Metro Health Med. Ctr., 58 F.3d 1130, 10 IER 1418 (6th Cir. 1995), *cert. denied,* 116 S. Ct. 1041 (1996) *26:* 33

Wrightson v. Pizza Hut of Am., Inc., 99 F.3d 138, 72 FEP 186 (4th Cir. 1996) *20:* 27

Wyatt v. City of Boston, 35 F.3d 13, 65 FEP 1441 (1st Cir. 1994) *17:* 4, 23, 40

Wygant v. Jackson Bd. of Educ, 476 U.S. 267, 40 FEP 1321 (1986) *27:* 44

Wyoming; EEOC v., 460 U.S. 226, 31 FEP 74 (1983) *16:* 33

Y

Yatvin v. Madison Metro. Sch. Dist., 840 F.2d 412, 45 FEP 1862 (7th Cir. 1988) *36:* 19

Yeary v. Goodwill Indus. Knoxville, Inc., 107 F.3d 443, 73 FEP 146 (6th Cir. 1997) *20:* 26

Yeldell v. Cooper Green Hosp., 956 F.2d 1056, 66 FEP 607 (11th Cir. 1992) *24:* 36

Yenkin-Majestic Paint Corp.; EEOC v., 112 F.3d 831, 73 FEP 1317 (6th Cir. 1997) *2:* 30

Yerdon v. Henry, 91 F.3d 370, 71 FEP 1733 (2d Cir. 1996) *22:* 1

Yin v. California, 95 F.3d 864, 5 AD 1487 (9th Cir. 1996), *cert. denied,* 116 S. Ct. 64 (1997) *9:* 2

Yniguez v. Arizonans for Official English, 69 F.3d 920 (9th Cir. 1995), *vacated and remanded,* 117 S. Ct. 1309 (1997) *11:* 20–27

Yodice v. Metropolitan Dade County, 4 AD 1384 (S.D. Fla. 1995) *9:* 245–46

Yoonessi v. State Univ. of N.Y., 862 F. Supp. 1005 (W.D.N.Y. 1994), *cert. denied,* 516 U.S. 1075, 69 FEP 1504 (1996) *31:* 20

York v. American Tel. & Tel., 95 F.3d 948, 73 FEP 1654 (10th Cir. 1996) *4:* 11–12

Young
—v. Easter Enters., Inc., 915 F. Supp. 58 (S.D. Ind. 1995) *16:* 57
—v. General Foods Corp., 840 F.2d 825 (11th Cir. 1988) *16:* 112
—v. Lukens Steel Co., 881 F. Supp. 962, 71 FEP 739 (E.D. Pa. 1994) *16:* 219–20, 243; *41:* 26, 84
—v. Pennsylvania House of Reps., 1998 WL 76249 (M.D. Pa. Feb. 18, 1998) *16:* 35
—v. State Farm Mut. Auto Ins. Co., 868 F. Supp. 937, 69 FEP 1227 (W.D. Tenn. 1994) *19:* 11
—v. University of Kan. Med. Ctr., 1997 WL 150051 (D. Kan. Feb. 26, 1997) *16:* 35

Yusuf v. Vassar College, 35 F.3d 709 (2d Cir. 1994) *11:* 12

Z

Zambelli v. Historic Landmarks, Inc., 4 AD 308 (E.D. Pa. 1995) *16:* 104

Zapata v. IBP, Inc.
—1994 WL 649322, 1994 U.S. Dist. LEXIS 16285 (D. Kan. Nov. 10, 1994), *review denied,* 1994 U.S. Dist. LEXIS 18660 (D. Kan. Dec. 12, 1994) *38:* 12–13, 30, 57
—167 F.R.D. 147 (D. Kan. 1996) *37:* 3, 23, 50, 54, 63–64, 104–05

Zarate v. Younglove, 86 F.R.D. 80 (C.D. Cal. 1980) *37:* 90

Zarnoski v. Hearst Business Communications, 69 FEP 1514 (E.D. Pa. 1996) *30:* 55, 59

Zartic Inc., 315 NLRB 495, 147 LRRM 1201 (1994) *25:* 1

Zellars v. Liberty Nat'l Life Ins. Co., 907 F. Supp. 355, 69 FEP 1223 (M.D. Ala. 1995) *16:* 59

Zenni v. Hard Rock Cafe Int'l, Inc., 903 F. Supp. 644 (S.D.N.Y. 1995) *17:* 34; *19:* 4, 11

Zveiter v. Brazilian Nat'l Superintendency, 833 F. Supp. 1089, 68 FEP 1429, *opinion supplemented on reconsideration,* 841 F. Supp. 111 (S.D.N.Y. 1993) *20:* 39

Zimmerman v. Cook County Sheriff's Dep't, 96 F.3d 1017, 71 FEP 1537 (7th Cir. 1996) *20:* 102

Zirpel v. Toshiba Am. Info. Sys., 111 F.3d 80, 6 AD 929 (8th Cir. 1997) *9:* 47

Zolotarevsky v. General Elec. Co., 862 F. Supp. 659 (D. Mass. 1994) *18:* 10

Zorn v. Helene Curtis, Inc., 903 F. Supp. 1226, 70 FEP 371 (N.D. Ill. 1995) *20:* 67

Zughni v. Peña, 851 F. Supp. 300 (N.D. Ill. 1994), *aff'd,* 56 F.3d 82 (Fed. Cir. 1995) *33:* 47, 49